What People Just Like You Are Saying about *Using Excel*:

Using Excel for Windows helped me get beyond the basics with ease. The index was inclusive, and I could quickly find the information I needed. This book makes using Excel inviting.

John J. Boyle
Manager, Syndication Accounting
CBS, Inc.

The book helped me learn several things about Excel that I just didn't know existed.

Chris Dyer
Mallinckrodt Anesthesiology
Administrative Assistant

Que has done another bang-up job with *Using Excel for Windows*. The Que *Using* series is the best value for help in running software.

Gerald H. Denoncourt
Edgewood Center
Chemical Engineer

Que books are essential to accelerating my learning curve. The book is very clear and organized. When I am in trouble or need an answer fast, I just reach up and grab *Using Excel*.

Don Collyard
Hoffman Engineering Company
Manager, Marketing Communications

Que books give you the ability to use all of the capabilities that Excel offers.

William L. Dore
Zycon Corp.
Senior Process Engineer

The exercise on "Linking Cells by Pointing" helped me to thoroughly understand the process. After working with 1-2-3 for eight years, Excel can be confusing. This book enables me to adequately support the end-users in our company.

Connie Wagner
Montana-Dakota Utilities Co.
Support Center Instructor

The book's instructions are clear and easy to use. This book is fast and easy to use—we all appreciate fast help when we are in trouble or are trying to push a spreadsheet one step further.

Ann Kivimaki
Scott Paper Company
Maintenance Skills Assistant

Extremely well organized—depth of coverage is great.

Robert C. Ingram
Energy Conversion Devices, Inc.
Risk Manager

Everything is very detailed and easy to understand. The book is extremely well written.

Laura Hershey
Consulting, Etc.
Consultant (Sole Proprietor)

Que has done a great job with this book!

Daniel J. Williams
President
InterCoast Gas Services

Using Excel Version 5 for Windows™, Special Edition

Ron Person

que

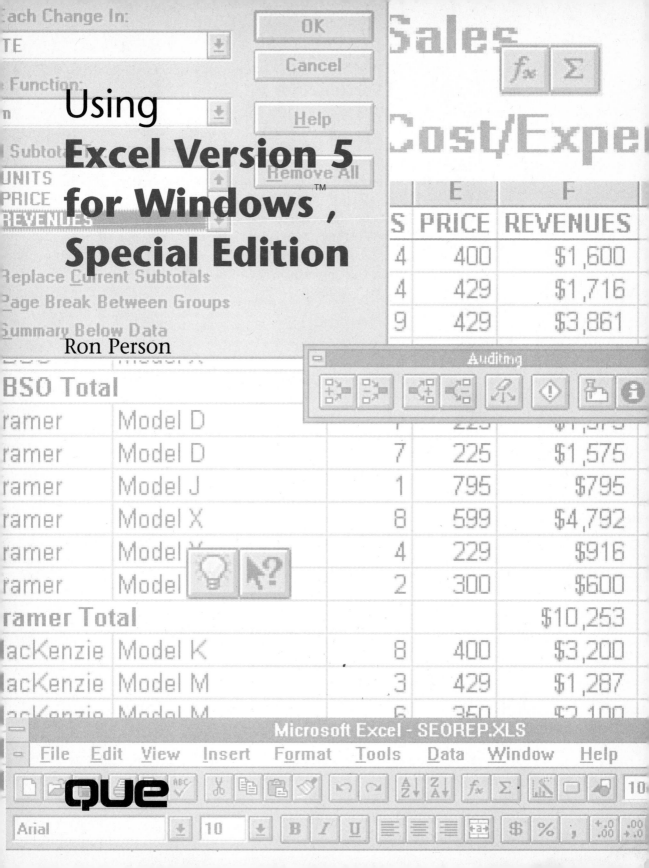

Using Excel Version 5 for Windows, Special Edition

Library of Congress Catalog No.: 93-86750

ISBN: 1-56529-459-9

96 95 94 8 7 6 5

Interpretation of the printing code: the rightmost double-digit number is the year of the book's printing; the rightmost single-digit number, the number of the book's printing. For example, a printing code of 93-1 shows that the first printing of the book occurred in 1993.

Using Excel Version 5 for Windows, Special Edition, is based on Microsoft Excel Version 5 for Windows.

Publisher: David P. Ewing

Director of Publishing: Michael Miller

Managing Editor: Corinne Walls

Marketing Manager: Ray Robinson

Credits

Publishing Manager
Don Roche, Jr.

Acquisitions Editor
Nancy Stevenson

Product Directors
Joyce J. Nielsen
Jim Minatel

Product Development
Kathie-Jo Arnoff
Robin Drake
Bryan Gambrel
Steven M. Schafer
Jill D. Bond

Production Editor
Don Eamon

Copy Editors
William A. Barton
Elsa Bell
Lori Cates
Chris Haidri
Tom Hayes
Patrick Kanouse
Susan Ross Moore
Cindy Morrow
Chris Nelson
Ginny Noble
Heather Northrup
Linda Seifert
Pamela Wampler

Technical Editors
Warren W. Estep
Robert D. Holtz
Patrick T. Irwin
Anne Poirson
Don Roche, Jr.
Michael Watson
Eric Bloom

Production Manager
Scott Cook

Proofreading/Indexing Coordinator
Joelynn Gifford

Production Analyst
Mary Beth Wakefield

Book Designer
Amy Peppler-Adams

Cover Designer
Dan Armstrong

Graphic Image Specialists
Dennis Sheehan
Susan VandeWalle
Jeff Shrum

Credits

Production Team

Angela Bannan
Claudia Bell
Danielle Bird
Charlotte Clapp
Paula Carroll
Anne Dickerson
Karen Dodson
Terri Edwards
Brook Farling
Michelle Greenwalt
Bob LaRoche
Elizabeth Lewis
Shelly Palma
Caroline Roop
Amy L. Steed
Donna Winter
Michelle Worthington
Lillian Yates

Indexers

Michael Hughes
Joy Dean Lee

Composed in *1Stone Serif* and *MCPdigital* by Que Corporation

About the Author

Ron Person has written more than 14 books for Que Corporation, including *Using Word Version 6 for Windows,* Special Edition; *Excel for Windows Hot Tips, Using Windows 3.1,* Special Edition, and *Windows 3.1 QuickStart.* Ron is one of the original twelve Microsoft Consulting Partners, Microsoft's highest rating for independent consultants. He is a Microsoft Solutions Provider. He has an M.S. in physics from The Ohio State University and an M.B.A. from Hardin-Simmons University.

Ron Person & Co., based in San Francisco, has attained Microsoft's highest rating for Microsoft Excel and Word for Windows consultants: Microsoft Consulting Partner. They are a Microsoft Solutions Provider. The firm is a recognized leader in training developers and support personnel in Visual Basic for Applications and the application languages used by Microsoft Excel, Word for Windows, and Microsoft Access. The firm's developer courses have enabled many corporations to develop their own financial, marketing, and business-analysis systems. If your company plans to develop applications using Microsoft's Visual Basic for Applications, Word Basic, or Microsoft Access Basic, you should contact Ron Person & Co. regarding on-site courses for support personnel, advanced users, and developers.

For information on course content, on-site corporate classes, or consulting, contact Ron Person & Co. at the following address:

Ron Person & Co.
P.O. Box 5647
Santa Rosa, CA 95409

(415) 989-7508 Voice (8 a.m. to 5 p.m. PDT)
(707) 539-1525 Voice (8 a.m. to 5 p.m. PDT)
(707) 538-1485 FAX

For telephone support for technical questions on Excel, please call Microsoft Support Services at:

(206) 635-7070

Microsoft Support Services is open from 6 a.m. to 6 p.m. PDT Monday through Friday. Additional support services and telephone numbers are in the Appendix.

Acknowledgments

The expertise, knowledge, and production that go into a book like *Using Excel Version 5 for Windows*, Special Edition, requires teams of talented people. A book of this size and detail can be updated only through conscientious and dedicated work from each person. To meet incredibly short deadlines, while covering Excel in the depth it deserves, everyone missed weekends and worked long nights. Thank you for your work and skill.

Thanks to Microsoft Excel's development teams and marketing managers. Excel is an amazing combination of power, flexibility, and accessibility that continues to redefine the limits of electronic spreadsheets. Thanks to **Eric Wells** for keeping the Consulting Partners informed and enthusiastic about Excel. And thanks to **Joel Spolsky** and **Ben Waldman** for presentations that clarified Visual Basic for Applications.

Que, the world's largest publisher of computer books, continues to stay ahead of the competition through the energy and skills of its people. I appreciate their grace and humor while under pressure.

Don Roche and **Nancy Stevenson** did one of the smoothest jobs I've ever seen of managing the high-speed turnaround on this book. They stayed ahead of the project through every twist and turn and had alternative plans for every unexpected corner.

Joyce Nielsen and **Don Eamon** and their teams worked the long hours necessary to get the book through development and editing. Their contributions give the book that Que style.

Thanks to the software consultants, professional writers, and technical editors who helped write and edit *Using Excel Version 5 for Windows,* Special Edition. However, the responsibility for errors that may have slipped through their knowledgeable gaze lies solely with me. There were weeks of 16-hour days and months of missed weekends required to finish this book, and I appreciate the work of the following people:

Robert Voss, Ph.D., deserves special thanks for his help in bringing this book together. Beyond applying his writing and training skills to the original writing, Bob made a significant contribution to this book and many of Que's best-selling books, including *Using Word Version 6 for Windows*, Special Edition. Bob is a senior trainer in Microsoft Excel and Word for Windows for Ron Person & Co.

Ralph Soucie, long-time contributing editor to *PC World*, and author of a popular book on Microsoft Excel, is also a Microsoft Excel consultant. Ralph's Excel consulting firm, Onset, Inc., is located in Jonesport, Maine. His Excel consulting and training practice includes Boston, the eastern seaboard, and Atlantic Canada.

William Orvis brought his considerable writing and Visual Basic skills to the chapters on Visual Basic for Applications. He is an engineer at Lawrence Livermore National Laboratories, part of the University of California. He has many years experience in programming in different languages and has written two books on programming in Visual Basic.

Matthew Harris is a computer consultant in Oakland, California who has been doing training, support, and technical writing since 1980 for corporations and non-profit organizations. He is the author of *The Disk Compression Book* and has made significant contributions to four other Que books. He can be reached on CompuServe at 74017,766.

Shelley O'Hara has written over 25 computer books and is one of Que's best-selling authors. Shelley is well known for having written most of Que's *Easy* series and a major portion of the new *Excel Version 5 for Windows Quick Reference*. She is an independent technical writer and consultant in Indianapolis. Shelley's high productivity and quality have always amazed me.

Rick Winter is the owner of PRW Computer Services in Denver. He does training and consulting on spreadsheets and word processing. He has contributed to or written numerous Que books. I appreciated his attention to detail and the quality of his writing.

Anne Poirson is a *Microsoft Consulting Channel Partner in Excel*. In addition to updating two chapters, Anne helped with technical editing. Anne owns the consulting firm, Computer Synergy, located in Cleveland, Ohio. She has over 20 years experience developing custom software applications for firms such as General Electric, Newport News Shipbuilding, and BP America. In addition to her computer science degree, Anne is a graduate of General Electric's Financial Management Program.

Tim Pyron is a trainer and consultant in database and spreadsheet applications who lives in San Antonio, Texas. He is the information systems manager for Squire Computer Services of Texas. His knowledge of linear and non-linear optimization systems was a real contribution.

Karen Rose came from a graphics and desktop publishing background to contribute her knowledge to the graphics portions of the book.

Cathy Kenny is the assistant editor for a computer magazine in Boston.

Brian Underdahl is a spreadsheet wizard living in Reno, Nevada who updated the Analysis ToolPak chapter. Brian is known for his Que book, *Using Quattro Pro 5.0 for Windows*, Special Edition.

Trademarks

Contents at a Glance

Introduction 1

Everyday Worksheet Tasks 11

1 What's New in Excel 5 for Windows 13
2 Getting Around in Excel and Windows 25
3 Navigating and Selecting in a Workbook 65
4 Entering and Editing Data 87
5 Working with Formulas 125
6 Using Functions 173
7 Moving or Copying Data and Formulas 235
8 Reorganizing Workbooks and Sheets 257
9 Managing Files 267
10 Formatting Worksheets 303
11 Printing Worksheets 369

Everyday Worksheet Tasks

Creating and Formatting Charts 401

12 Creating Charts 403
13 Modifying Charts 435
14 Formatting Charts 477
15 Building Complex Charts 505

Working with Charts

Optimizing Excel 531

16 Managing the Worksheet Display 533
17 Adding Graphics Elements to Sheets 553
18 Outlining Worksheets 593
19 Creating Automatic Subtotals 607
20 Publishing Worksheets and Charts 617
21 Creating Slide Show Presentations 659
22 Taking Advantage of Excel's Add-Ins 671

Optimizing Excel

Analyzing the Worksheet 683

23 Manipulating and Analyzing Data 685
24 Building Forms with Controls 719
25 Linking, Embedding, and Consolidating Worksheets 743
26 Auditing Workbooks and Worksheets 777
27 Solving with Goal Seeking and Solver 795
28 Testing Multiple Solutions with Scenarios 819
29 Using the Analysis ToolPak 837

Analyzing the Worksheet

Managing Lists or Databases 861
30 Designing a List or Database 863
31 Entering Data in a List or Database 875
32 Sorting Data 887
33 Finding, Filtering, and Editing Lists and Databases 901
34 Working with Filtered Data 933
35 Retrieving Data from External Databases 947
36 Using Pivot Tables 983
37 Analyzing and Reporting with Pivot Tables 1011

Managing Lists

Integrating Excel with Other Applications 1041
38 Using Excel with Windows Applications 1043
39 Using Excel with DOS and Mainframe Applications 1069

Integrating Excel

Customizing Excel
40 Customizing Excel 1093
41 Creating Custom Toolbars and Menus 1107
42 Creating Templates and Controlling Excel's Startup 1127

Customizing Excel

Automating with Visual Basic for Applications 1137
43 Introducing Visual Basic for Applications 1139
44 Recording and Modifying VBA Modules 1153
45 Programming in Visual Basic for Applications 1173
46 Exploring Visual Basic For Applications Examples 1223

Automating with VBA

Appendix 1239
Support Services 1239

Index 1241

Appendix

Contents

Introduction 1

Reviewing Excel Features 1
- Lotus 1-2-3 Capability 1
- Operating Ease 2
- Worksheet Publishing 3
- Analytical Tools 4
- Graphics Features 4
- Linking and Consolidating Features 5
- Charting Capabilities 6
- Database Capabilities 6
- Worksheet Outlines 7
- Visual Basic for Applications and Excel 4 Macro Language 7

Using This Book 8

Conventions Used in This Book 9
- Special Typefaces and Representations 9
- Margin Icons 10
- Special Sections 10

I Everyday Worksheet Tasks 11

1 What's New in Excel 5 for Windows 13

New Features That Provide Better Accessibility 13
- Simpler and Standardized Menus 13
- Tabbed Dialog Boxes 14
- TipWizard 15
- ToolTips 15
- Tear-Off Palettes 15
- Full Screen View 16

New Features That Simplify Everyday Tasks 16
- Workbooks That Contain Multiple Worksheets 16
- Better File Management 17
- Custom Data Series 17
- Function Wizard 18
- Individual Character Formatting 18
- Format Painter 18
- Drag and Drop Data onto Charts 18
- Worksheet Auditing 19

New Features That Provide More Analytical Capabilities 19
- OLE Automation 19

Drop-Down Lists, Check Boxes, and Option Buttons in Worksheets 20
Subtotal and Grand Total Reports 20
Custom Chart Elements 20
Automatic Chart Formatting 21
Automatic Chart Trendlines 21
AutoFilter 21
TextWizard 21
Microsoft Query 22
Pivot Tables 22
Visual Basic for Applications 23

2 Getting Around in Excel and Windows 25

Starting and Quitting Excel 25
Understanding the Excel Screen 27
Using the Mouse 31
Understanding Windows and Excel Terms 34
Mouse Actions 34
Keyboard Actions 35
Choosing Commands 38
Saving Time with Shortcut Menus 39
Choosing Commands with the Keyboard 40
Choosing Alternative Commands with Shift 41
Using Excel 4 Commands 41
Using the Toolbars 41
Getting Help on Tools 44
Displaying or Hiding Toolbars 45
Moving, Resizing, and Reshaping Toolbars 46
Using Tear-Off Palettes from Toolbars 47
Working in Dialog Boxes 48
Selecting a Tabbed Section of a Dialog Box 50
Selecting Option Buttons and Check Boxes 50
Editing Text Boxes 51
Selecting from List Boxes 52
Closing Dialog Boxes 54
Getting Help 55
Searching for a Topic in Help 56
Jumping between Help Topics 57
Getting Help in Dialog Boxes 57
Closing the Help Window 58
Using the TipWizard 58
Manipulating Windows 58
Switching between Applications 59
Switching between Workbook Windows 59
Minimizing, Maximizing, and Restoring Windows 60
Moving a Window 60
Sizing a Window 61
Closing a Workbook Window 61
From Here... 62

3 Navigating and Selecting in a Workbook 65

Understanding Workbooks and Worksheets ... 66
Moving between Workbooks ... 67
Selecting and Moving between Sheets ... 67
 Moving between Worksheets in a Workbook ... 68
 Selecting Multiple Worksheets in a Workbook ... 69
 Tips about Selecting Sheets ... 69
Moving Around in a Worksheet ... 70
 Scrolling with the Mouse ... 71
 Scrolling with the Keyboard ... 71
Selecting Cells and Ranges ... 72
 Selecting a Single Cell ... 73
 Moving to the Edge of a Block of Cells ... 74
 Using the Go To Command To Move or Select ... 75
 Selecting a Range ... 76
 Selecting Rows and Columns ... 82
 Selecting Cells by Type of Content ... 83
 Tips about Selecting ... 85
From Here... ... 86

4 Entering and Editing Data 87

Entering Data ... 87
 Entering Text ... 89
 Entering Numbers ... 90
 Entering Dates and Times ... 93
Editing Text and Formulas ... 94
 Editing in the Formula Bar ... 94
 Editing Directly in a Cell ... 95
 Undoing and Repeating Changes ... 97
Finding or Replacing in a Worksheet ... 97
 Finding Text, Numbers, and Formulas ... 97
 Replacing Text, Numbers, or Formulas ... 99
Clearing, Inserting, or Deleting in a Worksheet ... 101
 Clearing Cell Contents ... 102
 Inserting or Deleting Cells, Rows, and Columns ... 103
Entering a Series of Numbers or Dates ... 109
 Creating a Linear Series ... 110
 Creating Series of Text and Headings ... 116
Increasing Data-Entry Efficiency ... 120
 Entering Numbers with a Fixed Decimal Place ... 120
 Moving the Active Cell When Entering Data ... 121
 Using Data-Entry Shortcut Keys ... 121
 Working While Excel Recalculates ... 122
From Here... ... 123

5 Working with Formulas 125

Understanding Formulas 125
Entering Formulas 127
Working in the Formula Bar or In-Cell 127
Entering Cell References 128
Using Operators in Formulas 139
Pasting Names and Functions into Formulas 143
Entering Text, Dates, and Times in Formulas 144
Changing Formulas to Values 144
Defining Formula Errors 145
Calculating with Arrays 152
Entering Array Formulas 152
Selecting an Array Range 154
Calculating Array Results 155
Editing Array Formulas and Functions 156
Naming Cells for Better Worksheets 157
Creating Names 159
Creating Names from Worksheet Text 162
Creating 3-D Names 166
Pasting a List of Names 166
Changing or Deleting Names 167
Using Names in Formulas and Commands 167
Applying Names 168
Naming Formulas and Values 170
From Here... 171

6 Using Functions 173

Understanding Functions 173
Using Arguments within Functions 175
Viewing the Parts of the Screen that Help Create Functions 177
Entering Worksheet Functions 178
Typing Functions 179
Using the AutoSum Tool 179
Using the Function Wizard 180
Editing Functions 182
Getting Help 183
Excel Function Dictionary 184
Database Functions 185
Date and Time Functions 187
Financial Functions 192
Information Functions 201
Logical Functions 207
Lookup and Reference Functions 208
Mathematical Functions 215
Statistical Functions 221
Text Functions 226
Trigonometric Functions 232
From Here... 233

7 Moving or Copying Data and Formulas 235

Moving Cell Contents 235
Moving by Dragging 235
Moving with Commands 236
Dragging and Inserting Cells 237
Moving and Inserting with Commands 238
Making Moves Across a Workbook 239
Filling or Copying Cell Contents 241
Using the Fill Handle 241
Using Ctrl+Enter To Fill Cells 242
Using the Fill Commands 243
Creating a Custom Fill 244
Copying by Dragging and Dropping 245
Copying with Commands 247
Pasting Multiple Copies 247
Pasting Nonadjacent Multiple Copies 249
Inserting Copied Cells with Commands 251
Copying Data Across a Workbook 252
Pasting Formats, Values, or Transposed Data 252
From Here... 255

8 Reorganizing Workbooks and Sheets 257

Understanding Workbooks and Sheets 258
Changing the Default Number of Sheets in New Workbooks 258
Inserting and Removing Sheets 258
Inserting a Sheet 259
Removing a Sheet 260
Copying and Moving Sheets 260
Copying a Sheet 260
Moving a Sheet 262
Renaming a Sheet 264
Grouping Sheets for Editing, Formatting, and Reorganizing 264
From Here... 266

9 Managing Files 267

Creating a New Workbook 267
Opening an Existing Workbook 268
Listing Other File Types 270
Changing Drives and Directories 270
Changing the Default Directory 271
Opening Files on a Network 271
Opening Excel 4 Documents 272
Saving Workbooks 272
Saving Your Workbook 272
Saving Files with a New Name 274
Saving with Summary Information To Make Workbooks Easier To Find 275

Saving without Renaming 277
Automatically Saving Documents 277
Creating Automatic Backups 278
Password-Protecting Your Workbooks 279
Saving to Other File Formats 280
Saving a Workspace File 280
Closing Workbooks 282
Using the Find File Command 282
Finding Files 284
Using the Find File Command 284
Searching Different Drives or Directories 285
Searching for Specific Files or Different File Types 286
Searching by Summary Information or Text in the File 287
Searching by Date Saved or Created 290
Saving Search Criteria 291
Viewing Workbooks and File Information 292
Using Find File To View Workbooks and File Information 292
Sorting File Lists 293
Previewing Workbooks 294
Viewing File Information 296
Viewing Summary Information 296
Editing and Adding Summary Information 297
Working with Files 299
Selecting Files with Which To Work 299
Opening Found Files 300
Printing Found Files 300
Copying Found Files 301
Deleting Found Files 302
From Here... 302

10 Formatting Worksheets 303

Formatting with Autoformats 303
Formatting a Table Automatically 305
Using Only Part of an Autoformat 306
Tips about Autoformatting 307
Using TrueType Fonts 308
Understanding Screen, Printer, and TrueType Fonts 308
Enabling TrueType Fonts 309
Tips about TrueType Fonts 310
Copying and Pasting Formats 311
Understanding the Format Painter Button 311
Using the Format Painter Button 311
Changing Character Fonts, Sizes, Styles, and Colors 312
Formatting All Characters in a Cell or Range 314
Formatting Selected Characters in a Cell 315
Formatting Cells or Characters with Toolbars 316
Formatting Cells or Characters with Shortcut Keys 317
Tips about Formats 318

Aligning and Rotating Text and Numbers 319
Aligning Cell Entries 319
Centering Text across Cells 320
Wrapping Text To Fit in a Cell 322
Joining Together Text or Text and Numbers 323
Tabbing and Breaking Lines in a Cell 324
Justifying Text Lines 324
Rotating Numbers and Text 326
Tips about Aligning Characters 327
Formatting Numbers 328
Using Excel's Automatic Number Formatting 328
What You Need To Know about Number Formats 328
Understanding the Potential Danger in Formatted Numbers 330
Formatting Numbers 331
Designing Custom Numeric Formats 333
Formatting Conditionally 339
Hiding Zeros 339
Tips about Numeric Formatting 340
Formatting Dates and Times 341
Understanding Date and Time Formats 342
Formatting Dates and Times 344
Creating Custom Date and Time Formats 344
Tips about Date and Time Formatting 345
Formatting Rows and Columns 346
Adjusting Column Width 346
Hiding Columns 348
Adjusting Row Height 348
Hiding Rows 349
Tips about Rows and Columns 350
Adding Colors, Patterns, and Borders 350
Adding a Pattern or Color 351
Adding Borders and Lines 352
Tips about Borders, Patterns, and Colors 354
Applying Multiple Formats at One Time 354
Using a Style To Apply a Collection of Formats 355
Creating Styles 356
Redefining Styles 359
Redefining the Default (Normal) Style 361
Deleting Styles 361
Tips about Styles 361
Protecting Sheets and Workbooks 362
Unprotecting and Hiding Formulas 363
Turning On Protection 364
Tips about Protecting Sheets and Workbooks 365
Formatting a Group of Sheets in a Workbook 365
Setting Startup Formats 366
From Here... 367

11 Printing Worksheets 369

Reviewing the Printing Process 370
Setting Up Your Printer 371
Installing a Printer 372
Selecting the Printer 372
Defining the Page Setup 374
Setting the Paper Margins 375
Setting the Page Orientation and Paper Size 377
Turning Gridlines and Row or Column Headings On and Off 377
Creating Headers and Footers 378
Specifying the Page Layout Order 382
Reducing and Enlarging Prints 382
Printing Color or Black and White 383
Setting the Print Quality 383
Setting the Print Range 383
Setting a Print Area 384
Removing a Print Area 385
Adjusting How Pages Print 385
Setting Multiple Print Areas 387
Printing Titles 389
Previewing the Document 389
Adjusting Margins and Column Widths While Previewing 391
Compressing Reports To Fit the Paper Size 392
Compressing Reports to One Page 392
Compressing Longer Reports 394
Printing 395
Printing Report Manager Reports 396
Creating a Sequence of Reports 397
Reorganizing Report Sequences 398
Printing a Report Sequence 399
From Here... 399

II Creating and Formatting Charts 401

12 Creating Charts 403

Reviewing the Charting Process 403
Defining Chart Terms 405
Understanding How To Create a Chart 406
Creating an Embedded Chart 407
Creating an Embedded Chart Using the ChartWizard 407
Understanding ChartWizard Dialog Boxes 408
Verifying the Chart Data Range 409
Defining the Chart Type 410
Choosing a Chart Format 410
Changing How Excel Interprets Data Layout 411
Add Legends and Titles 412

Opening an Embedded Chart for Formatting 414
Creating a Chart in a Chart Sheet 415
Creating a Chart Automatically 415
Understanding How Excel Builds a Chart 416
Creating a Chart Automatically 418
Creating a Chart Manually 421
Understanding Non-Standard Data Layouts 421
How To Create a Chart Manually 423
Saving Charts 426
Changing Chart and Worksheet Links 427
Opening Charts 428
Printing Charts 429
From Here... 432

13 Modifying Charts 435

An Overview of Modifying Charts 435
Using Shortcut Menus 435
Selecting Chart Objects 436
Choosing a Chart Type 438
Using the Menu Command To Change a Chart Type 438
Using the Chart Toolbar To Change a Chart Type 440
Using Autoformats 441
Applying Autoformats to a Chart 441
Examining Types of 2-D Autoformats 442
Examining Types of 3-D Charts 447
Creating Custom Autoformats 451
Changing the Chart Type 452
Choosing Line or XY (Scatter) Charts 453
Choosing a Default Chart Format 454
Adding or Deleting Data 456
Adding Data to Embedded Charts 456
Adding Data with the Insert New Data Command 457
Adding Data from Multiple Worksheets 458
Adding Data with the Edit Copy and Edit Paste Commands 458
Changing the Data Range with the ChartWizard 459
Deleting Data 461
Working with the Series Formula 461
Understanding the Series Formula 461
Editing a Data Series 462
Rearranging the Markers 464
Inserting Text 465
Inserting Titles 466
Inserting Other Text 468
Checking Spelling in Charts 469
Inserting Data Labels 469
Inserting Legends 472
Inserting Arrows 474
Inserting Gridlines 475
From Here... 475

14 Formatting Charts 477

Learning the Basic Chart Formatting Procedure 477
Moving and Sizing Chart Objects 478
Changing Object Colors, Patterns, and Borders 480
Formatting Text and Numbers 483
    Understanding How To Format Text and Numbers 483
    Changing Fonts and Styles 485
    Changing Text Alignment 486
    Formatting Numbers 486
Formatting Data Series 488
    Understanding Data Series Formatting 488
    Formatting Trendlines 490
    Formatting Error Bars 491
Formatting Data Markers 491
Scaling and Customizing an Axis 492
    Customizing the Format of an Axis 493
    Changing the Scaling of an Axis 494
Formatting Arrows 496
Formatting 3-D Charts 497
    Rotating a 3-D Chart by Dragging 497
    Rotating a 3-D Chart by Command 500
Clearing Chart Formats or Contents 501
Changing and Modifying Chart Types 502
Transferring Chart Formats 503
From Here... 504

15 Building Complex Charts 505

Creating Combination Charts 505
    Creating a Combination Chart from the Predefined Chart Types 508
    Creating a Combination Chart with the Format Chart Command 508
    Changing Chart Types 509
    Adding a Secondary Axis 509
Using Charts To Analyze Data 510
    Analyzing Charts for What-If Analysis 510
    Moving Markers To Change Worksheet Values 511
Automatically Analyzing Trends with Charts 513
    Adding a Trendline to a Data Series 514
Adding Error Bars to a Chart 517
    Inserting Error Bars 518
Creating Charts from Outlines 519
Creating Hierarchical Charts 522
Linking Chart Text to Worksheet Cells 523
Creating Picture Charts 524
From Here... 529

III Optimizing Excel 531

16 Managing the Worksheet Display 533

Controlling the Worksheet Display 533
Displaying the Worksheet Full Screen 533
Hiding Row and Column Headings 535
Turning Scroll Bars On and Off 535
Hiding the Formula Bar, Status Bar, and Sheet Tabs 536
Hiding or Coloring Gridlines 536
Displaying Formulas 537
Magnifying Worksheet Displays 538
Saving Frequently Used View and Print Settings 540
Naming and Saving a View 540
Displaying a Named View 543
Deleting a Named View 543
Viewing a Window through Multiple Panes 544
Dividing a Window into Multiple Scrolling Panes 544
Freezing Headings into Position 546
Activating Different Panes 546
Working with Multiple Windows 546
Opening Additional Documents 547
Switching to a Window 547
Displaying Worksheets in Separate Windows 547
Arranging Multiple Windows 548
Hiding and Unhiding Windows and Sheets 550
Locking Windows in Position 551
Saving and Closing Multiple Windows 552
From Here... 552

17 Adding Graphics Elements to Sheets 553

Understanding Uses of Graphics Elements 553
Using Graphics and Clip Art from Other Applications 556
What Is Clip Art? 556
Understanding Graphic File Formats 556
Inserting Graphics 557
Copying Graphics onto a Sheet 558
Creating Graphic Objects 560
Using the Drawing Tools 561
Using Drawing Shortcut Menus 563
Drawing Lines, Ellipses, Rectangles, and Arcs 564
Drawing Freehand Objects 565
Drawing Text Boxes 567
Drawing Macro Buttons 568
Combining Data and Charts on the Same Page 571
Deciding between Pasting and Embedding Charts 571
Embedding Linked Pictures of Charts in a Worksheet 572
Pasting Unlinked Pictures of Charts in a Worksheet 573
Linking Pictures of Cells in a Worksheet 574

Learning Basic Skills for Editing Graphic Objects 577
Selecting Graphic Objects 577
Deleting Graphic Objects 579
Formatting Graphic Objects 579
Formatting Lines and Arrows 579
Formatting Borders and Patterns 581
Changing Object Size, Shape, and Position 583
Sizing, Moving, and Copying Graphic Objects 583
Reshaping a Freehand Object 584
Fixing Object Positions 584
Grouping and Layering Graphic Objects 588
Grouping Graphic Objects 588
Reordering Layers of Graphic Objects 589
Protecting, Printing, and Hiding Graphic Objects 590
Protecting Graphic Objects 590
Printing Graphic Objects 591
Hiding Objects 591
From Here... 592

18 Outlining Worksheets 593

Benefits of Outlining 593
Understanding Outline Layout 595
Outline Symbols 597
Creating an Outline 598
Using Excel's Automatic Outlining To Create an Outline 598
Creating Outlines Manually 599
Clearing an Outline 600
Manipulating the Display of an Outline 600
Hiding Outline Symbols 600
Displaying or Hiding Outline Levels 600
Formatting Outlines 602
Copying and Charting from Specific Outline Levels 603
From Here... 605

19 Creating Automatic Subtotals 607

What Are Automatic Subtotals? 607
Creating Simple Subtotals 607
Preparing for the Subtotals 608
Creating a Subtotal 608
Removing a Subtotal 610
Creating Advanced Subtotals 610
Creating Nested Subtotals 611
Using Multiple Summary Functions 611
Changing the Detail Level 612
Using Subtotals on Filtered Data 613
Formatting and Printing the Report 614
From Here... 615

20 Publishing Worksheets and Charts 617

Preparing the Worksheet for Presentation-Quality Output 619
Understanding Format and Layout 620
Giving Your Worksheet a Professional Look 620
Designing the Layout of Your Worksheet 623
Using White Space 624
Displaying the Page Border 624
Creating a Single- versus Multiple- Page Report 626
Laying Out and Formatting Your Worksheet 627
Using an Existing Worksheet versus Creating a New Worksheet 628
Using Columns and Rows Effectively 633
Using Different Levels of Label Headings 634
Using Columns and Rows for White Space 635
Centering Headings in the Worksheet 636
Centering Symbols Vertically in a Row 638
Determining Fonts and Point Sizes for Worksheets 638
Using Boldface, Italic, and Underlining for Emphasis 643
Using Lines, Boxes, and Shading for Emphasis 644
Publishing Your Worksheet in Color 646
Adding Charts to Your Worksheet 648
Using Named Styles and Automatic Formatting 651
From Here... 656

21 Creating Slide Show Presentations 659

Setting Up a Slide Show 660
Activating the Slide Show Add-In 660
Creating a New Slide Show 661
Editing Transitions 665
Reordering a Slide Show 665
Running a Slide Show 666
Starting a Slide Show 666
Stopping, Pausing, or Restarting a Slide Show 667
Putting the Final Polish on a Slide Show and Saving It 667
Saving a Slide Show 668
Modifying an Existing Slide Show 668
From Here... 669

22 Taking Advantage of Excel's Add-Ins 671

Installing Add-Ins 672
Using Add-In Programs 675
Starting Add-Ins 675
Using the Tools Add-Ins Command 676
Using the Analysis ToolPak 676
Adding an AutoSave Feature 677

Adding the Report Manager 678
Adding a Slide Show 678
Adding Optimization with the Solver 679
Adding the View Manager 679
From Here... 680

IV Analyzing the Worksheet 683

23 Manipulating and Analyzing Data 685

Manipulating Text 685
Using Formulas To Make Decisions 687
Making Simple Decisions 688
Making Complex Decisions 689
Checking Data Entry 690
Using Formulas To Look Up Data in Tables 693
Using LOOKUP Functions on Tables 693
Finding Exact Matches 695
Using MATCH and INDEX Functions 695
Calculating Tables of Answers 697
One Changing Variable and Many Formulas 698
Two Changing Variables and One Formula 700
Editing Data Tables 701
Calculating Data Tables 703
Analyzing Lists with Database Functions 703
Using Basic Database Functions 704
Summarizing Specific Data in a List 705
Combining Database Functions with Data Tables 707
Analyzing Trends 710
Calculating Trends with Fill Handles 711
Calculating Trends with the Data Series Command 713
Calculating Trends with Worksheet Functions 715
From Here... 717

24 Building Forms with Controls 719

What You Need to Know About Controls 720
Differences between Controls in a Worksheet and in a Dialog Box 720
Using the Forms Toolbar 721
How Controls Affect Cell Content and Calculations 723
Making Worksheets Appear Like Forms 723
Adding Controls to a Worksheet 724
Drawing the Control 725
Changing a Control's Format 725
Adding Check Boxes for TRUE/FALSE Responses 727
Adding Option Buttons for Multiple Choice 728
Adding Scrolling or Pull-Down Lists for Limited Text Choices 730

Adding Spinners To Change Numbers Quickly 733
Adding Scroll Bars To Enter Widely Ranging Numbers 734
Modifying Controls 736
Reshaping, Copying, or Deleting a Control 736
Enhancing Controls 737
Controlling Recalculation 737
Dimming or Blanking Controls 739
Printing Forms without the Control 739
Protecting a Form 740
From Here... 741

25 Linking, Embedding, and Consolidating Worksheets 743

Linking Pictures of Worksheet Cells 744
Desktop Publishing Layouts with Linked Pictures 744
Linking Cell Pictures 745
Updating Linked Cell Pictures 747
Changing Links to Linked Cell Pictures 749
Linking Workbook Cells and Ranges 750
What You Need To Know about Links 750
Linking Cells with Copy and Paste Link Commands 753
Linking Cells by Pointing 755
Linking Cells by Typing 757
Opening Linked Workbooks 758
Changing and Updating Links 759
Editing a Link Manually 761
Editing Arrays Made with Paste Link 762
Freezing Links 763
Saving Linked Workbooks 763
Consolidating Worksheets 763
Consolidating with 3D Formulas 765
Understanding Consolidation 766
Consolidating Worksheets by Physical Layout 767
Consolidating Worksheets by Row and Column Headings 770
Deleting or Editing Links 772
Linking Consolidated Worksheets 774
Formatting Consolidated Worksheets 774
Consolidating Worksheets Manually 776
From Here... 776

26 Auditing Workbooks and Worksheets 777

Troubleshooting Error Messages 777
Viewing Worksheet Information 779
Viewing Formulas 779
Viewing Cell Information 780
Finding Errors by Selecting Special Cells 781

Using Excel's Auditing Tools 783
    Tracing the Flow of Data and Formulas 783
    Using the Auditing Toolbar 786
Checking Spelling 787
    Using the Standard Dictionary 787
Adding Notes and Voice Messages 789
    Using Text Notes 790
    Using Sound Messages 792
From Here... 794

27 Solving with Goal Seeking and Solver 795

Deciding Which Tool To Use 795
Using the Goal Seek Feature 796
    Solving for a Single Solution 796
    Moving a Chart Marker To Seek a Goal 798
Finding the Best Solution with Solver 800
    Understanding When To Use Solver 801
    Creating the Sample Worksheet 802
    Installing Solver 804
    Solving for the Best Solution 805
    Changing a Limited Resource 809
    Changing Constraints 810
    Setting Integer Constraints 810
    Changing Operational Settings 811
    Printing Solver Reports 812
    Saving and Loading Solver Data 815
    Understanding the Solver Samples 816
From Here... 817

28 Testing Multiple Solutions with Scenarios 819

Creating Scenarios 819
    Using Named Cells 821
    Adding Named Scenarios 822
Switching between Scenarios 826
Editing a Scenario 826
Using Multiple Scenario Sets 828
Summarizing Scenarios in Tables 830
    Creating a Scenario Summary Report 830
    Creating a Scenario Pivot Table Report 831
Managing Scenarios 832
    Merging Scenarios 833
    Managing Scenario Names 834
    Using Scenario Manager in a WorkGroup 834
From Here... 836

29 Using the Analysis ToolPak 837

Using Data Analysis Tools Commands 838
    Creating Realistic Sample Data 838
    Creating Histograms and Frequency Distributions 842

Smoothing Time-Series Data 846
Overview of ToolPak Commands and Functions 850
From Here... 859

V Managing Lists or Databases 861

30 Designing a List or Database 863

What Is a List? 863
Identifying the Parts of a List 866
Identifying the Database Range 867
Identifying the Criteria Range 869
Identifying the Extract Range 870
Choosing the Contents for a List 871
Organizing Your List 872
From Here... 873

31 Entering Data in a List or Database 875

Entering the Field Names 876
Naming the List or Database Range 877
Entering the Data 879
Using the Data Form 879
Entering Data Directly 881
Speeding Up Data Entry 884
Formatting Your List or Database 885
From Here... 886

32 Sorting Data 887

What You Need To Know about Sorting 887
Sorting by Command 890
Sorting with the Toolbar 892
Returning a Sort to the Original Order 892
Sorting in a Special Order 893
Sorting by Date and Time 894
Sorting Account Codes, Service Codes, or Part Numbers 895
Sorting on More Than Three Fields 896
Sorting Calculated Results 897
Rearranging Worksheet, List, or Database Columns 897
From Here... 900

33 Finding, Filtering, and Editing Lists and Databases 901

Specifying Criteria 902
Finding Simple or Exact Matches 902
Using Numeric Comparisons 904
Finding Date and Time Matches 905

Finding Near Matches with Wild Cards 906
Matching Multiple Criteria with AND and OR Conditions 907
Choosing the Best Search Method 908
Using the Data Form 909
Finding Data with the Data Form 909
Editing with the Data Form 912
Using the AutoFilter 913
Finding Data with the AutoFilter 914
Finding Near Matches or AND/OR Matches 916
Using the Advanced Filter 916
Understanding the Advanced Filter 918
Finding Data with the Advanced Filter 919
Using Multiple Comparisons in a Criteria Range 921
Calculating What You Want To Find 923
Viewing and Editing Filtered Lists 928
From Here... 931

34 Working with Filtered Data 933

Editing, Sorting, Subtotaling, and Charting the Filtered Data 933
Editing Filtered Data 934
Sorting, Subtotaling, and Printing Filtered Data 934
Charting Filtered Data 934
Copying Filtered Data to a New Location 935
Creating a Copy with AutoFilter 936
Copying to the Same Sheet with an Advanced Filter 936
Copying Filtered Data between Worksheets or Workbooks 942
Maintaining Data 945
Backing Up Data 945
Deleting a Group of Records 946
From Here... 946

35 Retrieving Data from External Databases 947

Understanding Microsoft Query and ODBC 947
Database Types and Terms 949
Data Sources and Result Sets 950
What Databases Can You Query? 951
Starting Microsoft Query 951
Installing Microsoft Query and the Microsoft Query Add-In 951
Installing the Microsoft Query Add-In in Excel 952
Starting Microsoft Query from Excel 953
Starting Microsoft Query from Program Manager 953

Creating a Query 954
- Specifying or Creating the Data Source 954
- Understanding the Query Window 956
- Creating the Query Definition 958
- Executing a Query 963
- Saving a Query 963
- Closing a Query 964
- Opening a New Query Window 964
- Using a Saved Query Definition 964

Working with SQL Queries 965
Joining Multiple Tables 965
- Adding Join Lines 967
- Removing Join Lines 968

Working with Data in the Result Set 968
- Working with Columns and Rows 968
- Sorting Data 970
- Working with Records and Fields 972
- Formatting Data 973
- Editing Data 973

Transferring Data to Excel 975
- Returning Data from Microsoft Query 976
- Pasting or Linking Data from Microsoft Query 977
- Opening Worksheets Linked to Databases 980

Closing Microsoft Query 980
Moving Data and Query Definitions to Another Worksheet or Workbook 980
Editing Existing Query Results in a Worksheet 981
Updating Query Results 981
From Here... 982

36 Using Pivot Tables 983

Working with Pivot Tables 984
Understanding Pivot Tables 986
Creating a Pivot Table 988
Editing Your Pivot Table 994
Updating a Pivot Table 995
Specifying the Source Data 996
- Using a List or Database in the Workbook 996
- Using a List or Database in Another Workbook 997
- Using External Databases 997
- Converting Crosstab Tables from Version 4 998

Filtering Data by Creating Page Fields 999
Consolidating Data Using a Pivot Table 1001
Using More Than One Data Field 1005
Creating a Pivot Table from Another Pivot Table 1006
Creating a Chart from a Pivot Table 1007
Saving Files with Pivot Tables 1008
From Here... 1009

37 Analyzing and Reporting with Pivot Tables 1011

Adding and Removing Data 1011
- Adding New Rows, Columns, or Pages 1012
- Removing Rows, Columns, or Pages 1014
- Adding Data To Analyze 1014

Reorganizing the Pivot Table 1015
- Flipping the Orientation 1015
- Moving Individual Items within a Field 1016
- Moving Data Fields 1017
- Grouping Items 1018

Analyzing the Data 1027
- Analyzing Pivot Table Data with Charts 1027
- Sorting Items 1028
- Paging or Filtering a Pivot Table 1028
- Managing Totals and Subtotals 1030
- Using Other Functions for Data Analysis 1033

Formatting the Pivot Table 1037
- AutoFormatting Pivot Tables 1037
- Formatting Numbers 1038
- Changing Field and Item Names 1039

From Here... 1039

VI Integrating Excel with Other Applications 1041

38 Using Excel with Windows Applications 1043

Understanding the Clipboard 1044

Copying Data between Applications 1045
- Copying and Pasting Text 1045
- Copying and Pasting Charts, Images, and Screens 1046

Linking Data between Applications 1047
- Linking Excel to Data in Other Windows Applications 1048
- Turning Links On and Off 1049
- Saving External Link Values 1049

Embedding Data from Other Applications into Worksheets 1050
- Inserting New Embedded Objects 1051
- Inserting Existing Files as Embedded Objects 1054
- Pasting Embedded Objects 1055
- Embedding Objects as Icons 1057
- Converting Embedded Objects 1057
- Printing Embedded Objects 1057

Editing Linked and Embedded Objects 1058

Examples of Transferring and Linking Data 1059
- Copying Excel Screen Shots into PageMaker 1060

Linking Charts and Tables into Word for Windows 1061
Embedding Objects in a Worksheet 1066
From Here... 1068

39 Using Excel with DOS and Mainframe Applications 1069

Understanding How Windows Runs DOS Applications 1070
Copying and Pasting between Applications 1070
Copying and Pasting in Standard Mode 1070
Copying and Pasting in 386 Enhanced Mode 1072
Exporting Data 1074
Understanding File Formats 1074
Saving Excel Worksheets in a Different Format 1076
Exporting Text 1077
Linking Excel Data to WordPerfect 6 1077
Exporting Files to Macintosh Excel 1079
Importing Data 1079
Opening Files Saved in Another File Format 1079
Importing Data from Mainframe Computers 1080
Importing Text Files with the Convert Text Import Wizard 1081
Separating (Parsing) Text into Columns with the Text Wizard 1086
From Here... 1089

VII Customizing the Excel Screen

40 Customizing Excel 1093

Exploring Customization Features 1093
Creating Your Own Colors 1095
Setting Preferences 1098
Operating with 1-2-3 Keys 1098
Moving the Active Cell after Entering Data 1099
Editing Data Directly in a Cell 1099
Customizing Excel with the Windows Control Panel 1099
Changing the Screen Appearance 1101
Changing the Desktop 1102
Customizing the Mouse 1103
Changing International Character Sets 1104
From Here... 1106

41 Creating Custom Toolbars and Menus 1107

Customizing and Creating Toolbars 1108
Adding Buttons 1108
Reorganizing Buttons 1110
Creating Your Own Toolbar 1111

Assigning a Macro or Visual Basic Procedures to a Button ... 1112
Drawing Your Own Button Faces ... 1113
Transferring Toolbars to Other Users ... 1115
Creating Custom Menus ... 1117
Running the Menu Editor ... 1117
Understanding Menu Terms ... 1118
Building Menus from the Top Down ... 1120
Creating a New Menu ... 1120
Adding Items to a Menu ... 1121
Creating a Submenu ... 1122
Assigning a Procedure to an Item ... 1123
Creating a New Menu Bar ... 1124
From Here... ... 1125

42 Creating Templates and Controlling Excel's Startup 1127

Creating Workbook and Worksheet Templates ... 1128
Understanding the Concept of Templates ... 1128
Creating and Saving a Workbook Template ... 1128
Creating Workbooks from Templates ... 1129
Creating Autotemplates ... 1129
Editing Templates ... 1130
Inserting Sheet Templates ... 1130
Controlling How Excel Starts ... 1132
Controlling How Excel Starts in the Windows Program Manager ... 1133
Creating Custom Icons for Startup ... 1134
Starting Excel with a Group of Workbooks ... 1135
Running Macros and Procedures on Startup ... 1136
From Here... ... 1136

VIII Automating with Visual Basic for Applications 1137

43 Introducing Visual Basic for Applications 1139

Major Differences ... 1140
Understanding the Visual Basic Object Model ... 1141
Using Containers To Specify Objects ... 1142
Using `With` To Reduce Code Size ... 1143
Changing Objects without Selecting Them ... 1144
Getting and Giving Information Using Parallel Syntax ... 1144
Referencing Ranges and Cells Is Easier in Visual Basic ... 1145
Using Variables To Store Information ... 1147
Storing Objects ... 1147
Creating Dialog Boxes in Visual Basic for Applications ... 1148
Creating Menus and Toolbars ... 1149

Getting In-Depth Help On-Line 1150
Debugging Tools 1150
Running Excel 4 Macros in Visual Basic 1151
From Here... 1151

44 Recording and Modifying VBA Modules 1153

Automating with Visual Basic for Applications 1153
Starting the Recorder 1155
Recording a Macro 1157
Stopping the Recorder 1158
Examining the Procedure 1159
Running the Procedure 1161
Attaching Procedures to Buttons, Menus, and Objects 1162
Understanding and Editing the Procedure 1163
Using Comments 1164
Procedure Headers and Footers 1165
Controlling Characteristics 1165
Accessing Worksheet Cells 1166
Getting Data with a Data-Entry Box 1168
Displaying a Message 1169
From Here... 1171

45 Programming in Visual Basic for Applications 1173

Learning More with On-Line Help 1173
Understanding Objects 1174
Accessing Objects 1175
Understanding Classes and Collections 1177
Accessing Collections 1178
Understanding Properties 1179
Accessing Properties 1180
Understanding Methods 1182
Accessing Methods 1183
Finding Objects with the Object Browser 1184
Understanding Functions and Procedures 1184
Subprocedures 1184
User-Defined Functions 1185
Creating an Application 1188
Understanding Variables and Assignment Statements 1194
Using Declarations and Visual Basic Data Types 1194
Arrays 1196
User-Defined Types 1197
The Scope of Variables 1198
Constants 1198
Branching and Decision Making 1198
Block If Statements 1199
Logical Formulas 1200
`Select Case` 1201

Accessing Worksheet Cells 1201
Calling Procedures 1203
Using Loops 1204
`For/Next` 1204
`While/Wend` 1205
`Do/Loop` 1206
`For Each` 1207
Accessing Disk Files 1207
Using Excel's Dialog Boxes 1211
Creating Custom Dialog Boxes 1212
Using the Debugging Tools 1217
Using Break Mode 1218
Setting Breakpoints 1218
The Debug Window 1219
The Immediate Pane 1219
The Watch Pane and Watch Variables 1220
The Step Commands 1220
The Calls Window 1221
From Here... 1221

46 Exploring Visual Basic for Applications Examples 1223

Creating Command Procedures 1223
Examining Procedures 1224
Examining Worksheet Data with If Statements 1224
Entering Data with a Location and Offset 1225
Printing Worksheet Cells with a Procedure 1227
Testing for an Open Workbook and Opening It 1228
Moving Objects on the Worksheet 1229
OLE Automation 1231
Creating User Defined Functions 1232
Using Worksheet Functions in Visual Basic 1232
Selecting a Calculation with an Index 1233
Passing Excel Arrays 1234
From Here... 1236

IX Appendix 1239

Support Services 1239

Microsoft Corporation 1239
CompuServe 1239
Que Corporation 1240
Ron Person & Co. 1240

Index 1241

Introduction

Windows has created almost as much change in the use of computers as the introduction of IBM's first personal computer. At the printing of this book, Windows is selling more than one million copies per month, and the most productive and powerful of applications used on personal computers is the electronic spreadsheet.

Excel is now the best-selling spreadsheet in the world, for Windows-, Macintosh-, and DOS-based computers combined. When Excel 5 was released, more than four million copies of Excel were in use. Major magazines and consultants have proclaimed Microsoft Excel as the easiest worksheet to use and yet the most powerful.

With the release of Excel 5 and Pentium-based computers, you can have desktop computational power that rivals dedicated minicomputers and mainframe Executive Information Systems of just five years ago.

Reviewing Excel Features

The following sections present Excel's major strengths and capabilities. Features new to Excel 5 are indicated by the version 5 icon in the margin. New features are described in the first chapter, "What's New in Excel 5 for Windows."

Lotus 1-2-3 Capability

You don't need to worry about converting from 1-2-3 to Excel—the task is easy. Excel reads and writes all versions of 1-2-3 worksheets, including formatting. Excel even runs 1-2-3 Release 2.01 macros, so you can continue to use 1-2-3 macros. Excel also loads 1-2-3 graphs and 3-D worksheets; you don't lose productivity, you gain significantly more.

You can set up Excel to accept 1-2-3 navigation keys, database methods, or menu choices. When you use the 1-2-3 command demonstrator, Excel accepts 1-2-3 menu choices and then demonstrates how to perform the equivalent process in Excel. As you watch the Excel demonstration, you learn how to use the program. By using your 1-2-3 knowledge with new Excel worksheets, you can continue to perform productive work and learn Excel simultaneously.

Operating Ease

Excel is one of the easiest worksheets to use, and it remains the most powerful worksheet. This paradox is possible because of Excel's toolbar and shortcut menus. Microsoft has one of the world's largest software-usability testing laboratories.

Microsoft's Office Suite Strategy guarantees that the most frequently used Microsoft applications can work together sharing data, using common menus and toolbars, as well as using a common user programming language—Visual Basic for Applications.

Drag and drop is a concept so beneficial that, when you see it work, you wonder why it didn't become a standard years ago. With drag-and-drop technology, you can select a group of cells and then use the mouse to drag the cells (or a copy of the cells) to a new location. When you release the mouse button, the cells drop onto the cells beneath the mouse pointer. In Excel 5, you can even drag and drop between applications compatible with OLE 2.

A concept similar to drag and drop is the *fill handle*. By dragging the fill handle, you can copy formulas to adjacent cells. The fill handle reduces a multiple-step process to a quick drag with the mouse.

Toolbars are strips or rectangles of tools (buttons). Each button represents a familiar command. By just clicking a button, you can shortcut many keystrokes. When you use a mouse with the toolbars, you have quick access to the most frequently used commands in a worksheet. Microsoft Excel comes with a predefined set of toolbars, but you can add buttons to, or remove them from, the toolbars and even create toolbars to which you can add buttons you create.

Shortcut menus enable you to click the right mouse button (in this book, the term, *right click* is used) on a worksheet or chart item; the most relevant commands appear immediately under the mouse pointer; and the commands you use most frequently are immediately accessible.

Data entry controls what you are used to seeing in dialog boxes, such as pull-down lists, check boxes, and option buttons can be placed directly on a worksheet. An intermediate-level user can create sophisticated data entry forms. You don't need to know programming. It's as easy as drawing a button and then making selections in a dialog box.

Workbooks enable you to keep collections of related worksheets, charts, and programming in one file. You no longer need to be concerned about having a complete collection of all interlinking files.

Worksheet Publishing

Excel is easily the leader in worksheet publishing capabilities. Besides having all the formatting capability of desktop publishing software, Excel is the first worksheet to include a built-in spelling checker. By using the spelling checker, you can feel confident that the quality of your analysis isn't compromised by poor spelling.

Layout and worksheet design also are easy in Excel, because Excel includes a zoom feature. Zooming enables you to reduce or magnify the view of the worksheet so that you can see a close-up view to adjust formats or a compressed view to see the big picture. If you frequently view different areas of the document by using different display settings or print different areas with various print settings, you also may be interested in the new View Manager, which enables you to give different names to each view or printing setup.

The templates and cell styles available in Excel can help you greatly if you need to create a frequently used worksheet or a worksheet that presents a standardized appearance. Templates act as master documents that contain worksheet layouts, text, formulas, cell styles, custom menus, and macros. When opened, a template produces a new worksheet that contains everything in the original template. You must save the document to a new name, which preserves the template as a master.

Styles are a powerful feature found in professional-level word processors. With a style, you can name a collection of formatting commands and apply all the formats by selecting this style name. A style named Total, for example, may contain the formats Arial 12 point, bold, right align, currency with two decimal places, and a double-line upper border. Changing the definition of a style changes all cells formatted with this style.

Excel 5 includes AutoFormat, a collection of predefined formatting combinations that you can apply to tables of data. AutoFormat saves you a great deal of time when formatting budgets, forecasts, or lists.

If you need a numeric or date format that isn't on the list of formats, you can design custom formats. You also can add text in a format so that numbers include abbreviations, such as 5.678 kph. You also can design formats so that numbers or dates within ranges appear in different colors.

Excel's printing preview capabilities show you how print is positioned on the page. You can zoom in to see the detail of character and drawing positions. While in the preview, you also can drag column and margin markers to reposition columns and change print margins.

Analytical Tools

Although Excel always has been known for offering more analytical tools than other worksheets, new analytical tools in Excel make analysis easier for novice users and expand the upper limits for scientists, engineers, and financial analysts.

Anyone who occasionally tests many different inputs and their results can easily appreciate the Scenario Manager. By using the Scenario Manager, you can name a set of input variables. After you have multiple names of inputs you want tested, you can run the Scenario Manager, which generates a report that shows all the different inputs and their results.

Some problems must be solved for an optimum solution. For these problems, Excel includes the Solver. The Solver is an add-in program provided with Excel that uses linear and nonlinear programming techniques to find the best solution to a problem.

Excel's hundreds of built-in functions, which are predefined formulas, were expanded with the addition of the Analysis ToolPak. The Analysis ToolPak is another add-in program provided with Excel. If a job requires extensive statistical or financial and investment analysis, install the Analysis ToolPak when you install Excel.

Graphics Features

You can perform many kinds of drawing on Excel worksheets. By using the drawing tools on the toolbars, you can draw lines, arrows, rectangles, ovals, circles, and arcs. You also can draw freehand and then reshape the freehand drawing by dragging lines and corners into new locations. You can create text boxes that you can position anywhere on the page. All the colors in the custom color palette and many shades of gray are available for emphasis. The graphic features are like getting a high-level drawing program with Excel.

You can embed charts or cell pictures in a worksheet. You can take the cell pictures or charts from the same or from a different worksheet. When you change data, the embedded charts or cell pictures update, which enables you to position pieces of worksheet or charts in any arrangement on a worksheet. You can arrange these pieces in the same way that a desktop publisher builds newsletters or annual reports.

With Object Linking and Embedding (OLE), you can embed drawings and graphics from dedicated graphics programs. Embedded graphics are more than images in the worksheet; these images include the actual data necessary to re-create the graphic. Excel works with both OLE 1- and OLE 2-compatible applications. You can edit an OLE 1 object by double-clicking the embedded graphic to start and open the application that originally created this graphic. When you double-click an object from an OLE 2 application, Excel's menus and toolbars actually change to the menus and toolbars of the application that created the object. When you click outside the object, the Excel menus and toolbars return.

Linking and Consolidating Features

Excel is flexible enough to adapt to many business situations. Within Excel, you can link worksheets to fit the way you work. You can link cells or ranges of cells between open worksheets or worksheets on disk.

When you need to gather data from multiple divisions or different times to a single worksheet, you can use the new 3-D formulas in Excel 5 or Excel's consolidation feature. With Excel's 3-D formulas, you can insert many worksheets into one workbook. One 3-D formula can give a consolidated total from all the sheets by *spearing* through all the cells at the same location in each sheet. You also can use Excel's consolidation feature. Excel can consolidate data from Excel or 1-2-3 worksheets. By using one method, you can link worksheets according to the contents of cells in a specific location. All cells at the top left corner of a range, for example, move together. One competing worksheet uses this method, but the feature is not flexible because all worksheets must be designed in exactly the same manner—a rare occurrence in the real world.

Excel's more flexible method uses the row and column labels to the left of and above the areas to consolidate. Excel examines the row and column name of each item in all the worksheets and works with the items that are identical. Unique items are given a unique position in the consolidation. This flexibility is helpful when some divisions or departments have different budget line times or different products.

Charting Capabilities

Excel has over one hundred chart formats from which to choose, but building a chart is extremely simple when you use Excel's ChartWizard. The ChartWizard guides you through the process of building charts. As you select alternatives, you can see the effect of the choices you make. At any time, you can back up and make an alternative selection.

When you format your chart, you can use Excel's AutoFormat feature for charting, which makes it easy to see how a chart will appear before you are finished. You even can create user-defined chart types. After you select a type of chart and basic format, you can use all of Excel's charting tools. You can drag the legend to any position on the chart, orient text sideways, use up to 256 different fonts, and link numbers and text back to worksheet cells. Excel's charting capability rivals the capability of dedicated charting programs. You can even draw on a chart.

By using a chart as the data entry device, Excel even enables you to solve worksheet problems. In line, bar, and column charts, you can drag a *chart marker* (line symbol or top of bar or column) to a new location. If the marker reflects the result of a formula in a worksheet, Excel asks for the cell that you want to manipulate to accomplish the desired result. This feature provides a way to back into solutions and uses the chart to specify the final answer.

Database Capabilities

A database is like a card-file system that stores information. Because so many worksheet problems involve a collection of historical sales, marketing, engineering, or scientific information, Excel has both built-in database capabilities and the capability of linking to external databases of many different formats. Excel's new database features filter information directly in the worksheet, hiding data you don't want to see and displaying information you are interested in.

Besides Excel's previous capability of doing statistical analysis of a database's contents, you now have the power of the pivot table. Pivot tables enable you to view statistics about the contents of your data in a table format. With simple drag-and-drop procedures, you can completely change the topics being analyzed, the time span in which you are interested, and so on.

When you need to work with extremely large databases or databases stored on a mainframe computer or a local area network server, you may want to use Microsoft Query, a program that comes with Excel. Microsoft Query adds commands to Excel that enable you to link worksheets to large databases outside of the worksheet.

Worksheet Outlines

Excel contains an outlining feature, which is valuable to anyone who must create extensive reports. The outline enables you to quickly expand and collapse databases and worksheets so that you see only the level of information you need to print or display on-screen.

Outlining also enables you to *drill down*. When you build a summary report by consolidating other worksheets, you have the choice of maintaining links from the source worksheets to the summary. When you double-click a summary number in the consolidation worksheet, Excel drills down and opens the source worksheet.

Visual Basic for Applications and Excel 4 Macro Language

Excel is the first application to include Microsoft's Visual Basic for Applications, a user-oriented language with a foundation in BASIC. Eventually, all Microsoft applications in Office Suite either will contain Visual Basic or will be controllable by Visual Basic. If you have an investment in existing Excel 4 macros or macro knowledge, you have plenty of time for transition. Excel 5 and future Excel versions will continue to support Excel 4 macros. In fact, in Excel 5 you can either program in Visual Basic for Applications or record in a manner similar to Excel 4 macros.

You can easily customize Excel by recording commands and procedures and then assigning those commands and procedures to a shortcut key combination or to button on a toolbar that you can select. You also can go far beyond the easy-to-use Macro Recorder, however.

If you are inexperienced with programming, you can use Excel's recorder to create automated procedures to save time. To run these procedures, you press a shortcut key, choose the macro or procedure name from a list, or click a *button* on the worksheet.

Using This Book

Using Excel Version 5 for Windows, Special Edition, contains eight parts and an appendix. The following list presents an overview of the parts in *Using Excel Version 5 for Windows*, Special Edition:

Part I, "Everyday Worksheet Tasks," presents the basics of using Excel, how to enter data and formulas, copy and move contents, organize worksheets within the workbooks, format using Excel's powerful formatting capability, and print the results.

Part II, "Creating and Formatting Charts," shows you how to create, format, and manipulate charts. The chapters in this section cover topics that range from basic charts, to charts embedded in worksheets, to advanced charting tricks.

Part III, "Optimizing Excel," teaches you how to use Excel's graphics and reporting features to present your results with a memorable impact.

Part IV, "Analyzing the Worksheet," explains how to use some of the powerful analytical and reporting capabilities in Excel. You learn how to analyze databases, create data entry forms, solve complex worksheets for the best answer and more.

Part V, "Managing Lists or Databases," shows you how to create and maintain a database. The chapters in this section teach you how to enter, edit, sort, find, and copy information from a database. One chapter explains how to retrieve data from databases outside of Excel by using Microsoft Query.

Part VI, "Integrating Excel with Other Applications," shows you how to use Excel with other popular applications, whether you use Windows- or DOS-based applications.

Part VII, "Customizing Excel," explains how to customize the toolbars, create buttons on toolbars, and modify the menus. You also see how to create templates so you don't have to re-create frequently used worksheets or charts.

Part VIII, "Automating with Visual Basic for Applications," shows you how to record and modify simple Visual Basic procedures. You learn how to ask users for input, display custom dialog boxes, and perform more advanced programming.

The Appendix explains where to get additional support via telephone or training.

Conventions Used in This Book

Certain conventions are used in *Using Excel Version 5 for Windows*, Special Edition, to help you more easily use this book and understand Excel's concepts. The following sections include examples of these conventions to help you distinguish among the different elements.

Special Typefaces and Representations

Special typefaces in *Using Excel Version 5 for Windows*, Special Edition, include the following:

Type	Meaning
italics	New terms or phrases when initially defined; function and Visual Basic syntax placeholders
boldface	Information you are asked to type, including menu and dialog box options that appear underlined on-screen
`special type`	Direct quotations of words that appear on-screen or in a figure; Visual Basic code

Elements printed in uppercase include names such as SALES, functions such as `SUM( )`, and cell references such as A1:G20. Also presented in uppercase are file names such as STATUS.XLS.

In most cases, keys are represented as they appear on the keyboard. The arrow keys usually are represented by name (for example, the *up-arrow key*). The Print Screen key is abbreviated PrtSc; Page Up is PgUp; Insert is Ins; and so on. On your keyboard, these key names may be spelled out or abbreviated differently.

When two keys appear together with a plus sign, such as Shift+Ins, press and hold the first key as you press the second key. When two keys appear together without a plus sign, such as End Home, press and release the first key before you press the second key.

Note

This paragraph format indicates additional information that may help you avoid problems or that should be considered in using the described features.

Tip

This paragraph format suggests easier or alternative methods of executing a procedure.

Caution

This paragraph format warns the reader of hazardous procedures (for example, activities that delete files).

Margin Icons

This book uses a special margin icon to indicate new Excel 5 features or tasks you can perform only in the current version. If the icon appears next to the first paragraph in a section, all the information in that section is new.

Additional icons appear in the margin to indicate that the procedure described in the text includes instructions for using the appropriate toolbar buttons in Excel 5.

Special Sections

Using Excel Version 5 for Windows, Special Edition, uses cross-references, called "For Related Information," to help you access other parts of the book. At the end of major topic sections, related tasks you may need to perform are listed in the margin by section name and page number.

In addition, troubleshooting sections are provided in most chapters to help you find solutions to common problems encountered with the Excel procedures covered in that section of the book.

Part I

Everyday Worksheet Tasks

1 What's New in Excel 5 for Windows

2 Getting Around in Excel and Windows

3 Navigating and Selecting in a Workbook

4 Entering and Editing Data

5 Working with Formulas

6 Using Functions

7 Moving or Copying Data and Formulas

8 Reorganizing Workbooks and Sheets

9 Managing Files

10 Formatting Worksheets

11 Printing Worksheets

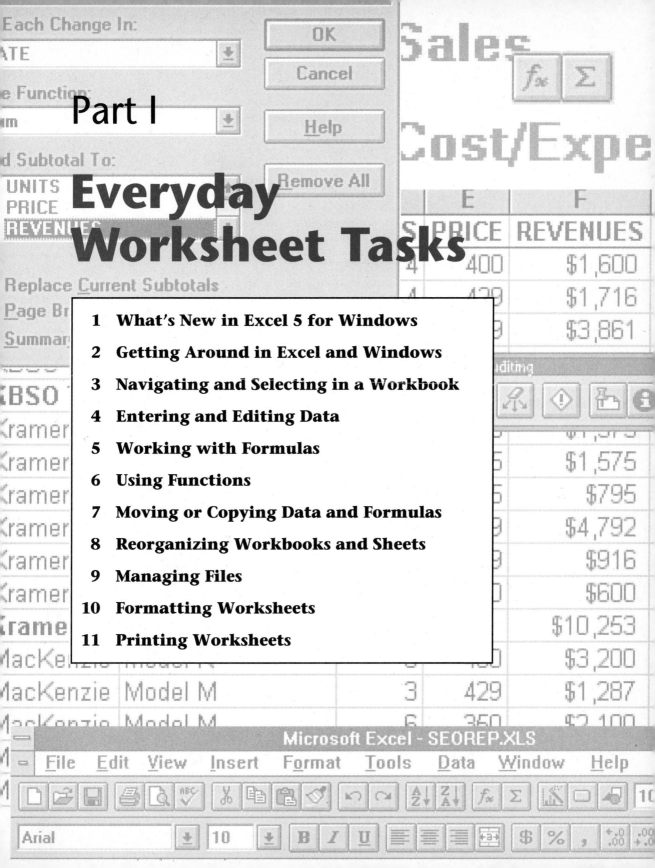

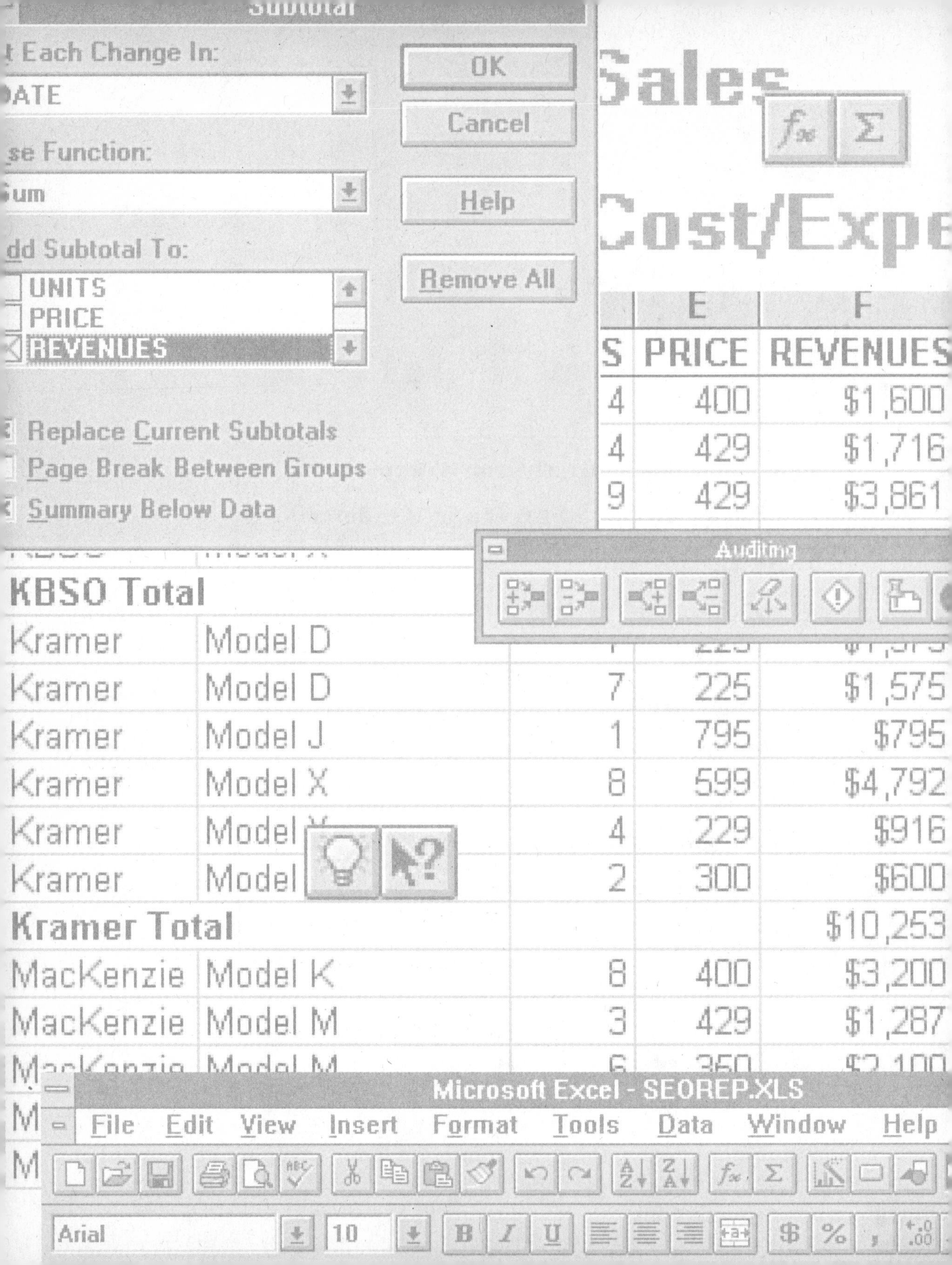
Subtotal
t Each Change In:
DATE
OK
Cancel
se Function:
Sum
Help
dd Subtotal To:
UNITS
PRICE
REVENUES
Remove All
Replace Current Subtotals
Page Break Between Groups
Summary Below Data
Sales
Cost/Expe
E
F
S PRICE REVENUES
4 400 $1,600
4 429 $1,716
9 429 $3,861
Auditing
KBSO Total
Kramer Model D
Kramer Model D 7 225 $1,575
Kramer Model J 1 795 $795
Kramer Model X 8 599 $4,792
Kramer Model 4 229 $916
Kramer Model 2 300 $600
Kramer Total $10,253
MacKenzie Model K 8 400 $3,200
MacKenzie Model M 3 429 $1,287
Microsoft Excel - SEOREP.XLS
File Edit View Insert Format Tools Data Window Help
Arial
10
B I U

Chapter 1

What's New in Excel 5 for Windows

Excel Version 5 for Windows is a major upgrade of the previous release of Excel for Windows. Excel Version 5 for Windows offers many impressive new features.

Microsoft has made three kinds of changes in Excel 5—features that improve accessibility, that simplify everyday tasks, and that were made more powerful. Of course, some improvements do not easily fall into one category or another because all the new features combine power with accessibility.

Some new Excel 5 features covered in this chapter include the following:

- A redesigned user interface with simpler and standardized menus
- Workbooks that contain multiple worksheets
- Simpler database extracts with AutoFilter
- Worksheet auditing capabilities
- Capability of examining data from different points of view using pivot tables

New Features That Provide Better Accessibility

Microsoft understands that program features are not important unless you can use them. In Excel 5, the features you use most often have been made more accessible and much easier to use.

Simpler and Standardized Menus

The menu for Excel 5 has been completely redesigned. The new menu looks very much like the Word 6 for Windows menu. Because many people who use Excel also use Word for Windows, this similarity makes learning both applications easier. In figure 1.1, notice the similarity of menus and toolbars between the applications.

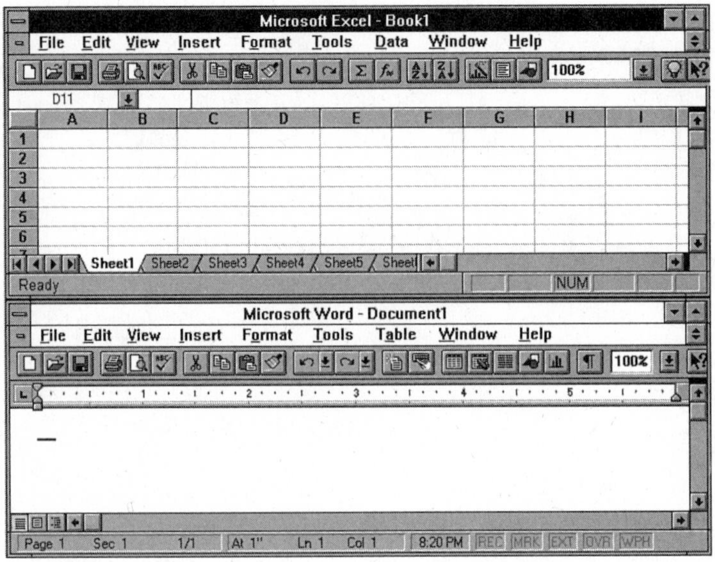

Fig. 1.1
Menus in Microsoft's major applications are becoming simpler and standardized.

Tabbed Dialog Boxes

For Related Information

- "Choosing Commands," p. 38

Excel has so many features and options that there is no way that all the features can be available from the menu. Instead, Microsoft kept the menus short and made hundreds of options available in dialog boxes. Because so many options are available, many dialog boxes now have options grouped together into tabbed *cards* within the dialog box. You can switch among groups of options by clicking the appropriate card's tab, or by pressing the Tab key until a tab is selected and then pressing the left- or right-arrow keys to activate a different tab.

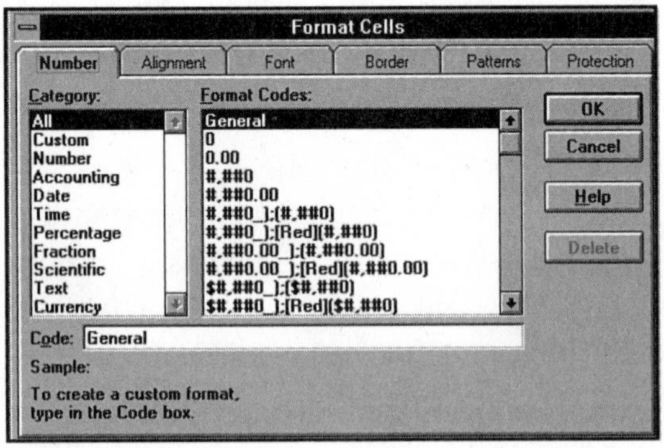

Fig. 1.2
With Excel's new tabbed dialog boxes, you have quick access to many options.

TipWizard

Applications such as Excel, with pull-down menus and tabbed dialog boxes, are becoming easier to use, but when you gain proficiency in certain tasks, you may find that you want faster, more productive ways to work. Although you can use the Search button in Help to learn about Excel's many shortcuts, a fun way to learn shortcuts is to watch the TipWizard, located in the Standard toolbar. The TipWizard resembles a light bulb. When the bulb in the Standard toolbar is lit, the TipWizard has been "watching you work" and has a tip to make your work easier or faster. Click the TipWizard button to see its current tip. Figure 1.3 shows the TipWizard button and one of its tips.

For Related Information

- "Working in Dialog Boxes," p. 48
- "Getting Help," p. 55

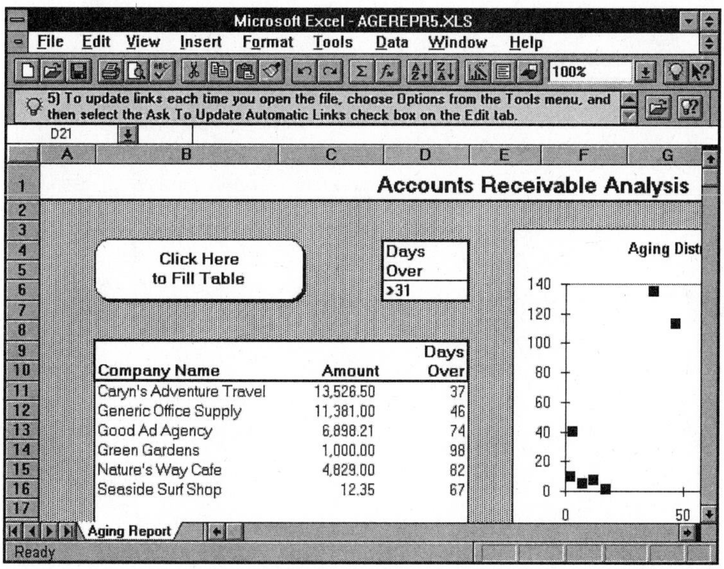

Fig. 1.3
Learn helpful tips about Excel from the TipWizard to make your work easier and faster.

ToolTips

Because so many buttons are on the toolbars in Excel 5, you may have trouble remembering them at first. Fortunately, the ToolTips feature is available. Just poise the pointer over a tool, and a brief caption is displayed beside the pointer, telling you what the button does.

For Related Information

- "Customizing and Creating Toolbars," p. 1108

Tear-Off Palettes

Some of Excel 4's formatting features seem cumbersome to use because you have to continually go back and rechoose the same commands. In Excel 5, you can drag a palette from the borders, colors, patterns, or font colors buttons. Just click the button and drag down to *tear off* a palette that contains the options. The palette stays on-screen so that you can click a cell and then click a color. This feature makes formatting remarkably quick.

For Related Information

- "Using Tear-Off Palettes from Toolbars," p. 47

Full Screen View

Some computer users are distracted by menus, toolbars, and scroll bars. If you feel this distraction, you may want to work in Excel's new Full Screen view. To display the full screen, choose the **V**iew F**u**ll Screen command. Return to the previous view by clicking the Full Screen button that appears, or by choosing the **V**iew F**u**ll Screen command again. Figure 1.4 shows a full screen view. Notice that minimal screen elements appear.

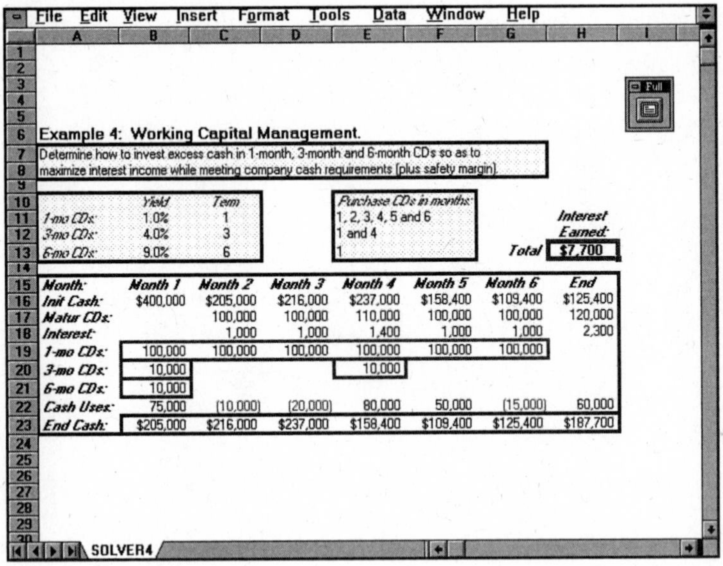

Fig. 1.4
The new full screen view makes your workbook appear as though you are working on a spreadsheet that fills the entire screen.

New Features That Simplify Everyday Tasks

For Related Information

- "Displaying the Worksheet Full Screen," p. 533

Making Excel easier to use makes your work life a little easier. Although Excel's more powerful features are useful for an occasional special project, the majority of work is done by repeating the same common tasks. Excel 5 has improved many of these common tasks, such as finding files and grouping worksheets.

Workbooks That Contain Multiple Worksheets

For Related Information

- "Selecting and Moving between Sheets," p. 67

One of the most significant changes to Excel 5 is the incorporation of workbooks. *Workbooks* are containers that hold one or more sheets. The different types of sheets available are worksheets, charts, Excel 4 macro sheets, Visual Basic modules, and dialog sheets. Keeping all sheets related to a given project or model in one file reduces file management and the need to use linking formulas. Figure 1.5 shows the tabs at the bottom of a workbook that enable you to switch sheets.

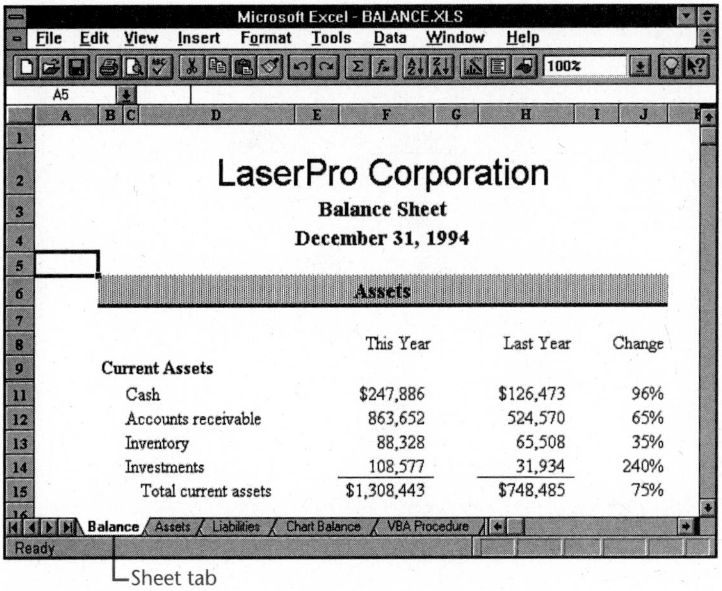

Fig. 1.5
Click a tab at the bottom of a workbook to change sheets.

Better File Management

It doesn't take long to accumulate hundreds of workbooks on your hard disk, which makes finding a specific workbook tedious and frustrating. Excel's new Find File command lets you find files according to various characteristics so that you no longer have to decipher inscrutable eight-letter file names. You even can preview a file's contents. This feature works exactly as Find File does in Word 6 for Windows. Figure 1.6 shows the Find File dialog box when previewing files.

For Related Information

- "Finding Files," p. 284

Custom Data Series

Excel 4's AutoFill feature amazed everyone with its ability to fill in the labels of the months in a year or quarters in a business cycle. Excel 5 goes a step beyond this by letting you create your own custom series that it recognizes and fills in. For example, if you type in the name of one regional office from a series you defined and then drag across additional cells, Excel fills in the other regional offices.

For Related Information

- "Creating Series of Text and Headings," p. 116

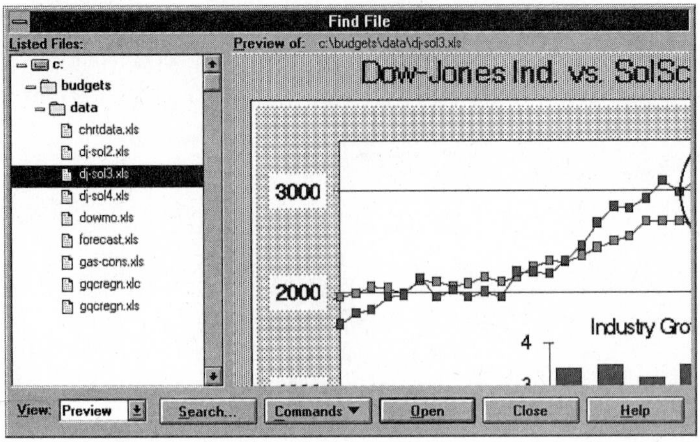

Fig. 1.6
Finding and previewing files is significantly easier with the new Find File feature.

Function Wizard

Excel has over 400 built-in formulas, known as functions. Excel 4 would help you by pasting into a formula the name and arguments required for the function, but still required you to know the argument definitions and how the function worked. In Excel 5, the Function Wizard guides you by prompting for the type of data needed.

For Related Information

- "Pasting Names and Functions into Formulas," p. 143

Individual Character Formatting

You can now mix character formatting within a cell. Just select the text in the formula or text string, and choose a font formatting command.

For Related Information

- "Formatting Selected Characters in a Cell," p. 315

Format Painter

The Format Painter tool on the Standard toolbar looks like a paintbrush. With this tool you can copy a font and other attributes from one cell onto other cells. It lets you *paint* a format across a spreadsheet, rather than painstakingly apply multiple attributes.

For Related Information

- "Copying and Pasting Formats," p. 311

Drag and Drop Data onto Charts

Adding data to a chart in earlier versions required editing the chart's series formula or rerunning the ChartWizard. Now, you simply *drag and drop*. Just select the data you want to add to an existing chart, and then drag the selected cells until the mouse pointer is over the chart. Release the mouse button, and the chart redraws to accommodate the new data.

For Related Information

- "Adding or Deleting Data," p. 456

Worksheet Auditing

Two major surveys have found that approximately 30 percent of all corporate worksheets have significant errors. You can reduce this number (and your own chances of personal embarrassment) by using Excel's auditing tools, available through the **T**ools **A**uditing command. Figure 1.7 shows how you can use auditing tools to indicate relationships among formulas in cells.

For Related Information

- "Auditing Workbooks and Worksheets," p. 777

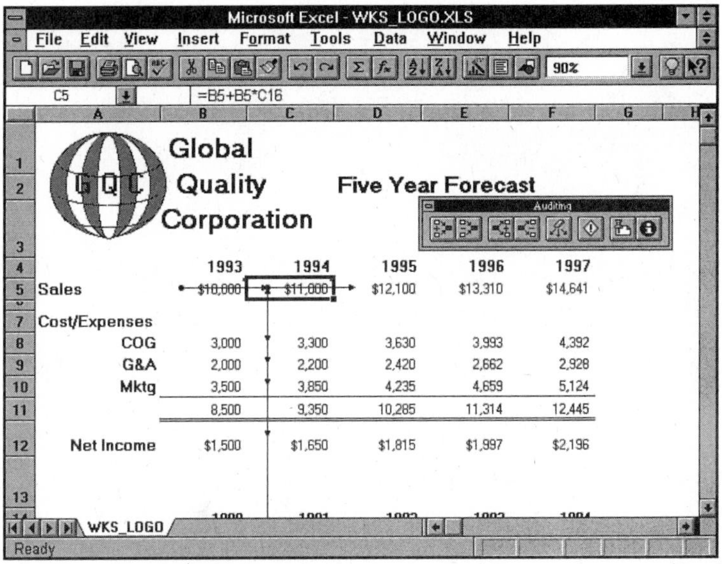

Fig. 1.7
Audit tools can help you find errors and can show relationships among formulas.

New Features That Provide More Analytical Capabilities

Excel 5 has additional analytical capabilities, especially for working with lists.

OLE Automation

When working in conjunction with other Windows applications, Excel 5 has more flexibility and power than ever before. Besides Excel 4's previous capability of copying and pasting or of linking to data in other Windows applications, Excel now includes OLE (Object Linking and Embedding) automation, which means that within an Excel worksheet, you can edit or modify embedded objects from applications such as Word 6 for Windows. Notice that in figure 1.8 the Excel menu and toolbar reflect the Word textual document that is embedded in the Excel worksheet.

For Related Information

- "Embedding Data from Other Applications into Worksheets," p. 1050

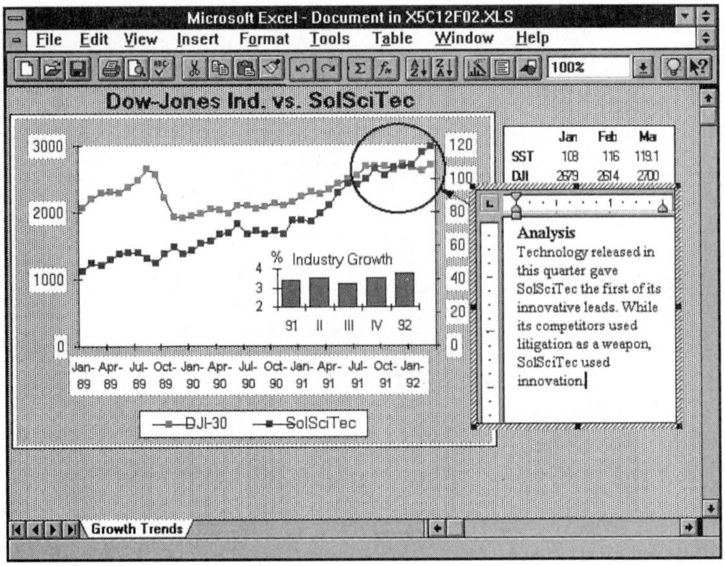

Fig. 1.8
Excel now works better with other Windows applications. You can edit data from OLE 2 applications, such as Word 6 for Windows and Microsoft Project, without leaving the Excel worksheet.

Drop-Down Lists, Check Boxes, and Option Buttons in Worksheets

For Related Information

- "Making Worksheets Appear Like Forms," p. 723

Many Excel users who create worksheets want to be able to use the data-entry features available in dialog boxes. These scrolling lists, drop-down lists, check boxes, and option buttons make data entry easier and less error-prone. Most people, however, are stopped because they need to learn programming to create dialog boxes. Excel 5 has changed this. You can easily draw scrolling lists, drop-down lists, check boxes, and option buttons directly on a worksheet. When someone makes a selection from one of these *controls*, the result shows up in a worksheet cell, where you can use normal worksheet formulas to work with it.

Subtotal and Grand Total Reports

For Related Information

- "Creating Automatic Subtotals," p. 607

Many companies download data from a mainframe, and then tie someone to his or her desk to filter out unwanted data and insert formulas for subtotals and grand totals. With Excel 5's new **D**ata **S**ort, **F**ilter, and Su**b**totals commands, such jobs are done in a few minutes. The Su**b**total command automatically enters subtotals and grand totals under headings you indicate and figures where to insert the necessary rows. You can remove the subtotals and grand totals later with a single command.

Custom Chart Elements

For Related Information

- "Adding Graphics Elements to Sheets," p. 553

With Excel 4, you still occasionally needed a graphics program to add a custom element to a chart. This is unlikely to happen with Excel 5 because you can use built-in drawing tools directly on a chart. In addition, you can select and drag almost any chart element to a new location.

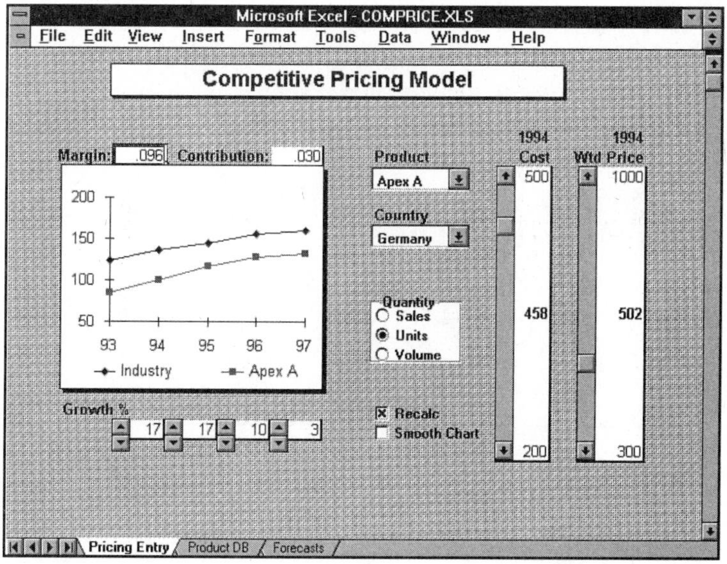

Fig. 1.9
Excel now allows scrolling lists, drop-down lists, check boxes, and option buttons directly in a worksheet.

Automatic Chart Formatting

Excel initially gained recognition among electronic spreadsheets for its high-quality charts. With the new chart AutoFormatting feature, creating charts is even easier. In Excel 4, you used the chart gallery and chart templates to select a type of chart. AutoFormats guides you through this process and even enables you to create custom formats.

For Related Information

- "Using Autoformats," p. 441

Automatic Chart Trendlines

Previously, if you wanted to create a chart that had trendlines, you had to use array functions to analyze the data and plot trendline data points. Excel 5 offers automated trendline charts that can calculate different types of trendlines, chart the data and the trendlines, and show the trend statistics.

For Related Information

- "Automatically Analyzing Trends with Charts," p. 513

AutoFilter

Although it wasn't *extremely* difficult, learning how to create and use an Excel 4 list could take a new user a few hours. Excel 5's new users can find and filter information from a list within minutes. The new AutoFilter feature pinpoints the list's location and then inserts drop-down lists over the names at the top of each list column. You choose the information you want to see from these drop-down lists.

For Related Information

- "Using the AutoFilter," p. 913

TextWizard

Many business people use Excel to analyze business information they receive as text files from an accounting or sales system, often a system on a large

For Related Information

- "Importing Data," p. 1079

corporate computer. These text files may be column delimited, meaning each type of data is in a known column. Unused columns are filled with blank characters. Excel's new Text Import Wizard shown in figure 1.10 makes it easy to separate long strings of imported text into individual worksheet cells.

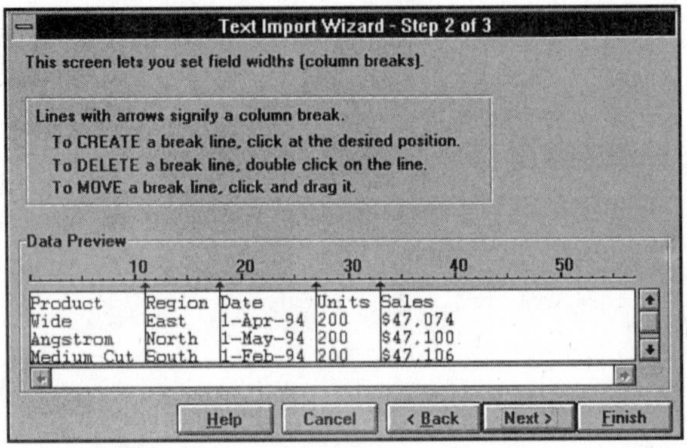

Fig. 1.10 Separating long strings of text into individual worksheet cells is much easier with the Text Import Wizard.

Microsoft Query

For Related Information
■ "Retrieving Data from External Databases," p. 947

Whether you are in a major corporation or a small business, you probably have information in a database that you would like to analyze and chart with Excel. For example, you may need to analyze growth rates, sales forecasts versus actual sales, new product contributions to the bottom line, and so on. Excel 5 comes with Microsoft Query to retrieve information from most databases found on PCs, SQL Server, or mainframes. Microsoft Query can be run separately or as an Excel add-in.

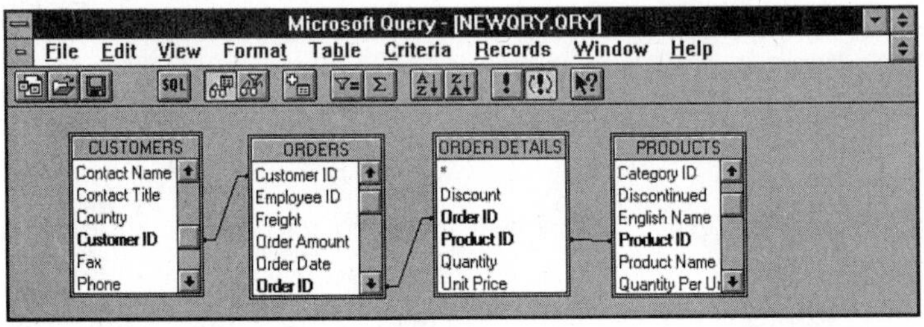

Fig. 1.11 Excel can retrieve data from most major database applications using Microsoft Query.

Pivot Tables

For Related Information
■ "Using Pivot Tables," p. 983

The most powerful analytical tool added to Excel 5 is the pivot table. This feature enables you to create a table that shows the relationships among different data in a list. Pivot tables also use drag-and-drop technology, so if you want to examine the data in a table from a different point of view—for example, to look at regions by month, rather than sales by month—all you have to do is drag and drop labels onto the appropriate table heading. Users of crosstabs in Excel 4 should find pivot tables significantly more powerful, yet as easy to use.

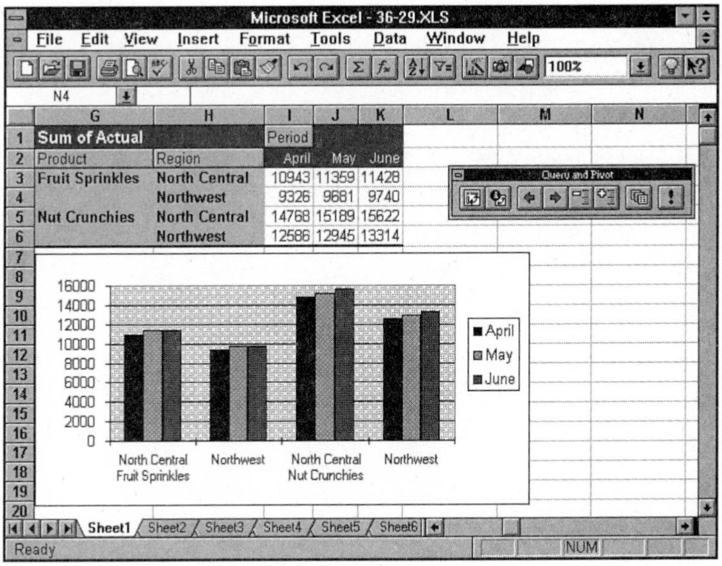

Fig. 1.12
Analyze your list or database from different perspectives with pivot tables.

Visual Basic for Applications

Microsoft has a vision that all its major applications will use or be controlled by one user programming language, Visual Basic for Applications. Visual Basic is the most widely used Windows programming language, and Microsoft has embedded this programming language inside Excel 5. The skills and procedures you develop in Visual Basic for Excel soon will be transferable to other Microsoft applications. If you have much experience with Excel 4 macros, or use macros created with the Excel 4 macro language, you need not be concerned. You can continue to program and use the Excel 4 macro language in Excel 5.

For Related Information

- "Introducing Visual Basic for Applications," p. 1139

Chapter 2

Getting Around in Excel and Windows

This chapter is the place to start if you are not familiar with Microsoft Windows or Microsoft Excel. You can use the ideas and concepts that you learn here in all your Excel operations. In fact, what you learn in your first Windows application carries over to other Windows applications.

You learn how to control Excel's menus and dialog boxes and the windows that contain Excel and its worksheets, charts, and macro workbooks. By the end of this chapter, you should be able to choose commands from menus, select options from dialog boxes, and manipulate windows on-screen. You need to know these techniques to run the application. Beyond such basic tasks, you should be able to organize windows so that you can access and use multiple worksheets at once, and be able to clear off your desktop so that you can concentrate on one job.

In this chapter, you to do learn the following:

- Start and quit Excel
- Choose commands and making select in dialog boxes
- Operate Excel using the keyboard or the mouse
- Manipulate windows
- Use toolbars

Starting and Quitting Excel

To start the Excel application, follow these steps:

1. Start Windows from the DOS prompt by typing **win** and pressing Enter.
2. Activate the group window that contains Excel. This is the Microsoft Office group, the Microsoft Excel group, or another group in which an Excel application item icon has been created. Figure 2.1 shows the Microsoft Office group window, with the title of the Microsoft Excel icon highlighted.

Activate the group window by clicking the window if the window is open, or double-clicking the window's icon if the window is closed. To use the keyboard to activate the group window if it is already open, press Ctrl+Tab until the desired window becomes active. To use the keyboard to activate the group window when it is closed, press Ctrl+Tab until the title of the group icon is highlighted, and then press Enter to open and activate the group window.

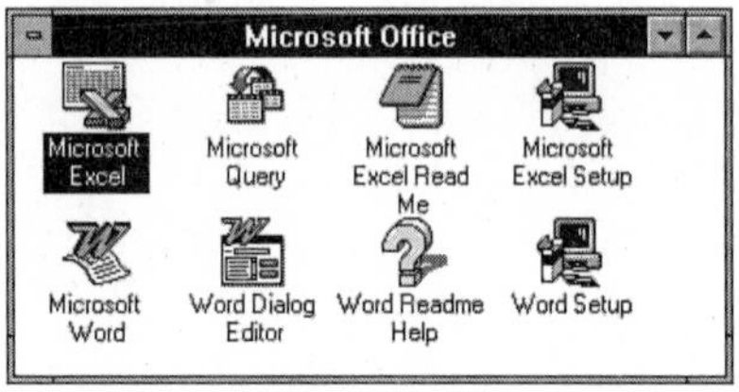

Fig. 2.1
Double-click the Excel icon to start Excel.

3. To use the mouse to start Excel, double-click the Excel application icon. To use the keyboard to start Excel, press the arrow keys until the title of the Excel application icon is highlighted, and then press Enter.

Note

To start Excel automatically when Windows starts, add a copy of the Excel application icon to the StartUp program group. Any program in the StartUp program group starts up automatically whenever Windows starts. To copy the Excel application icon into the StartUp program group, press Ctrl and drag the Excel application icon into the StartUp program group window.

Tip
Another way you can start Excel is by starting the File Manager, displaying the EXCEL.EXE file, and double-clicking the file.

You also can start Excel by choosing an Excel workbook, chart, or macro file from the File Manager. To start Excel and load one of these items automatically, double-click the file name, or select the file name and press Enter. If this procedure does not work, check to see whether the PATH command in the AUTOEXEC.BAT file includes the directory in which the EXCEL.EXE file is located. If the procedure still does not work, you may need to *associate* Excel files with Excel. The **F**ile **A**ssociate command in the File Manager associates file extensions with specific applications. The association process is described in the Windows manual and in Que's *Using Windows 3.1,* Special Edition.

Close or quit Excel when you are finished working for the day or when you need to free memory for other applications. To quit Excel, perform the following steps:

1. Choose the **F**ile E**x**it command. To choose this command using the keyboard, press Alt+F and then press X. Alternatively, press the shortcut key combination Alt+F4, which closes Excel without using the **F**ile menu. To choose this command using the mouse, click the **F**ile menu and then click the E**x**it command.

2. If you made changes to any workbook, Excel displays an alert box asking whether you want to save your current work. Choose the **Y**es command (click its command button, or press Enter) to save your work, or choose the **N**o command (click its command button, or press Tab and then Enter) to quit without saving.

3. Repeat step 2 for any other alert boxes that appear. An alert box appears for each workbook you have open on-screen that has been changed.

Tip

To quit Excel, you also can double-click the Control menu box.

When all workbooks are closed, the Excel window closes, and the application is terminated.

Troubleshooting

You can't find the Excel application icon.

Normally, the Excel application icon appears in the Excel program group. If you can't find the application icon, it may be in a different program group. Open the other program groups to find the Excel application icon. If you don't find this icon in any program group, it might have been deleted. In this case, you need to reinstall Excel.

For Related Information

- "Opening an Existing Workbook" p. 268
- "Saving Workbooks," p. 272

Understanding the Excel Screen

One advantage of Windows applications is the capability to run several applications and display them on-screen simultaneously. Chapters 38 and 39 describe how to run Excel and other Windows or DOS applications together and transfer information among them. This can save you time when you transfer data into or out of Excel, transfer charts to graphics programs for further enhancements, create updatable links between Excel worksheets and Windows applications, or embed Excel data into other Windows application workbooks.

Each Windows application, such as Excel, runs in its own application window. Because some application windows can contain multiple workbook windows, you can work simultaneously with more than one worksheet, chart, or Visual Basic module sheet. Figure 2.2 shows the Excel application window containing a worksheet window and a chart sheet window.

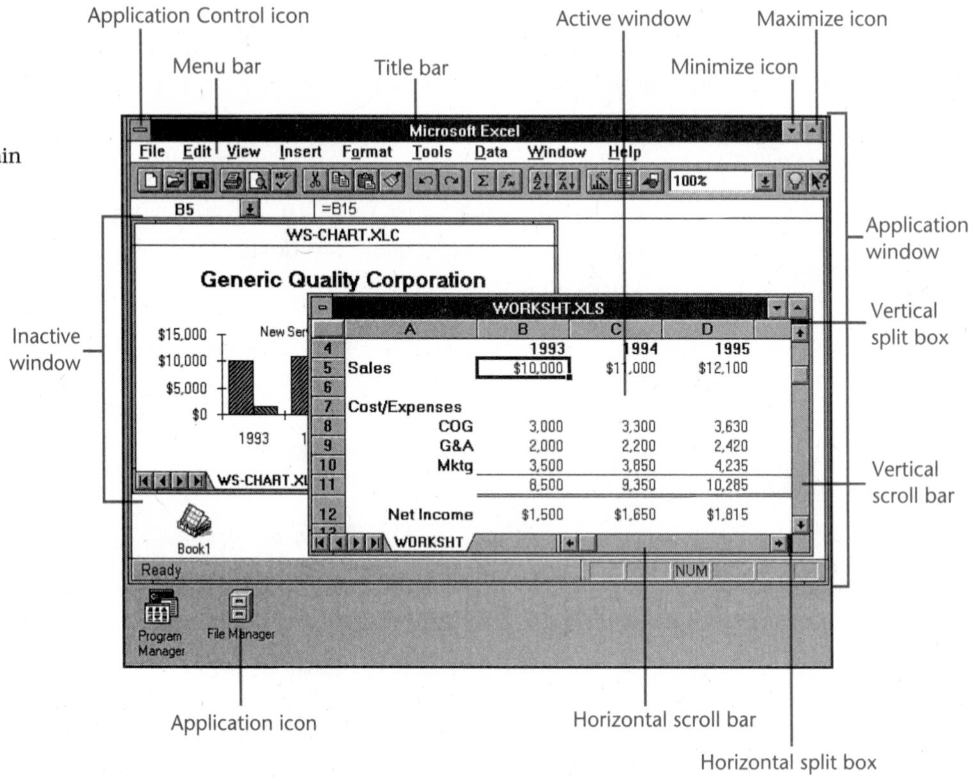

Fig. 2.2
Excel may contain more than one workbook window.

Table 2.1 lists and describes the parts of an Excel screen.

Table 2.1 Parts of Excel and Windows Screens

Part	Description
Application window	The window within which Excel runs.
Application icon	The icon of a running application.
Application Control icon	Opens a menu that enables you to manipulate the application window.

Part	Description
Active window	The window that accepts entries and commands; this window is shown with a solid title bar and is normally the top window.
Inactive window	A window that is open, but currently is unaffected by commands; such a window normally has a gray title bar and is behind the active window.
Mouse pointer	The on-screen arrow, cross, or I-beam that indicates the current location affected by your mouse actions. (Not shown in figure.)
Title bar	The bar at the top of an application or workbook window; it usually contains the title of the window, or the name of the file upon which the window is based, and also can contain Minimize, Maximize, and Restore icons.
Menu bar	A list of menu names displayed below the title bar of an application.
Menu	A pull-down list of commands. (Not shown in figure.)
Command	A function or action chosen from a pull-down menu. (Not shown in figure.)
Minimize icon	An arrowhead facing downward, located at the right end of a title bar. Clicking this stores an application as an application icon at the bottom of the screen; equivalent to the application control menu's Mi**n**imize command.
Maximize icon	An arrowhead facing upward, located at the right end of a title bar. Clicking this fills all available screen display space with the workbook or application; equivalent to the application control menu's Ma**x**imize command.
Restore icon	A double arrowhead at the right end of a title bar that, when clicked, restores an application or workbook into a sizable window; equivalent to the application control menu's **R**estore command. (Not shown in figure.)
Scroll bar	A gray horizontal or vertical bar that enables you to scroll the screen horizontally or vertically using the mouse; a scroll box in the bar shows the current display's position relative to the entire workbook contained in that window.
Split box	A dark bar at the end of a scroll bar that you drag to a new location along the scroll bar to split a window into two views of the same workbook.
Status bar	A bar at the bottom of the screen that explains a selected command or prompts you with guidance or instructions.

Figure 2.3 shows the elements of the Excel application window and an open Excel workbook in more detail. The workbook window, WORKSHT.XLS, has a solid title bar, indicating that it is the active workbook window. You can have multiple workbooks, worksheets, charts, or programming module sheets open at the same time. Most entries and commands affect only the active window. Inactive windows are normally behind the active window and have a lighter colored or cross-hatched title bar.

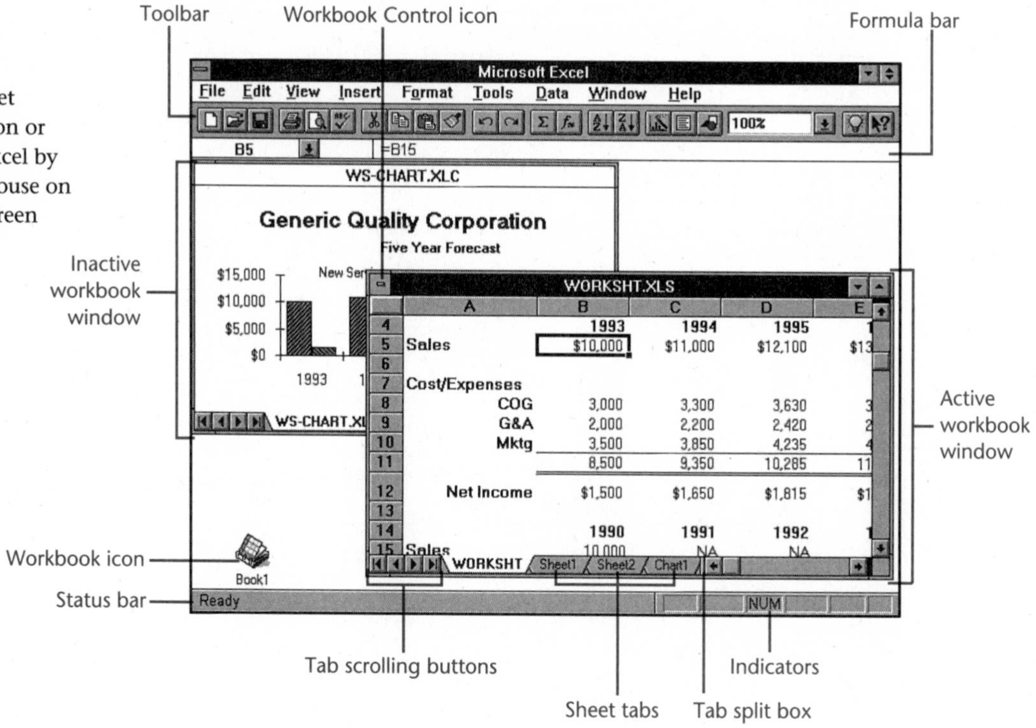

Fig. 2.3
You can get information or control Excel by using a mouse on various screen elements.

Various objects that appear on an Excel screen are described in table 2.2.

Table 2.2 Objects on the Excel Screen

Object	Description
Workbook window	A window within the Excel application window in which a worksheet, macro sheet, chart, or dialog box is displayed.
Active workbook window	The Excel workbook window that currently accepts entries and commands; this window has a solid title bar and is normally the top window.

Object	Description
Inactive workbook window	An open window that contains Excel information, but currently is unaffected by commands; such a window normally has a gray title bar and is behind the active workbook window.
Workbook icon	The icon of a minimized workbook within the Excel application window.
Workbook Control icon	This icon opens a menu that enables you to manipulate the active workbook window.
Sheet tabs	These tabs enable you to switch to a specific sheet in a workbook.
Tab scrolling buttons	These VCR-like controls help you to move quickly through the sheets in a workbook.
Tab split box	This box is dragged left or right to adjust the sizes of the area to display sheet tabs and the area to display the horizontal scroll bar on the bar that these objects share.
Toolbar	A bar containing buttons giving quick access to commands and tools, such as bold, italic, create chart, styles, and drawing tools. A toolbar can be moved to a different location and reshaped.
Formula bar	The area of the screen where you enter text, numbers, or formulas. The formula bar is below the menu bar or toolbar.
Status bar	A bar at the bottom of the screen that shows what Excel is prepared to do next; watch the status bar for prompts, explanations of the current command, or guidance.
Indicators	These display modes of operation, such as NUM when the numeric keypad is on, SCRL when the Scroll Lock key has been pressed, or EXT when Extend mode is on.

Using the Mouse

The mouse is an optional piece of hardware that attaches to your PC and enables you to move the on-screen pointer in synchronization with the movements of the mouse by your hand. In Excel, you can control the program using either keystrokes or mouse movements. Some Excel actions, such as drawing graphical objects, require the use of a mouse; other actions, such as manipulating charts, are significantly easier when you use a mouse.

Basic worksheet and list management features are accessible through the use of the keyboard. You might find, however, that combining mouse actions, touch-typing, and shortcut key combinations is the most productive way to work.

Note

Left-handed users can customize the left and right mouse buttons in the Windows Program Manager. Activate the Control Panel and click the Mouse icon to set up mouse options. Choose the Swap Left/Right Buttons option.

Depending on location, the mouse pointer changes appearance. You usually see the mouse pointer as an arrow when it is among the menus and as a thick cross in the worksheet. When located over an area of text that you can edit, the pointer becomes an I-beam. For drawing graphical objects or embedding objects on a worksheet, the mouse pointer's shape changes to a cross hair (a thin cross). The mouse pointer's shape at a given location indicates actions that you can perform.

Table 2.3 shows and explains the different shapes of the pointer.

Table 2.3 Mouse Pointer Shapes

Pointer Shape	Location(s)	To Use
	Menu, scroll bar, toolbar	Select by moving the tip of the arrow on a name or icon and then clicking the mouse button.
	Text boxes, formula bar	Repositions the flashing cursor (insertion point) within editable text. To move the insertion-point location, move the I-beam to the new desired location, and click.
	Appears during placement, resizing, or drawing of placement command objects	Select object and drag across sheet or move to square handle on object and drag to resize.
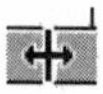	Appears between column headings	Drag to change column width.
	Appears between row headings	Drag to change row height.

Pointer Shape	Location(s)	To Use
	Appears on window edge	Drag to change position of window edge.
	Window corners	Drag to reposition two window edges at one time.
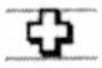	Inside worksheet	Click to select cells in worksheet.
 	Split bar at ends of scroll bar	Drag to split window into two views.
	Print Preview	Select workbook area for closer view.
	Help window, macro buttons	Click for help or to run macro.
	Appears at corner of selected cells	Drag to contiguous cells to copy cell contents to the contiguous cells.
	Appears at corner of selected cell(s) when you press Ctrl	Drag to copy and increment to contiguous cells.
	Appears after you click the Help button	Click any part of the Excel screen to get help information about that area.
	Appears when you are specifying where you want Excel to display a chart	Drag to select the desired height and width of the chart.
	Appears when you are resizing an object	Drag to resize the object.
	Appears when you are resizing an object	Drag to place the control where you want it.
	Appears at the edge of selected object	Drag to move the object.
	Any screen	Means "Please wait."

For Related Information

- "Setting Preferences," p. 1098
- "Customizing Excel with the Windows Control Panel," p. 1099

Troubleshooting

The mouse moves either too fast or too slow across the screen.

Windows, not Excel, controls the rate at which the mouse moves across the screen. To change the mouse acceleration, double-click the Mouse icon from the Control Panel program group. In the dialog box that appears, select Slow, Moderate, or Fast, depending on the acceleration rate that you desire.

Understanding Windows and Excel Terms

All Windows applications, including Excel, require the same keyboard and mouse actions to select what is changed on-screen, or to give commands. By learning the following two actions, you learn how to operate menus and to select items within any Windows application.

Action	Description
Select	Highlight or mark a menu name, command, dialog box option, cell location, or graphical object, using specific keystrokes or mouse actions.
Choose	Execute and complete a command. Some commands are executed when you choose a command from the appropriate menu. Other commands are executed when you choose a command button from the appropriate dialog box.

Mouse Actions

Mouse techniques are simple to learn and to remember. These techniques make using Excel much easier. In fact, for such work as moving and copying cells, charting, drawing, and embedding objects, the mouse is nearly indispensable. Table 2.4 describes mouse actions you use to carry out Excel operations.

Some mouse actions have a different effect when you hold down the Shift or Ctrl key while you click, double-click, or drag with the mouse. As a general rule, holding down the Shift key as you click selects text or cells between the current location and the location where you Shift+click. Holding down the Ctrl key as you click nonadjacent areas and then drag across adjacent areas enables you to select areas that are not contiguous (next to each other). By selecting with this method, you can format multiple areas with one command.

Table 2.4 Mouse Actions

Action	Description
Click	Place the tip of the mouse pointer or the lower portion of the I-beam pointer at the desired location and then quickly press and release the left mouse button **once**. This action selects a menu, command, cell, or graphical object so that you can work with it; in text boxes and formula bars this action places the insertion point.
Right click	Position the tip of the mouse pointer in the desired location on a worksheet, chart, or toolbar and then click the right mouse button. This action displays a *shortcut menu* appropriate to the item you clicked.
Drag	Position the tip of the mouse pointer, center of the cross-hair, or lower portion of the I-beam on an item; then hold down the left mouse button as you move the mouse pointer. This action selects multiple items, cells, or text characters, or moves graphical objects.
Double-click	Position the tip of the mouse pointer or the lower portion of the I-beam pointer at the desired location and then quickly press the left mouse button **twice**. This action is usually a shortcut for manually selecting the item you click (for example, double-clicking selects an entire word, without you dragging across it letter by letter).

Keyboard Actions

The keyboard is most useful for entering text and numbers, performing fast operations with shortcut keys, and operating with portable or laptop computers that do not have a mouse. Don't forget, however, that the best way of operating Excel and other Windows applications is through the combined use of mouse and keyboard. Table 2.5 lists and describes keyboard actions you use in Excel.

Table 2.5 Keyboard Actions

Action	Description
Type	Type, but do not press the Enter key.
Enter	Type and then press the Enter key.
Alt	Press the Alt key.
Alt, *letter*	Press the Alt key, release it, and then press the underlined letter or number shown. The active letters that appear underlined on-screen appear in bold print in this book.

(continues)

Table 2.5 Continued

Action	Description
Letter	Press only the underlined letter shown in the menu, command, or option.
Alt+*letter*	Hold down the Alt key while you press the underlined letter.
Alt, hyphen	Press the Alt key, release it, and then press the hyphen key.
Alt, space bar	Press the Alt key, release it, and then press the space bar.
Tab	Press the Tab key.
Esc	Press the Esc key.

Throughout this book, you see combinations of keys indicated with a plus sign (+), such as Ctrl+F. This combination means that you must hold down the Ctrl key while you press the F key. After pressing the F key, release both keys. (This book uses capital letters, but you do not need to hold down the Shift key unless instructed to do so.)

Keystrokes that appear separated by commas should be pressed in sequence. Alt, space bar, for example, is accomplished by pressing and releasing Alt and then pressing the space bar.

If you have a mouse, try using both mouse actions and keystrokes to perform commands and tasks. You soon should find that the keyboard works better for some commands and features, and that the mouse works better for others. A combination of mouse and keyboard techniques usually is the most efficient approach to Excel. The Quick Reference card bound inside the back cover of this book shows the keyboard shortcut methods.

The keyboard also is useful for many shortcut keys. These shortcut keys are listed in appropriate areas throughout this book.

The 12 function keys offer you a shortcut method of choosing commands that are normally chosen from a menu. Some function keys used in combination with other keys result in different commands. When two or more keys in an instruction are joined by a plus sign, hold down the first key(s) as you press the next key. Table 2.6 lists the function keys and their equivalent menu commands.

Table 2.6 Function Keys and Menu Command Equivalents

Excel Application Window Function Keys	Menu Command
Alt+F4	Close
Excel Workbook Window Function Keys	**Menu Command**
F1	Help
Shift+F1	Context Choosing Help
F2	Activate Formula Bar
Shift+F2	Formula Note
Ctrl+F2	Window Show Info
F3	Insert Name Paste
Shift+F3	Insert Function
Ctrl+F3	Insert Name Define
Ctrl+Shift+F3	Insert Name Create
F4	Repeats last action/Switch Reference
Ctrl+F4	Control Close (workbook window)
Alt+F4	File Exit
F5	Edit Goto
Shift+F5	Edit Find (cell contents)
Ctrl+F5	Control Restore (workbook window)
F6	Next Pane
Shift+F6	Previous Pane
Ctrl+F6	Control Next Window
Ctrl+Shift+F6	Previous Workbook Window
F7	Spelling
Ctrl+F7	Control Move (workbook window)
F8	Extend Mode (toggles on/off)

(continues)

Table 2.6 Continued

Excel Workbook Window Function Keys	Menu Command
Shift+F8	Add Mode (toggles on/off)
Ctrl+F8	Control Size (workbook window)
F9	Tools Options Calculate Now
Shift+F9	Tools Options Calculate Sheet
Ctrl+F9	Control Minimize workbook
F10	Activate Menu Bar
Shift+F10	Display Shortcut Menu
Ctrl+F10	Control Maximize (workbook window)
F11	Insert New Chart
Shift+F11	Insert New Worksheet
Ctrl+F11	Insert New Excel 4 Macro Sheet
F12	File Save As
Shift+F12	File Save
Ctrl+F12	File Open
Ctrl+Shift+F12	File Print

Notice that key combinations are listed on the right side of some pull-down menus. These key combinations are used to execute the commands without using menus. Rather than choosing the **F**ile Save **A**s command, for example, you can press the F12 key.

If you are working in Excel and forget a function key or shortcut key combination, choose the **H**elp **C**ontents command, and then, under the Reference section, choose the Keyboard Guide topic for keyboard listings and shortcuts.

Choosing Commands

Excel uses the same menu-selection methods used by all Windows applications. You can control commands with the mouse, keystrokes, directional keys, or shortcut keys. You often can mix your methods of menu selection by starting with one method and finishing with another.

You may notice that some commands in a menu are dimmed. These commands are unavailable at that point in Excel's operation.

Commands that are followed by an ellipsis (...) need more information after you choose them before they can execute. These commands display dialog boxes that ask you for more information.

Tip

You cannot use a shortcut key while a menu is pulled down or a dialog box is displayed.

Some Excel menus have submenus that appear to the side of the main menu. Commands that display submenus appear with a small arrowhead to the side. To display a submenu using the mouse, drag down to the command, then continue to hold down the mouse button while you drag to the side of that command. Using the keyboard, press the activating letter for the command to see the submenu; or press the down-arrow until the command is selected, and then press Enter. Figure 2.4 shows the F**o**rmat menu with the **R**ow command selected. Its submenu appears to the right.

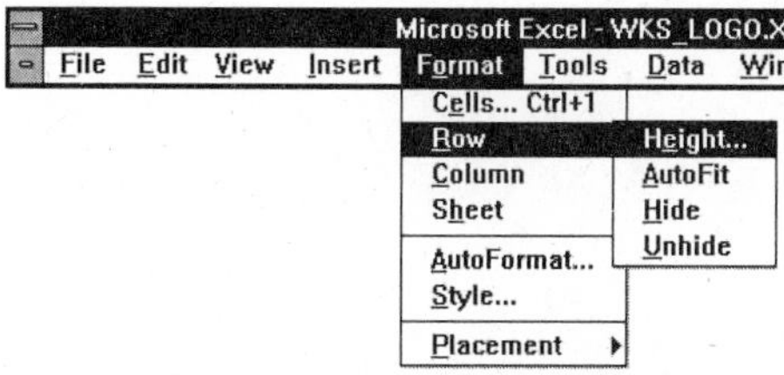

Fig. 2.4

Arrowheads indicate a submenu. An ellipsis indicates that a dialog box follows to ask for more information before the command executes.

In Excel, you can back out of any pull-down menu or dialog box by pressing Esc. If you are using a mouse, you can back out of a menu by clicking the menu name a second time or back out of a dialog box by clicking the Cancel button.

Saving Time with Shortcut Menus

You can save yourself time by using shortcut menus. Shortcut menus display the most frequently used commands that relate to the selected item or object.

To display a shortcut menu, click—with the right mouse button—the item or object for which you need a shortcut menu. If you are using a keyboard, select the item and then press Shift+F10.

Shortcut menus appear under the mouse pointer or at the top-left corner of the display, if activated by the keyboard. Select a command by clicking it, or by pressing the up- or down-arrow key and then pressing Enter. To remove a shortcut menu, click outside the menu or press Esc.

Tip

Some toolbar areas, such as the Fonts list, don't respond to a right-click. To display the toolbar shortcut menu, right-click a button or the toolbar background.

Figures 2.5 and 2.6 show a few shortcut menus; the captions indicate with which items the menus appear.

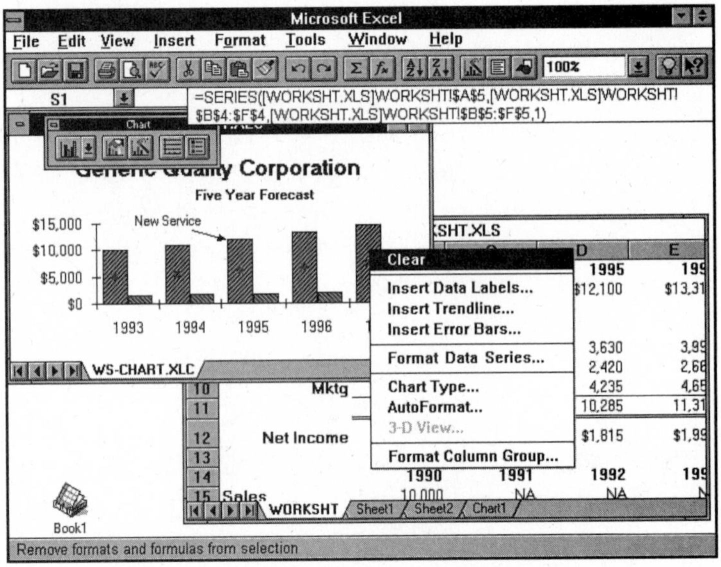

Fig. 2.5
A right-click on a bar chart displays a shortcut menu to change charts.

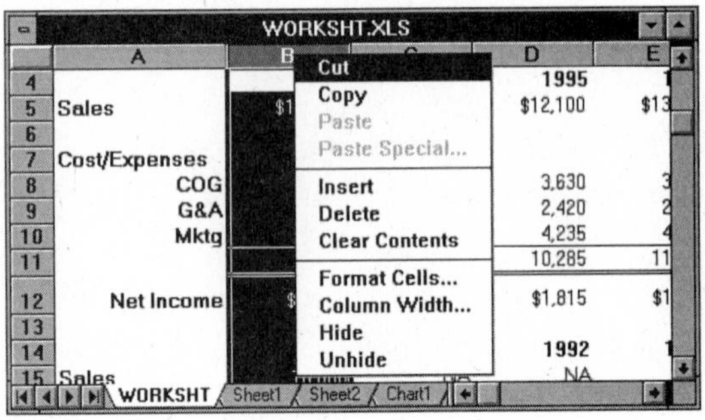

Fig. 2.6
A right-click on a column displays a shortcut menu to change the column and contents.

Choosing Commands with the Keyboard

When you are familiar with the Excel menus, you can perform the following steps to touch-type commands:

1. Press Alt to select the menu bar.

2. Press the underlined letter in the menu name; for example, press the F key for **F**ile. The menu pulls down.

3. Press the underlined letter in the command name; for example, press the O key for **O**pen.

You do not need to wait for the menu to appear when you touch-type commands.

Choosing Alternative Commands with Shift

You can choose alternative commands from certain menus. To display these additional commands, hold down the Shift key while you choose the menu. The following table lists the normal and shifted commands:

Normal Command	Alternative Command
File **C**lose	**F**ile **C**lose All
Edit **C**opy	**E**dit **C**opy Picture
Edit **P**aste	**E**dit **P**aste Picture
Edit Paste **S**pecial	**E**dit Paste Picture Li**n**k

Note

To use an alternative command, hold down the Shift key while pressing Alt+F or Alt+E. Continuing to hold down the Shift key while pressing the second letter of the command is unnecessary.

Using Excel 4 Commands

If you are upgrading from Excel 4, you may want to use Excel 4 menus. Choose the **T**ools **O**ptions command. Select the General tab and then select Microsoft E**x**cel 4.0 Menus.

If you go ahead and work with the Excel 5 menus, but at some point need to do an action for which you know only the Excel 4 command, you easily can learn the corresponding Excel 5 command. Switch to Excel 4 menus as explained in the previous paragraph, click the Help button on the Standard toolbar, and then choose the command using the Excel 4 menus. A help screen gives you Excel 5 instructions so that after you return to Excel 5 menus, you know how to do the operation.

Using the Toolbars

The toolbars in Excel give you quick access to frequently used commands and procedures. Tools on toolbars can only be used with a mouse or similar pointing device. To use a tool on a toolbar, click the button that represents the command or procedure you need. You decide which toolbars are displayed and where they appear on-screen. Toolbars are always accessible because they float above worksheets.

In Excel, you can display and work with more than one toolbar at a time. Excel has 13 predefined toolbars that appear automatically when needed or when displayed using the **V**iew **T**oolbars command. The toolbars are described in the following list:

- *Standard toolbar.* The Standard toolbar contains the buttons most frequently used for formatting, file handling, and printing (see fig. 2.7).

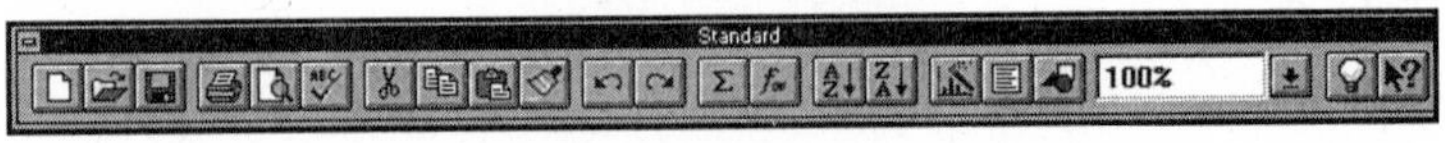

Fig. 2.7
The Standard toolbar.

- *Formatting toolbar.* The Formatting toolbar contains buttons used for formatting fonts, setting alignment, applying numeric formats, formatting borders, and applying shading (see fig. 2.8).

Fig. 2.8
The Formatting toolbar.

- *Query and Pivot.* The Query and Pivot toolbar contains buttons to help you create, update, and manipulate pivot tables (see fig. 2.9).

Fig. 2.9
The Query and Pivot toolbar.

- *Chart toolbar.* The Chart toolbar contains the buttons to add or remove the legend, arrows, and text boxes (see fig. 2.10).

Fig. 2.10
The Chart toolbar.

- *TipWizard.* The TipWizard toolbar displays a useful tip about Excel that can increase your productivity (see fig. 2.11).

Fig. 2.11
The TipWizard toolbar.

- *Drawing toolbar.* The Drawing toolbar contains buttons for drawing, filling, reshaping, and grouping objects in the worksheet (see fig. 2.12).

Fig. 2.12
The Drawing toolbar.

- *Forms toolbar.* The Forms toolbar contains buttons with which you can draw and format controls such as check boxes, option buttons, and drop-down lists. These controls can be used on worksheets or dialog sheets (see fig. 2.13).

Fig. 2.13
The Forms toolbar.

- *Stop Recording toolbar.* The Stop Recording toolbar contains a button to stop macro recording (see fig. 2.14).

Fig. 2.14
The Stop Recording button.

- *Visual Basic toolbar.* The Visual Basic toolbar contains buttons to increase your productivity when programming in Visual Basic for Excel (see fig. 2.15).

Fig. 2.15
The Visual Basic toolbar.

- *Auditing toolbar.* The Auditing toolbar contains buttons to help you find the most common types of errors in Excel worksheets (see fig. 2.16).

Fig. 2.16
The Auditing toolbar.

- *WorkGroup toolbar.* The WorkGroup toolbar contains buttons, such as Find File and Send Mail, that are useful for working with others on a network (see fig. 2.17).

Fig. 2.17
The WorkGroup toolbar.

- *Microsoft toolbar.* The Microsoft toolbar displays buttons that enable you to quickly switch to other Microsoft Windows business applications (see fig. 2.18).

Fig. 2.18
The Microsoft toolbar.

- *Full Screen.* The Full Screen toolbar appears when you display the Excel workspace full-screen. Click the button to return to the previous view (see fig. 2.19).

Fig. 2.19
The Full Screen button.

Tip
Customize a toolbar by adding or removing buttons as described in Chapter 41, "Creating Custom Toolbars and Menus."

Caution

If someone has used Excel before you, the predefined toolbars may be modified. You also may find custom toolbars available that previous users created for themselves or that someone has created to assist you with specific tasks.

Note

Toolbars throughout this book occasionally were modified to suit the text. Your toolbars may look different from those shown in figures.

Getting Help on Tools

To see what a tool does, move the mouse pointer to the related toolbar button and read the description in the status bar at the bottom of the Excel window. When you need help using a tool, click the Question Mark (**?**) button, if it is available, and then click the tool to use. If the **?** button is not visible, press Shift+F1 and then click a tool. A help window appears to show you how to use the tool. Press Alt+F4 or choose the **F**ile E**x**it command to close the Help window.

In many cases the buttons on toolbars are small, and if you don't use them often, you may forget the name or function of a button. To help you remember each button, Excel comes with ToolTips. ToolTips are small labels that appear next to a button when you move the pointer onto the button but don't click. You can turn ToolTips on or off by choosing the **V**iew **T**oolbars command and then selecting or deselecting the **S**how ToolTips check box in the Toolbars dialog box.

Displaying or Hiding Toolbars

You can use the **V**iew **T**oolbars command or the toolbar shortcut menu to display or hide toolbars.

To display additional toolbars, follow these steps:

1. Choose the **V**iew **T**oolbars command. The Toolbars dialog box shown in figure 2.20 appears.

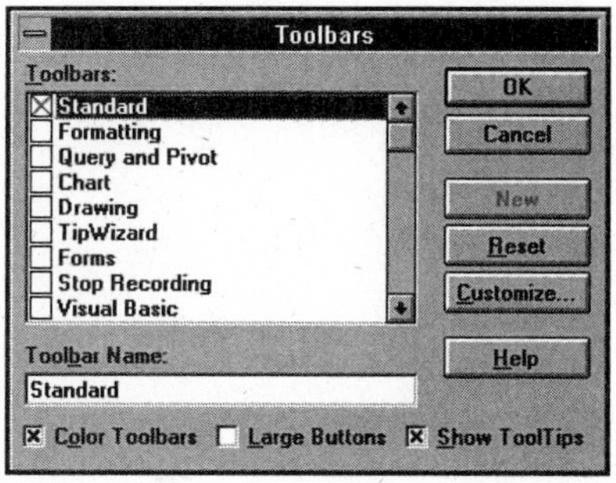

Fig. 2.20
Display a list of toolbars by choosing the **V**iew **T**oolbars command.

2. Select the toolbar you want to display. A selected check box indicates that the toolbar is already displayed.

3. Choose OK.

Excel displays the toolbar you select. The toolbar is displayed in the position in which it was last used.

To display an additional toolbar using the mouse, follow these steps:

1. Click with the right mouse button on an already displayed toolbar to display a shortcut menu.

2. Click the name of the toolbar you want to display. The shortcut menu does not list all available toolbars. If the name of the toolbar you want to display is not on the list, choose Toolbar from the list, and the Toolbars dialog box described in the preceding set of steps appears.

You can close (hide) a toolbar in three ways. First, you can click the toolbar with the right mouse button to display the toolbar shortcut menu. In the shortcut menu, displayed toolbars appear with a check mark. Click to deselect the name of the toolbar that you want hidden.

Second, you can choose the **V**iew **T**oolbars command. In the Toolbars dialog box, deselect the toolbar name, and then choose OK.

Third, if a toolbar displays a control menu icon in its top-left corner, you can close the toolbar without using menus, simply by clicking the control menu icon.

Excel records the toolbars, their locations, and which ones are open. When you restart Excel, the toolbars you last used are available to you.

Moving, Resizing, and Reshaping Toolbars

You can move or reshape toolbars to fit the way you want to work. Toolbars can be *docked* in a position along an edge of the window or they can *float* free in their own window. Docked toolbars are one tool wide or high. You can reshape toolbars that float in a window and drag them wherever they are most convenient to use. Figure 2.21 shows floating and docked toolbars.

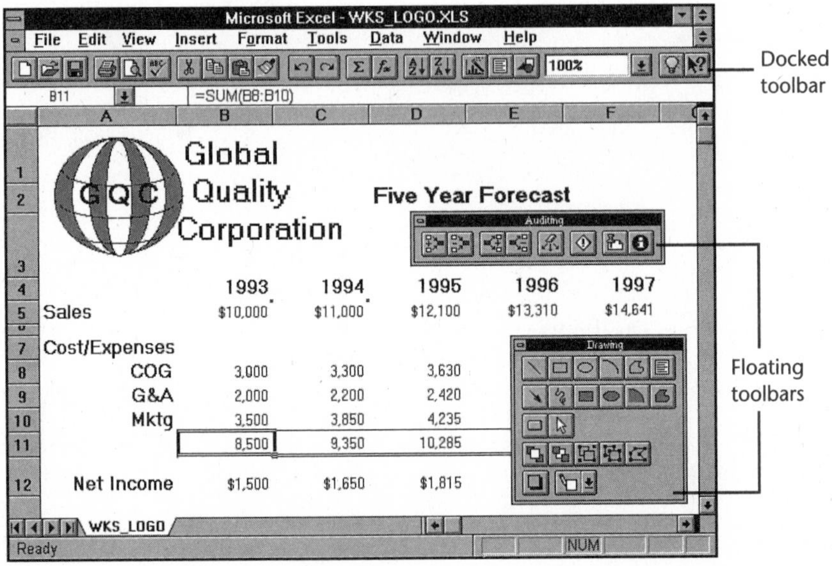

Fig. 2.21
You can drag toolbars to an edge to dock them, or you can use them as floating palettes.

To move a toolbar, click the gray area around the edge of the toolbar and drag. If you drag the toolbar to the bottom of the Excel window, the toolbar docks against the edge. A toolbar is ready to dock when the gray outline becomes thinner. Toolbars that contain drop-down list boxes, such as the Formatting toolbar, cannot dock against a left or right edge because the list cannot fit in the width of the toolbar.

Toolbars also can float free in a window. To move a floating toolbar, drag its wide edge. You can resize a floating toolbar window by clicking its border and dragging, as shown in figure 2.22. To return the toolbar to a dock, drag the floating toolbars title bar to an edge of the screen and then release the mouse button. To dock a floating toolbar in the last place it docked before becoming a floating toolbar, double-click the toolbars title bar.

Tip
To move a docked toolbar back to the last floating position, double-click the toolbar background.

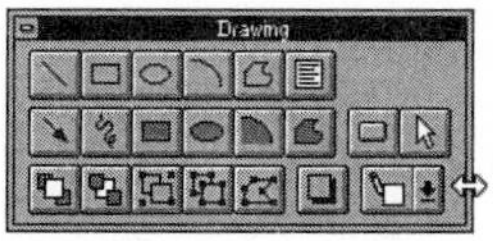

Fig. 2.22
Drag the edge of a toolbar to reshape it.

If you use a super VGA monitor, the on-screen tool size may seem too small to easily distinguish. You can switch between normal tools and larger tools by choosing the **V**iew **T**ools command, selecting the **L**arge Buttons option, and choosing OK.

Toolbars with colored tools display in color if you select the C**o**lor Buttons check box in the Toolbars dialog box. When this check box is unmarked, colored tools appear in shades of gray.

Using Tear-Off Palettes from Toolbars

Some toolbars contain drop-down lists to make selecting from a wide range of options an easy task. A few of these drop-down lists may be ones you use frequently enough that you want to *tear off* the list and keep it displayed in a palette that floats over your worksheet. This makes the selections very accessible while you are formatting. Figure 2.23 shows four tear-off palettes floating over the worksheet. At the upper-right corner of the figure, you can see the border button displaying a palette before it is torn off. The palettes you can tear off are Border, Font Color, Pattern, and Color from the Formatting and Drawing toolbars.

To tear off a palette, follow these steps:

1. Click the border, font color, pattern, or color button on the toolbar. This displays the palette.

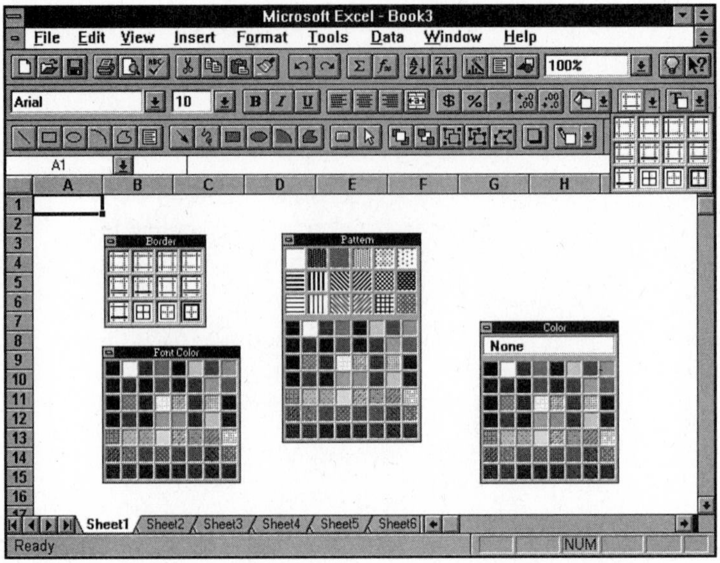

Fig. 2.23
Tear off frequently used palettes and let them float over the worksheet.

2. Continue to hold down the mouse button as you drag down and away from the toolbar. The palette detaches and stays with the mouse pointer.

3. Release the mouse pointer to drop the palette.

Unlike toolbars, palettes cannot be reshaped. You can close a palette by clicking its control icon in the top left corner.

For Related Information

■ "Creating Your Own Toolbar," p. 1111

Troubleshooting

The buttons appear large, and you can't see all the buttons on the toolbar.

You may have chosen the option to display the toolbar larger than normal. To remedy the problem, choose **V**iew **T**oolbars and deselect the **L**arge Buttons option.

Working in Dialog Boxes

In the pull-down menus, commands that require additional information are followed by ellipses (...). Choosing one of these commands displays a dialog box in which you enter information needed before the command is executed. The **T**ools **O**ptions command opens a dialog box containing 12 tabbed sections, for which the tabs show across the top of the dialog box.

Each tabbed section contains a different type of option that you can use to customize Excel. If you select the General tab, the dialog box appears as in figure 2.24.

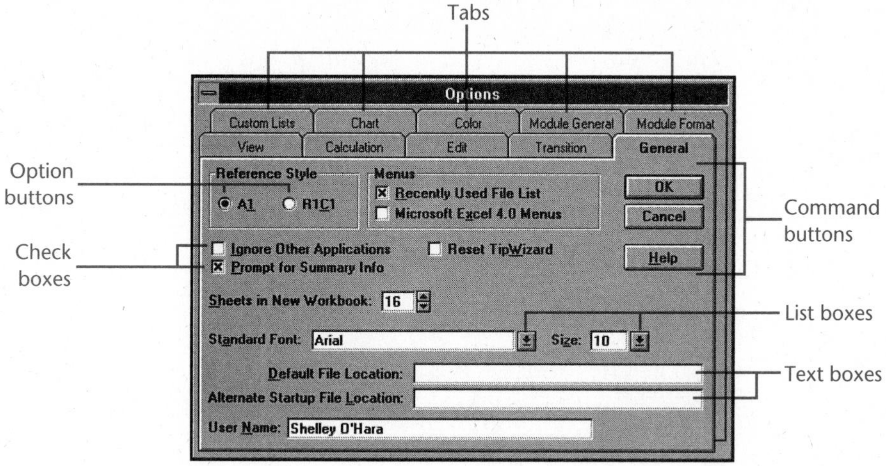

Fig. 2.24
Tabs in dialog boxes give you easy access to groups of options.

Dialog boxes contain different types of items. These items are described in more detail in the sections immediately following. To familiarize yourself with Excel dialog box items, read the following list:

- *Tabs.* In multiple part dialog boxes only. Each tab you select changes the dialog box to display a related group of options. Only one tab at a time can be selected.
- *Text box.* A box in which you can type and edit text, dates, or numbers. Some text boxes have up and down arrows next to them. You can click on these arrows to increment or decrement the value.
- *Option button.* A button that you use to select one choice from a group of two or more options.
- *Check box.* A square box that can be selected (turned on) or deselected (turned off).
- *List box.* A list or drop-down list that scrolls to display available alternatives.
- *Command buttons.* Buttons that complete or cancel the command; some buttons give you access to additional options.

Selecting a Tabbed Section of a Dialog Box

A dialog box may contain more than one section, as figure 2.24 shows. If so, *tabs* appear within the dialog box as if they are cards within a card file. All options grouped on the same card are related, and the titles of the option groups appear on tabs across the top of the dialog box. When you select the Chart tab of the Options dialog box, for example, all options that appear are related to charts.

To select a tab by using the keyboard:

Select the tab to the right	Press Ctrl+Tab or Ctrl+Page Down
Select the tab to the left	Press Ctrl+Shift+Tab or Ctrl+Page Up

To select a tab by using the mouse:

Click the tab title.

Selecting Option Buttons and Check Boxes

Figure 2.25 shows check boxes and a group of option buttons. You can select only one option button from a group, but you can select none, one, or several of the check boxes that are offered.

Fig. 2.25
You can select only one option from within a group.

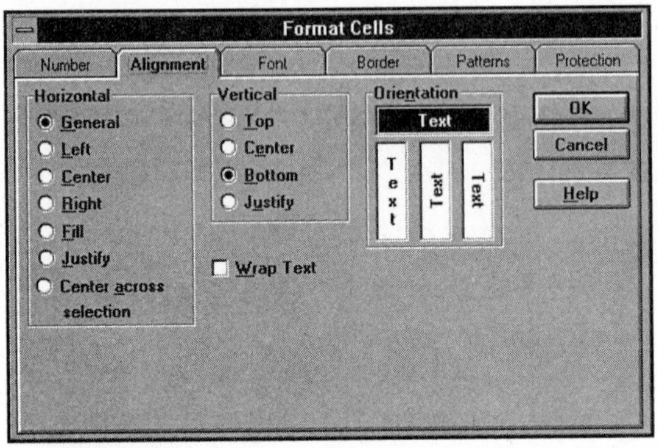

To select an option button using the mouse, click the button. To clear an option button, you must click another in the same group. A dot within the option indicates that the option is on. Remember that you can select only one button in a group.

To select an option button by using the keyboard, hold down the Alt key and then press the underlined letter of the option group you want. Alternatively, press Tab until an option in the group is enclosed by dashed lines. After you select the group, press the arrow keys to select the option button you want from within the group.

Check boxes are square boxes that you can turn on or off and use in combination with other check boxes. A check box is selected (on) when an × appears in the box.

To select or deselect a check box, click the check box that you want to change. From the keyboard, press Alt+*letter,* where *letter* is the underlined letter in the name of the check box.

When you are making a succession of changes in a dialog box, pressing the Tab key is probably the easiest way to move between items in the box (Shift+Tab moves in reverse). The active item is enclosed in a dashed line or contains the flashing insertion point for text editing. To change a check box that is enclosed by the dashed line, press the space bar. To change an option button in a group enclosed by the dashed line, press the arrow keys.

Editing Text Boxes

You use text boxes to type information, such as file names and numbers, into a dialog box. You can edit the text within a text box the same way you edit text elsewhere in Excel.

When the mouse pointer is on a text box, it appears in the shape of a capital I, which is known as an I-beam. The actual location where typing will appear is indicated by a flashing vertical bar, as shown in figure 2.26.

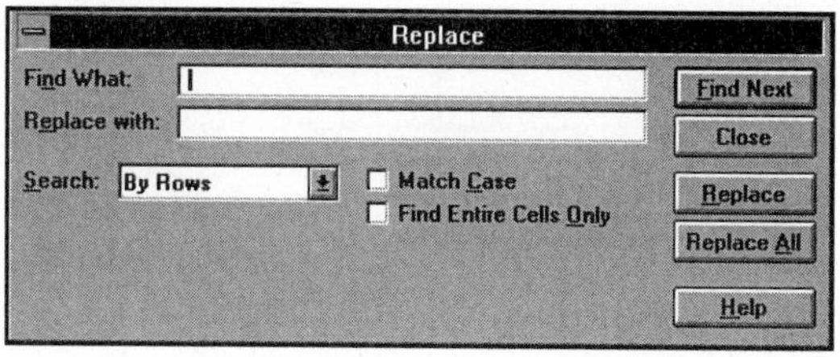

Fig. 2.26
An insertion point indicates where typing and editing occur in an edit box.

To select characters using a mouse, click in the text wherever you want the insertion point, and then drag across text to select as many characters or words as you want. Double-click a word to select the entire word.

To select	Mouse Action
Multiple letters	Drag across letters
Word	Double-click word
Words or formula terms	Double-click word; then drag

To select text with the keyboard, press the Alt+*letter* combination for the text box. Press the left- or right-arrow keys to move the flashing insertion point and then type the text you want to insert.

Delete characters to the right of the flashing insertion point by pressing Del. Delete characters to the left of the insertion point by pressing Backspace.

To select multiple characters using the keyboard so that you can delete or replace them by typing, perform these actions:

To select	Keyboard Action
Multiple letters	Shift+arrow key
Words	Shift+Ctrl+arrow key
To the beginning of the current line	Shift+Home
To the end of the current line	Shift+End
From the active cell to A1	Shift+Ctrl+Home
From the active cell to the last workbook cell	Shift+Ctrl+End

Selecting from List Boxes

In some cases, Excel has multiple alternatives from which to choose. The Font tab of the Format Cells dialog box, for example, shows you lists of fonts (see fig. 2.27).

Some list boxes show only the current selection in what appears to be a text box. To see the entire list of alternatives, you must drop down the list. Figures 2.28 and 2.29 show the Border tab of the Format Cells dialog box before and after the Color list has been dropped down.

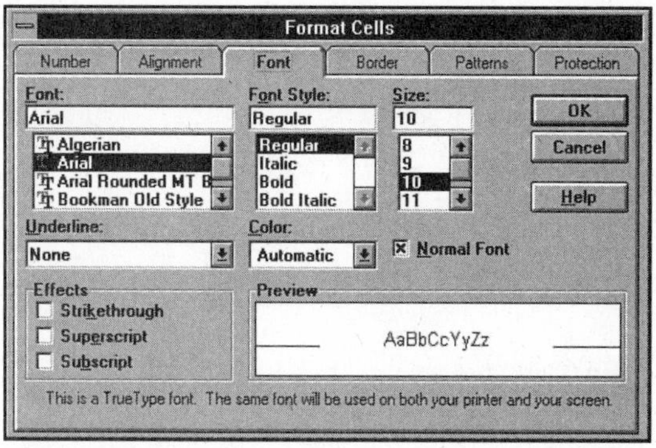

Fig. 2.27
A list box gives you a list of alternate selections.

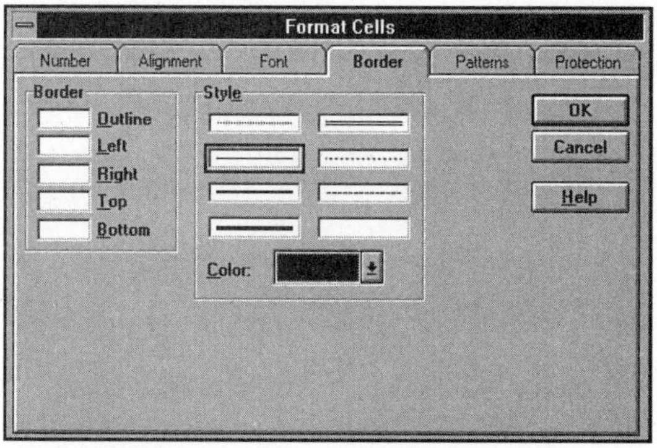

Fig. 2.28
The Borders tab with the Color list not dropped down.

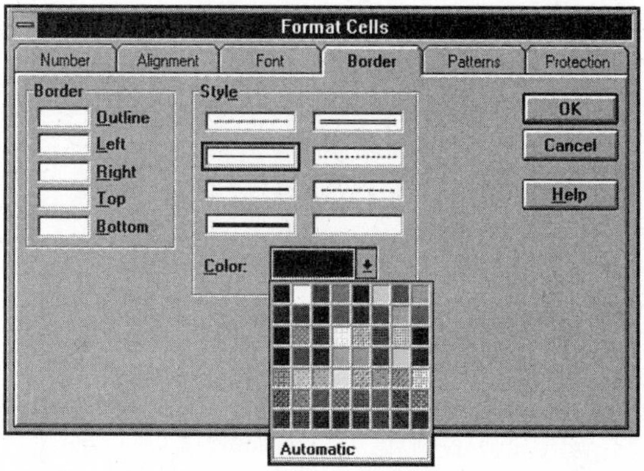

Fig. 2.29
The Borders tab with the Color list dropped down.

To select an item from a list box, follow these steps:

1. If the list is not displayed, click the down arrow to the side of the list or activate the list box by pressing Alt+*underlined letter*. If you are using the keyboard and the box is a drop-down list box, press Alt+down-arrow key.

2. When the list displays, click the arrowheads in the scroll bar to scroll to the name you want, and then click the name. Alternatively, scroll to the name you want by pressing the up-arrow, down-arrow, Home, or End key.

3. Click OK if you are in a dialog box, or press Enter to complete the command.

In most dialog boxes, you can double-click a name in a list box to select the name and choose OK in one operation. (You cannot double-click a name in a drop-down list box.)

Before you select a command button such as OK, make sure that the name you want to select from the list box is highlighted, not just surrounded by a dashed line.

Note

You can find names in a list box quickly because they appear in alphabetical order. Select the box by clicking in it once or by pressing Alt+down-arrow key. Then press the first letter of the name for which you are searching. The list scrolls to the first name beginning with that letter. You also can scroll with the up- and down-arrow keys and the Home, End, PgUp, and PgDn keys.

Closing Dialog Boxes

Command buttons usually appear at the top-right corner or down the right side of dialog boxes. You usually use these buttons to execute or cancel a command. The right side of the dialog box in figure 2.29 contains the command buttons OK, Cancel, and Help.

Using a mouse, you click a command button to choose it. From the keyboard, you can choose a command button in three different ways. If the command button contains an underlined letter, press Alt+*letter*. If a button name is enclosed in dashed lines, press Enter to choose the button. In most cases, pressing Enter initially chooses OK. You can select any command button by pressing Tab until the button name is enclosed in dashed lines, and then pressing Enter. Choose Cancel by pressing Esc.

Getting Help

Windows and Excel provide Help information to guide you through new commands and procedures. Excel's Help files are extensive and explain topics that range from parts of the screen to commands, dialog boxes, and business procedures.

To get help in Excel or another Windows application, choose a command from the **H**elp menu, press F1, or choose the **H**elp button when it appears in a dialog box. The **H**elp **C**ontents command or F1 displays the window shown in figure 2.30. From this window, you can learn how to use Help or you can see the contents of all Help topics. Notice that you can access or control Help information in different ways. You can use the menus at the top of the Help window or you can use the buttons under the menu bar to **S**earch for a topic or to see a His**t**ory of all the previous topics you have viewed.

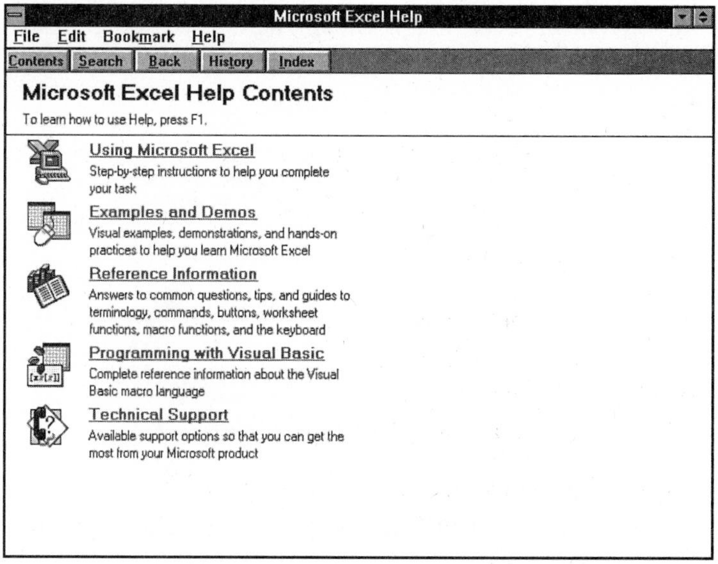

Fig. 2.30
Press F1 to get help related to an open dialog box or alert window. At other times, press F1 to display all contents of Help.

You can use the command buttons located under the menu to move through the Help topics. Choose a button by clicking it or by pressing Alt+*letter*. The following command buttons help you move through information:

Button	Action
Contents	Shows the index or contents of Help at the highest level.
Search	Displays a list of key words. Choosing a key word displays a list of Help topics related to that key word. Choosing from the topics displays the specific help for that topic.
Back	Returns to the preceding Help topic. With this button, you can retrace the topics you have viewed, all the way back to the initial Help Index.
History	Shows a list of previously selected topics. Double-click a topic to return to it; or press the up- or down-arrow key to select the topic, and then press Enter.
Index	Shows an alphabetical list of topics.

Searching for a Topic in Help

The Search dialog box enables you to find topics related to the subject on which you need help. To use Search, choose the **H**elp **S**earch command. If the Help window is already displayed, choose the **S**earch button. The dialog box shown in figure 2.31 appears.

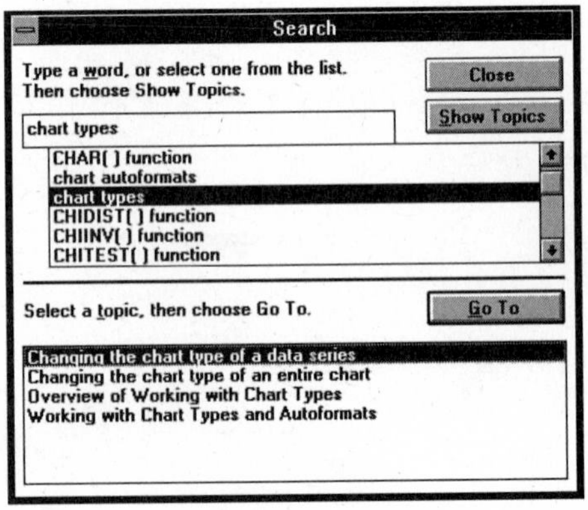

Fig. 2.31
Use the Search button to quickly find topics related to the subject on which you need help.

If you are using a mouse, click the **S**earch button to display the Search dialog box. Type a word in the top text box or select a topic from the top list box, and then choose the **S**how Topics command. The bottom list box displays topics related to the word. Select a topic from the bottom list box and then choose the **G**o To command.

If you are using the keyboard, press Alt+S to activate Search mode, and then press Alt+W to choose the top list. Type a topic in the text box. As you type, the list scrolls to topics that begin with the letters you type. To scroll through the list, press Tab so that a topic in the list is enclosed with dashes, and then press the up- or down-arrow key. Press Enter to choose the **S**how Topic button, and the Go To list is filled with related topics. Press the up- or down-arrow key to select a topic and then press Enter to choose the **G**o To command.

Jumping between Help Topics

Hot words or phrases appear within the actual Help text. Words or phrases linked to additional help information have a solid underline. Words or phrases linked to a definition have a dashed underline.

To jump to the topic related to a word with a solid underline, click the word; or press Tab until the word is selected, and then press Enter.

To display the definition of a word that appears with a dashed underline, click the word; or press Tab until the word is selected, and then press Enter. Click again or press Enter to remove the definition.

Getting Help in Dialog Boxes

You can get help for any dialog box or error message that appears in Excel. When any dialog box from a command or an error message appears, press F1 to get help. Figure 2.32 shows the error dialog box that appears when you attempt to enter a formula containing an error. Figure 2.33 shows the Help window that appears if you choose the **H**elp button or press F1 after the error dialog box appears.

Fig. 2.32
Choose the Help button to get help on any dialog box or error message.

To learn what action a command performs or how a portion of the screen works, press Shift+F1 and then click the command or portion of the screen. Alternatively, click the Help button and then click the command or portion of the screen. Notice that after pressing Shift+F1 or clicking the Help button, the mouse pointer changes to a question mark that overlays the pointer. You use this modified pointer to ask a question about the next item you click.

Tip
To print a copy of any of the Help window contents, choose the **F**ile **P**rint Topic command.

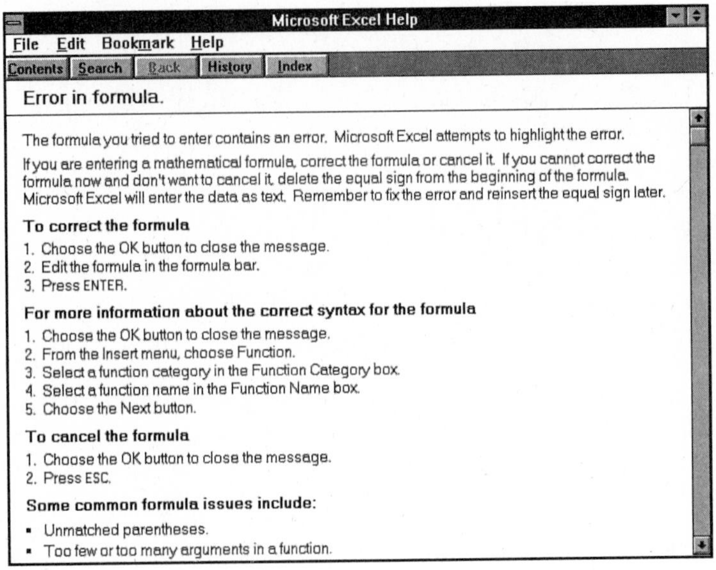

Microsoft Excel Help
File Edit Bookmark Help
Contents Search Back History Index
Error in formula.
The formula you tried to enter contains an error. Microsoft Excel attempts to highlight the error.
If you are entering a mathematical formula, correct the formula or cancel it. If you cannot correct the formula now and don't want to cancel it, delete the equal sign from the beginning of the formula. Microsoft Excel will enter the data as text. Remember to fix the error and reinsert the equal sign later.
To correct the formula
1. Choose the OK button to close the message.
2. Edit the formula in the formula bar.
3. Press ENTER.
For more information about the correct syntax for the formula
1. Choose the OK button to close the message.
2. From the Insert menu, choose Function.
3. Select a function category in the Function Category box.
4. Select a function name in the Function Name box.
5. Choose the Next button.
To cancel the formula
1. Choose the OK button to close the message.
2. Press ESC.
Some common formula issues include:
▪ Unmatched parentheses.
▪ Too few or too many arguments in a function.

Fig. 2.33
An explanation of the error appears in the Help window.

Closing the Help Window

Because Help actually is an application, you need to close the Help window when you are done. To remove the Help window, either double-click the control menu icon at the left of the Help title bar; press Alt, space bar, C; or press Alt+F4.

Using the TipWizard

To tell Excel to display tips based on the action you are performing, choose the TipWizard button. This displays the TipWizard toolbar. When Excel has a tip, the TipWizard light bulb turns yellow (it usually is white). Use the scroll bars to scroll through the tips.

Manipulating Windows

Windows allows you to display and run one or more other applications besides Excel, and to use multiple worksheets, charts, and macros within Excel. Seeing this much information on your screen can be confusing unless you keep your windows organized. Just as you organize folders and papers on your desktop, you can organize your Windows applications and Excel workbooks.

You see two types of windows on-screen. An *application window* contains an application, such as File Manager, Excel, or Microsoft Word for Windows. A *workbook window* contains an Excel workbook. You can open multiple workbook windows within the Excel application window.

Switching between Applications

You can work in an application or workbook only when the window is active. The active window has a solid title bar. In most cases, the active window also is the top window. In a few instances, however, such as during the process of linking worksheets together, the active window may not be on top.

If you are running Excel with other Windows or non-Windows applications, you can switch between application windows by activating the application whose window you want. Press Ctrl+Esc to display the Task List. To choose an application from the Task List, double-click its name; or press the up- or down-arrow key to select the application, and then press Enter.

You also can cycle between applications by holding down the Alt key and pressing Tab. A dialog box or a title bar shows which application will be activated. Release all keys when you see the title of the application you want to activate.

If you can see an inactive application window open on-screen, you can switch to the application by clicking any part of it.

Switching between Workbook Windows

Because Excel makes working with several workbooks and their worksheets easy, you frequently may have more than one window on-screen. This *workbook window* may contain different types of documents, worksheets, charts, modules, and so on. You can, however, affect only the active workbook window. If you can see an inactive workbook window open on-screen, you can make it active by clicking any part of it. If you know a workbook window is open, but you cannot see it, move the other workbook windows so that you can see the one you want to click.

To switch to another window using the keyboard, pull down the **W**indow menu. The name of each workbook appears in the menu. Press the number of the workbook window you want to activate. You can cycle between workbook windows by pressing Ctrl+F6.

Minimizing, Maximizing, and Restoring Windows

You soon may find that your computer desktop has become as cluttered as your real desktop. To gain more space, you can store applications or workbook windows by minimizing them so that they become small symbols (icons) at the bottom of the screen.

When you need one of the applications or workbooks that has been minimized, you can restore the icon to its former window location and size. When you want a window to fill the entire available display area, you can maximize it. The icons for minimizing and maximizing space are shown in figure 2.2, earlier in this chapter.

To maximize an application or workbook window using the mouse, click the maximize icon for the active window or double-click the title bar of the window. To maximize an application or workbook window using the keyboard, press Alt, hyphen to display the workbook control menu, or press Alt, space bar to display the application control menu, and then choose the Ma**x**imize command.

You can minimize application or workbook windows so that they are stored temporarily at the bottom of the screen. To minimize a window using the mouse, click the minimize icon. Using the keyboard, press Alt, hyphen to display the workbook control menu or press Alt, space bar to display the application control menu, and then choose the Mi**n**imize command. You can minimize the active workbook window by pressing Ctrl+F9.

You can restore Excel and workbook windows from their maximized or minimized sizes to their preceding window size and location. If Excel or a workbook has been converted to an icon at the bottom of the screen, double-click the icon. If Excel or a workbook window is maximized, click the double-headed icon at the right of the Excel or workbook title bar to restore it to its earlier window size. Using the keyboard, press Alt, space bar to select the Excel control menu or press Alt, hyphen to select the workbook control menu, and then choose the **R**estore command.

Moving a Window

With multiple applications or multiple Excel workbooks on-screen, you probably want to move windows for the same reasons that you shuffle papers on your desk.

Using a mouse, activate the window you want to move. Drag the title bar until the shadow outline is where you want the window to be located. Release the mouse button to fix the window in its new location.

Using the keyboard, press Alt, space bar to select the application control menu or press Alt, hyphen to select the workbook control menu. Choose the **M**ove command. A four-headed arrow appears in the title bar. Press the arrow keys to move the shadow outline of the window. Press Enter to fix the window in its new location, or press Esc to retain its original location.

Sizing a Window

You often want to see only part of an application or workbook window. The following steps show you how to change the size of the window using the mouse or the keyboard.

To resize a window using the mouse, drag the window edge or corner to the location you want, and then release the mouse button.

To resize a window using the keyboard, follow these steps:

1. Activate the window.
2. Press Alt, then space bar to select the application control menu; or press Alt, then hyphen to select the workbook control menu.
3. Choose the **M**ove command.
4. Press the arrow key that points to the edge you want to move.
5. Press the arrow keys to move that edge to its new location.
6. Press Enter to fix the edge in its new location, or press Esc to cancel.

Closing a Workbook Window

When you finish using an application, worksheet, or chart, you should close its window to remove it from the screen and to free memory. If you have made any changes since the last time you saved the workbook, Excel displays an alert dialog box, as shown in figure 2.34, asking whether you want to save your work before closing.

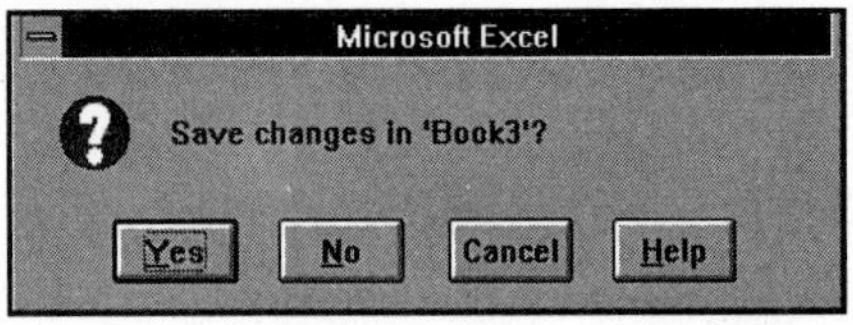

Fig. 2.34
Choose **Y**es if you want to save your most recent changes before closing the window.

> **Caution**
>
> The difference between closing a workbook window and closing an entire workbook is important. If more than one window is open on a workbook, you can close the active window without closing the file. However, if there is only one workbook window or if you choose **F**ile **C**lose, you also close the file that contains the workbook.

Tip
To close all visible workbooks, hold down Shift as you choose **F**ile, and choose **C**lose All, which closes all visible workbooks.

To close the active workbook using a mouse when more than one window is open on a workbook, double-click the workbook control menu icon at the left side of the workbook title bar.

To close the active workbook window using the keyboard when more than one window is open on a workbook, press Alt, hyphen to select the workbook control menu, and then choose the **C**lose command.

For Related Information

- "Saving Workbooks," p. 272
- "Closing Workbooks," p. 282
- "Viewing a Window through Multiple Panes," p. 544
- "Working with Multiple Workbooks," p. 546

To close the file so that all windows for a given workbook close, follow these steps:

1. Choose the **F**ile **C**lose command. The window closes if no changes have been made to the workbook since the last save.
2. If you have made changes to the workbook since the last save, a dialog box appears, asking you whether you want to save your changes.

   In the dialog box, choose **N**o if you do not want to save a changed version of the file or choose **Y**es if you do want to save your changes.

   If you choose **Y**es and the file has not been saved before, a Save As dialog box appears. If this happens, type a new file name and choose OK.

From Here...

For information related directly to controlling Excel and working with workbook windows you can refer to the following chapters:

- Chapter 9, "Managing Files." Covers how to open and close new or existing workbooks.
- Chapter 16, "Managing the Worksheet Display." Explains how to control the worksheet's window display.
- Chapter 40, "Customizing the Excel Screen." Covers how to set your personal work and keystroke preferences.

Chapter 3

Navigating and Selecting in a Workbook

Many business projects on which you work require multiple sheets of paper containing related information. It's rare that a budget, model, or financial projection can be done on a single large sheet of paper. In fact, putting all that information on a single sheet may make the work difficult to grasp.

Microsoft Excel 5 for Windows is designed around the concept that you probably work with multiple sheets of related information. In fact, a new workbook opened using the default settings contains 16 worksheets.

To enter and format information or formulas in an Excel sheet, you must be able to move around in the sheets and move between sheets in the workbook. Excel worksheets can be very large. If one worksheet were a piece of paper, the entire sheet would measure as wide as two cars and stand as tall as a 30-story building! To find and select things on a worksheet, you need to know how to get around efficiently.

Excel has many different methods of moving and selecting in workbooks and worksheets. Use whichever method fits best with what you are doing at the moment, as shown in figures 3.1 and 3.2.

In this chapter, you learn how to:

- Move between and select sheets within a workbook
- Scroll the contents of a sheet
- Move to locations on a worksheet
- Select a cell or range of cells
- Customize keyboard or mouse for easier use

Fig. 3.1
Select worksheets from within a workbook by clicking the tab.

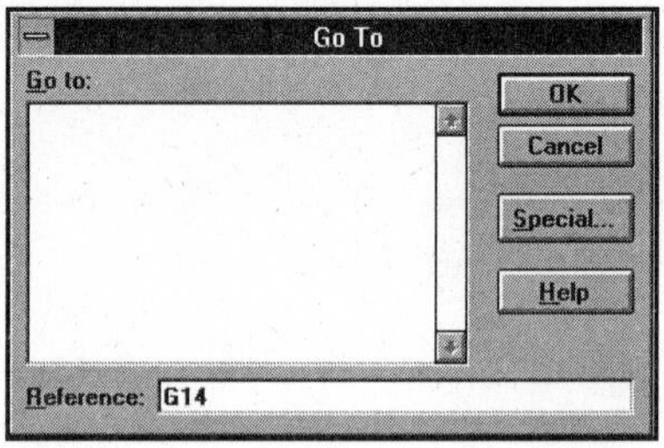

Fig. 3.2
Move to or select cells or ranges with F5, the Go To key.

Understanding Workbooks and Worksheets

Workbooks are collections of sheets stored in the same file on disk. Sheets may contain different types of information; usually the sheets in a workbook contain related information, such as budgets, with each sheet containing the budget for a different sales region within the division. By keeping related sheets in the same workbook, it is easy to make simultaneous changes and edits to all a workbook's sheets at one time, or to consolidate related sheets, or to do math involving numbers from multiple worksheets.

For Related Information

- "Entering Data," p. 87
- "Formatting a Group of Sheets in a Workbook," p. 365
- "Consolidating Worksheets," p. 763

Worksheets contain 256 columns and 16,384 rows. The intersection of a row and column forms a *cell* in which you can enter information or a formula. Column headings start at A and go to IV; when they reach the letter Z column headings restart with AA, AB, and so on. Row headings, down the left side of a sheet, go from 1 to 16,384. In most cases, you do not want to build a giant worksheet that contains all the information. Instead, you want to separate related information onto its own worksheet within the workgroup. It is very easy for formulas to refer to information in another worksheet of the same group.

Workbooks can contain up to 255 sheets. Besides worksheets, a workbook can include chart sheets, Visual Basic modules, dialog box sheets, Microsoft Excel 4.0 macro sheets, and Microsoft Excel 4 international macro sheets. Figure 3.3 shows a workbook that contains multiple worksheets. Notice the tabs across the bottom of the document window. These tabs enable you to see the names of worksheets in the workbook and select the sheet that you want active.

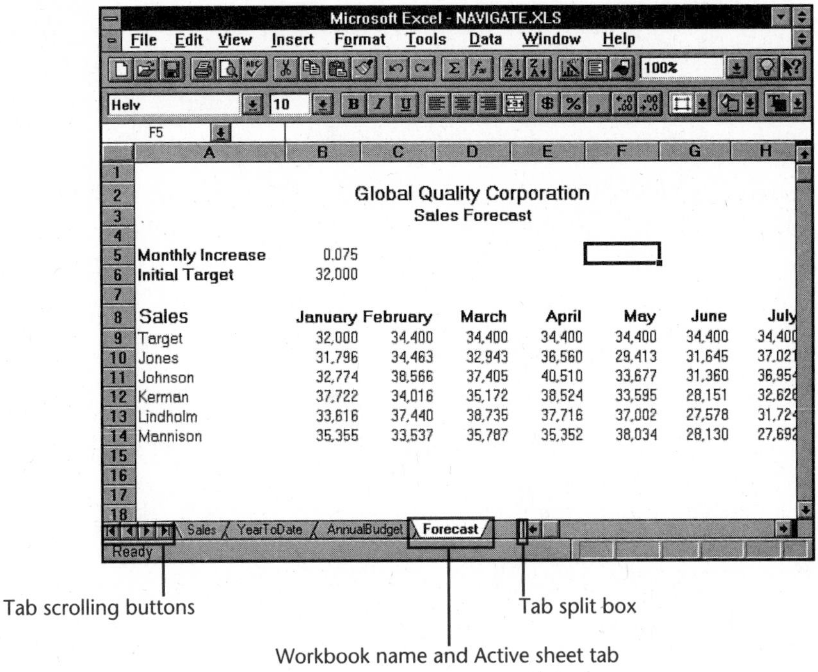

Fig. 3.3
Tabs and Tab scrolling buttons make it easy to move between worksheets.

Moving between Workbooks

When you open an Excel file from disk, you open a workbook that can contain multiple sheets. You can have multiple workbooks open, each in their own document window. You need to *activate*—bring to the top—the workbook in which you want to work.

To activate an open workbook, choose **W**indow and, at the bottom of the menu, select the name of the document window you want to activate.

To switch between workbooks with a shortcut key, press Ctrl+F6 and cycle between open workbook documents.

To activate an open workbook with a mouse, click the document window you want on top.

Selecting and Moving between Sheets

When multiple sheets are in a workbook, you need a quick and easy way to select or move between the sheets. When you select a single sheet, that sheet moves to the top of the window so you can work there. You also can select multiple sheets. Selecting multiple sheets is useful if you want to insert or delete multiple sheets. Chapter 8, "Reorganizing Workbooks and Worksheets," describes inserting and deleting sheets.

Moving between Worksheets in a Workbook

If you want to work within a specific worksheet, activate the workbook that contains the worksheet, and then activate the worksheet in which you want to work. The name on the tab of the active sheet is bold. The active sheet is the sheet in which you can work. You can switch between worksheets by using either keys or mouse actions.

At the bottom of a workbook, the tab scrolling buttons (which look like VCR controls) enable you to use a mouse to move quickly through the names in a workbook. The tab scrolling buttons don't actually select a sheet—they only scroll the names. Clicking the left-end or right-end button scrolls to the first or last worksheet in the workbook. Clicking the left or right button moves one worksheet left or right in the workbook.

Tip
If you move to a sheet that is distant in a workbook and contains many sheets, use the F5 (Go To) key. To select a nearby sheet, click the named tabs or use Ctrl+Page Up/Down.

To move across many sheets in a large workbook, follow these steps:

1. Press F5 to display the Go To dialog box.
2. In the **R**eference text box, type the name and cell of the sheet to which you want to go. For example,

   BUDGET.XLS!B12

3. Choose OK.

To move forward or backward through sheets using the keyboard, use these shortcut keys:

Ctrl+PgUp	Activate previous sheet
Ctrl+PgDn	Activate next sheet

To move to a worksheet within a workbook when using a mouse, follow these steps:

1. Click the tab scrolling buttons to scroll the workbook until you can see the name of the worksheet in which you want to work.
2. Click the tab containing the name of the worksheet you want to activate.

Selecting Multiple Worksheets in a Workbook

Before you can insert, delete, enter, or edit in multiple sheets, you must select all the sheets involved in the work you want to do.

> **Note**
>
> To select multiple sheets, you must use a mouse.

To select multiple, adjacent sheets, follow these steps:

1. Click the scroll buttons to display the first sheet name you want to select.
2. Click the named tab of the first sheet you want to select.
3. Click the scroll buttons to display the last sheet name from the group you want to select.
4. Shift+Click the last sheet name.

All sheets between the first and last that you clicked are selected.

To select multiple, non-adjacent sheets, follow these steps:

1. Click the scroll buttons to display one of the sheet names you want to select.
2. Click a sheet's named tab.
3. Click the scroll buttons to display another sheet name from the group you want to select.
4. Ctrl+click the next sheet name.
5. Return to step 3, and continue using Ctrl+click to select additional sheets.

Tips about Selecting Sheets

When you are constantly switching between two or three sheets in a workbook, you may find the preceding methods of selecting sheets tedious. You can change between two or three worksheets by pressing F5 and typing the name and reference or cell name of the sheet and reference to which you want to go. As shown in figure 3.4, the Go To dialog box remembers the last four locations you went to. To return to one of these previous sheets, press

F5, check the top of the Go To dialog box for where you want to go, and double-click the sheet you want.

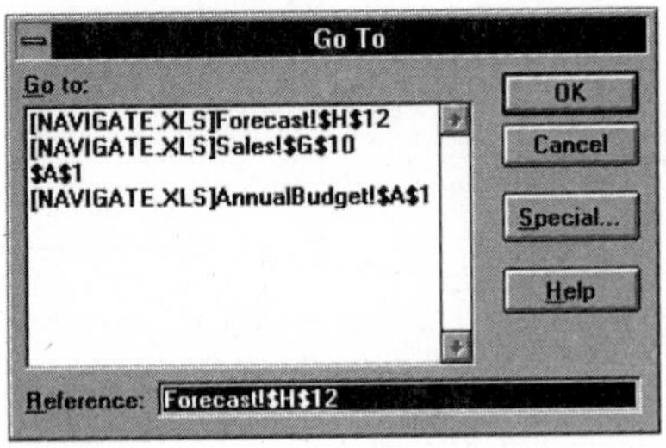

Fig. 3.4
Press F5 to see the names of the sheets to which you can quickly go to by double-clicking.

To see more tab names, drag the tab split box to the right. To see more of the horizontal scroll bar, drag the tab split box to the left. Figure 3.3 shows the tab split box.

Troubleshooting Worksheet Viewing

Excel doesn't display the tabs that contain sheet names along the bottom edge of the workbook.

Displaying tabs in a workbook is an option, which may be turned off. To display tabs with the sheet names, choose the **T**ools **O**ptions commmand, select the View tab and the Sheet Ta**b**s check box.

*Although the Sheet Ta**b**s check box is selected in the View tab of **T**ools **O**ptions, the tabs still are not displayed.*

The sheet in which you are working may have split screens so that no room is available on-screen to display both the horizontal scroll bar and the tabs. To reposition the split on the horizontal scroll bar, look for the tab split box, a double-vertical line, located at the left end of the horizontal scroll bar. When you position the pointer over the tab split box, the pointer changes to two vertical lines. Double-click the tab split box to restore the default split between tabs and the horizontal scroll bar.

Moving Around in a Worksheet

An Excel worksheet can be extremely large. If the worksheet were a piece of paper, the entire sheet may measure as wide as two cars and stand as tall as a 30-story building. To find things on a worksheet, you need to know how to get around efficiently. You can scroll with the mouse or the keyboard.

Scrolling with the Mouse

When you scroll a window, imagine that the worksheet stays still and you move the window over the top of the worksheet. To scroll the window with the mouse, use the scroll bars located at the right and bottom of each worksheet (see fig. 3.5). The arrows in the scroll bars show the direction the window moves over the worksheet.

The position of the scroll box in the scroll bar shows the relative position of the window on the area where data has been entered into the worksheet. Look at the vertical and horizontal scroll boxes to see where you are on the worksheet.

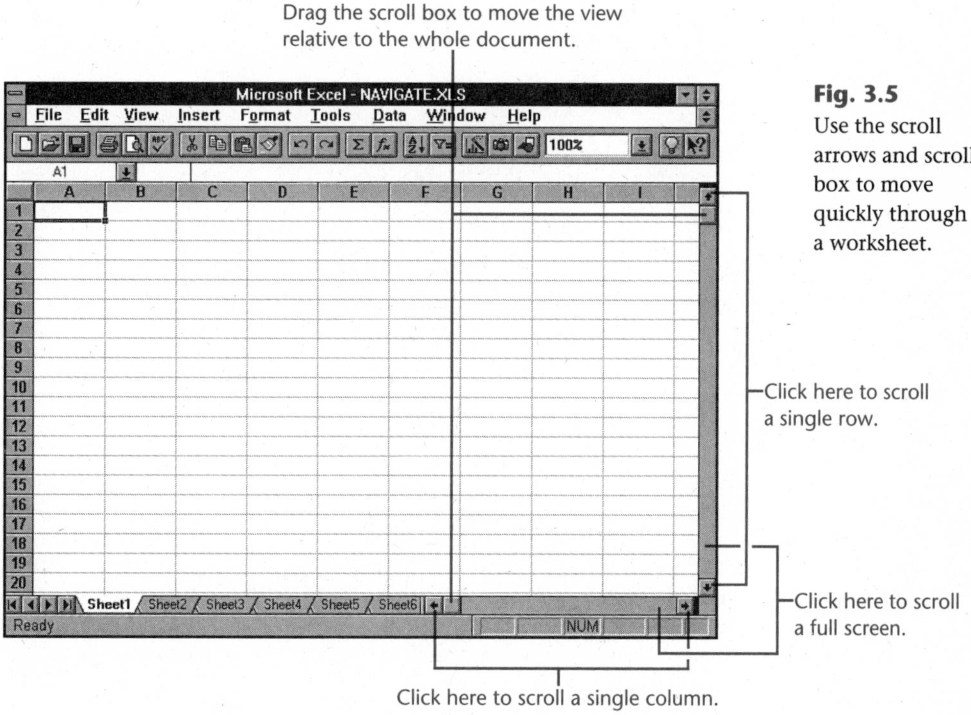
Drag the scroll box to move the view relative to the whole document.
Microsoft Excel - NAVIGATE.XLS
File Edit View Insert Format Tools Data Window Help
100%
A1
Sheet1 Sheet2 Sheet3 Sheet4 Sheet5 Sheet6
Ready
NUM
Click here to scroll a single row.
Click here to scroll a full screen.
Click here to scroll a single column.

Fig. 3.5
Use the scroll arrows and scroll box to move quickly through a worksheet.

Scrolling with the Keyboard

If you press arrow or page keys on the keyboard, you move the selected cell. If you move past the window, the area displayed in the window also changes. In some cases, you want to scroll the window without moving the selected cells.

From the keyboard, you can scroll the window over the worksheet without changing the selection by pressing normal movement keys, but you must

Tip
Watch the reference area at the top left of the screen (next to the formula bar) as you drag the scroll box to see how far you are moving.

press the Scroll Lock key first. When Scroll Lock is activated, you see SCRL at the bottom of the screen. This indicator means that if you press the arrow or movement keys, the screen scrolls without moving the cells you have selected. On many keyboards, a light appears on the key or keyboard when Scroll Lock is enabled. After you finish scrolling, do not forget to press the Scroll Lock key a second time to return the movement keys to their normal function.

Table 3.1 lists the keys that scroll the window.

Table 3.1 Keys that Scroll the Window

Key*	Movement
Up arrow	Scrolls up one row
Down arrow	Scrolls down one row
Right arrow	Scrolls right one column
Left arrow	Scrolls left one column
PgUp	Scrolls up one window
PgDn	Scrolls down one window
Ctrl+PgUp	Scrolls right one window
Ctrl+PgDn	Scrolls left one window
Home	Moves to the top left cell in the window
Ctrl+Home	Moves to cell A1
Ctrl+End	Moves to lower right corner of the worksheet

**Press Scroll Lock until the SCRL indicator appears at the bottom of the screen, and then press one of the keys.*

Selecting Cells and Ranges

Before you can enter, edit, or modify the contents of a cell, you must select the cell or cells you want to change. The single cell that receives the data or formula you enter is the *active cell*. A selection of multiple cells is referred to as a *range*.

The cell defined by a bold border and white background is the active cell. Commands affect all selected cells; data and formulas are entered in the active cell.

Selected cells are highlighted. If you select a range of cells, all the cells are highlighted, but one cell has a bold border and white background.

Selecting a Single Cell

Use either the mouse or the arrow keys to select cells. Selecting a cell with the mouse is easiest; just move the mouse pointer over the cell and click the mouse button.

To select a single cell from the keyboard, press the appropriate movement key to move the active cell. Table 3.2 shows the keys that move the active cell. To issue key combinations, such as Ctrl+PgUp, hold down the first key (Ctrl) as you press the second key (PgUp).

Tip
If you want to see the active cell, but it is not visible in the window, press Ctrl+Backspace. The window scrolls to show the active cell. Selected ranges remain selected.

Table 3.2 Keys that Move the Active Cell

Key	Movement
Up arrow	Moves the active cell up one cell
Down arrow	Moves the active cell down one cell
Right arrow	Moves the active cell right one cell
Left arrow	Moves the active cell left one cell
Tab	Enters data and moves the active cell right
Shift+Tab	Enters data and moves the active cell left
Enter	Enters data and moves the active cell down (when a range is selected or when the **M**ove Selection after Enter option is selected on the Edit tab in the Options dialog box)
Shift+Enter	Enters data and moves the active cell up in the selected range
Ctrl+arrow End+arrow	Moves the active cell in the direction indicated until the edge of a block of data is reached
Home	Moves the active cell to column A of the current row
Ctrl+Home	Moves the active cell to the first cell in the worksheet (A1)

(continues)

Table 3.2 Continued

Key	Movement
Ctrl+End	Moves the active cell to the last cell in the used portion of the worksheet
PgUp	Moves the active cell up one full window
PgDn	Moves the active cell down one full window
Ctrl+PgUp	Moves the active cell one screen left
Ctrl+PgDn	Moves the active cell one screen right

Moving to the Edge of a Block of Cells

If you have a large worksheet, database, or list, you need a way to accelerate your moves across blocks of data. With Excel's accelerator techniques, you can use the mouse or keyboard to move the active cell quickly across a filled row or up or down a filled column.

When using a mouse, double-click the side of a cell in the direction you want to move (see fig. 3.6). If the current cell is full, the active cell moves to the edge of the full area on the side you double-clicked. If the current cell is empty, the active cell moves to the first blank cell at the edge of the next full cell in the direction you click. Just double-click the side of a cell in the direction you want to go. You may find this technique easier if you turn the gridlines on by choosing the Tools Options command and selecting the View tab and the Gridlines check box.

The Ctrl or End key can save you time when you move across a filled row in a worksheet or when you move up or down a filled column. The Ctrl+arrow or End+arrow key combinations act as express keys that move the active cell as if the cell were on an expressway or an elevator. These key combinations move the active cell in the direction of the arrow until the active cell reaches the edge of a block.

To use these keys, select a cell, and hold down the Ctrl key as you press an arrow key in the direction you want to move. To use the End key, press the End key, release it, and press the arrow key in the direction you want to move.

If the current cell is full, the active cell moves in the direction of the arrow key to the edge of the filled area. If the current cell is empty, the active cell moves in the direction of the arrow to the first blank cell at the edge of the next filled area.

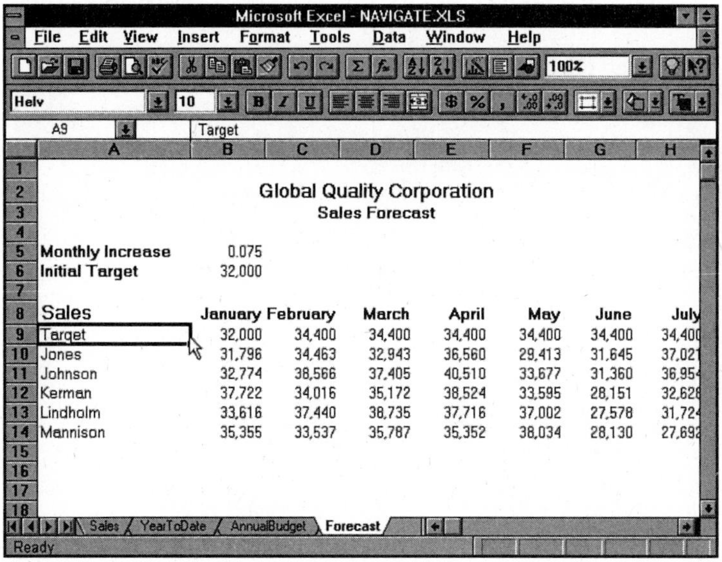

Fig. 3.6
Double-click the edge of the highlighted cell in the direction you want to move across filled cells.

Using the Go To Command To Move or Select

The **E**dit **G**o To command moves the active cell to any address you request. (Remember that an address is the indicator of the cell and is formed by combining the column letter and row number.) If you choose a named cell or range with **G**o To, the entire range is selected. (Named ranges are cells or ranges given a text name, such as *Revenue.*)

To use the **G**o To command, follow these steps:

1. Choose Edit Go To or press F5 to display the Go To dialog box (refer to fig. 3.4).
2. In the Reference text box, type the cell address or range you want to go to, or select from the list box the named location you want to go to.
3. Choose OK or press Enter.

To go to a named location on the active worksheet when you are using a mouse, follow these steps:

1. Click the down-arrow to the right of the reference area to display a list of names on the worksheet, as shown in figure 3.7.

2. Click the name of the range to which you want to go.

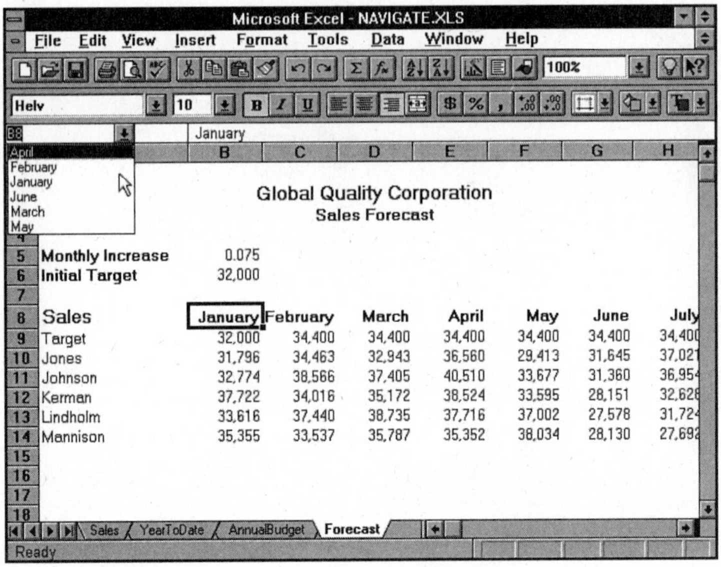

Fig. 3.7
Click the pull-down arrow next to the reference area to see a list of named ranges to which you can go.

Selecting a Range

Select a range of cells when you want to apply a command to all the selected cells or enter data into the cells in the range.

To select a range of cells with the mouse, follow these steps:

1. Click the cell at one corner of the range.

2. Drag to the opposite corner of the range and release the mouse button.

A rectangular range of cells is selected, as shown in figure 3.8. The pointer can wander on-screen as it moves to the opposite corner; make sure that the pointer is on the correct cell when you release the mouse button.

If a corner of the range is off the screen, drag the mouse pointer against the document window's edge in the direction you want to move. The window scrolls over the worksheet.

To select cells by using the keyboard, hold down Shift as you press movement keys, or press F8, movement keys, and F8 again to turn off Extend mode.

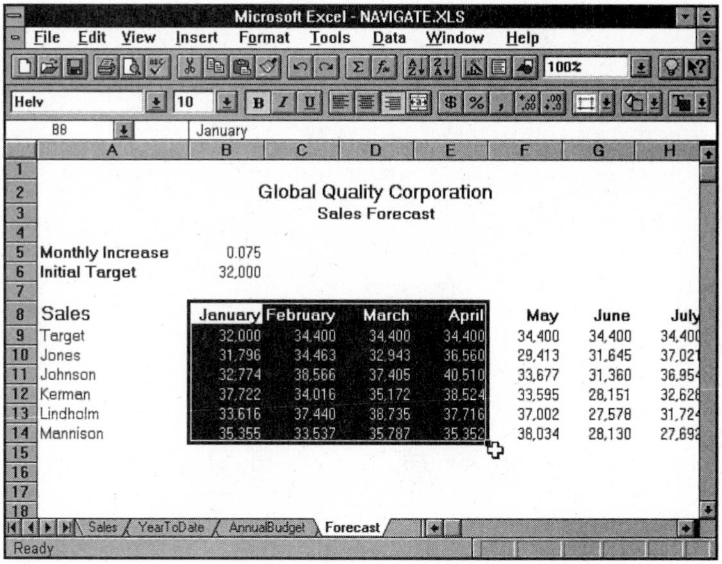

Fig. 3.8
Select a range by clicking the cell at one corner and dragging to the opposite corner.

If the opposite corner is outside the edge of the window, continue to hold down Shift and press the cursor-movement keys. The window scrolls to let you see the direction you are selecting.

At the left end of the formula bar, the Reference Area shows you how many rows and columns you are selecting as you drag the mouse or press the arrow keys.

Selecting a Large Range. In some cases, a range is so large that dragging or pressing keys from one corner to another takes a long time. You can use quicker methods for selecting large areas.

To select a large range using the keyboard, follow these steps:

1. Select one corner of the range.

2. Choose the **E**dit **G**o To command, or press F5.

3. Type the cell reference of the opposite corner in the **R**eference text box.

4. Hold down Shift as you choose the OK button, or press Enter.

   To select a range different from where you are located, choose the **E**dit **G**o To command. You can also press F5 and type a range address in the **R**eference box, such as A5:F12, and then choose OK or press Enter. In this case, the active cell is A5 and the range selected is from A5 to F12.

To select a large area with a mouse, follow these steps:

1. Select one corner of the range.
2. Scroll the window so that the opposite corner appears. (Do not click in the worksheet. The original corner must remain active.)
3. Hold down Shift as you click the opposite corner. All cells between the two corners are selected.

You also can select ranges by using the F8 key to turn on Extend mode. Extend mode produces the same result as continuously holding down the Shift key.

To select a range by using Extend mode, follow these steps:

1. Select a corner of the range by using the mouse or keyboard.
2. Press F8 to enter Extend mode. Extend mode acts the same as pressing Shift as you move. Notice the EXT indicator at the bottom of the window.
3. Select the opposite corner of the range by clicking it or moving to it with the movement keys.
4. Press F8 again to turn off Extend mode.

As long as EXT appears in the status bar, the first corner selected remains anchored.

Keep in mind that you can use all the mouse actions or movement keys combined with Shift or F8 to select a range with the keyboard. Table 3.3 lists shortcut keys for selecting ranges.

Table 3.3 Shortcut Keys for Selecting Ranges

Key	Extend selection from active cell to
F8	Next cell selected
Shift+arrow	Next cell selected
Shift+Home	Beginning of row
Shift+Ctrl+Home	Beginning of worksheet (A1)
Shift+Ctrl+End	End of worksheet

Key	Extend selection from active cell to
Shift+End	Lowest right cell used in worksheet
Shift+space bar	Entire row of active cell
Ctrl+space bar	Entire column of active cell
Shift+Ctrl+space bar	Entire worksheet
Shift+PgUp	Cell in same column one window up
Shift+PgDn	Cell in same column one window down
Shift+Ctrl+PgUp	Cell in same row one window right
Shift+Ctrl+PgDn	Cell in same row one window left
Shift+Ctrl+arrow	Edge of the next block of data in the direction of the arrow key

Selecting Multiple Ranges. Excel has the capability to select multiple non-adjacent (noncontiguous) ranges simultaneously. This enables you to format multiple ranges with a single command, print different parts of the worksheet with a single command, or erase multiple data-entry cells with a keystroke.

To select multiple ranges using the keyboard, follow these steps:

1. Select the cell at the corner of a range.
2. Select the first range.
3. Press Shift+F8 to enter Add mode. The ADD indicator shows at the bottom of the screen.
4. Repeat steps 1, 2, and 3 if you want to select an additional range.

To select multiple ranges using F5, follow these steps:

1. Press F5.
2. In the **R**eference text box, type the names or references you want to select, separating each with a comma as shown in figure 3.9. Do not uses any spaces.
3. Choose OK.

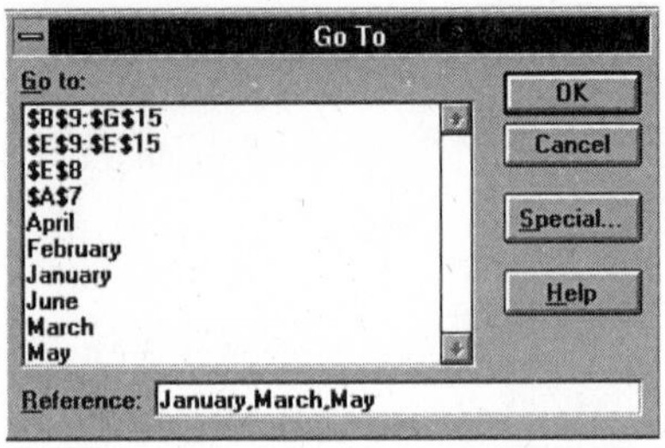

Fig. 3.9
Select multiple locations by pressing F5 and typing the locations separated by commas.

To select multiple ranges by using the mouse, follow these steps:

1. Select the first range.

2. Press Ctrl as you select each additional range.

3. Release Ctrl.

Figure 3.10 shows an example of selecting multiple ranges.

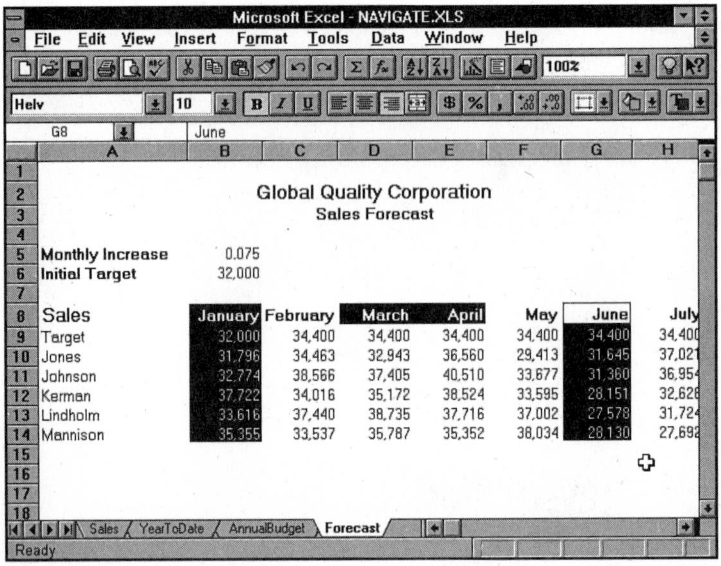

Fig. 3.10
Press Ctrl as you drag the mouse across each additional selection.

Selecting Blocks of Adjacent Cells. Often, the data that you want to copy or format lies in a contiguous block of cells, such as the rows in a filled budget sheet or the filled columns in a database. Selecting all the cells in such a row or selecting a column can be easy with mouse shortcuts or shortcut keys (see fig. 3.11). For these shortcuts, remember that pressing Shift as you move selects the cells you move across.

With the mouse, you can select contiguous cells by pressing Shift as you double-click the edge of the cell in the direction you want to select. In figure 3.11, for example, the active cell is cell A5. To select cells A5:F5, press Shift and double-click the vertical cell edge between A5 and B5.

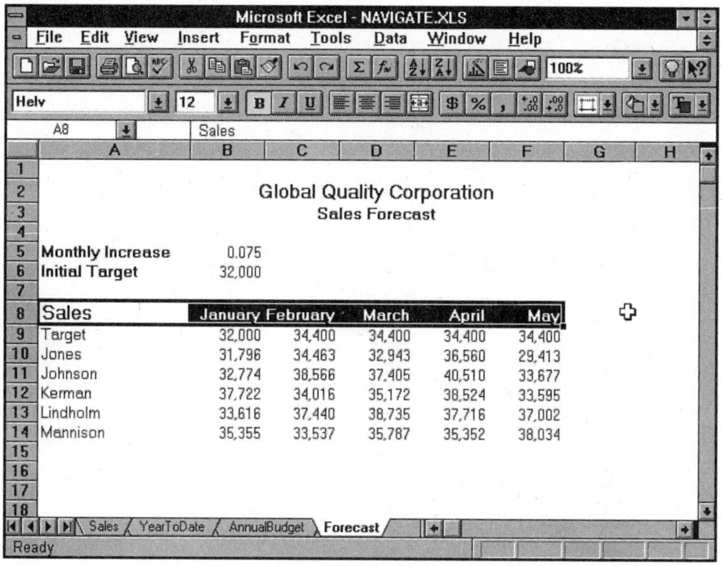

Fig. 3.11
Shift+double-click a cell edge to select a filled row or column.

With the keyboard, you can select contiguous cells by selecting a cell at one corner of a block, and pressing Shift+Ctrl as you press the arrow key that points in the direction you want to select. Filled cells are selected until a blank cell is reached.

> **Caution**
>
> Be careful in using these selection techniques! While fast, they may cause you to miss part of a selection. For example, if you are on a full cell and you select a row or a column with this technique, the selection stops as soon as a blank cell is reached, which can cause problems in a database where one or more blank cells may be in a column. You may think that you selected the entire column, but the selection is discontinued part way by a blank cell.

Another method for selecting a rectangular block around all touching full cells is to select one of the filled cells, and press Ctrl+*. This is the shortcut key for choosing the **E**dit **G**o To command, selecting **S**pecial, and selecting Current **R**egion. A following section, "Selecting Cells by Type of Content," discusses other options in the **E**dit **G**o To **S**pecial command.

After you select cells with the **E**dit **G**o To **S**pecial command, you can maintain the selections and move between the cells by pressing Tab, Shift+Tab, Enter, or Shift+Enter. This technique enables you to move the active cell between selected cells and see the contents, such as formulas, in the formula bar while maintaining the selected range.

Selecting Rows and Columns

Some operations are quicker if you select an entire row or column at one time. Formatting is also more memory efficient if you select and format an entire row or column instead of formatting each cell in the row or column (see fig. 3.12).

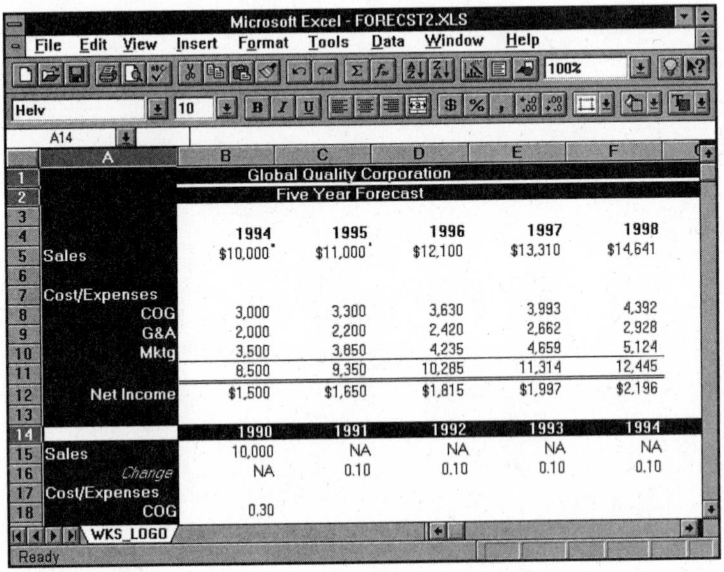

Fig. 3.12
Select multiple rows or columns to format more quickly and save memory.

To select an entire row or entire column with the mouse, click the row or column heading. Click the number 5 at the left edge of the document, for example, to select row 5. You can select adjacent rows or columns by dragging across the headings or by clicking the first and Shift+clicking the last. Select multiple nonadjacent rows or columns by holding down the Ctrl key as you click each heading.

To select the row or column containing the active cell with the keyboard, use the following shortcut keys:

Shift+space bar	Selects the row
Ctrl+space bar	Selects the column

After you select a row or column, you can select additional adjacent rows or columns by holding down Shift as you press the arrow keys.

Figure 3.12 shows how you can select multiple rows and columns before you give a single bold command or click bold in the toolbar. By pressing Ctrl and clicking each row or column heading, you select these rows and columns.

Selecting Cells by Type of Content

Excel contains a valuable command that enables you to select cells by content or relationship to formulas. This command is useful if you need to select the following:

- Cells containing values within an area of formulas or vice versa
- Related formulas
- Notes
- A rectangular region that surrounds all touching filled cells
- Array formulas
- Errors
- Embedded, graphical, or charting objects

To select cells according to their content, follow these steps:

1. If you want to check the entire worksheet for a specific cell content, select a single cell, or select a range of cells to check cells within a range.
2. Choose the **E**dit **G**o To command, or press F5.
3. From the Go To dialog box, choose **S**pecial. The Go To Special dialog box appears (see fig. 3.13).

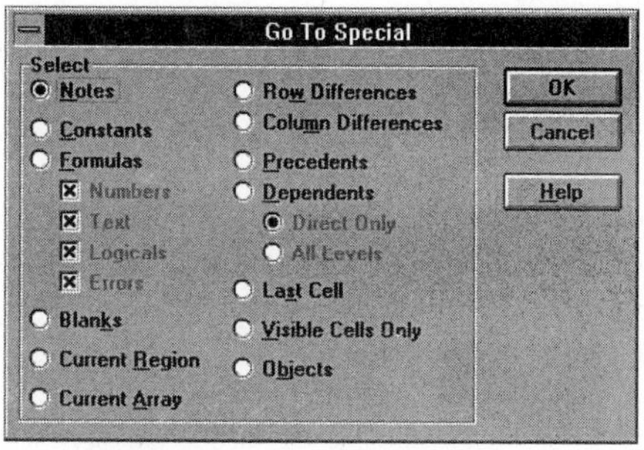

Fig. 3.13
After pressing F5 and choosing **S**pecial, you can select different types of cell contents.

4. Select one of the following options:

   Notes: Selects cells containing notes. (Shortcut: Ctrl+Shift+?).

   Constants: Selects cells containing constants of the type specified in the check boxes below.

   Formulas: Selects cells containing formulas that produce a result of the type specified in the check boxes below.

   Check Boxes

   > Numbers: Selects cells containing numbers.
   >
   > Text: Selects cells containing text.
   >
   > Logicals: Selects cells containing logical values.
   >
   > Errors: Selects cells containing errors.

   Blanks: Selects blank cells.

   Current Region: Selects a rectangular block of cells that includes all touching non-blank cells. (Shortcut: Ctrl+*).

   Current Array: Selects the array containing the active cell. (Shortcut: Ctrl+/).

   Row Differences: Selects cells containing formulas that have different relative references than other formulas in the row.

   Column Differences: Selects cells containing formulas that have different relative references than other formulas in the column.

   Precedents: Selects cells that feed into the formula in the selected cell. Select one of the following check boxes to define the depth of precedent.

   Dependents: Selects cells containing formulas that depend upon the result from this cell. Select one of the following check boxes to define the depth of dependence.

   Check Boxes

   > Direct Only: Selects only the first precedent or dependent cell.
   >
   > All Levels: Selects all precedent or dependent cells.

Last Cell: Selects the lowest, rightmost cell used by the active worksheet.

Visible Cells Only: Selects the visible cells; prevents changes to collapsed outline data or hidden rows or columns.

Objects: Selects all graphical objects.

5. Choose OK.

Tips about Selecting

Use the **E**dit **G**o To command to select frequently used ranges quickly. Name the cells or ranges you use frequently with the Insert Name Define command. After you name the cells, you can go to and select these cells or ranges by pressing F5, selecting the name, and choosing OK. For a shortcut when going to a name, press F5 and double-click the name.

When you work with large lists, databases, or print ranges, it may be impossible to see and check the area around a corner. You can move the active cell around the corners while keeping the range selected by selecting a range and pressing Ctrl+. (period).

You don't need to redo an entire selection when you select an area that is slightly different from the selection you want. Instead use the following steps to adjust the current selection:

1. Press Ctrl+. (period) until the active cell is diagonally opposite the corner you need to move. Each press of Ctrl+. moves the active cell clockwise to the next corner.

2. Press Shift and an arrow key. The window changes to show you the corner you want to move. Press Shift+arrow to move the corner you want while keeping the rest of the selection the same.

You can quickly return to one of the last four locations you selected by using F5. To return to one of the previous locations, press F5 to display the Go To dialog box. As shown in figure 3.14, the last four locations selected by using the Go To dialog box are at the top of the list. Double-click the location you want to return to or select a location and choose OK.

When you know the text, number, or formula you are looking for but don't know the location, use the Edit Find command, which locates numeric or text values, partial or whole formulas, or the contents of a note attached to a cell. Chapter 4, "Entering and Editing Data," contains more information about the Find command.

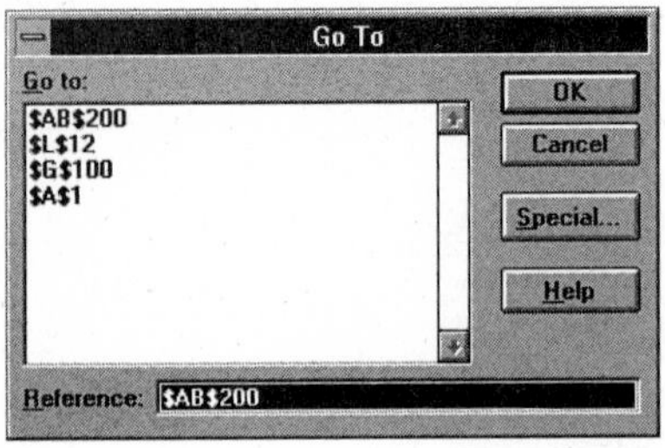

Fig. 3.14
Press F5 and double-click one of the last four locations you selected with the Go To command.

For Related Information

■ "Naming Cells for Better Worksheets," p. 157

After you select cells with the Edit Go To Special command, you can maintain the selections and move between the cells by pressing Tab, Shift+Tab, Enter, or Shift+Enter. This technique enables you to move the active cell between selected cells and see the contents, such as formulas, in the formula bar while maintaining the selected range.

From Here...

For information relating directly to moving and selecting in workbooks and worksheets, review the following major sections of this book:

- Chapter 5, "Working with Formulas," for information on creating range names.
- Chapter 8, "Reorganizing Worksheets and Workbooks," for information on managing sheets and clearing, inserting, and deleting cell contents.
- Chapter 26, "Auditing Workbooks and Worksheets," for information on auditing your workbooks.

Chapter 4

Entering and Editing Data

4

Excel's value lies in storing, manipulating, and displaying data. Before you can use data in Excel, however, you must enter it. This chapter discusses the types of data a cell can contain, and explains how to enter data.

In this chapter, you learn how to:

- Enter text, numbers, and dates
- Edit the contents of a cell
- Find and replace text, numbers, and formulas
- Insert and delete cells, rows, and columns
- Enter a series of numbers and dates
- Improve your data-entry efficiency

Entering Data

Excel worksheet cells can contain values or formulas. The constant values that cells can contain are numbers, text, dates, times, logical values, and errors. A *logical value*, such as `TRUE` or `FALSE`, is the result displayed after a condition is tested. *Error values*, such as `#NUM!`, occur when Excel cannot properly evaluate a formula in a cell.

When you type a value or formula in the active cell, your entry appears at the insertion point, or cursor, in the formula bar near the top of the screen. The entry appears in the long text box on the right side of the formula bar. You can also type and edit directly in a cell if you turn on in-cell editing. Even if what you type exceeds the width of the cell, the full contents of the cell are displayed so that you can see what you are doing. Figure 4.1 shows editing in the formula bar and in cell C5.

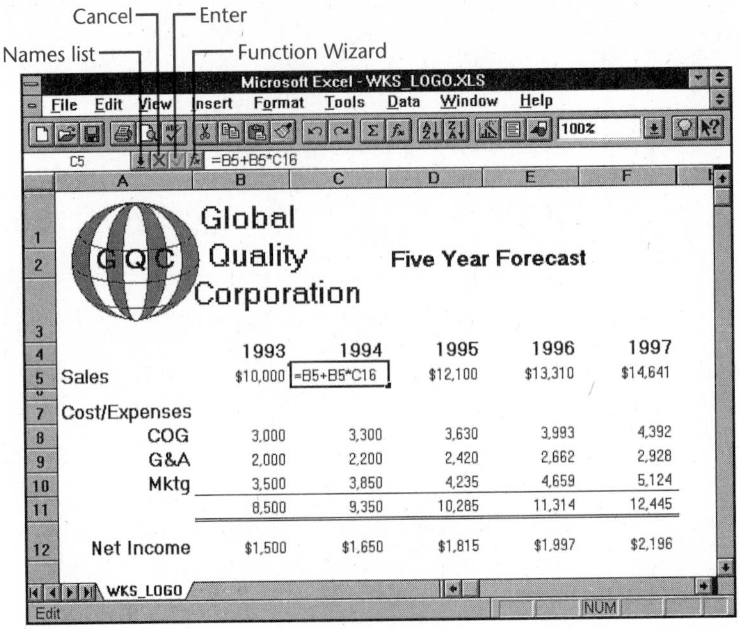

Fig. 4.1
Type or edit in the formula bar at the top of the screen. With in-cell editing, you can type or edit directly within a cell.

The *insertion point,* a flashing vertical line in the formula bar or cell, indicates where characters you type will appear. When you type or edit in the formula bar, boxes appear to the left of the formula bar. If you are using a mouse, clicking the Cancel box (the box with an × in it) cancels an entry; clicking the Enter box (the box with a check mark in it) enters the contents of the formula bar into the active cell. The Function Wizard box enables you to paste a function directly into the cell. The Names List box enables you to paste a named cell reference into formulas.

To enter data in a worksheet by typing in the formula bar, follow these steps:

1. Select the cell in which you want to enter data.
2. Type the entry.

   The entry appears in the formula bar as you type. If you decide that you want to cancel the entry, click the Cancel box in the formula bar or press Esc.
3. Enter what you have typed by clicking the Enter box in the formula bar or by pressing Enter.

You can also enter and edit data directly in a cell. This may be more convenient if you have the formula bar turned off or if the worksheet is built to look like a form where in-cell editing is expected.

To turn on in-cell editing, follow these steps:

1. Choose the **T**ools **O**ptions command to display the Options dialog box.
2. Select the Edit tab.
3. Select the **E**dit Directly in Cell check box.
4. Choose OK.

To enter data directly in a cell, follow these steps:

1. Double-click the cell in which you want to enter data.
2. Begin typing.

   As you type the entry, the cell contents extend, if necessary, beyond the cell's right boundaries.

If you want to back out before the value or formula is entered in a cell, press Esc or click the Cancel box in the formula bar.

You have learned the basic procedure for entering data in a worksheet. In the following sections, you will learn many shortcuts for entering data and formulas.

Entering Text

Text entries can include alphabetical characters, numbers, and symbols. To enter text in a cell, select the cell, type the text entry, and then enter the text by clicking the Enter box in the formula bar or by pressing Enter.

You can type as many as 255 characters in a cell. (Note that all the characters may not be displayed if the cell is not wide enough and if the cell to the right contains data.) When you enter text in a cell that still has the original General format, the text automatically aligns on the left side of the cell.

As you are working in Excel, you may find that you need to enter a number as text. For example, you may need to create a text heading—such as ($000)—that Excel would normally treat as a number. You can make Excel accept numbers as text by typing an apostrophe (') followed by the number—for example, **'45,000**. You also can enter numbers as text by placing an equal sign in front of the numbers and enclosing the numbers in quotation marks. To enter the number 45,000 as text, for example, you type **="45,000"**. Notice that in a cell with the General format, numbers entered as text will align on the left like text. When you enter a number as text, you can still use the number if it is needed in a numeric formula.

Note

You can quickly format a range of numbers as text in your worksheet by using the Text numeric format. To use this format, select the range of cells containing the numbers, click the right mouse button, choose the F**o**rmat C**e**lls command, select the Number tab, select Text from the Category list, select @ from the Format Codes list, and click OK.

Another method used to enter a number as text is to use the TEXT() function. The TEXT() function enables you to enter a number in a format you specify and then converts the formatted number into text. This can be very useful for numbers that need to appear as titles or numbers that must exceed the column width. The use of TEXT() is described in Chapter 23, "Manipulating and Analyzing Data."

Entering a number as text enables the number display to exceed the cell's width. If you enter a number in the normal way and the cell is not wide enough to display it, the cell fills with # signs or in some cases may display the number in scientific notation.

If you need to display quotation marks on-screen within a formula involving text, you must enclose the quotation marks you want within quotation marks. Enclosing the quotation marks rather than the text results in three quotation marks on either side of the text, as in the following example:

="""The Absolute Best"""&" the worst"

Excel enables you to type phrases that begin with a number directly into the worksheet. For example, the following address is accepted by Excel as text because it contains letters:

45 Oak Ridge Trail

Entering Numbers

Numbers are constant values containing only the following characters:

1 2 3 4 5 6 7 8 9 0 _ + / . E e

To enter a number, you select the cell, type the number, and then press Enter or click the Enter box in the formula bar. You can enter integers, such as 135 or 327; decimal fractions, such as 135.437 or 327.65; integer fractions, such as 1 1/2 or 2/3; or scientific notation, such as 1.35437E+2.

As you create worksheets, Excel may display newly entered numbers or formulas as `2.67E+9`, for example, or as ######### (see fig. 4.2). Scientific notation is another way of representing the same number. For example, 2.67E+9 represents 2.67 times 10^9 (1 with 9 zeroes behind it).

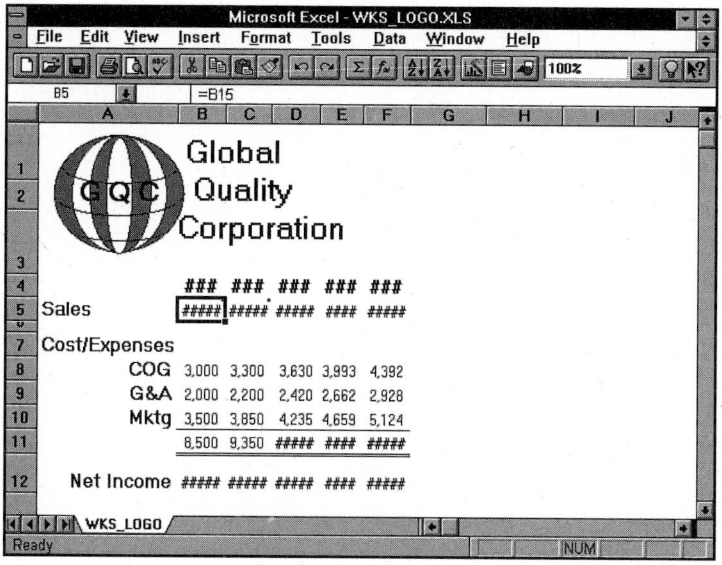

Fig. 4.2
Scientific format or the signs ### appear when a column is not wide enough to display a number or date.

A cell filled with # signs indicates that the column is not wide enough to display the number correctly. In this case, you need to change the numeric format or widen the column. Formatting worksheets is described in Chapter 10, "Formatting Worksheets."

Note

You may need to convert a numeric or date result into text for use in a title or so that it will fit into a narrow cell. To do so, use the TEXT( ) function. The TEXT( ) function also formats numeric or date results using any of the predefined or custom numeric and date formats. The TEXT( ) function is described in Chapter 23, "Manipulating and Analyzing Data."

Electronic worksheets like Excel store both the number typed into a cell and the format or appearance in which the number should be displayed. When you enter a number into a cell, Excel tries to establish how the number should be formatted. For example, Excel accepts and displays the entries listed in table 4.1 with the formats indicated.

Table 4.1 Excel's Automatic Formats

Typed Entry	Excel's Automatically Chosen Format	Displayed Result
897	Number, General	897
7999 Knue Rd.	Text, left aligned	7999 Knue Rd.
$450.09	Number, dollar format	$450.09
54.6%	Number, percent format	54.60%
2 3/4	Number, fraction	2 3/4
0 3/4	Number, fraction	3/4
45,600	Number, comma format	45,600
–678	Number, negative	–678
(678)	Number, negative	–678
1/5/93	Date, m/d/yy	1/5/93
4/5	Date, m/d/yy (current year assumed)	5-Apr

The second example, 7999 Knue Rd., illustrates that if an entry is not a number or date, Excel stores it as text. This feature is convenient when you are entering database or list information, such as inventory codes or street addresses.

To enter a fraction, you must type an integer, a space, and then the fraction. If you are entering only the fractional part, type a zero, a space, and then the fraction; otherwise Excel will interpret the entry as a date. The result is a number that can be used in calculations.

Entering Dates and Times

Excel recognizes dates and times typed in most common ways. When you type a date or time, Excel converts your entry to a *serial number*. The serial number represents the number of days from the beginning of the century until the date you type. Time is recorded as a decimal fraction of a 24-hour day.

If Excel recognizes your entry as a valid date or time format, you see the date or time on-screen. Correctly entered dates appear in the formula bar with the format m/d/yyyy, regardless of how the cell is formatted.

A valid date entry typed into an unformatted cell is aligned as a number, to the right. A valid date entry typed into a cell that has been previously formatted with a numeric format appears as a serial number. If, for example, you type **5 Nov 93** in a cell formatted to show numbers with a comma and two decimal places (#,##0.00), you will see that date as `34,278.00`.

Tip
To format a date in the default date format, select the cell containing the date and press Ctrl+#.

If Excel does not recognize your entry as a valid date or time format and you type a text date, such as **Sept 5 93**, Excel treats the entry as text and, in an unformatted cell, aligns it to the left.

To enter a date, type the date into the cell with any of these formats:

7/8/93

8-Jul-93

8-Jul (The year from the system date is used.)

Jul-93 (Only the month and year show.)

6/8/93 09:45

Tip
To quickly enter the current date in a cell, select the cell and press Ctrl+; (semicolon). To enter the current time in a cell, press Ctrl+: (colon).

In any of these date formats, you can use either a /, -, or space to separate elements.

Enter times in any of these formats:

13:32

13:32:45

1:32 PM

1:32:45 PM

6/8/93 13:32

Tip
To format a time in the default time format, press Ctrl+@.

For Related Information

- "Changing Character Fonts, Sizes, Styles, and Colors," p. 312
- "Formatting Numbers," p. 328
- "Formatting Dates and Times," p. 341

The first two examples are from a 24-hour clock. If you use a 12-hour clock, follow the time with a space and A, AM, P, or PM (in either upper- or lowercase). Be sure that you leave a space before the AM or PM. Do not mix a 24-hour clock time with an AM or PM. As the last format shows, you can combine the date and time during entry.

For information about formatting or changing the formats of dates and times, refer to Chapter 10, "Formatting Worksheets."

Note

In some cases when you enter a correctly formatted date or time, the displayed result appears as a number, not in a date or time format. This occurs when the cell's format has been previously changed from the default, General. To reformat for the correct display, select the cell, choose the F**o**rmat **C**ell command, or press Ctrl+1, choose the Number tab, select the appropriate date or time format from the list box, and then choose OK.

Editing Text and Formulas

When the time comes for you to edit a cell entry, you can either edit the text in the formula bar or in the cell itself. If you are used to using the formula bar, you may want to continue editing in the formula bar. For worksheets built like data-entry forms, the users often expect to type directly into a cell.

Editing in the Formula Bar

To edit in the formula bar, perform the following steps:

1. Select the cell containing the data you want to edit.

2. Move the insertion point into the text.

   Move the pointer over the text until it changes into an I-beam. Position the pointer in the text you want to edit, and then click. A flashing insertion point indicates where typing and editing take place.

   If you have selected a cell, press F2. Press the movement keys to move the insertion point to where you want to edit the text.

3. Edit the formula.

EXCEL 5

Editing Directly in a Cell

To edit directly in a cell, perform the following steps:

1. Double-click the cell.
2. Press the arrow keys to move to where you want to edit.
3. Press Enter to enter the information, or press Esc to leave the contents unchanged.

> **Caution**
>
> If you know that a formula contains an error, but you cannot find it, do *not* press Esc—the formula bar will clear and you will lose the formula. Instead, delete the equal sign and press Enter. The formula becomes text in the cell. Later, when you know how to fix the formula, reselect the cell, re-enter the equal sign, and correct the formula.

Table 4.2 lists shortcut keys and mouse actions you can use for editing.

Table 4.2 Shortcut Keys and Mouse Actions for Editing Formulas

Key(s)	Mouse	Action
F2	Click formula bar	Moves the cursor into the formula bar for editing.
N/A	Double-click	Displays in-cell editing.
F4		Cycles the cell reference through all combinations of absolute and relative references.
F9	N/A	Calculates the selected part of a formula.
Ins	N/A	Toggles between Insert and Typeover modes.
Del	N/A	Clears the selected characters or character to the right of the insertion point.
Backspace	N/A	Clears the selected character(s) to the left of the insertion point.

(continues)

Table 4.2 Continued

Key(s)	Mouse	Action
Ctrl+Del	N/A	Clears all characters from the insertion point to the end of the line.
Ctrl+X	**E**dit Cu**t**	Cuts the character or selection to the right of the insertion point.
Ctrl+C	**E**dit **C**opy	Copies the selection to the Clipboard.
Ctrl+V	**E**dit **P**aste	Pastes the text at the insertion point, or replaces the selected characters.
Ctrl+Z	**E**dit **U**ndo	Reverses many editing actions.
Home	N/A	Moves the insertion point to the front of the formula bar.
End	N/A	Moves the insertion point to the end of the formula bar's contents.
Shift+Home	Drag up and left	Selects all characters from the insertion point to the front of the current line of the formula bar.
Shift+End	Drag down and right	Selects all characters from the insertion point to the end of the current line of the formula bar.
Shift+Ctrl+ Home	Drag up and left	Selects all characters from the insertion point to the beginning of the formula (even in multiple-line formulas).
Shift+Ctrl +End	Drag down and right	Selects all characters from the insertion point to the end of the formula (even in multiline formulas).
Shift+arrow	Drag across	Selects characters the insertion point crosses over.
Ctrl+left/ -right arrow	N/A	Moves a word or formula a term at a time.
Shift+Ctrl+ left/right arrow	Double-click, Double-click+drag	Selects a word or formula a term at a time.

When you need to insert the same text in several places, select the text and copy it with the **E**dit **C**opy command. Then move the insertion point to each spot where you want to place the text and choose the **E**dit **P**aste command.

Excel normally is in Insert mode, so what you type inserts itself at the insertion point. If you want to type over existing text, press Ins (Insert) to enter Typeover mode, and then type. Pressing Ins a second time toggles back to Insert mode.

You can delete single characters to the left of the cursor by pressing Backspace. Delete single characters to the right of the cursor by pressing Del.

Note

When Excel beeps and prohibits you from editing a cell's contents, the cell may be protected against changes. Protection is described in Chapter 10, "Formatting Worksheets."

Undoing and Repeating Changes

When you want to undo your last entry or last executed command, choose the **E**dit **U**ndo command or click the Undo tool. The **U**ndo command changes to show you the last command it can undo. After you have chosen the **U**ndo command, you can choose it again to undo the undo. To use the **U**ndo command, you must choose it immediately after the action you want to undo. If you want to repeat the last command, choose the **E**dit **R**epeat command or click the Repeat tool. Not all commands can be repeated.

For Related Information

- "Entering Formulas," p. 127
- "Moving Cell Contents," p. 235
- "Filling or Copying Cell Contents," p. 241

Finding or Replacing in a Worksheet

When you must change a lot of data or formulas that contain the same terms, use the **E**dit **F**ind or **E**dit R**e**place commands. These commands enable you to find text, numbers, or formula terms that are anywhere on the worksheet. R**e**place enables you to search and replace in a worksheet just as you do in a word processor. You also can use Find and Replace on formulas or portions of formulas.

Finding Text, Numbers, and Formulas

The **E**dit **F**ind command finds whatever you want in the worksheet (or list), including text or formulas. You can use the **E**dit **F**ind command to locate formulas that contain a unique term, a specific text label, a cell note containing a specific word, or error values. The **E**dit **F**ind command is especially helpful when you are correcting a worksheet you may not be familiar with.

To find text or a value with the **E**dit **F**ind command, perform the following steps:

1. Select the cells you want to search. Select a single cell to search the entire worksheet.
2. Choose the **E**dit **F**ind command or press Shift+F5 to display the Find dialog box (see fig. 4.3).

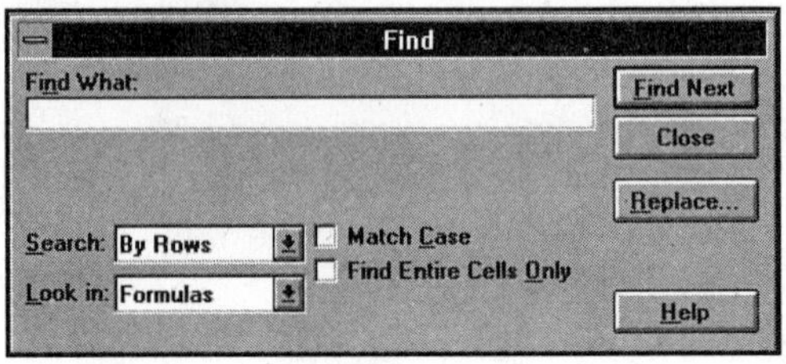

Fig. 4.3
Use **E**dit **F**ind to look for text, numbers, or formula terms in the worksheet or in notes.

3. Type what you are searching for in the Fi**n**d What box.
4. In the **L**ook In drop-down list box, select the name of the items you want to search through:

Option	Description
Formulas	Search through formulas in the cells indicated.
Values	Search through values in the cells indicated.
Notes	Search through notes attached to the cells indicated. (Notes are hidden descriptive text that can be attached to cells.) See Chapter 26, "Auditing Workbooks and Worksheets," for related information on notes.

5. Select the Find Entire Cells **O**nly check box if you want to find matches where only the entire cell contents match the contents in the Fi**n**d What text box. If this option is not selected, you will also find matches where only part of the cell contents match.
6. In the **S**earch drop-down list box, select the option that describes the direction in which you want the search to proceed:

Option	Description
By Rows	Search across rows starting at the current cell.
By Columns	Search down columns starting at the current cell.

7. Select the Match **C**ase check box if you want to exactly match upper- and lowercase.

8. Choose **F**ind Next to find the next match, or press Shift and choose **F**ind Next to find the previous match. Choose Close to stop finding items.

After you have completed step 8 and find the item, edit the formula with normal editing procedures.

To quickly find the next cell that satisfies the same conditions, press F4 to find the next occurrence. You can open the Replace dialog box from the Find dialog box by choosing the **R**eplace button. For more information on using the **E**dit R**e**place command, see the next section.

Edit **F**ind cannot be used with comparative operators, such as =, <, and >=. Entering **<12** in the Fi**n**d What box, for example, creates a search for the text <12 rather than for numbers less than 12. If your data is laid out properly, you can search on many different criteria using the techniques described in the database chapters.

You can search for *near misses* by using wild cards. You can use an * in the Fi**n**d What box to search for any group of characters, numbers, or cell references, and use a ? to search for any single character or part of a cell reference. If you type **=B12~*(C3+*)** in the Fi**n**d What box, for example, Excel looks for formulas that have anything as the last term in the parentheses. If you type **=B?**, Excel finds formulas with first terms that are relative references in the B column. Note that the first asterisk is preceded by a tilde (~). This tilde tells Excel to treat the asterisk as normal text, not as a wild card.

Replacing Text, Numbers, or Formulas

The **E**dit R**e**place command is a big help when you overhaul a worksheet. The command works the same way as a search-and-replace command does in a word processing application. You tell Excel what the new text is and what text it should replace. You can replace selectively or replace throughout the entire worksheet.

Note

Find cells linked to other cells, worksheets, or Windows applications by searching for occurrences of an exclamation mark. In the Find dialog box, select Formulas in the **L**ook In drop-down list box, and deselect the Find Entire Cells **O**nly check box.

To find cells that feed into the current formula or cells that depend on the current formula, use the **E**dit **G**o To **S**pecial command and select the **P**recedents or **D**ependents options. The D**i**rect Only and All **L**evels options indicate how many levels of precedents or dependents should be selected.

Edit R**e**place can save you from financial mistakes. If you must make major changes to a term or formula used throughout a worksheet, missing a single formula can have dire consequences. With **E**dit R**e**place, you can be sure that you have found and replaced all the incorrect formulas or terms.

To search and replace, perform the following steps:

1. Select the cells you want to search. Select a single cell to search the entire worksheet.

2. Choose the **E**dit R**e**place command to display the Replace dialog box (see fig. 4.4).

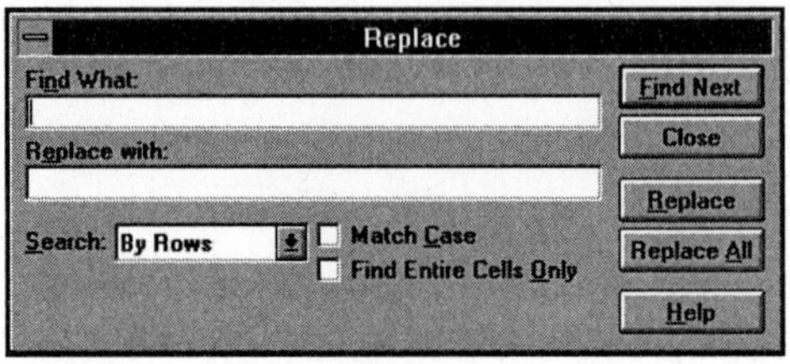

Fig. 4.4
The **E**dit R**e**place command is invaluable for making changes quickly throughout your worksheet or database.

3. In the Fi**n**d What box, type the text, cell reference, or formula term to be replaced.

4. Select the R**e**place With box, and type the replacement text.

5. Select the Find Entire Cells **O**nly check box if you want to specify that the text in the Fi**n**d What text box must match the entire cell contents. Clear this check box if the text in the Fi**n**d What box can match any part of the cell contents.

6. Select the option in the **S**earch drop-down list box that describes the direction in which you want the search to proceed:

Option	Description
By Rows	Search across rows starting at the current cell.
By Columns	Search down columns starting at the current cell.

7. Select the Match **C**ase check box if you want to find and replace only those words that exactly match upper- and lowercase.

8. Choose the Replace **A**ll button to find and replace all matches, **F**ind Next to find the next match, or **R**eplace to replace the current found item. Choose Close to stop the search. Choosing Close does not undo replacements that already have occurred.

If you need to undo changes you have made, choose the **E**dit **U**ndo Replace command.

To search for items to replace, you can use the * and ? wild cards as described in the previous section on the **E**dit **F**ind command. This method can be a very efficient way to change formulas or database contents in a portion or in the entire worksheet.

For Related Information

- "Finding Errors by Selecting Special Cells," p. 781
- "Using Text Notes," p. 790

Note

You can use the Edit Replace command to recalculate only selected cells on a worksheet. To do so, select all the cells you want to recalculate, and then use the **E**dit R**e**place command to replace the equal signs (=) with equal signs (=). This causes each formula to recalculate as though it were re-entered. However, the results of this method may be inaccurate if you do not include all cells involved in the calculations.

Clearing, Inserting, or Deleting in a Worksheet

After you have drafted and tested your worksheet, you may find that you need to reorganize or restructure the layout of the worksheet. This need is especially true if you inherit old worksheets or if you want to convert old 1-2-3 spreadsheets. When you restructure, you may need to insert or delete cells, rows, or columns.

Shortcut keys that are very helpful to reorganizing the worksheet layout are shown in table 4.3.

Table 4.3 Shortcut Keys for Changing the Worksheet Layout

Key(s)	Action
Del	Clears selected formulas; same as the **E**dit Cle**a**r **C**ontents command.
Backspace	Clears the formula bar; activates and clears the formula bar.
Ctrl+C	Copies the selection so that it can be pasted; same as the **E**dit **C**opy command.
Ctrl+X	Cuts the selection so it can be pasted; same as the **E**dit Cu**t** command.
Ctrl+V	Pastes at the selected cell; same as the **E**dit **P**aste command.
Ctrl+Z	Undoes last command from **E**dit menu.
Ctrl+Backspace	Repositions the worksheet so that the active cell is in view.

Clearing Cell Contents

Excel gives you alternatives when clearing or erasing cells. You can clear or erase everything in a cell or range, erase the format only, erase the formulas only, or erase the notes only.

Caution

When many people first use Excel, they make the mistake of choosing the **E**dit **D**elete command to remove the contents of a cell. They should use the **E**dit Cle**a**r command. The **E**dit **D**elete command removes the actual cell from the worksheet, like pulling a brick out of a wall. **E**dit Cl**e**ar leaves the cell in place, but erases the cell's contents.

Note

Novice worksheet users commonly think they can type a blank space, and then press Enter to erase a cell's contents. *Cells with spaces create problems.* For example, in most worksheet functions and database commands, Excel does not see that cell as blank, but as a cell containing a space character. Uncovering this problem can be difficult.

The quickest way to clear the contents of a cell is to select the cells, and then press the Del key. Only the contents are deleted. Formats and notes remain.

To clear the contents of a cell, perform the following steps:

1. Select the cell or range of cells you want to clear.
2. Choose the **E**dit Cle**a**r command to display the Clear cascading menu.
3. Select the command that describes what you want cleared:

Command	Description
All	Clears cell contents and notes; returns the format to General format.
Formats	Returns the format to General format.
Contents	Clears contents but does not change formats or notes.
Notes	Clears notes but does not change contents or formats.

To clear the contents of a cell or range of cells, select the cell(s), click the right mouse button and choose Clear Cells.

If you want to clear other cells immediately after this, you can save steps by pressing F4 or choosing the Repeat tool.

If you accidentally clear a cell's contents, immediately choose the **E**dit **U**ndo command (or press Ctrl+Z). This command undoes your most recent edit.

Note

If you clear the contents of a cell and find that formulas in a worksheet result in an error, you can use the Go To command to locate the errors in the worksheet. Choose the **E**dit **G**o To command or press F5. From the Go To dialog box, select the **S**pecial option. From the Go To Special dialog box, select the **F**ormula option. Turn off all the check boxes, but leave the **E**rrors check box selected; then choose OK. All cells that contain error values (such as #NAME?) are selected. Press Tab to move among the selected cells.

Inserting or Deleting Cells, Rows, and Columns

With Excel, you can delete or insert entire rows or columns. You also can easily delete or insert cells, leaving the surrounding rows or columns unaffected. This technique enables you to add or remove cells without having to change entire rows or columns.

Deleting Cells, Rows, and Columns. The Edit **D**elete command removes cells, rows, or columns from the worksheet. This command is useful when rearranging your worksheet to give it a more suitable layout.

Edit **D**elete is different from the Edit Cle**a**r command. Edit Cle**a**r clears a cell's contents, format, or note, but it leaves the cell intact. Edit **D**elete completely removes cells, rows, or columns; it doesn't just remove their contents.

When the Edit **D**elete command deletes cells, it completely removes the selected cells and *slides in* other cells to fill the gap. You can choose the direction in which the remaining cells move. Figures 4.5 and 4.6 show a worksheet before and after cells were deleted. The lower cells were moved up to fill the gap. Notice that the worksheet area to the right of the deleted cells was not affected. Edit **D**elete is an excellent command for sliding rows or columns into a new location without affecting adjacent cells.

> **Caution**
>
> Commands such as Clear, Insert, and Delete work differently when Excel is filtering information in a list or database. When Excel is filtering a list, the words `Filter Mode` appear in the status bar. To learn more about editing, inserting, and deleting when you are filtering a list or database, refer to Chapter 33, "Finding, Filtering, and Editing Lists and Databases."

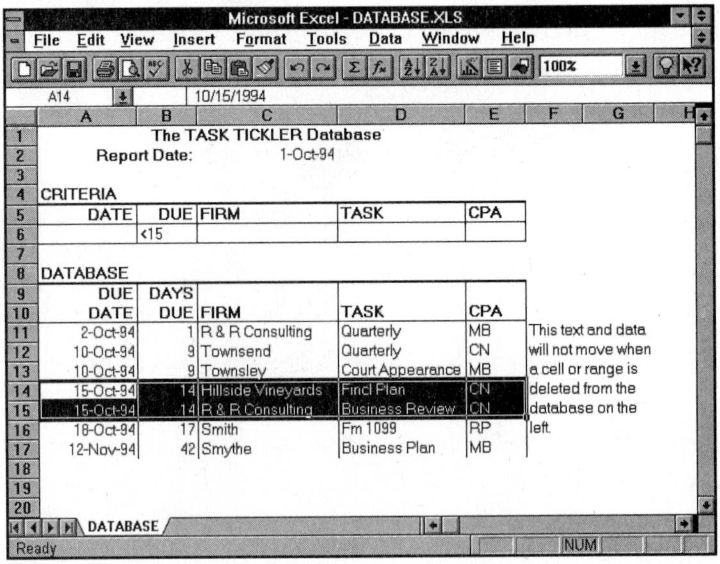

Fig. 4.5
A worksheet before cells are deleted.

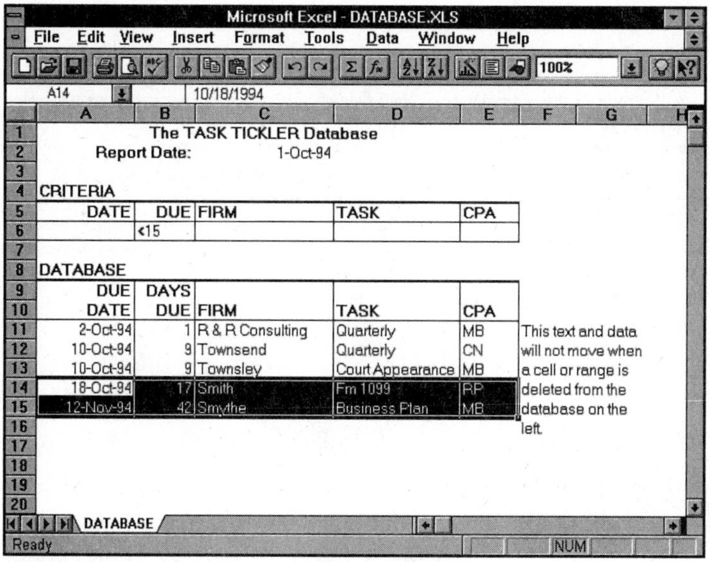

Fig. 4.6
Surrounding cells fill in the gap after cells have been deleted.

When you need to remove cells, rows, or columns from the worksheet, perform the following steps:

1. Select the cells or range to be deleted, or select cells in the rows or columns to be deleted.

2. Choose the **E**dit **D**elete command, or press Ctrl+– (minus), or click the right mouse button and select Delete. The Delete dialog box appears (see fig. 4.7).

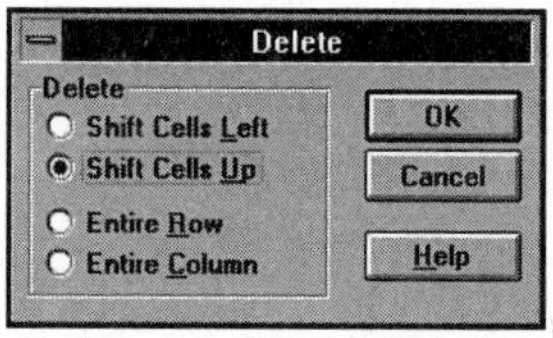

Fig. 4.7
The Delete dialog box displays options that enable you to control how surrounding cells are affected by a deletion.

If you selected a whole row or column, the dialog box does not appear.

3. If you want to delete cells, select the direction in which you want remaining cells to move:

Option	Description
Shift Cells **L**eft	Cells to the right of the deleted cells move left.
Shift Cells **U**p	Cells below the deleted cells move up.

If you want to delete the row(s) or column(s) containing the selected cells, select one of the options:

Option	Description
Entire **R**ow	Deletes each row containing a selected cell.
Entire **C**olumn	Deletes each column containing a selected cell.

4. Choose OK.

To undo an incorrect deletion, either choose the **E**dit **U**ndo Delete command, press Ctrl+Z, or click the Undo tool immediately.

You can delete rows or columns quickly by selecting the entire row or column, and then using the **E**dit **D**elete command or pressing Ctrl+– (minus). Click row or column headings to select the entire row or column, or press Shift+space bar to select a row and Ctrl+space bar to select a column.

Note

In 1-2-3, if you delete a row or column that contains a range boundary, formulas and functions that depend on that range are lost. If you delete a row or column on a range boundary in Excel, Excel reduces the range to compensate. In other words, with Excel, you can delete the last row of a database or SUM( ) column without producing errors and destroying your worksheet.

Inserting Cells, Rows, or Columns. Sometimes you must insert cells, rows, or columns to make room for new formulas or data. You can insert cells, rows, or columns as easily as you can delete them.

To insert cells, rows, or columns, perform the following steps:

1. Select a cell or range of cells where you need new cells inserted. Or select cells in the rows or columns where you want to insert new rows or columns.

2. Choose the **I**nsert C**e**lls command, or press Ctrl++ (plus) or click the right mouse button and select Insert. The Insert dialog box appears (see fig. 4.8).

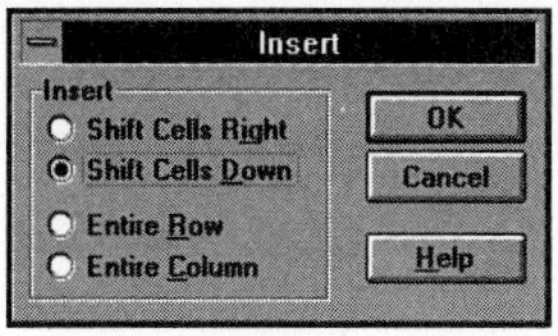

Fig. 4.8
The Insert dialog box enables you to control how surrounding cells are affected when you insert.

3. If you want to insert cells, select the direction you want selected cells to move when blank cells are inserted:

Option	Description
Shift Cells R**i**ght	Selected cells move right.
Shift Cells **D**own	Selected cells move down.

If you want to insert rows or columns, select the option button desired:

Option	Description
Entire **R**ow	Insert a row at each selected cell.
Entire **C**olumn	Insert a column at each selected cell.

4. Choose OK.

Another way to insert rows, or columns, is to select cells in the rows or columns where you want to insert new rows or columns. Then choose **I**nsert **R**ows or **I**nsert **C**olumns.

In figure 4.9, a range of cells has been selected where blank cells will be inserted. Figure 4.10 shows the results after insertion. Notice that the data in the cells to the right of the inserted area has not moved. Only the cells below the insertion move down to make room for the inserted cells.

Excel takes some of the work out of inserting. In most cases, when you insert a row or group of cells, you want each inserted cell to have the same format as the cell above. Excel automatically formats the inserted row or cells with the format above. If you don't want this format, use the method described in Chapter 10, "Formatting Worksheets," to format the new cells.

For Related Information

- "Moving Cell Contents," p. 235
- "Filling or Copying Cell Contents," p. 241
- "Inserting and Removing Sheets," p. 258
- "Copying and Moving Sheets," p. 260
- "Selecting Cells and Ranges," p. 72
- "Linking Pictures of Cells in a Worksheet," p. 574

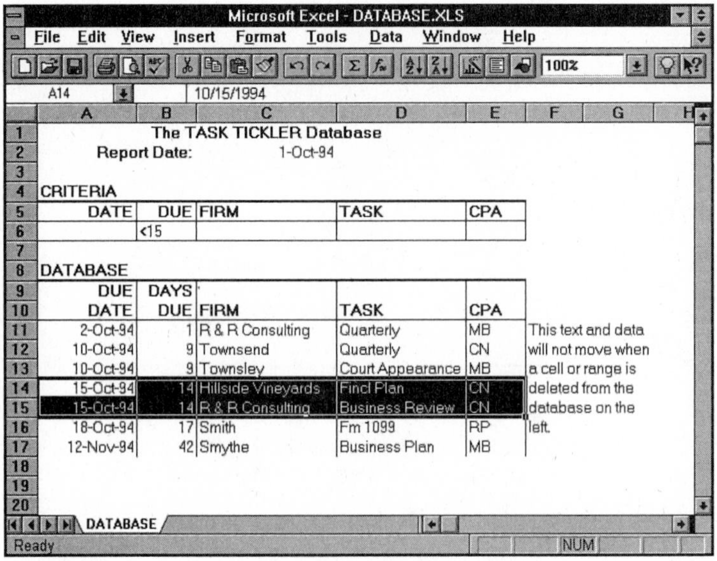

Fig. 4.9
Blank cells will be inserted in the selected range.

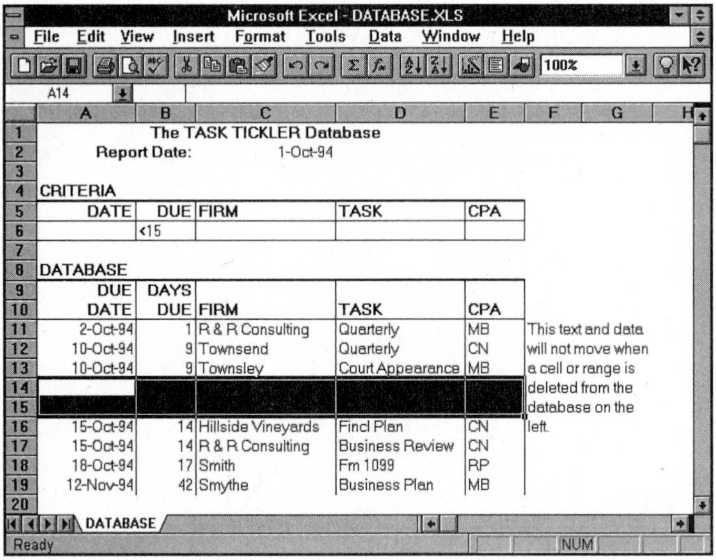

Fig. 4.10
Blank cells are inserted in the selected range and cells below the insertion move down.

Entering a Series of Numbers or Dates

When you build forecasts, budgets, or trend analyses, you often need a series of dates, numbers, or text. You can enter a series quickly with the **E**dit F**i**ll **S**eries command or by dragging the fill handle. A data series can number the items in a database, enter a series of consecutive dates, create quarterly or dated headings, or create a series of data-entry values for a table of solutions that you generate with the **D**ata **T**able command.

Note

You can use series techniques for trend analysis. To perform a trend analysis on data, you can use series techniques to create the forecasted series and produce trend parameters. To learn how to perform a linear or growth best-fit analysis by using data series techniques, read the section "Analyzing Trends" in Chapter 23, "Manipulating and Analyzing Data."

Figure 4.11 shows examples of numeric and date series, entered with the **E**dit F**i**ll **S**eries command or by dragging the fill handle. Note that the dates for the days and months are created with a custom date format. Custom date and numeric formatting is described in Chapter 10, "Formatting Worksheets."

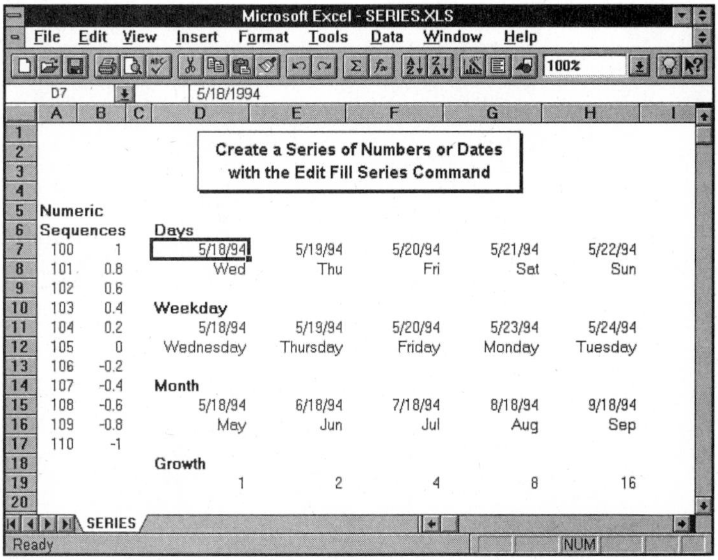

Fig. 4.11
Use the fill handle with the right mouse button or the **E**dit F**i**ll **S**eries command to fill in different types of sequential data.

You can create a series in two ways. The easiest method uses the mouse to drag the fill handle. The second method uses a command and gives you the capability to create many kinds of series.

Creating a Linear Series

To create a series that increments in equal steps, perform the following steps:

1. Enter the first two pieces of data in the series in adjacent cells, as shown in figure 4.12.

   Excel uses these two data to determine the amount to increment in each step and the starting number for the series.

Fig. 4.12
Select the first two numbers in the series.

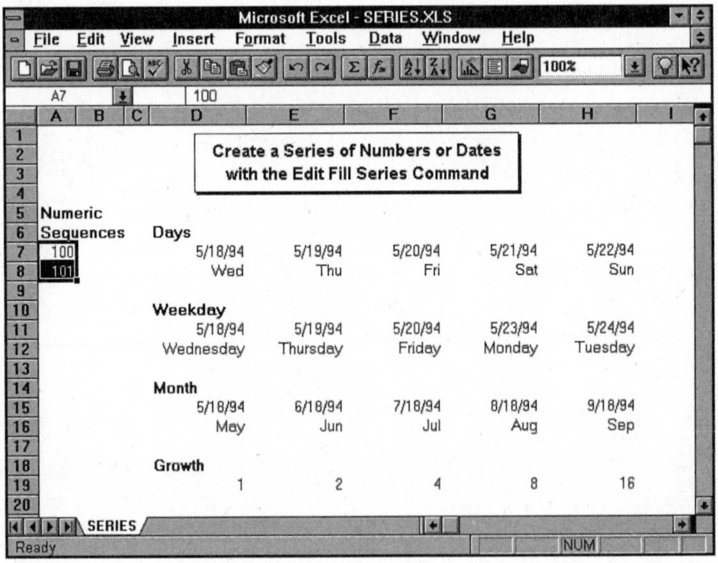

2. Select these two cells, as shown in figure 4.12.

3. Drag the fill handle down or right to enclose the area you want filled with a series of numbers. Figure 4.13 shows the fill handle dragged down to prepare for creating a series. The fill handle is the small square located at the lower right corner of a selection.

4. Release the mouse button.

The area enclosed with the gray border fills with a series determined by the first two cells you selected.

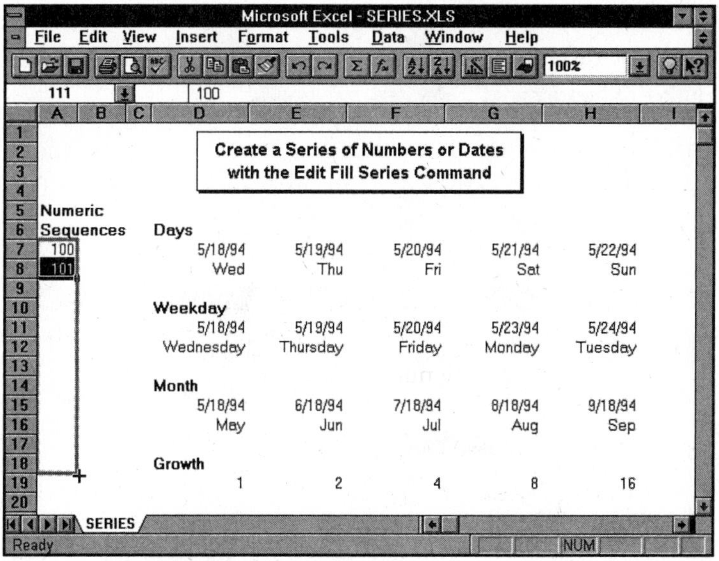

Fig. 4.13
Drag the fill handle across cells you want filled with a series.

You can create a series up or left by dragging the fill handle up a column or left across a row if you need a series that goes up or left from the two starting *seed* cells. Make sure that you end the selection outside the original cells, however, or part of the original selection will be cleared.

Note

If you select more than two cells that contain data and drag the fill handle, Excel will replace the cells dragged across with values that fit the straight trend line (linear regression). To learn how you can create a trend line with the fill handles, see "Analyzing Trends" in Chapter 23. To learn how to create charts that automatically display a trend line, see Chapter 15, "Building Complex Charts."

To use the AutoFill shortcut menu to fill a series of dates or numbers, follow these steps:

1. In the first cell, enter the starting number or date if you want the range to be filled with values that increment by one. If you want the range filled with values that increment differently, fill the first cells in the range with values that increase or decrease as you want the series to increase or decrease.

2. Select the range of cells containing dates or numbers used as starting values for the series. At the lower right corner of the selection is the square fill handle.

3. Select the range to be filled by dragging the fill handle with the right mouse button. Release the right mouse button to display the shortcut fill menu shown in figure 4.14.

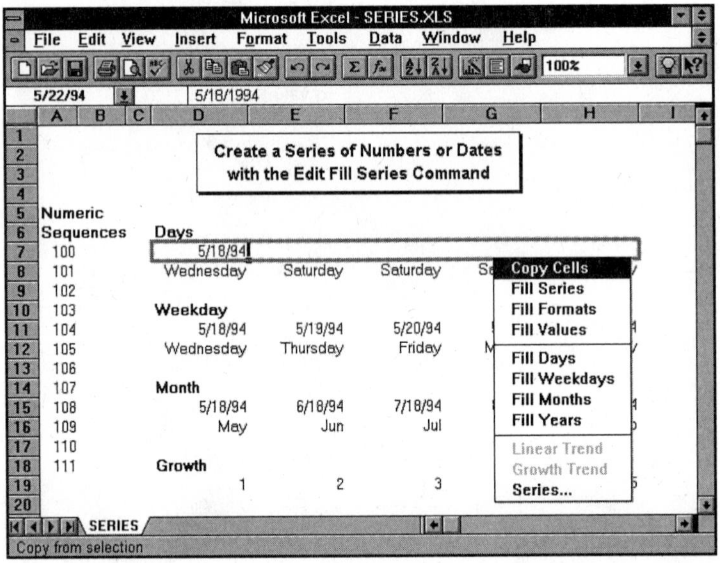

Fig. 4.14 Drag the fill handle with the right mouse button, then release to display the fill shortcut menu.

4. Click one of the following commands from the shortcut menu:

Command	Description
Fill Series	Fills the selection with values that increase by one from the value in the first cell.
Fill Days	Fills the selection with days that increase by one beginning with the day in the first cell.
Fill Weekdays	Fills the selection with weekdays that increase by one beginning with the day in the first cell.
Fill Months	Fills the selection with months that increase by one beginning with the month in the first cell.

Command	Description
Fill Years	Fills the selection with years that increase by one beginning with the year in the first cell.
Linear Trend	Fills the blank cells in the selection with linear regression (best fit) values. Starting values are not overwritten. This command is only available when more than one cell is filled with a starting value.
Growth Trend	Fills the blank cells in the selection with values calculated from a growth (exponential) regression. Starting values are not overwritten. This command is only available when more than one cell is filled with a starting value.
Series	Displays the Series dialog box described in the following procedure.

Your selection will fill with values that increase or decrease according to your starting values and the shortcut command you chose.

To create a series of numbers or dates by using the **E**dit F**i**ll **S**eries command, perform the following steps:

1. In the first cell, enter the first number or date.
2. Select the range of cells you want filled (see fig. 4.15).
3. Choose the **E**dit F**i**ll **S**eries command to display the Series dialog box (see fig. 4.16).
4. Verify that the **R**ows or **C**olumns option matches the type of range you want filled. This is normally automatically selected to match the orientation of the cells you selected.
5. Select the **T**rend check box if you want selected values to be replaced by values for a linear or exponential best-fit. This selection limits step 6 to **L**inear or **G**rowth options.

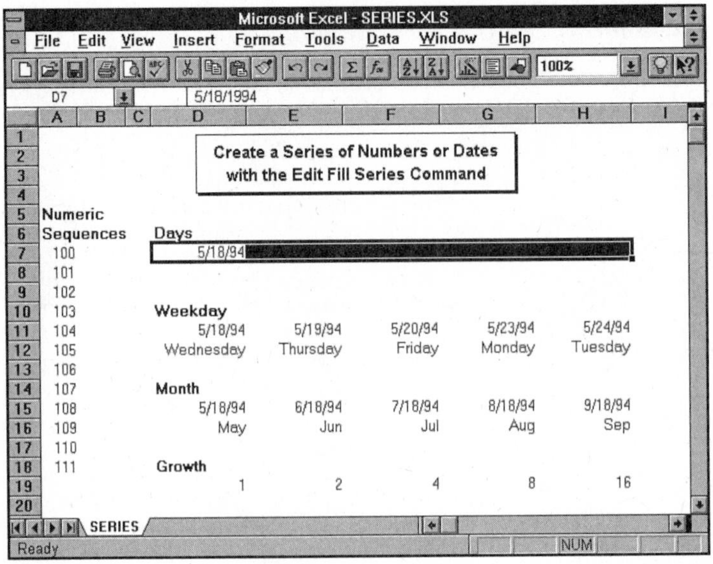

Fig. 4.15
Select the cell containing the starting data and the cells to be filled with the series.

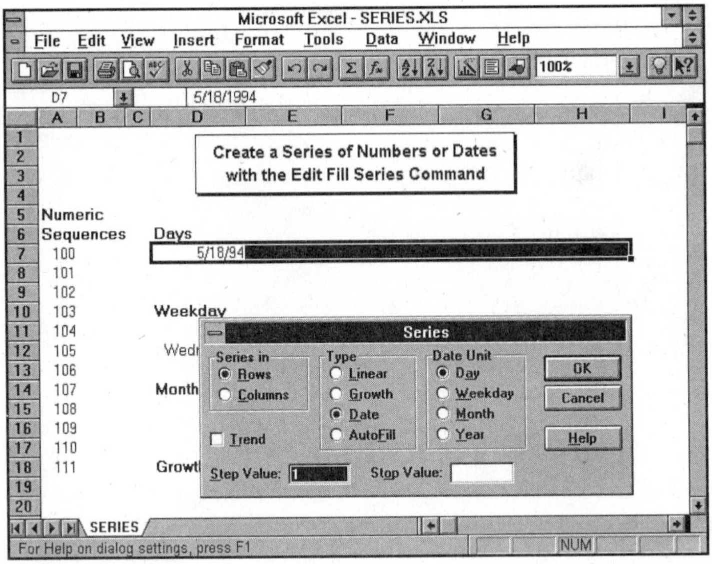

Fig. 4.16
After choosing **E**dit F**i**ll **S**eries, select the type of series as well as its start and stop points.

6. Select one of the following Type options:

Option	Description
Linear	Adds the **S**tep Value to the preceding number in the series. If **T**rend is selected, the trend values will be a linear trend.

Option	Description
Growth	Multiplies the **S**tep Value by the preceding number in the series. If **T**rend is selected, the trend values will be an exponential growth trend.
Date	Enables the Date Unit group so that the increment applies to a D**a**y, **W**eekday, **M**onth, or **Y**ear.
Auto**F**ill	Creates automatic series that may include text dates and labels. This is described in the next section, "Creating Series of Text and Headings."

Now, depending on the kind of series you want to create, use one of the following sets of steps.

If, in step 6, you are entering a series of numbers and you choose either **L**inear or **G**rowth, continue with the following steps:

1. Enter the **S**tep Value. This number is the constant amount by which the series changes from cell to cell. The **S**tep Value may be positive or negative.

2. Enter the St**o**p Value only if you think that you highlighted too many cells when you selected the range to fill.

3. Choose OK.

When the series reaches either the end of the selected range or the St**o**p Value, Excel stops. If you use a negative **S**tep Value, the St**o**p Value must be *less* than the starting value. You can type a date or time as the stop value if you type in a format that Excel recognizes.

If, in step 6, you are entering a series of dates and you choose **D**ate, complete the following steps:

1. From the Date Unit area of the Series dialog box, select either D**a**y, **W**eekday, **M**onth, or **Y**ear to designate the date increment. (**W**eekday gives you dates without Saturdays and Sundays.)

2. To specify the increment amount, enter the **S**tep Value. If the starting value is 12/1/93, for example, and you choose Month as the Date Unit and 2 as the **S**tep Value, the second date in the series becomes 2/1/94, and the third date becomes 4/1/94.

3. If you think that you highlighted too many cells, enter the **Stop** Value.

   The St**o**p Value indicates the last date in the series. You also can use one of Excel's predefined date formats as the St**o**p Value.

4. Choose OK.

Creating Series of Text and Headings

Some headings or series you create may not be dates or numbers. These items, for example, may be a text heading that includes a number, such as Quarter1, QTR3, Task1, Project 52, or Tuesday (see fig. 4.17). Excel also can extend these kinds of series.

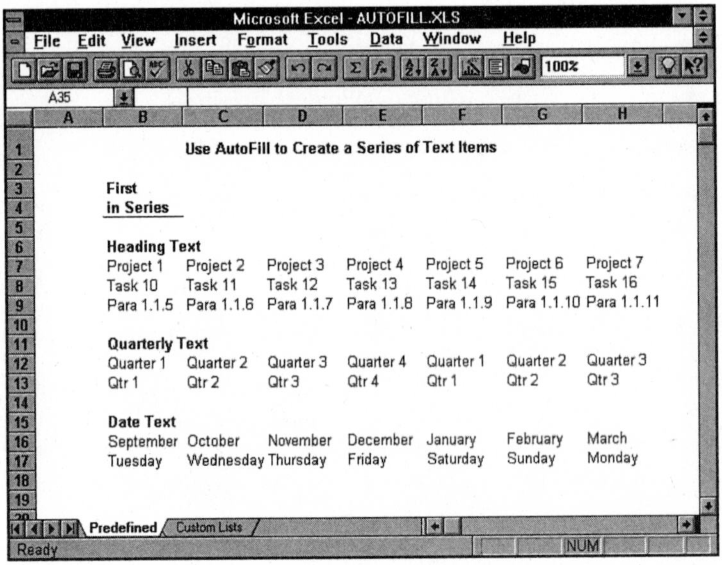

Fig. 4.17
Excel can extend predefined or custom series of labels or text.

Excel can fill in the remaining members from one of its predefined lists or from a custom list that you have created. The text series that Excel recognizes includes the text shown in the following table:

Type	**Example**
Day	Tuesday, Wednesday, or Tue, Wed
Month	September, October, or Sep, Oct
Text	Project, Task

Type	Example
Text *number*	Task 1, Task 2 Paragraph 1.2, Paragraph 1.3
Quarterly	Quarter 1, Quarter 2 Qtr 2, Qtr 3 Q1, Q2

Excel's AutoFill feature recognizes key words, such as days of the week, month names, and Quarterly abbreviations. Excel knows how these series run and repeat and extends a series to repeat correctly; for example, Qtr1 follows Qtr4 and then the series continues.

If you use two data cells to start a series, like rows 8 and 9 in figure 4.17, Excel determines how the number used with the text is incremented. Cells B9 and C9, for example, dictate that the legal Paragraph numbering in row 9 increments by 0.0.5 with each new number.

To use the fill handles to create a series that increases by one increment in each cell, complete the following steps:

1. Select the first cell that contains data.
2. To outline the cells you want filled, drag across or down.
3. Release the mouse button.

Tip
To prevent a series from incrementing or to fill a range with the same value, hold down the Ctrl key while you drag the fill handle.

To use a command to create a series that increases by one increment in each cell, complete the following steps:

1. Select the first cell and the cells that you want to fill.
2. Choose the **E**dit F**i**ll **S**eries command.
3. Select the Auto**F**ill option.
4. Choose OK.

When you need to fill in a series that increments by a value that is different from one unit, you need to enter two seeds in adjacent cells. To create a series that increments by an amount different from one unit per cell, complete the following steps:

1. Enter the starting value in the first cell.

2. Enter the second value in the adjacent cell. This value should already be increased or decreased by the amount of change you want in the series.

3. Select both seed cells.

4. To select the cells you want filled, drag the fill handle.

5. Release the mouse button.

To use the **E**dit F**i**ll **S**eries command to fill with increments of more than one unit, make sure that both seed cells are the first two cells of the selection before you choose the **E**dit F**i**ll **S**eries command and select the Auto**F**ill option.

Although the predefined lists in Excel are useful, you will find the ability to create your own custom lists even more useful. After you have created a custom list, you can use it to fill a range of cells.

To type in a custom list for use with AutoFill, follow these steps:

1. Choose the **T**ools **O**ptions command.

2. Select the Custom Lists tab shown in figure 4.18.

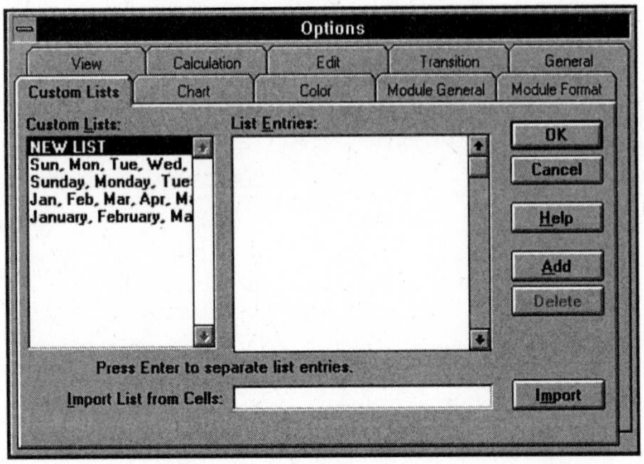

Fig. 4.18
Create your own custom lists in the Custom Lists tab.

3. Select NEW LIST in the Custom Lists box.

4. Select the List **E**ntries list box, and type each item you want in the list. Press Enter to separate items. You can delete and edit as you would in the formula bar or a word processor.

5. To add the list to the Custom **L**ists list box, choose the **A**dd button.

   Your list appears in the Custom **L**ists list box as shown in figure 4.19.

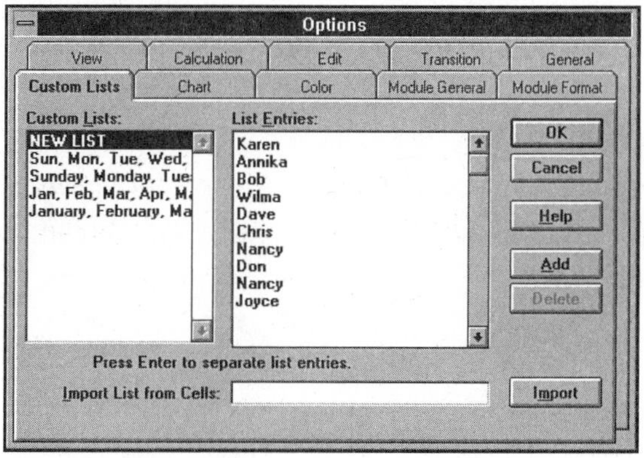

Fig. 4.19
You can review, edit, or delete your custom list.

6. Choose OK if you have no more lists to enter. If you have additional lists to enter, select NEW LIST from the Custom **L**ists list box, and then begin typing your list in the List **E**ntries list box.

To add a list that is in a range of cells on the worksheet, follow these steps:

1. Select the cells containing the list.

2. Choose the **T**ools **O**ptions command, and then select the Custom Lists tab.

   The range appears in the **I**mport List from Cells box. You can reselect it or edit it if it is incorrect.

3. Choose the I**m**port button, and then choose OK.

The list you create is stored with Excel. It can be used in other worksheets.

You can edit a list by displaying the Custom Lists tab, selecting the list from the Custom **L**ists list box, and editing its contents in the List **E**ntries list box. When you finish editing, choose the **A**dd button to add the edited list. If you want to delete a list, select it from the Custom **L**ists list box, and then choose the **D**elete button. You will be asked whether you want to delete the list. Choose OK if you do.

For Related Information

- "Filling or Copying Cell Contents," p. 241
- "Formatting Numbers," p. 328
- "Automatically Analyzing Trends with Charts," p. 513
- "Analyzing Trends," p. 710
- "Entering Data in a List or Database," p. 875

Increasing Data-Entry Efficiency

Data entry usually is tedious, but it must be done correctly. The following sections show you how to speed up the data-entry process.

You can make editing easier by dragging editing buttons to the toolbars with which you work. Customizing toolbars is described in Chapter 41, "Creating Custom Toolbars and Menus." The editing buttons are available by choosing the **V**iew **T**oolbars command, and then selecting the **C**ustomize button. Select Edit from the **C**ategories list. Following are the edit buttons you can drag onto toolbars:

Undo Last Command	*Repeat Last Command*
Cut	Copy
Paste	Clear Formulas
Clear Formats	Paste Formats
Paste Values	Format Painter
Edit Delete	Delete Rows
Insert	Delete Columns
Insert Rows	Insert Columns
Fill Right	Fill Down
Create Button	

Entering Numbers with a Fixed Decimal Place

If you are accustomed to using a 10-key keypad that enters decimal points automatically, you will appreciate the fixed decimal feature of Excel. You can make Excel automatically enter the decimal by choosing the **T**ools **O**ptions command. When the Options dialog box appears, select the Edit tab, and then select the Fi**x**ed Decimal check box. In the **P**laces text box, enter the number of decimal places you want (two is normal). Choose OK.

To enter the number 345.67, for example, you can type **34567**. When you press Enter, Excel enters the number and inserts the decimal point. You can override the automatic decimal placement by typing the decimal in the number you enter.

The feature continues to work until you turn it off by clearing the Fi**x**ed Decimal check box.

Moving the Active Cell When Entering Data

To quicken the data-entry process, select the range in which you want to enter data; the active cell will move automatically after pressing a data-entry key. This feature is especially convenient for data-entry forms and lists.

To enter data in a selected area, press the appropriate key:

Key(s)	Action
Tab	Enters data and moves right in the selected area; at the right edge of the selected area, wraps to the left.
Shift+Tab	Enters data and moves left in the selected area; at the left edge of the selected area, wraps to the right.
Enter	Enters data and moves down in the selected area; at the bottom of the selected area, wraps to the top.
Shift+Enter	Enters data and moves up in the selected area; at the top of the selected area, wraps to the bottom.

When the active cell reaches the edge of the selected area, it automatically wraps around to the next appropriate cell. If, for example, you press Tab repeatedly, the active cell reaches the right edge, and then jumps to the first cell in the next row of the left edge.

Using Data-Entry Shortcut Keys

As you enter data in a list, you may want to copy information from the cell above the active cell or insert the current date and time. Excel has shortcut keys that make these tasks easy and convenient to do.

Key(s)	Action
Ctrl+' (apostrophe)	Copies the formula from the cell above (cell references are not adjusted to the new location).
Ctrl+" (quotation mark)	Copies the value from the cell above.
Ctrl+; (semicolon)	Inserts the date.
Ctrl+: (colon)	Inserts the time.

Working While Excel Recalculates

When Excel recalculates, it calculates only those formulas involved with the data that has changed. Your worksheet recalculates faster, and you spend less time waiting.

For Related Information

- "Setting Preferences," p. 1098
- "Customizing and Creating Toolbars," p. 1108

When it recalculates, Excel incorporates two additional features that can increase your productivity. First, you can continue entering data, changing formulas, or giving commands as the worksheet recalculates. Excel incorporates the changes you make as it recalculates. Second, you can start a recalculation on a worksheet, activate other Windows applications, and work in them as Excel continues recalculating the worksheet.

Troubleshooting

Number signs are appearing in a cell where a value should be.

If a cell is too narrow to display a number in its entirety, Excel may display number signs or may display the value in scientific notation instead. You must use the Format Column Width command to make the cell wider.

Excel converted a date to a number.

You must enter dates in a format that Excel recognizes (for example, 4/2/94 or 2 Apr 94.) Other characters may not produce a valid date. Sometimes a cell in which you enter a date may already contain a numeric format. Use the Format Cells command to assign a different format.

Nothing happens when the Edit Undo command is chosen.

In order for the Edit Undo command to undo your changes, you must choose the command immediately following the action you performed.

Excel deletes the entire cell when deleting just the contents of a cell.

You used the Edit Delete command instead of the Edit Clear command. You should use the Edit Clear command when you need to delete the contents of a cell.

The formulas result in an error when deleting a row in the worksheet.

Depending on the design and layout of the worksheet, deleting cells, rows, or columns that contain information used by formulas can cause errors. Because the cell and its contents no longer exist, formulas that used that cell cannot find a cell to reference. These cells produce a #REF! error. To make sure that you do not delete rows or columns containing formulas or values, first select the cells, rows, or columns that you want to delete, and then choose the Edit Go To command. Select the Special option. Then select the Dependents Direct Only option, and choose OK. If you are presented with the No cells found message, you can safely delete the cells.

Troubleshooting (Continued)

Excel adds decimals to every value entered in a worksheet.

The Fixed Decimal option has been enabled. To disable the feature, choose the Tools Options command, select the Edit tab, select Fixed Decimal to remove the ×, and click OK or press Enter.

The Edit Fill Series command fills the entire range with the same label entered in the first cell of the range.

If Edit Fill Series cannot recognize the correct pattern to use for incrementing labels, it copies the starting label to the entire range. Make certain that the starting label is one that Edit Fill Series can recognize (for example, Qtr 1 or January), or create a custom list so that Edit Fill Series knows how you want to fill a range.

From Here...

For information relating directly to entering and editing data, you may want to review the following major sections of this book:

- Chapter 3, "Navigating and Selecting in a Workbook." This chapter shows you how to move to different areas in a workbook and select cells and worksheet ranges.
- Chapter 5, "Working with Formulas." In this chapter, you learn how to calculate and troubleshoot worksheet formulas.
- Chapter 6, "Using Functions." This chapter details Excel's built-in functions to help you create complex calculations.
- Chapter 7, "Moving or Copying Data and Formulas." When you need to modify worksheets, refer to this chapter to learn how to rearrange your data.
- Chapter 10, "Formatting Worksheets." This chapter shows you how to apply and create your own custom numeric and date formats.
- Chapter 23, "Manipulating and Analyzing Data." In this chapter you learn advanced techniques such as creating formulas to help you make decisions, analyzing trends in data, and using database functions to pull information from Excel data tables.

- Chapter 30, "Designing a List or Database." Create and manage lists of information using Excel's data management features covered in this chapter.
- Chapter 40, "Customizing the Excel Screen." In this chapter, you find out how to change Excel settings to suit your personal work style.
- Chapter 41, "Creating Custom Toolbars and Menus." This chapter teaches how to customize the toolbar and add your own buttons as well as how to change the menu by using the Menu Editor.

Chapter 5

Working with Formulas

In this chapter you learn how to:

- Understand formulas
- Enter formulas
- Edit formulas
- Calculate with arrays
- Control calculations
- Name cells

Formulas are at the core of an Excel worksheet. Formulas do the work, that is, the calculations, that we used to do by hand or with a calculator. Without formulas, there would be no point to using an electronic worksheet such as Excel.

You can use formulas to do simple calculations involving addition, subtraction, multiplication, and division, as well to carry out very complex financial, statistical, or scientific calculations. You also can use formulas to make comparisons and to manipulate text. When you need to carry out any calculation whose result you want to appear in a worksheet, use a formula.

Understanding Formulas

After you enter a formula in a cell in a worksheet, the results of the formula usually appear on the worksheet. To view the formula that produces the results, select the cell and the formula appears in the formula bar (see Chapter 4, "Entering and Editing Data," for detailed information on working with the formula bar). To view the formulas in-cell, double-click the cell or press F2. Figure 5.1 shows the results of a formula in C11, and the formula that produced the result is in the formula bar.

Formulas in Excel always begin with an equal sign (=) and can include numeric and text values (constants), arithmetic operators, comparison operators, text operators, functions, parentheses, cell references, and names. By combining these components, you can calculate the result you want by using the information in the worksheet. A formula's components are discussed in detail in the following section.

> **Note**
>
> You can display the formulas on a worksheet, instead of the results of the formulas, by choosing the **T**ools **O**ptions command, selecting the View tab, selecting the Fo**r**mulas option, and choosing OK. The shortcut key for toggling between viewing formulas and viewing the results of formulas is Ctrl+'. Although you won't usually want to view the formulas in worksheets, it is helpful to do this when debugging a worksheet. Figure 5.2 shows the same worksheet as shown in figure 5.1, but with the formulas displayed.

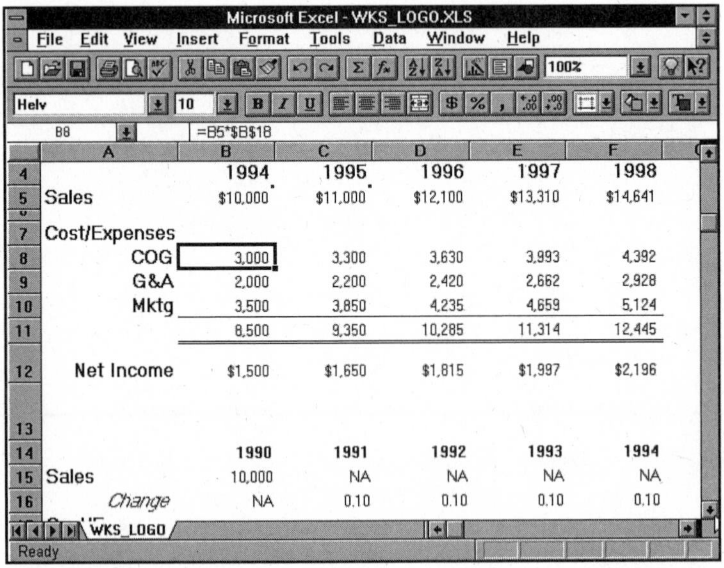

Fig. 5.1
The formula bar displays the formula in the active cell.

Formulas automatically recalculate and produce current results after you update data used by the formulas. Formulas refer to the contents of a cell by the cell's reference, such as B12. In formulas, you can use math operators such as + or – and also built-in formulas, called *functions*, like SUM( )or PMT( ) (payment).

A simple formula may appear in the *formula bar* under the menu as the following:

=B12*D15

This formula multiplies the contents of cell B12 by the contents of cell D15.

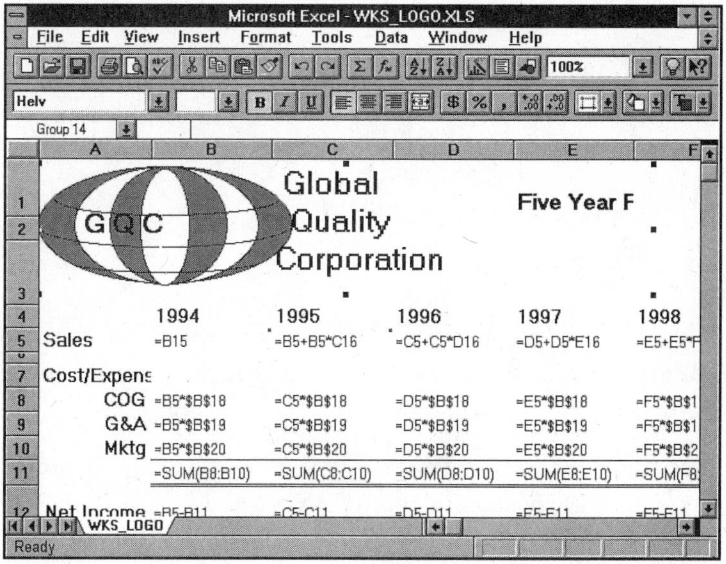

Fig. 5.2
Formulas are displayed in the worksheet by pressing Ctrl+‘.

> **Caution**
>
> Make sure you remember to start the formula with an equal sign (=). If you forget the equal sign, Excel does not interpret the entry as a formula. If you enter B12*D15 (no equal sign), then B12*D15 is actually entered into the cell. To get the result of multiplying the contents of cells B12 and D15, you must enter =B12*D15.

Entering Formulas

When you enter a formula in Excel, you can work in either the formula bar or in-cell. You begin a formula with an equal sign (=) and then construct the formula piece-by-piece, using values, operators, cell references, functions, and names to calculate the desired result. This section explains in detail the steps involved in entering a formula into a cell, including how to use cell references, operators, functions, and names in formulas.

Working in the Formula Bar or In-Cell

You can enter formulas either in the formula bar or in-cell, in the same way that you enter text or values. You enter a formula using the formula bar by simply typing it in and pressing Enter. If you turn on in-cell editing, you can enter a formula directly in the cell and bypass the formula bar. The benefit of using in-cell entry is that you don't have to look to the top of the screen, the location of the formula bar, when you are entering the formula.

You enter formulas directly in the cell by simply double-clicking the cell, or by selecting the cell and pressing F2. See Chapter 4, "Entering and Editing Data," for more information on entering data.

To enter a formula in the formula bar, take these steps:

1. Select the cell to contain the formula.
2. Type an equal sign (=).
3. Type a value, cell reference, function, or name.
4. If the formula is complete, press Enter or click the Enter box (a check mark) in the formula bar. If the formula is incomplete, go to step 5.
5. Type an operator. There are many types of operators. The most common operators are math symbols, such as + and –.
6. Return to step 3.

To enter a formula in-cell:

1. Double-click the cell in which you want to enter the formula, or select the cell and press F2.
2. Type an equal sign (=).
3. Type a value, cell reference, function, or name.
4. If the formula is complete, press Enter. If the formula is incomplete, go to step 5.
5. Type an operator. There are many types of operators. The most common are math symbols, such as + and –.
6. Return to step 3.

Always separate terms in a formula with operators or parentheses.

Before you enter a formula, you can clear it by clicking the Cancel box, an X to the left of the formula bar, or by pressing Esc. Remember that a formula isn't actually put in the cell until you enter it into the cell.

Entering Cell References

Cell references are used in a formula to refer to the contents of a cell or a group of cells. Cell references allow you to use values from different parts of a worksheet and execute a desired calculation. You can use any cell or group of cells in a formula, and any cell or group of cells can be used in as many formulas as you want.

A cell is always referred to by the row and column heading. For example, the cell at the intersection of column A and row one has the cell reference of A1. The reference of the active cell is displayed in the name box at the left end of the formula bar.

> **Note**
>
> You can refer to cells in the same worksheet, in other worksheets in the same workbook, or to cells in other workbooks. You also can enter 3-D references that refer to cells that span a series of worksheets. In this section you learn how to enter and work with all the types of cell references.

Entering Cell References by Pointing. The least error prone method of entering cell references in a formula is by pointing to the cell you want to include in a formula. Although you can type an entire formula, you often can make a typing error or misread the row or column headings and end up with D52 in a formula when it should be E53. When you point to a cell to include in a formula, you actually move the pointer to the cell you want in the formula. It is obvious when you select the correct cells.

To enter a cell reference into a formula by pointing:

1. Select the cell for the formula.

2. Type an equal sign (=).

3. Point to the cell you want in the formula and click, or press the movement keys to move the dashed marquee to the cell you want in the formula.

   The address of the cell you point to appears at the cursor location in the formula bar.

   You also can enter ranges into formulas by pointing. Rather than clicking on a cell, point to a corner cell of the range and drag across the range to the opposite corner. To use the keyboard, move to a corner of the range and hold down the Shift key as you move to the opposite corner.

4. Enter an operator, such as the + symbol.

5. Point to the next cell.

6. Repeat the steps from step 4 to continue the formula, or enter the formula by clicking the Enter box or pressing Enter.

Tip
You do not need to type the last parenthesis if you are creating a formula composed of a function that encloses all other terms.

Entering Cell References in Existing Formulas. Using the same techniques you used to create formulas, you can edit formulas to change or add new cell references. You can enter new cell references by typing them, pointing to and clicking them, or moving to them with the movement keys.

To insert a new cell reference or range into an existing formula, take these steps:

1. Position the insertion point in the formula bar where you want the new cell reference or range.

   You also can double-click the cell that contains the formula you want to edit (or select the cell and press F2) and position the insertion point where you want the new cell reference or range.

2. Select a cell reference or range you want to replace completely. (Drag across it with the pointer or use Shift+arrow keys.)

3. Type or click the new cell reference. If the new reference is a range, click one corner and drag to the opposite corner. From the keyboard, type the new cell reference or press the movement keys to move to the cell you want as the new reference. To include a range in the formula, press F2 to change to Enter mode, use the movement keys to move to one corner of the range, hold down Shift, and move to the opposite corner of the range. Press F2 again to return to Edit mode.

   Watch the formula bar or in-cell contents as you perform step 3. The new cell reference replaces the old.

4. Add cell references, or choose OK. Press Esc to back out of the changes.

Note

If you are adding cell references to a formula by pointing to them, you can go to the distant location by pressing the F5 key. Once there, you can select that cell or another close by. If the cell or range you want to add is in the Go To dialog box that appears after pressing F5, choose the name from the list box and choose OK. The name appears in the formula, and a marquee appears around the named cells.

Using Cell References in Formulas. You can refer to a cells location in Excel with a relative reference or an absolute reference. Be careful to use the correct type of cell reference in each formula you create. If you understand the difference between the two types of cell references used in Excel, you can avoid creating formulas that change incorrectly when copied to new locations.

You use relative and absolute references in your daily life. Suppose that you are in your office, and you want someone to take a letter to the mailbox. Using a relative reference, you tell the person: "Go out the front door; turn left and go two blocks; turn right and go one block." These directions are relative to your office location at the time you give the instructions. If you move to a different location, these directions no longer work.

To make sure that the letter gets to the mailbox no matter where you are when you give the directions, you must say something like this: "Take this letter to the mailbox at 2700 Mendocino Avenue." No matter where you are when you speak, the mailbox is at one absolute location: 2700 Mendocino Avenue. The address absolutely does not change.

Using Relative References. Unless you specify otherwise, Excel uses relative referencing for cell addresses when you enter a formula. This means that cell references in a formula change after you copy the formula to a new location or after you fill a range with a formula. You usually want formulas to use relative cell references.

In figure 5.3, the formula in cell C5 is =B5+B5*C16. All these references are relative. The formula, translated into English, would read as follows:

> "In cell C5, multiply the number in the cell one column to the left in same row (cell B5 in this example) and the number in the cell 11 rows down in same column (cell C16). Add the number contained in the cell one column to the left in the same row (cell B5)."

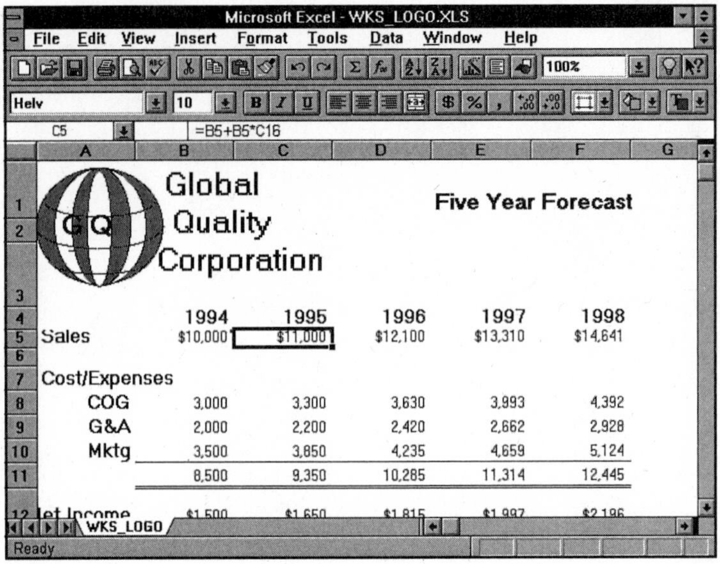

Fig. 5.3 The relative reference formula in C5 is shown in the formula bar.

You can see the equivalent formula in R1C1, row-column format, by choosing the **T**ools **O**ptions command, selecting the General tab, and then selecting the R1**C**1 option. If you change the formula display to R1C1 format, the formula in the same cell, R5C3, is =RC[–1]+RC[–1]*R[11]C. The R1C1 format makes relative references more obvious because the cell references are presented as the relative change from the current cell. For example, C[–1] means one column left, and R[11] means 11 rows down from the active cell. For more information on using the R1C1 reference style, see "Changing Cell Reference Style," later in this chapter.

When you copy either formula across row 5, the formulas adjust their cell references to their new positions. The copied formulas are as follows:

Cell Containing Formula	A1 Format	R1C1 Format
D5 or R5C4	=C5+C5*D16	=RC[–1]+RC[–1]*R[11]C
E5 or R5C5	=D5+D5*E16	=RC[–1]+RC[–1]*R[11]C
F5 or R5C6	=E5+E5*F16	=RC[–1]+RC[–1]*R[11]C

Notice how the formula that uses A1 format changed to give the cell references the same relative position from the cell that contains the formula. Formulas with R1C1 format do not change when copied because the formula always shows the relative position of the cell being used.

Usually, you want cell references to change when copied. Occasionally, however, these changes can cause problems. What happens if the worksheet lacks a row of values all the way across row 16? What if row 16 had a single value that each copied formula had to use? What if the worksheet had only a single change number in row 20, used for each years revenue increase? Each copied formula in these cases would be wrong. If you copy a formula and you want to make sure that some terms in the formula don't adjust to the new locations, you designate those terms as absolute references.

Using Absolute References. To keep cell references from changing when you copy a formula to new locations, use absolute references. If you use the A1 formula format, indicate absolute references by putting a dollar sign ($) in front of the column letter or row number that you want to freeze. Put the dollar sign ($) in front of both the column letter and row number if you want neither to change. In R1C1 format, indicate an absolute cell reference by typing a specific row or column number; do not enclose the number in square brackets.

In figure 5.4, the COG factor is referred to by using an absolute reference address of $B$18 in A1 format or R18C2 in R1C1 format. In A1 format, the dollar sign in front of each part of the address, B and 18, prevents the cell reference from changing during a copy; in R1C1 format, the specific row and column numbers without brackets prevent the cell reference from changing during a copy or fill operation.

The formula in B8, for example, was copied into cells C8, D8, E8, and F8. Cell B8s formula is =B5*$B$18 in A1 format or =R[–3]C*R18C2 in R1C1 format. When copied, only the first term changes in each new cell that the formula is copied into. The second term remains absolutely the same. This was necessary because there was a value in B18, but no corresponding values in C18, D18, E18, and F18. Had the formula used B18 instead of $B$18, all the copied formulas would have referenced the blank cells C18, D18, E18, and F18.

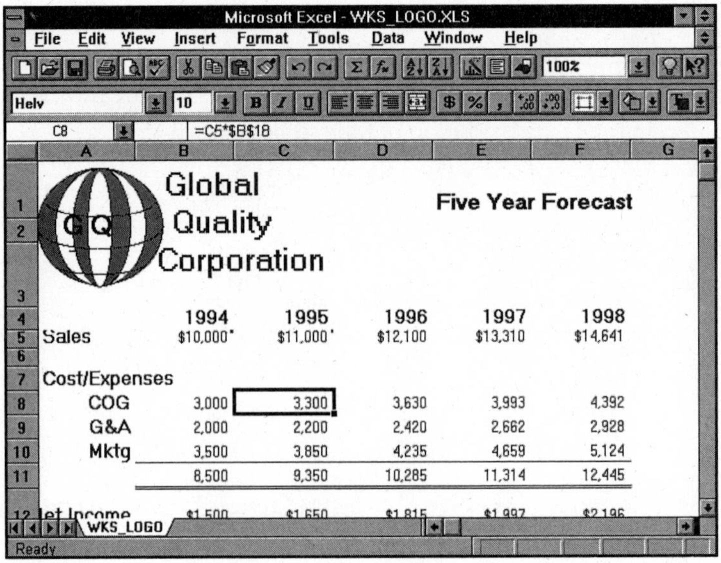

Fig. 5.4
Absolute reference formulas use a $ to freeze a row or column reference.

You can enter an absolute reference the following two ways:

- As you enter the formula, type the dollar sign in front of the row or column that you want to remain the same. In R1C1 format, delete the square brackets.

- Move the flashing insertion point in the formula bar so that it is inside the cell reference, and press F4, the absolute reference key. (If the formula was entered already, select its cell and press F2 to edit.) Each time you press F4, the type of reference changes. The first time you press F4, both the column and row reference become absolute. Press F4 again to make only the row reference absolute. Press F4 a third time to make just the column reference absolute.

To enter an absolute reference by using the F4 key, perform the following steps:

1. Type an equal sign (=) and the cell reference you want to be absolute.

2. Press F4, the absolute reference key, until the correct combination of dollar signs appears. For R1C1 format, type the specific row or column number without brackets, or press F4.

3. Type the next operator and continue to enter the formula.

You can use the F4 key when editing an existing formula.

Using Mixed References. On some occasions, you want only the row to stay fixed when copied or only the column to stay fixed when copied. In these cases, use a mixed reference, one that contains both absolute and relative references. For example, the reference $B5 prevents the column from changing, but the row changes relative to a new copied location; the dollar sign keeps the column from changing. In B$5, just the opposite occurs. The column adjusts to a new location but the row always stays fixed at 5; the dollar sign keeps the row from changing.

A mixed reference in R1C1 style may look like R[1]C2, where the R[1] means one row down from the formula and C2 means the absolute second column. R2C[–1] means the absolute second row and the column one left of the formula.

You can create mixed references the same way you can create absolute references. Type the dollar signs or specific row and column numbers without brackets or press F4. Each press of F4 cycles the cell reference to a new combination.

Each time you press F4, Excel cycles through all combinations of relative and absolute references. Press F4 four times, for example, and you cycle from B22 through $B$22, B$22, $B22, and B22.

Changing Cell Reference Style. An Excel worksheet is composed of 256 columns and 16,384 rows. The intersection of each row and column creates a cell. Cell A5 is the intersection of column A and row 5. Within a cell, you can place text, a number, or a formula.

You can refer to ranges, or rectangular groups of cells, with the notation D7:F10. The opposite corners of the range (D7 and F10) are separated by a colon (:). In Excel, you can select multiple ranges at one time. You use ranges if you want a command to affect multiple cells or if you use a formula involving the contents of multiple cells.

The R1C1 style indicates a cell by its row number, R1, and its column number, C1. You also can designate a range in R1C1 style. This style is familiar to users of Multiplan and is easier to use in complex formulas involving relative positions and in macro programming.

You can switch the worksheets row and column headings between the A1 and R1C1 styles by choosing the **T**ools **O**ptions command, selecting the General tab and selecting the desired option. After you change the reference style, formulas throughout the worksheet change to reflect the new style. This book uses the A1 style of references, except where indicated in complex formulas or in macros. Figure 5.5 shows a worksheet its row and column headings in R1C1 style.

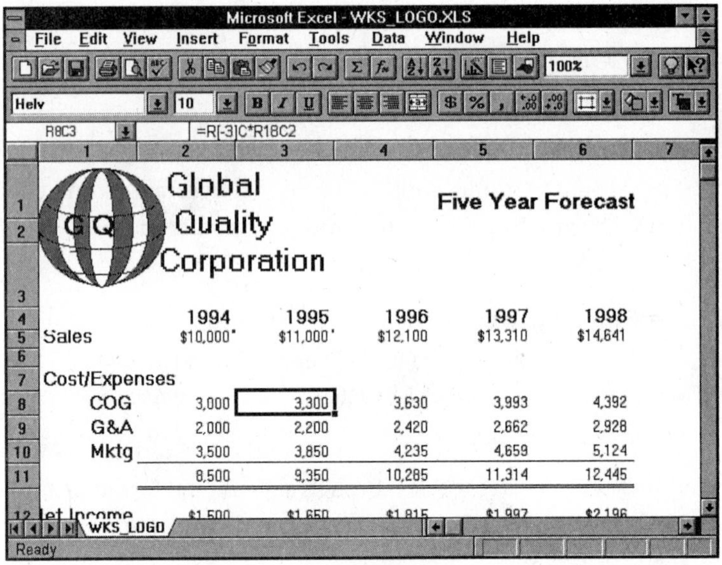

Fig. 5.5
A worksheet with its row and column headings in R1C1 style.

Editing Absolute and Relative References. To change an absolute or relative cell reference that is already entered in a formula:

1. Select the formula (either in the formula bar or in-cell).
2. Move the insertion point so it is within or next to the formula you want to change.
3. Press F4 to cycle through combinations of absolute and relative cell references.
4. When the formula is displayed correctly, press Enter.

Figure 5.6 shows a formula bar with the insertion point in a cell reference before F4 was pressed. Figure 5.7 shows the effect of pressing F4 one time.

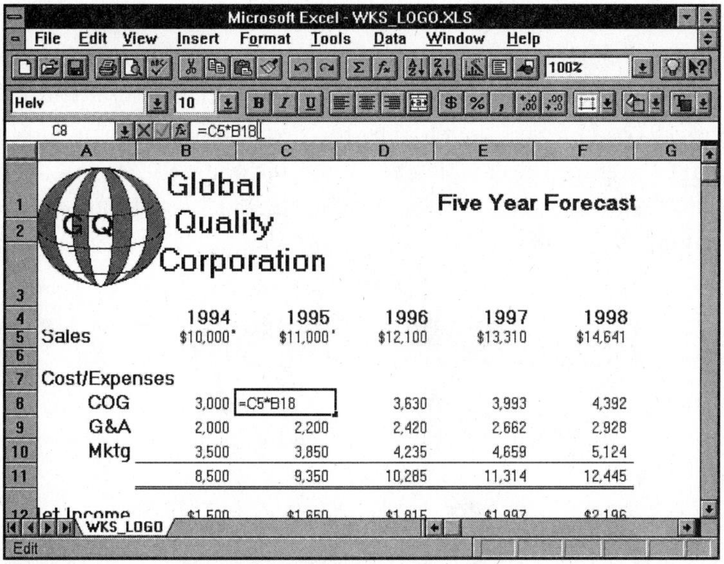

Fig. 5.6
Move the insertion point next to the cell reference you want to change.

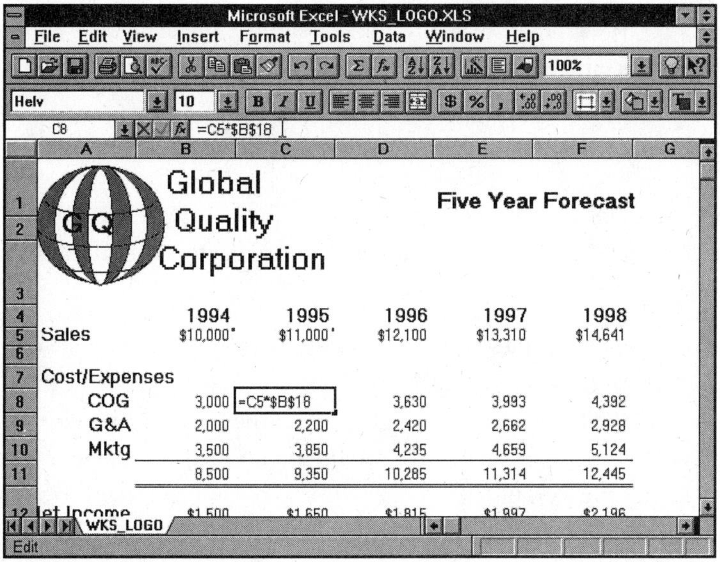

Fig. 5.7
Each press of the F4 key changes the mix of absolute and relative cell references.

Referring to Other Sheets in a Workbook. You can refer to other sheets in a workbook by including a sheet reference as well as a cell reference in a formula. For example, to refer to cell A1 on Sheet6, you would enter Sheet6!A1 in the formula. Notice the exclamation mark that separates the sheet reference from the cell reference. If you have named the sheet, simply use the sheet name and then the cell reference. If the sheet name includes spaces, you must surround the sheet reference with single quotation marks.

You also can use the mouse to enter a reference to a cell or range on another worksheet in a workbook. To do this, start entering the formula in the cell where you want the result to appear and then click the tab for the worksheet with the cell or range you want to refer to. Next, select the cell or range that you want to refer to. The complete reference, including the sheet reference appears in the formula bar. If the sheet name includes spaces, Excel inserts surround the sheet reference with single quotation marks. Finish the formula and press Enter.

Note

You also can make *external references* to cells in other workbooks. See Chapter 25, "Linking, Embedding, and Consolidating Worksheets," for more information on using external references to link workbooks.

Entering 3-D References. You can use 3-D references to refer to a cell range that includes two or more sheets in a workbook. A 3-D reference consists of a sheet range, specifying the beginning and ending sheets, and a cell range specifying the cells being referred to. The following is an example of a 3-D reference:

=SUM(Sheet1:Sheet2!$E$1:$E$6)

This reference sums up the values in the range of cells $E$1:$E$6 in each of the sheets from Sheet1 to Sheet6, and adds the sums together resulting in a grand sum.

Using the same techniques you use for entering regular references, you can enter 3-D references. You can either type the references directly in the formula bar (or in-cell), or you can use the mouse the select the worksheet tabs and cell ranges for the reference. To use the mouse to enter the reference, begin entering the formula in the cell where you want the result to appear, click the tab for the first worksheet you want to include in the reference, hold down the Shift key and click the last worksheet you want to include in the reference, and then select the cells you want to refer to. Finish the formula and press Enter.

You can use 3-D reference to pull together the information from several worksheets into a consolidation worksheet. For example, you may have a worksheet that records sales for each of several regional offices. If these worksheets are arranged identically, you can consolidate the sales for the regional offices into a summary worksheet using 3-D references.

You also can use 3-D references when defining names. See the following section, "Naming Cells for Better Worksheets," in this chapter to learn how to name cells.

Several functions built-in to Excel can use 3-D references. The following list shows the functions that can use 3-D references:

AVERAGE	STDEV
COUNT	STDEVP
COUNTA	SUM
MAX	VAR
MIN	VARP
PRODUCT	

Using Operators in Formulas

Operators tell formulas what operations to perform. Excel uses four types of operators:

Operators	Signs
Arithmetic	+, – *, /, %, ^
Text	&
Comparative	=, <, <=, >, >=, <>
Reference	colon (:), comma (,), space ( )

Table 5.1 illustrates how you can use each of the arithmetic operators in formulas.

Table 5.1 Arithmetic Operators

Operator	Formula	Result	Type of Operation
+	=5+2	7	Addition
–	=5–2	3	Subtraction
–	–5	–5	Negation (negative of the number)

(continues)

Table 5.1 Continued

Operator	Formula	Result	Type of Operation
*	=5*2	10	Multiplication
/	=5/2	2.5	Division
%	5%	.05	Percentage
^	=5^2	25	Exponentiation (to the power of)

Excel can work with more than just arithmetic formulas. Excel also can manipulate text, perform comparisons, and relate different ranges and cells on the worksheet. The ampersand (&) operator, for example, joins text within quotation marks or text contained in referenced cells. Joining text is known as concatenation. Table 5.2 illustrates how you can use text operators.

Table 5.2 Text Operators

Operator	Formula	Result	Type of Operation
&	="Ms. Gibbs" results	Ms. Gibbs	Text is joined
&	=A12&" "&B36	Ms. Gibbs	Text is joined when A12 contains Ms. and B36 contains Gibbs

To compare results, you can create formulas using comparative operators. These operators return a TRUE or FALSE result, depending on how the formula evaluates the condition. Table 5.3 lists the comparative operators.

Table 5.3 Comparative Operators

Operator	Type
=	Equal to
<	Less than
<=	Less than or equal to
>	Greater than
>=	Greater than or equal to
<>	Not equal to

The following are examples of comparative operators in formulas:

Formula	Result
=A12<15	TRUE if the content of A12 is less than 15; FALSE if the content of A12 is 15 or more.
=B36>=15	TRUE if the content of B36 is 15 or more; FALSE if the content of B36 is less than 15.

Another type of operator is the reference operator (see table 5.4). Reference operators make no changes to constants or cell contents. Instead, they control how a formula groups cells and ranges of cells when the formula calculates. Reference operators enable you to combine absolute and relative references and named ranges. Reference operators are valuable for joining cells (union) or referring to a common area shared between different ranges (intersect).

Note

Use the range operator (:) to reduce your work in formulas. If you want a formula to refer to all cells in column B, type B:B. Similarly, the range that includes all cells in rows 5 through 12 is entered as 5:12.

Table 5.4 Reference Operators

Operator	Example	Type	Result
:	SUM(A12:A24)	Range	Evaluates as a single reference the cells in the rectangular area between the two corners.
,	SUM(A12:A24,B36)	Union	Evaluates two references as a single reference.
space	SUM(A12:A24 A16:B20)	Intersect	Evaluates the cells common to both references (if no cells are common to both, then #NULL results).
space	=Yr92 Sales	Intersect	Cell contents at the intersect of the column named Yr92 and the row named Sales.

Note

Excel uses a colon (B12:C36) to designate a range like 1-2-3 uses two periods (B12..C36). You can use a comma to select multiple ranges (B12:C36,F14:H26) for many functions.

Excel follows a consistent set of rules when applying operators in a formula. Working from the first calculation to the last, Excel evaluates operators in the order shown in table 5.5.

Table 5.5 The Order in Which Excel Evaluates Operators

Operator	Definition
:	Range
space	Intersect
,	Union
–	Negation
%	Percentage
^	Exponentiation
* and /	Multiplication and division
+ and –	Addition and subtraction
&	Text joining
=, <, and <= >, >=, and < >	Comparisons

You can change the order in which calculations are performed by enclosing in parentheses the terms you want Excel to calculate first. Notice, for instance, the difference between these results:

Formula	Result
=6+21/3	13
=(6+21)/3	9

Pasting Names and Functions into Formulas

You can use English names in formulas to reference cells or ranges. You also can reduce the formula size to operate faster and with less chance of typographical error by using the built-in formulas, called *functions*, that are part of Excel. Names and functions can be pasted into formulas. Excel enables you to choose the name or function from a list to paste into a formula. This process is easier and more accurate than typing. Naming cells, ranges, formulas, and values is described later in this chapter. For a discussion of functions, see Chapter 6, "Using Functions."

To paste a name into an existing formula, take these steps:

1. Move the insertion point in the formula bar (or in-cell) to where you want to paste the name.

2. Activate the worksheet or workbook that holds the named reference to paste.

3. Choose the **I**nsert **N**ame **P**aste command to display the Paste Name dialog box (see fig. 5.8).

   If you have not named any cells, ranges, formulas, or values, the **P**aste command in the **N**ame submenu is grayed.

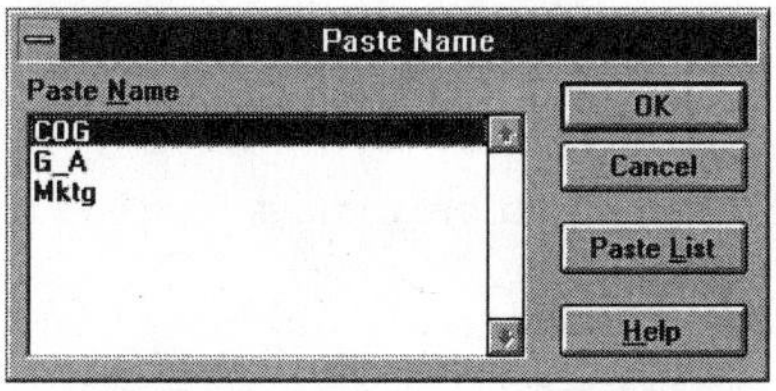

Fig. 5.8
The Paste Name dialog box.

   You also can click the down arrow to the right of the Name box at the far left of the formula bar to display a list of named cells.

4. Select the name you want to paste.

5. Choose OK, then complete the formula with additional terms, if necessary, and press Enter.

To paste a function into a formulas, take these steps:

1. Move the insertion point in the formula bar (or in-cell) to where you want the function.

2. Choose the **I**nsert **F**unction command or click the Function Wizard button immediately next to the formula bar to start the Function Wizard.

3. Follow the instructions that appear in the Function Wizard dialog boxes.

   See Chapter 6, "Using Functions," for more information on using the Function Wizard.

Tip
You can select from most list boxes and choose the OK button simultaneously by double-clicking a selection in the list.

Entering Text, Dates, and Times in Formulas

Enter text, dates, and times in formulas by including the data in quotation marks. For example:

="The Total Budget is " & TOTAL_BUDGET

displays The *Total Budget is $1,200,000* if the number $1,200,000 is in the cell named TOTAL_BUDGET.

If you want to perform date math on explicit dates, which are dates that are not in cells, use a formula such as

="5/14/93"–"5/14/91"

or

="14 May, 93"–"14 May, 91"

These formulas produce the number of days between the two dates.

When you need numeric or date results from a formula or reference to appear as text, use the TEXT( ) function with a predefined or custom format. For example, **use ="Today is " & TEXT(A13,"mmm dd, yy")** to produce a text date from the contents of cell A13.

Changing Formulas to Values

In some situations, you may want to freeze a formulas results so the formula changes to a value. To freeze a formula into its resulting values, take these steps:

1. Select the cell of an existing formula and press F2 (the Edit key), or click the formula bar, or double-click the cell if you are using in-cell editing.

2. Press F9.

   The formula in the formula bar is replaced by its calculated value.

3. Choose OK.

Defining Formula Errors

When Excel cannot evaluate a formula or function, the program displays an error value in the offending cell. Error values begin with a pound sign (#). Excel has seven kinds of error values with self-explanatory names (see table 5.6). You can use the **T**ools **A**uditing Trace **E**rror command to help you find the source of an error. This command is described in detail in Chapter 26, "Auditing Workbooks and Worksheets."

Table 5.6 Excel Error Values

Value	Meaning
#DIV/0!	The formula or macro is attempting to divide by zero.
	Check to see whether cell references are blanks or zeros. You may have accidentally deleted an area of the worksheet needed by this formula. An incorrectly written formula may be attempting to divide by zero.
#N/A	The formula refers to a cell that has a #N/A entry.
	Check to see whether you can type #N/A in mandatory data-entry cells. Then, if data isn't entered to replace the #N/A, formulas that depend on this cell display #N/A. This error value warns that not all the data was entered. An array argument is the wrong size, and #N/A is returned in some cells. HLOOKUP( ), VLOOKUP( ), LOOKUP( ), MATCH( ), or other functions have incorrect arguments. Often, these functions return an error value when they cannot find a match. You omitted an argument from a function. If Excel cannot evaluate the arguments that you entered, some functions return #N/A. See the functions description in Chapter 6 for more information on the function.
#NAME?	Excel doesn't recognize a name.
	Check by using the Insert Name Define command to see if the name exists. Create a name, if necessary. Verify the spelling of the name. Make sure that no spaces exist.

(continues)

Table 5.6 Continued

Value	Meaning
	Verify that functions are spelled correctly. Use no spaces between the function name and the opening parenthesis. Novice users frequently type a space between the last character in the function name and the first parenthesis.
	Check whether you used text in a formula without enclosing the text in quotation marks. Excel considers the text as a name rather than as text. Check whether you forgot to replace one of the Paste Arguments prompts pasted into a function. Check whether you mistyped an address or range, making this information appear to Excel as a name, such as the cell ABB5 (two Bs) or the range B12C45 (a missing :). Check whether you referred to an incorrect or nonexistent name in a linked worksheet.
#NULL!	The formula specifies two areas that don't intersect.
	Check to see whether the cell or range reference is entered incorrectly.
#NUM!	The formula has a problem with a number.
	Check to see whether the numeric argument is out of the acceptable range of inputs, or whether the function can find an answer given the arguments you entered.
#REF!	The cell reference is incorrect.
	Check to see whether you deleted cells, rows, or columns referenced by formulas. Other causes may include indexes that exceed a range used in a function or offsets that reach outside worksheet boundaries. See whether external worksheet references are still valid. Use the File Links command to open source worksheets. If you need to change a link to a worksheet with a different name or directory, use the File Links command with the Change button on, described in Chapter 26, in the section on linking worksheets. See whether a macro returned a #REF! value from an unopened or incorrect function macro. See whether a Dynamic Data Exchange (DDE) topic is incorrectly entered or is unavailable.
#VALUE!	The value is not the type expected by the argument or the result from an intersect operation when the ranges being evaluated do not intersect.
	Verify that values used as arguments are of the kind listed in Chapter 6, "Using Functions."

Troubleshooting

After pressing Enter to enter a formula, Excel beeps and displays an alert box warning that an error exists in the formula.

Press the F1 key for Help when you see this kind of alert box. Excel displays a Help window that lists the most common errors that occur in formulas. If, after reading the Help, you cannot find the error in the formula, delete the equal sign (=) at the front of the formula and press Enter. This step enters the formula as text so that you can return later and work on it. To turn the text back into a formula, just reenter the equal sign at the front of the formula and press Enter.

When typing a complicated formula that includes many pairs of parentheses, you miss, and cannot locate, one of the parentheses.

Excel highlights matching pairs of parentheses as you move the insertion point across one parenthesis of a pair. To see these highlighted, move the insertion point to the formula bar, and then press the right- or left-arrow keys to move the insertion point across a parenthesis. Watch for an opposing parenthesis to highlight. If the highlighted parenthesis doesnt enclose the correct term in the formula, you have found the terms that require another parenthesis.

Everything within a function appears correct, but Excel doesn't accept the entry.

A frequent mistake when typing functions is to miss or delete a comma between arguments. You can reduce the chance of omitting commas and entering arguments incorrectly by entering functions with using the Function Wizard. Invoke the Function Wizard by choosing the **I**nsert **F**unction command or using the Function Wizard button in the formula bar. The Function Wizard prompts you to enter the arguments needed in the proper order and take care of entering commas for you. See Chapter 6, "Using Functions," for more information on using the Function Wizard.

When auditing a worksheet, you want to see more than one formula or determine the range names that a cell is part of.

You can switch the worksheet to display formulas by choosing the **T**ools **O**ptions command, selecting the View tab, and selecting the Fo**r**mulas option. The shortcut key is Ctrl+' (grave accent). Open a second window to the worksheet with the **W**indow **N**ew Window command; then format one worksheet to show results and the other to show formulas.

To see the range names, formulas, and formats that involve a cell, select the cell and then choose the **T**ools **O**ptions command, select the View tab, and select the Info **W**indow check box to display an Info window. A new menu appears while the Info Window is active. Select from the Info menu the attributes you want to see about the active cell. When troubleshooting a worksheet, leave the Info window open. When you select a new cell, you can switch to the Info window for this cell by pressing

(continues)

Troubleshooting (Continued)

Ctrl+F6 to display the Info window updated for the current cell. You can use the Window Arrange command to arrange the Info window and the worksheet window so that you can view them simultaneously.

If you selected exactly the same cells used by a range name, the name appears in the Reference area at the top-left corner of the worksheet.

Large Excel worksheets are difficult to understand without a map that shows areas and regions.

Use Excel's **V**iew **Z**oom command to shrink the worksheet so that you can see more. This shows the actual worksheet results. You also can create a map showing text, values, and formulas. See Chapter 26, "Auditing Workbooks and Worksheets," for more information on using Excel's audit tools.

The Circular (Circ) indicator appears at the bottom of the worksheet. Although no data has changed, with every recalculation of the worksheet, some of the results grow larger or grow smaller.

The worksheet has a circular error—a formula that refers to another cell that contains a formula that refers to the first. This error may happen through a chain involving many cells. The formula feeds on itself with progressing recalculations. Therefore, like a snake devouring its tail, each recalculation reduces the results; or the results can grow larger, depending on how the formula is built. To find all the cells involved in a circular error, use Excel's auditing tools. See Chapter 26, "Auditing Workbooks and Worksheets," for more information on using Excel's audit tools.

In a long formula that contains many parts, one of the smaller terms in the formula is incorrect. You cannot find the part of the formula that produces these incorrect results.

To see how a term or function within a formula evaluates, complete the following steps:

1. Select the cell that produces the incorrect result or an error value.
2. In the formula bar, select the smallest portion of the formula that may cause this problem. The term you select must be a complete function or portion of a formula that is calculated by itself. Figure 5.9 shows a portion of an IF() function selected. Notice that the complete AND() function, including both parentheses and all arguments, is selected.
3. To calculate the portion you selected, press the F9 key. Figure 5.10 shows how the selected portion in the formula changes to the related calculated result, FALSE. If the selected portion results in a number, text, error, or array you see these values.

Troubleshooting (Continued)

4. Select and calculate other parts of the formula until you find the portion causing the error.

5. To return the formula to the original form, press Esc or click the Cancel box in the formula bar. If you press Enter, the result of the formula replaces the formula.

6. Correct the portion of the formula that returned the incorrect answer.

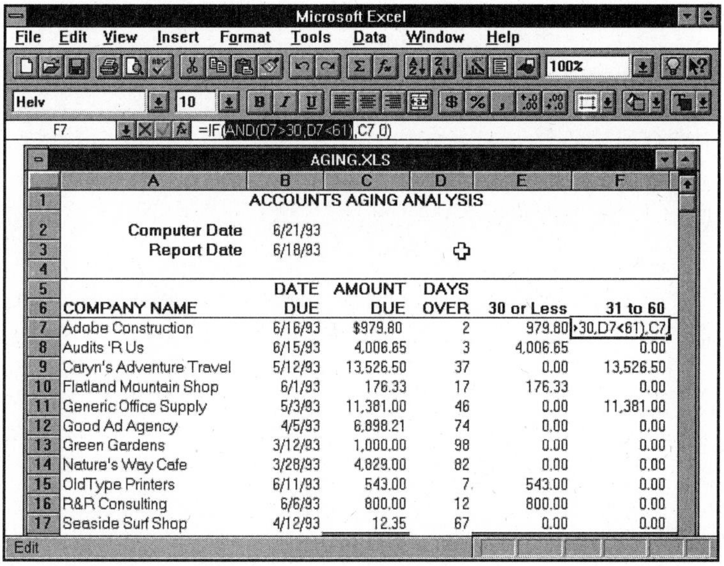

Fig. 5.9
Select the portion of the formula that you want to check.

The preceding method of calculating part of a formula displays the contents of arrays. If, in the formula bar, you select a function that returns an array of values and press F9, you see the values within the array, as in the following example:

{2,3,"four";5,6,"seven"}

Commas separate array values into columns. Semicolons separate rows.

Searching individual formulas for errors or related formulas takes too long. You want to quickly select cells that contain errors, feed into the formula in the active cell, or depend on the result of the active cell.

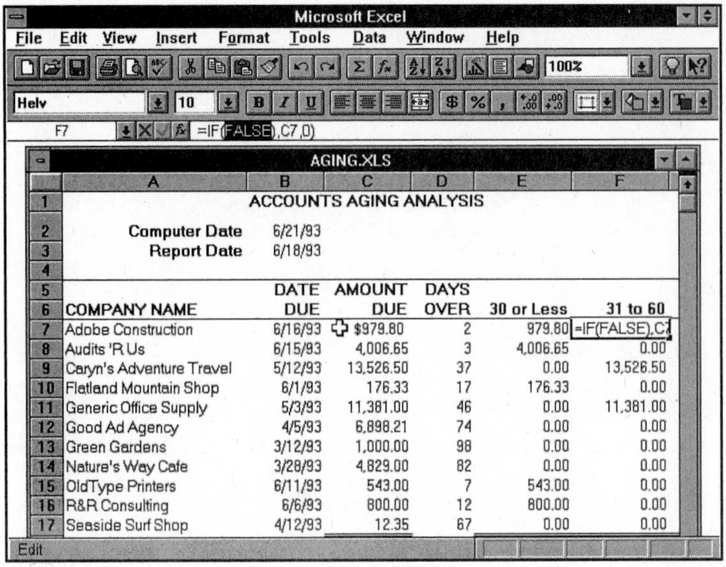

Fig. 5.10
Only the selected portion is calculated.

Chapter 26, "Auditing Workbooks and Worksheets," describes techniques that enable you to trace both formulas feeding into a cell (precedents) and formulas that depend upon a cell (dependents). Another technique is to use the Go To Special feature.

The **E**dit **G**o To **S**pecial command is a powerful ally in auditing and trouble-shooting a worksheet. Form the Go To Special dialog box (see fig. 5.11), you can select specific parts of a worksheet of cell contents.

Table 5.7 describes the Go To Special options you can use when auditing a worksheet. Finding errors, such as #REF! or #N/A, in a worksheet or in a range is easy. Select the **F**ormulas option and deselect all check boxes except the **F**ormulas option, and select **E**rrors.

Table 5.7 Edit Go To Special Options Used in Auditing

Option	Action
Constants	Specifies that constants of the type you specify are selected. Available types are numbers, text, logicals, and errors.
Formulas	Specifies that formulas with results of the type you specify are selected.
Numbers	Selects constants or formulas that result in numbers.

Option	Action
Text	Selects constants or formulas that result in text.
Logicals	Selects constants or formulas that result in logicals (true/false).
Errors	Selects cells with error values.
Precedents	Selects cells that support the active cell.
Dependents	Selects cells that depend on the active cell.
Row Differences	Selects cells in the same row that have a different reference pattern.
Column Differences	Selects cells in the same column that have a different reference pattern.

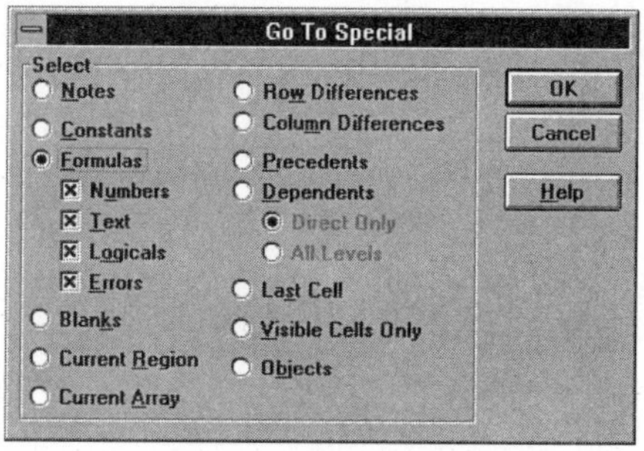

Fig. 5.11
The Edit Go To Special command is a valuable ally in troubleshooting worksheets.

When debugging a worksheet, find the cells that feed information in the active cell and the cells that depend on the results in the active cell. To see which cells feed into the active cell, select the **P**recedents option; select the **D**ependents option to see cells that depend upon the active cell. The D**i**rect Only option selects cells that immediately feed or depend on the active cell. The All **L**evels option selects cells that feed into or depend on the active cell at all levels. The **D**irect Only option is like selecting only your parents or your children. The All **L**evels option is like selecting the entire family tree, backward or forward.

For Related Information

- "Working in the Formula Bar or In-Cell," p. 127
- "Entering Worksheet Functions," p. 178
- "Excel Function Dictionary," p. 184
- "Displaying Formulas," p. 537
- "Linking Worksheet Cells and Ranges," p. 750

Typing a number over a formula is a common error in worksheets. To see cells that contain formulas and cells that contain values, select the range you want to troubleshoot and select the **C**onstants or **F**ormulas options from the Select Special dialog box. Usually, you leave all the related check boxes selected. You may be surprised to find a constant value in the middle of what you believed were formulas!

Press Tab or Shift+Tab to move the active cell between the selected cells, while keeping all other cells selected. Read each cells contents in the formula bar until you find the cell that contains an error.

Calculating with Arrays

Arrays are rectangular ranges of formulas or values that Excel treats as a single group. Some array formulas or functions return an array of results that appear in many cells. Other formulas or functions affect an entire array of cells, yet return the result in a single cell.

Arrays are a powerful method of performing a large amount of calculation in a small space. When used to replace repetitive formulas, arrays also can save memory. Some Excel functions, such as the trend analysis functions discussed in Chapter 23, "Manipulating and Analyzing Data," require some knowledge of arrays.

Entering Array Formulas

Rather than entering or copying a repetitive formula in each cell of a range, you can save memory by entering an array formula. Excel stores an array of formulas in memory as a single formula even if the array affects many cells. Some Excel functions also must be entered as arrays that span a range of cells because the function produces multiple results and each result appears only in one cell.

Figure 5.12 shows a worksheet for cost estimating with Price in column D and Quantity in column E. Using standard formulas, you find the result of the products in column D times column E by entering a formula, such as =D5*E5 in F5, and copy it down column F. This method requires a formula for each cell that produced a result.

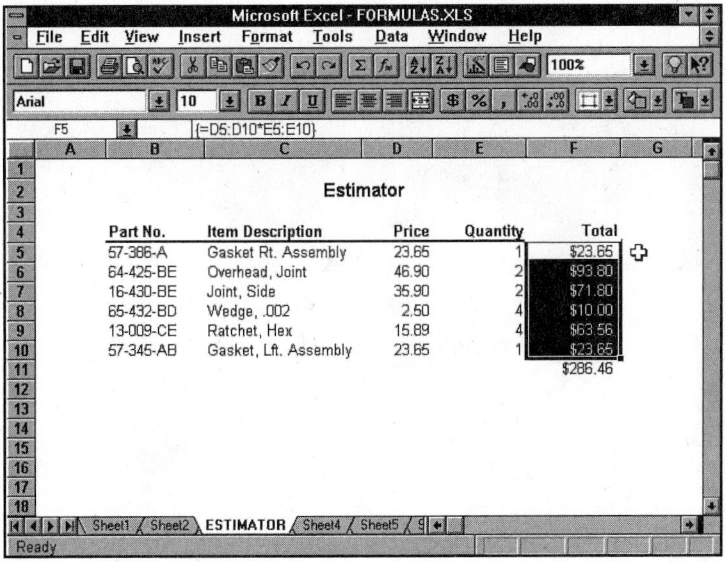

Fig. 5.12
Entering a repetitive formula as an array formula.

Instead, you can enter a single array formula in cell F5 that fills the range from F5 through F10 and uses only the memory and storage required for a single formula. Notice that the entire range F5:F10 reflects a different kind of formula shown in the formula bar. This array formula appears enclosed in curly braces, ({ }).

To enter a single array formula:

1. Select the range to contain the array formula—F5:F10 (see fig. 5.13).
2. Enter the formula that uses ranges by typing the formula or pointing with the mouse. The formula in cell F5 is =D5:D10*E5:E10.
3. To enter the formula or function as an array, press Shift+Ctrl+Enter.

Rather than multiplying two cells, the formula shown in the formula bar of figure 5.11 multiplies the two arrays D5:D10 and E5:E10 by taking each corresponding element from the two arrays and multiplying them in pairsfor example, D5*E5, then D6*E6, and so on. The corresponding result is placed in each cell of the range F5:F10, that was selected before entry.

Notice that the formula in figure 5.11 is enclosed in braces ({ }). Each cell in the array range F5:F10 contains the same formula in braces. The braces signify that the formula is an array formula and that the array range must be treated as a single entity. You cannot insert cells or rows within the array range, delete part of the range, or edit a single cell within the range. To change an array, you must select and change the entire array.

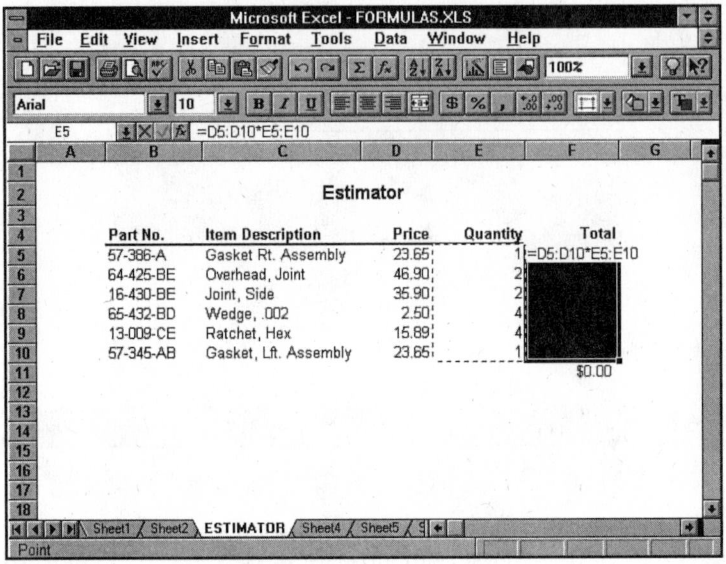

Fig. 5.13
Select the range and then enter the array formula with Shift+Ctrl+Enter.

You can enter functions that operate on corresponding values in ranges with array math. Array functions use an array of values as an input and produce an array of results as an output. Enter array functions the same way you enter an array formula. Select a range of the correct size to hold the results of the array function and enter the array formula or function specifying the ranges on which the formula or function works. Then press Shift+Ctrl+Enter.

Suppose that you want only the total in cell F11 of figure 5.11 and do not need the total price for each part. You can calculate and sum the products in a single cell with an array formula. To see this result, type the following formula in cell F11:

=SUM(D5:D10*E5:E10)

Enter the formula by pressing Shift+Ctrl+Enter so that Excel treats the formula as an array formula. Excel calculates the sum of the array product. The SUM() formula appears in the formula bar, enclosed in braces.

Selecting an Array Range

Usually, the range you select in which to enter an array formula or function should be the same size and shape as the arrays used for input. If the array range you select for the result is too small, you cannot see all the results. If the array range is too large, the unnecessary cells appear with the #N/A message. If an array of a single cell, a single row, or a single column is entered in too large a selection, this element, row, or column is repeated to expand the array to the appropriate size.

In figure 5.13, the array range for each column is 6-by-1 (six rows by one column). The result of multiplying these two arrays is a 6-by-1 array. Therefore, the range from F5 through F10 is selected.

Calculating Array Results

Figure 5.14 shows how a single array formula can perform the work of multiple formulas in a range of extensive database analysis. The formulas in cells C15 and D15 match the entry in cell B15 against the list of Part No. In the formula in cell C15, for example, when the part number in cell B15 matches a part in the range B5:B10, the corresponding value from E5:E10 is added to a total. The result of the total displays in cell C15.

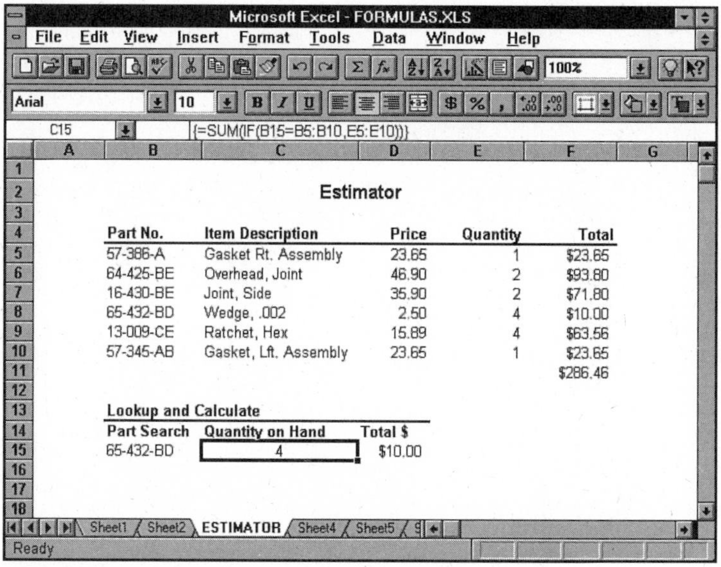

Fig. 5.14
Array formulas can do extensive lookups and calculations in a single cell.

The following line shows the formula in cell C15:

{=SUM(IF(B15=B5:B10,E5:E10))}

This formula was entered as an array formula in C15 by typing the formula and pressing Shift+Ctrl+Enter.

The formula in cell C15 uses the IF() function to compare the contents of cell B15 with each cell in the range B5:B10. When a match is found, the corresponding cell in the range E5:E10 is added to a total kept by SUM(). For this formula to work, you must enter the formula as an array formula.

The following line shows the formula in cell D15:

=SUM(IF(B15=B5:B10,D5:D10*E5:E10))

This formula is entered as an array formula in C15 by typing the formula and pressing Shift+Ctrl+Enter.

The formula in cell D15 works almost exactly as the formula in C15 but adds an extra calculation. When a match is found between the contents of B15 and a cell in the range B5:B10, the calculation of the corresponding cells in columns D and E are multiplied. The result of this multiplication is totaled by the SUM( ) function. This formula must be entered as an array formula.

Note

There are two new database functions in Excel 5, SUMIF and COUNTIF, used to sum and count data that meet specified criteria. You can use these functions rather than the method outlined previously when you want to find the sum of or count up specified subsets of data. To carry out other types of calculations, however, such as averaging, on subsets of data, you still must use the method for calculating array results just discussed. For more information on using the SUMIF and COUNTIF functions, see Chapter 23, "Manipulating and Analyzing Data."

For Related Information

- "Entering Functions," p. 178
- "Logical Functions," p. 207
- "Using the Analysis Toolpak," p. 676

Editing Array Formulas and Functions

To edit an array formula or function, take these steps:

1. Move the pointer within the array range.
2. Click in the formula bar, or press F2 (the Edit key), or double-click the cell if you are using in-cell editing.
3. Edit the array formula or function.
4. To reenter the array, press Shift+Ctrl+Enter.

Naming Cells for Better Worksheets

If you get tired of trying to decipher the meaning of B36 or F13:W54 in a formula, you should use names. If you get tired of selecting the same ranges over and over for reports that you need to print each day or each week, you should use names.

You can, for example, give an area to be totaled the name Sales_Total. You can give the print range F19:L65 an easily recognizable name, such as Sales_Report. Named cells and ranges in Excel are similar to range names in Lotus 1-2-3, but in Excel, you can paste names into formulas, create compound names, and even assign frequently used formulas and constants to names.

Using names in worksheets has the following advantages:

- Names reduce the chance for errors in formulas and commands. You are likely to notice that you mistyped **Sales.Report** when you meant to type Sales_Report, but you may not notice an error when you type F19:L65. When you enter an unrecognizable or undefined name, Excel displays a #NAME? error.

- Names are easier to remember than cell references. After you name cells or ranges, you can look at a list of names and paste the names you want into formulas with the **I**nsert **N**ame **P**aste command or using the Name box next to the formula bar (see Pasting Names and Functions into Formulas earlier in this chapter).

- Names make formulas easy to recognize and maintain. For example, the following formula:

  =Revenue–Cost

  is much easier to understand than the following formula

  =A12–C13

- You can redefine a named reference, and all formulas that use that reference are updated.

- You can name any frequently used constant or formula and use the name in formulas. (The named constant or formula does not have to reside in a cell.) You can, for example, enter a name, such as RATE, into a formula, and then at any later time use the **I**nsert **N**ame **D**efine command to assign a new value to the name RATE. The new assignment changes the value of RATE throughout the worksheet. Nowhere in the worksheet does the value of RATE need to be typed. This technique enables you to create predefined constants and formulas that others using the worksheet can use by name.

- Named ranges expand and contract to adjust to inserted or deleted rows and columns. This feature is important for creating print ranges, charts, databases, macros, and linked worksheets that continue to work no matter how a named range is expanded or contracted.

- Names make finding your way around the worksheet easy. You can choose the **E**dit **G**o To command, or press F5 and select the name of the location you want to go to. Choosing the **E**dit **G**o To command and then selecting Data.Entry or Report.Monthly is a time-saver.

- Using names in macros when referring to specific locations on worksheets helps make your macros more versatile. The macros continue to work on rearranged worksheets.

- Names make typing references to worksheets in other workbooks easy. You do not need to know the cell reference in the other worksheet. If the other workbook has a named cell reference, then you can type a formula such as

  =YTDCONS.XLS!Sales

  This formula brings the information from the Sales cell in the workbook with the file name YTDCONS.XLS into the cell in your active worksheet.

- One set of names can be used throughout a workbook, so that when you need to reference a named cell or cell range in another sheet in a workbook, you don't need to include the worksheet reference.

- You can define names that are unique to a worksheet, so that the same name can be used in different worksheets in a workbook.

Creating Names

When the time comes to create names, you must remember a few rules. Names must start with a letter or an underscore, but you can use any character after the initial letter except a space or a hyphen. Do not use a space in a name; instead, use an underline (_) or a period (.).

Incorrect Names	Correct Names
SALES EXPENSES	SALES_EXPENSES
SALES-EXPENSES	SALES_EXPENSES
Region West	Region.West
1993	YR1993
%	Rate

Although names can be as long as 255 characters, you want to make the names shorter. Because formulas also are limited to 255 characters, long names in a formula leave you less room for the rest of the formula, and the full name does not show in a dialog box. Names of as many as 15 characters display in most scrolling list boxes.

You can type names in either upper- or lowercase letters. Excel recognizes and continues to use the capitalization used to create the name. Don't use names that look like cell references, such as B13 or R13C2.

Defining Names with the Insert Name Define Command. You can define names on a worksheet in two ways—you can use the **I**nsert **N**ame **D**efine command or the name box in the formula bar. An advantage to using the **I**nsert **N**ame **D**efine command is that you can define several names at once without having to close the Define Name dialog box.

To name a cell, range of cells, or multiple range using the **I**nsert **N**ame **D**efine command, take these steps:

1. Select the cell, range, or multiple ranges you want to name.
2. Choose the **I**nsert **N**ame **D**efine command.
3. If Excel proposes an acceptable name, leave the name or type the name you want in the Names in **W**orkbook box.

4. Leave the cell reference in the **R**efers to box, if it is acceptable, or type an equals sign (=) followed by the correct reference. (This procedure is described later.)

5. Choose OK to define the name and close the dialog box.

   You also can choose **A**dd to define the name and leave the dialog box open.

   At this point, you can select the Names in **W**orkbook box and type another name in, and then select the **R**efers to box and either type in a cell reference or select the cell or range of cells on the worksheet. Choose the **A**dd to define the new name. This process can be repeated as many times as you like. Choose OK when you want to close the dialog box.

You can see in figure 5.15 that Excel often proposes a name for the cells you select. Excel looks at the left edge for a text name of a row or looks above for a text name of a column. If you select a range, Excel checks for a name in the upper-left corner of the range. If the text contains a blank space, as figure 5.15, Excel replaces the blank with an underscore to make the name legal. Excel has done this in the following figure.

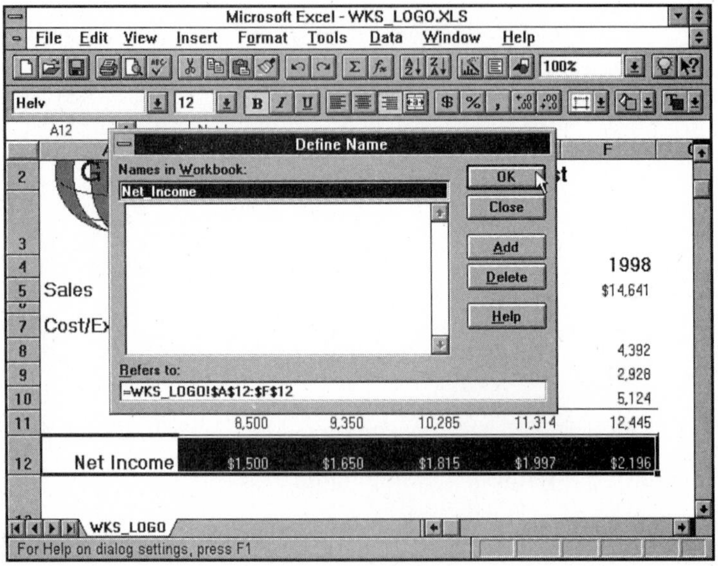

Fig. 5.15
Insert Define Name attempts to propose names for the cell or range you select.

Defining Names by Using the Name Box. The name box appears at the left end of the formula bar. The reference area displays the cell reference for the active cell or the name of the currently selected cell or cells, if they are named. If you click the arrow to the right of the name box, you display an alphabetical list of all defined names in the workbook (see fig. 5.16). You can select a named cell or range by clicking the arrow and selecting the name from the list. You also can use the name box to define a name and to insert a name in a formula (see "Pasting Names and Functions into Formulas," earlier in this chapter).

Fig. 5.16
The name box can be used to quickly select a named cell or range or to define a name.

To define a name using the name box, follow these steps:

1. Select the cell or range of cells you want to name.
2. Click the arrow to the right of the name box. The active cell appears in the name box and is highlighted.
3. Type in the name for the selected cell or cells.
4. Press Enter.

   If you enter a name that is already being used, the cell or range with that name is selected, rather than the current selection being given that name. If you want to redefine an existing name, you must use the **I**nsert **N**ame **D**efine command.

Note

Excel doesn't immediately replace existing cell references in formulas with range names. You have the advantage of specifying the areas of the worksheet where formulas show the range names. This procedure is described in the section, "Applying Names," later in this chapter.

Workbook-level Versus Sheet-level Names. Unless you specify otherwise, names that you define by using the **I**nsert **N**ame **D**efine command or the name box are at the workbook level and apply to all the sheets in the workbook. For example, if a cell on Sheet1 is named Net_Income and you are working in Sheet2, if you open and select the name box, you see Net_Income in the list, Sheet1 becomes the active sheet and the cell named Net_Income is selected. When used in any formula, Net_Income refers to the contents of the named cell on Sheet1. If you define a cell or range with the name Net_Income on another sheet, the name is redefined. Using the method described here, the same name cannot be used to define cells or ranges on different sheets in the same workbook.

To use the same name to define cells or ranges on more than one sheet in a workbook, you can create sheet-level names. In this way, you can use the same name to designate related cells in different worksheets. For example, each of several worksheets representing regional sales can have a cell named Net_Income.

To create sheet-level names, you must use the **I**nsert **N**ame **D**efine command. Follow the same procedure outlined in the section "Defining Names with the Insert Name Define Command," earlier in this chapter, but when you enter the name for the cell or range in the Names in **W**orkbook box (refer to fig. 5.16), proceed the name with the name of the sheet followed by an exclamation mark. For example, to define a cell with the name Net_Income in Sheet2, you would enter Sheet2!Net_Income in the Names in **W**orkbook box.

When you use the sheet-level name on that name's sheet, you don't need to specify the sheet. You can use the name alone. To refer to a sheet-level name from another sheet, you must include the sheet name. To refer to the cell named Net_Income on Sheet2 in a formula on Sheet1, for example, type **Sheet2!Net_Income**. Sheet-level names take precedence over book-level names, so a name in a sheet defined at the sheet-level is used even if the same name is defined at the workbook-level. When you open the Define Name dialog box, only names for the active sheet appear in the Names in **W**orkbook list. You can paste names from another Sheet into a formula by following the steps described in the previous section, "Pasting Names and Functions into Formulas."

Creating Names from Worksheet Text

If you have built a text skeleton consisting of row and column headings for your worksheet, you can use the text names on the worksheet to assign names to adjacent cells. Moreover, by selecting a range of cells, you can assign a number of names at the same time. This technique of creating multiple names from text labels is important to creating well-written macros.

To assign a number of names at the same time, use the **I**nsert **N**ame **C**reate command. You can choose whether Excel uses as names the existing text along one or more edges of the selected area.

To create names using text in the worksheet, take these steps:

1. Select the range of cells you want to name. Be sure to include the row or column of text cells that are used as names (see fig. 5.17).

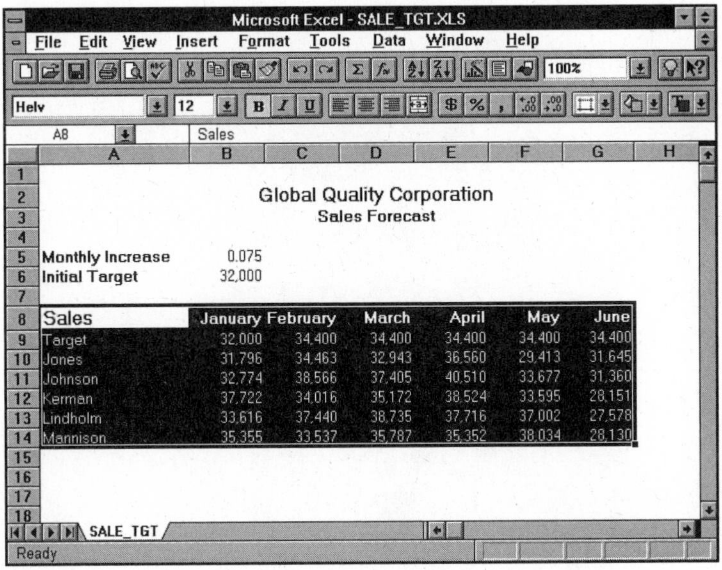

Fig. 5.17
Include text you want to use as names in the range you select.

2. Choose the **I**nsert **N**ame **C**reate command. The Create Names dialog box appears (see fig. 5.18).

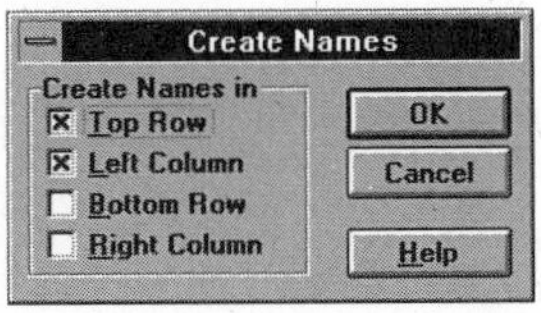

Fig. 5.18
The Create Names dialog box enables you to choose the location of text that is used as names.

3. Select the **T**op Row check box to use text in the top row of the selection as names for the columns. Similarly, the **B**ottom Row check box uses

the bottom row of text as names for the columns. The **L**eft Column check box uses text in the left column to name the rows to the right of the text; and the **R**ight Column check box uses the text in the right column to name the rows to the left of the text.

4. Choose OK.

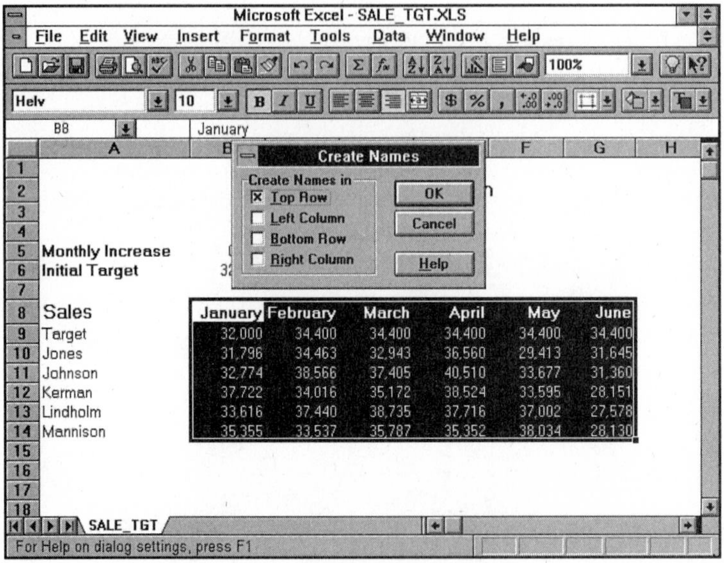

Fig. 5.19 Use the names at the top of these columns to name the cells going down.

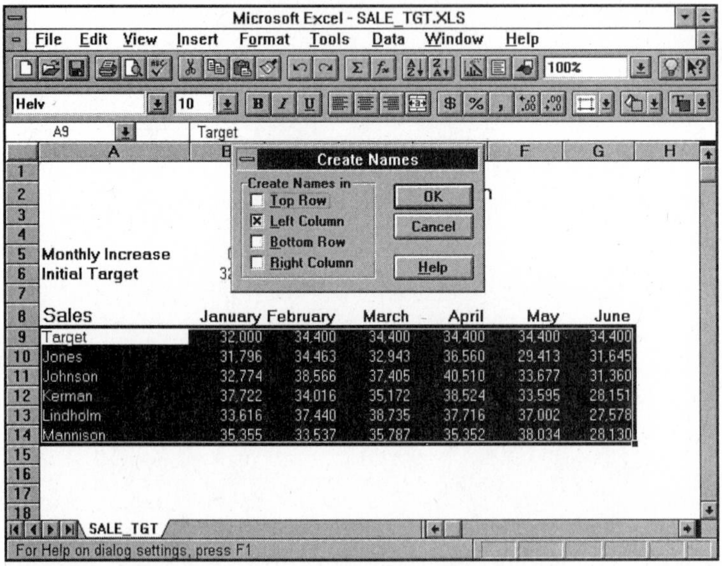

Fig. 5.20 Use names at the left of rows to name the selected cells in the rows.

In figure 5.19, the range under the columns is selected. The names at the top of the column can be assigned by selecting the **T**op Row check box. In figure 5.20, the rows are selected. The names at the left edge of the selection can be assigned to the rows by selecting the **L**eft Column check box.

If you try to assign a duplicate name, a dialog box appears, warning you that the name is already in use. Choose the **Y**es button to update the name to the new references; choose the **N**o button to retain the old name and references; or choose the Cancel button to retain the old name and back out of creating new names.

Text in cells used as names can include spaces. Excel automatically replaces the space with an underscore in the created name. For example, SALES RATE in a cell becomes the name SALES_RATE. You can fit longer names in a tighter space if you use a period as a separator rather than an underscore.

If you use **I**nsert **N**ame **C**reate to name cells, try to use names that do not violate the rules for names. Remember that names cannot begin with numbers. Illegal characters are replaced with underscores, so a text label such as North %Margin results in the name North__Margin, substituting underscores for the blank and the illegal %.

Note

You can create both row and column names at the same time in the selection shown in figure 5.19. Just select both the **T**op Row and **L**eft Column check boxes. Both row and columns names are created. The entire range of data, not including the names, is named with the name at the top-left corner.

You can select more than one box from the Create Names dialog box. As a result, you can name cells in different orientations with different names. If you select two options that overlap, then any text in the cell at the overlap is used as the name for the entire range. If you select both the **T**op Row and **L**eft Column options, then the text in the cell at the top left of the selected range is the name for the entire range. In figure 5.19, the name SALES applies to the range B9:H14, the names on the left apply to the rows, and the names at the top apply to the columns.

You can create intersecting names using row or column headings. For example, if you select a range with text labels along the top and down the left edge, you can select the **T**op Row check box and the **L**eft Column check box. This uses the names along the top row to name each column in the selected range. The names down the left column name each row in the selected range. For example, assigning names using the names in the top row and left column in figure 5.21 would enable you to use the following formula to see Januarys sales amount for Jones:

=Jones January

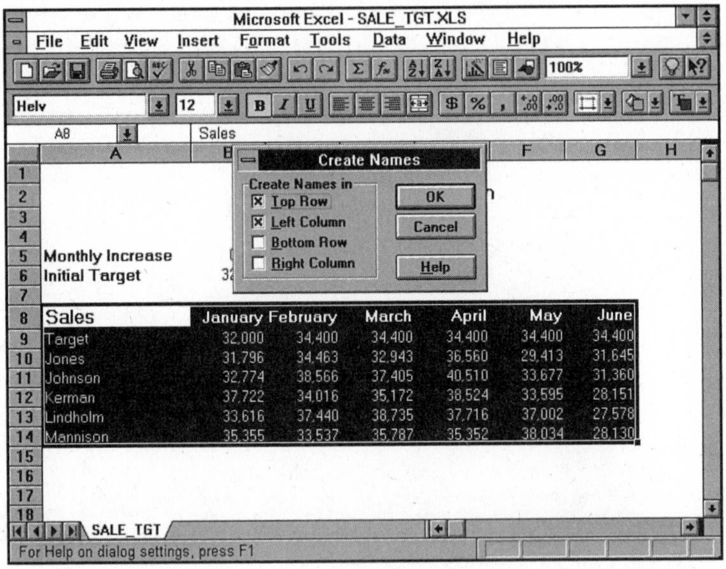

Fig. 5.21
You can use both row and column headings to name cells at the same time.

The space between Jones and January acts as the intersect operator. This formula selects the cell that is common to both the row named Jones and the column named January. The result in the cell containing the formula is 31,796.

Creating 3-D Names

You can use 3-D references when you define a name. When you enter the reference in the **R**efers to box in the Define Name dialog box, you include a 3-D reference of the definition. For example, to define a name that refers to cells A1:A12 in sheets Sheet1 to Sheet6 in a workbook, type =Sheet1:Sheet6!A1:A12. For more information on using 3-D references, see "Entering 3-D References," earlier in this chapter.

Pasting a List of Names

As part of your worksheet documentation, you should include a list of the names used. Excel can paste into your worksheet a complete list of names and the cells they name. Move the active cell to a clear area; be careful to select an area without data, or the list overwrites any existing data. Choose the **I**nsert **N**ame **P**aste command and choose the Paste **L**ist button. A list of all the names and corresponding cell addresses appears in your worksheet.

Changing or Deleting Names

Sometimes you may want to change a name or the cells that the name refers to. Also, from time to time, you may want to delete unneeded names. Deleting unneeded names keeps your list of names free of clutter.

To change a name or the cells that the name references, take these steps :

1. Choose the **I**nsert **N**ame **D**efine command, which is the same command you use to name a cell or range of cells manually. The Define Name dialog box appears.
2. Select from the list box the name you want to change.
3. Select the Names in **W**orkbook box or the **R**efers to box.
4. Edit the name or cell reference in the appropriate text box. Use the arrow keys, Backspace, and Delete keys to edit in the text box.
5. Choose OK.

To delete a name, select the name you want to delete and choose the **D**elete button.

When you change a name, formulas that used the old name are not updated to reflect the new name. For a more extensive name change, use the Change Name add-in.

The CHANGER.XLA file found in the LIBRARY directory under Excel adds the command Formula Change Name. For a complete description of this additional command see Chapter 22s discussion of Excel add-ins.

> **Caution**
>
> After you have deleted a name, selecting Cancel does not undelete it.

Using Names in Formulas and Commands

Names can be used wherever you use cell or range references. In formulas, you can type a name. You also can paste a name into a formula by moving the insertion point in the formula bar where you want the name to appear, and then choosing the **I**nsert **N**ame **P**aste command (or pressing F3). Select the name from the Paste **N**ame list and choose OK. You also can paste a name using the name box. Click the arrow to the right of the name box and select the name you want to paste.

Names also can be used in dialog boxes to indicate a cell reference or range. Just type the name in the edit box requiring the reference.

If you use a name in a formula that Excel cannot find, the #NAME? error value is returned. There are several things to check for if this happens:

- The name is typed correctly in the formula
- Names of functions are typed correctly in the formula.
- The name you are using in the formula has actually been defined.
- The name you are using was deleted.
- The name should not be enclosed in quotation marks.
- References to a cell range must include a colon., otherwise, Excel interprets the range reference as a name.

Note

If you copy a formula that uses a name into another workbook and that workbook already has a cell or range defined with the same name, a message box asks you if you want to use the existing definition of the name, that is, the one in the destination workbook. Answer **Y**es if you want to use this definition or **N**o if you want to use the definition from the workbook you are copying the formula from. If you choose **N**o, you must enter a new name for the cell or range in the source worksheet in the **N**ew Name box of the Name Conflict dialog box that appears.

Applying Names

When you create or define names, they do not automatically appear in existing formulas in the worksheet. If you create formulas before names, you need to apply the names to the formulas. With the **I**nsert **N**ame **A**pply command, Excel gives you the capability to select where you want names applied (see fig. 5.22).

To apply existing names to formulas containing named cell references, follow these steps:

1. Select a single cell if you want to apply names to the entire worksheet, or select a range to apply names to formulas in the range.

2. Choose the **I**nsert **N**ame **A**pply command. The Apply Names dialog box appears.

   The most recently created name(s) are selected in the Apply Names list box, but you can choose whatever names you want to apply.

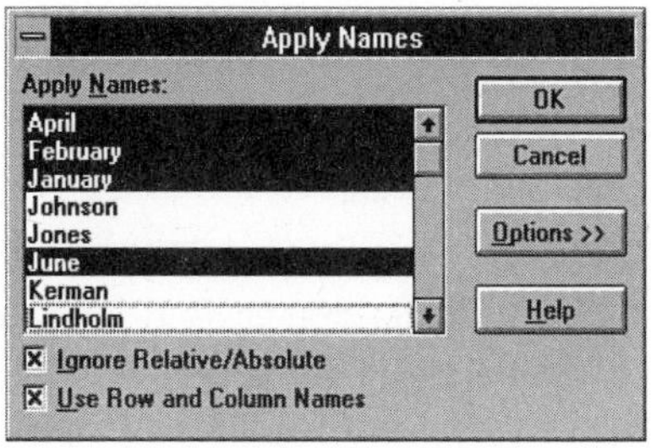

Fig. 5.22
To apply names to existing formulas, use the Insert Name Apply command.

3. You select the names you want applied from the Apply Names list box by clicking each name you want to apply. To select a range of adjacent names, click the first name, press the Shift key, and click the last name. To select multiple non-adjacent names, press the Ctrl key as you click the names. To select adjacent names with the keyboard, press the Shift key and use the arrow keys to select names.

   To select multiple non-adjacent names, press space to select or deselect a name, and hold down Ctrl to keep from deselecting the selected names as you use the arrow keys to move through the list.

4. Select the **I**gnore Relative/Absolute check box if you want names to replace absolute and relative references. Normally this box should be selected. Clearing this box applies absolute names to absolute references and relative names to relative references.

5. Select the **U**se Row and Column Names check box if you want Excel to rename cell references that can be described as the intersect of a named row and a named column. In figure 5.22, cell G10 can be referenced as Jones June. (A space character is the intersect operator.) Clear this box if you want only individual cell names to apply to cell references.

6. Select the **O**ptions button to omit row or column names when the cell containing the formula is in the same row or column as the name. The following options are available:

   Omit **C**olumn Name if Same Column

   Omit **R**ow Name if Same Row

   After selecting **O**ptions, you also can select the order in which you want row and column names to appear. Simply select or clear the options for Name Order: Ro**w** Column and Co**l**umn Row.

7. Choose OK.

Naming Formulas and Values

Your worksheets are much more readable and understandable if you create names for commonly used constants or frequently used formulas. You can name any number or formula, and then use that name in a cell or formula. The number or formula does not need to be in a cell.

Named formulas and values (constants) differ from named cells and ranges. In named cells and ranges, the name references a worksheet location. In named formulas and values, the name references a formula or value that doesn't exist on the worksheet.

To name a value or formula you enter, take these steps:

1. Choose the **I**nsert **N**ame **D**efine command. The Define Name dialog box appears.

2. Select the Names in **W**orkbook text box and enter the name.

3. Select the **R**efers to box.

4. Type the constant number or the formula. Enter the formula or constant as you would in the formula bar. You can edit in the **R**efers to box as you edit in the formula bar.

   If you need to use the arrow keys to move around within the formula, press F2 to change to Edit mode. Otherwise, arrow keys point to cells on the worksheet.

5. Choose OK.

Figure 5.23 illustrates how a formula is assigned a name. Because the formula or constant stored in the name does not need to be stored in a cell, your worksheets stay neater and are easier for inexperienced users to work with.

If you build formulas in the **R**efers to box by pointing to cell references (clicking them or moving to them), Excel supplies only absolute references, such as $D$15. These references are absolute because a name usually applies to one specific location on a worksheet. You can type relative references or edit out the dollar signs to create names that act like relative references. (Named relative reference formulas can be confusing to use, so be careful.) If the active cell is C6, you can type the formula =C12 in the Refers to box. You could give the formula the name RIGHT6. You then can use the name RIGHT6 in a formula or cell to indicate the contents of the cell six cells to the right of the cell containing =RIGHT6. You can move the Define Name dialog box if it is in the way of the cell you need in a formula.

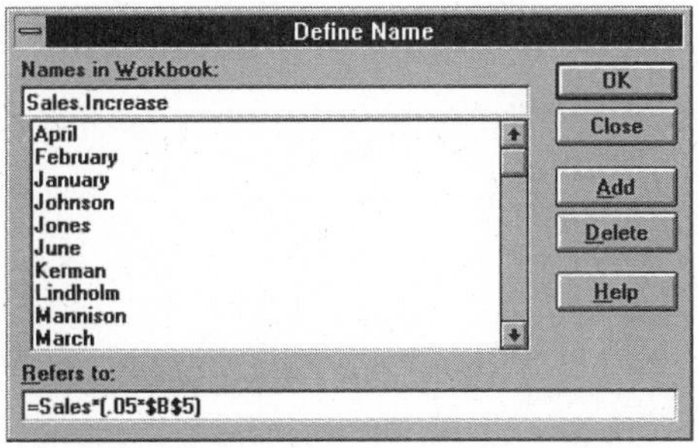

Fig. 5.23
Assign frequently used formulas or constant values to a name.

> **Note**
>
> Deleting all the rows or columns that make up a named range does not delete the name. These names simply refer to cell references that no longer exist. In the Define Name dialog box, selecting an invalid name like this displays a #REF! error in the **R**efers to box.

For Related Information

- "Linking Workbook Cells and Ranges," p. 750

From Here...

Now that you learned how to work with formulas, you can move on to some of the other chapters in this book that take you further in learning the skills you need to learn to create and maintain worksheets in Excel:

- Chapter 6, "Using Functions," to learn how to use Excel's built-in functions, that can save you the time and trouble of writing you own formulas to carry out many types of calculations.
- Chapter 7, "Moving or Copying Data and Formulas," to learn how to rearrange the contents of your worksheets.
- Chapter 10, "Formatting Worksheets," to learn how to use Excel's powerful and easy-to-use formatting features that allow you to create worksheets with a rofessional look.
- Chapter 26, "Auditing Workbooks and Worksheets," to learn how to use Excel's auditing tools to troubleshoot your worksheets.

Chapter 6

Using Functions

In this chapter, you will learn:

- What functions and arguments are
- How to write and edit a function
- How to use the AutoSum tool and Function Wizard
- How to find help on a function
- The required syntax and arguments for Excel's functions

As seen earlier in this book, a cell can contain text, numbers, formulas, or functions. Both formulas and functions allow you to put a calculated value in the cell. Formulas allow you to do addition, subtraction, multiplication, division, and can contain functions. Excel uses prebuilt worksheet functions to perform math, text, or logical calculations or to find information about the worksheet. Functions allow you to speed up your calculations compared to writing a formula. For example, you could create a formula =(A1+A2+A3+A4+A5+A6+A7+A8)/8 or use the function =AVERAGE(A1:A8) to do the same thing. Whenever possible, use functions rather than writing your own formulas. Functions are fast, take up less space in the formula bar, and reduce the chance for typographical errors.

Functions act on data in much the same way that formulas act on numbers. Functions accept information, referred to as *arguments*, and return a result. In most cases, the result is a math calculation, but functions also return results that are text, references, logical values, arrays, or information about the worksheet. The functions listed in this chapter can be used in worksheets and in Excel 5 macro sheets.

In the first part of the chapter, you learn what functions are and how to use them. The latter part of the chapter is a directory of the majority of Excel's approximately 200 worksheet functions with descriptions of the arguments that the functions use. The directory is divided by types of functions and includes examples for many of the functions.

Understanding Functions

Functions accept data through arguments. You enter arguments, enclosed in parentheses, after the function name. Each function takes specific types of arguments, such as numbers, references, text, or logical values. Functions use these arguments in the same way that equations use variables.

If, for example, you want to write an equation to determine a mortgage or loan payment, you need the following information:

Argument	Description
rate	Interest rate per period
nper	Number of periods
pv	Present value (starting value of loan)
fv	Future value (ending value at loan completion)

Because the equation for an amortized loan payment requires many complex terms, you are likely to make typographical errors if you write your own equation. Excel also solves a formula you enter more slowly than it solves a built-in function for the same operation.

Instead of manually entering a long formula to calculate the loan payment, you can use the Excel worksheet function, PMT( ) for this kind of calculation. You can type a function into a cell or insert it into a cell with the guidance of the Function Wizard.

In parentheses, you enter the values or references for the information needed to do the calculation. These terms inside the parentheses are known as *arguments*. The PMT( ) function is entered in this form:

=PMT(*rate*,*nper*,*pv*,_fv_,_type_)

Note

Arguments in bold and italic such as ***rate***, ***nper***, and ***pv*** are required. Those arguments in italic only are optional.

The arguments give the information needed to solve for a calculation for a payment, with the addition of the argument *type*. Some functions return different answers depending on the value of *type*. In the case of PMT( ), Excel can calculate payments for different types of loans depending on the value used for *type*. An actual PMT( ) function may look like this:

=PMT(Mo.Int,A12,B36)

Here, Mo.Int is the name of the cell that contains the monthly interest rate (*rate*), A12 contains the number of months (*nper*), and B36 contains the present value (*pv*). The arguments *fv* and *type* are optional and are not used in this calculation of a simple mortgage payment.

Using Arguments within Functions

Most functions contain one or more arguments within the parentheses. If the function contains more than one argument, separate the arguments with commas. When you write a function, never include a space unless the space is in quoted text. In order to give the appearance of words, you can instead include an underscore, as in *num_chars*.

Excel uses various types of arguments for different types of information. As shown in table 6.1, you can often tell the required types of data for an argument by the name of the argument.

Table 6.1 Types of Arguments

Argument	Type	Sample Function and Argument Names
text	text	**LEFT(*text*,*num_chars*)** (in quotation marks or a reference)
value	value	**LOOKUP(*lookup_value,array*)** (text in quotation marks, a number, or a reference)
num	numeric	**RIGHT(*text*,*num_chars*)** (a number or a reference)
reference	cell reference	**COLUMN(*reference*)**
serial_number	date/time number	**DAY(*serial_number*)** (or a reference)
logical	logical	**OR(*logical1*,*logical2,...*)** (or a reference)
array	array	**TRANSPOSE(*array*)** (or a reference)

If you have a long function or formula, you can enter carriage returns (Alt+Enter) and tabs (Ctrl+Tab) to make the function more readable.

Some functions can have up to 30 arguments. This chapter shows these functions, such as the OR( ) function, with an ellipsis (...) to indicate that there are more arguments possible.

Some functions have optional arguments, which are shown in the directory in *italic type*. Mandatory arguments are shown in ***bold italic type***. If you leave out optional arguments, you do not need to enter their commas if there are no additional arguments. Commas act as place holders so that Excel understands the position of the optional arguments that you do enter. For example, the following is the format of the PMT( ) function with all its arguments:

PMT(*rate*,*nper*,*pv*,*fv*,*type*)

If you omit the *fv* optional argument, but use the *type* argument, you would enter the function as

PMT(*rate*,*nper*,*pv*,*type*)

While the PMT function requires values, other functions, such as LEFT, require text. Be certain that you enclose text in quotation marks (" "). Text contained in a cell and referenced by the cell address does not have to be in quotation marks. Do not enclose range names in quotation marks, and do not type spaces between the quotes. Text values in a cell, including the quotation marks, can be up to 255 characters long. If your text includes a quotation, use two quotation marks to begin and end each internal quotation. For example, to find the length of the following phrase:

She said, "So!"

You must use

=LEN("She said,""So!""")

Note

To produce a blank cell display, use two quotation marks with nothing between them, as in the following example:

=IF(A12>15,"","Entry must be greater than 15!")

When A12 is greater than 15, the cell displays nothing because the TRUE portion of the IF( ) function returns "". When A12 is 15 or less, the cell displays the following message:

```
Entry must be larger than 15!
```

Viewing the Parts of the Screen that Help Create Functions

Figure 6.1 shows the different parts of the screen that you can use to create functions. The function aids are in two basic places: on the Standard toolbar and on the formula bar. Both the formula bar and the Standard toolbar appear when you first load Excel. If the formula bar has been turned off, select **V**iew **F**ormula Bar to turn it on. If the Standard toolbar has been turned off, select **V**iew **T**oolbars, check the Standard toolbar box, and choose the OK command button.

When you begin entering information in a cell, four buttons appear on the formula bar. These buttons as well as the function-related buttons on the Standard toolbar are explained in table 6.2 and shown in figure 6.1.

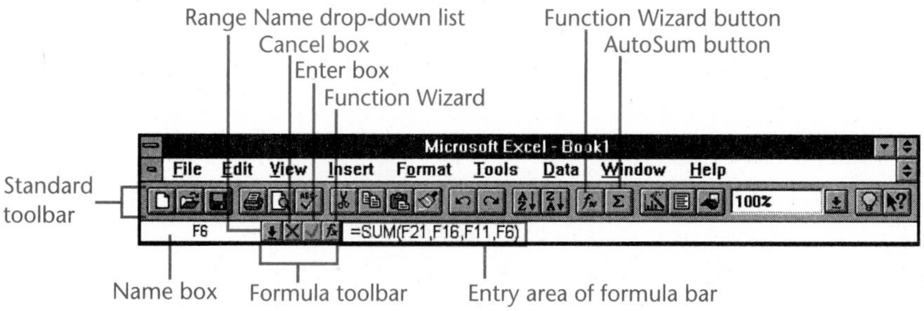

Fig. 6.1
The Standard toolbar and formula bar contain many parts relating to functions.

Table 6.2 Standard Toolbar and Formula Bar Parts Related to Creating Function

Standard Toolbar	
Name	**Description**
AutoSum	Allows you to total a range. Places the SUM( ) function in a cell or number of cells.
Function Wizard	Guides you through the process of creating any function.

(continues)

Table 6.2 Continued

Formula Bar

Name	Description
Name box	Shows cell reference or name of active cell.
Range Name drop-down list	Displays a list of named cells or ranges.
Cancel box	Click to cancel the function.
Enter box	Click to enter the function in the cell.
Function Wizard	Works like Function Wizard on the toolbar.
Entry area	Displays formula function as you create or edit it.

Entering Worksheet Functions

You can enter worksheet functions as a single entry in the formula bar, such as this:

=PMT(A12,B36,J54)

Or, worksheet functions can be part of a much larger formula, including nested functions that are within other functions, as in this example:

=IF(LEFT(A12,4)="VDT",SUM(B36:B54),SUM(C36:C54))

Note

This function looks at the first three characters of the text in cell A12. If the first three characters contain VDT, the function will sum cells in column B, otherwise, the function will sum column C.

You can enter functions by manually typing the function or by pasting the function into the formula bar (which is below the toolbar). One function, SUM( ), also can be pasted from the toolbar.

Typing Functions

You can type any function into the formula bar just as you would type in a formula. If you remember the function and its arguments, typing may be the fastest method. If you are unsure of the function's spelling or its arguments, paste in the function with the Function Wizard.

Using the AutoSum Tool

The most frequently used function is SUM( ). This function totals the numeric value of all cells in the ranges it references. For example, SUM( ) can total all the cells between two endpoints in a column or row. Because SUM( ) is used so frequently, an AutoSum button, which you can use to total adjacent columns or rows automatically, appears on the standard toolbar. As well as entering the SUM( ) function, the AutoSum tool selects the cells in the column above the SUM( ) or in the row to the left of the SUM( ). SUM( ) is useful for totaling columns of expenses or rows of sales by region. SUM( ) can even total subtotals while disregarding the numbers that created the subtotals.

If the Standard toolbar does not show on-screen, turn on the Standard toolbar by choosing the **V**iew **T**oolbars command and clicking the Standard check box. If another toolbar already is displayed, you can click it anywhere except over a drop-down list box to display a shortcut menu from which you can choose Standard. Figure 6.2 shows how to enter a SUM( ) function in cell D12 by using a mouse. Select cell D12B11, below the column you want to total, and then click the AutoSum button. Excel inserts the SUM( ) function and enters that column's range between parentheses, as shown in the figure. You can continue the formula by adding more terms, or you can enter the SUM( ) function into the cell by clicking the AutoSum button a second time.

If you want to select the range of cells to total, highlight the range to sum including blank cell(s) to the right or below the range. When you select the AutoSum tool, Excel fills in totals. Sum totals appear in blank cells below and to the right of a range of numbers.

You can enter multiple SUM( ) functions at one time by clicking the AutoSum tool an a preselected range.

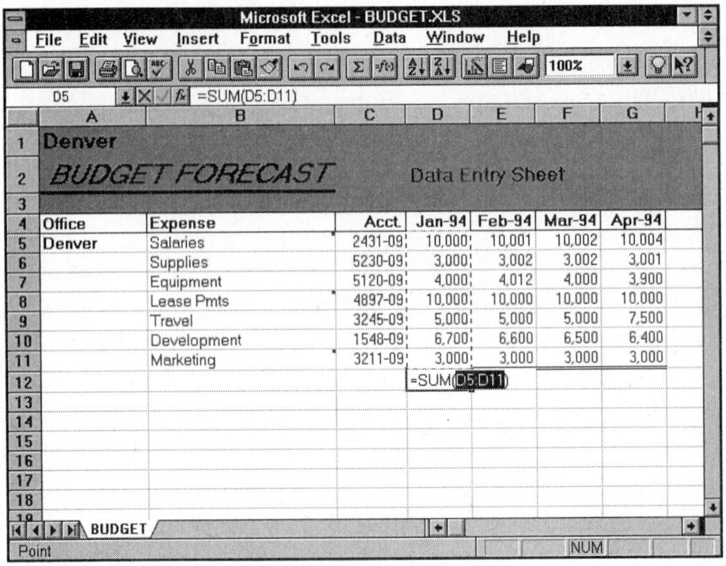

Fig. 6.2
Double-click the AutoSum button to total the column above or to the left of the active cell.

EXCEL 5

Note

You can quickly enter totals at the bottom of a table of any size. If you have a table that is surrounded by blank cells, you can select the entire table, no matter how large, by clicking on a cell in the table and pressing Ctrl+* (asterisk). With the table selected, click the AutoSum button. The AutoSum enters a total under each column in the table.

EXCEL 5

If you have tables of data containing subtotals, you can use AutoSum to total the subtotals. Figure 6.3 shows a simple table that contains subtotals in cells F7, F11, F15, and F19. When you click on cell F20 and then click the AutoSum button, AutoSum enters a grand total in cell F20 by looking at the filled cells above the range and creating the function SUM(F19,F15,F11,F7). Cells that contain numbers are ignored so they are not counted twice.

Tip
In the Function Wizard, use the Most Recently Used category to quickly get to functions you use frequently.

Using the Function Wizard

Creating functions can seem difficult, especially with the potentially different ways to spell a function name (AVG, AVE, AVERAGE) and the potential number of arguments possible. Use the Function Wizard to make your job much easier. The Function Wizard will guide you through the process and explain each function as well as each argument within a function.

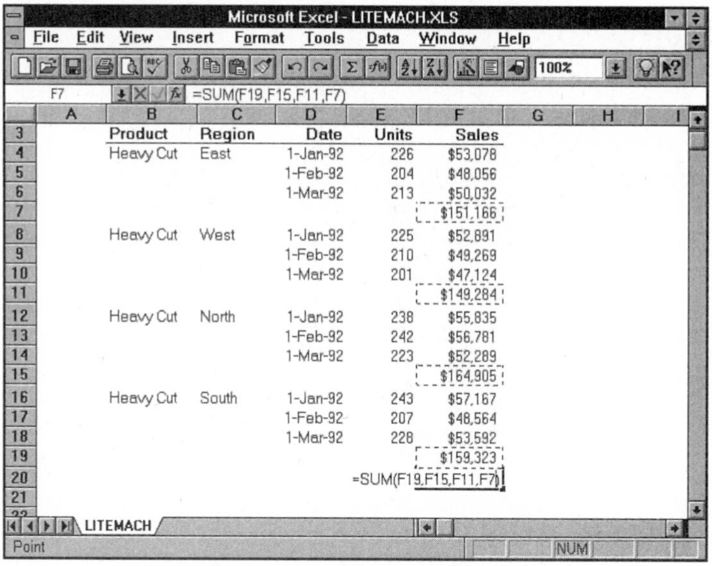

Fig. 6.3
AutoSum also totals subtotals.

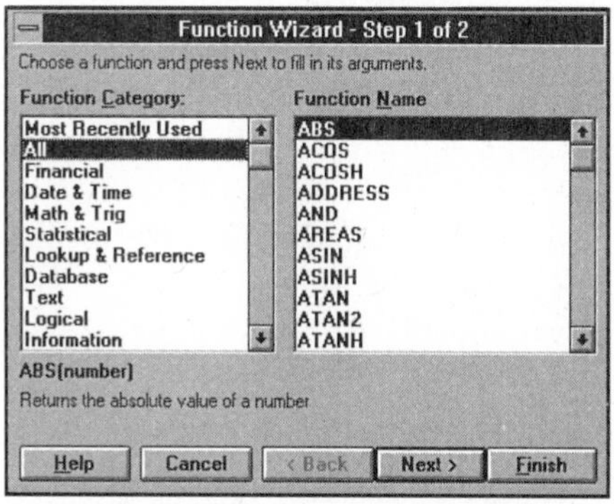

Fig. 6.4
The first step of the Function Wizard shows function names for each function category.

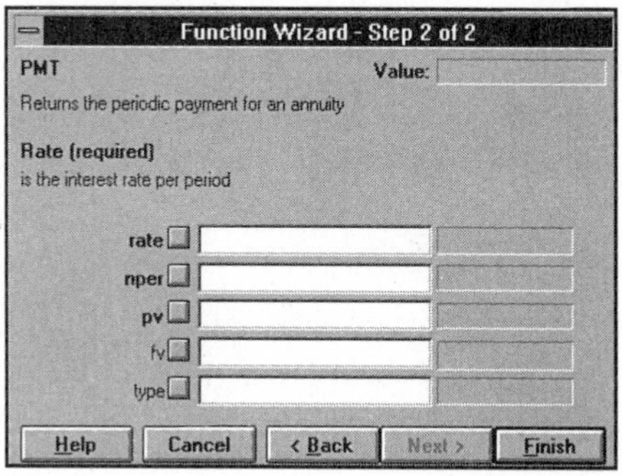

Fig. 6.5
The second step of the Function Wizard shows the required arguments in bold and the optional arguments in normal typeface.

To insert a function and its arguments into the worksheet:

1. Select the cell where you want to enter the function. If you are entering a formula in the formula bar, move the insertion point to where you want the function inserted.

2. Choose **I**nsert **F**unction or click the Function Wizard button to display the Step 1 dialog box in the Function Wizard.

Tip
Add custom functions by creating a Visual BASIC function as shown in Chapter 45, "Programming in Visual Basic for Applications."

Tip
Engineering, finance, and statistics functions are available with the Analysis ToolPak add-in described in Chapter 29.

Tip
Scroll quickly to a function by clicking in the list and typing the first letter.

3. Select the type of function you want from the Function **C**ategory list. These categories segment the large number of functions into smaller lists. If you are unsure of the category, check Most Recently Used or All.

4. Choose the specific function that you want from the Function **N**ame list box. Read the description in the lower part of the Step 1 window to check that you want this function.

5. Choose the Next button.

6. In the Step 2 dialog box of the Function Wizard, in each argument text box: type the cell references or numbers; click on the cell to enter; or drag across multiple cells to enter. Notice the description of each argument as you select the text box.

   If you want to use range names in an argument text box, type the range name or select **I**nsert **N**ame **P**aste.

   You can also create more complex functions where each argument is a function itself. Click on the Function Wizard button indicated by *fx* next to the argument name and complete the Function Wizard dialog boxes.

7. Choose the **B**ack button to return to the Step 1 dialog box. Choose **F**inish to complete the function and insert it in a cell.

   You also can choose Cancel to not insert the function.

Editing Functions

After you enter functions into a formula in the formula bar, you can edit them in two ways. You can use the Function Wizard to step through the functions in a formula, or you can manually edit the formula and functions.

To edit functions using the Function Wizard:

1. Select the cell containing a function.

2. Choose **I**nsert **F**unction or click the Function Wizard button in the Standard toolbar. The Function Wizard appears and shows the first function in the formula.

3. Change any arguments necessary in the first function.
4. When you finish making changes, choose **F**inish. If there is another function in the same formula you want to edit, choose Next.
5. Repeat steps 3 and 4 for each function you wish to edit.

To edit functions manually:

1. Select the cell containing the formula.
2. Press F2 to edit the Formula bar or click in the Formula bar.
3. Select the argument or term in the formula you want to change.
4. Enter the new argument by typing, dragging, pasting a name, or inserting a function.
5. Choose OK.

Tip
Select a term or argument in the Formula bar by double-clicking it. With the keyboard, press Shift+Ctrl+arrow.

You can move across arguments by pressing Ctrl+left- or right-arrow. To select as you move, hold down Shift. Chapter 4, "Entering and Editing Worksheet Data," describes other editing shortcuts.

Getting Help

Excel contains extensive on-line Help for functions. If you forget how to use a function or want to see an example, use the Help files that are always available. To get help while you are building a function choose **H**elp in the Function Wizard. To get help about a function that is in the formula bar, select the name of the function, for example PMT, then press the help key: F1. To access Help about functions, choose **H**elp **S**earch for Help On. Type the phrase, **About Worksheet Functions**, in the top text box, or type the name of a specific function you want help with; then choose **S**how Topics. Select a more specific topic from the lower window, then choose **G**o To to display a help window on that topic. If you are looking for help on a specific function, a help screen similar to the one in figure 6.6 appears. Press Alt+F4 to close the Help window.

For Related Information

- "Getting Help," p. 55
- "Entering Formulas," p. 127
- "Working in the Formula Bar or In-Cell," p. 127
- "Using Excel's Auditing Tools," p. 783

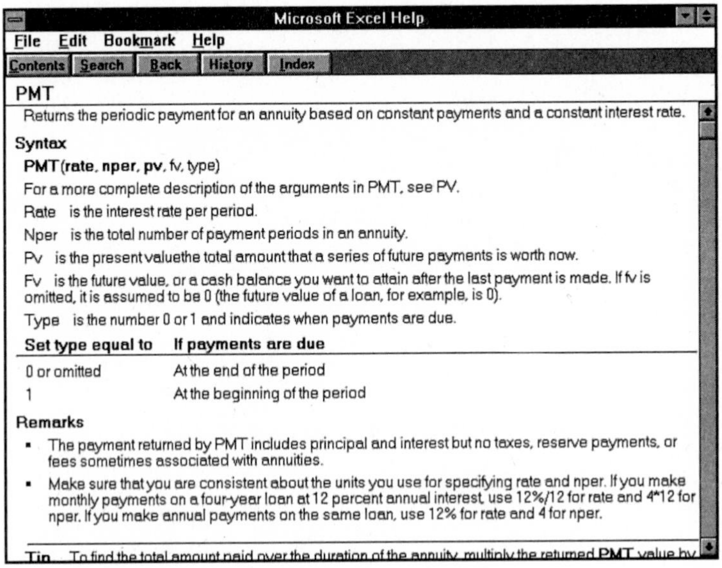

Microsoft Excel Help
File Edit Bookmark Help
Contents Search Back History Index
PMT
Returns the periodic payment for an annuity based on constant payments and a constant interest rate.
Syntax
PMT(rate, nper, pv, fv, type)
For a more complete description of the arguments in PMT, see PV.
Rate is the interest rate per period.
Nper is the total number of payment periods in an annuity.
Pv is the present valuethe total amount that a series of future payments is worth now.
Fv is the future value, or a cash balance you want to attain after the last payment is made. If fv is omitted, it is assumed to be 0 (the future value of a loan, for example, is 0).
Type is the number 0 or 1 and indicates when payments are due.
Set type equal to If payments are due
0 or omitted At the end of the period
1 At the beginning of the period
Remarks
The payment returned by PMT includes principal and interest but no taxes, reserve payments, or fees sometimes associated with annuities.
Make sure that you are consistent about the units you use for specifying rate and nper. If you make monthly payments on a four-year loan at 12 percent annual interest, use 12%/12 for rate and 4*12 for nper. If you make annual payments on the same loan, use 12% for rate and 4 for nper.

Fig. 6.6
The Help window for the PMT function.

Excel Function Dictionary

In the function directory that follows, the most commonly used Excel functions are listed with their arguments. The directory also includes explanations, limitations, examples, and tips. Function definitions are grouped by type and are listed in alphabetical order within each group. The function groups include the following:

- Database
- Date and Time
- Financial
- Information
- Logical
- Lookup and Reference
- Math & Trig (includes matrix)
- Statistical
- Text

Database Functions

Each of Excel's database functions uses the same arguments: *database*, *field*, and *criteria*. The descriptions of these arguments in the discussion of DAVERAGE( ) apply to all the database functions.

The *criteria*, *field*, and *database* arguments used in D*functions* can be of any range on the worksheet. You can have several D*functions* working at the same time on different ranges of data, and each function can have its own criteria range.

For the *database* argument, you can specify a range (such as B36:D54), a range name (such as INVENTORY), or the name DATABASE (which you create with the **I**nsert **N**ame **D**efine command). The *field* argument specifies the column to average. You can specify the *field* by its field name in quotation marks ("Sales"), by a reference to a cell containing the field name, or by a number (1 is the first field [column], 2 the second, and so on). The *criteria* argument can be a reference (such as B12:D13), a name (such as Crit.Sales), or the name CRITERIA, which you create with the **I**nsert **N**ame **D**efine command.

The database functions work on a list or database. The functions provide summary statistics about the database. On the other hand, the list commands in Chapters 30–35 allow you to find items on lists, extract records based on criteria, and link Excel to databases outside the program. You often work with the database functions and list commands together in one workbook.

DAVERAGE(*database,field,criteria*)

This function averages the numbers in the *field* of the *database* for records that match the query in *criteria*.

The *database*, *field*, and *criteria* arguments do not have to be the same as those used for the **D**ata F**o**rm and **D**ata **F**ilter **A**dvanced Filter commands. This means that you can analyze multiple databases on the same worksheet. If you want to analyze multiple databases with range names, give each database and criteria a unique name, such as Crit.Sales.1 and Crit.Sales.2.

The following examples are valid DAVERAGE( ) functions:

=DAVERAGE(Database,2,Criteria)

where Database and Criteria are set with the **I**nsert **N**ame **D**efine command, and the second field is averaged.

=DAVERAGE(B12:H534,"Days",Crit.Sales)

where the *database* being analyzed is in B12:H534, the *field* being averaged has the heading Days, and the *criteria* is in a range with the name Crit.Sales. Notice that when the name of a field heading is used, it is enclosed in quotation marks.

DCOUNT(*database,field,criteria*)

Counts the numeric records in the *database field* that satisfy the *criteria*.

Limits: If the *field* argument is omitted, DCOUNT( ) counts all records in the *database* that satisfy the *criteria*.

DCOUNTA(*database,field,criteria*)

Counts the number of nonblank cells in the *field* of the *database* for those records that satisfy the *criteria*.

Limits: If the *field* argument is omitted, DCOUNTA( ) counts all nonblank records in the *database* that satisfy the *criteria*.

DGET(*database,field,criteria*)

Extracts from the *database* the single record that matches the *criteria*. If no records match the *criteria*, #VALUE! is returned. If more than one record matches the *criteria*, #NUM! is returned.

DMAX(*database,field,criteria*)

Finds the largest number in the *database field* for records that satisfy the *criteria*.

DMIN(*database,field,criteria*)

Finds the smallest number in the *database field* for records that satisfy the *criteria*.

DPRODUCT(*database,field,criteria*)

Multiplies all values in the *field* of the *database* for records that satisfy the *criteria*. This function is similar to DSUM( ), but the values are multiplied rather than added.

DSTDEV(*database,field,criteria*)

Calculates the standard deviation of a sample population, based on the numbers in the *field* of the *database* for records that satisfy the *criteria*.

DSTDEVP(*database,field,criteria*)

Calculates the standard deviation of the entire population, based on the numbers in the *field* of the *database* for records that satisfy the *criteria*.

DSUM(*database,field,criteria*)

Totals all numbers in the *field* of the *database* for records that satisfy the *criteria*.

DVAR(*database,field,criteria*)

Calculates the estimated variance (how the sample deviates from the average) of a sample population, based on the numbers in the *field* of the *database* for records that satisfy the *criteria*.

DVARP(*database,field,criteria*)

Calculates the variance of an entire population, based on the numbers in the *field* of the *database* for records that satisfy the *criteria*.

Date and Time Functions

Excel records dates and times as serial numbers. A date is the number of days from January 1, 1900, to the date you specify; a time is a decimal fraction of 24 hours. Serial numbers provide the capability to calculate elapsed days, future times, and so on. For example, the serial number for January 1, 1992, 6:30 p.m., is 34335.7708333, where 34335 is the number of days from the beginning of the century and .7708333 is the decimal fraction of 24 hours representing 6:30 p.m.

Windows Excel usually counts dates from the beginning of the year 1900. On the Macintosh, however, Excel uses a date system based on 1904. You can change the date system by choosing the **T**ools **O**ptions command, selecting the **C**alculation tab, and choosing the 1904 **D**ate System option. You may need to select this option when you are reading Excel worksheets created on the Macintosh. The following definitions and examples assume that the 1904 **D**ate System is not selected.

Note

The same date and time formats that you type into a worksheet, such as *10/12/93* or *9-Sep-94*, can be used with worksheet functions. When a function's argument is *serial_number*, you can use the serial date number or a reference to a cell containing a date or time, or you can enter a date as text in the argument, such as *"24-Dec-94"*. Remember to enclose the text date in quotation marks because it is treated as text.

DATE(*year,month,day*)

Produces the serial number for a specific date. Use the DATE( ) function to calculate a serial number from formulas that produce a numeric year, month, or day. Enter numbers for the *year*, *month*, and *day* or reference cells that contain numeric values or formulas.

Tip
Calculate the last day of a month by using =DATE (year,month=1,0). Calculate the last day of the last day of the previous month by using =DATE (year,month,0).

Limits: Excel returns serial numbers for dates between January 1, 1900, and December 31, 2078. Enter years between 1900 and 2078 (or 00 and 178), months from 1 to 12, and days from 1 to 31.

Example: DATE(1988,7,B11) produces the serial number 32336 if B11 contains the day number 12.

Note

DATE(1994,CHOOSE(*QTR*,1,4,7,10),1) produces serial numbers for the first day of each quarter when *QTR* refers to a cell that contains a number between 1 and 4. Choose Forma**t** C**e**lls and select the Number tab to format the cell containing a serial number so that it appears as a date.

Do not use Excel's DATE( ) and DATEVALUE( ) functions to enter dates as you would with the @DATE and @DATEVALUE functions in Lotus 1-2-3. Cells in Excel directly accept dates in the format used by the country set in the International Program in the Control Panel.

DATEVALUE(*date_text*)

Converts a date written as text into a serial number. The *date_text* can be in any of Excel's predefined date formats. These formats are found in the list box of the Forma**t** C**e**lls command Number tab dialog box. Excel accepts text dates entered in formulas or directly into cells.

Limits: Excel returns serial numbers for dates between January 1, 1900, and December 31, 2078. Enter years between 00 and 178, months from 1 to 12, and days from 1 to 31.

Example: DATEVALUE("24-Dec-94") produces 34692.

Note

If you need to combine (concatenate) dates, numbers, and text into a single text line, or if you want to format a date so that it can exceed the width of a cell, use the TEXT( ) function to convert the date or cell reference to text; then join the date and text together with the concatenation operator: & (ampersand).

DAY(*serial_number*)

Converts a *serial_number* to the number of the day of the month between 1 and 31. Format the cell as a number.

Limits: The serial number must be in the 0 to 65380 range.

Examples: DAY(32501) produces 24.

DAY("24-Dec-94") produces 24.

DAY(B11) produces 24 when B11 contains 24-Dec-94.

DAYS360(*start_date,end_date*,*method*)

Produces the number of days between the *start_date* and the *end_date* in a 360-day year. These calculations are necessary for accounting and finance systems based on twelve 30-day months. The optional *method* argument is a number (1 or blank for U.S. or 2 for European) that changes the value if the starting date is the 30th or 31st of the month.

Limits: If the *end_date* occurs before the *start_date*, Excel returns a negative number.

Example: DAYS360("4/1/94",B12) produces 90 when B12 contains the date 7/1/94.

EDATE(*start_date,months*)

Produces the serial number date that has the same day of the month at the number of *months* from the *start_date*. Format the cell as a number. This function is good for calculating maturity dates on loans.

Example: EDATE("5/15/94",12) will return 5/15/95 if the cell is formatted as a date.

EOMONTH(*start_date,months*)

Produces the serial number date of the last day of the month at the number of *months* from the *start_date*. Format the cell as a number.

Example: EOMONTH("5/15/94",12) will return 5/31/95 if the cell is formatted as a date.

HOUR(*serial_number*)

Hours are the fractional part of a day in a serial number. HOUR( ) returns the number of hours (based on a 24-hour clock) for the fractional day in the *serial_number*. Format the cell as a number.

Examples: HOUR(32501.75) produces 18.

HOUR("24-Dec-94 18:00") produces 18.

MINUTE(*serial_number*)

Returns the number of minutes from a *serial_number*. The fractional part of a day is based on a 24-hour clock. The number of minutes returned is between 0 and 59. Format the cell as a number.

Example: MINUTE(32501.75456) produces 6 minutes.

MONTH(*serial_number*)

Converts the *serial_number* to the number of the month (from 1 to 12). Format the cell as a number.

Examples: MONTH(32501.7546) produces 12.

MONTH(B14) produces 12 if B14 states "24-Dec-94".

NETWORKDAYS(*start_date,end_date,*holidays)

Produces the number of working days between *start_date* and *end_date*. The number of working days excludes weekends and any set of one or more serial number *holidays*).

Example: NETWORKDAYS("10/10/93","10/17/93") produces 5 (10/10 and 10/17 are Sundays, so there are 5 workdays between these two dates).

NOW( )

Calculates the serial number of the date and time in the computer's clock. Excel updates the date and time only when the worksheet is opened or recalculated.

Limits: Include the empty parentheses when entering this function. NOW( ) does not use an argument.

> **Note**
>
> Use the NOW( ) function to stamp a worksheet with the date and time of printing. Enter NOW( ) in a cell. If the result doesn't appear as a date, format the cell with the F**o**rmat C**e**ll command and Number tab as a date/time format. Each time you retrieve the worksheet or recalculate, the cell contents are updated. To freeze a date or time, copy the cell with **E**dit **C**opy, then paste over the cell you copied with **E**dit Paste **S**pecial with the **V**alues option selected. Do not use NOW( ) in a header or footer; use the &D and &T codes for date and time.

SECOND(*serial_number*)

Returns the number of seconds (between 0 and 59) in the fractional part of the *serial_number*.

Examples: SECOND(32501.753) produces 19.

SECOND("24-Dec-94 18:04:19") produces 19.

TIME(*hour,minute,second*)

Calculates the serial number when given the *hour, minute,* and *second* of time on a 24-hour clock.

Example: TIME(18,4,19) produces .752998.

TIMEVALUE(*time_text*)

Converts a time written as text into a serial number. The *time_text* must be enclosed in quotation marks and must use one of Excel's predefined time formats.

Limits: You must enclose the text in quotation marks and use one of Excel's predefined date or time formats. The date is not converted.

Examples: TIMEVALUE("18:04:19") produces .752998.

TIMEVALUE("12:00 PM") produces .5.

TODAY( )

Calculates the serial number of the computer's current date. This acts the same as the NOW( ) function but does not return the time portion of the serial number. Excel updates the serial number when the worksheet is opened or recalculated.

WEEKDAY(*serial_number*,*return_type*)

Converts the *serial_number* to the day of the week. The result is a number from 1 (Sunday) to 7 (Saturday).

Examples: WEEKDAY("23-Dec-93") produces 5 (Thursday).

WEEKDAY(B12) produces 5 when cell B12 contains 23-Dec-93.

The optional *return type* determines what day of the week to start with. With a return type of 1 (or no return type), number 1 is Sunday and 7 is Saturday. With a return type of 2, number 1 is Monday and 7 is Sunday. With a return type of 3, number 0 is Monday and 6 is Sunday.

YEAR(*serial_number*)

Converts the *serial_number* into the year.

Example: YEAR(33962) produces 1992.

YEARFRAC(*start_date,end_date*,*basis*)

Produces the fraction of the year between the *start_date* and *end_date*. The optional argument *basis* is a number that represents the type of day count with 0 representing a 360 day year and 30 day month and 1 representing the actual number of days in the month and year. 2, 3, and 4 are other arguments for the number of days (actual, actual, and European 30) in a month and year (360, 365, and European 360).

Example: YEARFRAC("1/1/94","7/1/94") produces 0.5.

Financial Functions

Rather than typing financial equations, you can use Excel's financial functions. Excel functions operate faster and with less chance of error than typed formulas.

Excel provides a family of functions that solve annuity problems. An annuity is a series of regular cash flows over a period of time. For example, cash flows may be rent payments coming in according to a regular time period or payments that you make to a retirement fund. A few of the functions that involve annuities include the following:

FV(*rate,nper,pmt*,*pv,type*)

NPER(*rate,pmt,pv*,*fv,type*)

PMT(*rate,nper,pv*,*fv,type*)

RATE(*nper,pmt,pv*,*fv,type,guess*)

The *rate* is the periodic interest. The interest period must have the same unit as *nper*—the number of periods (such as months) in the life of the cash flow. For example, the annual interest rate should be divided by 12 if payments or receipts are monthly.

The *pmt* (payment) is the constant amount paid or received in each period on an investment or amortized loan such as a mortgage. Normally, *pmt* contains both principal and interest. Enter cash you pay out, a negative *pmt* (payment), as a negative amount in the function. The worth of something at the end of the last period is the *fv* (future value), and *pv* (present value) is the worth of something at the beginning of the period.

Some functions perform different tasks depending on the number you enter as the *type* argument. When *type* equals zero, cash flow is assumed to be at the end of the period. If *type* equals 1, cash flow is assumed to be at the beginning of the period. If no value is entered for *pv* or *type*, each is assumed to be zero.

guess is your best estimate of the final rate. Usually, a *guess* between 0 and 1 will produce an answer. If *guess* is not entered, a *guess* of 10 percent (.1) is assumed. If your *guess* is too far off, Excel cannot find an answer and the #NUM! error is returned.

Note

If #NUM! appears after you enter one of the financial functions, you may have incorrectly entered the positive or negative signs for pmt, pv, or fv. Remember that money you are paying out should appear as a negative number.

Excel also includes functions to analyze uneven cash flows and to calculate depreciation. A few of these functions follow:

IRR(*values*,*guess*)

MIRR(*values*,*finance_rate*,*reinvest_rate*)

Note

If you do work with any form of financial analysis, make sure that you review the additional financial analysis tools that can be added to Excel with the Analysis ToolPak. The Analysis ToolPak comes free with Excel and is described in Chapter 29, "Using the Analysis ToolPak."

Additional financial functions include the following:

DB(*cost*,*salvage*,*life*,*period*,*month*)

DDB(*cost*,*salvage*,*life*,*period*,*factor*)

VDB(*cost*,*salvage*,*life*,*start_period*,*end_period*,*factor*,*no_switch*)

These calculate the depreciation for the *period* you indicate, using the double-declining balance depreciation method. You must indicate the initial *cost*, the *salvage* value at the end of depreciation, and the *life* of the item. In DB( ), declining balance, *month* is the number of months in the first year. The default for *month* if it is not used is 12. In DDB( ) and VDB( ), *factor* is how quickly the balance declines. If omitted, *factor* is assumed to be 2 for double-declining depreciation. In VDB, variable declining balance, the *start_period* and *end_period* define the period for which you want to calculate the depreciation. Both start_period and end_period must be in the same units as life.

Limits: The *periods* and economic *life* must be in the same units (such as months or years). See an accountant to determine the appropriate economic life.

The function uses the following equation in its calculations:

DDB=((*cost*_prior total depreciation)**factor*)/*life*

Example: The lathe in your factory costs $130,000 and will be worth $4,800 at the end of its economic life in 15 years. What is the depreciation amount at different points in the life?

DDB(130000,4800,15,12)

results in $3,591.33 for year 12.

DDB(130000,4800,15*12,12)

results in $1,277.39 for month 12 in the first year.

FV(*rate,nper,pmt*,*pv,type*)

Calculates the future value of a series of cash flows of equal *pmt* amounts made at even periods for *nper* periods at the constant interest *rate*. A lump sum, *pv*, can be invested at the beginning of the term.

Limits: If no values are entered for *pv* and *type*, they are considered to be zero.

Example: You invest $2,000 as a lump sum and add $100 at the start of each month for 5 years (60 months) at an interest rate of 8 percent compounded monthly. Use the following function to find the worth of the investment at the end of the term:

FV(.08/12,60,–100,–2000,1)

The result is $10,376.36. Notice that amounts you pay out are negative, and amounts you receive are positive.

IPMT(*rate,per,nper,pv*,*fv,type*)

Calculates the interest portion of a payment on an annuity. You can use this function to calculate the interest paid on a mortgage at some period, *per*, within the term of the mortgage, *nper*.

Limits: The value of *per* must be in the range 1 to *nper*. If no values are entered for *fv* and *type*, they are considered to be zero.

Example: A flat-rate mortgage of $150,000 is made at 10 percent interest for 30 years. How much was paid toward interest in the fourteenth month? Use this function to calculate the answer:

IPMT(.10/12,14,360,150000,0,0)

The result is $–1,242.44. The result rate is negative because it is the amount you paid out.

IRR(*values*,*guess*)

Produces the internal rate of return for the series of periodic cash flows found in *values*. The function uses your *guess* as to the rate of return as a starting point for estimation. The result is the rate of return for a single period.

The *values* can be positive and negative cash flows of uneven amounts contained in a range or array of referenced cells. The cash flows must be in the order received. The array or range of values must include at least one sign change, or Excel returns a #NUM! error. If you paid money out at time zero in the investment, the initial value should be a negative number.

The guess is your best estimate of the final rate. Usually, a *guess* between 0 and 1 will produce an answer. If *guess* is not entered, a *guess* of 10 percent is assumed. If your *guess* is too far off, Excel cannot find an answer and a #NUM! error is returned.

The IRR( ) function makes continuous estimates of the rate of return until two estimates differ by no more than .00001%. If this resolution cannot be reached after 20 tries, IRR( ) produces the error value #NUM!. If this occurs, change the *guess* and recalculate.

Limits: The IRR( ) method used by all spreadsheets can produce a different solution for each change of sign in the cash flow. You must try different guesses to find the most accurate solution. The IRR( ) method does not allow you to reinvest positive cash flows or save for negative cash flows at realistic rates. The MIRR( ) function produces more realistic results.

Example: Figure 6.6 shows the forecasted cash flows from an apartment complex. Year 0 is the purchase price plus rehabilitation costs. The internal rate of return function in cell G6 is

IRR(D5:D15,0.1)

The result of the function is 0.111166, or 11 percent return. (Cell G6 shows a text version of the function used in cell G5.)

MIRR(*values*,*finance_rate*,*reinvest_rate*)

Calculates the modified internal rate of return from a series of positive and negative cash flows in the range *values*. The *finance_rate* specifies the cost of the investment funding. The *reinvest_rate* is the safe rate at which positive cash flows can be reinvested.

Limits: At least one positive and one negative cash flow must be specified.

Example: Consider the same forecasted cash flows from an apartment complex as those used for the IRR( ) function in figure 6.7. For this example, a finance rate of 12 percent and a reinvestment rate of 7 percent are used to make the calculation more realistic. (Finance rate is the rate charged to you on money that you borrow for the investment; reinvestment rate is the rate at which you can reinvest positive cash flows in a safe instrument, such as a CD.) The function in cell G10 is

MIRR(D5:D15,G8,G9)

The result is .104732. This result is a half percent less than it was with the IRR( ) method. On projects with different cash flows or with large amounts, the difference between the IRR( ) method and MIRR( ) method can be substantial. The MIRR( ) method is more realistic.

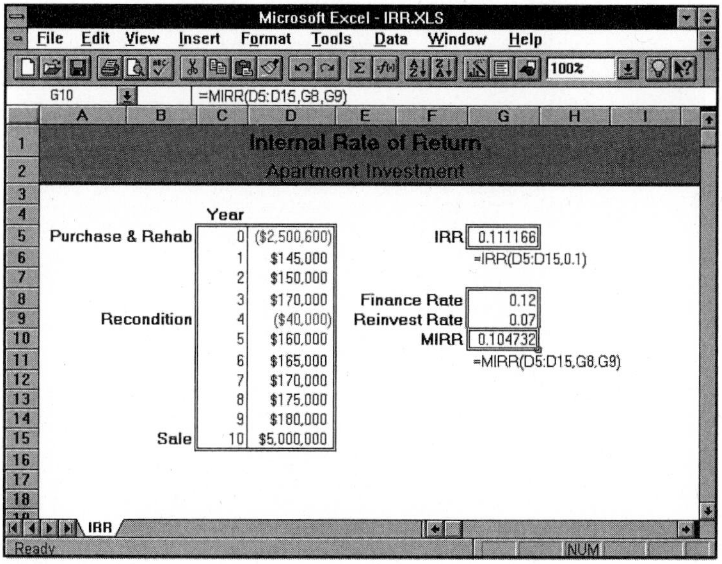

Fig. 6.7
Although IRR is commonly used to analyze cash flows, MIRR returns a more accurate result.

NPER(*rate,pmt,pv*,*fv,type*)

Calculates the number of periods required to create the annuity specified by the given arguments.

Limits: If no values are entered for *fv* and *type*, they are considered to be zero.

Example: NPER(0.10/12,–500,10000) produces 21.969, or 22 payments.

NPV(*rate,value1*,*value2,...*)

Calculates the net present value of a series of cash flows found in the range or array of *value1*, *value2*, and so on, given a discount rate equal to *rate*. The net present value of a series of cash flows is the value that a future stream of cash represents in terms of cash today, given the fact that future cash can be invested to earn the *rate* percentage.

Limits: The cash flows are considered to be at the end of each period. Cash flows do not have to be equal amounts. The rate must be the rate per period. You can have a maximum of 13 values.

Example: You purchase a piece of equipment for $40,000 cash. You could have invested the cash at 8 percent. At the end of each year for the next five years, the equipment saves you $9,000, $6,000, $6,000, $5,000, and $5,000, respectively. At the end of the sixth year, the equipment saves you $5,000, and you sell the equipment for $20,000. Is the purchase worth making?

The net present value of the purchase is

NPV(0.08,9000,6000,6000,5000,5000,25000)

If the values were entered in an array or range of cells the formula also could be NPV(.08,C15:H15).

The result is $41,072.67. The purchase saves you $1,072.67 over what an equivalent amount invested at 8 percent would earn.

PMT(*rate,nper,pv*,*fv,type*)

Calculates the periodic payment for different *types* and future values (*fv*) of investments given the investment's *rate*, term (*nper*), and present value (*pv*).

Limits: If no values are entered for *fv* and *type*, they are considered to be zero.

Example: Suppose that you want to purchase a one-room bungalow in California with a mortgage amount of $190,000 and a flat-rate mortgage of 30 years at 10 percent. If the annual interest is in B12, the annual term in B13, and the mortgage amount in B14, the function would appear in this form:

PMT(B12/12,B13*12,B14)

The result is $–1667.39. The amount is negative because you will be paying out the mortgage. Make sure that the interest rate and term are in the same units as your payment frequency, for example: term in months, interest per month, and one payment per month.

PPMT(*rate,per,nper,pv*,*fv,type*)

Calculates the principal portion of a payment made on an amortized investment. This portion is the part of the PMT( ) function that reduces a loan balance.

Limits: If no values are entered for *fv* and *type*, they are considered to be zero.

Example: Consider the mortgage described in the PMT( ) function example. The payment toward principal in the 12th month will be

PPMT(B12/12,12,B13*12,B14)

The result is $–92.09, which is negative because you are paying out the money.

PV(*rate,nper,pmt*,*fv,type*)

Calculates the present value of a series of future cash flows of equal *pmt* amounts made at even periods for *nper* periods at the constant interest *rate*. PV( ) is the amount in current dollars that equals an even cash flow in the future. If the amounts of the cash flow are uneven, use the NPV( ) function.

Limits: If no values are entered for *fv* and *type*, they are considered to be zero.

Example: You know that you can afford a car payment of $220 per month for the next four years. Current loans are at 9 percent. How large a loan can you afford? The function you need for the calculation is

PV(0.09/12,48,–220)

The result is $8,840.65.

RATE(*nper,pmt,pv,* *fv,type,guess***)**

Calculates the interest rate for the annuity that you define with the arguments.

Limits: If no values are entered for *fv* and *type*, they are considered to be zero. If you do not enter an estimated interest rate for *guess*, Excel uses 10 percent (.1). RATE( ) can return more than one solution, depending on the value used for guess. If *guess* is too far from the correct value, Excel may not be able to make an estimate and may return #NUM!.

Example: RATE(12,–800,9000) results in an interest rate of 1.007 percent per month (12.09 percent per year).

SLN(*cost,salvage,life*)

Returns the annual amount of straight-line depreciation when given the initial *cost* of an item, the *salvage* value at the end of the item's economic life, and the economic *life* of the item.

Example: SLN(40000,12000,5) produces $5,600 per year depreciation.

SYD(*cost,salvage,life,per*)

Calculates the depreciation for the period, *per*, using the sum-of-the-years' depreciation method. You must indicate the initial *cost*, the *salvage* value at the end of the economic life, and the *life* of the item.

Examples: SYD(40000,12000,5,1) produces $9,333 depreciation for the first year.

SYD(40000,12000,5,2) produces $7,467 depreciation for the second year.

VDB(*cost,salvage,life,start_period,end_period*,*factor,no_switch*)

The variable declining-balance depreciation function returns the depreciation on an asset for the period you indicate. The *cost, salvage,* and *life* arguments have the same definitions as described in earlier functions.

Start_period is the period at which you want to start calculating depreciation and *end_period* is the ending period for the calculation. Both must be in the same units as the *life*.

Factor is the rate at which the balance declines. If *factor* is omitted, it is assumed to be 2 (for double-declining balance).

No_switch is a logical argument indicating whether VDB should switch to straight-line depreciation when it is greater than the declining-balance depreciation. Using TRUE for *no_switch* prevents the switch to straight-line method. FALSE, or omitting the *no_switch* argument, switches to the straight-line method. All arguments must be positive.

Information Functions

The information functions listed here are primarily for compatibility with worksheets from other vendors. Excel's macro functions contain extensive information gathering capabilities giving you the ability to test for conditions ranging from which worksheets are open, to whether a cell is formatted with Helvetica bold, to whether the worksheet is running on a Mac or PC and how much memory is available.

CELL(*info_type,reference*)

Returns information about the cell contents of the active cell, or the *reference* cell. The *info_type* determines what the cell contents are checked for. The possible values of *info_type* and the result returned by the function are listed in table 6.3.

This function is primarily included for compatibility with other worksheets. Refer to the IS.*functions* for more commonly accepted Excel functions. In macros, use Excel's GET.*functions*.

Table 6.3 Results Returned by the CELL Function

<table>
<tr><th>info_type</th><th>Returned value</th></tr>
<tr><td>"width"</td><td>The column width in integer numbers, measured in terms of the currently selected font</td></tr>
<tr><td>"row"</td><td>The row number of the reference</td></tr>
<tr><td>"col"</td><td>The column number of the reference</td></tr>
<tr><td>"protect"</td><td>0 if the cell is not locked; 1 if it is locked</td></tr>
<tr><td>"address"</td><td>The first cell in the reference, given in text form; for example, $B$2</td></tr>
<tr><td>"contents"</td><td>The value in the reference</td></tr>
<tr><td>"format"</td><td>The text value showing the cell format; examples:
<table>
<tr><td>Format</td><td>Text Value</td></tr>
<tr><td>General</td><td>G</td></tr>
<tr><td>0</td><td>F0</td></tr>
<tr><td>#,##0</td><td>,0</td></tr>
<tr><td>0.00</td><td>F2</td></tr>
<tr><td>#,##0.00</td><td>,2</td></tr>
<tr><td>$#,##0_);($#,##0)</td><td>C0</td></tr>
<tr><td>$#,##0_);[Red]($#,##0)</td><td>C0_</td></tr>
<tr><td>$#,##0.00_);($#,##0.00)</td><td>C2</td></tr>
<tr><td>$#,##0.00_);[Red]($#,##0.00)</td><td>C2_</td></tr>
<tr><td>0%</td><td>P0</td></tr>
<tr><td>0.00%</td><td>P2</td></tr>
<tr><td>0.00E+00</td><td>S2</td></tr>
<tr><td>#?/? or #??/??</td><td>G</td></tr>
<tr><td>m/d/yy or m/d/yy h:mm</td><td>D4</td></tr>
<tr><td>d-mmm-yy</td><td>D1</td></tr>
<tr><td>d-mmm</td><td>D2</td></tr>
<tr><td>mmm-yy</td><td>D3</td></tr>
<tr><td>h:mm AM/PM</td><td>D7</td></tr>
<tr><td>h:mm:ss AM/PM</td><td>D6</td></tr>
<tr><td>h:mm</td><td>D9</td></tr>
<tr><td>h:mm:ss</td><td>D8</td></tr>
</table>
In addition, _ is returned for negative formats that use color and ( ) is returned for negative formats that use parentheses</td></tr>
<tr><td>"prefix"</td><td>The label prefix for alignments:
<table>
<tr><td>'</td><td>Left alignment</td></tr>
<tr><td>"</td><td>Right alignment</td></tr>
<tr><td>^</td><td>Center alignment</td></tr>
<tr><td>""</td><td>All other alignments</td></tr>
</table></td></tr>
<tr><td>"type"</td><td>The text value showing the cell format:
<table>
<tr><td>b</td><td>Blank</td></tr>
<tr><td>l</td><td>Text constant (label)</td></tr>
<tr><td>v</td><td>Value (all other values)</td></tr>
</table></td></tr>
<tr><td>"color"</td><td>1 if cell is formatted for color with negative number; 0 if it is not</td></tr>
</table>

info_type	Returned value
"filename"	The path and file name of the file that contains the reference; nothing is returned if the sheet has not been saved
"parentheses"	1 is returned if the cell is formatted so that positive numbers display in parentheses; 0 if positive numbers are displayed without parentheses

Limits: The CELL( ) function is used primarily with macros translated from Lotus 1-2-3. For more capabilities with Excel macros, use the GET.CELL macro.

Example: CELL("type",B36) results in b if B36 is blank.

Note

Create a prompt for users to type into an adjacent cell by entering a formula such as IF(CELL("type",B12)="b","Enter a name here","") in the cell next to the data cell. The formula results in the text *Enter a name here* whenever cell B12 is blank.

ERROR.TYPE(*error_val*)

Produces a number depending upon the type of error in the cell referenced by *error_val*. Use ISERROR( ) or ISERR( ) to first detect an error. Then, use an IF( ) function with ERROR.TYPE( ) to handle different types of errors differently. The values returned by different errors are as follows:

Error	Value Returned
#NULL!	1
#DIV/0!	2
#VALUE!	3
#REF!	4
#NAME?	5
#NUM!	6
#N/A	7
Other values	#N/A

Other functions described later in this section that evaluate errors are ISERROR( ) and ISERR( ).

INFO(*type_text*)

Determines information about the operating system and environment. *type_text* indicates what information you want to learn, as in the following list. If you are using a macro, use GET.*functions*, DOCUMENTS( ), and other functions to examine the worksheet and environment. The following table indicates specific arguments.

type_text	Returned Value
"directory"	Current directory
"memavail"	Memory available
"numfile"	Number of active worksheets
"osversion"	Operating system version
"recalc"	Recalculation mode: Automatic or Manual
"release"	Microsoft Excel version
"system"	Operating system name: Windows = pcdos; OS/2 = pcos2; Macintosh = Mac
"totmem"	Memory available, in bytes; includes memory in use
"memused"	Memory used for data, in bytes

IS*function*(*value*)

Excel has 11 worksheet functions that determine whether a cell meets certain conditions, such as whether it is blank or contains an error value. Depending on the status of the cell, the IS*function* produces either a TRUE or FALSE *value*.

The IS*functions* can be entered into worksheet cells—adjacent to a data-entry cell, for example—or used in a macro to control macro flow.

IS*functions* are most useful when used with the IF( ) function to test whether a cell or range is blank or contains numbers, text, or errors. For example, you might want to prevent the division by zero error, #DIV/0!. Consider the following formula entered in a cell next to C13:

```
=IF(ISERROR(B12/C13),"C13 must not be zero",B12/C13)
```

This formula determines whether B12/C13 produces an error. If an error is produced, the formula prints the message `C13 must not be zero`. If an error is not produced, the division result appears.

You also can use IS*functions* to test for the proper type of entry. This example tests to make sure that B36 contains a number:

=IF(ISNUMBER(B36),"Good entry","Entry not a number")

The IS*functions* and their results are listed in table 6.4.

Table 6.4 Excel ISfunctions

Function	Result
ISBLANK(*value*)	TRUE if *value* is a blank reference; FALSE if *value* is nonblank
ISERR(*value*)	TRUE if *value* is any error other than #N/A; FALSE for any other *value*
ISERROR(*value*)	TRUE if *value* is any error value; FALSE if *value* is not an error value
ISEVEN(value)	TRUE if the integer portion of the *value* is an even number; FALSE if the value is odd
ISODD(value)	TRUE if the integer portion of the *value* is an odd number; FALSE if the value is even
ISLOGICAL(*value*)	TRUE if *value* is a logical value; FALSE if *value* is not a logical value
ISNA(*value*)	TRUE if *value* is the #N/A error value; FALSE if *value* is not #N/A
ISNONTEXT(*value*)	TRUE if *value* is not text; FALSE if *value* is text
ISNUMBER(*value*)	TRUE if *value* is a number; FALSE if *value* is not a number
ISREF(*value*)	TRUE if *value* is a reference; FALSE if *value* is not a reference
ISTEXT(*value*)	TRUE if *value* is text; FALSE if *value* is not text

N(*value*)

Translates *value* into a number. N( ) translates numbers or numbers as text ("9") into numbers, and logical TRUE into 1. Any other value becomes 0. The

N( ) function is used primarily to provide compatibility when converting other worksheets. A related function is VALUE( ) which is described in the "Text Functions" section later in this chapter.

Examples: N("9 nine") produces 0.

N(A12) produces 1 if A12 is TRUE.

Note

Numbers entered into Lotus 1-2-3 worksheets preceded by a ',", or ^ are actually text. In Excel when the worksheets are open, these *numbers* may not be evaluated as numbers. Use the VALUE( ) or N( ) function to convert the text numbers into numbers that Excel can evaluate.

NA( )

Tip
Enter **#N/A** into blank data-entry cells. If a data-entry cell is not filled, the formulas that depend on this cell result in #N/A.

Always produces the error value #N/A, which means "No value Available." NA( ) does not take an argument. You can type **#N/A** directly into a cell for the same result. Include the parentheses after NA( ).

TYPE(*value*)

Determines the type of a cell's contents and produces a corresponding code, as shown in table 6.5.

Table 6.5 Results of the TYPE Function

Value	Result
Number	1
Text	2
Logical value	4
Formula	8
Error value	16
Array	64

Examples: TYPE(B36) results in 1 if B36 contains a number.

TYPE(B36) results in 16 if B36 contains #N/A.

Logical Functions

The logical functions are powerful worksheet functions that enable you to add decision-making and logical preferences to your worksheets results. The IF( ) statement is useful for testing conditions and making decisions. AND( ) and OR( ) functions can test multiple *criteria* or test conditions for use in IF functions.

AND(***logical1***,*logical2,...*)

Joins test conditions: Returns TRUE if all *logical* arguments are TRUE; FALSE if any *logical* argument is FALSE. Logical arguments include statements such as C12>20 or A4+A5=6. The answer would be true or false.

Limits: Arguments must be single logical values or arrays that contain logical values. AND( ) cannot contain more than 30 *logical* values. The #VALUE! error results if there are no logical values in the arguments.

Example: AND(B36,C12>20) is TRUE only when B36 is not zero and C12 is greater than 20.

FALSE( )

Always produces a logical FALSE. Type the parentheses without an argument. Excel also recognizes FALSE without parentheses.

IF(***logical_test,value_if_true***,*value_if_false*)

Produces the *value_if_true* when the *logical_test* evaluates as TRUE; produces the *value_if_false* when the *logical_test* evaluates as FALSE. If *value_if_false* is omitted, Excel returns the value FALSE when *logical_test* evaluates as FALSE.

IF( ) is one of the most valuable functions in Excel; this function can test cells and make decisions based on the cell contents.

Note

Use the AND( ), OR( ), and NOT( ) functions with the IF( ) function to make complex decisions. For example,

```
=IF(AND(B12>5,B12<20),"Good","Invalid")
```

If the contents of B12 is more than 5 and less than 12, the text *Good* appears; otherwise, the text *Invalid* appears.

NOT(*logical*)

Reverses the result of the *logical* argument from TRUE to FALSE or from FALSE to TRUE. Use this function to return the opposite condition of the logical_test in an IF( ) statement.

Example: IF(NOT(OR(B36=12,B36=20)),"Not a 12 or 20","Is a 12 or 20"). This statement determines whether B36 contains a 12 or 20 and produces the message `Not a 12 or 20` when the cell does not.

OR(*logical1*,*logical2,...*)

Joins test conditions: Returns TRUE if one or more *logical* arguments is TRUE; FALSE only when all *logical* arguments are FALSE.

Limits: OR( ) is limited to 30 or fewer arguments. Arguments cannot be blank cells, error values, or text. Use IS*functions* in OR( ) functions to test for blank cells, error values, or text.

Example: IF(OR(B36=12,B36=20),"Is a 12 or 20","Not a 12 or 20"). This statement checks whether B36 contains either 12 or 20 and produces the message `Is a 12 or 20` when it does. If B36 contains anything else, the message `Not a 12 or 20` appears.

TRUE( )

Always produces TRUE. Type the parentheses without an argument. Excel also recognizes TRUE without parentheses.

Lookup and Reference Functions

The LOOKUP( ) and MATCH( ) functions enable your worksheets to retrieve a value from within a table. INDEX( ) functions enable you to extract specific values from within an array. The OFFSET( ) function, listed later with Reference Functions, enables you to retrieve information that is offset a specified distance from a base reference.

Reference functions are necessary when you need to determine cell contents, ranges, or selected areas. Some of them, such as OFFSET( ) also are used in macro sheets and are a necessity for more advance macros.

ADDRESS(*row_num,column_num*,*abs_num,a1,sheet_text*)

Produces a cell reference in text form for the cell indicated by the *row_num* and *col_num*. Use one of four values in *abs_num* to specify the type of reference:

Absolute reference (default)

Absolute row, relative column

Relative row, absolute column

Relative reference

If the *a1* argument is TRUE, or omitted, Excel returns A1 style references. FALSE returns the R1C1 style reference. *sheet_text* is the name of the worksheet or macro sheet used by the reference.

Other functions related to ADDRESS( ) are CELL( ), ACTIVE.CELL( ), OFFSET( ), INDEX( ), ROW( ), COLUMN( ), and SELECTION( ).

Examples: ADDRESS(15,4,2,TRUE) returns D$15.

ADDRESS(Counter.Row,4,4,FALSE,"ASSETS.XLS") returns ASSETS.XLS!R[25]C[4] where Counter.Row is a name containing the value 25.

AREAS(*reference*)

Returns the number of areas in *reference*. Use the AREAS( ) function to find how many selections are within an area.

Example: AREAS(PRINTOUT) results in 2 when the range named PRINTOUT is defined as the two ranges A1:F55 and G56:O210.

CHOOSE(*index_num,value1*,*value2,...*)

Chooses from the list of *value*s a value that corresponds to the *index_num*. For example, when the *index_num* is 2, the function chooses *value2*. When used in a macro, the CHOOSE( ) function can have values that are GOTO( ) or action functions.

Limits: CHOOSE( ) displays #VALUE when the *index_num* is less than one or greater than the number of items in the list.

Examples: CHOOSE(B12,5,12,32,14) produces 32 when B12 contains 3.

DATE(1992,CHOOSE(*QTR*,1,4,7,10),1) produces the serial number for the first day of each quarter when *QTR* refers to a cell containing a number from 1 to 4.

COLUMN(*reference*)

Produces the column number of the *reference* cell. If *reference* is an array or a range, then the column numbers of each column in the range return as a horizontal array. If the *reference* argument is not specified, COLUMN( ) produces the column number of the cell that contains the function. *Reference* cannot contain multiple areas. Use the INDEX( ) function to read values from an array.

Examples: COLUMN(C15) returns 3.

If Print is the range name of the range C5:E20, COLUMN(Print) returns the array {3,4,5}.

COLUMNS(*array*)

Returns the number of columns in *array*.

Example: COLUMNS(E4:G6) produces 3.

HLOOKUP(*lookup_value,table_array,row_index_num,range_lookup*)

Looks across the top row of the range defined by *table_array* until the *lookup_value* is met; then looks down that column to the row specified by *row_index_num*. Range_lookup is a logical value (TRUE or FALSE). If the value is TRUE or omitted, HLOOKUP will return an approximate match. If FALSE, HLOOKUP will return an exact match or #N/A if no match is found.

Limits: Values in the first row of *table_array* must be in ascending order, both alphabetically (A-Z) and numerically (0-9). The *lookup_value* and the values in the first row of the *table_array* can be text, numbers, or logical values.

If the *lookup_value* is not found, HLOOKUP( ) uses the largest value that is less than or equal to the *lookup_value*. This results in the return of a value even though an exact match for the *lookup_value* is not found. If you want to find an exact match in a table, use the *range_lookup* argument or MATCH( ) and INDEX( ) functions in combination, as described in Chapter 23, "Manipulating and Analyzing Data."

row_index_num begins with 1. To return a value from the first row, use 1, and from the second row, use 2, and so on. If *row_index_num* is less than 1, HLOOKUP( ) produces the #VALUE! error. If *row_index_num* is greater than the number of rows in the table, #REF! is displayed.

Examples: Refer to Chapter 23, "Manipulating and Analyzing Data," for examples using the HLOOKUP( ) function.

INDEX(*array*,*row_num,column_num*)

In the array form of INDEX( ), *row_num* and *col_num* return the value of a cell in the array. The definitions of *row_num* and *col_num* are the same as described in the reference version of INDEX( ).

Examples: INDEX({3,4,5;8,9,10},2,3) produces 10.

INDEX({3,4,5;8,9,10},0,3) produces the single-column matrix {5;10} when the INDEX( ) function is entered as an array formula by using Shift+Ctrl+Enter.

INDEX(*reference,*row_num,column_num,area_num*)

In the reference form, INDEX( ) produces a cell reference from within the *reference* specified and at the intersection of the *row_num* and *column_num*. If *reference* is a single row or column, then the *column_num* or *row_num* argument can be omitted: =INDEX(A1:A10,5), for example. Other functions convert the value returned by INDEX( ) to a cell reference or value as needed.

The referenced area is *reference*. If this area contains multiple ranges, enclose the reference in parentheses, as in (B36:D45,G56:H62). If *reference* contains more than one area, *area_num* can choose between areas. In the preceding example, an *area_num* of 2 will choose G56:H62. If you do not include an *area_num*, Excel assumes that it is 1.

The arguments *row_num* and *column_num* choose a cell in the area specified. The first row or column is 1. Omitting the *row_num* or *column_num* or using 0 returns a reference for the entire row or column. A second form of the INDEX( ) function is used with arrays.

Limits: If either *row_num* or *column_num* is outside the specified area, INDEX( ) results in the message #REF!.

Example: INDEX((B2:C5,E7:G9),1,2,2) produces a reference or value in F7, the second area, first row, second column.

INDIRECT(*ref_text*,*a1*)

Returns the contents of the cell whose reference is in the cell indicated by *ref_text*. The *ref_text* argument must be an A1 or R1C1 reference or a cell name or a name defined as a reference; otherwise, an error is returned. Ref_text can be a string of formulas, =INDIRECT("range" & B5), and even an external reference, =INDIRECT(sheet&"!Range"). When *a1* is TRUE, 1, or omitted, INDIRECT( ) expects *ref_text* to be A1 style. When *ref_text* is FALSE, or 0, INDIRECT( ) expects R1C1 style.

Example: INDIRECT(A20) results in 5 if A20 contains the cell reference B35 (without quotation marks) and cell B35 contains 5.

LOOKUP(*lookup_value*,*lookup_vector*,*result_vector*)

LOOKUP( ) can be either a vector or an array function. This description applies to the vector function. This function is useful for looking up values from a table with incremental numbers, such as discount schedules and tax tables. A *lookup_vector* contains a single row or column. This function searches through the *lookup_vector* until the *lookup_value* is found. The function then produces the value that is in the same location in the *result_vector*. If the *lookup_value* cannot be found, LOOKUP( ) returns a value corresponding to the largest value less than or equal to the *lookup_value*. If the *lookup_value* is smaller than any value in *lookup_vector*, the message #NA is returned.

Limits: Values in *lookup_vector* can be text, numbers, or logical values. They must be sorted in ascending order to give the correct return.

LOOKUP(*lookup_value*,*array*)

The array form of LOOKUP( ) is similar to HLOOKUP( ) and VLOOKUP( ). LOOKUP( ) searches for a match to *lookup_value* in the first row or the first column of the *array*, depending on the shape of the array. If the array is square, or wider than tall, LOOKUP( ) searches across the first row for the *lookup_value*. If the array is taller than it is wide, the search proceeds down the first column.

If LOOKUP( ) cannot find the *lookup_value*, it finds the largest value less than the *lookup_value*. If *lookup_value* is smaller than the smallest value in the row or column being examined, the message #N/A is returned.

The value returned is taken from the last row or column in the *array* that matches the *lookup_value*.

Limits: The row or column being examined for the *lookup_value* must be sorted in ascending order.

MATCH(*lookup_value,lookup_array*,*match_type*)

MATCH( ) returns the position of the match for *lookup_value* in the *lookup_array*. The type of match is determined by *match_type*. The *lookup_value* can be a number, text, logical value, or cell reference.

When combined with the INDEX( ) function, as shown in Chapter 29, the MATCH( ) function enables you to find exact matches to a *lookup_value* or return an error. This prevents the possible use of an incorrect value returned by VLOOKUP( ), HLOOKUP( ), or LOOKUP( ).

The types of matches are given here with a description of what each match type finds:

match_type	Finds
1, or omitted	Largest value less than or equal to *lookup_value*. The *lookup_array* must be in sorted order. The default is 1 if *match_type* is omitted.
0	First value that is an exact match.
–1	Smallest value greater than or equal to *lookup_value*. The *lookup_array* must be in sorted order.

Limits: MATCH( ) returns the row or column position in the array of the found item, not its value or cell reference.

OFFSET(*reference,rows,cols*,*height,width*)

Returns the cell reference "offset" from a reference by a number of rows and a number of columns. The reference used is the *reference* argument. The reference may be a single cell or a range. The height and width of an offset range can be controlled by the *height* and *width* values. If *height* and *width* are omitted, OFFSET( ) uses the height and width of the *reference*.

In a worksheet, OFFSET( ) is an excellent way to retrieve data from a historical table of information. The second example shows how this function can be used to retrieve data from a table of sales histories.

Use OFFSET( ) with the SELECTION( ) and FORMULA( ) functions in Excel macros to select ranges or to enter values on worksheets. Using OFFSET( ) to specify the cell to act on is much faster than concatenating text references.

Limits: If the offset extends beyond the edge of the worksheet, or if the row or height is less than one, the function returns the #REF! error.

Examples: OFFSET(C3,1,2) entered in a worksheet results in the value stored in E4.

OFFSET(Sales.History,A3,B3) entered in a worksheet returns the value stored in the cell that is offset from the cell named Sales.History by the number of rows in cell A3 and the number of columns in cell B3.

OFFSET(C3,1,2,3,4) returns an array of values three rows high and four columns wide. These values are returned from a range of cells of the same size and whose upper left corner is specified as offset from C3 by one row and two columns, or E4. When OFFSET( ) is used in this manner it returns more results than fit in one cell—in this case 12 results (3 X 4). An *array formula* like this must be entered as an array into a range that is the same size (3 rows by 4 columns). Enter array formulas by selecting the cells on the worksheet (3 rows by 4 columns), typing the formula and pressing Shift+Ctrl+Enter instead of just Enter. If you select a cell range larger than the three-by-four range in which to enter the array, unneeded cells return the #N/A error.

You also can retrieve information from the array returned by an offset by putting the OFFSET( ) function inside of an INDEX( ) function. The INDEX( ) function retrieves data from one result out of the three-by-four array.

ROW(*reference*)

Results in the row number of the *reference* cell. If *reference* is a range, ROW( ) produces a vertical array of the row numbers. If you don't specify the *reference* argument, ROW( ) produces the row number of the cell in which the function is entered. Use the INDEX( ) function to extract a row number as a specific element within ROW( ).

Examples: ROW(D5) results in 5.

ROW(D5:F7) results in {5;6;7}. When entered into a single cell, the result displays as 5. When entered by selecting three cells in a column and pressing Shift+Ctrl+Enter, the result displays each row number.

The formula =INDEX(ROW(D5:F7),3,1) entered in a single cell finds the row number in the third row of the first column of the array. The array {5;6;7} has only one column and three rows, so the value returned is 7.

ROWS(*array*)

Produces the number of rows in *array*.

Example: ROWS(B12:D35) results in 24.

TRANSPOSE(*array*)

Transposes the current *array* so that the first row in the current *array* becomes the first column of the new array, the second row of the current *array* becomes the second column of the new array, and so on.

Because the TRANSPOSE( ) function produces an array as a result, you must enter the TRANSPOSE( ) function as an array formula. Entering the TRANSPOSE( ) function is described in Chapter 5, "Working with Formulas."

VLOOKUP(*lookup_value,table_array,col_index_num,*range_lookup)

Looks down the left column of *table_array* until the *lookup_value* is met, and then looks across that row to the column specified by *col_index_num*. Values in the first column can be text, numbers, or logical values in ascending order. Upper- and lowercase text are considered the same. *Range_lookup* is a logical value (TRUE or FALSE). If the value is TRUE or omitted, VLOOKUP will return an approximate match. If FALSE, VLOOKUP will return an exact match or #N/A if no match is found.

Limits: If VLOOKUP( ) cannot find *lookup_value,* the function searches for the next largest value in the first column. Other limits are the same in the discussion of the HLOOKUP( ) function.

Mathematical Functions

Mathematical functions provide the foundation for the majority of worksheet calculations. Most scientific and engineering functions are found under mathematical functions.

> **Note**
>
> For additional mathematical tools, such as Fourier transforms, review the Analysis ToolPak described in Chapter 29, "Using the Analysis ToolPak." It adds additional analysis tools into Excel. The Analysis ToolPak comes free with Excel.

ABS(*number*)

Returns the absolute (positive) value of the *number*.

Examples: ABS(–5) produces 5.

ABS(5) produces 5.

CEILING(*number,significance*)

Produces a number that has been rounded up to the level of significance you specify. If you want to round down, use the FLOOR( ) function later in this section.

Examples: CEILING(A12,.10) rounds the number in cell A12 up to the nearest dime.

CEILING(145321,100) rounds the number 145321 up to 145400.

COMBIN(*number,number_chosen*)

Produces the combination of items without regard to order. For example, if there are 23 socks in a drawer and you pull out two socks, there are COMBIN(23,2) different combinations you could choose from. The answer is 253.

EVEN(*number*)

Rounds a number up to an even number.

Examples: EVEN(4.6) produces 6.

EXP(*number*)

Returns e, the base of the natural logarithm, raised to the power of *number*. EXP( ) is the inverse of the LN( ) function.

Limits: The value of e is 2.71828182845904.

Examples: EXP(0) produces 1.

EXP(LN(10)) produces 10.

FACT(*number*)

Returns the factorial of the *number*. A noninteger *number* is truncated.

Example: FACT(4) produces 24 (4*3*2*1).

FLOOR(*number,significance*)

Rounds a number down to the level of significance that you specify.

Example: FLOOR(5432,100) produces 5400.

INT(*number*)

Rounds the *number* down to the nearest integer.

Examples: INT(7.6) produces 7.

INT(–7.6) produces –8.

Note

Use INT( ) to round a number down to the nearest integer. Use TRUNC( ) to truncate a number by removing the decimal portion. Use ROUND( ) to round a number to a specific number of places to the left or right of the decimal.

LN(*number*)

Returns the natural log of the *number* in base e. LN( ) is the inverse of EXP( ).

Limits: The value of the *number* must be positive.

Example: LN(3) produces 1.098612289.

LOG(*number*,*base*)

Returns the logarithm of the *number* in the *base* specified.

Limits: The value of the *number* must be positive. LOG( ) uses base 10 if the *base* argument is omitted.

Examples: LOG(10) produces 1.

LOG(64,2) produces 6.

LOG10(*number*)

Returns the logarithm of the *number* in base 10.

Examples: LOG10(10) produces 1.

LOG10(100) produces 2.

MDETERM(*array*)

Produces the determinant of *array*. The array can be a reference, such as B36:C37, or an array constant, such as {1,2,3;5,6,7;8,9,10}.

MINVERSE(*array*)

Produces the inverse of *array*. The array can be a reference, such as B36:C37, or an array constant, such as {1,2,3;5,6,7;8,9,10}.

Because the MINVERSE( ) function produces an array as a result, you must enter this function as an array formula by selecting a square range of cells of equivalent size, typing the formula, and then pressing Shift+Ctrl+Enter.

MMULT(*array1,array2*)

Produces the product of *array1* and *array2*. The number of columns in *array1* must be the same as the number of rows in *array2*. The arrays must contain only numbers.

Because the MMULT( ) function produces an array as a result, you must enter the MMULT( ) function as an array formula, as described under MINVERSE( ).

MOD(*number,divisor*)

Produces the remainder (modulus), of the *number* divided by the *divisor*.

Limits: The #DIV/0! error appears if the *divisor* is zero.

Examples: MOD(7,6) produces 1.

MOD(32,15) produces 2.

ODD(*number*)

Produces a number rounded up to the closest odd number.

Example: ODD(455.5) produces 457.

PI( )

Returns the value of π.

Limits: An estimate of π, 3.14159265358979, is used. The parentheses must be included even though the function does not take an argument.

PRODUCT(*number1*,*number2,...*)

Multiplies *number1* by *number2* by the rest of the arguments.

Limits: You can specify up to 14 arguments. Arguments that are blank cells, logical values, error values, or text are ignored. Text that can be converted into a numeric value is converted.

Example: PRODUCT(B12:C14) produces 24 when cells B12 through C14 contain the numbers 1, 2, 3, and 4.

RAND( )

Produces a random decimal number from 0 to 1. The function does not take an argument between the parentheses. Press F9 to produce new random numbers. Freeze random numbers by copying them with **E**dit **C**opy and pasting them on top of themselves. For this operation, choose **E**dit Paste **S**pecial and select the Paste **V**alues and Operations N**o**ne options.

ROUND(*number,num_digits*)

Rounds the *number* to the number of digits, *num_digits*, specified. If *num_digits* is positive, the number rounds to the specified decimal places to the right of the decimal point. If *num_digits* is zero, the number rounds to an integer. If *num_digits* is negative, the number rounds upward to the left of the decimal point.

Examples: ROUND(456.345,2) produces 456.35.

ROUND(546789,–3) produces 547000.

SIGN(*number*)

Produces 1 when the *number* is positive, 0 when it is 0, and –1 when it is negative.

Example: SIGN(B12) produces 1 when B12 contains 5, and –1 when B12 contains –23.

Tip
If you need to round up or down to a given number of decimals, use the CEILING( ) or FLOOR( ) functions.

SQRT(*number*)

Returns the square root of the *number*.

Limits: The value of the *number* must be positive.

Example: SQRT(25) produces 5.

SUM(*number1*,*number2,...*)

Calculates the sum of the arguments. Arguments can be individual values or ranges and are limited to 30 arguments. Arguments that cannot be converted from text to numbers or error values are ignored.

Example: SUM(B36:B40) produces 25 if the range includes the numbers 3, 4, 5, 6, and 7.

SUMPRODUCT(*array1,array2,...*)

Results in the sum of the product of the arrays. All the arrays must have the same size and shape. You can specify 2 to 30 arguments.

Example: SUMPRODUCT(B8:B10,C8:C10) results in 32 where B8:B10 contains 1, 2, and 3 and C8:C10 contains 4, 5, and 6.

SUMSQ(*number1*, *number2...*)

Produces the sum of the squares for all numbers in the range ***number 1,*** *number 2....*

SUMX2MY2(*array_x,array_y*)

Produces the sum of the difference of squares of values in two arrays.

Limits: The values in arrays must be numbers, blanks, or #N/A! values. Other values produce #VALUE! errors. Arrays that do not have the same number of elements produce #N/A! errors.

SUMX2PY2(*array_x,array_y*)

Produces the sum of the squares of values in two arrays.

Limits: The values in arrays must be numbers, blanks, or #N/A! values. Other values produce #VALUE! errors. Arrays that do not have the same number of elements produce #N/A! errors.

SUMXMY2(*array_x,array_y*)

Produces the sum of the squared differences from values in two arrays.

Limits: The values in arrays must be numbers, blanks, or #N/A! values. Other values produce #VALUE! errors. Arrays that do not have the same number of elements produce #N/A! errors.

TRUNC(*number*,*num_digits*)

Changes the *number* to an integer by cutting off, or *truncating*, the decimal fraction portion. If *num_digits* is omitted, it is assumed to be zero.

Example: TRUNC(5.6) produces 5.

Statistical Functions

Statistical functions can help you with simple problems, such as finding an average or counting items. Statistical functions also can do simple statistical analysis, such as biased or nonbiased standard deviation. Not all of the worksheet statistical functions are explained in the listings in this section. Table 6.6 lists the additional statistical functions that are not explained. You can learn more about these functions from the Help files and from the Microsoft function reference manual.

Note

In addition to the worksheet statistical function, make sure that you examine the Analysis ToolPak, described in Chapter 29, "Using the Analysis ToolPak." The Analysis ToolPak contains many more statistical and analytical tools. The Analysis ToolPak comes free with Excel.

Explanations for some of the more commonly used statistical functions are listed here.

AVERAGE(*number1*,*number2,...*)

Returns the average (mean) of the arguments. Arguments may be single values or ranges. The ranges can contain numbers, cell references, or arrays that contain numbers. Text, logical values, errors, and blank cells are ignored.

Limits: AVERAGE( ) can take from 1 to 30 arguments.

Examples: AVERAGE(B12:B15) produces 3.5 when B12:B15 contains the numbers 2, 3, 4, and 5.

AVERAGE(B12:B15,20) produces 6.8 when B12:B15 contains the numbers 2, 3, 4, and 5.

Table 6.6 Additional Statistical Functions

AVEDEV( )	GAMMADIST( )	PEARSON( )
BETADIST( )	GAMMAINV( )	PERCENTILE( )
BETAINV( )	GAMMALN( )	PERCENTRANK( )
BINOMDIST( )	GEOMEAN( )	PERMUT( )
CHIDIST( )		
CHIINV( )HARMEAN( )		POISSON( )
CHITEST( )	HYPGEOMDIST( )	PROB( )
CONFIDENCE( )	INTERCEPT( )	QUARTILE( )
CORREL( )	KURT( )	RANK( )
COVAR( )	LARGE( )	RSQ( )
CRITBINOM( )	LOGINV( )	SKEW( )
DEVSQ( )	LOGNORMDIST( )	SLOPE( )
EXPONDIST( )	MEDIAN( )	SMALL( )
FDIST( )	MODE( )	STANDARDIZE( )
		STEYX( )
		TDIST( )
FINV( )	NEGMINOMDIST( )	TINV( )
FISHER( )	NORMDIST( )	TRIMMEAN( )
FISHERINV( )	NORMINV( )	TTEST( )
FORECAST( )	NORMSDIST( )	WEIBULL( )
FREQUENCY( )	NORMSINV( )	ZTEST( )
FTEST( )		

COUNT(*value1*,*value2,...*)

Produces a count of the numbers in the arguments. The *value* arguments can be numbers, cell references, or arrays that contain numbers. Text, logical values, errors, and blank cells are not counted.

Limits: You can include from 1 to 30 arguments in COUNT( ).

Example: COUNT(B12:B15) produces 4 when B12 to B15 contains the numbers 2, 3, 4, and 5. The statement produces 3 if B12 is blank instead of containing 2.

COUNTA(*value1*,*value2,...*)

Produces a count of the values in the arguments. This function counts text values as well as numbers. Empty cells in arrays or references are ignored. COUNTA( ) determines the number of nonblank cells.

Limits: You can include from 1 to 30 arguments in COUNTA( ).

Example: COUNTA(A12:A20) produces 8 if cell A13 is the only blank cell.

COUNTA(B12:B15) produces 4 when B12:B15 contains the values 2, "Tree", 4, and "Pine".

GROWTH(*known_y's*,*known_x's,new_x's,const*)

Calculates the exponential growth curve that best fits the test data contained in the ranges *known_y's* and *known_x's*. GROWTH( ) then uses the *new_x's* values to calculate new *y* values along the calculated curve. If *const* is TRUE or omitted, the constant term is calculated. If *const* is FALSE, 1 is used for the constant term.

Because the GROWTH( ) function produces an array, you must enter the GROWTH( ) function as an array formula.

LINEST(*known_y's*,*known_x's,const,stats*)

LINEST( ) calculates the straight line equation that best fits the data and produces an array of values that define the equation of that line. If *known_x's* is omitted, an array equal in size to *known_y's* is used with values of {1,2,3,...}.

The line has the following equation:

y=b+m1*x1+m2*x2+....

Excel uses a least-squares fit to find the best straight-line fit to the data. The array returned is of the form {m1,m2,...,b}. The constants within that array can be used to calculate *y* values on the line for any given set of x1, x2, and so on.

If *const* is TRUE or omitted, the constant term is calculated; if FALSE, the constant is zero. If *stats* is FALSE or omitted, the slope and y-intercept are returned. If *stats* is TRUE, the following statistics are returned:

Standard error for each coefficient

Standard error for the constant b

Coefficient of determination (r-squared)

Standard error for the y-estimate

F-statistic

Degrees of freedom

Regression sum of squares

Residual sum of squares

LOGEST(*known_ y's*,*known_x's,const,stats*)

Calculates the exponential curve of the form

y=b*(m1^x1)*(M2_^x2)*....

that best fits the data. When given the data *known_ y's* and *known_x's*, the values for *b* and *m* are returned in a horizontal array of the form {m1,m2,...,b}.

If *const* is TRUE or omitted, the constant term is calculated. If *const* is FALSE, the constant is 1. If *stats* is FALSE or omitted, only the slope and y-intercept are returned. If *stats* is TRUE, the function returns the following statistics in an array:

Standard error for each coefficient

Standard error for the constant b

Coefficient of determination (r-squared)

Standard error for the y-estimate

F-statistic

Degrees of freedom

Regression sum of squares

Residual sum of squares

MAX(*number1*,*number2,...*)

Produces the largest value among the arguments.

Limits: MAX( ) can take up to 30 arguments. Arguments that are error values or text that cannot be interpreted as a number are ignored. Within a referenced array or range, any empty cells, logical values, text, or error values are ignored.

Example: MAX(C2:D4) produces 32 if the numbers in these cells are –2, 4, 32, and 30.

MEDIAN(*number1*,*number2,...*)

Returns the median value of the arguments.

MIN(*number1*,*number2,...*)

Produces the smallest value among the arguments.

Limits: MIN( ) can take up to 30 arguments. Arguments that are not numbers are ignored. If the arguments contain no numbers, MIN( ) produces 0.

Example: MIN(C2:D4) produces –2 if the numbers in these cells are –2, 4, 32, and 30.

STDEV(*number1*,*number2,...*)

Calculates an estimate of the standard deviation of a population from a sample of the population.

Limits: STDEV( ) can take up to 30 arguments. If the arguments include the entire population, use STDEVP.

Example: STDEV(B2:B12) produces 12.12 when the range from B2 to B12 contains 98, 67, 89, 76, 76, 54, 87, 78, 85, 83, and 90.

STDEVP(*number1*,*number2,...*)

Calculates the standard deviation of a population, where the entire population is listed in the arguments.

Limits:	STDEV( ) can take up to 30 arguments. If the arguments do not include the entire population, use STDEV.
Example:	STDEVP(B2:B12) produces 11.55 when the range from B2 to B12 contains 98, 67, 89, 76, 76, 54, 87, 78, 85, 83, and 90.

TREND(*known_y's*,*known_x's,new_x's,const*)

Returns the values along a straight line that best fit the data in the arrays *known_y's*. If a *known_x's* array is omitted, an array of the same size is used that contains the values {1,2,3,...}. For each value in the *new_x's* array, the TREND function produces an array of corresponding *y* values. If *const* is TRUE or omitted, the constant term is calculated. If FALSE, the constant term is zero.

VAR(*number1*,*number2,...*)

Calculates an estimate of the variance in a population from a sample given in the arguments.

Limits:	Use VARP( ) if the arguments contain the entire population.

VARP(*number1*,*number2,...*)

Calculates the variance when given the entire population as arguments.

Limits:	Use VAR( ) if the arguments contain only a sample of the population.

Text Functions

Text functions enable you to manipulate text. You can abbreviate text to pull-out portions you need from long strings of text, or you can change numbers and dates to text so that they can exceed a cell's width without producing a cell filled with #####. Numbers or dates converted to text can be concatenated (joined) to text in titles, sentences, and labels. Text functions are also very important for manipulating text that is converted to ASCII files and loaded into mainframe computers.

CHAR(*number*)

Produces the character corresponding to the ASCII code *number* between 1 and 255.

Example: CHAR(65) is A.

CLEAN(*text*)

Removes from the specified *text* argument any characters that are lower than ASCII 32 or above ASCII 127. These characters are not printed. This function is useful for removing control codes, bells, and non-ASCII characters from imported text.

CODE(*text*)

Produces the ASCII code of the first letter in the specified *text.*

Example: CODE("Excel") produces 69.

CONCATENATE(*text1*,*text2*,...,*text30*)

Joins text1 to text2 (and up to 30 arguments).

Example: CONCATENATE("Enter choice ","A"," Here") produces Enter choice A Here.

DOLLAR(*number*,*decimals*)

Rounds the *number* to the specified number of *decimals* to the right of the decimal point and converts the number to text in a currency format. This text can be concatenated with other text phrases.

Use the DOLLAR( ) function to incorporate numbers in text. For example, consider the following statement:

="Your reimbursement is "&DOLLAR(A12,2)&"."

When A12 contains the number 2456.78, this is the result:

```
Your reimbursement is $2,456.78.
```

If you specify a negative number for the *decimal* argument, the function rounds the *number* to the left of the decimal point. If you omit the *decimal* argument, the function assumes two decimal places.

Examples: DOLLAR(32.45,2) results in $32.45.

DOLLAR(5432.45,–3) results in $5,000.

EXACT(*text1,text2*)

Compares *text1* and *text2*: if they are exactly the same, returns the logical TRUE; if they are not the same, returns FALSE. Upper- and lowercase text are considered to be different.

Example: EXACT("Glass tumbler", A12) produces TRUE when A12 contains the text 1 "Glass tumbler," but produces FALSE when A12 contains 1 "glass tumbler."

FIND(*find_text,within_text*,*start_num*)

Beginning at *start_num*, FIND( ) searches the text specified by *within_text* to locate *find_text*. If *find_text* is found, the FIND( ) function produces the character location where *find_text* starts. If *start_num* is out of limits or a match is not found, the #VALUE! error value is displayed. If *start_num* is not specified, it is assumed to be 1.

Example: FIND(B12,"ABCDEFGHIJKLMNOPQRSTUVWXYZ") produces 3 if B12 contains "C".

FIXED(*number*,*decimals,no_commas*)

Rounds the *number* to the specified *decimals* and displays it as text in fixed decimal format with commas. If you omit *decimals*, the *number* is rounded to two decimal places. If you specify a negative number of *decimals*, the function rounds the *number* to the left of the decimal point. When *no_commas* is TRUE, commas are removed from the result.

Examples: FIXED(9876.543) produces 9,876.54.

FIXED(9876.543,-3) produces 10,000.

LEFT(*text*,*num_chars*)

Produces the leftmost number of characters from *text*.

Limits: The value of *num_chars* must be greater than zero. If the value is omitted, it is assumed to be 1.

Example: LEFT(A17,3) produces Que if A17 contains "Que Corporation."

LEN(*text*)

Produces the number of characters in *text*. The LEN( ) function is particularly useful when paired with the LEFT( ), MID( ), and RIGHT( ) functions so that portions of long text can be separated.

LOWER(*text*)

Changes *text* to all lowercase.

Example: LOWER("Look OUT!") produces look out!.

MID(*text,start_num,num_chars*)

Produces characters from the specified *text*, beginning at the character in the *start_num* position and extending the specified *num_chars*.

Example: MID("Excel is THE worksheet",10,3) produces THE.

PROPER(*text*)

Changes *text* to lowercase with leading capitals.

Example: PROPER("excel, the worksheet") produces Excel, The Worksheet.

REPLACE(*old_text,start_num,num_chars,new_text*)

Replaces the characters in *old_text* with *new_text*, starting with the character at *start_num* and continuing for the specified *num_chars*. The first character in *old_text* is character 1.

Example: REPLACE(A12,8,11,"one") takes the phrase in cell A12

```
We are many people on an island in space.
```

and changes it to

```
We are one on an island in space.
```

REPT(*text,num_times*)

Repeats the *text* for *num_times*.

Limits: The value of *num_times* must be positive and nonzero. The maximum number of resulting characters is 255.

Example: REPT("__..",3) produces __..__..__..

RIGHT(*text*,*num_chars*)

Results in as many characters as specified by *num_chars* from the right end of *text*. The value of *num_chars* defaults to 1 when omitted.

Examples: RIGHT("San Francisco, CA",2) produces CA.

RIGHT(B12,2) produces 02 when B12 contains the numeric ZIP code 95402.

SEARCH(*find_text,within_text*,*start_num*)

Begins at *start_num* in the specified *within_text*, searches through it for the *find_text*, and produces the character number where *find_text* begins. The first character position in *within_text* is 1. If *start_num* is omitted, it is assumed to be 1. SEARCH( ) ignores case differences. If *find_text* is not found or if *start_num* is out of limits, #VALUE! is returned.

The wild card ? can be used in *find_text* to specify any single character at that location within the text being found. The wild card * can be used in *find_text* to specify any group of characters at that location within the text being found.

Examples: SEARCH("an","Marathoners run long distances",14) produces 26.

SEARCH("l*g","Marathoners run long distances") produces 17.

SUBSTITUTE(*text,old_text,new_text*,*instance_num*)

Substitutes *new_text* for *old_text* within the specified *text*. If *old_text* occurs more than once, *instance_num* specifies which occurrence to replace. If *instance_num* is not specified, every occurrence of *old_text* is replaced.

Example: SUBSTITUTE("The Stone Age by Earl Stone","Stone","Information",1) produces The Information Age by Earl Stone.

T(*value*)

Returns text when *value* is text; returns blank when *value* is not text.

Examples: T(B12) produces Top if B12 contains "Top."

T(57) produces blank.

TEXT(*value, format_text*)

Converts the numeric *value* to text and displays it with the format specified by *format_text*. The result appears to be a formatted number, but actually is text. Use one of the predefined or custom numeric or date formats to specify the format for the *value*. These formats and custom formats are described in Chapter 10, "Formatting Worksheets." The format cannot contain an asterisk (*) or be in the General format.

Example: TEXT(4567.89,"$#,##0.00") produces $4,567.89.

Enter a title with date or number in a cell narrower than the width that would normally display the date or number by using a formula such as the following:

"Today's date is "&TEXT(NOW( ),"mmm d, yyyy")

TRIM(*text*)

Deletes all spaces from *text* so that only one space remains between words. This can be useful for *cleaning* text used in databases or imported to or exported from Excel.

Example: TRIM("this   is   the   breathy   look") produces this is the breathy look.

UPPER(*text*)

Changes *text* to all uppercase.

Example: UPPER(B2) produces ENOUGH! when B2 contains "enough!"

VALUE(*text*)

Converts text numbers or dates in one of Excel's predefined formats into numbers that are usable in formulas. Because Excel normally converts numeric text into numbers when necessary, this function is used primarily to ensure compatibility with other spreadsheets.

Limits: The text number must be in one of the predefined numeric formats available in Excel.

Example: VALUE(B2) produces 52 when B2 contains the text "$52.00."

Trigonometric Functions

Trigonometric functions use angles measured in radians. Convert between radians and degrees with these equations:

Radians = Degrees*p/180

Degrees = Radians*180/p

ACOS(*number*)

Produces the arc cosine of the *number* in radians. ACOS( ) is the inverse of the COS( ) function. The *number* must be in the range –1 to 1. The resulting angle is in the range 0 to p radians (0 to 180 degrees).

Example: ACOS(.2) produces 1.369438406 radians.

ACOSH(*number*)

Produces the inverse hyperbolic cosine of the *number*. The *number* must be greater than or equal to 1.

ASIN(*number*)

Produces the arc sine of the *number* in radians. When given a *number*, the result of a sine function, ASIN( ), produces the original angle measured in radians. The *number* must be in the range –1 to 1. The resulting angle will be in the range –p/2 to p/2 radians (–90 to 90 degrees).

Example: ASIN(.2) produces .201357921 radians.

ASINH(*number*)

Produces the inverse hyperbolic sine of the *number*.

ATAN(*number*)

Produces the arc tangent of the *number* as a radian angle. ATAN( ) is the inverse of the TAN( ) function. The resulting angle will be in the range –p/2 to p/2 radians (–90 to 90 degrees).

ATAN2(*x_number,y_number*)

Produces the arc tangent for coordinate values of *x_number* and *y_number*. The resulting angle is in the range –p to p radians (–180 to 180 degrees) excluding –p (–180 degrees). If *x_number* and *y_number* are both 0, the function produces the message #DIV/0!.

ATANH(*number*)

Produces the inverse hyperbolic tangent of the *number*. The *number* must be between, but not including, –1 and 1.

COS(*number*)

Produces the cosine of the radian angle *number*.

COSH(*number*)

Produces the hyperbolic cosine of the *number*.

SIN(*number*)

Produces the sine of the radian angle *number*.

Example: SIN(.5) produces .479425539.

SINH(*number*)

Produces the hyperbolic sine of the *number*.

TAN(*number*)

Produces the tangent of the radian angle *number*.

TANH(*number*)

Produces the hyperbolic tangent of the *number*.

From Here...

For information relating to functions and their use in formulas review the following chapters of this book:

- Chapter 23, "Manipulating and Analyzing Data." See examples of many of the more frequently used functions and how you can use them to analyze worksheet and database information.

- Chapter 29, "Using the Analysis ToolPak." The ToolPak contains many additional functions in the areas of engineering, finance, and statistics.

For Related Information

- "Using Formulas to make Decisions," p. 687
- "Using Formulas To Look Up Data in Tables," p. 693

Chapter 7

Moving or Copying Data and Formulas

Your worksheet wouldn't be easy to work with if rearranging the data was impossible or if you had to enter every number or formula. With Excel, you can move data around, if necessary. You also can enter data or a formula once and then copy it to other rows and columns.

In this chapter, you learn how to:

- Move data
- Fill data
- Copy data
- Do special pastes
- Copy data across a workbook group

Moving Cell Contents

Cutting and pasting is a valuable function for reorganizing your worksheet. You *cut out* a range of cells to *paste* elsewhere. This operation moves cell contents, the format, and any note attached to the moved cells.

Formulas remain the same when moved by cutting and pasting. You do not need to worry about relative and absolute cell references. (For more information on cell references, see Chapter 5, "Working with Formulas.")

Moving by Dragging

If you have a mouse, the easiest and most intuitive way to move a cell or range is to drag the cell or range to the new location and drop it. Excel moves the cell contents and format.

To drag cells to a new location, perform the following steps:

1. Select the cell or range you want to move.
2. Move the mouse pointer over the selections border. The pointer changes to an arrow.
3. Drag the pointer and the gray outline of the selection to the new location. Drag past the edge of a window to make the window scroll.

Figure 7.1 shows the wide gray border that encloses the area to be moved.

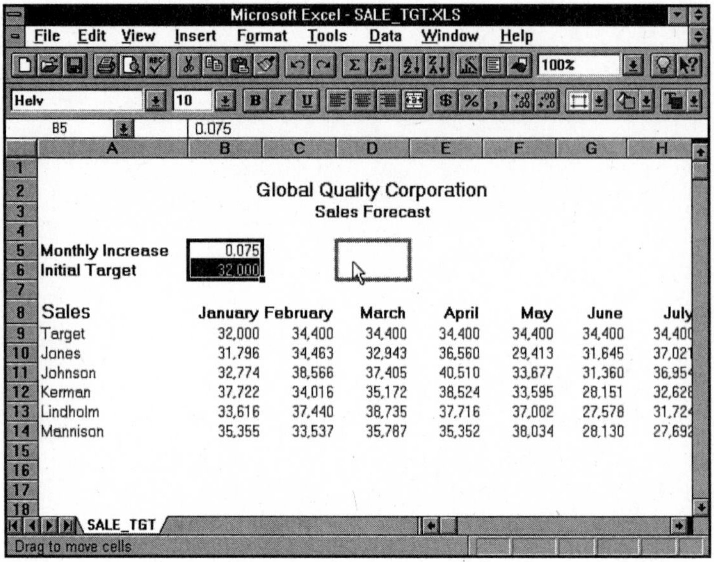

Fig. 7.1
As you drag the range, you see a gray outline. After the data is in the right spot, release the mouse button.

4. Release the mouse button when the gray outline is where you want to place the selected range.

The cell contents you selected in step 1 are pasted over the contents of the receiving cells. Choose **E**dit **U**ndo (or press Ctrl+Z) if you need to undo the command.

> **Note**
>
> If the pointer doesn't change to an arrow when you move it to the selection's border, choose the **T**ools **O**ptions command. Select the Edit tab; then select the Allow Cell **D**rag and Drop option. Choose OK.

Moving with Commands

Although the drag-and-drop technique is useful, you cannot use it to move data between different worksheets, between panes in a split worksheet, or to another application. You can make these moves with menu commands or shortcut keys.

To move a cell or a range to a new location, perform the following steps:

1. Select the cell or range you want to move.

2. Either choose the **E**dit Cu**t** command, click the Cut button on the Standard toolbar, or press Ctrl+X. The cells you selected appear surrounded by a *marquee*, a moving dashed line.

3. Select the cell at the upper-left corner of where you want the pasted cells.

4. Either choose the **E**dit **P**aste command, click the Paste button, or press Ctrl+V.

The cells you selected in the first step are cut and moved to the location you indicated. The area from which the cells were cut is blank and has a General format. If you accidentally paste over existing data or formulas, choose the **E**dit **U**ndo command. (Pasting over existing cells replaces the cell's previous contents and format with the pasted contents and format.)

Tip
You also can select the range and click the right mouse button to display a shortcut menu. Choose the command you want from the menu.

You need to select only the upper-left corner of the new location. The move procedure is similar to moving a picture from one place on a wall to another. You do not need to describe where all four corners of the picture go; you need to specify only the upper-left corner.

As you select the range to cut, notice the reference area at the left of the formula bar, which shows the size of the range you are cutting (for example, 8R × 4C). This information helps you determine whether you can move the data without pasting over existing cells and replacing their contents.

Dragging and Inserting Cells

You also can drag and insert a cell or range so that existing cells move aside. With this procedure, you do not need to insert cells to make room for new data, and then move in the new data. This method is an excellent way to rearrange a list or move individual records in a database.

To move and insert data so that existing data moves aside, take the following steps:

1. Select the cell or range you want to move.

2. Move the mouse pointer over the selection's border. The pointer changes to an arrow.

3. Hold down the Shift key and drag the pointer to where you want the data inserted. The location where the data is inserted appears as a grayed partial cell boundary, as shown in figure 7.2.

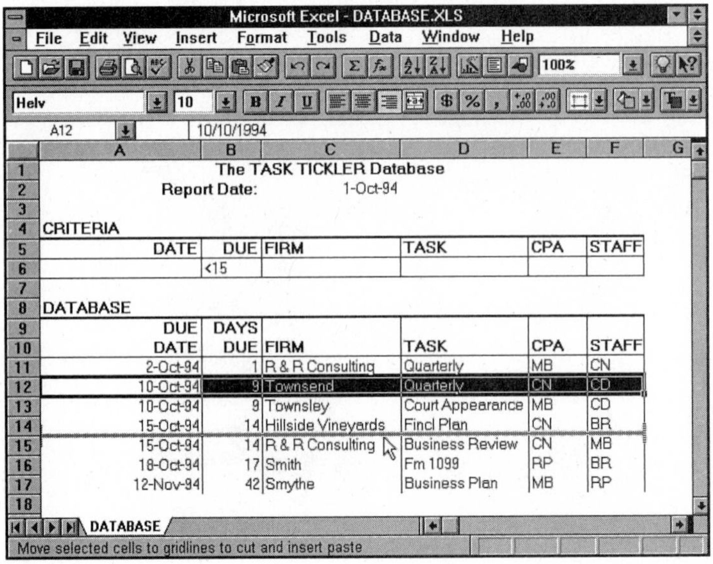

Fig. 7.2
The grayed cell boundary shows where the moved data will be inserted.

4. Continue holding the Shift key as you release the mouse button.

5. Release the Shift key.

The cells you dragged are inserted at the location of the grayed boundary. Other cells move down or right.

Moving and Inserting with Commands

In some cases, you can move cells to a new location and move existing cells aside. This technique uses the Insert Cut C**e**lls command.

To insert pasted cells, perform the following steps:

1. Select the cells you want to move.

2. Either choose the **E**dit Cu**t** command, click the Cut button, or press Ctrl+X.

3. Select a cell in which to insert the cut cells.

   You cannot place an insert into a cell that will cause the source range of the copy to shift.

Figure 7.3 shows a cut range and where it will be inserted.

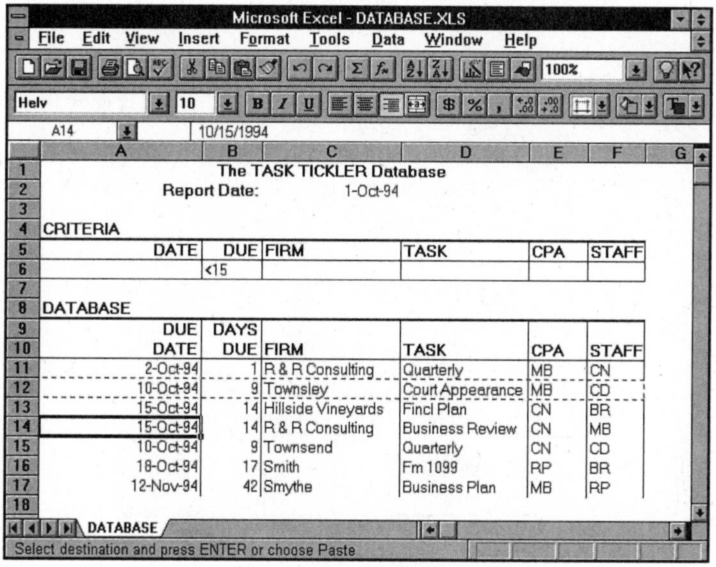

Fig. 7.3
The marquee encloses cells to be cut out. Select where you want to insert the cut cells.

4. Choose the **I**nsert Cut C**e**lls command.

5. If the Insert Paste dialog box appears, select the Shift Cells **R**ight option to shift existing cells right. Select the Shift Cells **D**own option to shift existing cells down. Choose OK.

   The cut range is inserted in the worksheet, shifting cells down or to the right. Figure 7.4 shows the database record from figure 7.2 after it was inserted. Notice that the other cells have shifted down.

Tip
To display a shortcut menu with **C**opy, Cu**t**, and **P**aste commands, select the range you want to copy. Then click the right mouse button.

Making Moves Across a Workbook

You aren't limited to moving from just one worksheet area to another. If you need to, you also can move information among worksheets within the workbook.

EXCEL 5

To move information among worksheets in a workbook, follow these steps:

1. Select the cell or range you want to move.

2. Either choose the **E**dit Cu**t** command, click the Cut button, or press Ctrl+X. The cells you select appear surrounded by a *marquee*, a moving dashed line.

3. Select the worksheet to which you want to move data.

   For information on moving among worksheets, see Chapter 3, "Navigating and Selecting in Excel."

4. Select the cell at the upper-left corner of where you want the pasted cells.

5. Either choose the **E**dit **P**aste command, click the Paste button, or press Ctrl+V.

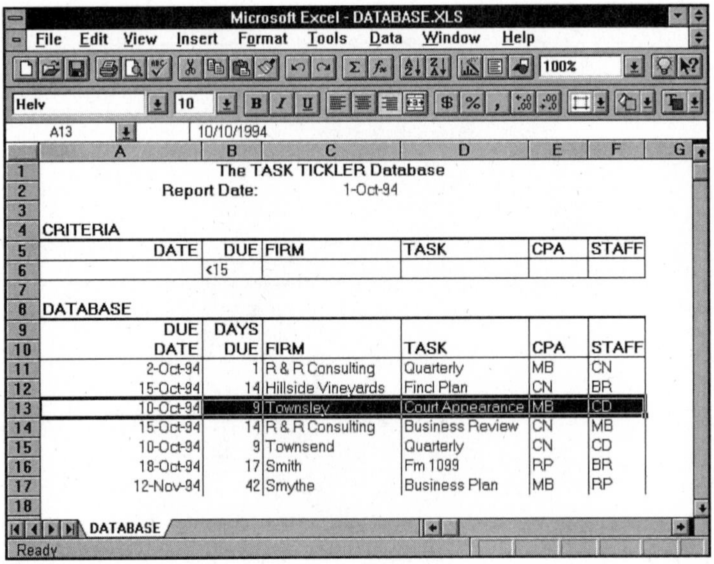

Fig. 7.4
The selected range from figure 7.2 is moved to a new location. Existing cells are shifted down to make room for the data.

The data is pasted in the selected worksheet. If formulas are included in the move, all references are adjusted so that the references refer to the same cells in the new location. If you want to refer to cells in the original worksheet, add the sheet name to the formula. See Chapter 5, "Working with Formulas," for information on referencing cells in other worksheets in a workbook.

If you see a #REF error message, Excel cannot find a reference used in a formula. See Chapter 26, "Auditing Workbooks and Worksheets," for help on tracing error messages.

Troubleshooting

Some of the cells now display #REF.

When you move cells, any formulas are adjusted to reflect the new location. One of the formulas is probably referring to a cell that is no longer valid. Check all formulas. If necessary, adjust cell references so that they are absolute. See Chapter 5, "Working with Formulas."

The pasted data overwrote existing data in the worksheet.

When you paste data, it overwrites the existing data. Choose the **E**dit **U**ndo command to undo the paste, and then select a blank area of the worksheet for the paste. Or insert the cells, as described in the section "Dragging and Inserting Cells."

Filling or Copying Cell Contents

You can save a great deal of data-entry time with Excel's **C**opy and F**i**ll commands and the many shortcuts that copy or fill. Rather than typing each formula in a worksheet, you can type a few formulas and copy or fill them into other cells. You even can copy the formula and format at the same time.

For Related Information

- "Entering Formulas," p. 127
- "Selecting and Moving between Sheets," p. 67
- "Troubleshooting Error Messages," p. 777

Caution

Because cell references in the formulas change relative to the new cell locations, some formulas don't produce the correct results when copied. Always cross-check copied or filled formulas to ensure that these formulas produce reasonable results. If you suspect an error, review the descriptions of relative and absolute cell references in Chapter 5, "Working with Formulas."

Using the Fill Handle

If you use a mouse and need to fill data or formulas into adjacent cells, you need to learn how to use the *fill handle*. The fill handle is a black square at the lower-right corner of the selected cell or range. Dragging the fill handle across cells can fill the cells with copies or a data series. A *data series* is a series of data that continues a repeating pattern. To learn more about creating a math or date series, see Chapter 4, "Entering and Editing Data."

To fill adjacent cells, perform the following steps:

1. Select the cell or range that contains the data or formulas.

2. Drag the fill handle so that the wide gray border encloses all cells to fill. Figure 7.5 shows an area being filled by using the mouse. Notice the shape of the pointer.

3. Release the mouse button.

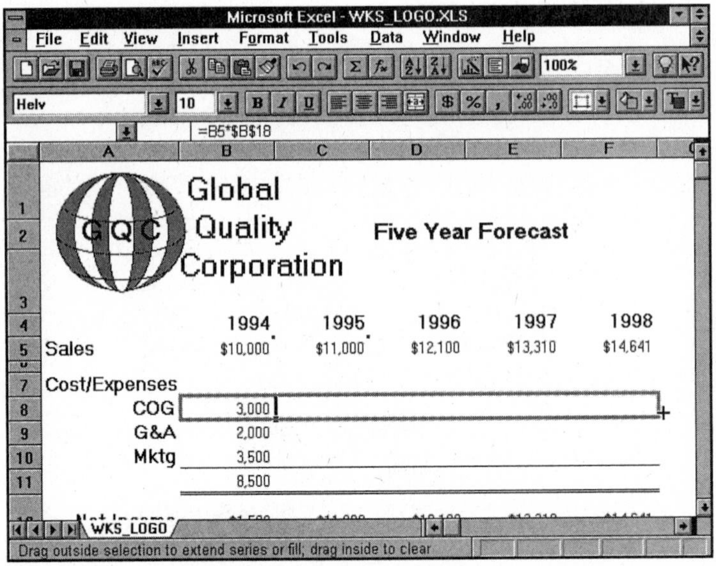

Fig. 7.5
Drag the fill handle to copy formulas into selected cells.

Tip
To fill multiple rows or columns at one time, select all the original cells, and then use the Ctrl+drag procedure to fill all the cells at one time. See the section "Copying by Dragging and Dropping."

Filling formulas into an area produces the same result as copying and pasting. Relative reference formulas adjust as though they were copied.

If you select two cells and then drag the fill handle, Excel uses the values in the two cells as seeds to create a series of data that fills the selection. A *series* is a sequence of data that has a mathematical, date, or text pattern. Series are useful for filling in a sequence of dates or a list of numbers. Series are described in Chapter 4, "Entering and Editing Data."

Tip
To turn off AutoFill, choose the **T**ools **O**ptions command. Select the Edit tab; then select the Allow Cell **D**rag and Drop option. After you turn off this option, AutoFill is turned off. Choose OK.

Using Ctrl+Enter To Fill Cells

You can fill cells as you enter data or formulas if you first select the adjacent cells or ranges to fill. Next, type the formula or value in the active cell. Rather than pressing Enter, press Ctrl+Enter. Formulas and values fill into all selected cells just as though you used a F**i**ll or **C**opy and **P**aste command. This method also works with nonadjacent multiple selections.

Using the Fill Commands

If you don't have a mouse, you need to use the F**i**ll commands on the **E**dit menu to fill formulas or data into adjacent cells. You can fill cells left or right across a row and up or down a column.

To use the menu F**i**ll commands, perform the following steps:

1. Select the row or column you want to fill. The cell that contains the formula or value used to fill other cells must be on the outside edge. Figure 7.6 shows cells in the worksheet selected before filling.

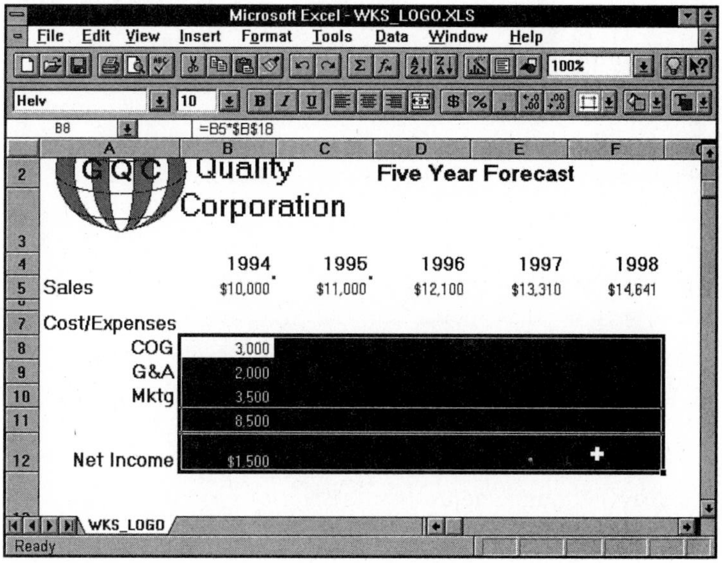

Fig. 7.6
Select both the original cells and the cells you want filled.

2. Choose the **E**dit F**i**ll command. Then choose the direction to fill: **R**ight, **L**eft, **U**p, or **D**own. Figure 7.7 shows the resulting filled cells.

3. Check to see that the filled formulas produced reasonable answers.

Tip
Shortcut keys for filling are Ctrl+R to fill right and Ctrl+D to fill down.

The result of an **E**dit F**i**ll command is the same as copying. Relative references adjust to the new locations. Duplicated formulas or values replace all cell contents they cover. The formatting of the original cells also copies to the filled cells.

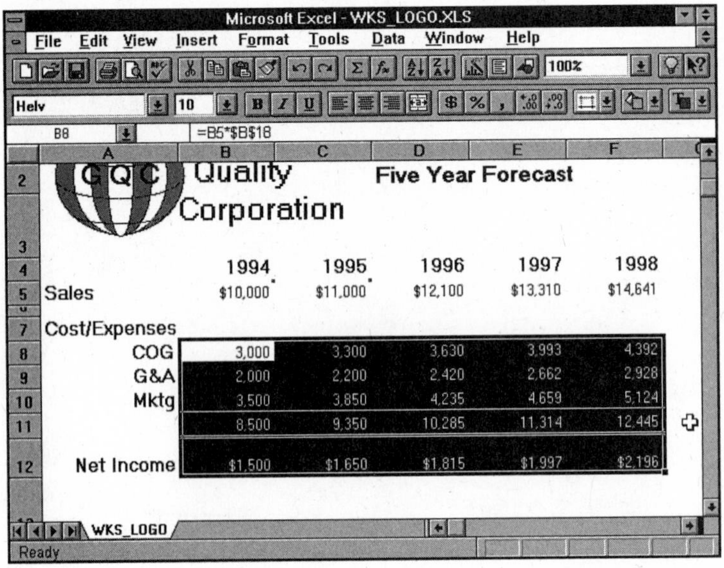

Fig. 7.7
The Fill commands fill the original formula or value into the rest of the range.

Creating a Custom Fill

If you enter the same series of data, you can create and insert a custom list. Suppose that you enter the same salespeople's names in a worksheet. You can define these names as a list, enter the first name, and then have Excel fill in the rest.

To create the custom list, follow these steps:

1. If you already typed the list in a worksheet, select the list. You then can import the list. Alternatively, you can skip this step and wait until later in this procedure to type the list manually in the Custom Lists tab.

2. Choose the **T**ools **O**ptions command.

3. Select the Custom Lists tab (see fig. 7.8).

4. If you selected text in step 1, choose the I**m**port button. The **I**mport List from Cells text box should list the selected range. Continue with step 5.

   If you didn't select text for step 1, type the list items in the List **E**ntries text box. Press Enter after each entry.

5. To add this list and keep the dialog box open, choose **A**dd, or choose OK to add the list and close the dialog box.

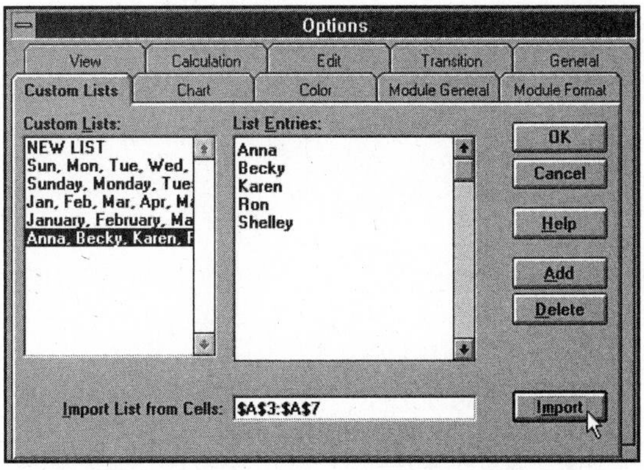

Fig. 7.8
Type the list items in the List **E**ntries text box, or import selected data from the worksheet.

To insert the list, type the first item in the list and then fill, using the drag and drop technique (see fig. 7.9). Or you can enter the first value, select the range you want filled, and then choose the **E**dit F**i**ll **S**eries command. In the Series dialog box, select Auto**F**ill as the type. Then choose OK.

To delete a list item, display the Custom Lists tab. Select the list you want to delete. Then choose the **D**elete button.

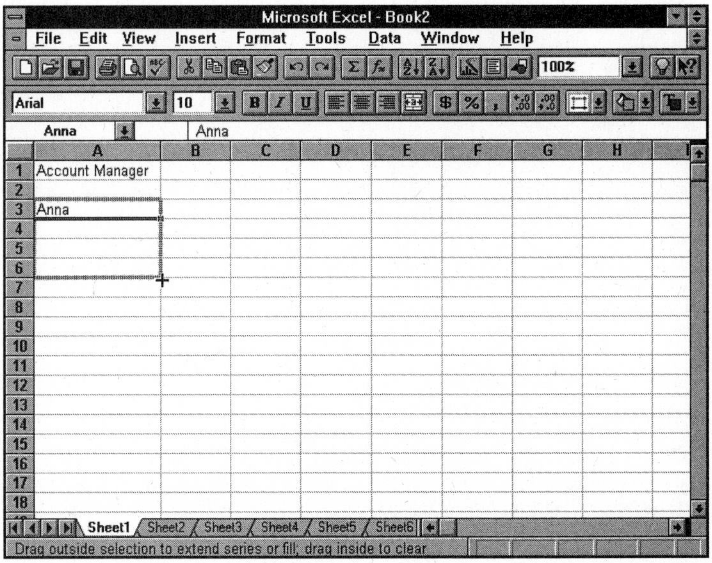

Fig. 7.9
Filling in a custom list.

Copying by Dragging and Dropping

Using the mouse, you can copy by making a selection and dragging the selection to where you want it.

To copy formulas or data with the mouse, perform the following steps:

1. Select the range of cells you want to copy.
2. Hold down the Ctrl key and move the pointer over an edge of the selection. The pointer becomes an arrow with a + (plus) sign.
3. Continue holding Ctrl as you drag the edge of the selection to where you want the copy. The copy's location appears enclosed by a wide gray border, as shown in figure 7.10.

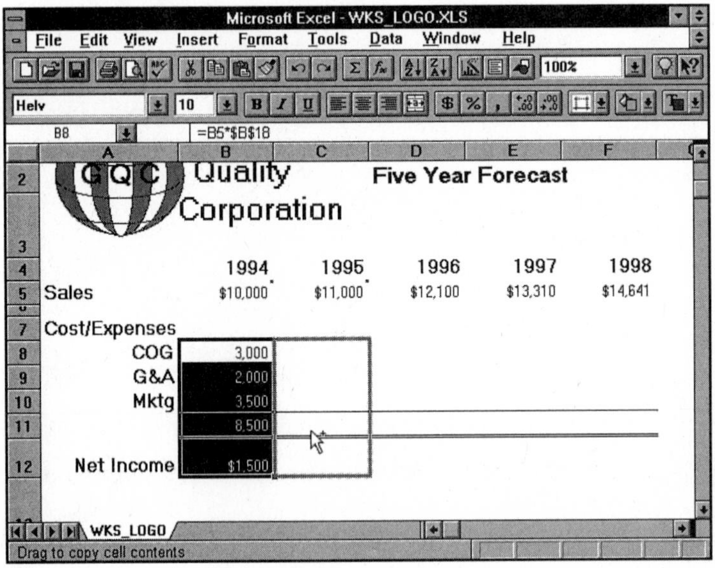

Fig. 7.10
Use Ctrl+drag to drag copies to a new location. The plus sign next to the arrow tells you that you are copying (rather than moving).

4. When the gray border is where you want the copy, release the mouse button first, and then release the Ctrl key.

Using the drag and drop method, you can make only a single copy. You cannot copy to multiple locations or fill a range. See some of the preceding mouse shortcuts if you need to perform this kind of copy.

If you release the Ctrl key before you release the mouse button, the copy operation becomes a move operation; the plus sign next to the arrow disappears. You can press Ctrl again to switch back to a copy operation. As long as you don't release the mouse button, you can change your mind about whether to copy or move the selection.

Copying with Commands

Copying works well for duplicating values or formulas to cells that are not adjacent to the original cell. Copying adjusts formulas to the new locations. Other chapters in this book describe how you can use copying to transfer information to other Windows applications (see Chapter 38, "Using Excel with Windows Applications"), link worksheets together (see Chapter 25, "Linking, Embedding, and Consolidating Worksheets"), and link worksheets and charts (see Chapter 12, "Creating Charts," and Chapter 15, "Building Complex Charts").

Tip
As you copy, check the size of the range you are copying by watching the reference area to the left of the formula bar.

To copy a cell or range to a new location, perform the following steps:

1. Select the cell or range of cells you want to copy.

2. Either choose the **E**dit **C**opy command, click the Copy button on the Standard toolbar, or press Ctrl+C. The cells to copy are surrounded by a marquee, a moving dashed line.

3. Select the cell at the top-left corner of where you want the duplicate to appear. Check to see whether other cell contents will be overwritten. If needed cells will be overwritten, see the following section on inserting copied cells.

4. Either choose the **E**dit **P**aste command, click the Paste button, or press Ctrl+V to paste and retain the copy in memory. Press Enter to paste only one time.

Because you already established the size and shape of the copied area, you need to indicate only the upper-left corner of the paste location. Selecting the wrong size area into which you are pasting prevents Excel from pasting and displays an alert box.

Pasting Multiple Copies

You can make multiple copies of a range with a single command. Remember to select only the top-left corners of where you want each of the duplicate ranges to go. Figure 7.11 shows the marquee around a copied column of formulas and the top of each column where you are pasting the original column. Notice that pasting in multiple columns is like hanging wallpaper; you need to indicate only where the tops of each roll of wallpaper go; the wallpaper hangs down correctly. Figure 7.12 shows the pasted columns.

Tip
To remove the marquee or cancel the copy in progress, press the Esc key.

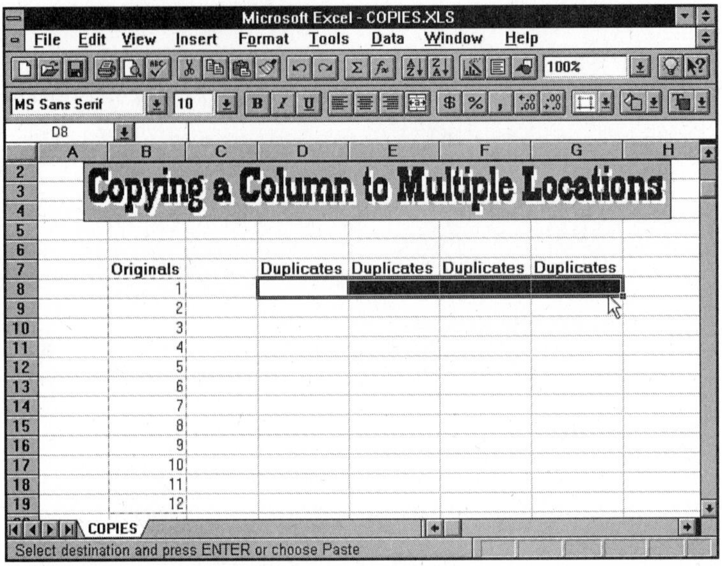

Fig. 7.11
Select the top cell where you want duplicated columns to appear.

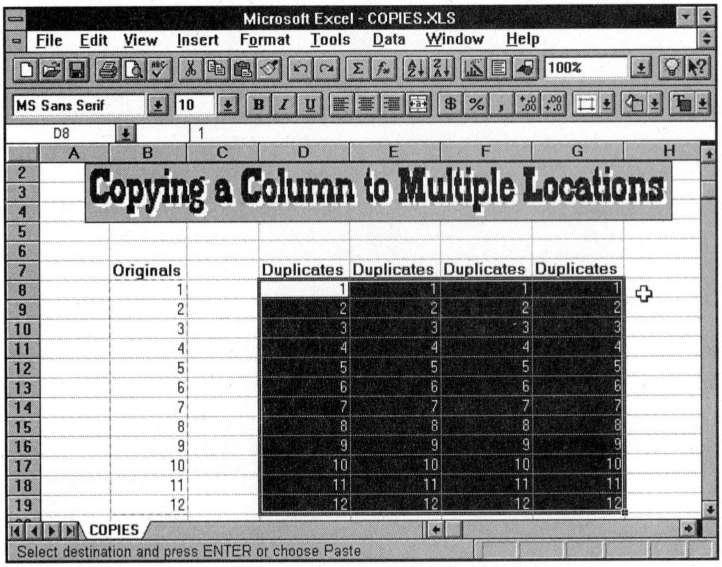

Fig. 7.12
The columns are pasted.

Figures 7.13 and 7.14 show how to copy an original row into multiple rows. Notice that only the left cell is selected where each duplicated row will be pasted.

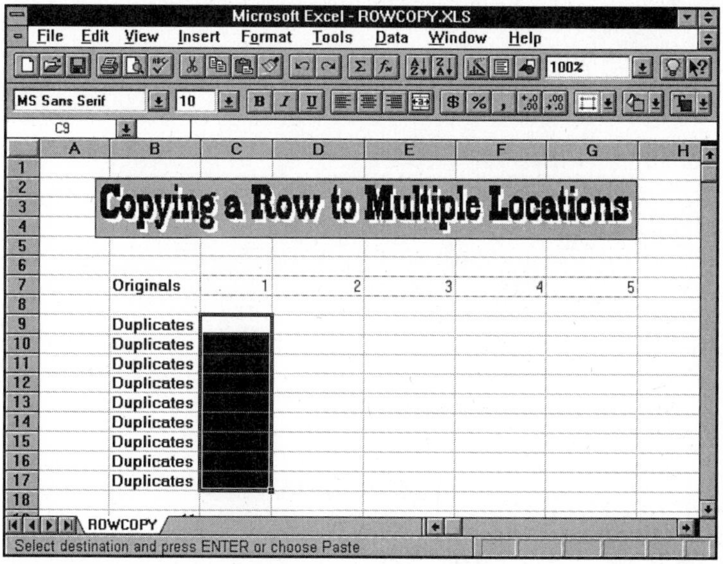

Fig. 7.13
Select the left cells where you want duplicated rows to appear.

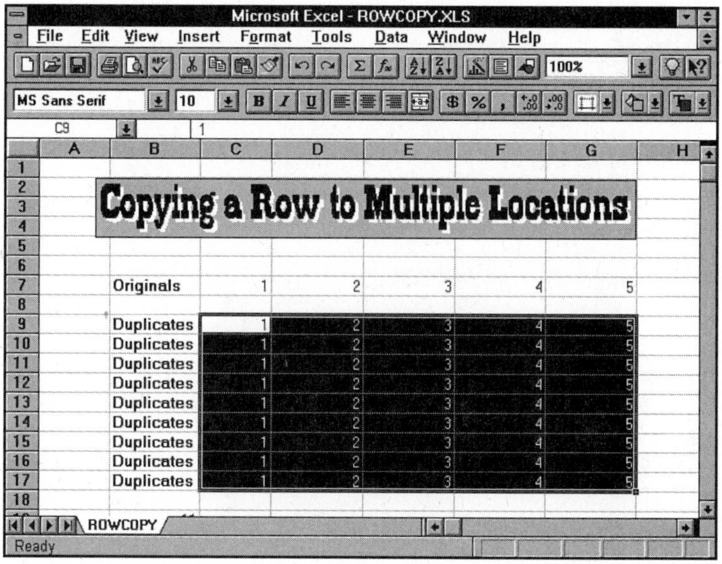

Fig. 7.14
The rows are pasted.

Pasting Nonadjacent Multiple Copies

Well-formatted worksheets may interfere with some of the previous methods of copying or filling formulas into a range, because worksheets may need blank rows or columns as separators for appearance. These blank rows and columns, however, prevent filling data with a single command.

Using noncontiguous selections, such as the selections shown in figure 7.15, you can paste multiple copies even if the areas into which you are pasting are not adjacent.

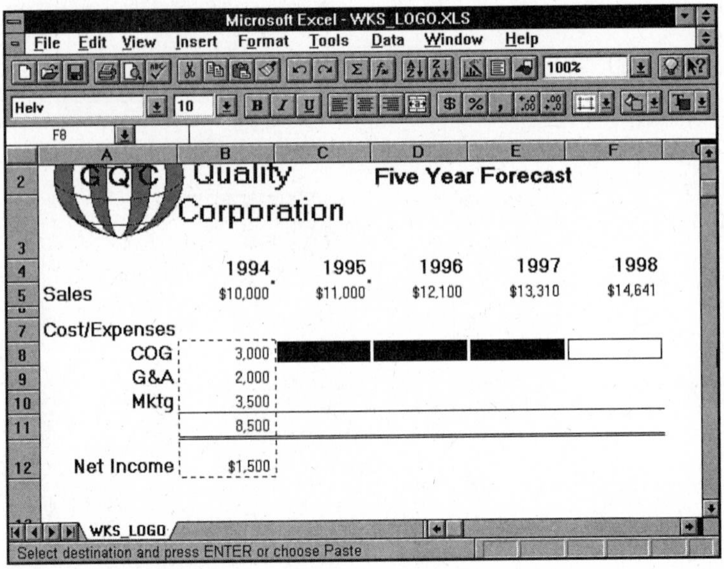

Fig. 7.15
You can paste into multiple areas even if they aren't next to each other.

To paste into nonadjacent areas, perform the following steps:

1. Select the cells or ranges you want to copy.

2. Either choose the **Edit Copy** command, click the Copy button, or press Ctrl+C.

3. Select the top-left corner where you want each copy to paste. With the mouse, hold down the Ctrl key as you click each cell to receive a pasted copy.

   With the keyboard, move to the first cell to receive a copy and press Shift+F8 so that the ADD indicator appears in the status bar. Move to the next cell to receive data and press Shift+F8 until ADD disappears, then reappears. Move to the next cell, and so on.

4. Either choose the **Edit Paste** command, click the Paste button, or press Ctrl+V.

Notice that the target cells are separated by blank columns. Figure 7.16 shows the result of the paste operation.

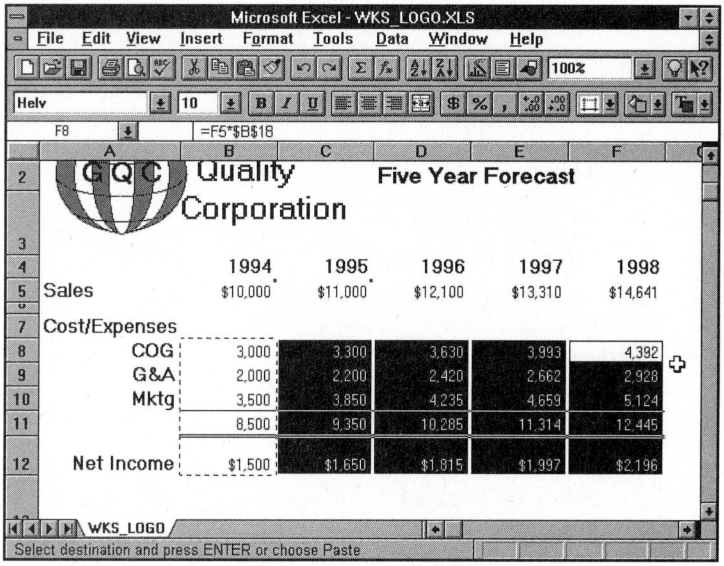

Fig. 7.16
Pasted data is entered in nonadjacent ranges.

Inserting Copied Cells with Commands

Pasted cell contents usually replace the cell contents they paste over. In some cases, you may want to copy and paste to insert the copied material into the worksheet so that existing cell contents are moved aside. You can perform this technique with the **I**nsert Copied C**e**lls command.

To copy and then insert cells or a range of cells into another location, perform the following steps:

1. Select the cells or range of cells you want to copy.
2. Choose the **E**dit **C**opy command.
3. Select the cell at the top-left of where you want to insert your copies.
4. Choose **I**nsert Copied C**e**lls.

   If Excel needs information about which direction to shift existing cells, the Insert Paste dialog box shown in figure 7.17 appears.

Tip
You must recopy the original data each time before you do an insert paste.

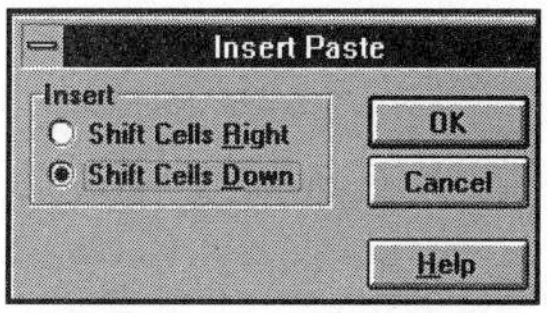

Fig. 7.17
Select which way you want to shift existing cells.

5. Select the Shift Cells **R**ight option if you want cells being pasted over to move right. Select the Shift Cells **D**own option if you want cells being pasted over to move down.

6. Choose OK.

You cannot perform an insert paste over the original data. You also cannot perform an insert paste so that the original data is forced to move. If you attempt an illegal paste, Excel displays an alert box.

Copying Data Across a Workbook

To copy a cell or range to a new location, perform the following steps:

1. Select the cell or range of cells you want to copy.

2. Either choose the **E**dit **C**opy command, click the Copy button, or press Ctrl+C. The cells to copy appear, surrounded by a marquee (a moving dashed line).

3. Select the worksheet to which you want to move data.

   For information on moving among worksheets, see Chapter 3, "Navigating and Selecting in a Workbook."

4. Select the cell at the top-left corner of where you want the duplicate to appear.

5. Either choose the **E**dit **P**aste command, click the Paste button, or press Ctrl+V to paste and retain the copy in the Clipboard. Press Enter to paste one time.

The range is pasted in the new worksheet. Keep in mind that the formula references are adjusted to refer to the new location, and absolute references refer to the same cells. For 3-D moves, you may need to insert the sheet name as part of the reference. See Chapter 5, "Working with Formulas," for more information on cell references.

Tip
To copy formats, select the cells with the formats that you want to copy. Click the Format Painter button on the Standard toolbar. Then select the range to copy the formats to.

Pasting Formats, Values, or Transposed Data

The **E**dit Paste **S**pecial command is handy to copy and paste part of a cell's attributes, such as the format or value, but not both. With this command you can reorient database layouts into worksheet layouts and vice versa. The command also enables you to combine the attributes of cells by pasting them together. This feature is useful when you need to combine or consolidate different parts of a worksheet. Consolidation is covered extensively in Chapter 25, "Linking, Embedding, and Consolidating Worksheets."

To use the **E**dit Paste **S**pecial command for any of its many operations, perform the following steps:

1. Select the cell or range of cells.

2. Choose the **E**dit **C**opy command or click the Copy button.

3. Select the upper-left corner of where you want to paste.

   When transposing (flipping) rows and columns, be sure to consider which cells are covered when the pasted area is rotated 90 degrees.

4. Choose the **E**dit Paste **S**pecial command to display the Paste Special dialog box, shown in figure 7.18.

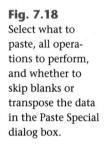

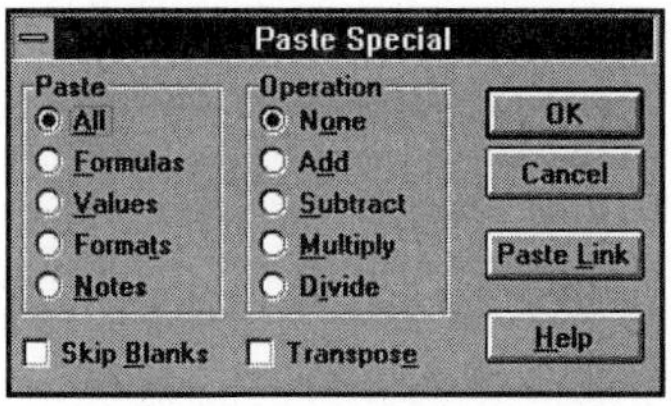

Fig. 7.18
Select what to paste, all operations to perform, and whether to skip blanks or transpose the data in the Paste Special dialog box.

   If a Paste Special dialog box that shows a Data Type list appears, the last copy you completed was from an application other than Excel. Return to step 1 to copy and paste within Excel.

5. Select the characteristics you want transferred:

Option	Function
All	Transfer all of the original contents and characteristics.
Formulas	Transfer only the formulas.
Values	Transfer only the values and formula results. This option converts formulas to values.
Forma**t**s	Transfer only the cell formats.
Notes	Transfer only note contents.

6. Select from the dialog box how you want the transferred characteristics or information combined with the cells being pasted into:

Option	Function
None	Replace the receiving cell.
Add	Add to the receiving cell.
Subtract	Subtract from the receiving cell.
Multiply	Multiply by the receiving cell.
Divide	Divide into the receiving cell.

7. Select the Skip **B**lanks check box if you do not want to paste blank cells on top of existing cell contents.

8. Select the Transpos**e** check box to change rows to columns or to change columns to rows.

9. Choose OK.

By copying the range of formulas you want to freeze, you can convert formulas into their results so that they do not change. After copying, without moving the active cell, use Paste **S**pecial with the **V**alues and **N**one check boxes checked to paste the values over the original formulas.

The Transpos**e** option in the Paste Special dialog box can save time and work if you use database information in worksheets or worksheet data in a database.

For Related Information

- "Entering Formulas," p. 127
- "Understanding Workbooks and Sheets," p. 258
- "Entering and Editing Data," p. 87

The Transpos**e** option rotates a range of cells between row orientation and column orientation, which is useful for switching between a database row layout and a worksheet column layout. You cannot transpose over the range that contains the original data. Figure 7.19 shows an original range on the left and its transposition on the right.

The Paste **L**ink button enables you to link the pasted data to the original source. Chapter 25, "Linking, Embedding, and Consolidating Worksheets," covers linking data.

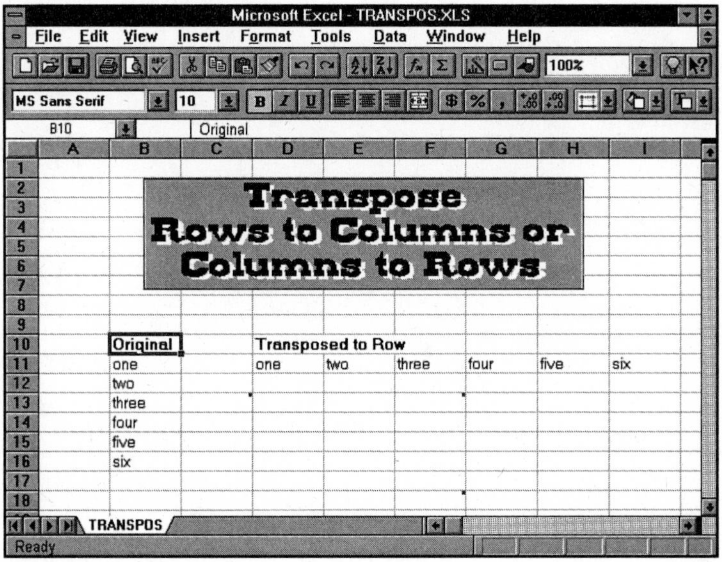

Fig. 7.19 Transposing changes rows to columns or vice versa.

Troubleshooting

*The **P**aste command is not available.*

You haven't selected anything to paste. You must select the range and choose the **E**dit **C**opy or **E**dit Cu**t** command. Then the **P**aste command is available.

Nothing happens when I drag.

Drag and drop may not be enabled. Choose the **T**ools **O**ptions command. Select the Edit tab; then select the Allow Cell **D**rag and Drop option. Choose OK.

From Here...

One of the benefits of using Windows is that you can share data among applications. If you use another Windows application, perhaps a word processing program or a presentation program, you can cut and copy Excel data in that application.

- See Chapter 38, "Using Excel with Windows Applications," and Chapter 39, "Using Excel with DOS and Mainframe Applications," for more information on these topics.
- Another time-saving feature is the capability to link and consolidate worksheets. Chapter 25, "Linking, Embedding, and Consolidating Worksheets," covers this topic.

Chapter 8

Reorganizing Workbooks and Sheets

Workbooks and the sheets they contain are the foundation for the work you do in Excel. Within a workbook you can place the sheets containing formulas, databases, charts, slides, macros, and Visual Basic procedures.

Workbooks make it easy to group all the pieces related to a job you are doing in Excel. Because sheets are grouped into one file, you can give a file to a co-worker and know that all information and automation necessary for a particular Excel job is in the file.

Use some thought when designing your workbooks. You may want to create a workbook template to give to all the plant accountants so their reporting procedures are consistent and it will be easier to consolidate numbers.

Caution

When you organize a workbook, keep in mind that all sheets within the workbook open with the workbook and that you use memory for each sheet. So if you have a large worksheet that you use only on occasion, you may want to keep it in a separate workbook.

When you first open a new workbook, it has a default number of worksheets. You do not need to keep all of them. You can insert or delete additional Excel sheets of any type, and you can copy or move sheets within or between workbooks.

In this chapter, you learn how to:

- Change the default number of sheets in new workbooks
- Insert and remove sheets
- Copy and move sheets
- Rename sheets
- Group sheets for editing, formatting, and reorganizing
- Troubleshoot 3-D references when sheets have been reorganized

Understanding Workbooks and Sheets

In Excel 5, a workbook is the file where you work and store data. Each workbook can contain many sheets. These sheets may be worksheets, charts, slides, Excel 4 macros to let you use macros developed for earlier versions of Excel, dialog sheets, or Visual Basic modules to let you use Visual Basic to develop macros for Excel 5. When you open, close, save, copy, or delete a file in Excel, you open, close, save, copy, or delete a workbook.

For Related Information

- "Managing Files," p.267

The default workbook opens with 16 worksheets, but you can change this number. The number of worksheets in a workbook is limited by available memory. Sheet names appear on *sheet tabs* at the bottom of the workbook window. You move from sheet to sheet by clicking the sheet tabs or by pressing Ctrl+PgUp or Ctrl+PgDn. The active sheet has a bold sheet tab.

Changing the Default Number of Sheets in New Workbooks

To change the number of sheets included in new workbooks, take these steps:

1. Choose the **T**ools **O**ptions command to display the Options dialog box shown in figure 8.1.

2. Select the General tab.

3. Select the **S**heets in New Workbook option and then select the number of sheets you want (up to 255) by clicking the arrows to the right of the option box. To use the keyboard, press Alt+S and then the up- or down-arrow key, or just type the new number.

4. Choose OK.

For Related Information

- "Managing Files," p. 267

All new workbooks now are created with the adjusted number of sheets, until you change the **S**heets in New Workbook setting again.

Inserting and Removing Sheets

As you create and revise workbooks, you will want to insert and remove sheets for the same reasons you insert and remove sheets in a manual workbook. The following section shows how to perform these tasks with Excel.

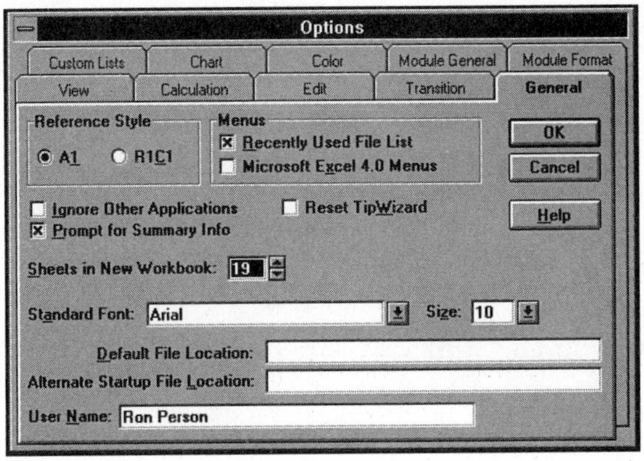

Fig. 8.1
Change the **S**heets in New Workbook amount to control how many sheets are in each new workbook.

Inserting a Sheet

Whenever you need more sheets in a workbook, just insert them.

To insert a sheet into your workbook, take these steps:

1. Activate the workbook into which you want to insert the sheet.
2. Select the existing sheet before which you want the new sheet inserted, by clicking on its sheet tab at the bottom of the workbook, or by pressing Ctrl+PgUp or Ctrl+PgDn.
3. Choose the insert command appropriate to the sheet type:

Type	Insertion Method
Worksheet	Choose the **I**nsert **W**orksheet command, or press Shift+F11
Chart sheet	Choose the **I**nsert C**h**art **A**s New Sheet command, or press F11
VB module	Choose the **I**nsert **M**acro **M**odule command
VB dialog sheet	Choose the **I**nsert **M**acro **D**ialog command
Microsoft Excel	Choose the **I**nsert **M**acro MS **E**xcel 4.0 macro sheet Macro command, or press Ctrl+F11

Note

You can use a shortcut menu to insert new sheets. Point to the selected sheet tab and click the right mouse button. Choose Insert, and when the Insert dialog box appears, choose Worksheet, Chart, MS Excel 4.0 Macro, Module, or Dialog.

You can insert several sheets of the same type at once. Group several adjacent sheets using the method described in a following section of this chapter, "Grouping Sheets for Editing, Formatting, and Reorganizing." Then follow the preceding step 3 to insert the sheets. The number of sheets inserted equals the number in your group. If you grouped two existing sheets, for example, two new sheets are inserted.

Removing a Sheet

To remove a sheet from a workbook, take these steps:

1. Select the sheet you want to delete.
2. Choose the **E**dit De**l**ete Sheet command.

> **Note**
>
> To delete the sheet using a shortcut menu, point to its selected sheet tab, click the right mouse button, and then choose Delete.

The message `Selected sheets will be permanently deleted. Continue?` is displayed on-screen.

3. Choose OK.

For Related Information

- "Navigating and Selecting in a Workbook," p.65
- "Managing Files," p. 267

You can delete several sheets at once by grouping sheets (using the technique described in the section "Grouping Sheets for Editing, Formatting, and Reorganizing," later in this chapter) and then following the preceding steps 2 and 3.

Copying and Moving Sheets

Just as you want to insert and remove sheets while you work with workbooks, you also want to move or copy sheets to different workbooks. For example, your workbooks may reflect the organization of divisions within the corporate structure, and you want to update the workbooks when a corporate reorganization occurs.

Copying a Sheet

To copy a sheet within or between workbooks by using the mouse, take these steps:

1. Select the sheet you want to copy.
2. If you are copying within the workbook, hold down Ctrl while dragging the sheet tab across the sheet tabs at the bottom of the workbook.

If you are copying between workbooks, arrange the display so that you can see both workbooks. Hold down Ctrl while dragging the sheet tab from one workbook onto the tabs in the other workbook.

A black triangle appears above the receiving tabs, to show the location for the copy's insertion. Figure 8.2 shows the triangle above the tabs.

3. Release the mouse button.

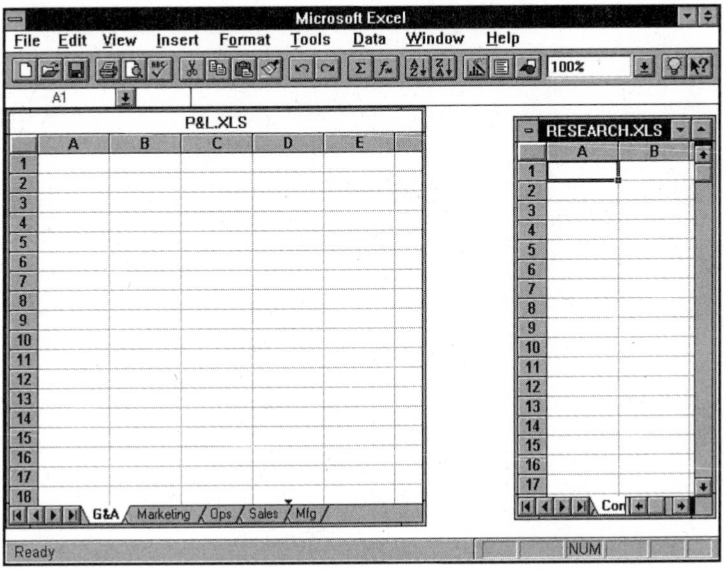

Fig. 8.2
When you drag a sheet tab, a cursor shows the copied sheet's intended location before the copy occurs.

A copy of the sheet is inserted at the new location. The name of the copy is the original sheet name. If a sheet with the same name is already in the workbook, the name is followed by a number in parentheses indicating which copy it is. For instance, the first copy of a sheet named April Expense Report is named April Expense Report (2).

To copy a sheet to another workbook by using the keyboard, take these steps:

1. Activate the workbook from which you want to copy a sheet. The workbook to which you want to copy also must be open.

2. Select the sheet you want to copy.

3. Choose the **E**dit **M**ove command or Copy Sheet. This displays the Move or Copy dialog box shown in figure 8.3.

4. From the **T**o Book drop-down list, select the name of the workbook to which you want to copy.

5. Select from the **B**efore Sheet list the name of the sheet before which you want the inserted sheet placed.

6. Select the **C**reate a Copy check box.

7. Choose OK.

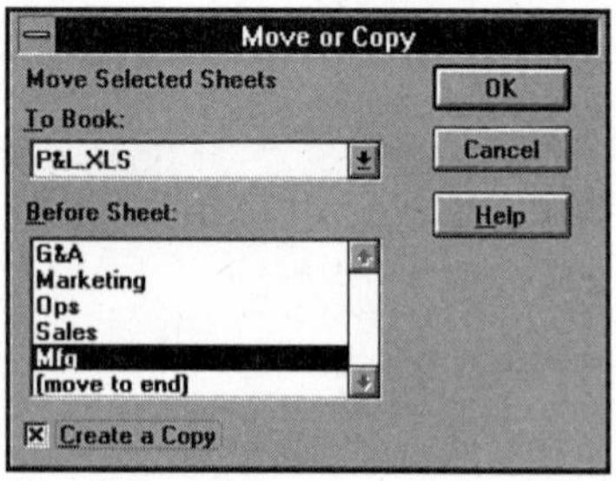

Fig. 8.3
The Move or Copy dialog box appears when you use the **E**dit **M**ove or Copy Sheet command.

To copy a sheet into a workbook that contains no other sheets, using the mouse, hold down Ctrl while you drag the sheet tab onto Excel's background, and release the mouse button. A copy of the sheet appears in its own workbook.

To copy a sheet into a new workbook by using the keyboard, take these steps:

1. Select the sheet you want to copy.

2. Choose the **E**dit **M**ove command or Copy Sheet.

3. From the **T**o Book drop-down list, select (new book).

4. Select the **C**reate a Copy check box.

5. Choose OK.

Moving a Sheet

To move a sheet within or between workbooks with the mouse, take the following steps:

Tip
You can copy several sheets at once by selecting and copying a group, using the preceding steps. The copied sheets are inserted contiguously.

1. Select the sheet you want to move.

2. If you are moving the sheet within the original workbook, drag the sheet tab across the other sheet tabs at the bottom of the workbook.

   If you are moving the sheet to another workbook, drag the sheet tab onto the tabs at the bottom of the other workbook (the display must be arranged to show both workbooks).

A black triangle above the sheet tabs shows where the sheet is to be inserted.

3. Release the mouse button.

The sheet is inserted at the new location. If a sheet with the same name is already in the destination workbook, the moved sheet name has a copy number enclosed in parentheses.

Tip
The techniques for copying and moving sheets using the mouse are very similar. The difference is that you press the Ctrl key while you copy sheets.

To move a sheet to another workbook by using the keyboard, take these steps:

1. Activate the workbook from which you want to move the sheet. The workbook to which you want to move the sheet also must be open.
2. Select the sheet you want to move.
3. Choose the **E**dit **M**ove command or Copy Sheet. The Move or Copy dialog box appears (refer to fig. 8.3).
4. From the **T**o Book drop-down list, select the name of the workbook to which you want to move the sheet.
5. From the **B**efore Sheet list, select the sheet before which you want the moved sheet to appear.
6. Deselect the **C**reate a Copy check box.
7. Choose OK.

To move a sheet into a new workbook by using the mouse, drag the sheet tab onto Excel's background, and release the mouse button. The sheet disappears from the original workbook and reappears in its own workbook.

To move a sheet to a new workbook by using the keyboard, follow these steps:

Tip
You can move several sheets at once by creating and moving a group using these steps. The moved sheets are inserted contiguously.

1. Select the sheet you want to move.
2. Choose **E**dit **M**ove or Copy Sheet.
3. From the To Book drop-down list, select (new book).
4. Deselect the **C**reate a Copy check box.
5. Choose OK.

Renaming a Sheet

For Related Information

- "Navigating and Selecting in a Workbook," p. 65
- "Managing Files," p. 267

To rename your sheet, take these steps:

1. Select the sheet you want to rename.

2. Choose the F**o**rmat S**h**eet **R**ename command.

> **Note**
>
> To rename the sheet using a shortcut menu, point to the selected sheet tab, and click the right mouse button; then choose Rename.

   The Rename Sheet dialog box appears as shown in figure 8.4.

3. Type the new sheet name, using up to 31 characters including spaces, in the **N**ame text box.

4. Choose OK.

The new sheet name appears on the sheet tab.

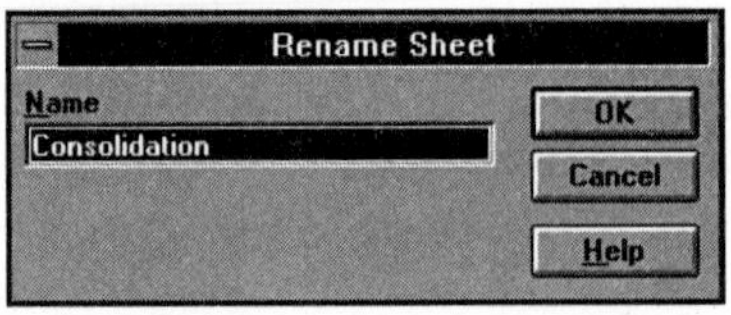

Fig. 8.4
Use the Rename Sheet dialog box to rename the Consolidation worksheet.

Grouping Sheets for Editing, Formatting, and Reorganizing

Tip
Double-click the sheet tab to display the Rename Sheet dialog box.

You can perform operations on several sheets at once by creating a *group selection*. This feature is useful to edit or format a group of sheets identically or to reorganize a group of sheets.

To edit or format a group of sheets, follow the instructions to create a group selection as discussed in the following steps, then edit or format as described in Chapters 4 and 7. To insert, remove, copy, or move a group of sheets, create a group selection and then follow the appropriate steps provided earlier in this chapter to perform the respective operation.

To select a group of sheets that are contiguous, take these steps:

1. Select the first sheet tab.
2. Hold down Shift while selecting the last sheet tab in the group.

To deselect the group, choose Ungroup Sheets from the sheet tab shortcut menu, or click any sheet tab that is not selected.

To select a group of sheets that are not contiguous, follow these steps:

1. Select the first sheet tab.
2. Hold down Ctrl while selecting the other sheet tabs in the group.

To deselect the group, choose Ungroup Sheets from the sheet tab shortcut menu, or click any sheet tab that is not selected.

To select all sheets in a workbook, take the following steps:

1. Point to any sheet tab.
2. Click the right mouse button to open the sheet tab shortcut menu, and then choose Select All Sheets.

To deselect the group, Choose Ungroup Sheets from the sheet tab shortcut menu, or click any sheet tab.

After you create a group selection, `[Group]` appears in the title bar of the workbook.

For Related Information

- "Navigating and Selecting in a Workbook," p. 65

Troubleshooting

After adding a worksheet within the range of a 3-D formula, the new numbers were not reflected in the formula.

Make sure that the numbers you expected to be reflected in the formula are at the exact row and column referenced in your formula. If they are in another location, the 3-D formula will not include them.

After reorganizing the sheets in a workbook, the 3-D formulas are wrong.

Most of the rules for formulas when sheets are inserted or deleted are obvious. Suppose that this formula is in the workbook: `=SUM(Sheet2:Sheet4!C2)`. If you insert a sheet between Sheet2 and Sheet4, the value at C2 in the inserted sheet is included in the sum. If you remove a sheet between Sheet2 and Sheet4, the value at C2 in the removed sheet is removed from the sum.

Caution

Use caution when you insert, remove, or move sheets included in 3-D references because the reorganization of sheets can affect the results of calculations.

For Related Information

- "Working with Formulas," p. 125
- "Moving or Copying Data and Formulas," p. 235
- "Auditing Workbooks and Worksheets," p. 777

When you move a sheet within a workbook, however, you may affect formulas of which you are not aware. This is especially true if the sheet being moved is an *anchor* (one end of a range of sheets). Continuing with the current example, if you move Sheet2 or Sheet4, and Sheet2 still is at a location before Sheet4, the sum includes the values of C2 for all sheets between the same anchors, using the same formula as before the move. If you move Sheet4 to a location before Sheet2, however, the formula changes to `=SUM(Sheet2:Sheet3!C2)`. If you move Sheet2 to a location after Sheet4, the formula changes to `=Sum(Sheet3:Sheet4!C2)`.

From Here...

For more information about using and reorganizing workbooks and worksheets, see the following chapters:

- Chapter 3, "Navigating and Selecting in a Workbook." This chapter discusses basic techniques for using workbooks and sheets.
- Chapter 5, "Working with Formulas." This chapter shows you how to reference other sheets in a workbook.
- Chapter 7, "Moving or Copying Data and Formulas." This chapter discusses moving or copying cell contents across workbooks.
- Chapter 9, "Managing Files." This chapter tells you how to manage workbooks.
- Chapter 25, "Linking, Embedding, and Consolidating Worksheets." This chapter shows you how to manage data from more than one worksheet.
- Chapter 26, "Auditing Workbooks and Worksheets." This chapter shows you how to use tools from Excel's Auditing toolbar to examine a worksheet for errors.

Chapter 9

Managing Files

In this chapter, you learn all you need to know to work with files in Excel. You first learn how to create a new workbook, then how to open existing workbook files, and finally how to save and close workbooks. In the remainder of the chapter, you learn how to use Excel's powerful new **F**ind File command, which allows you to quickly find the files you created in Excel, if you forget where the files are located or if you want to find a group of related files. You also learn how to use the **F**ind File command to preview files and to open, print, copy, and delete files.

In this chapter you learn how to:

- Create a new workbook
- Open a workbook
- Save a workbook
- Close a workbook
- Use the **F**ind File command to find and work with files

Creating a New Workbook

When you start Excel, the program opens with a blank *workbook* titled Book1. A workbook can contain one or more *sheets* of varying types. You can have, for example, *worksheets*, *chart sheets*, and *macro sheets* combined in a single workbook. The default workbook that appears when you open Excel contains 16 worksheets. If you want, you can change the default number of worksheets contained in a new workbook (see Chapter 8, "Reorganizing Workbooks and Sheets"). A *file* in Excel is the same as a workbook, so when you save or open a file in Excel, you are saving or opening a single workbook that may contain many sheets.

To create a new workbook, choose the **F**ile **N**ew command, press Ctrl+N, or click the New Workbook button on the Standard toolbar. If you have templates stored in the \XLSTART directory, a dialog box opens when you choose the **F**ile **N**ew command. In the **N**ew list, Workbook is selected by default; but, if you want, you can select a template from the list. To learn more about templates, see Chapter 42, "Creating Templates and Controlling Excel's Startup."

Opening an Existing Workbook

After you save a workbook, you may want to retrieve this workbook at a later time to continue working on it. This procedure involves opening the workbook file you saved and closed when you were previously working with the workbook.

To open an existing workbook, take the following steps:

1. Choose the **F**ile **O**pen command, press Ctrl+O, or click the Open File button on the Standard toolbar. The Open dialog box appears (see fig. 9.1).

   When you choose **F**ile **O**pen, you may not be in the directory that contains the file you want. To change to the directory that contains the file, follow the next step.

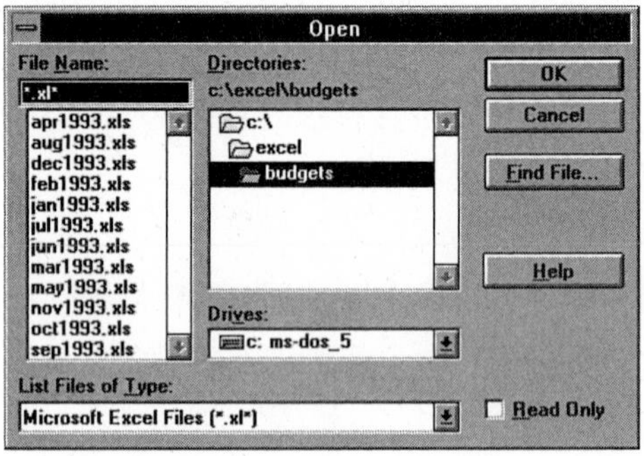

Fig. 9.1
Select a file to open in the Open dialog box.

2. Open the drive and, if necessary, the directory that contains the file you want.

   Select the drive that contains the file in the Dri**v**es drop-down list. Select the directory that contains the file in the **D**irectories list box.

3. Select the kind of file you want to open by typing in a different file extension in the File **N**ame text box, or select the type of file in the List Files of **T**ype drop-down list.

   See the following section for more information on file types.

4. Select the file from the File **N**ame list box, or type the name of the file in the File **N**ame text box.

5. Choose OK.

You can open multiple workbooks simultaneously. To open files whose names are adjacent, select the first file name, and then hold down the Shift key as you click the last. With the keyboard, hold down the Shift key as you move to the last file name. To open files whose names are not together, hold down the Ctrl key as you click each name. Nonadjacent files cannot be opened with the keyboard.

To quickly change directories and open files, press Ctrl+F12 or click the File Open button. Double-click the directory to which you want to change in the Open dialog box, and then double-click the file you want to open. Double-clicking selects the name and chooses OK.

At the bottom of the **F**ile menu, Excel displays the names of the four most recently opened documents so that you can open these files quickly without accessing the Open dialog box. If you want to open one of these files, click the file name at the bottom of the menu. This action opens the file, but does not change the directory. If you do not see the names listed at the bottom of the **F**ile menu, choose the **T**ools **O**ptions command and select the General tab. Select the **R**ecently Used File List option and choose OK.

Note

When you open an Excel file on the network, other users cannot open the same file. To allow others to open the same file, select the **R**ead Only check box in the Open dialog box before opening the file. You must save your changes to the file under a different name, but while you work on the file, others will also be able to open it.

Workbooks can have two types of password protection. The password can protect the workbook against unauthorized opening, and the password can protect against changes saved back to the original name. If the file you want to open is protected, you are prompted for the password. Type the password, using the exact upper- and lowercase letters as the original password, and then choose OK.

If the workbook has been saved with the read-only option, you are asked whether you really need to make changes. Choose **Y**es to open the file as read-only; choose **N**o to open the file so that you can make changes; or choose Cancel if you decide not to open the file.

Listing Other File Types

The file extension can help you find the file you want. Excel files use different file extensions for each type of file. Changing the file extension in the File **N**ame text box or in the List Files of **T**ype list and choosing OK displays files that contain the extension you want. To see chart files, for example, use *.XLC; to see Lotus 1-2-3 files, use *.WK*; to see all files, use *.*. Some of the more frequently used file extensions that Excel reads are described in table 9.1.

Table 9.1 File Extensions Read by Excel

Extension	File Type
.	All files
XLS	Excel workbook
XLC	Excel chart
XLM	Excel macro sheet
CSV	Comma-separated values
TXT	Tab-delimited text
WKS	1-2-3 Release 1A
WK1	1-2-3 Release 2
WK3	1-2-3 Release 3

Changing Drives and Directories

Excel displays files, directories, and drives in the Open and Save As dialog boxes. With these dialog boxes, you can change the directory and drive that Excel uses for saving and retrieving. The current drive and directory appear as text at the top of the **D**irectories list box.

Use the Dri**v**es list box to select a new drive. This procedure is discussed earlier in this section. You do not have to select a file to change directories or disk drives. When you reach the step to select a file, you can choose Cancel or press Esc and remain in the new disk or directory that you selected.

Use the **D**irectories list box to select a new directory. Daughter directories are indented to the right from the parent directory in which they reside.

Changing the Default Directory

When you first choose the **F**ile **O**pen or **F**ile Save **A**s command, you see a listing of files in the \EXCEL directory. Because you should reserve this directory for the Excel program files and store the files you create in Excel in other directories, you need to switch to some other directory to find the file you want. After you have switched directories in the Open dialog box (or the Save As dialog box), that directory becomes the current directory until you close Excel; when you choose either the **F**ile **O**pen or **F**ile Save **A**s command, the files in that directory are listed.

You can change the default directory so that when you first choose either the **F**ile **O**pen or the **F**ile Save **A**s command, that directory is the current directory. You can make the directory where you store your most-used files the default directory.

To change the default directory, follow these steps:

1. Choose **T**ools **O**ptions and select the General tab.
2. Type in the full path name for the directory you want to use as the default in the **D**efault File Location text box.
3. Choose OK.

Opening Files on a Network

If your computer is connected to a network, you can open any Excel files stored in directories on the network to which you are granted access. To open a file on a network, choose the **N**etwork button in the Open dialog box and use the Connect Network Drive dialog box to connect to the network drive. After you connect to a network drive, you can open a file on that drive by selecting the drive from the Dri**v**es list in the Open dialog box, as previously discussed. The Excel files on that drive are displayed in the File **N**ame list box, as with any other drive. Select the file you want to open and choose OK.

If another user is accessing the file when you try to open it, a message box informs you that the file is in use. You can open the file as a read-only file, which means you can view the file but cannot make changes to the file and save it with the same name. You also are given the option of being notified when the file is available for use.

If you only want to view a workbook file on a network and don't need to make changes to the file, you can select the **R**ead Only option in the File Open dialog box, which allows other users to have read-and-write access to the file while you are viewing it.

Opening Excel 4 Documents

You need to know exactly what happens when you open files that were created in Excel 4 or earlier versions. When you open a worksheet, it is converted to an Excel workbook with a single worksheet. Both the workbook and the single worksheet in the workbook are given the name of the original worksheet.

For Related Information

- "Using the Toolbars," p. 41
- "Importing Data," p. 1079

When you open a chart or macro sheet, a new workbook with a single chart sheet or macro sheet is created. Excel 4 templates are converted into workbook templates (see Chapter 42, "Creating Templates and Controlling Excel's Startup," for more information on working with templates). Excel 4 workbooks are converted to Excel 5 workbooks. Only bound sheets from an Excel 4 workbook are kept together in the new workbook. Unbound sheets must be opened separately, just as you would open any other Excel 4 worksheet.

Saving Workbooks

Tip

You can use version numbers in file names, such as FORCST03.XLS and FORCST04.XLS, when you save so that you always can return to previous versions of a work.

You should save your workbooks every 15 to 20 minutes so that if your computer crashes or the power fails, you lose a minimal amount of work. If you save to the same file name each time, the previous work is replaced. The **F**ile Save **A**s command is used to save a file with a new name. The **F**ile **S**ave command saves a file with the same name as it already has. (Delete old versions of work with the **F**ile **F**ind File command or with the File Manager from Windows.)

The **F**ile Save **A**s command also is the easiest method of saving the worksheet data in formats readable by other Windows and DOS programs. Chapters 38, "Using Excel with Windows Applications," and 39, "Using Excel with DOS and Mainframe Applications," explain how to save Excel files in formats you can use with other programs: 1-2-3, dBASE, or many forms of text files. To learn how to save a workbook as a template, see Chapter 42, "Creating Templates and Controlling Excel's Startup."

Saving Your Workbook

The first time you save a workbook, you need to name it and decide where you want to store it.

To save and name a workbook:

1. Activate the workbook you want to save. (The workbook window on top is the file that is saved.)

2. Choose the **F**ile Save **A**s command, press F12, or choose the Save button on the toolbar (the third button from the left). The Save As dialog box appears (see fig. 9.2).

> **Caution**
>
> If you already saved the file, clicking the Save button on the Standard toolbar saves the file with the same file name instead of opening the Save As dialog box. The old version of the file is replaced with the new version.

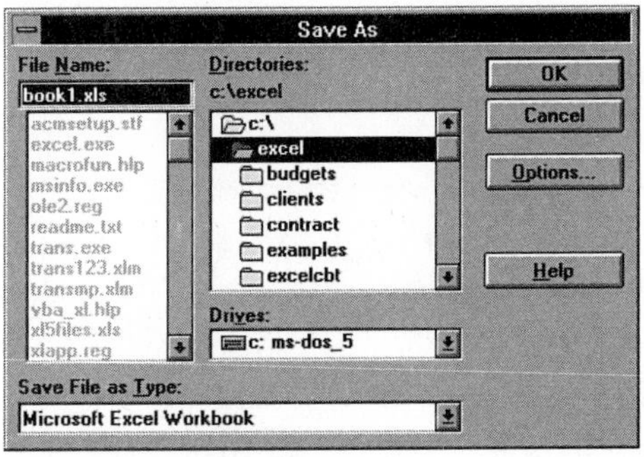

Fig. 9.2
Use the Save As dialog box to name a file and assign where you want it stored.

3. Type a file name in the File **N**ame box.

4. In the Dri**v**es list, select the drive where you want to save your file. Use this option to save your file to a floppy disk in drive A or B, for example, or to save the file to a different drive on your hard disk. (See "Changing Drives and Directories" earlier in this chapter.)

   If you are connected to a network, you can use the Network button to connect to a network drive and save files in a network directory. See "Opening Files on a Network" earlier in this chapter for more information on sharing workbooks on a network.

5. In the Directories list box, select the directory where you want to save your file. (See "Changing Drives and Directories" earlier in this chapter.)

6. Choose OK.

7. If you selected the option to display the Summary Info dialog box when you first save a file (see "Saving with Summary Information To Make Workbooks Easier To Find" in a following section of this chapter), fill in the dialog box when it appears and choose OK. You can bypass the dialog box by choosing OK without entering any information.

You can change the default directory that is listed when you first choose the **F**ile **S**ave or **F**ile Save **A**s command. See "Setting the Default Directory" earlier in the chapter.

If you are familiar with directory path names, you can save a file into another directory by typing the path name and file name in the File **N**ame box of the Save As dialog box. To save a file named REPORTS into the CLIENTS directory on drive C, for example, type the following path name and then choose OK:

C:\CLIENTS\REPORTS

Use DOS file names with one to eight characters. File names can include letters, numbers, and some symbols. Because only some symbols can be used in file names, the best practice is to use only the underline (_) and the hyphen (-).

Caution

File names can never include spaces. Spaces confuse DOS's capability of storing the file with the name you want. Also, don't use periods in file names, other than the period before the extension.

Note

If you ever need to save a sheet in a workbook as its own file, select the sheet and choose the **F**ile Save **A**s command. Select Microsoft Excel 4.0 Worksheet from the Save File as **T**ype list and choose OK. A message box informs you that only the current worksheet is saved; choose OK. Now, reopen the file, choose the **F**ile **S**ave command, and choose **Y**es when asked if you want to update the file to Excel 5.0 format.

Saving Files with a New Name

You can use the **F**ile Save **A**s command to save a named file with a new name, which creates a backup of your file. If you have a file called

BUDGET1.XLS, for example, you can save your file a second time, giving it the name BUDGET2.XLS. You then have two versions of the same file, each with a different name. You can save the new version of your file in the same location as the original, or in any other directory or drive.

Revising your file before saving it with a new name is a common practice. You then have the original file and the second, revised file, each with a unique name. Using this method, you can store successive drafts of a document on disk. You can always return to an earlier draft if you need to.

To save a named file with a new name, choose the **F**ile Save **A**s command, change the file name in the File **N**ame box, change the drive or directory if you want, and then choose OK.

You can use the **F**ile Save **A**s command to make sequential backups of important documents. The first time you save a file, name the file with a number, such as FILE01. Then each time you save the file again, rename the document with the next higher number: FILE02, FILE03, and so on. The file with the highest number is always the most recent version. And when you finish the project, you can delete the files with low numbers.

Be sure that you name the files FILE01 and FILE02—including the zero—so that the files stay in order in dialog box lists. If you don't, FILE11 is listed before FILE3 because files are listed alphabetically and numerically. This rule is especially important in the Open dialog box, where you want to be sure that you open the most recent version of your file.

For safety, you may want to use the Save **A**s command instead of the **S**ave command. The Save **A**s command shows you the directory and gives you a chance to change the file name for each save. The **F**ile **S**ave command or File Save button saves the document under the name last used.

Saving with Summary Information To Make Workbooks Easier To Find

Summary information includes descriptive notes that can ease the task of organizing and finding files after you have created many files. You can attach summary information to your workbook at two different times—while you work on the file or when you save the file. No matter which method you choose, including summary information is a wonderful time-saver. Later in this chapter, you learn how to use this information to locate misplaced files or files whose names you don't quite remember. The Summary Info dialog box also helps you cope with the limited file-naming rules of DOS. Although you still must limit the names of files to eight characters, you can attach a title to any document and then list the files in any subdirectory along with the titles, using the **F**ind File command. You can include any text—up to 255 characters—in any Summary Info field. No naming or character restrictions exist.

Filling in the Summary Info box may seem a nuisance, but try using the box—it may be worth your while. When you learn how to use the powerful **F**ind File command, you will see that summary information helps you find files more easily than using the cryptic eight-letter DOS file name.

To add summary information to a workbook with which you are working, take these steps:

1. Choose the **F**ile Summary **I**nfo command to display the Summary Info dialog box shown in figure 9.3.

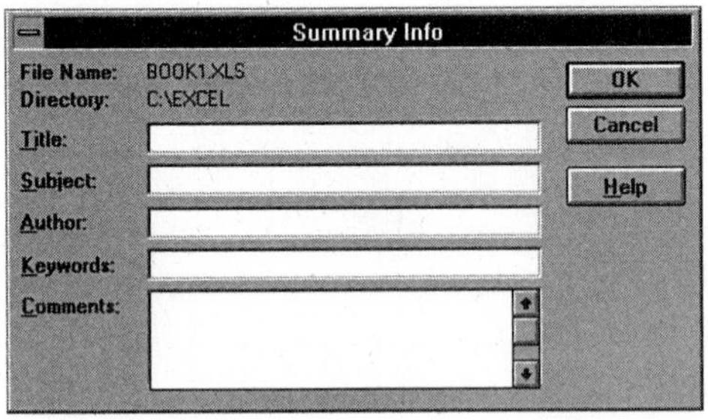

Fig. 9.3
Use the Summary Info dialog box to attach descriptive notes to workbook files.

2. Fill in any of the fields with descriptive text. Include as much (up to 255 characters) or as little information as you like. The following tables describes each of the fields:

Field	Description
Title	Type a descriptive title in this field. Even if you use only this field, you can overcome the limitations of DOS file names.
Subject	Enter the subject of the worksheet.
Author	Enter the author of the workbook in this field. The name that appears in the User Name box in the General tab of the Tools Options dialog box appears by default in this field.
Keywords	Enter some words or phrases that can be used to locate the workbook by using the **F**ind File command.
Comments	Enter any comments that you want in this field.

3. Choose OK.

You can add, edit, or view the summary information at any time by choosing the **F**ile Summary **I**nfo command to display the Summary Info dialog box. If you want to be prompted to enter summary information when you save a file, you can select an option to display the Summary Info dialog box whenever you choose the **F**ile Save **A**s command. Choose the **T**ools **O**ptions command and select the General tab. Select the **P**rompt for Summary Info option and choose OK. Now, when you first save a file, the Summary Info dialog box appears. If you don't want to enter summary information for the file, choose OK to bypass the dialog box.

Saving without Renaming

Every time you save a workbook with a unique name, you create a new file on disk—a good way to keep backups of your workbook. Not all files are so important, however, that you need multiple backups. If you don't need multiple backups of a workbook, you can save the workbook to the file's existing file name, replacing the current version of the file.

> **Caution**
>
> Remember that when you save without renaming, you erase and replace the existing file with the new file.

To save without renaming, choose the **F**ile **S**ave command, press Shift+F12, or click the Save button on the toolbar (the third button from the left). See "Creating Automatic Backups," a following section, for information on how to have Excel automatically save files.

Automatically Saving Documents

As you work in a workbook, you can have Excel periodically save your workbook automatically. A message in the status bar indicates that your file is being saved.

To have Excel automatically save workbooks, take these steps:

1. Choose the **T**ools A**u**tosave command.

   If the A**u**tosave command doesn't appear in the **T**ools menu, choose the **T**ools Add-**I**ns command, select AutoSave in the **A**dd-ins Available list, and choose OK. If AutoSave doesn't appear in the **A**dd-ins Available list, you must run the Excel Setup program to install the AutoSave add-in. See Chapter 22, "Taking Advantage of Excel's Add-Ins," for more information on working with the add-in features that come with Excel.

2. Select the Automatic **S**ave Every option.
3. Enter a value for time interval between automatic saves in the **M**inutes text box.
4. Select either the Save Active Workbook Only or the Save All Open Workbooks option in the Save **O**ptions group.
5. If you want Excel to prompt you before automatically saving a document, select the **P**rompt Before Saving option.
6. Choose OK.

You can find out quickly if the A**u**tosave command is turned on by selecting the **T**ools menu and looking for a check mark next to the A**u**tosave command. If no check mark shows, the Autosave feature is turned off. If a check mark shows, Autosave is turned on.

Creating Automatic Backups

You can tell Excel to create a backup copy of your workbook every time you save the workbook. When you choose this option, Excel saves the previous version of the workbook as a backup file, and gives it the same file name as the original, but with the extension BAK.

To create backup copies of your workbooks, follow these steps:

1. Choose the **F**ile Save **A**s command or press F12. The Save As dialog box appears.
2. Choose the **O**ptions button. The Save Options dialog box appears.
3. Select the Always Create **B**ackup option.
4. Choose OK.
5. Choose OK to save the file or choose Cancel to return to the workbook without saving the file.

If the file is lost or damaged due to a power failure or some other problem, you can open the backup copy of the file so that you can at least recover all the work you did up until you last saved the file. Backups also enable you to get back to where you started before you revised and saved a file, in case you decide you want to discard all revisions or you need to see what the file looked like before you revised it. You must save a file more than once before a backup copy is created. The backup copy is stored in the same directory as the original workbook.

Password-Protecting Your Workbooks

You can protect your workbooks against unauthorized opening or unauthorized changes by saving them with different types of passwords. To add protection to a file, choose the **O**ptions button in the Save As dialog box. The dialog box shown in figure 9.4 appears.

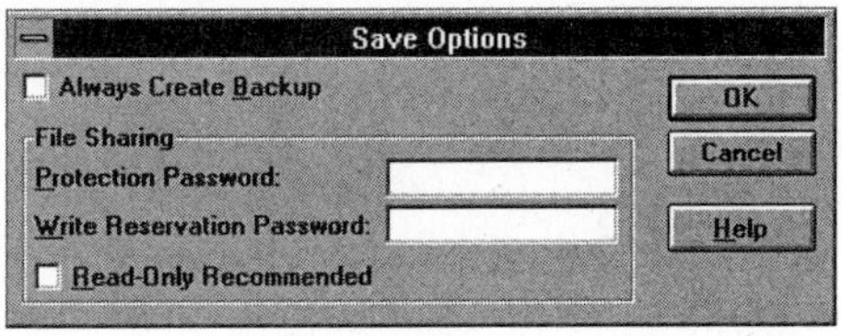

Fig. 9.4
The Save Options dialog box.

To protect a file so that a password is requested before the file can be opened, type a password of up to 15 characters in the **P**rotection Password text box. The password can contain text, numbers, spaces, and symbols. Remember to note upper- and lowercase letters. When you try to open the file later, you are asked for the exact upper- and lowercase letters that you used originally. Because asterisks show on-screen in place of the password, you are asked to enter the password to ensure that you typed it correctly. You can use passwords to protect workbooks, templates, and charts.

To ensure that only authorized users can change a file, type a password in the **W**rite Reservation Password text box. When the file is opened, users are prompted for the Write Reservation password. Without the password, users can open the file only as a read-only file. This restriction forces users to save the file with a new file name and preserves the original file. If users know the Write Reservation password, they can make changes to the file and save the file over the original file.

To recommend that users open a file as read-only, but not force them to, select the **R**ead-Only Recommended check box. This selection enables operators to make changes to the original without a password, but reminds them to check the **R**ead Only check box for normal work. This option is best when you want to protect files against accidental changes, but you want all users to have open access to the files.

> **Caution**
>
> The Excel protection options do not prevent you from deleting or erasing a file. Make backup copies of your important work.
>
> If your work is important, keep the original and backup copies in two different physical locations. When you keep copies apart, a fire or vandal cannot destroy both your original and your backup copies.

Saving to Other File Formats

Microsoft Excel 5 opens worksheets, macros, and charts from earlier versions of Excel. When you save one of these older files from Excel 5, you are asked if you want to update the file to Excel 5 format. Choose **Y**es if you want to save the file as an Excel 5 file. Otherwise, choose **N**o to keep the file in its original format.

To save an Excel file in a previous Excel format, choose the **F**ile Save **A**s command, select the type of file you want to save it as in the Save File as **T**ype list, enter the name for the file in the File **N**ame text box, and choose OK.

If you use a worksheet feature not supported by the earlier version of Excel, the value result of that feature is calculated and used in the worksheet. Chart characteristics found only in Excel 5 are not saved. A chart format that does not exist in earlier versions of Excel is changed to a format that does exist.

You also can save an Excel workbook in other file formats. You can save an Excel workbook, for example, as a Lotus 1-2-3 file. To save a file in another file format, select the file type from the Save File as **T**ype list in the Save As dialog box.

Saving a Workspace File

EXCEL 5

Excel provides a convenient way to save information about what workbooks are open and how they are arranged on-screen. The **F**ile Save **W**orkspace command enables you to save this information as a workspace file. The workspace file contains information on the name and location of each workbook in the workspace and the position of the workbook when the workspace was saved. When you open the workspace file, all the workbooks in the workspace are opened and arranged as they were when the workspace file was created. Workspace files can save you the trouble of having to reopen all the workbook files and rearrange them the way they were when you closed them.

To create a workspace file, take these steps:

1. Open and arrange the workbooks as you want them to be saved in the workspace.
2. Choose the **F**ile **W**orkspace command to display the Save Workspace dialog box.
3. Accept the default file name, RESUME.XLW, or type in a new file name in the File **N**ame text box.
4. Choose OK.

You open a workspace file just as you open any other Excel file (see "Opening an Existing Workbook" earlier in this chapter). You must not move the workbook files that are included in a workspace file, or Excel will not be able to find the files when you open the workspace file.

After you have opened a workspace file, you can save and close the individual workbooks in the workspace as you normally would. In fact, if you make changes in a workbook in the workspace, you must save it; the **F**ile Save **W**orkspace command saves information only on which workbooks are opened and how they are arranged and does not save workbook data. To change the workbooks included in the workspace file or the positioning of the workbooks, use the **F**ile Save As **W**orkspace command to save the workspace again—see the preceding steps.

If you want Excel to open the workspace file when you start Excel, transfer the workspace file to the Excel startup directory (usually, \EXCEL\XLSTART). You need to transfer only the workspace file to the startup directory. You should leave the workbook files in the original locations.

For Related Information

- "Saving Frequently Used View and Print Settings," p. 540
- "Saving and Closing Multiple Windows," p. 552
- "Saving Excel Worksheets in a Different Format," p. 1076

Closing Workbooks

You can close the active workbook window by choosing the **F**ile **C**lose command. The mouse shortcut for closing a workbook window is to double-click the workbook Control menu button to the left of the workbook's title bar. Be certain that you double-click the Control menu button to the left of the workbook's title bar (to the left of the File menu name when the workbook is maximized), not to the left of the Excel title. By keyboard, you can press Ctrl+F4.

If you made changes since the last time you saved the workbook, an alert box appears (see fig. 9.5). If you want to save the workbook before closing, choose **Y**es.

Fig. 9.5
The Close and Save alert box.

To close all the workbook windows with a single command, hold down the Shift key as you choose the **F**ile menu. The command **C**lose All appears. Choosing **C**lose All closes all workbooks; you can confirm whether you want to save workbooks that you have changed.

Using the Find File Command

The **F**ind File command is a powerful new feature in Excel 5 that enables you to search for files by file name, location, author, and the date the files were created or last saved. Alternatively, you can use the information you entered in the Summary Info dialog box (refer to "Saving with Summary Information To Make Workbooks Easier To Find" previously in this chapter). You also can search for specific text that occurs in a workbook. You can specify search criteria as broadly or narrowly as you want. The more you narrow the search, the fewer the files that will be found.

The files found by using the criteria you specified are listed in the Find File dialog box (see fig. 9.6). From there, you can browse through the directories that you included in the search, sort the files in the list, and preview any file without opening it in Excel. Further, you can view information about a file, specifically the file name, title, size, author, and date last saved; or you can view the summary information you entered for a file.

You can accomplish many other file-related tasks from the Find File dialog box. You can select as many files as you want in the list, and then open, print, copy, or delete the files. The capability of working with multiple files is a powerful feature of the **F**ind File command and a great time-saver.

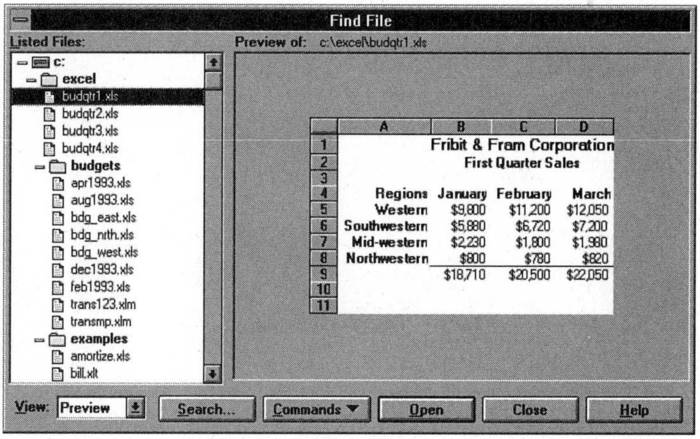

Fig. 9.6
All the files that meet the search criteria you specify are listed in the Find File dialog box.

When you save a file, you give it a file name and then decide where you want to store the saved file. As the number of files you create in Excel increases, you may want to come up with some system for organizing files. The easiest way is to set up directories on the hard disk that contain related files. For example, you might have a directory for budget workbooks and another one for sales workbooks. You also might have a directory for each of the projects on which you are working. When you save a workbook, be sure that you do so in the appropriate directory. In this way, it is easier to retrieve the workbook if you need to work with it again. For more information on working with file names and directories, refer to "Changing Drives and Directories" earlier in this chapter.

After you have decided where your files are stored, you still need to locate them when you want to work with them again. If you haven't worked with a workbook for a long time, you can easily forget its name or location when you want to reopen it. Or you may want to look over a group of related workbooks without having to open each one in Excel. You can use the **F**ind File command to bring together a list of related files or to find a specific file.

After you have found the files that match the criteria you specified, you can browse through the directories included in the search until you find the file or files with which you want to work. You can preview any file to make sure that it is the one you want and then open, print, copy, or delete the file. To act on several files at once, you can select them first and then issue one of the commands that acts on these files. You can select a group of files, for example, and then copy them to a floppy disk to back them up, or print several files at once without opening the files in Excel.

Finding Files

Before you can use the **F**ind File command to manage files, you need to find the files with which you want to work. The search can be narrow; for example, you can look for a particular file with a familiar file name. You also can search for a group of files that match whatever criteria you specify. This section shows you the ways you can search for files.

Using the Find File Command

You begin a search for files by using the **F**ile **F**ind File command. Alternatively, you can choose the **F**ind File button in the Open dialog box. To find files, you must specify the *search criteria* that **F**ind File uses to look for the files. The first time you use the **F**ind File command, Excel displays the Search dialog box so that you can describe the files or directory you want to search. After you complete the first search with **F**ind File, when you next choose the **F**ind File command, the Find File dialog box shows the list of files that match the criteria for which you last searched.

To change the found files shown in the listing, you must specify new or additional criteria and then initiate a new search in the Search dialog box (see fig. 9.7). You can limit the search to a file with a specific file name; to all Excel files that end with the extension XL*; or to all types of files, regardless of extension. To limit the scope of the search to one disk drive or to certain directories on a disk, you can specify the location for the search.

Using the **A**dvanced Search command, you can narrow the list of files that must be found (see fig. 9.8). You do this by specifying additional criteria, such as the file creation or save date, author name, summary information, or specific text strings (such as a word or phrase).

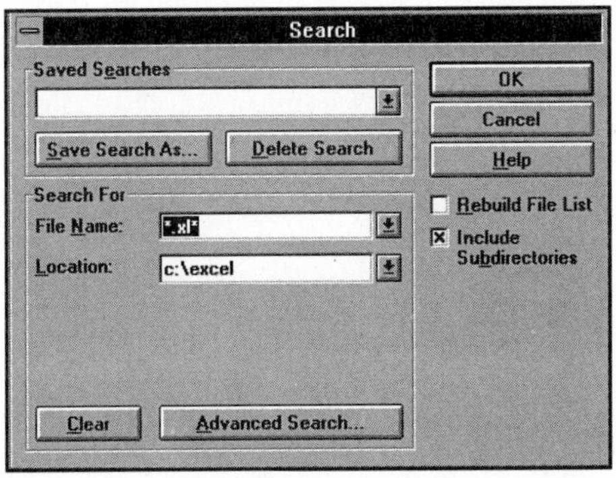

Fig. 9.7
You specify the criteria for a simple file name or directory search in the Search dialog box.

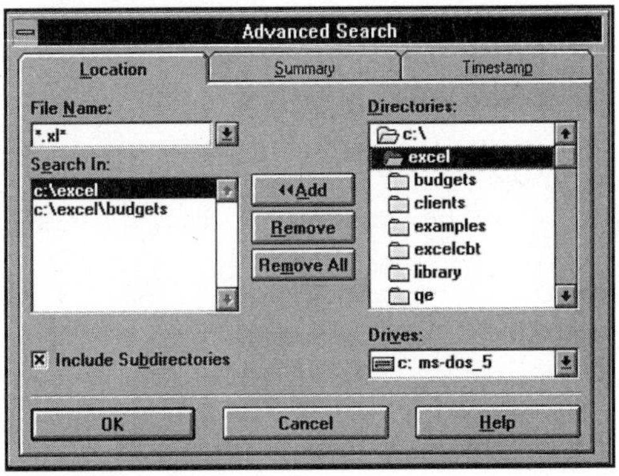

Fig. 9.8
You can enter additional search criteria in the Advanced Search dialog box.

After you specify search criteria, you initiate a new search by choosing OK in the Search dialog box. If you must cancel a search before it is completed, choose Cancel. The files meeting the new search criteria are listed in the Find File dialog box. For instructions on how to view file information and preview the files in the list, see the following section, "Viewing Workbooks and File Information," in this chapter.

Searching Different Drives or Directories

If you know where the files you are looking for are located, you can specify to search certain directories. This technique speeds up the process of finding the files because **F**ind File does not have to search the entire hard disk. For example, you may know that the files you want to find are in one or more of the subdirectories of the \EXCEL directory. In this case, you can limit the search to these subdirectories. You also can specify a different drive for a search, such as a floppy drive.

To specify the directories to search, take these steps:

1. Choose the **F**ile **F**ind File command or the **F**ind File button in the Open dialog box. The Find File dialog box appears, listing the files that meet the current search criteria (refer to fig. 9.6).

2. Choose the **S**earch button in the Find File dialog box. The Search dialog box appears (refer to fig. 9.7).

3. From the **L**ocation list, select the drive you want to search.

4. Choose the **A**dvanced Search button and select the **L**ocation tab. The Location tab in the Advanced Search dialog box is displayed (refer to fig. 9.8).

   The directories that are currently searched are listed in the S**e**arch In list.

5. To add a directory to the S**e**arch In list, select the directory in the **D**irectories box and choose the **A**dd button.

6. To remove a directory from the S**e**arch In list, select the directory in the list and choose the **R**emove button. To remove all directories from the S**e**arch In list, choose the Re**m**ove All button.

   If you are connected to a network, you can use the Net**w**ork button to connect to a network drive, and select the network drive from the Dri**v**es list. The directories for the network drive are listed in the **D**irectories list, and you can select which directories you include in the search as described in steps 5 and 6. If you aren't connected to a network, the Net**w**ork button doesn't appear.

7. To include all the subdirectories of the directories listed in the S**e**arch In list, select the Include Su**b**directories check box.

8. Choose OK in the Advanced Search dialog box, and then choose OK in the Search dialog box to begin the search.

The files matching the location criteria and other criteria specified are listed in the Find File dialog box.

Searching for Specific Files or Different File Types

By default, Excel searches for all Excel files in the specified directories (or on the entire drive if no path has been specified). However, you also can search for a specific file or different types of files. If the files are compatible with

Excel, you can open or print the files; you can copy or delete the files you find, even if they are not compatible with Excel.

To search for different file types, take these steps:

1. Choose the **F**ile **F**ind File command or the **F**ind File button in the Open dialog box. The Find File dialog box appears, listing the files that meet the current search criteria (refer to fig. 9.6).

2. Choose the **S**earch button. The Search dialog box appears (refer to fig. 9.7).

3. In the File **N**ame box, type the name of the file for which you want to search. Be sure to include the file extension.

4. To search instead for a file type, pull down the File **N**ame list and select the type of file for which you want to search.

   In the File **N**ame box, type also the extension of the file type for which you want to search. You can use wild-card characters. An asterisk (*) represents any string of characters; you can search for all files ending with the extension WK3 by typing ***.WK3**. A question mark (?) represents any one character; you can search for BUDGET?.XLS to find all files named BUDGET1.XLS, BUDGET2.XLS, BUDGET3.XLS, and so on.

   By default, Excel replaces the existing file list with a new list of files matching the current search criteria. To add the files that match the new criteria to the existing list, choose the **A**dvanced Search button and select the **S**ummary tab. Next select Add Matches to List from the **O**ptions list and choose OK.

5. Choose OK.

Searching by Summary Information or Text in the File

One of the best advantages to including summary information in all Excel files is that you can search for files by text contained in any of the summary information fields. You can add a title to a workbook, for example, and then use it to search through files. In this way, Excel enables you to override the DOS limitation of an eight-character file name. You also can search for a file based on any of the text contained in it. To learn how to add summary information to your Excel files, refer to "Saving with Summary Information To Make Workbooks Easier To Find."

To search by summary information or any text in the file, follow these steps:

1. Choose the **F**ile **F**ind File command or the **F**ind File button in the Open dialog box. The Find File dialog box appears, listing the files that meet the current search criteria (refer to fig. 9.6).

2. Choose the **S**earch button to display the Search dialog box (refer to fig. 9.7).

3. Choose the **A**dvanced Search button. The Advanced Search dialog box appears (refer to fig. 9.8).

4. Select the **S**ummary tab. The Summary tab appears (figure 9.9 shows a partially complete Summary tab).

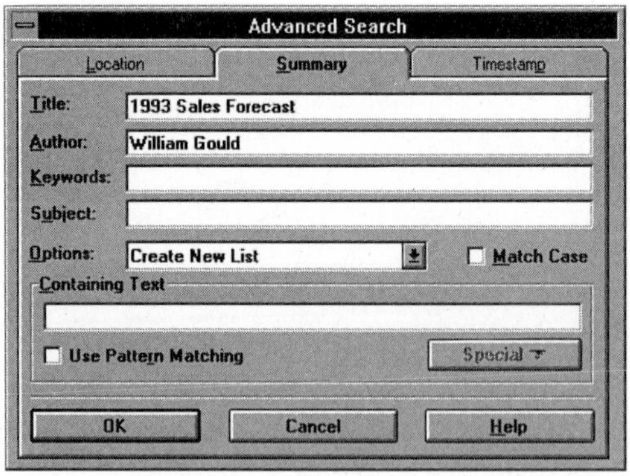

Fig. 9.9
You can use summary information to help you find files.

5. In the appropriate text boxes, type the summary information for which you want to search:

Text Box	Searches For
Title	Text you enter in the Title box
Author	Text you enter in the Author box
Keywords	Text you enter in the Keywords box
S**u**bject	Text you enter in the Subject box

6. Select **M**atch Case to match upper- and lowercase exactly.

7. To search the contents of a Excel workbook, enter the text to search for in the **C**ontaining Text box. To add special symbols or wild cards to the searched text, select the Use Patte**r**n Matching check box and choose the Sp**e**cial button to display a list of special characters. Select a character to insert in the search text.

8. From the **O**ptions list, select one of the the following options:

Option	**Description**
Create New List	Replaces the existing list.
Add Matches to List	Adds the new list to the exiting list.
Search Only in List	Searches for criteria only in the existing list. (This option doesn't apply when you search a different drive or directory.)

9. Choose OK twice.

A few rules exist for searching files by summary information or text in the file. You can type as many as 255 characters in any of the summary information fields in the **S**ummary tab (shown in fig. 9.9). You can use partial words or any combination of upper- and lowercase letters. If you type **an** or **An** in the **T**itle field, for example, you get a list of files that contains the words annual or *bank*, as well as any other files that have the letters *an* in their titles. (Select the **M**atch Case option to match upper- and lowercase exactly.) To search for a phrase, such as *sales forecast loan*, enclose it in double quotation marks, as in **"sales forecast"**. You can use wild cards in the search, and you can combine words, as the following examples show:

To Search for	**Type in the Text Box**
Any single character	? (question mark) *Example:* type **an??** to find *Andy*
Any string of characters	* (asterisk) *Example:* type **an*** to find any word that begins with the letters *an*
A phrase (such as *bank loan*)	" " (quotation marks enclosing the phrase) *Example:* type **"sales forecast"**

(continues)

To Search for	Type in the Text Box
One word or another word	, (comma) *Example:* type **sales,forecast** to find files containing *sales* or *forecast*
One word and another word	& (ampersand or space) *Example:* type **sales & forecast** or **sales forecast** to find files containing *sales* and *forecast*
Files not containing	~ (tilde) *Example:* type sales~forecast to find files containing *sales* but not *forecast*

Searching by Date Saved or Created

You can search for files based on the last date you created or saved the file. This feature is convenient, especially when used with other search criteria. You can search for files, for example, containing the title words *bank* and *letter* that were created between June 1 and June 30 of last year.

To search for files by date created or saved, take these steps:

1. Choose either the **F**ile **F**ind File command or the **F**ind File button in the Open dialog box. The Find File dialog box appears, listing the files that meet the current search criteria (refer to fig. 9.6).

2. Choose the **S**earch button to display the Search dialog box (refer to fig. 9.7).

3. Choose the **A**dvanced Search button. The Advanced Search dialog box appears (refer to fig. 9.8).

4. Select the Timestam**p** tab. The Timestamp tab appears (see fig. 9.10 for a completed Timestamp tab).

5. To search files by date last saved, in the **F**rom box type the beginning date of the range of dates for which you want to search. In the **T**o box, type the ending date. Use the format *mm/dd/yy* (for example, 6/1/93).

   You cannot search files by the dates created in Excel for Windows.

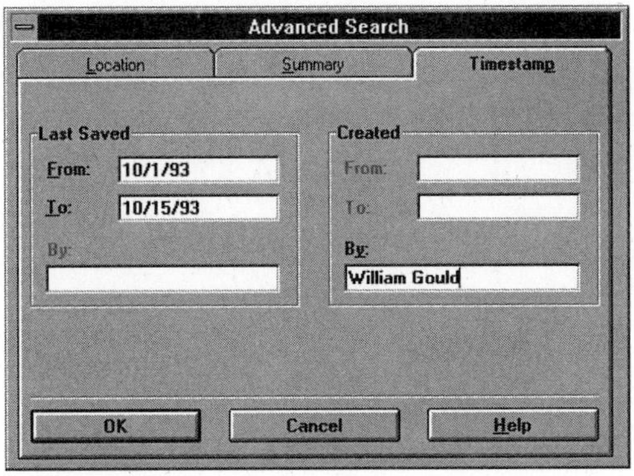

Fig. 9.10
You use the Timestamp tab to date criteria for a search.

6. You can specify the author of the file by typing the name in either the **B**y or the B**y** box.

7. Choose OK.

Saving Search Criteria

If you have entered a set of search criteria and you want to reuse it for future searches, you can save the criteria with a name. When you want to reuse the criteria, you select the named set of criteria from the Search dialog box and then initiate a new search.

To save search criteria, take these steps:

1. Choose either the **F**ile **F**ind File command or the **F**ind File button in the Open dialog box. The Find File dialog box appears, listing the files that meet the current search criteria (refer to fig. 9.6).

2. Set up the search criteria you want, as outlined in the preceding sections.

3. Choose the **S**ave Search As button in the Search dialog box. The Save Search As dialog box appears (see figure 9.11 to see the dialog box with text filled in).

Fig. 9.11
You can name a set of search criteria, save it, and reuse it.

4. In the **S**earch Name text box, type a name for the search criteria.

5. Choose OK.

6. To start a search with these criteria, choose OK.

To reuse saved search criteria, follow these steps:

1. Select the set of criteria you want to use from the Saved S**e**arches list in the Search dialog box.

2. Choose OK to begin the search using the saved criteria.

The name of the set of search criteria used in the search appears at the top of the listed files.

Viewing Workbooks and File Information

After you find the files with which you want to work, you can sort the list of found files and view file information or preview a file. Viewing file information and previewing files can help you manage your workbooks. You can preview a file, for example, before you open or print it so that you know you are working with the right workbook. You also can view file information to find out which is the most recent version of a workbook on which you are working.

Using Find File To View Workbooks and File Information

After you complete a search by using the criteria you specify, all the files matching the criteria are listed in the **L**isted Files box in the Find File dialog box (see fig. 9.12). The matching files are listed by directory, starting with the root directory. Each directory that contains files that match the criteria is represented by a folder in the **L**isted Files box. The name of the directory appears on the right side of the folder icon. Closed folders have a plus sign (+) beside them and can be opened to display the files in the folder. To do this, click the plus sign or use the arrow keys to move the highlight to the folder and press Enter. Open folders are displayed with a minus sign (–) next to them. To close a folder, click the minus sign or use the arrow keys to move the highlight to the folder and press Enter.

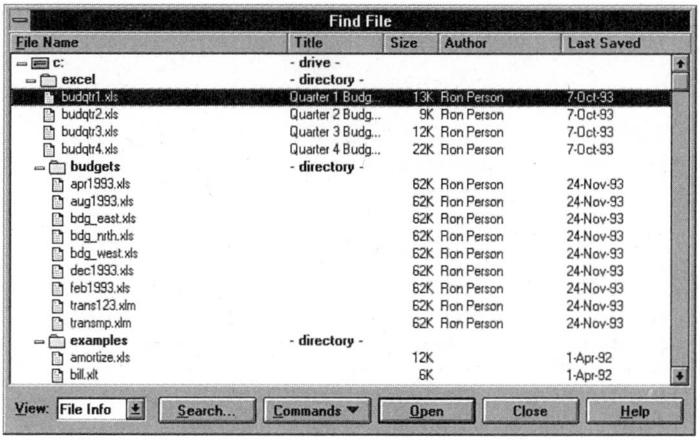

Fig. 9.12
The Find File dialog box displays a list of files matching your search criteria.

Before you can view a file or its information, you must select the file. To select the file, click the file name with the mouse or press the Tab key until the focus (the dotted lines) is in the box with the list of files. Then use the up- and down-arrow keys to select the file.

The rest of this section describes how to sort a list of files, preview a file, and view file information.

Sorting File Lists

If the list of files in a directory is long, you may want to sort the listed files. You can sort by file name, author, size, creation date, or date last saved. You also can sort by using the name of the person who most recently saved the file. You can list the files by file name or by title entered in the Summary Info dialog box (refer to "Searching by Summary Information or Text in the File" earlier in this chapter).

To sort a list of files, take these steps:

1. Choose the **F**ile **F**ind File command or the **F**ind File button in the Open dialog box.

2. Choose the **C**ommands button in the Find File dialog box. Then choose Sor**t**ing. The Options dialog box is displayed (see fig. 9.13).

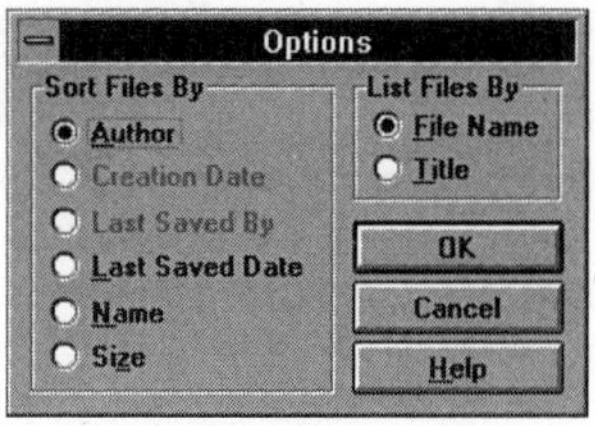

Fig. 9.13
In the Options dialog box, you can select how you want to sort and list files.

3. In the Sort Files By list, select one of the following sorting options:

Option	How Files Are Listed
Author	Alphabetically by author
Creation Date	Not available in Microsoft Excel for Windows
Last Saved By	Not available in Microsoft Excel for Windows
Last Saved Date	Chronologically by the date files are saved (most recent date first)
Name	Alphabetically by name (default choice)
Size	Numerically by file size

4. Select one of the following List Files By options:

Option	How Files Are Listed
Filename	By file name
Title	By title used in the Summary Info for each file

5. Choose OK.

The files in all the directories in the Find File dialog box are sorted.

Previewing Workbooks

Among the most useful features in the Find File dialog box is the capability of previewing a workbook. When you make decisions about what files you want to open, copy, print, or delete, it is helpful to preview files' contents quickly, without having to open them.

To preview a file, take these steps:

1. Choose **F**ind File from the **F**ile menu or the **F**ind File button in the Open dialog box.

2. From the **V**iew list in the Find File dialog box, select Preview (see fig. 9.14).

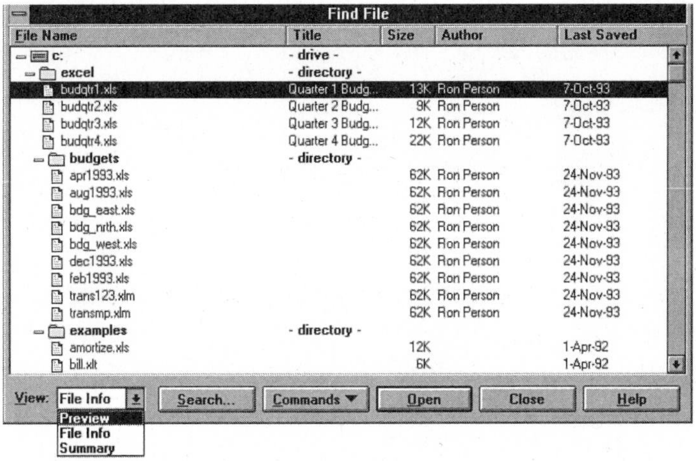

Fig. 9.14
You can view files listed in the Find File dialog box with one of three methods.

3. Select the file you want to preview from the list of files.

   A reduced view of the file contents is displayed in the **P**review Of box (see fig 9.15).

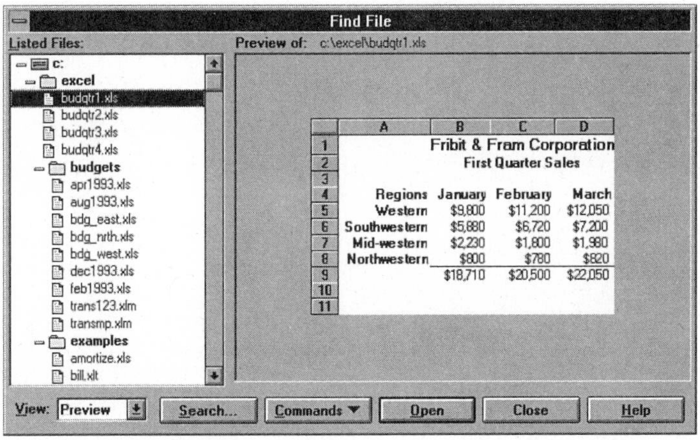

Fig. 9.15
You can view the contents of a file without opening it.

If you select a non-Excel file, it is converted, providing the necessary converter has been installed. You can run the Excel Setup program to install additional converters (see Chapter 39, "Using Excel with DOS and Mainframe Applications").

Note

Selecting Preview as the view in the Find File dialog box can slow you down if you don't have a fast computer because the Preview area is redrawn each time you select a new document from the file list. Use the File Info or Summary view to speed up things.

Viewing File Information

You can view information for a file rather than view the file's contents. When you select the File Info view, information for each file in the file list is displayed next to the name of the file. You see different information, depending on how you have sorted the file list. For example, if you sort by name, the title, size, author, and date last saved are displayed. If you sort by creation date, the Last Saved field is replaced by the Created field.

To view file information, follow these steps:

1. Choose the **F**ile **F**ind File command or the **F**ind File button in the Open dialog box.

2. Select File Info in the **V**iew list at the bottom of the Find File dialog box (refer to fig. 9.14).

The file information for each file in the list is displayed in columns adjacent to the list (see fig. 9.16). You can change the width of any of the columns. To do this, move the mouse pointer over the right border line of the column heading for the column whose width you want to change. When the mouse pointer changes to a double-headed arrow, drag the border to a new position.

Viewing Summary Information

If you chose to add summary information to Excel files (refer to "Saving with Summary Information To Make Workbooks Easier To Find"), you can view this information in the Find File dialog box. The information can include title, author name, subject, keywords, and comments you enter in the Summary Info dialog box. The summary information automatically includes other statistics about the file, including the creation date, date last saved, and size of the file. Therefore, even if you don't add summary information when you save the file, you see some information when you view the summary information.

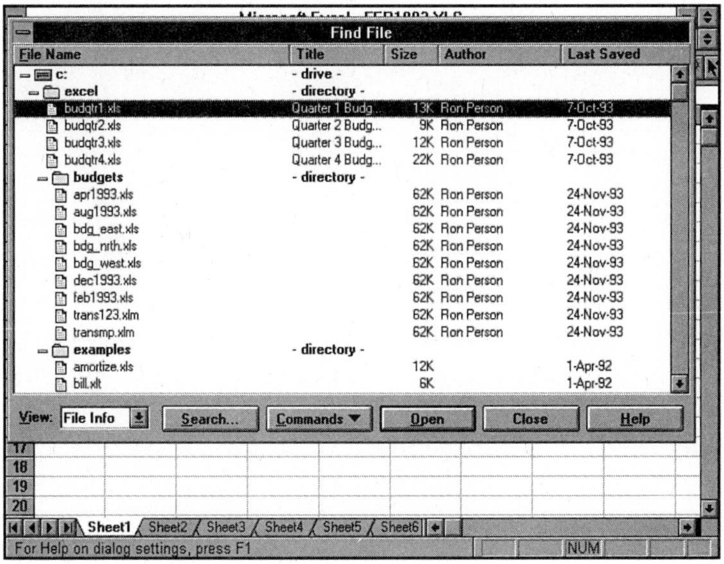

Fig. 9.16
You can use the File Info view to view information about the files listed in the Find File dialog box.

To view summary information, take these steps:

1. Choose the **F**ile **F**ind File command or the **F**ind File button in the Open dialog box.

2. Select Summary in the **V**iew list at the bottom of the Find File dialog box (refer to fig. 9.14).

The summary information and document statistics are displayed for the file selected in the **L**isted Files box (see fig. 9.17).

Editing and Adding Summary Information

If you didn't add summary information to an Excel file when you created or saved it (refer to "Saving with Summary Information To Make Workbooks Easier To Find" previously in this chapter), or if you want to edit the summary information for a file, you can do so from the Find File dialog box.

Tip
If you already opened a document, you can view and edit summary information by choosing the **F**ile Summary **I**nfo command.

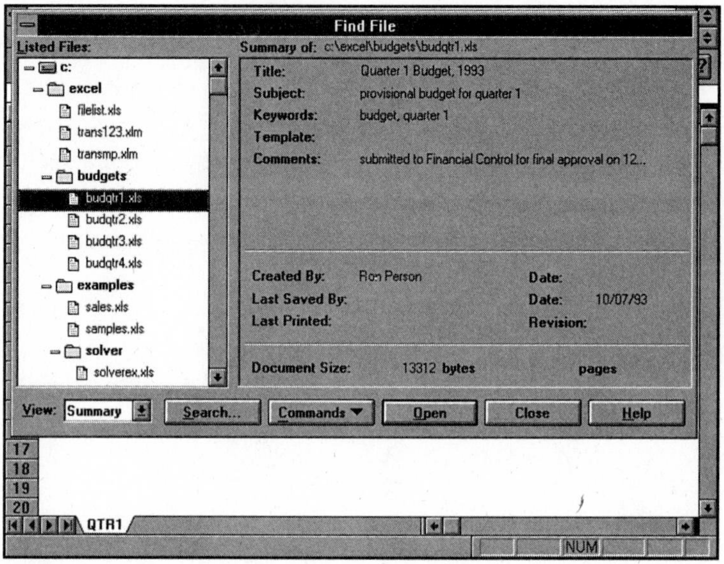

Fig. 9.17
You can view the summary information for a file in the Find File dialog box.

To edit or add summary information, take these steps:

1. Choose the **F**ile **F**ind File command or the **F**ind File button in the Open dialog box. The Find File dialog box appears.

2. From the **L**isted Files box, select the file with which you want to work.

3. Choose the **C**ommands button, and then choose **S**ummary from the submenu.

4. Fill in or edit any of the fields. Include as much information (up to 255 characters) or as little as you want.

5. Choose OK.

For Related Information

■ "Viewing a Window through Multiple Panes," p. 544

Note

Use the Summary Info box to attach a descriptive title to all the Excel documents. Then list the files by title in the Find File dialog box. This makes it easier to identify your files in the file list, and helps you work around the eight-character limitation for DOS file names.

Working with Files

After you find the files that meet the search criteria you specify, you can accomplish many tasks with these files by using the commands in the Find File dialog box. You can open, print, copy, or delete a file or group of selected files—all from this dialog box. Selecting more than one file at a time from the **L**isted Files list is a tremendous time-saver. For example, if you want to print several files at once, you can find all of them with the **F**ind File command. Then you can select all the files you want to print, and issue one print command. This approach is much simpler and quicker than opening each of the files, one by one, from within Excel and printing them separately. You can use the same approach to copy or delete groups of files. This capability, along with being able to preview the contents of a file without having to open it, greatly facilitates the process of managing your files.

Selecting Files with Which To Work

Before you issue various commands to manage files, you need to select one or more of the files with which you want to work. To select a file with the mouse, click the name of the file you want; or press and hold down the Ctrl key and click multiple file names (see fig. 9.18). If you want to select several sequential files, press and hold down the Shift key and then click the first and last file you want. (Press and hold down the Ctrl key and click a second time to deselect any file you select by mistake.)

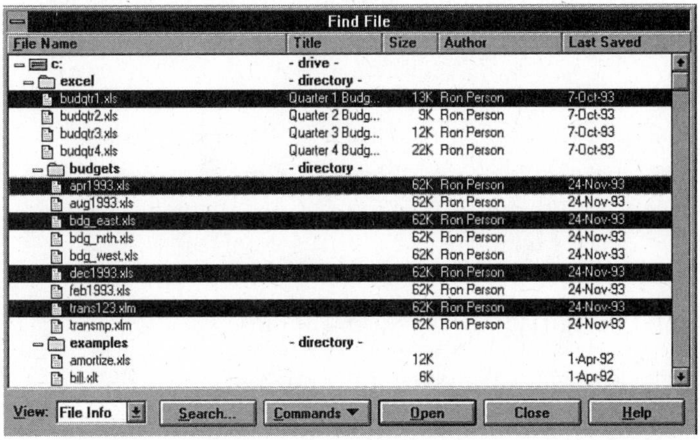

Fig. 9.18
Multiple files selected in the file list.

To select a file with the keyboard, press the Tab key until the focus (the dotted line) is in the **L**isted Files box. Then use the up- or down-arrow key to move to the file you want to select. To select multiple files that are not contiguous, press Shift+F8. Then move to each file you want to select, and press the space bar. Press Shift+F8 again to turn off the multiple-selection mode. To select multiple contiguous files, press the up- or down-arrow key to select the first file. Next, press and hold down Shift and then press the up- or down-arrow key to extend the selection.

Opening Found Files

After you use the **F**ind File command to find and select a file, you can open it from the Find File dialog box. You can also open more than one file.

To find and open documents, take these steps:

1. Choose the **F**ile **F**ind File command or the Open dialog box.
2. Select the file or files you want to open.
3. Choose the **O**pen button.
4. If you want to prevent yourself from modifying any of the files you open, choose the **C**ommands button. Then choose the Open **R**ead Only command from the submenu.

When you choose the **O**pen button, all files open, each in a separate document window. For more information on working with multiple workbooks, refer to Chapter 3, "Navigating and Selecting in a Workbook."

Printing Found Files

You can use the **F**ile **P**rint command to print the open workbook. If you want to print several workbooks with the same printing parameters at once, however, use the **F**ind File command to first find and then print the files.

To print documents from the Find File dialog box:

1. Choose the **F**ile **F**ind File command or the Open dialog box.
2. Select one or more files you want to print.
3. Choose the **C**ommands button and then the **P**rint command from the submenu. The Print dialog box appears.
4. Select the printing options.
5. Choose OK.

If you select multiple documents to print, they all print with the parameters you identify in the Print dialog box. For more information on printing, see Chapter 11, "Printing Worksheets."

Note

If you routinely need to print the same set of worksheets, such as the worksheets you use in a report, set up a search criteria set that finds only these files. Then save the search criteria set. When you need to print these documents, select the set of criteria from the Saved Searches list. Next, run the search and select all the found files. Then issue the **P**rint command.

Copying Found Files

You can use **F**ind File to copy selected files from one location to another. Similarly, you can use a combination of techniques to move files. You must first copy them to their new location and then delete them from their original location.

To find and copy files, follow these steps:

1. Choose the **F**ile **F**ind File command or the Open dialog box.

2. Select one or more files you want to copy.

3. Choose the **C**ommands button, and then the **C**opy command from the submenu. The Copy dialog box appears (see fig. 9.19).

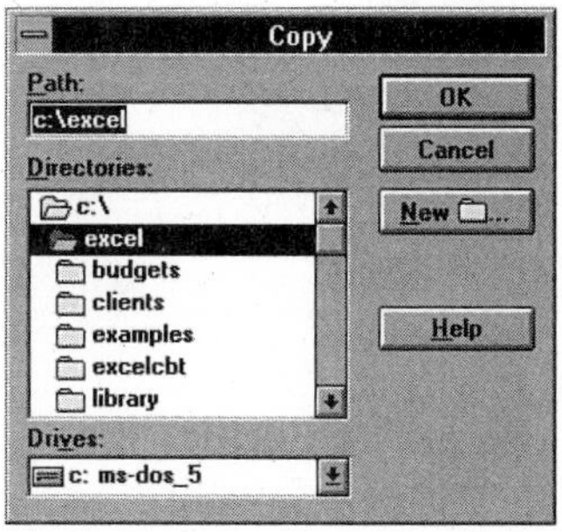

Fig. 9.19
You can copy files to another location by using the Copy dialog box.

4. If the destination is on another drive, select the drive from the Dri**v**es list.

5. If you want to create a new directory to copy the files to, select the directory you want the new directory to be a subdirectory of, and choose the **N**ew button. Type the name for the new directory and choose OK.

6. In the **D**irectories box, select the directory to which you want to copy the file(s), or type the path name in the **P**ath text box.

7. Choose OK.

Files are copied to a new location with their original name and extension. Using the **F**ind File command to copy files is a good way to make backups on a floppy disk.

For Related Information

- "Previewing the Document," p. 389
- "Printing," p. 395

Deleting Found Files

To find and delete files, take the following steps:

1. Choose the **F**ile **F**ind File command or the Open dialog box.

2. Select the files you want to delete.

3. Choose the **C**ommands button and then the **D**elete command from the submenu. A dialog box asks you to confirm the deletion.

4. Choose **Y**es to delete the files, or choose **N**o if you don't want to erase them. (Select **H**elp to learn more about deleting files.)

From Here...

Now that you learned the basic skills you need to create, open, save, close, and find workbook files, you can look through the following chapters to learn more about working with workbooks:

- Chapter 10, "Formatting Worksheets." You learn how to format your worksheets to get them to look the way you want.

- Chapter 11, "Printing Worksheets." You learn how to produce professional-quality printouts of your worksheets.

- Chapter 16, "Managing the Worksheet Display." You learn how to control the on-screen appearance of your worksheets; how to use the View Manager to save views of your worksheets; and how to work with multiple panes, multiple windows, and multiple workbooks.

Chapter 10

Formatting Worksheets

In this chapter, you learn how to:

- Format with Autoformats
- Copy and paste formats
- Change character fonts, sizes, styles, and colors
- Format numbers, dates, times, rows, and columns
- Add colors, patterns, and borders
- Apply multiple formats
- Protect sheets and workbooks
- Format sheets in a workbook

Appearance isn't everything, but it counts for a great deal when you need to communicate with confidence. Your work may be excellent, but it may make a poor impression if important information is obscured or has a slipshod appearance.

Excel has formatting features that make reports, worksheets, and databases easier to read and understand. One of these powerful features is the capability to use TrueType fonts. With these fonts, you can see on-screen how a font will look when printed. Another useful formatting feature is autoformatting, which enables you to format tables and reports in one step with preset combinations of numeric formats, alignments, borders, and shading.

In addition to changing column widths or selecting preset numeric and date formats, you can create your own numeric and date formats; change the height of rows; change the font, size, color, and style of characters; control the placement of text within cells; hide columns, rows, and grid lines; and shade, color, and border ranges. You also can use styles to simplify your formatting tasks and can protect portions of your document that you don't want changed. With Excel, your printed worksheet or database can look as though it just came from the typesetter. You can drive your point across with emphasis and elegance.

Formatting with Autoformats

Excel's AutoFormat feature lets you create great-looking documents with the click of a few buttons. Even if you are a first-time Excel user, you can create beautifully formatted reports, tables, and lists without resorting to complex formatting operations. If you are an advanced Excel user, you also will appreciate the amount of time you can save by using AutoFormat. Figures 10.1, 10.2, and 10.3 show a few of the 16 formats available through the use of a single F**o**rmat **A**utoFormat selection.

Fig. 10.1
The Simple autoformat gives this table a clean, professional look.

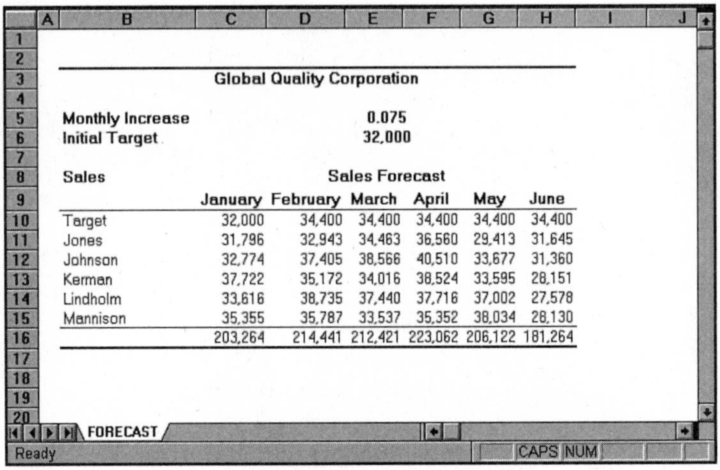

Global Quality Corporation

Monthly Increase 0.075
Initial Target 32,000

Sales — Sales Forecast

Sales	January	February	March	April	May	June
Target	32,000	34,400	34,400	34,400	34,400	34,400
Jones	31,796	32,943	34,463	36,560	29,413	31,645
Johnson	32,774	37,405	38,566	40,510	33,677	31,360
Kerman	37,722	35,172	34,016	38,524	33,595	28,151
Lindholm	33,616	38,735	37,440	37,716	37,002	27,578
Mannison	35,355	35,787	33,537	35,352	38,034	28,130
	203,264	214,441	212,421	223,062	206,122	181,264

Fig. 10.2
The Classic autoformats add visual impact to a table.

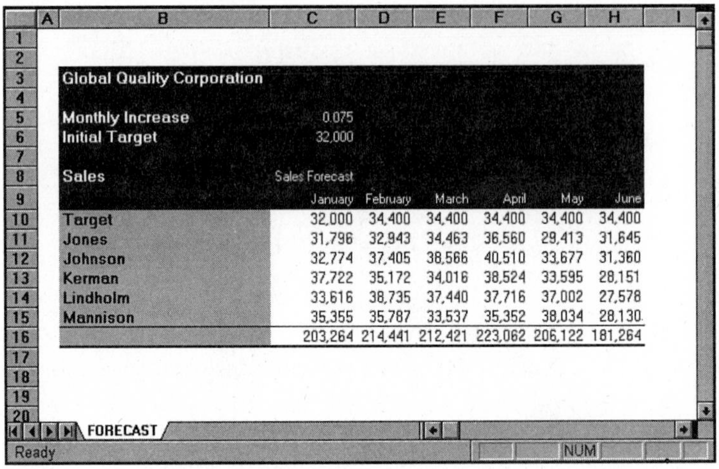

Global Quality Corporation

Monthly Increase 0.075
Initial Target 32,000

Sales — Sales Forecast

Sales	January	February	March	April	May	June
Target	32,000	34,400	34,400	34,400	34,400	34,400
Jones	31,796	32,943	34,463	36,560	29,413	31,645
Johnson	32,774	37,405	38,566	40,510	33,677	31,360
Kerman	37,722	35,172	34,016	38,524	33,595	28,151
Lindholm	33,616	38,735	37,440	37,716	37,002	27,578
Mannison	35,355	35,787	33,537	35,352	38,034	28,130
	203,264	214,441	212,421	223,062	206,122	181,264

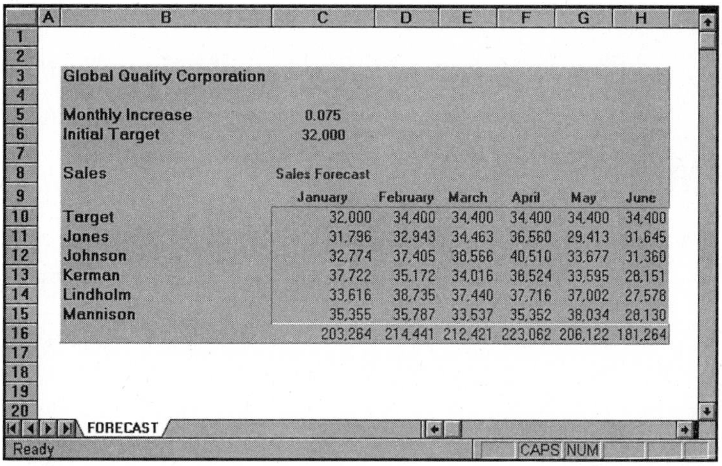

Fig. 10.3
Add another dimension to your tables with one of the 3-D Effects autoformats.

Formatting a Table Automatically

With AutoFormat, you can apply preset formats to the labels, backgrounds, lines, totals, and numbers in Excel tables. These formats are designed for tables of information in which labels run down the left column and across the top rows. SUM( ) functions or totals are expected in the bottom row or right column. These preset formats include formatting for numbers, borders, font, pattern, alignment, column width, and row height. You have the option of selecting which of these formatting elements is used when you format with the F**o**rmat **A**utoFormat command.

To apply an autoformat to a table, follow these steps:

1. Select the range containing the table. If the table is a block of contiguous cells surrounded by clear rows and columns, select a single cell within the table.

2. Choose the F**o**rmat **A**utoFormat command. The AutoFormat dialog box appears, as shown in figure 10.4.

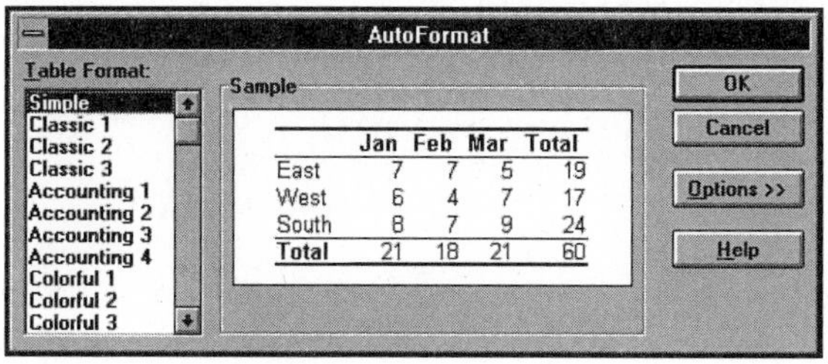

Fig. 10.4
You can select and preview from among 16 formats in the AutoFormat dialog box.

3. Select the format you want from the **T**able Format list.

4. Review the Sample box to see whether this table format is the one you want. If not, return to step 3 and select a different table format.

5. Choose OK.

If the format does not appear as you expected, immediately choose the **E**dit **U**ndo AutoFormat command to restore the table to its previous format.

After you format a table with AutoFormat, the formatting in the cells is the same as if you had applied normal formatting. Use the techniques described throughout this chapter to change cell formatting to enhance or remove the formatting applied by AutoFormat.

Using Only Part of an Autoformat

You don't need to accept the AutoFormat formats exactly as they are. You can decide which types of formatting in the autoformat are applied to your table. This capability can be useful, for example, if you have formatted with different colors or have applied custom numeric or date formats that you do not want autoformatting to change.

To accept or reject different parts of autoformatting, follow these steps:

1. Select the range or a cell within a table.

2. Choose the F**o**rmat **A**utoFormat command.

3. Select a format from the **T**able Format list.

4. Choose the **O**ptions button. The dialog box expands to include a Formats to Apply group of options as shown in figure 10.5.

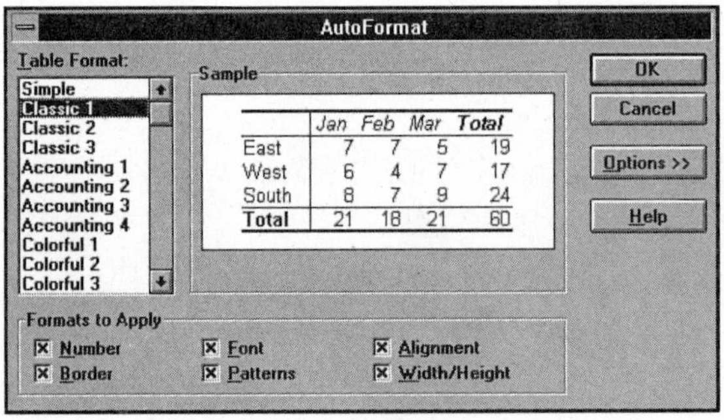

Fig. 10.5
Choose the **O**ptions button when you need to apply only parts of an autoformat.

5. Clear formats in the Formats to Apply group that you do not want applied.

6. Review your changes in the Sample box.

7. Choose OK or press Enter.

Note

Changes in a format after using the **O**ptions button *do not* carry over to the next time you use AutoFormat. Make the changes every time to modify the AutoFormat default settings.

Tips about Autoformatting

If the autoformats do not produce the result you need, try creating styles to format your tables or rows or columns within a table. *Styles* are collections of formats that you assign to a name. You can apply all the formats at one time by selecting the style's name from a list. You might need a combination of styles—one for the table body, one for cells in the total at the bottom of a table, and another for totals at the right edge of a table.

If you need to manually apply a format to a table before you apply the autoformat, there is an easy way to select the entire table with a single keystroke. Select a cell within the table, and then press F5. This is the same as choosing the **E**dit **G**o To command, choosing the **S**pecial button, and selecting the Current **R**egion option. For this technique to work, the table must be surrounded by a *moat* of blank cells on all sides.

Troubleshooting

Wide titles within the table cause the column widths to be too wide when the autoformat is applied.

If you include wide titles within the formatted area the width may cause automatic column-width adjustments to make columns too wide. To create wide titles that do not affect automatic column-width adjustments, center the title across selected cells, as described in this chapter's section "Centering Text across Cells." You also can choose the **O**ptions button in the AutoFormat dialog box and deselect the **W**idth/Height option. This keeps row height and column width from changing.

For Related Information

■ "Creating Styles," p. 356

Using TrueType Fonts

Windows 3.1 includes *TrueType* technology. This technology enables your computer and printer to display and print a variety of *fonts* that display on-screen almost exactly as they print from the printer—no matter what printer you have. A wide variety of fonts come preinstalled with Windows 3.1, and you can add additional TrueType fonts to your system by way of third-party font software. With TrueType fonts, it's easy to produce great-looking documents from Excel!

Understanding Screen, Printer, and TrueType Fonts

Windows applications use screen fonts and printer fonts. In Windows 3.1, you have the choice of using many screen and printer fonts.

Screen fonts are used to display characters on-screen. *Printer fonts* are used to print your spreadsheets and charts. Some laser and dot-matrix printers come with built-in sets of printer fonts that can be stored in permanent memory in the printer. You also may be able to plug in cartridges containing printer fonts. Some printers contain PostScript, an application that generates fonts of different styles and sizes. And some printers have sets of fonts downloaded to the printer's memory from a computer.

Although you may be using a built-in printer font to print your spreadsheets, a separate screen font is used to display the characters on-screen. When you installed your printer in Windows, a set of screen fonts to match your printer should have been installed. These screen fonts represent your printer fonts so that what you see on-screen is close to what prints. Screen fonts are limited to certain styles and sizes, however, so not all screen representations match the printed results.

When you choose the F**o**rmat C**e**lls command and select the Font tab, the fonts available with your printer are listed in the **F**ont list with printer icons next to them (see fig. 10.6). After you select a new font from the **F**ont list, read the description of the font below the Preview box. The description explains the font you have selected and how it affects printing.

Screen fonts that do not match any font in your printer also can be used in your worksheets or charts. Because the printer doesn't have a matching font, however, Windows selects a similar type and size of font when you print. Occasionally, the printer font may be close; often, it may be very different. Screen fonts that do not match a printer font appear in the **F**ont list without an icon.

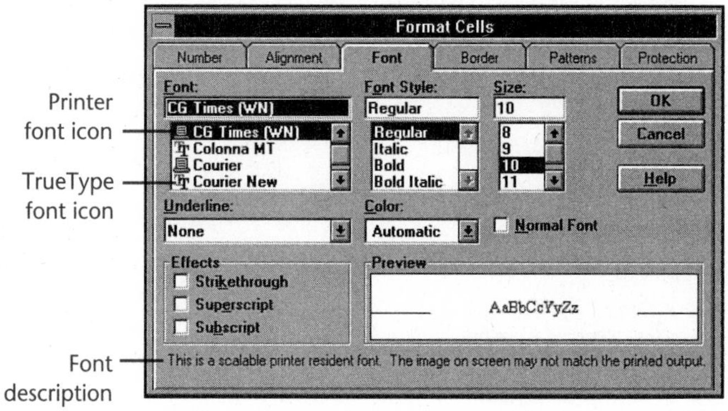

Fig. 10.6
Printer fonts appear with a printer icon and a description.

With *TrueType fonts,* the character shapes, sizes, and styles for both the screen and the printer are generated as they are needed. Because they are generated by the same application and because Windows knows the type of screen and printer you are using, what you see on-screen is very close to what prints. TrueType fonts appear in the **F**ont list of the Font dialog box preceded by a TT icon. TrueType fonts give you a wide range of sizes and styles, and you can purchase additional typefaces designed for TrueType. The disadvantage is that the time needed to create the screen fonts and download the characters slows system performance slightly. This slowdown is noticeable only on older systems.

Enabling TrueType Fonts

A basic set of TrueType fonts is installed automatically for you during the installation of Windows 3.1 or later. Some applications, such as CorelDRAW!, install additional TrueType fonts. To make sure that you have these fonts available for applications such as Excel, you need to enable TrueType fonts. If the **F**ont list in the Font dialog box shows the TT icons with the font names Arial, Courier New, Symbol, and Times New Roman, you have TrueType fonts enabled. If the list does not show these fonts, you need to enable TrueType.

To enable TrueType fonts, follow these steps:

1. Open the Control Panel from the Main group window in the Program Manager.

2. Start the Fonts application by double-clicking the Fonts icon or selecting the icon with the arrow keys and pressing Enter. The Fonts dialog box appears (see fig. 10.7).

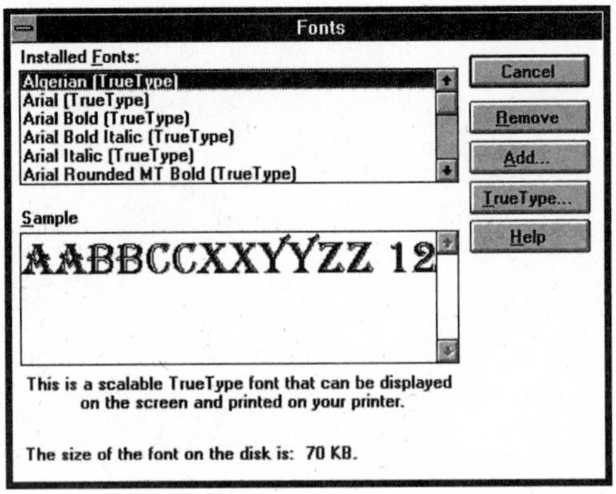

Fig. 10.7
You can view the installed fonts and enable TrueType with the Fonts program from the Main group.

3. Choose the **T**rueType button. The TrueType dialog box appears.

4. Select the **E**nable TrueType Fonts check box.

5. Select the **S**how Only TrueType Fonts in Application check box if you want to see only TrueType fonts and not screen or printer fonts in the **F**ont list.

6. Choose OK.

7. If you changed the setting for the **E**nable TrueType Fonts check box, another dialog box appears. Choose the **D**on't Restart Now button if you want to return to your Windows applications to finish work and save documents. Choose the **R**estart Now button if you want to restart Windows immediately. (Excel asks whether you want to save any changed worksheets.) Keep in mind that changing the **E**nable TrueType Fonts check box does not take effect until you exit and restart Windows.

Tips about TrueType Fonts

There are numerous software packages available that let you add new TrueType fonts to your system. You can find font packages that range from the serious (with a variety of fonts that work well in business documents) to the whimsical (with "fun" fonts for special occasions) and everything in-between. Remember, when you add new TrueType fonts to Windows, they're available for all of your Windows applications—including Excel.

If your system includes a Hewlett-Packard LaserJet printer, you may want to invest in the Windows Printing System from Microsoft. This is a kit that consists of a special cartridge to plug into the front of your LaserJet, along with a special software program that you install and run from Windows. The software program replaces the Windows Print Manager, and gives you additional control over the printing process. The cartridge includes 79 different TrueType fonts. When you use the Windows Printing System, you can actually speed up the Windows printing process!

Troubleshooting

The printer doesn't print the right fonts.

There are two common causes for this problem. First, you may not have the same fonts installed for both your screen display and your printer; check your font setup to make sure the fonts you've chosen are actually installed for printing. This problem may also occur when you try to print a document created on another PC; it's possible that the original PC had fonts installed that aren't on the second PC. If this is the case, you'll need to change the fonts in your document to match the fonts installed for your current printer.

For Related Information

- "Setting Up Your Printer," p. 371
- "Determining Fonts and Point Sizes for Worksheets," p. 638

Copying and Pasting Formats

While you can always start from scratch by changing the formatting of particular cells, Excel offers an easy way to reuse formats you've already created. With the Format Painter tool, you can copy formats from one cell to another with the click of a mouse button.

Understanding the Format Painter Button

The Format Painter button is designed to let you pick up formatting information from a selected cell or range and apply that formatting to another cell or group of cells. All formats attached to the selected cells are copied, including number, text, background, and border formats.

Using the Format Painter Button

To use the Format Painter button to copy information from a single cell, follow these steps:

1. Select the cell you want to copy from (the source cell).

2. Click the Format Painter button on the toolbar. A "paintbrush" picture is added to your normal on-screen pointer.

3. Select the cell or group of cells you want to receive the new format (the destination cells) by dragging the on-screen pointer over the cells while pressing the mouse button. As you *paint* over the selected cells, they automatically receive the formatting from the source cell.

When you release the mouse button, the on-screen pointer returns to normal and the paint operation is complete.

To copy information from a range of cells to another range of cells, follow these steps:

1. Select the source range by dragging your mouse across the selected cells while pressing the mouse button.

2. Click the Format Painter tool on the toolbar.

3. Select the first cell in the destination range and release the mouse button.

The new range now appears with the formatting of the source range.

Changing Character Fonts, Sizes, Styles, and Colors

You see different character fonts and styles every day. Fonts are the various typefaces used in printed materials. Font heights are measured in points, and there are 72 points per inch. Fonts also appear in different styles: plain, bold, italic, underline, and strikethrough. With Excel, you also can change font colors, which appear on-screen. If you have a color printer, you can print these colors.

Note

Technically, the words "font" and "typeface" are not exactly the same—although, for our purposes, it's safe to use the terms interchangeably. Figures 10.8, 10.9, and 10.10 show some of the different fonts, sizes, and styles available in Excel 5 with TrueType.

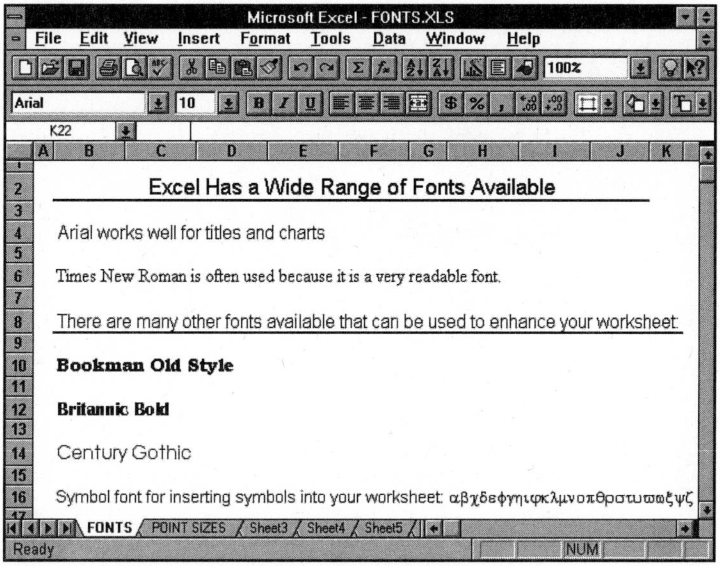

Fig. 10.8 You can select from a range of fonts in Excel.

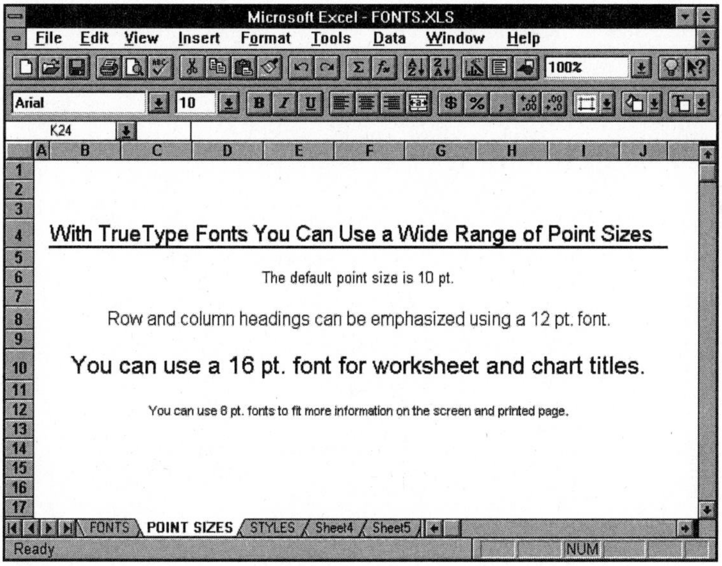

Fig. 10.9 TrueType fonts allow you to use a wide range of point sizes.

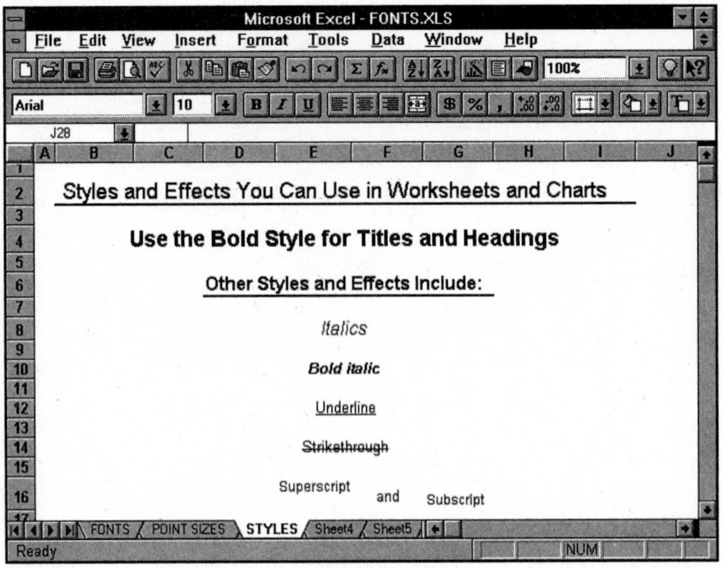

Fig. 10.10
You can use different font styles to emphasize parts of your worksheets.

Excel can use up to 256 different fonts on a worksheet. If you use more than a few fonts per worksheet, however, your worksheet may look like a ransom note made from assorted magazine clippings.

You can use one of three methods to change the appearance of your data: a button on a toolbar, a menu command, or a shortcut key.

See "Applying Multiple Formats at One Time" later in this chapter to learn how to consolidate several formatting options into a single style.

Formatting All Characters in a Cell or Range

In most cases, you want to select a cell or range of cells and format all of their contents with the same font, style, and size.

Tip
To format quickly, select the cells, and then click the *right* mouse button to display the shortcut menu. Choose the Format Cells command, and then click the tab you want.

To change the appearance of characters within a cell or range, follow these steps:

1. Select the cell, range, or multiple ranges.
2. Choose the Format Cells command. The Format Cells dialog box shown in figure 10.11 appears.

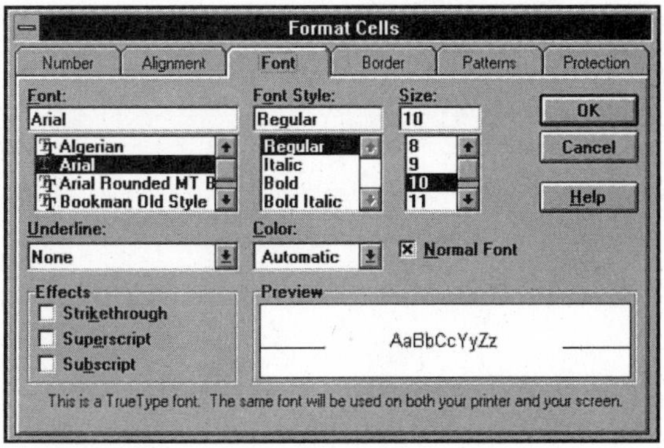

Fig. 10.11
From the Font tab of the Format Cells dialog box, you can change the appearance of individual cells.

3. Select the Font tab if it is not already on top.
4. From the **F**ont list, select the font.
5. From the F**o**nt Style list, select the font style.
6. From the **S**ize list, select the point size. Remember that approximately 72 points equal one inch of height.
7. From the **U**nderline list, select the style of underline. You can select underlines of None, Single, Double, Single Accounting, and Double Accounting.

8. From the **C**olor list, select a color. Use Automatic for black-and-white printers.
9. From the Effects group, select any combination of Stri**k**ethrough, Sup**e**rscript, or Su**b**script check boxes.
10. Check the Preview box to see if the sample text appears as you want. If it does not, return to step 4 and select different options.
11. Choose OK or press Enter.

To return the selected cells to the default font style and size, use the same procedure and select the **N**ormal Font check box.

Tip
To quickly apply a font selection, a size, or character formatting, see "Formatting Cells or Characters with Toolbars" later in this chapter.

Formatting Selected Characters in a Cell

You can change the appearance of part of the text within a cell just as easily as changing the appearance of a cell or range of cells. Formatting selected characters in a cell can be useful for emphasis on specific words, titles, or in cells containing wrapped text, as shown in figures 10.12 and 10.13.

EXCEL 5

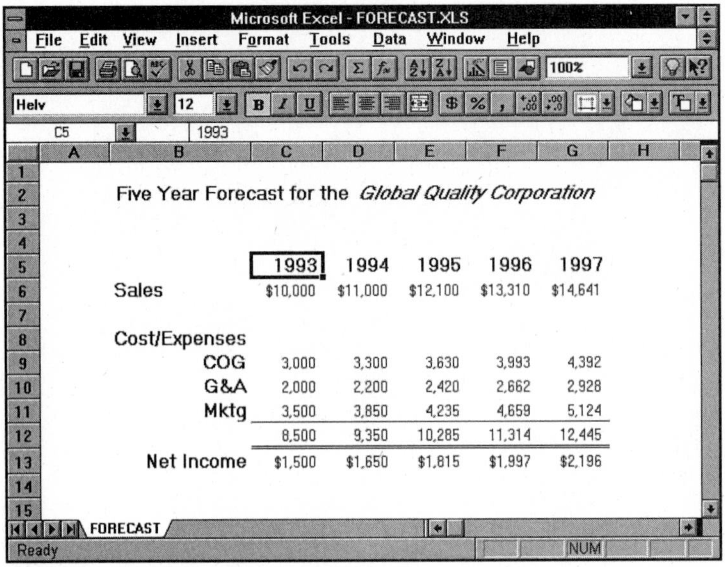

Fig. 10.12
Format selected characters in a title for additional emphasis.

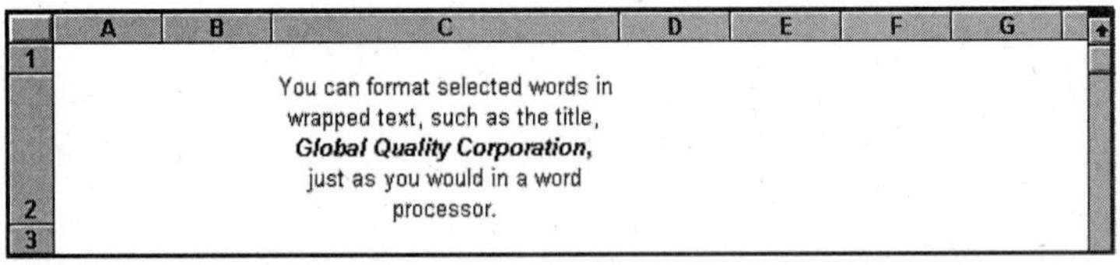

Fig. 10.13
Format characters in a cell as though they were in a word processor.

To change the appearance of individual characters within a cell, follow these steps:

1. Select the cell containing the text you want to change.
2. Select the text in the formula bar that you want to change by dragging across it with the mouse or by pressing Shift and the right- or left-arrow key.
3. Choose the F**o**rmat C**e**lls command.
4. Select the Font tab.
5. Select the font appearance you want.
6. Choose OK.

Tip
Access a cell's contents by using the mouse or pressing F2. When you press F2, you can edit cell contents directly in the worksheet cell.

Formatting Cells or Characters with Toolbars

The toolbars give you quick access to frequently used formatting commands. To use a formatting button, select the cell or range you want to format, or select the text in a text box or button. Then click the appropriate formatting button. When a button is turned on, the button appears depressed. When you click a depressed button, you turn off the button—and the button returns to the normal *up* position.

The Formatting toolbar contains many formatting buttons, including Font, Size, Bold, Italic, and Underline. Figure 10.14 shows the formatting buttons that are available. You can add these formatting buttons to a predefined toolbar or your own custom toolbar using the techniques described in Chapter 41, "Creating Custom Toolbars and Menus."

Tip
If you don't know what a toolbar button does, move the pointer over the button and read the status bar message at the bottom of the screen.

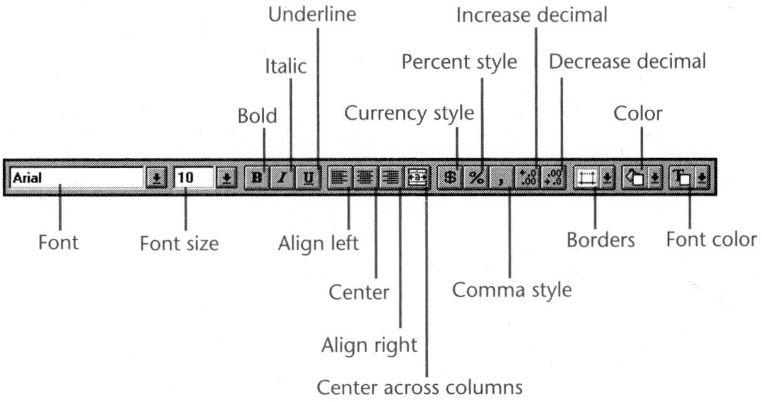

Fig. 10.14
The Formatting toolbar contains many buttons to help you format worksheets.

Formatting Cells or Characters with Shortcut Keys

To format cells or selected characters in a cell quickly with shortcut keys, select the cell, range, or text. Then press the appropriate shortcut key combination. The following chart explains which shortcut key combination applies which format.

Tip
To return to a normal format, turn off all Bold, Italic, Underline, or Strikethrough formatting by pressing the appropriate shortcut keys again.

Format	Shortcut Keys
Bold (toggle on/off)	Ctrl+2 or Ctrl+B
Italic (toggle on/off)	Ctrl+3 or Ctrl+I
Underline (toggle on/off)	Ctrl+4 or Ctrl+U
Strikethrough (toggle on/off)	Ctrl+5
Font (toggle on/off)	Ctrl+F

Tips about Formats

If you find that you frequently use the same combination of text and numeric formatting, borders, patterns, and alignments, you should learn about styles. *Styles* are combinations of formats that are assigned to a word. Selecting that word from a style list reformats characters with the entire combination of formats. There are other advantages to using styles. See the section titled "Applying Multiple Formats at One Time" later in this chapter.

When you are selecting individual words or characters in the formula bar, remember that the formula bar works like a miniature word processor, with many of the shortcuts of Word for Windows. The following list shows some tips for selecting words or phrases in the formula bar:

Select this Amount	With this Action
Word	Double-click word or Shift+Ctrl+left/right arrow
Phrase	Double-click first word, and then drag right
From insertion point to end	Press Shift+End key
From insertion point to beginning	Press Shift+Home key

When creating slides within Excel sheets for use in a slide show, you can use colors, bold, or italic on individual words in a bulleted item to add emphasis to key words within a line. This same emphasis can be useful when formatting text in a report.

Using color in formatting can help differentiate parts of the screen as well as make your documents more pleasing to work in. Some printers, however, may not print colored text with enough darkness to read. If you want to ensure that colors print black, choose **F**ile Page Set**u**p and select the Sheet tab. Select the **B**lack and White check box.

If you need single or double underlines for accounting totals and subtotals, you may want to use borders rather than character underlining. Using character underlining creates an underline that is only as wide as the number of characters in the cell. This means the width of the underline changes with different-sized numbers. Some companies prefer that all total and subtotal underlines have the same width. If you need underlines with all the same width, use one of the top or bottom underlines described in the section "Adding Borders and Lines" later in this chapter.

> **Troubleshooting**
>
> *Characters appear OK on-screen, but they do not print as shown.*
>
> Use TrueType fonts in your sheets and charts. TrueType fonts come with Windows 3.1. In the **F**ont list of the Font tab, you will see the names of TrueType fonts preceded by a TT. TrueType fonts are designed to appear on-screen as they will when printed. It is likely that you used a font on-screen that your printer could not exactly reproduce. TrueType takes care of this problem.
>
> *Character formatting appeared correct the last time the document was opened, but now the character formatting has changed. In some cases, formatting is missing.*
>
> The printer for the document may have been changed from the printer that was set during the original formatting. If the current printer is not capable of reproducing the fonts, sizes, or styles that were originally formatted, Windows will show you the best that the current printer can do. Correct this problem by reselecting a printer capable of printing the formats. Choose the **F**ile **P**rint command, and then choose the P**r**inter button and select a new printer.

For Related Information

- "Entering Numbers," p. 90
- "Entering a Series of Numbers or Dates," p. 109

Aligning and Rotating Text and Numbers

In an unformatted cell, text aligns against the left edge of the column, and numbers align against the right edge. To enhance your worksheet, you can align values or formula results so that they are left, right, or centered in a cell. You also can align a title across a selection of cells, which enables you to easily center a heading over a table or report. You can fill cells with a character that you specify, such as a dash or an equal sign, to create lines across your worksheet. You can rotate text within a cell. Excel also wraps words within a cell so that you can put a readable paragraph within one cell.

Aligning Cell Entries

To align cell contents using the Format menu, follow these steps:

1. Select the cell or range you want to format.
2. Choose the F**o**rmat C**e**lls command.
3. Select the Alignment tab (see fig. 10.15).

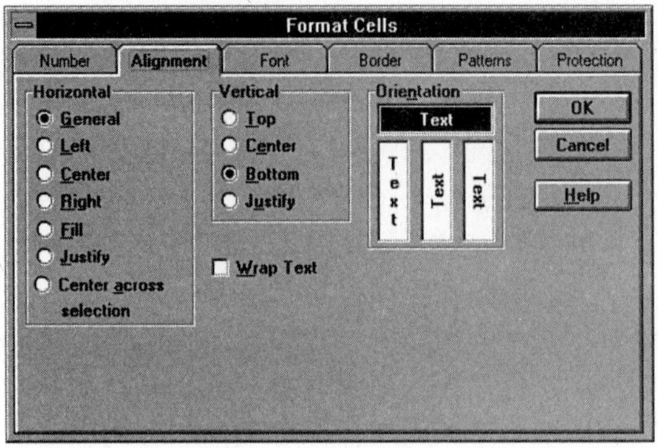

Fig. 10.15
Align or rotate text using options in the Alignment tab.

4. Select one of the following alignment buttons in the Horizontal group:

   Select **G**eneral, the default setting, to align text to the left and numbers to the right.

   Select **L**eft to align cell contents at the left edge.

   Select **C**enter to center the cell contents within the cell. Characters may extend outside the cell.

   Select **R**ight to align cell contents at the right edge.

   Select **F**ill to repeat the text to fill the cell.

   Select **J**ustify to align cell contents to both edges.

   Select Center **a**cross selection to align cell contents in the center of a selected group of cells (see the following section for details).

5. Choose OK.

To align cell contents using the Formatting toolbar, follow these steps:

1. Select the cell or range containing the contents you want to align.

2. Click the Left, Center, or Right Align button in the toolbar.

Centering Text across Cells

One problem you may face when building worksheets and databases in other software applications is not being able to center titles across multiple cells. With Excel's Center **a**cross selection option or Center Text in Selection button in the Formatting toolbar, centering titles becomes easy.

Figure 10.16, for example, shows the new title Sales Forecast entered in cell C8. After centering across the selected cells, the title appears as shown in figure 10.17.

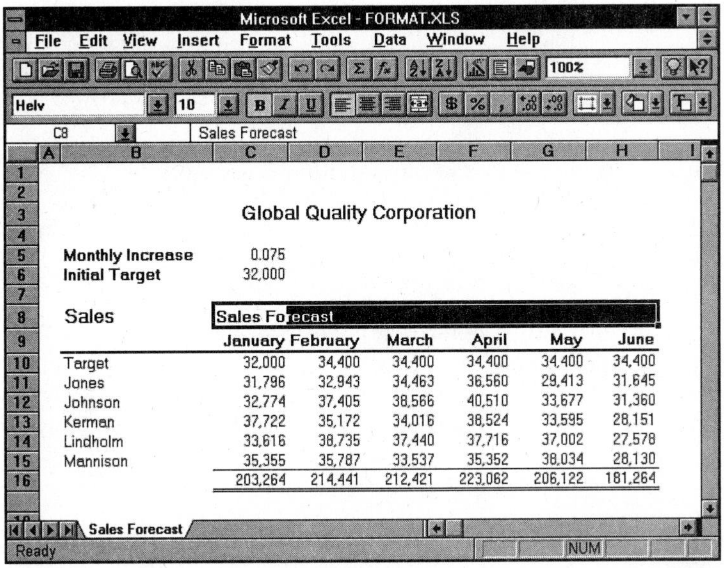

Fig. 10.16
Select the title and the cells in which you want the title centered.

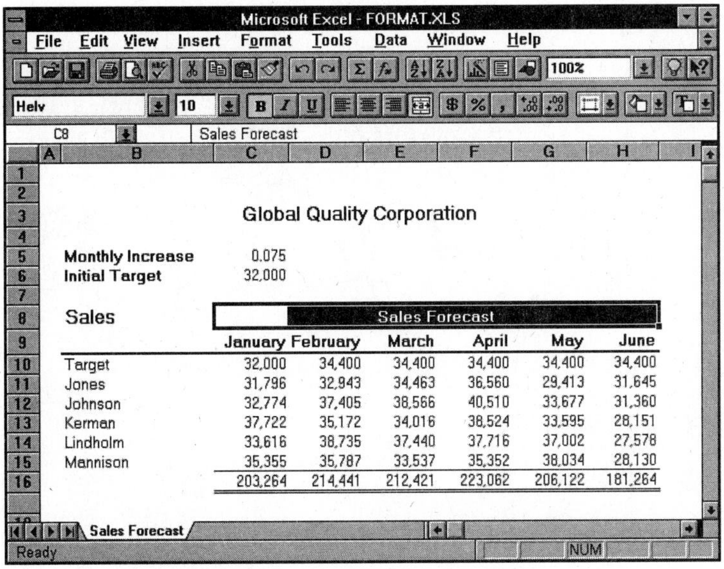

Fig. 10.17
Click the Center Across Selection button found in the Formatting toolbar.

To center a title across multiple cells using the Alignment tab, follow these steps:

1. Type and format the title in the left cell of the range in which you want the title centered.
2. Select the cells across which you want the text centered.
3. Choose the F**o**rmat C**e**lls **A**lignment command.
4. Select the Center **a**cross selection option.
5. Choose OK or press Enter. The text centers between the cell where the text is entered and the final cell you selected.

To center a title using the Center Text in Selection button from the Formatting toolbar, follow these steps:

1. Type and format the title in the left cell of the range in which you want the title centered.
2. Select the range.

3. Click the Center Text in Selection button.

Wrapping Text To Fit in a Cell

If you have made a lengthy text entry in a cell, you can have Excel wrap the text so that it forms a paragraph that fits in a cell. The cell's height increases to contain multiple lines. Figure 10.18 illustrates how the **W**rap Text option works. Notice that the text in cell B4 extends outside the cell. The text in cell B7, however, where the **W**rap Text option has been selected, wraps within the cell to form a single paragraph.

Tip
To readjust row height, move the pointer into the header numbers at the window's left edge and double-click the line under the row number.

To wrap text within cells, follow these steps:

1. Select the cell or range containing the text you want to wrap.
2. Choose the F**o**rmat C**e**lls command.
3. Select the Alignment tab.
4. Select the **W**rap Text check box.

If you change the length of the text in the cell formatted as wrapped text, the row height for the row containing that cell automatically adjusts to accommodate the next text length.

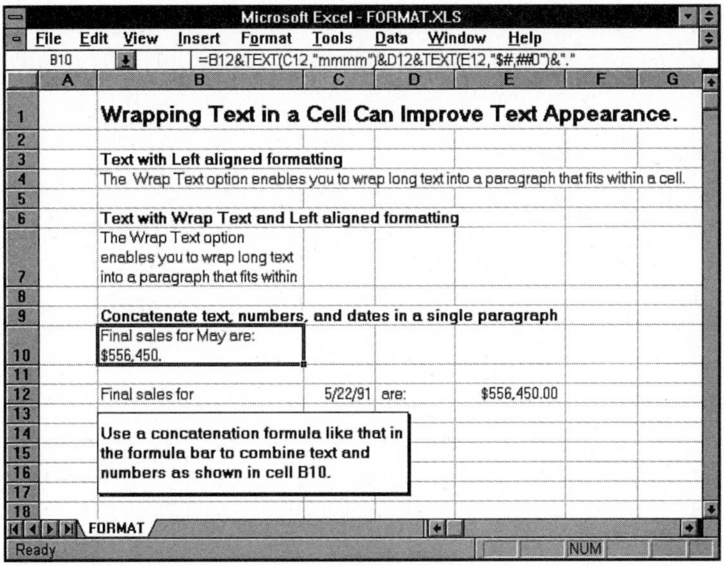

Fig. 10.18
Use the **Wrap Text** check box in the Alignment tab to wrap text within a cell.

Joining Together Text or Text and Numbers

In some reports, you may need to join together the contents of two cells, for example, joining a text phrase such as "You owe: " with the dollar amount found in cell B36. Another way joining text with a number or date is helpful is being able to put a date within a title or subtitle, such as "Today's date is May 12, 1994."

Figure 10.18 shows you an example of *concatenation*—the combining of text, numbers, and dates within a single cell. The formula in the formula bar illustrates how to combine the text, numbers, and dates from cells B12, C12, and D12 into the single cell B10. The formula is the following:

```
=B12&TEXT(C12,"mmmm")&D12&Text(E12,"$#,##0")&"."
```

The & is a concatenation operator that joins text, numbers, and dates into one long text string. The contents of B12 and D12 are text. The TEXT( ) functions format the contents of C12 to appear as a month and E12 to appear as currency. The TEXT( ) function can use any custom numeric format that Excel recognizes. These formats are described in the following section, "Designing Custom Numeric Formats."

Tabbing and Breaking Lines in a Cell

Long formulas or text wrapped within a cell as a paragraph can be difficult to read. Inserting tabs and line breaks can give lengthy text entries and formulas a structure that makes them easier to read and understand.

To enter a line break within text in a cell, begin typing in the formula bar. When you need to break a line, hold down the Alt key as you press Enter. To enter a tab in the formula bar, hold down the Alt and Ctrl keys as you press the Tab key. Enter the cell contents by pressing the Enter key. Delete the tab and carriage-return characters as you would any character in the formula bar.

Justifying Text Lines

Excel's J**u**stify option provides you with elementary word processing capability. This option takes long strings of text, divides them into lengths that you specify, and reenters each length in its own cell. Lines are broken so that words stay together. The result appears as a paragraph with each line starting in the next lower cell. You can use justification to join and wrap strings of text that are not in the same cell. Cell heights do not change as they do with the **W**rap Text option.

Tip
For a text box with formatting beyond justification, see the text boxes in Chapter 17 or use an application such as Microsoft PowerPoint.

The worksheet shown in figure 10.19 contains strings of text in cells A2, A3, A4, A6, and A7 that would look better if they were of similar length. Figure 10.20 shows the results of the justification. Notice that blank lines occurring in the text remain blank after justification. This feature keeps paragraphs separated as they were before justification. Text in adjacent rows, no matter how short a line, merges to form continuous sentences and paragraphs. Data outside the range that you specify does not move when you justify the text.

To justify strings of text so that they become paragraphs, follow these steps:

1. Select the range that contains the cell entries you want to justify. Extend the range to the right and down to define how much space the text can occupy after justification. In the example, the range A2 through D12 is selected.

2. Choose the F**o**rmat C**e**lls command.

3. Select the Alignment tab.

4. Select the J**u**stify option.

5. Choose OK.

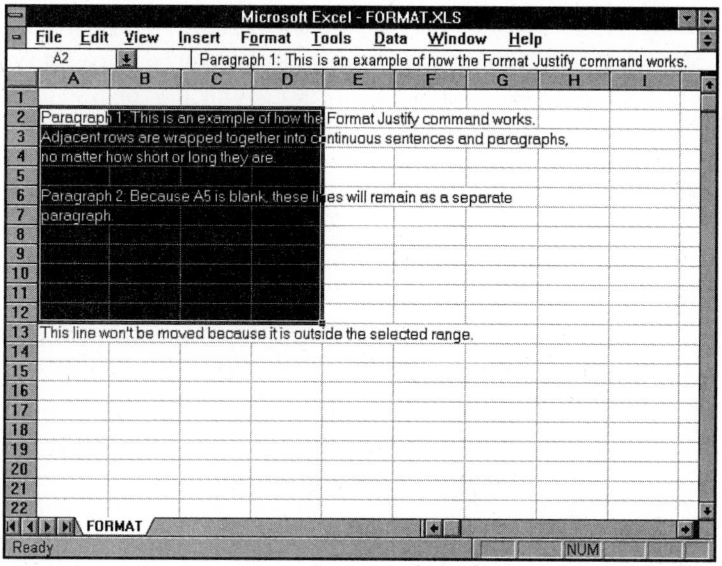

Fig. 10.19 Adjacent filled rows become paragraphs. Blank rows separate paragraphs.

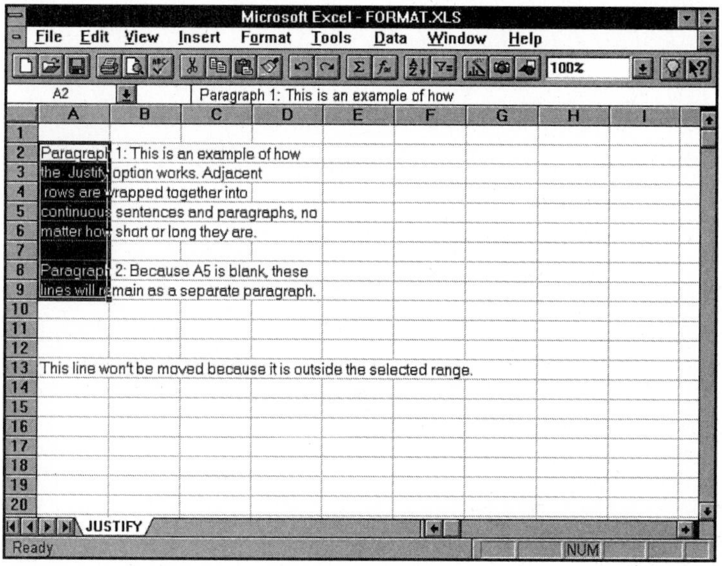

Fig. 10.20 Adjacent filled rows wrap to form paragraphs within the width of the selected range.

Caution

If the text cannot justify and fit within the range you specify, Excel displays an alert box. If you choose OK rather than Cancel, the text justifies even though it will not fit into the specified area. The **J**ustify option doesn't move numbers or formulas down to make way for text, so existing numbers or formulas may be overwritten.

If you accidentally cover information with justified text, immediately choose the **E**dit **U**ndo Justify command. When you have insufficient space to justify text, either shorten the text, select a larger area in which to justify the text, or move the obstructing information.

Rotating Numbers and Text

When you need vertical titles for reports or to label the sides of drawings or embedded charts, use Excel's F**o**rmat C**e**lls command with the Alignment tab to rotate the text or numbers. You can use rotated text effectively beside tables or embedded charts.

To rotate text or numbers, follow these steps:

1. Select the cells containing the title or label to be rotated.

   Until you are familiar with this feature, you may want to do one cell at a time so that you can see what happens step by step.

2. Choose the F**o**rmat C**e**lls command.

3. Select the Alignment tab. (See fig. 10.21.)

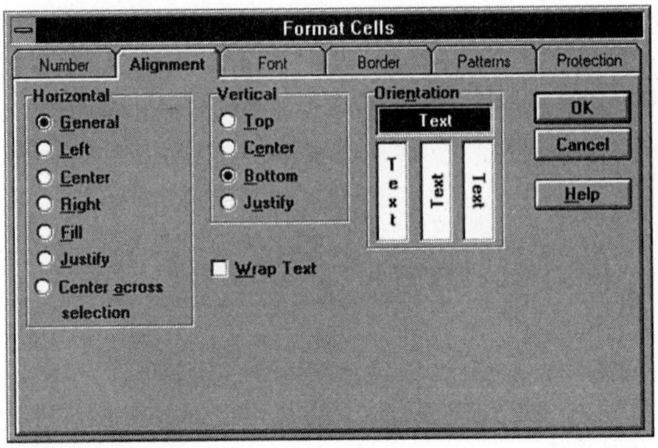

Fig. 10.21
Rotate text using the rotation options in the Alignment tab.

4. Select a text orientation from the Orie**n**tation group.

   If you are using the keyboard, press Alt+N, and then use the arrow keys to move between different orientations.

   The default Text orientation is horizontal, reading left to right. You also can align text so that the letters are stacked, reading top to bottom; rotated 90 degrees counter-clockwise, reading top to bottom; or rotated clockwise, reading top to bottom.

5. Choose OK.

Tip
You can add rotation buttons to a toolbar (see Ch. 41).

To rotate text by using buttons, follow these steps:

1. Select the cell or range containing the text.

2. Click the Vertical text, Left rotate, or Right rotate button.

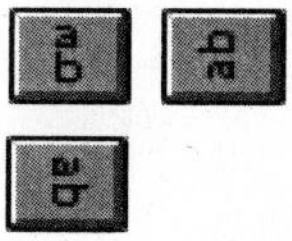

Tips about Aligning Characters

To save time when formatting, select multiple cells and ranges and give a single command. You can select nonadjacent ranges by holding down the Ctrl key as you drag the pointer across separate ranges; or press Shift+F8 to change to Add mode, and then move to another range and select it with Shift+arrow keys.

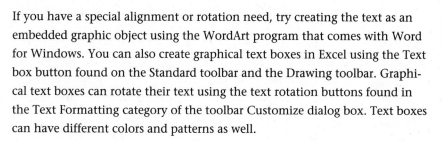

If you have a special alignment or rotation need, try creating the text as an embedded graphic object using the WordArt program that comes with Word for Windows. You can also create graphical text boxes in Excel using the Text box button found on the Standard toolbar and the Drawing toolbar. Graphical text boxes can rotate their text using the text rotation buttons found in the Text Formatting category of the toolbar Customize dialog box. Text boxes can have different colors and patterns as well.

Troubleshooting

There is a title on-screen, but when the cell behind it is selected, the text does not show in the formula bar. It is as though the text is invisible.

The title may have been centered using the Center Across Selection button or alignment option. If this is the case, the actual cell containing the text may be to the left of where the title appears. Another possible reason that you cannot find the text is that worksheet protection is turned on and the cell containing the text has been formatted as hidden. If this is the case, use the T**o**ols **P**rotection command to unprotect the worksheet, and then look for the text in a cell.

There is sideways text in a cell, but it isn't all visible.

Only a few characters of vertically rotated text display in a normal sized cell. If some characters are missing, display the entire rotated text entry by double-clicking the bottom line under the row heading number or by using the F**o**rmat **R**ow H**e**ight command to change the row height to best fit the row's contents.

For Related Information

■ "Entering Text," p. 89

Formatting Numbers

When you enter a number into a cell in Excel, the number may not appear in the sheet with the numeric appearance that you entered. For example, some trailing zeroes may have been dropped. Excel stores all numbers and dates as numbers. The appearance of the number or date on the screen is handled by numeric formatting.

Excel has many numeric and date/time formats that already are defined. In addition, you can design your own custom formats. These custom formats can contain characters and symbols that you specify, can designate the decimal precision you want, and can apply any one of 16 different colors. The format and color can even change according to the range of values in the cell.

Cells that have not been used or that have been cut or cleared have the General numeric format, which means that Excel displays a number to the greatest precision possible. If the number is too large or small, the display appears in scientific format, such as 5.367 E+05. If a number or date is still too large to fit in the specified format, the cell fills with # symbols.

Using Excel's Automatic Number Formatting

Numbers, dates, and times are stored in cells as pure numbers without formatting. Excel examines the format of the number you enter, however, to determine whether the application can format a cell for you. If you enter the number $12.95 into a General format cell, which is the default setting, for example, Excel formats the cell for currency ($X,XX0.00). Enter a percentage, such as 15%, into a cell with General format and you see it in the worksheet as 15%, although it appears in the formula bar as .15.

> **Caution**
>
> If a cell fills with # characters, the column is not wide enough for the number in its current format. To correct this problem, widen the columns. If widening the columns causes formatting problems elsewhere in the worksheet, use the TEXT() function to change the number to text. The number or date then can exceed cell width and can have any format, including custom formats.

What You Need To Know about Number Formats

Excel's predefined formats and the custom formats you create have four parts, as shown in the following syntax example:

positive format;negative format;zero format;text format

Notice that each of the parts is separated from the next by a semicolon. The first position specifies the format for positive numbers in the cell, the second for negative numbers, and so on. Although not all these format positions are used in the predefined formats, they are useful with custom formats.

The symbols used in the predefined numeric formats act as placeholders or format specifiers. Notice that the 0 acts as a placeholder and displays a 0 in that position when no number is in the position.

The symbols _) following a positive format ensure that positive numbers leave a space on the right that is the same width as the right parenthesis,), which is included with negative numbers. Positive and negative numbers then align evenly along the right edge of each column.

Table 10.1 shows how three entered sample numbers, 2500, –2500, and .5, display in the different predefined numeric formats Excel provides.

Table 10.1 Using Predefined Number Formats

Format Code		**Display Results**	
Entered Number:	***2500***	***–2500***	***0.5***
General	2500	–2500	0.5
Number			
0	2500	–2500	1
0.00	2500.00	–2500.00	0.50
#,##0	2,500	–2500	1
#,##0.00	2,500.00	–2500.00	0.50
#,##0_);(#,##0)	2,500	–2,500	1
#,##0_); (Red)(#,##0)	2,500	–2,500*	1
#,##0.00_); (#,##0.00)	2,500.00	–2,500.00	0.50
#,##0.00_); (Red){#,##0.00)	2,500.00	–2,500.00*	0.50

(continues)

Table 10.1. Continued

Format Code *Entered Number:*	*2500*	**Display Results** *–2500*	*0.5*
Currency			
$#,##0_);($#,##0)	$2,500	($2,500)	$1
$#,##0_); [RED]($#,##0)	$2,500	($2,500)*	$1
$#,##0.00_); ($#,##0.00)	$2,500.00	($2,500.00)	$0.50
$#,##0.00_); [RED]($#,##0.00)	$2,500.00	($2,500.00)*	$0.50
Percentage			
0%	250000%	–250000%	50%
0.00%	250000.00%	–250000.00%	50.00%
Scientific			
0.00E+00	2.50E+03	–2.50E+03	5.00E–01
Fraction			
# ?/?	2500	–2500	1/2

**This negative number displays in red.*

Understanding the Potential Danger in Formatted Numbers

The formatted values that appear on-screen may not be the same values used in calculations. This discrepancy can cause the displayed or printed results to be different from manually calculated answers (see fig. 10.22).

Figure 10.22 illustrates this problem. Worksheet columns C and D contain the numeric values. Columns E and G contain the same formula that multiplies the adjacent cells in C and D. Cells E15 and G15 contain SUM() functions that sum their respective columns. Notice that the totals for columns E and G do not agree. Column G has been formatted to appear with two decimal places, but the numbers used in calculation have three decimal places. That third decimal place causes the displayed and actual results to appear differently.

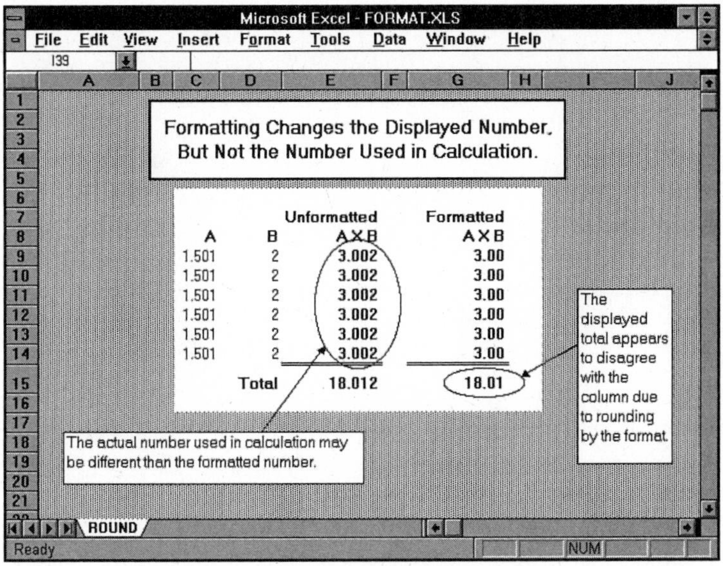

Fig. 10.22
The formatted number you see may not have the same precision as the number used in calculations.

You can resolve the problem either for the entire worksheet or for individual cells. In most cases you want to fix the *precision* of your calculations to ensure a consistency of calculations throughout your entire worksheet.

To set up your entire worksheet so that the numbers displayed match those used in the calculation, choose the T**o**ols **O**ptions command and select the Calculation tab. Choose the **P**recision as Displayed check box. (When you choose OK or press Enter, you are warned that constant numbers throughout the worksheet will be rounded permanently to match cell formatting.)

You can also *fix* the precision of selected cells by using Excel's ROUND() function. For the example in figure 10.22, you can use the formula =ROUND(C9*D9,2) in cell E9. This formula rounds the multiplied value before it is summed. Always round before doing further calculations.

Formatting Numbers

To format cells containing numbers using the menu commands, follow these steps:

1. Select the cell or range you want to format.
2. Choose the F**o**rmat C**e**lls command.
3. Select the Number tab shown in figure 10.23.

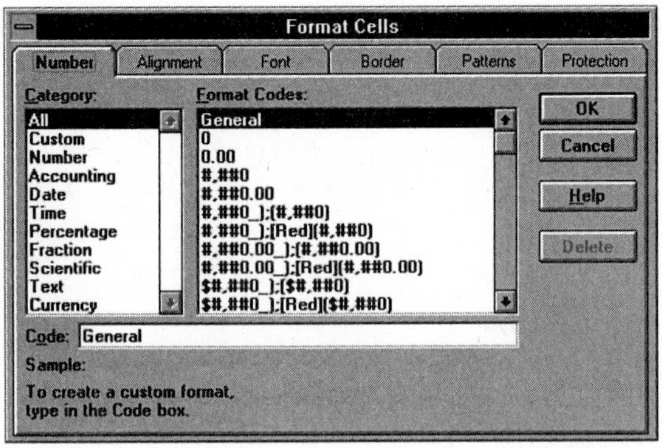

Fig. 10.23
Select predefined number, date, and time formats from the Number tab.

4. Select the type of number you want to format from the **C**ategory list. This selection limits what appears in the **F**ormat Codes list.

5. Select the format you want from the **F**ormat Codes list. Custom formats that you have created appear at the bottom of the list.

6. Choose OK.

If the active cell contains a number, the Sample area at the bottom of the Number tab shows you the appearance of the numeric format.

To format cells with shortcut keys, follow these steps:

1. Select the cell or range you want to format.

2. Press one of the following keystroke combinations:

Format	Shortcut Key
General	Shift+Ctrl+~
#,##0.00	Shift+Ctrl+!
$#,##0.00_);($#,##0.00)	Shift+Ctrl+$
0%	Shift+Ctrl+%
0.00E+00	Shift+Ctrl+^

The Formatting toolbar contains buttons to help you quickly format cells for numeric display.

To apply a numeric format using a button on the Formatting toolbar follow these steps:

1. Select the cell or range you want to format.

2. Click the button.

The Formatting toolbar offers buttons for currency, percentage, or comma format. Also, if you want to increase or decrease the decimals displayed, 2click the buttons that contain decimals and zeros. One increases and the other decreases the number of decimal places.

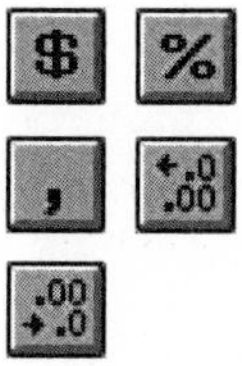

Designing Custom Numeric Formats

You can design your own numeric formats for financial or scientific tasks and create formats for catalog numbers, telephone numbers, international currency, and so on. Any time you need to display a number in a special way, consider using a custom numeric format.

Tip

Custom numeric formats are easy to create, and solve many problems. Don't be put off. Try them!

Figure 10.24 shows examples of custom formats and how they can be used. The format shown in column C was entered in the Number Format dialog box as a custom format. This format then was used to format the number in column D so that the number appears as shown in column E.

Figure 10.25 shows uses for custom numeric formats beyond just formatting numbers.

Understanding Custom Numeric Formats. Creating a custom numeric format is easy, but it does require that you understand the few symbols that Excel uses to define a numeric code. To create your own custom numeric format, you will need to type these symbols into the Code text box on the Number tab.

In a numeric format, Excel uses a semicolon (;) to separate the formats for positive, negative, zero, and text formats. The order for each of these formats is as follows:

positive format;negative format;zero format;text format

To understand how these parts work, examine this sample custom format:

$#,##0_);($#,##0); "Zero"

It displays a positive number in the $#,##0 format, a negative number in the ($#,##0) format, and the text *Zero* for a zero. For example, 3550 appears as `$3,550`, –3550 appears as `($3,550)`, and 0 appears as the word `Zero`.

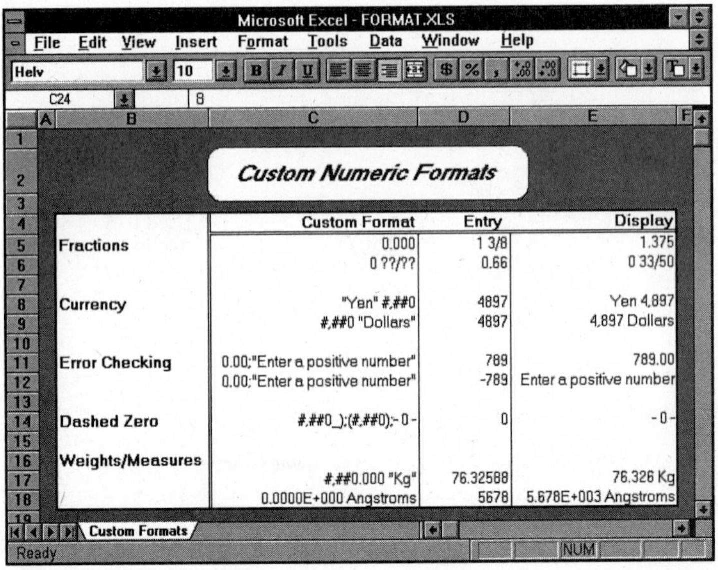

Fig. 10.24 Use custom numeric formats to display numbers the way you want.

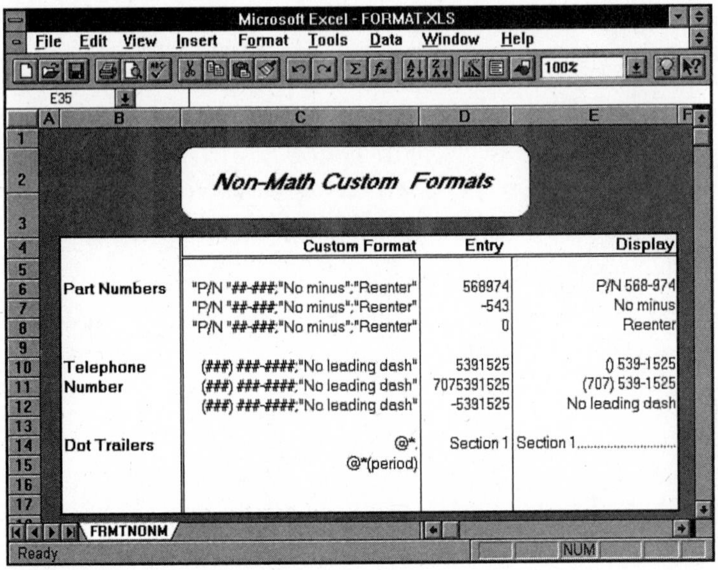

Fig. 10.25 Custom numeric formatting can include text or error messages.

Symbols that you can use when creating custom formats are described in table 10.2.

Table 10.2 Formatting Symbols for Custom Formats

Formatting Symbol	Function
General	Uses the default format for unformatted cells. Displays numbers as precisely as possible for column width. Displays in scientific format for large or small numbers.
#	Acts as a placeholder for digits. 0 is not displayed if a number is absent. Decimal fractions round up to the number of #s to the right of the decimal. The value 3.5 with format $#,###.##, for example, is displayed as $3.5, and the number .245 as $.25.
0	Acts as a placeholder for digits. Used to display a 0 if no number is entered. Decimal fractions round up to the number of 0s to the right of the decimal. The value 3.5 with a format $#,##0.00, for example, is displayed as $3.50, and the number .245 appears as $0.25.
?	Acts as a placeholder for digits in the same way the 0 does. Insignificant 0s are removed and spaces inserted so that numbers still align correctly. Use this symbol as the integer portion with fractional custom formats so that a number does not appear if you type a fraction such as 0 3/4.
_ (underscore)	Skips the width of the character following the underscore. Typing **_)** at the end of a positive format, for example, inserts a blank space that is the width of the). This feature enables you to align a positive number correctly with a negative number enclosed in parentheses. Without the _), the character at the far right of the positive number would align with the closing) of a negative number.
. (decimal)	Marks the location of the decimal point. Use a 0 to the left of the **.** (decimal) to indicate a leading 0.
, (comma)	Marks the position of thousands. You need to mark only the location of the first thousand.
%	Multiplies the entry by 100, and displays the number as a percentage with a % sign. A decimal number appears in the formula bar.
E_E+e_e+	Displays the number in scientific notation. One or more 0s or #s to the right of the E or e indicate the power of the exponent.
: **$** _ + ( )	Displays this character in the same position in the formatted number.

(continues)

Table 10.2 Continued	
Formatting Symbol	**Function**
/ (slash)	Serves as a separator in fractions. Type a decimal fraction, such as 1.667, into the cell; or type a leading integer followed by a fraction, as in 1 2/3, to produce a fractional display of 1 2/3.
\ (backslash)	Indicates a single text character or symbol when it precedes an entry.
"text"	Displays the specified text within quotation marks.
* *character*	Fills the remaining column width with the character following the asterisk (one asterisk per format).
@	Acts as a format code to indicate where user-input text will appear in the format.
[*color*]	Formats cell content with the color specified. For more information, see this chapter's section "Formatting Data with Color."
[*condition value*]	Uses conditional statements within the number format to specify when a format will be used. Conditions can be <, >, =, >=, <=, and <>. Values can be any number. For more information, see this chapter's section "Formatting Conditionally."

Creating Custom Numeric Formats. To create custom numeric formats you can use anywhere on the worksheet, follow these steps:

1. Select the cells for which you want to use the custom format.
2. Choose the Format Cells command.
3. Select the Number tab.
4. If an existing format is close to the custom format you want to create, select that format by choosing the appropriate category from the Category list and choosing the closest code from the Format Codes list.
5. In the Code text box, edit the custom formats pattern (see fig. 10.26).
6. Choose OK.

After you create a custom numeric format, type an appropriate number in a cell, and then test the custom format with positive, negative, and zero values.

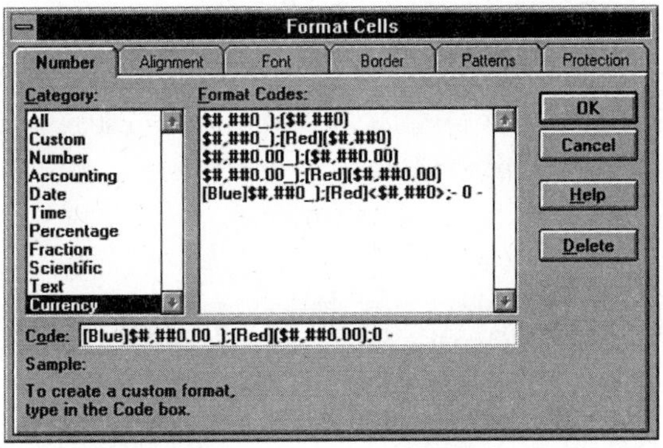

Fig. 10.26
Edit or enter a numeric format to fit your special needs in the Code text box.

You can reuse this custom format on any cell in the worksheet by selecting the same category as when you created the format, scrolling to the bottom of the Format Code list, and selecting the custom format as you would any predefined format.

Deleting Custom Formats. To remove a custom format, follow these steps:

1. Choose the Format Cells command.
2. Select the Number tab.
3. Select Custom from the Category list, and then select the format you want to delete from the Format Codes list.
4. Choose the Delete button.

You cannot delete built-in formats.

Displaying Text with Numbers. Display text in the same cell as the number by enclosing the text in quotation marks and inserting these text elements at appropriate locations between semicolons in the custom format. The number in the cell is still used in calculations as a number, but it displays with text. For example, if you want a part number always to be preceded by P/N and to show a hyphen before the last three numbers, create a custom format such as the following:

"P/N "####-###;"Use Positive";"Enter Number"

With this format, the number 5768953 is displayed as `P/N 5768—953`. Entering a negative number displays the text, `Use Positive`, and entering a zero produces the text, `Enter Number`.

Hiding Numbers Using a Custom Format. To hide numbers in your custom format, don't put a format code between semicolons where Excel expects one. Table 10.3 gives some examples of ways you can use text and the semicolon to your advantage. In the second example in table 10.3, negative numbers and zeros are hidden.

Table 10.3 Custom Formats that Hide Values

Custom Format	Positive	Negative	Zero
$#,###_);($#,###);	$2,500	($2,500)	
$#,###_);;	$2,500		
$#,### ;($#,###);"Zero"	$2,500	($2,500)	Zero
;;	All values hidden but used in calculation		

As you see in the table, a double semicolon hides all numbers. Hidden numbers are still in the worksheet and can be used by other formulas. You can see these numbers in the formula bar if you select a cell containing one of them. If you also want to hide the numbers shown in the formula bar, use the Protection tab under the F**o**rmat C**e**lls command to format cells as Hidden. When you turn on protection for the worksheet or workbook, the cell contents do not display in the formula bar. Select and reformat cells to redisplay hidden numbers.

Formatting Data with Color. Colored text or numbers can help you pick up discrepancies in data entry or flag numbers that are out of tolerance. The color format works on a cell along with the numeric or date formats.

Indicate the color you want by placing the color name within brackets in the proper portion of the custom number format. Color formats in the text format position, for example, change the color of text. And if you want the positive format to be blue and the negative format to be red, use a format such as this one:

[BLUE]$#,##0.00_0;[RED]($#,##0.00)

Colors that you can use include the eight named colors and any of the custom colors. Specify the color with one of the following color symbols:

[BLACK]

[WHITE]

[RED]

[GREEN]

[BLUE]

[YELLOW]

[MAGENTA]

[CYAN]

[COLOR#] (where # is a color numbered from 0 to 56 on the color palette)

You can see Excel's color palette by choosing the T**o**ols **O**ptions command and selecting the Color tab. Colors on the Standard Colors palette are numbered across the top from left to right, and then across the bottom. (The top left color is 1; the lower right color is 56.)

Formatting Conditionally

When you use the [*condition value*] formatting symbol in your custom format, you can format a cell so that numbers appear in different formats or colors, depending on the value of the number. This technique is especially valuable for error checking on data entry, for exception reporting from analysis, and for executive information systems.

The following format, for example, makes all numbers in the cell use the 0.00 numeric format. The numbers appear black when greater than or equal to 1,000; red when less than or equal to 500; and blue for any number between these values.

```
[BLACK][>=1000]0.00;[RED][<=500]0.00;[BLUE]0.00
```

Hiding Zeros

Hiding zeros often makes worksheets easier to read. In Excel, you have three options for hiding zeros: hiding them throughout the worksheet, creating a custom format, or using an IF() function.

To hide zeros throughout the entire worksheet, choose the T**o**ols **O**ptions command, select the View tab, and then clear the **Z**ero Values check box. Select the **Z**ero Values check box when you want to see the zeros again.

To hide zeros by using a custom format, use the semicolon in the appropriate position to indicate that a zero format follows, but do not enter a format for zero numbers, as in the following format:

$#,###_);($#,###);

In formulas, use an IF() function to hide a zero, as in the following example:

=IF(A12+B12=0,"",A12+B12)

This formula says that if A12+B12 equals zero, Excel displays what is between the quotation marks, which is nothing. (Beware of using a space to indicate a zero; a space causes problems in some databases or numeric and text functions.) If A12+B12 does not equal zero, Excel displays the result of the formula.

Tips about Numeric Formatting

You can use a comma format, for example #,##0, to make the displayed number appear divided by multiples of 1000. This is useful for displaying thousands or millions of dollars. For example, 123456789 formatted as $#,##0,"M" (where a comma ends the numeric portion of the format), displays as `$123,457M`. Notice that the displayed number is rounded rather than truncated. Calculations continue to use the actual number in the cell, not the displayed, truncated number.

When you need a number to fit into a narrow column, use the TEXT() function to convert the number or result of a formula into text. The number can then overlap cell edges instead of turning into ### signs. Numbers converted to text by the TEXT() function can still be referred to in other formulas and will calculate correctly. The numeric format used in TEXT() can be one of the custom numeric formats described earlier in this section. For example, if the result of A12*C35 is too large to fit in a narrow cell and it needs a currency format, you can use the following formula in the same cell in which you would have used A12*C35:

=TEXT(A12*C35,"$#,##0_);($#,##0);0")

Troubleshooting

After formatting, one of the longer numbers no longer fits in the cell. It's too wide and produces #### in the display.

Widen the column until the number appears. You can also use the TEXT() function to convert the number or formula result into text that can overlap cell edges. This number as text can be referenced by other formulas and will still work as a number. See the preceding section for more information.

For Related Information

- "Entering Numbers," p. 90
- "Creating Your Own Colors," p. 1095

Formatting Dates and Times

Excel can do date and time calculations, but to do so, you must enter dates and times in a way that Excel recognizes. You can usually type dates and times in cells the way you are accustomed to reading or writing them. Excel recognizes dates and times entered in any of the formats shown in table 10.4. If you type the date 1/12/92 into a cell with the default General format and then press Enter, for example, Excel formats the cell in the m/d/yy date format.

Dates and times in Excel are actually stored in cells as a number, the *serial-date* number. A date is the number of days from the beginning of the century, and a time is the percentage of a 24-hour clock. You can see a serial-date format by entering a date, and then formatting the cell with the General format.

Tip

You can use the serial number to perform date arithmetic such as calculating days between dates. Time is calculated as a decimal portion of 24 hours.

Table 10.4 Predefined Excel Date and Time Formats

Format	Example
m/d/yy	12/24/91
d-mmm-yy	24-Dec-91
d-mmm	24-Dec
mmm-yy	Dec-91
h:mm AM/PM	9:45 PM (12-hour clock)
h:mm:ss AM/PM	9:45:15 PM (12-hour clock)
h:mm	21:45 (24-hour clock)

(continues)

Table 10.4 Continued

Format	Example
h:mm:ss	21:45:15 (24-hour clock)
m/d/yy h:mm	12/24/88 21:45 (24-hour clock)
mm:ss	45:15
mm:ss.0	45:15.0
[h]:mm:ss	21:45:15 (24-hour clock)

If the cell is in the default General format before you enter a date, you do not need to format the cell. Excel changes the General format to agree with the date and time format that you first enter. You can change this format or create a custom format at any time.

If you enter a date or time and see it appear on the left side of the cell, Excel did not interpret your entry as a date or time but instead accepted the entry as text. Check to see whether the formula bar shows the date in the pattern m/d/yy. If so, the entry was accepted as a date.

Understanding Date and Time Formats

Excel uses a few simple codes to define how a date or time format will appear. You can use these codes to understand the built-in date and time formats listed in the Number tab, or you can use them to create your own custom date and time formats. The formatting characters you can use for date and time formats are described in table 10.5.

Table 10.5 Date and Time Symbols

Type/Symbols	Display Result
General	Serial date number of days from the beginning of the century. Dec 24, 1991, for example, is 33596. Times appear as decimal portions of 24 hours.
Days	
d	Day number from 1 to 31; no leading zero.
dd	Day number from 01 to 31; leading zero.
ddd	Day displayed as an abbreviation (Mon-Sun).

Type/Symbols	Display Result
dddd	Day displayed as a full name (Monday-Sunday).
Months*	
m	Month number from 1 to 12; no leading zero.
mm	Month number from 01 to 12; leading zero.
mmm	Three-letter month abbreviation from Jan to Dec.
mmmm	Full name of month from January to December.
Years	
yy	Two-digit year number from 00 to 99.
yyyy	Full year number from 1900 to 20714.
Hours	
h	Hour number from 0 to 24; no leading zero.
hh	Hour number from 00 to 24; leading zero.
Minutes	
m	Minute number from 0 to 59; no leading zero.
mm	Minute number from 00 to 59; leading zero.
Seconds	
s	Second number from 0 to 59; no leading zero.
ss	Second number from 00 to 59; leading zero.
[ ]	Hours greater than 24, minutes greater than 60, or seconds greater than 60.
AM/PM	
A/P	Displays the hour, using the AM/PM 12-hour clock.
Separators	
_	Places dash divider between parts.
/	Places slash divider between parts.
:	Places colon divider between parts.

**Excel interprets m characters that follow an h as minutes.*

Formatting Dates and Times

Regardless of how you enter or calculate the date and time, you can display the date and time in any of Excel's predefined formats. You also can select a different color for the cell's contents, or set a format for dates and times within a range.

To change the date and time format of a cell, follow these steps:

1. Select the cell or range.
2. Choose the F**o**rmat C**e**lls command.
3. Select the Number tab.
4. Select Date or Time from the **C**ategory list.
5. Select a format from the **F**ormat Code list.
6. Choose OK.

To enter dates and times and automatically format them using shortcut keys, follow these steps:

1. Select the cell.
2. Press one of the following keys:

Shortcut Key	Format Result
Ctrl+;	Inserts current date
Ctrl+Shift+:	Inserts current time
Shift+Ctrl+@	Formats in h:mm AM/PM
Shift+Ctrl+#	Formats in d-mmm-yy

Creating Custom Date and Time Formats

If you cannot find the date or time format you want, you can create it with the same process you use to create custom numeric formats: type the new format into the C**o**de edit box in the Number tab. The only difference is that you use different formatting symbols for date and time formatting.

Some examples of custom date formats are shown in table 10.6.

Table 10.6 Sample Custom Date and Time Formats

Format	Display
dddd	Friday
mmmm d, yyyy	April 1, 1994
d mmm, yy	1 Apr, 94
yy/mm/dd	94/12/01
[BLUE] d mmm, yy	1 Apr, 94 (in blue)
[RED][>=34691] d mmm,	24 Dec, 94 (in red)
yy;d mmm, yy	23 Dec, 94 (in black) (The number 33596 is the serial date number for 24 Dec, 91.)

Tips about Date and Time Formatting

You can use the TEXT() function along with concatenation to create titles that include the current date. For example,

="Today's date is "&TEXT(NOW(),"mmm d, yy")

produces text that looks like the following:

Today's date is May 25, 94

Whenever the worksheet recalculates or opens, the NOW() function updates the date.

You can also create custom date formats that include text like the preceding text. Just add the text you desire (such as "Today's date is") in the C**o**de edit box in the Number tab. Make sure that you include the text within quotation marks.

> **Troubleshooting**
>
> *Worksheets imported from Macintosh Excel show a different date.*
>
> Excel for the Macintosh starts counting its serial dates from a different date than Excel for Windows. If you are using worksheets that originated on the Macintosh and find the dates are incorrect, choose the T**o**ols **O**ptions command and select the Calculation tab. Select the 1904 **D**ate System check box.

For Related Information

■ "Entering Numbers," p. 90

Formatting Rows and Columns

You can improve the appearance of your worksheet or database by adjusting column widths and row heights. Appropriate adjustments also help you fit more data on a page. You even can hide confidential data in a row or column. The following pages describe these tasks.

Adjusting Column Width

You can adjust one or more columns in Excel to get the best appearance in your worksheet or to fit the maximum data on-screen or in a printout. If a column is not wide enough to display a number, date, or time, Excel lets you know by displaying # characters in the cell.

To change one or more columns widths by command, follow these steps:

1. Select cells in the columns that you want to change. Change multiple columns by selecting a cell in each column.

2. Choose the F**o**rmat **C**olumn command.

3. Use one of the following techniques to adjust column widths:

   Choose the **W**idth command to adjust columns to a specific width based on the width of the Normal font. The Column Width dialog box appears (see fig. 10.27). Type in the width, and then choose OK.

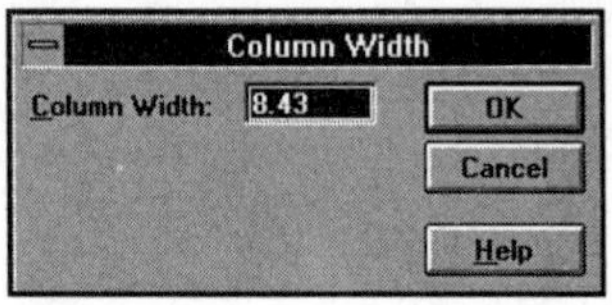

Fig. 10.27
Type widths based on the Normal font.

   Choose the **F**it Selection command to fit the column width to the widest cell contents in the selection.

   Choose the **S**tandard Width command and choose OK to accept the default standard column width for the selected column. (You can also use this dialog box to change the standard column width for *all* columns; note that the measurement in this dialog box is in inches.)

4. Choose OK or press Enter.

To change one or more column widths with the mouse, follow these steps:

1. Select multiple columns by dragging the pointer across the column headers, the letters at the top of each column. You do not need to select the column to change a single column. Select nonadjacent columns by pressing Ctrl and clicking the letter in each column's header (see fig. 10.28).

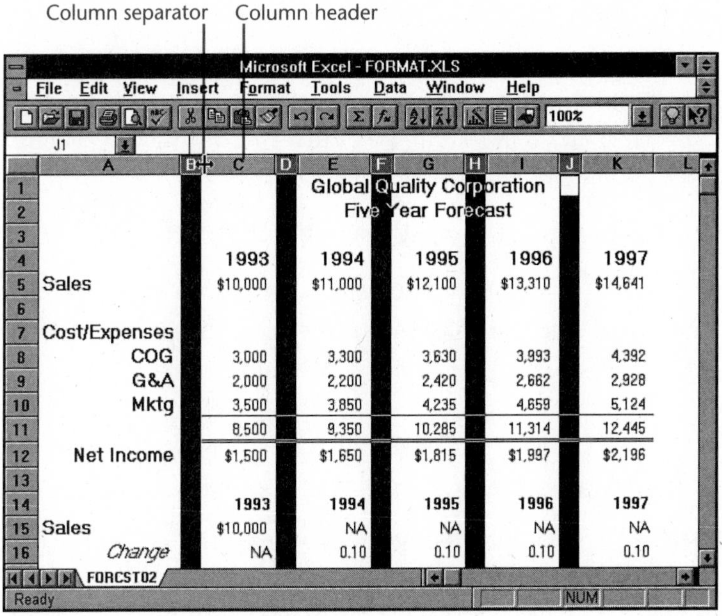

Fig. 10.28 Select non-adjacent columns with a Ctrl+click in the column header.

2. Move the pointer onto the column separator directly to the right of the column heading. To change the width of column B, for example, move onto the line between the B and C headers. The pointer changes to a two-headed, horizontal arrow.

3. Drag the column left or right until the shadow is where you want it; then release the mouse button. All selected columns drag to the same width.

To fit the column to its widest entry using the mouse:

Double-click the column heading separator—the vertical line between column headings—on the right side of the column you want adjusted.

The width of the column is based on the screen fonts. If you are using TrueType fonts, the column width should be correct for printing.

Hiding Columns

When you generate a database or worksheet for multiple users, you may not want to print all the information that you enter. You can hide columns temporarily so that they do not print or appear on-screen.

To hide selected columns using the keyboard, follow these steps:

1. Select cells in the columns you want to hide.

2. Choose the F**o**rmat **C**olumn **H**ide command.

Reveal hidden columns by selecting cells that span the hidden column; then choose the F**o**rmat **C**olumn **U**nhide command.

To hide a column using the mouse, follow these steps:

1. Move the mouse pointer over the column separator line that is directly to the right of the column header where the hidden column should be. The pointer changes to a two-headed pointer.

2. Drag the column separator left until it is past the separator on its left.

To unhide a column using the mouse, follow these steps:

1. Move the pointer so that its left edge touches the column separator on the right of a hidden column. The pointer changes to a two-headed pointer with space between the two heads.

2. Move the pointer so that its left tip touches the column separator.

3. Drag the column separator to the right, and then release.

Adjusting Row Height

You may want to change row heights to create more space for titles or more space between subtotals and grand totals. The procedure for changing the height of rows is similar to that for changing column widths. Row heights change automatically to accommodate the tallest font in the row. Before making a row height shorter, you may want to make sure that you do not cut off the tops of large characters.

To change row height by using the keyboard, follow these steps:

1. Select a cell in each row you want to change.

2. Choose the F**o**rmat **R**ow H**e**ight command to display the Row Height dialog box.

3. Enter the height in the **R**ow Height box.

4. Choose OK or press Enter.

To change the height of one or more rows with the mouse, follow these steps:

1. Select one or more rows. Figure 10.29 shows selected multiple rows.

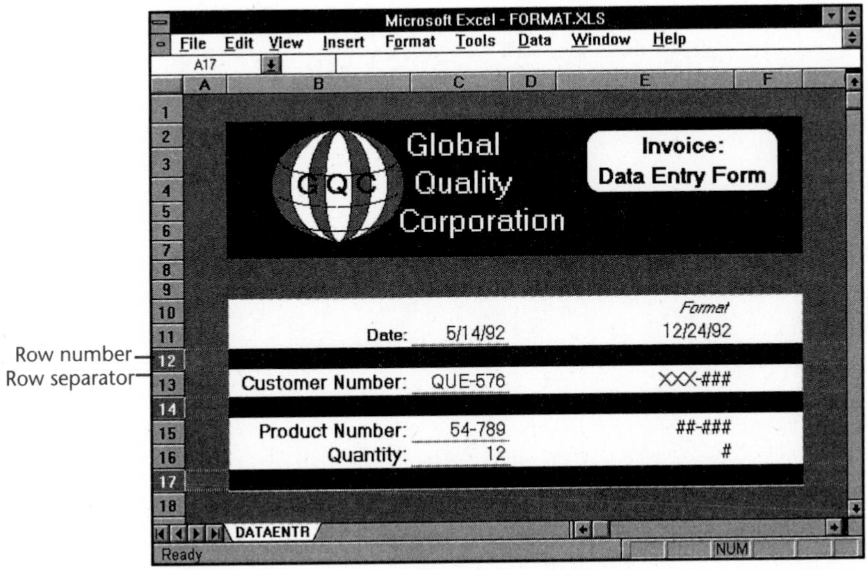

Fig. 10.29
Select multiple rows and adjust all their heights at the same time.

2. Move the mouse pointer to the line directly under the row header of the row you want to change. When correctly positioned, the mouse pointer changes to a two-headed vertical arrow.

3. Drag the two-headed arrow up or down until the shadow of the row bottom is where you want it. Then release the mouse button. You also can double-click the bottom of one of the row headers.

To adjust a row height to the best fit for the tallest characters in the row, double-click the separator line below the rows number in the row headings.

Hiding Rows

To hide rows of information, use steps similar to the ones you use to change the row height. Select the rows you want to hide, and choose the F**o**rmat **R**ow **H**ide button.

Reveal hidden rows by selecting cells that span the hidden row; then choose the F**o**rmat **R**ow **U**nhide command. Or you can unhide hidden rows by dragging the row heading separator down. To do this, move the pointer over the row number that is under the hidden rows. Move the pointer up slowly until it changes to a double-headed pointer with space in between the two heads. Drag the line down to reveal the hidden row.

Tips about Rows and Columns

Use the View Manager to help you switch between hidden and unhidden rows and columns.

If you frequently use different combinations of hidden rows or columns in worksheets, you should use the View Manager. The View Manager enables you to assign a name to different combinations of hidden rows and columns. You can then switch between these different *views* by selecting the name of the view you want displayed.

For Related Information

- "Selecting Cells and Ranges," p. 72
- "Adjusting Margins and Column Widths While Previewing," p. 391

Troubleshooting

I can't unhide a row or column.

Sometimes a row or column is hidden so well it's difficult to manually unhide. (That is, you can't get your pointer to change to the double-headed arrow with space in-between.) In such instances, your best bet is to highlight the columns surrounding the hidden column and choose the F**o**rmat **C**olumn **S**tandard Width command; click OK to accept the standard column width. This will resize all three selected columns to the standard column width. From there you can manually resize any of the columns to a different width.

Adding Colors, Patterns, and Borders

Shading, borders, and even colors can dress up your worksheet or reports to make important information stand out. These features create an impression of high-quality, polished work. This section explains the color and pattern changes you can make.

You can add emphasis and polish to your worksheets by using different shadings and patterns as backgrounds for tables of numbers, as shown in the examples throughout this book. Figure 10.30 shows the 18 black-and-white patterns available.

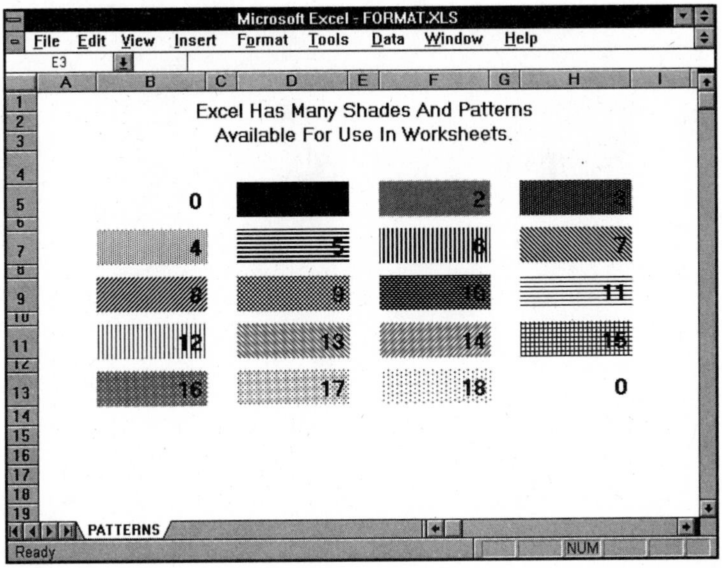

Fig. 10.30
Use patterns and shading to enhance worksheet appearance.

You also can create these shadings by using foreground and background colors within a pattern. Colors can emphasize screen display, output printed to any color-capable Windows-compatible printer, and output projected onscreen with a color screen projector.

Another way to add shading is with the Light Shading and Dark Shading buttons. These buttons are in the Customize dialog box for the Formatting toolbar, and you can add them to any toolbar. (See Chapter 41, "Creating Custom Toolbars and Menus," for directions on adding buttons to toolbars.) To use a shading button, just select the cells you want shaded and then click the button.

Adding a Pattern or Color

To add a pattern in black and white or color to your worksheet, follow these steps:

1. Select the cell(s) to which you want to add color or a pattern.
2. Choose the F**o**rmat C**e**lls command.
3. Select the Patterns tab (see fig. 10.31).
4. Select the main color for your pattern from the Color grid.
5. Select a pattern from the **P**attern pull-down list.

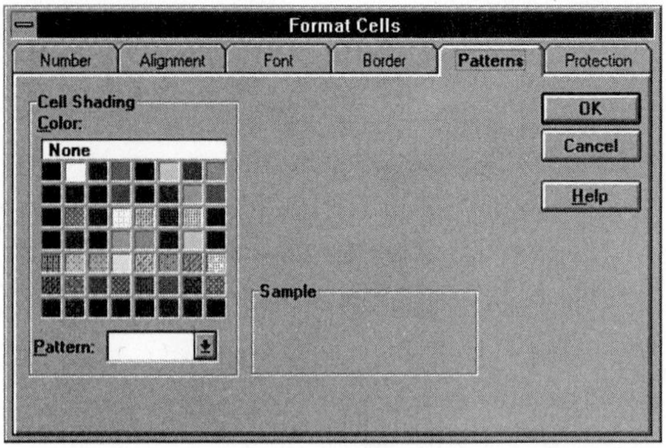

Fig. 10.31
The Patterns tab enables you to view samples of colors and patterns before you use them.

6. If you want a colored pattern, select a background color from the **P**attern pull-down list. Check the Sample area at the bottom right of the dialog box to see the color and pattern.

7. Choose OK.

You can add custom buttons to a toolbar that apply dark or light shading. The dark and light shading buttons are located in the Formatting category of the Customize dialog box. Customizing the toolbar is described in Chapter 40, "Customizing the Excel Screen."

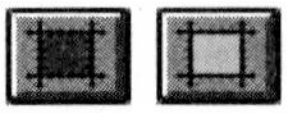

To add a pattern to selected cells using the dark and light shading buttons, click the dark or light button.

To add a foreground color to a selected cell, follow these steps:

1. Click the Color Palette button found on the Formatting toolbar.

2. Continue clicking to cycle forward through the palette. Shift+click to reverse the direction through the color palette.

Tip
Borders are more visible with no gridlines. Choose T**o**ols **O**ptions and deselect **G**ridlines.
On-screen, borders are more visible with no gridlines. Choose T**o**ols **O**ptions and deselect **G**ridlines.

Adding Borders and Lines

You can place borders around cells or use borders as lines and double lines under cells to add emphasis, to define data-entry areas, or to mark totals and subtotals. When combined with shading, borders make your documents easier to read and give them flair (see fig. 10.32).

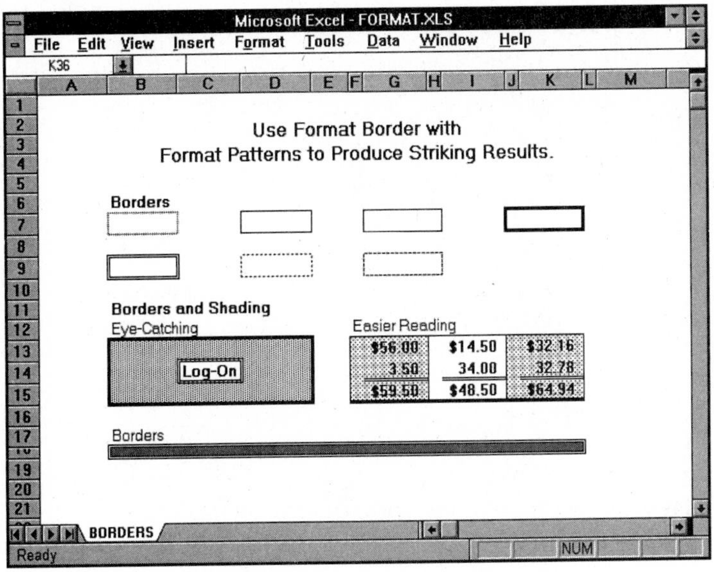

Fig. 10.32
Excel has a wide variety of shading and border combinations.

To add borders using a command, follow these steps:

1. Select the cell or range.
2. Choose the F**o**rmat C**e**lls command.
3. Select the Border tab.
4. In the Border group, select the parts of the cell or range that you want bordered. You can choose **O**utline, **L**eft, **R**ight, **T**op, or **B**ottom. **O**utline puts a border around the outside of the selected cells. To put lines inside a range, select one or more of the other edges.
5. In the Styl**e** group, select the style of line you want for the border. If you are using the keyboard, press Alt+E and then use the arrow keys to move between the different styles. Use the double-underline style for totals.
6. Select the color you want for the border from the **C**olor drop-down list box. If you are using the keyboard, press Alt+C, and then press the down arrow. Use the arrow keys to move to the color you want.
7. Choose OK.

You can also use the Borders button on the Formatting toolbar to add borders to selected cells. Follow these steps:

1. Select the cell or range.

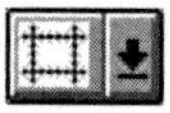

2. Click the Borders button to pull down the Borders list.

3. Click the desired border.

The selected cell or range now is bordered with the selected border.

Tips about Borders, Patterns, and Colors

For the finest resolution of a gray pattern, use the next to the last gray color on the Color grid in the Patterns tab. With this color, use a solid pattern. This light gray color prints very evenly on laser printers.

You can use as many as 16 colors for your cell patterns. The 16 colors available are specified on the color palette. Use the T**o**ols **O**ptions command, and select the Color tab to see the palette of available colors. This command is described in Chapter 40, "Customizing the Excel Screen."

If you don't like the colors available for patterns or characters, you can redefine the color palette by choosing the T**o**ols **O**ptions command and selecting the Color tab. In this tab, you can select a color, and then select the **E**dit button to display a palette that enables you to redefine the color you selected.

For Related Information

- "Creating Graphic Objects," p. 560

To create a border that acts as an underline for subtotals, put narrow columns between columns with borders, or format left and right borders with thick, white borders. Refer back to figure 10.32 to see how columns F, H, and J are used as separators between border underlines.

Applying Multiple Formats at One Time

Styles are a powerful formatting feature in Excel that can save you time and help you apply a group of formats consistently. By giving a set of combined formats a style name, you can apply that combination to one or more cells by choosing the style name rather than all the individual formats. If you later change the definition of formats associated with that style, all cells having that style immediately change to the new definition. A style name is defined for all sheets in a workbook.

Styles are helpful because they eliminate the need to choose multiple commands for repetitive formats, and they reduce the need to reformat worksheets. If you work in a company in which a standard appearance for proposals and presentations is important, styles can ensure that everyone uses consistent formatting. The company can create preferred styles for titles, headings, bodies of financial reports, and totals. Everyone then can use these styles to reduce the workload and produce a consistent corporate image.

A style can contain all the formatting you use for numbers, font, alignment, borders, patterns, and cell protection. You can even specify *not* to include a format type in a specific style! A style, for example, can specify a numeric format and font but leave the existing color unchanged.

Using a Style To Apply a Collection of Formats

You can use styles in different sheets in a workbook. All sheets in a workbook have the same style names available. The default Excel worksheet comes with a few predefined styles: Comma, Comma (0), Currency, Currency (0), Normal, and Percent. Normal is the default style for the entire worksheet. Redefining the formats associated with the Normal style changes the format used throughout a worksheet in those cells not affected by special formatting.

Tip
You can add the Style list to any toolbar by dragging the Style button from the Text Formatting **C**ategories list in the Customize toolbar dialog box. See Chapter 41.

You can apply a style in two ways. Both ways require that you first select the cell(s) to which you want the styles formats applied. Then you choose the style from the Style list on the toolbar or from the Style dialog box.

To apply a style using the Style list on the toolbar, follow these steps:

1. Select the cell or range you want to format.
2. Select the Style list in the toolbar by clicking the down arrow.
3. Click the name of the style that defines the formats you want to apply.

Tip
If you have many style names in the worksheet, it's quicker to select the Style list in the toolbar, type a style name, and press Enter.

To apply a style using the command, follow these steps:

1. Select the cell(s) to which you want the style applied.
2. Choose the F**o**rmat **S**tyle command to display the Style dialog box.
3. Select the **S**tyle Name list box, and then select the style name from the list. Alternatively, you can type the name in the box. When you select or type the name, the Style Includes box shows the formats that are contained in that style.

4. If you want to use some of a style's formatting but exclude some of the formats in a style, deselect the check box of the formats you do not want applied. The check boxes you can deselect are **N**umber, **F**ont, A**l**ignment, **B**order, **P**atterns, and P**r**otection.

5. Choose OK.

Tip
You can see quickly which style was applied to a selected cell by looking at the style listed in the toolbar's Style box.

Whether a style's formats overwrite existing formats in a cell depends on whether check boxes in the Style Includes group were selected to override conflicting styles. For example, in step 4, if you cleared the **P**atterns check box in the Style Includes group, you can use the style on any cell without changing the existing pattern in the cell.

Creating Styles

You can create styles in three different ways. You can create them by using the existing format in a cell as an example; you can create them by choosing formats from dialog boxes; or you can merge styles that exist in another workbook.

Creating a Style by Example. If a cell on the sheet already has the formats you want associated with a style, you can use the formats in that cell to define a new style. You can use this method of *style by example* to create styles with either the toolbar and mouse or with the Forma**t** **S**tyle command. If you have multiple cells selected, the style includes only formatting attributes that are common to all of the cells.

To use menu commands to create a style by example, follow these steps:

1. Select a cell containing the formats you want to include in a style.

2. Select the F**o**rmat **S**tyle command. The Style dialog box appears (see fig. 10.33).

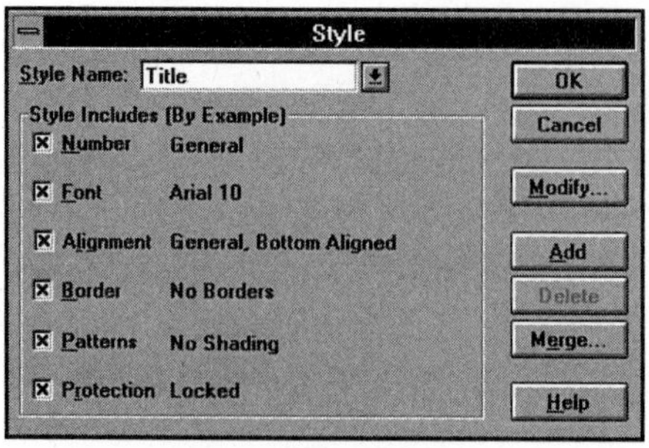

Fig. 10.33
Type a new style name into the **S**tyle Name text box to create a style by example.

3. Select the **S**tyle Name text box and type a new name.

4. Choose OK.

Notice that you can read a description of what the current cell's formatting contains, and what the new style will contain, in the Style Includes box.

Creating a Style by Defining It. If you do not have a mouse or if an example of your style does not exist in the workbook, you can define a style by selecting formats just as you select formats from the F**o**rmat commands.

To define a style by using the Format Style command, follow these steps:

Tip
It's usually easier to create a style by example than to define it by menu choices. You also see results on the sheet before you create the style.

1. Choose the F**o**rmat **S**tyle command.

2. Select the **S**tyle Name list box and type a new name.

> **Caution**
>
> Excel does not warn you if you are about to change an existing style. To make sure that you are not using an existing name, click the down arrow and scroll through the list; or press Alt+S, and then press the down arrow and scroll down.

3. Choose the **M**odify button to display the Format Cells dialog box (see fig. 10.34).

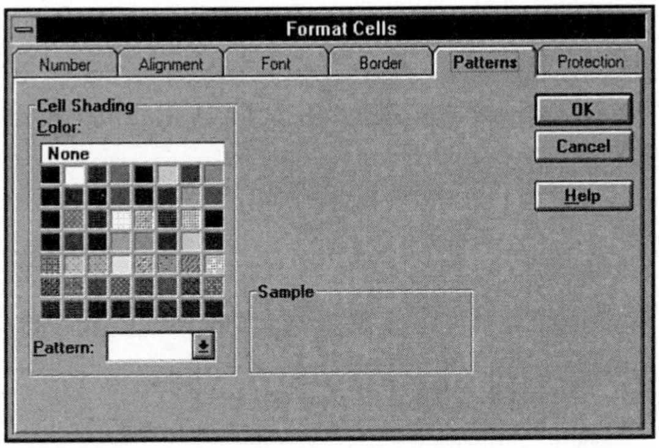

Fig. 10.34
Use the tabs in the Format Cells dialog box to define a new style.

4. Select the formats you want to associate with this style by selecting the appropriate tabs and options from the Format Cells dialog box. Choose OK.

5. If you do not want the style to include a type of formatting, such as patterns, deselect the appropriate check box in the Style Includes box. (The style you are defining changes only the formats that have check boxes selected in the Style Includes box.)

6. If you want to keep this style and define additional styles, choose the **A**dd button. If you want to keep this style and apply it to the selected cells, choose OK or press Enter. If you want to keep this style but not apply it to the selected cells, choose **A**dd and then Close.

Clearing a format check box in the Style Includes group affects the formats a style changes when applied to a cell. If a check box is deselected when the style is defined, when you apply the style to a cell already containing formats, the cell keeps its original formatting for those deselected formats.

Merging Styles. You may have worksheets or macro sheets that contain styles you want to use on other worksheets and macro sheets. You can copy styles between workbooks through a process called *merging*. You must take into consideration, however, the fact that *all* styles from the source workbook are merged into the target sheet; they replace styles in the target sheet having the same name.

To copy styles from a source workbook to a target workbook, follow these steps:

1. Open both workbooks and activate the workbook that will receive the styles.

2. Choose the F**o**rmat **S**tyle command.

3. Choose the M**e**rge button. The Merge Styles dialog box is displayed (see fig. 10.35).

Tip
When merging styles from another workbook, the source workbook must be open.

4. Select from the **M**erge Styles From list the source workbook that contains the styles you want to copy.

5. Choose OK. You may see an alert box as shown in figure 10.36.

   You see the alert box only if the source and target workbooks have styles with the same names and the styles with the same names have different definitions.

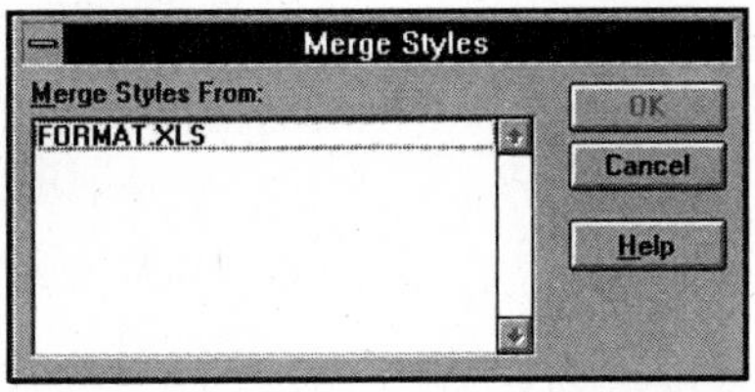

Fig. 10.35
Merging styles from another workbook.

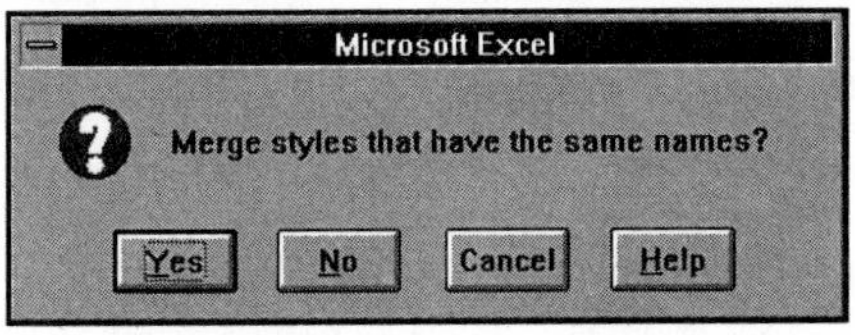

Fig. 10.36
You are warned if styles being copied into a workbook could replace styles with the same names.

6. If the source workbook contains styles with the same names as styles in the target workbook, select one of the following alternatives from the alert box:

   Select **Y**es if you want the source styles to replace styles with the same name in the target workbook.

   Select **N**o if you want to merge all styles except those with the same name.

   Select Cancel if you don't want to merge styles after all.

   Excel returns you to the Style dialog box.

7. Choose the Close button in the Style dialog box to close the dialog box without applying a style to the current selection.

Redefining Styles

In addition to saving time used in applying multiple formats, styles also save you time when you need to reformat a document. If your document uses styles, you need only to redefine the style. All cells in the workbook using that style immediately reformat to match the style's new definition.

> **Caution**
>
> Be careful when you redefine a style. Redefining the appearance of a style on one sheet redefines the appearance of cells using that same style on other sheets in the same workbook.

If you decide that you need a format different from the one used in an existing style, you have two choices: create a new style for use with new formatting, or redefine an existing style. The advantage to redefining an existing style is that all cells currently assigned to that style update to use the new formats in the redefined style. This feature makes reformatting all the headings, titles, dates, or totals in a document an easy task. If you redefine the formats associated with a style named Headings, for example, all cells that use the Headings style take on the new format definition.

Redefining a Style by Example. To redefine a style by using an example, follow these steps:

1. Select a cell that is formatted with the style you want to redefine.
2. Format the cell so that it has the new formats you want for the style's definition.
3. Use either the toolbar or the F**o**rmat **S**tyle command to reapply the same style name to the cell.
4. An alert box appears asking if you want to redefine the style. Choose one of the following alternatives:

   Select **Y**es to redefine the existing style.

   Select **N**o to keep the existing style and apply it again to the cell.

   Select Cancel to make no changes to the style or cell.

Tip
Remember, the Styles button does not appear on any default toolbar. You must customize a toolbar to display this button.

Redefining a Style by Format Commands. If a style is complicated or if you know exactly how you want to redefine the style, you probably want to redefine the style through Excel's format commands.

To redefine a style through Excel's format commands and dialog boxes, follow these steps:

1. Choose the F**o**rmat **S**tyle command.
2. Choose the **M**odify button to display the Format Cells dialog box.
3. Select the tab for the type of formatting you want to redefine.
4. Change the options you have selected in the tab to match the changes you want in the style.
5. Choose OK to return to the Style dialog box.

6. Choose OK to redefine the style and apply it to the current cell. Choose **A**dd to redefine the style and keep the dialog box open for more definitions. Choose Close to close the dialog box without applying the style to the selected cell.

Redefining the Default (Normal) Style

The default (standard) format is stored in Excel's Normal style format. If you type in an unformatted cell, Excel uses the Normal style. If you redefine the Normal style, all the cells that you did not format with a style change to match the new Normal definition. If you delete formats from a cell, the cell is reset to the Normal style. Normal style is used also for the column and row headings, fonts, and as the default font for print headers and footers.

To redefine the Normal style and thus the formatting used as the standard when you insert new sheets in the workbook, use one of the previously described methods to redefine the Normal style.

Deleting Styles

If you no longer use a style, delete it to avoid clutter, prevent incorrect use, and to make other styles easier to find.

To delete a style, follow these steps:

1. Choose the F**o**rmat **S**tyle command.
2. From the **S**tyle Name list, select the style you want to delete. You cannot delete Excel's predefined styles.
3. Choose the **D**elete button.
4. If you want the cell to return to Normal style, choose OK or Close. If you want to apply a new style, select the style and choose OK.

Tips about Styles

A style is used by all sheets in a workbook—if you redefine a style in one sheet, you change the definition of that style in other sheets of the same workbook. In some cases, you may have multiple sheets in a workbook that need similar style names, but you don't want the potential problems that can arise if a style in one sheet is redefined. To prevent confusion, assign your style names a prefix that identifies the sheet on which they are to be used. For example, you may have a budget workbook containing sheets from Divisions A, B, and C. This same workbook contains two different final reports.

Because subtotals may be formatted in each of these types of sheets, you may want to assign style names of DivSubTotal, YTDSubTotal, and EOMSubTotal.

If most of the sheets in a workbook need Normal style defined one way, but a few sheets need Normal defined a different way, don't despair. You can't have a different Normal style on the few sheets that are different, but you can apply one style to the entire worksheet before you start work. To apply a style to an entire worksheet, click the rectangle that is to the left of the column headings and above the row headings. If you are using the keyboard, press Shift+Ctrl+space bar. Now apply a style to the entire worksheet. This has nearly the same effect as redefining Normal for that specific sheet. Be aware that if you clear the formatting from a range, the style for that range returns to the Normal style used in the workbook.

Also note that you can start up Excel with a worksheet customized to your liking preloaded. Simply set the styles on a worksheet the way you want them, and then save the worksheet as a *template* with the file name SHEET1.XLT in the EXCEL\XLSTART directory. Whenever you launch Excel, the SHEET1.XLT template will load automatically; you can then save the worksheet under a different name when ready. (Any worksheet or template located in the XLSTART directory will automatically load when you launch Excel.)

Protecting Sheets and Workbooks

If you develop Excel worksheets for use by inexperienced operators, if you create worksheets for sale, or if you work in the mistake-filled hours after midnight, you will find this section helpful. With Excel, you can protect cells, graphical objects, sheets, windows, and entire workbooks. If you need to protect confidential or proprietary information, you also can hide formulas so that they do not appear in the formula bar. And you can use a password to prevent unauthorized people from changing the protection status or the display of hidden information.

The procedure for protecting a worksheet and its contents involves two commands. The first command formats the cells or objects that you want unprotected. The second command turns on protection for a sheet or the entire workbook.

Unprotecting and Hiding Formulas

Cell protection is a valuable feature that prevents someone from accidentally entering data on top of a formula and prevents unauthorized users from changing your formulas. You also can specify whether a cell's contents are visible in the formula bar. Even when the cell contents are hidden from the formula bar, the cell's value or formula results still appear in the worksheet.

The default format for all cells is protected and visible. Using the following steps, you can format specific cells that you want users to enter data in or where you want cell contents hidden from the formula bar. Protection and hiding do not take effect until you choose the T**o**ols **P**rotection command.

To unprotect a cell so that it can be changed, or to hide a cell's contents from the formula bar, follow these steps:

1. Select the cell or range that you want to unprotect or whose contents you want to hide from the formula bar.
2. Choose the F**o**rmat C**e**lls command.
3. Select the Protection tab of the Format Cells dialog box (see fig. 10.37).

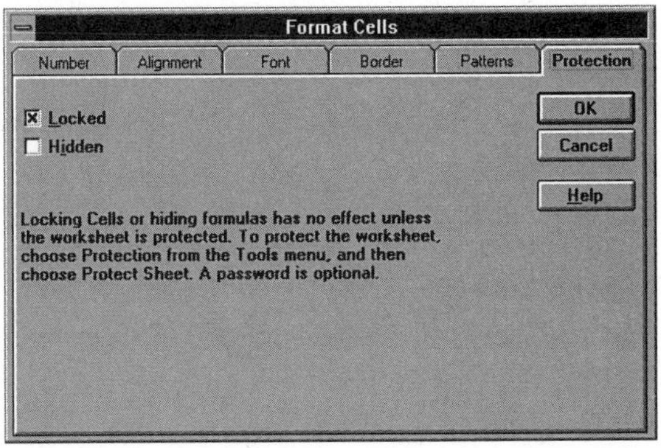

Fig.10.37
First format cells as unlocked or hidden, and then turn on protection for the entire sheet or workbook.

4. Clear the **L**ocked check box to mark the cell or range as one that can be changed, or select the H**i**dden check box to mark the cell or range as one whose contents do not show in the formula bar.
5. Choose OK.

You can continue to change all cells on the worksheet and see any cell contents until you turn on protection for the worksheet.

Turning On Protection

To turn on protection for a sheet or workbook, follow these steps:

1. Choose the T**o**ols **P**rotection command. Choose either the **P**rotect Sheet or Protect **W**orkbook subcommand.
2. If you choose to protect the active sheet, select what you want to protect: **C**ontents, **O**bjects, or **S**cenarios.

   Or

   If you choose to protect the workbook, select what you want to protect: **S**tructure or **W**indows.
3. If you prefer, enter a password in the **P**assword text box. You can include numbers, spaces, and upper- and lowercase characters.
4. Choose OK.

Protected windows, contents, and objects cannot be moved, sized, or formatted. Protect objects that you want to lock into place on a worksheet, and protect windows that are prepositioned for use by novice users. Protecting contents prevents the user from changing a cell unless you formatted it as unlocked. Protecting scenarios keeps users from changing the sets of data in scenarios. Protecting a workbook's structure prevents sheets from being inserted, deleted, or moved.

You can turn on protection without using a password. If you do enter a password, you are asked to retype it just to ensure that you typed it correctly the first time. Remember both the spelling and the case you use; the password is case-sensitive.

To unprotect your sheet or workbook, choose the T**o**ols **P**rotection command, and then the Un**p**rotect Sheet or Unprotect **W**orkbook subcommand. If you entered a password, you are asked to type it. Re-enter it exactly the same as the original, including spelling and capitalization.

After you protect the worksheet, look through some of the menus. Notice that most of the commands are grayed and unusable. The only commands available on a protected sheet or workbook are those commands that affect items that are not protected.

Tips about Protecting Sheets and Workbooks

You can make data-entry forms that are easier to use if you unlock cells in which you want users to type data and turn off gridlines. Before entering data, protect the contents of the sheet. Pressing the Tab or Shift+Tab key moves the active cell only between unlocked cells.

Don't forget your password. If you do, you cannot get back in and make changes. Here are a few helpful hints for choosing passwords:

- Remember the characters that you capitalize in a password. Excel passwords differentiate between upper- and lowercase letters.
- Avoid using passwords that are easy to figure out, such as the following commonly used choices: your mother's maiden name, your spouse's maiden or middle name, your birthdate, or your employee number.
- Don't stick your password to the computer with a piece of tape. (Some people do.)
- Use symbols or uncommon capitalization that you will not forget.
- Have a senior officer in the company keep a confidential list of passwords to ensure that a password is accessible if the original guardian isn't.
- Change passwords whenever you doubt security.

For Related Information

- "Password-Protecting Your Workbooks," p. 279

Formatting a Group of Sheets in a Workbook

You can save time by formatting a group of sheets in a workbook. As you format the active sheet in the group, the formatting passes through to the same cells in the other sheets in the group. Sheets that you want to group together must be in the same workbook.

Before you can do group formatting, you must group together sheets by selecting all the sheets in a workbook that will belong to the same group. To do so, you must use a mouse. To group sheets that are adjacent in a workbook, click the first sheet tab, and then scroll to display the last sheet tab and Shift+click the last sheet tab. To group sheets that are not adjacent, click the sheet tab, and then Ctrl+click all other sheet tabs you want selected. Notice

For Related Information

- "Selecting and Moving between Sheets," p. 67

that the title bar now contains `[Group]`. All formatting you do on the active worksheet also applies to other sheets in the group. When you want to separate the group into individual sheets, click just one sheet's tab.

Setting Startup Formats

There are two different reasons you may want to change how Excel opens new worksheets and workbooks. The most common reason for wanting to modify a new workbook or worksheet is to change the standard font, Normal style, used in unformatted cells. The second reason is that you may want new workbooks or worksheets that already contain titles, text, data, formulas, and formats. These *templates* also can contain formatting styles that you create, as well as macros or Visual Basic modules to automate work. If you are interested in learning how to create and use templates or styles, refer to Chapter 42, "Creating Templates and Controlling Excel's Startup."

To change the standard font used by Excel when it opens new sheets, follow these steps:

1. Choose the T**o**ols **O**ptions command.
2. Select the General view.
3. Select a new standard font from the St**a**ndard Font list and a new size from the Si**z**e list.
4. Choose OK.
5. An alert box appears, warning you that you must restart Excel before the new standard font can take effect. Choose OK.

The next time you start Excel, the standard font you selected is used as the new Normal font for all new worksheets and workbooks, unless a worksheet or workbook template take priority. Worksheet and workbook templates are described in Chapter 42, "Creating Templates and Controlling Excel's Startup."

Troubleshooting

Changing the Standard font has no effect on other worksheets in a workbook.

You may need to close the workbook and reopen for a universal change like this to take effect. You also may be using a different or customized template for one or more of the worksheets in your workbook that is unaffected by this change—in which case you have to change the font in each worksheet individually.

Changing the Normal style does not effect new worksheets.

The Normal style only impacts the active worksheet. Change the Normal style separately in each new worksheet.

For more information about working with the Normal style, see Chapter 42, "Creating Templates and Controlling Excel's Startup."

From Here...

For information relating directly to this chapter, you may want to review the following chapters:

- Chapter 17, "Adding Graphics Elements to Sheets." In this Chapter, you learn how to place clip art, charts, and other graphics objects in Excel.
- Chapter 20, "Publishing Worksheets and Charts." This chapter teaches you how to add desktop publishing layout elements to your Excel information.

Chapter 11

Printing Worksheets

Excel enables you to use the full capabilities of your printer. Using Excel, you can achieve better quality with your printer than you ever could before. Excel reports printed from laser printers can look as though they have been typeset.

Figures 11.1 and 11.2 give you some idea of what you can produce. Excel can produce the equivalent of preprinted invoices or annual report-quality financial statements.

Excel saves you from the trial and error process of printing to see the result. You can preview the printed page on-screen before you send it to the printer. You also can adjust margins and column widths in the preview.

When you have many different reports or *views* to print from a worksheet, you can use the **V**iew **V**iew Manager command to assign a name and print settings to each different view. Views and the View Manager are described in Chapter 16, "Managing the Worksheet Display."

If your work involves multiple sheets or views that need to be printed in sequence, including sequential page numbers, use the Report Manager. The Report Manager enables you to list the different views and scenarios that you want printed. These views and scenarios are then printed as a single document. (*Scenarios* are stored collections of input values that enable you to print multiple test results. The Scenario Manager is described in Chapter 28, "Testing Multiple Solutions with the Scenarios.") The Report Manager is described near the end of this chapter.

Windows' Print Manager also increases your work efficiency. The Print Manager stores the material you want to print in a temporary disk file called the *print spool* or the *print queue*. This process enables the computer to print while you continue working on other projects. Use the Windows Control Panel to activate the Print Manager.

In this chapter, you learn how to:

- Set up your printer
- Define the page setup
- Preview a document
- Print Report Manager reports
- Print documents

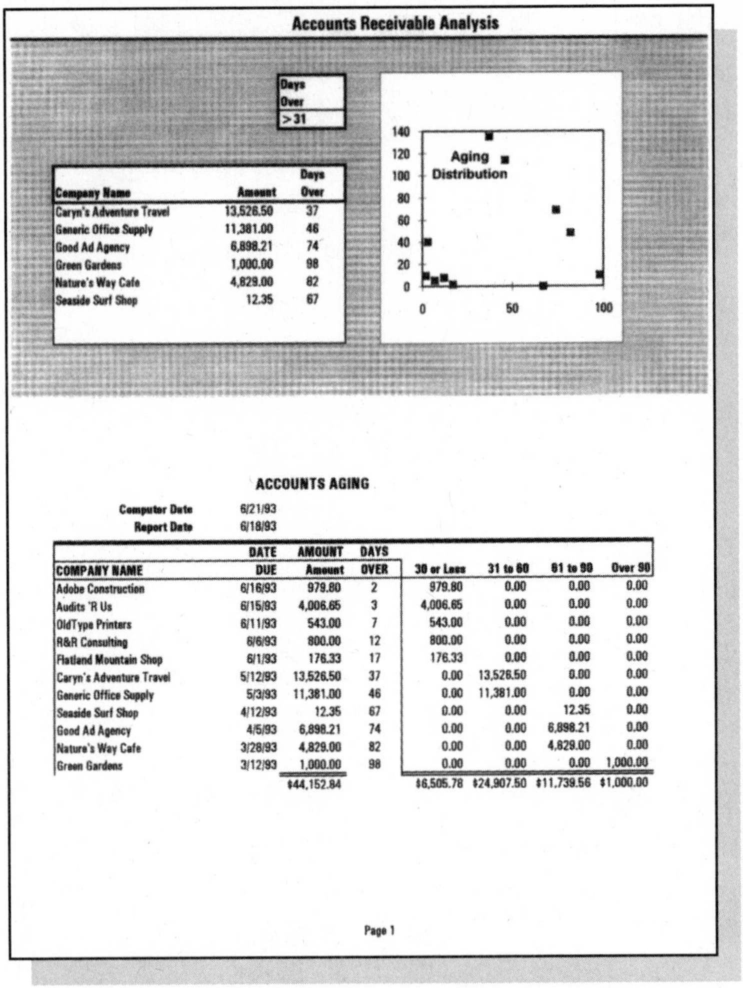

Accounts Receivable Analysis

Days
Over
>31

Company Name	Amount	Days Over
Caryn's Adventure Travel	13,526.50	37
Generic Office Supply	11,381.00	46
Good Ad Agency	6,898.21	74
Green Gardens	1,000.00	98
Nature's Way Cafe	4,829.00	82
Seaside Surf Shop	12.35	67

ACCOUNTS AGING

Computer Date 6/21/93
Report Date 6/18/93

COMPANY NAME	DATE DUE	AMOUNT Amount	DAYS OVER	30 or Less	31 to 60	61 to 90	Over 90
Adobe Construction	6/16/93	979.80	2	979.80	0.00	0.00	0.00
Audits 'R Us	6/15/93	4,006.65	3	4,006.65	0.00	0.00	0.00
OldType Printers	6/11/93	543.00	7	543.00	0.00	0.00	0.00
R&R Consulting	6/6/93	800.00	12	800.00	0.00	0.00	0.00
Flatland Mountain Shop	6/1/93	176.33	17	176.33	0.00	0.00	0.00
Caryn's Adventure Travel	5/12/93	13,526.50	37	0.00	13,526.50	0.00	0.00
Generic Office Supply	5/3/93	11,381.00	46	0.00	11,381.00	0.00	0.00
Seaside Surf Shop	4/12/93	12.35	67	0.00	0.00	12.35	0.00
Good Ad Agency	4/5/93	6,898.21	74	0.00	0.00	6,898.21	0.00
Nature's Way Cafe	3/28/93	4,829.00	82	0.00	0.00	4,829.00	0.00
Green Gardens	3/12/93	1,000.00	98	0.00	0.00	0.00	1,000.00
		$44,152.84		$6,505.78	$24,907.50	$11,739.56	$1,000.00

Page 1

Fig. 11.1
An aging analysis.

Reviewing the Printing Process

EXCEL 5

Usually, printing consists of the following steps (these steps, along with the available options, are described in detail later in this chapter):

1. Select the area to be printed.
2. Set manual page breaks, if necessary, with the **I**nsert Page **B**reak command.
3. Choose the **F**ile **P**rint command.
4. Choose the P**r**inter button and select your printer. You only need to do this once unless you change printers.

5. Choose the Page Set**u**p button to set margins, page orientation, print quality, headers and footers, page titles, and other options.

6. Choose the OK button to print your document, or choose the Print Previe**w** command to see how the printed document will appear. While in the preview mode, choose the Prin**t** button when you want to print.

LaserPro Corporation
Balance Sheet
December 31, 1994

	This Year	Last Year	Change
Assets			
Current Assets			
Cash	$247,886	$126,473	96%
Accounts receivable	863,652	524,570	65%
Inventory	88,328	65,508	35%
Investments	108,577	31,934	240%
Total current assets	$1,308,443	$748,485	75%
Fixed Assets			
Machinery and equipment	$209,906	$158,730	32%
Vehicles	429,505	243,793	76%
Office furniture	50,240	36,406	38%
(Accumulated depreciation)	(101,098)	(64,394)	57%
Total fixed assets	$588,553	$374,535	57%
Total Assets	**$1,896,996**	**$1,123,020**	**69%**

	This Year	Last Year	Change
Liabilities and Shareholders' Equity			
Current Liabilities			
Accounts payable	$426,041	$332,845	28%
Notes payable	45,327	23,486	93%
Accrued liabilities	34,614	26,026	33%
Income taxes payable	88,645	51,840	71%
Total current liabilities	$594,627	$434,197	37%
Noncurrent Liabilities			
Long-term debt	$488,822	$349,253	40%
Deferred federal tax	147,844	92,101	61%
Total noncurrent liabilities	$636,666	$441,354	44%
Shareholders' Equity			
Common stock	$1,000	$1,000	0%
Retained earnings	664,703	246,469	170%
Total shareholders' equity	$665,703	$247,469	169%
Total Liabilities and Equity	**$1,896,996**	**$1,123,020**	**69%**

Fig. 11.2
A balance sheet.

Setting Up Your Printer

Before you can print, you need to install and set up your printer. Usually, you install and set up your printer only once, unless you change printers or use more than one printer. The printer you select and set up becomes the default printer for all Windows applications. The *default printer* is the printer that is used automatically, so you don't have to select a printer every time you print.

Installing a Printer

When you install Windows, you are asked to select the printer(s) you use. To install or remove printers after installing Windows, open the Main window in the Program Manager and start the Control Panel application. Start the Printers application and press F1 for Help about the Printers application. Windows needs to read the original Windows disks to install the printer driver files; Windows also may need to read supplemental disks supplied with your printer.

Selecting the Printer

You may have installed more than one printer when you installed Windows, or you may have added more printers by using the Printers application in the Control Panel. Previous versions of Excel required you to use the Windows Control Panel to change printers; with Excel 5, however, you can change printers without leaving Excel. To change between printers while in Excel, follow these steps:

1. Choose the **F**ile **P**rint command. Excel displays the Print dialog box.

2. Choose the P**r**inter button. Excel displays the Printer Setup dialog box.

3. Select the printer you want to use from the **P**rinter list in the Printer Setup dialog box.

4. Choose the **S**etup button if you have not used this printer previously or if you want to change the printer's paper size, paper orientation, or print resolution.

   A Setup dialog box similar to the box shown in figure 11.3 appears. You establish the default settings for your printer in this dialog box. After you establish these settings, you should rarely have to use this dialog box again.

5. Select Paper Si**z**e, Paper **S**ource, and Orientation (**P**ortrait or **L**andscape). Also, select options appropriate to additional memory or font cartridges available in your printer. The Setup dialog box is different for various printers. Table 11.1 lists some of the available options.

   If necessary, choose the **O**ptions button to make more selections specific to your printer. Choose OK to close the Options dialog box.

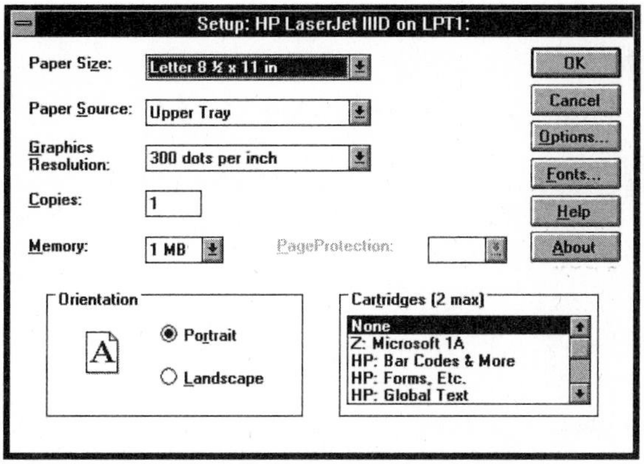

Fig. 11.3
Setup dialog boxes vary with each printer.

Table 11.1 Printer Setup Options

Option	Description
Resolution	Specifies print quality; printing at high resolution slows the printer speed but produces better graphic images.
Paper Si**z**e	Lists the sizes and types of paper available.
Paper **S**ource	Lists the bins from which your printer may input paper.
Memory	Specifies the exact model of printer and its memory capacity (to ensure that Windows uses all the features of this model).
Orientation	Specifies the placement of print on the page. Po**r**trait prints characters on the page as they appear in a normal letter; **L**andscape prints sideways on the paper and is useful for making transparencies and charts.
Car**t**ridges	Specifies the types of font cartridges available.

6. Choose OK to close the Setup dialog box and return to the Printer Setup dialog box.

7. Choose OK a second time to close the Printer Setup dialog box and return to the Print dialog box. This section and the following sections of this chapter describe how to define the page setup, page layout, and printing range. Choose Cancel if you do not want to print now.

The printer and printer settings you choose in the Printer Setup dialog box are the default printer and printer settings. These settings remain in effect for all documents, even those in other applications, until you change these settings.

If you have questions about the settings available for your printer, choose the **H**elp button in the Setup dialog box.

Defining the Page Setup

The **F**ile Page Set**u**p command (and the Page Set**u**p button in the Print dialog box) controls all the settings you usually need in order to print. A few items controlled from the Page Setup dialog box include the position of print on the page, paper orientation (vertical or sideways), headers and footers, gridlines, color or black and white, and row and column headings.

To change the page setup for the printed page, complete the following steps:

1. Choose the **F**ile Page Set**u**p command, or choose the Page Set**u**p button from the Print dialog box.

2. Change the page options as needed in the Page Setup dialog box (see fig. 11.4). The following sections describe these options in more detail. (Notice that the Page Setup dialog box opens with whatever tab was last used as the active tab; it will not always open with the Page tab active, as shown in fig. 11.4.)

3. Choose the OK button.

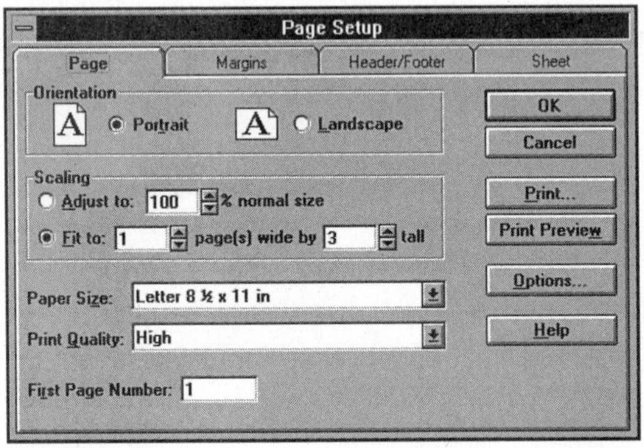

Fig. 11.4
Use the Page Setup dialog box to set options for page orientation, paper size, margins, headers and footers, and the printing range for the spreadsheet.

The options available in the Page Setup dialog box are grouped into separate options tabs: Page, Margins, Header/Footer, and Sheet. Usually, you need to set options on several of these tabs to set up the page.

The Page tab enables you to select the paper size, the print quality, and the page orientation. The Page tab of the Page Setup dialog box also enables you to reduce or enlarge the size of the report or sheet that you are printing.

The Margins tab enables you to set the top, bottom, left, and right margins for the printed page, and also enables you to select how far from the top or bottom edge of the page the headers or footers are printed. The Margins tab also enables you to select whether the printed page should be centered vertically or horizontally, or both.

The Header/Footer tab enables you to choose the content of the headers and footers that are printed on each page. The Header/Footer tab also enables you to create custom headers and footers.

Finally, the Sheet tab enables you to set the print area, the print titles, and the order in which pages are printed. The options on the Sheet tab also enable you to choose whether to print gridlines, notes, change colors to black and white, or print row and column headings. You can also use the Sheet tab to select draft quality printing.

The remaining parts of this section describe how to use the Page, Margins, Header/Footer, and Sheet tabs to accomplish specific tasks.

Setting the Paper Margins

Excel's character width changes with each different font size. Consequently, you need to measure your margins in inches rather than by a count of characters. Table 11.2 shows the default settings for margins.

Table 11.2 Default Margin Settings

Margin	Default in Inches
Left	0.75
Right	0.75
Top	1
Bottom	1

Measure the margins from the edge of the paper inward. When you set the top and bottom margins, keep in mind that headers and footers automatically print 1/2 inch from the top or bottom of the paper, unless you change the header or footer distance from the edge of the page.

Many laser printers are unable to print to the edge of the paper. Because of this limitation, you may not be able to set margins of less than 1/4 inch.

Many inkjet printers also cannot print to the edge of the paper and limit the left and right margins to a minimum of 1/4 inch, while the top and bottom margins are limited to a minimum of 1/2 inch.

To set or change the margins, follow these steps:

1. In the Page Setup dialog box, select the Margins tab to bring the margins options forward, as shown in fig. 11.5.

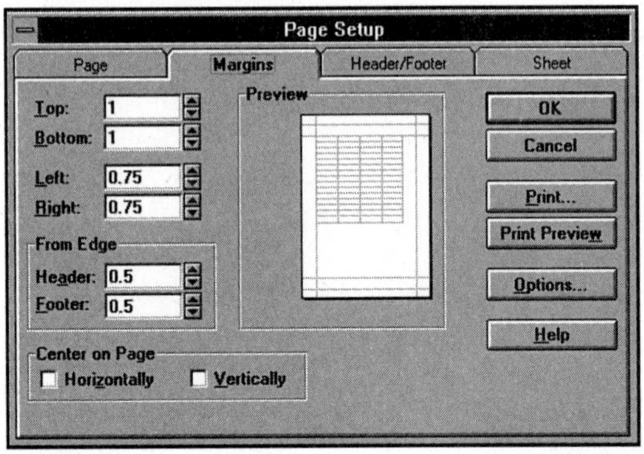

Fig. 11.5
Changing the margin settings in the Page Setup dialog box.

2. Set the margins options in any combination. The following table describes the available options (remember that distances are measured in inches):

Option	Description
Top	Sets the size of the margin at the top of the page.
Bottom	Sets the size of the margin at the bottom of the page.
Left	Sets the size of the margin at the left edge of the page.
Right	Sets the size of the margin at the right edge of the page.
He**a**der	Sets the distance from the top edge of the page at which the header (if any) will print.
Footer	Sets the distance from the bottom edge of the page at which the footer (if any) will print.
Hori**z**ontally	Selecting this check box (so that an × appears) causes Excel to center the spreadsheet horizontally on the printed page.
Vertically	Selecting this check box (so that an × appears) causes Excel to center the spreadsheet vertically on the printed page.

The Preview area shows how the changes you make in the margins affect the printed page.

3. Choose OK if you have finished making changes to the Page Setup options.

Setting the Page Orientation and Paper Size

If the spreadsheet document is wider than tall, you may want to use a landscape orientation when you print. (*Landscape* means printing across the long edge of the page.) Alternatively, if your printer can handle different paper sizes, you may want to print some documents on legal-sized (or some other size) rather than the standard letter-sized documents.

To change the page orientation and paper size, select the Page tab in the Page Setup dialog box to display the page options. In the Orientation area of the Page options, select Por**t**rait or **L**andscape, as desired.

To change the paper size, select the Page tab in the Page Setup dialog box, and then use the Paper Si**z**e drop-down list to select the desired paper size. The choice of paper sizes available to you depends on the printer you have selected.

Turning Gridlines and Row or Column Headings On and Off

For most printed reports, you don't want to print gridlines or the row and column headings. If you turn off gridlines in the worksheet by using the **T**ools **O**ptions command, the gridlines also turn off for printed copies. You also can turn on or off the printing of gridlines in the Page Setup dialog box. To turn on or off printing gridlines or row and column headings, follow these steps:

1. In the Page Setup dialog box, select the Sheet tab to bring the Sheet options forward (see fig. 11.6).

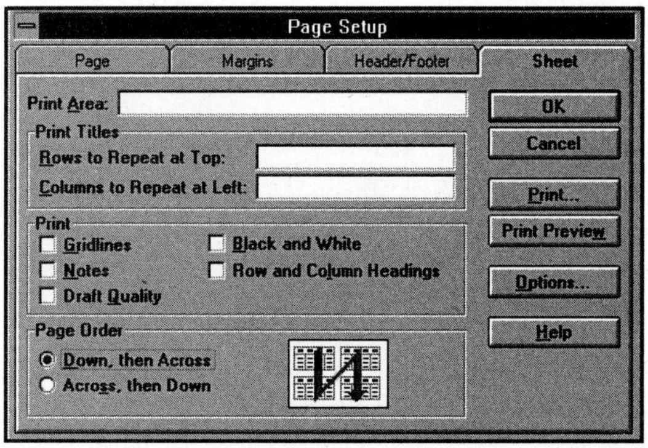

Fig. 11.6
Changing the print titles, print options, and page order settings in the Page Setup dialog box.

2. Set or clear the **G**ridlines check box in the Print area to turn on or off gridline printing.

3. Set or clear the Row and Co**l**umn Headings check box in the Print area to turn on or off printing the row and column headings.

4. Choose OK when you finish making changes to the Page Setup options.

You probably will want to print row and column headings when you print worksheet documentation showing formulas or when you print notes entered in cells in your spreadsheet. If you use the **T**ools **O**ptions command with the Fo**r**mulas check box on the View tab selected, you can display the formulas on-screen so that they print.

Creating Headers and Footers

You can create headers and footers that place a title, date, or page number at the top or bottom of each printed page of your worksheet. You also can format them with different fonts, styles, and sizes. Use headers and footers to enter a confidentiality statement, to document the worksheet's creator, to show the printout date, or to note the source of worksheet and chart data.

Excel uses the sheet name as the header and uses the word *Page* and the page number as the footer. You can delete or change these.

Headers and footers always use a 3/4-inch (.75) side margin and a default 1/2-inch (.5) margin at the top and bottom. You can change the distance of the header or footer from the top or bottom edge of the page; follow the instructions on changing margins in the preceding part of this section. If you specify page setup margins that cross the header and footer boundaries, the document may print over a header or footer.

To create or change a header or footer, use the Page Setup dialog box. Open the Page Setup dialog box by choosing the **F**ile Page Set**u**p command or by choosing the Page Set**u**p button in the Print dialog box. In the Page Setup dialog box, select the Header/Footer tab to display the header and footer options, shown in figure 11.7. The Header/Footer tab displays a sample of the currently selected header and footer.

EXCEL 5

Excel provides several predefined formats for the headers and footers. To select one of the predefined header or footer formats, use the He**a**der or **F**ooter drop-down lists, and choose the desired format. The same formats are available for both headers and footers.

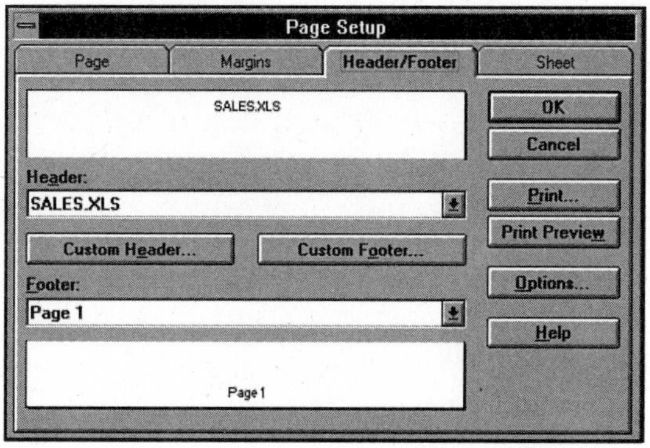

Fig. 11.7
Changing the headers and footers for a printed spreadsheet.

You also can create customized headers and footers using special fonts, symbols, and text you type. To create a custom header or footer, follow these steps:

1. In the Page Setup dialog box, select the Header/Footer tab to display the header and footer options (refer to fig. 11.7).

2. Choose the Custom Header button to create a customized header, or choose Custom Footer to create a customized footer. Figure 11.8 shows the Header dialog box as it first appears; the Footer dialog box, except for its title, is identical.

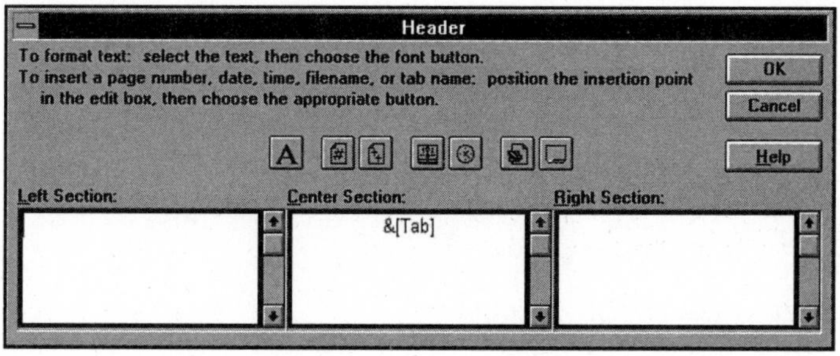

Fig. 11.8
Creating a customized header.

The Header dialog box contains three sections for left-, center-, or right-aligned data. You enter text or codes, such as the date code, into the three sections. The sections are labeled **L**eft Section, **C**enter Section, and **R**ight Section.

3. Enter the text and codes you want for each section of the header or footer. The following paragraphs describe how to use the mouse and the keyboard to select each section and to enter codes.

4. Choose OK.

To enter information into a section with the mouse, click a section and type. Click a code button to enter a code at the insertion point. To format text, select the text and click the Font button to display the font dialog box; select your font formatting options and choose OK. The code buttons and their results are listed in table 11.3.

To enter information from the keyboard, press Alt+*letter* (the L, C, or R key) to move the insertion point into the corresponding section (**L**eft, **C**enter, or **R**ight). Type the text and codes listed in table 11.3, or select code buttons by pressing Tab until the button is selected, and then pressing Enter. Use the **H**elp button if you forget the codes. You can create multiple-line headers or footers by pressing Alt+Enter to break a line.

As the following examples illustrate, you can combine the codes shown in table 11.3 with your own text to create the header and footer you need:

Code:

Left	&L&D Page &P of &N
Center	&C&"Tms Rmn"&14&BABC Investment Corp.
Right	&RMortgage Banking Div.

Result:

12/24/92 Page 1 of 3 **ABC Investment Corp.** Mortgage Banking Div.

When you print or preview the document, the result appears as shown in figure 11.9. Notice that the character-formatting codes cause the text to display with the attributes and fonts you selected; the codes themselves do not display, except when you first type them.

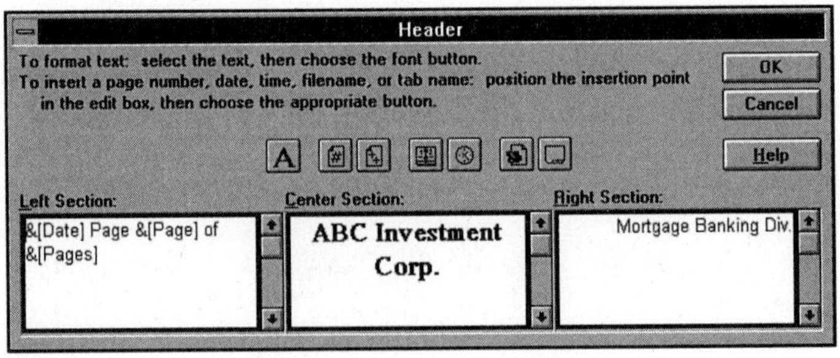

Fig. 11.9
A completed custom header.

Table 11.3 Header and Footer Codes

Button	Code	Effect
	&"fontname"	Prints text that follows (or selected text, if you choose the button) in the font specified. Use the same spelling as in the Format Font dialog box and enclose it in quotes.
	&nn	Prints text that follows (or selected text, if you choose the button) in the font size specified by nn. Use a two-digit point size: 08, 12, or 14.
	&B	Prints text that follows (or selected text, if you choose the button) in bold.
	&I	Prints text that follows (or selected text, if you choose the button) in italic.
	&U	Prints text (or selected text, if you choose the button) that follows as underlined.
	&S	Prints text that follows (or selected text, if you choose the button) with strikethroughs.
	&[Date]	Calendar; inserts the computer's date.
	&[Time]	Clock; inserts the computer's time.
	&[File]	Excel sheet; inserts the name of the file.
	&[Tab]	Excel Tab; inserts the name of the tab in the workbook.
	&[Page]	Inserts the page number.
	&[Page]+#	Inserts the page number plus an amount you specify (#). Use the page code with the plus sign (+) to start printing at a page number greater than the actual page number.
	&[Page]-#	Inserts the page number minus an amount you specify (#). Use the page code with the minus sign (–) to start printing at a page number smaller than the actual page number.
	&[Pages]	Inserts the total number of pages. For example, the header Page &P of &N produces the result, `Page 6 of 15`.
N/A	&&	Prints an ampersand.

By default, headers are printed 1/2 inch from the top of the page, and footers are 1/2 inch from the bottom. If text overlaps the header or footer, use the

Margins tab in the Page Setup dialog box to change the top or bottom margin or to change the distance of the header and footer from the edge of the page.

> **Note**
>
> If you directly type a font name, size, and style, make sure that the font name is in quotation marks and spelled the same as it appears in the Font dialog box. Use TrueType fonts, or use font styles and sizes that are available in your printer.

Specifying the Page Layout Order

When Excel prints a range larger than will fit on one sheet of paper, it prints down the range, and then goes to the columns to the right of the first page and prints down those. In some cases—wide landscape reports, for example—you may want to print so that Excel prints across the wide range first and then goes to the next lower area and goes across it.

To select how you want Excel to print pages, select the Sheet tab in the Page Setup dialog box. From the Page Order group, select either the **D**own, then Across option or the Acro**s**s, then Down option.

Reducing and Enlarging Prints

If the printer supports scalable type or if you use TrueType fonts, you can print a document proportionally reduced or enlarged. By making a proportional reduction, you can fit a document to a page without losing or redoing the formatting. To scale a document, select the Page tab in the Page Setup dialog box (refer to fig. 11.4) and select the **A**djust to option or the **F**it to option.

Use the **A**djust to option to print the document at full size or to scale the document to a specified percentage of full size. Enter the desired size in the **A**djust to text box. Entering a number smaller than 100 reduces the page to that percentage of the original. Entering a number larger than 100 enlarges the page. If the printer is incapable of scaling the print job to fit the page, the **A**djust to and **F**it to boxes are gray.

Use the **F**it to option to tell Excel to scale the document to fit a specified number of pages. In the first text box in the **F**it to option, enter the number of page widths you want the document fit to. In the second text box, enter the number of pages tall that you want the document fit to. If you have a document that usually prints three pages wide and two pages tall, for example, and you want to fit it on a single page, you would enter **1** in both the first and second text box.

Printing Color or Black and White

Although worksheets and charts may use color on-screen, you need to make sure that they will look good on your black-and-white printer. To substitute grays for colors, white background for patterns, and black text for colored text, select the Sheet tab in the Page Setup dialog box, and then select the **B**lack and White check box.

Tip
To print a sheet large enough to use as a wall chart or presentation poster, use the **F**it to or **A**djust to options.

Setting the Print Quality

For many printers, high quality graphics images and smooth text take quite a while to print. You often can save a great deal of printing time by using a lower printing quality. Some printers have a draft quality setting; for other printers, you select the print quality by choosing the number of dots per inch (dpi) that the printer can print. The higher the number of dpi, the higher the printing quality; a print quality setting of 300 dpi is better than a print quality setting of 150 dpi.

Tip
Leave Print **Q**uality set to a high quality and select draft quality printing by selecting the Draft **Q**uality check box on the Sheet tab.

To change the print quality, select the Page tab in the Page Setup dialog box, and then use the Print **Q**uality drop-down list to select the desired print quality. The choice of print qualities available to you depends on the printer that you have selected. If the printer has only one quality setting, then the Print **Q**uality drop-down list is grayed.

For Related Information

- "Using TrueType Fonts," p. 308

Setting the Print Range

By default, Excel prints the entire worksheet unless you specify otherwise. When you need to print only a portion of the worksheet, you must define that area by using either the **F**ile Page Set**u**p command or choosing the Page Set**u**p button in the Print dialog box. The print area can include more than one range.

If you have many print ranges on one worksheet, you may want to create named views of these print ranges and settings. You then can print a range with its settings by returning to that view. If you have many views that you want to print, even from multiple documents, make sure that you read about the Report Manager, described briefly at the end of this chapter and in Chapter 19.

> **Note**
>
> When you work with databases or large worksheets, you may be tempted to put field names or column headings in the header so that you can see the labels on each page of the printout. *Don't!* Labels in the header are difficult to align with columns and cannot be positioned close to the body of the report. Instead, use the options in the Sheet tab of the Page Setup dialog box to set print titles.

Setting a Print Area

The options in the Sheet tab in the Page Setup dialog box control how much of the document is printed; these options also control which cell notes are printed.

To define a single print area, follow these steps:

1. Choose the **F**ile Page Set**u**p command, and then select the Sheet tab to display the Sheet options in the Page Setup dialog box.

2. Place the insertion point in the Print **A**rea text box.

3. Select the range of cells you want to print (drag the Page Setup dialog box out of the way, if necessary).

   Excel enters the cell coordinates in the Print **A**rea text box as you select the printed area.

4. Choose OK to close the Page Setup dialog box.

Cell notes that are in the selected range will print if you select the **N**otes check box in the Print section of the Sheet options.

You also can set the print area by typing the cell coordinates for the top left corner of the print area and the bottom right corner of the print area, separated by a colon, directly into the Print **A**rea text box in the Sheet options of the Page Setup dialog box. To set a print area to print the first three rows and the first three columns of a worksheet, for example, you type **$A$1:$C$3** in the Print **A**rea text box.

After you set the print area, Excel marks the edges of the print area with dashed lines. In figure 11.10, you can see the dashed lines that mark the edges of the print area after the appropriate Page Setup options are chosen. Dashed lines also indicate manual and automatic page breaks. A *page break* indicates the bottom or right edge of the sheet of paper that the document prints on, and shows you where a new printed page begins.

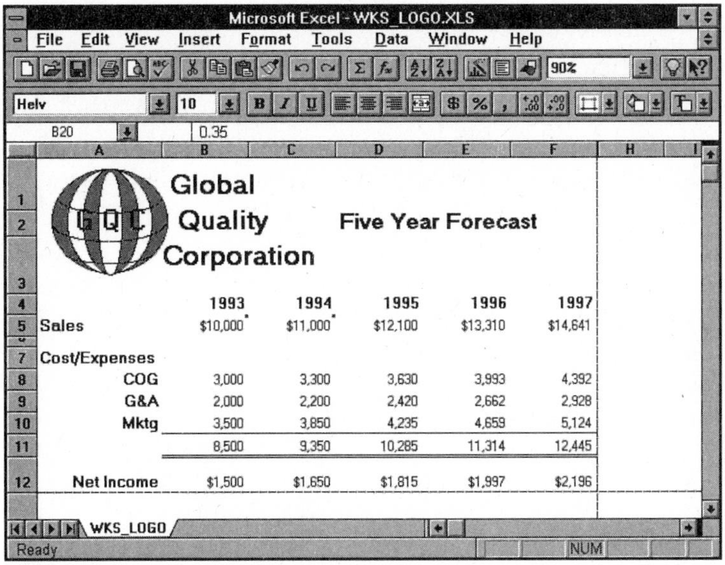

Fig. 11.10
Dashed lines mark the page breaks and the edges of a print area.

Setting the print area with the **F**ile Page Set**u**p command creates a named range called *Print_Area*. You can display this range name and its cell references with the **I**nsert **N**ame **D**efine command.

Removing a Print Area

If you want to return to printing the entire worksheet, remove the print area. To remove a print area, choose the **F**ile Page Set**u**p command, and select the Sheet tab to display the Sheet options. Delete all the text in the Print **A**rea text box to print the entire document, or delete only the cell coordinates for the print area you want to remove.

Adjusting How Pages Print

After you select a print area, you may want to make adjustments to fit the information on the page. You may, for example, want to change the page breaks to keep related data together. You also may want to change the margins or font size so that you can fit the information on the page.

When you set a print area with the **F**ile Page Set**u**p command, Excel displays dashed lines to mark the page boundaries and automatic page breaks. Automatic page breaks are determined by how much of the print area you have selected will fit within the printable area of the page.

Setting Manual Page Breaks. Sometimes you may need to insert a manual page break to override an automatic page break. When you insert manual page breaks, the automatic page breaks reposition automatically.

When you choose the **I**nsert Page **B**reak command, the manual page breaks appear above and to the left of the active cell. Figure 11.11 shows page breaks above and to the left of the active cell. Manual page breaks appear on-screen with a longer and bolder dashed line than the automatic page breaks. Page breaks are easier to see on-screen when you remove gridlines with the **T**ools **O**ptions command (clear the check box on the View tab in the Options dialog box).

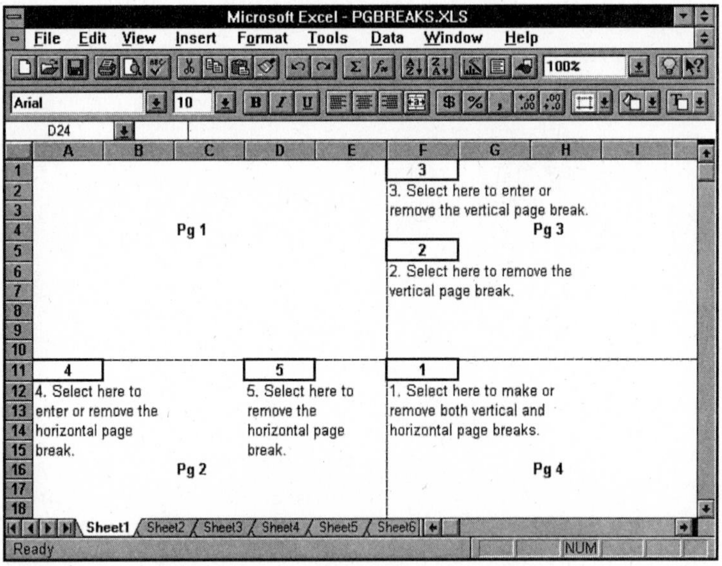

Fig. 11.11
Manual page breaks appear above and to the left of the active cell.

To insert manual page breaks, move the active cell beneath and to the right of the place you want the break, and then choose **I**nsert Page **B**reak. If you want to set vertical page breaks (that affect only the sides), make sure that the active cell is in row 1 before you choose the **I**nsert Page **B**reak command. If you want to set horizontal page breaks (the breaks for only the tops and bottoms of pages), move the active cell to the correct row in column A, and then choose **I**nsert Page **B**reak.

A manual page break stays at the location that you set until you remove it. Remove manual page breaks by first moving the active cell directly below or immediately to the right of the manual page break. Then choose **I**nsert Remove Page **B**reak. This command appears on the menu only when the active cell is positioned correctly. Remove all manual page breaks by selecting the entire document and choosing the **I**nsert Remove Page **B**reak.

Note

Be sure that you try to remove only manual page breaks. You can go crazy trying to remove an automatic page break that you mistake for a manual one.

Fitting More Data on a Page. You can fit more information on a page by decreasing the margins, decreasing the column widths or row heights, or choosing a smaller font size. You also can use the fit-to-page feature described in "Reducing and Enlarging Prints" earlier in this chapter.

If you used styles to format a document, you can change fonts throughout the entire worksheet by redefining the style names used in your worksheet. Normal is the style used in cells that have not been formatted. Use a small font size to fit more data on a page. Save the document before you change fonts so that you can return to the original document easily.

Smaller margins produce more room on the paper. Some laser and inkjet printers can print only within 1/4 inch of the paper's edge.

You also can narrow columns and reduce row height to fit more data on a page. To make sure that all adjustments are the same, select multiple columns before you narrow a column. All the columns will reduce simultaneously.

To fit more of a document on the page, you also can use the **A**djust to option or the **F**it to option found on the Page tab of the Page Setup dialog box. The **F**it to and **A**djust to options are described earlier in this chapter in "Defining the Page Setup."

Setting Multiple Print Areas

Excel can print multiple ranges with a single print command. Although these ranges print sequentially, each range prints on its own sheet.

EXCEL 5

To select multiple print areas, follow these steps:

1. Choose the **F**ile Page Set**u**p command, and select the Sheet tab to display the Sheet options.

2. Place the insertion point in the Print **A**rea text box.

3. Select the first area you want to print (drag the Page Setup dialog box out of the way, if necessary).

   Excel enters the cell coordinates for the selected area in the Print **A**rea text box of the Sheet tab.

4. Type a comma (,) in the Print **A**rea text box, and select the next area you want to print. Select areas in the order that you want them to print.

5. Repeat step 4 until you have selected all the areas you want to print.

6. Choose OK.

This technique works well for creating a single printed report from different areas of a worksheet. Each print area prints on a separate page.

You can also set multiple print ranges by typing the cell coordinates for the top left corner and bottom right corner of each print area (separated by a colon) directly into the Print **A**rea text box in the Sheet tab of the Page Setup dialog box. Separate each set of coordinates for the different print ranges with a comma. For example, typing **$A$1:$C$3,$A$10:$C$13** in the Print **A**rea text box sets two print ranges. The first is for the first three rows and columns of the worksheet, and the second print area contains the first three columns of rows 10 through 13 of the worksheet.

Note

If you frequently print the same parts of a document, save time by learning the **V**iew **V**iew Manager command. The View Manager enables you to assign names to print settings and frequently printed ranges. To print multiple views or to print the same output with different sets of input data, learn about the Report Manager at the end of this chapter. The **V**iew **V**iew Manager command is described in Chapter 16, "Managing the Worksheet Display."

For Related Information

- "Choosing Commands," p. 38
- "Moving Around in a Worksheet," p. 70
- "Selecting Cells and Ranges," p. 72
- "Saving Frequently Used View and Print Settings," p. 540

Troubleshooting

I get only one print area whenever I try to select multiple print areas.

Be sure to type a comma in the Print **A**rea text box in between print areas. If you do not type the comma, Excel assumes that you are redefining the print area(s) and replaces the existing print area with the single new selection.

I get only one print area when I try to add another print area to an existing print area.

To add one or more new print areas to an existing print area, type a comma at the end of the list of cell coordinates already in the Print **A**rea text box *before* you select the additional print area(s). Otherwise, Excel assumes that you are redefining the print area and replaces the existing print area(s) with the single new selection.

Printing Titles

Repeating printed titles on each page can make large worksheet or database printouts easier to read. When the worksheet is wider than one page, for example, you can repeat row titles along the left margin of each page. You can repeat column titles at the top of each page of a database that spans multiple pages. The Sheet options available through the **F**ile Page Set**u**p command specifies that selected rows or columns will print at the top or left side of each printed page.

To specify titles, complete the following steps:

1. Choose the **F**ile Page Set**u**p command, and then select the Sheet tab to display the Sheet options (refer to fig. 11.6).
2. Place the insertion point in the **R**ows to Repeat at Top text box or the **C**olumns to Repeat at Left text box, depending on whether you are setting row or column titles.
3. Select the row(s) or columns(s) of titles you want on each page. The rows or columns must be adjacent.
4. Choose OK.

To display the currently selected titles, press the Goto key (F5) and select Print_Titles. To delete Print_Titles, choose the **F**ile Page Set**u**p command, select the Sheet tab, and then clear the **R**ows to Repeat at Top and **C**olumns to Repeat at Left text boxes.

You don't have to limit yourself to one row or column of titles. As long as the title rows or columns are adjacent, you can include as many as you want.

For Related Information

- "Entering Data," p. 87
- "Editing Text and Formulas," p. 94
- "Changing Character Fonts, Sizes, Styles, and Colors," p. 312
- "Formatting Rows and Columns," p. 346
- "Controlling the Worksheet Display," p. 533

Previewing the Document

Instead of printing to check the appearance of your worksheet, you can view a display of the printout with miniature pages such as the page shown in figure 11.12. When you want to examine a preview page up close, you can zoom into the area you want to see.

To preview pages, choose the **F**ile Print Pre**v**iew command. The preview screen shows you how the page will look when printed.

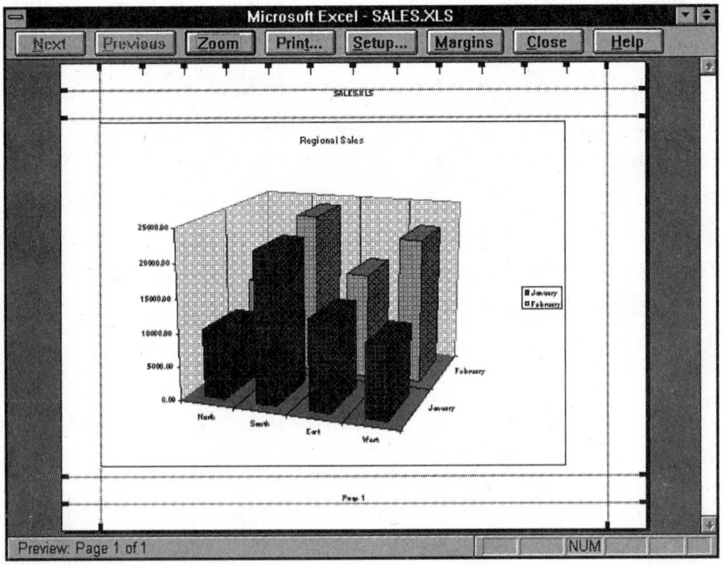

Fig. 11.12 Previewing enables you to see how the document is positioned on the printed page.

To zoom into a portion of the page, choose the **Zoom** button or click the mouse pointer—a magnifying glass—over the portion that you want to magnify. Use the cursor keys or scroll bars to move around in the zoomed-in view. Figures 11.13 and 11.14 show the zoom-in and zoom-out views of the document. To zoom out, choose **Zoom** a second time, or click a second time.

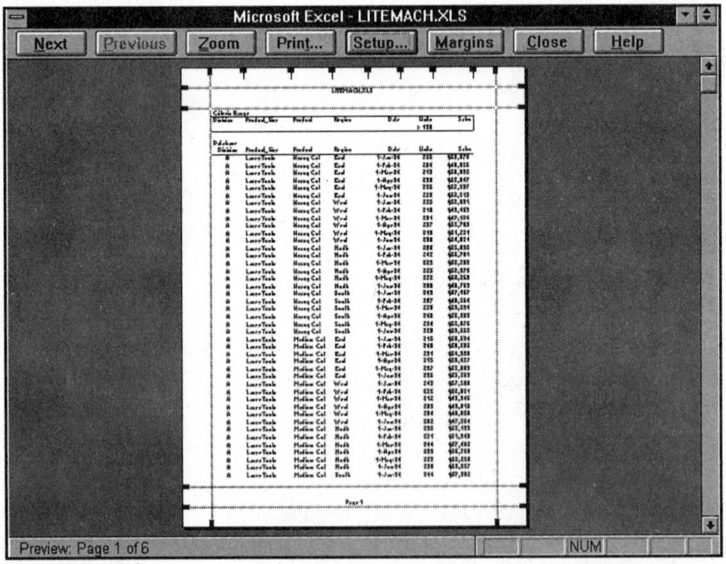

Fig. 11.13 Get the big picture of the page fit when you adjust margins and columns.

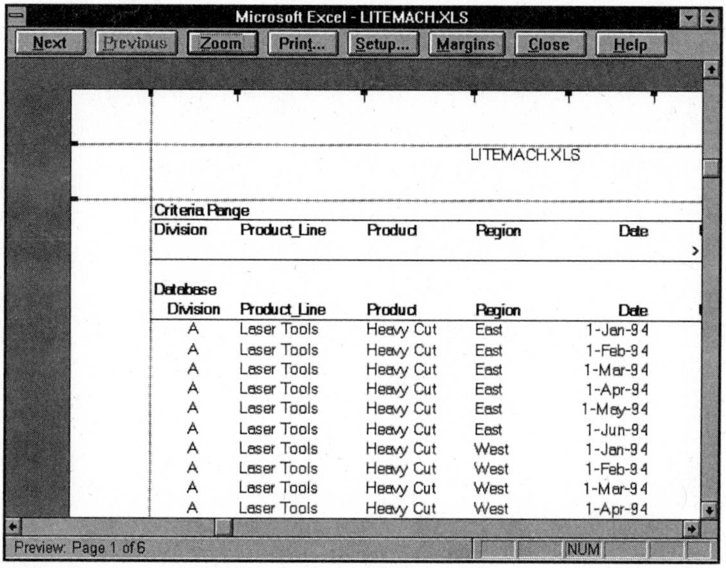

Fig. 11.14
Zoom in for a precise positioning of margins and column widths.

To change pages in the preview mode, use the **N**ext or **P**revious buttons. These buttons appear dimmed if there is no next or previous page.

After you preview the worksheet, you can print it from the preview screen by choosing the Prin**t** button. If you want to change or see the Page Setup settings, choose the **S**etup button. To return to the worksheet, choose the **C**lose button.

For Related Information

- "Using the Mouse," p. 31
- "Choosing Commands," p. 38

Adjusting Margins and Column Widths While Previewing

You can adjust margins and column widths while in the preview screen. Before adjusting margins with this method, save your document so that you can return to the original settings easily, if needed.

To adjust margins or column widths, complete the following steps:

1. Choose the **F**ile Print Pre**v**iew command.

2. Choose the **M**argins button. Column and margin markers appear on the preview page in full page view or when zoomed in.

3. Choose the **Z**oom button or click the magnifying glass pointer to zoom in or out of the preview for more accurate viewing.

4. Drag the margin handles (black squares) or the dotted line to a better position.

5. Drag column handles (black Ts) or the column gridline to adjust column widths.

6. Choose **C**lose to return to the document with these new settings, or choose Prin**t** to print the document with these settings.

For Related Information

- "Choosing Commands," p. 38

Figures 11.13 and 11.14, in the preceding section, show column and margin adjustment from either a magnified or full view.

Compressing Reports To Fit the Paper Size

You may have faced the problem of adjusting row heights, column widths, or margins so that your document would not have a few columns lapping over to an adjacent page or three lines hanging over at the bottom. With Excel's print-to-fit feature, you can compress a report so that it fits snugly in the space you demand.

Compressing Reports to One Page

The most basic way of using the print-to-fit feature is to compress the report enough so that a few lines from a second page move to the first page. This can turn a two-page report into a single-page report.

Figure 11.15 shows a split-window view of a worksheet that can generate long, multiple page reports.

If you print the data from Division A for Heavy Cut and Medium Cut tools at 100 percent of its size (Excel's default), five lines will extend to the next page (see fig. 11.16).

The Page Setup dialog box in figure 11.17 shows how you can compress the five lines on the second page of the report to the first page. In the Scaling area, select the **F**it to option button. The two text boxes after the **F**it to button indicate that the print area will shrink to 1 page wide by 1 page tall.

The Print Pre**v**iew screen in figure 11.18 shows that the whole report, all the sales data for Heavy and Medium Cut tools from Division A, now fits on a single page.

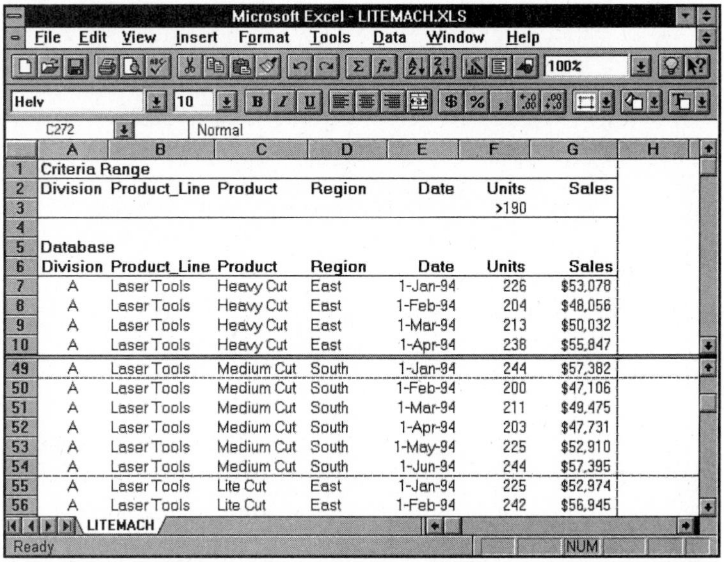

Fig. 11.15
A split-window view of LITEMACH.XLS, containing sales data from several company divisions.

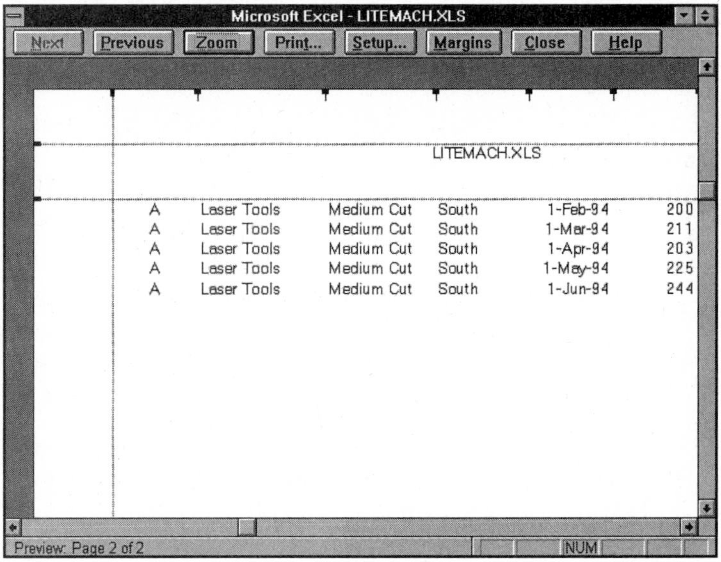

Fig. 11.16
A Print Preview screen showing that the report has a few lines on the second page.

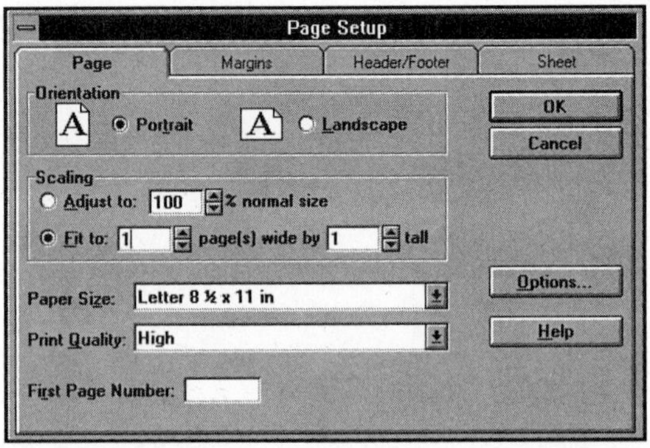

Fig. 11.17
The printed area will be reduced to fit in an area one page tall by one page wide.

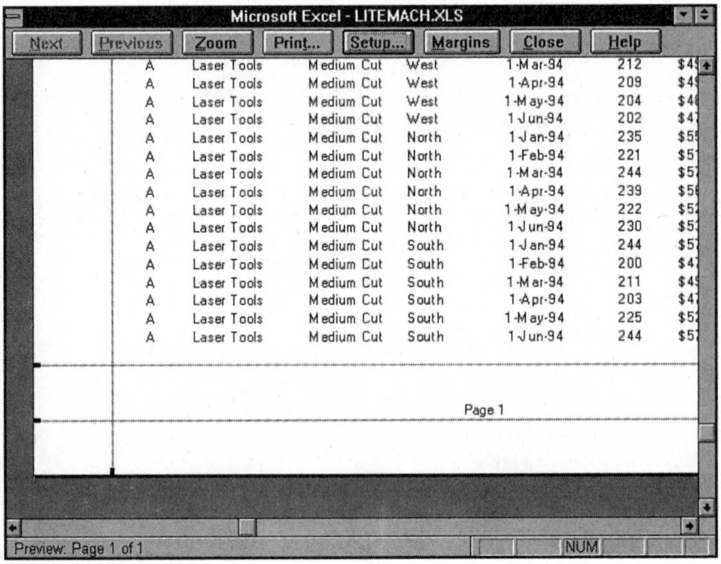

Fig. 11.18
The report now fits on one page.

Compressing Longer Reports

Long reports also can be compressed so that they fit exactly on the final page. This prevents the last few lines from dropping over to the last page.

To compress a tall report that is one page wide and 8 1/4 pages long so that it fits on eight pages, enter the following settings in the **F**it to boxes:

Fit to: 1 pages wide by 8 tall

To print a report that is three pages long but one column too wide so that it fits on three pages, enter the following in the **F**it to boxes:

Fit to: 1 pages wide by 3 tall

Printing

With Excel, you can select the range of pages and the number of copies that you want to print. In addition, you can preview the printout on-screen before printing to paper.

After you are ready to print, choose the **F**ile **P**rint command to display the print options in the Print dialog box, as shown in figure 11.19.

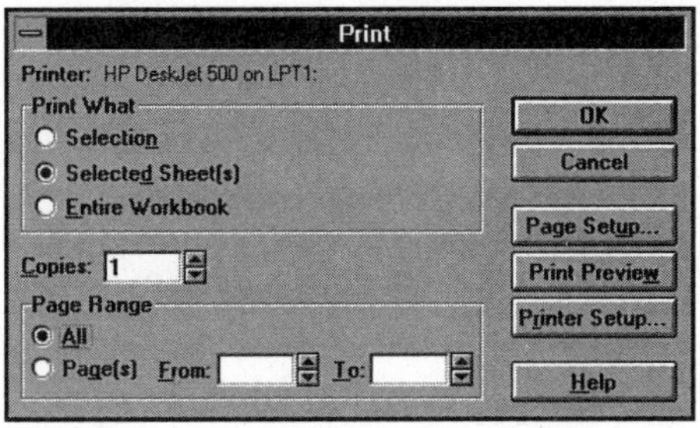

Fig. 11.19
The Print dialog box.

In the **C**opies text box, enter the number of copies you want to print. Specify the range of pages that you want to print; select the **A**ll option to print the entire print area, or you can select the Pa**g**e(s) option and enter page numbers in the **F**rom and **T**o text boxes.

When you need a quick print, choose the Page Set**u**p button, and then select the Sheet tab to display the Sheet options. Next, select the Draft **Q**uality check box, and then choose OK. Printing is faster when you select Draft **Q**uality, but the appearance of the printout is not high quality. To see a preview before printing, choose the Print Pre**v**iew button.

Note

Selecting or deselecting the Draft **Q**uality check box may have little or no effect if Print **Q**uality (on the Page tab of the Page Setup dialog box) is already set to a low quality of printing. See "Setting the Print Quality," a previous section in this chapter.

Specify what you want to print by selecting the Selectio**n**, Selecte**d** Sheets, or **E**ntire Workbook options. Selectio**n** prints only the selected cells in the selected worksheets; selecting this option overrides the print area defined in the Page Setup dialog box. Selected areas that are not adjacent are printed on separate pages. Selecte**d** Sheets prints the defined print areas on each of the selected worksheets; if no print area for a selected sheet is defined, then the entire sheet is printed. **E**ntire Workbook prints all of the print areas on all sheets in the workbook; if a sheet in the workbook does not have a defined print area, the entire sheet is printed.

For Related Information

- "Choosing Commands," p. 38
- "Selecting Cells and Ranges," p. 72

To print notes in the spreadsheet, make sure that the **N**otes check box on the Sheet tab of the Page Setup dialog box is selected. If you want to print cell references along with each note, also make sure that the Row and Co**l**umn Headings check box on the Sheet tab of the Page Setup dialog box is selected.

To print, just choose the OK button. Make sure that your printer is turned on and is on-line.

Printing Report Manager Reports

The Report Manager automates the printing of worksheets that may have unique print ranges and different sets of input data. The finished product from the Report Manager is a report that appears to have been compiled from one all-encompassing worksheet. Read Chapter 19, "Creating Automatic Subtotals," for helpful tips on building and printing reports.

You can compile, print, and edit sequences of reports with the **F**ile Print R**e**port command. The individual reports, which are compiled into report sequences, must be created from views of a worksheet and input scenarios. Views include named print areas and their associated print settings. Views are described in Chapter 16, "Managing the Worksheet Display." The Scenario Manager controls multiple sets of data used as inputs for your worksheet. The Scenario Manager is described in Chapter 28, "Testing Multiple Solutions with Scenarios."

Note

The Report Manager is an add-in installed during Excel installation. If you do not see the Print R**e**port command under the **F**ile menu, refer to Chapter 22, "Taking Advantage of Excel's Add-Ins," to learn how to add the Report Manager.

The Report Manager enables you to put together a collection of views that print in sequence as one large report. You also can print sequential page numbers. If you also have specified sets of data to be controlled by the Scenario Manager, the reports can print the result from each set of data.

Creating a Sequence of Reports

Before you can create a report, you must have already created the views you want to print. You don't need to create scenarios to use the Report Manager. Follow these steps to create a sequence of reports:

1. Choose the **F**ile Print R**e**port command.

   The Print report dialog box appears (see fig. 11.20).

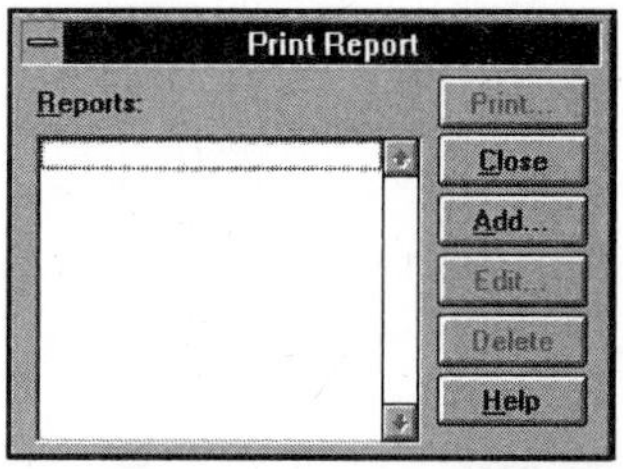

Fig. 11.20
The Print Report dialog box.

2. Choose the **A**dd button. You see the Add Report dialog box (see fig. 11.21).

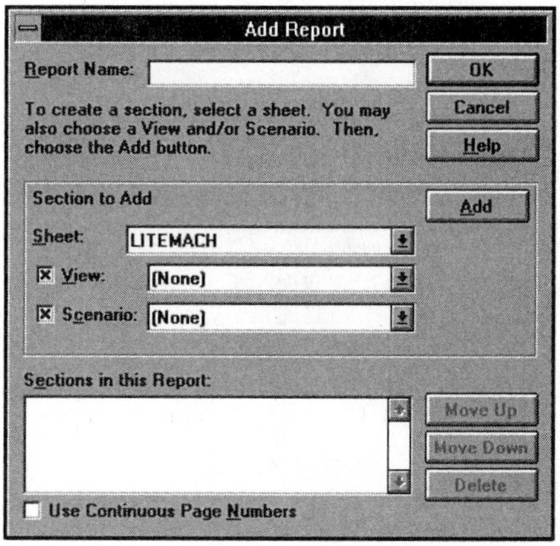

Fig. 11.21
The Add Report dialog box.

3. Type the name of the report you are creating in the **R**eport Name box.
4. Select the sheet name in the **S**heet pull-down list.
5. Select the name of the view from the **V**iew pull-down list.
6. Select the name of the scenario from the **S**cenario pull-down list. You do not need a scenario for a report.

Enter views and scenarios in the order in which you want them to print in the report. You can reorder items after you have built your list.

7. Choose the **A**dd button to add the view and scenario to the bottom of the Current **S**ections list.

8. If you want the report to print with continuous page numbers, select the Continuous Page **N**umbers check box.

9. Return to step 4 if you want to add more views and scenarios.

10. Choose OK.

Figure 11.22 shows a complete Current Selection list. Views appear as the first item followed by the associated scenario.

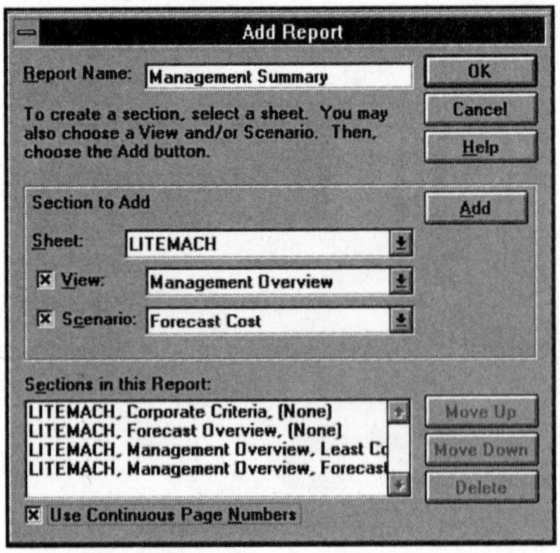

Fig. 11.22
A complete Current Selection list showing views and scenarios and their order in the report.

Reorganizing Report Sequences

After a sequence of views and scenarios is created, you may need to edit and reorganize it. For example, a client may prefer to see reports printed in a different order, or you may need to add or delete reports.

To edit a report sequence, choose the **F**ile Print R**e**port command. When the Print Report dialog box appears, choose the **E**dit button. When the Add Report dialog box appears, select from the Current **S**ections list the view and scenarios you want to change. To delete a scenario, choose the De**l**ete button. To move the selected item up or down in the list, choose the Move **U**p or Move **D**own button. Choose OK when you are finished.

Printing a Report Sequence

You can create several different report sequences. When you are ready to print one of them, complete the following steps:

1. Choose the **F**ile Print R**e**port command.
2. Select the name of the report you want to print.
3. Choose the **P**rint button.
4. Enter the number of copies and choose OK.

For Related Information

■ "Creating Scenarios," p. 819

From Here...

With the power for views, scenarios, and the Report Manager, you can automate the printing of reports you must do frequently. Don't forget to use Excel's print preview so that you can see what's going to print without wasting a trip to the printer and a ream of paper. Other areas that relate to printing include the following:

- Chapter 16, "Managing the Worksheet Display." See this chapter for information on worksheet views.
- Chapter 19, "Creating Automatic Subtotals." See this chapter for information on the Report Manager and building scenarios.

Part II

Creating and Formatting Charts

12 Creating Charts

13 Modifying Charts

14 Formatting Charts

15 Building Complex Charts

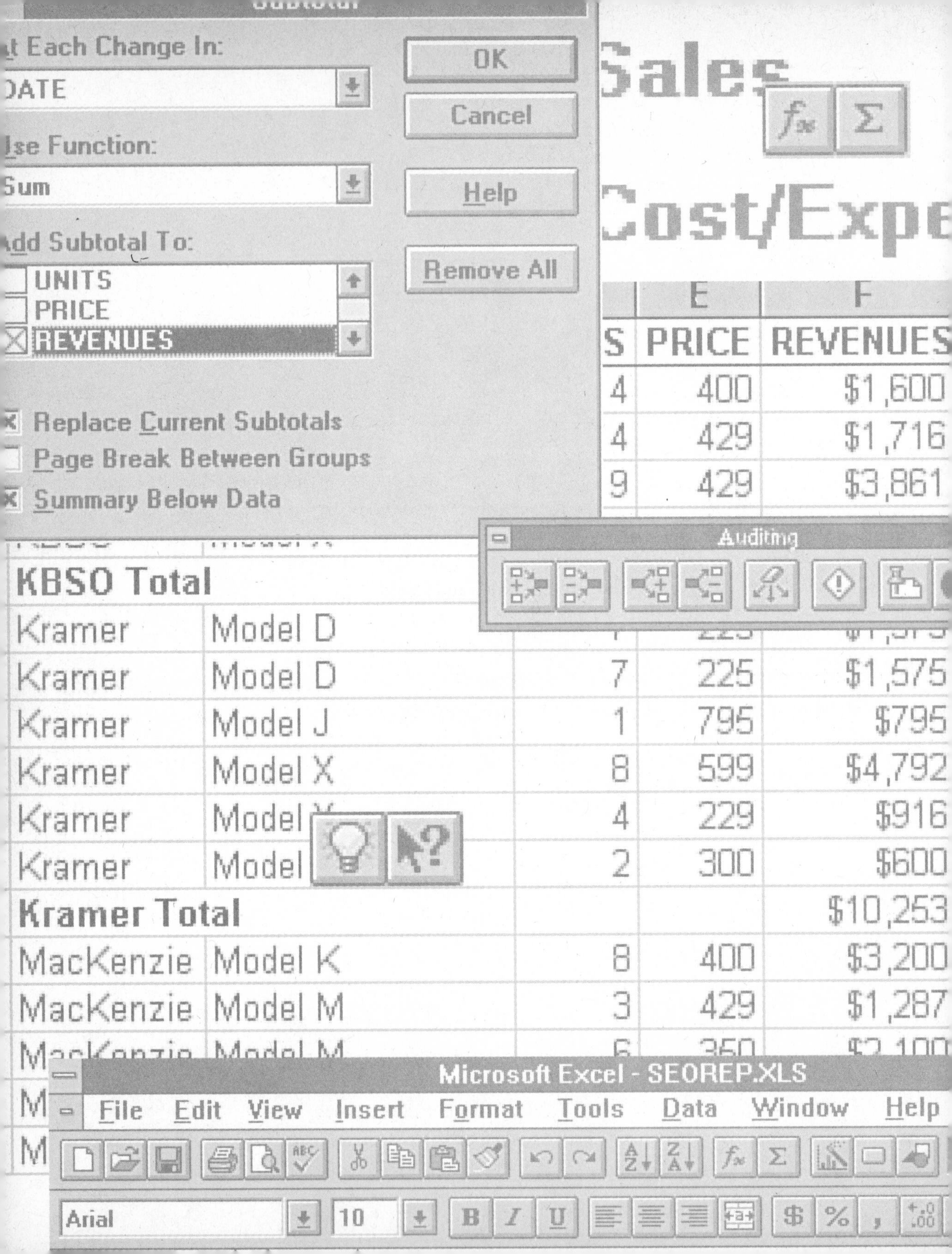
Subtotal
At Each Change In:
DATE
Use Function:
Sum
Add Subtotal To:
UNITS
PRICE
REVENUES
Replace Current Subtotals
Page Break Between Groups
Summary Below Data
OK
Cancel
Help
Remove All
Sales
Cost/Expe
E
F
S
PRICE
REVENUES
4 400 $1,600
4 429 $1,716
9 429 $3,861
Auditing
KBSO Total
Kramer Model D
Kramer Model D 7 225 $1,575
Kramer Model J 1 795 $795
Kramer Model X 8 599 $4,792
Kramer Model 4 229 $916
Kramer Model 2 300 $600
Kramer Total $10,253
MacKenzie Model K 8 400 $3,200
MacKenzie Model M 3 429 $1,287
Microsoft Excel - SEOREP.XLS
File Edit View Insert Format Tools Data Window Help
Arial
10

Chapter 12

Creating Charts

Using Excel, you can create charts appropriate for any boardroom presentation. When you analyze a worksheet or database and need to visually present the results, you can use any of Excel's predesigned formats or completely customize the chart by adding text, arrows, titles, and legends as well as change shading, overlay, patterns, and borders. When you print the chart on a laser printer or plotter, the quality rivals charts created by graphic art firms.

This chapter explains the details of creating a chart. The following two chapters explain how to modify and format charts by using the custom formatting features available for Excel charts. After finishing these three chapters, you will be able to meet the majority of business charting needs. The final charting chapter shows some techniques for creating more complex charts and for using charts to analyze your data.

Figures 12.1 and 12.2 show examples of charts you can create by using Excel. Figure 12.1 shows a chart in its own document. Figure 12.2 illustrates how you can embed charts on a worksheet. Embedded charts display and print with the worksheet.

EXCEL 5

In this chapter, you learn the following:

- Creating an embedded chart
- Using the ChartWizard
- Creating a chart in a chart sheet
- Creating a chart automatically
- Creating a chart manually
- Printing charts

Reviewing the Charting Process

Excel creates charts from data you select. You can use the ChartWizard to guide you through the process of creating a chart step-by-step. In many cases, you can have Excel draw a chart for you from the selected data. To draw the chart, the application uses certain rules based on how the data is configured. The data orientation determines which cells are used for the *category axis*, the labels along the bottom or x-axis, and which cells are used for the *legend* labels. In most cases, the rules fit standard data layout, so Excel charts come out correctly without intervention from you. You can customize the chart by using the many chart commands.

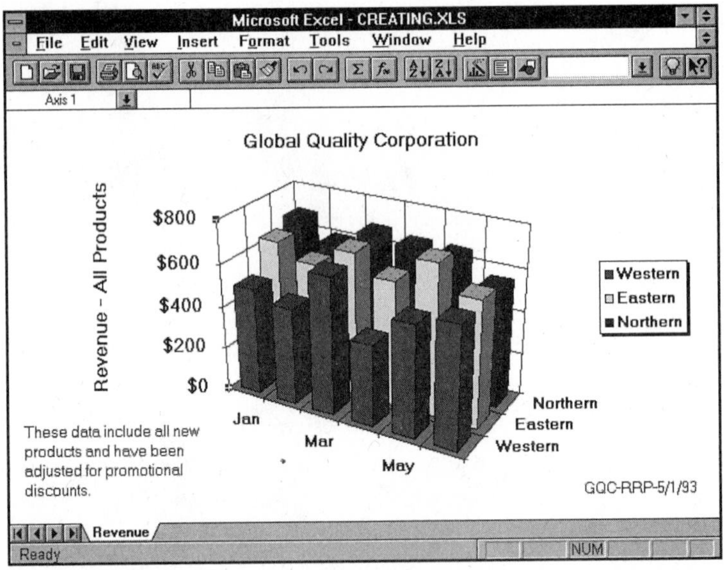

Fig. 12.1
A sample Excel chart inserted in its own chart sheet.

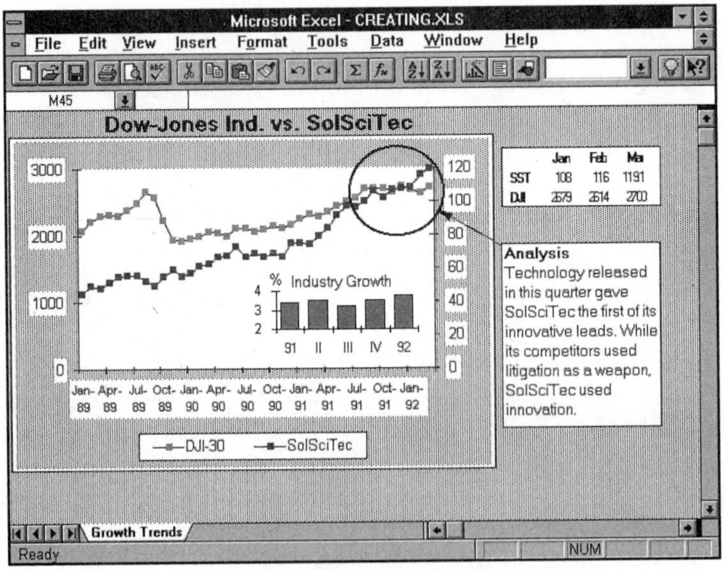

Fig. 12.2
Embed or paste charts on worksheets for better understanding.

You can embed a chart in a worksheet or insert a chart in its own chart sheet. In either case, the chart is linked to the data from which it was created, so if the data changes, the chart is automatically updated.

Defining Chart Terms

Excel charts contain many objects that you can select and modify individually. Figure 12.3 shows some of these objects, and each object is described in table 12.1.

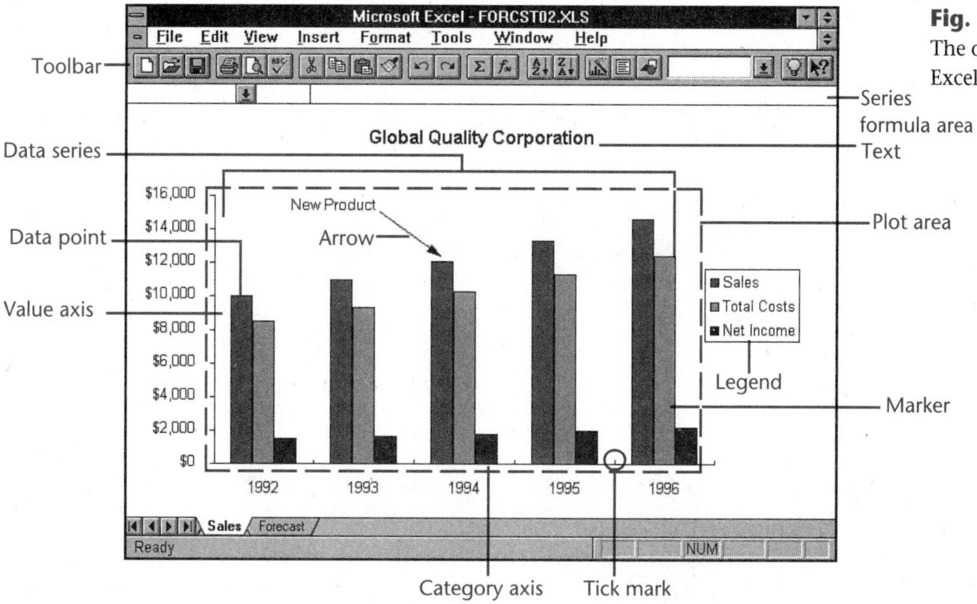

Fig. 12.3
The objects in an Excel chart.

Table 12.1 The Parts of an Excel Chart

Object	Description
Arrow	A movable and sizable object that you can format as an arrow or a line. Charts can use multiple arrows.
Axis	The category axis (the horizontal or x-axis along the bottom of most charts, frequently refers to time series) and value axis (the vertical or y-axis against which data points are measured) form the boundaries of a chart and contain the scale against which data plots. A z-axis is used for the third dimension on 3-D charts. (Axes for bar charts are reversed. Pie charts have no axes.)
Data point	A single piece of data, such as sales for one year.

(continues)

Table 12.1 Continued

Object	Description
Data series	A collection of data points, such as sales for the years from 1991 to 1995. In a line chart, all points in a data series are connected by the same line.
Legend	A guide that explains the symbols, patterns, or colors used to differentiate data series. The name of each data series is used as a legend title. You can move legends anywhere on a chart.
Marker	An object that represents a data point in a chart. Bars, pie wedges, and symbols are examples of markers. All the markers that belong to the same data series appear as the same shape, symbol, and color. In 2-D line, bar, column, and XY scatter charts, Excel can use pictures drawn in Windows graphics programs as markers.
Plot area	The rectangular area bounded by the two axes. This area also exists around a pie chart. A pie chart does not exceed the plot area when wedges are extracted.
Series formula	An external reference formula that tells Excel where to look on a specific worksheet to find the data for a chart. You can link a chart to multiple worksheets.
Text	You can edit and move titles (chart, value, and category) and data labels (text associated with data points). Unattached or free-floating text can be moved, and the box containing the text can be resized.
Tick mark	A division mark along the category (X) and value (Y and Z) axes.
Toolbar	A special toolbar is available with charting tools.

Understanding How To Create a Chart

You can create two kinds of charts in Excel—embedded charts and charts that appear in a chart sheet. An embedded chart appears in the worksheet next to tables, calculations, and text. Figure 12.2 shows an embedded chart. Embedded charts make sense when you want to include a chart side-by-side with the data for the chart, such as in a report.

A chart also can appear in its own chart sheet within a workbook and then be printed separately from the data you used to create the sheet. When you insert a chart in a sheet, you add the chart to the active workbook and save the chart with the workbook. Charts are named Chart1, Chart2, Chart3, and so on, and can be renamed by using the F**o**rmat S**h**eet **R**ename command or by double-clicking the tab for the chart sheet and typing in a new name. If you need to print the chart on its own, for example, to use in a presentation, this method is best to use.

You can easily create both embedded charts and charts in chart sheets by using the ChartWizard. The ChartWizard guides you through the process of creating the chart step-by-step and gives you a preview of the chart before creating it, so you can make any needed changes.

If you select data and press the F11 key, Excel inserts a chart in a chart sheet, using the default chart type. You then can use the chart commands to modify the chart.

You also can create a chart manually by inserting a blank chart and pasting data into it. This technique is useful when creating complex XY scatter charts or when creating charts with data from different worksheets. The section "Creating a Chart Manually" describes this procedure.

Creating an Embedded Chart

Using the mouse and ChartWizard is the easiest method of creating an embedded chart. The ChartWizard guides you through the creation process and shows a sample of the chart you are creating, so that you can see the effect of your choices before the chart is complete. This method is helpful when you use data not arranged in a layout that Excel recognizes by default.

The ChartWizard button looks like a magic wand inside a chart. When docked under the menu, you see the ChartWizard button on the right side of the Standard toolbar (refer to fig. 12.3).

Creating an Embedded Chart Using the ChartWizard

Before you use the ChartWizard button, select the data in your worksheet that you want to chart. Although the ChartWizard allows you to select the data you want to chart, doing so is easier before starting the ChartWizard.

To create an embedded chart with the ChartWizard, follow these steps:

1. Select the data you want to chart.

2. Choose the **I**nsert C**h**art **O**n This Sheet command or click the ChartWizard button.

3. Drag across the cells you want to contain the chart, and then release the mouse button (see fig. 12.4).

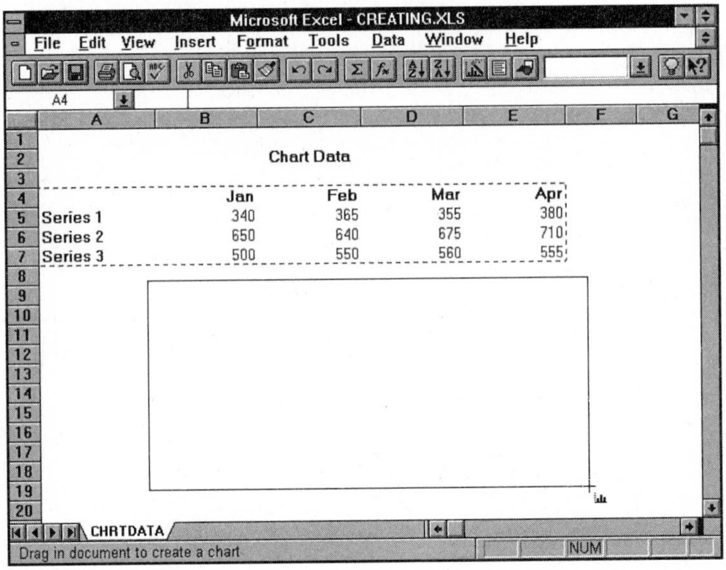

Fig. 12.4
You can use the ChartWizard to embed a chart in a worksheet.

Tip
To align a chart with cell edges, hold down Alt as you drag across where you want to establish the chart. To make the chart square, hold down Shift as you drag.

You can drag to the edges or the middle of cells. You are not restricted to keeping the chart aligned with cell boundaries.

The first of a series of ChartWizard dialog boxes appears. Follow the directions in these boxes. The following sections describe each ChartWizard dialog box.

The following rules cover selecting cells for the ChartWizard:

- Select noncontiguous data, if necessary, by holding down the Ctrl key as you drag across each additional series of data.
- If one series of data includes a cell with a label, then all series must include a cell in the same position, even if the cell is blank.

For clarification of how Excel builds a chart from different data layouts, see the sections, "Understanding How Excel Builds a Chart" and "Understanding Non-Standard Data Layouts," in this chapter.

Understanding ChartWizard Dialog Boxes

The ChartWizard dialog boxes display control buttons similar to VCR controls. Figure 12.5 shows one of the ChartWizard dialog boxes with the buttons labeled.

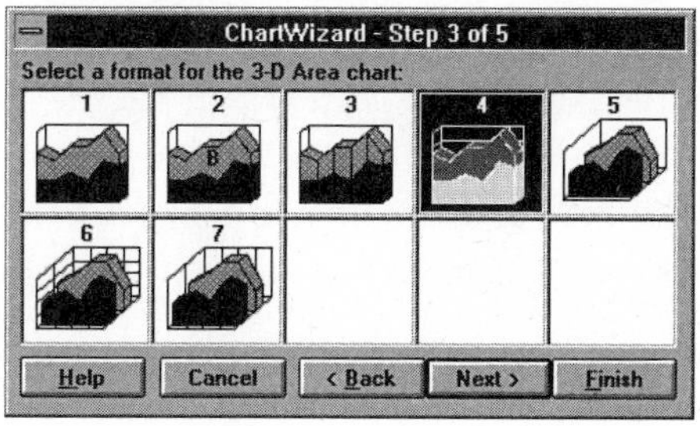

Fig. 12.5
ChartWizard dialog boxes use buttons similar to buttons found on a VCR.

The ChartWizard buttons control the following actions:

Button	Action
Next>	Go to the next step in the ChartWizard. You also can press the Enter key.
<**B**ack	Go to the previous step in the ChartWizard.
Finish	Fast forward; complete the chart by using the selections made so far.
Cancel	Return to the worksheet without creating a chart. You also can press the Cancel key.
Help	Display a Help window that describes what to do at this point.

Verifying the Chart Data Range

The ChartWizard displays a series of dialog boxes that guide you through chart-making. The first dialog box (see fig. 12.6) enables you to correct an incorrect data selection. You can edit the data range in the **R**ange edit box. Edit as you do in the formula bar. Click in the reference range, or press F2, the edit key. You can re-enter ranges or cells by dragging across the worksheet behind the dialog box. Ranges of noncontiguous data are separated in the **R**ange box by a comma.

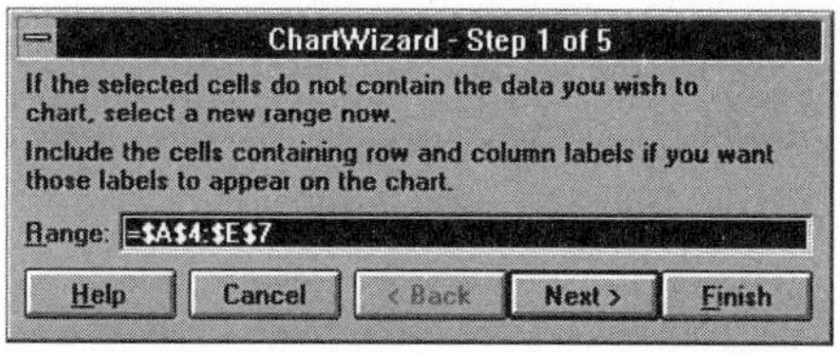

Fig. 12.6
The first dialog box enables you to change the range.

Add a data series to a chart by extending the reference in the **R**ange edit box in the Step 1 dialog box. Click the insertion point at the end of the existing range and type a comma, and then drag across the cells you want included. (A comma separates a series of data.) If the original data ranges included a cell with a label, the added range should include a cell.

After you select the range the way you need it, choose Next to move to step 2 of the ChartWizard.

Note

Choosing **F**inish in the first step of the ChartWizard creates the chart by using the default chart format. If you didn't set a default chart format, Excel creates a chart in the default format, 2-D column. See "Choosing a Default Chart Format," in Chapter 13, to learn how to set the default chart format.

Defining the Chart Type

After you verify the range and choose the Next button or press Enter, the second dialog box shown in figure 12.7 appears. This dialog box enables you to choose among the many types of Excel charts. In figure 12.7, the 3-D C**o**lumn type is selected. These chart types are described in the following chapter. Click the chart type you want or press the arrow keys to select a format, and then choose Next. The default chart type is the preferred chart format.

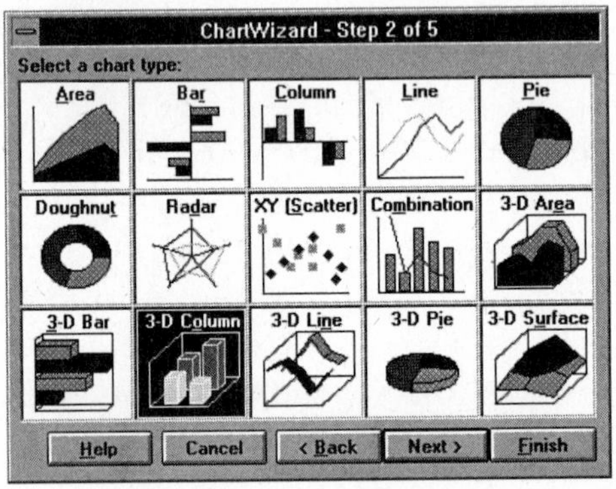

Fig. 12.7
In the second dialog box, you can choose from many basic chart types.

Choosing a Chart Format

The third ChartWizard dialog box enables you to choose from among the defined formats for the chart type that you selected. In figure 12.8, 3-D C**o**lumn is selected. Each of the 15 chart types has many defined formats.

You can find examples of these defined formats in the following chapter in the section, "Using Autoformats." Predefined formats may include gridlines, marker overlaps, and labeling.

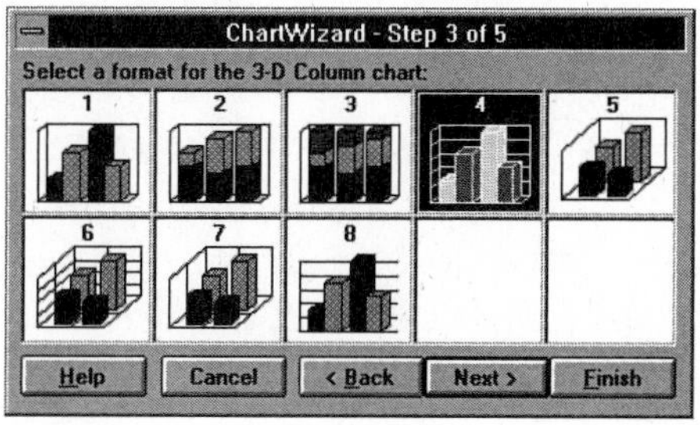

Fig. 12.8
Choose a predefined format for your basic chart type from dialog box 3.

Changing How Excel Interprets Data Layout

After you define the chart type and the predefined format, the fourth dialog box appears. This dialog box displays a sample chart that uses the data and labels you selected (see fig. 12.9).

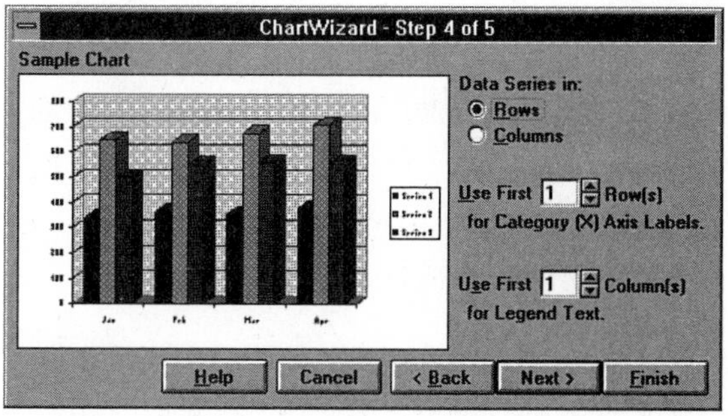

Fig. 12.9
Change a chart's orientation if Excel did not understand the data layout.

In this dialog box, you can make corrections if Excel has incorrectly drawn the chart. Excel may not draw a chart correctly if the data is not in a layout that Excel understands. The sections "Understanding How Excel Builds a Chart" and "Understanding Non-Standard Data Layouts" describe how Excel expects data to be laid out on a worksheet.

If the sample chart doesn't correctly portray the data and labels, select the unmarked option in the Data Series in group to reverse how Excel interprets the data selection. When you change the option selected in the Data Series in group, the labels for the following two options change. You must make sure that you selected the correct option here before changing the next two options. Changing the options haphazardly can create a confusing chart.

Begin at the top option group and work down. Choose Next to move to the next dialog box after you have made the correct selections. If your chart doesn't appear correct, consider the following troubleshooting guidelines:

- If Category (X) Axis Labels appear in the legend, and vice versa, select the other option Data Series.
- If the sample chart displays numbers as Category (X) Axis Labels and it should display labels, type or select 1 in the **U**se First Row(s) for Category (X) Axis Labels option. If your category axis labels appear in more than just the first row, type or select a higher number.
- If you didn't include a series of Category (X) Axis Labels and the sample chart is missing a series of data, type or select 0 in the **U**se First Row(s) for Category (X) Axis Labels option.
- If you included a label in each data series you selected but no labels appear on the Series (Y) Axis or in the legend, type or select 1 in the Use First Column(s) Series (Y) Axis Labels option. If the series axis labels appear in more than just the first column, type or select a higher number.
- If you didn't include a label in each data series you selected and your sample chart is missing one data point, type or select 0 in the U**s**e First Column(s) Series (Y) Axis Labels option.

Add Legends and Titles

The final ChartWizard dialog box enables you to add or remove a *legend*, which is a box that labels colors or patterns used (see fig. 12.10). Legends also contain text edit boxes so that you can add titles that you fix in locations on the chart. If the preferred chart format uses a legend, then a legend is preselected. Depending on the type of chart you are making, some titles may not be available.

You add a title just as you usually edit in a dialog box. Click the **C**hart Title box and type, or press Alt+C and type.

When you type a title in one of the title text boxes, do not press Enter. Type the title, and then tab to the next title; the title appears in the sample chart. You can edit in these text edit boxes. After you're satisfied with the titles, choose **F**inish. The Next button is grayed out because this is the last step in the ChartWizard.

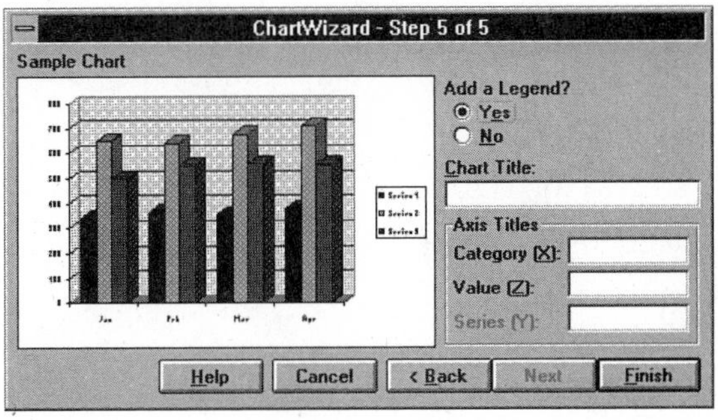

Fig. 12.10
Add legends and fixed titles in the final ChartWizard dialog box.

After you choose **F**inish in the final ChartWizard dialog box, Excel embeds the chart you created in the area you selected on the worksheet (see fig. 12.11).

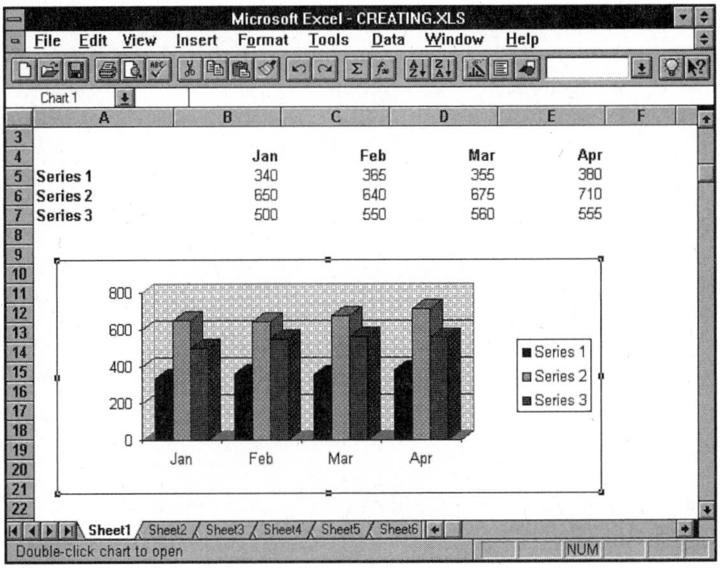

Fig. 12.11
The ChartWizard embeds its chart in the worksheet.

The embedded chart now is part of the worksheet and is saved and opened with the workbook. You can position and size the chart exactly as you want. To move the chart, select it by clicking the chart with the mouse. When selected, *black handles* appear around the borders of the chart. Point anywhere within the chart and click, and drag the chart to the desired position.

To change the size or proportions of the chart, grab the black handles along the borders (the pointer changes to a double-headed arrow) and drag until the chart is sized and proportioned the way you want. Be sure that you change the size and proportions of the chart before you open the chart to format it. If you format and enhance the chart with titles, a legend, text, and so on, and then change the size, the formatting and enhancements will be out of proportion with the chart.

To delete an embedded chart, select the chart and press Del or choose the **E**dit Cle**a**r **A**ll command.

To enhance the chart or make formatting changes, open the chart into a separate window, as described in the following section.

For Related Information

- "Mouse Actions," p. 34
- "Combining Data and Charts on the Same Page," p. 571

Troubleshooting

Excel doesn't update or redraw the chart after you change data on the worksheet.

Excel may be set for manual recalculation. To update the chart by using new worksheet data, choose the **T**ools **O**ptions command, select the Calculation tab, and choose the Calc **N**ow command. The shortcut key for recalculating is F9. You can also reset the workbook to automatically recalculate by choosing the **A**utomatic option in the Calculation tab.

Opening an Embedded Chart for Formatting

A chart embedded in a worksheet prints with the worksheet and is saved with the workbook. You must *activate* an embedded chart if you want to edit or format the chart.

To activate the embedded chart so that you can edit it, double-click it. A hatched-border appears around the chart, and the charting menu replaces the worksheet menu. You can use all the editing or enhancing techniques described in the remaining chart chapters while the chart is activated. After you finish enhancing or editing an embedded chart, return to the worksheet by clicking outside the chart in the worksheet or pressing Ctrl+F6.

Troubleshooting

Selecting the embedded chart in a worksheet does not make the chart menu appear.

To change or format an embedded chart, double-click the embedded chart to activate it. While the chart is activated, you can format it. To return to the worksheet, click in the worksheet or press Ctrl+F6.

Creating a Chart in a Chart Sheet

You can create a chart that appears in a separate sheet in a workbook by using the **I**nsert C**h**art command. You can print a chart sheet separately from the worksheet that contains the chart data and is saved with the other sheets in the workbook. When you use the **I**nsert C**h**art **A**s New Sheet command, the ChartWizard appears to guide you through the process of creating the chart.

To create a chart in a chart sheet, follow these steps:

1. Select the data you want to chart.

2. Choose the **I**nsert C**h**art command, and then choose **A**s New Sheet.

3. Move through the steps in the ChartWizard, as described in "Creating an Embedded Chart Using the ChartWizard," a previous section of this chapter.

The finished chart appears in its own chart sheet, which is part of the active workbook. You can rename the chart by using the F**o**rmat S**h**eet **R**ename command or double-clicking the tab for the sheet and typing a new name in the Rename Sheet dialog box.

You can embed into a worksheet a chart that exists in its own chart sheet. Select the chart sheet, and then select the entire chart by clicking along the outside of the chart. Black handles appear around the outside border of the chart. Choose **E**dit **C**opy, select the worksheet in which you want to embed the chart, select the cell that will be the upper-left corner of the chart, and choose **E**dit **P**aste. The chart is embedded into the worksheet as a full-sized chart and can be resized, moved, and formatted just like any embedded chart. See "Creating an Embedded Chart," a previous section of this chapter.

For Related Information

- "Selecting and Moving between Sheets," p. 67
- "Copying and Moving Sheets," p. 260

Creating a Chart Automatically

Although using the ChartWizard is the easiest and most foolproof method for creating charts, you also can create a chart automatically by using the chart shortcut key. If the data is in a layout that Excel can interpret, you need only select the data and press F11 to create a chart. (Press Alt+F1 if you don't have an F11 key.)

Excel uses several rules to decide how to create a chart from the selected cells. If the cells you selected do not meet these rules, you must create the chart by using the ChartWizard, described in "Creating an Embedded Chart Using the ChartWizard," previously in the chapter, or by using the procedure outlined in "Creating a Chart Manually."

Understanding How Excel Builds a Chart

Excel can build a chart automatically from selected data and labels if the selected area follows rules. Excel uses these rules to understand what information goes on the horizontal Category (X) axis, what information goes on the vertical Value (Y) axis, and where cell labels used for legend titles are located.

Before you learn the rules, you must understand the terms, *series* and *point.* These terms describe how the data is used by a chart. Understanding how Excel builds a chart from the data on a worksheet can prevent you from building charts with reversed axes or labels.

A *series* is a collection of associated data, such as the dollar amounts sold of the Global Quality bicycle, the forecast in units for specific products, or the readings from each of three specific medical instruments. When charted, the data from a series appears as a single line or as bars or columns of the same color.

A *point* is a single piece of data within any of the series. Examples of points in most charts are time sequences, such as years, quarters, or months. A point appears in a chart as a single dot on a line or one column out of a series.

You can enter labels for the Category (X) axis and legends in cells in the worksheet, and Excel uses them as labels in the chart. When charted correctly, the label for each point—month, for example—appears on the horizontal Category (X) axis. The series labels appear as titles in the legend (see fig. 12.12).

Excel uses the following rules to interpret how series and points are laid out on the worksheet:

- When Excel examines the data you selected, the program assumes that the Category (X) axis runs along the longest side of the selection. If the selection is square or wider than it is tall, as in figure 12.12, then Excel assumes that the category labels run across the top row of the selection. If the selection is taller than wide, as in figure 12.13, Excel assumes that the category labels run down the left column of the selection.

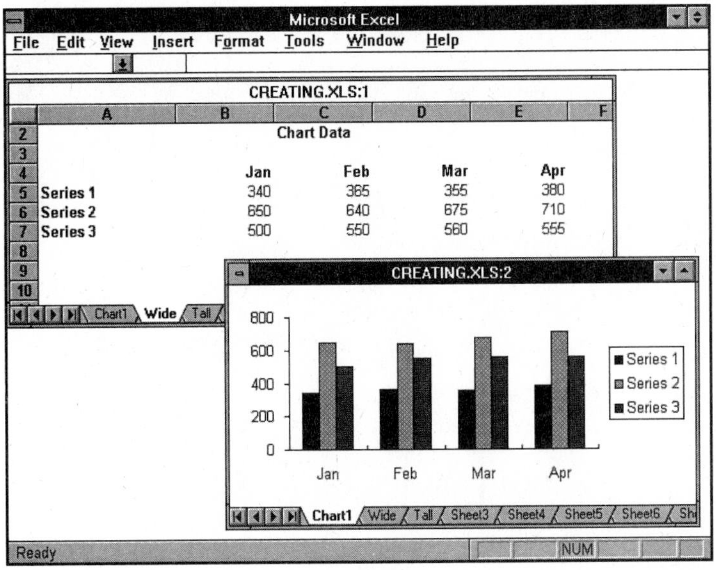

Fig. 12.12
A selection wider than it is tall plots its graph with category labels from the top row.

- Excel assumes that labels in cells along the short side of the selection should be used as titles in the legend for each data series. If only one data series exists, Excel uses this label to title the chart. If you select more than one data series, Excel uses the labels in these cells to title the legend.

- If the contents of the cells that Excel wants to use as category labels are numbers (not text or dates), Excel assumes that these cells contain a data series and plots the graph without category (X) labels, numbering each category instead.

- If the contents of the cells that Excel wants to use as series labels are numbers (not text or dates), then Excel assumes that these cells are the first data points in each of the data series and assigns the names Series 1, Series 2, and so on, to each of the data series.

- If the contents of all the selected cells contain numbers, Excel invokes the ChartWizard when you press F11, because Excel cannot determine how the data is laid out in this situation. You then can use the ChartWizard to specify how the data is arranged.

If the ChartWizard appears, follow the steps presented in the dialog boxes as described in the previous section, "Creating an Embedded Chart Using the ChartWizard." See "Changing How Excel Interprets Data Layout," a previous section in this chapter, for information on how to tell Excel to interpret the data correctly.

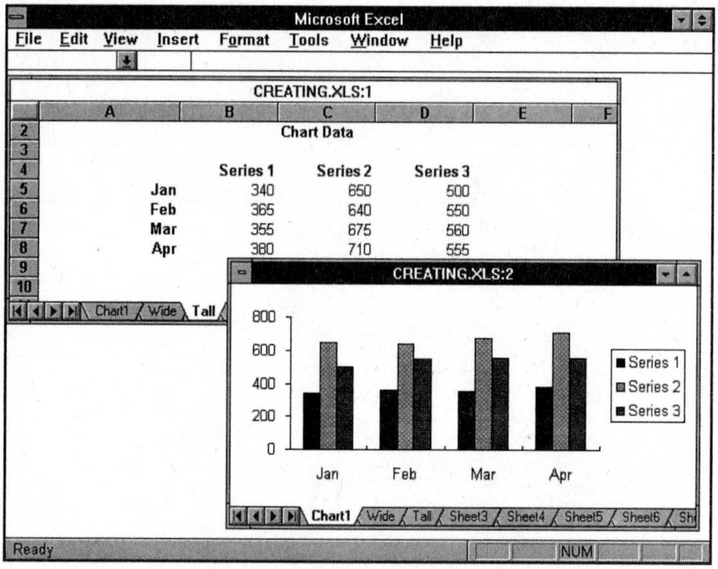

Fig. 12.13
A selection taller than it is wide plots with category labels from the left column.

Creating a Chart Automatically

To build a chart that has the correct orientation of category data along the longest side, complete the following steps:

1. Select the data and labels, as shown in figure 12.14.

   Notice that the selected range includes more data points— the months—than data series; the range has three series and four data points in each series. A data series in this example is a collection of related data—for example, all the sales for one product.

2. Press F11. (If you dont have an F11 key, press Alt+F1.)

Excel plots the data in the preferred chart type; the default is the 2-D column chart. Figure 12.15 shows a column chart created with the preceding steps.

In the chart in figure 12.15, notice that the points (months from the top row of the worksheet data) are used as category labels below the Category (X) axis.

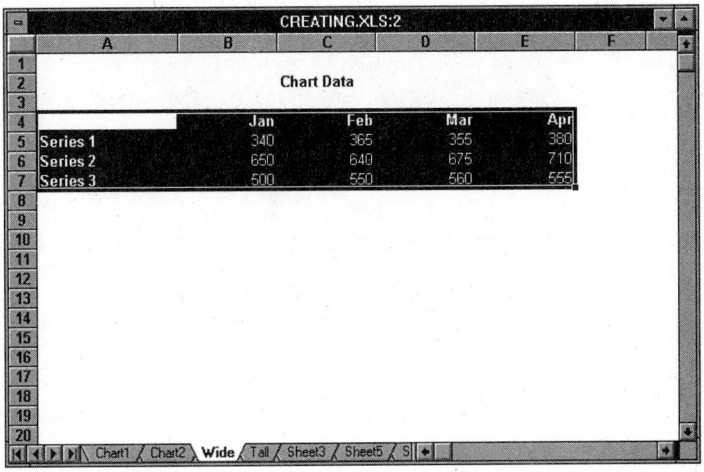

Fig. 12.14
A worksheet with three data series.

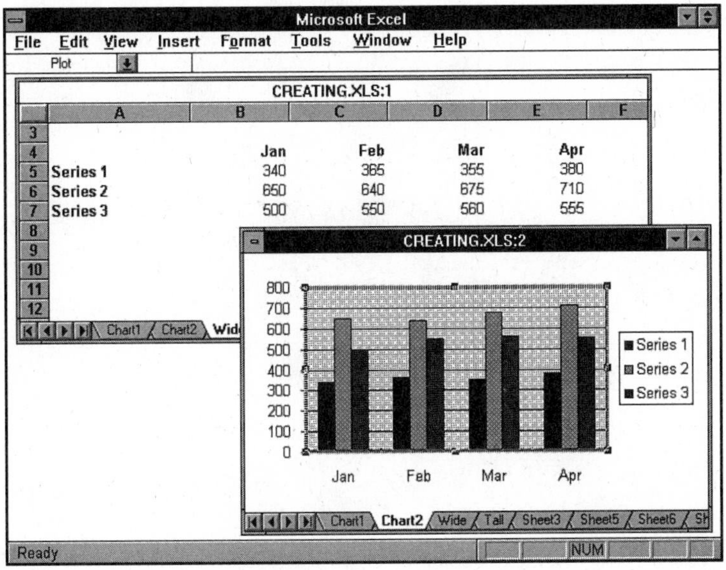

Fig. 12.15
An example of a column chart.

What happens if a series of data was listed down a column, as in figure 12.16? If you select the data shown in figure 12.16 and press F11, the chart in figure 12.17 appears. Notice that the chart still is drawn correctly. Here, however, Excel assumes that the data series again goes in the long direction. Because the long direction is in columns, Category (X) axis labels are taken from the left column.

In the preceding two examples, Excel drew a correct chart. Excel, however, can create an incorrectly oriented chart if the data is laid out so that it doesn't match the rules Excel uses. When this happens, you need to create the chart manually, as described in the following section, or use the ChartWizard, described previously in the chapter.

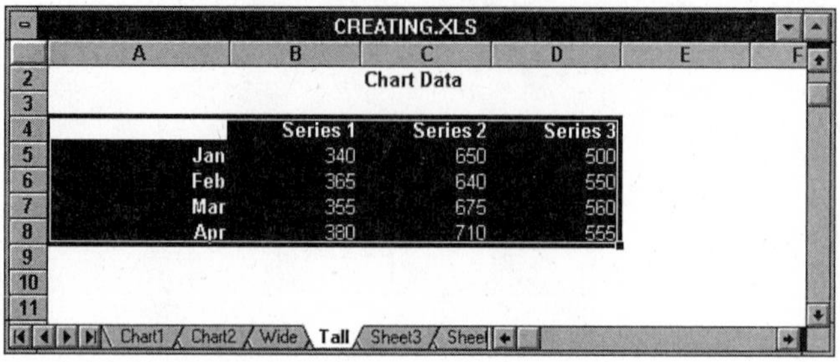

Fig. 12.16
A worksheet with the data series down a column.

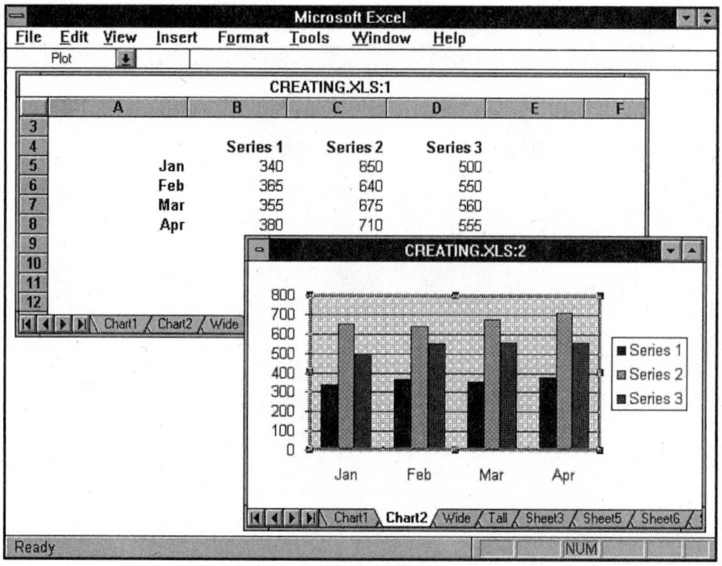

Fig. 12.17
The chart created from the vertical data series.

> **Note**
>
> Numbers along the category axis indicate that you forgot to select category labels. If you didn't include a row or column of labels for the Category (X) axis, the chart shows a sequence of numbers that begin with 1 along this axis.

If you want to create a chart from data not in adjacent rows or columns, such as the selection shown in figure 12.18, select the rows or columns by using the Ctrl and drag method with the mouse or by pressing Shift+F8 on the keyboard. Select the Category (X) axis cells; then select Value (Y) data cells in the same order in which you want the value series to appear on the chart.

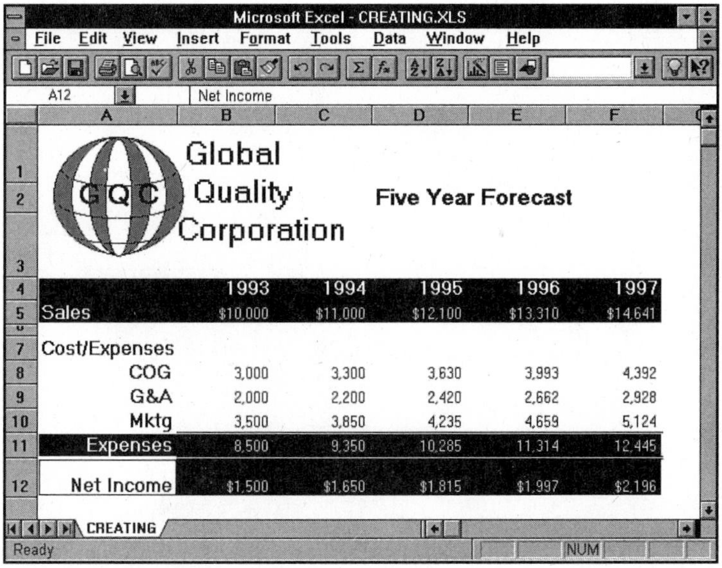

Fig. 12.18
Select nonadjacent cells to chart nonadjacent data.

For Related Information

- "Selecting Cells and Ranges," p. 72
- "Controlling the Worksheet Display," p. 533
- "Outlining Worksheets," p. 593

Note

If data exists in a table that you do not want to include in a chart, you can hide the rows or columns that contain the data, or if the data is in outline form, you can collapse levels in the outline that you don't want to include in a chart.

Creating a Chart Manually

When the data is laid out in a nonstandard way, so that Excel cannot automatically create a chart, you can use the ChartWizard to create the chart as described in "Creating an Embedded Chart," or you can create the chart manually. The following sections describe how to create charts by copying data from the worksheet and pasting the data into a blank chart.

Understanding Non-Standard Data Layouts

When the data you select for a chart doesn't meet Excel's rules for charting, Excel still creates a chart, but it may not be correct. If the chart's horizontal

Category (X) labels appear in the legend and labels used for the series appear in the Category (X) axis, you need to create a chart manually (see fig. 12.19).

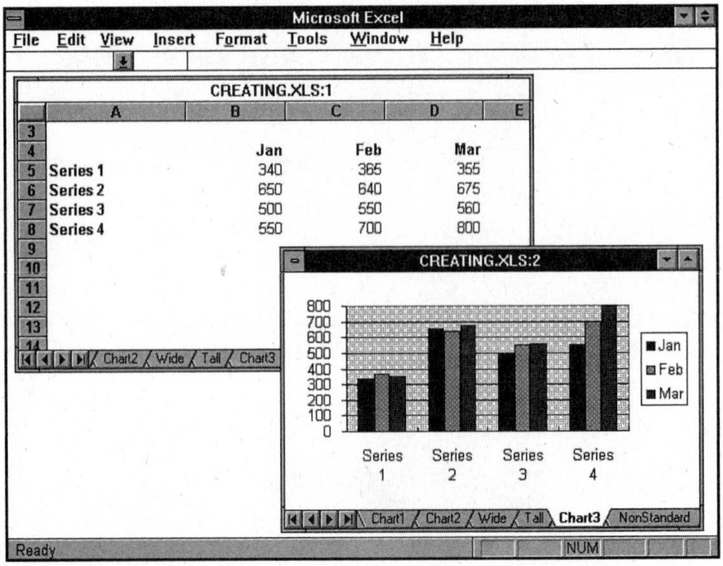

Fig. 12.19
A chart where series and points are reversed.

Another problem occurs if Excel cannot find cell contents on the long side of the selection to use as Category (X) labels. When this error happens, the Category (X) axis displays a series of integers—1, 2, 3, and so on. Figure 12.20 shows how such a chart looks.

The following rules help determine when you need to create a chart manually or use the ChartWizard:

- When the Category (X) axis labels, such as months, are along the short side of the selection, create the chart manually or use the ChartWizard.
- When the labels along the long side of the selection should be used in the legend, create the chart manually or use the ChartWizard.
- When a number appears in the upper left corner of the selection, Excel may misinterpret whether the first row or column is data or labels; you may need to create the chart manually or use the ChartWizard.
- When you try to create a chart and don't get what you want, create the chart manually by using the procedures for a nonstandard data layout or use the ChartWizard.

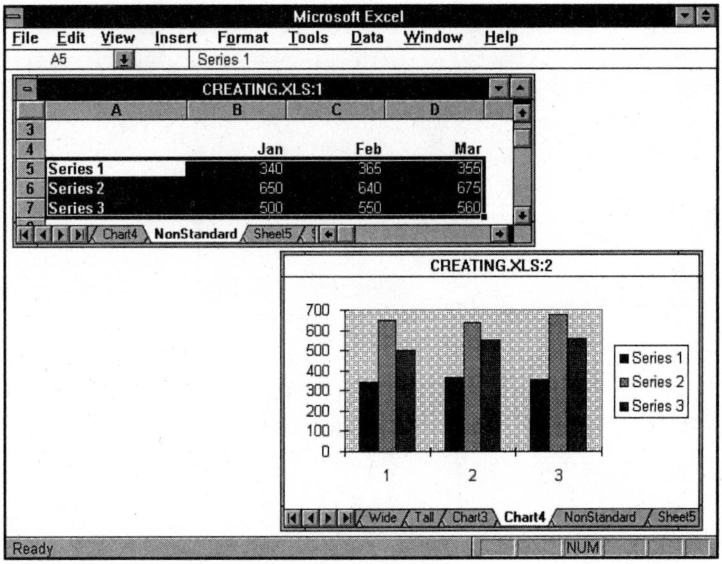

Fig. 12.20
A chart that did not have labels for use along the category axis.

How To Create a Chart Manually

To create a chart manually, you copy the selected data from the worksheet and then paste the data in a blank chart document. When you paste data into the blank chart, you use the **E**dit Paste **S**pecial command to call up a dialog box where you can specify the correct orientation of data series and where labels are located.

Suppose that you have a column chart with more series than data points—the Category (X) axis is along the short side of the selection. Also, suppose that the selection includes series labels that you may need later for legend titles. If created automatically, the chart appears as shown in figure 12.21. The series labels appear on the Category (X) axis and the point labels appear in the legend, which is the reverse of the configuration you want.

Note

Use the ChartWizard with nonstandard data layout when possible. When creating charts from the ChartWizard, you can specify whether series are in columns or rows and whether a row contains Category (X) labels or legend titles. When you try these alternatives in the ChartWizard, the effect appears in the sample chart, and the chart uses your data.

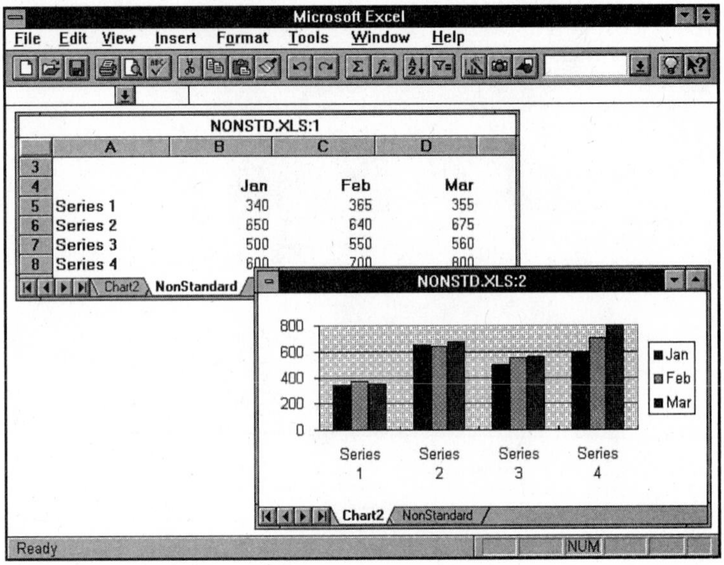

Fig. 12.21
An automatically created chart with series and points reversed.

Before you start the process of creating a chart manually, make a note of the following pieces of information about your data to help you make the correct choices in the Paste Special dialog box:

- Which way are Y values (a plotted line) oriented: across rows or down columns? These are the series.
- If Category (X) labels exist, are the labels across the top row or down the left column?
- If series (legend) labels exist, are these items across the top row or down the left column?

To create a chart manually, follow these steps:

1. Select the data, as shown in figure 12.22.

   Notice that the data selected violates rules for automated charting. The actual Category (X) axis side of the data is narrower than the number of series.

2. Either choose the **E**dit **C**opy command, press Ctrl+C, or click the Copy button on the Standard toolbar.

3. Press F11 or choose the **I**nsert C**h**art **A**s New Sheet command.

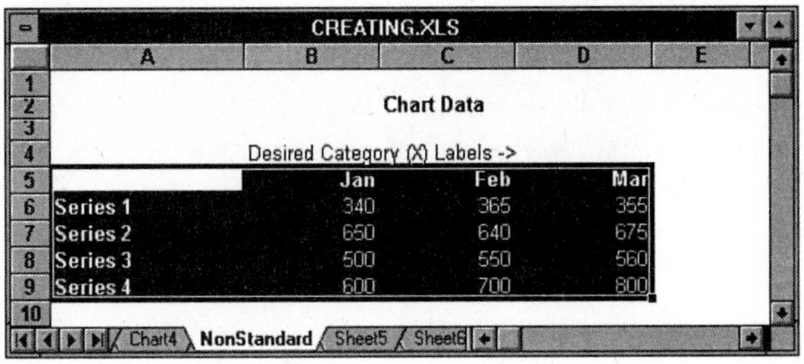

Fig. 12.22
A layout of data from which Excel doesn't create the correct chart automatically.

4. Choose the **E**dit Paste **S**pecial command to display the dialog box shown in figure 12.23.

   The Paste Special dialog box appears, with options selected that create a chart automatically. If the automatically created Excel chart has the series and data labels reversed, select the opposite option from the one that appears selected in Values (Y) in **R**ows/**C**olumns.

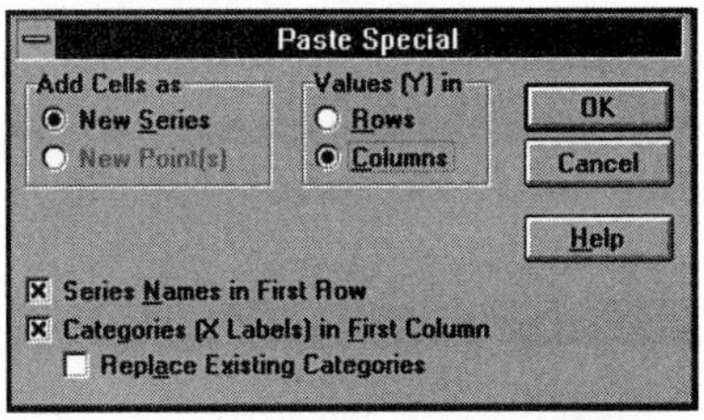

Fig. 12.23
The Paste Special dialog box enables you to change chart orientation and determine which labels are used.

5. If each series of Y data goes across a row, select Values (Y) in **R**ows. If each series of Y data goes down a column, select Values (Y) in **C**olumns.

6. If the selection includes series names (used in legend titles) for each set of Y values, select Series **N**ames in First Column (Row).

> **Note**
>
> Depending on your selection in step 6, the text in the Paste Special dialog box changes between Column and Row. For example, if you select the **R**ows option in the Values (Y) in group, the Series **N**ames option reads Series **N**ames in First Column. If you select the **C**olumns option, the Series **N**ames option reads Series **N**ames in First Row.

7. If your selection encloses Category (X) labels, select the Categories (X Labels) in **F**irst Row (Column) option.

> **Note**
>
> The option text here changes between Row and Column, depending on your selection in step 6. For this example, you select Categories (X Labels) in **F**irst Row.

8. Choose OK.
9. Choose the **V**iew Sized with **W**indow command to fill the window with the chart.
10. Choose the F**o**rmat Chart **T**ype command and select the type of chart you want.

Figure 12.24 shows a completed column chart and data.

Fig. 12.24
The manually created chart.

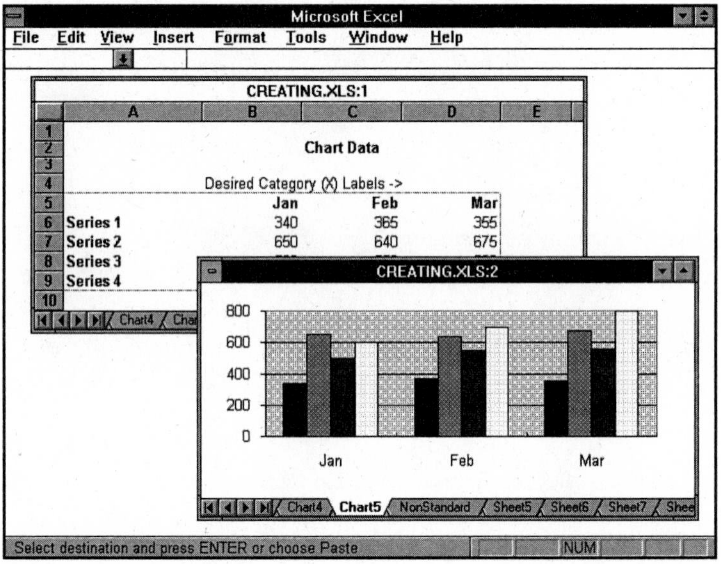

For Related Information

- "Filling or Copying Cell Contents," p. 241

Saving Charts

A chart that you embedded in a worksheet is saved when you save the workbook that contains the worksheet. A chart in its own sheet also is saved when you save the related workbook. See Chapter 9, "Managing Files," for more information on saving workbooks.

When you open a chart that was created with an earlier version of Excel, it appears in its own workbook in a chart sheet. When you save the chart, you can save it in the original format, or you can update it to Excel 5.0 format. When you save the file, a dialog box appears and asks if you want to update the chart to Excel 5.0 format. Choose **Y**es to update the file or **N**o to save the file in original format. Be aware that when you format and enhance a chart in Excel 5 and save it as an earlier version file, you may lose some of the formatting or enhancements due to incompatiblities between Excel 5 and earlier versions of Excel.

For Related Information

- "Opening Excel 4 Documents," p. 272
- "Saving to Other File Formats," p. 280

Changing Chart and Worksheet Links

All charts are linked to data in a worksheet. If a chart is embedded in a worksheet or if a chart in a chart sheet is linked to data in a worksheet that is part of the same workbook as the chart, then you don't have to worry about maintaining the link between the chart and the worksheet. If, on the other hand, you have linked a chart to data in a worksheet from another workbook, it is possible to break the link, for example, if you move the source workbook to a different directory, change the name of the worksheet, or delete the worksheet.

If one chart loses its link to its worksheet or if you need to link a chart to a different worksheet, perform the following steps:

1. Open the chart.
2. To establish a link with a different worksheet, open the workbook that contains the worksheet and activate the worksheet.
3. Activate the chart.
4. To display the dialog box shown in figure 12.25, choose the **E**dit Lin**k**s command.
5. Select the worksheet link you want to change in the Source File list.
6. Chose the **C**hange Source button.
7. Select from the File **N**ames list box the name of the worksheet with which you want to establish or reestablish a link. You may need to change directories or disks to find the file. Use the same directory and drive-changing techniques you use in the **F**ile **O**pen or **F**ile Save **A**s dialog box.

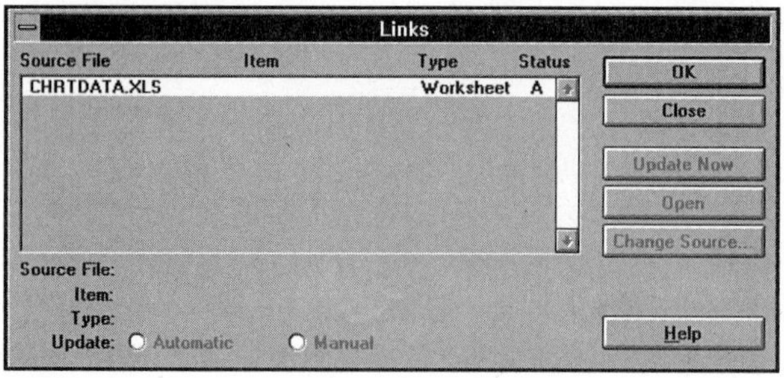

Fig. 12.25
Use the **E**dit **L**inks command to open or change source worksheets.

8. Choose OK.

9. Save the workbook.

To learn more about understanding and working with links, see Chapter 25, "Linking, Embedding, and Consolidating Worksheets."

For Related Information

- "Linking Workbook Cells and Ranges," p. 750
- "Opening an Existing Workbook," p. 268

Troubleshooting

You opened a chart that is linked to data in another workbook without updating it to see the chart using old data. Now you want to update the chart without opening the workbook.

Choose the **E**dit Lin**k**s command, select the source workbook from the Source File list in the Links dialog box, and choose the **U**pdate Now command. Choose Close to return to the chart.

Opening Charts

EXCEL 5

A chart can be in a separate document window or embedded in a worksheet. You can reformat either chart.

To open or activate a chart embedded in a worksheet, double-click the embedded chart; a hatched-border appears around the chart when it is activated. After you finish formatting the embedded chart, return to the worksheet by clicking outside the chart in the worksheet or pressing Ctrl+F6.

To open a chart that exists in a separate chart sheet, choose the **F**ile **O**pen command, select the workbook file that contains the chart, and choose OK. When you open a chart that is linked to data in an unopened workbook, a dialog box asks whether you want to update the chart (see fig. 12.26). If you choose **Y**es, the chart uses the current values stored in the worksheet file. If you choose **N**o, however, the chart uses the values with which it was saved.

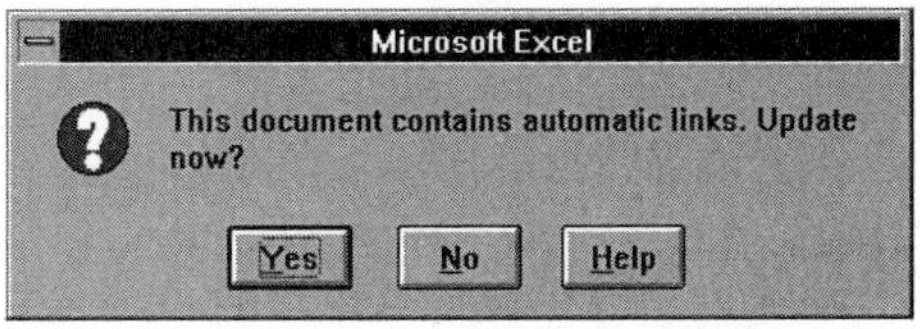

Fig. 12.26
This dialog box asks whether you want to update the chart with the information linked to the worksheet on disk.

To open the worksheets linked to open charts, choose the **E**dit Lin**k**s command. Select the worksheet file name in the Source File box and choose the **O**pen button.

Printing Charts

Printing charts is similar to printing worksheets. You can print directly from the screen, or you can preview the chart before printing. Previewing a chart gives you a more accurate view of how the chart appears when printed. Charts embedded on worksheets print with the worksheets.

Note

You can print charts embedded on a worksheet by using the same techniques you use to print worksheets. You can store views and scenarios that involve the embedded charts, and then use the **F**ile Print R**e**port command to print views with different scenarios.

Before you print a chart that is in a separate chart sheet, decide how large you want the chart to appear on the page. Set the size of the chart on the page by choosing the **F**ile **P**age Set**u**p command or choosing the **S**etup button in the **F**ile Print Pre**v**iew dialog box and selecting the Margins tab to display the dialog box shown in figure 12.27. You also can change margins by choosing the **M**argins button in the **F**ile Print Pre**v**iew dialog box and dragging the margin lines to a new setting.

Note

If you choose fonts that the printer cannot print, the printed chart will differ from the on-screen image. To ensure that charts use fonts available in the printer, select fonts from the Font tab in the Format dialog box that show a printer icon or the TT icon that indicates TrueType.

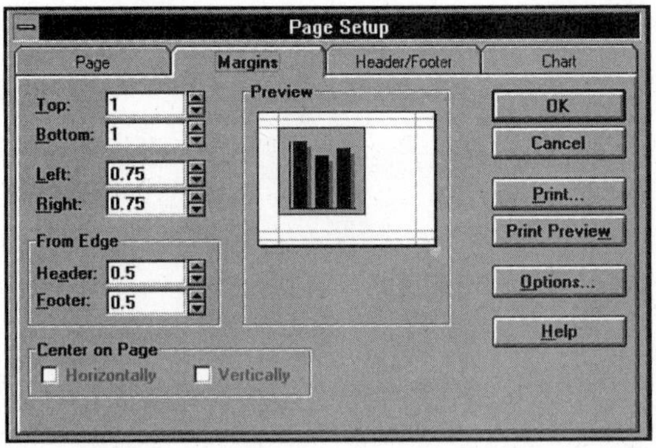

Fig. 12.27
Use the Page Setup dialog box to set a chart size and other print options.

Use the chart options in the Page Setup dialog box to determine how charts react to print area margins. Choose the **F**ile Page Set**u**p command or the **S**etup button in the **F**ile Print Pre**v**iew dialog box, and select the Chart tab to display the dialog box shown in figure 12.28. To expand the chart proportionally until margins are touched, select Scale to **F**it Page. The results of a Scale to Fit Page setting are shown in figure 12.29. To expand the chart in both height and width until margins in all directions are reached, select **U**se Full Page. The same chart in figure 12.29 is shown with the **U**se Full Page option in figure 12.30.

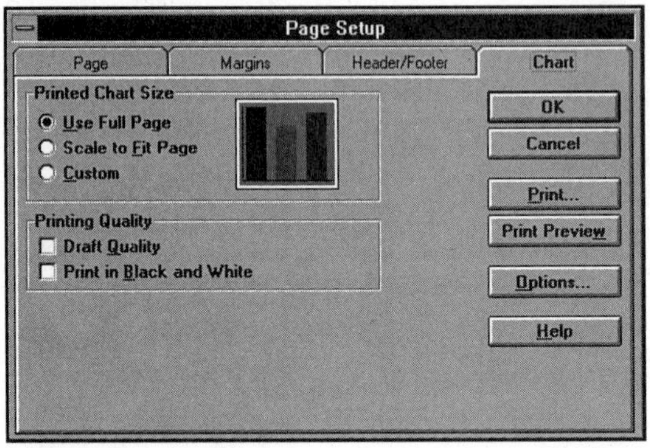

Fig. 12.28
Specify how the chart will be fitted to the page in the Page Setup dialog box.

To preview your chart before printing or to use the mouse to visually adjust chart size or margins, take the following steps:

1. Choose the **F**ile Print Pre**v**iew command.

2. Examine detail and positioning on the chart by zooming in or out on the page. To zoom in, move the pointer, a magnifying glass symbol, over an area of interest and click. Click the zoomed page to return to

the expanded view. With the keyboard, choose the **Z**oom button to zoom and unzoom by keyboard.

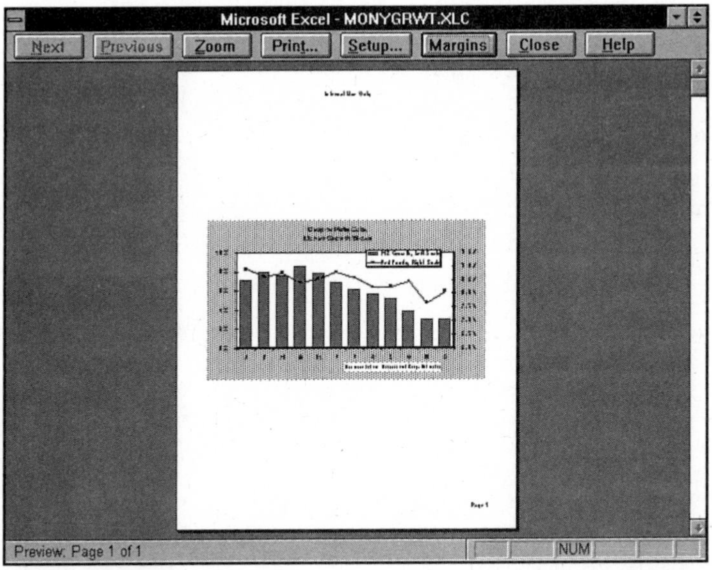

Fig. 12.29
Scale to Fit Page expands a chart proportionally until a page margin is reached.

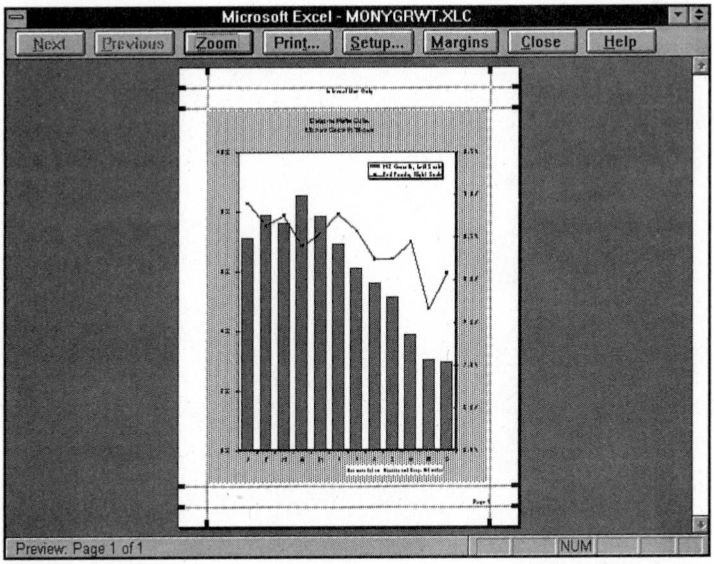

Fig. 12.30
Use Full Page expands a chart on all sides until page margins are reached.

3. Return to the Page Setup dialog box by selecting the **S**etup button. To expand the chart in height and width, select the Chart tab and then select the **U**se Full Page option from the Page Setup dialog box.

4. Choose OK.

5. Adjust margins and the size of the chart by clicking the **M**argins button. To change margins and to change the chart size, drag the black handles shown in figure 12.29.

6. To display the Print dialog box, choose **P**rint. To return to the chart document, choose **C**lose.

To print the chart, choose the **F**ile **P**rint command or press Ctrl+P and complete the dialog box. Follow the same described procedures as you follow for printing a worksheet as in Chapter 11, "Printing Worksheets."

For Related Information

- "Defining the Page Setup," p. 374
- "Previewing the Document," p. 389
- "Combining Data and Charts on the Same Page," p. 571

Troubleshooting

The printed copies of the chart do not look the same as the chart looks in the window. Why does this difference exist, and what can be done about it?

Always use printer fonts or TrueType fonts in your charts. Printer fonts have a small printer icon next to them in the Font list, and TrueType fonts have a small TT icon. If you create a chart with fonts unavailable to your printer, the printer makes a substitution, which can cause problems with spacing, style, and size.

From Here...

For more information related directly to creating and using charts, you can review the following chapters of this book:

- Chapter 11, "Printing Worksheets." This chapter explains how to print Excel worksheets.
- Chapter 13, "Modifying Charts." In this chapter, you learn about customizing the charts that you created in Excel by changing the chart type and adding other enhancements.
- Chapter 14, "Formatting Charts." This chapter explains how to format the objects in charts to make them look the way you want.
- Chapter 15, "Building Complex Charts." This chapter teaches advanced techniques for creating combination charts, using charts to analyze data, adding error bars to charts, and other special purpose procedures.

- Chapter 17, "Adding Graphics Elements to Sheets." This chapter covers adding graphical objects to a chart to add visual impact.
- Chapter 21, "Creating Slide Show Presentations." Here, you learn how to use charts in a slide show presentation to add impact to your message.

Chapter 13

Modifying Charts

After you have created a chart in Excel, you can modify the chart in many ways. The first modification you may want to make is to change the type of chart you are using. You may decide that you can present your data more effectively with a 3-D column chart than with the default 2-D column chart. You also can add titles, a legend, and other text to your chart to make it easier to understand. If you need to, you can add new data series or data points, or delete existing data series.

In this chapter, you learn how to modify the charts you have created in Excel. In the following chapter, you learn how to format different objects in your chart so that you have a custom chart that looks exactly the way you want.

In this chapter, you learn how to:

- Select chart objects
- Choose a chart type
- Use autoformats
- Add and delete data
- Work with data series formulas
- Insert text and other objects into a chart

An Overview of Modifying Charts

The first step in modifying a chart is selecting the type of chart you want to use to present your data most effectively. You may already have selected the appropriate chart type if you used the ChartWizard to create your chart. After the chart is created, you can change the chart type, if you want.

After you have selected the proper type of chart, you can start inserting titles and other text, data values, a legend, gridlines, arrows, and other graphical objects to enhance your chart and make it easier for the viewer to interpret your data. You also can add data points and data series to an existing chart, or delete them from an existing chart.

Using Shortcut Menus

In chart sheets and worksheets, clicking an object using the right mouse button displays a shortcut menu containing the most frequently used commands for that object. Figure 13.1 shows a shortcut menu for the value axis on a 3-D surface chart.

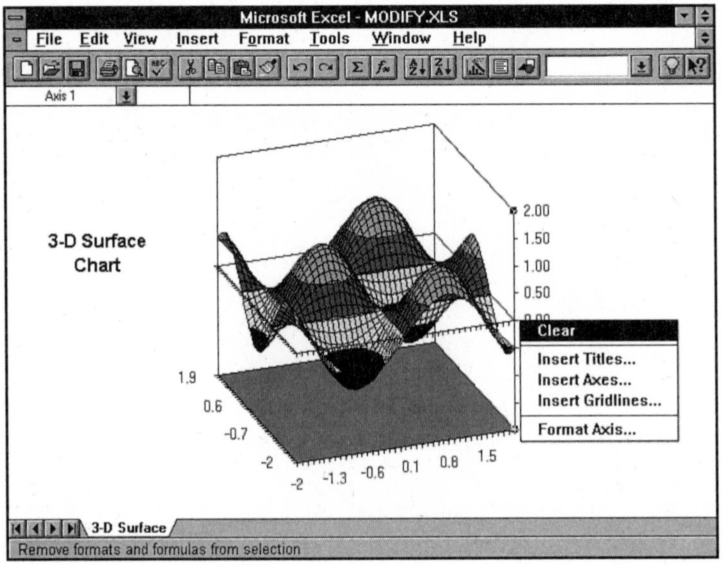

Fig. 13.1
The shortcut menu for a value axis.

After the shortcut menu appears, you can click the left or right mouse button to choose a command. An easier way to choose a command is to click with the right mouse button (to open the shortcut menu), drag down to the command you want, and then release the mouse button.

Selecting Chart Objects

Charts are composed of objects such as markers, legends, axes, and text. When you customize charts, you either add objects—which you learned how to do in Chapter 12—or you format existing objects with a new appearance. Before you can format a chart object, you must select it.

To select an object on the chart with the mouse, click the object. To select a single data point in a series, click the point once to select the series, and a second time to select the point. The same procedure works with legend elements and data labels. Click the legend once to select it, and then click a legend entry or legend key to select it. Click an individual data label once to select all labels in the data series, and click a second time to select just that label. If you double-click an object, you open a dialog box that presents formatting options for that object. Just use a single click to select an object.

You can select the two largest chart objects—the plot area and the chart background—by using the mouse. Click inside the rectangle formed by the axes to select the plot area, or click outside this rectangle to select the chart background.

To select an object on the chart with the keyboard, select the object's class by pressing the up- or down-arrow key. Following are the classes of chart objects:

Chart background

Plot area

Axes

Data series

Legend

Arrows

Hi-lo lines

Markers

Drop lines

Gridlines

Text

Next, select the specific object from within its class by pressing the left- or right-arrow key. When you reach the first or last object in a class, the selection skips to objects in the adjacent class.

A selected object has small squares around or on top of it, and its name appears in the left end of the formula bar. Some objects can be moved and resized. If the mouse pointer changes to a double-headed arrow when you position it over any edge of the square around a selected object, you can resize that object by dragging the edge. In figure 13.2, the plot area has been selected and the mouse pointer is positioned to resize the plot area. Titles (chart, value, and category) and data values can be moved but not resized. Press Esc to clear any selection.

For Related Information

- "Saving Time with Shortcut Menus," p. 39
- "Selecting Cells and Ranges," p. 72

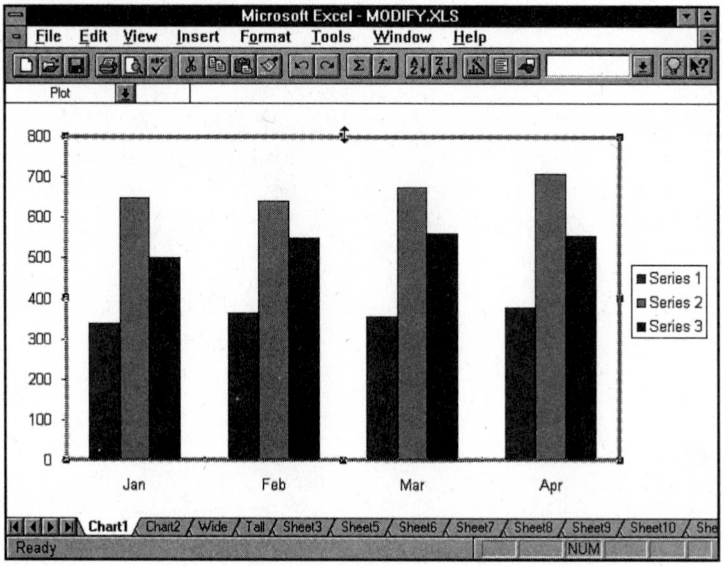

Fig. 13.2
You can resize an object if the mouse pointer changes to a double-headed arrow.

Choosing a Chart Type

Excel offers you eight different 2-D chart types and six different 3-D chart types. Within each of these general types, you can select a format or subtype. The easiest way to create charts is to select the chart type and subtype closest to the type you want. Then you can customize the predefined chart until it fits your exact needs. You should select the most appropriate chart type before you begin customizing your chart.

You can apply a chart type to the entire chart, a single data series in the chart, or to a group of data series. You can create a combination chart by applying different chart types to various data series in a chart. You can combine a line chart with a column chart, for example, to separate different types of data. See Chapter 15, "Building Complex Charts," for details on how to create a combination chart.

Using the Menu Command To Change a Chart Type

You can use the F**o**rmat Chart **T**ype command to change the chart type for all data series in your chart, or just for certain series. After you choose the F**o**rmat Chart **T**ype command, you can choose from among the subtypes for the chart type you choose. When you click the Chart Type tool to choose the chart type, you always get the default subtype.

To change the chart type by using the Format Chart Type command, follow these steps:

1. Activate the chart you want to change by clicking the tab for the chart sheet, or by double-clicking the chart if it is embedded in a worksheet.

2. Choose the F**o**rmat Chart **T**ype command; or choose Chart Type from the shortcut menu.

   If you select a data series before you choose the Format Chart Type command, or if you click a data series with the right mouse button and then choose Chart Type from the shortcut menu, you have the option of applying a chart type to just the selected series.

   The Chart Type dialog box displaying the chart types appears (see fig. 13.3).

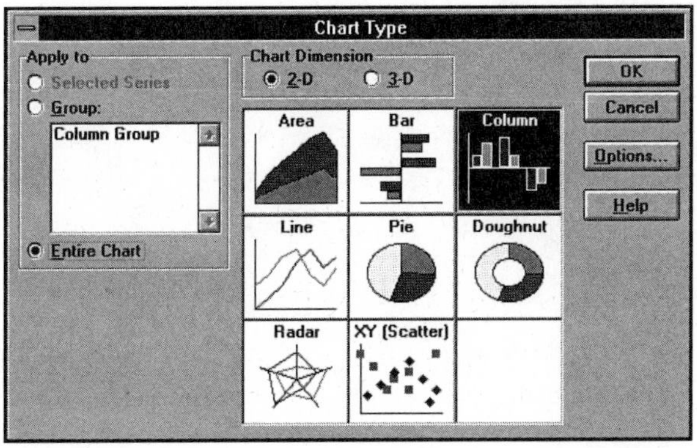

Fig. 13.3
Select the type of chart you want in the Chart Type dialog box.

3. Select one of the Apply to options.

   If you selected a data series in step 1, you can apply the chart type to this series by choosing the S**e**lected Series option. You also can apply the chart type to all data series by selecting the **E**ntire Chart option, or to one of the chart type groups (if there is more than one), by selecting one of the groups in the **G**roup list box. See Chapter 15, "Building Complex Charts," for more information on chart type groups.

4. Select either the **2**-D or **3**-D option and then select a chart type.

5. To display subtypes for this chart type, choose the **O**ptions button, and then choose the Subtype tab (see fig. 13.4).

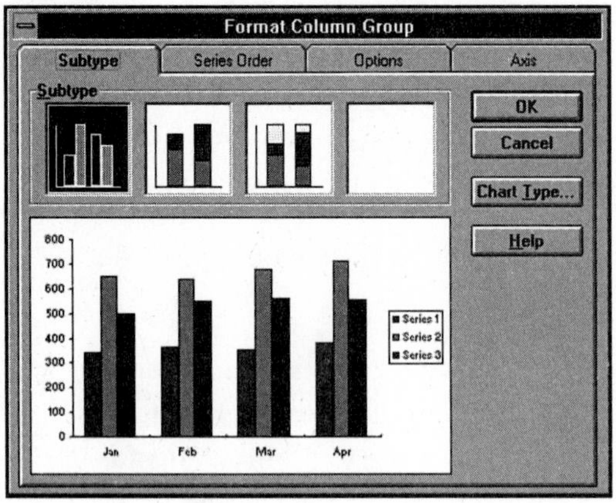

Fig. 13.4
Each chart type has at least one subtype you can select.

Tip
If you double-click the kind of chart you want in the Chart Type dialog box, you select the default subtype for the chart and close the dialog box without choosing OK.

6. Select a subtype and choose OK.

7. Choose OK to close the Chart Type dialog box.

Using the Chart Toolbar To Change a Chart Type

You can add the chart toolbar to your screen, and click the Chart Type button to change the chart type. The Chart Type button uses the default subtype for each chart type. To select other subtypes, use the F**o**rmat Chart **T**ype command, as explained earlier.

To use the Chart Toolbar to change the chart type, follow these steps:

For Related Information

- "Using the Mouse," p. 31
- "Using the Toolbars," p. 41

1. Choose the **V**iew **T**oolbars command; or, with the right mouse button, click any toolbar displayed on-screen, and then choose Chart from the shortcut menu.

2. If you use the **V**iew **T**oolbars command in step 1, select Chart from the **T**oolbars list box in the Toolbars dialog box, and then choose OK.

3. Click the arrow next to the Chart Type button on the Chart toolbar to drop down a list of chart types (see fig. 13.5). Select a chart type from the list.

   If you selected a data series before this step, the selected chart type is applied only to that series.

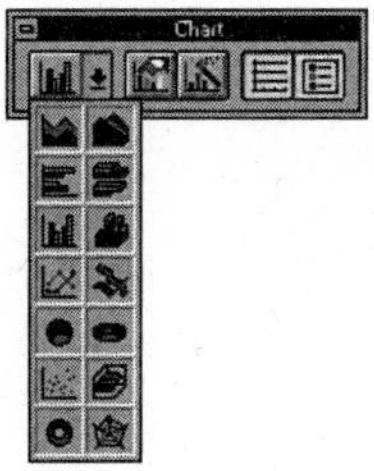

Fig. 13.5
You can select a chart type by using the Chart Type button on the Chart toolbar. The button's icon is a column chart.

Using Autoformats

Autoformats enable you to apply predefined chart formats to your data. For each chart type, several autoformats make it easy to select exactly the type of chart you want. Autoformats are similar to the subtype options that are available when you use the Format Chart Type dialog box (see the preceding section "Using the Menu Command to Change a Chart Type"), except that you have many more choices. In fact, you have the same choices available to you as when you use the ChartWizard to create a chart (see Chapter 12, "Creating Charts," for more information on using the ChartWizard). You can also create custom autoformats, using as templates other charts you have created and customized. See "Creating Custom Autoformats," later in this chapter, to learn how to create your own autoformats.

Applying Autoformats to a Chart

You can apply any of the built-in autoformats to an existing chart. When you apply an autoformat, it is applied to every series in the chart. To change the chart type of just one series in a chart, select that series, and then choose the F**o**rmat Chart **T**ype command or click the Chart Type button on the Standard toolbar.

To apply an autoformat to a chart, follow these steps:

1. Activate the chart to which you want to apply an autoformat.
2. Choose the F**o**rmat **A**utoFormat command or choose AutoFormat from the shortcut menu. The AutoFormat dialog box appears (see fig. 13.6).
3. Select a chart type from the **G**alleries list box.
4. Select a chart format from the **F**ormats box and choose OK; or double-click the chart format you want.

   The chart type and format are applied to the active chart.

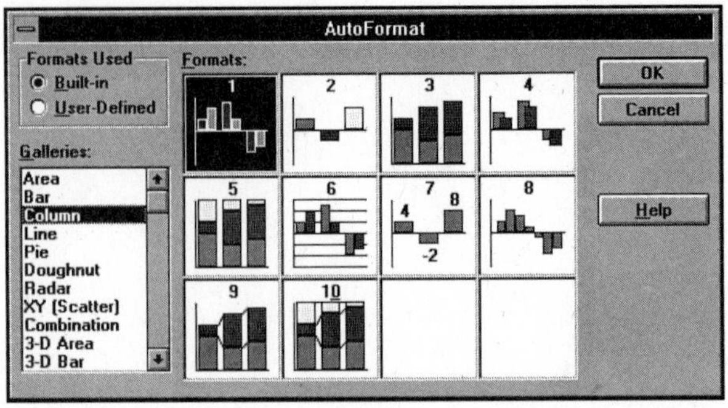

Fig. 13.6
You can select one of Excel's autoformats to apply to a chart.

> **Note**
>
> If you want to change the chart type for a series or entire chart you have already customized, do not use the **A**utoFormat command; if you do, you lose all custom formatting. Change the chart type by choosing the F**o**rmat Chart **T**ype command.

Examining Types of 2-D Autoformats

Excel's seven 2-D chart types give you many options for presenting your data most effectively. For each of these chart types, there are several autoformats you can apply to your charts. This section examines how each type of chart is generally used. This information helps you to select the chart type that matches your data correctly.

Area Charts. The area chart autoformats are shown in figure 13.7. An area chart compares the continuous change in volume of multiple data series. This type of chart sums the data from all the individual series to create the top line that encloses the area, giving the viewer an impression of how different series contribute to the total volume. Use the area chart for sales and production figures, to show how volume changes over time, and to emphasize the amount or volume of change. The subjects of area charts are similar to those of line charts, such as units shipped per day, or the volume of orders over time.

Bar Charts. The bar chart autoformats are shown in figure 13.8. A bar chart is used for comparing distinct (noncontinuous), unrelated objects over time. This chart type gives little impression of time but uses horizontal bars to show positive or negative variation from a center point. You can use a bar chart to give a snapshot of budget variance for different items at a single point in time. Bars to the left of the center have negative variance, and those to the right have positive variance.

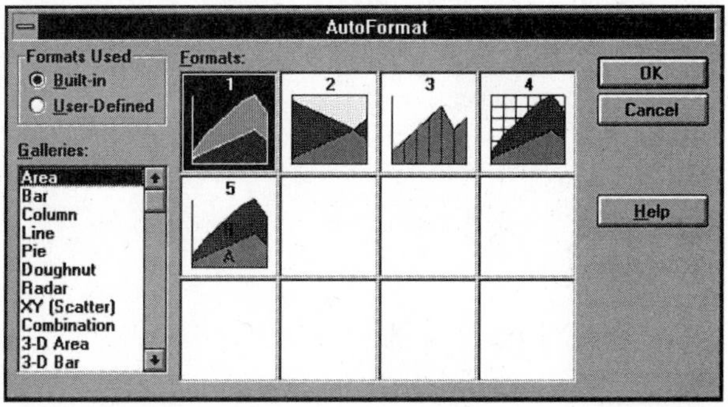

Fig. 13.7
The area chart autoformats.

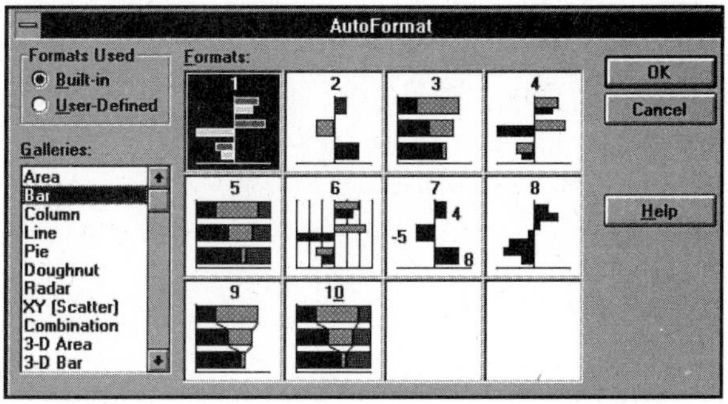

Fig. 13.8
The bar chart autoformats.

In 2-D bar charts, you can drag a point to a new position, and the corresponding value in the worksheet changes. If the data point plots the result of a formula in the worksheet, Excel executes the **T**ools **G**oal Seek command to find the input value in the worksheet required to give the new result you plotted by dragging the data point. See Chapter 15, "Building Complex Charts," for more information on moving data points.

Column Charts. The column chart autoformats are shown in figure 13.9. Column charts often compare separate (noncontinuous) items as they vary over time. This chart type uses vertical columns to give the impression of distinct measurements made at different intervals. Column charts frequently are used for comparing different items by placing them side-by-side.

In 2-D bar charts, you can drag a point to a new position, and the corresponding value in the worksheet changes. If the data point plots the result of a formula in the worksheet, Excel executes the **T**ools **G**oal Seek command to find the input value in the required worksheet to give the new result you plotted in the chart by dragging the data point. See Chapter 15, "Building Complex Charts," for more information on moving data points.

Fig. 13.9
The column chart autoformats.

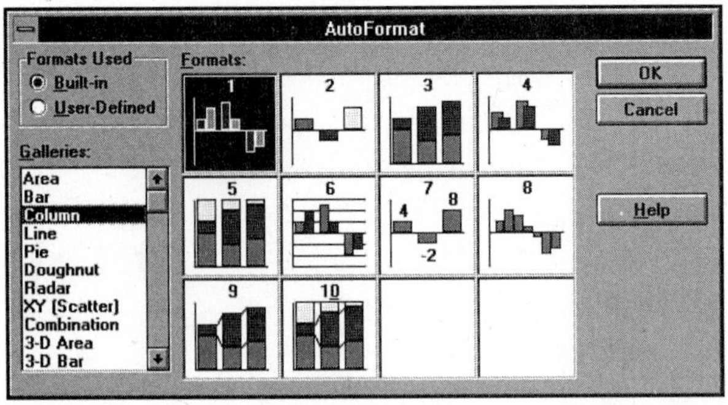

Line Charts. The line chart autoformats are shown in figure 13.10. A line chart compares trends over even time intervals (or other measurement intervals) plotted on the category axis—if your category data points are at uneven intervals, use an XY [scatter] chart. Use the line chart in production, sales, or stock market situations to show the trend of revenue or sales over time. In the hi-lo and hi-lo-close charts, autoformat numbers 7 and 8, point lines extend from the highest to the lowest value in each category. In the stock market, hi-lo-close charts show the high, low, and closing stock prices on each plotted day.

In 2-D bar charts, you can drag a point to a new position, and the corresponding value in the worksheet changes. If the data point plots the result of a formula in the worksheet, Excel executes the **T**ools **G**oal Seek command to find the input value in the worksheet required to give the new result you plotted in the chart by dragging the data point. See Chapter 15, "Building Complex Charts," for more information on moving data points.

Fig. 13.10
The line chart autoformats.

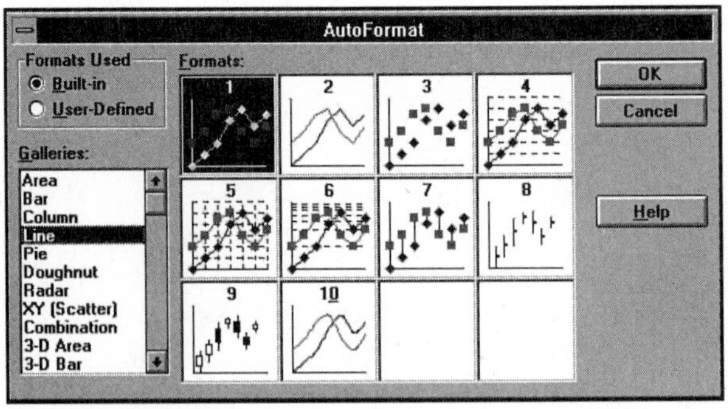

Pie Charts. The pie chart autoformats are shown in figure 13.11. A pie chart compares the sizes of pieces in a whole unit. Use this type of chart when the parts total 100 percent for a single series of data. Only the first data series in a worksheet selection is plotted. Pie charts work well to show the percentage of mix in products shipped, mix in income sources, or mix in target populations. Wedges in pie charts can be pulled out from the pie to emphasize the data point they represent. To pull out, or "explode," a slice of a pie chart, point to the slice, then click and drag the slice away from the pie. Release the mouse button when the slice is positioned where you want it.

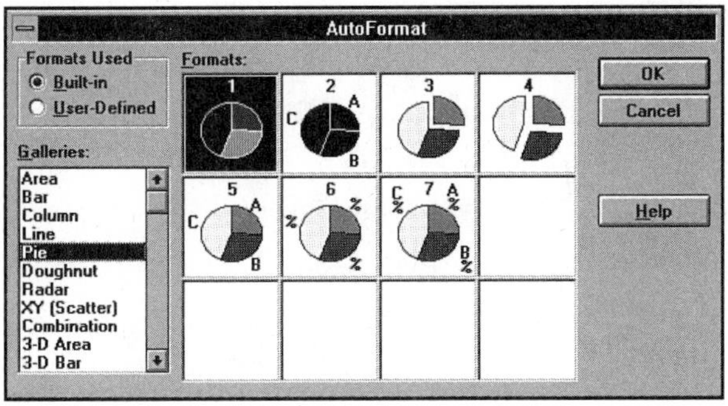

Fig. 13.11
The pie chart autoformats.

If you want to compare many data points, you are better off using a column chart, as it becomes difficult to make accurate comparisons when there are more than six or eight pieces in a pie. Also, if you need to distinguish precise percentages, use a column chart so that you have a value (Y) axis from which to read percentage values.

Doughnut Charts. The doughnut chart autoformats are shown in figure 13.12. Similar to pie charts, doughnut charts compare the sizes of pieces in a whole unit. The arrangement of the doughnut chart, however, allows you to show more than one data series.

Again, as with pie charts, if you need to make precise distinctions between percentage values, use a column chart rather than a doughnut chart so that you have a value (Y) axis from which to read percentage values.

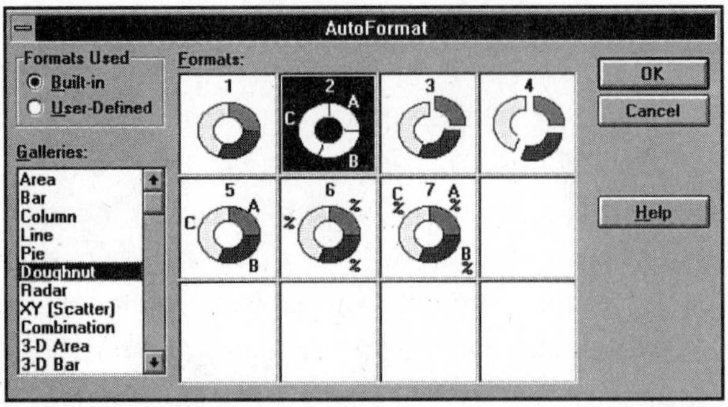

Fig. 13.12
The doughnut chart autoformats.

Radar Charts. The radar chart autoformats are shown in figure 13.13. Use radar charts to show the relationships between individual data series, and between a specific series and the whole of the other series. Unless you and those who view these are accustomed to working with radar charts, avoid this chart type. Radar charts are difficult to read and interpret.

Each category (data series label) in the chart has its own axis (spoke). Data points appear along the spoke. Lines that connect the data points define the area covered by the items. Radar charts in which each data series is a task in a given project, for example, can show how much time is spent on each task.

Each spoke on the radar chart represents time spent on a specific task. If all tasks require the same time, the chart creates a near circle. The larger the total area covered by the plot, the more total time is spent on the project.

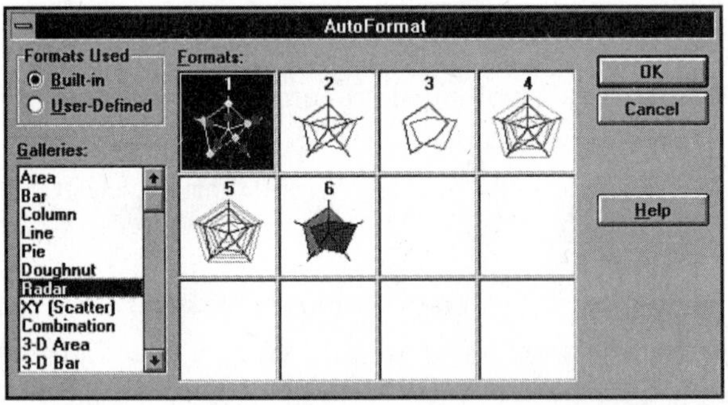

Fig. 13.13
The radar chart autoformats.

XY (Scatter) Charts. The XY (scatter) chart autoformats are shown in figure 13.14. A scattergram or XY chart compares trends over uneven time or measurement intervals plotted on the category axis (if your category data is at even intervals, use a line chart). Scatter charts also display patterns from discrete X and Y data measurements. Use scatter charts when you must plot data in which the independent variable is recorded at uneven intervals, or the category data points are specified in uneven increments. For example, survey data plotted with responses on the value axis, and ages on the category axis, can reveal opinion clusters by age. Much scientific and engineering data is charted with scatter charts.

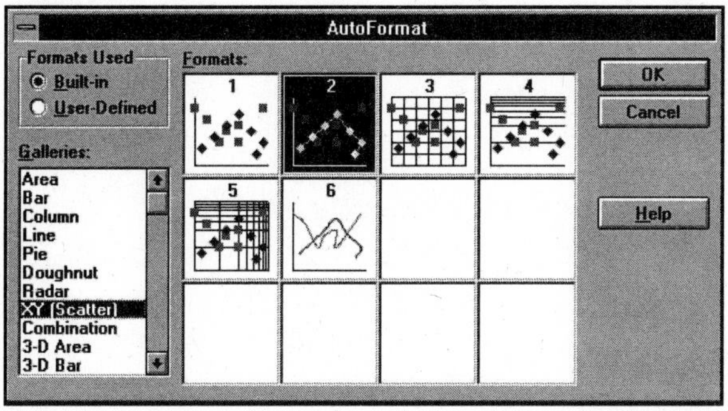

Fig. 13.14
The XY (Scatter) chart autoformats.

Combination Charts. The combination chart autoformats are shown in figure 13.15. A combination chart places one chart type over another. This type of chart is helpful to compare data of different types, or data requiring different axis scales. After a combination chart is created, you change the type of chart to be used for the main (overlaid) chart by choosing the F**o**rmat Chart **T**ype command. See "Creating Combination Charts," in Chapter 15, for further information.

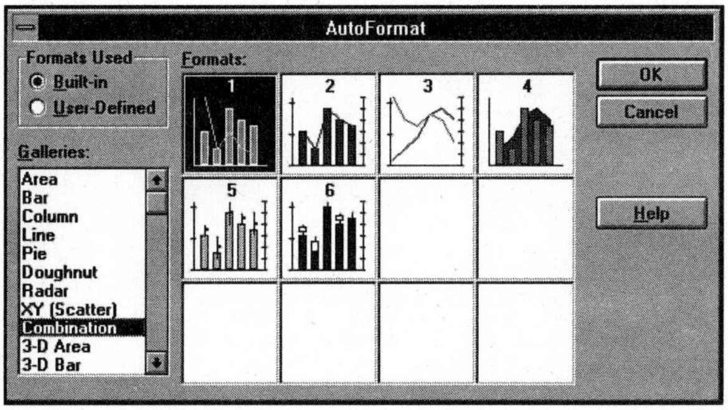

Fig. 13.15
The combination chart autoformats.

Examining Types of 3-D Charts

Excels 3-D charts are attractive and work well for presentations or marketing materials. Most of the 3-D chart types do not actually add any information regarding your data. Instead, they are used to add visual depth and impact to the presentation of your data. They work well in reports, and work well to make overhead slides for presentations. When you use charts for analytical work, however, you may find exact data comparison easier on 2-D charts.

3-D surface charts do add another dimension of information. Surface charts can illuminate relationships between data that would not otherwise be easy to ascertain. Colors and patterns are used to indicate areas of the same value in a surface chart, similar to the way that shading and colors are used in a topographical map. These charts are useful for visually representing high and low points in a data set that result from two changing variables.

3-D Area Charts. 3-D area charts are similar to 2-D area charts. The 3-D area chart autoformats are shown in figure 13.16. Use 3-D area charts for the same types of data used in 2-D area charts.

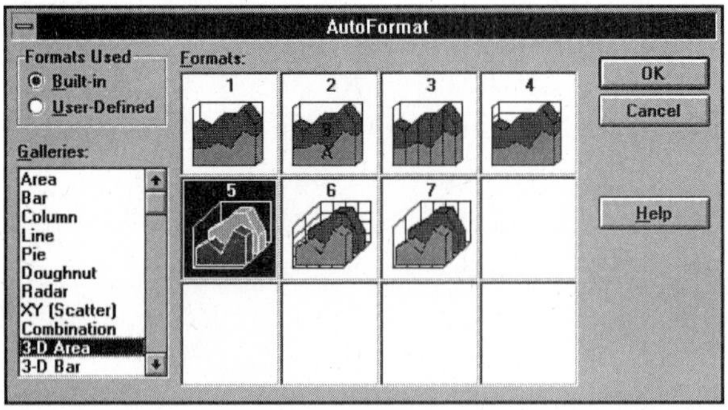

Fig. 13.16
The 3-D area chart autoformats.

3-D Bar Charts. 3-D bar charts are used to compare data series over time or against each other. The 3-D bar chart autoformats are shown in figure 13.17.

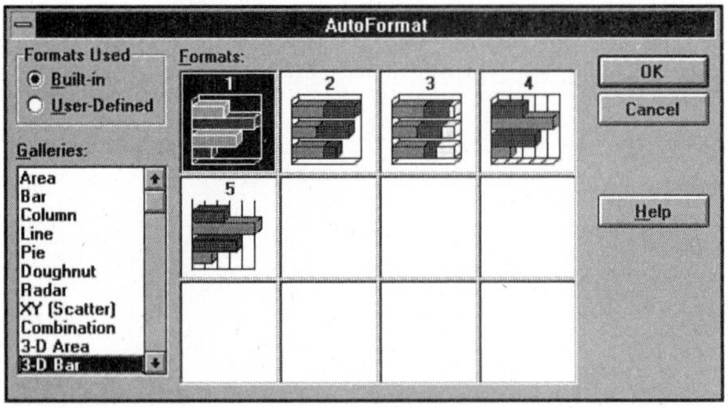

Fig. 13.17
The 3-D bar chart autoformats.

3-D Column Charts. You can create 3-D column charts with columns adjacent to each other, or layered into the third dimension. The 3-D column chart autoformats are shown in figure 13.18. Use 3-D column charts for the same types of data as in 2-D column charts.

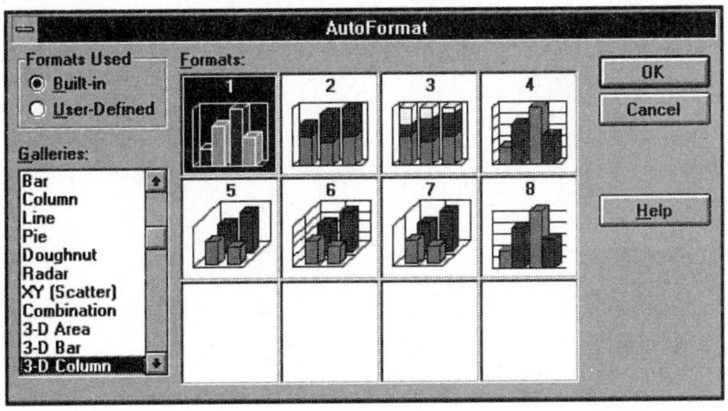

Fig. 13.18
The 3-D column chart autoformats.

3-D Line Charts. 3-D line charts are known also as *ribbon charts*. The 3-D line chart autoformats are shown in figure 13.19. Use 3-D line charts for the same types of data as those used in 2-D line charts.

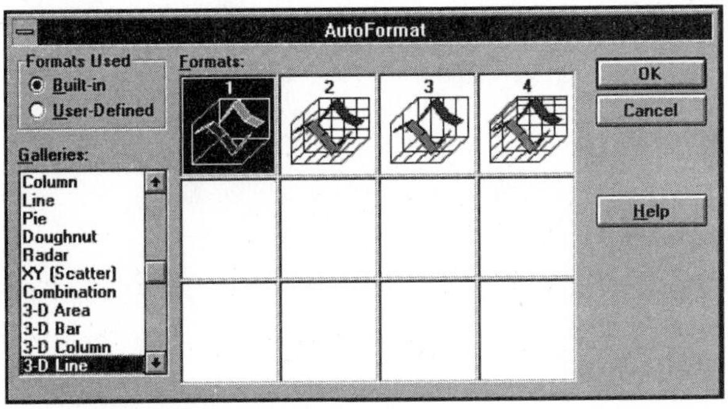

Fig. 13.19
The 3-D line chart autoformats.

3-D Pie Charts. The 3-D pie chart autoformats are shown in figure 13.20. These charts work well for marketing materials or presentations in which an overall impression is required. You can pull a wedge from the pie when you need to discuss that wedge's contents. Excel can show labels or calculate percentages for wedges. As with a 2-D pie chart, only the first data series in a selection is charted as a pie.

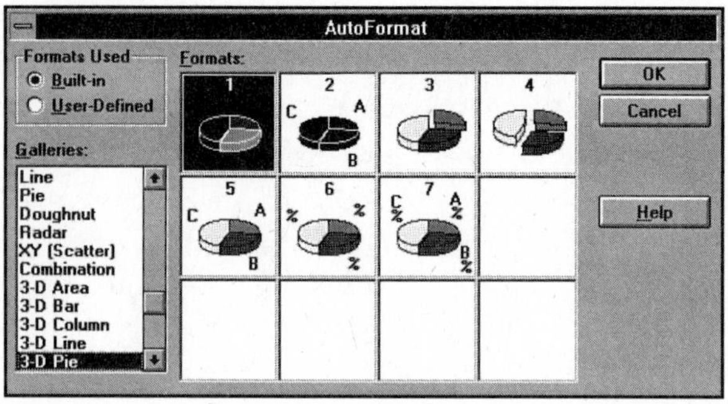

Fig. 13.20
The 3-D pie chart autoformats.

3-D Surface Charts. Surface charts are like topographical maps—they show high and low points along a surface. Surface charts are an excellent way of visually locating high and low points resulting from two changing variables.

The autoformats offer both wire frame and surface displays (see fig. 13.21). The surface chart, choice 1, shows a surface stretched between points. The color of the surface helps to indicate its value. A color contour chart, choice 3, acts like a topographical map by showing elevations according to color. If you want to see the surface map from a different point of view, click one of the chart axis corners. When black handles appear at the corners (it may take a moment), drag the handles to rotate the chart. This procedure is described in more detail in Chapter 14, "Formatting Charts."

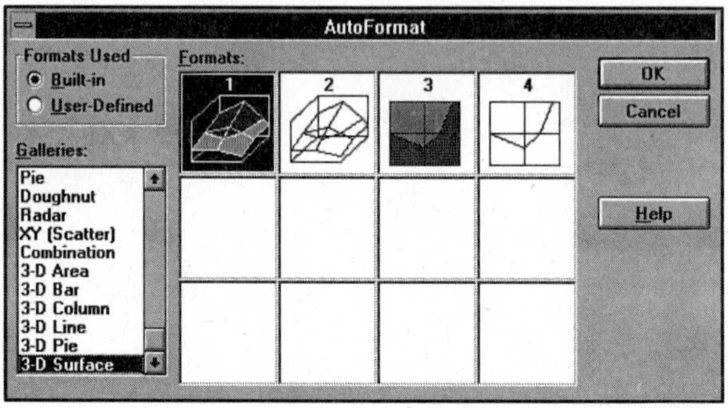

Fig. 13.21
The 3-D surface chart autoformats.

Surface chart types 1 and 2 display a three-dimensional view of the surface. Types 3 and 4 appear more like topographical maps, which show changes in elevation with contour lines and colors. Type 2 displays data in a wire frame. The wire frame enables you to more easily compare data points that may be hidden in the 3-D chart.

The colors used in 3-D surface maps are defined by the current palette. The number of colors used depends on the scaling of the vertical axis.

Creating Custom Autoformats

You can easily create custom autoformats, which are added to the **G**alleries list in the AutoFormat dialog box. If you have already created a chart that is formatted the way you want, use it as a template for a custom autoformat. Otherwise, create from scratch a chart that is formatted the way you want, and then use it as a template for a custom autoformat.

To create a custom autoformat, follow these steps:

1. Activate the chart you want to use as a basis for the autoformat.

2. Choose the F**o**rmat **A**utoFormat command, or choose AutoFormat from the shortcut menu, to display the AutoFormat dialog box shown in figure 13.22.

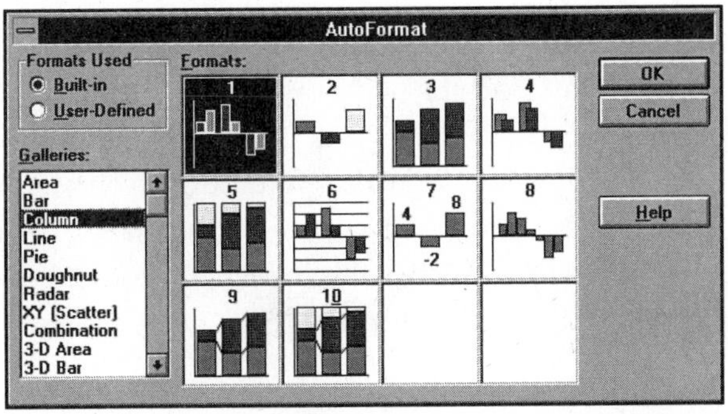

Fig. 13.22
The AutoFormat dialog box.

3. Select the **U**ser-Defined option in the Formats Used box.

4. Choose Custo**m**ize. The User-Defined AutoFormats dialog box appears (see fig. 13.23).

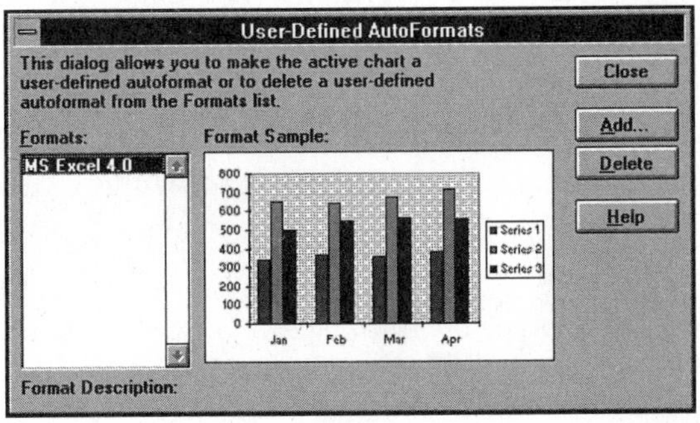

Fig. 13.23
Add custom autoformats in the User-Defined AutoFormats dialog box.

5. Choose **A**dd. The Add Custom AutoFormat dialog box appears (see fig. 13.24).

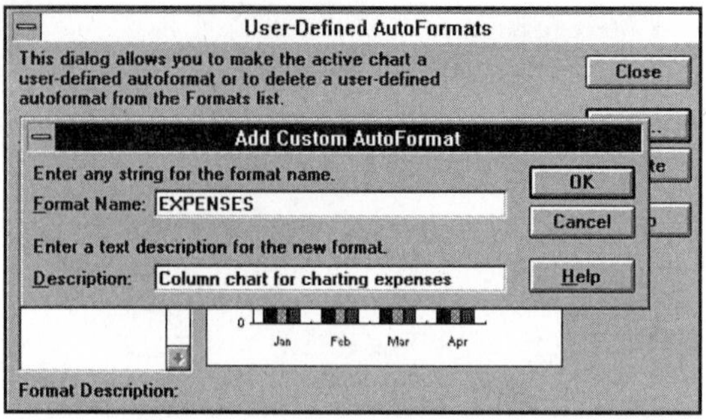

Fig. 13.24
Name a new custom autoformat in the Add Custom AutoFormat dialog box.

6. Type a name for the new custom format in the **F**ormat Name text box, and type a description of it in the **D**escription text box.

7. Choose OK.

The new format is added to the **F**ormats list in the AutoFormat dialog box and can be applied to any chart the same way built-in formats are applied. When you open the AutoFormat dialog box, select the **U**ser-Defined option to display the list of custom autoformats. Select the one you want to apply to the current chart, and choose OK. To delete a custom autoformat, select **U**ser-Defined in the Autoformat dialog box, choose Custo**m**ize, select the format to be deleted in the **F**ormats list, and then choose **D**elete.

Changing the Chart Type

Choosing the F**o**rmat **A**utoformat command to change the chart type in an existing chart removes custom formatting you may have added and returns the chart to its default colors and patterns. If you need to change the chart type on an existing chart, or for a series or group of series on an existing chart, choose the F**o**rmat Chart **T**ype command to display the Chart Type dialog box shown in figure 13.25. If you want to change the chart type for the entire chart, select the **E**ntire Chart option in the Apply to box. If you want to change the chart type for just a selected series, select the S**e**lected Series option. To change the chart type for a group of series that are using the same chart type in a combination chart, select the **G**roup option, and then select the group whose chart type you want to change. To display the subtypes for that chart type in its Group Options dialog box, choose **O**ptions and then choose the Subtype tab (see fig. 13.26). Select a subtype from the **S**ubtype box, examine the sample in the preview box to verify that you have made the right selection, and then choose OK.

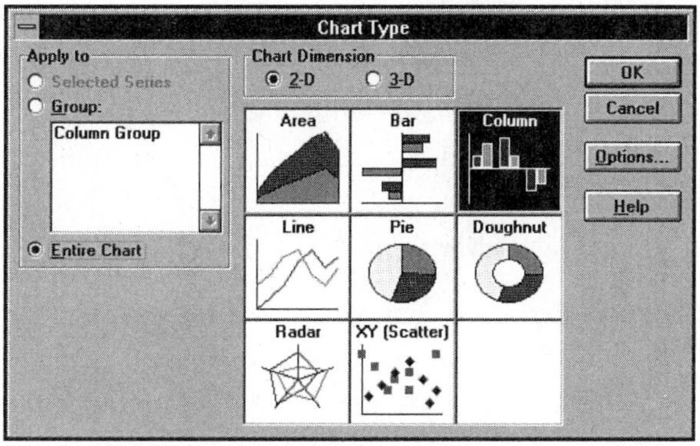

Fig. 13.25
The Chart Type dialog box enables you to change the chart type of existing charts, but also to preserve custom formatting.

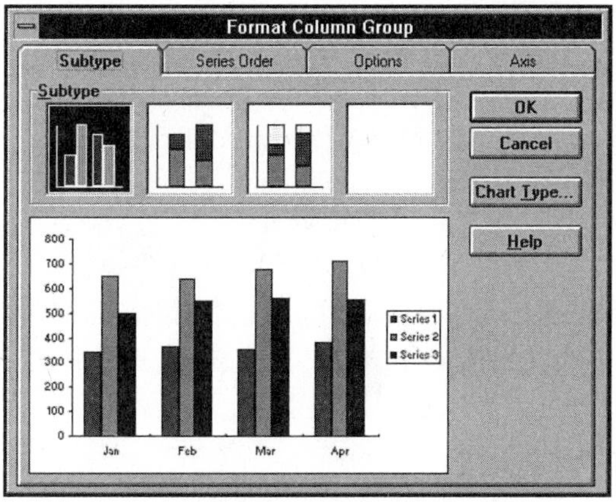

Fig. 13.26
Select the subtype for a selected chart type in its Group Options dialog box.

For Related Information

- "Formatting with AutoFormats," p. 303
- "Creating Workbook and Worksheet Templates," p. 1128

Troubleshooting

Changing the chart type removes custom formats.

If you apply one of the autoformats to a chart that has already been custom formatted, you lose some or all of the chart's custom formatting. To change the chart type of an existing chart, yet retain its custom formatting, use the F**o**rmat Chart **T**ype command. Refer to "Choosing a Chart Type," earlier in this chapter, for more information on this command.

Choosing Line or XY (Scatter) Charts

Line and XY (scatter) charts can be similar in appearance, but they treat data differently. You need to be aware of the differences if you want accurate charts.

You should use a line chart when the category (X) data points are evenly spaced or when the category data points are text, and spacing does not matter. Category data should be in ascending or descending order. Line charts are most commonly used for business or financial data that is distributed evenly over time or in such categories as Sales, Costs, and so on. Category data such as time should be sequential, with no data missing.

You should use an XY (scatter) chart when data is intermittent or unevenly spaced. When Excel creates a scatter chart, the program reads the lowest and highest values in the category data and uses these values as the end points for the category axis (X). The tick marks are placed at even intervals between the end points. The data is plotted along the category axis according to the X data value, not at evenly spaced intervals as it would be in a line chart.

Figure 13.27 shows data plotted in a line chart that should have been plotted in an XY (scatter) chart. The correctly plotted data in an XY (scatter) chart appears in figure 13.28. Notice the difference in the spacing of missed days in the two charts.

Fig. 13.27
Intermittent data plotted in a line chart, giving an incorrect impression.

Incorrect spacing of missed days

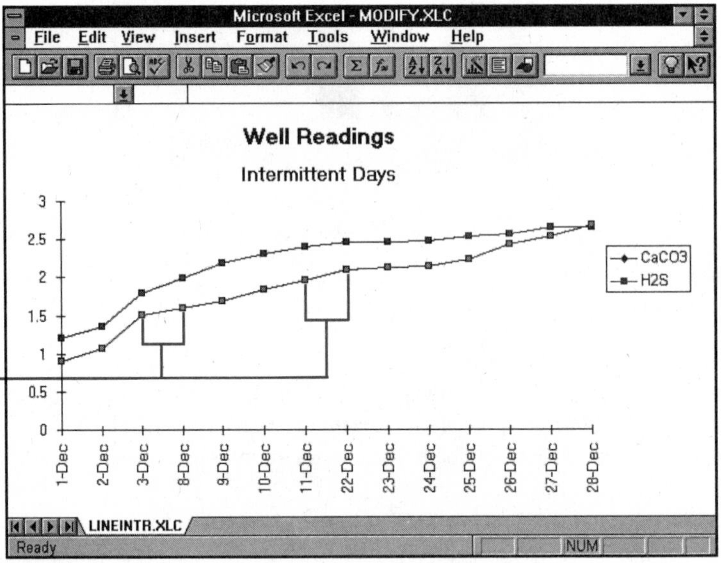

Choosing a Default Chart Format

EXCEL 5

If you deal with the same chart type and format regularly, you may want to designate a specific type and format for Excel to use as the default for newly created charts. Usually, Excel's preferred chart type is the first predefined 2-D column chart. To change Excel's default chart type, activate a chart that has the type and custom formatting you want to use as the default. Choose the **T**ools **O**ptions command and choose the Chart tab to display the Options dialog box shown in figure 13.29. Select a chart from the Default Chart Format drop-down list (your custom autoformats also appear in this list—see "Creating Custom Autoformats," earlier in this chapter, for more information), and then choose OK.

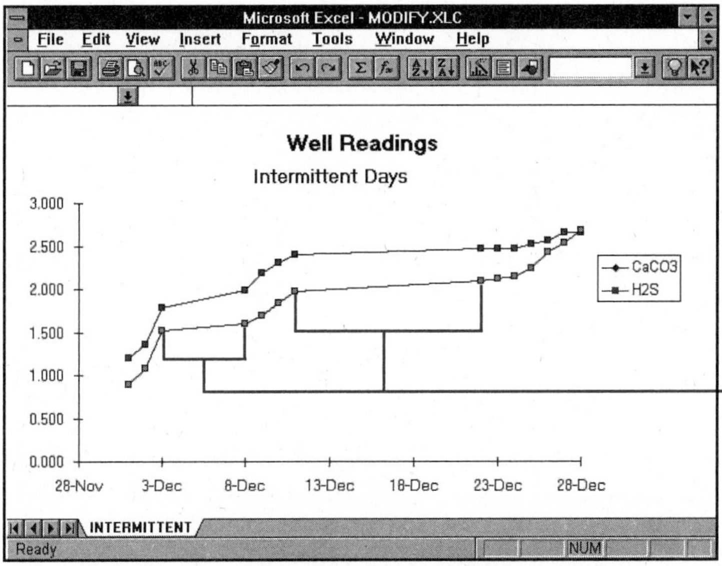

Fig. 13.28
The same data plotted in an XY (scatter) chart, showing the correct relationship.

Correct spacing of missed days

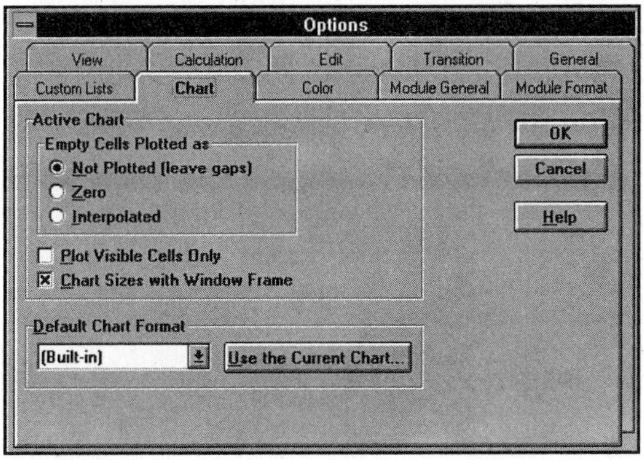

Fig. 13.29
Change the default chart format in the Options dialog box.

You can also select the **U**se the Current Chart option to make the active chart the default chart format. When you choose this command, the Add Custom AutoFormat dialog box appears. Type a name and description for the format, and choose OK. Choose OK again to return to your chart. Future charts created during this work session begin with your preferred format. To return to the original default chart, choose the **T**ools **O**ptions command, choose the Chart tab, select Built-In from the Default Chart Format drop-down list, and choose OK. As an alternative method, while working with any chart, you can click the Default Chart button on the Chart toolbar to make that chart's format the default format.

When you change the default chart type, it stays in effect only for the current work session. When you reopen Excel, the normal default type is in effect. Use the steps just outlined to change the default for the current work session.

Adding or Deleting Data

You can add data to existing charts, regardless of whether they were created automatically or manually (see Chapter 12, "Creating Charts"). You can add new data series, add new data points to existing series, or change the range of data used by a chart.

There are several methods for adding data to a chart. If you are working with an embedded chart, you can select the data you want to add in the worksheet, and then drag-and-drop the selection onto the embedded chart. If you are working in a chart window with either an embedded chart that you have opened, or with a chart sheet, you can use the **I**nsert **N**ew Data command. You can use the **E**dit Cu**t**/**E**dit **C**opy and **E**dit **P**aste commands to add data to either kind of chart. You can also edit the chart's data series formula in the Format Selected Series dialog box.

Adding Data to Embedded Charts

You can add data to an embedded chart quickly by using the mouse. To add data using the mouse, follow these steps:

1. Select the data you want to add to the embedded chart.

2. Drag the data onto the chart and release the mouse button.

   To drag the selected data, move the mouse pointer up to the bottom edge of the selected data. The mouse pointer changes to an arrow. If the pointer changes to a cross, you have moved too far into the selection—move back toward the edge of the selection until you see the arrow. Hold down the left mouse button and drag the data into the chart.

If the data you select has the same layout as the original data used to create the chart, the new data is added immediately to the chart. If the data you select is such that Excel cannot determine how it should be placed in the chart, the Paste Special dialog box appears (see fig. 13.30). Specify the layout for the data, and choose OK. Refer to "How to Create a Chart Manually," in Chapter 12, for detailed information on how to work with this dialog box.

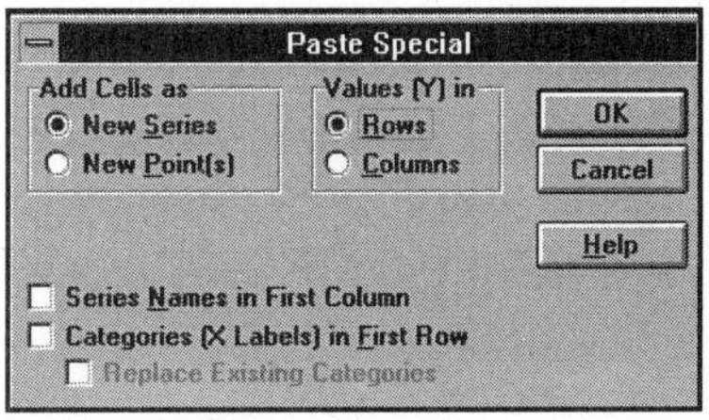

Fig. 13.30
The Paste Special Dialog box can be used to specify how data is used in a chart.

Adding Data with the Insert New Data Command

When you are working with an embedded chart that has been activated or with a chart on a chart sheet, you can add new data to the chart with the **I**nsert command.

To add new data using this command, follow these steps:

1. Activate the embedded chart or activate the chart sheet for the chart to which you want to add data.

   To activate an embedded chart, double-click it. To activate a chart on a chart sheet, click the tab for the chart sheet.

2. Choose the **I**nsert **N**ew Data command. The New Data dialog box appears (see fig. 13.31).

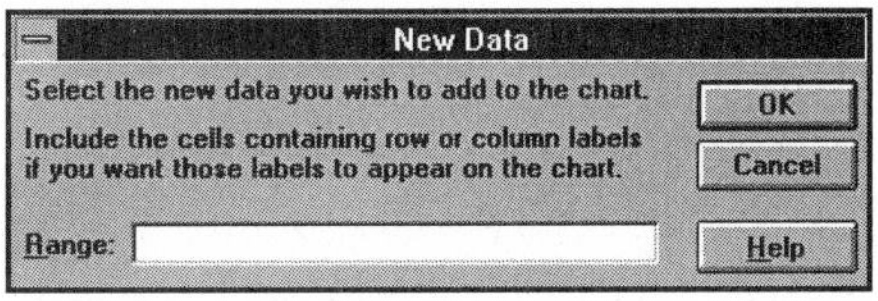

Fig. 13.31
Specify the data you want to add to a chart in the New Data dialog box.

3. Select the worksheet that contains the data you want to add to the chart by clicking the tab for the worksheet.

4. Select the data in the worksheet, just as you would select data in a worksheet when you first create a chart.

Include row and column headings in the selection, if you want them to appear in the chart. The reference for the data range you select appears in the **R**ange text box, or type the cell references for the data you want in the **R**ange edit box.

5. Choose OK.

If the data you select has the same layout as the original data used to create the chart, the data is added immediately to the chart. If the data you select is such that Excel cannot determine how it should be placed in the chart, the Paste Special dialog box appears. Specify the layout for the data, and choose OK.

Adding Data from Multiple Worksheets

By choosing the **I**nsert **N**ew Data command, you easily can combine data from multiple worksheets into one chart. You can, for example, create a chart that reflects data from four different quarters, although each quarter is on a different worksheet.

To combine data from multiple worksheets into one chart, follow these steps:

1. Create a chart from the worksheet data you want as the first series in the chart.
2. Choose the **I**nsert **N**ew Data command.
3. Activate a different worksheet.
4. Select a data series. Include labels if the original data selection includes labels. (If you are adding to an XY [scatter] chart, the number of data points does not need to be the same, but you must include both X and Y data, as described earlier.)
5. Choose OK.
6. Repeat steps 2-4 for each data series you want to add to the chart.

Adding Data with the Edit Copy and Edit Paste Commands

To add data to charts with the **E**dit **C**opy and **E**dit **P**aste commands, simply copy the data from the worksheet and then paste the data onto the chart. If the original data to create the chart includes cells containing labels, the new data you copy also must include cells for labels, even if those cells are blank.

To add data with the Copy and Paste commands, follow these steps:

1. Activate the worksheet containing the data you want to add, and select the data.

2. Choose the **E**dit **C**opy command.

3. Activate the chart into which you want to copy the data.

4. Choose the **E**dit **P**aste command if you are adding data with a standard layout.

   If you are adding a new series that uses a standard layout and has the same number of data points as the original series in the chart, or if you are just adding new data points, the **E**dit **P**aste command works.

   You also can choose the **E**dit Paste **S**pecial command if the data you want to add uses a nonstandard layout and its category axis (X) is along the short side of the selection, or if a data series you are adding has fewer data points than the original data series.

   Select from the Paste Special dialog box the options that describe the layout of the data, and whether the new data should be added as a new series or as new data points. You usually must select the opposite option button from the one selected under Values (Y) in group when the box first displays. If the box appears with **R**ows selected, for example, you select **C**olumns. After you change the option button, select the appropriate check boxes to describe where labels are located.

5. Choose OK.

You can use the **E**dit **C**opy and **E**dit **P**aste (or **E**dit Paste **S**pecial) commands to add data from multiple worksheets. Simply activate the worksheet that has the data you want to add, choose the **E**dit **C**opy command, activate the chart to which you are adding the data, and choose the **E**dit **P**aste command (or the **E**dit Paste Special command). Repeat this procedure for each worksheet that has data you want to add to the chart.

Changing the Data Range with the ChartWizard

One of the easiest ways to change the data range used in a chart is by using the ChartWizard. To change the data range used in a chart, follow these steps:

1. Open the workbook containing the data and chart with which you want to work. Activate the chart.

2. If the Standard and Chart toolbars are not displayed, choose the **V**iew **T**oolbars command, choose Standard or Chart from the Toolbars dialog box, and choose OK.

   or

   Click any existing toolbar using the right mouse button, and then select Standard or Chart from the shortcut menu.

3. Click the ChartWizard button.

   The worksheet containing the data activates, with the current chart data selected. A ChartWizard dialog box appears over the worksheet, as shown in figure 13.32.

Fig. 13.32
Drag across the worksheet to select the new data range you want for the chart.

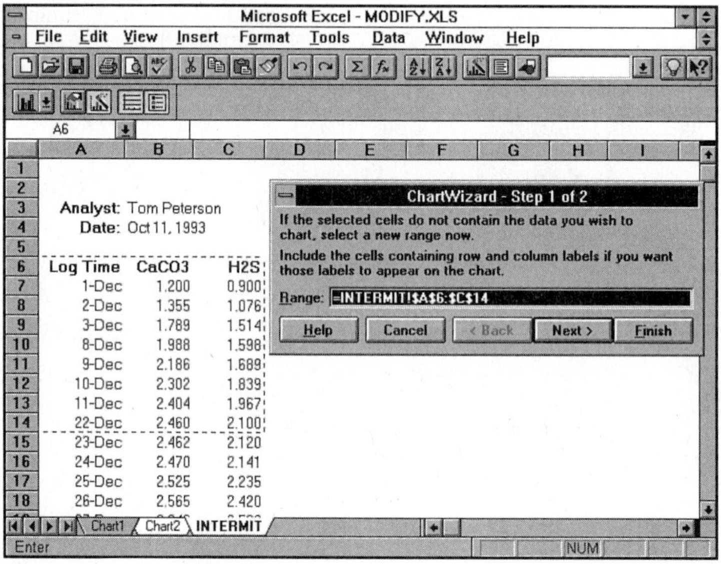

4. Edit the range or reselect the data range so that the ChartWizards **R**ange text box displays the new range you want for the chart.

5. Choose Next. A second dialog box displays and gives you the opportunity to change the chart orientation and labels for the new data layout.

6. Make selections as described in the section "Creating an Embedded Chart Using the ChartWizard," in Chapter 12.

7. Choose OK.

Excel redraws your chart using the new data you selected, but keeping the previous data type and formatting.

Deleting Data

You can delete an entire data series or points in a data series. To delete a data series, select the series in the chart. Then choose the **E**dit Cle**a**r **S**eries command, or press Del.

To delete points in a data series, delete them in the worksheet that is the source for the chart, or redefine the data range used by the chart. The latter can be done using the ChartWizard, as described in the previous section.

For Related Information

- "Filling or Copying Cell Contents," p. 241
- "Working with Multiple Windows," p. 546
- "Analyzing Pivot Table Data with Charts," p. 1027

Working with the Series Formula

When you create a chart, or add a data series to a chart, Excel links each data series in the chart to a data series on a worksheet. Excel creates this link with a series formula. If you use the ChartWizard or the F**o**rmat S**e**lected Series command to change the data used by a chart, you should understand how to use a series formula.

Understanding the Series Formula

A series formula tells the chart several things: where the worksheet is located on the disk or network, which worksheet to use, and which cells of that worksheet contain data to be charted. Each data series has a series formula. When you select one of the markers in the data series, the series formula is displayed in the formula bar. The formula that appears in the formula bar in figure 13.33, for example, belongs to the first data series, which is shown with squares inside the columns.

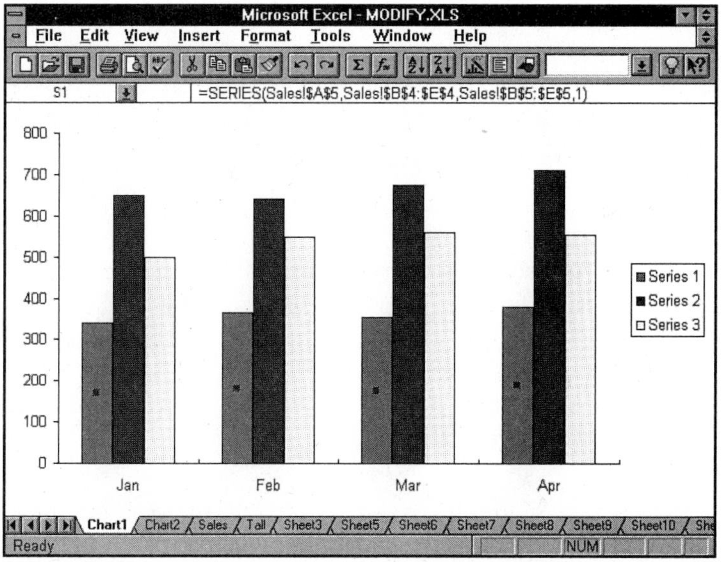

Fig. 13.33
When you select a data series in a chart, the series formula appears in the formula bar.

When you examine the worksheet and the related chart, you can see how the series formula works. All series formulas are constructed on the following pattern:

```
=SERIES("series_name",worksheet_name!category_reference,
worksheet_name!values_reference,marker_order_number)
```

The `series_name` is text in quotation marks or an external reference to the cell that contains the text label for the data series. An external reference to a text label in a cell is not enclosed in quotation marks. The `series_name` is used in the legend.

The `worksheet_name!category_reference` is an absolute reference to the worksheet cells that contain the category labels for the X-axis. The `worksheet_name!values_reference` specifies which worksheet cells contain the Y values for the data series.

The `marker_order_number` dictates the order of the data series. In the example in figure 13.33, the `marker_order_number` is 1. The first series appears first in the legend and appears as the first series of columns in column charts. A `marker_order_number` of 2 would make the markers for this data series the second series of markers on the chart.

Editing a Data Series

When you extend a series of data on a worksheet, you probably want to extend the related chart as well. You can use the ChartWizard to make these changes, as described earlier. Another method is to choose the F**o**rmat S**e**lected Series command to extend the range of the data series by editing the series formula.

To edit the data series used in a chart, follow these steps:

1. Open the workbook containing the worksheet and chart. Activate the chart.

2. Select the data series you want to edit.

3. Choose the F**o**rmat S**e**lected Series command to display the Format Data Series dialog box.

4. Choose the X Values tab to reach the choices shown in figure 13.34.

5. Select the **X** Values text box, and then manually edit the external reference formula or select the new data range in the worksheet by dragging across it using the mouse.

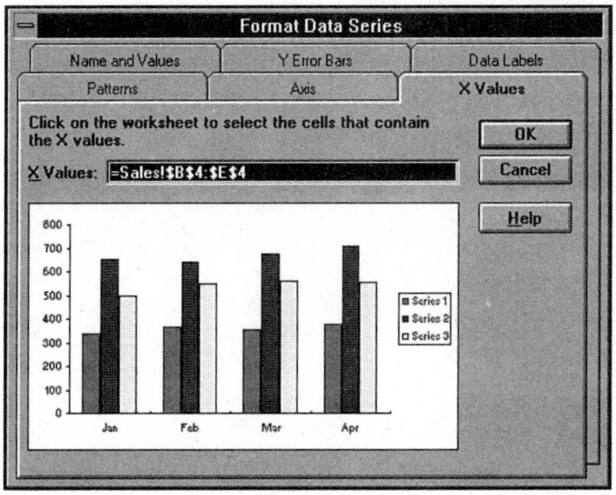

Fig. 13.34
The Format Data Series dialog box, before the external references are extended to include more cells.

The **X** Values text box contains the external reference formula for data used to create the category axis. Excel uses the X Values for the first data series to determine category axis labels. If you select the second or subsequent data series, no X Values tab appears in the Format Data Series dialog box.

Manually edit the reference if it needs only minor changes. For significant changes, such as referencing a worksheet range you cannot remember or using a data series from a different worksheet or workbook, activate the worksheet and scroll to the data area. The Format Data Series dialog box remains on top, but can be moved by dragging the title bar with the mouse if necessary. Select the text you want to change in the **X** Values text box. Select the cells you want to reference in the worksheet.

6. Select the Name and Values tab and repeat step 5 to edit the references in the **N**ame and **Y** Values text boxes.

The **N**ame text box references the cell from which the legend name is taken. You can type a legend name directly instead of using a reference to an external cell that contains text.

The **Y** Values text box contains an external reference formula for the value represented by chart markers.

7. Choose OK.

8. Repeat steps 2-7 for each data series in the chart.

Note

Usually, Excel uses the names associated with each data series in the worksheet to create the names used in the chart legend. To create your own names without changing the text in the worksheet, use the F**o**rmat S**e**lected Series command, choose the Names and Values tab, and replace the reference in the **N**ame text box. To perform the replacement, select the external reference in the **N**ame text box, type the text you want to appear instead in the legend, and then choose OK. Repeat this procedure for each data series in the chart.

Rearranging the Markers

You can rearrange the order in which data series that use the same chart type are plotted in a chart.

To change the order in which data series are plotted, follow these steps:

1. Select the series group you want to reorder from the list at the bottom of the F**o**rmat menu. An options dialog box for that group is displayed.

2. Select the Series Order tab to display the dialog box area shown in figure 13.35.

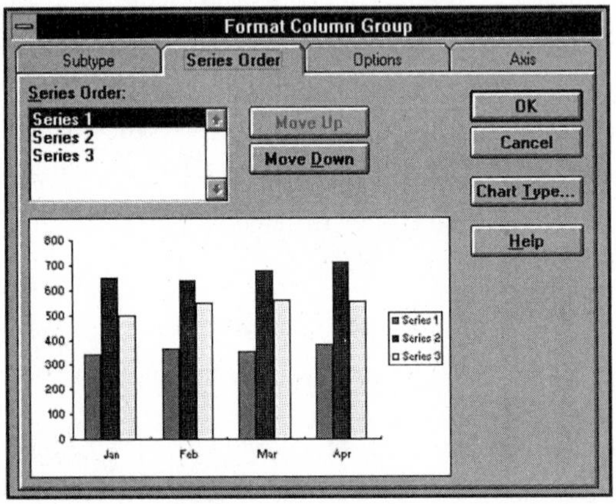

Fig. 13.35
You can change the order in which data series are plotted in a chart.

3. Select a series you want to move in the **S**eries Order list box.

4. Choose Move **U**p or Move **D**own to move the series to the desired position.

   View the chart mock-up at the bottom of the dialog box to make sure the data series appear in the order you want.

5. Choose OK.

For Related Information

- "Understanding Formulas," p. 125
- "Entering Cell References," p. 128

Inserting Text

When you create a chart, Excel automatically includes labels along the category and value axes if, when you select your data, you include cells containing labels. Depending on how you select your data and what choices you make if you use the ChartWizard to create your chart, you may also have labels for the legend and the title. You probably want to add other text to your charts—for example, a title and text annotations—to help clarify the data being presented. In this section, you learn how to add text associated with specific objects in the chart, as well as "free-floating" text.

There are two types of text you can add. The first type of text is associated with specific objects in a chart, such as the title, axes, or data points. After you insert this type of text, you can select it and revise it whenever you want, and you can reposition it. The second type of text is not associated with objects in the chart. Unattached text appears in a box that can be resized, so that the text wraps around exactly the way you want, and can be repositioned anywhere on the chart. Unattached text is useful as text labels or comments beside a chart, or for hiding portions of the screen.

You can insert titles associated with the chart and chart axes by choosing the **I**nsert **T**itles command. You can insert data labels that are associated with data points in the chart by choosing the **I**nsert **D**ata Labels command. These labels can be either the value for a data point or the category label associated with the point.

You need no command to insert unattached text. Just select any nontext object in the chart—for example, the chart itself—and type the desired text. You can then move the box that contains the text to any position on the chart.

All the text you use in an Excel chart can be formatted. In the next chapter, you learn how to format text and other chart objects.

Inserting Titles

You probably want to add to the text that Excel automatically attaches to the axes in your charts. For example, you likely want to add a chart title, and you might want to add titles to the category and value axes as well. The chart shown in figure 13.36 has text attached to the title position and to each of the three axes.

Fig. 13.36
In this chart, text is attached in the form of a chart title and axis titles.

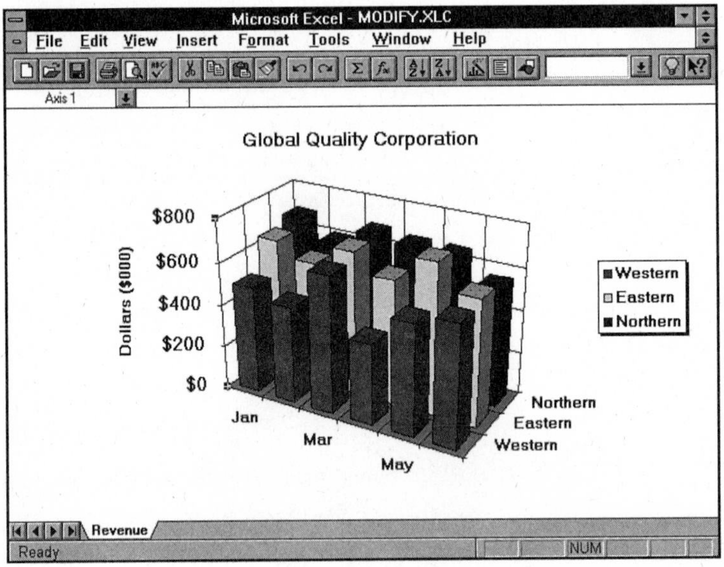

To insert titles, follow these steps:

1. Choose the **I**nsert **T**itles command—or click the right mouse button in the chart or plot area, and select Insert Titles from the shortcut menu—to display the Titles dialog box shown in figure 13.37.

Fig. 13.37
You can attach text to a chart's titles and axes.

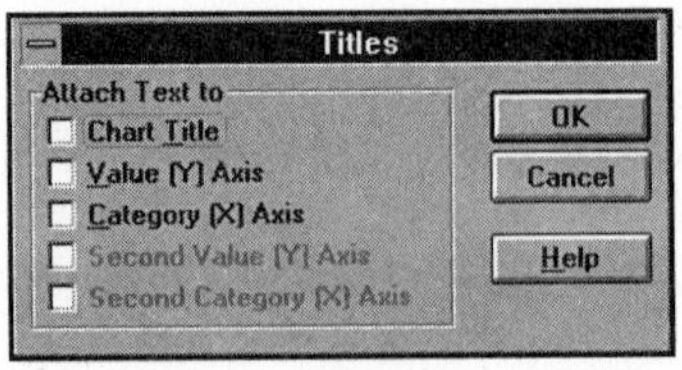

2. Select from the following list the location for the title text.

Item	Location
Chart **T**itle	Centers the temporary text `Title` above the chart.
Value (Z) Axis	Centers the temporary text Y beside the Y-axis in 2-D charts or beside the Z-axis in 3-D charts.
Category (X) Axis	Centers the temporary text X under the X-axis.
Second Value (**Y**) Axis	Centers the temporary text Y2 beside the Y-axis, in charts with two value axes.
Second Category (**X**) Axis	Centers the temporary text X2 below the X-axis, in charts with two category axes.

Not all selections listed in the table above always appear in the Titles dialog box. The selections that appear vary depending on the type of chart selected.

3. Choose OK.

Temporary text is attached to the point you specify, and remains selected. The surrounding black squares indicate that the text is selected and can be moved. You can edit the text or type over it.

4. To replace the temporary text, simply start typing. As long as the title is selected, you can simply type over the existing text.

5. Press Enter or click the Check button on the formula bar.

To edit a title by using the mouse, click the title to select it and then click inside the box that contains the text. The insertion point appears where you click. You can then use the arrow keys to move around the text, the Backspace and Del keys to delete characters, and the keyboard to enter new text.

To edit a title by using the keyboard, use the arrow keys to select the title (see Chapter 14, "Formatting Charts," for more information on how to select objects in a chart), and press F2 to open the formula bar. Edit the text in the formula bar as you would edit any cell contents, and then press Enter.

To make a line break to create a two-line title, or to break unattached text into separate lines, press Alt+Enter. You can remove the line break by positioning the insertion point to the right of it and pressing Backspace.

Inserting Other Text

In Excel, creating text that can be placed anywhere on a chart is easy and extremely useful. Figure 13.38 illustrates how you can use floating text in a comment box to label an arrow. See "Inserting Arrows," later in this chapter, for information on how to add arrows to a chart.

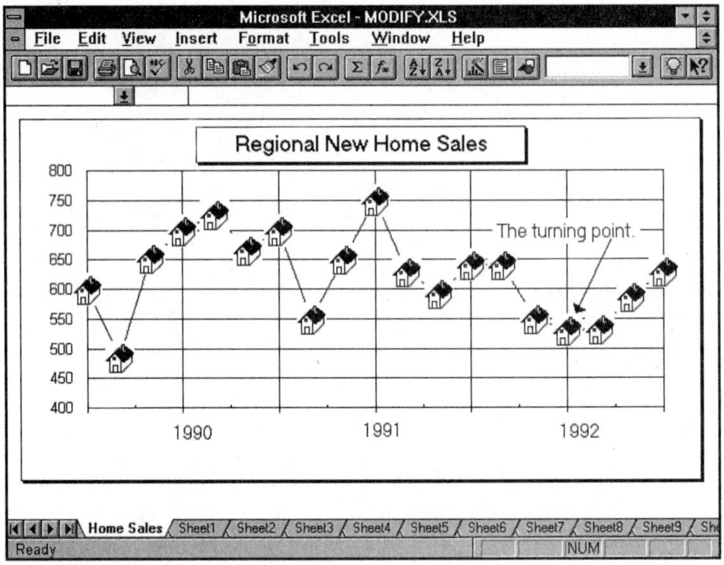

Fig. 13.38 Floating text can be used to comment on a data point.

To add unattached text to a chart, follow these steps:

1. Select a nontext object. You can click the outside border of the chart or click one of the data series.

2. Type the unattached text. This text appears on the formula bar, where you can edit it using normal editing procedures.

3. Press Enter or click the Check button when the text is complete.

Small black squares and a hatched border surround the text on the chart. You can move and resize the text background.

To move unattached text with the mouse, click the text and then point to one of the borders. The mouse pointer should be shaped like an arrow. If the mouse pointer is shaped like an I-beam, move the pointer down slightly until it appears as an arrow. Drag and drop the text to the desired position. Size text blocks by selecting the text and dragging one of the black squares to expand or contract the block. Drag a corner to change two dimensions at the same time. Words within the text box wrap to fit the new block size.

To edit unattached text, click the text to select it and then click inside the box that contains the text. The insertion point appears wherever you click, and the text background turns white. You can now edit the text directly on the chart. Use the arrow keys to move around the text, the Backspace and Del keys to delete characters, and the keyboard to enter new text. When you have finished editing the text, click outside the text box.

To edit text with the keyboard, use the arrow keys to select the text, press F2 to open the formula bar, edit the text in the formula bar as you edit any cell contents, and then press Enter.

Checking Spelling in Charts

To check the spelling of attached and unattached text in your charts, choose the **T**ools **S**pelling command. The spelling checker works the same as it does in a worksheet. For a description of how to operate the spelling checker, see Chapter 26, "Auditing Workbooks and Worksheets."

The spelling checker checks attached and unattached text. If any text in a chart is linked to a worksheet, as described in Chapter 14, use the spelling checker in the worksheet to check that text. You can check the spelling in an entire workbook by selecting all its sheets and then running the spelling checker.

Inserting Data Labels

You can insert a label that is associated with a data point on your chart. This label can either be the value for that data point, or the category axis label associated with the data point. You can attach labels to as many data points as you want. Attaching labels to data points can help the viewer interpret the data in a chart more easily.

For Related Information

- "Entering Formulas," p. 127
- "Formatting Text and Numbers," p. 483
- "Sizing, Moving, and Copying Graphic Objects," p. 583

To insert data labels, follow these steps:

1. Activate the chart to which you want to add data labels.
2. Select the data point or points to which you want to add labels.

   To select an entire data series, click any point in the series. All data points in that series are selected, as indicated by squares that appear on each data point (see fig. 13.39). To select an individual point in the series, click a second time on that data point. The squares now appear on only that data point (see fig. 13.40).

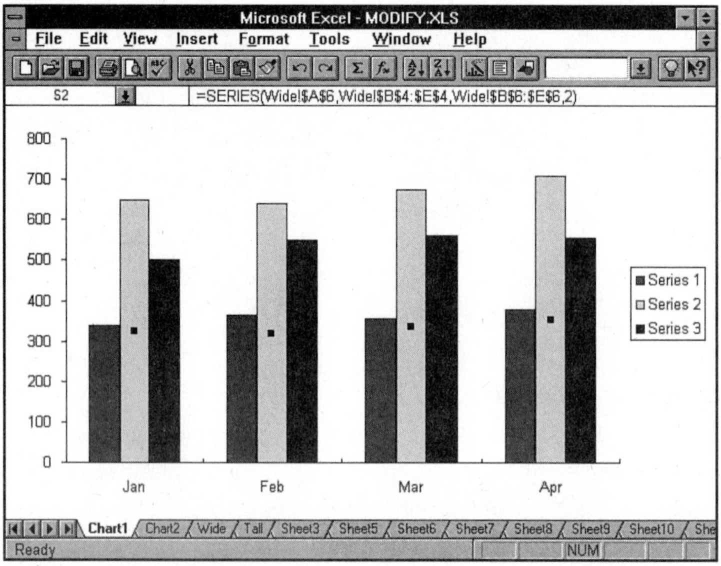

Fig. 13.39
When you select a data series, boxes appear on each data point.

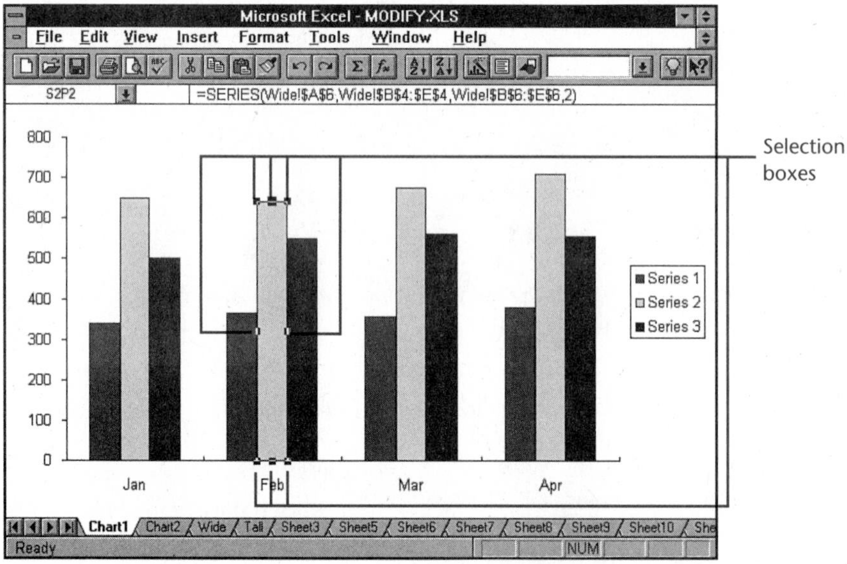

Fig. 13.40
When you select one data point, a box appears on just that data point.

To insert labels on all data points for all series, select any object in the chart that is not a data point. For example, click outside the chart to select the entire chart.

3. Choose the **I**nsert **D**ata Labels command. The Data Labels dialog box appears (see fig. 13.41).

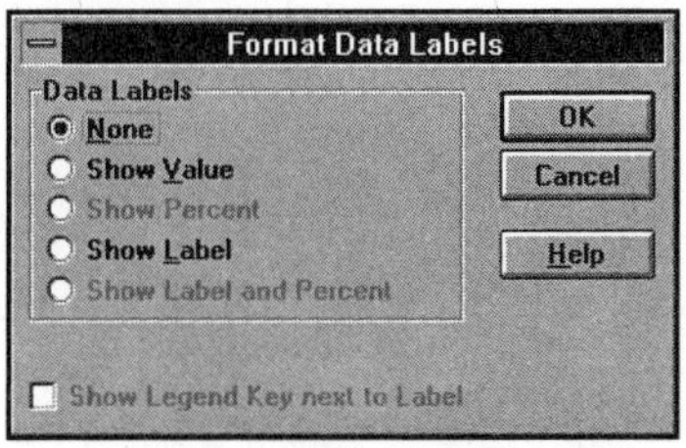

Fig. 13.41
You can insert values or labels on data points in a chart, using the Format Data Labels dialog box.

4. Select an option from the following list:

Item	Result
None	No labels are inserted with the selected data points. Previously inserted labels are removed.
Show **V**alue	The values for selected data points are inserted.
Show **P**ercent	The percentages for selected data points are inserted (this option is available only with pie and doughnut charts).
Show **L**abel	The category (X) labels associated with selected data points are inserted.
Show Label **a**nd Percent	The percentages and associated category labels for selected data points are inserted (this option is available only with pie and doughnut charts).

5. If you want the key from the legend to be displayed along with the data value, select the Show Legend **K**ey next to Label option.

6. Choose OK.

The chart appears with data labels at the selected data points. Figure 13.42 shows a chart with data labels attached to one data series. These labels have been formatted to show dollar signs. You learn how to format chart objects in Chapter 14, "Formatting Charts."

Fig. 13.42
Data labels can make a chart easier to read.

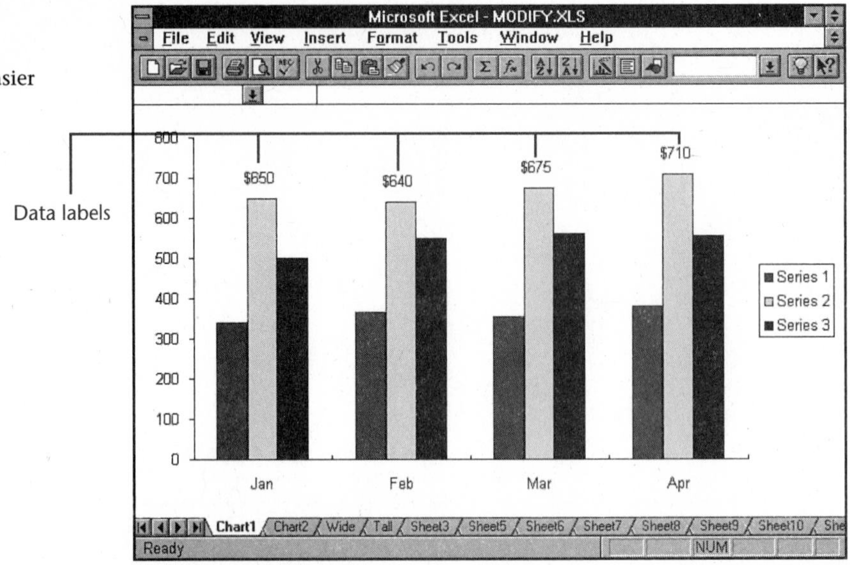

Note

The data point values that attach to markers use the format of the corresponding cell in the worksheet. To change a number's format in the chart, you can format its worksheet cell. You can also format the data values directly in the chart using the F**o**rmat S**e**lected Labels command. See Chapter 14, "Formatting Charts," for more information on formatting data labels.

Inserting Legends

For Related Information

- "Formatting Numbers," p. 328

A *legend* explains the markers or symbols used in a chart. Excel creates legends from the labels on the shorter side of the worksheet data series. Figure 13.43 shows an example of a legend. The legend in the figure was customized with border, pattern, and font selections. To learn about working with borders, patterns, and fonts, see Chapter 14, "Formatting Charts."

If you use the ChartWizard to create the chart, you can add a legend by choosing Yes in response to the Add a legend question in step 5 (for additional information on the ChartWizard, see Chapter 12). At any time, you can add a legend by choosing the **I**nsert **L**egend command, or by clicking the Legend button on the Chart toolbar. The legend appears on the right side of the chart. To delete a legend, select it and press Del; or click the Legend button on the Chart toolbar.

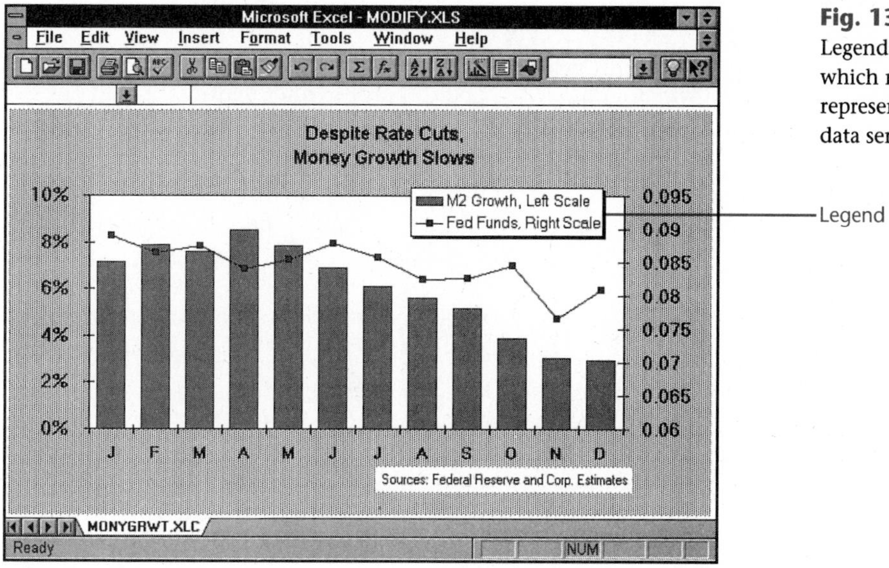

Fig. 13.43
Legends explain which marker represents each data series.

You can move the legend to any location on the chart by selecting and then dragging the legend with the mouse. If you move the legend to a central part of the chart, the legend stays where you leave it. Figure 13.43 shows a legend over a central area of the chart. You can resize the box that contains the legend by selecting the legend, and then grabbing any of the black handles that surround the legend. Drag the box to resize the legend.

You can use the F**o**rmat S**e**lected Legend command to move the legend to one of the predefined positions. Select the legend and choose the F**o**rmat S**e**lected Legend command to open the Format Legend dialog box. You can also click the legend with the right mouse button and then choose Format Legend from the shortcut menu. Select the Placement tab to display the area shown in figure 13.44. Select a location from the Type box and choose OK.

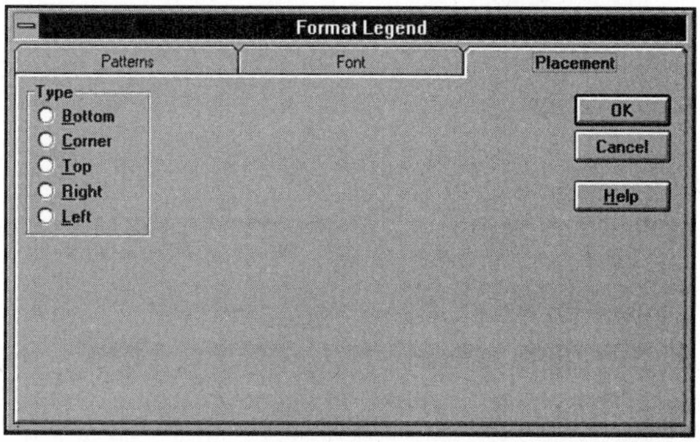

Fig. 13.44
Select the position for the legend in the Format Legend dialog box.

Inserting Arrows

Tip

You can add, resize, and position graphic objects onto a chart. You can also draw on a chart. See Chapter 17, "Adding Graphics Elements to Sheets."

Use arrows and unattached text to point to and identify (or explain) specific places on a chart. Headless arrows serve as straight lines. Click the Arrow button on either the Standard or Drawing toolbar to add arrows to a chart.

To add an arrow or a straight line to an active chart, follow these steps:

1. Choose the **V**iew **T**oolbars command, select Drawing in the **T**oolbars list box, and choose OK. Alternatively, you can click the Drawing button on the Standard toolbar to display the Drawing toolbar, or click with the right mouse button any toolbar displayed on-screen and then select Drawing from the shortcut menu.

2. Click the Arrow button on the toolbar. The mouse pointer changes to a crosshair.

3. Click the mouse in the chart where you want the tail of the arrow, hold down the mouse button while you drag across the chart to where you want the head of the arrow, and then release the mouse button (see fig. 13.45).

To remove an arrow, select the arrow you want to remove, and then press Del.

Move an existing arrow by dragging its middle with the mouse. You can drag on the black square at either end of the arrow to change the arrow's size and position.

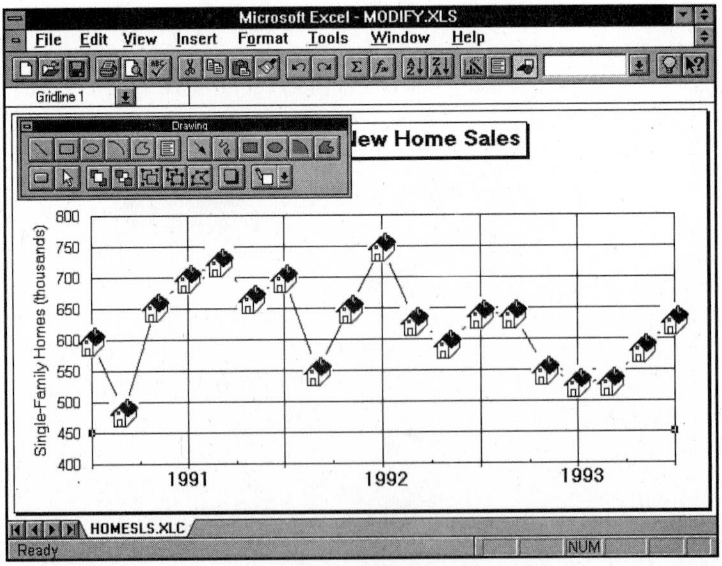

Fig. 13.45
Use the mouse to place an arrow on a chart.

For Related Information

- "Creating Graphic Objects," p. 560

Inserting Gridlines

Gridlines help viewers compare markers and read values. You can add gridlines that originate from either the category or value axis, or both. You can choose also whether gridlines originate from only major divisions on an axis, or from points between major divisions.

To add or delete horizontal gridlines from the major value axis (Y), click the Horizontal Gridlines button on the Chart toolbar. The Horizontal Gridlines button looks like a miniature chart with horizontal lines.

If you are using a keyboard, choose the **I**nsert **G**ridlines command. Select the type of gridlines you want from the Gridlines dialog box, shown in figure 13.46; then choose OK.

Too many gridlines obscure the chart, making it messy and confusing. In general, do not use gridlines if the chart is for overhead projection. You should use gridlines in printed material, in which readers need to read charts more precisely.

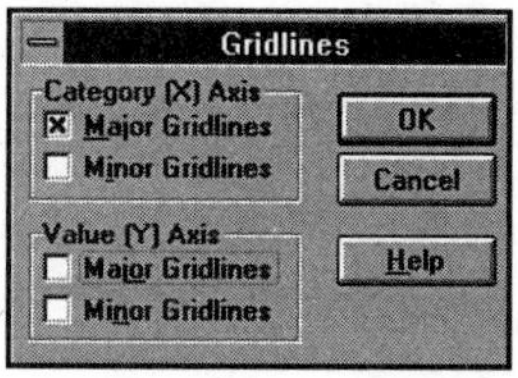

Fig. 13.46
Add gridlines to either axis with the Gridlines dialog box.

From Here...

For additional information on using charts in Excel effectively, see the following chapters:

- Chapter 14, "Formatting Charts." Shows you how to custom format a chart. You learn how to do the following: format text and numbers; add colors, patterns, and borders to the objects in a chart; customize your axes; and format 3-D charts.

- Chapter 15, "Building Complex Charts." Teaches you advanced techniques for creating combination charts, using charts to analyze data, adding error bars to charts, and other special purpose procedures.

Chapter 14

Formatting Charts

In the preceding two chapters, you learned how to create a chart and then to modify the predefined charts produced by Excel. In this chapter, you learn how to format your charts to give them the professional look you need for your reports and presentations.

After you select a predefined chart format, you can change the colors and patterns of the objects in your chart. You can add borders to the chart and to the text, legends, and other objects in your chart to increase the visual effect of your chart. You can customize the font and color of text as well as the format of numbers. By selecting an axis and then a format command, you can change the scale and the appearance of tick marks and labels. There are many enhancements you can make to data series as well as to individual data markers. You also can rotate 3-D charts to give the best view of your data.

In this chapter, you learn how to:

- Move and size chart objects
- Change the colors, patterns, and borders of chart objects
- Format data series and data markers
- Format 3-D charts
- Create a chart template

Learning the Basic Chart Formatting Procedure

After you select one of the predefined chart types, you can customize your chart. You can make it more attractive and easier to understand while emphasizing the point you want to make.

Customize charts by using the same concept you use with worksheets: select, then do. The following procedure applies to any object in a chart. The exact formatting changes you can make vary depending on what object in the chart you have selected. Perform the following steps to customize a chart:

1. Select the chart object you want to customize by clicking it or by pressing an arrow key. (Refer to Chapter 13, "Modifying Charts," to learn how to select objects in a chart.)

2. To open the Format dialog box, either choose the F**o**rmat S**e**lected object command, click the selected object with the right mouse button and select the Format command from the shortcut menu, or double-click the object.

   The F**o**rmat S**e**lected command changes depending on the object that is selected. If a data series is selected, for example, the F**o**rmat S**e**lected Series command appears in the menu.

   The Format dialog box for the selected object appears. The Format Data Series dialog box is shown in figure 14.1.

3. If the dialog box contains tabs, select the tab that contains the options you want to change.

4. Choose OK.

These steps are explained in the following sections.

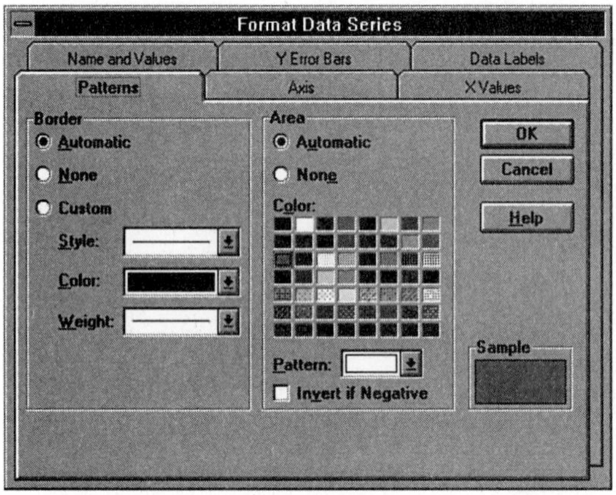

Fig. 14.1
You can customize the data series in a chart using the options in the Format Data Series dialog box.

Moving and Sizing Chart Objects

You can move or resize some objects in a chart. You can move the plot area, chart and axis titles, the legend, data labels, slices in both pie and doughnut charts, and graphic objects that you have added to a chart, such as arrows and text boxes. Objects that can be resized include the plot area, legend, and graphic objects.

To move an object using the mouse, click the object to select it and then point to the selected object and hold down the left mouse button. Drag the object to its new location and release the mouse button.

If you are moving the plot area, legend, or an arrow, drag from the center of the selected object. Do not drag on a any of the black boxes that appear when the object is selected or you may change the size of the object. A rectangle shows the position of the object as you move it.

To move a title, data value, or text box, position the mouse pointer just beneath the hatched gray border that appears around the selected object (see fig. 14.2). The mouse pointer should appear as an arrow. If you move the mouse pointer just inside the box, the mouse pointer changes to an I-beam. If you click the mouse button at this point, an insertion point appears inside the box, enabling you to edit the text. Press the Esc key to display the box again, and move the pointer until you see the arrow. Then drag the title or value to a new location.

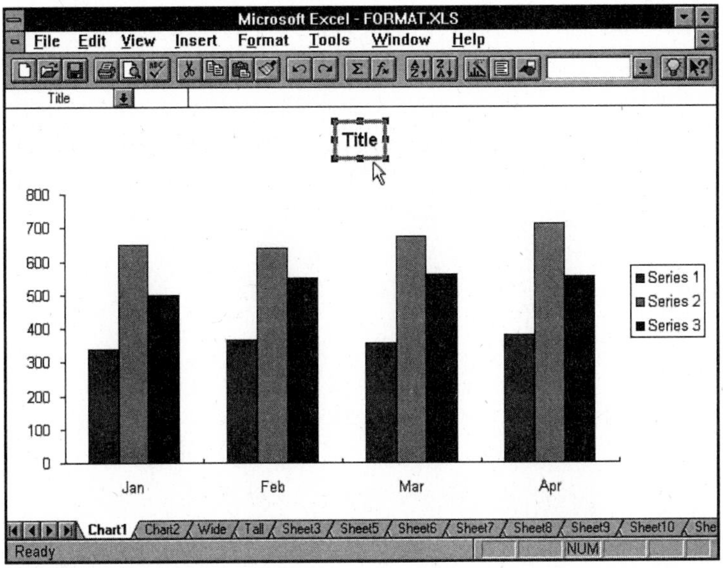

Fig. 14.2
The mouse pointer positioned to move the title in this chart.

To resize an object using the mouse, select the object by clicking it. Drag one of the black boxes that appear around the selected object to expand or contract the object. Drag a handle on the edge of a text box to keep the objects other dimension the same. Drag a handle on the corner of a text box to change two dimensions at the same time. Words in a text box wrap to fit the new size.

Excel resizes pie wedges when you move them. The farther you move the wedges from the center, the smaller the wedges and pie become.

For Related Information

- "Sizing, Moving, and Copying Graphic Objects," p. 583

Resizing unattached text changes the size of the box the text is inside of, not the text itself. You can determine how text will wrap by changing the size of the box around the text. To resize the text itself, you need to use the Font tab in the Format dialog box to change the point size (see "Formatting Text and Numbers," later in this chapter).

Changing Object Colors, Patterns, and Borders

You can change the appearance of every object in a chart by using the formatting commands. For many objects, changing appearance consists of adding borders to the object and changing the fill pattern and color of the area around the object. You can add a shadowed border, for example, around a title and change the background color behind the title, or you can change the patterns and colors of the columns in a column chart. With the axes, you can change the appearance of the axis line and modify the tick marks.

Note

To use different colors than the 56 default colors, you can use the **T**ools **O**ptions Color command to select your own set of 56 colors from a wide range of colors. This command and the Options Color Palette for worksheets are described in Chapter 40, "Customizing the Excel Screen."

In this section, you learn the general procedures for changing the patterns, colors, and borders of objects in a chart. In the following sections, you learn how to make other changes in the appearance of specific objects in a chart; for example, modifying the tick marks on the axes, or changing the spacing between the columns in a chart.

To change the borders, colors, and patterns of selected objects, follow these steps:

1. To display the Format dialog box, double-click the object, or click with the right mouse button on the object and choose the Format command. Alternatively, select the object and then choose the F**o**rmat S**e**lected object command.

The **Fo**rmat **Se**lected command changes depending on the object that is selected. If a data series is selected, for example, the F**o**rmat S**e**lected Series command appears in the menu.

The Format dialog box for the selected object appears. The Format Data Series dialog box is shown in figure 14.1.

2. Select the Patterns tab if it isn't already selected.
3. Make selections from the dialog box. The lists in pattern boxes are drop-down list boxes, so the list appears only when you select the list box. Click the down arrow or press Alt+down arrow. Figure 14.3 shows a pattern box with the Area Pattern list dropped down.
4. Choose OK.

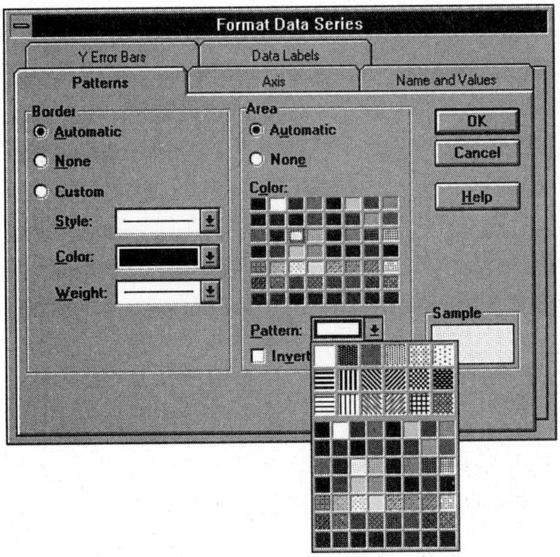

Fig. 14.3
Click the down-arrow to open a drop-down list in the Patterns tab.

Pattern dialog boxes are similar for all objects except the axes. The left group in the dialog box displays formatting alternatives for the border or line in the object. The right group in the box displays formatting alternatives for the fill pattern in the object. A sample of the completed format appears in the bottom right corner. The options in the Pattern dialog boxes are described in table 14.1.

Tip
To format one marker, click the marker to select the data series; click again to select the marker, and follow the steps to the left.

Table 14.1 The Pattern Dialog Box Options

Option	Description
Border	
Automatic	Uses default settings.
None	Uses no border.
Custom	
Style	Changes type of line.
Color	Changes color of line. Choose from 16 alternatives.
Weight	Changes the thickness of line.
Area	
Automatic	Uses default settings.
None	Uses no fill (background shows through).
Custom	
Color	Changes the color of the background color of the object. If no pattern is selected, this will be the color of the object.
Pattern	Changes the pattern and color of the pattern.
Sample	Shows you how your selections will appear.

Pattern boxes for objects such as arrows and axes include options that specifically affect the objects. Formatting these objects is discussed in a following section of this chapter.

If you choose the Invert if Negative option, the data markers for column, bar, and pie charts display with the background and foreground colors reversed.

The largest areas in a chart are the chart background and the plot area. The chart background includes the entire chart; the plot area includes only the area within the axes. You can change the colors, patterns, and boundaries of both areas. Click the background area before choosing the format command. Figure 14.4 shows a chart with patterns for the chart background and plot area and with the text for the axes in boldface.

Formatting Text and Numbers

You can format any text that appears in a chart, including the axes and legend labels, any titles or data values that you have inserted, or any unattached text that you placed in a chart. You also can format the numbers that appear in a chart. You can, for example, add dollar signs to the numbers on the value (Y) axis.

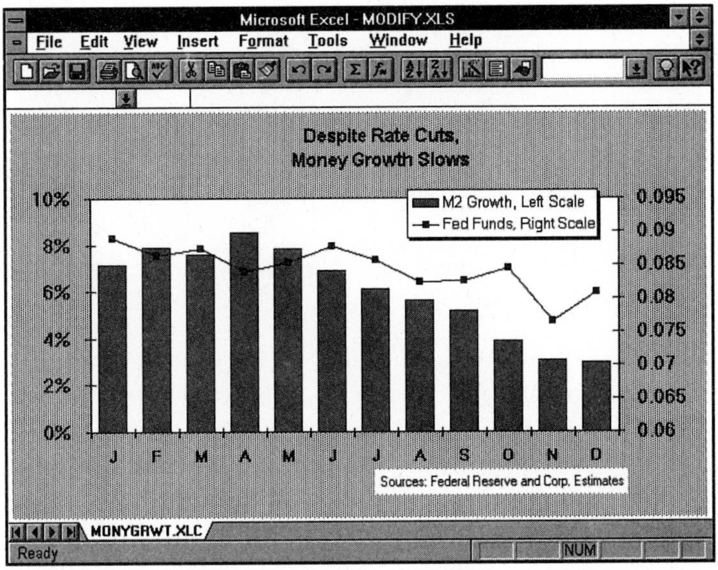

Fig. 14.4
A chart and plot area formatted for a standout appearance.

Understanding How To Format Text and Numbers

To reach format commands quickly, display a shortcut menu by clicking the text with the right mouse button, and then click the Format command. Figure 14.5 shows the shortcut menu displayed for an attached title.

Tip
If you make a change to a chart pattern or color and don't like the results, you can use the **E**dit **U**ndo command to change it back.

Note

Several tools are available for formatting text. You can use formatting tools for changing alignment, adding bold and italic formatting, and selecting the font and font size. To add the Formatting toolbar to your screen, choose the **V**iew **T**oolbars command, select Formatting from the **T**oolbars list, and choose OK. Or click an existing toolbar with the right mouse button and select Formatting from the menu. Then select the text in the chart and click the tool you want to use.

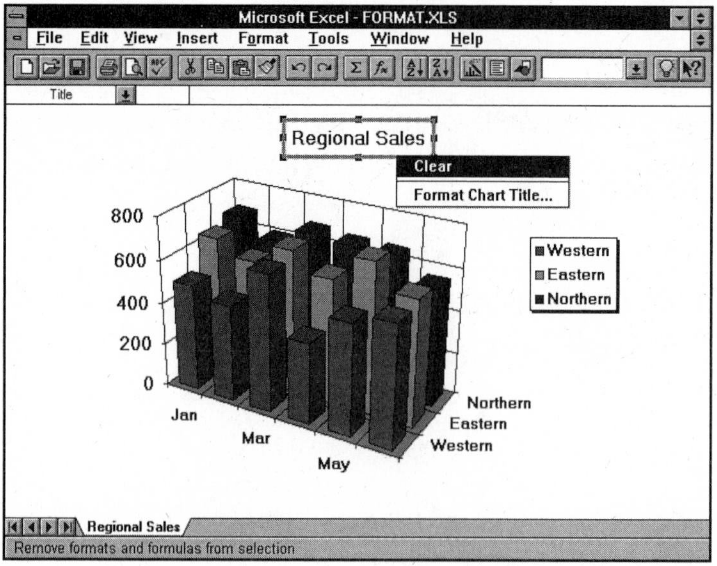

Fig. 14.5
A shortcut menu is displayed by clicking an object with the right mouse button.

For Related Information

- "Adding Colors, Patterns, and Borders," p. 350
- "Creating Your Own Colors," p. 1095

As an alternative to the shortcut menus, you can select the text and then choose the Format Selected object command or double-click the text. When the Format dialog box opens, choose the Font tab to view the options for formatting text. If you have selected an object that has numbers—for example, the value axis—you can select the Number tab to format the numbers.

After you open the Format dialog box for a selected object and change the formatting for the text or numbers, you can select the Patterns tab to change the borders, patterns, and colors for that object without leaving the dialog box, and you can select the Alignment tab to change text alignment.

Note

The procedure for hiding selected parts of a chart is similar to the procedure for creating unattached text. Create an empty, unattached text box by making an unattached text box that contains only one space character. (If the space appears as a blank character in the pattern, select the text and choose Format Selected Object and select the Font tab. Next, choose Background Transparent to make the characters background invisible.) Select the Patterns tab and select a Foreground and Background color that match the area being covered. Move the box in front of what you want to hide.

Changing Fonts and Styles

To change the fonts and font style for text in a chart, follow these steps:

> **Tip**
> If you choose fonts unavailable in your printer, the printed chart will differ from the on-screen chart. Use only TT (TrueType) or printer fonts.

1. Select the object whose text you want to change.
2. Choose the F**o**rmat S**e**lected object command, click the object with the right mouse button and select the Format command from the shortcut menu, or double-click the object to open the Format dialog box.
3. Select the Font tab. The dialog box shown in figure 14.6 appears.
4. From the **F**ont list, choose the font you want. Check the sample box to see how that font looks.
5. From the Font Style list, choose the font style.
6. From the **S**ize list, choose the point size. Remember that approximately 72 points equal one inch of height.
7. Choose one of the **U**nderline options, if you want.
8. If you prefer, select one of the Stri**k**ethrough, Sup**e**rscript, or Su**b**script options.
9. From the **C**olor list, choose a color. Use Automatic for black-and-white printers.
10. Choose one of the B**a**ckground options.

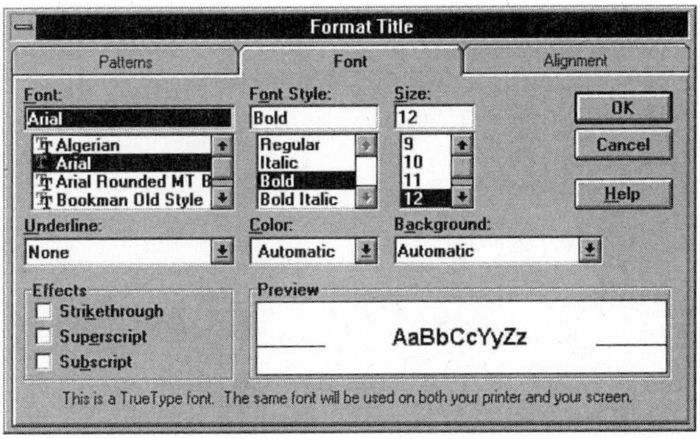

Fig. 14.6
Select the font, font style, and point size for the selected object in the Font tab of the Format Title dialog box.

Tip
To change the default font used for all text in a chart, double-click outside the border of the chart and choose the Font tab. Select the font, font style, size, and choose OK.

You also can change the immediate background behind the text, which is useful for text that overlaps lines or patterns. Select Automatic to use the default background pattern, Transparent to let the area show through, and Opaque to remove any pattern behind characters but keep the foreground color.

11. Choose OK.

Changing Text Alignment

You can align the text in charts. For some text objects—for example, titles—you can change both the horizontal and vertical alignment, as well as the orientation of the text. For other objects, such as the labels on the axes, you can change only the orientation. The capability of changing the texts orientation enables you to rotate axis titles or text boxes that contain explanations.

To change text alignment, follow these steps:

1. Select the object whose alignment you want to change.
2. Choose the F**o**rmat S**e**lected object command, click the object with the right mouse button and select the Format command from the shortcut menu, or double-click the object to open the Format Title dialog box.
3. Select the Alignment tab. The Alignment tab for titles is shown in figure 14.7.
4. Select the desired alignment options from the Horizontal and Vertical option groups.
5. Select another option in the **O**rientation if you want to change the orientation of the text.
6. Choose OK.

Formatting Numbers

You can format the numbers in a chart just as you format the numbers in a worksheet. If the numbers in the worksheet you used to create the chart are formatted, the numbers used in the value axis in the chart are formatted the same way. You can override this formatting, however, or add formatting if the numbers in the chart are unformatted.

To format the numbers in a chart, follow these steps:

1. Select the object whose numbers you want to format.
2. Choose the F**o**rmat S**e**lected object command, click the object with the right mouse button and select the Format command from the shortcut menu, or double-click the object to open the Format Axis dialog box.
3. Choose the Number tab. The dialog box shown in figure 14.8 appears.
4. Choose the kind of number you want to format from the **C**ategory list. This selection limits what appears in the **F**ormat Codes list.
5. Choose the format you want from the **F**ormat Codes list. Custom formats that you created appear at the bottom of the list.
6. To return the formatting to the numbers in the source worksheet, select the **L**inked to Source option.
7. Choose OK.

For Related Information

- "Changing Character Fonts, Sizes, Styles, and Colors" p. 312
- "Aligning and Rotating Text and Numbers," p. 319
- "Formatting Numbers," p. 328
- "Inserting Text," p. 465

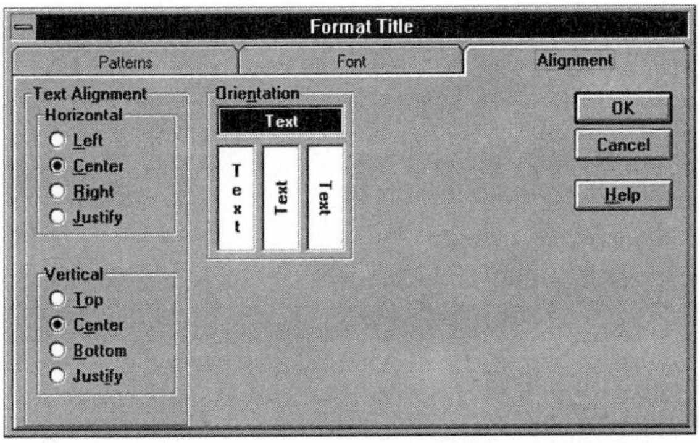

Fig. 14.7
You can change text alignment and orientation in the Alignment tab of the Format Title dialog box.

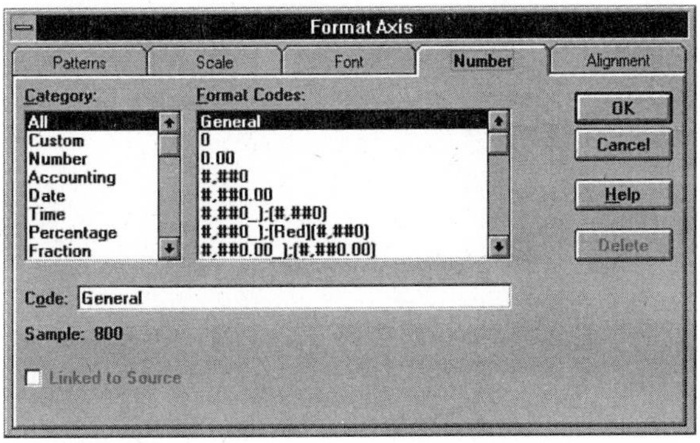

Fig. 14.8
You can custom format the numbers that appear in your charts in the Number tab of the Format Axis dialog box.

Formatting Data Series

Besides formatting the borders, patterns, and colors for the data series in your charts, you can enhance the presentation of your data by adding error bars, drop lines, hi-lo lines, and up and down bars. You also can change the gap width between the columns in a column chart, and make other formatting changes. The available options depend on the type of chart with which you are working. You access some of the options from the Format dialog box, and you access others using the F**o**rmat Group command.

Understanding Data Series Formatting

A range of options is available for all the chart types and formats, which you access by using the F**o**rmat Group command. To change the options for a data series or group of data series using the same chart type, choose the F**o**rmat command and, from the bottom of the menu, select the group with which you want to work (see fig. 14.9). Unless you applied different chart types to the series in the chart, you have only one group. When you select a group from the bottom of the F**o**rmat menu, the Format dialog box for that group opens. If you select a column group, for example, the Format Column Group dialog box appears. Select the Options tab to display the options available for the chart type you are working with. Figure 14.10 shows the options available for column charts.

The various options that are available for the different chart types and formats are described in table 14.2. Not all of these options are available for any one chart type. Which options are available depends on the chart type you work with. The table specifies to what chart types each option applies.

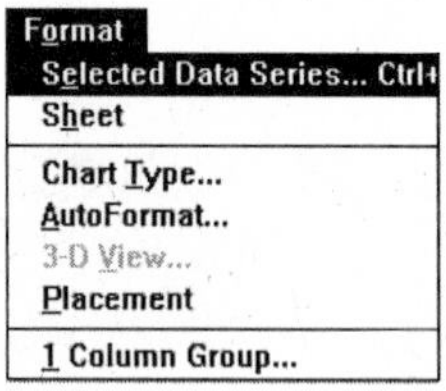

Fig. 14.9
Select the group you want to format from the bottom of the F**o**rmat menu.

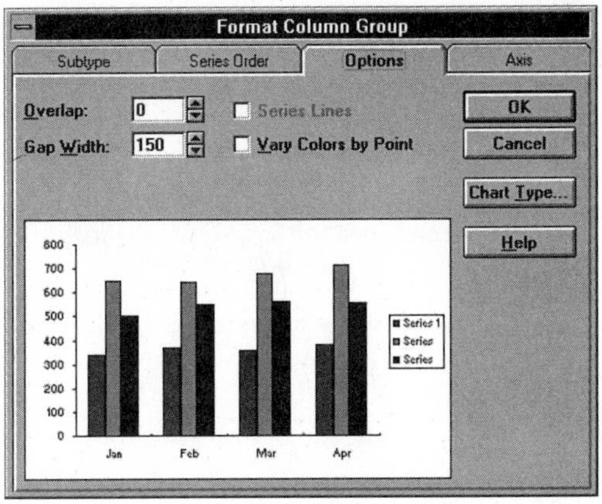

Fig. 14.10
The Options tab displayed in the Format Column Group dialog box vary depending on the type of chart you are working with.

Table 14.2 Chart Formatting Options

Option	Description
Overlap	Specifies how much bars or columns overlap. Enter a positive number as the percentage of overlap. 100 is full overlap. A negative number separates individual bars or columns.
Gap **W**idth	Specifies the space between groups of bars or columns. Measured as a percentage of one bar or column width.
Gap Depth (3-D charts only)	Specifies the spacing in depth between markers as a percentage of a marker. 50 changes the space of the depth between markers to 50 percent of a marker width. Because the chart depth has not changed, this action makes markers thinner. The number must be between 0 and 500.
Chart Depth (3-D charts only)	Specifies how deep a 3-D chart is relative to its charts width. Enter a number as a percentage of the chart width. 50 makes the depth 50 percent of the width. The number must be between 20 and 2000.
Series Lines	Draws a line between types of markers in stacked bar and stacked column charts.
Vary Colors by Point/Slice	Specifies a different color or pattern by category for each marker in all pie charts or any chart with one data series.
Drop Lines	Drops a vertical line from a marker to the category (X) axis. Used on line or area charts.
High-Low Lines	Draws a line between the highest and lowest lines at a specific category. Used on 2-D line charts.

(continues)

Table 14.2 Continued

Option	Description
Up-Down Bars	Used in stock market charts to draw a rectangle between opening and closing prices. Creates an open-high-low chart. Use only on line charts. If series are in rows, Hi data should be in the first row; Open data in the second row; and Close data in the third row.
Category Labels	Creates labels for the category axis (spokes) on radar charts.
A**n**gle of First Slice	Specifies the starting angle in degrees for the first wedge in a pie chart. Vertical is zero degrees.
Doughnut Hole Size	Changes the size of the hole in the center of doughnut charts. 50 makes the diameter of the hole 50 percent of the diameter of the doughnut. The number must be between 10 and 90.

Formatting Trendlines

You can add a trendline to a series of data points to analyze the direction your data is moving, based on regression or moving average analysis. You learn how to add a trendline to a data series in Chapter 15, "Building Complex Charts." After you add a trendline, you can format it just like any other object in a chart.

To format a trendline, follow these steps:

1. Select the trendline.
2. Choose the F**o**rmat S**e**lected item command, click the object with the right mouse button and select the Format command from the shortcut menu or double-click the object to open the Format dialog box.
3. Choose the Patterns tab.
4. Choose the Line options you want to use for the trendline. See table 14.1 for a description of the options.
5. Choose OK.

If you need to make any changes in how the trendline is derived and displayed, you can access the same options you used to create the trendline by selecting the Type and Options tabs.

Formatting Error Bars

You can use error bars to give a visual indication of your data's margin of error. The margin of error is a measure of the degree of uncertainty or variation in a data set. Learn how to add error bars to a data series in Chapter 15, "Building Complex Charts." You can change the patterns of the error bars by using the Format dialog box.

To format error bars, follow these steps:

1. Select the error bars by clicking one of the bars with the mouse.
2. Choose the F**o**rmat S**e**lected item command, click the object with the right mouse button and select the Format command from the shortcut menu or double-click the object. The Format dialog box appears.
3. Choose the Patterns tab.
4. Choose one of the Line options. See table 14.1 for a description of the options.
5. Select the type of marker you want to use in the Marker box.
6. Choose OK.

   You can select the Y Error Bar tab to make changes in how the error bars are set up.

For Related Information

- "Adding or Deleting Data," p. 456
- "Working with the Series Formula," p. 461
- "Automatically Analyzing Trends with Charts," p. 513
- "Adding Errors Bars to a Chart," p. 517

Formatting Data Markers

Besides customizing the color, weight, and style of the lines used in line charts, you can modify the color and style of the markers used to mark the data points.

To format the markers in a line chart, follow these steps:

1. Select the line you want to modify.
2. Choose the F**o**rmat S**e**lected item command, click the object with the right mouse button and select the Format command from the shortcut menu, or double-click the object, to open the Format Data Series dialog box.
3. Choose the Patterns tab to display the dialog box shown in figure 14.11.

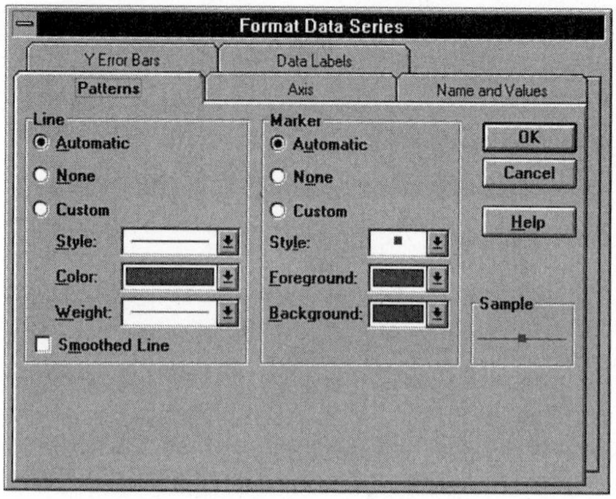

Fig. 14.11
You can format the markers used to mark data points in a line chart in the Patterns tab of the Format Data Series dialog box.

4. Choose a Line option. See table 14.1 for a description of the options.

5. Choose among the following options from the Marker group:

Option	Description
Automatic	Uses default setting.
None	No markers used at data points.
Custom	
Style	Changes the type of marker used.
Foreground	Changes the color of the outline of the marker.
Background	Changes the color of the fill in the marker.

6. Choose the Smoothed Line option to have Excel smooth the line between data points.

7. Check the Sample box to see if the data point looks the way you want, and then choose OK.

Scaling and Customizing an Axis

When you create a chart, Excel uses the default settings for the axis style, tick marks, and scaling. You can customize the axis, changing the style of the line used for the axis, the tick marks, the positioning of the tick-mark labels, and the scaling of the axis.

Customizing the Format of an Axis

To customize the axes in a chart, follow these steps:

1. Select the axis by clicking one of the axis lines or by pressing the arrow keys until the axis is selected. Black handles appear at either end of the axis.

2. Choose the Format Selected item command, click the object with the right mouse button and select the Format command from the shortcut menu, or double-click the object, to open the Format Axis dialog box.

3. Select the Patterns tab to display the dialog box shown in figure 14.12.

4. Choose one of the Line options. See table 14.1 for a description of the options.

5. Choose the desired options from the Major and Minor boxes.

   Tick marks intersect the value and category axes and are used to divide the axes into equal units. They facilitate reading values from the axes. You can have both major tick marks, which display next to the labels for the value and category labels for the axes, and minor tick marks, which indicate subunits between the major tick marks.

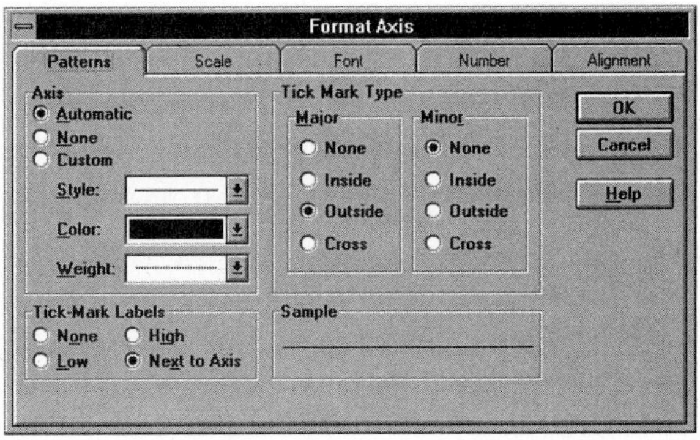

Fig. 14.12 You can customize the appearance of the axes in the Format Axis dialog box.

   Select the None option to remove tick marks, the Inside option to have tick marks displayed inside the axis, the Outside option to display tick marks on the outside of the axis, or the Cross option to have tick marks cross the axis.

6. Choose an option from the Tick-Mark Labels box to specify where the tick-mark labels are to be positioned.

Tick-mark labels are used to identify the values and categories in a chart and are displayed along the axes. You can select from among four options for where the tick-mark labels are positioned. Select N**o**ne to remove the tick-mark labels or Ne**x**t to Axis to place the labels next to the axis, regardless of where the axis is positioned. Select **L**ow to position the labels on the bottom (category) or to the left (value) of a chart, even if the corresponding axis is at the opposite side. Select H**i**gh to position the labels at the top (category) or to the right (value) of the chart, even if the corresponding axis is at the opposite side.

7. Check to see if the line in the sample box looks like you want, and then choose OK.

To change the formatting of the axis text and numbers, see "Formatting Text and Numbers," previously in the chapter.

Changing the Scaling of an Axis

Tip

When you change multiple axis settings, change one setting at a time, see the result, and then change another. Otherwise, the results can become confusing.

You can modify the scaling of the category (X) and value (Y) axes to enhance the presentation of your data. The dialog box to change the scale of an axis is different for the category and the value axes.

The Scale tab for the category (X) axis in the Format Axis dialog box, shown in figure 14.13, enables you to change the appearance of the category (X) axis. To change the point at which the value (Y) axis crosses the category (X) axis, change the number in the Value (Y) Axis **C**rosses at Category Number text box. To display fewer or more labels or tick marks along the category axis, change the values in the Number of Categories between Tick-Mark **L**abels and Number of Categories between Tick Mar**k**s text boxes.

You can have the value (Y) axis cross either between or within categories, using the Value (Y) Axis Crosses **b**etween Categories option. To reverse the order in which the categories are displayed, select the Categories in **R**everse Order. Select the Value (Y) Axis Crosses at **M**aximum Category to move the value (Y) axis to the high end of the category (X) axis.

In a Scatter (XY) chart, the Scale tab in the Format dialog box for the category (X) axis (see fig. 14.14) enables you to specify the range of the scale, by changing the values in the Mi**n**imum and Ma**x**imum text boxes. By default, these values are determined automatically. To return to the default values, select the Auto check boxes.

To change the major and minor units used for the major and minor tick marks, enter new values in the M**a**jor Unit and M**i**nor Unit text boxes. You also can change where the value (Y) axis crosses by changing the value in the Value (Y) Axis **C**rosses At text box.

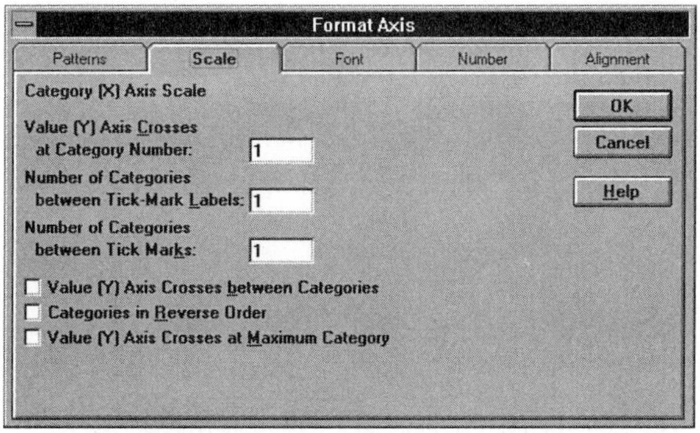

Fig. 14.13
You can change the scaling of the category (X) scale in the Scale tab of the Format Axis dialog box.

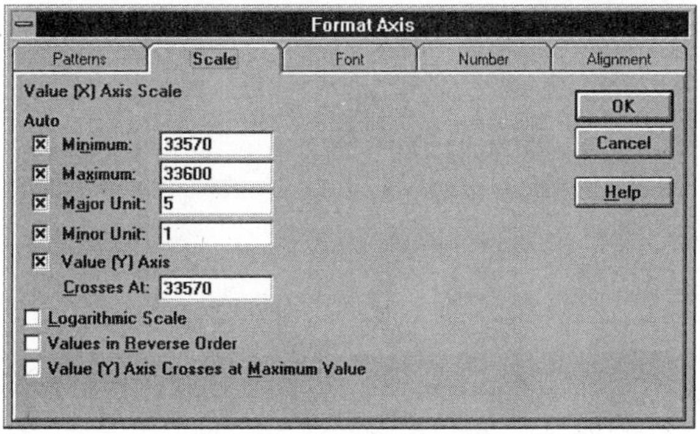

Fig. 14.14
The Scale tab in the Format Axis dialog box for a Scatter (XY) chart.

To plot data on a logarithmic scale, select the **L**ogarithmic Scale option. Select the Values in **R**everse Order option to plot the values from high to low instead of low to high. To move the value (Y) axis to the high end of the category (X) axis scale, select the Value (Y) Axis Crosses at **M**aximum Value.

In figure 14.14, notice that dates on the category (X) axis appear as numbers in the Mi**n**imum and Ma**x**imum text boxes. These numbers are the numbers of days from the beginning of the century to the specified starting and ending dates. Because months have an unequal number of days, no M**a**jor Unit

For Related Information

- "Inserting Arrows," p. 474
- "Creating Graphic Objects," p. 560
- "Using Graphics and Clip Art from Other Applications," p. 556

value is available to produce the same date on the axis for each month. One way to create evenly spaced month/day labels on the category (X) axis is to use a M**a**jor Unit value of 29.5. After the axis is scaled, you can correct any month that has a day different from the others by using a floating text label to cover month/day combinations that arent exact.

The Scale tab in the Format Axis dialog box used for formatting the value (Y) axis is shown in figure 14.15. You can change the minimum and maximum values, the major and minor scaling units, and where the category (X) axis crosses the value (Y) axis. You also can choose to use a logarithmic scale, plot values in reverse order, and have the category (X) axis cross at the maximum value on the value (Y) scale. See the descriptions of the category (X) axis tabs above for a more detailed discussion of these options.

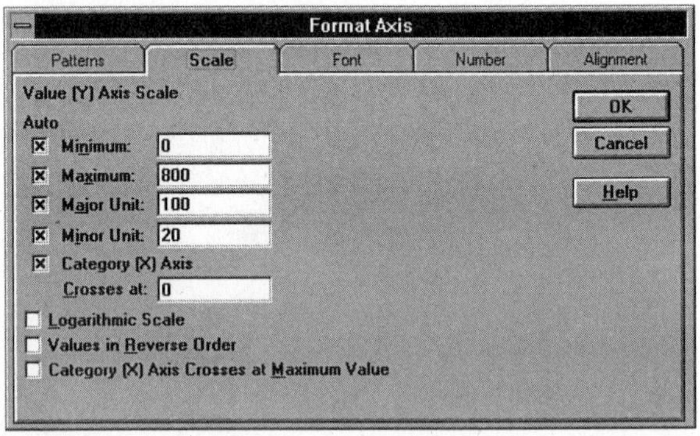

Fig. 14.15
You can change the scaling of the value (Y) scale in the Scale tab of the Format Axis dialog box.

Note

Don't crowd tick marks and axis labels. Some charts, such as charts of stock prices or instrument readings, contain so many data points that the labels and tick marks crowd one another. To reduce this clutter, choose the category (X) axis and open the Format Axis dialog box. Choose the Scale tab and enter larger numbers into the text boxes for Number of Categories between Tick-Mark **L**abels and for Number of Categories Between Tick Mar**k**s. The larger the numbers you enter, the more distance between individual labels and individual tick marks.

Formatting Arrows

You can change an arrow's appearance by double-clicking the arrow to display the Format Object dialog box, by choosing Format Object from the shortcut menu, or by selecting the arrow and choosing the F**o**rmat S**e**lected Object command. Select the Patterns tab to modify the appearance of the arrow (see fig. 14.16). Notice that the Arrow Head drop-down list boxes enable you to use many different arrowhead shapes and to change an arrow into a line.

Note

Change an arrow to a line by selecting the arrow and then displaying the Format Object dialog box. The dialog box in figure 14.16 has many alternatives for the color, weight, and style of the arrows shaft and head. To make a straight line, select the straight line from the Arrow Head Style drop-down list.

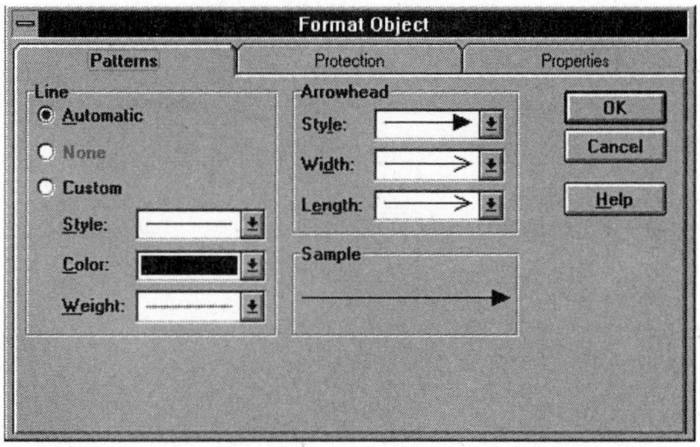

Fig. 14.16
You can change the appearance of an arrow in the Patterns tab of the Format Object dialog box.

Formatting 3-D Charts

Some 3-D charts may display data in such a way that some series are difficult to see. In figure 14.17, for example, the second and third series are blocked from view. To avoid this problem, you can rotate and adjust 3-D charts by using the F**o**rmat 3-D **V**iew command. After rotation, the same 3-D chart appears as shown in figure 14.18.

Rotating a 3-D Chart by Dragging

With a mouse, you can rotate a 3-D chart in any direction by dragging one end of an axis. To rotate a 3-D chart by dragging, perform the following steps:

1. Click at the tip of one of the axes.

   Black handles appear at the end of all eight tips (see fig. 14.19).

2. Drag one of the handles on the side close to you. Drag in the direction you want the chart to rotate. Imagine that the chart is in a sphere and that you are dragging the mouse along the surface of this sphere.

As you drag, a wire-frame outline of the chart depicts the charts orientation, as shown in figure 14.20.

3. Release the mouse button when the outline appears in the correct orientation. Excel redraws the chart, as shown in figure 14.18.

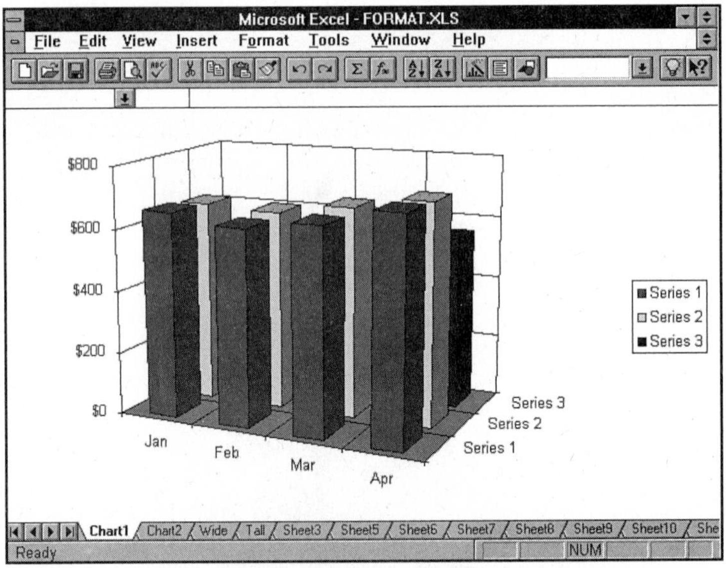

Fig. 14.17
A 3-D chart with data series blocked from view.

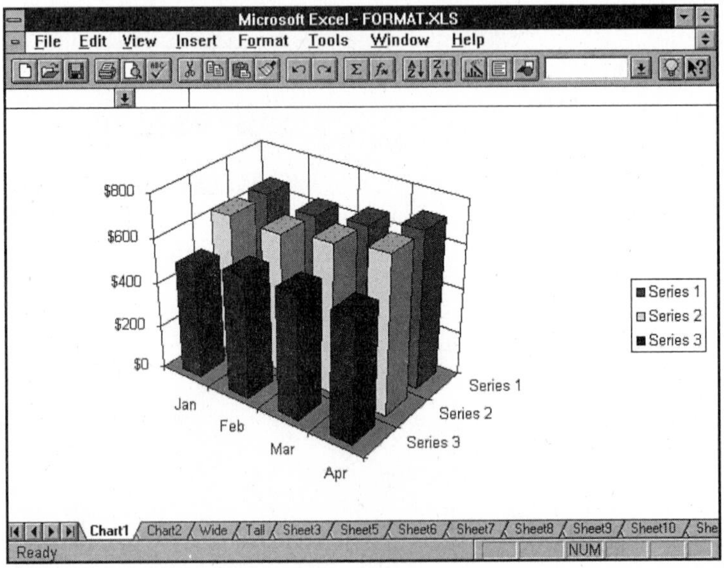

Fig. 14.18
Rotating and adjusting the perspective of a 3-D chart displays the series from a better angle.

Note

Drag different handles as the chart rotates. Use one of the handles closest to you when you begin dragging the chart. After the chart passes approximately 90 degrees of rotation, you may have difficulty visualizing how the chart is rotating. Release the handle you were dragging and begin dragging one of the handles that is now in front.

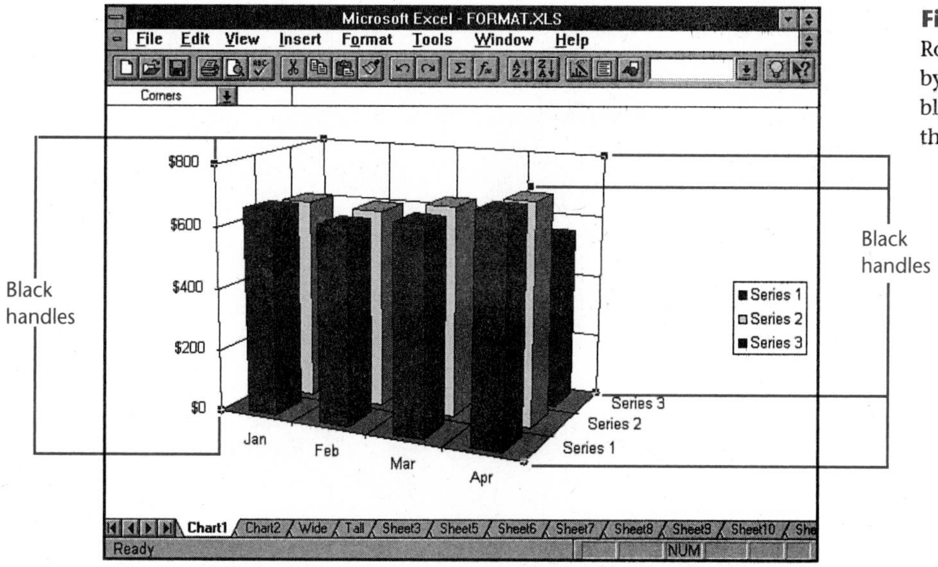

Fig. 14.19 Rotate 3-D charts by dragging a black handle at the tip of an axis.

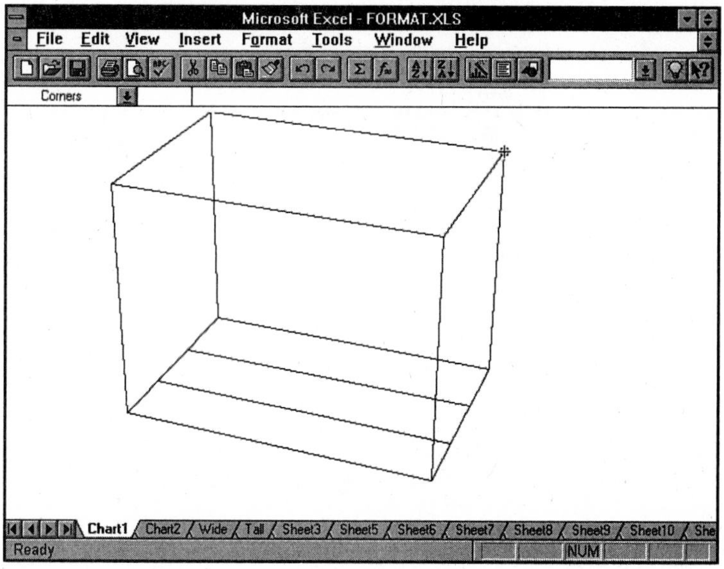

Fig. 14.20 Rotate the wire frame as though inside a sphere to change the view of 3-D charts.

Rotating a 3-D Chart by Command

Tip
Use the mouse to get the basic rotation and perspective for your 3-D charts and use Format 3-D View to fine-tune the settings.

Tip
See the previous section, "Understanding Data Series Formatting," for adjusting chart depth and the depth and width of the gaps in 3-D column and bar charts.

You also can use the Format 3-D View command to change the perspective on 3-D charts. Using the dialog box is helpful when you need to apply the same perspective to several 3-D charts. You can use the mouse the get the exact rotation and perspective for the first chart, and then use the Format 3-D View dialog box to read and record the settings for that chart. Next, use the Format 3-D View command to apply those same settings to your other charts.

When you choose the Format 3-D View command, the dialog box shown in figure 14.21 appears. Selections in this dialog box change the angle and perspective from which the 3-D chart is drawn.

You can use a mouse or a keyboard to rotate or adjust the viewpoint shown in the 3-D View dialog box. Using the mouse is faster and easier.

If you are using the mouse to rotate or adjust the viewpoint, click the appropriate directional button to rotate or adjust the viewpoint.

To rotate or adjust the viewpoint with the keyboard, select a text box and then type a number within the range. The following table lists the available options.

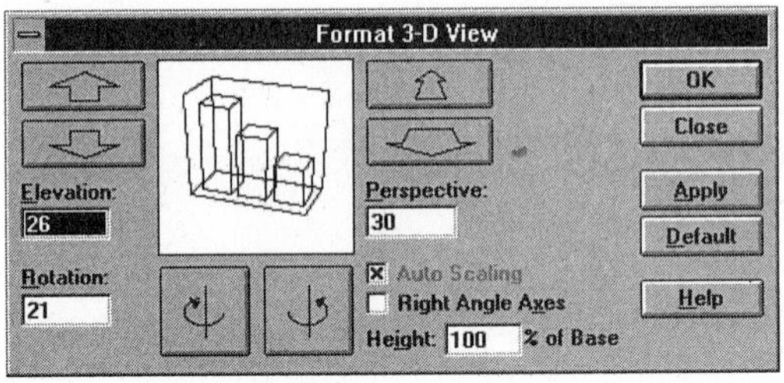

Fig. 14.21
Rotate the wireframe chart to rotate your 3-D chart.

Option	Effect on Chart
Elevation	Changes the height from which you see the chart. Use an angle from -90 to +90 degrees for all charts except pie charts. Use an angle from 10 to 80 degrees for pie charts.
Rotation	Rotates the chart around the vertical (Z) axis. The range is from 0 to 360 degrees.
Perspective	Controls the vanishing point or the sense of depth in the chart. Use a number between 0 and 100 to specify the ratio of the front of the chart to its back.
Height % of Base	Controls the height of the vertical (Z) axis as a percentage of the chart width (X) axis. Enter a number between 5 and 500.
Right Angle Axes	Freezes axis angles at 90 degrees. Perspective is turned off.

When the wire-frame chart has the orientation you want, choose OK. By choosing the Apply button, you can keep the dialog box on-screen and apply the current settings to the chart so that you can see how they look. Choose the **D**efault button to return all dialog box settings to default values.

Note

You can format the floor and walls of a 3-D chart using the same procedures discussed in "Changing Object Colors, Patterns, and Borders," a previous section of this chapter. You can change the border and area formatting in the Pattern tab of the Format dialog box. To open the Format dialog box, either choose the F**o**rmat **Se**lected item command, click the object with the right mouse button and select the Format command from the shortcut menu, or double-click the object.

Clearing Chart Formats or Contents

You don't have to create a new chart from the worksheet when you want to change all the data or formats. Use the Edit Cle**a**r command to selectively remove chart objects and data series or to remove just the formatting from a data series.

To remove a chart object and its formatting, follow these steps:

1. Select the chart object.
2. Choose the **E**dit Cle**a**r **A**ll command or press the Delete key.

   If you select the entire chart, all objects in the chart—including the data series—are removed, leaving a blank chart sheet or embedded chart. If you select an embedded chart, the chart is removed from the worksheet.

   You can copy and paste new data on top of a chart whose contents you deleted. The new data uses the format of the preceding chart.

To remove a data series, trendline, or error bars, follow these steps:

1. Select the data series, trendline, or error bars.
2. Choose the **E**dit Cle**a**r command and then choose either **S**eries, **T**rendline, or **E**rror Bars from the submenu, or press the Delete key.

   The command in the submenu changes depending on the type of object that you selected.

To remove just the formatting for a selected series, follow these steps:

1. Select data series.

2. Choose the **E**dit Cle**a**r **F**ormats command.

   This command clears any custom formatting that has been applied to a data series and restores the default formatting that is defined by the default chart format.

Note

To retrieve an accidentally deleted object or data series, use the **E**dit **U**ndo command or the Undo button on the Standard toolbar to undo your mistake.

Troubleshooting

When I select a single data point and use the ***E****dit Cle****a****r command or Delete key to try to delete that data point, the entire data series is deleted. How can I delete a single data point?*

You cannot truly delete a single data point on an existing chart. You can delete either the data for the point in the worksheet that is the source for the chart, or you can format the data point so you don't see it. Select the data point and choose the F**o**rmat S**e**lected Point command. Select the Patterns tab, and select the None options on both sides of the dialog box. Depending on the type of chart, you may have to select none for both the Border and Area groups, as in a column chart, or the Line and Marker groups, as in a line chart. Formatting a data point with the None options effectively removes the point from the chart. Note that in line charts, if you remove a data point, the line connecting the adjacent points also is removed.

For Related Information

- "Using Autoformats," p. 441
- "Choosing a Default Chart Format," p. 454

Changing and Modifying Chart Types

If you use the AutoFormat command to change the chart type, Excel erases some of your custom formatting. To change the type of an existing chart and retain custom colors and other formatting, choose the F**o**rmat Chart **T**ype command or choose Chart Type from the shortcut menu. Select the new chart type from the Chart Type dialog box (see fig. 14.22). If you have created a customized column chart, for example, and you want to switch to a bar chart, select Bar in the Chart Type dialog box and choose OK. Your custom formatting is preserved, if it is appropriate for the new type of chart.

You have many options in the Chart Type dialog box. After you have chosen a chart type, you can choose the **O**ptions button and select the Subtype tab to select the subtype you want to use, and you can select the Options tab to select various options for that chart type. These options are discussed in "Formatting Data Series" earlier in the chapter.

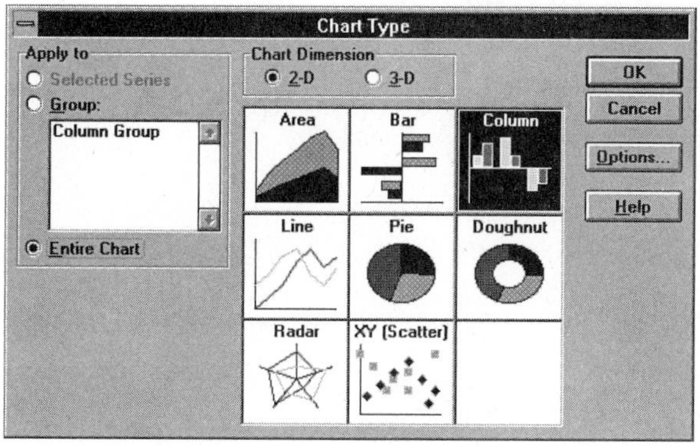

Fig. 14.22
Use the Chart Type dialog box to change chart type in a chart that you have already customized.

Transferring Chart Formats

After you create a chart, you can apply formatting from another chart. To transfer a chart format, use the Paste **S**pecial command to copy the formatting from one chart and paste it onto another chart.

To transfer a chart format, perform the following steps:

1. Activate the chart that has the format you want to copy.
2. Select the entire chart by clicking near the outside of the chart or pressing the up or down arrow key until the chart is selected. Black handles appear around the outside of the chart.
3. Choose the **E**dit **C**opy command.
4. Activate the chart you want to format.
5. Choose **E**dit Paste **S**pecial to display the Paste Special dialog box (see fig. 14.23).
6. Choose Forma**t**s from the Paste Special dialog box.
7. Choose OK.

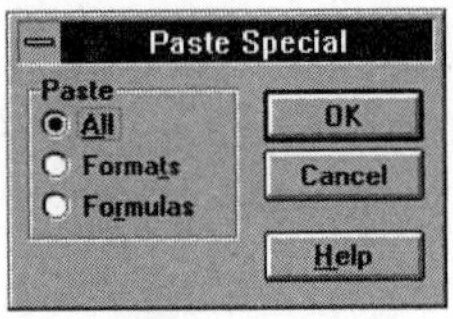

Fig. 14.23
Use the Paste Special dialog box to copy formatting from one chart to another.

From Here...

- Chapter 7, "Moving or Copying Data and Formulas," shows you how to paste formats and transpose data.
- Chapter 15, "Building Complex Charts," shows you how to create combination charts and use charts to analyze data.
- Chapter 21, "Creating Slide Show Presentations," shows you how to use charts in slide show presentations.

Chapter 15

Building Complex Charts

In this chapter, you learn how to:

- Create combination charts
- Analyze data with charts
- Add trendlines to a chart
- Add error bars to a chart
- Create charts from outlines
- Create picture charts

When you have a situation that requires special charts or you need to go beyond the fundamentals in modifying and formatting charts, the techniques in this chapter will help you. You can use Excel's powerful charting features to plot individual data sets differently on the same chart, making it easy to compare different types of data (see fig. 15.1). Two new features in Excel—trendlines and error bars—can make your charts even more informative. Add visual impact to your charts by replacing data points with graphics (see fig. 15.2).

Creating Combination Charts

Combination charts present two or more data series on the same chart and use different chart types for the data series. For example, you may plot one series using a column chart, and a second series using a line chart, to make it easier to compare the two sets of data or to look for possible interactions between the data sets. You can also use a combination chart if you need to use a different axis with a different scale for plotting one or more of the data series in a chart. This might be the case if one of the data series in the chart has a range of values that differs substantially from the other data series in the chart.

Figure 15.1 shows a combination column chart and line chart created by pasting in a data series, and then using the F**o**rmat Chart **T**ype command to change the added data to a line chart. The goal data series is plotted as a line to separate it from the actual data for the western and eastern regions. This combination enables you to easily compare more than one type of data.

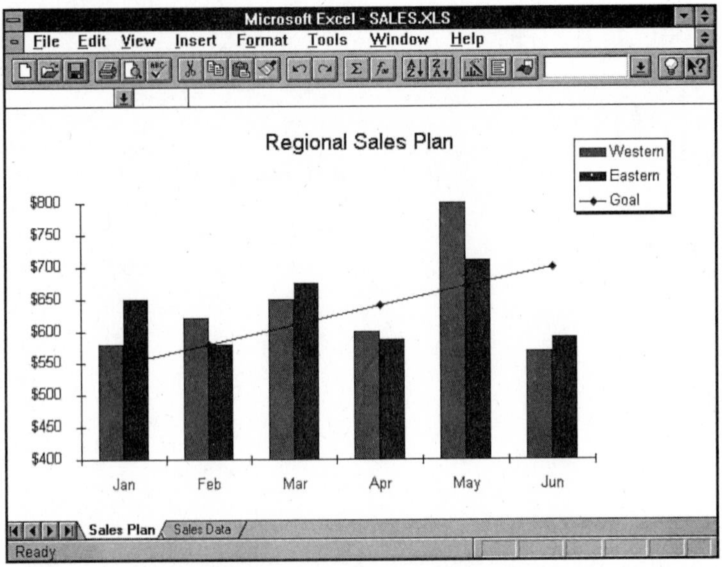

Fig. 15.1
Use combination charts to show different chart types in the same chart.

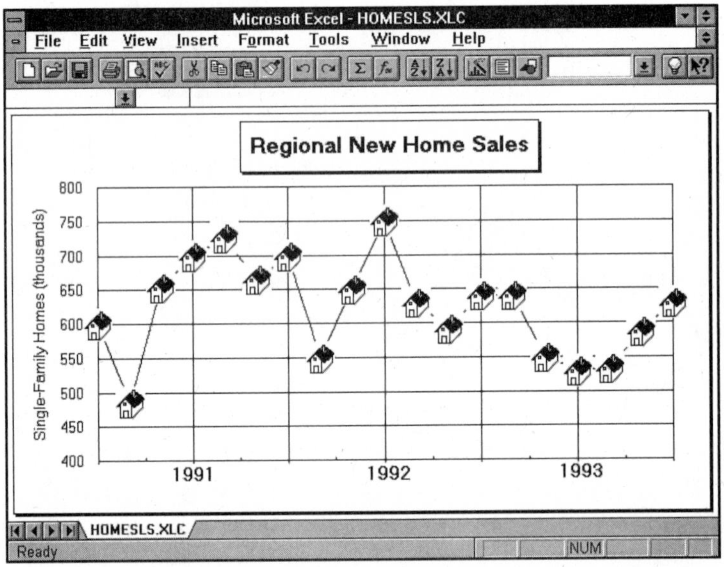

Fig. 15.2
Graphics can be used to mark data points in a chart to add visual impact.

Figure 15.3 shows a combination chart where both charts are line charts. This combination enables you to use two value (Y) axes with different scales.

You can create a combination chart in three ways: when you are creating a new chart, you can use the ChartWizard to create a combination chart; you can apply one of the combination chart autoformats to an existing chart; or you can select a data series in an existing chart and change the chart type for that series. If you have already customized a chart, you should not apply an autoformat because you will destroy the custom formatting. Instead, change the chart type for individual data series in the chart.

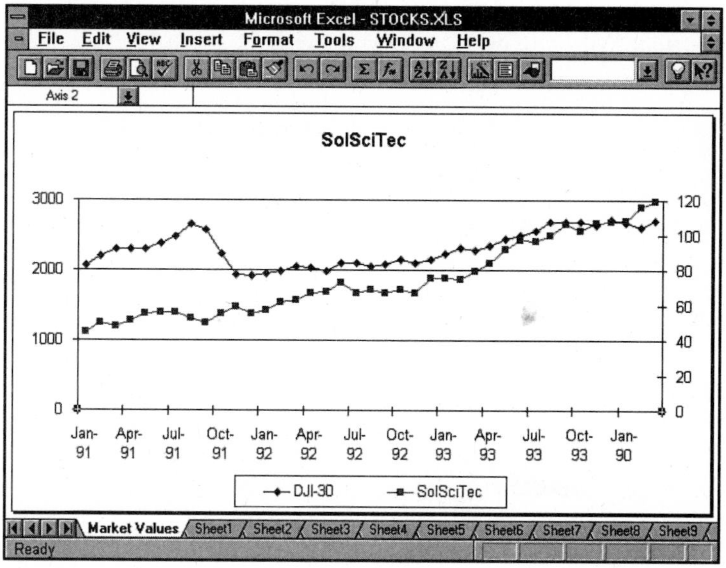

Fig. 15.3
Combination charts enable you to create two axes on the same chart.

You can choose six combination types in the ChartWizard or the Autoformat dialog box. When you use a predefined combination chart, the data series are divided evenly, with the first half of the data series becoming one chart type group and the second half of the data series becoming the other chart type group. If the chart has an odd number of data series, the extra series is included in the first chart type group.

The third method involves selecting one of the data series and then using the F**o**rmat Chart **T**ype command to change the chart type for the selected series. This is the method you must use if you want to create a combination chart from an existing chart that has been customized. When you select a data series and change its chart type, the series becomes a *chart type group*. For example, you may have a line chart type group and a column chart type group in a combination chart. More than one data series can belong to a chart type group. You can work with the two chart type groups separately, applying different formatting to each of the groups. Each chart type group is listed at the bottom of the Format menu. When you select one of the groups, you can make changes that will apply only to that group. For example, you can change the chart subtype for that group or plot the data series along a secondary axis, which is how the chart in figure 15.3 was created.

Creating a Combination Chart from the Predefined Chart Types

If you are creating a new combination chart or working with an existing chart that was not customized, you can apply one of the combination chart types to quickly create a combination chart.

To create a new combination chart using the ChartWizard, perform the following steps:

1. Select the data you want to chart and start the ChartWizard (see Chapter 12, "Creating Charts," for more details on using the ChartWizard).
2. Select the Co**m**bination option in step 2 of the ChartWizard.
3. Select one of the combination chart formats in step 3 of the ChartWizard.
4. Complete the remaining steps of the ChartWizard.

EXCEL 5

To create a combination chart from an existing chart, using the combination chart autoformats, perform the following steps:

1. Activate the chart.
2. Choose the F**o**rmat **A**utoFormat command, or click near the outside border of the chart, and choose AutoFormat from the shortcut menu.
3. Select Combination in the **G**alleries list box.
4. Select one of the combination chart formats in the **F**ormats box.
5. Choose OK.

Whether you use the ChartWizard or the F**o**rmat **A**utoformat command, Excel applies one of the chart types to half the data series and the other chart type to the other half of the data series. If an odd number of data series exists, the first chart type receives the greater number of data series.

You can change the chart type used by either one of the data series groups created when you apply one of the predefined combination chart types. Choose the F**o**rmat Chart **T**ype command and select the group you want to change in the **G**roup list box. Select the type of chart you want to use for the selected group and choose OK.

Creating a Combination Chart with the Format Chart Command

You can create a combination chart easily from any existing chart that has two or more data series. Initially, the chart consists of one series group.

However, you can select any individual data series and use the F**o**rmat Chart **T**ype command to change the chart type for the selected series. The chart then becomes a combination chart. You can use this same method to change the type of chart used by any of the series in an existing combination chart.

To create a combination chart using the F**o**rmat Chart **T**ype command, perform the following steps:

1. Open the chart from which you want to create the combination chart.
2. Select the data series whose chart type you want to change.
3. Choose the F**o**rmat Chart **T**ype command, or choose Chart Type from the chart shortcut menu.
4. Select the type of chart you want to use for the selected series in the Chart Type dialog box.
5. Choose OK.

Changing Chart Types

You can easily change the chart type used by any one of the chart type groups in a combination chart. To change the chart type, choose the F**o**rmat Chart **T**ype command and select the group you want to modify in the **G**roup box of the Chart Type dialog box. Select the type of chart you want to apply to the selected group, and if you want to select the subtype of chart, choose the **O**ptions button, select one of the subtypes in the **S**ubtype box, and choose OK.

Adding a Secondary Axis

Sometimes you may want to compare two sets of data whose value ranges differ substantially. In this case, using the same category axis for both data sets will obscure the data points for the data set with the lower range of y-values. This problem can be corrected by adding a secondary category axis for one of the data sets. You can also add a secondary axis when you are comparing data sets with different units of measure—for example, dollars and number of units.

To add a secondary axis for a single data series, perform the following steps:

1. Select the series you want to plot along a secondary axis by clicking a data point in the series or by using the up- and down-arrow keys until the series is selected.

2. Choose F**o**rmat S**e**lected Series, or choose Format Series from the shortcut menu, and select the Axis tab.

3. Select the **S**econdary Axis option.

4. Choose OK.

To add a secondary axis for a data series group, perform the following steps:

For Related Information

- "Choosing a Chart Type," p. 438
- "Using Autoformats," p. 441
- "Scaling and Customizing an Axis," p. 492

1. Choose the F**o**rmat menu, and select the chart type group you want to plot on a secondary axis from the bottom of the menu.

   or

   Select the series you want to plot on a secondary axis, click the right mouse button, and choose the Format Group command at the bottom of the menu.

2. Select the Axis tab.

3. Select the **S**econdary Axis option and choose OK.

Using Charts To Analyze Data

Besides lively presentations, charts make excellent analytical tools. Excel charts are linked to one or more worksheets, so playing *what-if* games on the worksheets updates the charts linked to them. Updating can reveal profit-loss crossover points, forecast inventory quantities, or quantify trends for different scenarios.

Excel also has the powerful capability of finding a worksheet value to match changes in the chart. If you drag a bar, column, or line to a new location in the chart, Excel seeks a new worksheet input that produces the result shown in the chart. This feature provides a quick and easy way to make a visual estimate of a situation and have Excel determine the numbers that correspond.

Analyzing Charts for What-If Analysis

You can use Excel to make changes to your worksheet and watch the chart immediately reflect those changes. This capability is valuable for performing what-if types of analysis. Because you can see the effects of your worksheet changes, you can determine emerging trends, crossover points between profit and loss, and mistakes made during data entry.

As figure 15.4 illustrates, you can position worksheet and chart windows so that all windows are visible. As you change a variable in the worksheet, the Sales versus Costs and the Itemized Cost charts reflect the changes immediately. To arrange chart and worksheet windows side by side, choose the **W**indow **N**ew Window command to open a new window for the current workbook. Next, choose the **W**indow **A**rrange command, select one of the options in the Arrange group, and choose OK. You can also drag the sides and title bars to arrange the windows. In one of the windows, activate the worksheet, and in the other window activate the chart.

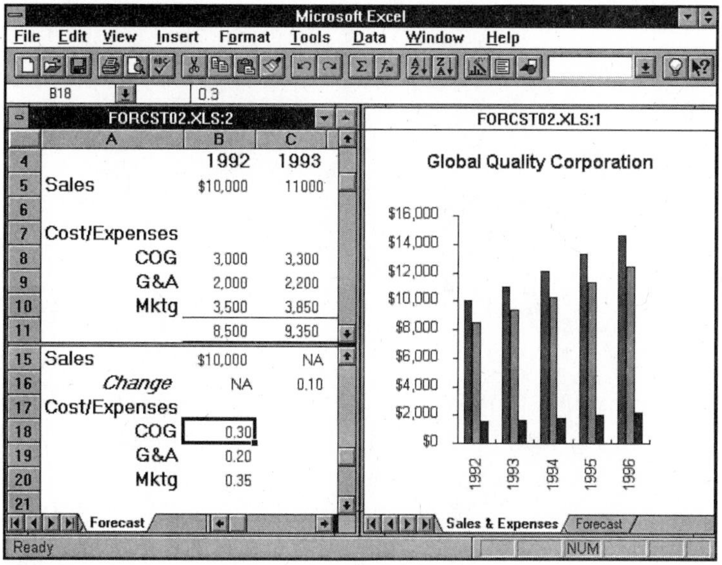

Fig. 15.4
Open new windows and arrange them when you need to see chart and data simultaneously.

Moving Markers To Change Worksheet Values

Excel enables you to move column, bar, or line markers on a chart and cause the corresponding data in the worksheet to change. If the data is not a value but a formula, Excel executes the **T**ools **G**oal Seek command to find the input value that makes the worksheet correspond to the chart.

To change values on the worksheet from the chart, perform the following steps:

1. Open the workbook containing the worksheet and chart with which you want to work. Activate the chart. The chart must be a two-dimensional column, bar, line, or XY scatter chart.

2. Click once on the data point you want to change; the entire series will be selected. Click a second time on the same data point. Handles appear on the marker as shown in figure 15.5.

Fig. 15.5
The handles for the selected data point indicate that this column can be dragged to a new height.

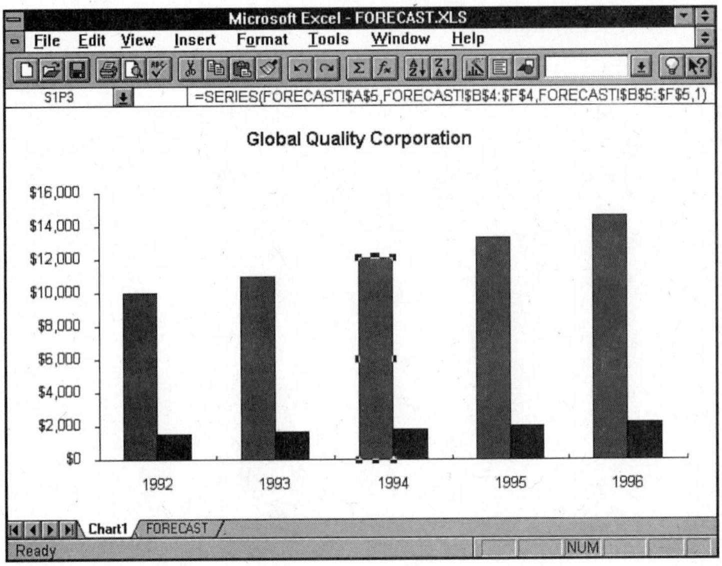

3. Drag the handle at the top of the data point to the location you want. Watch the reference area to the left of the formula bar to see the changing numeric value for the marker. A sliding marker shows the position on the value (Y) axis. You can drag the marker past the top of the value (Y) axis if you want.

4. Release the mouse when the marker is at the location you want.

For Related Information

- "Manipulating Windows," p. 58
- "Using the Goal Seek Feature," p. 796

If the column, line, or bar references a number on the worksheet, that number changes in the worksheet. If the column, line, or bar references the result of a formula, Excel activates the **T**ools **G**oal Seek command. This command activates the worksheet for the marker and displays the Goal Seek dialog box, as shown in figure 15.6.

To operate Goal Seek, perform the following steps:

1. In the By **c**hanging cell text box, select the cell (or type the cell reference of the cell) that you want to change to produce the result in the chart. The cell you select must not contain a formula.

2. Choose OK.

   Goal Seek iterates through input values to find the value that produces the result in the chart. Then, the Goal Seek dialog box displays the solution.

3. Choose OK to enter the new input value, or choose Cancel to return to the original worksheet.

When Goal Seek is complete, Excel reactivates the chart. (The Goal Seek command is described in detail in Chapter 27, "Solving with Goal Seeking and Solver.")

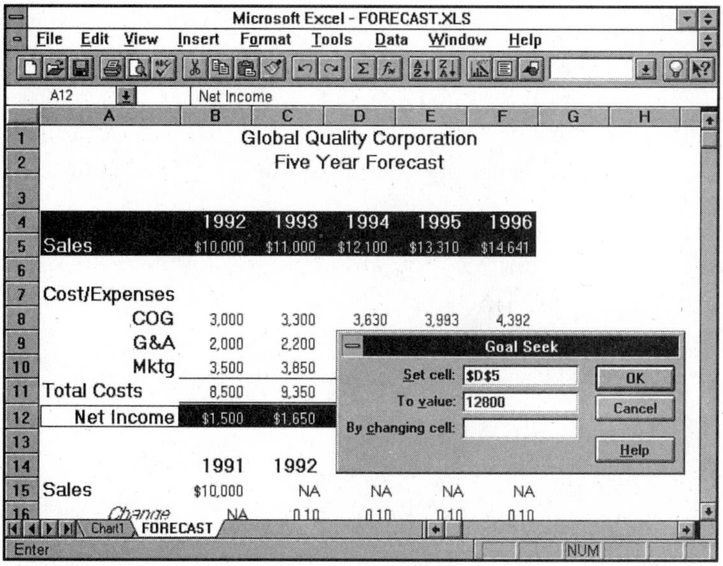

Fig. 15.6
The Goal Seek dialog box asks which worksheet cell should be changed to achieve the result in the chart.

Automatically Analyzing Trends with Charts

In previous versions of Excel, you could analyze trends and make forecasts using either the fill handles or worksheet commands. In Excel 5, you can also analyze trends by adding a trendline to a chart, using the **I**nsert T**r**endline command. The trendline will show you the direction of the plotted data and can also be used to make predictions. Regression analysis is used to create the trendline from the chart data, and you can select from among five types of regression lines or calculate a line that displays *moving averages*. Moving averages smooth out fluctuations in a data series by basing a given data point on the trendline on the average of a specified number of prior data points.

Caution

Trendlines are a statistical tool and, like any statistical tool, can be misused or abused. If you are going to use trendlines to analyze the data in your charts, be sure that you understand the theory behind their use and that the trendlines represent a real trend in your data. It is very easy, especially with the aid of computers, to fit a trendline to data that doesn't necessarily have any statistical validity.

You can select any series of data in a chart and add a trendline, as long as the selected data is an area, bar, column, line, or scatter (XY) chart. When you add a trendline to a data series, it is linked to the data, so that if you change the values for any of the data points in the series, the trendline is automatically recalculated and redrawn in the chart. If you change the chart type for the data series to a chart type other than one listed previously, the trendline is permanently deleted.

You have the option of setting the y-intercept value for the trendline and adding the regression equation and r-squared value for the regression to the chart. You can also make backward and forward forecasts for the data, based on the trendline and its associated regression equation.

Adding a Trendline to a Data Series

Adding a trendline to a data series is a simple process of selecting the data series and choosing the **I**nsert T**r**endline command. You do need to know what type of regression analysis you want to use on the data.

To add a trendline to a data series, perform the following steps:

1. Select the data series to which you want to add the trendline.

2. Choose the **I**nsert T**r**endline command or select Inserts Trendline from the shortcut menu, and select the Type tab to display the Trendline dialog box, shown in figure 15.7.

3. Select from among the six trend/regression types. The following table describes each of the regression types and how they are derived:

Type	Description
Linear	Produces a linear regression line using the equation: $y = mx + b$ where *m* is the slope of the line and *b* is the y-intercept of the line.
Logarithmic	Produces a logarithmic regression line using the equation: $y = c\ln x + b$ where *c* and *b* are constants, and *ln* is the natural logarithm.
Polynomial	Produces a polynomial regression line using the equation: $y = b + c_1x + c_2x^2 + c_3x^3 + \ldots c_6x^6$ where *b* and c_1 through c_6 are constants. Select the order of the polynomial equation in the Order text box. The maximum order for a polynomial trendline is 6.
Power	Produces a power regression line using the equation: $y = cx^b$ where *c* and *b* are constants.
Exponential	Produces an exponential regression line using the equation: $y = ce^{bx}$ where *c* and *b* are constants and *e* is the base of the natural logarithm.
Moving Average	Produces a moving average, where the value for each data point on the trendline is based on the average of a specified number of prior data points (periods). The more the number of periods used to calculate the moving average, the smoother but less responsive is the resulting trendline. The equation used to calculate the moving average is: $F_t = \frac{A_t + A_{t-1} + \ldots A_{t-n+1}}{n}$

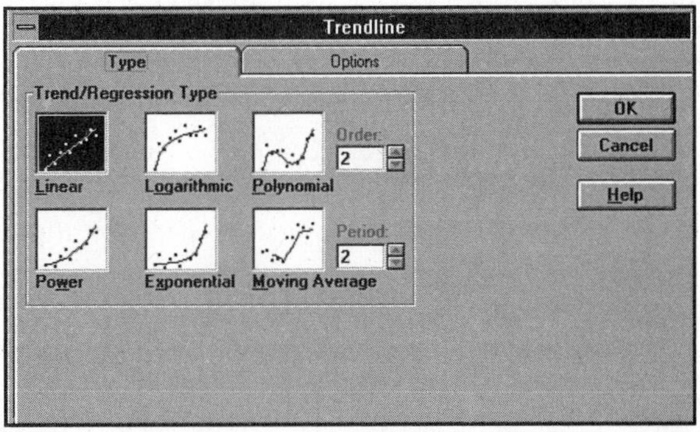

Fig. 15.7
You select the type of trendline you want to add to the selected data series in the Trendline dialog box.

4. Select the Options tab if you want to select any of the options that are available for trendlines (see fig. 15.8).

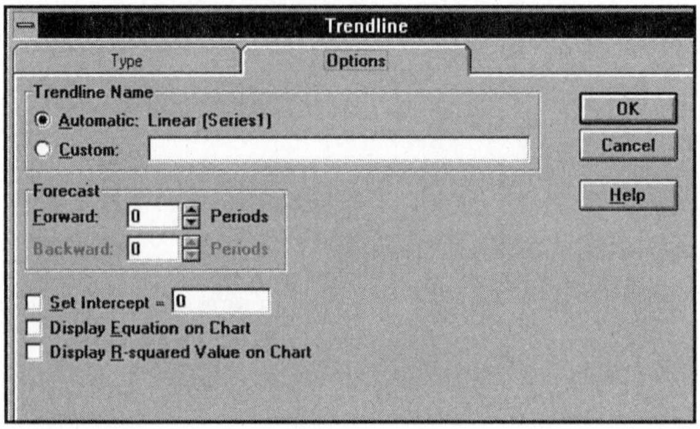

Fig. 15.8
The Options tab in the Trendline dialog box.

The trendlines options are described in the following table:

Option	Description
Trendline Name	
Automatic	Applies the data series name to the trendline.
Custom	Types a new name in the Custom text box.
Forecast	
Forward	Projects the trendline forward for the number of periods specified in the Periods text box.
Backward	Projects the trendline backward for the number of periods specified in the Periods text box.
Set Intercept	By default, the Y-intercept is calculated based on the data. You can set the Y-intercept to a specific value.
Display **E**quation	When selected, the regression on Chart equation for the trendline is displayed as free-floating text on the chart.
Display R-squared Value on Chart	When selected, the r-squared value is displayed as free-floating text on the chart.

For Related Information

- "Formatting Trendlines," p. 490
- "Analyzing Trends," p. 710

5. Choose OK.

Figure 15.9 shows a line chart with a linear regression trendline. The regression equation and r-squared value are displayed in the chart.

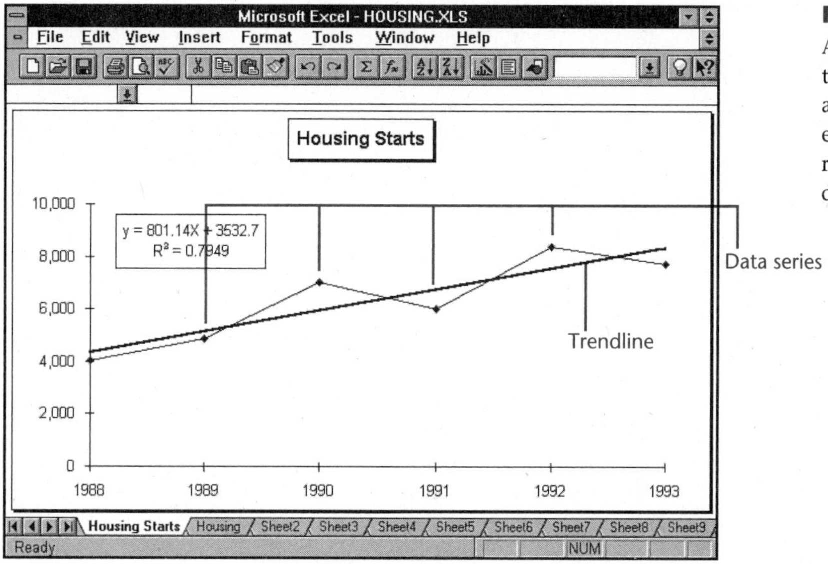

Fig. 15.9
A data series with a trendline inserted and the regression equation and r-squared value displayed.

Adding Error Bars to a Chart

Error bars are used in charts to visually represent the margin of error or degree of uncertainty in a data series. Error bars are commonly used in plots of statistical and engineering data to give the viewer an indication of how reliable the data being presented is. The greater the uncertainty associated with the data points in a data series, the wider are the error bars. Figure 15.10 shows a chart with error bars inserted.

EXCEL 5

Caution

As with trendlines, do not use error bars unless you understand how to apply them correctly. Error bars should only be added to a chart if they accurately represent the statistical error in your data.

Excel 5 enables you to associate error bars with any data series of the area, bar, column, line, or scatter (xy) chart type. If you change the data series to a 3-D, pie, doughnut, or radar chart, the error bars will be permanently lost. Scattergrams (xy-charts) can have error bars associated with both the x- and y-values.

II Working with Charts

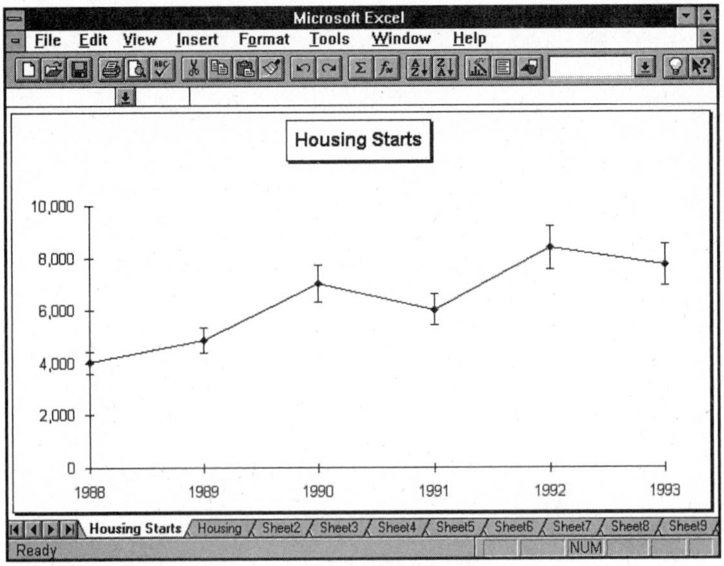

Fig. 15.10
Error bars show the degree of uncertainty in a data point.

Several options are available for deciding how Excel calculates the error bars (see table 15.2 in the next section). After you add error bars to a data series, they continue to be associated with the series, even if you change the order in which the data series are plotted; if the values for the data points change, the error bars are automatically recalculated.

Inserting Error Bars

To insert error bars for a data series, perform the following steps:

1. Select the data series to which you want to add error bars.

2. Choose **I**nsert Error **B**ars, or choose Insert Error Bars from the shortcut menu to display the dialog box shown in figure 15.11.

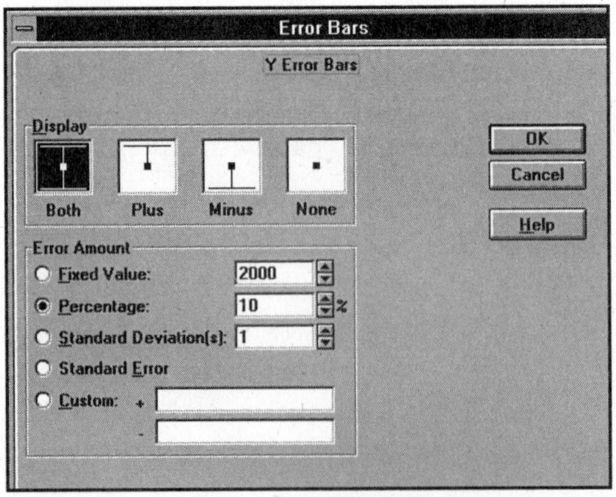

Fig. 15.11
Format the scale and appearance of error bars using the Error Bars dialog box.

3. Select the type of error bars you want to display from the **D**isplay group.

4. Select the method you want Excel to use for calculating the error amounts in the Error Amount group. The following table describes these options:

Option	Description
Fixed Value	You enter a value that is used for the error amount for all of the data points.
Percentage	You enter a percentage that is used to calculate the error amount for each of the data points.
Standard Deviation(s)	You enter the number of standard deviations to use to calculate the error amount. The standard deviation for the plotted data is calculated automatically.
Standard **E**rror	The standard error for the data is used for the error amount for all the data points. The standard error is automatically calculated from the plotted data.
Custom	You can either enter ranges from a worksheet in which the positive and negative error values are stored or enter the desired values for the error amounts as an array. Whether you use a range or an array, you must have the same number of error values as you have data points. Use this option if you want to specify different error amounts for each data point.

5. Choose OK.

Creating Charts from Outlines

EXCEL 5

When you create a chart from data in an outline, you can choose to include just the visible data in the chart or data that is not visible in the worksheet because some of the levels in the outline are collapsed. Fig. 15.12 shows an outline in which level 3, both vertically and horizontally, has been collapsed; data in the outline was selected for creating a chart. The resulting chart is shown in figure 15.13. Only the visible data appears in the chart.

To plot all the data in the selection, including the data that is not visible because the outline is partially collapsed, choose the **T**ools **O**ptions command and select the Chart tab. Deselect the **P**lot Visible Cells Only option and choose OK. The chart in figure 15.14 shows the results of turning off the **P**lot Visible Cells Only option.

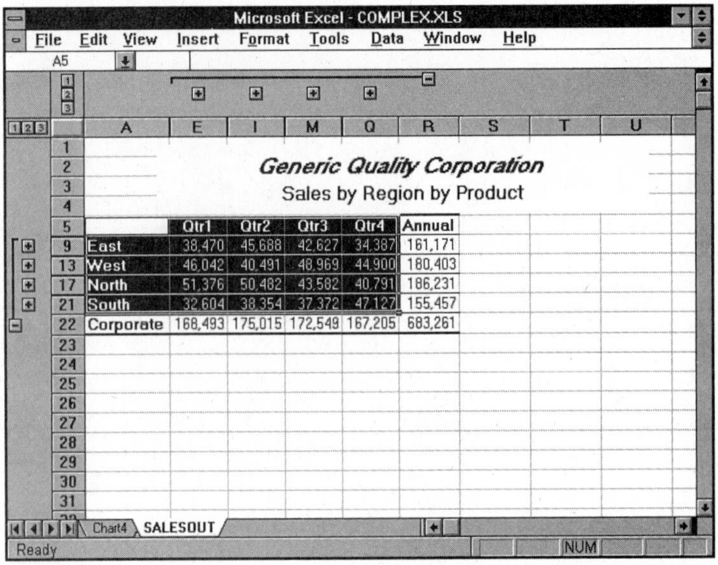

Fig. 15.12
Level 3, collapsed both vertically and horizontally.

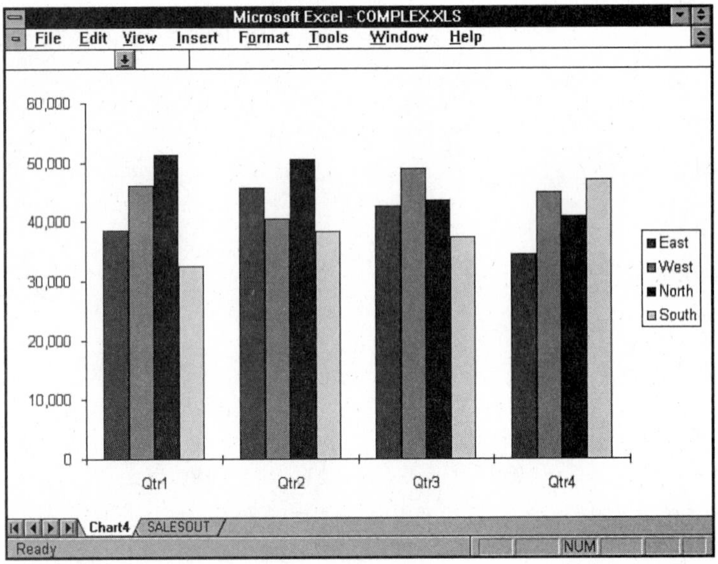

Fig. 15.13
The chart that results from the collapsed levels shown in figure 15.12.

If the **P**lot Visible Cells Only option is turned on and you expand the outline, the chart updates. Figure 15.15 shows the outline from figure 15.12 expanded to level 3 vertically. The resulting chart is shown in figure 15.16.

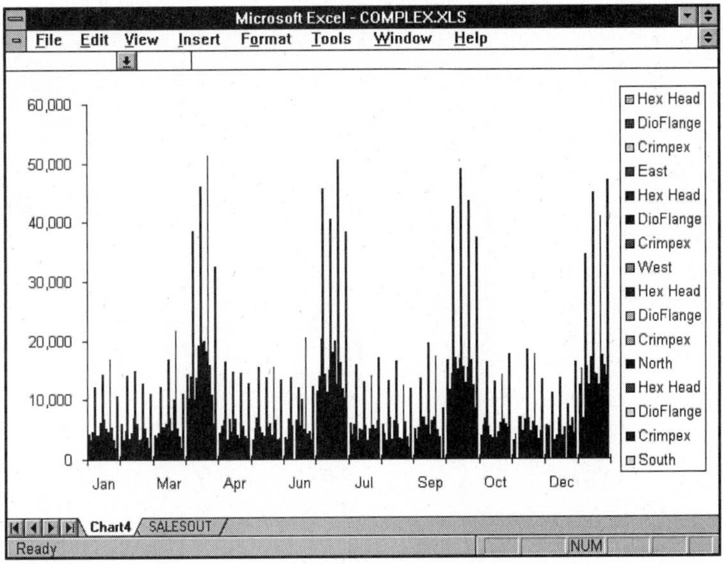

Fig. 15.14
With the **P**lot Visible Cells Only option turned off, the resulting chart shows too much data.

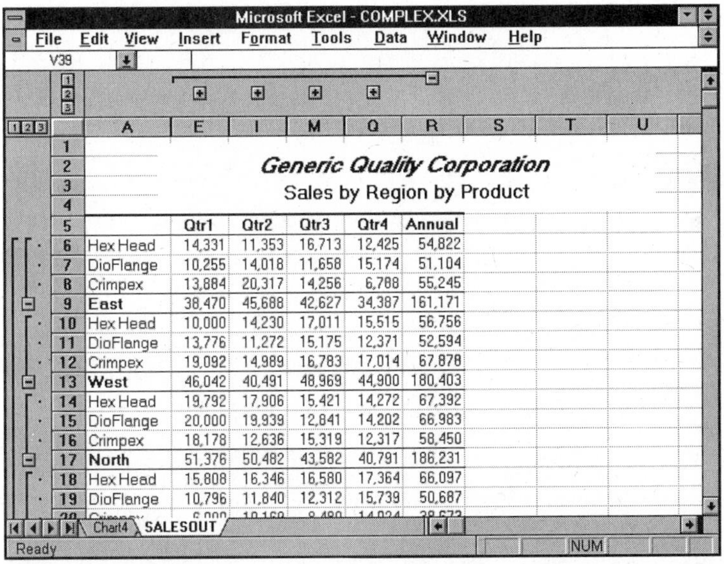

	Qtr1	Qtr2	Qtr3	Qtr4	Annual
Hex Head	14,331	11,353	16,713	12,425	54,822
DioFlange	10,255	14,018	11,658	15,174	51,104
Crimpex	13,884	20,317	14,256	6,788	55,245
East	38,470	45,688	42,627	34,387	161,171
Hex Head	10,000	14,230	17,011	15,515	56,756
DioFlange	13,776	11,272	15,175	12,371	52,594
Crimpex	19,092	14,989	16,783	17,014	67,878
West	46,042	40,491	48,969	44,900	180,403
Hex Head	19,792	17,906	15,421	14,272	67,392
DioFlange	20,000	19,939	12,841	14,202	66,983
Crimpex	18,178	12,636	15,319	12,317	58,450
North	51,376	50,482	43,582	40,791	186,231
Hex Head	15,808	16,346	16,580	17,364	66,097
DioFlange	10,796	11,840	12,312	15,739	50,687

Fig. 15.15
The information from figure 15.12, expanded to level 3 vertically.

Note

To prevent a chart created from an outline from updating when the outline is collapsed or expanded, click the Select Visible Cells button (or choose **E**dit **G**o To **S**pecial and select the **V**isible Cells Only option) after you select the cells for creating a chart but before you start creating the chart.

Fig. 15.16
The resulting chart of the expansion shown in figure 15.15.

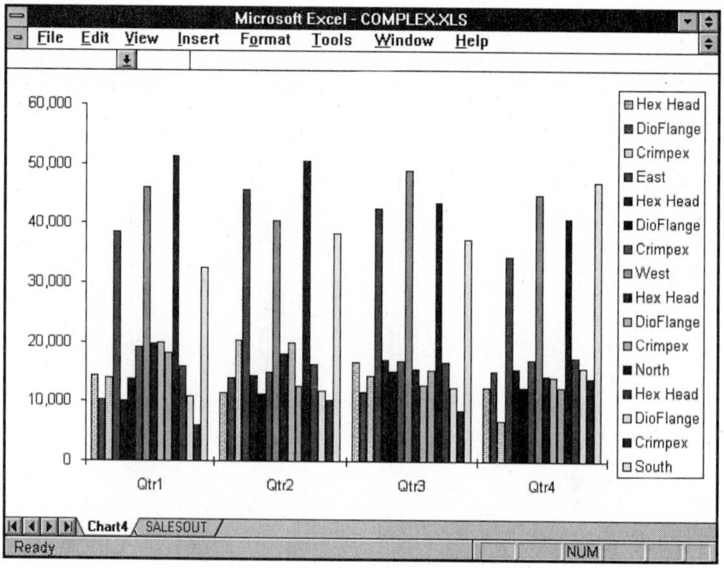

For Related Information

- "Creating an Outline," p. 598
- "Manipulating the Display of an Outline," p. 600

Creating Hierarchical Charts

You can create charts that display more than one level of categories or series on the same chart.

When you create a multilevel chart, examine the dialog box in step 4 of the ChartWizard carefully to be sure that the correct rows and columns are being used to plot the categories and series. Change the settings in this dialog box if necessary. See Chapter 12, "Creating Charts," for detailed information on using the ChartWizard. When you add data to a multilevel chart, always use the ChartWizard to be sure that you maintain existing category and series levels.

For Related Information

- "Verifying the Chart Data Range," p. 409
- "Changing the Data Range with the ChartWizard," p. 459

You also can create charts that show the multilevel categories and series in a pivot table. When you change the view of the pivot table, the chart updates. See Chapter 36, "Using Pivot Tables," to learn how to create and use pivot tables and how to create charts from a pivot table.

Linking Chart Text to Worksheet Cells

The capability of linking worksheet text or numbers to attached or unattached (free-floating) chart text is helpful. You can use this technique to update chart or axis titles when titles on the worksheet change or to link comments in a worksheet cell to a chart. Figure 15.17 shows a text box that displays the contents of a worksheet cell.

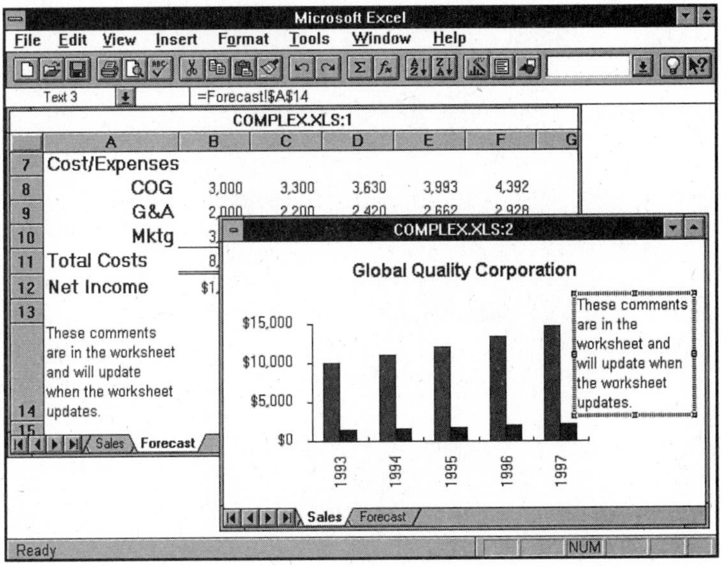

Fig. 15.17
Comments, dates, or numbers in a worksheet can be linked to a chart text box.

When you edit the worksheet comments, the change appears in the chart text. You also can link a worksheet cell's contents to the data series numbers that are attached to the top of columns or bars. The worksheet cell's contents then also appear at the top of the column or end of the bar.

To link a worksheet cell's contents to attached or unattached text in a chart, perform the following steps:

1. Open the worksheet and the chart. Activate the chart.

2. Create attached text, such as titles or data series numbers, if you want the cell contents to appear at these points.

3. If you want to link a worksheet cell's contents to unattached text, be certain that no text object is selected and enter an equal (=) sign; the formula bar opens.

If, on the other hand, you want to link a cell's contents to an attached text object, say the chart title, select the attached text and type an equal (=) sign; the formula bar opens.

4. Activate the worksheet containing the cell whose contents you want to link to the chart by clicking its tab at the bottom of the window.

5. Select the cell that contains the text to link. You also can select cells that contain numbers.

   If the worksheet cell is named, you can enter the name by choosing the **I**nsert **N**ame **P**aste command, selecting the name in the Paste **N**ame list box, and choosing OK, or by selecting the name from the name drop-down list at the left end of the formula bar.

6. Press Enter.

7. Position, resize, and format the text as you usually do.

For Related Information

■ "Linking Workbook Cells and Ranges," p. 750

Figure 15.17 shows a worksheet containing information linked to a chart. The unattached text in the chart is selected so that the external reference formula that links the text box in the chart to the worksheet appears in the formula bar.

Creating Picture Charts

Excel charts can use pictures as markers in place of columns, bars, or lines. You can use this feature to make picture charts that grab the eye and then communicate the information. Figure 15.18 shows how you can use pictures in column charts. Figure 15.19 shows a drawing created in Windows Paintbrush used as a replacement for line markers.

To replace columns, bars, or lines, you can use pictures from any Windows graphics or drawing program that can copy graphics to the Clipboard in the Windows Metafile format. Examples of such programs are Windows Paintbrush (the free program that comes with Windows), CorelDRAW!, and Micrografx Designer. You also can use Excel's worksheet drawing tools to create pictures to copy and paste into charts. Chapter 17, "Adding Graphics Elements to Sheets," describes how to draw on the worksheets and chart sheets.

You can store frequently used pictures in a worksheet used as a picture scrapbook. Chapter 17 explains how to paste pictures in worksheets. Copy pictures from the worksheet by selecting them and choosing the **E**dit **C**opy command.

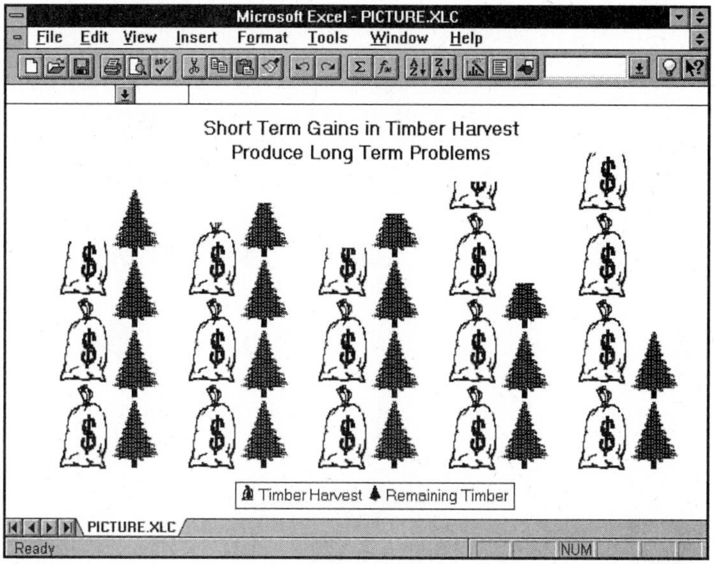

Fig. 15.18
Pictures can replace columns or bars.

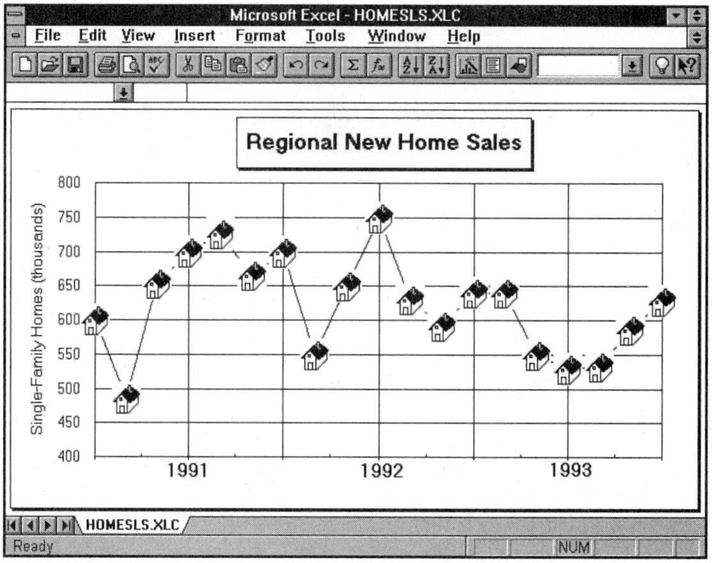

Fig. 15.19
Pictures can replace the markers on lines.

To create a picture chart, perform the following steps:

1. Activate a column, bar, or line chart in Excel.

2. Switch to the Windows graphics program in which you want to draw. Press Ctrl+Esc to see the Task List, or press Alt+Tab to cycle between programs.

3. Draw or open the picture you want to use in the chart. (Some graphics programs come with extensive libraries of graphics, called *clip art*.)

4. Select the picture by using the graphic selection tool for that program, and then choose **E**dit **C**opy. Figure 15.20 shows a picture about to be copied from Windows Paintbrush.

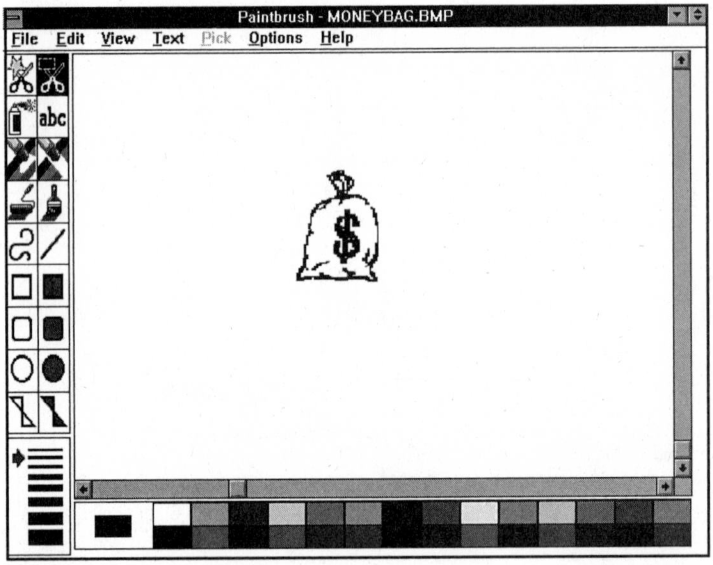

Fig. 15.20
Draw the picture in a Windows graphics program, such as Paintbrush.

5. Switch back to Excel. Press Ctrl+Esc to see the Task List, or press Alt+Tab to cycle between programs.

6. Select the column, bar, or line series (as shown in fig. 15.21) you want to contain the picture. Click the series, or press the arrow keys to select the series.

7. Choose the **E**dit **P**aste command or click the Paste button. The picture replaces the series markers, as shown in figure 15.22. The picture may stretch to fit. You can adjust the picture later.

To stretch, stack, or stack and scale the pictures in column or bar charts, select the series containing the picture, choose the F**o**rmat S**e**lected Series command, or choose the Format Series command from the shortcut menu, and select the Patterns tab. From the dialog box shown in figure 15.23, select one of the picture-formatting options. A stacked picture appears in figure 15.24.

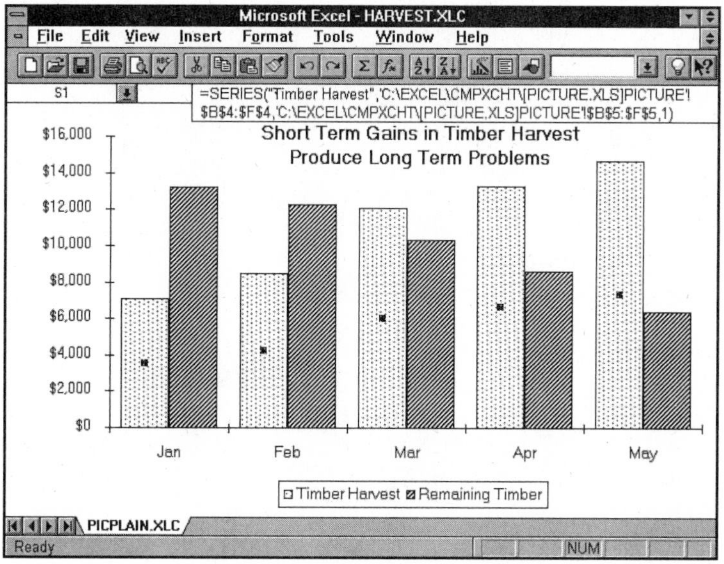

Fig. 15.21
Select the series you want to represent with the picture.

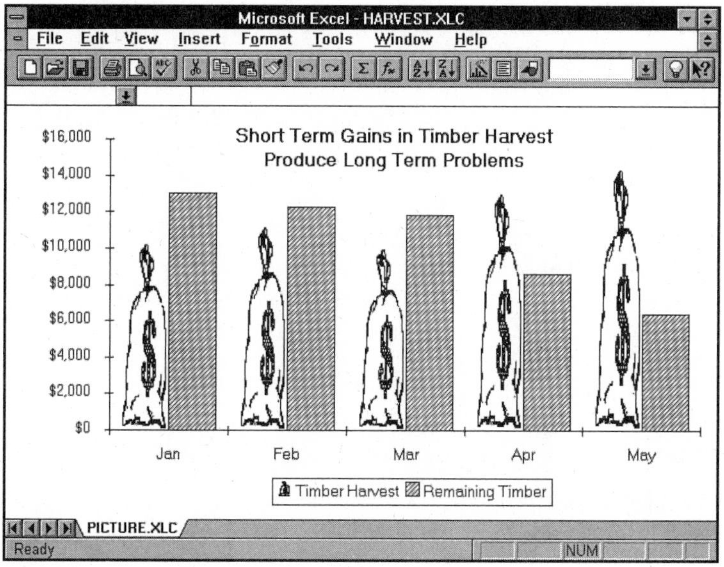

Fig. 15.22
The pasted picture replaces the series markers.

Fig. 15.23
The Patterns tab in the Format Data Series dialog box when a picture is selected.

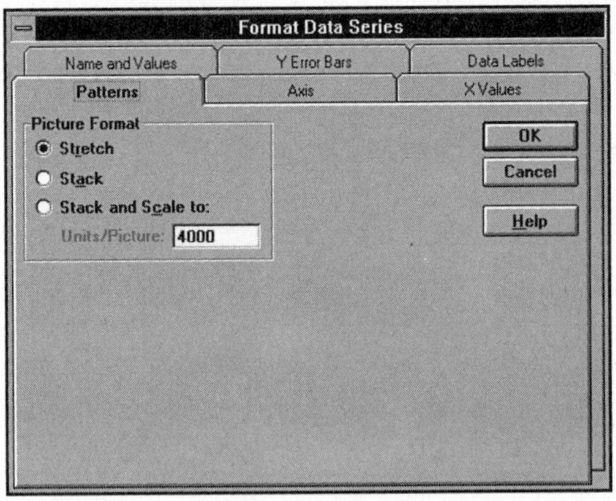

Fig. 15.24
A stacked picture for a different representation.

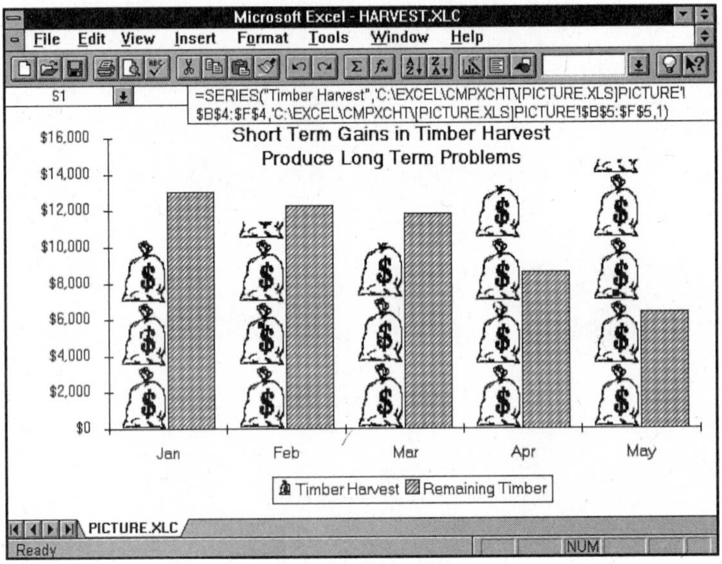

For Related Information

- "Using Graphics and Clip Art from Other Applications," p. 556
- "Creating Graphic Objects," p. 560
- "Embedding Data from Other Applications into Worksheets," p. 1050

The Patterns tab of the Format Data Series dialog box contains the following options:

Option	Effect
Stretch	Stretches the picture to match the value for each data point.
Stack	Stacks the picture in its original proportions to match the value for each data point.
Stack and Scale	Scales the picture's height to equal the value in the Units/Picture text box, and then stacks the picture to match the value for each data point.

To remove a picture from a series, perform the following steps:

1. Select the series.

2. Choose the **E**dit Cle**a**r **F**ormats command.

From Here...

To learn more about other features in Excel that help you create impressive, professional-looking graphics for presentations, look over the following chapters:

- Chapter 17, "Adding Graphics Elements to Sheets." Learn how to insert graphic objects into worksheets and chart sheets, how to create graphic objects using Excel's drawing tools, and how to work with graphic objects.

- Chapter 21, "Creating Slide Show Presentations." Learn how to create slide show presentations, using Excel in combination with Microsoft Powerpoint and using the slide show add-in that comes with Excel.

Part III

Optimizing Excel

16 Managing the Worksheet Display

17 Adding Graphics Elements to Sheets

18 Outlining Worksheets

19 Creating Automatic Subtotals

20 Publishing Worksheets and Charts

21 Creating Slide Show Presentations

22 Taking Advantage of Excel's Add-Ins

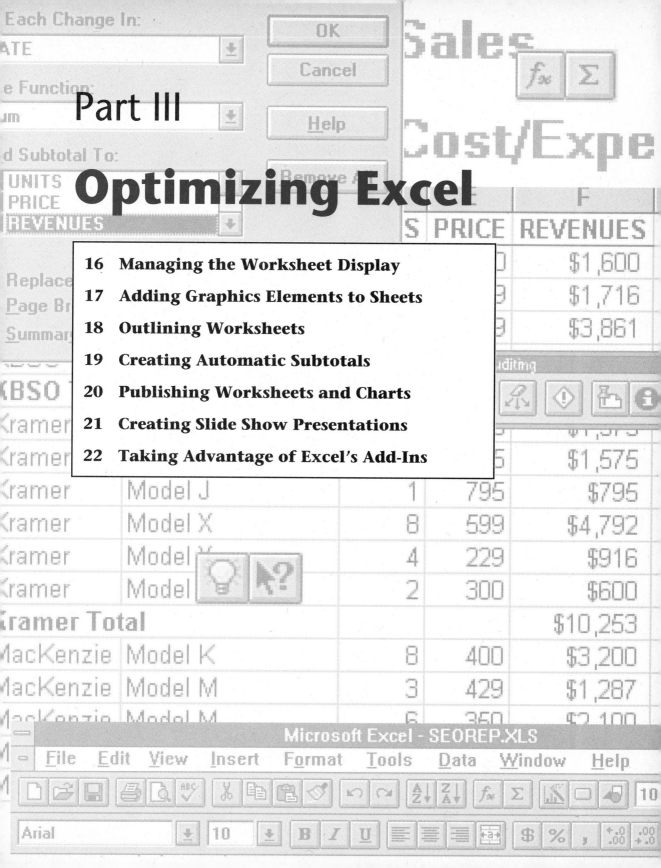

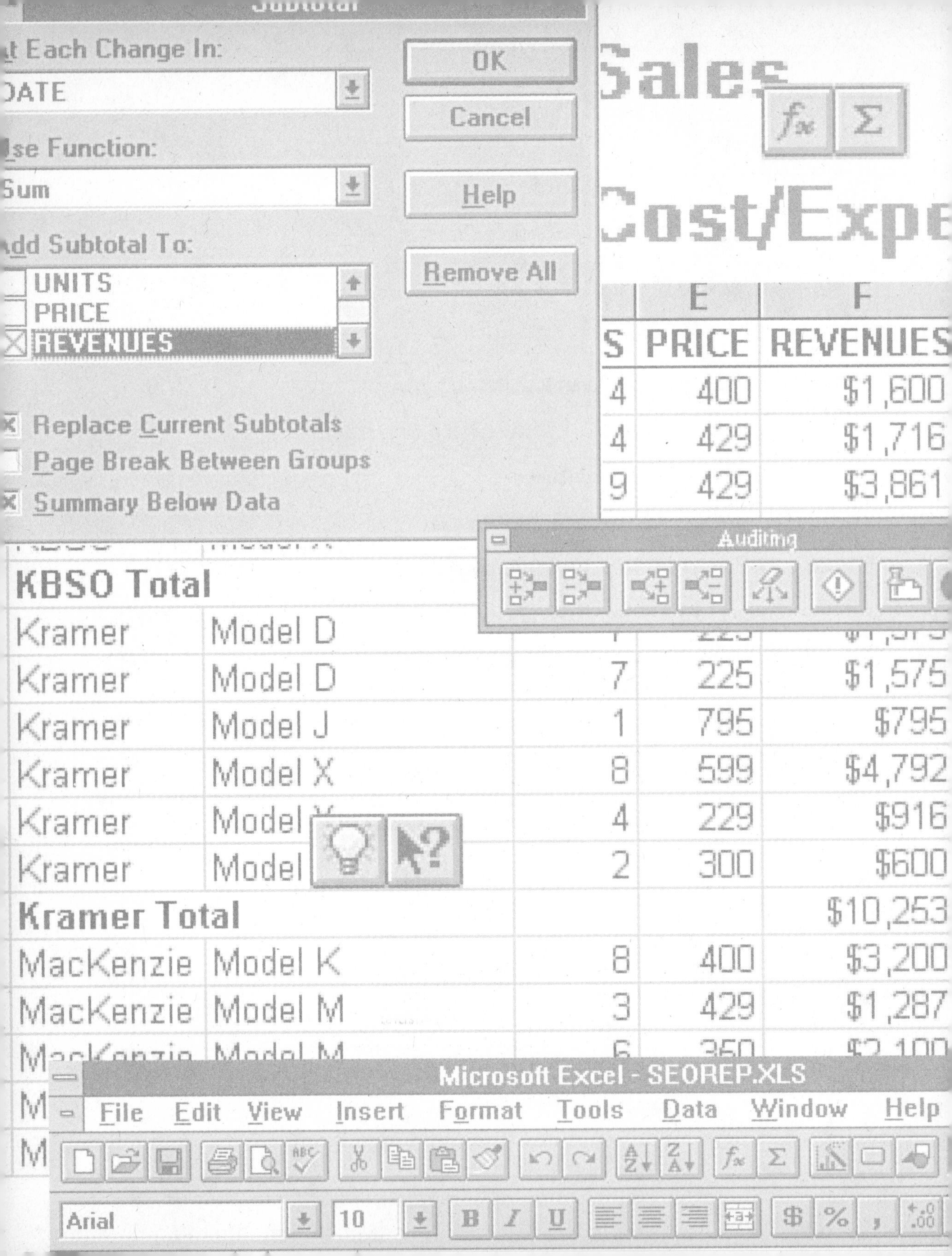

Subtotal
At Each Change In:
DATE
Use Function:
Sum
Add Subtotal To:
UNITS
PRICE
REVENUES
Replace Current Subtotals
Page Break Between Groups
Summary Below Data
OK
Cancel
Help
Remove All
Sales
Cost/Expe
E
F
S
PRICE
REVENUES
4
400
$1,600
4
429
$1,716
9
429
$3,861
Auditing
KBSO Total
Kramer
Model D
Kramer
Model D
7
225
$1,575
Kramer
Model J
1
795
$795
Kramer
Model X
8
599
$4,792
Kramer
Model
4
229
$916
Kramer
Model
2
300
$600
Kramer Total
$10,253
MacKenzie
Model K
8
400
$3,200
MacKenzie
Model M
3
429
$1,287
Microsoft Excel - SEOREP.XLS
File
Edit
View
Insert
Format
Tools
Data
Window
Help
Arial
10

Chapter 16

Managing the Worksheet Display

16

With very little effort, you can change the way Excel displays its sheets. If you like to see a lot of the worksheet, you can reduce the size of a worksheet to see more landscape. If you need to arrange multiple workbooks or worksheets so you can see and move between them easily, you can. You can split a worksheet and freeze parts so that they don't scroll.

One of Excel's most important display features is how the View Manager can save and restore different *views* of a worksheet. This enables you to set up display and print settings and assign those settings to a name. Whenever you want to return to the Data Entry view, for example, you can select Data Entry from the View Manager. If you have certain print settings and ranges for one report that are different from the print settings and ranges for another report, assign each of these combinations of views and settings to a name in the View Manager. When you want to return to that view and settings, just select the appropriate name from the View Manager. Let it handle the job of changing display settings and moving to the correct locations.

In this chapter, you learn how to:

- Manage the screen display
- Display Excel in Full Screen view
- Assign a name to combinations of display and print settings
- View a workbook in multiple panes
- Work with multiple windows

Controlling the Worksheet Display

You can change many characteristics of Excel's worksheet display, giving worksheets and databases a custom appearance. By removing gridlines, row and column headings, and scroll bars, you can create windows that appear like dialog boxes or paper forms.

Displaying the Worksheet Full Screen

EXCEL 5

To work with the maximum amount of worksheet and reduce screen clutter, you need to know about Full Screen. In a normal view, like the view shown in figure 16.1, screen elements such as formula bars and status bars take up on-screen space. As figure 16.2 shows, the Full Screen mode rids Excel of the title bar, the formula bar, and the status bar. Toolbars are reduced to the standard toolbar unless you intentionally add another toolbar.

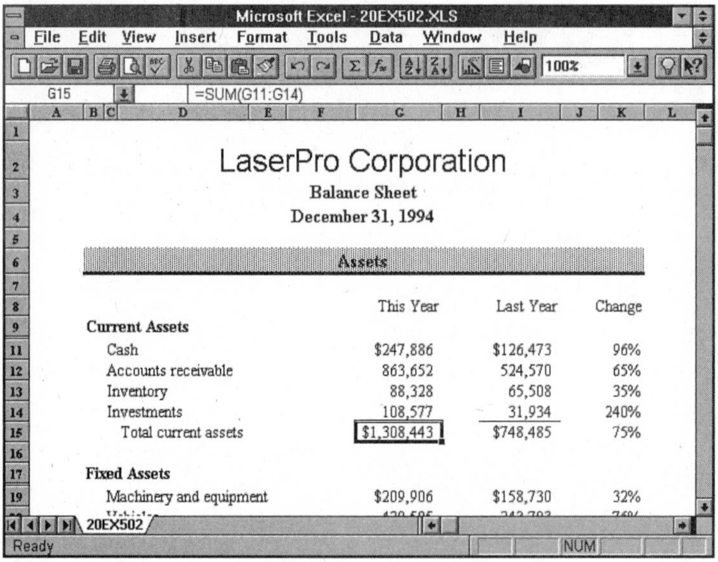

Fig. 16.1 In a normal display, your visible work area is reduced by the title bar, formula bar, status bar, and so on.

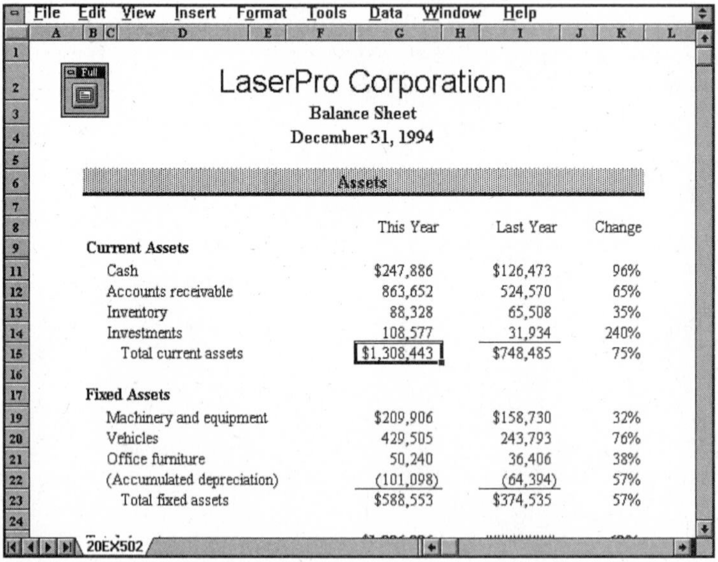

Fig. 16.2 The Full Screen display eliminates some screen elements, letting you see more of your work.

To display the active worksheet in full screen, choose the **V**iew **F**ull **S**creen command.

When Full Screen is on, a check mark appears alongside the command. To turn off Full Screen, select the option again.

While you are in Full Screen mode, you want to make sure that you have in-cell editing turned on. This enables you to type or edit long entries directly into cells and see the typing or editing in the cell. To turn on in-cell editing, choose the **T**ools **O**ptions command. Select the Edit tab and **E**dit Directly In-Cell.

Tip
To hide or display screen elements, choose the **T**ools **O**ptions command and select the View tab.

Hiding Row and Column Headings

You can create special displays in Excel for data-entry forms, on-screen information, and help screens. By removing row and column headings and gridlines, you can make windows appear as if they are not based on a spreadsheet.

When you hide row and column headings, you only hide them in the active worksheet. If you want row and column headings hidden for the workbook, you must change them in each worksheet.

To remove row and column headings on the active worksheet, follow these steps:

1. Choose the **T**ools **O**ptions command.
2. Select the View tab.
3. Deselect the Row & Columns H**e**aders check box.
4. Choose OK.

This action doesn't affect the row and column headings for printing. Use the Sheet tab from the **F**ile Page Set**u**p command to turn off row and column headings for printing.

Turning Scroll Bars On and Off

To make a window appear like a data-entry form and not allow the user to scroll in it, turn off the horizontal or vertical scroll bars. When you hide scroll bars, you are hiding them only in the active workbook.

To hide scroll bars on the active worksheet, follow these steps:

1. Choose the **T**ools **O**ptions command.
2. Select the View tab.
3. Deselect the Horizon**t**al Scroll Bar or **V**ertical Scroll Bar check box.
4. Choose OK.

Turn the scroll bars back on in a sheet by selecting the Horizon**t**al Scroll Bar or **V**ertical Scroll Bar check box.

Hiding the Formula Bar, Status Bar, and Sheet Tabs

When you need more space on-screen for the display, you want to hide the formula bar, status bar, or sheet tabs. Even with sheet tabs hidden, you can change between sheets with the Ctrl+PgUp and Ctrl+PgDn keys, under the control of a Visual Basic program, or with the Excel 5 macro.

When you hide the formula bar and status bar, you hide these bars for all sheets in Excel. When you hide sheet tabs, you hide them only on the workbook that is active when you give the command.

To hide the formula bar, status bar, or sheet tabs, choose the **T**ools **O**ptions command, select the View tab, and then deselect the **F**ormula Bar, **S**tatus Bar, or Sheet Ta**b**s check boxes.

Hiding or Coloring Gridlines

Turning off the on-screen gridlines, gives a better appearance to data-entry forms and on-screen reports. But you may want the gridlines on while you build formulas or place text boxes and objects. To turn the screen gridlines off, choose the **T**ools **O**ptions command, select the View tab, and deselect the **G**ridlines check box. Select the check box to turn them back on.

Figure 16.3 shows several of the options you can take to display or hide screen elements.

To change the color of your gridlines and headings, follow these steps:

1. Choose the **T**ools **O**ptions command.
2. Select the View tab.

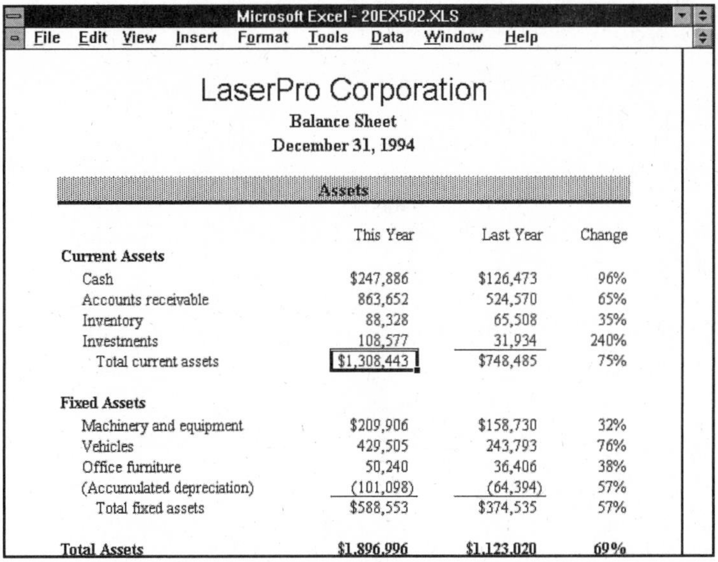
Microsoft Excel - 20EX502.XLS

File Edit View Insert Format Tools Data Window Help

LaserPro Corporation

Balance Sheet

December 31, 1994

Assets

	This Year	Last Year	Change
Current Assets			
Cash	$247,886	$126,473	96%
Accounts receivable	863,652	524,570	65%
Inventory	88,328	65,508	35%
Investments	108,577	31,934	240%
Total current assets	$1,308,443	$748,485	75%
Fixed Assets			
Machinery and equipment	$209,906	$158,730	32%
Vehicles	429,505	243,793	76%
Office furniture	50,240	36,406	38%
(Accumulated depreciation)	(101,098)	(64,394)	57%
Total fixed assets	$588,553	$374,535	57%
Total Assets	$1,896,996	$1,123,020	69%

Fig. 16.3
Turn off scroll bars, gridlines, and other screen elements to make the display appear less like a spreadsheet and more like a graphic or paper display.

3. Make sure that the **G**ridlines check box is on, and select a color from the **C**olor pull-down menu by clicking the down arrow, or pressing Alt+C and Alt+down arrow, and selecting the color.

4. Choose OK.

To color individual cells, borders, or range contents, choose the F**o**rmat C**e**lls command. Select the Font tab to color content, the Border tab to color borders, and the Patterns tab to color background.

Displaying Formulas

You need to display formulas on-screen or in your printout at the following times: when debugging your worksheet (finding and correcting problems), when reviewing an unfamiliar worksheet, or when printing a documentation copy of the worksheet for future reference. To show the formulas in a worksheet, choose the **T**ools **O**ptions command, select the View tab and the Fo**r**mulas check box.

When printing a worksheet to show formulas, choose the **F**ile Page Set**u**p command and select the Sheet tab; then select the Row & Co**l**umn Headings check box.

Troubleshooting

The worksheet doesn't display a formula bar, scroll bars, or other worksheet elements. How can the worksheet be returned to normal?

Excel may be in Full Screen mode or individual elements may have been turned off. To see whether Excel is in Full Screen mode, choose the **V**iew menu and look at the F**u**ll Screen command. If there is a check mark next to it, it is in Full Screen mode. Turn off Full Screen mode by choosing the **V**iew F**u**ll Screen command again. If this isn't the problem, individual screen elements probably were turned off. To control the individual screen elements, choose the **T**ools **O**ptions command and select the View tab. In this tab you can select or deselect whether to show or hide the formula bar, scroll bars, status bar, and so on.

The worksheet displays without row and column headings, but it still prints with row and column headings. Why?

Row and column headings are controlled separately on the screen and on the printer. To turn row and column headings on or off when printing, choose the **F**ile Page Set**u**p command, select the Tab sheet, and then deselect the Row and Co**l**umn Headings check box.

When I hide scroll bars it hides them for the entire workbook, but I need scroll bars on for some sheets and off for others.

To hide scroll bars on some sheets and display them on other sheets in the same workbook, you need to open a second window on the same workbook. Open a second window by activating the workbook and then choosing the **W**indow **N**ew Window command. You can then use the **T**ools **O**ptions command with the View tab to set one window to scroll bars off and the other to scroll bars on. If you save the file with the two windows open, it reopens with the same settings in the two windows.

For Related Information

- "Adding Colors, Patterns, and Borders," p. 350
- "Defining the Page Setup" p. 374
- "Viewing Worksheet Information," p. 779
- "Customizing and Creating Toolbars," p. 1108

Magnifying Worksheet Displays

Large worksheets or worksheets that present many different display and print areas can be difficult to get around in. If you work with large amounts of information, you need to see as much as possible on-screen. Excel's **V**iew **Z**oom command can help you in both cases. It magnifies or reduces the amount you see on-screen so that you can see more or less. This command doesn't change the printed result, but it does enable you to reduce a worksheet so that you can see more of it or magnify one part to make formatting easier. Although **V**iew **Z**oom changes how much of a document appears on-screen, it does not alter the font, column widths, or related features when the document prints.

Note

Magnifying the worksheet by zooming also makes a screen easier to read when it needs to be read from a distance—for example, when it is projected onto a screen with an LCD projection panel, projection system, or large screen monitor. Instead of reformatting the fonts in your worksheet, you can leave everything as it is and magnify the zoom so that everyone can read the content.

To change the zoom with the mouse and the Standard toolbar, pull-down the Zoom pull-down list located to the left of the Helpful tip light bulb. Select the magnification you want. If you want a custom magnification, click in the Zoom box, type the percentage, and press Enter. You can enter a custom zoom from 10 percent to 400 percent.

To change the zoom with the keyboard, choose the **V**iew **Z**oom command, from the Zoom dialog box select one of the five magnifications or select one of the two custom zooms. The Zoom dialog box includes five standard zoom settings and two custom settings. The standard view has 100 percent magnification. The 200-percent magnification setting doubles the size of characters. The 75-percent setting presents about 30 percent more rows and columns than the standard view.

To select one of the standard zooms, select the option button and choose OK or press Enter. The new view appears immediately. Figure 16.1 shows a document with 85 percent magnification.

Tip
On a VGA display, try using the custom settings of 85 percent for working and 150 percent for audience display.

When you need to magnify or reduce a screen by a percentage different than the predefined settings, choose the **V**iew **Z**oom command and **F**it Selection, or choose the **V**iew **Z**oom command and type a percentage in the **C**ustom edit box. If you have a range you want to expand or contract to fit within Excel's boundaries, select the range and choose the **V**iew **Z**oom command and then the **F**it Selection option. The range expands or contracts to fit in the boundaries. If you know approximately how much you want the normal view magnified or condensed, choose the **V**iew **Z**oom **C**ustom command and enter a percentage in the **C**ustom edit box. To return to the normal view, select 100 percent.

Saving Frequently Used View and Print Settings

You probably use certain areas on worksheets again and again. You may need to display these areas differently or print them differently. You may be wasting a lot of time if you don't use Excel's View Manager.

The View Manager has the capability of storing the range, and the display and print settings for worksheet areas you frequently view or print. You can set up the areas with the display or print settings, position the worksheet onscreen as you want to view it, and then assign the view and settings to a name. When you save the workbook, the name and settings are saved so that you can use them later. The next time you want to see that view with the same settings, you can choose its name from the Views dialog box.

To print an area that has an assigned view name, you can select and then print the view. Excel sets the print settings assigned to the name. If you have many views to print, use Excel's Report Manager to select and order the views you want printed. The named view stores the print settings saved with each view, so you don't need to change print settings with each view. You also can print views in sequence and include sequential page numbers to create a large report. The Report Manager is described in Chapter 11, "Printing Worksheets."

Note

The **V**iew command is available only when the View Manager add-in is installed in Excel. (The View Manager add-in comes free with Excel.) You can install the View Manager add-in installation or add it to Excel at any time by using the Add-In Manager. If you did a standard installation, the View Manager is installed. To learn how to add or delete add-ins from Excel by using the Add-In Manager, read Chapter 22, "Taking Advantage of Excel's Add-Ins."

Naming and Saving a View

Worksheets are dynamic. You move between locations and print different areas. By using the View Manager, you can name different views with their display and print settings. To return to the same view or print setup, you only need to select the desired named view.

Saving views or print areas and settings with a name can be helpful in many situations, as in the following list:

- You can store the page setup, print ranges, headers, and footers for printed reports.
- You can look at the data-entry view with display settings that make the entry form appear like a paper form.
- You can set up on-screen views for reports that turn off screen elements that may clutter viewing final results. You may want to show the view—for example, with gridlines, status bar, formula bar, and scroll bars turned off.
- You can set up formula debugging views and large-area overviews.

Figures 16.4 and 16.5 show before and after examples of switching between different views and settings on the same worksheet.

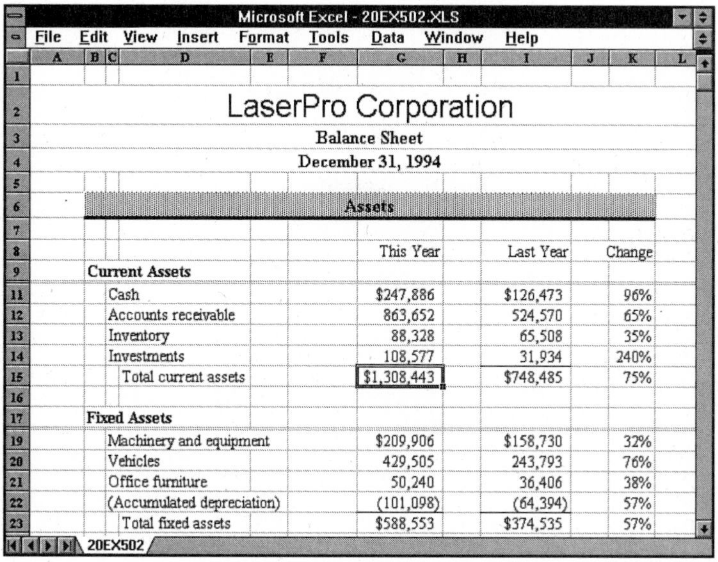

Fig. 16.4
You can assign a view such as this one a name like Working View.

To create a named view, follow these steps:

1. Create the worksheet or macro sheet.
2. Position the window, add panes by splitting the window, size or hide rows and columns, and set display settings as you want them in the view. If you are naming an area you will use for printed reports, specify the print area, print titles, and page setup settings.

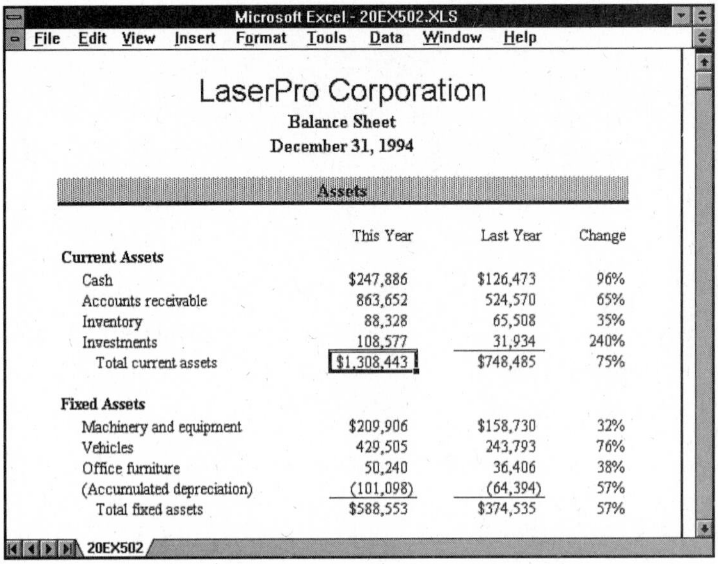

Fig. 16.5
You can assign a view like this one a name like Presentation View.

3. Select the cells or ranges you want selected when the view appears.

4. Choose the **V**iew **V**iew Manager command.

   The View Manager dialog box appears, as shown in figure 16.6.

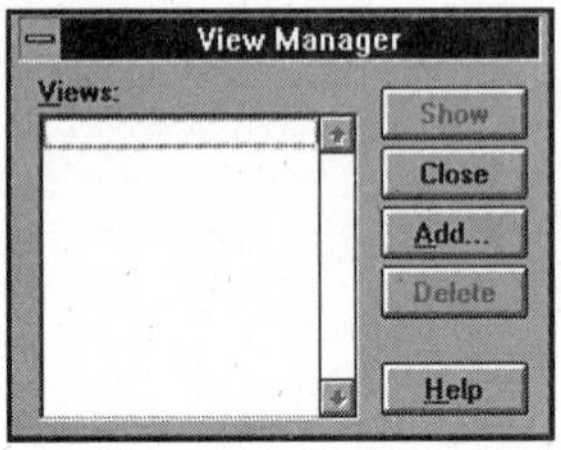

Fig. 16.6
Choose the **V**iew **V**iew Manager command to see or add named views.

5. Choose **A**dd. The Add View dialog box appears (see fig. 16.7).

6. Type the view's name in the **N**ame text box.

7. Select or clear the **P**rint Settings and Hidden **R**ow & Column Settings check boxes.

8. Choose OK or press Enter.

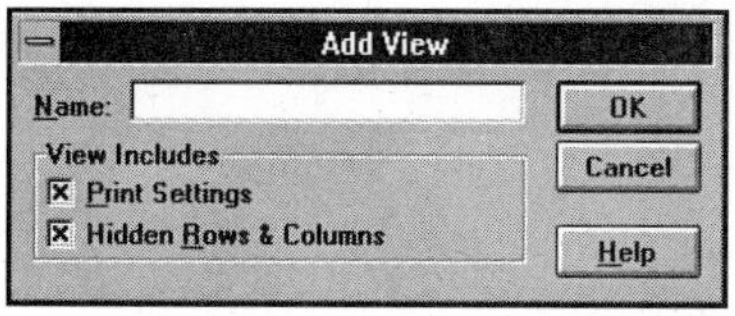

Fig. 16.7
Enter the name you want assigned to the current display and print settings.

To store the print and title ranges as well as the page setup settings, select **P**rint Settings. If you have rows and columns hidden when you record the view and you want these rows or columns hidden when you redisplay or print the view, select Hidden **R**ows & Columns.

To change a view you have already named, display the view. Then modify the window, display settings, or print settings as needed. Repeat the process of choosing the **V**iew **V**iew Manager **A**dd command. Enter the same name you used originally to name the view.

Displaying a Named View

To display a named view, complete the following steps:

1. Choose the **V**iew **V**iew Manager command.
2. Select the **V**iews list, and then select the name of the view you want, as shown in figure 16.8.

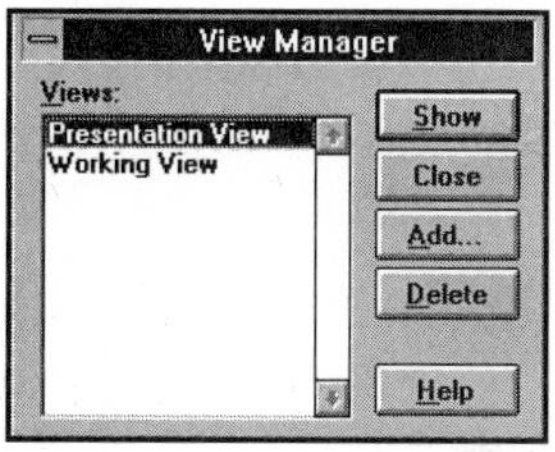

Fig. 16.8
The **V**iews list shows all the names to which you assigned display and print settings.

3. Choose **S**how.

When your named view is displayed, you can work in the worksheet or print by using the **F**ile **P**rint or **F**ile **P**re**v**iew commands.

Deleting a Named View

To delete a view, choose the **V**iew **V**iew Manager command. Select the name from the **V**iews list of the view you want to delete. Choose **D**elete. Select and delete additional names, or choose Close.

For Related Information

- "Defining the Page Setup," p. 374
- "Using Add-In Programs," p. 675

Viewing a Window through Multiple Panes

Dividing an Excel window into sections enables you to see two or four parts of a worksheet. Appropriately, each section of the window is referred to as a *pane.* Multiple panes are particularly useful when you work with databases or large worksheets. The views in each pane are synchronized so that scrolling through one pane scrolls its counterpart in the same direction.

As an illustration, you can display both the list and criteria range for an Advanced Filter at the same time even if they are many rows apart. In figure 16.9 the criteria range and the viewed portion of the list are over 260 rows apart. This technique enables you to enter a criterion in one pane and see the resulting filtered data in the other pane.

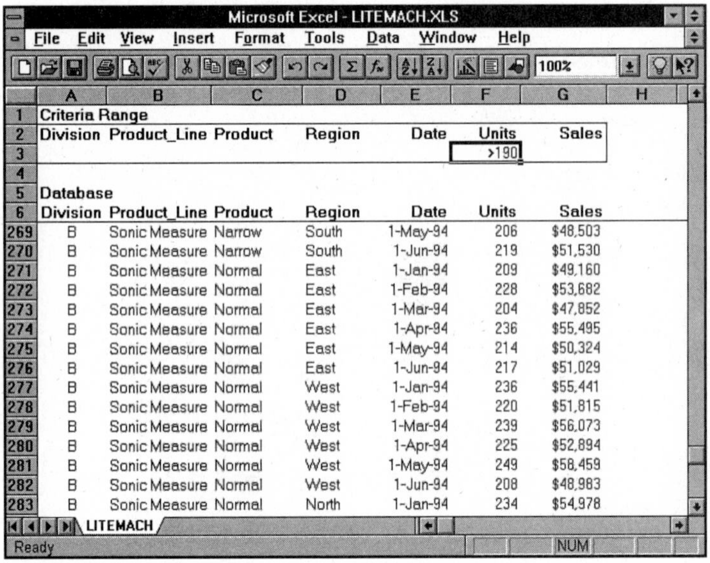

Fig. 16.9
The split windows are used for viewing both the list and criteria range of an Advanced Filter at the same time.

If you need to scroll through a long list or database, you can divide the worksheet into four panes and freeze the panes. You can scroll through the worksheet and still see the worksheet's row and column headings. As another example, you can place the data-entry area of a large worksheet in one pane and the results in another.

Dividing a Window into Multiple Scrolling Panes

Figure 16.9 shows a worksheet divided into two panes. Notice how the row numbers jump from 6 to 269. The upper pane shows the criteria range, the database headings; the lower pane shows the database. With this arrangement, you never lose sight of the column headings as you scroll through a database.

To split a worksheet window, follow these steps:

1. Activate the window you want to split.
2. Select a cell below and to the left of where you want the window split.
3. Choose the **W**indow **S**plit command. The window splits above and to the left of the active cell.

   To split the window horizontally into two sections, move the active cell to column A in the cell below where you want the split, and then choose the **W**indow **S**plit command.

   To split the window vertically into two sections, move the active cell to the first row in the column to the right of where you want the split, and then choose the **W**indow **S**plit command.

To remove a split window with the keyboard, choose the **W**indow Remove **S**plit command. The active cell can be in any location.

Before you create panes with the mouse, notice that a solid black bar appears at the top of the vertical scroll bar and at the right edge of the horizontal scroll bar. This solid black bar is the split-screen bar.

To create panes with the mouse, follow these steps:

1. Drag the solid black bars down the vertical scroll bar or across the horizontal scroll bar. As you drag, a gray pane divider shows where the window splits.
2. Position the gray pane divider where you want the window to split, and release the mouse button.

Caution

Your row or column headings may appear to have disappeared if you do not drag a split bar completely to the end of its scroll bar. If the split bar goes through the middle of either the row or column headings, the headings seem to disappear.

To resize panes, drag the split line to a new location. To remove the split, drag the solid black bar past the arrow on the scroll bar, and release the mouse button.

Tip

If you want to split a window into panes quickly, double-click one of the solid black bars. To remove one of the splits, double-click the solid black bar creating the split.

Freezing Headings into Position

You can freeze the panes in position so that you cannot change them accidentally. To freeze panes you already have positioned, choose the **W**indow **F**reeze Panes command.

When panes are frozen, the gray split bar becomes a thin solid line and you cannot scroll into the frozen area. The top or left pane cannot scroll. You can move the active cell into the frozen area by pressing the arrow keys or clicking a cell. To *thaw* the frozen panes, choose the **W**indow Un**f**reeze Panes command.

Note

If you have not split a worksheet into panes, you can split the window and freeze the panes with a single command. Select a cell positioned below and to the right of where you want the panes to split and freeze, and choose the **W**indow **F**reeze Panes command. Choose the **W**indow Un**f**reeze Panes command to remove the panes.

For Related Information

■ "Manipulating Windows," p. 59

Activating Different Panes

Using the keyboard, you can move the active cell clockwise among panes by pressing F6; press Shift+F6 to move counterclockwise among the panes. The active cell moves to the same cell it occupied the last time it was in the pane. With the mouse, you can shift among panes by clicking in the pane you want to activate. Note that jumping between panes often causes windows to reposition. You cannot move between panes like this if the panes are frozen.

Working with Multiple Windows

Excel enables you to have multiple windows on-screen. You can use this to display more than one workbook at a time or to arrange the worksheets contained in one workbook. Working with multiple documents is a great convenience and time-saver when you want to link worksheets, view worksheets and graphs simultaneously, or see multiple documents at the same time.

Opening Additional Documents

When you need to work with the contents of other workbooks or data files, open additional files with the **F**ile **O**pen command, just as you opened the first document. These new workbooks appear in separate windows.

Switching to a Window

If you have multiple workbooks or windows on-screen, you can switch to the one you want to work on. Using the mouse, click anywhere in the window you want to work on. This window appears on top. If you cannot see the window, move the other windows out of the way by dragging their title bars.

With the keyboard, press Ctrl+F6 until the window you want is active; or you can choose the **W**indow command and select the window's name from the menu.

Displaying Worksheets in Separate Windows

When a workbook opens, all its sheets appear in the same window. When you select a sheet's tab, that sheet becomes active in the workbook's window. This leaves you able to only see one sheet at a time in a workbook.

To display worksheets from the same workbook in separate windows, activate the workbook containing the sheets. Choose the **W**indow **N**ew Window command one time for each additional worksheet you want to see. This opens a new window onto the workbook each time you choose the command.

Note

If you save a workbook while it is open in multiple windows, the next time you open the workbook with the **F**ile **O**pen command, multiple windows appear onto the same workbook. This is a time-saver when you want to keep sheets in separate windows, but it's a shock if you don't know what to expect.

After opening multiple windows onto the same workbook, you can display a different worksheet in each window. To do this, activate a workbook's window and then activate within it the worksheet you want in that window. To activate a worksheet in the window, click the worksheet's tab or press Ctrl+PgUp or Ctrl+PgDn. Activate the next window and use the same procedure to display a different worksheet in it.

> **Note**
>
> With many windows open on worksheets, a lot of space is taken by all the sheet tabs that are visible. After you display the worksheets that you need, you may want to hide the sheet tabs by choosing the **T**ools **O**ptions command, selecting the View tab, and then deselecting Sheet Ta**b**s.

Arranging Multiple Windows

You can arrange windows manually by moving and sizing them as explained in Chapter 2, "Getting Around in Excel and Windows." If you have many windows to reorganize, you can take advantage of some automated assistance. Choose the **W**indow **A**rrange command, and from the Arrange Windows dialog box, select how you want the windows arranged. If you want to only arrange windows that contain sheets from the active workbook, choose the **W**indows of Active Workbook option. The windows are resized and rearranged. Figure 16.10 shows three windows before using the **W**indow **A**rrange command and the Arrange Windows dialog box, and figure 16.11 shows the same three windows after they are arranged, using the settings shown in figure 16.10.

Fig. 16.10
Manually arranged windows can become disorganized.

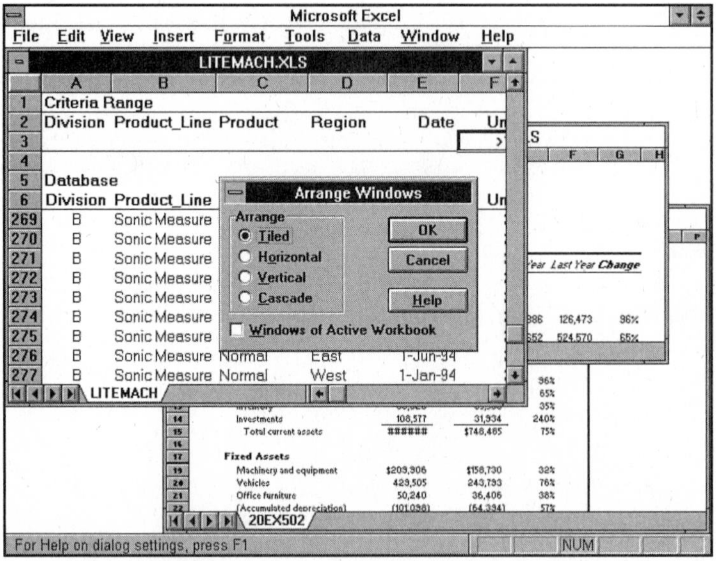

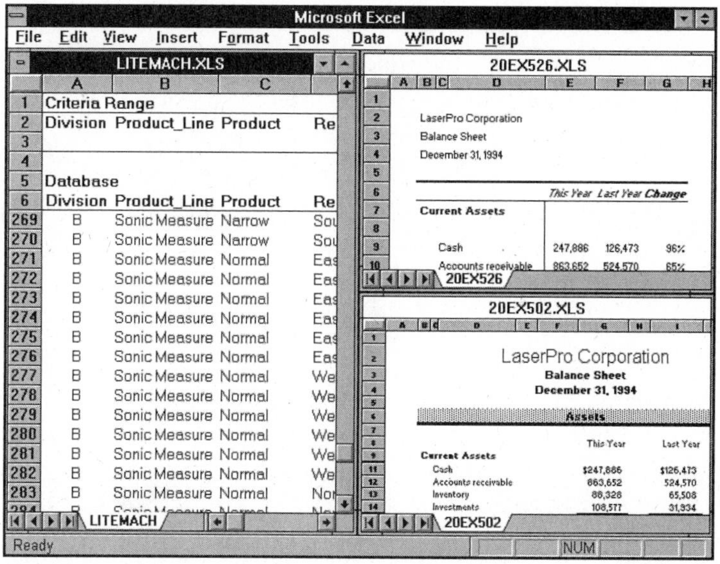

Fig. 16.11
Arranging Windows with the Arrange Windows dialog box can keep them organized.

Note

The **W**indow **A**rrange command doesn't put the worksheets in a workbook into their own separate windows. If you want to view a worksheet in its own window, open a new window on the workbook and activate that worksheet in the window.

The different Arrange Windows options include the following:

Option	Function
Tiled	Arranges an even number of windows to divide the screen so that the active window becomes the top-left window. Arranges an odd number of windows so that the active window appears vertically along the left edge.
H**o**rizontal	Arranges all the windows in horizontal strips. The active window moves to the top.
Vertical	Arranges all the windows in vertical strips. The active window moves to the far left.
Cascade	Stacks the windows from the top of the screen down so that their title bars are visible.
Windows of Active Workbook	Places all windows of the active workbook in the fore-ground; all others in the background.

Hiding and Unhiding Windows and Sheets

You do not need to keep all your windows on-screen at one time. Or keep all your sheets displayed in a workbook. You can hide windows from view so that the screen appears more organized and less confusing. If only one workbook is open on a window, when you hide the window, the entire workbook is hidden. The sheets in a hidden window remain available to other documents with which it is linked.

To hide a window, follow these steps:

1. Activate the window.
2. Choose the **W**indow **H**ide command.

> **Note**
>
> To move a worksheet out of the way but to keep it accessible, minimize the worksheet to an icon. To minimize a worksheet, click the worksheet's minimize icon (a double-headed arrow) at the top-right corner of the worksheet. To restore the worksheet icon into a window, double-click the icon.

To reveal hidden windows, follow these steps:

1. Choose the **W**indow **U**nhide command. The Unhide dialog box appears.
2. From the **U**nhide Workbook list box, select the title of the hidden window you want to reveal.
3. Choose OK.

   The hidden windows reappear in their former position and size.

If you attempt to unhide a window that is protected, you are asked for a password. The following section explains how to hide a window with a password.

If all windows are hidden, the **W**indow menu is not available, so the **U**nhide command appears under the **F**ile menu.

> **Note**
>
> To hide a worksheet or macro so that it cannot be unhidden, you need to create an add-in document with a write-reservation password.

To hide a sheet within a workbook, follow these steps:

1. Activate the sheet within the workbook. You cannot hide the only visible sheet in a workbook.

2. Choose the F**o**rmat S**h**eet command.

3. Select **H**ide from the submenu.

To unhide a sheet within a workbook, follow these steps:

1. Activate the workbook containing the sheet.

2. Choose the F**o**rmat S**h**eet command to display the Unhide dialog box.

3. Select the sheet you want to display from the **U**nhide Sheet list.

4. Choose OK.

Locking Windows in Position

After your windows are sized and in the proper positions, you can make sure that they stay there. Locking windows in position is a good idea, particularly if the worksheets are used by inexperienced operators or displayed by macros.

To keep a window from moving or changing size, follow these steps:

1. Position and size the window as you want it.

2. Choose the **T**ools **P**rotection Protect **W**orkbook command.

3. Select the **W**indows check box.

4. Enter a password if you do not want others to remove protection. (A password can be any combination of letters and numbers; letters are case-sensitive. Make sure that you don't forget your password—you cannot unprotect your document if you do.)

5. Choose OK. If you entered a password, the Confirm Password dialog box prompts you to retype it.

You can scroll through locked windows, but you cannot resize or move them (notice that the sizing border disappears from a protected window). You cannot rearrange, insert, or delete sheets in a workbook if the **S**tructure check box is selected during workbook protection.

To unlock a workbook, activate its window and choose the **T**ools **P**rotection Unprotect **W**orkbook command. If a password locks the window's position, you are asked to enter the password.

Tip
Hold the Shift key as you choose the **F**ile command to display **C**lose All.

For Related Information

- "Manipulating Windows," p. 58
- "Password-Protecting Your Workbooks," p. 279
- "Saving a Workspace File," p. 280

Saving and Closing Multiple Windows

When you save a workbook to disk, all the open windows on this workbook, with the current sizes and shapes, are saved. You can set up multiple windows on a workbook in the arrangement that you use most frequently, and then save the workbook to disk. When you open the workbook from disk, all the windows are arranged and sized as you left them.

To save a workbook with only one window, make sure that you close the extra windows. To close unwanted windows, first activate the window that you want to close. Then double-click in the document Control menu to the left of the document title. To close the entire file and the multiple windows that may be looking at it, choose the **F**ile **C**lose command.

From Here...

For information relating directly to displaying workbooks and customizing Excel to the way you work, you may want to review the following chapters of this book:

- Chapter 2, "Getting Around in Excel and Windows." Learn how to maximize, minimize, or restore windows. You also learn how to display, hide, or reshape toolbars.
- Chapter 11, "Printing Worksheets." Learn how to control borders, row and column headings, headers and footers, and other aspects of printing.
- Chapter 40, "Customizing the Excel Screen." Learn how to set screen colors, mouse controls, and other features.
- Chapter 41, "Creating Custom Toolbars and Menus." In this chapter, you learn to create toolbars that contain buttons with the commands you use most frequently.
- Chapter 42, "Creating Templates and Controlling Excel's Startup." This chapter describes how to create partially completed worksheets that contain settings, format, and content. You can use these *templates* over and over.

Chapter 17

Adding Graphics Elements to Sheets

Excel gives you the power to communicate with emphasis and polish. Your Excel worksheets can contain more than just numbers; the layouts can include any of the following elements that add information and value to your reports:

- Drawings composed of lines, arrows, ellipses, circles, rectangles, and squares
- Text boxes containing titles or paragraphs of word-wrapped text; rotated text
- Embedded charts and text from other Windows applications
- Pictures of charts or worksheet ranges that are updated when you update the charts or ranges
- Professional graphics, illustrations, or logos from Windows drawing programs, clip art, or scanned artwork
- Macros linked to graphic objects so that selecting an object runs a macro

In this chapter, you learn how to:

- Insert pictures and clip art into sheets
- Create graphic objects
- Combine data and charts
- Edit graphic objects
- Format graphic objects

Understanding Uses of Graphics Elements

Excel's information and analysis systems can perform more functions—in less time and at a fraction of the cost—than many high-end executive or management information systems. Excel's analytical and charting power, combined with worksheet graphics and macros, gives you professional-quality publishing and design capabilities.

Figures 17.1, 17.2, and 17.3 show how you can enhance information displays, program controls, and printed reports by using the tools described in this chapter and in the charting sections.

Figure 17.1 shows an Excel worksheet that is the front-end to a management information system. This system enables users to retrieve business information from global divisions. Two graphics have been inserted from other Windows applications: the globe and the world map. Text boxes create the title at the top and the instructions at the bottom.

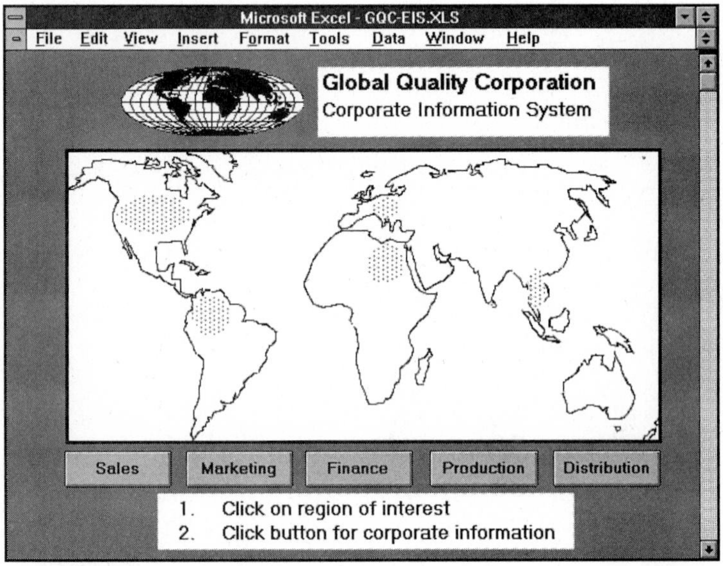

Fig. 17.1
Link graphics and inserted pictures to macros to create an executive information system front-end.

Figure 17.2 shows the use of charts, linked cell pictures, text boxes, ellipses, and arrows. Shading sets off screen areas. The chart titles and analysis box are created with text boxes. The arrow and ellipse are drawn with tools from the Drawing toolbar. The two charts are embedded charts. The small bar chart below the line chart was drawn on top of the larger chart. This chart was created by using a picture of cells from the stock data worksheet and embedding and expanding the cell picture on the worksheet.

Figure 17.3 shows an accounts receivable database. The worksheet is set up so that all the aging analysis is in one screen. Light shading helps differentiate parts of the screen. A database below the screen contains accounts receivable information.

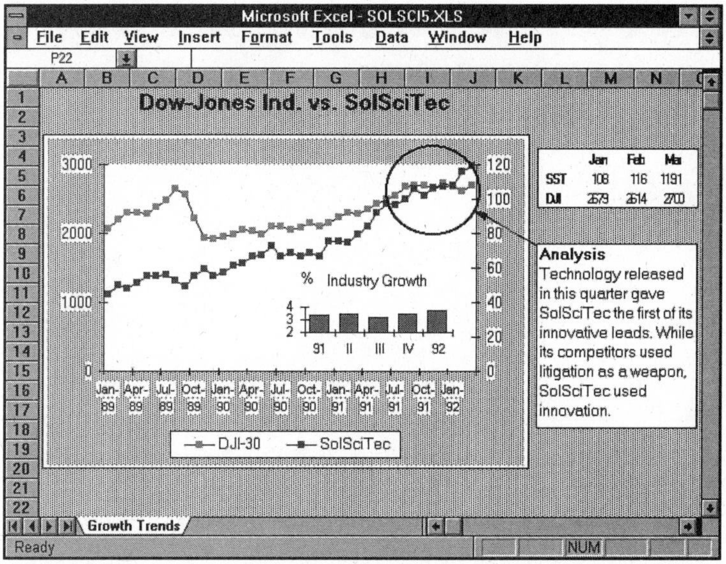

Fig. 17.2
Combine embedded and overlapped charts and cell pictures for a concise display of a large amount of information.

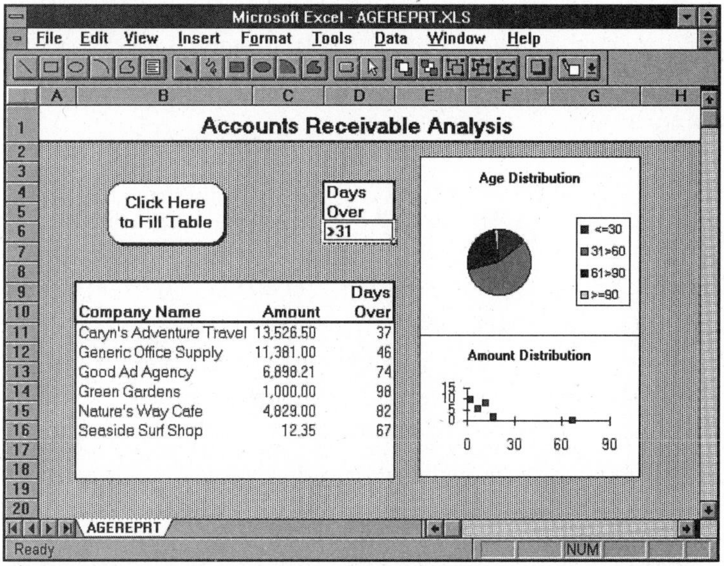

Fig. 17.3
Get the big picture quickly by combining different views of the same information.

The two charts are linked to the same data to display aged receivables in two different ways.

Using Graphics and Clip Art from Other Applications

In Excel, you can illustrate your ideas with pictures. Pictures you insert into your Excel worksheets come from many sources. Some come from stand-alone graphics programs, which you can use to create illustrations ranging from the simple to the sophisticated. Some—including photographs—come from scanners that digitize artwork for use in a computer. Some pictures come from clip art packages that provide you with ready-to-use artwork.

All the pictures you insert come from a source outside of Excel (and can be used in many programs besides Excel). That makes them different from the graphic objects you create using tools on Excel's Drawing toolbar; using the Drawing toolbar, you create a graphic that exists only as a part of your Excel worksheet.

Stand-alone graphics programs often are more powerful than the tools on the Drawing toolbar. Therefore, Excel gives you the flexibility to include a range of graphics in your documents—from simple drawings you create yourself without leaving Excel, to sophisticated graphics you (or someone else) create by using a powerful stand-alone graphics program.

What Is Clip Art?

Clip art comes on a disk and includes graphics and pictures that you use to illustrate documents you create using programs like Excel. Clip art collections are usually sold by category—business graphics, medical graphics, educational graphics, and so on. Prices, style, and file format vary. To locate clip art, look in the ads in the back of computer magazines, and particularly desktop publishing magazines. You can call clip art manufacturers for samples of their work before spending the money to buy a package. Before you buy, be sure the collection includes the type of illustrations you want, in the style you need, and in a format Excel can use.

Some programs come with free clip art collections. Word for Windows, for example, includes in the CLIPART subdirectory images that you can use with Excel. CorelDRAW!, a graphics program, includes a vast library of clip art on CD-ROM.

Understanding Graphic File Formats

Excel is compatible with many of the most frequently used graphics programs. You can import pictures created by any of these programs, or that are in any of these formats:

Program Format	File Extension
PC Paintbrush	PCX
Tagged Image File Format	TIF (scanned images)
Windows Metafile	WMF
Encapsulated PostScript	EPS
Windows Paintbrush	BMP
Windows Bitmaps	BMP
Computer Graphics Metafile	CGM
HP Graphic Language	HGL
DrawPerfect	WPG
Micrografx Designer	DRW
Macintosh Picture	PCT

Don't despair if your favorite graphics program isn't listed. Many programs easily export a graphic (or even part of a graphic) from its native format to a commonly used format. If your graphics program isn't listed, see if it can save a graphic in one of the formats listed above so you can use it in Excel.

If you attempt to insert a picture and Excel warns you that the appropriate graphics filter is not available, rerun the Excel installation program. Choose the Custom installation, and only install the graphics filter you need. You do not need to reinstall all of Excel.

Inserting Graphics

You can insert a picture into your document without ever opening the program you used to create the picture. As when opening or saving an Excel file, you must locate the picture or clip art file to insert it.

After a picture is inserted, you can move it, resize it, reshape it, or change its border or fill color or pattern.

To insert a picture, follow these steps:

1. Select the cell where you want the top left of the picture to appear. If no cell is selected, the picture appears in the top left cell.

2. Choose the **I**nsert **P**icture command. The Picture dialog box appears (see fig. 17.4).

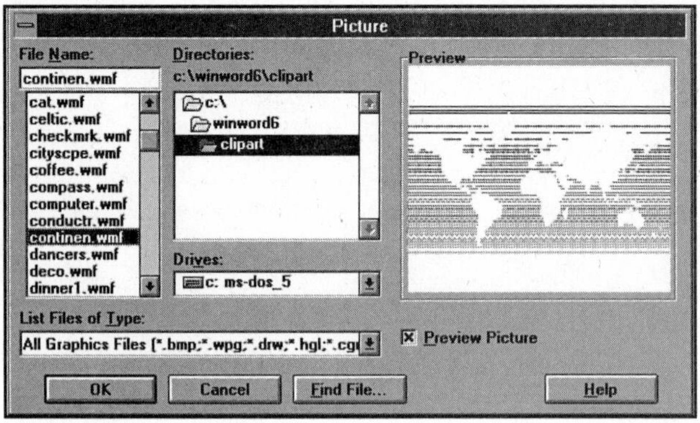

Fig. 17.4
You can insert many types of picture files from the Picture dialog box.

3. By default, all graphics file types are listed. If you want to restrict the type of files listed, select the type of file you are looking for in the List Files of **T**ype list box.

4. Locate your file. If the drive containing your picture file is different from the current drive, select the drive containing your file from the Dri**v**es list. From the **D**irectories list, select the directory containing your picture file.

5. From the File **N**ame list, select the picture file you want to insert.

6. If you want to see the picture before you insert it, select the **P**review Picture option. A miniature version of your picture appears in the Preview box.

7. If you want help finding your file, choose **F**ind File.

8. Choose OK.

Copying Graphics onto a Sheet

If you aspire to produce worksheets that any graphic artist would be proud of, you aren't limited to the drawing tools in the Drawing toolbar. You can create drawings in almost any Windows graphics program, copy the drawings, and then paste them into your worksheet where you can resize and move them. You also can add pictures, photos, or hand drawings to your worksheet by scanning them with a digital scanner, copying the image, and pasting the image into the worksheet. Excel accepts any graphic that can be copied into the Clipboard in the Windows Metafile or bit-map format.

Note

Many Windows applications come with *applets,* small window applications designed to enhance a major application. These applications are available by choosing **I**nsert **O**bject and selecting the applet you want to run. Chapters 25, "Linking, Embedding, and Consolidating Worksheets," and 38, "Using Excel with Windows Applications," describe some applets and their use with Excel.

Putting graphics in your worksheets can do more than just make the worksheets more attractive. Now you can put your company logo on worksheets; add architectural or engineering symbols to specifications, plans, or bids; add schematics or drawings that explain proposals; or create graphic buttons that run macros when clicked.

Note

If you frequently use the same graphics or pictures, you can save time by collecting them in an Excel worksheet. You can, for example, draw graphics and pictures with programs like Windows Paintbrush or CorelDRAW!, and then copy the graphics and paste them into a worksheet that acts as a scrapbook.

Storing your graphics and pictures in a worksheet used as a scrapbook makes it easy to find the graphic you want, copy it, and paste it into the worksheet on which you are working. There's no need to start the Windows graphics program. Figure 17.5 shows part of an Excel worksheet serving as a scrapbook. You can store images in reduced size in a worksheet, and resize the images after you paste them into the worksheet.

To copy graphics from another Windows program for use in Excel worksheets or macro sheets, follow these steps:

1. Activate the drawing program and select the graphic you want to copy.
2. Choose the **E**dit **C**opy command or the appropriate program procedure to copy the selected graphic to the Clipboard.
3. Activate Excel and select the cell or object where you want the graphic to appear.
4. Choose the **E**dit **P**aste command.

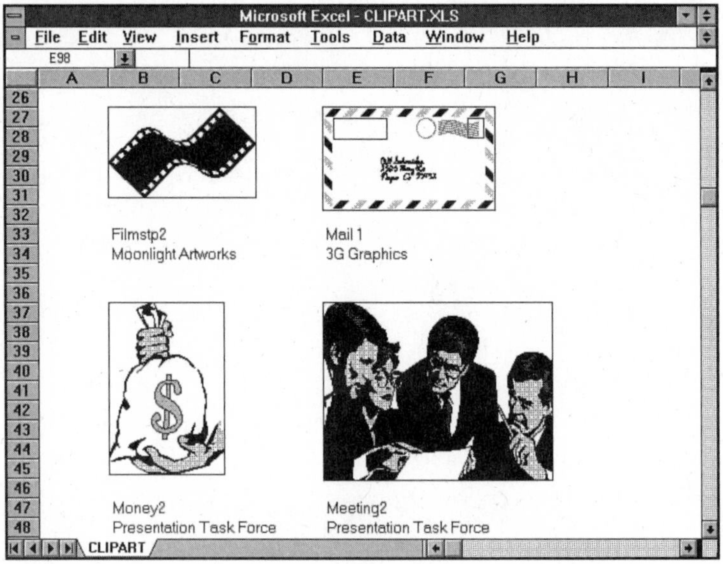

Fig. 17.5
Use a worksheet as a scrapbook to store frequently used graphics or symbols.

For Related Information

- "Linking Pictures of Worksheet Cells," p. 744
- "Linking Workbook Cells and Ranges," p. 750
- "Embedding Data from Other Applications into Worksheets, p. 1050

After the graphic is on the Excel worksheet or macro sheet, you can treat it like any other graphic object. You can link a macro to it, resize or move it, or change its borders.

To learn more about copying and pasting graphical objects between Windows applications, refer to Chapter 38, "Using Excel with Windows Applications." Chapter 38 also discusses how to use the **E**dit Paste **S**pecial command to paste graphics in different formats.

Creating Graphic Objects

Excel worksheets can contain graphic objects that appear on-screen and print on the worksheet printout. These objects reside in layers that cover the worksheet.

> **Note**
>
> Nearly all work with worksheet graphics requires a mouse. Few features are available for graphic objects without the mouse. One of the few tasks you can perform with a keyboard is to take a picture of a worksheet range or chart and paste it onto the worksheet.

Using the Drawing Tools

The Excel Drawing toolbar comes with a collection of drawing tools to help you produce an attractive worksheet. The toolbar enables you to click a button, and then immediately draw, shade, or outline on the worksheet. The section "Using the Toolbars" in Chapter 2, "Getting Around in Excel and Windows," describes how to use toolbars. You can customize toolbars as described in Chapter 41, "Creating Custom Toolbars and Menus."

Note

You can paste graphic objects (for example, drawings of cars or trains) into charts, creating a picture chart in which objects replace column, bar, or line markers. This Excel feature is covered in detail in Chapter 15, "Building Complex Charts."

Tip
Some drawing tools perform two functions. If you Shift+click a button, you will see the alternate function for the button in the status bar at the bottom of the window.

Note

You can draw on a chart just as you draw on a worksheet. To draw on a chart, the chart must be in a window or on its own sheet. If the chart is embedded in a worksheet, double-click it to put it in a window. Use drawing buttons from the Drawing toolbar just as you would use them on a worksheet.

The Drawing toolbar (see fig. 17.6) contains many drawing tools (see table 17.1). Some tools on other toolbars, such as font formatting and alignment tools, also are helpful. If you need a specialized collection of drawing tools, see Chapter 41, "Creating Custom Toolbars and Menus," to learn how to create a custom toolbar.

Fig. 17.6
Buttons on the Drawing toolbar give you instant access to tools for drawing.

If the Drawing toolbar is not displayed, choose the **V**iew **T**oolbars command, select Drawing, and choose OK. Or click the Drawing button on the Standard toolbar. If a toolbar is displayed, click with the right mouse button on the toolbar, and select the toolbar you want from the shortcut menu.

Table 17.1 describes each of the tools available on the Drawing toolbar.

Table 17.1 Drawing Tools

Button	Name	Function
	Line tool	Draws a straight line.
	Rectangle tool	Draws a rectangle or square.
	Ellipse tool	Draws an ellipse or circle.
	Arc tool	Draws an arc.
	Freeform tool	Draws a polygon or freeform shape.
	Text Box tool	Draws boxes for word-wrapped text.
	Arrow tool	Draws an arrow.
	Freehand tool	Draws smooth curves.
	Filled Rectangle tool	Draws a filled rectangle or square.
	Filled Ellipse tool	Draws a filled ellipse or circle.
	Filled Arc tool	Draws a filled arc.
	Filled Freeform tool	Draws a polygon or freeform shape that closes end points.
	Create Button tool	Creates a button to which you can assign a macro.
	Select tool	Selects groups of objects by dragging a rectangular marquee around them.
	Bring to Front tool	Brings selected object above other objects.
	Send to Back tool	Sends selected object behind other objects.
	Group tool	Groups together selected objects.

Button	Name	Function
	Ungroup tool	Separates the selected group into individual objects.
	Reshape tool	Reshapes a freehand line by dragging at points along the line.
	Drop Shadow tool	Draws a shadow behind text boxes and most shapes.
	Pattern tool	Adds pattern and color to filled shapes.

To draw with the drawing tools, you click the desired button and drag the mouse pointer across the worksheet to create the object. After you create the object, the easiest way to change borders and colors is to click the object with the right mouse button to display a shortcut menu. Detailed directions for using the individual tools are given later in this section.

Using Drawing Shortcut Menus

Shortcut menus help save time when you are drawing and formatting in Excel. To display a menu applicable to any changeable item—the worksheet background, an object you are drawing, or even the toolbar—use the right mouse button to click the item. A shortcut menu, like the one in figure 17.7, appears under the pointer. Then click the command you want.

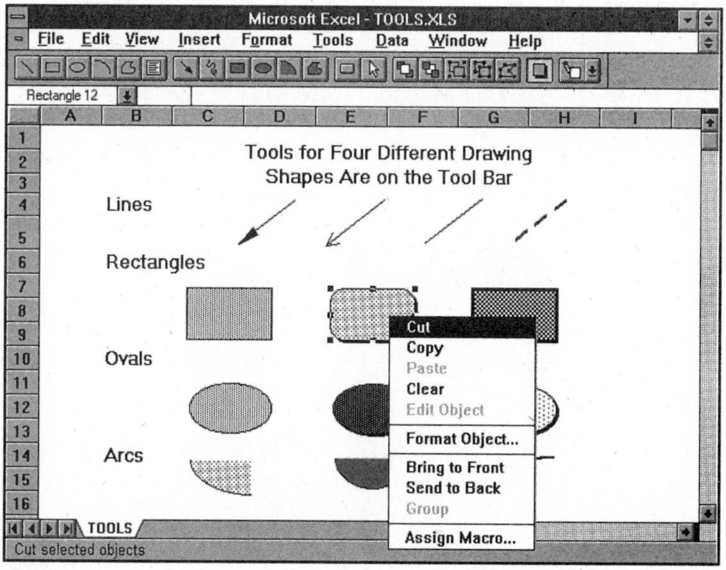

Fig. 17.7
Click any drawing object with the right mouse button to display a shortcut menu.

Drawing Lines, Ellipses, Rectangles, and Arcs

With the drawing tools available in the toolbar, you can add enhancements including boxes, ellipses, and arcs to your worksheet.

Lines, ellipses, rectangles, and arcs are basic drawing elements in Excel. After formatting your worksheets with patterns and line widths, you can layer and combine these simple shapes to create more complex drawings. If the Excel drawing tools don't produce the result you need, you can insert or paste in drawings created with Windows programs, such as Windows Paintbrush, CorelDRAW!, or Micrografx Designer.

The process of pasting drawings from other applications into Excel is explained in Chapter 38, "Using Excel with Windows Applications," and earlier in this chapter under the heading, "Using Graphics and Clip Art from Other Applications."

To draw a line, ellipse, rectangle, or arc, follow these steps:

1. Select the drawing tool you want by clicking its button. The mouse pointer symbol is replaced with a cross hair symbol.

2. Move the cross hair to where you want to start the drawing.

3. Follow these procedures if you want to constrain drawing to certain positions:

   Hold down the Shift key to keep lines vertical, horizontal, or at 45 degrees; ellipses and arcs circular; and rectangles square.

   Or hold down the Alt key to align the corner of the object with cell gridlines.

4. Drag the cross hair until the object has the size and orientation you want.

5. Release the mouse button to complete the object.

Tip
To draw an arrow, click the Arrow button in the Drawing toolbar, drag from where you want the foot of the arrow to the tip, and release.

Figure 17.8 shows a few of the shapes, patterns, borders, and shadows you can draw with Excel tools.

The object is selected when you finish. A selected object displays black handles at the edges and corners of an invisible rectangular frame enclosing the object. Objects must be selected before you can format or change them (if your object becomes deselected, you can select it again by clicking it).

You can use commands and tools explained in the section "Formatting Graphic Objects" to change the lines, borders, and patterns used in an object.

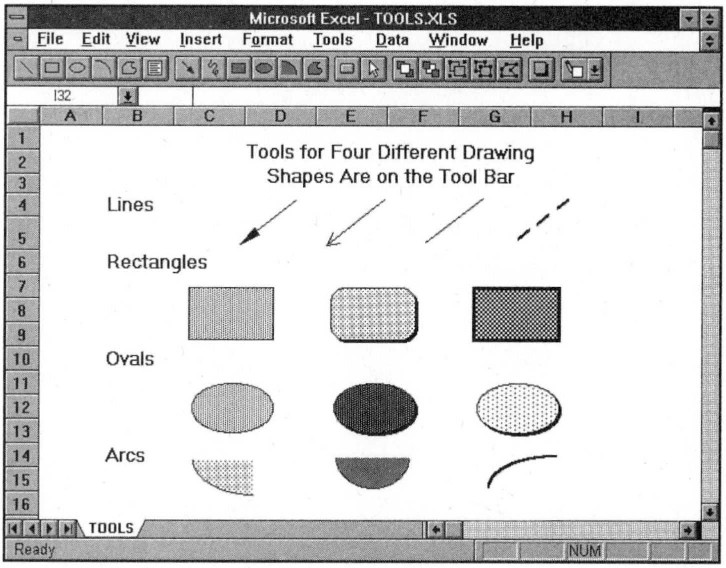

Fig. 17.8
Drawing tools produce many different shapes.

To remove a graphic object, you must select and delete it. You can learn how to select and delete later, in the section "Learning Basic Skills for Editing Graphic Objects."

If you want to draw multiple objects using the same tool, double-click the tool. The tool stays selected when you finish drawing an object. To return to the normal pointer, click the same tool again or press Esc.

Drawing Freehand Objects

Excel has freehand drawing tools that enable even the non-artist to produce good work. The program offers three freehand drawing tools—the Freehand tool, the Freeform tool, and the Filled Freeform tool—and one tool that enables you to reshape a freehand drawing after it's completed. The three freehand drawing tools enable you to draw smooth freehand shapes, polygons, (which are shapes with many straight sides), or filled polygons. Freehand shapes can be filled too.

Tip
If objects print in a slightly different location than they appear on-screen, preview by using the **F**ile Print Pre**v**iew command.

The Reshape tool enables you to drag an existing line end point in a freehand shape to a new position. (The Reshape tool is covered in "Reshaping a Freehand Object," later in this chapter.)

Figure 17.9 shows freehand drawing with each of the three tools. Notice that you can draw smooth curves with either of the polygon tools as well as the Freehand tool. You can draw smooth curves by dragging the tool rather than clicking at end points.

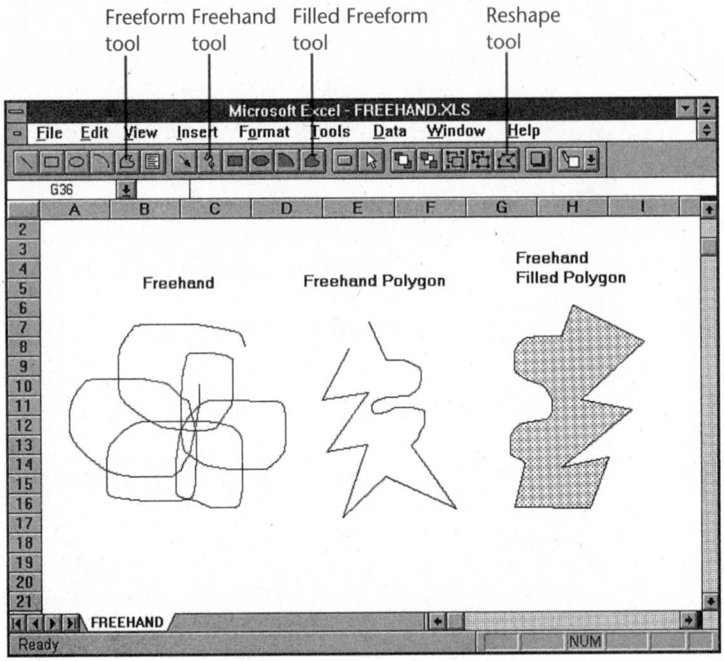

Fig. 17.9
You can draw three types of freehand shapes.

To use one of the freehand tools, follow these steps:

1. Click one of the freehand tool buttons.

   The pointer changes to a cross hair.

2. Move the cross hair to where you want to begin drawing.

3. Draw with one of the following techniques:

Technique	Description
Freehand tool	Hold down the mouse button and move the pointer to draw any shaped line.
Freeform tool	Click to set a line end, move to where you want the next end, and click. Click another end and so on. Excel draws a straight line between each click. Draw smooth lines by holding down the mouse and dragging the cross hair.
Filled Freeform tool	Follow the same technique as used for drawing a freehand polygon.

4. End the drawing by double-clicking at the last point.

Drawing Text Boxes

Excel enables you to place text boxes of word-wrapped text anywhere on the worksheet. You can edit and format the text in these miniature pages just as you edit and format text in most Windows word processing software.

When positioned over worksheet tables, text boxes make excellent titles. Because text boxes *float* in a layer over the worksheet, you can position a title of any size anywhere without affecting worksheet row or column positions.

To draw a text box, follow these steps:

1. Click the text box button. The mouse pointer becomes a cross hair.

   Hold down the Shift key if you want a square text box.

   Hold down the Alt key if you want the text box aligned with the cell grid.

2. Drag from one corner to the opposite corner where you want the text box.

3. Release the mouse button.

When you release the mouse button, a flashing insertion point appears in the text box, indicating that you can begin typing text. Type continuously (as you would with word processing software); the text wraps when you reach the margin. If you type more text than will fit in the box, the box contents scroll so that you can see what you are typing; the full contents may not be visible (to display all the text, make the box larger as described in the later section "Sizing, Moving, and Copying Graphic Objects"). If you later decide to change the size or shape of the text box, the text inside wraps to fit the new shape.

Tip
The Format Cells command (Alignment tab, Center Across Selection option) or the Center button on the Formatting toolbar can help you center a title across selected cells.

To edit material in the text box, use the arrow keys to move the insertion point in the text. Press Ctrl+left arrow or right arrow to move by whole words. Use Del or Backspace to delete a character or selected characters. To insert new material, begin typing at the insertion point. To replace existing text, select the text to be replaced and type the new text. To select with the keyboard, hold down Shift as you move with the arrow keys. Select entire words by double-clicking the word or by pressing Shift+Ctrl+left arrow or right arrow.

Text in a text box is different from text in a cell. In a cell, all the words and characters must have the same format. In a text box, formats can vary. To change the format of text in a text box, select the text to be changed, and then format it by clicking the box with the right mouse to display a shortcut menu, or by choosing the F**o**rmat Obj**e**ct command. You also can click the Bold and Italic buttons in the Formatting toolbar to change characters, or click the Left, Right, or Center buttons to change alignment of all text in the box.

Tip

When you want to frame worksheet contents and include text, use a text box that has its pattern formatted with a fill of None.

Notice in figure 17.10 that you can rotate text in a text box. To rotate text, you must select the text box—not the text—and then choose the F**o**rmat Obj**e**ct command (or click the text box with the right mouse button and select Format Object from the shortcut menu). To select a text box, click its border. Figure 17.11 shows the Format Object dialog box (Alignment tab) used to rotate text and align it vertically or horizontally in the box. When you click a rotated text box to edit the text, the text box positions itself so that it can be read while you edit. Selecting the A**u**tomatic Size option makes the text box fit tightly around the text. Click outside the text box when you are finished editing.

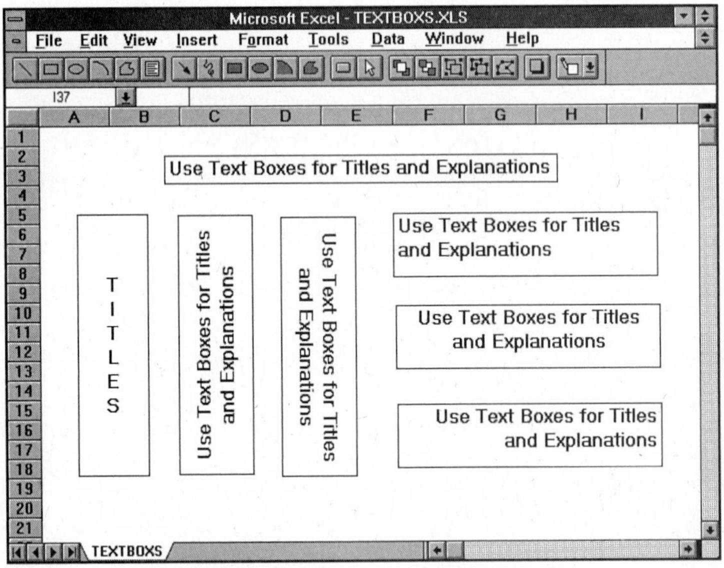

Fig. 17.10
You can format, align, and rotate text boxes.

Drawing Macro Buttons

Using the Create Button tool on the Drawing toolbar, you can draw a button that you can click to activate an Excel 4 macro or Visual Basic procedure (hereafter referred to as a macro). When you draw the button, you either assign it to an existing macro, or you record a new macro. Alternatively, you can edit an existing button and change the assigned macro. When the button is complete, you can click it to activate the assigned macro. To learn more about creating macros, see Chapters 44, "Recording and Modifying VBA Modules," and 45, "Programming in Visual Basic for Applications."

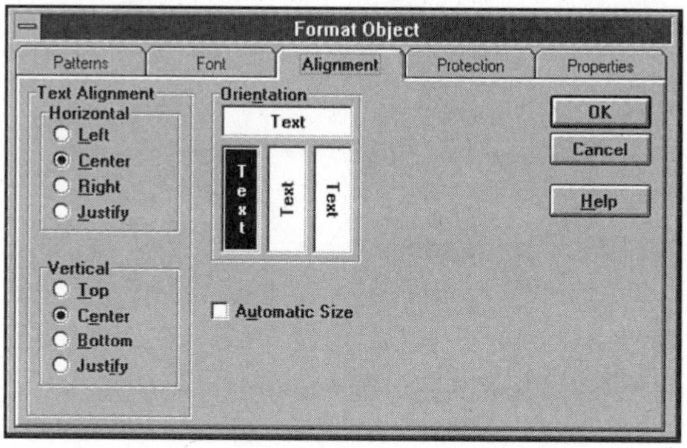

Fig. 17.11
Using the Format Object dialog box, you can rotate text in a text box.

To draw a macro button, follow these steps:

1. Click the Create Button button. The mouse pointer becomes a cross hair.

2. Drag the cross hair to draw the button. When you release the mouse button, the Assign Macro dialog box appears (see fig. 17.12).

3. To assign an existing macro to the button, select the macro from the **M**acro Name/Reference list and choose OK.

   To record a macro or Visual Basic procedure, type its name in the **M**acro Name/Reference box and choose **R**ecord. Record the macro or procedure as usual.

   To edit an existing macro, select the macro from the Macro Name/Reference list and choose **E**dit.

The new macro button appears on-screen, selected (see fig. 17.13) and is named with the word `Button` and a number. Buttons are numbered sequentially as you create them. While the macro button is selected, you can move or resize it like other graphic objects (moving and sizing are described later in this chapter). You also can rename a selected button by selecting its current name and typing a new name.

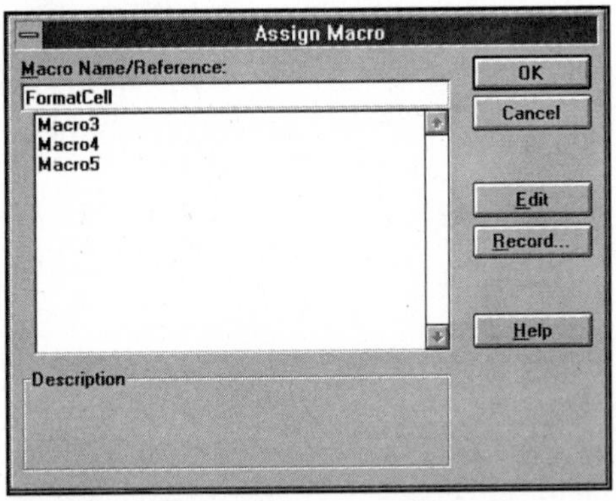

Fig. 17.12
Use the Assign Macro dialog box to assign a button to a macro.

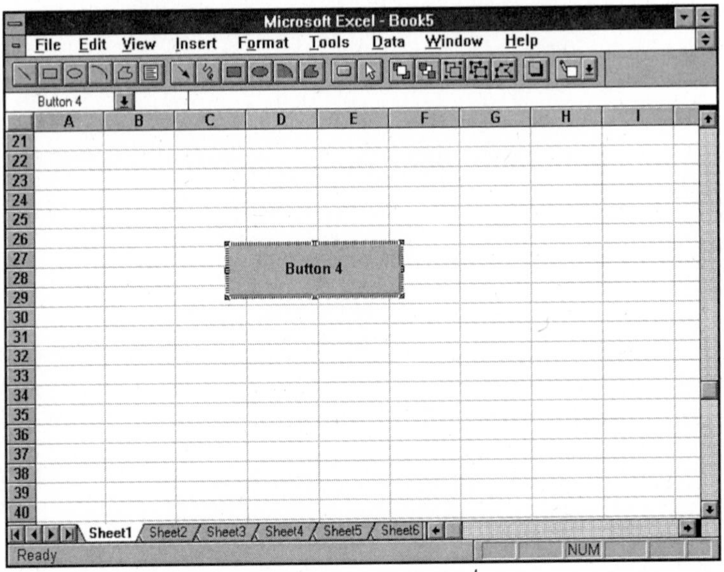

Fig. 17.13
A completed macro button is selected, and you can change its name, move it, or resize it.

After a macro button is completed, clicking it activates the assigned macro (if no macro is assigned to the button, clicking the button selects it). However, you can select it so that you can change its name, move it, or resize it. To select a completed button, hold Ctrl as you click it.

You can change the macro assigned to a completed button. Select a completed button by holding Ctrl as you click it. Then choose the **T**ools Assig**n** Macro command, or click the button with the right mouse button and select Assign Macro from the shortcut menu. The Assign Macro dialog box appears (see fig. 17.12). Complete step 3 in the preceding steps to assign a different macro to the button.

You can assign a macro to a different type of graphic object by selecting the object and choosing the **T**ools Assig**n** Macro command. The Assign Macro dialog box appears (see fig. 17.12). Complete step 3 in the preceding steps to assign a macro to the graphic object.

For Related Information

- "Saving Time with Shortcut Menus," p. 39
- "Using the Toolbars," p. 41
- "Changing Character Fonts, Sizes, Styles, and Colors," p. 312
- "Attaching Macros to Buttons, Menus, and Objects," p. 1162

Combining Data and Charts on the Same Page

You can make worksheet information easier to understand by presenting related data and charts on the same page. With numeric forecasts, for example, you may need to show a table of census data and a chart of those forecasts; these related items can appear on the worksheet. You also probably have faced the problem of wanting to print multiple areas on the same page. Using the techniques described in this section, you learn how to take pictures of worksheet ranges, and then arrange them however you want on a printed page—much like a desktop publishing program.

You can combine worksheet ranges and charts on the same page in two ways. You can create a picture of a worksheet range or chart and paste it in the appropriate spot on a worksheet, or you can embed the picture in a worksheet. Pasted pictures are not updated when the original changes. Embedded pictures can be reformatted and updated when the original worksheet range or chart changes. Chapter 25, "Linking, Embedding, and Consolidating Worksheets," goes into more detail about embedding data from other Windows applications.

Displaying or printing charts and worksheets together on the same page is an important Excel feature. This feature enables you to create printouts that illustrate your point with a chart, along with presenting details in a worksheet. You also can add a text box on the same page to give a written explanation. Figures 17.2 and 17.3 illustrate the use of charts on a worksheet.

Deciding between Pasting and Embedding Charts

You can put two types of chart pictures on an Excel worksheet: an *unlinked* picture of a chart and an *embedded* picture of a chart. Use unlinked pictures when you do not want the chart picture to change, even when the data changes.

Embedded charts contain external references linking the embedded chart to the worksheet cells it was created from. When the data changes on the worksheet, the embedded chart changes. You can double-click an embedded chart to open the chart into a window, where you can use normal charting techniques to reformat the chart. Creating embedded charts is described in the section "Creating an Embedded Chart" in Chapter 12. Formatting charts is described in Chapter 13, "Modifying Charts."

Note

To format or change an embedded chart, you double-click the chart to put it in a window. While it is in a window, you may be tempted to maximize the window during your formatting. You can, but don't. With the window maximized, you might use larger fonts and add arrows, legends, and gridlines that will not display well in the smaller size of the embedded chart.

Embedding Linked Pictures of Charts in a Worksheet

You can create embedded charts directly on the worksheet by using the ChartWizard and the procedures described in Chapter 12, "Creating Charts."

If you already have an embedded chart you want to reuse, or you have a chart in its own window that you want to embed, follow these steps:

1. Select the chart.
2. Choose the **E**dit **C**opy command.
3. Activate the worksheet in which you want to paste the chart.
4. Select a cell that will be the upper-left corner for the picture.
5. Choose the **E**dit **P**aste command.

The picture appears on the worksheet, selected and ready for formatting. Figure 17.14 shows two charts pasted into a worksheet.

Embedded charts remain linked to the worksheet data they use. Even if you create an embedded chart by copying a chart from a document window, the embedded chart is linked to the worksheet that supplied the original data. Refer to the section, "Opening an Embedded Chart for Formatting," in Chapter 12 to learn how to activate and reformat embedded charts.

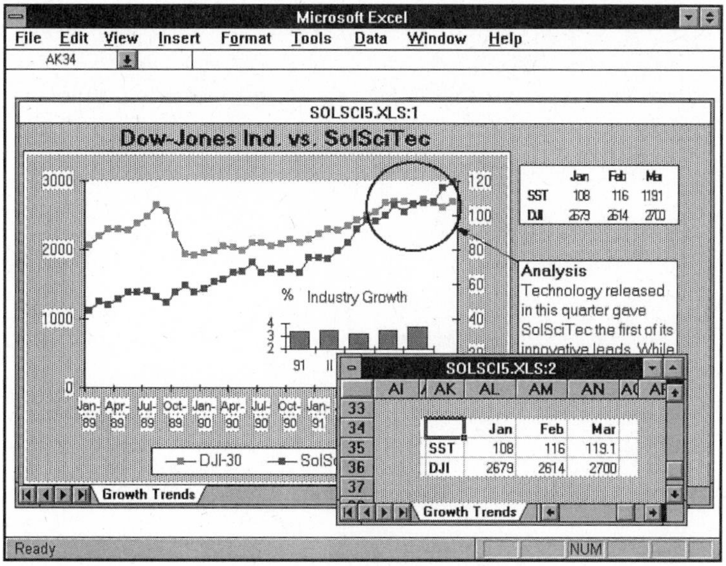

Fig. 17.14
Charts can be embedded on a worksheet so that they display and print on the same page.

Pasting Unlinked Pictures of Charts in a Worksheet

If you want a picture of a chart that will not change when data changes and that is not linked to a worksheet, paste a chart picture.

To paste pictures of charts to a worksheet, follow these steps:

1. Select the chart.
2. Choose the **E**dit **C**opy command.
3. Choose OK.
4. Activate the worksheet in which you want to paste the chart.
5. Select a cell that will be the upper-left corner for the picture.
6. Choose **E**dit Paste **S**pecial command.
7. Select the **A**s Picture item from the list.
8. Choose OK.

These steps paste the chart as a picture. Pictures require less memory and print better than the bit maps used in previous versions of Excel. The picture appears on the worksheet, selected and ready for formatting.

Linking Pictures of Cells in a Worksheet

Linked or unlinked pictures of cells can help you get past layout or formatting obstacles you may face when building reports or displays. By using linked cell pictures, you can put different parts of one or more worksheets next to each other on the same screen or the same printed page.

Pictures of cells are like snapshots of a selected worksheet or macro range. You can put those snapshots anywhere on the same or a different worksheet or macro sheet. Figure 17.15 shows a picture of cells at the top-right corner of the background worksheet. The smaller window shows the area of the worksheet the cell picture came from. Each picture appears and can be formatted, sized, or moved separately.

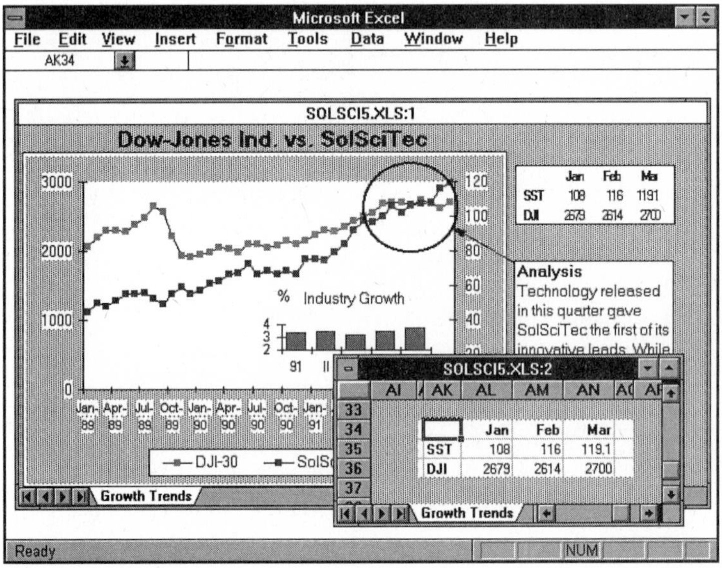

Fig. 17.15
Pictures of cells link to original data even if the data is on a different worksheet.

Cell pictures give you the flexibility to organize your macro sheet or worksheet in the best way for data entry, analysis, or programming. You can copy reporting and print areas as pictures and arrange them on pages alongside text boxes and charts. You can have separate print areas all printed on the same page. If the cell pictures are linked, they will be updated when the source cells are changed.

Deciding between Linked or Unlinked. Pictures can be linked or unlinked. Linked cell pictures are updated when their original data is changed.

An advantage of linked cell pictures is that you can use them to create tables or boxes containing information from another area of the worksheet or macro. You can size the linked picture into a small box and double-click the box to display the source worksheet. It's like having a telescopic window to other parts of the worksheet.

Note

If you double-click a linked cell picture, you are taken to the source of that picture, even if it is on another worksheet. To return to the last active cell before you double-clicked, press the Goto key, F5, and choose OK. Excel remembers the preceding location.

Creating Linked Cell Pictures. Before you can use the Camera Button to link a cell picture, you must add the Camera button to a toobar. To add the Camera button to a toolbar, choose the **V**iew **T**oolbars command, and then select the Customize button from the Toolbars dialog box. When the Customize dialog box appears, select Utility from the Categories list. The Camera button will now be visible in the Buttons area of the Customize dialog box. Drag the Camera button onto a toolbar, and then choose Close. To create linked pictures of cells using the Camera button and mouse, follow these steps:

1. Select the cells you want to use for the picture.
2. Click the Camera button. The pointer changes to a cross hair when it is over the sheet.

3. Drag in the sheet from the top left corner of where you want the picture to the bottom right corner, and then release the mouse button.

The picture appears.

To create linked pictures of cells using commands, follow these steps:

1. Select the cells you want to use for the picture.
2. Choose the **E**dit **C**opy command.
3. Activate the worksheet or macro sheet in which you want the picture to appear.
4. Hold down the Shift key and choose the **E**dit Paste Picture Li**n**k command.

Linked cell pictures are updated when data changes or when you change the worksheet display of the source cells. For example, Excel will update linked picture cells when you change the display of the source cells by turning gridlines on or off.

To return to your original location, press the Goto key, F5, and then immediately choose OK. Goto remembers the preceding location.

Copying Unlinked Cell Pictures. To copy unlinked pictures of cells, follow these steps:

1. Select the cells you want to use for the picture.
2. Hold down the Shift key and choose the **E**dit **C**opy Picture command.
3. Select the copy options you want, depending on which picture appears better when pasted:

   As Shown on **S**creen copies the picture as it appears on-screen.

   As Shown when **P**rinted copies the picture as it appears when printed.
4. If you select As Shown on **S**creen, you have the choice of selecting Format Pic**t**ure or Format **B**itmap.
5. Choose OK.
6. Activate the worksheet or macro sheet and select the cell or object where you want the picture to appear.
7. Choose the **E**dit **P**aste command.

Note

You can edit a bit-map image by copying it into Paintbrush. A bit-map image has lower resolution when printed. You can edit a picture image with programs using the Windows Metafile format through the Clipboard. You can edit a picture image by copying it into the Microsoft Draw applet that comes with many Microsoft applications. Editing and modifying embedded objects, such as these charts, is explained in Chapter 12, "Creating Charts."

> **Note**
>
> Unlinked pictures can display gridlines as well as row and column headings. If you do not want row and column headings or gridlines to appear on pictures of a worksheet, use the **T**ools **O**ptions command (View tab) to clear the **G**ridlines and Row & Column H**e**aders options in the original document.

Learning Basic Skills for Editing Graphic Objects

After you have created graphic objects or taken a picture of cells or a chart, you will need to know how to select these objects in order to modify or delete them. Excel offers several techniques for selecting graphic objects.

Selecting Graphic Objects

You must select an item before you can change or delete it. Graphic objects that have been selected are enclosed in an invisible rectangular *frame*. You can move a selected object by dragging its frame. The corners and edges of the frame display black squares, or *handles*, that you use to resize the object. Figure 17.16 shows a selected graphic object with frame and handles.

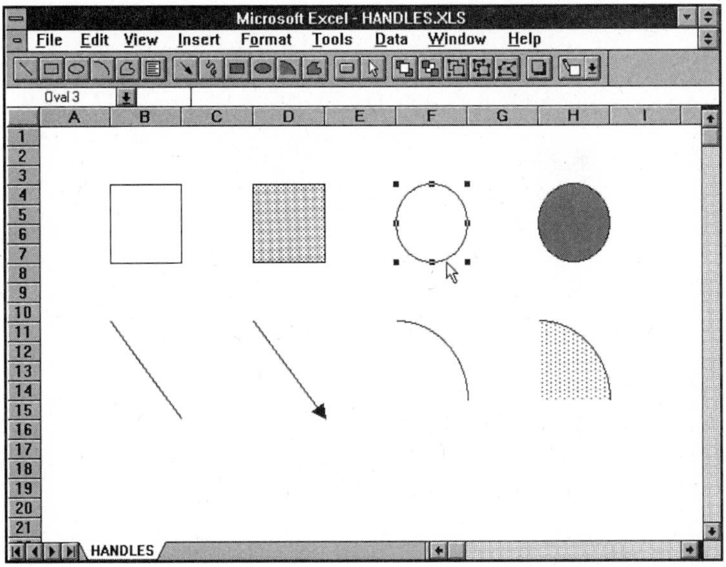

Fig. 17.16
Selected objects are enclosed by an invisible rectangular frame, and have square selection handles on each side and corner.

Each graphic object is identified by its type and a number that indicates the order in which it was created. The identifier of the selected object is displayed in the reference area to the left of the formula bar. Examples of identifiers include Rectangle 1, Arc 2, Oval 5, and Picture 8.

When you move the mouse to select an object, watch the mouse pointer. It must be shaped like an arrow to select the object. The pointer changes to an arrow over the inside of a filled object or picture and on the border of transparent objects, pictures, or text boxes.

To select a single object, move the mouse pointer over the objects border (or center if the object is filled), and then click. To select multiple objects, click the first object, and then hold down the Shift key as you click additional objects.

Using the keyboard, select all objects by choosing the **E**dit **G**o To command, and then choosing the **S**pecial button. In the Go To Special dialog box, select the O**b**jects button, and then choose OK. After all objects are selected, you can move the selection between them by pressing Tab or Shift+Tab.

Figure 17.17 shows a group of selected objects. If multiple objects are grouped closely together, you can select them by enclosing them with the Selection tool. To use this method, click the Selection button in the toolbar and drag the cross hair to surround all the objects. As you drag, a rectangular marquee encloses the objects. You must completely enclose an object to include it in

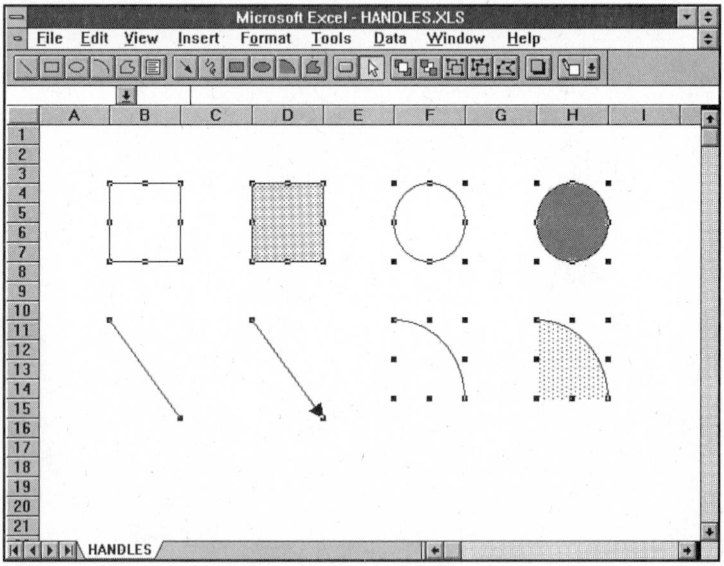

Fig. 17.17
You can select a group of objects by holding Shift as you click each one or by enclosing them with the Selection tool.

the selection. When you release the mouse button, all enclosed objects are selected and the marquee disappears. If an object is not selected, redraw the marquee to completely enclose it.

To enlarge the area enclosed with the Selection tool, make sure that the Selection tool is still selected and hold down the Shift key as you drag across additional objects. To select all graphic objects in a worksheet, choose the **E**dit **G**o To command, choose the **S**pecial button, and then select O**b**jects and choose OK.

If you want to exclude a few objects from a large group you have already selected, hold down the Shift key and click the individual objects you want to deselect. You can exclude a group of objects by clicking the Selection button, holding down the Shift key, and dragging the mouse pointer across the group. To deselect all objects, press the Esc key or click a cell in the worksheet.

Graphic objects can have macros assigned to them. Clicking such an object causes the macro assigned to it to run. To select an object without running its assigned macro, press and hold the Ctrl key when you click the object.

Deleting Graphic Objects

Deleting graphic objects is straightforward. Select the object and then press Del or Backspace or choose the **E**dit Cle**a**r **A**ll command. When deleting text boxes, make sure that you have the box selected and not the text (otherwise you delete the text and leave the box). Select a text box by clicking its edge.

Tip
You can delete several objects at once by using any selection technique and then deleting as described previously.

If you accidentally delete an object that you want to keep, immediately choose the **E**dit **U**ndo command, or press Ctrl+Z.

Formatting Graphic Objects

Excel gives you a wide array of colors, patterns, and line styles to use for formatting objects. You can change lines to arrows with heads of different weight and size. You also can change the thickness, style, and color of borders, and the fill pattern and color used in objects. Some objects even can use rounded corners or shadow box options.

Formatting Lines and Arrows

You can format lines for thickness, line style, and color. You also can put arrowheads on your lines. To format a line, follow these steps:

Tip
The quickest way to display a formatting dialog box is to double-click with the left mouse button the object you want to format.

1. Select the line you want to format.

2. Click the line with the right mouse button and choose Format Object from a shortcut menu, or choose the F**o**rmat Obj**e**ct command. Or, press Ctrl+1, or double-click the line you want to format.

3. Select the Patterns tab (if it is not selected already). Figure 17.18 shows the Patterns tab in the Format Object dialog box.

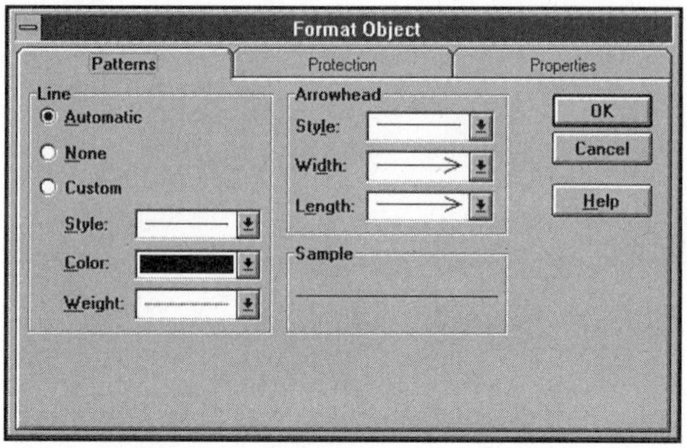

Fig. 17.18
You can customize lines and arrows using the Format Object dialog box.

4. Select from the Line options. To use the default line format, select **Au**tomatic. Select **N**one for an invisible line. Select Custom to select **S**tyle, **C**olor, and **W**eight of line from the pull-down list.

5. Select from the Arrowhead options if you want an arrow. Select from the Sty**l**e, Wi**d**th, and L**e**ngth pull-down lists to choose the type of arrowhead. You must choose an arrowhead from Sty**l**e, or Wi**d**th and L**e**ngth will not affect the line. Figure 17.19 shows the list for different arrowhead lengths.

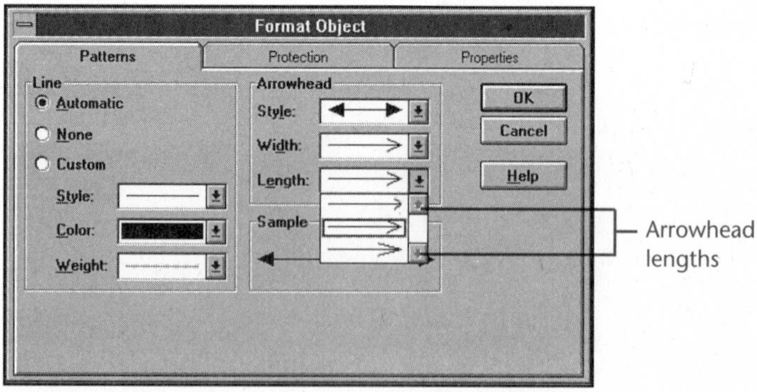

Fig. 17.19
Select the length of arrowhead you prefer.

6. Check the selection in the Sample box at the lower-right corner of the Patterns tab. Change the selections if necessary.

7. Choose OK.

Figure 17.20 shows examples of different lines, weights, and arrowheads.

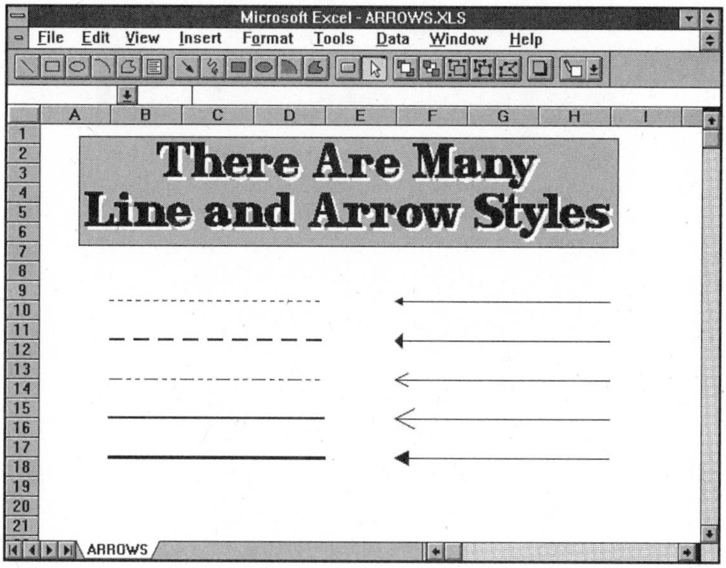

Fig. 17.20
You can create lines with different weights, colors, and arrowhead styles.

Formatting Borders and Patterns

All the graphic objects you draw in Excel can be formatted with different colors, patterns, and line styles or weights.

To change the fill, pattern, or border of an object, follow these steps:

1. Select the object or objects.

2. Choose the F**o**rmat Obj**e**ct command, or press Ctrl+1. Hold down the Ctrl key while clicking if the object has an assigned macro.

3. Select the Patterns tab (if it is not selected already). Figure 17.21 shows the Patterns tab in the Format Object dialog box.

4. Select from the Border options. To use the default border format, choose **A**utomatic. Choose **N**one for an invisible border. Choose Custom to select **S**tyle, **C**olor, and **W**eight of the border from the pull-down list. Click the down arrow to the right of a pull-down box to see the full list of selections.

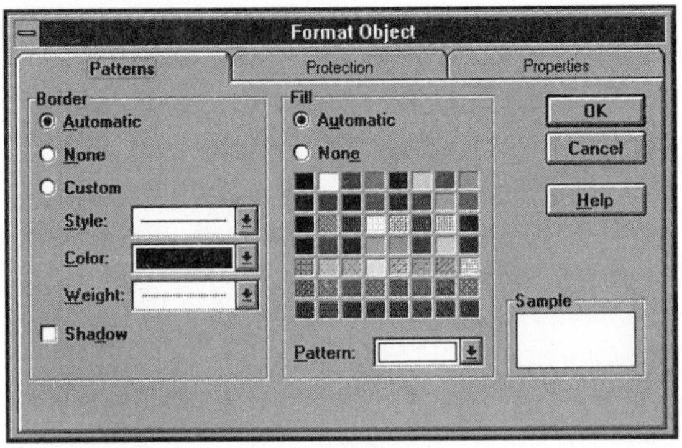

Fig. 17.21 The Patterns tab in the Format Object dialog box gives you many options for formatting objects.

5. Select the Shadow check box if the object needs a shadow.
6. Select the color for the fill from the color palette in the Fill group. Choose Automatic for an automatic fill color, or choose the None option if you want an invisible fill that lets the background show through.
7. From the **P**attern list, select a pattern and a color for the pattern. The pattern and its color are superimposed over the fill and its color.
8. Review the selection in the Sample box at the lower-right corner of the Patterns dialog box. Change your selections if necessary.
9. Choose OK.

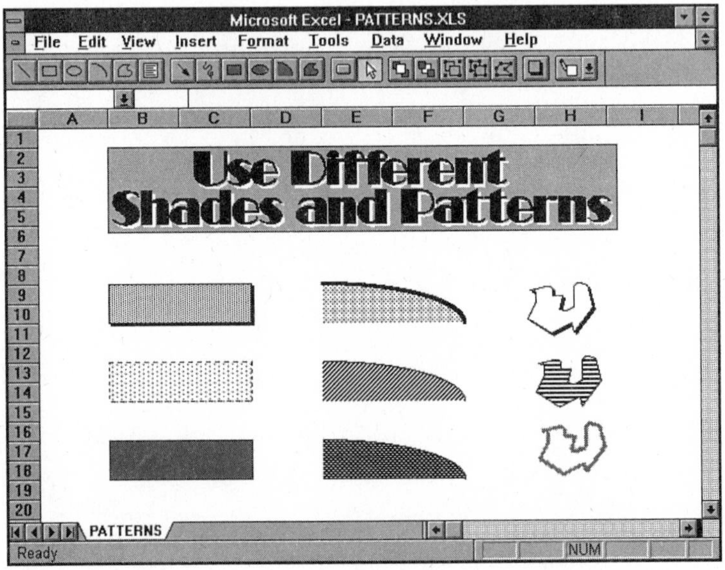

Fig. 17.22 You can fill an object with different patterns and colors, and change its border.

Figure 17.22 shows examples of patterns you can use to fill objects.

If you are unsure which colors, weights, or patterns to use, or if you want to return to default colors, choose the A**u**tomatic option for these commands.

To quickly add a pattern to an object, select the object and then select the Pattern button on the Drawing toolbar. From the drop-down palette that appears, select a pattern and a color. These selections become defaults; the next filled object you draw will be formatted with the pattern and color you chose previously using the Pattern tool.

Tip
To quickly add a drop shadow to a selected object in Excel 5, click the Drop Shadow button on the Drawing toolbar.

To format the internal portion of objects that are pictures linked to other documents, you must reformat the source document for the link. Open the source document by double-clicking the object. Then reformat the source document as you like. Use normal object formatting to format a picture's border or shadow.

Note

To highlight important results, draw rectangles or ellipses around cells and use the Non**e** option to fill the rectangle or ellipse, letting the worksheet data show through the rectangular or round border.

You can display the Format Object dialog box for an inserted picture by selecting the picture and choosing the **E**dit **O**bject command.

Changing Object Size, Shape, and Position

You do not need to worry too much about creating an object with the exact shape in the exact position you need when you first draw it. It is very easy to reshape, size, and move objects. If you need multiple copies of the same object, you can draw it once and then make as many copies as needed.

Sizing, Moving, and Copying Graphic Objects

To resize an object, select it so that you can see the black handles. Move the mouse pointer over a handle until the pointer becomes a cross hair. To change the size in one dimension (height or width), drag a handle in the middle of one side. To resize two sides, drag a corner handle.

To resize an object while keeping its proportions, hold down the Shift key and drag a corner handle.

To move an object, select it and drag the object to its new location. Be sure to drag objects that have an invisible (Non**e**) fill and all text boxes by the edges. If you drag an object by its black handle, you will resize it. If you need to move an object a long distance, cut the object to the Clipboard, move to the new location, and paste the object in place.

Move multiple objects by selecting them together, and then dragging them to the new location.

Tip
To keep several objects together, group them before moving them. See "Grouping Graphic Objects" in this chapter for more information.

To constrain movements to vertical or horizontal, hold down the Shift key while dragging. If you want the object to align on underlying cells, hold down the Alt key as you drag an object.

To cut or copy objects, select them and choose the **E**dit Cu**t** or **C**opy command. Select the new location for the object, and choose the **E**dit **P**aste command.

Reshaping a Freehand Object

Reshaping a freehand line is amazing the first time you see it done. After you draw a shape and then click the Reshape tool, you find that the shape is composed of small lines connected by movable handles called *nodes*. You can drag any one of these nodes to change the shape.

To reshape a freehand or polygon object, follow these steps:

1. Select the freehand or polygon object by clicking it.

2. Click the Reshape button.

3. Move the cross hair to a handle, and drag the handle to a new location.

4. Click the background when you are done.

Figure 17.23 shows a shape selected with the Reshape tool. Figure 17.24 shows its corner being *stretched* to a new location.

Fixing Object Positions

You can position objects relative to their underlying cells in three ways. These three ways enable you to specify how an object behaves when you insert, delete, or change the dimensions of underlying rows and columns.

Drawn objects, such as text boxes, rectangles, and ellipses, are attached to underlying cells; when you change the underlying cells, the objects move and change shape.

When first created, an embedded chart or pasted graphic is attached to the underlying cell at the upper-left corner of the object. An object moves with the cell during insertions, deletions, or dimension changes, but the size and

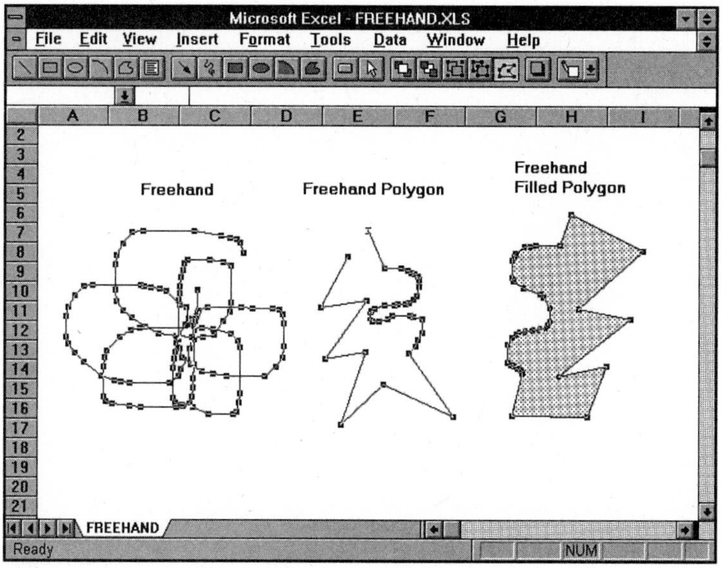

Fig. 17.23
Freehand objects selected with the Reshape tool show nodes that can be moved.

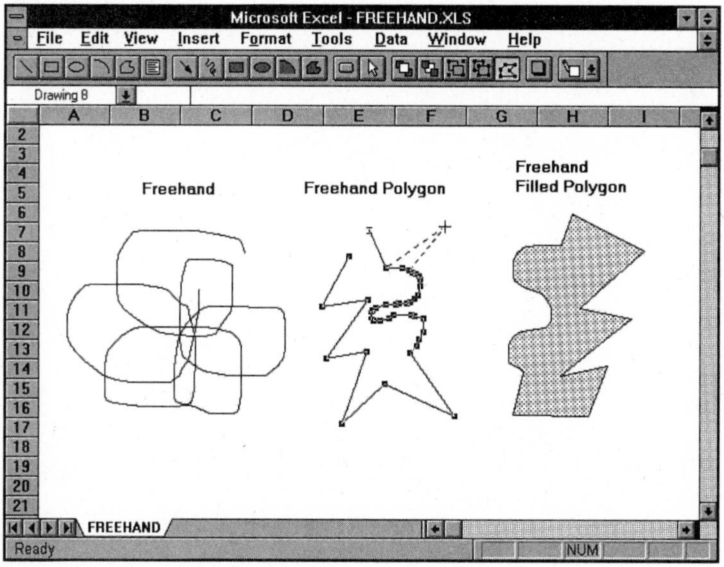

Fig. 17.24
After selecting a freehand object with the Reshape tool, you can drag nodes to reshape the object.

proportion of the object remain the same. During cell changes, pictures and charts stay proportional, and they continue to look the way you want them to look.

Use the Move and **S**ize with Cells option if you want an object to change size and shape relative to the worksheet cells it covers.

To change how an object is attached to underlying cells, follow these steps:

1. Select the object.
2. Choose the F**o**rmat Obj**e**ct command, or click the object with the right mouse button and choose Format Object. Alternatively, double-click the object or press Ctrl+1.

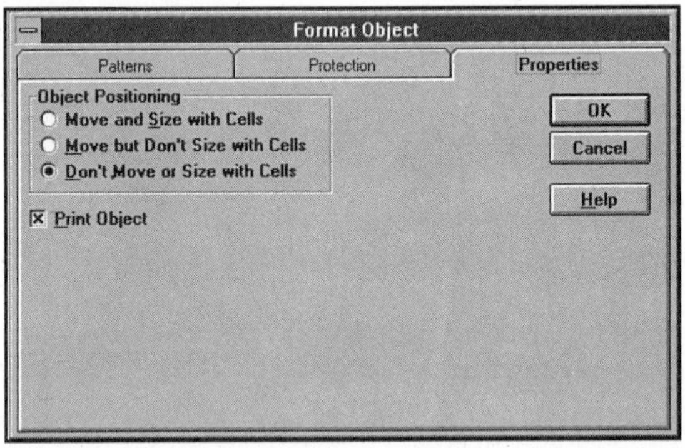

Fig. 17.25
You can decide whether you want graphic objects to change when the cells beneath them change.

3. Select the Properties tab. Figure 17.25 shows the Format Object dialog box with the Properties tab selected.
4. Select one of the following attachment options:

Move and **S**ize with Cells	Attaches an object to cells under the object's top-left and lower-right corners. The object moves or changes size with the underlying cells, rows, or columns. The normal attachment when objects are first drawn.
Move but Don't Size with Cells	Attaches the object to only the cell underlying the top-left corner of the object. The object moves with the cell during insertions or deletions, but it keeps its original size and proportions. The normal attachment when graphics are pasted or charts are embedded.

Don't Move or Size with Cells	Objects are not attached to the underlying worksheet. They must be moved and sized by themselves.

5. Choose OK.

The Move and **S**ize with Cells option is selected with drawn objects; this option attaches the object to the cells under the object's top-left and lower-right corners. The Move and **S**ize with Cells option is useful when you draw rectangles or ellipses around specific data on the worksheet, or when you use lines or arrows drawn between two points. As the underlying sheet changes, the end-points of the object remain fixed, enclosing the data if the object is a rectangle or ellipse, and pointing to the correct items if the object is a line or arrow.

Use the **M**ove but Don't Size with Cells option for charts, pasted graphics, groups of lines, and rectangles and ellipses you have created a logo or design with. It is the default option for inserted graphics. This option keeps the graphics in position but prevents them from stretching.

If you don't want objects to change shape or move, use the **D**on't Move or Size with Cells option. This option preserves an object's shape and keeps it fixed in position relative to the top-left corner of the worksheet.

Figure 17.26 shows objects with different object properties. Figure 17.27 shows the same worksheet after a column is inserted.

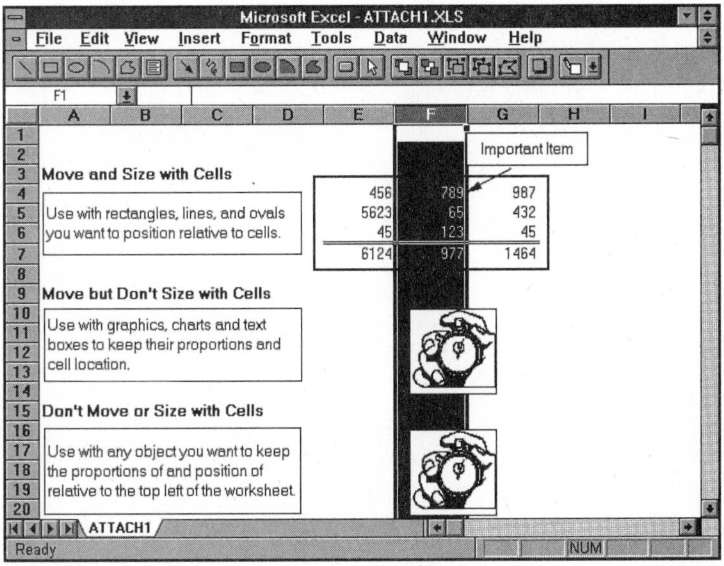

Fig. 17.26
You can use three methods of attaching objects to the underlying worksheet.

Grouping and Layering Graphic Objects

After you have drawn, formatted, and edited you graphic objects and have them looking exactly as you need them, you may want to group several of them so that the spacing and arrangement won't change. You may also find that an object is on top of another and it needs to be under it. Changing this order is accomplished with layers.

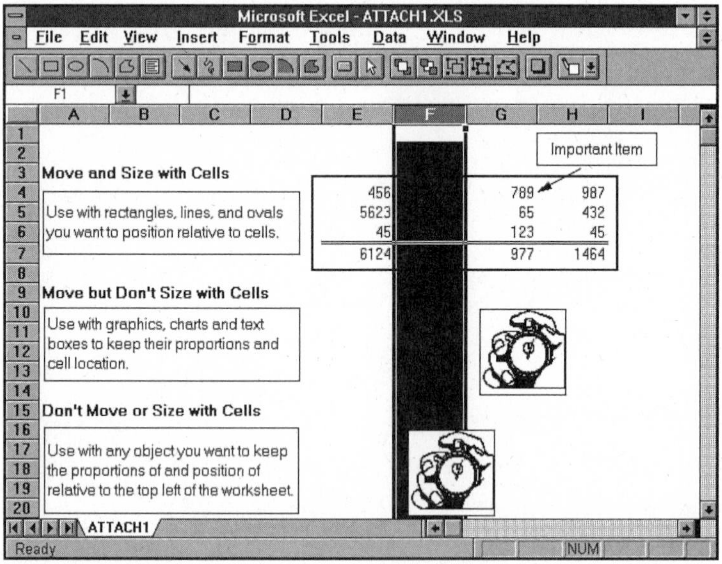

Fig. 17.27 Attachment methods work differently when the underlying worksheet changes shape.

Grouping Graphic Objects

Grouping objects together fuses them into a single object. When related objects are fused, they are easier to move and size. You can ungroup objects if you later need to separate them.

To group objects together, select the objects you want to group by using one of the multiple-selection techniques, and then choose the F**o**rmat **P**lacement **G**roup command or select the Group button on the Drawing toolbar. Alternatively, click with the right mouse button on one of the selected objects and select Group from the shortcut menu.

To separate a group into individual elements, select the group and choose the F**o**rmat **P**lacement **U**ngroup command or select the Ungroup button. Alternatively, click with the right mouse button on the group and select Ungroup from the shortcut menu.

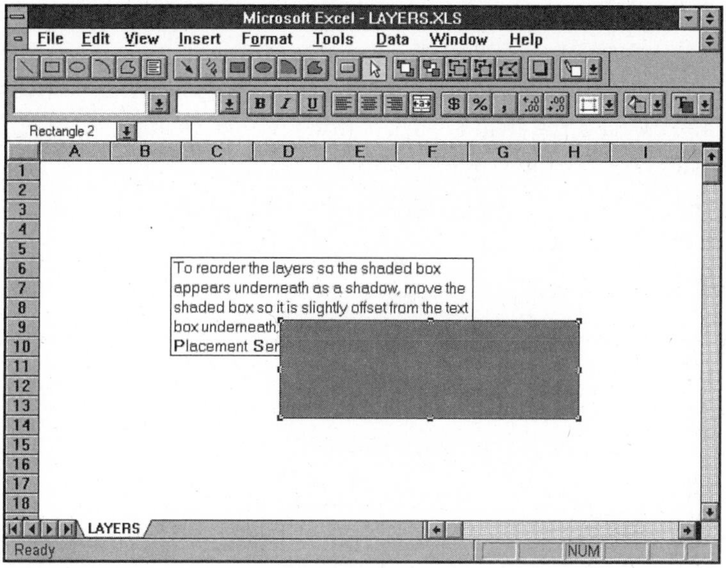

Fig. 17.28
The most recently created object appears in front.

Reordering Layers of Graphic Objects

Objects in Excel overlap each other in layers. Because objects overlap in the order in which they were created, the most recently drawn or pasted object appears in front. Figure 17.28 shows a text box that was created before the shaded box that partially covers it.

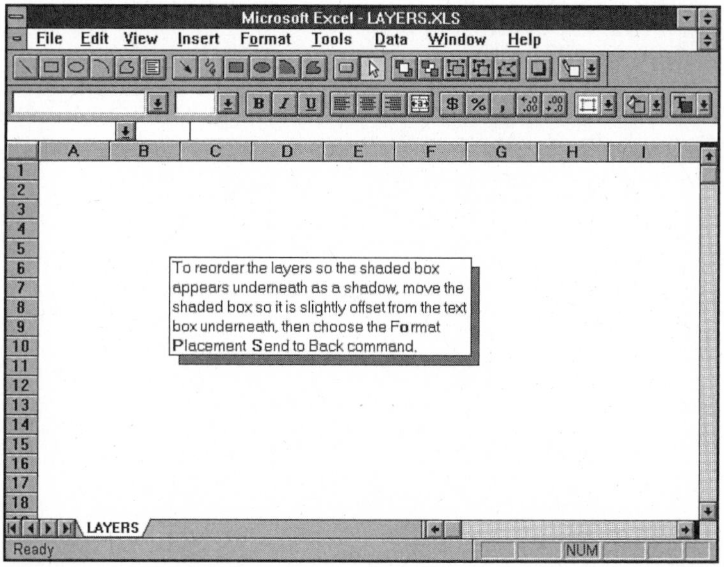

Fig. 17.29
Reorder layers of graphic objects by bringing one to the front or sending one to the back.

To reorder the layers so that the shaded box appears behind the text box as a shadow, move the shaded box to be slightly offset from the text box. With the shaded box still selected, choose the F**o**rmat **P**lacement **S**end to Back command or select the Send to Back button on the Drawing toolbar. Alternatively, click with the right mouse button on the object and select Send to Back from the shortcut menu. Figure 17.29 shows the text box in front with a shadow box background.

To bring an object to the front, select it and choose the F**o**rmat **P**lacement **B**ring to Front command or select the Bring to Front button. Alternatively, click with the right mouse button on the object and select Bring to Front from the shortcut menu. To preserve these two as one object, use grouping, which is described in the previous section.

Protecting, Printing, and Hiding Graphic Objects

Excel provides several ways you can control graphic objects on your worksheet. You can protect them, so they aren't accidentally changed. You can designate them as non-printing. You also can choose not to display them to save time as you're working with a sheet that contains many or complex graphics.

Tip
You can hide all graphics so that you can see the worksheet underneath the graphic objects. See "Hiding Objects" later in this chapter for directions.

Protecting Graphic Objects

You can protect objects to keep other people from changing them (or to keep you from accidentally changing them!). You protect objects just as you protect cells. Mark the objects you want to remain unprotected by selecting them and choosing the F**o**rmat Obj**e**ct command, selecting the Protection tab, and deselecting the **L**ocked check box. To activate protection for the worksheet, choose the **T**ools **P**rotection **P**rotect Sheet command and enter a password, if desired. Choose OK. Only those objects that were unlocked prior to document protection can be changed when the document protection is turned on (you can't even select locked objects in a protected worksheet). To unprotect a worksheet, choose the **T**ools **P**rotection Un**p**rotect Sheet command (entering the password and pressing OK if necessary).

Printing Graphic Objects

In most cases when you print, you want graphic objects to display, but you don't want macro buttons on worksheets to display. And that's exactly how Excel sets its defaults. All graphic objects print, except macro buttons.

If you want to change whether a graphic object or macro button prints, select the object, choose the F**o**rmat Obj**e**ct command, and select the Properties tab. Select or clear the **P**rint Object check box.

Hiding Objects

When you scroll windows or recalculate a worksheet that contains graphic objects, Excel redraws the objects. Because redrawing objects requires extra computer power, Excel's performance may slow down. Excel can show all objects, show placeholders for better performance, or hide all objects so that you can see the underlying worksheet. To speed up Excel's performance, change the display of objects. You may also want to use this option if you need to see the entire worksheet to work on it and graphic objects obscure your view.

To change the display of objects, choose the **T**ools **O**ptions command, select the View tab, and select the Hi**d**e All option or the Show **P**laceholders option. Toggle between these display modes by pressing Ctrl+6. Behind the Options dialog box, you can see the shaded placeholders that take the place of graphic objects. Figure 17.30 illustrates the display options.

For Related Information

- "Protecting Sheets and Workbooks," p. 362
- "Previewing the Document," p. 389

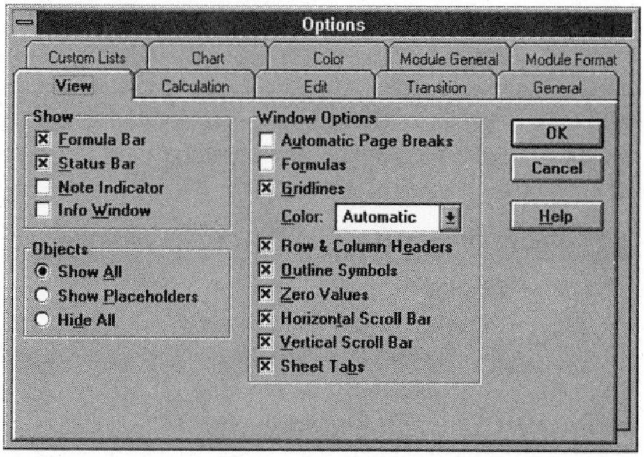

Fig. 17.30
For increased performance, choose to display object placeholders or hide objects.

From Here...

- Chapter 12, "Creating Charts." This chapter on creating and embedding charts shows you how to put charts into a worksheet. Once a chart is on a worksheet, you can use the graphic techniques described in this chapter to format the chart border or resize it.

- Chapter 14, "Formatting Charts." You can use the drawing techniques from this chapter to draw directly onto a chart which enables you to embellish and enhance your charts.

- Chapter 25, "Linking, Embedding, and Consolidating Worksheets." In some worksheets you may need a picture of a group of cells and their results. You can treat this picture as a graphic object and resize it, yet the picture updates when the cell results change.

- Chapter 38, "Using Excel with Windows Applications." When you need greater drawing or graphics capability than are found in Excel, use a dedicated Windows drawing or graphics application and insert or copy the graphic into Excel.

Chapter 18

Outlining Worksheets

Outlining enables you to expand or contract worksheets or reports so that you see more or less detail. In a sales report, for example, you may need two levels of detail depending upon who will read it. For a regional sales manager reviewing the performance of salespeople, you may want a report with full detail. But a report for the divisional manager may only include summary information. With the outline feature, you can hide or display up to eight levels of detail in rows or columns.

The Data Subtotals feature in Excel uses outlining to organize different levels of subtotals. By using the outline feature directly, you can gain even more organizing ability.

In this chapter, you learn how to:

- Understand an outline and what symbols and buttons are used when outlining
- Create an outline automatically or manually
- Expand or contract an outline to show more or less detail
- Format an outline's results
- Copy from or make charts from an outline's different levels of detail

Benefits of Outlining

Figure 18.1 shows a report on product sales by region and by month. This report has not had an outline applied. Notice how hard it is to determine where summary information is. The report also requires a lot of scrolling to see the summary rows for each region or the summary columns for each quarter.

Figure 18.2 shows the history of sales as an outline with three outline levels for rows and three outline levels for columns. East, West, North, and South rows summarize products within the region. The Corporate row summarizes the East, West, North, and South rows.

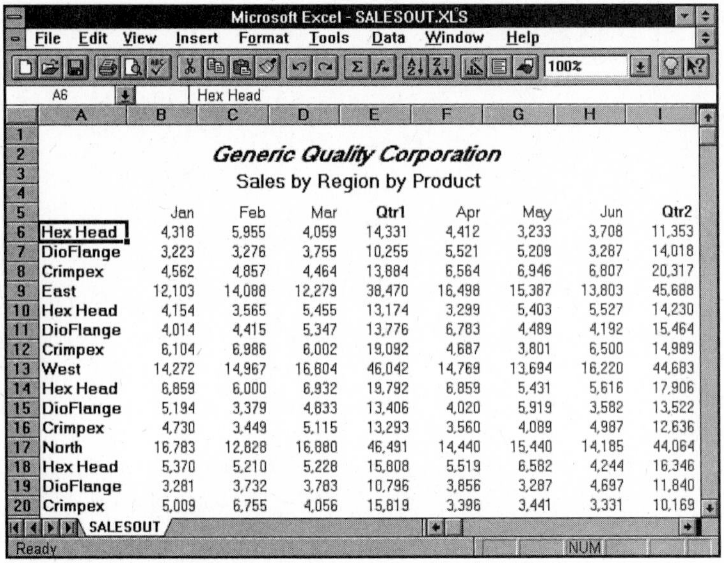

Fig. 18.1
Before applying an outline, there may be so much detail showing that it is hard to see the information you need.

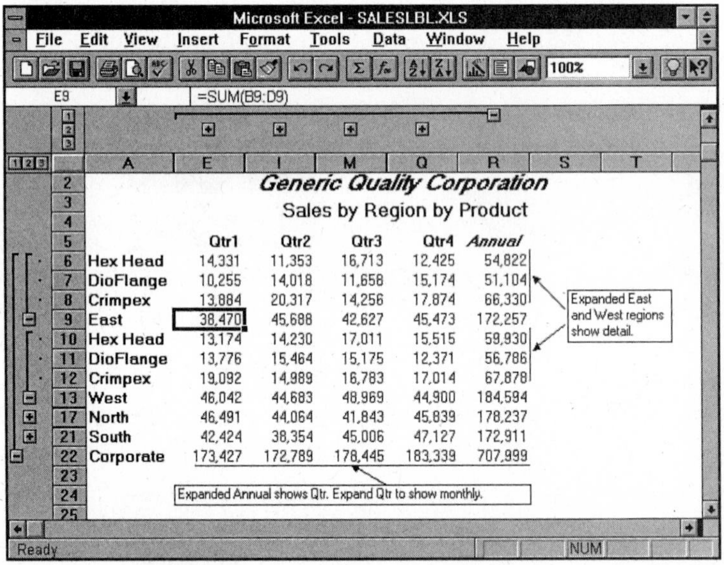

Fig. 18.2
With an outline, you can hide or display detail in rows or columns.

The columns shown have three outline levels. Notice that the monthly columns visible in figure 18.1 are hidden in figure 18.2 to show only quarterly summary columns. The highest column outline level is the Annual column, which summarizes the quarterly columns.

Using an outline like this makes information easier to read and compare. To hide or display a level of the outline, you can click the outline buttons that appear across the top or across the left side. If you are using a keyboard, you can hide or display details by using the Data Group and Outline commands.

Understanding Outline Layout

Excel can create an outline automatically if the data is laid out in a consistent manner. You also can create an outline manually. Manually created outlines may be necessary if Excel cannot understand the pattern of summary and detailed information on a worksheet or if you want to manually group detail rows or columns.

When Excel creates an outline, it examines the contents of each cell in the range to be outlined. Using the default settings, Excel looks to see if formulas are summarizing rows above and rows to the left. The direction of summary must be consistent throughout the area of the outline. If there are summaries of summary information, Excel also notes these and creates additional levels for the outline. The outline can have up to eight levels of rows and columns. You can place only one outline on a worksheet.

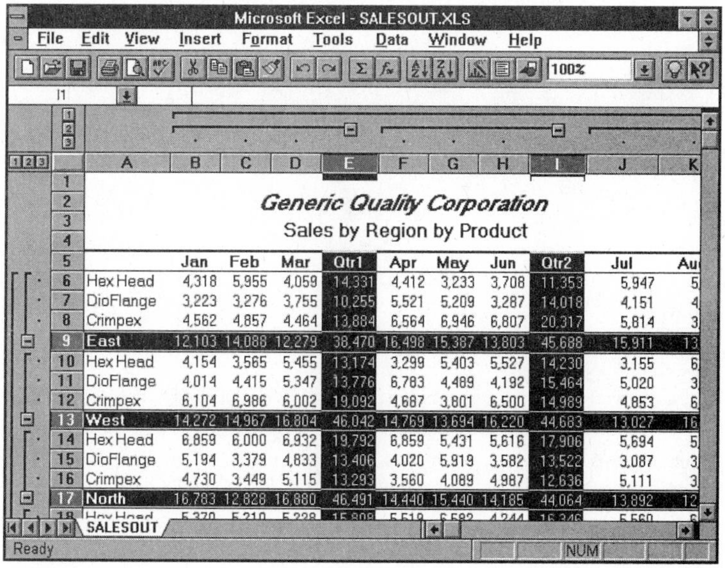

Fig. 18.3
Excel examines the layout of summary formulas to determine an outline's organization.

Figure 18.3 shows the selected rows and columns that contain summary formulas. The outline symbols at the left or top edge show these rows and columns as a higher level in the outline. For example, cells in column E use SUM( ) to total the cells in B, C, and D to the left. Cells in row 9 use SUM( ) to total the cells in rows 6, 7, and 8 above.

The highest levels in the outline are row 22 and column R, shown in figure 18.2. These levels summarize the regional and quarterly subtotals.

Note

All summary directions must be consistent. For automatic outlining to work, all summary columns must have the data on the same side, and all summary rows must have the data either all above or all below. If the outline mixes the direction in which data is summarized, use the manual method to create an outline.

When you create an outline automatically, Excel assumes that summary rows are below detail rows and summary columns are to the right of detail columns. If you use the **D**ata **G**roup and Outline S**e**ttings command to create the outline, you can specify that summary rows are above detail and summary columns are to the left of detail. The summary functions must summarize in the directions specified by the options for the outline to work correctly.

Note

A worksheet can contain only one outline, but the outline can be disjointed and spread over different parts of a worksheet.

Caution

Collapsing and expanding an outline can affect other parts of the worksheet. Rows that expand or collapse do so throughout the entire width of the worksheet. Columns that expand or collapse do so throughout the entire height of the worksheet, which means that you usually want an outline in rows and columns not shared with other cells from the worksheet. If other parts of the worksheet overlay rows or columns used by the outline, these other parts also expand and collapse when you change the outline.

Outline Symbols

While an outline is displayed, you see outlining symbols along the left edge and top of the worksheet that contains the outline. These outlining symbols and tools show or hide levels of the outline to let you see more or less detail.

Figure 18.4 shows the different buttons and elements used in working with outlines.

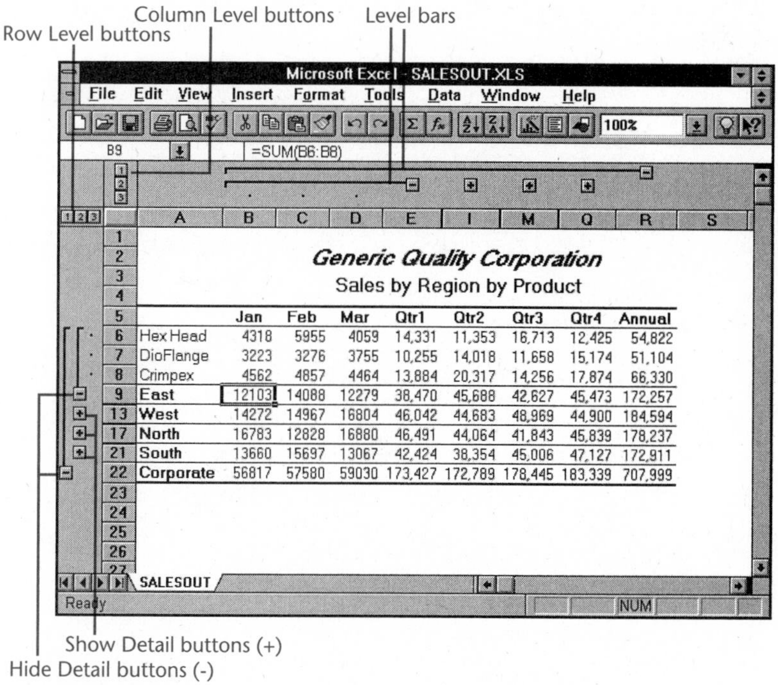

Fig. 18.4
Use these buttons and outline elements to control your outline.

The outlining symbols are described in the following list:

Symbol	Description
Show Detail (+)	Click this button to show the detail one level under this button
Hide Detail (–)	Click this button to hide all levels under this button
Row or Column Level buttons	Specifies the number of the row or column level to display throughout the outline
Level bars	Specifies all rows or columns at a specific level

Creating an Outline

Excel can create an outline, or you can manually create the outline. Excel's Automatic Outlining feature offers automated speed and convenience. Automatic outlining works well in most situations, and is useful if you haven't created an outline before and your outline has a consistent layout. Manual Outlining is necessary if the data is organized in a way that Excel doesn't understand. If you are experienced in creating outlines, manual outlining offers additional flexibility in designing your outline.

Using Excel's Automatic Outlining To Create an Outline

Before you use automatic outlining on a worksheet, check to see the direction in which summary formulas refer to cells. Summary formulas must be consistent in the direction in which they *point.* All summary formulas in rows, for example, should summarize cells above and all summaries in columns should summarize cells to the left. Automatic outlining works on summaries that refer to cells below or to the right *if all the summaries are consistent in the direction in which they point.*

If you cannot get automatic outlining to work because Excel cannot understand the direction in which summary formulas point or because no consistent direction exists, you can change the automatic settings or manually group rows and columns. These methods are described in this chapter in following sections.

To apply formatting styles associated with outlining automatically, see the following section, "Formatting Outlines," before you create an automatic outline.

To create an outline of the entire worksheet or a range on the worksheet, follow these steps:

1. If you want to outline data within a part of the worksheet, select the range you want to outline. If you want to outline the entire worksheet, select a single cell.
2. Choose the **D**ata **G**roup and Outline command.
3. Choose the **A**uto Outline command from the submenu.

To create an outline using the mouse, select the range containing the data or a single cell if you want to outline the entire worksheet. Click the Show Outline Symbols button. This button is available as a custom button from the Utility category on the Customize toolbars dialog box. (Chapter 41, "Creating Custom Toolbars and Menus," describes how to add this button to the toolbar.) If an outline doesn't already exist, the following message appears: `Cannot show outline symbols. No outline exists on the current worksheet. Create one?`. Choose OK to create the outline.

If Excel can determine a consistent direction of summarizing, it creates an outline. If Excel doesn't create an outline, it displays a warning message.

Creating Outlines Manually

If summary formulas are inconsistent in the direction in which they refer to detail or if no summary formulas exist, you still can outline by using manual methods. Manual outlining is also important as a way of promoting or demoting levels within an existing outline.

You can use the mouse or keyboard to create an outline or change the levels in an outline by selecting rows or columns and then promoting or demoting the rows or columns.

To group rows or columns into a new outline level, follow these steps:

1. Select cells in the rows or columns that you want to change. Select up to but not including the cell that contains the summary formula.

2. Either choose the **D**ata **G**roup and Outline **G**roup command, press Alt+Shift+right arrow, or click the Group button to group items on a level.

   The Group and Ungroup buttons are located on the Query and Pivot toolbar.

3. From the Group dialog box that appears, select **R**ows or **C**olumns, depending upon what you want to group.

4. Choose OK.

Tip
Press Ctrl+' (the ~ key) to display formulas so you can see which direction formulas point.

Clearing an Outline

You may want to remove an outline if it is no longer necessary or remove one so that you can create one in a different location on the same worksheet.

To remove a portion of an outline, select cells in the row or columns at the level you want removed, and then choose the **D**ata **G**roup and Outline **C**lear Outline command. Clear the entire outline by selecting the entire outline and choosing **D**ata **G**roup and Outline **C**lear Outline. If the outline covers the entire worksheet, you can select the entire worksheet by clicking the button to the left of the A column heading and above the 1 row heading or by pressing Shift+Ctrl+space bar.

Manipulating the Display of an Outline

The main benefit of creating an outline is that you can control the way data appears in the outline. The next few sections show you how to control the display of the outlining symbols, determine which levels of the outline are displayed, and reformat your outline.

Hiding Outline Symbols

You can keep an outline on the worksheet and hide the outline symbols by choosing the **T**ools **O**ptions command and selecting View tab. Clear the **O**utline Symbols check box. From the keyboard, press Ctrl+8, or use a mouse to click the Outline Symbols check box. (The Show Outline Symbols button must be added to a toolbar by dragging it from the Utility category in the Customize dialog box. You can learn how to customize a toolbar in Chapter 41, "Creating Custom Toolbars and Menus.") If no outline exists when you click this button, an alert box asks if you want to create an outline.

Displaying or Hiding Outline Levels

The real value of an outline is apparent when you expand and collapse the outline to display or work with different levels of data or summary. Although using the mouse is the easiest method to display or hide different levels, you also can use the keyboard.

Troubleshooting

The outline generated with the Data Group and Outline Auto Outline command is incomplete. The outline level bars and buttons are inconsistent or missing.

Use the audit tools described in Chapter 26, "Auditing Workbooks and Worksheets," to see which way formulas refer within the outlined area. If all the row formulas do not refer to the same direction or if all the column formulas do not refer to the same direction, you get unusual results. To remedy this situation, use the techniques described in "Creating Outlines Manually" to create your outline.

Someone created a subtotal on top of an already existing outline. The outline was modified to incorporate the subtotals.

Yes. That happens. Remove the subtotals by repeating the Data Subtotals command and choosing the Remove All button. Then re-create the outline.

Portions of the worksheet have disappeared.

When rows or columns in an outline are hidden to hide detail, they are hidden across the entire worksheet. This may hide other parts of the worksheet.

After creating an outline on part of my worksheet, it seems that there are row or column level buttons and lines throughout other parts of the worksheet.

If you select only a single cell in the worksheet, the entire worksheet is outlined. If Excel finds other parts of the worksheet where the formulas have a consistent direction of reference, then it outlines those parts of the worksheet as well. To outline part of a worksheet, select the range you want outlined, and then complete the outline procedure.

For Related Information

- "Creating Charts from Outlines," p. 519
- "Creating Simple Subtotals," p. 607
- "Reorganizing the Pivot Table," p. 1015

Note

Titles you place in cells above an outline may disappear if the column that contains the title is hidden when you hide a detail level for the outline. One way to prevent titles from disappearing is to make outline titles by using graphic text boxes created from the Drawing toolbar. Graphic objects can be made to float above cells and remain in place as rows and columns are hidden. Text boxes and graphic objects that overlap an outline may become distorted or disappear when you expand or collapse the outline. To prevent this distortion, format the text boxes or graphic objects with the F**o**rmat Obj**e**ct command. Select the Properties tab and format objects that overlap the outline with **D**on't Move or Size with Cells. Format arrows with Move and **S**ize with Cells. Text boxes that explain data in the outline usually use **M**ove but Don't Size with Cells.

If you are using graphics or text boxes as titles for an outline, this procedure keeps them over the correct areas, adjusts the length of arrows appropriately, and moves explanatory text boxes without distorting the text inside.

To display or hide levels using commands, follow these steps:

1. Select a cell in the summary row or column you want to display or hide.
2. Choose the **D**ata **G**roup and Outline command.
3. Select either **H**ide Detail or **S**how Detail.

You must be on a cell that contains a summary formula. These cells are in the rows or columns that contain the Display or Hide buttons.

Note

Before you can use the Show Outline button to show or hide outline symbols, you must add the button to a toolbar. The button is located in the Utility category of the Customize dialog box when you are customizing a toolbar. Chapter 41, "Creating Custom Toolbars and Menus," describes how to customize a toolbar.

To display or hide levels in an outline with the mouse, follow these steps:

1. If outline symbols are not displayed, click the Show Outline button or press Ctrl+8.
2. Display or hide levels of detail in specific rows or columns with one of the following actions:

   Expand a specific row or column by clicking the related Display (+) symbol.

   Expand to an entire level by clicking the appropriate Level number button. To display all levels, click the highest numbered button.

   Collapse a specific row or column by clicking the related Hide (-) symbol.

   Collapse to a level by clicking the appropriate Level number button. To collapse all levels, click the lowest numbered button.

Formatting Outlines

You can format outlines easily. Excel can apply a different format style to each level of heading. Styles are names that are assigned a combination of numeric, font, alignment, border, pattern, or protection formats. Besides applying many formats at once, styles enable you to change the format of all cells using a style by redefining the collection of formats assigned to the style name. To learn how to redefine styles, refer to Chapter 10, "Formatting Worksheets."

If you are creating a new outline, you can apply outline styles when Excel creates the outline by choosing the **D**ata **G**roup and Outline S**e**ttings command. Select **A**utomatic Styles. Now when you create an automatic outline, the styles are applied for you.

If you already created an outline and want to apply outline styles to it, select the cells to which you want to apply styles, choose the **D**ata **G**roup and Outline S**e**ttings command and choose Apply **S**tyles.

For Related Information

- "Formatting with AutoFormats," p. 303
- "Applying Multiple Formats at One Time," p. 354

The style names that Excel uses are of the form RowLevel_1, RowLevel_2, ColLevel_1, ColLevel_2, and so on. If you want styles to appear differently, you can redefine the collection of formats assigned to each style, which is described in Chapter 10.

If you clear an outline, the styles remain.

Copying and Charting from Specific Outline Levels

When an outline has details hidden, the worksheet still contains all the data at different levels. You can create charts from the visible data in an outline or from all the data in an outline. If you usually work one way, you can set your preference so that Excel charts visible data or all data.

To set a default preference whether all data or only visible data are charted, follow these steps:

1. Display a chart in its own window or sheet so that the chart menus are available.
2. Choose the **T**ools **O**ptions command.
3. Select Chart tab.
4. Select **P**lot Visible Cells Only. For most business situations you want this check box selected.
5. Choose OK.

Note

One way to select or chart visible data in a worksheet is to select the outline, and then click the Visible Cells button in a toolbar. You must customize a toolbar if you want the Visible Cells button available. The Visible Cells button is found in the Utility category of custom buttons. Chapter 41, "Creating Custom Toolbars and Menus," describes how to customize toolbars.

To manually specify that you want to only work with visible cells, follow these steps:

For Related Information

- "Creating an Embedded Chart," p. 407
- "Moving Cell Contents," p. 235
- "Filling or Copying Cell Contents," p. 241

1. Display the outline so that it shows the levels of detail and summary you need.
2. Select the cells with which you want to work.
3. Choose the **E**dit **G**o To **S**pecial command, select the **V**isible Cells Only option, and choose OK.

You see a separation between cells that contain nonvisible data, as shown in figure 18.5. The separation between cells is shown as white lines between the visible cells in the figure.

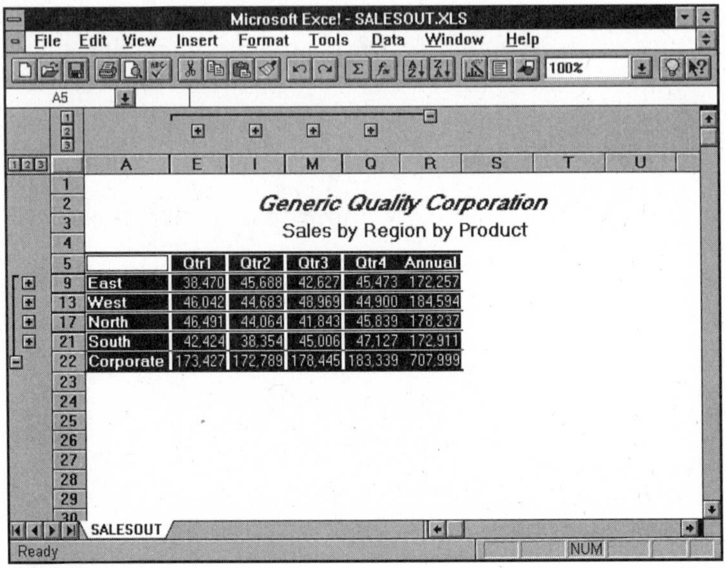

Fig. 18.5
Selecting only the visible data in an outline enables you to chart only visible data.

Now that you have only the visible data selected, continue working as you usually do. You may want to create a chart, for example, using only visible data. You cannot use drag-and-drop mouse techniques with visible data selected.

From Here...

For information relating directly to using an outline or other features that incorporate an outline, you may want to read the following chapters:

- Chapter 19, "Creating Automatic Subtotals." Learn how Excel automatically creates subtotals and grand totals in lists of data. As part of the bargain, it includes outlines so that you can show or hide detail.

- Chapter 37, "Analyzing and Reporting with Pivot Tables." Pivot Tables are one of Excel's most powerful features. With a Pivot Table you can create a report that analyzes the contents of large lists or databases. You can use outlines to enhance Pivot Tables.

Chapter 19

Creating Automatic Subtotals

In previous versions of Excel, you had to perform some fancy tricks to create subtotals and grand totals. Excel 5 provides an easy way to create subtotals. This feature is useful if you need to group data into separate groups—for example, group sales by account or group projects by team leader.

EXCEL 5

In this chapter you learn how to:

- Create simple subtotals
- Create more complex subtotals
- Display different levels of detail in the report
- Format and print the report
- Remove the subtotals

What Are Automatic Subtotals?

Subtotals are a quick and easy way to summarize data in a list. Suppose that you have a list of sales. The list includes the date, account, product, unit, price, and revenue. If you want to see subtotals by account, you can do so. If you want to see subtotals by product, you also can.

With Excel's Subtotals command, you don't need to create the formulas. Excel creates the formula, inserts the subtotal and grand total rows, and outlines the data automatically. The resulting data are easy to format, chart, and print.

Creating Simple Subtotals

The subtotals provide a great deal of flexibility in the way you can summarize data. Using subtotals, you can do the following:

- Tell Excel how to group the data
- Display subtotals and grand totals for one set of groups in the list

- Display subtotals and grand totals for several sets of groups in the list
- Perform different calculations on the grouped data—count the items, total the items, average the items

After you create the subtotals, you can quickly format and print the resulting report.

Preparing for the Subtotals

For the subtotals to work correctly, you need to organize the data into labeled columns. Excel uses the column labels to determine how the data are grouped and how the totals are calculated.

You also need to sort the data into the groups that you want. If you want to group the data by account, for example, then sort the data by account. You can sort by more than one criterion.

Tip

To select only certain rows in the data list, use a filter to display the desired rows. See "Creating Subtotals for Filtered Data" later in this chapter.

For more information on sorting data, see Chapter 32, "Sorting Data."

Creating a Subtotal

After the data is sorted in the way you want, you can create the subtotals quickly by following these steps:

1. Make sure that the cursor is within the list. Then choose the **D**ata Su**b**totals command. You see the Subtotal dialog box (see fig. 19.1).

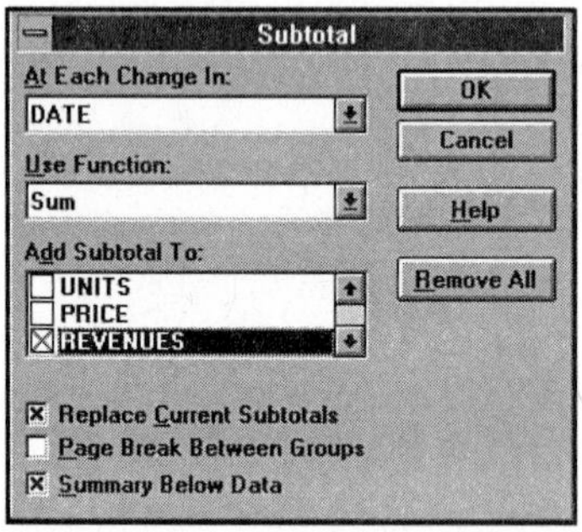

Fig. 19.1
Enter the column to group by and the column you want to calculate.

2. Select how to group the data by selecting the **A**t Each Change in drop-down list. This list displays the columns in your database or list. Select the column you want. If you were totaling net sales by account, for example, select Account.

   If this is the first time you selected the command, Excel selects the left-most column automatically. If you used the command before, the column you used last time is selected.

3. Select the calculation that you want performed by displaying the **U**se Function drop-down list and selecting the function you want. The most common function is Sum, but you also can select Count, Average, Max, Min, Product, Count Nums, StdDev, StdDevp, Var, and Varp. For more information on functions see Chapter 6, "Using Functions."

   Based on the type of data you are summarizing, Excel suggests a function. If the column you are summarizing contains numbers, for example, Excel enters the Sum function. If the column contains text, Excel enters the Count function.

4. Select data that you want calculated by selecting the check boxes in A**d**d Subtotal to list box. This list box displays the columns in the data list. You select the column you want calculated. For example, if you want to total revenue by account, select Revenues.

   To create summary functions for more than one column, select each of the columns you want. (To perform different calculations on the same columns, see the section, "Creating Additional Subtotals," which follows in this chapter.)

5. To replace any existing subtotals, select the Replace **C**urrent Subtotals check box so that an X appears.

6. To insert a page break before each group, select the **P**age Break Between Groups check box so that an X appears.

7. By default, the subtotal and grand totals appear at the end of the data group. If you prefer to show these totals before the data group, select the **S**ummary Below **D**ata to unmark the check box.

8. Choose OK.

Excel inserts subtotal rows for each group and performs the selected calculation (step 3) on the selected column (step 4). A grand total row is also inserted. The grand total is always the result of the detail data (not just a result of each subtotal).

Excel labels each inserted row with an appropriate title. For example, if you were totaling by Account, Excel displays the *Account Name* Total (*Account Name* would be the actual account name).

For Related Information

- "Excel Function Directory," p. 184
- "Sorting Data by Command," p. 890
- "Using the AutoFilter," p. 913

Excel also outlines the data. The outline symbols displayed after you create the subtotals enable you to quickly hide and show detail data. See the section, "Changing the Detail Level," that follows in this chapter for information on showing detail levels.

Figure 19.2 shows an example of subtotaling revenue by account.

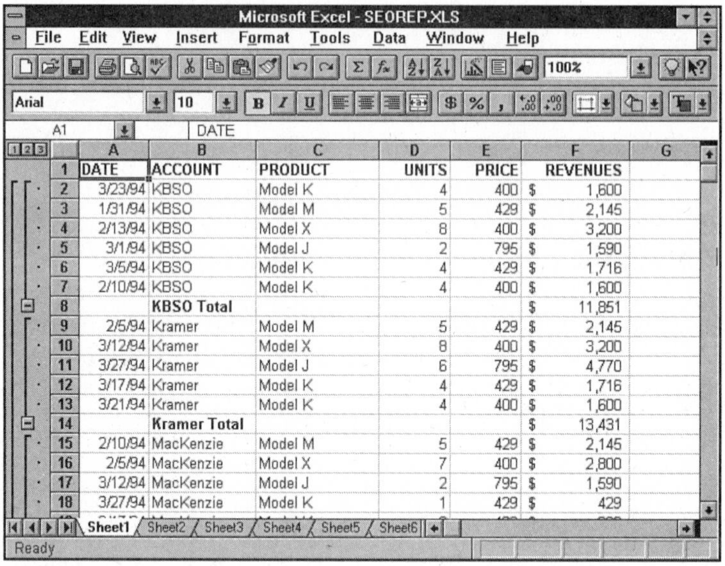

Fig. 19.2
Here, the entries are grouped by account. The revenue for each account is totaled.

Removing a Subtotal

If you immediately realize you don't want the subtotals, choose the **E**dit **U**ndo command to undo the subtotals. If Undo is unavailable because you made other changes, choose the **D**ata Su**b**totals command and choose the **R**emove All button.

Creating Advanced Subtotals

You aren't limited to just one calculation on one set of groups. You can create subtotals for groups within the first group. For example, you may want to display subtotals for account and then for product within the account.

You also can perform multiple calculations on the columns in a group. For example, you may want to count the number of sales in a group and then total the dollar amount.

Creating Nested Subtotals

If you want additional subtotals within each group (a nested subtotal), you can create two sets of subtotals. For instance, you might want to total all accounts and also include subtotals for each product within an account.

To create a nested subtotal, be sure that the data is sorted on the 2nd key. Then choose the **D**ata Su**b**totals command. Then choose the options for the first group (the largest group). Excel inserts subtotals for the first group.

Next, choose the **D**ata Su**b**totals command and choose the options for the next group. Be sure that Replace **C**urrent Subtotals check box is not selected (does not contain an X). Excel inserts a subtotal for the next set of groups.

Figure 19.3 shows revenue totals by account and unit totals by product.

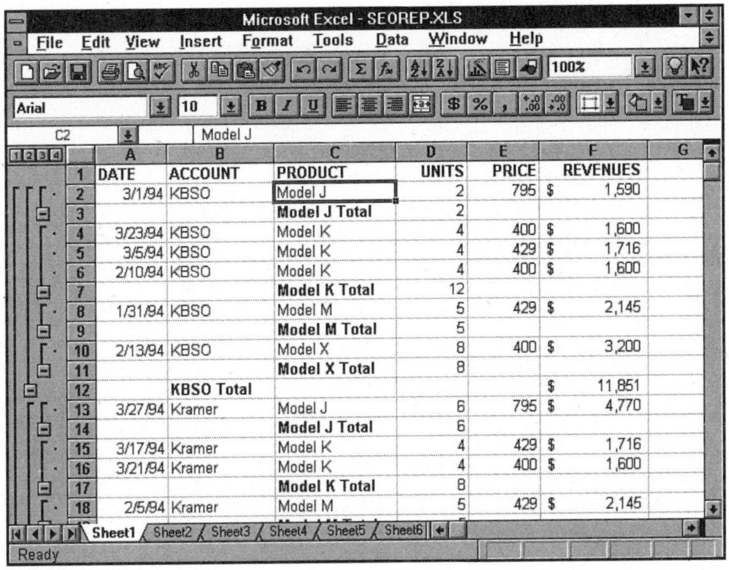

Fig. 19.3
Excel created revenue subtotals for each account. The accounts then were grouped by product and a unit total was calculated.

Using Multiple Summary Functions

For some lists of data, you might want to do more than one calculation. For instance, you might want to total the sales (using the SUM function) and show an average of the sales (using the AVG function). You can do so with Excel.

To display two or more summary functions for the same set of data, choose the **D**ata Su**b**totals command and select the first function. Choose OK. Excel

Tip
To perform a summary calculation on more than one column, just select the columns in the A**d**d Subtotal to drop-down list in the Subtotal dialog box.

inserts the subtotal rows. Then choose the command again and select another function. Be sure that Replace **C**urrent Subtotals check box is not selected. Excel inserts an additional subtotal row with the new calculation.

Figure 19.4 shows revenue totals by account and average revenue by account.

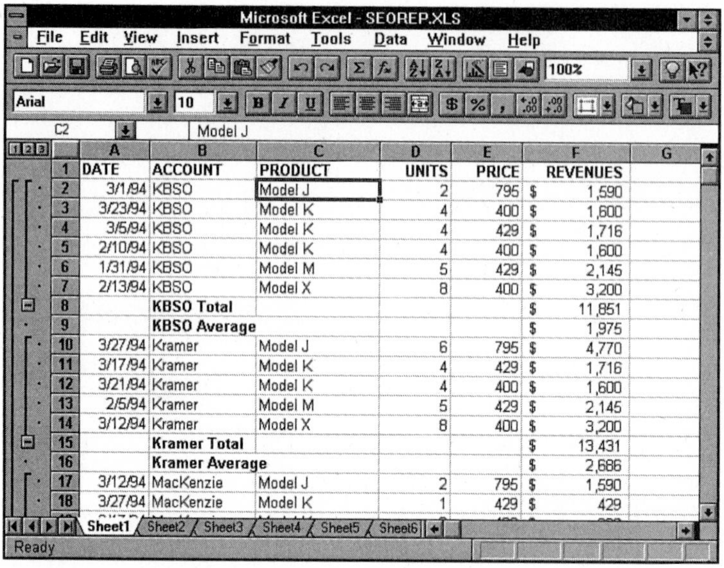

Fig. 19.4
Two calculations—a sum and an average—performed on the account groups.

Changing the Detail Level

For Related Information

- "Excel Function Directory," p. 184
- "Creating a Chart Automatically," p. 415

Depending on the level of subtotals you created, Excel creates an outline with different levels. In outline view, you can quickly display summary information. To display just the grand total and column labels, click the row level 1 symbol. If you want to display just the subtotals and grand total, click the row level 2 symbol.

You also can click on the Hide Detail (–) or Display Detail (+) symbol to collapse and expand the outline.

Changing the row levels is useful when you want to perform the following procedures:

- Create a chart of just the subtotals. Collapse the detail level of the data list to show just the subtotals. Then select and chart the subtotals.
- Sort the subtotals. Display the subtotals you want to sort and then sort the data with the **D**ata **S**ort command. All hidden rows are sorted with the associated subtotal row.

Figure 19.5 shows only the subtotal and grand total rows. All other rows are hidden.

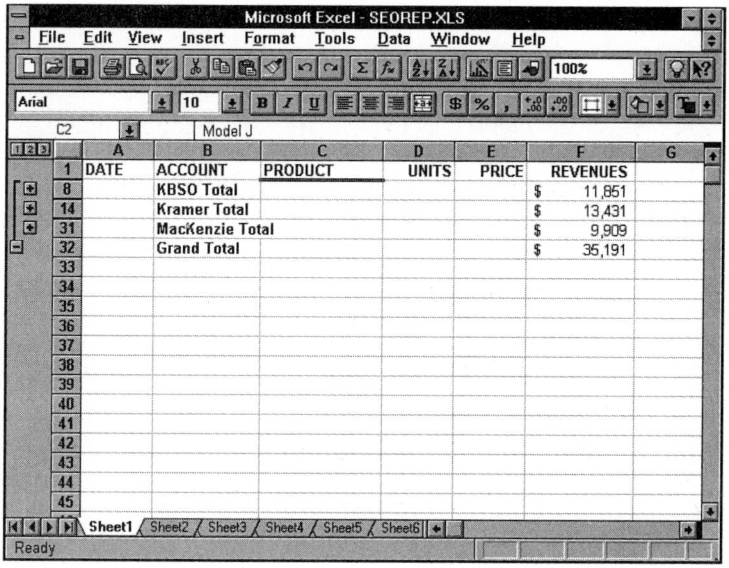

Fig. 19.5
You can change the level of detail shown in the outline so that only the subtotals and grand total are displayed.

Using Subtotals on Filtered Data

There may be some rows that you want to exclude from the list. Suppose that you want to summarize only sales over five units or summarize only the sales of a particular product. The easiest way to summarize only certain rows is to filter the database.

To filter the database, follow these steps:

1. Choose the **D**ata **F**ilter command.

2. Choose the Auto**F**ilter command. You should see a check mark beside the command, which indicates that the command is selected.

   Drop-down arrows appear next to each column head. Using these drop-down lists, you can specify the filter you want to use.

3. Click the arrow next to the column you want to use as the filter. For example, if you want to display only a certain product, click the down arrow next to Product.

You see a list of predefined filters in parentheses, and you see each unique entry in the column listed. (All) selects all the entries in this column. (Blanks) selects blanks. (Non Blanks) selects all non-blank cells. (Custom) enables you to create a custom filter. (See Chapter 33, "Finding, Filtering, and Editing Lists and Databases," for more information on filters). Selecting one of the entries in the column tells Excel to match this entry. If you select Model M in the Product column, for example, Excel displays only Model M products.

After you select the filters you want, Excel hides all rows that don't meet the criteria. Now you can create the subtotals for just the displayed rows.

Tip
You can filter on more than one column. Just continue selecting the filters you want.

Note

To turn off the AutoFilter, choose the **D**ata **F**ilter Auto**F**ilter command. When the filter is activated, a check mark appears next to the command.

4. Use the **D**ata Su**b**totals command to choose the subtotals you want calculated.

Figure 19.6 shows a database filtered by the Product column (only Model M products are displayed). The resulting list is then subtotaled by account.

Formatting and Printing the Report

The most likely reason for inserting subtotal rows is to produce a printed report. You can format the report quickly by using one of Excel's automatic formats. Choose the F**o**rmat **A**utoFormat command. Then select the format you want and choose OK. See Chapter 10, "Formatting Worksheets," for more information on this feature.

Tip
To print each group on a separate page, select the **P**age Break Between Groups check box.

To print the report, choose the **F**ile **P**rint command.

To print different versions of the same data, investigate creating views and using the Report Manager. Chapter 11, "Printing Worksheets," covers this topic.

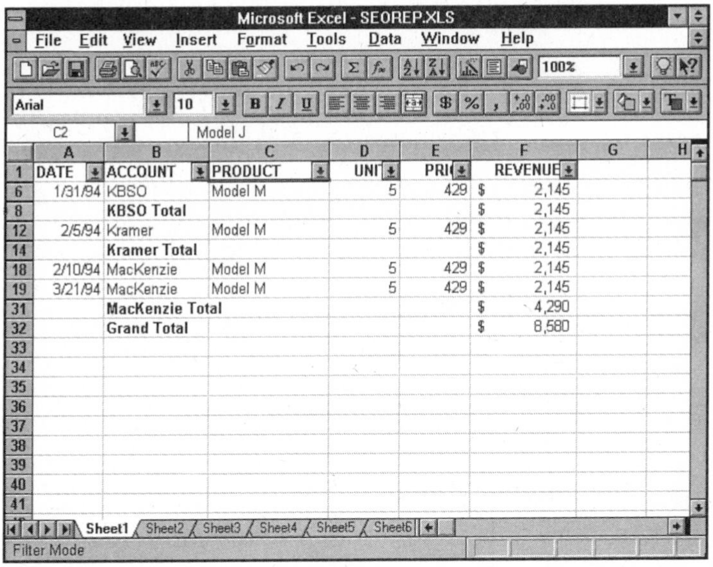

Fig 19.6
If you want to select only certain rows in your data list, filter the data first. Then do the subtotals.

From Here...

Excel has powerful features for working with databases. You can create data-entry forms; sort, search, filter, and extract data; and link up with external databases. If you work with databases, you should investigate Excel's database features, and these chapters may interest you:

- Chapter 30, "Designing a List or Database"
- Chapter 31, "Entering Data in a List or Database"
- Chapter 32, "Sorting Data"
- Chapter 33, "Finding, Filtering, and Editing Lists and Databases"

For Related Information

- "Formatting with Auto-Formats," p. 303
- "Printing," p. 395
- "Creating a Sequence of Reports," p. 397

Chapter 20

Publishing Worksheets and Charts

Like any other document, a worksheet or chart must communicate information. The content, of course, is the most important part of the document. If your worksheet or chart is among many competing documents that someone looks at, however, how do you get that person to review the document in the first place? Also, because of the large amount of information on many worksheets, it is easy for the reader to get lost in the detail. How do you show what is important in the mass of data?

To handle these questions, you can take advantage of the desktop publishing features of Excel. You can produce professional quality worksheets and charts that are inviting to read. With the enhanced features of Excel, you can also highlight important parts of the worksheet or chart so that anyone reviewing your work can quickly get to the point and save time. Figure 20.1 shows a worksheet printed with the standard capabilities of Excel; figure 20.2 shows a worksheet printed with the desktop publishing features of Excel.

This chapter helps you learn how to apply the desktop publishing capabilities of Excel to your worksheets and charts to achieve improved print quality that makes your worksheets easier to read and understand.

In this chapter you learn to:

- Prepare the worksheet to produce the printed output you want
- Format the worksheet for a professional look and make the worksheet easy to read and understand
- Add charts to your worksheet
- Create user-named formats, templates, and autoformats to automate the process of producing desktop-publishing-quality worksheets

Fig. 20.1
A worksheet printed with the standard capabilities of Excel.

LaserPro Corporation
Balance Sheet
December 31, 1994

Assets	This Year	Last Year	Change
Current Assets			
Cash	$247,886	$126,473	96%
Accounts receivable	863,652	524,570	65%
Inventory	88,328	65,508	35%
Investments	108,577	31,934	240%
	------------	-------------	
Total current assets	$1,308,443	$748,485	75%
Fixed Assets			
Machinery and equipment	$209,906	$158,730	32%
Vehicles	429,505	243,793	76%
Office furniture	50,240	36,406	38%
(Accumulated depreciation)	(101,098)	(64,394)	57%
	------------	-------------	
Total fixed assets	$588,553	$374,535	57%
Total Assets	$1,896,996	$1,123,020	69%
Liabilities and Shareholders Equity			
	This Year	Last Year	Change
Current Liabilities			
Accounts payable	$426,041	$332,845	28%
Notes payable	45,327	23,486	93%
Accrued liabilities	34,614	26,026	33%
Income taxes payable	88,645	51,840	71%
	------------	-------------	
Total current liabilities	$594,627	$434,197	37%
Noncurrent Liabilities			
Long-term debt	488,822	349,253	40%
Deferred federal tax	147,844	92,101	61%
	------------	-------------	
Total noncurrent liabilities	$636,666	$441,354	44%
Shareholders' Equity			
Common stock	1,000	1,000	0%
Retained earnings	664,703	246,469	170%
	------------	-------------	
Total shareholders' equity	$665,703	$247,469	169%
	------------	-------------	
Total Liabilities and Equity	$1,896,996	$1,123,020	69%
	============	=============	

LaserPro Corporation
Balance Sheet
December 31, 1994

Assets	This Year	Last Year	Change
Current Assets			
Cash	$247,886	$126,473	96%
Accounts receivable	863,652	524,570	65%
Inventory	88,328	65,508	35%
Investments	108,577	31,934	240%
Total current assets	$1,308,443	$748,485	75%
Fixed Assets			
Machinery and equipment	$209,906	$158,730	32%
Vehicles	429,505	243,793	76%
Office furniture	50,240	36,406	38%
(Accumulated depreciation)	(101,098)	(64,394)	57%
Total fixed assets	$588,553	$374,535	57%
Total Assets	**$1,896,996**	**$1,123,020**	**69%**

Liabilities and Shareholders' Equity	This Year	Last Year	Change
Current Liabilities			
Accounts payable	$426,041	$332,845	28%
Notes payable	45,327	23,486	93%
Accrued liabilities	34,614	26,026	33%
Income taxes payable	88,645	51,840	71%
Total current liabilities	$594,627	$434,197	37%
Noncurrent Liabilities			
Long-term debt	$488,822	$349,253	40%
Deferred federal tax	147,844	92,101	61%
Total noncurrent liabilities	$636,666	$441,354	44%
Shareholders' Equity			
Common stock	$1,000	$1,000	0%
Retained earnings	664,703	246,469	170%
Total shareholders' equity	$665,703	$247,469	169%
Total Liabilities and Equity	**$1,896,996**	**$1,123,020**	**69%**

Fig. 20.2
A worksheet using the desktop publishing features of Excel.

Preparing the Worksheet for Presentation-Quality Output

One of the great advantages of Excel is that you can see and evaluate the desktop publishing changes you make to your worksheet as you enter the worksheet data and add different formatting and layout features. Another advantage of Excel is its capability to set up the worksheet so that you can tell immediately whether the formatting and layout elements will produce a printed worksheet exactly as you want (for example, to make sure that your worksheet prints on one page). Setting up your worksheet before entering text and numbers helps you determine what your worksheet will look like. The following sections present techniques and tricks for preparing your worksheet for the kind of printed output you want with Excel.

Understanding Format and Layout

The terms *format* and *layout* are used throughout this chapter. To help you understand the references to format and layout, remember these definitions:

- *Format* refers to the form of the numeric and text information on the page—the type and size of font, including the use of bold or italic. Format also refers to the use of capitalization, underlining, or special graphical characters within the text.

- *Layout* refers to the position of numeric and text information on the page. Layout includes, for example, how information is presented in blocked, columnar fashion or how information is indented. Layout also refers to how information is positioned in relation to white space, including left, right, top, and bottom margins.

Giving Your Worksheet a Professional Look

You will have the most success using Excel if you remember to use its capabilities to communicate information presented in your worksheet. Although using the desktop publishing features of Excel to impress your readers may be helpful, you get the most impact from Excel by using its features to draw the reader's attention to certain information, to show how information is organized and subordinated to other information, and to make finding and reading information easy. This chapter presents a few key concepts that help you produce impressive-looking worksheets that communicate the information in an easy-to-follow form. The key ingredients to producing a professional looking worksheet include the following guidelines of good desktop publishing design and layout:

- Determine how you want the worksheet information communicated (what should be emphasized or de-emphasized, and how you want to indicate the relationships between information).

- Opt for simplicity; for example, avoid using too many different fonts or formatting elements.

- Establish consistency in the format and layout of your worksheets so that regular readers of your work can more easily and quickly find and understand information. Special elements will also have the desired effect.
- Use page format and layout to show contrast when you want certain elements on a worksheet to stand out in relation to all other information or whenever you want one worksheet to stand out in relation to other worksheets.

Following these basic guidelines helps you make the right choices when you are trying to decide what desktop publishing elements to include on your worksheets. The sample worksheet shown in figure 20.2 illustrates these basic concepts.

The layout and format of figure 20.2 illustrate the developer's intention to show clearly two main parts of the balance sheet—the Assets section and the Liabilities and Shareholders' Equity section.

First, the use of bold, shading, solid black rule, and large font for Assets and Liabilities and Shareholders' Equity segment shows the two main parts of the balance sheet. Second, bold calls attention to each of the main sections of the Assets and Liabilities and Shareholders' Equity parts of the balance sheet. Third, bold and underlining call attention to the rows of the balance sheet that contain totals for the overall Assets and Liabilities and Shareholders' Equity sections.

To achieve simplicity, the balance sheet in figure 20.2 uses one type of font for everything other than the company name at the top of the worksheet. Also, except for the company name, the worksheet uses only two different sizes of fonts—12 point for the main information and 14 point for the headings.

Maintaining consistency in the format and layout of the balance sheet in figure 20.2 is important for the following reasons. A consistency in format and layout conventions helps readers more easily read and understand other reports you produce. Consistency in the way you present the main headings of your worksheets, such as the Current Assets heading in the balance sheet in figure 20.2, helps readers see quickly the structure of your worksheet. Consistency in a worksheet like the balance sheet in figure 20.2 is also important whenever you plan to develop a series of balance sheets over time or need to develop many balance sheets for different divisions of your company.

Tip

For consistent-looking worksheets, learn to use templates as described in Chapter 42, "Creating Templates and Controlling Excel's Startup."

Contrast is used within the elements of a single worksheet and distinguishes one worksheet from another. The balance sheet in figure 20.2 shows contrast through bold, point size, position of headings, and underlining in the balance sheet. To distinguish one balance sheet among a series of others, you may, for example, box the contrasting balance sheet with a drop shadow to call attention to the balance sheet. Figure 20.3 shows how one balance sheet can stand out from others by using the Excel features for creating rounded boxes and drop shadows.

Fig. 20.3

Contrasting one balance sheet from others by placing a box and drop shadow around it.

LaserPro Corporation

Balance Sheet

December 31, 1994

Assets	This Year	Last Year	Change
Current Assets			
Cash	$247,886	$126,473	96%
Accounts receivable	863,652	524,570	65%
Inventory	88,328	65,508	35%
Investments	108,577	31,934	240%
Total current assets	$1,308,443	$748,485	75%
Fixed Assets			
Machinery and equipment	$209,906	$158,730	32%
Vehicles	429,505	243,793	76%
Office furniture	50,240	36,406	38%
(Accumulated depreciation)	(101,098)	(64,394)	57%
Total fixed assets	$588,553	$374,535	57%
Total Assets	**$1,896,996**	**$1,123,020**	**69%**

Liabilities and Shareholders' Equity	This Year	Last Year	Change
Current Liabilities			
Accounts payable	$426,041	$332,845	28%
Notes payable	45,327	23,486	93%
Accrued liabilities	34,614	26,026	33%
Income taxes payable	88,645	51,840	71%
Total current liabilities	$594,627	$434,197	37%
Noncurrent Liabilities			
Long-term debt	$488,822	$349,253	40%
Deferred federal tax	147,844	92,101	61%
Total noncurrent liabilities	$636,666	$441,354	44%
Shareholders' Equity			
Common stock	$1,000	$1,000	0%
Retained earnings	664,703	246,469	170%
Total shareholders' equity	$665,703	$247,469	169%
Total Liabilities and Equity	**$1,896,996**	**$1,123,020**	**69%**

Box and drop shadow

By following the simple desktop publishing guidelines for professional worksheets presented in this chapter, you can use Excel's capabilities to your best advantage.

Designing the Layout of Your Worksheet

The initial step for developing a desktop-published-quality worksheet with Excel includes spending time planning the layout and format for your worksheet before entering data. First, make a mental or written note of what you want to communicate through the information presented in the worksheet. What do you want to emphasize? What do you want readers to grasp easily? What do you want to persuade readers of? How do you want to communicate organization of the worksheet? Second, how can you keep the format and layout of your worksheet simple, but also show contrast and consistency?

After you make decisions about what information the worksheet should convey and how to format and lay out your worksheet, you can use Excel's Border Button or F**o**rmat C**e**lls Border option to create a grid on-screen so that you can easily lay out the worksheet on the page. This grid can be as simple as showing only the boundaries of your page so that you can tell whether your worksheet will fit on one page, or where the best place is to break information if you must print on two or more pages.

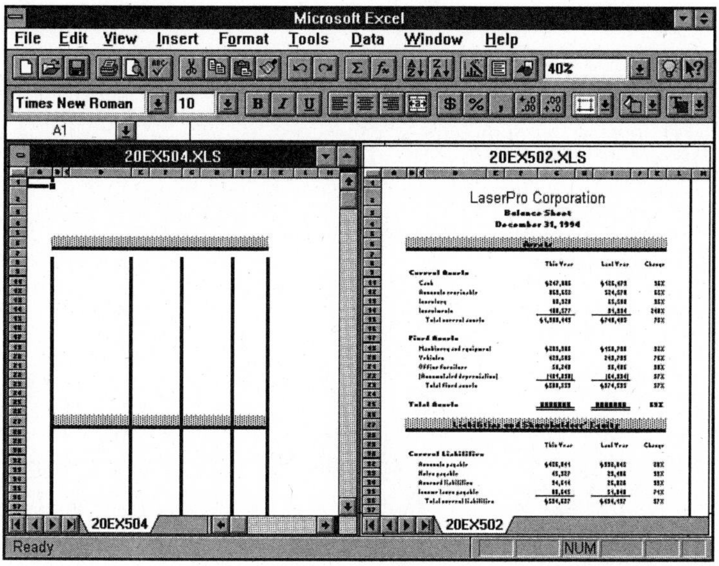

Fig. 20.4
An outline grid for the LaserPro balance sheet displayed in a window next to a reduced version of the balance sheet.

To keep the length of the worksheet to one page, you can use a small font size for all or parts of the worksheet. You can do this automatically by choosing **F**ile Page Set**u**p and then choosing the Page tab from the dialog box. On the Page tab, choose the **F**it to option. Avoid using too many different point sizes, and make certain that the worksheet will be readable, even if a poor photocopy blurs or lightens the characters on the page. A more complex grid can show the center points of your page to help you balance different parts of the worksheet on the page (see fig. 20.4).

Using a grid to lay out the worksheet shown in figure 20.2, for example, helps to determine how much space to give to the information at the top of the page and how to position the two major sections of the balance sheet. If you create a page border (see "Displaying the Page Border" later in this chapter) before you begin to enter data, you can avoid the need to move data on the page because it does not fit or because information is not balanced. Creating a page border before entering your worksheet data also helps you determine how much white space you can include.

Using White Space

If you have enough room on the page, reserve columns of *white space* between columns of data, and reserve rows of white space to divide sections of the worksheet. White space is really another name for blank areas—such as blank columns, blank row, or extra wide columns with short lines of text. White space between columns of data can also help create balance when columns of data vary in column width.

Figure 20.5 shows the layout of the balance sheet in figure 20.2, which contains 10 columns. Two columns are used for the labels on the left side of the balance sheet; three columns for numerical data; and five columns for white space (two of these are used for additional margin space on the left and right sides of the worksheet).

Displaying the Page Border

Excel provides three ways of knowing whether your worksheet data will fit on one page. First, Excel displays dashed lines around the borders of page breaks when you activate the A**u**tomatic Page Breaks option. To activate this option, choose **T**ools **O**ptions, choose the View tab from the dialog box, and then select A**u**tomatic Page Breaks in the Window Options area (see fig. 20.6). Second, the **F**ile Print Pre**v**iew command displays a picture of the printed page on-screen so that you can preview the page before it is printed. Finally, when you print, Excel brings up a dialog box that says how many pages will be printed with a `Page 1 of x` message where `x` is the number of pages. If you are quick, you may be able to stop printing by selecting Cancel on the dialog box or turning off the printer.

LaserPro Corporation
Balance Sheet
December 31, 1994

	This Year	Last Year	Change
Assets			
	This Year	Last Year	Change
Current Assets			
Cash	$247,886	$126,473	96%
Accounts receivable	863,652	524,570	65%
Inventory	88,328	65,508	35%
Investments	108,577	31,934	240%
Total current assets	$1,308,443	$748,485	75%
Fixed Assets			
Machinery and equipment	$209,906	$158,730	32%
Vehicles	429,505	243,793	76%
Office furniture	50,240	36,406	38%
(Accumulated depreciation)	(101,098)	(64,394)	57%
Total fixed assets	$588,553	$374,535	57%
Total Assets	**$1,896,996**	**$1,123,020**	**69%**
Liabilities and Shareholders' Equity			
	This Year	Last Year	Change
Current Liabilities			
Accounts payable	$426,041	$332,845	28%
Notes payable	45,327	23,486	93%
Accrued liabilities	34,614	26,026	33%
Income taxes payable	88,645	51,840	71%
Total current liabilities	$594,627	$434,197	37%
Noncurrent Liabilities			
Long-term debt	$488,822	$349,253	40%
Deferred federal tax	147,844	92,101	61%
Total noncurrent liabilities	$636,666	$441,354	44%
Shareholders' Equity			
Common stock	$1,000	$1,000	0%
Retained earnings	664,703	246,469	170%
Total shareholders' equity	$665,703	$247,469	169%
Total Liabilities and Equity	**$1,896,996**	**$1,123,020**	**69%**

Fig. 20.5
The white space used in the layout for the figure 20.2 worksheet.

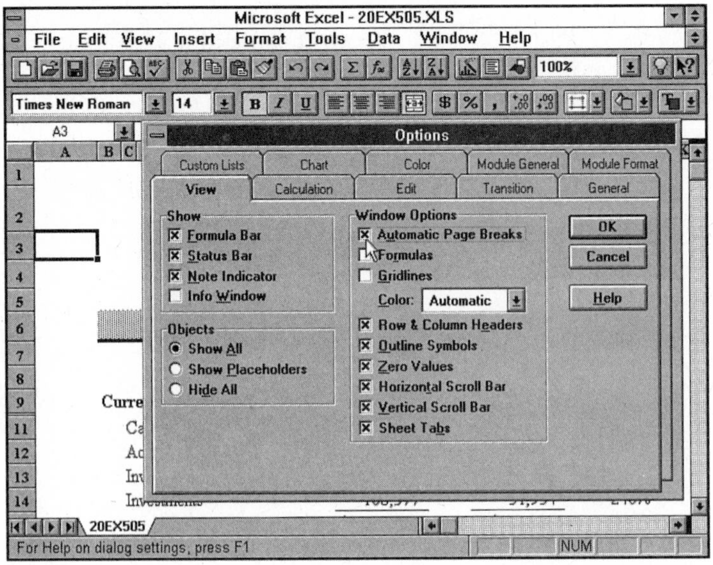

Fig. 20.6
Choose the **T**ools **O**ptions command, and on the View tab, mark the check box A**u**tomatic Page Breaks to display dashed lines where page breaks will occur.

If you find that your data range extends beyond the boundaries of the page break lines, you have a few choices. First, you can delete columns or rows or change the column widths. Second, you can split the document so that it fits on more than one page. Third, you can choose to have the worksheet automatically fit on one page with by choosing **F**ile Page Set**u**p and then selecting **F**it to on the Page tab. Keep in mind that when you shrink text or decrease column widths, however, you may sacrifice readability, balance, or enough white space in your document. In some cases, it may be appropriate to consolidate data.

Creating a Single- versus Multiple- Page Report

Before you enter data into a worksheet, you can select the A**u**tomatic Page Breaks option to help you determine what point sizes to use if you want to fit all information on one page. The A**u**tomatic Page Breaks option is also an advantage whenever you are creating multiple-page reports. This option helps you divide your worksheet into *page grids*. If you create one large worksheet with many columns and need to see at which column a new page will begin, select the A**u**tomatic Page Breaks option to show where these page breaks will occur. After you know how many columns of data fit onto a page, you can lay out columns appropriately. You can also use the **I**nsert Page **B**reak command to control manually where new pages should begin.

Suppose that you need to create a worksheet containing 18 columns of data. A sales report showing sales for each month, totals for each quarter, the yearly total, and labels for the product lines, for example, would need 18 columns. If you enter the data on a single worksheet, you can use the Automatic Page Breaks option to determine where page breaks will occur; you can then organize your data into quarterly sections according to the page divisions. Figure 20.7 shows a diagram of such a worksheet.

	Page 1				Page 2				Page 3				Page 4				
	Jan-94	Feb-94	Mar-94	1st Q	Apr-94	May-94	Jun-94	2nd Q	Jul-94	Aug-94	Sep-94	3rd Q	Oct-94	Nov-94	Dec-94	4th Q	Total
SERIES 1000																	
Model 1010	6,000	6,000	7,500	19,500	6,000	6,000	7,500	19,500	6,000	6,000	7,500	19,500	6,000	6,000	7,500	19,500	78,000
Model 1011	3,500	1,500	455	5,455	364	364	455	1,183	364	364	455	1,183	364	364	456	1,183	9,004
Model 1012	4,000	2,000	455	6,455	364	364	455	1,183	364	364	455	1,183	364	364	455	1,183	10,004
Model 1013	615	615	769	1,999	615	615	769	1,999	615	615	769	1,999	615	615	769	1,999	7,996
Model 1014	530	530	662	1,722	530	530	662	1,722	530	530	662	1,722	530	530	662	1,722	6,888
Model 1015	192	192	240	624	192	192	240	624	192	192	240	624	192	192	240	624	2,496
Model 1016	769	769	962	2,500	769	769	962	2,500	769	769	962	2,500	769	769	962	2,500	10,000
Model 1017	0	0	4,200	4,200	3,800	457	571	4,828	457	457	571	1,485	457	457	571	1,485	11,998
Model 1018	0	0	3,500	3,500	2,500	229	286	3,015	229	229	286	744	229	229	286	744	8,003
Model 1019	0	0	2,500	2,500	1,500	400	500	2,400	400	400	500	1,300	400	400	500	1,300	7,500
Model 1020	0	0	0	0	0	538	673	1,211	538	538	673	1,749	538	538	673	1,749	4,709
Model 1021	0	0	0	0	0	0	0	0	4,500	3,000	694	8,194	556	556	694	1,806	10,000
Total Series 1000	**15,606**	**11,606**	**21,243**	**48,455**	**16,634**	**10,458**	**13,073**	**40,165**	**14,958**	**13,458**	**13,767**	**42,183**	**11,014**	**11,014**	**13,767**	**35,795**	**166,598**
SERIES 2000																	
Model 2010	5,000	2,000	0	7,000	821	821	1,026	2,668	821	821	1,026	2,666	821	821	1,026	2,668	15,004
Model 2011	0	0	0	0	0	0	0	0	2,500	2,000	833	5,333	667	667	833	2,167	7,500
Model 2012	0	0	6,250	6,250	3,250	971	1,214	5,435	971	971	1,214	3,156	971	971	1,214	3,156	17,997
Model 2013	0	0	0	0	0	5,500	3,000	8,500	815	815	1,019	2,649	815	815	1,019	2,649	13,798
Model 2014	0	0	0	0	0	3,500	3,500	7,000	615	615	769	1,999	615	615	769	1,999	10,998
Total Series 2000	**5,000**	**2,000**	**6,250**	**13,250**	**4,071**	**10,792**	**8,740**	**23,603**	**5,722**	**5,222**	**4,861**	**16,805**	**3,889**	**3,889**	**4,861**	**12,639**	**65,297**
SERIES 3000																	
Model 3010	0	0	0	0	0	0	1,875	1,875	1,875	682	852	3,409	682	682	852	2,216	7,500
Model 3011	0	0	0	0	0	0	5,000	5,000	1,000	273	341	1,614	273	273	341	887	7,501
Model 3012	0	0	0	0	0	0	0	0	3,500	2,500	556	6,556	444	444	556	1,444	8,000
Model 3013	0	0	0	0	0	0	0	0	2,500	2,000	556	5,056	444	444	556	1,444	6,500
Model 3014	0	0	0	0	0	0	0	0	0	2,000	1,500	3,500	215	215	269	699	4,199
Model 3015	0	0	0	0	0	0	0	0	0	625	625	1,250	43	43	54	140	1,390
Total Series 3000	**0**	**0**	**0**	**0**	**0**	**0**	**6,875**	**6,875**	**8,875**	**8,080**	**4,430**	**21,385**	**2,101**	**2,101**	**2,628**	**6,830**	**35,090**
TOTAL	20,606	13,606	27,493	61,705	20,705	21,250	28,688	70,643	29,555	26,760	23,058	79,373	17,004	17,004	21,256	55,264	266,985

Fig. 20.7
A single worksheet showing a multiple-page layout.

Using the Automatic Page Breaks option to show page borders enables you to organize your worksheet so that data is laid out on the worksheet exactly as you want it to flow from page to page. If, for example, you want each page to begin with data for a new quarter—first quarter on the first page, second quarter on the second, and so forth—you enter columns where appropriate according to the page borders.

For Related Information

- "Previewing the Document," p. 389
- "Compressing Reports To Fit the Paper Size," p. 392
- "Controlling the Worksheet Display," p. 533

Laying Out and Formatting Your Worksheet

So far, this chapter has covered the beginning steps of worksheet publishing. These steps include planning your worksheet by considering how you can best communicate its information and using the features available with Excel. This chapter also covers the mechanics of getting started to create a professional-looking, quality worksheet with Excel. You can show page breaks and even create divider lines separating sections of your worksheet to make laying out worksheet data easier. Through examples, the following sections present step-by-step instructions for creating professional worksheets.

Using an Existing Worksheet versus Creating a New Worksheet

Although you can achieve exactly the same output whether you apply Excel to an existing worksheet or create a new one, working with an existing worksheet may require some precautions. You need to be careful of the effect that adding new columns and rows and moving data may have on an existing worksheet. You need to make sure, for example, that formulas are not affected if you decide to insert columns for additional white space on the page. Using an existing worksheet can be a big time-saver, however, because you don't have to spend time creating a new worksheet.

When working with an existing worksheet, you also need to consider whether the changes you make by applying desktop publishing techniques will affect the way a worksheet is used by others. If the worksheet you are changing, for example, is used by others for combining data from many worksheets, make sure that your changes will not cause errors when the worksheet is combined. Be careful with worksheets containing formulas that refer to worksheets in other files. Similarly, be careful when you change one Excel worksheet that is linked to worksheets or documents.

Finally, remember that the more you use the desktop publishing features of Excel, the more likely you will move or erase data, sometimes erasing data accidentally. If you use an existing worksheet, keep a backup copy, and take precautions to avoid losing data or causing errors in a complex application—particularly an application consisting of linked files. In other words, look before you delete. Before you delete rows or columns, look at parts of the worksheet that do not show on-screen.

Tip

Use the End and arrow keys to see if any data appears in faraway places on your worksheet.

Throughout the remaining sections of the chapter, two examples show you how to lay out and format professional-looking worksheets. To help you follow the discussion and provide a single reference of page layout and design specifications, the following tables list all features used in the examples. Table 20.1 presents the specifications for the balance sheet example shown in figures 20.2 and 20.8. Table 20.2 presents the specifications for the one-page sales report shown in figures 20.9 and 20.10.

Table 20.1 Balance Sheet Layout and Format Specifications for Figures 20.2 and 20.8

Fonts	
Main Headings	
LaserPro Corporation	Arial, 24 point, bold
Balance Sheet	Times New Roman, 14 point, bold
December 31, 1994	Times New Roman, 14 point, bold
Assets	Times New Roman, 14 point, bold
Liabilities...	Times New Roman, 14 point, bold
Column Headings	Times New Roman, 12 point, normal
Labels	Times New Roman, 12 point, normal
Numeric Data	Times New Roman, 12 point, normal
White Space	
Rows	1, 5, 7, 10, 16, 18, 24, 26, 28, 31, 37, 39, 43, 45, 49, 51
Columns	A, E, G, I, K
Format Borders	
Thin Bottom	F15, H14, F22, H22, F35, H35, F41, H41, F47, H47
Double Bottom	F25, H25, F50, H50
Thick Bottom	B6:J6, B27:J27
Format Patterns (4th)	B6:J6, B27:J27
Row Height of 2 points	10, 18, 31, 39, 45

Fig. 20.8
A balance sheet with the column and row references displayed.

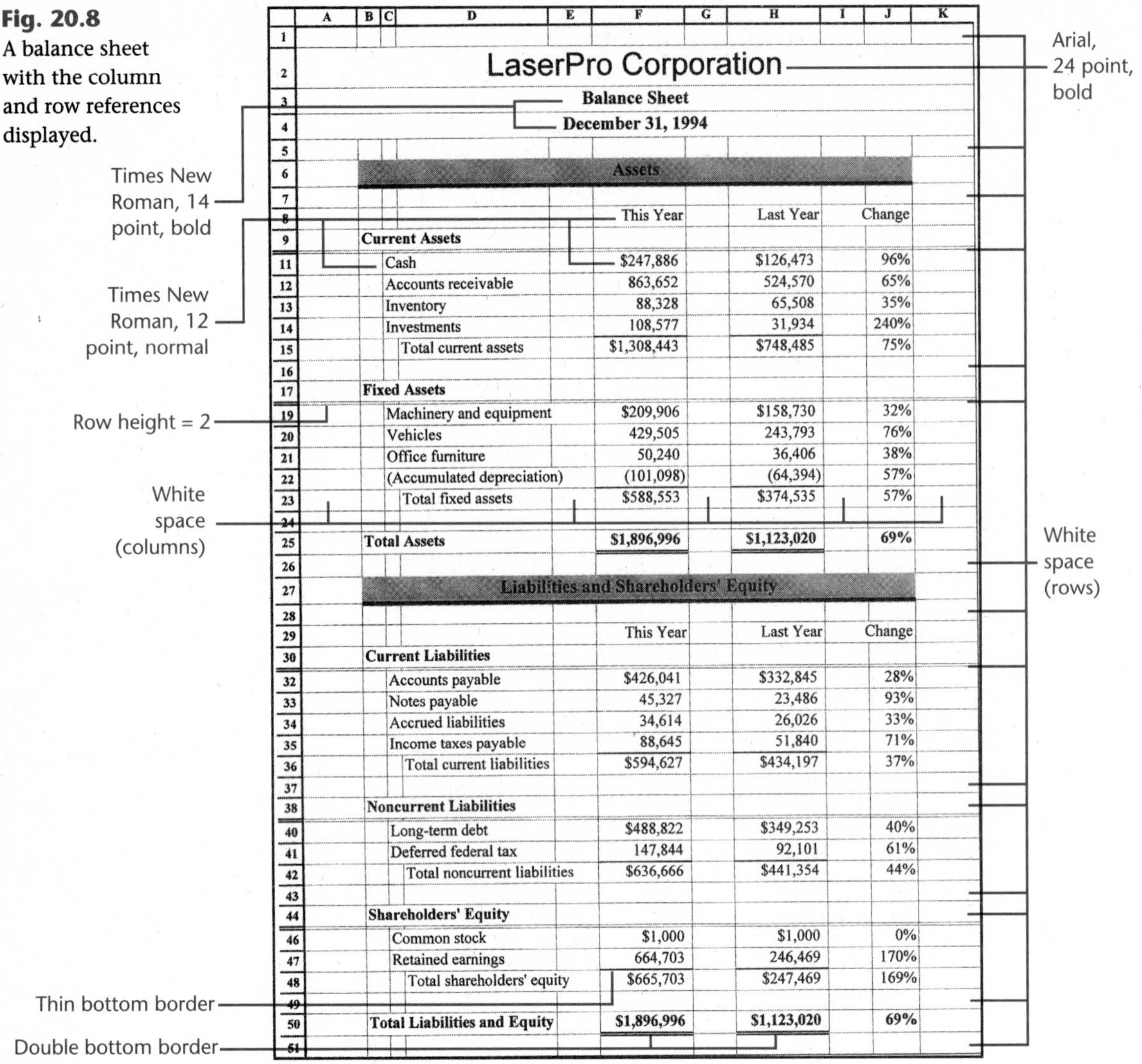

LaserPro Corporation

Balance Sheet
December 31, 1994

Assets

	This Year	Last Year	Change
Current Assets			
Cash	$247,886	$126,473	96%
Accounts receivable	863,652	524,570	65%
Inventory	88,328	65,508	35%
Investments	108,577	31,934	240%
Total current assets	$1,308,443	$748,485	75%
Fixed Assets			
Machinery and equipment	$209,906	$158,730	32%
Vehicles	429,505	243,793	76%
Office furniture	50,240	36,406	38%
(Accumulated depreciation)	(101,098)	(64,394)	57%
Total fixed assets	$588,553	$374,535	57%
Total Assets	**$1,896,996**	**$1,123,020**	**69%**

Liabilities and Shareholders' Equity

	This Year	Last Year	Change
Current Liabilities			
Accounts payable	$426,041	$332,845	28%
Notes payable	45,327	23,486	93%
Accrued liabilities	34,614	26,026	33%
Income taxes payable	88,645	51,840	71%
Total current liabilities	$594,627	$434,197	37%
Noncurrent Liabilities			
Long-term debt	$488,822	$349,253	40%
Deferred federal tax	147,844	92,101	61%
Total noncurrent liabilities	$636,666	$441,354	44%
Shareholders' Equity			
Common stock	$1,000	$1,000	0%
Retained earnings	664,703	246,469	170%
Total shareholders' equity	$665,703	$247,469	169%
Total Liabilities and Equity	**$1,896,996**	**$1,123,020**	**69%**

LaserPro Corporation

1994 Sales Report

(Units)

	Jan-94	Feb-94	Mar-94	1st Q	Apr-94	May-94	Jun-94	2nd Q	Jul-94	Aug-94	Sep-94	3rd Q	Oct-94	Nov-94	Dec-94	4th Q	Total
SERIES 1000																	
Model 1010	6,000	6,000	7,500	19,500	6,000	6,000	7,500	19,500	6,000	6,000	7,500	19,500	6,000	6,000	7,500	19,500	78,000
Model 1011	3,500	1,500	455	5,455	364	364	455	1,183	364	364	455	1,183	364	364	455	1,183	9,004
Model 1012	4,000	2,000	455	6,455	364	364	455	1,183	364	364	455	1,183	364	364	455	1,183	10,004
Model 1013	615	615	769	1,999	615	615	769	1,999	615	615	769	1,999	615	615	769	1,999	7,996
Model 1014	530	530	662	1,722	530	530	662	1,722	530	530	662	1,722	530	530	662	1,722	6,888
Model 1015	192	192	240	624	192	192	240	624	192	192	240	624	192	192	240	624	2,496
Model 1016	769	769	962	2,500	769	769	962	2,500	769	769	962	2,500	769	769	962	2,500	10,000
Model 1017	0	0	4,200	4,200	3,800	457	571	4,828	457	457	571	1,485	457	457	571	1,485	11,998
Model 1018	0	0	3,500	3,500	2,500	229	286	3,015	229	229	286	744	229	229	286	744	8,003
Model 1019	0	0	2,500	2,500	1,500	400	500	2,400	400	400	500	1,300	400	400	500	1,300	7,500
Model 1020	0	0	0	0	0	538	673	1,211	538	538	673	1,749	538	538	673	1,749	4,709
Model 1021	0	0	0	0	0	0	0	0	4,500	3,000	694	8,194	556	556	694	1,806	10,000
Total Series 1000	**15,606**	**11,606**	**21,243**	**48,455**	**16,634**	**10,458**	**13,073**	**40,165**	**14,958**	**13,458**	**13,767**	**42,183**	**11,014**	**11,014**	**13,767**	**35,795**	**166,598**
SERIES 2000																	
Model 2010	5,000	2,000	0	7,000	821	821	1,026	2,668	821	821	1,026	2,668	821	821	1,026	2,668	15,004
Model 2011	0	0	0	0	0	0	0	0	2,500	2,000	833	5,333	667	667	833	2,167	7,500
Model 2012	0	0	6,250	6,250	3,250	971	1,214	5,435	971	971	1,214	3,156	971	971	1,214	3,156	17,997
Model 2013	0	0	0	0	0	5,500	3,000	8,500	815	815	1,019	2,649	815	815	1,019	2,649	13,798
Model 2014	0	0	0	0	0	3,500	3,500	7,000	615	615	769	1,999	615	615	769	1,999	10,998
Total Series 2000	**5,000**	**2,000**	**6,250**	**13,250**	**4,071**	**10,792**	**8,740**	**23,603**	**5,722**	**5,222**	**4,861**	**15,805**	**3,889**	**3,889**	**4,861**	**12,639**	**65,297**
SERIES 3000																	
Model 3010	0	0	0	0	0	0	1,875	1,875	1,875	682	852	3,409	682	682	852	2,216	7,500
Model 3011	0	0	0	0	0	0	5,000	5,000	1,000	273	341	1,614	273	273	341	887	7,501
Model 3012	0	0	0	0	0	0	0	0	3,500	2,500	556	6,556	444	444	556	1,444	8,000
Model 3013	0	0	0	0	0	0	0	0	2,500	2,000	556	5,056	444	444	556	1,444	6,500
Model 3014	0	0	0	0	0	0	0	0	0	2,000	1,500	3,500	215	215	269	699	4,199
Model 3015	0	0	0	0	0	0	0	0	0	625	625	1,250	43	43	54	140	1,390
Total Series 3000	**0**	**0**	**0**	**0**	**0**	**0**	**6,875**	**6,875**	**8,875**	**8,080**	**4,430**	**21,385**	**2,101**	**2,101**	**2,628**	**6,830**	**35,090**
TOTAL	**20,606**	**13,606**	**27,493**	**61,705**	**20,705**	**21,250**	**28,688**	**70,643**	**29,555**	**26,760**	**23,058**	**79,373**	**17,004**	**17,004**	**21,256**	**55,264**	**266,985**

Fig. 20.9
A sales report formatted on one page.

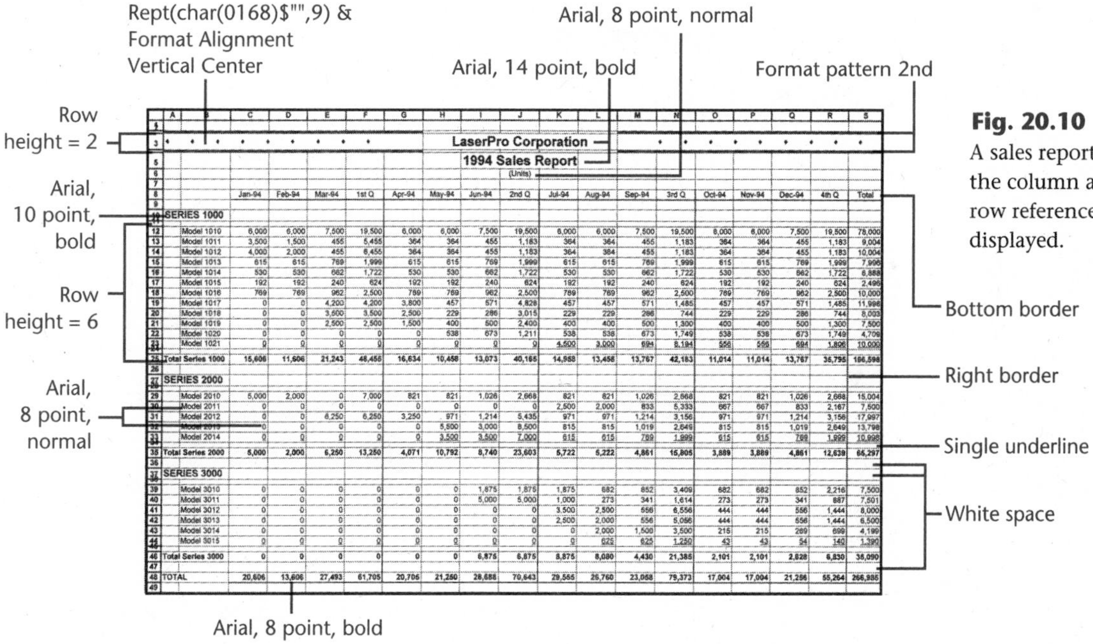

Fig. 20.10
A sales report with the column and row references displayed.

Table 20.2 Sales Report Layout and Format Specifications

Fonts	
Main Headings	
LaserPro Corporation	Arial, 14 point, bold
1994 Sales Report	Arial, 14 point, bold
(Units)	Arial, 8 point, bold
SERIES 1000	Arial, 10 point, bold
SERIES 2000	Arial, 10 point, bold
SERIES 3000	Arial, 10 point, bold
Column Headings	Arial, 8 point, normal
Labels (excluding totals)	Arial, 8 point, normal
Numeric Data (excluding totals)	Arial, 8 point, normal
Totals (labels and data)	Arial, 8 point, bold
Diamonds	Symbol (Char(0168))
Formulas for Diamonds	
Rept(Char(0168)&" ",9)	A3
Rept(" "&Char(0168),9)	M3
White Space	
Rows	1, 7, 9, 11, 24, 26, 28, 34, 36, 38, 45, 47
Underlining	
Single	C23:S23, C33:S33, C44:S44
Format Borders	
Bottom	C8:S8, C48:R48
Right	F8:F48, J8:J48, N8:N48, R8:R48
Format Pattern (2nd)	A2:G2, M2:S2 A4:G4, M4:S4

Format Borders		
	Row Height of 2 points	2, 4
	Row Height of 6 points	11, 24, 28, 34, 38, 45
	Format Alignment	A2, M2
	Vertical Center	

Note

The point sizes that result from printing these diagrams may not be the actual point sizes because you compress the worksheet to fit on one page.

Using Columns and Rows Effectively

Without the desktop publishing features of Excel, the options for using columns and rows on the worksheet are limited. Determining the number of columns your worksheet application should contain is a matter of determining how many columns of data you have and how many columns you need for labels. Similarly, determining the number of rows you need for your worksheet is a matter of knowing the type and amount of data your worksheet will include. The desktop publishing features of Excel, however, present many other ways for using rows and columns. You can use rows for creating solid black lines, space around boxes, graphics, or shaded elements. You can use columns for displaying graphs or graphics alongside worksheet data or for creating extra white space around and within the worksheet. This section describes the ways to use columns and rows when you lay out your desktop published worksheet.

Laying out a worksheet to achieve a high-quality, desktop published look includes using columns for white space, using columns to position labels, reserving columns for special text notations, and using columns for graphs and graphics. The worksheet shown in figure 20.8, for example, uses columns for positioning labels and for white space, in addition to using columns for numeric data.

Columns used for white space in the worksheet in figure 20.8 include columns A, E, G, I, and K. See "Using Columns and Rows for White Space," later in this chapter, for tips on how to use white space effectively in your worksheet design.

Determining how wide to make worksheet columns involves considering the width needed for data as well as the layout of the worksheet page. The column widths of the worksheet in figure 20.8, for example, were determined by four factors:

- The positions of the labels to the left of the numeric data
- The amount of white space needed to balance elements on the page
- The width needed to ensure that numeric and text data would have enough room to display and print
- The width needed for numbers to display in their columns

Using Different Levels of Label Headings

The columnar structure of Excel and the ability to change column widths make entering different levels of labels very easy in Excel. A worksheet that contains main headings with subheadings, such as the labels in the worksheet in figure 20.8, is very easy to create. For example, you can assign a new column for each new heading level rather than reserve one very wide column and create indentations by using the space bar to space labels to the right of the left margin. Notice in particular that columns B, C, and D help delineate different sections of information. Column C is used to indent the entries under each section of the Assets and Liabilities and Shareholders' Equity sections. Column D indents the total for each section.

If you cannot align your columns correctly, you may have used spaces before text to create an indented look. Using spaces before text is a poor alternative to using columns to delineate sections. However, you may be stuck with someone else's worksheet or a worksheet created before you read this paragraph. For example, you could type four spaces for the first indent and two spaces for the second indent in figure 20.8. However, typing spaces is not recommended. First, if you use a nonproportional font such as Arial or Times New Roman, spaces are not equivalent to characters, and you may have a problem lining up each section of data, especially if you change typefaces or point sizes. Second, it is difficult to tell how many spaces you typed. If you need to edit the worksheet later or if you make a mistake in the number of spaces, you may spend a significant amount of time correcting the worksheet. Third, if you need to change the spacing, it is much easier to change the column width than change the number of spaces for each label.

When you lay out your worksheet, remember to account for columns that you will use to enter various levels of indented information or to enter numbers, icons, or graphics preceding information.

Using Columns and Rows for White Space

Considering how much and where to use white space is an important part of designing and laying out professional-looking worksheets. White space plays an important part in giving a balanced look to the page and in conveying the contrast among elements. If used effectively, white space can contribute to making a worksheet, or any other document, easier to read.

Vertical White Space. The sample balance sheet in figure 20.8 shows columns and rows used for white space. Specifically, this worksheet uses columns A, E, G, I, and K for vertical white space and uses rows 1, 5, 7, 10, 16, 18, 24, 26, 28, 31, 37, 39, 43, 45, 49, and 51 for horizontal white space. White space borders the worksheet with blank columns A and K and blank rows 1 and 51. This white space helps make the box around the balance sheet stand out, and also helps make LaserPro Corporation and the headings in column B more distinct. The remaining blank columns, E, G, and I, help to set off the labels on the left and help to make the columns of numeric data easier to read—particularly when a reader is focusing on one column of data. Blank rows used for white space help to distinguish the separate sections of the balance sheet and also help to set off headings and rows containing totals.

Horizontal White Space. Excel users can also change the height of rows. You can change the height through the F**o**rmat **R**ow H**e**ight command or by dragging the bottom boundary of the row on the worksheet frame. One of the valuable uses for this capability is for varying white space between rows of data or lines of text. This feature makes it possible to have different leading (the space between lines of text) between blocks of text, headings and text, text and graphics, or boxed and unboxed text and graphics.

F**o**rmat **R**ow H**e**ight was used in the balance sheet in figure 20.8 to narrow rows that were added for white space between main headings and the labels that followed. Blank rows were inserted at rows 10, 18, 31, 39, and 45 to help make the headings in the rows above these rows stand out. In figure 20.10, narrowed rows were used to add white space and also to keep each series together. Narrow rows 11 and 24 keep the title SERIES 1000 and the Total for the series with the model numbers. The narrow rows still allow enough white space to allow the reader to focus on the title and the total; yet there is a difference in height between rows 26 and 36, which distinguish each series of models.

Notice the difference between figure 20.11 and the original balance sheet shown in figure 20.2. Figure 20.11 excludes the use of additional columns and rows for white space. Although still readable, the second balance sheet fails to show the contrast and readability of the original sheet.

Centering Headings in the Worksheet

Normally, centering headings is as simple as highlighting the characters that you want to center and the range over which you want them centered. You then select the Center Across Columns button. Additionally, follow these tips when you center headings in your worksheet:

- Enter the text in the far left column of the range.
- Use the A**u**tomatic Page Breaks command (accessed by choosing **T**ools **O**ptions and then choosing the Page tab on the dialog box) to determine the area within which you want to center your heading.
- Set the font size for your heading before you center it so that you can more accurately tell whether the heading is truly centered.
- If the centered heading is to be placed within a boxed area, or contains vertical lines on the left or any other entries in cells to the left of the centered heading, add these elements to the worksheet before you center the heading.

- When you center a heading with the Center Across Columns button, highlight the range inside the box or the range to the right of other entries left of the heading (see fig. 20.12).

LaserPro Corporation

Balance Sheet

December 31, 1994

Assets

	This Year	Last Year	Change
Current Assets			
Cash	$247,886	$126,473	96%
Accounts receivable	863,652	524,570	65%
Inventory	88,328	65,508	35%
Investments	108,577	31,934	240%
Total current assets	$1,308,443	$748,485	75%
Fixed Assets			
Machinery and equipment	$209,906	$158,730	32%
Vehicles	429,505	243,793	76%
Office furniture	50,240	36,406	38%
(Accumulated depreciation)	(101,098)	(64,394)	57%
Total fixed assets	$588,553	$374,535	57%
Total Assets	**$1,896,996**	**$1,123,020**	**69%**

Liabilities and Shareholders' Equity

	This Year	Last Year	Change
Current Liabilities			
Accounts payable	$426,041	$332,845	28%
Notes payable	45,327	23,486	93%
Accrued liabilities	34,614	26,026	33%
Income taxes payable	88,645	51,840	71%
Total current liabilities	$594,627	$434,197	37%
Noncurrent Liabilities			
Long-term debt	$488,822	$349,253	40%
Deferred federal tax	147,844	92,101	61%
Total noncurrent liabilities	$636,666	$441,354	44%
Shareholders' Equity			
Common stock	$1,000	$1,000	0%
Retained earnings	664,703	246,469	170%
Total shareholders' equity	$665,703	$247,469	169%
Total Liabilities and Equity	**$1,896,996**	**$1,123,020**	**69%**

Fig. 20.11
A balance sheet without extra white space added.

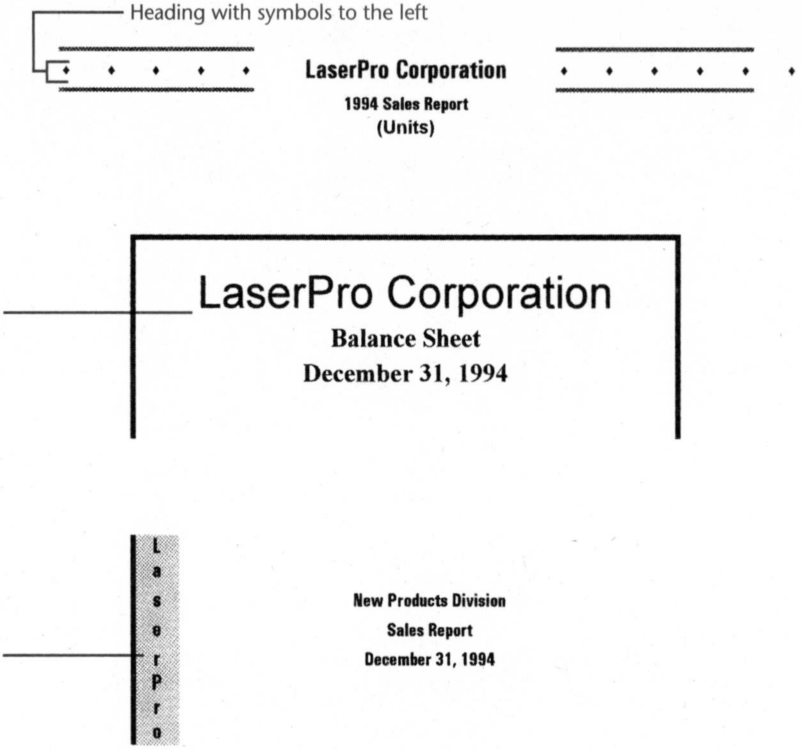

Fig. 20.12
Centering headings within boxes or to the right of other entries.

Centering Symbols Vertically in a Row

In addition to centering a heading horizontally, you also can center characters vertically within a cell. The diamond border for the Sales Report in figure 20.9 was centered by selecting Format Cells, choosing the Alignment tab on the dialog box, and marking Center in the Vertical box. You can also align characters on the top or bottom of the cell (see fig. 20.13).

Determining Fonts and Point Sizes for Worksheets

The number of fonts available to you on Excel depends on the printer and fonts you installed with Windows. With all the font and style choices available, you might think that selecting one for your worksheet or document is difficult. There are, however, some rules of thumb to help you create professional-quality printed output.

1. *Use a serif font (such as Times New Roman or MS Serif) for body text.* Serifs are cross strokes or embellishments on the feet and end of characters. The serifs tend to tie the text together, making it easier to read. Most people are accustomed to reading printed text and numbers in a serif font because it is commonly used.

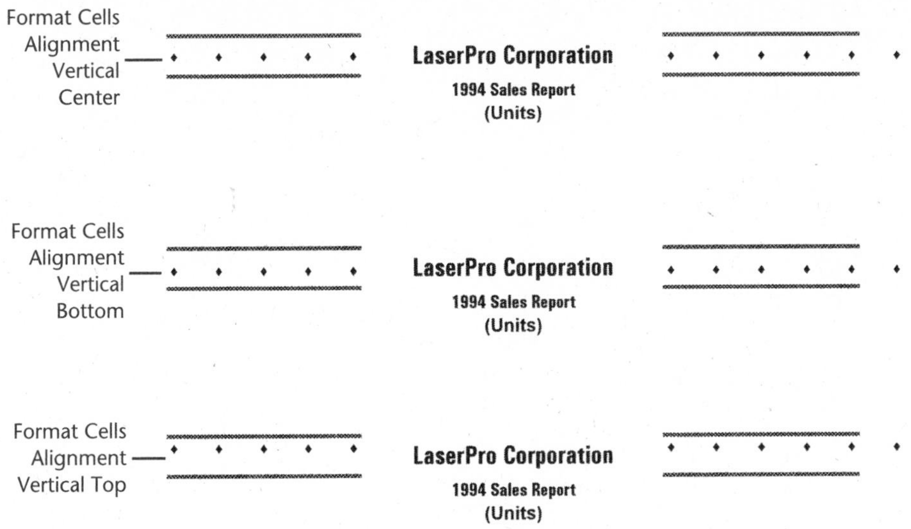

Fig. 20.13
The diamonds in this figure are aligned at the top, bottom, and centered vertically in each cell.

2. *Use a sans serif font (such as Arial or MS Sans Serif) for display text.* Sans serif typefaces have no serifs. Display text is a short text line, such as a title, headline, or subhead. A sans serif font helps this text stand out from the page, enabling readers to find key information quickly.

3. *Use a sans serif font for very small point sizes.* This rule is especially valid if you are going to copy the worksheet on a copier. For small text, the serifs tend to blend into each other, creating an illegible copy. However, if you have a decent printer and copier, a serif font is better for numbers.

4. *Use bold for emphasis and to help direct the reader.* In a long stretch of text, bold stands out and emphasizes a word or phrase. In table and chart titles, bold text draws attention to the main point of the document. Use bold to distinguish row or title headings from the body of a table.

5. *Use italic for subheadings or to indicate a quote or reference.* Italic can help differentiate titles from the body of a table. In a stretch of text, italic often gives the impression of speech. Also, use italic for instructions or for an introduction to new terminology, to distinguish it from other text.

6. *Use bold and italic together to make a point really stand out.* You also can use this combination in subheadings on charts and tables.

7. *Use bold and italic sparingly.* Too much use of bold type makes the page heavy and detracts from the words you really want to emphasize. Italic can be very light and seem to disappear into the page. Because of the increased white space, you can use bold and italic more in tables and charts.

8. *Use underline for numbers or for one or two capitalized words.* When you underline lowercase letters, the descenders (lower part of y, p, j) get lost in the underline. With underlining, readers have difficulty recognizing the shape of words and need more time to separate words from the underline. You can replace most underlines with bold or italic. In financial spreadsheets, however, underlines commonly separate data and totals. You can achieve the same affect with borders.

9. *Use strikeout to indicate text to be removed.* Strikeout is an editing tool that allows the reader to see text before and after editing.

10. *Although you have many available type styles, use them sparingly.* Excessively formatted pages are often called *ransom notes* because they seem to have been pieced together from many different sources. Pick a few text styles and use them consistently. This gives clarity and continuity to your page.

Notice the typefaces and type styles used in the two examples shown in figures 20.14 and 20.15. Figure 20.14 is the original balance sheet used throughout this chapter; the dominant typeface is Times New Roman, and the only changes in type style occur in the main headings. Figure 20.15 shows the same balance sheet with the Arial typeface used throughout. Although both are equally readable, the serif Times New Roman typeface in figure 20.14 is slightly lighter because characters do not have the same thickness at all points as does the sans serif Arial typeface.

Whether you use a serif or sans serif typeface as the primary typeface for your worksheet depends on a couple of factors. First, select a dominant typeface for the worksheet depending on the environment in which the worksheet will be presented. Your typeface decision may be very different if the worksheet is going to be read as a single, isolated document rather than as part of a report, newsletter, letter, or memo. If your worksheet will be presented with text around it (sentences and paragraphs), the text should use serif text, an easier to read typeface for body copy; you then can use a sans serif typeface for the dominant typeface for the worksheet data, making it distinct from the body copy around it.

LaserPro Corporation

Balance Sheet

December 31, 1994

Assets	This Year	Last Year	Change
Current Assets			
Cash	$247,886	$126,473	96%
Accounts receivable	863,652	524,570	65%
Inventory	88,328	65,508	35%
Investments	108,577	31,934	240%
Total current assets	$1,308,443	$748,485	75%
Fixed Assets			
Machinery and equipment	$209,906	$158,730	32%
Vehicles	429,505	243,793	76%
Office furniture	50,240	36,406	38%
(Accumulated depreciation)	(101,098)	(64,394)	57%
Total fixed assets	$588,553	$374,535	57%
Total Assets	**$1,896,996**	**$1,123,020**	**69%**

Liabilities and Shareholder's Equity	This Year	Last Year	Change
Current Liabilities			
Accounts payable	$426,041	$332,845	28%
Notes payable	45,327	23,486	93%
Accrued liabilities	34,614	26,026	33%
Income taxes payable	88,645	51,840	71%
Total current liabilities	$594,627	$434,197	37%
Noncurrent Liabilities			
Long-term debt	$488,822	$349,253	40%
Deferred federal tax	147,844	92,101	61%
Total noncurrent liabilities	$636,666	$441,354	44%
Shareholders' Equity			
Common stock	$1,000	$1,000	0%
Retained earnings	664,703	246,469	170%
Total shareholders' equity	$665,703	$247,469	169%
Total Liabilities and equity	**$1,896,996**	**$1,123,020**	**69%**

Fig. 20.14
A balance sheet using Times New Roman as the primary typeface.

A second factor to consider when you choose the typeface for your worksheet is readability. If you need to use a small type size to fit all the data onto one page, for example, you may want to use a sans serif typeface, because it is slightly more open between characters. This kind of typeface may increase readability, especially if you are going to photocopy the text (see fig. 20.16).

Fig. 20.15
A balance sheet using Arial as the primary typeface.

LaserPro Corporation
Balance Sheet
December 31, 1994

Assets	This Year	Last Year	Change
Current Assets			
Cash	$247,886	$126,473	96%
Accounts receivable	863,652	524,570	65%
Inventory	88,328	65,508	35%
Investments	108,577	31,934	240%
Total current assets	$1,308,443	$748,485	75%
Fixed Assets			
Machinery and equipment	$209,906	$158,730	32%
Vehicles	429,505	243,793	76%
Office furniture	50,240	36,406	38%
(Accumulated depreciation)	(101,098)	(64,394)	57%
Total fixed assets	$588,553	$374,535	57%
Total Assets	**$1,896,996**	**$1,123,020**	**69%**

Liabilities and Shareholders' Equity	This Year	Last Year	Change
Current Liabilities			
Accounts payable	$426,041	$332,845	28%
Notes payable	45,327	23,486	93%
Accrued liabilities	34,614	26,026	33%
Income taxes payable	88,645	51,840	71%
Total current liabilities	$594,627	$434,197	37%
Noncurrent Liabilities			
Long-term debt	$488,822	$349,253	40%
Deferred federal tax	147,844	92,101	61%
Total noncurrent liabilities	$636,666	$441,354	44%
Shareholders' Equity			
Common stock	$1,000	$1,000	0%
Retained earnings	664,703	246,469	170%
Total shareholders' equity	$665,703	$247,469	169%
Total Liabilities and Equity	**$1,896,996**	**$1,123,020**	**69%**

Note

As you may have guessed, much of this chapter consists of opinion rather than hard and fast rules. The choice of font, for example, depends on your sense of style and the circumstances of the surrounding document. On the other hand, how to choose a font is a rule (you select F**o**rmat C**e**lls and choose the Font tab). Experts themselves disagree as to the "best" font for small numbers on the worksheet. Some call for a serif font for small numbers, as opposed to the sans serif font that we recommend. It's easy to choose—go ahead and try different fonts yourself.

LaserPro Corporation
1994 Sales Report
(Units)

	Jan-94	Feb-94	Mar-94	1st Q	Apr-94	May-94	Jun-94	2nd Q	Jul-94	Aug-94	Sep-94	3rd Q	Oct-94	Nov-94	Dec-94	4th Q	Total
SERIES 1000																	
Model 1010	6,000	6,000	7,500	19,500	6,000	6,000	7,500	19,500	6,000	6,000	7,500	19,500	6,000	6,000	7,500	19,500	78,000
Model 1011	3,500	1,500	455	5,455	364	364	455	1,183	364	364	455	1,183	364	364	455	1,183	9,004
Model 1012	4,000	2,000	455	6,455	364	364	455	1,183	364	364	455	1,183	364	364	455	1,183	10,004
Model 1013	615	615	769	1,999	615	615	769	1,999	615	615	769	1,999	615	615	769	1,999	7,996
Model 1014	530	530	662	1,722	530	530	662	1,722	530	530	662	1,722	530	530	662	1,722	6,888
Model 1015	192	192	240	624	192	192	240	624	192	192	240	624	192	192	240	624	2,496
Model 1016	769	769	962	2,500	769	769	962	2,500	769	769	962	2,500	769	769	962	2,500	10,000
Model 1017	0	0	4,200	4,200	3,800	457	571	4,828	457	457	571	1,485	457	457	571	1,485	11,998
Model 1018	0	0	3,500	3,500	2,500	229	286	3,015	229	229	286	744	229	229	286	744	8,003
Model 1019	0	0	2,500	2,500	1,500	400	500	2,400	400	400	500	1,300	400	400	500	1,300	7,500
Model 1020	0	0	0	0	0	538	673	1,211	538	538	673	1,749	538	538	673	1,749	4,709
Model 1021	0	0	0	0	0	0	0	0	4,500	3,000	694	8,194	556	556	694	1,806	10,000
Total Series 1000	**15,606**	**11,806**	**21,243**	**48,456**	**16,634**	**10,458**	**13,073**	**40,165**	**14,958**	**13,458**	**13,767**	**42,183**	**11,014**	**11,014**	**13,767**	**35,795**	**166,598**
SERIES 2000																	
Model 2010	5,000	2,000	0	7,000	821	821	1,026	2,668	821	821	1,026	2,668	821	821	1,026	2,668	15,004
Model 2011	0	0	0	0	0	0	0	0	2,500	2,000	833	5,333	667	667	833	2,167	7,500
Model 2012	0	0	6,250	6,250	3,250	971	1,214	5,435	971	971	1,214	3,156	971	971	1,214	3,156	17,997
Model 2013	0	0	0	0	0	5,500	3,000	8,500	815	815	1,019	2,649	815	815	1,019	2,649	13,798
Model 2014	0	0	0	0	0	3,500	3,500	7,000	615	615	769	1,999	615	615	769	1,999	10,998
Total Series 2000	**5,000**	**2,000**	**6,250**	**13,250**	**4,071**	**10,792**	**8,740**	**23,603**	**5,722**	**5,222**	**4,861**	**15,805**	**3,889**	**3,889**	**4,861**	**12,639**	**65,297**
SERIES 3000																	
Model 3010	0	0	0	0	0	0	1,875	1,875	1,875	682	852	3,409	682	682	852	2,216	7,500
Model 3011	0	0	0	0	0	0	5,000	5,000	1,000	273	341	1,614	273	273	341	887	7,501
Model 3012	0	0	0	0	0	0	0	0	3,500	2,500	556	6,556	444	444	556	1,444	8,000
Model 3013	0	0	0	0	0	0	0	0	2,500	2,000	556	5,056	444	444	556	1,444	6,500
Model 3014	0	0	0	0	0	0	0	0	0	2,000	1,500	3,500	215	215	269	699	4,199
Model 3015	0	0	0	0	0	0	0	0	0	625	625	1,250	43	43	54	140	1,390
Total Series 3000	**0**	**0**	**0**	**0**	**0**	**0**	**6,875**	**6,875**	**8,875**	**8,080**	**4,430**	**21,385**	**2,101**	**2,101**	**2,628**	**6,830**	**35,090**
TOTAL	**20,606**	**13,606**	**27,493**	**61,705**	**20,705**	**21,250**	**28,688**	**70,643**	**29,556**	**26,760**	**23,058**	**79,373**	**17,004**	**17,004**	**21,256**	**55,264**	**266,985**

Fig. 20.16
Using sans serif typeface with small type size.

Using Boldface, Italic, and Underlining for Emphasis

Applying attributes such as boldface, italic, and underlining requires good planning to ensure that your worksheet highlights the information you want emphasized. To effectively call attention to parts of your worksheet, you need to follow the rules described in a previous section, "Giving Your Worksheet a Professional Look." Specifically, strive for simplicity, consistency, and contrast. Remember that these last two goals—consistency and contrast—are not contradictions. Italic type used sparingly can call attention to an important heading or important data, as long as a normal typeface is used consistently for most of the worksheet. This section explains how you can use underlining, bold, italic, and contrast effectively to emphasize different pieces of information.

When you determine what information to emphasize with bold, italic, and underlining, keep in mind the message you want to convey to those who review your worksheet. To emphasize the sales totals for the quarter rather than individual months, for example, use italic and bold together for the quarterly data to contrast and emphasize the information (see fig. 20.17).

Apart from the common use of underlining for totals lines, the only special use of underlining in the worksheet in figure 20.17 is the use of bold borders underlining to highlight months.

Fig. 20.17
Using italic and bold to emphasize quarterly sales data.

LaserPro Corporation

SALES REPORT

(Units)

	Jan-94	**Feb-94**	**Mar-94**	1st Quarter Total
SERIES 1000				
Model 1010	6,000	6,000	7,500	***19,500***
Model 1011	3,500	1,500	455	***5,455***
Model 1012	4,000	2,000	455	***6,455***
Model 1013	615	615	769	***1,999***
Model 1014	530	530	662	***1,722***
Model 1015	192	192	240	***624***
Model 1016	769	769	962	***2,500***
Model 1017	0	0	4,200	***4,200***
Model 1018	0	0	3,500	***3,500***
Model 1019	0	0	2,500	***2,500***
Model 1020	0	0	0	***0***
Model 1021	0	0	0	***0***
Total Series 1000	15,606	11,606	21,243	***48,455***
SERIES 2000				
Model 2010	5,000	2,000	0	***7,000***
Model 2011	0	0	0	***0***
Model 2012	0	0	6,250	***6,250***
Model 2013	0	0	0	***0***
Model 2014	0	0	0	***0***
Total Series 2000	5,000	2,000	6,250	***13,250***
SERIES 3000				
Model 3010	0	0	0	***0***
Model 3011	0	0	0	***0***
Model 3012	0	0	0	***0***
Model 3013	0	0	0	***0***
Model 3014	0	0	0	***0***
Model 3015	0	0	0	***0***
Total Series 3000	0	0	0	***0***
Product Total	20,606	13,606	27,493	***61,705***

Using Lines, Boxes, and Shading for Emphasis

Using bold, italic, and underlining may be effective for emphasizing a small number of elements in a worksheet. To emphasize a larger block of information, however, choose the F**o**rmat C**e**lls command and select the Border tab from the dialog box to create different kinds of bordering lines and boxes. Choose the F**o**rmat C**e**lls command, and then select the Patterns tab from the dialog box to create shaded or solid colored areas.

To emphasize the sales results of a new product line over the sales results of existing product lines, you can highlight the sales data for the new product line by boxing the data (see fig. 20.18).

LaserPro Corporation

SALES REPORT

(Units)

	Jan-94	Feb-94	Mar-94	1st Quarter Total
SERIES 1000				
Model 1010	6,000	6,000	7,500	19,500
Model 1011	3,500	1,500	455	5,455
Model 1012	4,000	2,000	455	6,455
Model 1013	615	615	769	1,999
Model 1014	530	530	662	1,722
Model 1015	192	192	240	624
Model 1016	769	769	962	2,500
Model 1017	0	0	4,200	4,200
Model 1018	0	0	3,500	3,500
Model 1019	0	0	2,500	2,500
Model 1020	0	0	0	0
Model 1021	0	0	0	0
Total Series 1000	15,606	11,606	21,243	48,455
SERIES 2000				
Model 2010	5,000	2,000	0	7,000
Model 2011	0	0	0	0
Model 2012	0	0	6,250	6,250
Model 2013	0	0	0	0
Model 2014	0	0	0	0
Total Series 2000	5,000	2,000	6,250	13,250
SERIES 3000				
Model 3010	0	0	0	0
Model 3011	0	0	0	0
Model 3012	0	0	0	0
Model 3013	0	0	0	0
Model 3014	0	0	0	0
Model 3015	0	0	0	0
Total Series 3000	0	0	0	0
Product Total	20,606	13,606	27,493	61,705

Fig. 20.18
Boxing data to emphasize sales of a new product.

Another way to emphasize sales data for the new product line in figure 20.18 is to use rules (publishing lingo for lines). Figure 20.19 shows this technique.

Fig. 20.19
Using rules to emphasize sales of a new product.

LaserPro Corporation
SALES REPORT
(Units)

	Jan-94	Feb-94	Mar-94	1st Quarter Total
SERIES 1000				
Model 1010	6,000	6,000	7,500	19,500
Model 1011	3,500	1,500	455	5,455
Model 1012	4,000	2,000	455	6,455
Model 1013	615	615	769	1,999
Model 1014	530	530	662	1,722
Model 1015	192	192	240	624
Model 1016	769	769	962	2,500
Model 1017	0	0	4,200	4,200
Model 1018	0	0	3,500	3,500
Model 1019	0	0	2,500	2,500
Model 1020	0	0	0	0
Model 1021	0	0	0	0
Total Series 1000	15,606	11,606	21,243	48,455
SERIES 2000				
Model 2010	5,000	2,000	0	7,000
Model 2011	0	0	0	0
Model 2012	0	0	6,250	6,250
Model 2013	0	0	0	0
Model 2014	0	0	0	0
Total Series 2000	5,000	2,000	6,250	13,250
SERIES 3000				
Model 3010	0	0	0	0
Model 3011	0	0	0	0
Model 3012	0	0	0	0
Model 3013	0	0	0	0
Model 3014	0	0	0	0
Model 3015	0	0	0	0
Total Series 3000	0	0	0	0
Product Total	20,606	13,606	27,493	61,705

Shading in figures 20.18 and 20.19 highlights the Product Total line at the bottom of the worksheet.

Publishing Your Worksheet in Color

For those of you lucky enough to have a color printer or plotter, you have an added potential and responsibility to make your worksheet look good. You can use colors in many ways in a presentation. The most used application for color is on charts. Each color represents a different set of data in pie slices, bars, or lines.

Another popular choice for color is to print negative numbers in red. Excel even has a cell format for negatives. Select F**o**rmat C**e**lls and choose the Number tab on the dialog box. Notice that some of the choices in the **F**ormat Codes list box indicate [Red] directly after the semicolon (;). This code indicates that negative numbers appear in red. Be careful when you use red for other numbers, however; accountants and bean counters will automatically assume you are losing money and may become red-faced in anger causing you to be red-faced in embarrassment.

As hinted at in the above paragraph, some colors have specific meanings to people. Red, orange, and yellow are warm, vibrant colors, indicating excitement. As seen above however, red can also suggest a negative, angry, or embarrassing picture. Use red, orange, and yellow sparingly on small areas of the page. Blue and violet are cool colors. They are easy on the eye. Use these colors for large areas of the page.

You have to be careful with your combination of colors, however. Black text on top of a blue background may be difficult to read because of a lack of contrast. Dark text on light backgrounds work the best, especially for work that is reproduced. For most of the body of the document, look for the widest contrast between your text and background—and guess what? Black text on a white background often works the best—even if you do have a color printer.

If you want to draw attention to a section of the worksheet, you can also set off a section with color. For example, just as you highlighted the 1st Quarter Total column with bold in figure 20.17, you can highlight the column by making the text green. In figures 20.18 and 20.19, you could make the lines highlighting SERIES 2000 a different color or shade the whole area with a color.

In addition to highlighting sections of your worksheet, color text sets off headlines and subheads and creates a more interesting page. You also can use color for column or row labels to distinguish them from the body of a table.

You should be aware, however, that color on the monitor is not always the same as it will be on your output. Because light reflects off a page instead of shining behind it, printed colors can differ greatly from projected colors. Be sure to test colors for your different output devices.

For Related Information

- "Changing Character Fonts, Sizes, Styles, and Colors," p. 312
- "Using TrueType Fonts," p. 308
- "Formatting Rows and Columns," p. 346
- "Adding Colors, Patterns, and Borders," p. 350

You can set colors in Excel by choosing the F**o**rmat C**e**lls command and then the **C**olor option on the Font, Border, or Patterns tab. The **C**olor option on the Border tab changes the outlines around the cells. In the Patterns tab, you can change the color of the different parts of the pattern with the **P**attern and **C**olor choices.

Because messing with inappropriate colors can cause headaches and eyestrain, be careful with mixing too many colors. To see complimentary colors that have been designed by professionals to work together on worksheets, look at the options under F**o**rmat **A**utoFormat.

Adding Charts to Your Worksheet

The desktop publishing capabilities of Excel let you display and print charts along with worksheets. You can position a chart created anywhere on the worksheet, and also use charting commands to enhance the chart you located on the worksheet. If you have not used charting commands, read Chapter 12, "Creating Charts," to learn how to place, edit, and enhance charts.

The guidelines to follow when adding charts to your worksheets are similar to those covered throughout this chapter for good worksheet layout and design. Use the chart to help communicate the information you need to your readers. Use the layout of the page and format the chart as either part of the overall consistent design of the page, or use the chart as a contrasting element to call attention to information not emphasized within the worksheet. Figures 20.20 and 20.21 show how you can use charts to extend and emphasize worksheet data.

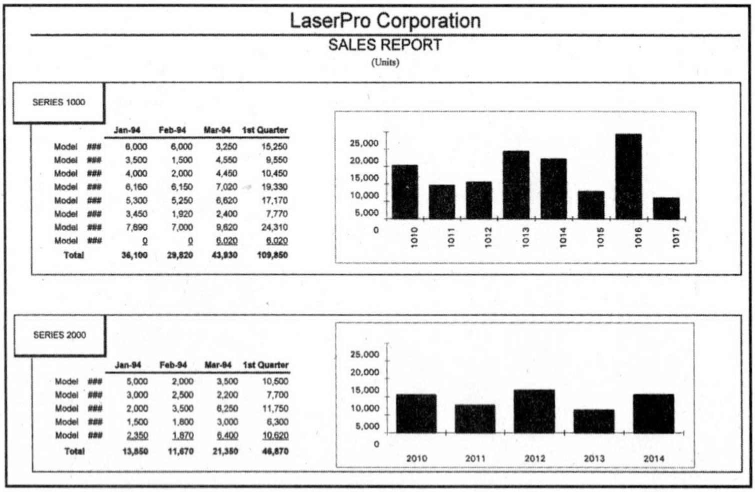

Fig. 20.20 Graphs used to complement worksheet data.

Note

Be careful when you change axis values on your charts. For example, on figure 20.20 the second chart values only go to approximately 15,000. It may be tempting to change the y-axis (left axis) to have the top value of 15,000. However, since both SERIES 1000 and 2000 are on one page, having both axes' maximum values at 25,000 gives you a comparison of the different series as well as the different models.

LaserPro Corporation

International Sales

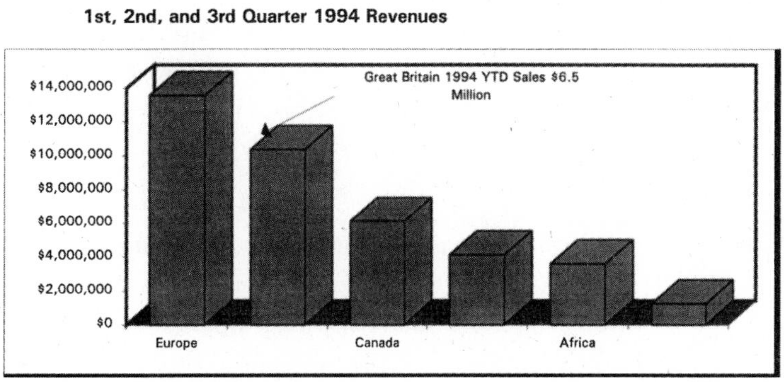

Region	*$ Sales*	*Units*	*% Increase*
Europe	$13,574,447	174,143	32%
Orient	$10,370,858	133,045	36%
Canada	$6,116,347	78,465	22%
South America	$4,121,762	52,877	28%
Africa	$3,595,989	46,132	24%
Mideast	$1,246,187	15987	-26%

Fig. 20.21
A graph positioned for emphasis.

The graphs in figure 20.20 are incorporated into the printout as part of the overall design. Notice that the layout of the page emphasizes two sets of data—first quarter sales of Series 1000 products and first quarter sales of Series 2000 products. The charts are placed within the boxes designed for the two categories of products. The charts show how sales of different products compare to each other at the end of the first quarter—a comparison not easily conveyed by the sales totals listed in the last column of each worksheet. The graph in figure 20.21, on the other hand, dominates the page and emphasizes the comparative sales of different international markets. The graph also notes the sales of Great Britain as part of the European market, which is information not shown by the worksheet.

Whether you have a chart as part of a worksheet or as a stand alone document (as in a transparency), the guidelines for charts are similar to those for worksheets.

- *Clarity*. This probably is the most important design consideration when creating an effective chart. Your audience perceives the message immediately from a well-planned chart. When you add enhancements and change default styles, clarity should be your utmost consideration.

- *Emphasis*. Through Excel's editing features, you can change any part of a chart. You can add arrows, boxes, and text. You can place emphasis on certain features of the chart to reinforce your message. Be careful not to inadvertently change the chart's message by emphasizing the wrong data, however.

- *White space*. You can create a well-planned chart by using white space effectively. Far too often, people cram too much information into a chart. The audience cannot find the message because too much information is portrayed. Special attention to white space helps you create a much more persuasive chart.

- *Proportion*. When you have limited space to express an idea, one aspect of the chart can get lost or dominate the chart.

- *Consistency*. Consistency must be present in a chart's design. Consistency allows frequent readers of your reports—your boss, for example—a way to quickly locate information they're interested in. Consistency also produces a well thought out, professional image. Keep fonts, patterns, colors, and borders consistent. Once you find the "best" design for your documents, consistency helps you maintain the good design. Lack of consistency can lead to a haphazard, unorganized image and can create the "ransom note" effect where many different fonts and design elements distract from the message. Excel offers templates to help keep consistency throughout your charts.

There are also some specific guidelines you should be aware of when you create charts:

- *Type size should reflect the importance of the various parts of your chart.* The title of the chart should be larger than the unattached text. Use large type to emphasize the main message of the chart.

- *Although the size of your fonts may change, limit the number of typefaces on each chart to two.* Generally, titles should appear in a sans serif font and the text in a serif font.

- *Be consistent in labeling.* Keep text in the chart as uniform as possible. Label text set in a larger size or bolder typeface can cause the audience to think that a column or pie slice is more important than others. If this is not your intent, you cause a misconception and the message is misunderstood. The column or slices have no greater significance than any others, but the viewer's eyes are drawn to them.

- *Use color appropriately.* When you use color, keep the whole design in mind. Your output must be supportive of color use. Red attracts your audience's eye and causes the message to stand out. Yellow is not suggested for text. It is a good idea to use dark, vibrant colors for your text.

For Related Information

- "Creating an Embedded Chart," p. 407
- "Changing Object Colors, Patterns, and Borders," p. 480
- "Formatting Text and Numbers," p. 483

Using Named Styles and Automatic Formatting

You can automate desktop publishing with Excel. As described in Chapter 10, these methods include creating styles with the F**o**rmat **S**tyle command, saving files as templates, and using the automatic formatting capabilities of Excel. This section describes examples of named styles and automatic formatting that you can use for worksheet publishing. See "Creating Styles" in Chapter 10 for more information.

File templates are helpful when you are preparing repetitive monthly reports or presentations. After you create the worksheet, you can use a template file whenever you are duplicating the layout and format of an original worksheet. To create a file template, follow these general guidelines:

1. Save the file as a normal Excel file.

2. Save the file again as a template file by selecting the template option on the Save File As **T**ype text box.

3. If you need to create new sales worksheets that follow the exact form of the template, open the template file and edit the template to include the new sales information.

4. When you save the file by clicking on the File Save button or choosing the **F**ile **S**ave command, Excel prompts you for a new file name.

See "Creating Workbook and Worksheet Templates" in Chapter 42 for more information on template files.

Named styles can make creating new worksheets much easier and much faster. The balance sheet discussed throughout this chapter is a good example of how to use the F**o**rmat **S**tyle **A**dd command to automate formatting different parts of the worksheet. Creating the six styles listed in table 20.3 for the balance sheet in figure 20.14 speeds up formatting the balance sheet and helps when you format other worksheets. Figure 20.22 shows the styles described in table 20.3.

Table 20.3 Worksheet Styles

Name	Description	Style
Title	Style for company name title	Arial font, 24 point, bold
Sub	Subtitles below the company name	Times New Roman font, 14 point, bold
Mhead	Main headings separating the two sections of the balance sheet border	Times New Roman font, 14 point, bold, 4th format pattern, thick bottom
Rtotal	Row total entries	Default font with single underline
Rhead	Outdented row headings	Default font (Times New Roman 12 point), bold
Stotal	Totals at the bottom of each main section	Default font in bold, double underline

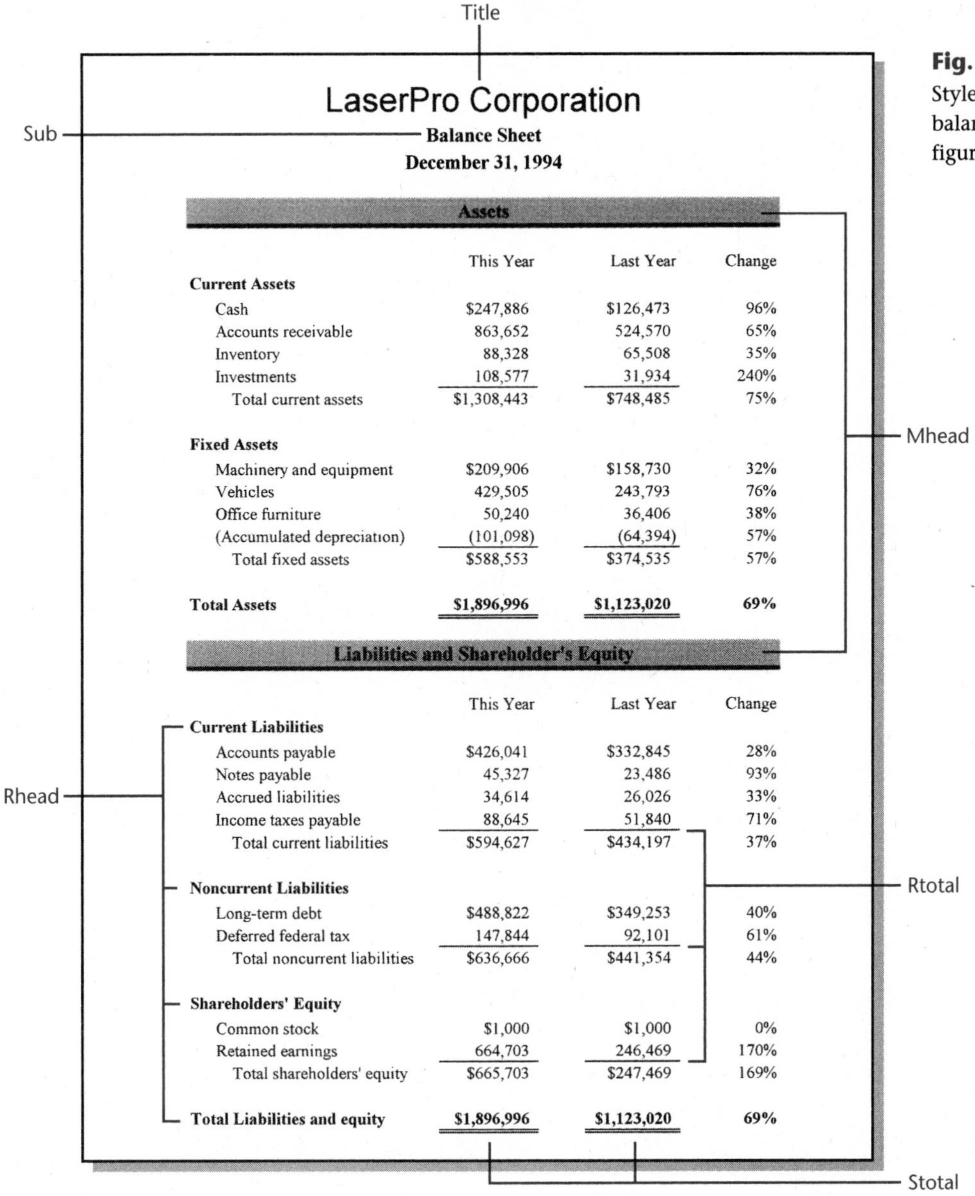

LaserPro Corporation

Balance Sheet

December 31, 1994

	This Year	Last Year	Change
Assets			
Current Assets			
Cash	$247,886	$126,473	96%
Accounts receivable	863,652	524,570	65%
Inventory	88,328	65,508	35%
Investments	108,577	31,934	240%
Total current assets	$1,308,443	$748,485	75%
Fixed Assets			
Machinery and equipment	$209,906	$158,730	32%
Vehicles	429,505	243,793	76%
Office furniture	50,240	36,406	38%
(Accumulated depreciation)	(101,098)	(64,394)	57%
Total fixed assets	$588,553	$374,535	57%
Total Assets	**$1,896,996**	**$1,123,020**	**69%**

	This Year	Last Year	Change
Liabilities and Shareholder's Equity			
Current Liabilities			
Accounts payable	$426,041	$332,845	28%
Notes payable	45,327	23,486	93%
Accrued liabilities	34,614	26,026	33%
Income taxes payable	88,645	51,840	71%
Total current liabilities	$594,627	$434,197	37%
Noncurrent Liabilities			
Long-term debt	$488,822	$349,253	40%
Deferred federal tax	147,844	92,101	61%
Total noncurrent liabilities	$636,666	$441,354	44%
Shareholders' Equity			
Common stock	$1,000	$1,000	0%
Retained earnings	664,703	246,469	170%
Total shareholders' equity	$665,703	$247,469	169%
Total Liabilities and equity	**$1,896,996**	**$1,123,020**	**69%**

Fig. 20.22
Styles for the balance sheet in figure 20.14.

For Related Information

- "Formatting with Autoformats," p. 303
- "Applying Multiple Formats at One Time," p. 354
- "Creating Workbook and Worksheet Templates," p. 1128

Besides using named styles, you also can use the automatic format capabilities available in Excel. Follow these steps:

1. Highlight the range of data you want to format, including column and row titles (see fig. 20.23).

2. Choose the F**o**rmat **A**utoFormat command.

   Excel then provides a dialog box that lists the possible formats and an example of each one (see fig. 20.24).

3. Select one of the formats.

Notice in figure 20.25 that most of the formatting is done for you. (Classic 1 was chosen as the **T**able Format in this example.) All you need to do is change the titles at the top of the page and possibly change the number format and column width.

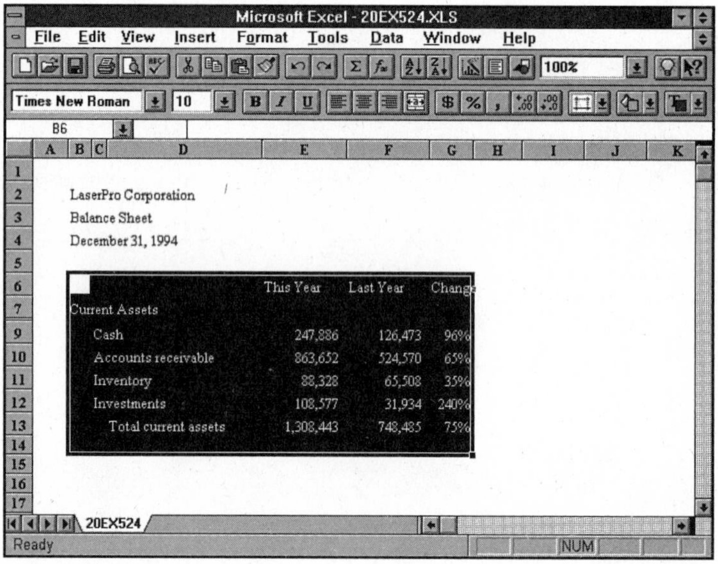

Fig. 20.23
A portion of the LaserPro balance sheet before using AutoFormat.

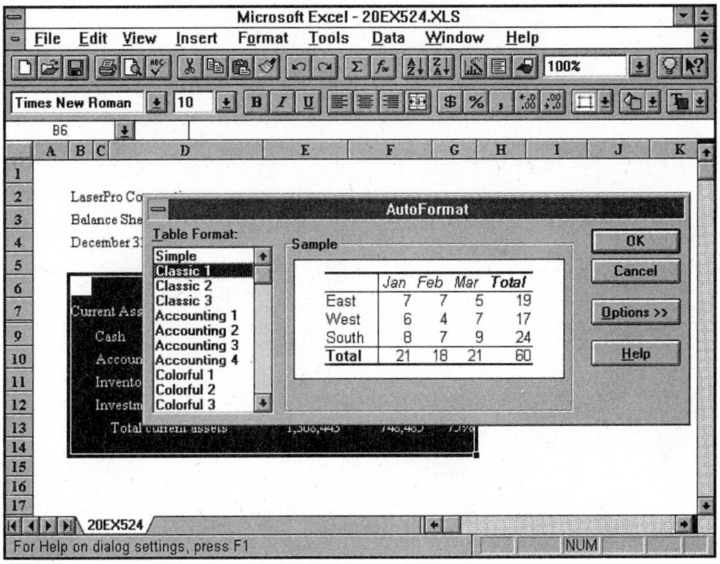

Fig. 20.24
The AutoFormat dialog box.

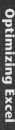

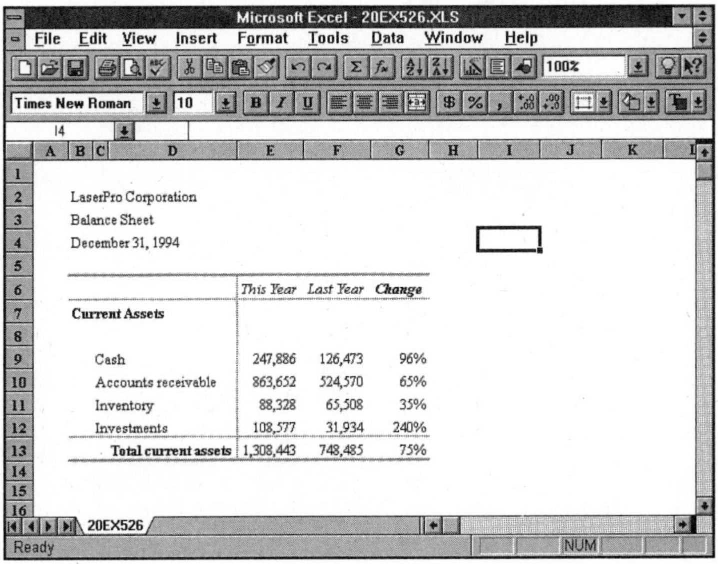

Fig. 20.25
The LaserPro balance sheet after using AutoFormat.

By looking at the many autoformats, you can get an idea of what the designers of Excel think are good worksheet designs (see fig. 20.26). Compare these designs to the desktop publishing basics you have learned so far.

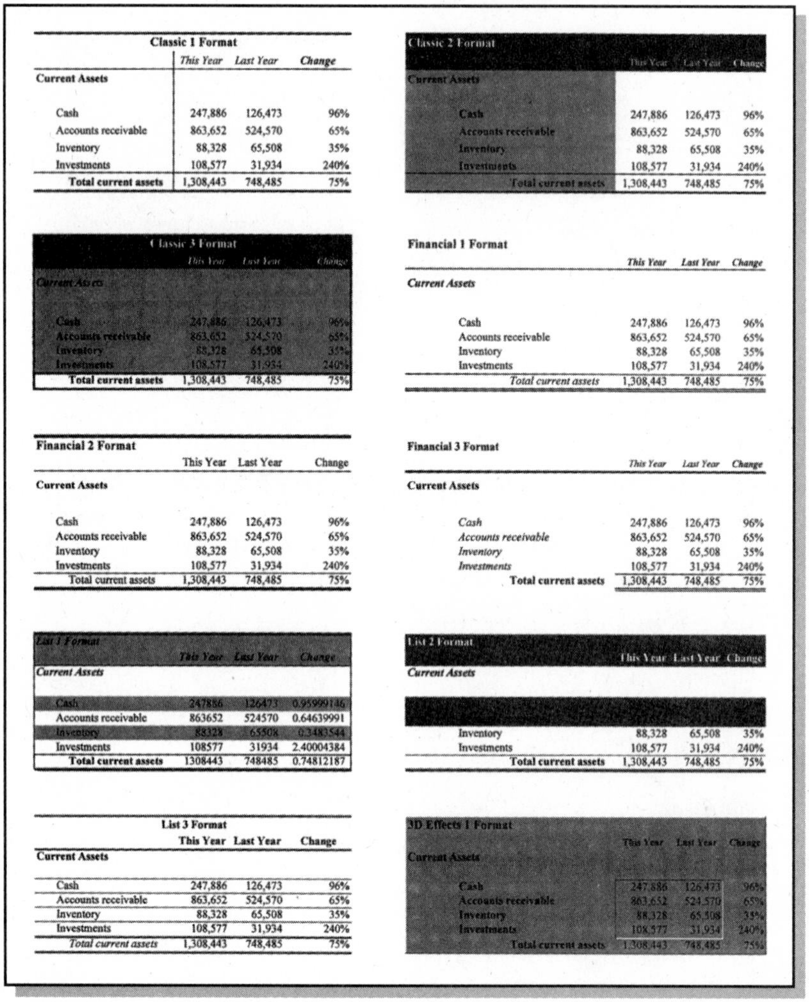

Fig. 20.26 Examples of different AutoFormat choices.

From Here...

For additional information that relates to desktop publishing, refer to the following chapters:

- Chapter 10, "Formatting Worksheets." This chapter introduces you to the fundamentals of using autoformats, fonts, borders, patterns, and styles.

- Chapter 11, "Printing Worksheets." This chapter introduces you to printing and previewing your worksheets and setting print ranges.
- Chapter 12, "Creating Charts." This chapter shows you how to create, save, and print a chart.
- Chapter 13, "Modifying Charts." This chapter shows you how to choose a chart type, select automatic formatting for your chart, and add data to your chart.
- Chapter 14, "Formatting Charts." This chapter shows you how to change fonts and styles of text in charts and format legends, arrows, and gridlines.
- Chapter 15, "Building Complex Charts." This chapter shows you how to create combination and picture charts.
- Chapter 16, "Managing the Worksheet Display." This chapter shows you how to turn on gridlines, magnify the display, and use the View Manager to save views.
- Chapter 17, "Adding Graphics Elements to Sheets." This chapter shows you how to add clip art, charts, and drawing objects to your worksheet.
- Chapter 21, "Creating Slide Show Presentations." This chapter shows you how to create a slide show in Excel.
- Chapter 38, "Using Excel with Windows Applications." This chapter shows you how to place Excel worksheets in word processing documents, how to capture graphic images from graphic applications, and how to link worksheet data to graphic applications.
- Chapter 42, "Creating Templates and Controlling Excel's Startup." This chapter shows you how to create and use Excel templates.

Chapter 21

Creating Slide Show Presentations

In this chapter, you learn:

- How to install the Slide Show add-in
- How to create a slide show
- How to add, delete, and modify a slide
- How to start and stop a slide show
- How to save a slide show

The Slide Show add-in enables you to create slide shows. With the Slide Show, you can display timed or manually controlled sequences of worksheets, charts, graphics, and text. Slide Show is perfect for making presentations through LCD overhead projectors or video projector systems. The slide shows you create can use special visual and audio effects when moving between slides. Figure 21.1 shows an example slide.

The Slide Show add-in gives you control over the following:

- A slide's display time
- Manually controlled slide changes
- Special visual transition effects
- Audio transition effects (available with soundboards)
- Which slide begins a presentation

If you want to use the special sound effects available when changing between slides, you need sound boards or multimedia boards and speakers compatible with Windows multimedia.

Note

Slide shows created with the add-in can appear only on a screen. You cannot direct slides to a printer, plotter, or other output device.

Fig. 21.1
Slide Show can help you make your point during presentations.

Setting Up a Slide Show

Before you can present a slide show, you need to make some preparations. You need to be sure the Slide Show add-in is installed and ready to use, and then you need to create the slides and paste them into the show. After you do this, you can edit the transitions and reorder the slides.

Activating the Slide Show Add-In

To determine whether the Slide Show add-in is available, choose the **F**ile **N**ew command and see if Slide is an available template in the New dialog box. If Slide is not shown in the list of templates or if the New dialog box does not appear, you may need to install or activate the Slide Show add-in.

Before you can create or run a slide show, you must install the Slide Show add-in. If you installed the add-ins during Excel installation, the appropriate files will be on your hard disk. If you choose Typical or Laptop setup, Excel doesn't install the Slide Show add-in. If you choose Complete setup, you need to make sure that you select Add-ins and that the Slide Show add-in option is selected. For more information on installing Excel, see the Excel 5 *User's Guide*. For more information on installing add-ins, see Chapter 22, "Taking Advantage of Excel's Add-Ins." If you did not install the add-ins, you can rerun Excel's Custom setup and elect to install only the add-ins or even just the Slide Show add-in.

Unlike other add-ins, you don't need to install Slide Show through **T**ools Add-Ins. Slide Show also doesn't add commands to the menus. Instead, the slide commands are accessed from buttons on a slide worksheet.

Two methods are available for opening a slide template. You can make the Slide template appear in the **F**ile **N**ew list of templates, or you can use the **F**ile **O**pen command to open the SLIDES.XLT template located in the LIBRARY\SLIDES directory located under Excel.

Creating a New Slide Show

You build slide shows by copying worksheets, charts, text, or graphics from Excel or other programs and then pasting them into the slide template. Any images included in a slide show must exist in the slide show template and in all original worksheets.

To create a slide show, open a new slide template by completing the following steps:

1. Choose the **F**ile **N**ew command.

2. Select Slides from the New dialog box.

3. Choose OK.

The slide template shown in figure 21.2 enables you to create, edit, and run slide shows. You will use the buttons at the top of a slide worksheet to manage the slide show. Table 21.1 describes the buttons.

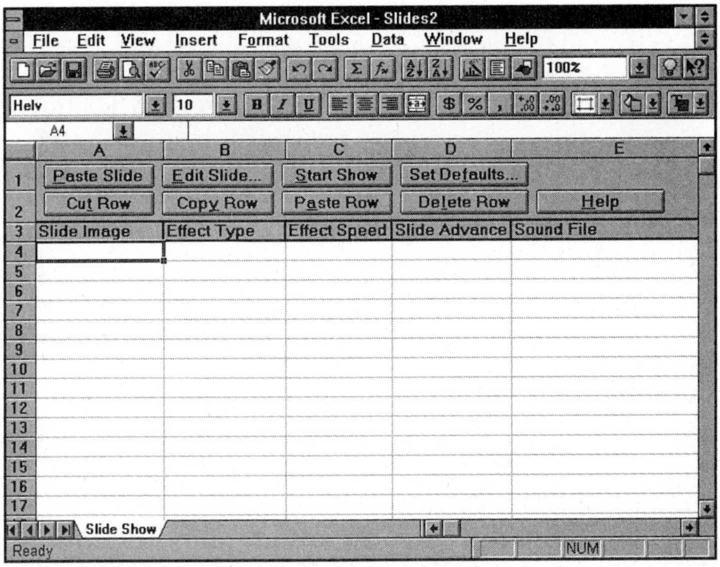

Fig. 21.2
The Slide Show command buttons appear on the Slide Show worksheet of your workbook.

Table 21.1 Slide Show Buttons

Button	Result
Paste Slide	Pastes the contents of the Clipboard into the slide worksheet. Data is captured for a slide by copying it into the Clipboard and then pasting it into the slide worksheet.
Edit Slide	Changes the transition from the current slide to the next slide.
Start Show	Starts the slide show and prompt for whether the show should be automatic or manually controlled.
Set De**f**aults	Changes the default settings for transition times and transition effects.
Cu**t** Row	Cuts a slide's information so that it can be moved to a different location in the slide show sequence.
Cop**y** Row	Copies a slide's information so that it can be moved to a different location in the slide show sequence.
P**a**ste Row	Pastes a row of slide information (from cut or copy) into the active row.
De**l**ete Row	Removes a slide from the slide show.
Help	Displays information about the Slide Show program.

You can add data to a slide worksheet after it is open. Figure 21.3 shows a slide worksheet containing data for a slide show. Each row in the slide worksheet contains information about a slide. From left to right, the cells contain a copy of the slide, the type of visual transition effect, the speed of transition, how long the slide is visible, and the audio transition effect.

Plan the slide show before you begin creating the slide show workbook. Although you can edit the order in which slides appear, initially pasting them into the slide sheet in approximately the correct order is faster.

To copy Excel cells, Excel charts, or graphics from a Windows application into a slide show, complete the following steps:

1. Select worksheet cells. Select all cells over which the characters you want to include extend. Format the worksheet, and choose the **T**ools **O**ptions command. On the View tab, set gridlines and colors as you want them to appear in the slide, select the chart you want as a slide, or select the object or graphic from another Windows application.

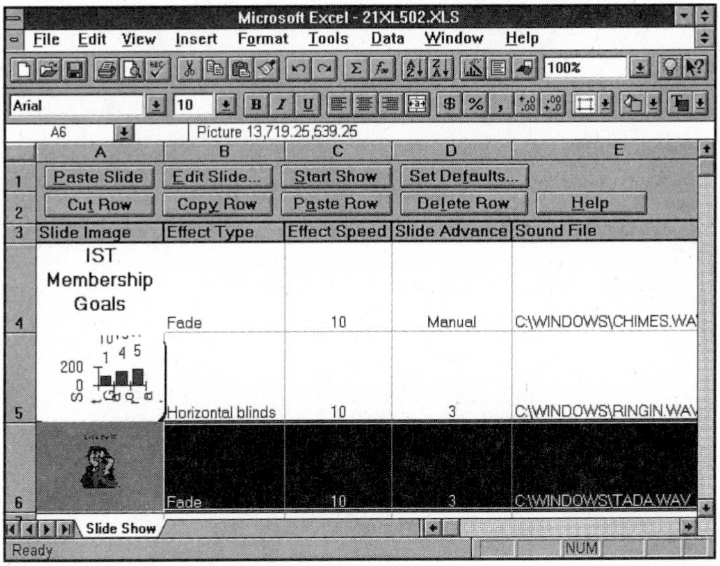

Fig. 21.3
The Slide Show worksheet shows a compressed image of the slide, and the transition type (effect type), speed, how the slide is advanced, and the name of the sound file.

2. Choose the **E**dit **C**opy command.

3. Activate Excel if you are in another application, and then activate the slide worksheet window.

4. Choose the **P**aste Slide button to copy the contents of the Windows Clipboard into the first free row on the slide worksheet.

   The Edit Slide dialog box appears, as shown in figure 21.4.

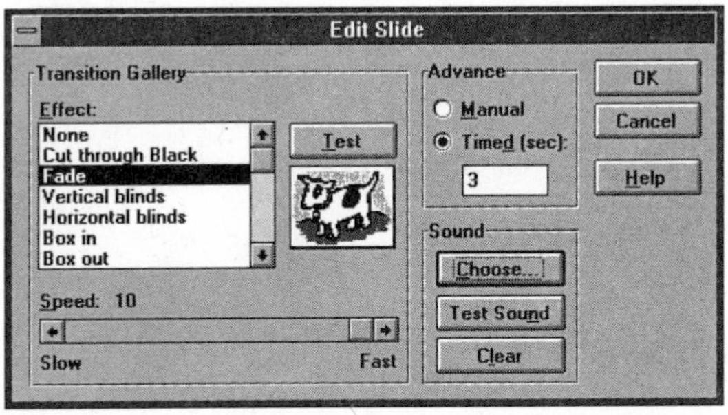

Fig. 21.4
Select the transition times and effects from the Edit Slide dialog box.

5. Select the options to control this slide, which are described in table 21.2.

6. Choose OK.

7. If you want to create another slide, return to step 1.

   Your slide and its options paste into the first available row in the slide worksheet.

> **Note**
>
> If text or a graphic from another application will not display in the slide show, paste it first into an Excel worksheet, and then save the worksheet. Now create a slide by using the text or graphic located on the Excel worksheet.

8. Change the defaults for transitions between all pairs of slides.
9. Edit transitions between individual pairs of slides.
10. Move, copy, or delete individual slides.
11. Save the slide show.
12. Start the slide show.

The Edit Slide dialog box controls three characteristics of the transition from the previous slide to the current one. Select the options you want for the transition from the current slide. Table 21.2 lists the options.

Tip
You also can use the **I**nsert **P**icture command to bring clip art from various packages into your Excel worksheet or into a program like Paintbrush.

Table 21.2 Edit Slide Options

Option	Description
Transition	**Gallery**
Effect	The visual transition effect between slides, such as fading from one to another, sliding one on and the other off, creating a venetian blind effect, or opening an iris or shutter.
Test	See a sample of how the effect works.
Speed	The speed of the transition in seconds.
Advance	
Manual	Begin transition to the next slide when you press the space bar or click a mouse button.
Time**d**	Begin transition to the next slide automatically in the number of seconds you enter in the edit box.

Option	Description
Sound	
Choose	Select a sound to play during the transition. (Only available with multimedia hardware and drivers installed.)
Test Sound	Play the selected sound.
Clear	Remove the sound for this transition.

Editing Transitions

The Edit Slide dialog box displays with default settings. If you frequently use different settings than those that appear, change the default settings. To change a slide show's defaults for transitions, choose the Set Defaults button on the slide template. The Sets Defaults dialog box appears. From this dialog box, you make selections as you would in the Edit Slide dialog box. When you next choose the Paste Slide button, the Edit Slide dialog box appears with the new default settings, which are Effect None, Manual Advance, and no sound.

To edit a slide's transition effects after it is pasted into a slide presentation, follow these steps:

1. Select a cell in the row with the slide you want to edit. The first cell containing a copy of the slide is protected. Select a cell to the right of the first cell or click the row number in the row header.
2. Choose the Edit Slide button on the slide template. The Edit Slide dialog box appears.
3. Select the options you want from the dialog box.
4. Choose OK.

Reordering a Slide Show

The steps for moving or copying one or more slides in a slide show are similar. In either case, you cut or copy a slide row from one location and paste it into another location.

For Related Information

- "Using Graphics and Clip Art from Other Applications," p. 556
- "Combining Data and Charts on the Same Page," p. 571
- "Starting Add-Ins," p. 675

To move one or more slides, perform the following steps:

1. Select a cell in the row with the slide you want to move. Select more than one row to move more than one slide. The first cell containing a copy of the slide is protected. Select a cell to the right, or click the row number in the row header.

2. Choose the Cu**t** Row or Cop**y** Row button on the slide template.

3. Select the slide above which you want to insert the slide(s).

4. Choose the P**a**ste Row button on the slide template.

To delete one or more slides, select them from the slide show template. Then choose the De**l**ete Row button from the template.

Running a Slide Show

After you have created your slide show and have all the slides in the correct order with the proper transitions between them, it is time to run the show. When you run it, you can control how it runs, much like you control a VCR by stopping, pausing, and restarting. Unlike with most VCRs, however, you also can start the slide show at a specific slide.

Starting a Slide Show

To run the slide show, perform the following steps:

1. Activate the slide workbook containing your slide show.

2. Choose the **S**tart Show button. The Start Show dialog box displays, as shown in figure 21.5.

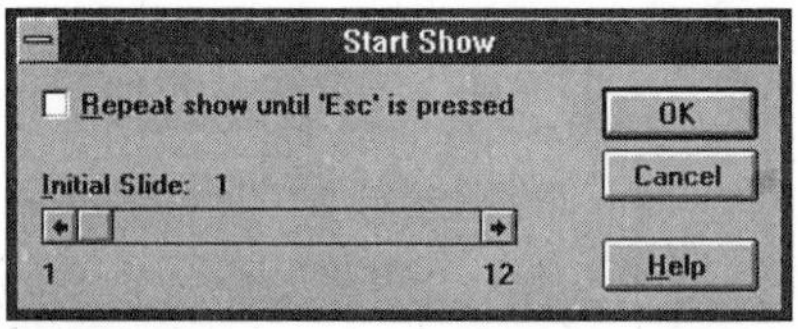

Fig. 21.5
Use the Start Show dialog box to control the start of your slide show.

3. Select the **R**epeat Show until 'Esc' Is Pressed check box if you want the show to run continuously. Otherwise the show runs through one time, then stops.

4. Select the **I**nitial Slide bar, and move the slide to the number at which you want the show to start. Drag the scroll box with the mouse, or use the scroll arrow keys to select a starting slide.

5. Choose OK.

Stopping, Pausing, or Restarting a Slide Show

To interrupt a slide show, press Esc. This action displays the Slide Show Options dialog box (see fig. 21.6), which enables you to stop the show, continue running the slide show, or go to a specific slide. The slide show pauses while this dialog box appears.

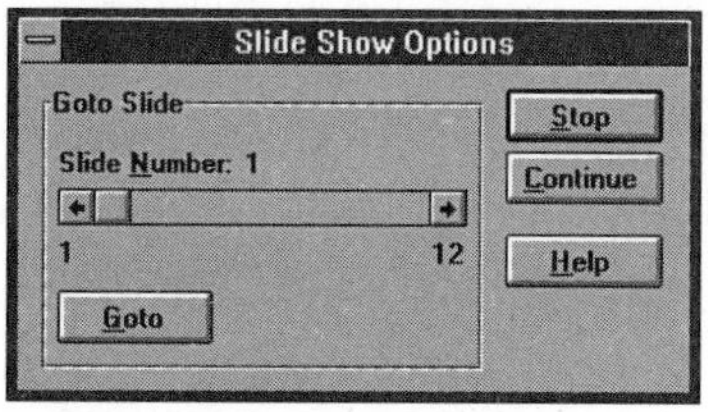

Fig. 21.6
You can stop, interrupt, or repeat slides from the Slide Show Options dialog box.

From the Slide Show options dialog box, you can stop the slide show by choosing the **S**top button. To continue the show, choose the **C**ontinue button.

If you want to return to a specific slide or restart the entire slide show, select the Slide **N**umber bar and move the box to the slide at which you want to begin. Use the mouse to drag the box, or press the arrow keys. Choose the **G**oto button to display the slide you have chosen and continue the show.

Putting the Final Polish on a Slide Show and Saving It

After you have viewed a slide show, you may decide that you need to edit some of the graphics or worksheet data you included. Or you may need to use the slide show on a regular basis with monthly updates—to reflect current sales, for example. With Slide Show you can modify the slides, save a Slide Show for later use, or edit a saved show.

When you select a chart in Slide Show, the Chart toolbar appears with five buttons as shown in figure 21.7. The buttons enable you to change the chart type, return to the default chart type, use the ChartWizard to edit the location of the data, add or remove gridlines, and add or remove a legend.

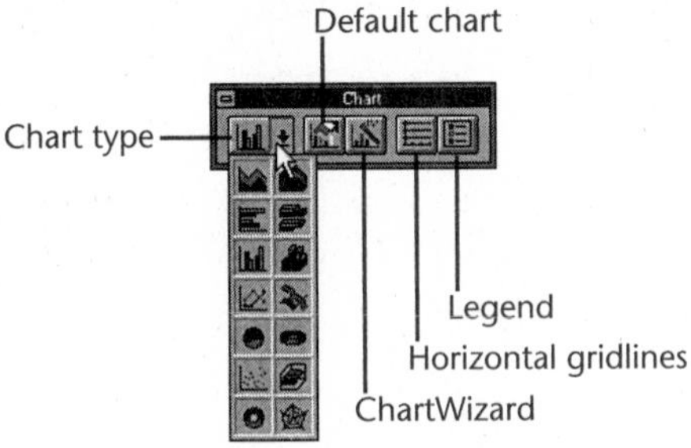

Fig. 21.7
The first button on the Chart toolbar enables you to select from a gallery of chart types.

Saving a Slide Show

After you design a slide show to match your specifications, or if you must move on to other activities, you need to save the slide show. To save a show, perform the same steps that you use to save a normal workbook:

1. Activate the slide show workbook.

2. Choose **F**ile **S**ave or click the Save button on the toolbar.
3. Type a name for the slide show in the File **N**ame text box of the File Save dialog box.
4. Choose OK.

Modifying an Existing Slide Show

Modifying an existing slide show is just like editing a new one—except that you open a previously composed slide show sheet instead of opening the template from **F**ile **N**ew.

To open an existing slide show, perform the following steps:

1. Choose the **F**ile **O**pen command.
2. Select the slide show worksheet you want to open.
3. Choose OK.

For Related Information

- "Saving a Workspace File," p. 280
- "Embedding Data from Other Applications into Worksheets," p. 1050

From Here...

For additional information that relates to creating slides and working with text, graphics, and color, browse through these chapters:

- Chapter 10, "Formatting Worksheets." This chapter shows you how to change fonts, add colors, patterns and borders, protect sheets, and define styles.
- Chapter 12, "Creating Charts." This chapters shows you how to create a chart with the ChartWizard or manually.
- Chapter 13, "Modifying Charts." This chapter shows you how to edit charts, add data, and use Autoformats.
- Chapter 14, "Formatting Charts." This chapter shows you how to change the font and style of titles, and how to work with data series, markers, legends, and work with 3-D charts.
- Chapter 17, "Adding Graphics to Sheets." This chapter shows you how to add and work with pictures and clip art.

Chapter 22

Taking Advantage of Excel's Add-Ins

Even with its ease of use, Excel has a more comprehensive set of features than other worksheets offer. But no matter how extensive Excel's features, special industries or special situations are bound to require more. With Excel, anyone who can record or write macros can add features, functions, and commands to Excel so that it works the way it's needed.

Excel ships with add-ins that enhance the way you work. After you install these add-ins on your hard disk during the installation process, you still need to activate the add-ins when you want to use them. These add-ins change Excel in different ways. Some add-ins provide additional items on menus. For example, figure 22.1 shows the View Manager added to the View menu. Other add-ins increase your number of options on an existing menu or dialog option. Figure 22.2 shows the Function Wizard dialog box. The Analysis ToolPak add-in adds a whole new function category, Engineering, that provides many engineering functions. The Analysis ToolPak add-in also adds functions to other function categories.

This chapter describes some of the add-in programs that come with Excel and add helpful, and sometimes extensive, capabilities. To learn how to create your own add-ins, see Chapters 44 and 45.

In this chapter, you learn:

- How to install add-ins
- How to remove add-ins
- General descriptions of some of the add-ins that come with Excel

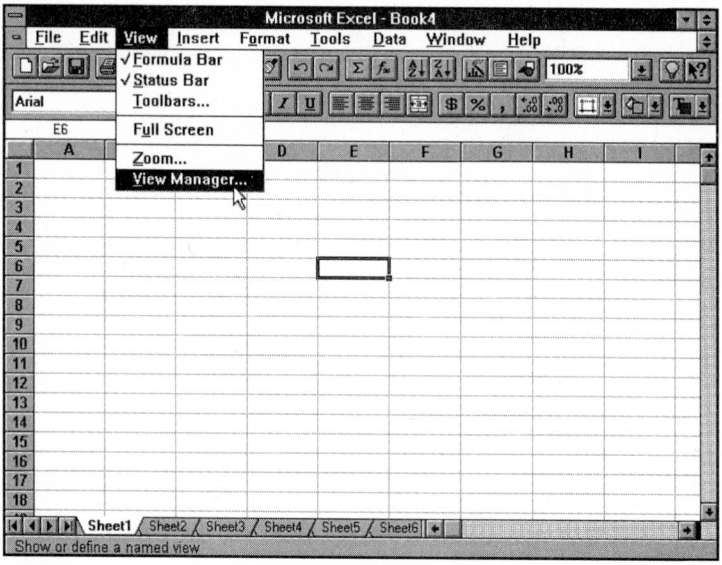

Fig. 22.1
Add-ins may add items on menus. The View Manager adds the command of the same name on the View menu.

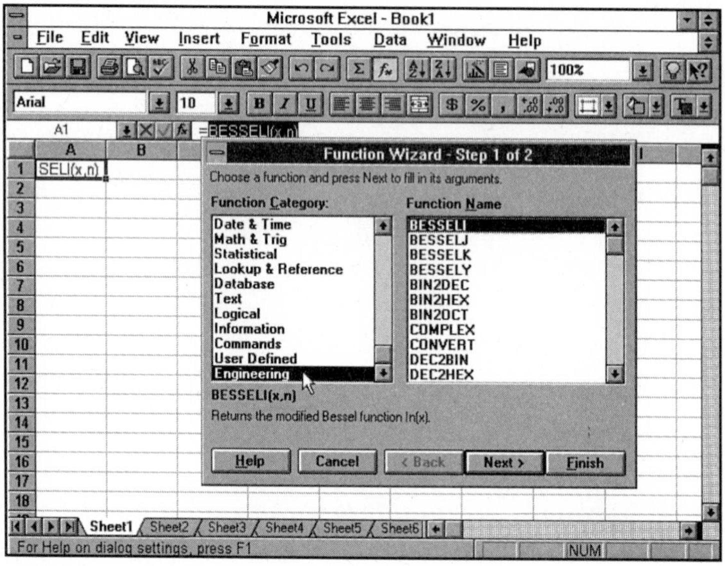

Fig. 22.2
Add-ins also can add functions. The Analysis ToolPak add-in adds a number of functions including a whole new category for engineering functions.

Installing Add-Ins

EXCEL 5

If you try to access an add-in and then get a `Cannot find` message with the name of the add-in file (with an XLA or XLL extension), you need to install the add-in. You can check which add-ins have been installed by looking at the dialog box that appears when you choose the **T**ools Add-**I**ns command (see the "Starting Add-Ins" section later in this chapter).

When you originally installed Excel, you had three install options: Typical, Complete/Custom, and Laptop (Minimum). The add-ins installed depend on which of these options you chose and whether any changes were made after the original installation. If you chose Laptop (Minimum) installation, no add-ins were installed. If you chose Typical installation, AutoSave, Report Manager, Solver, and View Manager were installed. The add-ins installed during Complete/Custom installation depend on which add-ins were deselected during the process. The default for Complete/Custom installation is for all add-ins to be installed. You can change the installed add-ins, however, within the Setup program.

Tip
For more information, choose the **H**elp **S**earch for Help on command, then type **add-ins** and select the **S**how Topics button. In the **t**opic area, select Add-ins included with Microsoft Excel and select the **G**o To button.

To install add-ins after you've installed the Excel program, follow these steps:

1. Exit Microsoft Excel if it is running.
2. In the Excel group, double-click the MS Excel Setup program icon (see fig. 22.3). The Microsoft Excel 5.0 Setup dialog box appears.

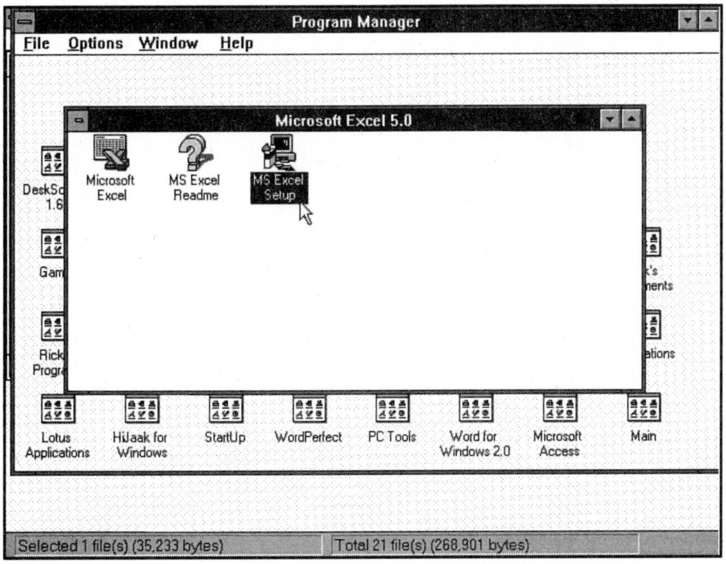

Fig. 22.3
The Microsoft Excel Setup program is separate from the Microsoft Excel program.

3. Choose the **A**dd/Remove button. The Microsoft Excel 5.0 - Complete/Custom dialog box appears.
4. In the **O**ptions section of the dialog box, select Add-ins, as shown in figure 22.4.

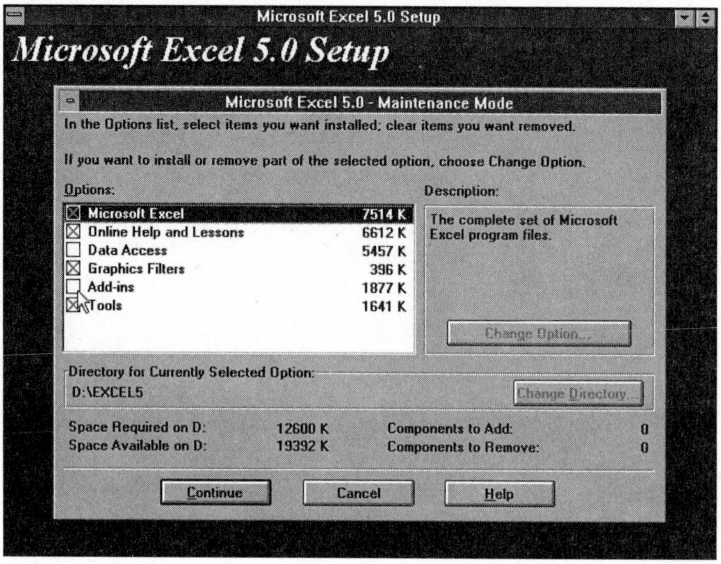

Fig. 22.4
In this dialog box, none of the add-ins are installed.

5. To choose the add-ins to install, choose the Chan**g**e Option button to the right of the list of options.

6. In the Microsoft Excel 5.0 - Add-ins dialog box, click on each option to install to check the box to the left of the option name as shown in figure 22.5.

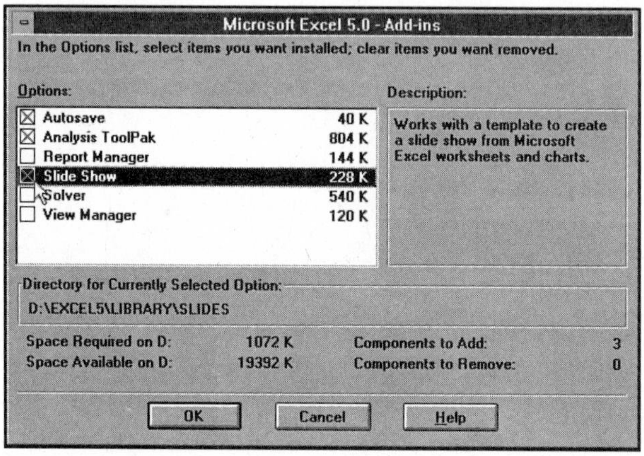

Fig. 22.5
In this example, Autosave, Analysis ToolPak, and Slide Show are selected for installation.

7. After you select the add-ins to install, choose OK.

8. Choose **C**ontinue in the Microsoft Excel 5.0 - Complete/Custom dialog box.

9. Insert the disks that the message box prompts you to insert.

10. At the end of the process, you should get a message that the setup was completed successfully. Choose OK. If the setup was not successful, you need to start over at step 2.

When you install the add-ins, you copy the files to your hard disk. You may still need to start the add-ins, using the procedure described in the "Starting Add-Ins" section.

Using Add-In Programs

The add-in programs that ship with Excel are stored in files ending with the XLA extension. Additional files needed by the add-ins use the extension XLL. You can find them in the LIBRARY subdirectory under the directory containing Excel. These XLA files are special macros that add features to Excel as though the features were built-in. To access the add-ins, you need to install the add-in files and also activate the add-ins. In this section, you learn how to start these add-in macros and how to manage them. To learn how you can make your own recorded or written macros into add-ins, read about Visual Basic programming in Chapters 43 through 46.

Starting Add-Ins

You start an add-in macro when you choose the add-in from the **T**ools Add-**I**ns menu. Excel opens add-in files with XLA extensions. When that add-in opens, special commands, shortcuts, functions, or features available through the add-in become accessible. Although you can open XLA files with the **F**ile **O**pen command, they are more manageable when added to menus with the **T**ools Add-**I**ns command. When you install an add-in with the **T**ools Add-**I**ns command, the new feature may appear on a menu, but the add-in file does not open until you choose the command. This process makes add-ins available without your using system resources unnecessarily. The add-in macros that come with Excel—except for Microsoft Query—are stored in the LIBRARY directory under the Excel directory. Some add-in macros have their own subdirectories under LIBRARY.

Using the Tools Add-Ins Command

The **T**ools Add-**I**ns command helps you by opening a collection of add-ins that you specify. The **T**ools Add-**I**ns command opens the Add-Ins dialog box (see fig. 22.6). Excel indicates active add-ins with a check mark in the check box next to the add-in name. Excel indicates available, yet inactive add-ins with a blank check box.

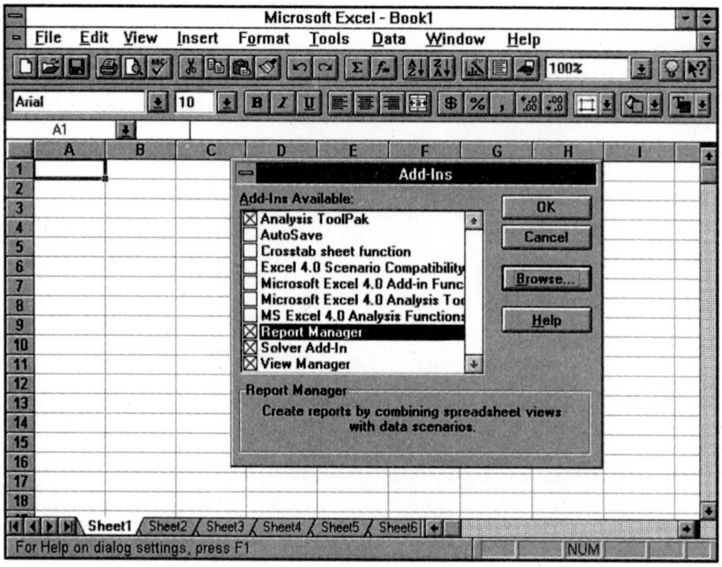

Fig. 22.6
This Add-Ins dialog box shows that the Analysis ToolPak Report Manager, Solver, and View Manager add-ins are active.

To add an add-in to Excel, follow these steps:

1. Choose the **T**ools Add-**I**ns command.
2. Select the add-in, or add-ins, that you want by marking the check box next to the add-in, as shown in figure 22.6.
3. If the add-in does not show on the Add-ins dialog box, select the **B**rowse button and search for the file. Files with XLA and XLL extensions are available as add-ins.
4. When you finish selecting add-ins, choose OK.

Using the Analysis ToolPak

The Analysis ToolPak is a must for financial, statistical, and some engineering and scientific analysis. It contains functions and models that a few years ago required minicomputers for solutions.

The Analysis ToolPak adds five Financial Functions, five Date & Time functions, seven Math & Trig functions, two Information functions, and a whole new category for forty Engineering functions. The Analysis ToolPak also allows you to add your own functions. To access these additional functions, choose **I**nsert **F**unction, select a Function **C**ategory and Function **N**ame on the Function Wizard dialog box (refer to fig. 22.2).

The Analysis ToolPak also adds the Data Analysis command on the **T**ools menu. When you choose this command, you get several statistical procedures to choose from, as shown in figure 22.7.

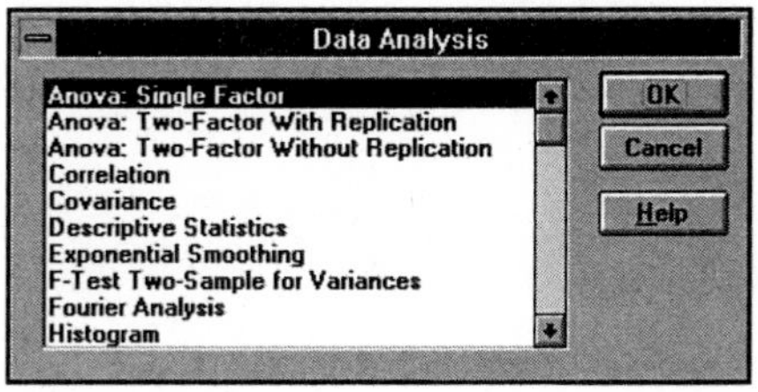

Fig. 22.7
This Data Analysis dialog box shows some of the statistical procedures available, including Anova, Correlation, and the F-Test.

For coverage of the added calculating capabilities available with the Analysis ToolPak, see Chapter 29, "Using the Analysis ToolPak."

Adding an AutoSave Feature

The AutoSave add-in saves Excel files for you at the frequency you specify. This macro helps you remember to save. When AutoSave loads, it adds the A**u**toSave command to the **T**ools menu. Choose the **T**ools A**u**toSave command to display the AutoSave dialog box, shown in figure 22.8

The first option on the AutoSave dialog box, Automatic **S**ave, allows you to turn the automatic save feature on or off. If you select this check box, you can enter the number of minutes between automatic saves in the Minutes text box. In the Save **O**ptions area, you can have Excel save all workbooks or only the active workbook. The last option, **P**rompt Before Saving, allows Excel to prompt you before saving workbooks.

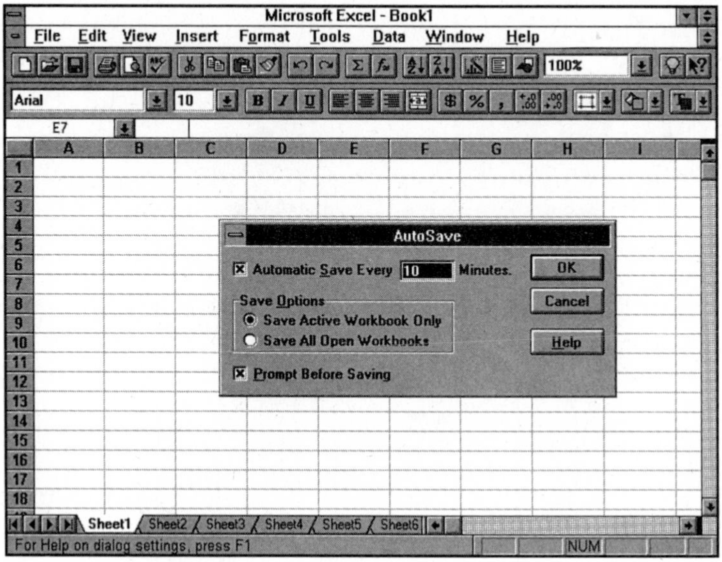

Fig. 22.8
The AutoSave feature allows you to save your work automatically or to have Excel prompt you to save your work.

Adding the Report Manager

The Report Manager is a major feature of Excel for anyone who must print charts and reports involving multiple worksheets, multiple views, or different sets of input data. If you need to do a job like this more than once, use the Report Manager. Add the Report Manager by using the **T**ools Add-**I**n Command. Use the Report Manager by choosing the **F**ile Print R**e**port command. The Print Report dialog box appears as shown in figure 22.9. The Report Manager is described in Chapter 19, "Creating Automatic Subtotals."

Adding a Slide Show

The Slide Show add-in, shown in figure 22.10, gives you access to the Slide Show program, which creates still images of Excel charts, worksheets, and graphics, or text from other applications. Slide Show allows you to show these still images or "slides" one after the other. Slide Show also includes sound capability and flashy slide transitions. You can view the *slides* that Excel displays only with a computer screen or screen projector. You cannot print them to 35mm or overhead transparency film with this add-in. You use the **F**ile **N**ew SLIDES command to start the show. Slide Show is described in Chapter 21.

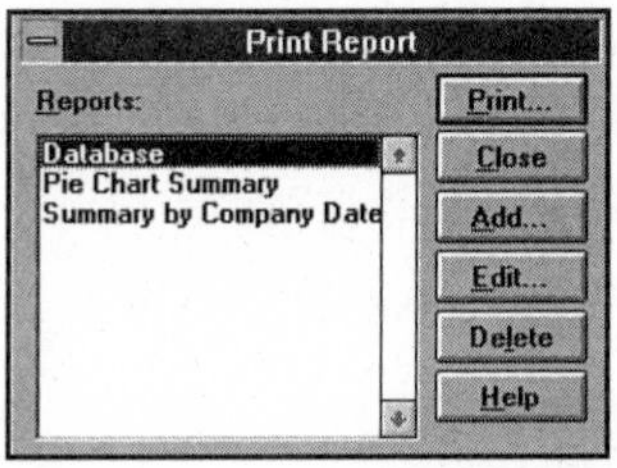

Fig. 22.9
The Report Manager add-in enables you to combine worksheets, charts, and views in one report.

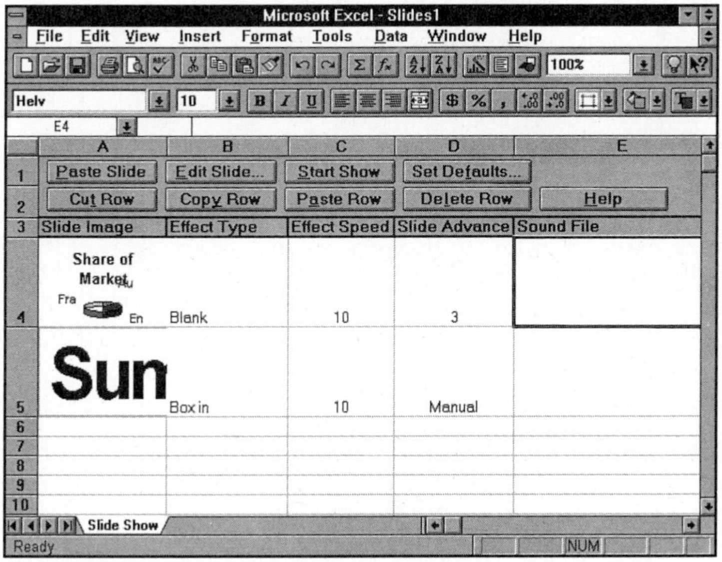

Fig. 22.10
Use Slide Show to create presentations with special effects.

Adding Optimization with the Solver

The Solver add-in, shown in figure 22.11, gives Excel the power of linear and nonlinear optimization. Solver not only finds an answer to a problem, but also finds the best answer, given a set of cells that it can change, a set of constraints that must be met, and one cell that must be optimized for the greatest, least, or equal to solution. Use **T**ools Add-**I**ns to add the Solver and the **T**ools Sol**v**er command to run the Solver. The Solver is described in Chapter 27, "Solving with Goal Seeker and Solver."

Adding the View Manager

The View Manager, shown in figure 22.12, enables you to name and save frequently used worksheet locations and their display settings. It also stores print areas and print settings by name. The View Manager is a real time-saver for frequently printed reports or for data-entry screens. You must use the View Manager if you want to use the Report Manager. Use **T**ools Add-**I**ns to add the View Manager and the **V**iew **V**iew Manager command to run the View Manager. The View Manager is described in Chapter 16, "Managing the Worksheet Display."

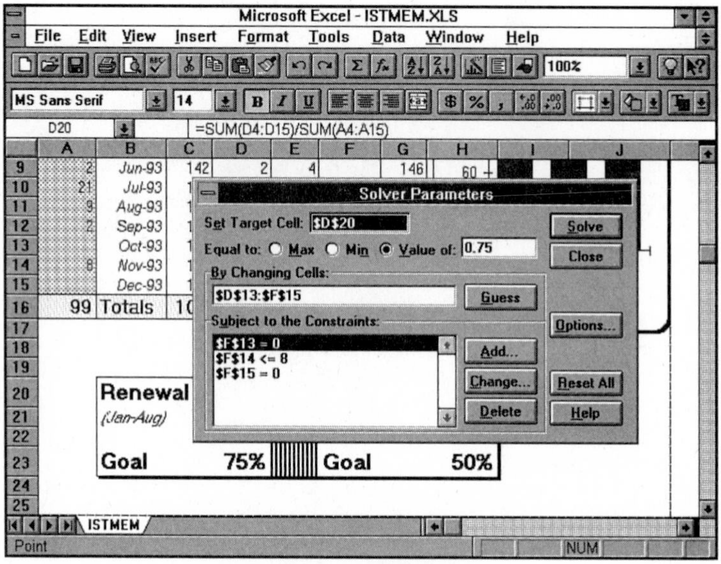

Fig. 22.11 Use the Solver to find the best possible solution even when there are multiple input values.

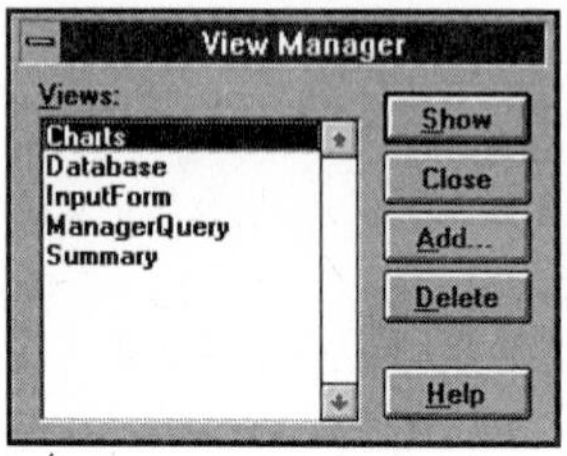

Fig. 22.12 The View Manager allows you to look at your worksheet in different ways.

From Here...

Add-ins are useful programs that extend and adapt Excel's capabilities. In addition to using the add-ins that come with Excel, you can create your own add-ins by using the Excel 4 macro language or Visual Basic for Applications.

- Chapter 11, "Printing Worksheets." Learn how to use the Report Manager to coordinate printing multiple page reports.

- Chapter 21, "Creating Slide Show Presentations." You can present your results as a slide show using special effects for transitions if you use the Slide Show add-in.

- Chapter 27, "Solving with Goal Seeking and Solver." The Solver add-in enables you to use linear and nonlinear optimization to find the best answer to complex worksheets.
- Chapter 28, "Testing Multiple Solutions with Scenarios." The Scenario Manager enables a workbook to remember different combinations of input values. You can reenter those input combinations just by selecting a name.
- Chapter 29, "Using the Analysis ToolPak." The Analysis ToolPak is an add-in that adds many advanced functions in the areas of finance, engineering, and statistics.
- Chapter 45, "Programming in Visual Basic for Applications." This chapter helps you get started in Visual Basic so you can create your own add-ins for your company or for commercial sale.

Part IV

Analyzing the Worksheet

23 Manipulating and Analyzing Data

24 Building Forms with Controls

25 Linking, Embedding, and Consolidating Worksheets

26 Auditing Workbooks and Worksheets

27 Solving with Goal Seeking and Solver

28 Testing Multiple Solutions with Scenarios

29 Using the Analysis ToolPak

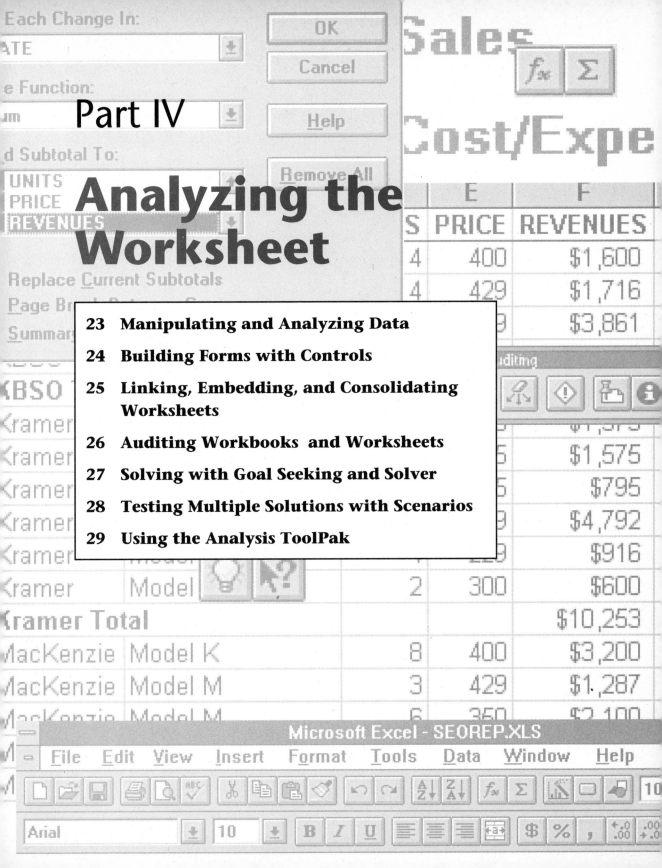

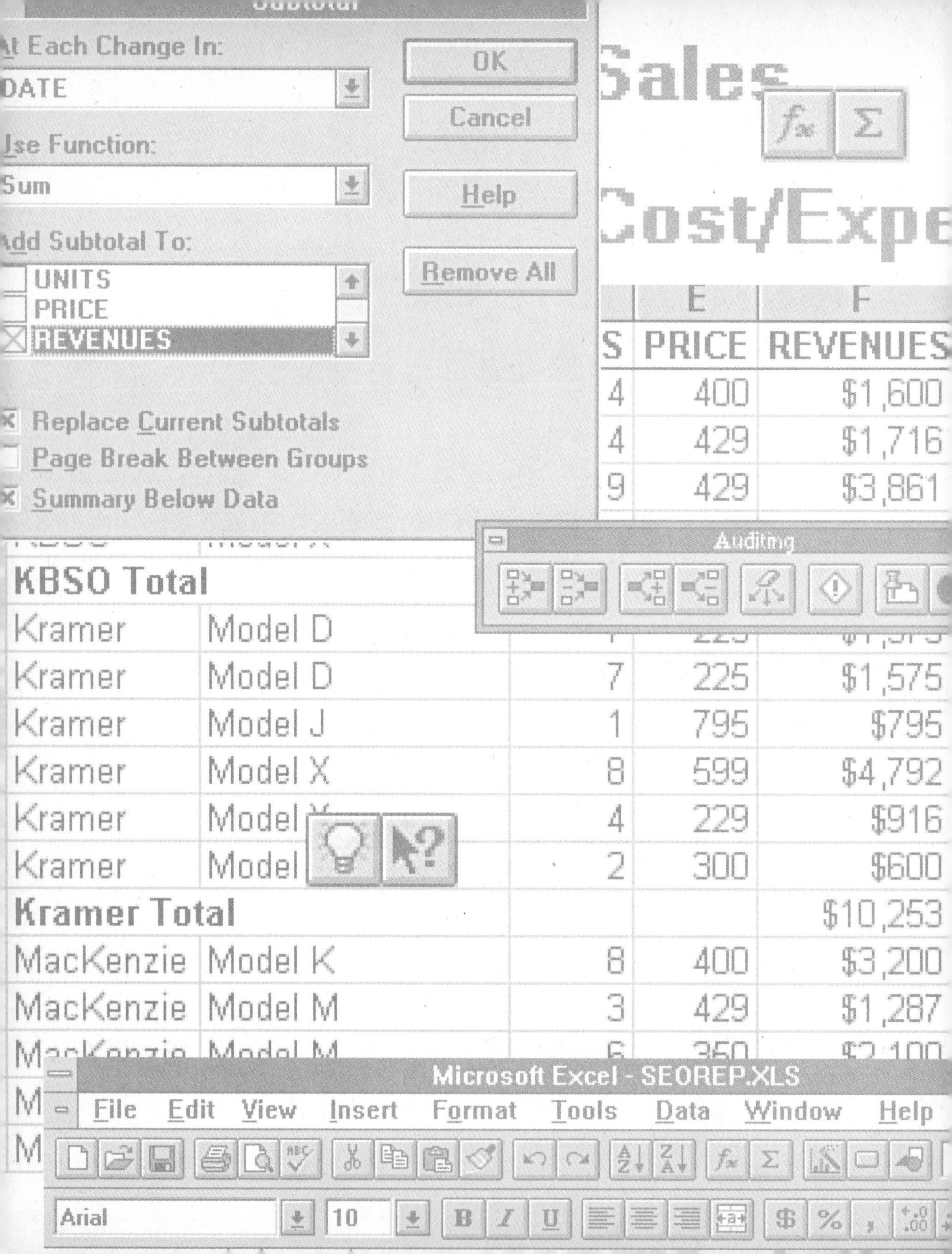
At Each Change In:
DATE
Use Function:
Sum
Add Subtotal To:
UNITS
PRICE
REVENUES
Replace Current Subtotals
Page Break Between Groups
Summary Below Data
OK
Cancel
Help
Remove All
Sales
Cost/Expe
E
F
PRICE
REVENUES
400
$1,600
429
$1,716
429
$3,861
Auditing
KBSO Total
Kramer Model D
Kramer Model D 7 225 $1,575
Kramer Model J 1 795 $795
Kramer Model X 8 599 $4,792
Kramer Model 4 229 $916
Kramer Model 2 300 $600
Kramer Total $10,253
MacKenzie Model K 8 400 $3,200
MacKenzie Model M 3 429 $1,287
Microsoft Excel - SEOREP.XLS
File
Edit
View
Insert
Format
Tools
Data
Window
Help
Arial
10

Chapter 23

Manipulating and Analyzing Data

If all Excel did was perform algebraic computations in worksheets, it would still be a powerful tool, but certain tasks need more than number-crunching. If you use Excel extensively, you will undoubtedly find situations where the result depends on different conditions. Some of these conditions may depend on specific values or a range of values in a given cell. In other situations, you may want Excel to look up an answer from a list. You may also need to summarize data in a list based on certain criteria. Excel provides a number of features to facilitate this kind of processing and analysis.

In this chapter, you learn how to:

- Use formulas to manipulate text
- Write formulas that make decisions based on conditions you specify
- Test input values to make sure that these values are in the correct range
- Use lookup tables to find such information as tax and commission rates
- Analyze data in lists with database functions

Manipulating Text

Excel enables you to manipulate text, numbers, and dates. Text manipulation is handy for combining text and numbers in printed invoices, creating titles from numeric results, and using data from a database to create a mailing list. With Excel, you can use formulas to manipulate text in the same way you use formulas to calculate numeric results.

Use the concatenation operator, the & (ampersand), to join text, numbers, or cell contents to create a text string. Enclose text in quotation marks. You don't need to enclose numbers in quotation marks. Do not enclose cell references in quotation marks. You can reference cells that contain text or numbers. For example, consider the following formula:

```
="This "&"and That"
```

This formula displays the following text:

```
This and That
```

Note

Text used in a formula must always be enclosed in quotes. Excel assumes that text not in quotes is a name. This situation causes a #NAME? error if a name with this spelling is not defined.

You also can join text by referring to the cell address. If A12 contains the text, `John`, and B12 contains the text, `McDougall`, you can use the following formula to combine the first and last names:

=A12&" "&B12

The result of the formula is the following:

```
John McDougall
```

Notice that a space between the two quotation marks in the formula separates the text contained in cells A12 and B12.

EXCEL 5

You also can use the CONCATENATE function to produce the same result. The formula =CONCATENATE(A12," ",B12) also returns `John McDougall`.

Excel also enables you to convert a number to text. You can refer to a number as you refer to a cell filled with text. If A12 contains `99` and B12 contains the text, `Stone St.`, use the following formula to create the full street address:

=A12&" "&B12

The result of the formula is the address:

```
99 Stone St.
```

When you refer to a number or date in a text formula, the number or date appears in the general format, not as the number or date appears in the formatted display. Suppose that cell B23 contains the date `12/24/94`, and you enter the following formula:

="Merry Christmas! Today is "&B23

The result of this formula is the following:

```
Merry Christmas! Today is 34692
```

You can change the format of the number with the FIXED( ), DOLLAR( ), and TEXT( ) functions. These functions change numbers and dates to text in the format you want. With dates, for example, you can use the TEXT( ) function to produce the following formula:

="Merry Christmas! Today is "&TEXT(B23,"mmm dd, yy")

The result appears as the following:

```
Merry Christmas! Today is Dec 24, 94
```

You can use any predefined or custom numeric or date format between the quotation marks of the TEXT( ) function.

The TEXT( ) function is a handy way to trick large numbers into exceeding the width of a column without producing the #### signs that indicate a narrow column. The TEXT( ) function also is useful for numeric titles. If you want the number $5,000,000 stored in A36 to fit in a narrow column, for example, use the following formula, which displays the formatted number as text so that the number can exceed the column width:

=TEXT(A36,"$#,##0")

For Related Information

- "Changing Character Fonts, Sizes, Styles, and Colors," p. 312
- "Aligning and Rotating Text and Numbers," p. 319
- "Text Functions," p. 226

Using Formulas To Make Decisions

Excels IF( ) function can make decisions based on whether a test condition is true or false. Use IF( ), for example, to test whether the time has come to reorder a part, whether data was entered correctly, or which of two results or formulas to use.

The IF( ) function uses the following format:

IF(*logical_test,value_if_true*,_value_if_false_**)**

If the *logical_test* (condition) is true, the result is *value_if_true*; but if the *logical_test* is false, the result is *value_if_false*. The result values can display text with an argument such as "Hello", calculate a formula such as B12*6, or display the contents of a cell such as D35. IF( ) functions are valuable in macros for testing different conditions and acting according to the results of the test conditions.

Consider the following formula:

=IF(B34>50,B34*2,"Entry too low!")

In this example, the IF( ) function produces the answer 110 if B34 is 55. If B34 is 12, however, the cell that contains the function displays this text:

```
Entry too low!
```

Making Simple Decisions

To make comparisons, use IF( ) functions. Figure 23.1 shows an Accounts Aging Analysis worksheet in which Excel checks how long an amount has been overdue. Using IF( ) functions and the age of the account, Excel displays the amount in the correct column.

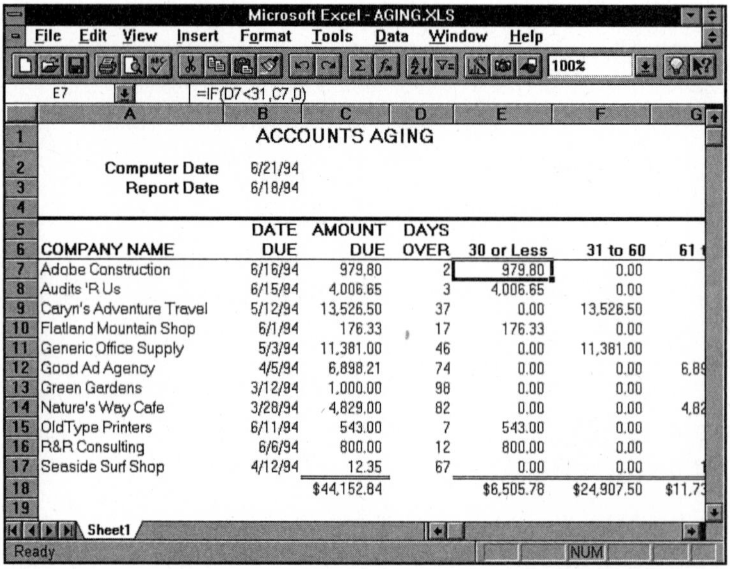

	A	B	C	D	E	F	G
1		ACCOUNTS AGING					
2	Computer Date	6/21/94					
3	Report Date	6/18/94					
4							
5		DATE	AMOUNT	DAYS			
6	COMPANY NAME	DUE	DUE	OVER	30 or Less	31 to 60	61 t
7	Adobe Construction	6/16/94	979.80	2	979.80	0.00	
8	Audits 'R Us	6/15/94	4,006.65	3	4,006.65	0.00	
9	Caryn's Adventure Travel	5/12/94	13,526.50	37	0.00	13,526.50	
10	Flatland Mountain Shop	6/1/94	176.33	17	176.33	0.00	
11	Generic Office Supply	5/3/94	11,381.00	46	0.00	11,381.00	
12	Good Ad Agency	4/5/94	6,898.21	74	0.00	0.00	6,89
13	Green Gardens	3/12/94	1,000.00	98	0.00	0.00	
14	Nature's Way Cafe	3/28/94	4,829.00	82	0.00	0.00	4,82
15	OldType Printers	6/11/94	543.00	7	543.00	0.00	
16	R&R Consulting	6/6/94	800.00	12	800.00	0.00	
17	Seaside Surf Shop	4/12/94	12.35	67	0.00	0.00	1
18			$44,152.84		$6,505.78	$24,907.50	$11,73
19							

Fig. 23.1
Use IF() functions to test ranges, such as the ages of these accounts.

The first few times you use IF( ) statements, you may want to write an English sentence that states the *logical_test,* or the question you want to ask. The question also should state both results if true and if false. For example, each cell from E7 through E16 uses an IF( ) statement equivalent to the following sentence:

> IF the value in the DAYS OVER column is less than 31, show the adjacent value in the AMOUNT DUE column, but if this condition is not true, then show zero.

The IF( ) function equivalent of this statement for cell E7 appears in the formula bar as the following formula:

=IF(D7<31,C7,0)

In this example, D7 contains the DAYS OVER for row 7, and C7 contains the AMOUNT DUE for row 7. To prevent displaying all zeros on the sheet, choose the **T**ools **O**ptions command, display the View tab, and clear **Z**ero Values.

> **Note**
>
> To display a blank cell for specific conditions, use a formula similar to the following:
>
> =IF(D7<31,C7,"")
>
> Nothing is entered between the quotation marks, so this function displays a blank cell for the false condition. Remember that Excel can hide zeros for the entire worksheet if in the Options dialog box, you deselect **Z**ero Values in the View tab.

Making Complex Decisions

In column F of the worksheet shown in figure 23.1, the IF( ) question needs to be more complex. The IF( ) functions in column F must test for a range of values in the DAYS OVER column. The DAYS OVER columns must be over 30 and less than 61:

> If the value in the DAYS OVER column is greater than 30 and the value in the DAYS OVER column is also less than 61, then show the value in the AMOUNT DUE column; if this is not true, show zero.

The IF functions in F7 through F17 use the following formula to check for DAYS OVER in the range from 31 to 60:

=IF(AND(D7>30,D7<61),C7,0)

The AND( ) function produces a TRUE response only when all the elements within the parentheses meet the conditions: D7>30 is true *AND* D7<61 is true. When the AND( ) function produces TRUE, the IF( ) formula produces the value found in C7.

When you want to check for a number within a range of values, use an AND( ) function as shown here, for the AND( ) function to be TRUE, all the arguments must be true. An AND( ) function is most frequently used to test whether a number or date is within a range.

For Related Information

- "Entering Formulas," p. 127
- "Entering Worksheet Functions," p. 178
- "Logical Functions," p. 207

An OR( ) function is another type of logical test. An OR( ) function produces a TRUE response when any one of its arguments is TRUE. OR( ) functions are usually used to match one value against multiple values. For example,

=IF(OR(B12=36,B12="Susan"),"OK","")

If the value in B12 is either 36 or Susan, then the formula results in the text OK. If the value in 36 is neither of these, then the result is nothing ("").

Checking Data Entry

Whether you enter data in a database form or make entries directly into the cells of a worksheet, you can prevent accidental errors by using formulas that automatically cross-check data as you enter it. Figure 23.2 shows an example of a data-entry form that uses formulas to cross-check entered data. The formula bar shows the formula used to check the data in cell D4. This formula produces no result, "", if the date entered in D4 is after 1/1/1994. However, if the date entered is prior to 1/1/1994, then the message appears in the formula's cell.

Note

If you are creating data entry worksheets and need to restrict the user to entering yes or no, multiple choices, or selections from a list, read Chapter 24, "Creating Worksheet Forms." Excel 5 worksheets can contain items seen in dialog boxes, such as scrolling lists, pull-down lists, check boxes, and groups of option buttons. Two new data entry devices also are available—a spinner to quickly *spin* through a range of numbers and scroll bars to let you drag across a wide range of numbers. The result from these devices appears in a worksheet cell where you can use it just as though it was typed.

Figure 23.3 shows the same form with incorrect data entered. Notice the warnings that appear to the side of the data-entry cells. The formulas used in those cells are given in the following table:

Cell	Cross-Check	Formula
G4	Date after 1/1/94	=IF(D4>DATEVALUE("1/1/1994") ,"","Enter date after 1/1/94")
G6	Item number in list	=IF(ISNA(MATCH D6,13:I11,0)), ("Invalid Number",")

Cell	Cross-Check	Formula
G8	Division name in list	=IF(ISNA(MATCH(D8, J3:J8,0)),"West, East, South, North","")
G10	Range of quantities	=IF(AND(D10>4,D10<21)," ","5 to 20 units")

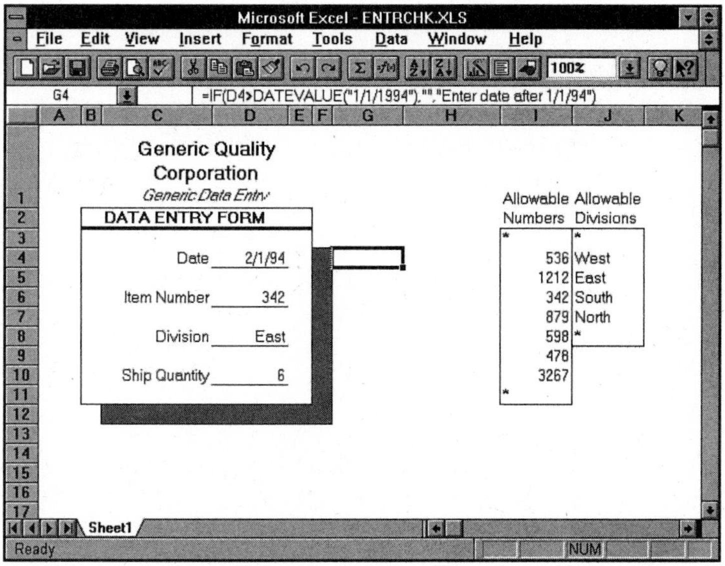

Fig. 23.2
In this data-entry form, the data in columns I and J serve as tables of valid inputs for the Item Number and Division entries in cells D6 and D8.

In each of these formulas, an IF( ) function combined with a conditional test decides whether the entry in column D is correct or not. The formula in cell G4 checks whether the date serial number from D4 is greater than the date in the IF( ) function. If the serial number is greater, the blank text " " is displayed. If the value in D4 is not greater, the function displays the prompting text.

Note

If the user needs to remember and type many different possible entries, an excellent data entry method is the use of a pull-down list or scrolling list placed on the worksheet. This Excel 5 feature is described in Chapter 24, "Building Forms with Controls."

In cell G6, the MATCH( ) function looks through the values in I3:I11 to find an exact match with the contents of D6. The 0 argument tells MATCH( ) to look for an exact match. When an exact match is not found, the function returns the error value `#N/A!`. The ISNA( ) function detects `#N/A!` values when a match is not found; it displays the text warning `Invalid Number`. When a match is found, `""` (nothing) is displayed on-screen.

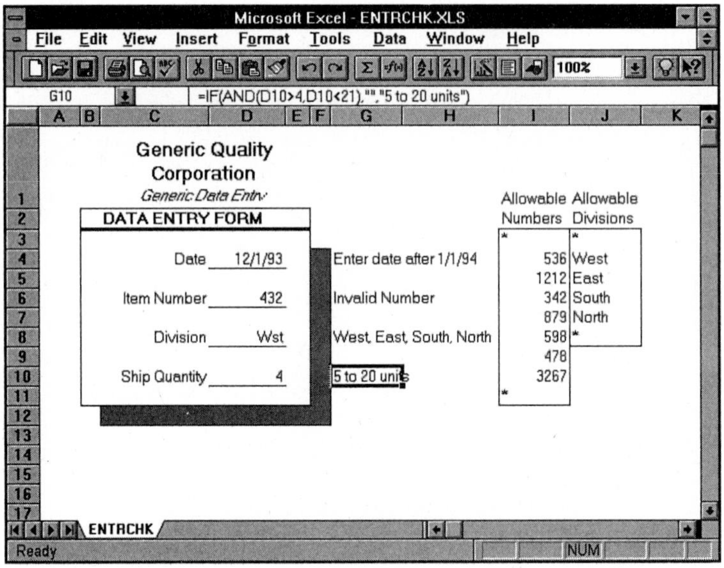

Fig. 23.3
In this data-entry form, formulas in column G display warnings when the user makes invalid entries.

Note that when you use MATCH( ), the items in the list do not need to be sorted if you use a 0 *match-type* argument as with the LOOKUP( ) functions. MATCH( ) also returns an error if an exact match is not found; whereas, a LOOKUP( ) function may return a near but incorrect result.

Cell G8 uses the same MATCH() method to check the division name against acceptable spellings. If you use large lists of possible entries, you may want to use the pull-down or scrolling lists that can be placed on a worksheet. Selecting from a list reduces the chance of typing an error or of forgetting an entry item. These pull-down or scrolling lists are described in chapter 24, "Building Forms with Controls."

For Related Information

- "Logical Functions," p. 207
- "Adding Controls to a Worksheet," p. 724

The value of Ship Quantity must be 5 to 20 units. Therefore, the formula in G10 uses an AND( ) statement to check that the number in D10 is greater than 4 *and* less than 21. When both checks are true, nothing is displayed. If the number is out of the range, the function displays the message `5 to 20 units`.

Using Formulas To Look Up Data in Tables

You can build a table in Excel and look up the contents of various cells within the table. Lookup tables provide an efficient way of producing numbers or text that you cannot calculate with a formula. For example, you may not be able to calculate a tax table or commission table. In these cases, looking up values from a table is much easier. Tables also enable you to cross-check typed data against a list of allowable values.

Excel has two techniques for looking up information from tables. The first method uses LOOKUP( ) functions. Although easy to use, these functions have the disadvantage of giving you an answer whether or not the function finds an exact match. The list in the table also needs to be in sorted order—another disadvantage. This method is good, however, in situations such as creating volume discount tables.

The second method uses a combination of the INDEX( ) and MATCH( ) functions to find an exact match in a table, regardless of whether the list in the table is sorted. If Excel cannot find an exact match, the function returns an error so that you know an exact match wasnt found. This method is good for exact matches, such as looking up the quantity on hand for a specific product. In this case, you need to find an exact part number, not the next closest item.

Using LOOKUP Functions on Tables

Excel has two functions that are useful in looking up values in tables. The VLOOKUP( ) function looks down the vertical column on the left side of the table until the appropriate comparison value is found. The HLOOKUP( ) function looks across the horizontal row at the top of the table until the appropriate comparison value is found.

The VLOOKUP( ) and HLOOKUP( ) functions use the following forms:

> **VLOOKUP(*lookup_value,table_array,col_index_num,range_lookup*)**
> **HLOOKUP(*lookup_value,table_array,row_index_num,range_lookup*)**

The VLOOKUP( ) function tries to match the value in the left column of the table; the HLOOKUP( ) function tries to match the value in the top row. These values are the *lookup_values*. The *table_array* describes the range that contains the table and lookup values. The *col_index* for the VLOOKUP( ) function or the *row_index_num* for HLOOKUP( ) tells the function which column or row, respectively, contains the result. The first column or row in the table always is numbered 1. The fourth argument, *range_lookup,* is optional and is explained in the next section.

The list you use for comparison in the table must be in ascending order. For the lookup function to work correctly, the cells in C11:C15, in figure 23.4, must be sorted in ascending order. The function searches down the first column of a VLOOKUP() table or across the first row of an HLOOKUP() table until it meets a value larger than the *lookup_value.* If the *lookup_values* are not in ascending order, the function returns incorrect results.

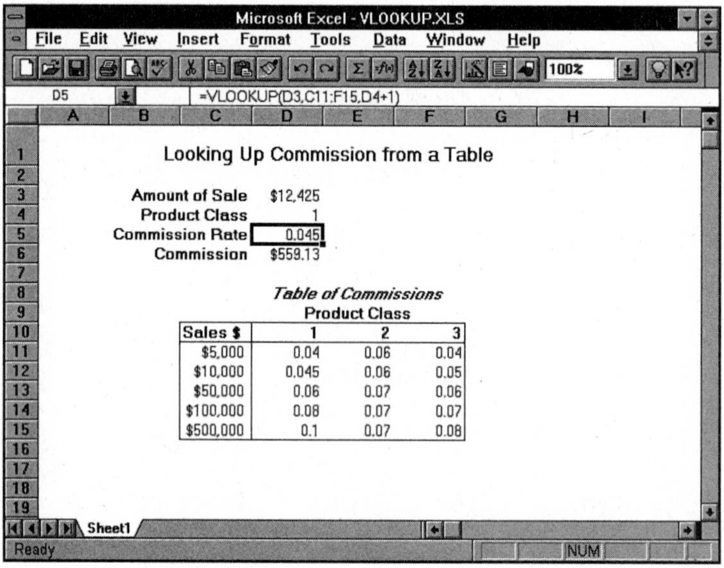

Fig. 23.4
The VLOOKUP() function finds information in a vertical table.

Figure 23.4 shows an example of a VLOOKUP() table that locates sales commissions. The VLOOKUP() and HLOOKUP() commands are helpful for looking up data in commission or tax tables because these tables contain data that can be difficult to calculate exactly. The sales on which a commission is based, for example, may fall between two numbers in the list. The formula that finds this sales commission is in cell D5. The VLOOKUP() function, as shown in the formula bar of the example, is used in the following formula:

=VLOOKUP(D3,C11:F15,D4+1)

The VLOOKUP() function looks down the left column of the table displayed in the range C11:F15 until a Sales $ amount larger than D3 ($12,425) is found. VLOOKUP() then backs up to the previous row and looks across the table to the column specified by D4+1. The formula D4+1 results in 2, the second column of the table. (Sales $ is column 1. The value 1 is added to D4 so that the lookup starts in the Product Class portion of the table.) The VLOOKUP( ) function returns the value .045 from the table. The commission is calculated by multiplying .045 by the amount of sale, which is $12,425.

The VLOOKUP( ) function doesn't use the headings in row 10. These headings are shown for the users benefit.

Finding Exact Matches

You can also use the VLOOKUP( ) and HLOOKUP( ) functions to look up data from a table and use an exact match to find the information. The data you are looking up can be text or numbers. If Excel doesn't find an exact match in the list, an error value warns you that the table contained no matches.

EXCEL 5

Using exact matches against a list is one way to prevent data-entry errors. Imagine a case in which an operator must enter an item number and an item description that belongs to this item number. To reduce data entry errors, you may want to have the operator enter the description using a pull-down list as described in chapter 24, "Building Forms with Controls." An Excel LOOKUP( ) function or INDEX(MATCH( )) function combination can then use the description to lookup the item number from a list. This technique not only reduces typing but cross-checks the item number by displaying either an accurate description or an error message if the number is incorrect.

The optional fourth argument (*range_lookup* in the Function Wizard) controls whether a VLOOKUP( ) or HLOOKUP( ) function looks for an exact match or the next largest value that matches. To find values that are an approximate match when an exact match is not available, use TRUE or omit the range_lookup argument. To specify an exact match, use FALSE as the fourth argument, as shown below:

```
=VLOOKUP(D3,C11:F15,D4+1,FALSE)
```

If you entered the preceding formula in cell D5, it would return the `#N/A` error value because an exact match for the $12,425 in cell D3 cannot be found in the Sales $ column.

Using MATCH and INDEX Functions

If your source list is not sorted, the lookup functions cannot work correctly. However, in this case you can use a combination of the MATCH and INDEX functions to look up values. In figure 23.5, Excel enters the item description if the item number is entered. If the item number is nonexistent, the worksheet displays `#N/A` in the Description cell (C8).

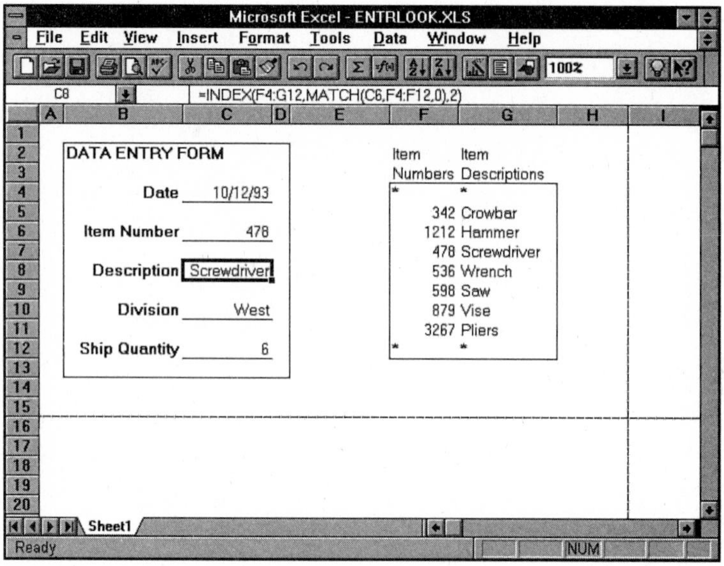

Fig. 23.5
Use a combination of INDEX and MATCH to find an exact match in an unsorted table.

The following formula found in cell C8 looks up and enters the description:

=INDEX(F4:G12,MATCH(C6,F4:F12,0),2)

The two functions used in this formula follow this syntax:

=INDEX(*array,row_num,column_num*)

=MATCH(*lookup_value,lookup_array,match_type*)

In the INDEX() function, *array* is the entire range that contains data. (It can also be an array constant.) If you enter the INDEX( ) function with the Function Wizard in working through these examples, select the set of arguments that match the INDEX( ) arguments shown above. The *row_num* and *column_num* arguments designate the row and column that specify a value in the *array*. For example, for the range F4:G12, a *row_num* of 5 and a *column_num* of 2 causes INDEX( ) to return Wrench.

In the MATCH( ) function, the *lookup_value* is the value for which you are searching. In the example, this value is the item number found in C6. The *lookup_array* is an array in a row or column that contains the list of values that you are searching. In the example, this array is the column of item numbers F4:F12. The *match_type* specifies the kind of match required. In the example, 0 specifies an exact match.

In the example, therefore, the MATCH( ) function looks through the range F4:F12 until an exact match for the contents of cell C6 is found. After an exact match is found, the MATCH( ) function returns the position of the match—row 4 of the specified range. Notice that the MATCH( ) function finds the first match in the range. For an exact match, the contents of the range F4:F12 do not need to be in ascending order.

You also can omit the *match_type* or specify *1* or *–1*. If the *match_type* is omitted or is 1, then MATCH( ) finds the largest value in the *lookup_array* equal to or less than the *lookup_value*. If *match_type* is omitted or is 1, the *lookup-array* must be in ascending order. If the *match_type* is –1, MATCH( ) finds the smallest value greater than or equal to the *lookup_value*. If the *match_type* is –1, the *lookup_array* must be in descending order.

In the formula shown in figure 23.5, the INDEX( ) function looks in the range F4:G12. The function returns the contents of the cell located at the intersection of column 2 and row 4, as specified by the MATCH( ) function. The result is `Screwdriver`.

For Related Information

- "Entering Worksheet Functions," p. 178
- "Lookup and Reference Functions," p. 208

The item numbers and descriptions in the table are outlined to identify the table. The asterisks (*) at the top and bottom of the table mark the corners of the ranges. The function continues to work correctly as long as you insert all new data item codes and descriptions between the asterisks.

Calculating Tables of Answers

Because of the *what if* game made possible by electronic worksheets, worksheets are extremely useful in business. Worksheets provide immediate feedback to questions, such as: "What if we reduce costs by .5 percent?," "What if we sell 11 percent more?," and "What if we don't get that loan?"

> **Note**
>
> If you find data tables useful, examine the Scenario Manager, described in Chapter 28, "Testing Multiple Solutions with Scenarios," along with other more advanced methods of analysis. If you need to test a set of data inputs and find the myriad of results, then look to the Scenario Manager.

When you test how small changes in input affect the result of a worksheet, you are conducting a *sensitivity analysis*. You can use Excels **D**ata **T**able command to conduct sensitivity analyses across a wide range of inputs.

Excel can create a table that shows the inputs you want to test and displays the results so that you don't need to enter all the possible inputs at the keyboard. Using a combination of a data table and the *Dfunctions*, you can do quick but extensive database analysis of finance, marketing, or research information.

You can have more than one data table in a worksheet so that you can analyze different variables or database statistics at one time.

You can use the **D**ata **T**able command in the following two ways:

- Change one input to see the resulting effect on one or more formulas.
- Change two inputs to see the resulting effect on only one formula.

One Changing Variable and Many Formulas

Among the best (and most frequently used) examples of sensitivity analysis is a data table that calculates the loan payments for different interest rates. The single-input data table described in this section creates a chart of monthly payments for a series of loan interest rates.

Before you create a data table, you need to build a worksheet that solves the problem you want to test. The worksheet in figure 23.6 calculates a house or car mortgage payment. The following formula in cell D8 handles that task:

```
=PMT(D5/12,D6*12,D4)
```

To build a data table, take the following steps:

1. Build the worksheet.
2. Enter the different values you want tested. You can enter the values in any sequence.

   Cells C11:C17 in figure 23.7 show the interest rates to be used as inputs in the sensitivity analysis.
3. In the top row of the table, row 10, above where the results appear, enter the address of each formula for which you want answers. In this cell, you also can enter the formula directly rather than reference a formula located elsewhere.

In figure 23.7, cell D10 contains `=D8`. Therefore, the results for the payment formula in D8 are calculated for each interest rate in the table. To see the results of other formulas in the table, enter these formulas in other cells across the top of the table. For example, you can enter more formulas in E10, F10, and so on.

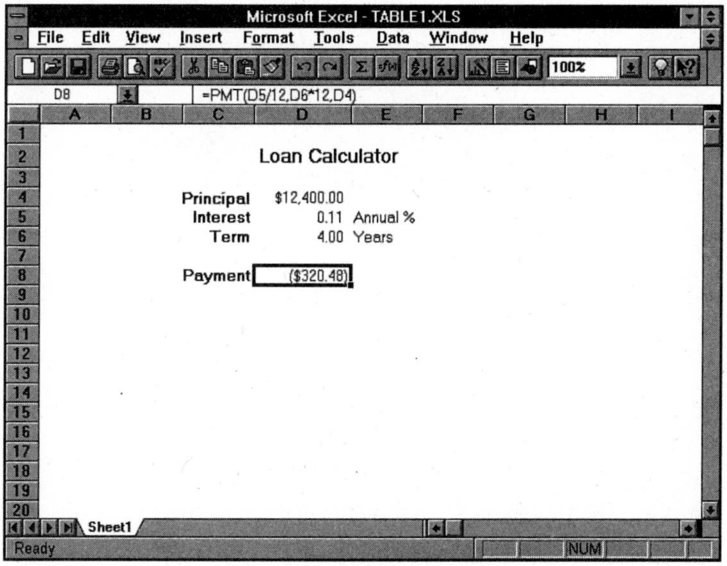

Fig. 23.6
Build a worksheet with a result you want to analyze.

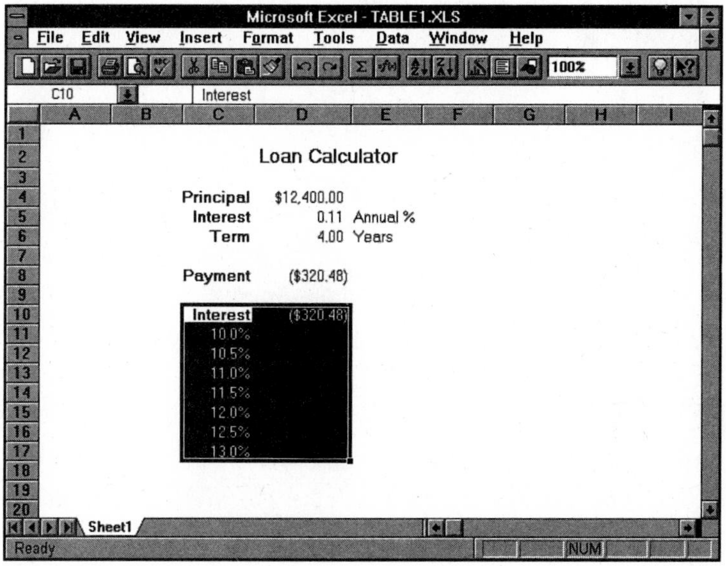

Fig. 23.7
The first step in creating this table of mortgage payments is to enter the range of interest rates to be evaluated.

4. Select the cells that enclose the table. Include the input values in the left column and the row of formulas at the top, as shown in figure 23.7. In figure 23.7 you should select C10:D17. The results fill into the blank cells in D11:D17.

5. Choose the **D**ata **T**able command to display the Table dialog box (see fig. 23.8).

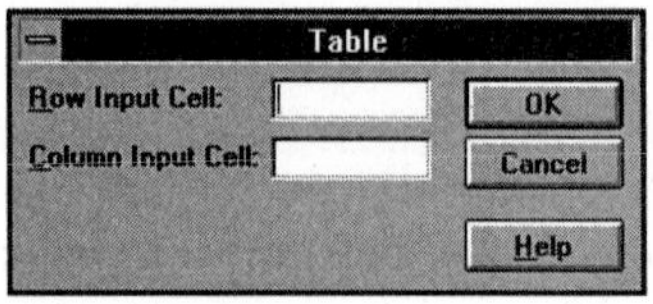

Fig. 23.8
Enter row or column input cells in the Table dialog box.

6. Enter **R**ow Input Cell or **C**olumn Input Cell. Click or point to the cell in which you want to type the variable numbers listed in the table.

   In this example the **C**olumn Input Cell is $D$5. You should enter $D$5 in the **C**olumn Input Cell text box. The **C**olumn Input Cell is used rather than the **R**ow Input Cell because in this table the values that are being tested in the table are the interest rates that go down the leftmost column. If you wanted to manually calculate payment amounts, you would type these interest rates into cell D5. By entering $D$5 into the **C**olumn Input Cell, you are telling Excel to test each interest rate in the left column of the table by entering that rate into cell D5. The resulting payment that is calculated for each interest rate is then placed in the adjacent cell in column D.

7. Choose OK.

The data table fills with the payment amounts that correspond to each interest rate in the table (see fig. 23.9).

Tip
Use the **E**dit F**i**ll **S**eries command or drag the fill handle across a series to fill incremental numbers for input values.

You can enter the **R**ow Input Cell or **C**olumn Input Cell by first clicking in the text box you want and then clicking on the appropriate cell in the worksheet. If the Table dialog box covers the cells that you want to select as the row or column inputs, move the dialog box.

Two Changing Variables and One Formula

Figure 23.10 shows how to create a data table that changes two input values, interest and principal (the loans starting amount). The worksheet calculates the result of a formula for all combinations of those values. The top row of the table, row 10, contains different principal amounts for cell D3, the **R**ow Input Cell. The left column of the table still contains the sequence of interest rates to use in cell D4. (If you are duplicating this example, notice that cell references in the example have changed by one row from the previous example.)

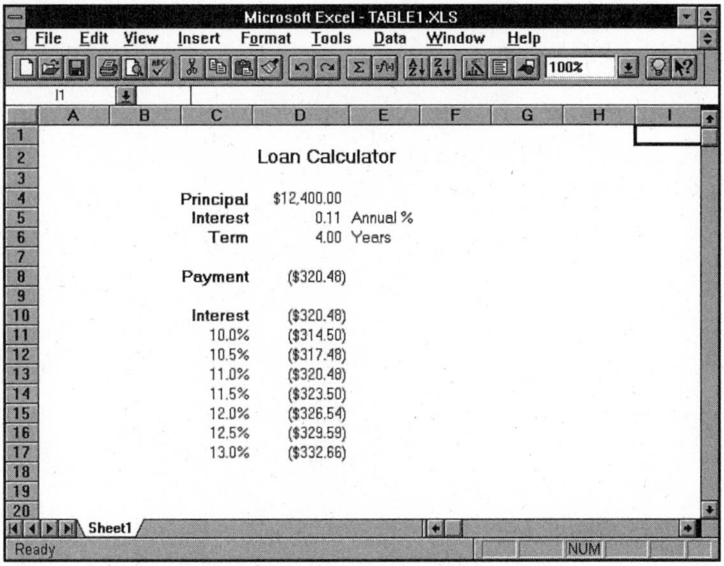

Fig. 23.9
The completed table, with results in column D for each value in column C.

Notice that when you use two different input values, you can test the results from only one formula. The formula or a reference to the formula must be in the top-left corner of the table. In figure 23.10, cell C10 contains the reference `=D7` to the payment formula to be tested.

The Table dialog box in figure 23.10 shows how the **R**ow Input Cell is $D$3 because the values from the top row of the table are substituted into cell D3. The **C**olumn Input Cell is $D$4 because the values from the left column of the table are substituted into cell D4.

Figure 23.11 shows the result of a two-input data table. Each dollar value is the amount you pay on a loan with this principal amount and annual interest rate. Because each monthly payment represents a cash outflow, the results appear in parentheses to show that the amounts are negative.

Editing Data Tables

After the data table is complete, you can change values in the worksheet on which the data table depends. Using the new values, the table recalculates.

In the example in figure 23.11, typing a new Term in D5 causes new Payment amounts to appear.

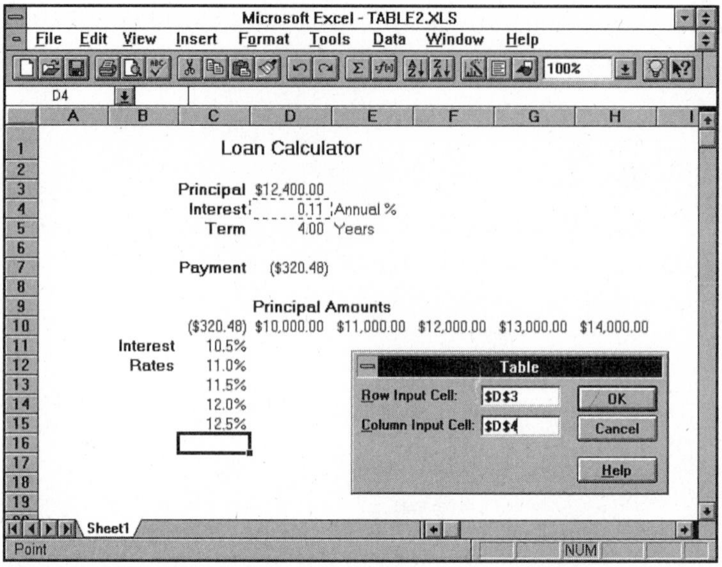

Fig. 23.10 Data tables also can change two input values used by one formula.

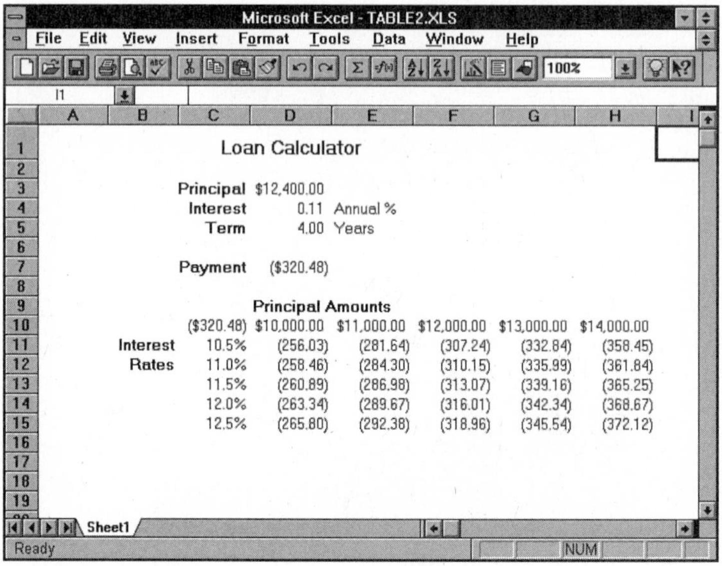

Fig. 23.11 The completed data table with the results of combinations from two input values, interest and principal.

You also can change the numbers or text in the rows and columns of input values and see the resulting change in the data table. In the example in figure 23.11, you can type new numbers or use the **E**dit F**i**ll **S**eries command to replace the numbers in C11:C15 or in D10:H10. If automatic recalculation is selected, the data table updates by default.

You cannot edit a single formula within the data table. All the formulas in this area are array formulas of the following form:

{=TABLE(*row_input,column_input*)}

To rebuild or just expand the data table, select all the cells that contain the {=TABLE( )} array formula and clear these cells by choosing **E**dit Cle**a**r **A**ll or pressing Del. Change the data table, select the table area, and choose **D**ata **T**able.

Calculating Data Tables

Large data tables or many data tables may slow down calculation. If you want the worksheet—but not the data tables—to recalculate, choose the **T**ools **O**ptions command, select the Calculation tab and select Automatic except **T**ables. Recalculate the tables by pressing F9 to calculate all worksheets or press Shift+F9 to calculate the active worksheet. If you are performing a large database analysis, you may not want the worksheet and the related tables to recalculate before saving, which is the normal process. To save without recalculating, choose the **T**ools **O**ptions command, select the Calculation tab then select **M**anual, and select Recalc**u**late Before Save.

For Related Information
- "Entering a Series of Numbers or Dates," p. 109

Analyzing Lists with Database Functions

If you have ever analyzed a database by hand, you know it can be a great deal of work. For example, if you have a small job-cost database, you may need to manually total amounts by job code. This can take hours. The techniques in this section reduce those hours to less than a minute. Excel can search your database for you and calculate totals, count items, and even perform statistical analysis on data in your database. For example, you can use Excel to count the number of client contacts by sales representative, total the amount for specific account codes by month, or see how repairs are distributed by type.

Note

Consider the advantages of pivot tables before using the data tables, especially if you expect to spend a significant amount of time analyzing a list. You may find that a pivot table gives you more flexibility and generates a more complex report with less effort than the data table method. Pivot tables are described in Chapters 36 and 37.

Using Basic Database Functions

Database functions can perform such operations as counting, averaging, or totaling the values in a field for only those records that meet your criteria. Three frequently used database functions are DSUM( ), DCOUNT( ), and DCOUNTA( ), which are similar to SUM( ), COUNT( ), and COUNTA( ). DSUM( ) totals items in a field; DCOUNT( ) counts only numeric values in a field; and DCOUNTA( ) counts all nonblank cells in a field.

Excel has many other database-analysis functions: DMIN( ), DMAX( ), DAVERAGE( ), DSTD( ), DSTDP( ), DVAR( ), DVARP( ), DGET( ), and DPRODUCT( ). Use the same procedure described in the following section for all these functions.

When you use database functions, you need to specify three arguments: the range where the source list or database is located, the column on which the function acts in the source list, and the range where the criteria is located. (As used in this section, the term *database* will refer to the source list that contains the data you want to analyze.) The format for database functions is as follows:

Dfunction(database,field,criteria)

The *field* argument in the function can be the column number in the database—the first column in the database is 1—or the field name at the top of the database. If you use a field name, such as CODE, be certain that you enclose it in quotation marks ("). If it is not in quotation marks, Excel expects it to be a name that refers to a cell with the field name.

In figure 23.12, the DSUM( ) formula in cell F18 totals the Amount column for all records having an Exp Code of 12. Notice the following formula in F18:

```
=DSUM(B5:F15,"Amount",B18:B19)
```

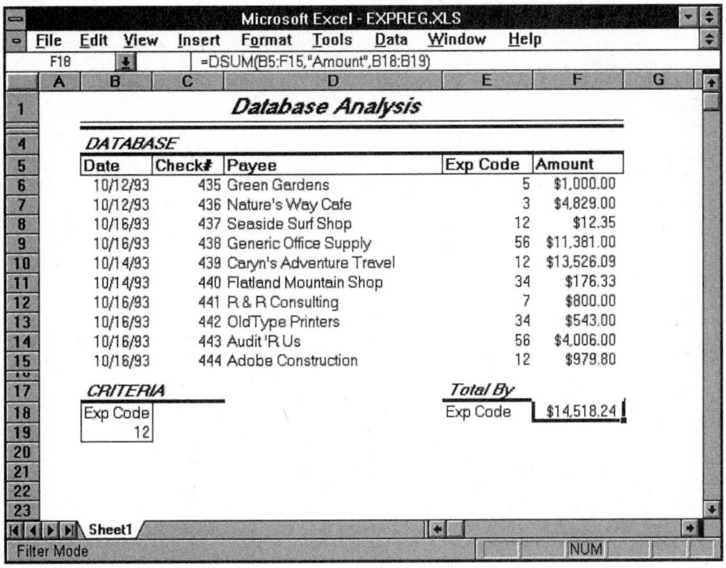

Microsoft Excel - EXPREG.XLS
File Edit View Insert Format Tools Data Window Help
F18
=DSUM(B5:F15,"Amount",B18:B19)
Database Analysis
DATABASE
Date Check# Payee Exp Code Amount
10/12/93 435 Green Gardens 5 $1,000.00
10/12/93 436 Nature's Way Cafe 3 $4,829.00
10/16/93 437 Seaside Surf Shop 12 $12.35
10/16/93 438 Generic Office Supply 56 $11,381.00
10/14/93 439 Caryn's Adventure Travel 12 $13,526.09
10/14/93 440 Flatland Mountain Shop 34 $176.33
10/16/93 441 R & R Consulting 7 $800.00
10/16/93 442 OldType Printers 34 $543.00
10/16/93 443 Audit 'R Us 56 $4,006.00
10/16/93 444 Adobe Construction 12 $979.80
CRITERIA
Exp Code
12
Total By
Exp Code
$14,518.24
Sheet1
Filter Mode
NUM

Fig. 23.12
A DSUM() formula in cell F18 totals the Amount column for all records having an Exp Code of 12.

The range B5:F15 is the database, which includes the field names. The range B18:B19 is the criteria to be used by this function only. The column being summed is "Amount". This argument also could be specified as 5, or the fifth column. If you used the Formula Define Name command to name the range B5:F15 as ChkDatabase and the range B18:B19 as ChkCriterial, you could enter the formula as the following:

=DSUM(ChkDatabase,"*Amount* ",ChkCriteria)

In figure 23.13, the criteria range has been reset to B18:C19, and the field name Date has been added to the criteria range. Now, only those records with an Exp Code of 12 and a Date of 10/16/93 are totaled.

Summarizing Specific Data in a List

Excel 5 includes two new database functions, SUMIF( ) and COUNTIF( ), that sum and count data that meets specified criteria. The SUMIF( ) and COUNTIF( ) functions produce a result that could be derived using the DSUM( ) or DCOUNT( ) functions, however, the SUMIF( ) and COUNTIF( ) functions do not require a criteria range. If you need many different SUMIF( ) or COUNTIF( ) calculations, they can be simpler to work with and require less room than DSUM( ) or DCOUNT( ).

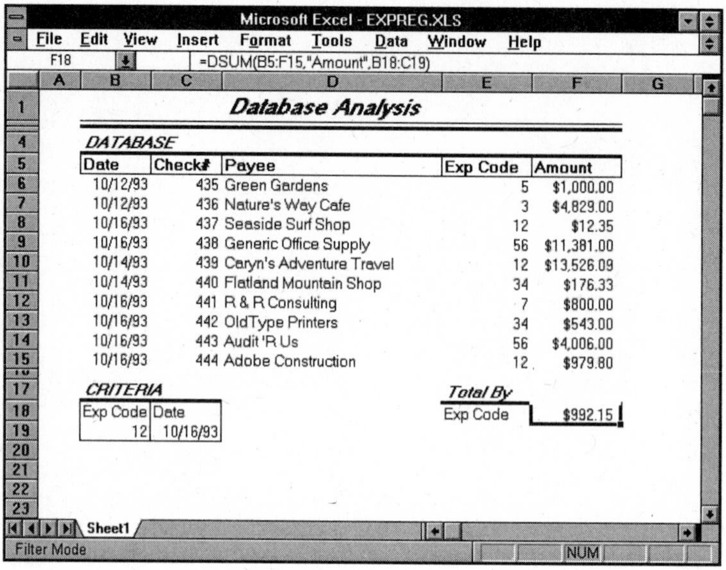

Fig. 23.13
The criteria range is now extended to total the Amount column for records that have an Exp Code of 12 and a date of 10/16/93.

To produce the sum of values in a given field for selected records, use the SUMIF( ) function, which takes the following form:

=SUMIF(range,criteria,sum_range)

where *range* contains the cells to be compared to the criteria; *criteria* is a constant, cell reference, or expression, and *sum_range* is the range (or field) containing the values you want to summarize.

Figure 23.14 illustrates how SUMIF( ) works. The formula in cell C17 is:

=SUMIF(B5:B10,B15,E5:E10)

In this formula, the range B5:B10 contains the comparison values. The criteria argument (B15) tells Excel to look in cell B15 for the selection criteria (part number 65-432-BD). The range argument (E5:E10) instructs Excel to sum the values in the Quantity field. The result, 4, is the total of the Quantity amounts in row 8—the only row containing a record for Part No. 65-432-BD.

The COUNTIF( ) function works in similar fashion, but takes only the *range* and *criteria* arguments.

Combining Database Functions with Data Tables

Although database functions are quite useful, they can require a great deal of time if you have many different criteria to type into the criteria range. In the check register shown in figure 23.15, if you want a total for each expense code, for example, you must type six different Exp Codes into the criteria range and then write down a total. Imagine that you were analyzing 50 or 150 codes. Wouldn't it be easier and faster to let Excel build a table for you that shows all the codes and all the database analysis results? By combining the database functions with **D**ata **T**able, you can have Excel build such a table.

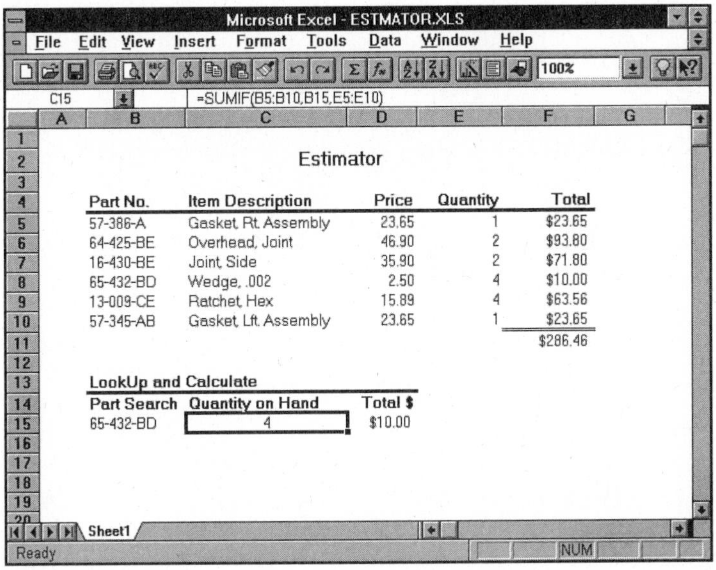

Fig. 23.14
The SUMIF( ) function sums values for records meeting specified criteria.

Data **T**able along with the DSUM( ) function in cell F18 takes the expense codes in E19:E24 and produces the total amounts for each expense code, as shown in F19:F24. **D**ata **T**able takes each code from column E and inserts it into the criteria in cell B19. The DSUM( ) result from that criteria is then placed under the DSUM( ) formula in the cell next to the appropriate expense code.

In figure 23.15, the DSUM( ) function combined with the Data Table command produces a table of expense codes and their totals. The table is in E18:F24, and the DSUM( ) formula is in cell F18. The left column lists each expense code, and the right column lists the resulting total amount for the corresponding expense code.

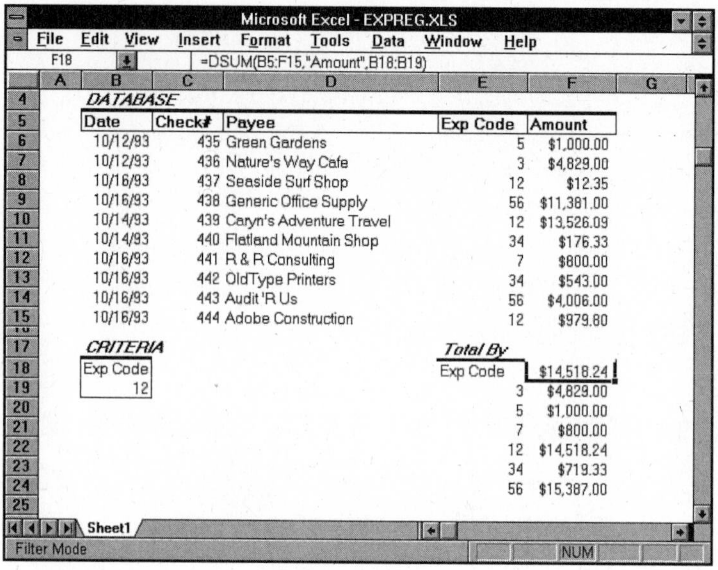

Fig. 23.15
The data table in the range E18:F24 lists expense codes and their totals.

The DSUM( ) formula in cell F18 is the following:

=DSUM(B5:F15,"Amount",B18:B19)

This is the same formula used in figure 23.12. The criteria range, B18:B19, again holds the criteria for the Exp Code field. **D**ata **T**able takes each value from the left side of the data table and places the values one at a time into the criteria cell B19. The command then records the DSUM( ) total for that criteria and puts it in the adjacent cell on the right side of the data table.

If figure 23.15 contained 537 different expense codes, the process of entering them in column E down the left side of the data table would be time-consuming. Instead, use **A**dvanced Filter to create a list of all the expense codes used in the database.

To create this list of codes, take these steps:

1. Choose **D**ata **F**ilter **A**dvanced Filter. The Advanced Filter dialog box appears (see fig. 23.16).
2. Select **C**opy to.
3. In the **L**ist Range text box, enter or select the single-column range in the list containing all the expense codes. Don't include the header label.

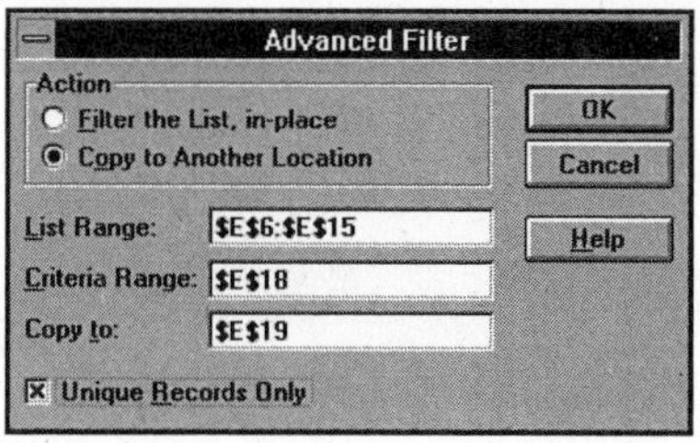

Fig. 23.16 The Advanced Filter dialog box.

4. In the **C**riteria Range text box, enter or select the cell that contains the header label.

5. Select Unique **R**ecords Only to remove duplicate records.

6. In the Copy **t**o text box, enter or select cell E19.

7. Choose OK.

Figure 23.17 shows the result of using the heading Exp Code as an extract range. Because Unique **R**ecords Only was selected, only one of each of the expense codes is extracted. You can choose the Sort buttons to rearrange the expense codes.

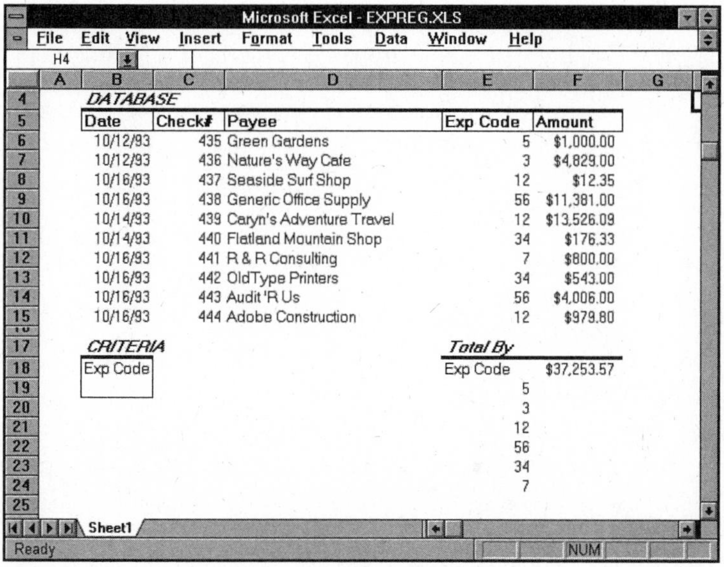

Fig. 23.17 After you use the Advanced Filter command, cells E19:E24 contain the expense codes extracted from the cells E6:E15.

You can now use the methods described in the section, "One Changing Variable and Many Formulas," to complete this check register analysis table. To complete the table, select cells E18:F24 as shown in figure 23.17. Then choose the **D**ata **T**able command. In the Table dialog box that appears, enter $B$19 in the **C**olumn Input Cell. Choose OK. The range F18:F24 fills with the total for each account code.

Note

Copying a filtered list to another location erases previously existing data in the extract range. Make sure you select a Copy **t**o range in a clear area of the worksheet. Then you can cut and paste the data to the appropriate place on your worksheet after the extraction. Large data tables or multiple data tables may require a long time to recalculate. If you want to recalculate the worksheet but not the tables, choose the **T**ools **O**ptions command, select the Calculation tab, and then select the Automatic Except **T**ables option. (Make sure that you return this to the **A**utomatic option when you recalculate the table.)

For Related Information

- "Database Functions," p. 185
- "Using the Advanced Filter," p. 916

Analyzing Trends

Excel can calculate a linear regression or best-fit line that passes through a series of data. You may be familiar with this simple form of forecasting a trend from high school biology or physics classes. In those classes, you may have plotted a series of points on a chart and then attempted to draw a straight line through the points such that the line had the least amount of difference from all the points.

In some cases, you can use the result of these calculations to analyze trends and make short-term forecasts. Two ways of calculating the data for these trends are available. You can drag across numbers by using the fill handles, or you can use worksheet functions.

If you need to extend existing data by a few periods (cells) but don't need the corresponding best-fit data for the existing cells, you can use the method of dragging fill handles to extend the data. You can also use the **E**dit F**i**ll **S**eries command to create a linear regression or best-fit line. If, however, you need both original data and the corresponding best-fit data for the same periods—for example, to show original data and a best-fit line through the data—then use the worksheet function method.

Note

Chart the data and trend to give trends more impact and make relationships more apparent. Excel has the ability to automatically create trend lines of different types directly on a chart. To learn how to create a chart that automatically shows a trend line, read "Automatically Analyzing Trends with Charts" in Chapter 15, "Building Complex Charts."

Calculating Trends with Fill Handles

Figure 23.18 shows known data for regional housing starts for the years 1990 through 1993. But the future housing starts for 1994 and 1995 are unknown. If the trend from 1990 through 1993 continues, you can use a linear regression to calculate the expected starts for 1994 and 1995.

You can project this data into the empty cells to the right, 1994 and 1995, by using a linear best-fit, select the cells as shown in figure 23.18. To fill the data in the empty cells, use the left mouse button to drag the fill handle to the right to enclose the area you want extended, then release the mouse button. Row 4 of figure 23.19 shows the results of this procedure.

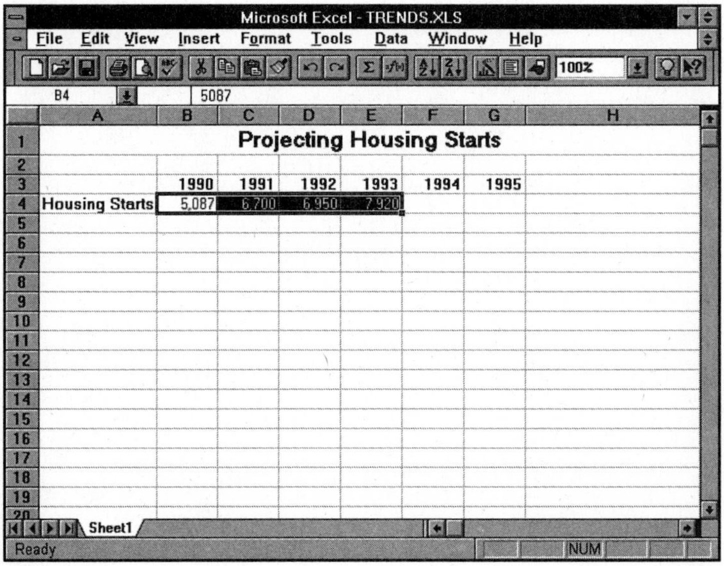

Fig. 23.18
Using linear best-fit, extend a series by dragging the fill handle.

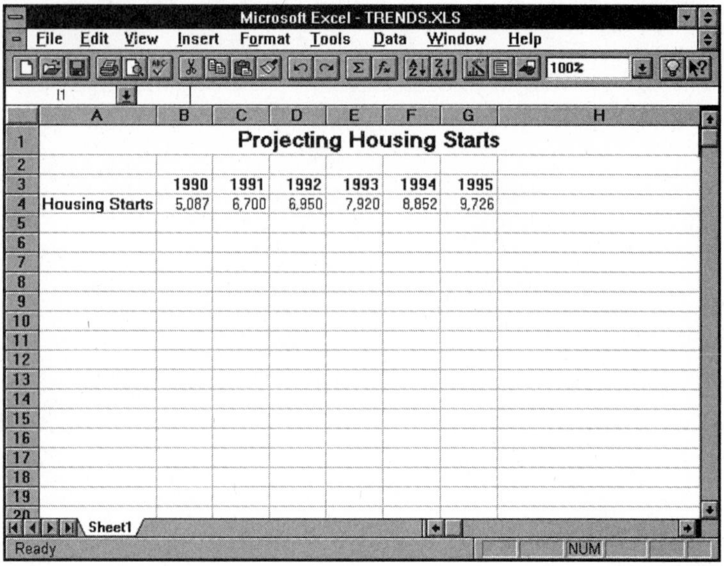

Fig. 23.19
The amounts shown for 1994 and 1995 are projections using linear best-fit.

To fill a range using a growth trend, take these steps:

1. Select the cells as shown in figure 23.18.
2. Drag the fill handle to the right with the right mouse button. Excel displays a shortcut menu with Linear Trend and Growth Trend as commands.

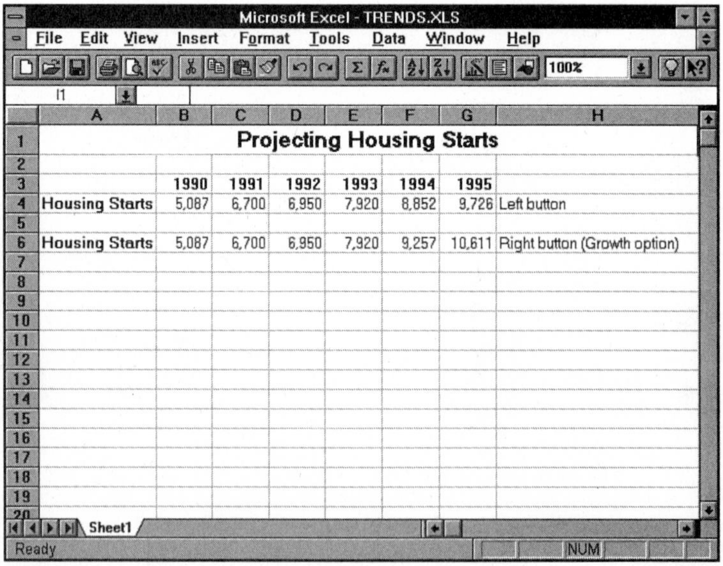

Fig. 23.20
Create the projections for 1994 and 1995 in row 6 by dragging the fill handle with the right mouse button, then choosing the Growth Trend command.

3. Select Growth Trend.

Row 6 of figure 23.20 shows the results of this procedure.

Calculating Trends with the Data Series Command

You may remember in science class recording a number of data points on a chart and then trying to draw a line through the points so that the line gave the trend of the data with the least errors. That line was a best-fit line. Points on that line are the best-fit data. Using Excel's **E**dit F**i**ll **S**eries command, you can create best-fit data to replace or extend the original data. You also can chart the best-fit data to create a best-fit line.

Edit F**i**ll **S**eries creates a linear (straight line) or exponential growth trend line. Using **E**dit F**i**ll **S**eries, you can create these two types of trend lines in two ways. Figure 23.21 illustrates the different types of trend data produced.

The original data used to produce the trends in the figure are the numbers 1, 5, and 12 shown in B4:D4. The selected range used with each command is in each of the rows from column B to column H. The different types of trend data produced use these combinations of settings in the Series dialog box:

Settings	Description of Resulting Trend
Default settings	A linear trend is produced starting with the original first data point. Calculated data replaces the original data. If charted, the trend line is forced to go through the first data point.
Auto**F**ill	A linear trend is produced. The original data remains. Selected cells beyond the original data fill with data points for the linear trend.
Trend and **L**inear	A linear trend is produced and the trend is not forced to pass through the first original data point. Original data is replaced with trend data.
Trend and **G**rowth	An exponential growth trend is produced and the trend is not forced to pass through the first original data point. Original data is replaced with trend data.

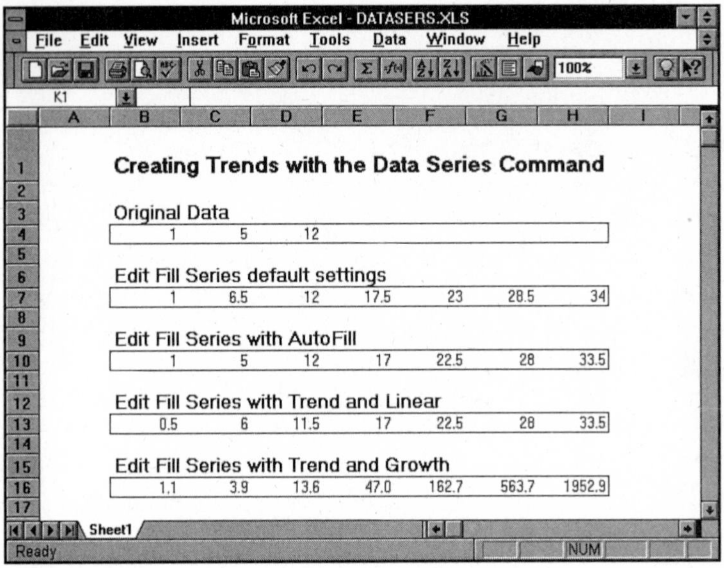

Fig. 23.21
Use the **Edit Fill S**eries command to produce any of the four types of trend data shown here.

To create a trend using **Edit Fill Series**, perform the following steps:

1. Select the original data and as many additional cells as you want the trend data to extend into. In figure 23.21, for example, the cells B4:H4 may be selected.

2. Choose the **Edit Fill Series** command.

3. Choose one of the following combinations of options:

Setting	**Result**
Default (no changes)	Linear trend through first data point. Trend replaces original data.
Auto**F**ill	Linear trend through first data point. Trend fills in blank selected cells.
Trend, Type **L**inear	Linear trend. Warning: this fills all cells. Select **T**rend check box, then **L**inear option.
Trend, Type **G**rowth	Exponential growth trend. Warning: this fills all cells. Select **T**rend check box, then **G**rowth option.

Note that, in addition to the four trend computations shown in figure 23.21, you can produce a fifth by dragging the fill handle with the right mouse button. This produces a growth trend that does not override the original data.

Calculating Trends with Worksheet Functions

Excel's trend functions work by calculating the best-fit equation for the straight line or exponential growth line that passes through the data. The LINEST( ) and LOGEST( ) functions calculate the parameters for the straight-line and exponential growth-line equations. The TREND( ) or GROWTH( ) functions calculate the values along the straight line or exponential growth line needed to draw a curve or forecast a short-range value.

Before you use the trend analysis functions, become familiar with dependent and independent variables. The value of a *dependent variable* changes when the *independent variable* changes. Frequently, the independent variable is time, but it also can be other items, such as the price of raw materials, the temperature, or a population size. The independent variables actual data is entered as the *known-x* argument in the function, and the dependent variables actual data is entered as the functions *known-y* argument.

Imagine that you own a concrete business that depends on new residential construction. You want to plan for future growth or decline so that you can best manage your firms assets and people.

After research with the help of local economic advisory boards, you assemble statistics on housing starts in the service area for the previous five years. In figure 23.18, row 4 shows the housing starts by year. After meeting with county planners, you are convinced that this area may continue to grow at the same or a slightly higher rate. You still need to estimate, however, the number of housing starts in 1994 and 1995.

In figure 23.18, the independent variables of time (*known_x*) are entered in B3:E3. The dependent variables of housing starts (*known_y*) are entered in B4:E4. If the trend from the past four years continues, you can project the estimated housing starts for the next two years with the following steps:

1. Select the range of cells that you want the straight-line projection to fill, B6:G6, as shown in figure 23.22.

2. Enter the TREND( ) function using either the keyboard or the Function Wizard.

3. Enter the arguments for the TREND( ) function. The following line shows the correct syntax:

   TREND(*known_y's, known_x's,new_x's*)

Tip

See "Entering Functions with the Function Wizard" in Chapter 6, "Using Functions," for detailed instructions on using the Function Wizard.

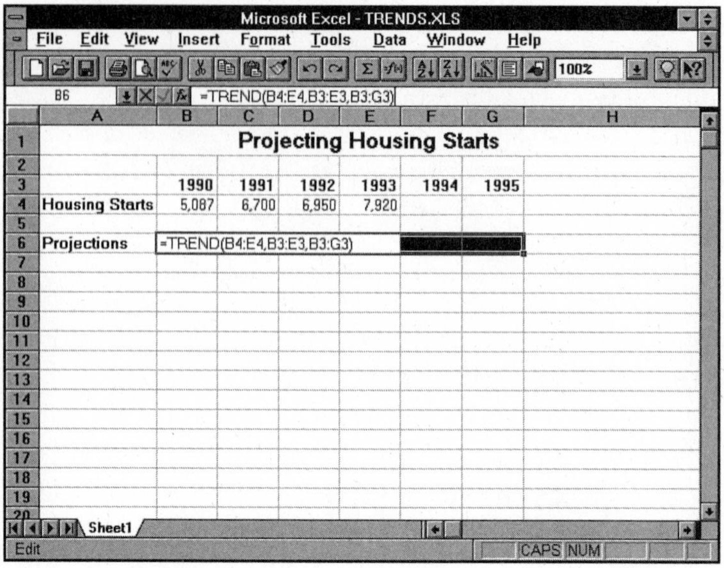

Fig. 23.22
Before entering an array formula such as TREND, select the entire range.

For this example: The *known_ys* argument is B4:F4. (Housing Starts are ys because these numbers are dependent on the Year value.)

The *known_xs* argument is B3:F3. (Year is the independent variable.)

The *new_xs* argument is B3:H3, which are the years for which you want to know the values that describe a trend line.

Notice that the selected area in figure 23.22 covers the room for the resulting calculated y values.

4. To enter the TREND( ) function as an array function in the selected range, press Shift+Ctrl+Enter.

If the present trend continues, the result shown in figure 23.23 illustrates that years 1994 and 1995 may have housing starts of about 8852 and 9726.

Notice that the new *y* values in cells B6:E6 don't exactly match the known *y* values in B3:E3 because the TREND( ) function calculated the housing starts for these years according to its trend equation (a linear regression). The real number of housing starts in each year undoubtedly will be different.

For Related Information

- "Entering Worksheet Functions," p. 178
- "Statistical Functions," p. 221
- "Using Data Analysis Tools Commands," p. 838

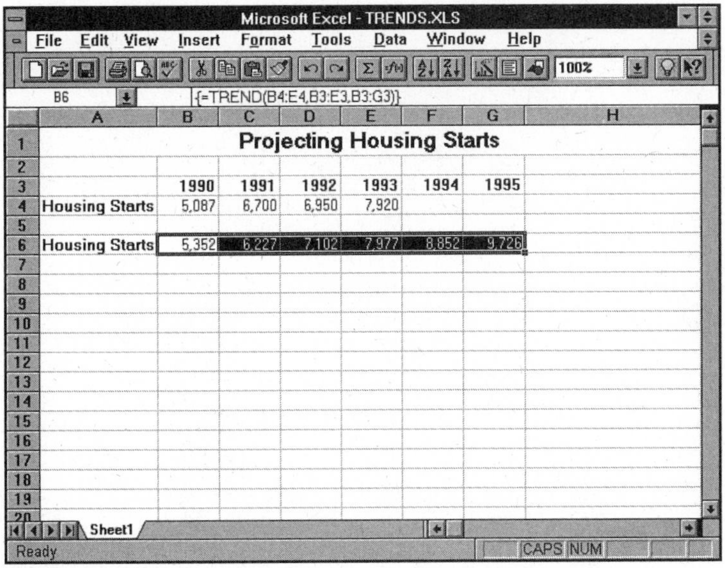

Fig. 23.23
The trend values in row 6 can help you make short-term projections. The TREND() function computes new values for the period of known values.

From Here...

For additional information on analyzing data and handling text, browse through these chapters:

- Chapter 6, "Using Functions," provides more detail on the database and statistical functions discussed in this chapter.
- Chapter 19, "Creating Automatic Subtotals," explains how to use Excel's subtotaling and reporting features to create reports.
- Chapter 27, "Solving with Goal Seeking and Solver," describes how to arrive at a desired solution: Goal Seek and the Solver.
- Chapter 28, "Testing Multiple Solutions with Scenarios," explains how to test multiple sets of data inputs and find the myriad of results with the Scenario Manager.
- Chapters 30 through 34 explain how Excel manages data in list form, and how to view and extract useful subsets of the data.
- Chapters 36, "Using Pivot Tables," and 37, "Analyzing and Reporting with Pivot Tables," show how to use Excel's pivot tables to summarize and view tabular data in a variety of ways.

Chapter 24

Building Forms with Controls

Excel is an excellent vehicle for creating forms that involve calculations. Excel's worksheets are easy to format so they appear as attractive as printed forms, yet Excel can calculate results and look up table information, which is impossible to do on a paper form.

In the past, a detriment to using a worksheet to enter data and do calculations was that complex formulas or macros often were needed to check data. Most worksheets traded the occasional data entry error against the time required to create data-checking formulas or data-entry macros or procedure. Also, making a worksheet data-entry area as appealing as a well-done dialog box was difficult.

With Excel 5, you can place on a worksheet the same type of data entry *controls* as you can place in a dialog box run by a macro or Visual Basic procedure. *Controls* are data entry objects, such as scrolling lists or check boxes. When you enter a value in a control or make a selection from a control, the entry appears in a worksheet cell, and the control makes sure that you can only make valid entries.

To use controls you don't need to know how to program, you only need to know how to make selections from a dialog box. You do need a mouse, however, to draw these controls onto a worksheet.

EXCEL 5

In this chapter, you learn how to:

- Format worksheets to resemble paper forms
- Create scrolling lists, pull-down lists, check boxes, and scroll bars
- Format pull-down lists and check boxes
- Enhance controls, so that choices from one control affect another control

What You Need To Know About Controls

Tip
You need a mouse or other pointing device to create controls on a worksheet.

Controls are data entry devices that can appear in a worksheet or in a dialog box. (The use of controls in dialog boxes is described in Chapter 45, "Programming in Visual Basic for Applications.") Figure 24.1 shows a form in a worksheet that uses controls for data entry.

Controls used in a worksheet are linked to a cell in a worksheet. When you enter data into a control or make a selection from the control, the result of the selection appears in the linked worksheet cell. The result in this cell then can be used in standard worksheet calculations, just as though the user had typed in the cell's value.

Besides being more attractive and easier to use, you can control the values a user selects from a control. If a control is a scrolling list, for example, you can control the items in the list, which reduces the amount of formula writing you must do and reduces or eliminates data entry errors.

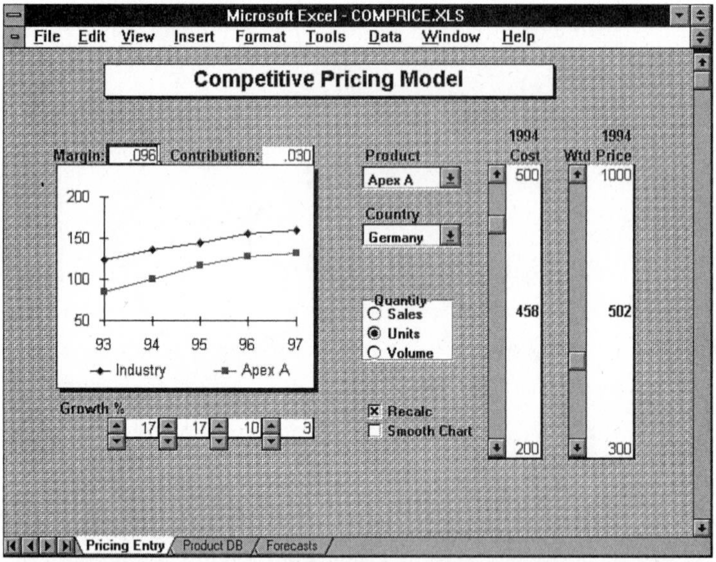

Fig. 24.1
Controls make data entry in a worksheet more attractive and less error prone.

Differences between Controls in a Worksheet and in a Dialog Box

The controls you use in a worksheet are just the same as the controls you place in a dialog box. However, more types of controls are available for use in a dialog box, some differences, advantages, and disadvantages exist between using a control on a worksheet to enter data and using a control in a dialog box. The following table compares some of these differences:

Difference	Worksheet Control	Dialog Box Control
Controls available	Labels, group box, edit command button, list box, drop-down, scroll bar, and spinner	Worksheet controls plus box, list edit box, drop-down list edit box
Ease of use	Intermediate user	Advanced user
Calculation	On any selection in control	Under Visual Basic control
Accelerator (Alt+) key	Not available	In dialog sheet, choose Format Object, then Control tab
Tab order	Not available	In dialog sheet, choose Tools Tab Order
Results data checking	Simple	Advanced
Data manipulation	In worksheet formulas	In worksheet formulas or in Visual Basic procedure
Runs macro or VBA procedure	No	Yes, when control changed or activated

Using the Forms Toolbar

You draw controls on a worksheet by clicking a button in the Forms toolbar and then dragging on the worksheet to indicate the size and location of the control. Once a control is drawn, you use a formatting command to assign properties to it such as allowed values, limits, protection properties, and so on.

To display the Forms toolbar, follow these steps:

1. Choose the **V**iew **T**oolbars command to display the Toolbars dialog box.
2. Select Forms from the **T**oolbars list.
3. Choose OK.

The buttons on the Forms toolbar are shown in Table 24.1.

Table 24.1 Buttons on the Forms Toolbar

Button	Name	Description
	Label	Text to name items or for intructions.
	Edit Box	Data entry box for text, numbers, dates, or cell references. Not available on a worksheet.
	Group	A border that groups option buttons. Only one option button in a group can be selected.
	Create Button	Creates a button to run a macro.
	Check Box	Check box produces True when selected; False when deselected.
	Option Button	Only one option button from a group can be selected. Returns the number of the selected button.
	List Box	A text list. Returns the number of the item selected.
	Drop-Down List	A drop-down list containing text. Returns the number of the item selected.
	List Edit Box	A text list with an edit box. Not available on a worksheet.
	Drop-Down Edit Box	A drop-down list with an edit box. Not available on a worksheet.
	Scroll Bar	A draggable scroll bar returns a number between the range limits of the top and bottom.
	Spinner	A counter whose returned number increases or decreases in integer amounts depending upon which arrow you click.

Button	Name	Description
	Properties	Displays a dialog box for the selected control. Use the dialog to set the control's behavior.
	Goto Macro	Use to edit the code assigned to the selected control. Used in a dialog box.
	Toggle Grid	Turns the alignment grid in a dialog sheet on or off. Turns grid lines on or off on a worksheet.
	Run Dialog	Displays the dialog box on the active dialog sheet. Used to test a dialog box you have drawn. Not available on a worksheet.

How Controls Affect Cell Content and Calculations

After you draw a control on a worksheet, you need to link the control to a cell in the worksheet. You use this link to transfer the value selected or entered in the control to a cell in the worksheet where the value can be used.

The control and the cell affect each other. If you make a selection in the control, the value in the cell changes. Conversely, if you change the content of the linked cell, the selection in the control changes. This linking is necessary to keep controls in synch with the worksheet. If someone manually changes a value in a cell, you expect a control linked to this cell to reflect the current state of the worksheet.

For Related Information

- "Creating Custom Dialog Boxes," p. 1212
- "Checking Data Entry," p. 690

Making Worksheets Appear Like Forms

With a little formatting, you can make worksheets appear more like a paper form. You probably want to start by having the form in the same workbook as the worksheets that do the calculations, which makes it easier creating and maintaining links from the controls on the form to the worksheets using the data.

To make a worksheet resemble a separate dialog box or form, but still be included within the workbook, choose the **W**indow **N**ew Window command. In the new window, select the worksheet tab to make the form worksheet active. Press Alt, hyphen (-), and choose the **R**estore command (if the command is available) to put this worksheet in a window. Now that the form is in a separate window, you need to make it look like a form.

To make the window look like a paper form, follow these steps:

1. Choose the **T**ools **O**ptions command to display the Options dialog box.

2. Select the View tab.

3. Select from the following check boxes in the Window Options group to affect the appearance of only the active window:

Check Box	Affect
A**u**tomatic Page Breaks	Deselect so automatic page breaks do not show.
Fo**r**mulas	Deselect so results show, not formulas.
Gridlines	Deselect so gridlines do not show.
Row & Column H**e**aders	Deselect so row and column headings are hidden.
Outline Symbols	Deselect unless your form is built in an outline.
Zero Values	Optional. Select to hide zeros.
Horizon**t**al Scroll Bar	Deselect to hide the scroll bar at the bottom.
Vertical Scroll Bar	Deselect to hide the scroll bar on the right edge.
Sheet Ta**b**s	Deselect to hide the worksheet tabs.

For Related Information

- "Adding Colors, Patterns, and Borders," p. 350
- "Controlling the Worksheet Display," p. 533
- "Saving Frequently Used View and Print Settings," p. 540
- "Hiding and Unhiding Windows and Sheets," p. 550
- "Laying Out and Formatting Your Worksheet," p. 627

You can color the background area of a form with a light grey to give it a more pleasing appearance. You also can use black and white lines or overlapping black and white rectangles to give pictures, charts, or text boxes the appearance of being raised or lowered.

Adding Controls to a Worksheet

EXCEL 5

You can use different controls on a worksheet or dialog sheet, but all controls are placed on the sheet in the same way. After you draw a control on the sheet, you must format the control. Formatting the control changes protection status, how the control moves when underlying cells move, and what the data entry items or limits are. In this section, you first learn how to draw a control on a sheet and then how to format each type of control.

Before you can draw a control on a worksheet or dialog sheet, you must display the Forms toolbar. To display the Forms toolbar, choose the **V**iew **T**oolbars command, select Forms from the **T**oolbars list, and then choose OK.

Drawing the Control

To draw a control on a worksheet or dialog sheet, follow these steps:

1. Click the button in the Forms toolbar that represents the control you want to draw. The pointer changes to a cross-hair. (These buttons are shown in table 24.1.)

2. Move the cross-hair to the top left corner of where you want the control to appear and drag down and right, to where you want the form's opposite corner.

3. Release the mouse button.

When you release the mouse button, the control appears on the form or dialog sheet. Black handles at the control's corners and edges show that the control is selected and can be moved, be resized, or have properties changed.

You can move a selected control by dragging an edge. Resize the control by dragging the black handle on a corner or the black handle on one edge. Delete a selected control by pressing the Delete key or by choosing the **E**dit Cle**a**r command.

Tip
Select a control and display the shortcut menu at the same time by clicking the control with the right mouse button.

You also can change the protection status of a selected control by formatting it. You can change how the control moves with cells, or you can set the defaults and limits for its data. To deselect a control, click a cell or object other than the selected control.

Changing a Control's Format

To set a control's format, follow these steps:

1. With the right mouse button, click the control that you drew on the worksheet, and then choose the Format Object command from the shortcut menu.

> **Note**
>
> The Format Object dialog box used to format controls on forms may contain a different number and type of tab depending on the control that you format.

2. To change the control, select one or more of the following tabs and select the options:

Font	Select the font, size, style, and color for fonts used on the macro button. Fonts on other controls cannot be formatted. This tab appears the same as font tabs used elsewhere in Excel.
Patterns	Select border type, size, and weight. Include a fill color or pattern. The Patterns tab is shown in figure 24.3.

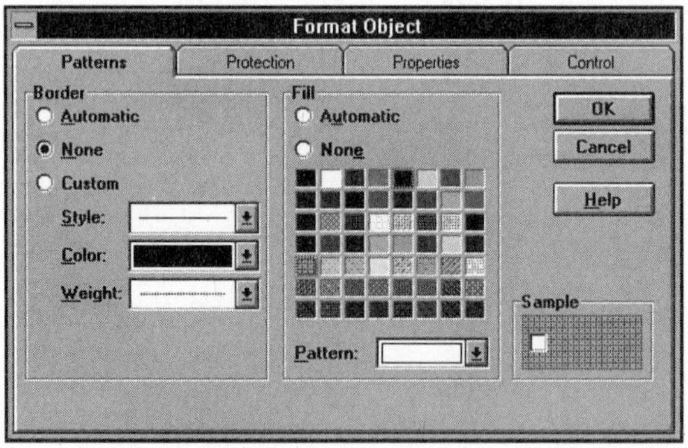

Fig. 24.3 Change the pattern and color on some controls with the Pattern tab.

Protection	Choose whether object can be moved, resized, or changed. Some controls can have text protected. Takes affect when protection is turned on, using the Tools Protection command, and then choosing Protect Sheet. A password is optional.

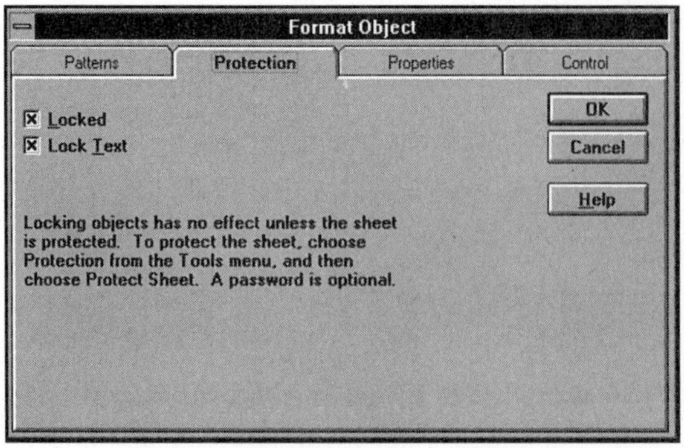

Fig. 24.4 Prevent a control from being changed by protecting it when worksheet protection is turned on.

Properties — Restrict how a control moves or resizes when the cells underneath are moved or resized. Described in detail in Chapter 17, "Adding Graphics Elements to Sheets." If you do not want a control to print, deselect the Print Object check box.

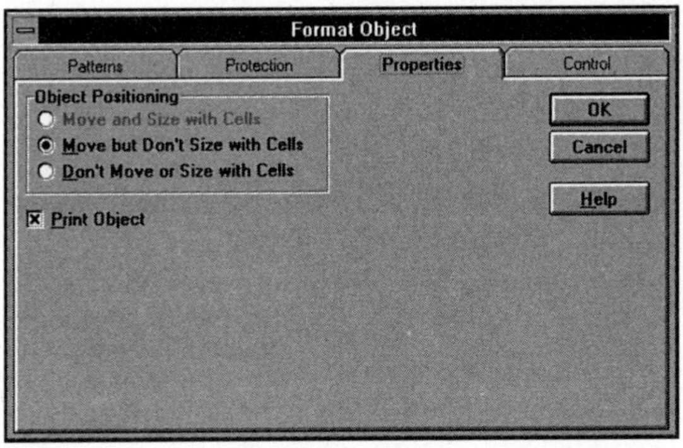

Fig. 24.5
Use these options to control how a control resizes when the cells underneath change.

Control — These settings determine the default value for a control, the control's data limits, and where the entered data will be passed. The options available depend on the control selected in step 1. The individual Control tabs for each type are shown in figures 24.6 and 24.7.

3. Choose OK.

Adding Check Boxes for TRUE/FALSE Responses

A check box gives the user only two choices, TRUE or FALSE. The check box is linked to a cell so that the result of the check box status appears as TRUE or FALSE in the linked cell. Selecting the check box makes the cell TRUE. Deselecting the check box makes the cell FALSE. You can use an IF function that examines the TRUE or FALSE status and produces two results, depending upon whether the check box is selected.

Tip
Double-click a selected control to display the Format Object dialog box.

To set the defaults and cell link on a check box that you draw, follow these steps:

1. Right click the check box you already drew on the worksheet and choose Format Object.

2. Select the Control tab shown in figure 24.6.

3. Select the default value of the check box, **U**nchecked for FALSE result, **C**hecked for TRUE result, and **M**ixed for #NA result. Choose the **3**D Shading check box to add an impression of depth to the check box.

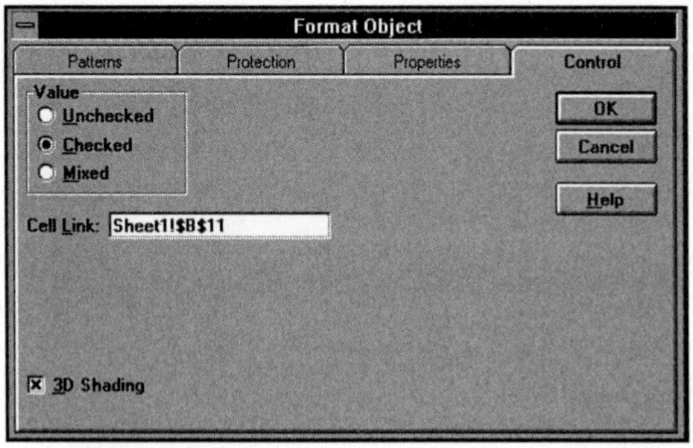

Fig. 24.6
The Control tab for check box describes the default value and the cell that is linked to the result.

4. Select the Cell **L**ink edit box, then click the cell in which you want to hold the results of the check box. You can use the **W**indow menu or tab names to display other sheets to which you want to link the control.

5. Choose OK.

Tip
For a more manageable system, type a range name in the Cell Link edit box rather than a cell reference.

When you need the user to choose between two values, use a check box combined with an IF function. Use an IF function to convert the TRUE/FALSE result in the linked cell to one of two results. The result from the IF function can be text, date, formula, or numeric. The syntax for IF is shown in the following example:

=IF(*LinkCell,TrueResult,FalseResult*)

If the linked cell is B35, for example the following formula produces LOCAL when the check box is selected (B35 is TRUE), and it produces INTERNATIONAL when the check box is deselected (B35 is FALSE). Make sure you put this formula in a different cell than cell B35 that the check box is linked to.

=IF($B$35,"LOCAL","INTERNATIONAL")

Adding Option Buttons for Multiple Choice

Options buttons are used most frequently to make one and only one choice from a group of choices. Option buttons are the round buttons that usually come in groups. Option buttons are exclusive of one another—select one option button and the others deselect, which means that you can select only one button in a group at a time.

If you just draw option buttons on a worksheet, all these buttons will belong to the same group, which means that you can select only one button at a time. You can have multiple groups of buttons, however, by enclosing each group in a group box drawn with the group tool. All option buttons in the same group use the same linked cell. Drawing a group of option buttons is slightly different from drawing other controls.

The result from a group of option buttons appears in one cell.

To create a group of option buttons, follow these steps:

1. Draw a group box by clicking the group box button and dragging from corner to corner where you want the box. While the box is selected, type a title to replace the default box title.

2. Click the option button tool and draw an option button within the group box. Type a title while the option button is selected.

3. Right mouse click the option button and choose Format Object to display the Format Object dialog box. Select the Control tab (a completed control tab is shown in figure 24.7). Then select the value for the option button: **U**nchecked, **C**hecked, or **M**ixed. Remember that only one option button in a group can be checked.

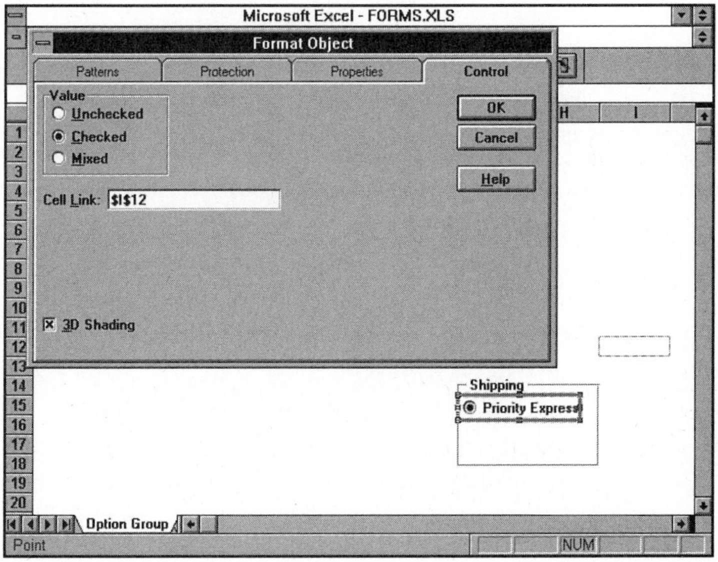

Fig. 24.7
The Control tab for an option button describes the default value for the button and the cell that was linked to the result.

4. Select the Cell **L**ink edit box, then click the worksheet cell that you want to contain the results from the group of option buttons.

5. Choose OK.

6. Return to step 2 to create another option button. All option buttons in a group box share the same cell reference. If you do not need to create another option button, click a cell outside the group.

When you create additional option buttons, you don't have to enter a cell reference for the Cell **L**ink. Only one linked cell exists for all option buttons in a group. If the first button drawn is selected, the linked cell becomes 1, if the second button drawn is selected, the linked cell becomes 2, and so on.

A group of option buttons usually are used to force the user to select only one choice from many. You can use a CHOOSE function to turn the choice into different results. The syntax for using CHOOSE is shown in the following line:

=CHOOSE(*LinkCell,Result1,Result2,Result3,...*)

Assume that a group box contains three option buttons linked to cell B35. Selecting option buttons then would produce the numbers 1, 2, or 3 in cell B35. To convert 1, 2, or 3 into three text results, use a formula, such as the following example:

=CHOOSE($B$35,"Monday","Tuesday","Wednesday")

If the cell that contains this formula is formatted to display dates, you can choose between yesterday, today, and tomorrow's dates by adding the following worksheet function:

=CHOOSE($B$35,NOW()-1,NOW(),NOW()+1)

Adding Scrolling or Pull-Down Lists for Limited Text Choices

A scrolling list or pull-down list restricts users to choosing from a defined list of items. The list may be product names, plant sites, employee positions, and so on. Restricting user selections prevents them from typing a mistake, entering nonexistent part numbers, or using old data. You even can use a choice from one list to look up a value from another list. Figure 24.8 shows a scrolling list and a pull-down list.

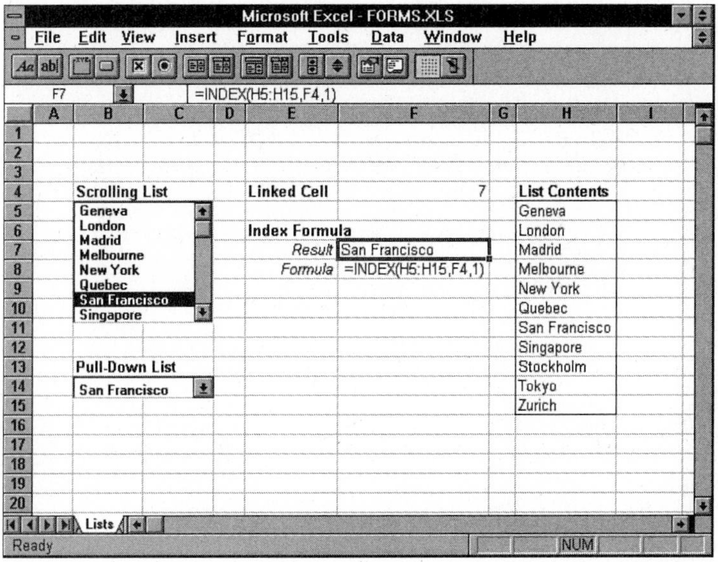

Fig. 24.8
Use scrolling lists or pull-down lists to restrict choices.

Scrolling lists and pull-down lists produce the same result, but the appearance of these lists differs. A scrolling list shows multiple items in the list, while the list stays the same height. A pull-down list is only one item high and has a pull-down arrow to the right side. Clicking the pull-down arrow displays the scrolling list. Pull-down lists usually are used when not enough room exists for a scrolling list.

To create a list, follow these steps:

1. On the worksheet enter a vertical list of items you want to appear in the list. Enter one item per cell as shown in range H5:H15 in figure 24.8.

2. Click the scrolling or pull-down list button and draw a list box on the worksheet. If the list box cannot be made wide enough for all of the items to remain fully visible, make the list wide enough to show a readable amount of each item. Make a scrolling list tall enough so that you can see multiple items. Make a pull-down list tall enough for one item.

3. Right mouse click the list and choose Format Object to display the Format Object dialog box. Select the Control tab.

4. If you are working on a pull-down list, the Control tab resembles figure 24.9. The Control tab looks the same for a scrolling list but doesn't have a **D**rop Down Lines edit box.

Tip
Use the **D**ata **S**ort command if you want the list to appear sorted within a control.

Tip
For a more manageable system, type a range name in the Input Range edit box rather than a range reference.

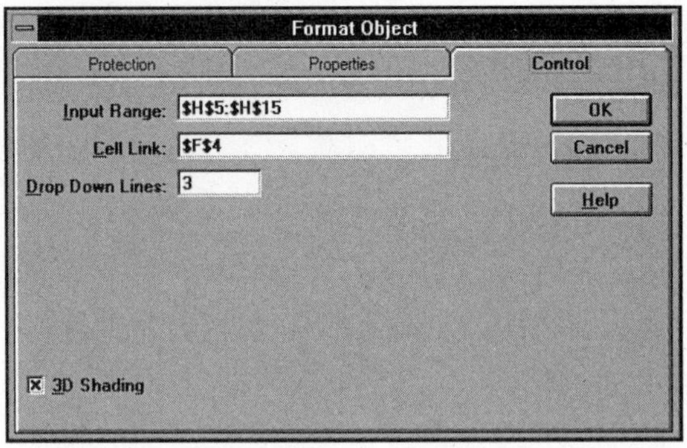

Fig. 24.9
For a list, you must indicate the cells where the list is located.

5. Select the **I**nput Range cell, then drag across the range that contains the list. This list appears in the scrolling list or pull-down list.

6. Select the **C**ell Link box and click the cell that will receive the results of the list. In figure 24.8, the cell link is to F4.

7. If you are formatting a pull-down list, enter in the **D**rop Down Lines box the number of lines displayed when the list appears.

8. Choose OK.

The result of a selection from a list is a number that is the position of the selected item in the list. If you selected the third item in the list, for example, the linked cell will contain the number 3. In most cases you don't want to convert this number into the actual item in the list. To do this, use the INDEX function. The syntax for the INDEX function is shown in the following line:

=INDEX(*ItemListReference,LinkCell,1*)

Assume that a list of cities in the range B12:B28 is used for the range in the **I**nput Range box. The link cell for the list is D15. This cell is where the numeric position of the item selected appears. In another cell you can show the city selected with the formula:

=INDEX($B$12:$B$28,$D$15,1)

This function looks down the list, B12:B28, to the row specified in cell $D$15. The item in that row of the list then is returned to the cell that contains the INDEX function.

As another useful technique, you can choose from one list but use a corresponding value from another list, which is useful for selecting easily recognizable named items from a list, but then letting Excel find the corresponding price for the item. You can use this technique to look up items by name or description but then return a more arcane result such as a part number, price, SKU, or weight.

To use an alternate list lookup, you need two lists (as shown in figure 24.10). One list, H5:H15, is used for the **I**nput Range to the control, which is the list users see. The other list is used to find the result you want to appear in the worksheet. In figure 24.10 the formula returns a price, after the user makes a selection of a city. The formula in cell F11 is shown in the following line:

=INDEX(I5:I15,F4,1)

This formula returns the item in a specific row of the price list, I5:I15. The row is specified in cell F4, the linked cell.

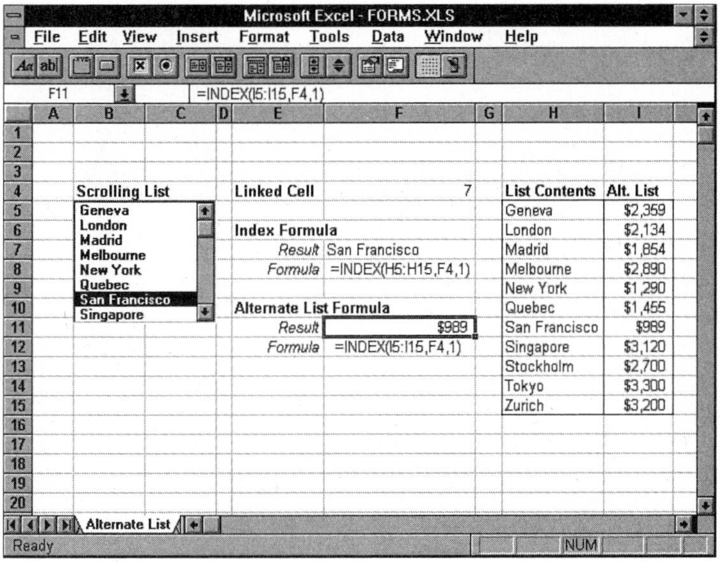

Fig. 24.10
You can choose one item from a list (San Francisco) and display an item from an alternate list ($989).

Adding Spinners To Change Numbers Quickly

Spinners are controls that show two arrow heads. Each click on an arrow head increases or decreases the amount in the cell linked to the spinner. Holding down the mouse button on a spinner causes the number to change continuously.

> **Caution**
>
> Unless you follow the tip described in the "Controlling Recalculation" section that follows in this chapter, the entire worksheet recalculates each time the link cell changes. When you spin through numbers with a spinner, this can cause a great deal of unnecessary recalculation, which slows both you and the computer.

To set the defaults and limits on a spinner, follow these steps:

1. Right mouse click the spinner control that you already drew on your worksheet, and then choose the Format Object command.
2. Select the Control tab shown in figure 24.11.

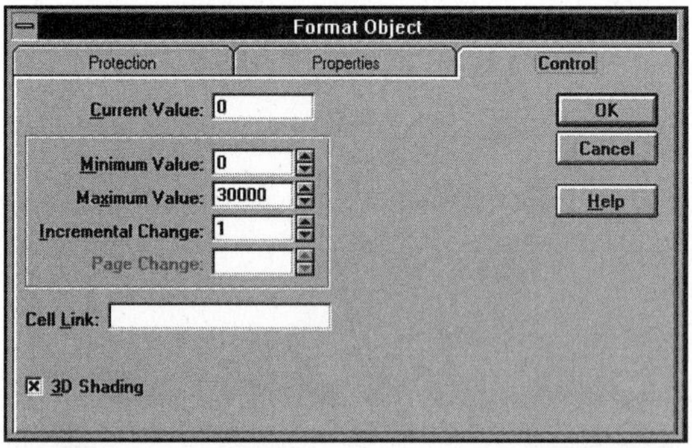

Fig. 24.11
You control the limits and change amounts on a spinner control.

3. In the **C**urrent Value edit box, enter the amount you want the linked cell to have when the worksheet opens.
4. Enter the lowest value you want the spinner to produce in the **M**inimum Value box. Enter the highest value you want in the Ma**x**imum Value box. Set the amount of change for each click on the control in the **I**ncremental Change box. The Page Change edit box is not used for the spinner control.
5. Select the Cell **L**ink edit box and then click the cell in the worksheet that you want to receive the spinner result.
6. Choose OK.

Adding Scroll Bars To Enter Widely Ranging Numbers

Scroll bars, also known as sliders, enable users to enter a widely ranging number while getting a visual impression of where their entry lies within the range. The scroll bar control looks like a vertical scroll bar. Like other controls, the scroll bar's output is linked to a worksheet cell. To enter a number, you can click the top or bottom arrowhead for incremental change, click the grey part of the bar for a page amount of change, or drag the square button in the scroll bar for a large change. The scroll bar works like the scroll bar on the right side of a window but enters numbers into a cell.

Caution

Unless you follow the tip in the following section, "Controlling Recalculation," the entire worksheet recalculates each time the link cell changes. When you enter data by clicking the scroll bar, this can cause a great deal of unnecessary recalculation, which slows both you and the computer.

To set the defaults and limits on a scroll bar that you already drew on the worksheet, follow these steps:

1. With the right mouse button, click the scroll bar control on the worksheet, then choose the Format Object command.
2. Select the Control tab shown in figure 24.12.

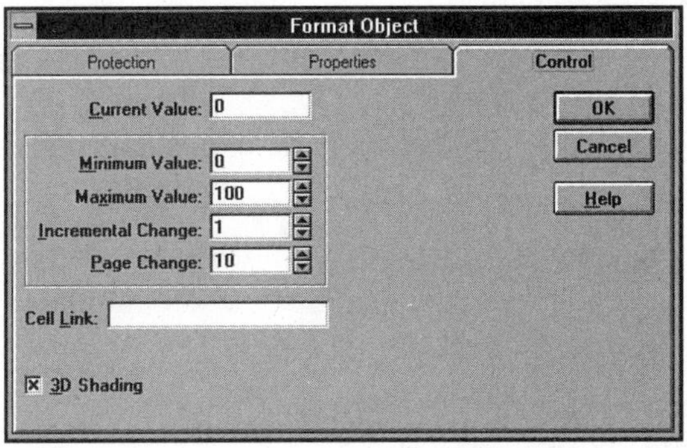

Fig. 24.12
Use scroll bars to enter widely varying values.

3. In the **C**urrent Value edit box, enter the amount you want the linked cell to have when the worksheet opens.
4. Enter the lowest value you want the spinner to produce in the **M**inimum Value box. Enter the highest value you want in the Ma**x**imum Value box. Set the amount of change for each click on the control in the **I**ncremental Change box. In the **P**age Change edit box, enter the amount of change you want when the user clicks the grey part of the scroll bar.

5. Select the Cell **L**ink edit box and then click the cell in the worksheet you want to receive the spinner result.

6. Choose OK.

For Related Information

- "Using Formulas To Make Decisions," p. 687
- "Using Formulas To Look Up Data in Tables," p. 693
- "Checking Data Entry," p. 690
- "Creating Custom Dialog Boxes," p. 1212

Settings for the minimum and maximum values must be in the range of 0 to 30000 and the Maximum edit box must be greater than the minimum. But this doesn't mean you have to accept these limits.

Most people are used to thermometers and having the highest number for a meter at the top of the vertical bar. The scroll bar gives results backwards to this—the top of the scroll bar results in zero. To reverse the scroll bar values, create a formula that subtracts the result from what you have set as the maximum. If the linked cell is C12 and the maximum value is 100, for example, you can reverse the minimum and maximum amounts by entering the following formula:

=100-C12

This formula belongs in cell D12.

Modifying Controls

After you create controls on a worksheet, you can return to and modify them with the Control Properties button. You must select the control before you can modify it. To select a control, hold down the Ctrl key, and then click the control. To select multiple controls, hold down the Shift and Ctrl keys as you click on each control you want selected. If you need to select multiple controls that are located near each other, click the Select button (an arrow) on the Drawing toolbar and drag a rectangle around the controls.

Note

To quickly display the Format Object dialog box, right click the object to display the shortcut menu, and then click the Format Object command.

Reshaping, Copying, or Deleting a Control

As you design a form, you probably may need to move or resize controls. You even may have to delete a control. To move a control, Ctrl+click to select the control, and then drag it to a new location by its edge. To resize a control, drag one of the handles at the corner or on the middle of a side. Delete a control by selecting the control and pressing the Delete key or choosing the **E**dit Cle**a**r **A**ll command.

To align a control's edges with the grid of a worksheet, hold down the Alt key as you drag the edge or handle of a selected control.

Tip
Hold down the Alt key while dragging or resizing a control to align the control with the worksheet grid.

To copy an image of a control, select the control with a Ctrl+click. Create a copy in two ways. To create a copy in close proximity to the original, Ctrl+click on the original to select it, and then hold down Ctrl as you drag an edge of the original. Release the mouse button to drop the copy, and then release the Ctrl key. To create a copy that you must place farther away, select the control, and then use the **E**dit **C**opy and **E**dit **P**aste commands to make a copy. Copies do not have the same linked cell as the original.

Enhancing Controls

Although controls are excellent for making worksheets easier to use, they work better and provide fewer management and training problems if you enhance the controls with a few design considerations.

Controlling Recalculation

When a control's result changes, the worksheet immediately recalculates. For selections from a list in a dialog box, this recalculation may not cause too much delay, because the selection probably is infrequent. Spinning through a series of numbers by holding the mouse button on a spinner, however, can cause significant delays. Each time you click a spinner, the result number changes and the worksheet recalculates.

One solution to this problem is to turn off automatic calculation by choosing the **T**ools **O**ptions command, selecting the Calculation tab, and then selecting **M**anual. To calculate, the user then presses the F9 key or repeats the command process and choose the **A**utomatic option. But this requires a number of manual steps.

One way to control recalculation is to *hide* changes until you are ready to recalculate. With this method, you can leave the worksheet in automatic calculation mode. You can hide the changed number resulting from a spinner, for example, by putting the spinner result inside an IF function. The IF function then is controlled by a check box control. When the check box control is selected, the IF reveals the changed spinner result. When the check box control is deselected, the IF produces the #NA error by using an NA() function.

Figure 24.13 shows the formulas that enable one check box to hide changed results from other controls. When the check box is selected, the results pass through the IF functions and the volume calculates. When the check box is deselected, the spinner results are stopped by the IF function and the #NA cascades through all formulas that use this spinner's results (see fig. 24.14).

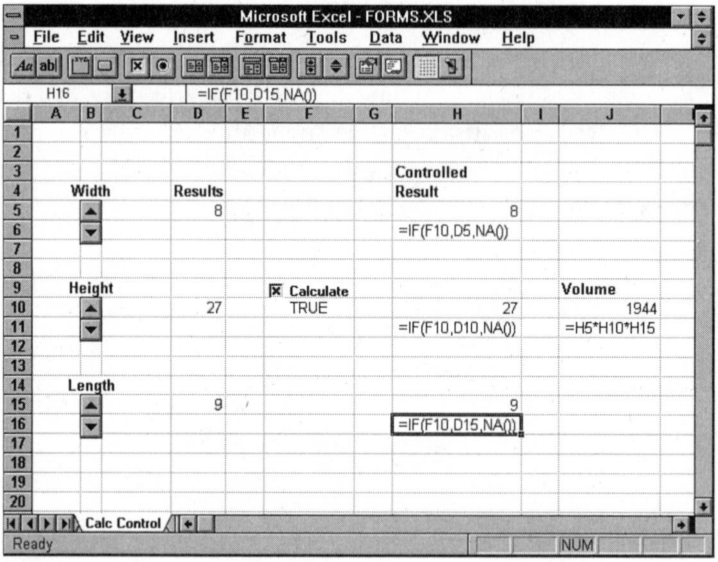

Fig. 24.13
Use formulas that enable calculation when the check box is selected.

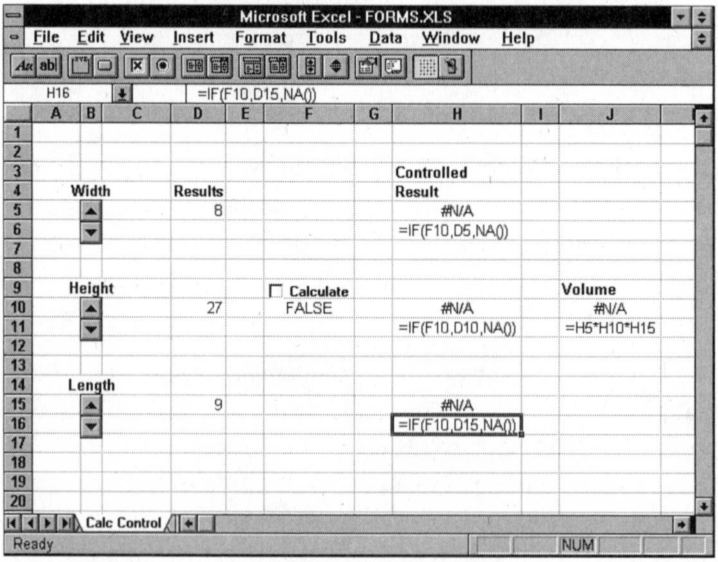

Fig. 24.14
When the check box is deselected, calculation is interrupted.

Dimming or Blanking Controls

Dimming—blanking a control so that it has no selection—is useful in a couple of ways. You can dim a control, such as a check box, to force the user to choose between selected (True) and deselected (False). You can create lists without a selected item to force the user to select rather than accept the default item. You even can display option buttons in a group, with no button selected so that the user is forced to make a choice.

To dim a check box or group of option buttons, type the following formula into the linked cell:

=NA( )

This function produces the #N/A error, which causes the check box to grey and removes all selections from a group of option buttons. The =NA() function also can produce a #N/A error in any formula that references the linked cell. This error lets users know that they haven't completed making selections from dimmed check boxes or option buttons.

To remove the selection from a list so that no item in the list is selected, type 0 or the following function into the linked cell:

=NA( )

Printing Forms without the Control

When you print a worksheet that contains controls, a graphic of the control prints. If you don't want to print this image, format the controls so they don't print. To format controls to not print, use a right mouse click on the control to display the shortcut menu, then choose the Format Object command. After the Format Object dialog box appears, select the Properties dialog box and deselect the **P**rint Object check box. While the **P**rint Object check box is deselected the control does not print. Cell contents under the control do print.

Note

A control can only link to one cell, but you may need to use the result in many locations. In that case, link the control to a single cell, and then enter formulas in other cells that reference the linked cell.

Protecting a Form

Forms are usually created as templates. Templates are used so a document can be opened and reused without concern for destroying or changing the original. However, even in a document created from a template, you probably will not want the user deliberately or accidentally changing formatting or erasing formulas. To prevent this, you need to protect the worksheet. Chapter 10, "Formatting Worksheets," describes in detail how to protect a worksheet.

When protecting a form on a worksheet, remember that the cells linked to controls cannot be protected. Linked cells must remain unprotected so the control can enter the new result. Having the linked cell unprotected is not much of a disability to good design and worksheet management.

> **Caution**
>
> Controls cannot be linked to protected cells. Because more forms are protected, it is a good idea to link a control to an unprotected cell on another sheet or at a distant location on the same sheet. If you need to display the value from the control next to the control, use a formula in a cell near the control to reference the unprotected cell. You may want to hide sheets that contain the unprotected linked cells. To hide them use the F**o**rmat S**h**eet **H**ide command.

To prevent users from accidentally altering the link cell, link all controls to cells on one sheet in the workbook. You may have controls on different sheets throughout the workbook, but all the linked cells for these controls are on the same sheet. To link a control between worksheets, display the Format Object dialog box, click the **C**ell Link box, activate the other sheet by clicking on the tab or choosing the other sheet from the **W**indow menu, and then click the cell in the other sheet.

For Related Information

- "Displaying Worksheets in Separate Windows," p. 547
- "Hiding and Unhiding Windows and Sheets," p. 550

After you place all the linked cells in one sheet, you can hide this sheet by activating the sheet and choosing the F**o**rmat S**h**eet **H**ide command. This action hides the sheet but keeps it in the workbook, which prevents accidental changes and less knowledgable users from making changes. Knowledgable users can unhide the sheet with the F**o**rmat S**h**eet **U**nhide command.

To hide the sheet so that users cannot get at it, you can use Visual Basic to change the sheet's Visible Property. For more information on this advanced technique, search the online Visual Basic Reference for Visible Property.

From Here...

Forms can be useful for any worksheet that requires control over data entry. Forms produce a much more appealing method of operation than typing in data. For additional information that will help you design forms you should take a look at the following chapters:

- Chapter 5, "Working with Formulas." This chapter describes how to enter and edit formulas.
- Chapter 6, "Using Functions." This chapter describes some functions you may want to use with the result in linked cells. Some of these functions are, INDEX(), MATCH(), VLOOKUP(), HLOOKUP(), CHOOSE(), and IF().
- Chapter 17, "Adding Graphics Elements to Sheets." This chapter describes how to dress up your forms with graphics so they print as well as preprinted forms.
- Chapter 20, "Publishing Worksheets and Charts." Creating forms for data entry and printing should require more design knowledge than putting together a simple spreadsheet for your use. You want them to look good, and this chapter describes how to do this.
- Chapter 23, "Manipulating and Analyzing Data." This chapter describes functions that you can use when working with lists.
- Chapter 45, "Programming in Visual Basic for Applications." If you need more control over how data is entered, you may need to use Visual Basic procedures and custom dialog boxes. Most of what you learn in this chapter can be used to to create custom dialog boxes.

Chapter 25

Linking, Embedding, and Consolidating Worksheets

In this chapter, you learn how to:

- Link pictures of worksheet cells
- Link worksheet cells and ranges
- Understand and use worksheet consolidation

Excel enables you to work with more than one worksheet and workbook at a time. You can copy a chart or worksheet range and embed it as a picture on the worksheet; you can link workbooks so that changes in one workbook update another workbook; and you can consolidate worksheets so that data from multiple worksheets accumulates into one worksheet.

You can use linking to divide a large business system into its component workbooks and worksheets. You can test each workbook and worksheet separately, and then link the workbooks together to produce an integrated system. You can create links that always update or that update only on your request.

Excel's capability of linking pictures enables you to bring together pictures of cells and charts from different documents and arrange them on one page. This capability gives you the power to work in separate documents but organize the printed results the way you want to present them. The results have the quality of desktop publishing.

Consolidation enables you to bring together data from multiple worksheets and workbooks into one worksheet. Consolidation is often used to accumulate budgets or forecasts from multiple divisions into a unified corporate budget or forecast. Excel enables you to fix these consolidations so that they don't change, or to link them so that the consolidations update when division data changes. Linked consolidations automatically build an outline.

Linking Pictures of Worksheet Cells

You can create two types of picture links within a worksheet. One type links a picture of a worksheet area into another worksheet. The linked picture can be updated. The second type links a cell or range in a supporting worksheet to a cell or range in another worksheet. The following sections describe how to link a picture of a worksheet area to another worksheet. The section "Linking Worksheet Cells and Ranges" describes how to link worksheet cells and ranges.

Many Windows programs, such as Excel, enable you to link objects from one document into another document. A linked object from Excel can be a cell, a range, a chart, or a complete Excel document. Embedded documents link an image of the original into another document. You can format and update the linked object whenever you want. The top-right corner of figure 25.1 shows a linked cell picture taken from a separate portion of the same worksheet. This single figure displays (and prints) two charts, a distant part of the worksheet, a text box containing explanation, and arrows and circles.

Fig. 25.1
A linked cell picture is an object that contains the data of the source worksheet.

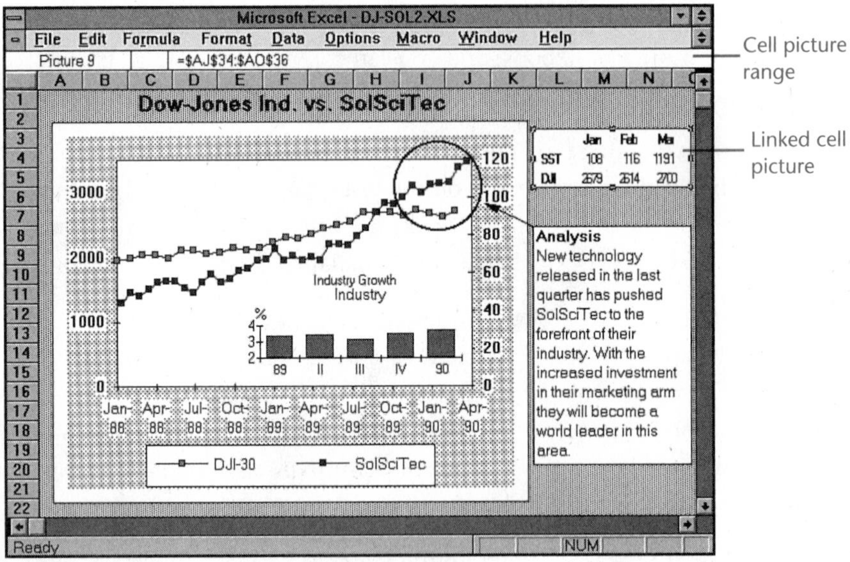

Desktop Publishing Layouts with Linked Pictures

To create page layouts displaying data from multiple worksheets and charts, you can link a picture of an Excel worksheet area into another worksheet. This linkage is an excellent way to create management information displays that bring together data from disparate sources. Linked cell pictures have the following advantages over cell or range links (described later in this chapter in the section "Linking Worksheet Cells and Ranges"):

- Linked cell pictures can be opened and updated quickly. When a linked cell picture is double-clicked, the entire supporting worksheet is activated and the pictured range is selected. If the worksheet is not open, Excel opens it and selects the range so that you can easily change data or make major corrections to the linked cell picture.
- Linked cell pictures can be formatted with most of the same features as text boxes (described in Chapter 17, "Adding Graphics Elements to Sheets"). This formatting makes the cell pictures attractive and easier to read.
- Linked worksheet objects can be resized and moved, unfettered by cell locations. This flexibility enables you to create attractive page layouts involving multiple linked worksheet ranges and charts.
- Linked cell pictures and charts print together on the page in which they appear.
- Linked cell pictures can be linked to macros; when such a cell picture is selected, it runs a macro.

Linked cell pictures have the following disadvantages:

- Linked cell pictures are not actual cells, so you cannot enter data in them.
- Linked cell pictures cannot be used in calculations. If you need to perform calculations with the information in the cells, use the methods in the following sections that describe linking cells and ranges.

Linking Cell Pictures

Embedding a range from one range on a worksheet in another area of the same or different worksheet involves *taking a picture* of the *source* range that supplies the data and pasting that picture in the *target* worksheet. One worksheet may be both a target and source if the linked picture appears on the same worksheet that supplied the cell picture.

Before you can use the Camera button to link cell pictures, you must add this button by choosing the **V**iew **T**oolbars command, selecting the **C**ustomize button, and when the **C**ustomize dialog box appears, selecting Utility from the list. The Camera button now is visible in the Button area. Drag the button onto a toolbar, and then choose Close.

To link a cell picture of the worksheet by using the toolbar and the mouse, follow these steps:

1. Select the range on the *source* worksheet that you want to take a picture of.

2. Click the Camera button. The cursor changes to a +.

3. Activate the *target* worksheet to receive the picture. If you are pasting the picture into the source worksheet, scroll the worksheet to where you want the picture.

4. Click the cell where you want the top left corner of the cell picture to appear. A picture with black handles around it appears on the worksheet.

To link a cell picture by using the keyboard, follow these steps:

1. Open the worksheet that supplies the picture (source) and the worksheet to receive the linked cell picture (target).

2. Activate the source worksheet.

3. Select the range of the worksheet to be copied.

4. Choose the **E**dit **C**opy command.

5. Switch to the target worksheet by clicking it or by choosing it from the **W**indow menu (or pressing Ctrl+F6). If you are pasting the picture into the source worksheet, then scroll the worksheet to where you want the picture.

6. Select the cell at the top-left corner of the area where you want the cell picture to appear.

7. Hold down the Shift key as you choose the **E**dit Paste Picture Li**n**k command.

A picture with black handles around it appears on the worksheet. Notice the black handles at the corners and edges of the picture in figure 25.1. Note that the reference formula linking this formula to the worksheet cells appears in the formula bar while the embedded worksheet is selected. In this figure, the cell picture is from the same worksheet that the picture is embedded on.

If the picture comes from a different worksheet in the same workbook, the formula bar shows a sheet reference. If the picture comes from a different workbook, the formula bar shows an external cell reference.

The cell reference formula that links the supporting workbook to the target workbook is known as an *external reference formula.* (External reference formulas are described in the section, "Linking Worksheet Cells and Ranges," later in this chapter.)

Note

Save the source worksheets before saving the target. By saving source worksheets first, the links in the target worksheet will contain the correct file names for the sources.

To format, resize, position, or protect the embedded cell picture, use the techniques described in the discussion of drawing, formatting, and placing graphics in Chapter 17, "Adding Graphic Elements to Sheets."

Updating Linked Cell Pictures

When you first open a worksheet that contains linked cell pictures, a dialog box asks whether you want the links updated from source files that are unopened. To update, choose **Y**es. To keep the pictures as they were when last saved, choose **N**o.

To update the cell picture or make changes to the source that supplied the picture, double-click the linked cell picture. Double-clicking the linked cell picture opens the source worksheet—if it is not already open—and activates the window. Excel selects the worksheet range in the picture. Make changes in this source worksheet range, save the changes, and then close the source worksheet if you do not need to make further changes. If the worksheet contains a cell picture from one of its own cells or ranges or from another worksheet in the same workbook, you don't need to close the worksheet.

If you have double-clicked a linked cell picture, the source worksheet and its range appear. If you double-click the picture and go to the source worksheet, you can return quickly to the linked cell picture by pressing the Goto key, F5. Notice that the **R**eference edit box in the Go To dialog box contains the address of the sheet and the location from which you came. Make no changes in the Go To box; choose OK or press Enter, and you return immediately to your original location.

Note

Excel has much of the power of executive information systems and management display systems. By using embedded pictures, linked worksheets, and linked outlines, you can create systems that enable short drill downs to underlying detail worksheets. Double-clicking a linked cell or linked cell picture or chart will open and activate the source if it is not already open. Excel also can support large executive information systems by linking Excel to an SQL Server or mainframe database Microsoft Query, or you can link to one of the many other access programs available for Windows.

If you are using a keyboard, you cannot open a source file and update a link to a closed source by double-clicking. You also may need to update multiple pictures simultaneously. Perform the following steps if you need to open and update multiple linked pictures:

1. Activate the worksheet containing linked pictures.
2. Choose the **E**dit Lin**k**s command. The Links dialog box appears (see fig. 25.2).

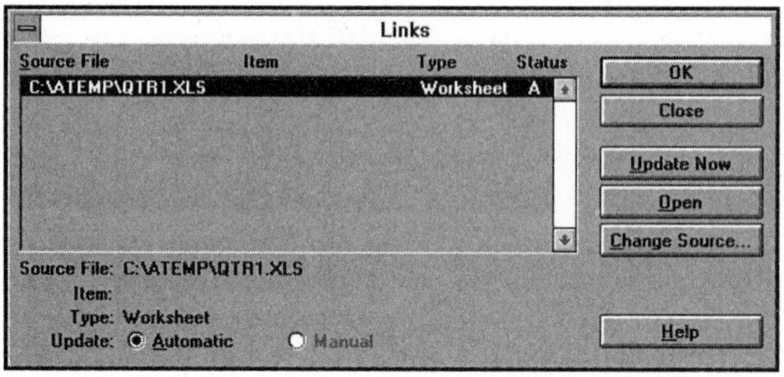

Fig. 25.2
Use the Links dialog box to manage linked files.

3. Select the source worksheet from the **L**inks list by clicking or by pressing the arrow keys. To select multiple worksheets, press Ctrl while you click more than one worksheet in the **L**inks list. Using the keyboard, select multiple worksheets by holding Ctrl as you press the up- or down-arrow keys. Press the space bar to select or clear a worksheet.
4. Choose **U**pdate Now to refresh the links from disk; then choose Close or press Esc.

   You also can choose **O**pen to open the selected worksheet.

Changing Links to Linked Cell Pictures

If you change the source workbook's name, move the workbook to a different directory, or want to change the source to a different workbook, you need to edit the embedded picture's cell reference formula. The external reference formulas used by linked cell pictures or objects are the same as those used by linked cells and ranges. You can see this reference formula by selecting a linked cell picture and looking at the formula bar.

> **Note**
>
> You can use the keyboard to select individual objects. Choose the **E**dit **G**o To command to get the Go To dialog box, select the **S**pecial option to get the Special dialog box, select the O**b**jects option, and then choose OK or press Enter. This procedure selects all objects on the active worksheet. Press Tab to select each object in turn or press Shift+Tab to cycle through the objects in reverse order.

To change or edit all links to the same source workbook, follow the procedures for the **E**dit Lin**k**s command in the following section on updating and editing linked workbooks. If you edit a linked cell picture and change it to a source workbook file that is not open, the linked cell picture appears blank. Use one of the update methods previously described to open the new source workbook and update the linked pictures. You can close the source workbook after you update the pictures. The linked cell picture continues to display data from the new source workbook.

To change the link to one embedded cell picture without changing other links to the same source workbook, select the individual linked cell picture. Edit the external reference formula in the formula bar to refer to the new source workbook's path, file, sheet, and cell references. Press Enter to reenter the formula. The linked cell picture is blank if the reference workbook is not open. Use the update techniques mentioned previously to update the linked picture.

To delete a linked cell picture, select it so that black handles appear along the picture's edges, and then press Del or Backspace, or choose the **E**dit Cl**e**ar command. Choose the **E**dit **U**ndo command immediately to restore a deleted embedded object.

For Related Information

- "Embedding Linked Pictures of Charts in a Worksheet," p. 572
- "Creating Graphic Objects," p. 560
- "Combining Data and Charts on the Same Page," p. 571
- "Grouping Graphic Objects," p. 588
- "Embedding Data from Other Applications into Worksheets," p. 1050

Linking Workbook Cells and Ranges

Linking data enables you to avoid the problems inherent in large, cumbersome workbooks. You can build small worksheets and workbooks to accomplish specific tasks, and then link all these *components* together to form a larger *system*.

The following list describes some of the advantages of building systems composed of smaller workbooks that share data by linking:

- Data linked between workbooks passes data, numbers, and text used by formulas in the receiving workbook.
- Linked data can be formatted by using the same formatting techniques you use on any cell contents.
- Systems require less memory because all workbooks may not need to be open simultaneously. Some workbooks can be linked to workbooks that remain on disk.
- Systems composed of workbook components are flexible and can be updated more easily. You can redesign, test, and implement one component without rebuilding the entire system.
- Smaller workbooks recalculate faster than single, large workbooks.
- You can create data-entry components that operate on separate computers or in separate locations. At a given time, filled-in components can be copied into a directory and given a file name expected by the link, which updates the spreadsheet that contains the link the next time it is opened. This arrangement has a number of advantages—more people can work on the system at once, people can work in separate locations, the work can be completed faster, and separate locations reduce the chance that an inexperienced operator can damage the overall system.
- Systems are easier to maintain and debug when assembled in components.
- Workbook components can be modified for use in different systems.

What You Need To Know about Links

Linking enables one workbook to share the data in another workbook. You can link one cell, a range of cells, and a named formula or constant and sheets. The workbook containing the original data—the source of information—is the *source workbook*. The workbook that receives the linked data is the *target workbook*. (You also may see the workbooks referred to as the *source* and the *target* or the *supporting* and the *dependent*.)

Source workbooks can be on-screen or on disk; the target workbook can get the information it needs through the link. When the target workbook opens, it updates linked data that is read from the source workbook, if the source workbook is open. If the source workbook is not open, the target workbook asks whether you want to use the data the target workbook had when it was saved or whether you want the target workbook to read in new data from the source workbook still on disk.

Note

If you have links from one workbook to a database in another workbook, the workbook that contains the link may open or close too slowly. The file size of the workbook also may become huge—too large to fit on a disk—because Excel actually is storing the last image of the database in the file, which enables you to open the workbook, not update the link to the database, and still use the workbook. Your workbook doesn't need to save this database image if the workbook that contains the database is always open with the linked sheet or if you will always be doing an update when you open the sheet. To turn off this saved image, choose the **T**ools **O**ptions command, select the Calculation tab, and deselect the Save External **L**ink Values check box. Choose OK.

Figure 25.3 shows workbooks linked by an external reference formula. QTR1.XLS is the source for the ANNUAL.XLS target workbook. The external reference formula in ANNUAL.XLS appears in the formula bar as `='[QTR1.XLS]QTR1 93'!$E$5`, which indicates that cell B5 on the ANNUAL 93 worksheet of the ANNUAL.XLS workbook is linked to the contents of cell E5 on the QTR1 93 worksheet of the QTR1.XLS workbook. When the contents of E5 in the QTR1 93 worksheet changes, the value of B5 of the ANNUAL 93 worksheet also changes.

External reference formulas use the following form:

```
='Path\[WorkbookName]SheetName'!CellRef
```

The following formula is an example of an external reference formula:

```
='[QTR1.XLS]QTR1 93'!$E$5
```

In this formula, QTR1.XLS is the name of the supporting workbook that contains the data, QTR1 93 is the specific worksheet in the workbook that contains the data, and $E$5 is the cell that supplies information to the link. An exclamation mark (!) separates the supporting workbook and worksheet name from the cell reference.

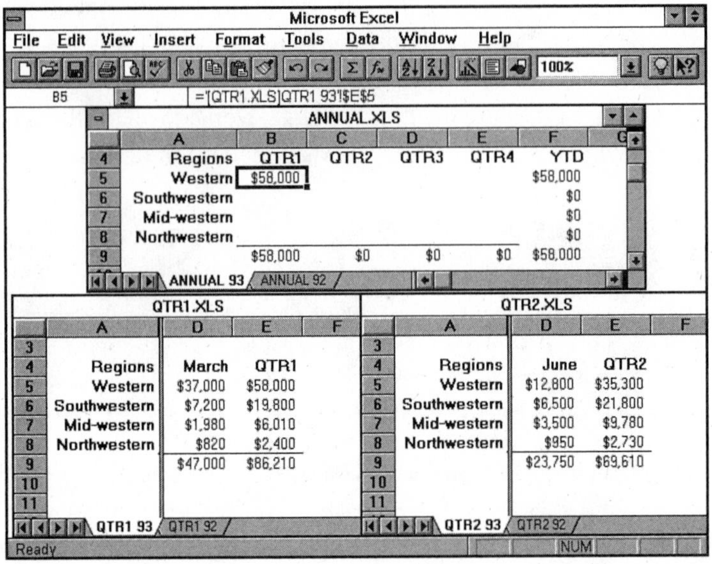

Fig. 25.3
The QTR1.XLS acts as the source for the ANNUAL.XLS workbook.

An external reference also can span a range of cells. The total in B9 on ANNUAL.XLS, for example, can be one formula that totals the range of cells from the QTR1 93 worksheet in the QTR1.XLS workbook. The formula may appear in the following way:

```
=SUM('[QTR1.XLS]QTR1 93'!$E$5:$E$8)
```

You can link a range of cells to another range of cells of the same size. These links use array formulas and are created with the **E**dit Paste **L**ink command. An external reference formula on ANNUAL.XLS that links B5:B8 to the supporting cells E5:E8 on QTR1.XLS appears as the following array:

```
{='[QTR1.XLS]QTR1 93'!$E$5:$E$8}
```

The braces, { }, around the formula indicate that it is an array formula. *Array formulas* act on multiple cells at one time. You must enter and edit array formulas differently than normal single-cell formulas. You cannot type the braces; you must enter them in a special way, described in a following section. Array formulas are described further in Chapter 5, “Working with Formulas.”

The external reference formula appears differently, depending on whether the source worksheet is open or closed. If the source worksheet is open, the external reference formula appears with only the worksheet name, as in the following example:

```
='[QTR1.XLS]QTR1 93'!$E$5
```

If the source worksheet is closed, the external reference appears with the full path name, disk, directory, and file name, enclosed in single quotation marks, as shown in the following example:

```
='C:\EXCEL\FINANCE\[QTR1.XLS]QTR1 93'!$E$9
```

Because open source workbooks don't include the path name in the external reference formula, you cannot have two workbooks open with the same name, even if both are from different directories. You can have links to source workbooks with the same names in different directories, but you can have only one workbook open at a time.

Linking Cells with Copy and Paste Link Commands

To link a cell or range in a supporting workbook to a cell or range in the target workbook, use the **E**dit Paste **S**pecial command with the Paste **L**ink Button. The range of E5:E8 on the QTR1.XLS workbook is linked to cells B5:B8 (the rows do not have to be the same) on the target ANNUAL.XLS workbook, as shown in the following steps:

1. Open the workbooks that you want to link.
2. Activate the source workbook.
3. Select the range of cells that provide the data you want linked (see fig. 25.4).
4. Choose the **E**dit **C**opy command.
5. Activate the target workbook to receive the data.
6. Select the top-left cell of the range where you want the link to appear.

   In this example, you would select cell B5 on the ANNUAL 93 worksheet of the ANNUAL.XLS workbook. Do not select an entire range to paste into; doing so is unnecessary and increases the chance that you may select the wrong size of range to paste into. You need to select only the single cell at the upper left corner of the area that you want to paste.
7. Choose the **E**dit Paste **S**pecial command. The Paste Special dialog box appears.

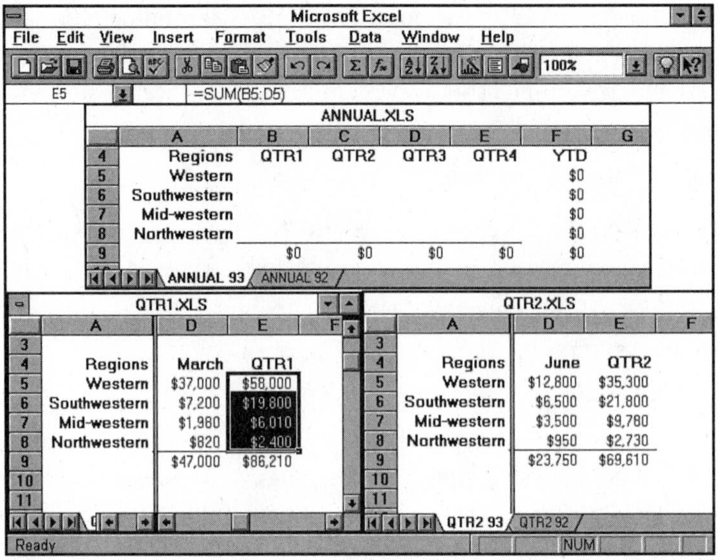

Fig. 25.4
Select the range on the source worksheet before copying.

8. Select the Paste **A**ll option and the Operation **N**one option.

9. Choose the Paste **L**ink command.

The link appears, as shown in figure 25.5.

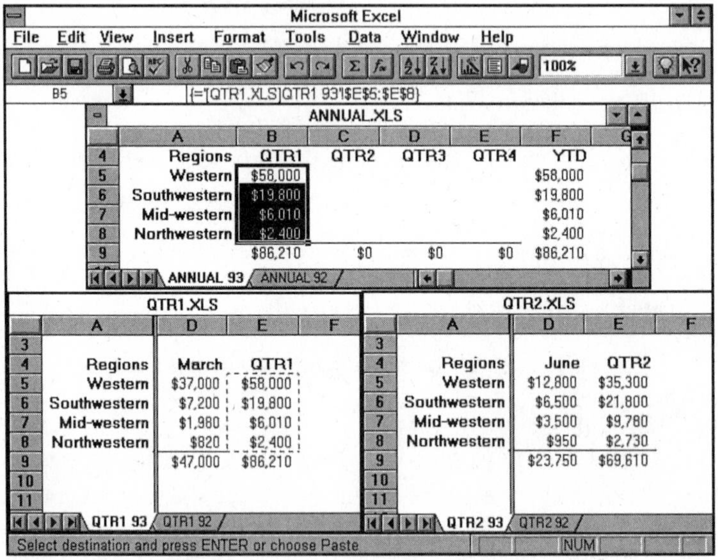

Fig. 25.5
The linked cells on ANNUAL.XLS act as a group, an array.

Notice that in the target workbook's formula bar, braces, { }, enclose cells in the linked range. The braces indicate that the linked range is one array. The entire range is linked, not the individual cells. You cannot change individual cells within the array, but you can edit the entire array, as described in the section "Editing Arrays Made with Paste Link."

If you use the **E**dit **C**opy and the **E**dit Paste **S**pecial command to link a single cell to another single cell, an external reference formula is created that is not an array. You can edit this formula like any other formula.

Linking Cells by Pointing

To create many links that are individual cells or are links within larger formulas, use the pointing method of creating links. You can enter external references in a formula in the same way that you build a formula within one workbook: by pointing to the cell references you want in the formula, even when the cells are on another workbook. To point to a cell or range so that it is included in a formula, click it as you build the formula, or drag across its range.

To link the target cell B5 on the ANNUAL 93 worksheet of the ANNUAL.XLS workbook to the source cell, E5 on the QTR1 93 worksheet of the QTR1.XLS workbook, perform the following steps:

1. Open the target and source workbooks.

2. Activate the target workbook.

3. Select the cell that you want to contain the link and start the formula. The formula may involve many terms and functions or be as simple as an equal sign (=) and the single linked cell.

   In figure 25.6, an equal sign (=) is typed in cell B5 on the ANNUAL 93 worksheet of the ANNUAL.XLS workbook.

4. Activate the source workbook, QTR1.XLS.

5. Select the source cell or range that supplies data to the link. In the example, click cell E5 on the QTR1 93 worksheet or press the arrow keys to enclose E5 in the dashed marquee.

6. Continue building the formula in the same way you build any formula, by typing another math operator (math sign) and continuing to select cells or to enter terms.

7. After you complete the formula, click the Enter box in the formula bar or press Enter.

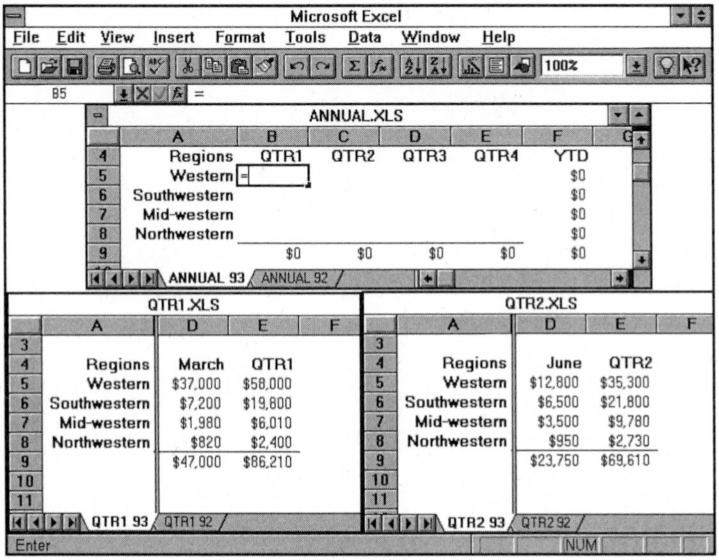

Fig. 25.6
Link cells by typing an = and clicking the source cell.

After you press Enter or type a math operator, the target worksheet reactivates. Figure 25.7 shows the result of the external reference formula in B5—`='[QTR1.XLS]QTR1 93'!$E$5`—just after pressing Enter.

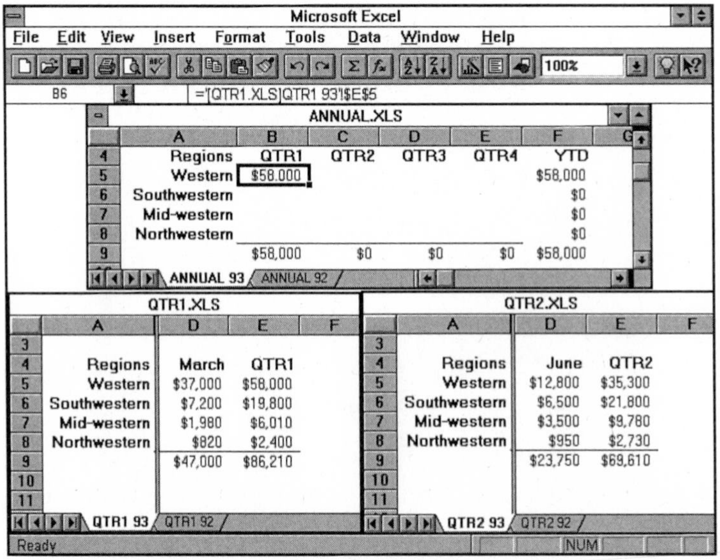

Fig. 25.7
The resulting link is created by pointing to a cell in another workbook.

You can use the pointing method to enter external references within complex formulas such as the following:

```
=2*SIN('[READINGS.XLS]TEST 1'!$AE$5)/(B12*56)
```

You also can point to ranges on other workbooks. Consider the following formula:

```
=SUM('[QTR2.XLS]QTR2 93'!$E$5:$E$8))
```

This formula was entered by typing **=SUM(** and then switching to the source workbook and dragging across the range E5:E8 with the mouse. To select the range with the keyboard, hold down the Shift key and press the arrow keys until the range is selected. Type the closing **)**, and press Enter.

Linking Cells by Typing

If you need to create links to workbooks on disk without opening the workbooks, you can type in the external reference formula. This technique can help you if the source file is too large to load with your existing workbook or if you are so familiar with the supporting workbook that you can type a reference faster than you can find and click the cell.

When you type an external reference to an open workbook, use syntax like that shown in the previous examples:

```
='[QTR1.XLS]QTR1 93'!$E$5
```

or

```
=SUM('[QTR1.XLS]QTR1 93'!$E$5:$E$8)
```

or

```
='[QTR1.XLS]QTR1 93'!RangeName
```

When you type an external reference to an unopened workbook on disk, enclose the full path name, workbook name, and worksheet name in single quotations, as in the following example:

```
='C:\EXCEL\FINANCE\[QTR1.XLS] QTR1 93'!$E$9
```

If the source file is in the current directory, Excel enters the path name. For example, type the following and press Enter:

```
='[QTR1.XLS]QTR1 93'!$E$9
```

Excel enters the path.

Typing external reference formulas is easiest when you use the **I**nsert **N**ame **D**efine or the **I**nsert **N**ame **C**reate command to name cells or ranges. Suppose that cell E5 in the QTR1 93 worksheet of the QTR1.XLS workbook is named Qtr1.Western. If both the ANNUAL.XLS and QTR1.XLS workbooks are open, you can link them by typing the following formula in the ANNUAL.XLS workbook:

```
='[QTR1.XLS]QTR1 93'!Qtr1.Western
```

This formula contains an external reference. When you type formulas that contain an external reference, the answer appears as soon as you enter the formula. (If you use a range name such as Qtr1.Western, this name must exist on the source workbook. In this example, the Qtr1 in the name Qtr1.Western is not related to the workbook name QTR1.XLS.)

Opening Linked Workbooks

When the workbook is opened, the linked data in a target workbook updates in different ways. If the source workbooks are already open, the target workbook updates immediately when opened. If the source workbooks are on disk when the target workbook opens, the alert box shown in figure 25.8 appears.

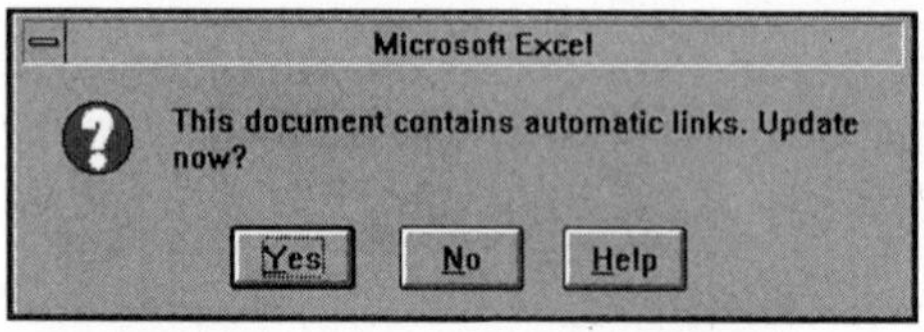

Fig. 25.8
When opening a target workbook, you can choose to keep the old values or update links to files on disk.

If you select **Y**es in the alert box, Excel reads the linked data off the files on disk and updates the target workbook. If you select **N**o, Excel retains the values the target workbook had when last saved.

If you already opened a target workbook and want to open the source workbooks that feed it, perform the following steps:

1. Activate the target sheet that contains the links.

2. Choose the **E**dit Lin**k**s command to display the Links dialog box, shown in figure 25.9.

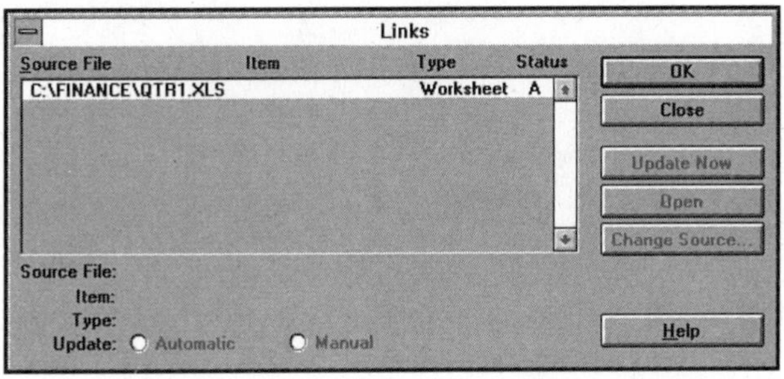

Fig. 25.9
Use the Links dialog box to change or update links between workbooks.

3. Select the files you want to open. Unopened files appear with their path name.

   To select multiple adjacent workbooks, click the first workbook and then Shift+click the last workbook. All workbooks between are selected. To select or clear nonadjacent workbooks, Ctrl+click the workbook names.

   Select multiple adjacent workbooks by pressing up- or down-arrow keys to select the first workbook, and then press Shift+arrow key to select adjacent names. Select nonadjacent workbooks by holding down Ctrl as you press the up- or down-arrow keys to move to different file names. Press the space bar to select or clear each file name.

4. Choose the **O**pen command.

Tip
Be sure that the target workbook is active. If a workbook without links is active, the **E**dit Lin**k**s command is grayed and the command is unavailable.

Changing and Updating Links

To maintain a system of linked workbooks properly, you need to know how to reestablish lost links and how to update a large system of links. If source workbooks are renamed or moved to other directories, target workbooks cannot find the needed data. These links are lost and must be reestablished.

To reestablish links to a workbook or to link a target workbook to a different supporting workbook, perform the following steps:

1. Open the target workbook.
2. Choose the **E**dit Lin**k**s command to display the Links dialog box.
3. Select the files to change or update (see fig. 25.10). Unopened files appear with their path name.

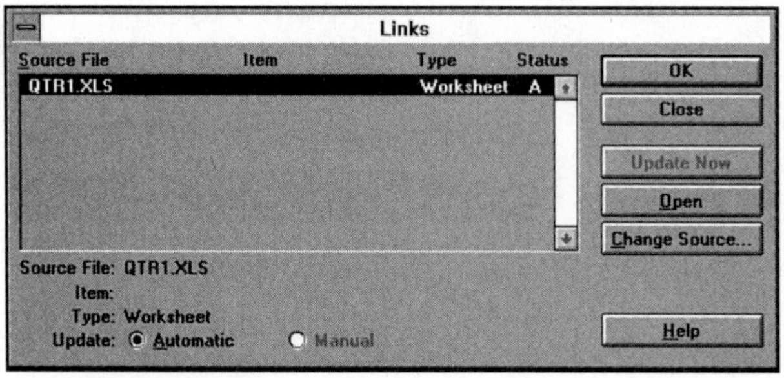

Fig. 25.10 Selected files whose links you want to reestablish or change.

4. Choose the **C**hange Source button to display the Change Links dialog box, shown in figure 25.11. The current link is displayed at the top of the dialog box.

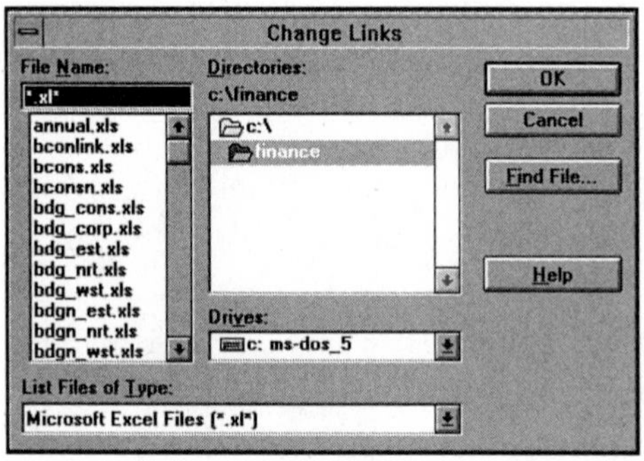

Fig. 25.11 Change links by using this dialog box.

5. Select a directory and file name to indicate the directory and file of the new supporting workbook, or type the directory and file name of the file you want to establish as the source.

6. Choose OK to link to the file name you selected, or choose Cancel to ignore the change.

7. If you selected multiple source files, repeat steps 5 and 6, noting at the top of the dialog box which source workbook you are changing.

To update an active target workbook when the source workbook is on disk, choose the **E**dit Lin**k**s command, select the source workbook from which the target workbook needs an update, and choose the **U**pdate Now button. You can select more than one source workbook by clicking the first workbook and then Shift+clicking the last workbook.

Note

You can unknowingly create linked workbooks where changed data doesn't get passed to all target workbooks. This situation occurs only when workbooks involved in the links aren't open. If workbook A passes data to B, and B passes data to C, in some cases a change in A may not occur in C. If you change workbook A, but never open and update B, B cannot have the updated data to pass on to C. Therefore, you must know and update the hierarchy of linked workbooks, in order, from the lowest source workbook to the highest target workbook.

Editing a Link Manually

You can edit an external reference formula that is linked to a cell or range. Consider the following example:

```
Frequently Used='[QTR1.XLS]QTR1 93'!$E$5
```

Edit the cell as you edit any formula. Select the cell, and then press F2 or click in the formula bar to edit.

Note

To find cells that contain external references, choose the **E**dit **F**ind command and select the Look in **F**ormulas option. Type an exclamation mark (!) in the Find **W**hat text box. Choose **F**ind Next to search. This method is helpful for finding cells containing external links that need to be edited selectively.

Links that link a range of cells use *array formulas*. When you select a cell that is part of an array, the external reference formula looks similar to the following example:

```
{='[QTR1.XLS]QTR1 93'!$E$5:$E$8}
```

Editing an external reference array formula requires more steps and a special entry keystroke. When you link a range of cells using **E**dit Paste **L**ink, you create an array formula in the dependent workbook that looks similar to {='[QTR1.XLS]QTR1 93'!$E$5:$E$8}. This formula spans multiple cells, linking a range in one workbook to another.

Consider, for example, the following formula:

```
{='[QTR1.XLS]QTR1 93'!$E$5:$E$8}
```

To edit this formula, select one cell on the dependent workbook that involves this array formula. You can select all cells manually or, for a large array, you can select one cell in the array and then choose the **E**dit **G**o To **S**pecial command. Select the Current **A**rray option and choose OK; or you can press the shortcut key, Ctrl+/.

Press F2 or click in the formula bar. Notice that the braces, { }, disappear. Edit the formula. You may want to replace the range $E$5:$E$8, for example, with a range name such as Qtr1.All. To reenter the formula as an array, press Shift+Ctrl+Enter; or hold down Shift and Ctrl as you click the Enter box in the formula bar.

To delete an array formula, such as the one just described, you must select and then delete all cells involving the array formula.

Editing Arrays Made with Paste Link

When you use **E**dit Paste **L**ink to link a range of cells, an array is created in the target workbook that looks similar to {='[QTR1.XLS]QTR1 93'!$E$5:$E$8}. An external reference array formula links a range of cells in one workbook to a range of cells in another workbook. Because an array is involved, you must edit the entire range that makes up the array. To edit the entire range, you must select the entire range and edit the formula. A special entry procedure is required, as described in "Editing a Link Manually." After you edit the array formula to include a named range, the array formula looks similar to the following example:

```
{='[QTR1.XLS]QTR1 93'!Qtr1.Totals}
```

To add a name to this formula, name the range in the supporting workbook. Look again at figure 25.5, for example; you can give the name Qtr1.Totals to $E$5:$E$8.

To add the name to the external reference formula in the target workbook, create the link by using **E**dit Paste **L**ink. With this command, you can paste the formula into a range such as B5:B8 in the ANNUAL.XLS workbook, as explained in the section, "Linking Cells with Copy and Paste Link Commands." Pasting creates the formula {='[QTR1.XLS]QTR1 93'! $E$5:$E$8} in cells B5:B8. Replace $E$5:$E$8 by selecting one of the linked cells that involve the range B5:B8. Click the formula bar and notice that the array formula changes to a normal formula. The array brackets disappear. Edit the formula to replace $E$5:$E$8 with Qtr1.Totals.

To reenter the external reference formula as an array in the selected cells, press Shift+Ctrl+Enter. The formula is {='[QTR1.XLS]QTR1 93'!Qtr1.Totals}. This link is preserved no matter where you move the range Qtr1.All on the QTR1.XLS workbook, even if you move the range while the target is not open.

Freezing Links

To preserve the values from a link but remove the external reference, you can freeze the external reference portion of a formula so that portion becomes a value. To freeze an external reference, select the cell so that the formula appears in the formula bar. Click in the formula bar or press the Edit Formula key, F2, and select the external reference part of the formula by dragging across it, or by pressing Shift+left or right arrow. Choose the **T**ools **O**ptions command, select the Calculation Tab and choose Calc **N**ow, or press F9 to change the selected reference into a value. Press Enter to reenter the formula.

You also can freeze formulas by selecting the cell or range that contains the formulas and choosing the **E**dit **C**opy command. Next, choose the **E**dit Paste **S**pecial command with the **V**alues option selected and paste directly on top of the original cell or range. This procedure replaces entire formulas with their values.

Saving Linked Workbooks

When you save linked workbooks, first save the source workbook that supplies the data. Next, save the target workbooks. This procedure ensures that the target workbooks will store the correct path name and file name of their source workbooks.

If you change the name of a source workbook, be sure that target workbooks that depend upon it also are open. Save the source workbook, and then resave the target workbooks. This procedure ensures that the target workbooks record the new path name and file name of their source workbook. If a target workbook becomes unlinked from its source workbook, you can relink the workbooks by using the **E**dit Lin**k**s command.

Consolidating Worksheets

When you consolidate worksheets, Excel performs calculations on similar data across multiple worksheets and workbooks and places the results of calculations in a consolidation worksheet. You can use this capability to

Tip
If you use consolidations, be sure to review outlining. A consolidation using the **D**ata Co**n**solidate command can produce an outline automatically. The details within the outline are the sources of the consolidation.

consolidate department budgets into one division budget; you then can consolidate the division budgets into the corporate budget. Consolidations can be more than just simple totals, however. Excel also can create consolidations that calculate statistical worksheet information such as averages, standard deviations, and counts.

The data in the multiple worksheets can have identical physical layouts or can have different layouts. If the physical layouts of the supporting worksheets are the same, Excel consolidates data by working with cells from the same relative location on each supporting worksheet. If the physical layouts of the source worksheets are different, you can ask Excel to examine the row and column headings in supporting worksheets to find the data to be consolidated. This method consolidates data by consolidating those cells having the same row and column headings, regardless of their physical location.

Tip
You can analyze and consolidate database data from different sheets by using the **D**ata **P**ivot Table command (see Chs. 36 and 37).

Note

Many systems involve integrating or consolidating sheets of data from different divisions or task areas. There are three basic approaches to building this kind of system. First, you can use Excel's **D**ata Co**n**solidate or **D**ata **P**ivot Table feature to consolidate data from different sheets and workbooks into one sheet. As a second approach, you can write a macro that copies updated worksheets into a workbook. The data sheets are copied into positions between the end points of 3D formulas that total all the data sheets. In the third method, you create a consolidation sheet that contains links to sheets with specific file names. Users then can copy new data sheets, with valid file names, into the directory. The next time the consolidation sheet opens it reads the new data sheets and updates its consolidation formulas.

A common example of a consolidation occurs in corporate budgeting. A corporation accumulates all the division budget forecast worksheets into one budget forecast worksheet for the entire corporation. Each division updates its own worksheets. Each month the corporation can consolidate the individual division budget worksheets into one corporate budget worksheet. Figure 25.12 shows 12 months of budget items from 3 sources, BDG_NRT.XLS, BDG_EST.XLS, and BDG_WST.XLS, which are consolidated with the SUM( ) function into the BCONS.XLS worksheet.

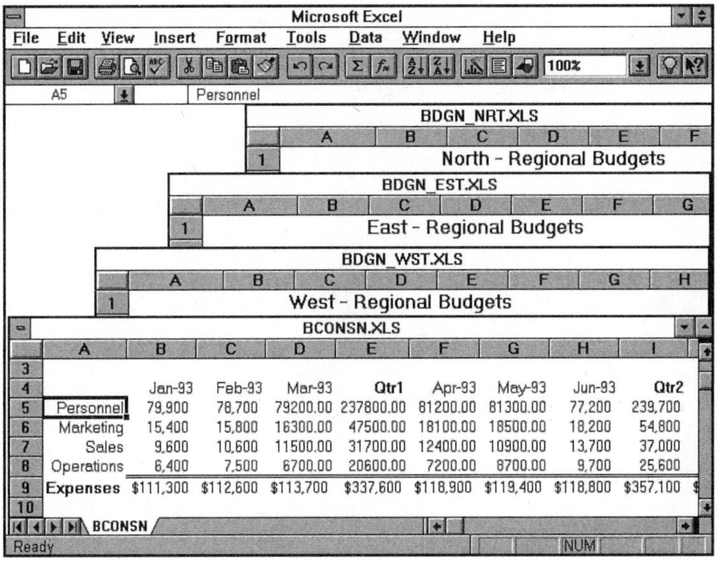

Fig. 25.12
BCONS.XLS contains a SUM( ) consolidation of three divisional budgets.

Other examples of business consolidation include sales forecasts and inventory reports. For scientific or engineering uses, consolidation can produce average or standard deviation reports. These reports can include data taken from multiple worksheets and workbooks, produced by various experiments, chromatograph analyzers, well readings, control monitors, and so on.

Tip
If your office uses a mixture of Excel and 1-2-3, remember that Excel can link and consolidate with 1-2-3 worksheets. Follow the same procedures you use for linking or consolidating with Excel workbooks.

Consolidating with 3D Formulas

You can create 3-D spearing formulas as shown in figure 25.13. In our example, there are three workbooks named SALES92.XLS, SALES93.XLS, and YTDSALES.XLS. There are four worksheets in SALES92.XLS and four in SALES93.XLS to represent each quarter's sales. There is one worksheet in YTD.SALES to represent consolidations and variances. At cell B5 in the YTD.SALES, we are consolidating first and second quarter sales for the Western region. Quarter1 sales (shown) are $58,000. Quarter 2 sales (not shown) are $35,300. The formula at B5 YTDSALES.XLS is:

```
=SUM([SALES93.XLS]QTR1:QTR2!$E$5)
```

That is, the sum of the values at E5 of worksheets QTR1 through QTR2 in the Sales93.XLS workbook is $93,000.

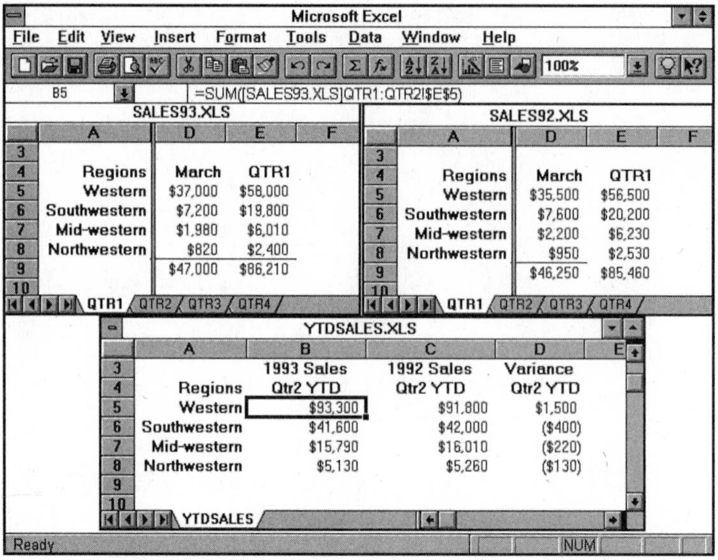

Fig. 25.13
Use 3D formulas to manually create consolidation formulas.

Understanding Consolidation

When you consolidate, Excel takes data from source areas on different worksheets and workbooks, calculates the data, and places that data onto a destination area in the consolidation worksheet. The following general steps provide an overview of consolidating multiple source areas into a destination area:

1. Select the destination area where you want the consolidation to appear.

2. Specify the source ranges that hold the data to be consolidated. A consolidation can have as many as 255 source ranges. The sources do not have to be open during consolidation.

3. Select the way that you want to consolidate the cells: by cell position with the source range or by the row or column headings in the source ranges.

4. Select what you want the destination area to contain: fixed values that do not change or links that update when the sources change.

5. Select one of the following types of consolidation:

   AVERAGE
   COUNT
   COUNTA

MAX
MIN
PRODUCT
STDEV
STDEVP
SUM
VAR
VARP

Consolidations are handled differently in the destination worksheet, depending on the layout of the destination area that you select, as shown in table 25.1.

Table 25.1 Destinations and Consolidation Results

Destination Selection	Consolidation Result
One cell	Uses as much room on the destination worksheet as needed to consolidate all the categories (items) from the sources.
Row of cells	Fills the consolidation down from the selection. The destination area is only as wide as your selection.
Column of cells	Fills the consolidation to the right of the selection. The destination area is only as tall as your selection.
Range	Consolidates as many categories into the destination as will fit. You are warned if the destination area is not large enough to hold the consolidation.

Consolidating Worksheets by Physical Layout

Consolidate worksheets by their physical layout if the data items, such as budget labels, are in the same position within each source range. The actual location of the source range may be different on each source worksheet. The destination range will have the same layout as the source range. To consolidate by layout, perform the following steps:

1. Select a destination range as described in table 25.1.

   Select only the data range, because text does not consolidate and because you won't want to consolidate dates used as headings.

2. Choose the **D**ata Co**n**solidate command to display the Consolidate dialog box, shown in figure 25.14.

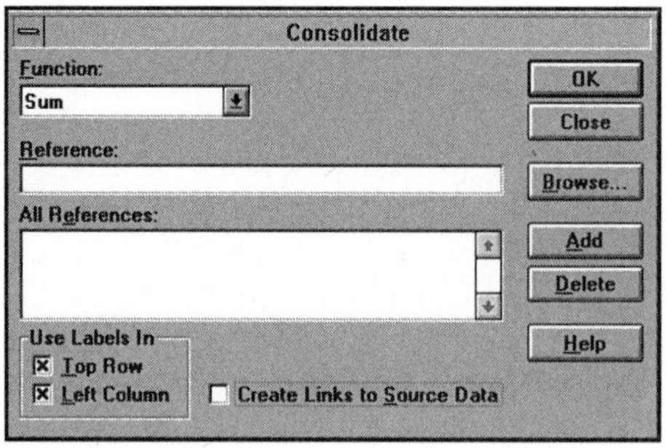

Fig. 25.14
Consolidate open or closed sheets using the Consolidate dialog box.

3. Select the **R**eference text box, and select or type a source area. Use an external reference of a form like =[BDG_WST.XLS]BDG_WST!$B$5:$Q$8. You can select an area in any open worksheet by clicking and dragging, although the destination worksheet remains the active worksheet. If the source worksheet is on disk, you can type its full path name and source area enclosed in single quotes.

   If the source worksheet is open and you use a mouse, click a source worksheet; or choose the **W**indow menu to activate the source worksheet. Select the source area on the worksheet by clicking it or dragging across it. Move the dialog box, if necessary.

   If the source worksheet is open and you use the keyboard, press Ctrl+F6; or choose the **W**indow menu to activate the source worksheet. Select the source area by moving to it and then holding the Shift key as you press arrow keys to select, or use the F8 key to extend the selection. Move the dialog box, if necessary.

   If the source worksheet is closed, choose the **B**rowse button. The standard File Open dialog box appears. Select the file name you want and choose OK. Excel enters the file name; you must type a range reference or range name.

4. Choose the **A**dd button to add the source entry to the All R**e**ferences list. The Excel screen will now look similar to the screen in figure 25.15, where the BCONSN.XLS worksheet is the destination and the source area is one of the BDGN_*.XLS division worksheets.

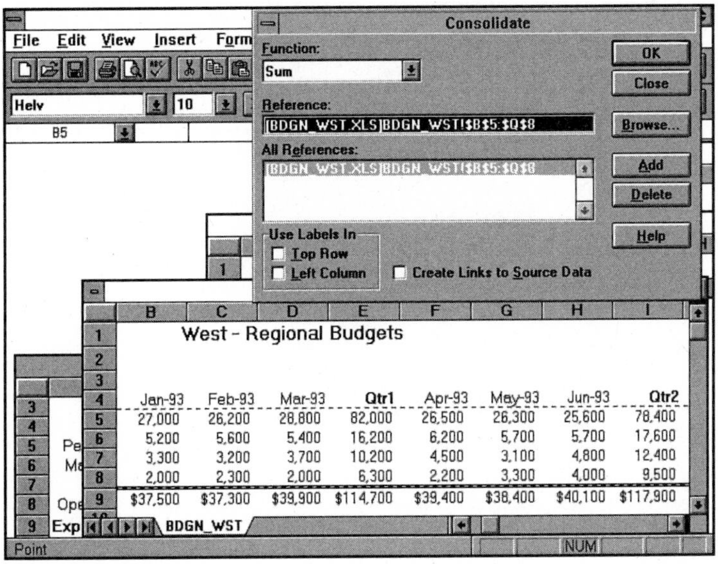

Fig. 25.15
The All **Re**ferences list shows the source sheets and ranges to be consolidated.

5. Repeat steps 3 and 4 to add all the source areas to the All **Re**ferences list. If you name all your source worksheets with similar file names and the source worksheets use the same range names, you only need to edit the **R**eference text box.

6. Select the type of consolidation you want from the **F**unction list.

7. Clear the Use Labels In **T**op Row and **L**eft Column check boxes.

   The consolidation in this procedure uses cell position within the source range, not labels in the row or column headings.

8. Select the Create Links to **S**ource Data check box if you want the destination range to be linked to the source range.

   Linking the source ranges to the destination ranges makes the consolidation an outline. Consolidation outlines are described at the end of this chapter.

9. Choose OK or press Enter.

The finished consolidation is shown in figure 25.16.

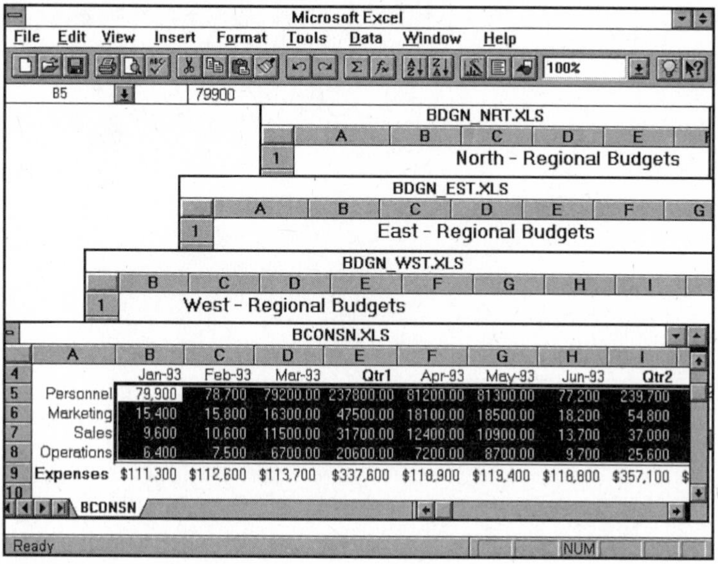

Fig. 25.16
The consolidation sheet will contain the totals derived from the source sheet.

Tip
To build identical worksheets, save a master worksheet under a different name. To create worksheets with matching text labels and layouts, or to make only a portion of different worksheets the same, create a Group Worksheet where edits and entries made in the active worksheet are repeated in other worksheets in the group. See Chapter 8, "Reorganizing Workbooks and Sheets."

Note

Do not include date headings in a consolidation by position. Excel treats the serial date number in a cell as a number to be consolidated. The serial date number throws off the consolidation of numeric data.

Be aware of how much space the consolidation will take if you select one cell as the destination area. One cell can use an unlimited destination area, which means that as many rows and columns are used for the consolidation as necessary. The consolidation may cover cells containing information you need.

Text and formulas within the source area are not brought into the destination area. Only values are brought in and formatted. If you are consolidating on a blank worksheet, copy text from divisional worksheets for use as headings.

You can reduce problems caused in moving or rearranging source areas. Use the **I**nsert **N**ame **D**efine command to name the source range on each source worksheet with the same range name. Edit the source areas in the **R**eference text box so that it references range names rather than cell references.

Consolidating Worksheets by Row and Column Headings

You usually don't want to consolidate worksheets by position. Doing so means that each division's worksheet must have exactly the same line items and column headings in the same order. The various divisions, for example, may have separate budget items or different sales territories selling different products. When you use the following method, source worksheets can contain different items and the headings can be ordered differently, yet the consolidation still works.

When source worksheets have data in different locations or when source worksheets contain different categories to be consolidated, use the names in row or column headings to consolidate. With this method, Excel consolidates data according to the row and column headings of a piece of data and not by the data's cell location. This method is the most flexible way to consolidate. The actual location of the data may be different on each source area.

To consolidate by headings, perform the following steps:

1. Select a destination area. If you want headings in a specific order, include the row or column headings that you want to use as consolidation categories. The headings must be spelled the same as in the source worksheets. If you do not enter headings, Excel will create them for you.

2. Choose the **D**ata Co**n**solidate command.

3. Select the **R**eference text box, and then select or type a source range. Include row and column headings in the source range. You can select the source range from an open worksheet. If the source worksheet is on disk, you can type its full path name and source range enclosed in single quotes. Use the form =[BDGN_EST.XLS]BDGN_EST!$A$4:$R$8.

   If the source worksheet is open and you are using a mouse, click a source worksheet; or choose the **W**indow menu and select a worksheet. Select the source area on the worksheet by clicking it or dragging across it. Move the dialog box, if necessary.

   If the source worksheet is open and you are using the keyboard, press Ctrl+F6; or choose the **W**indow menu to activate the source worksheet. Select the source area by moving to it and then holding the Shift key as you press arrow keys to select, or use the F8 key to extend the selection. Move the dialog box, if necessary.

If the source worksheet is closed, choose the **B**rowse button. The standard File Open dialog box appears. You then can select the file name you want and choose OK. Excel enters the file name; you must type a range reference or range name.

4. Choose the **A**dd button to add the source entry to the All R**e**ferences list.

5. Repeat steps 3 and 4 to add all the source areas to the All R**e**ferences list.

6. Select the type of consolidation that you want from the **F**unction list.

7. Select the headings in the source areas by which you want to consolidate. Select one or both of the following: the Use Labels In **T**op Row and the **L**eft Column check boxes.

8. Select the Create Links to **S**ource Data check box if you want the destination area to be linked to the source areas. This step makes the consolidation an outline. (Consolidation outlines are described at the end of this chapter.)

9. Choose OK or press Enter.

When you use headings to consolidate, you can specify which categories to consolidate and the order in which you want categories placed in the destination area. Enter the headings in the top row or left column of the destination area. Then include those headings in the selection you make before you start consolidation (step 1 in the preceding instructions).

Figure 25.17 shows a destination area with headings down the left column in an order different from the headings in the source areas. Notice that after consolidation, Excel has arranged the consolidated data in the correct rows by headings (see fig. 25.18).

Reduce problems caused by moving or rearranging source areas by editing the source areas in the **R**eference text box to use range names instead of cell references.

Deleting or Editing Links

You can add new source ranges to the All R**e**ferences list by opening the Consolidate dialog box, selecting the **R**eference text box, and then selecting the source range on a worksheet. Choose the **A**dd button to add the new range area to the All R**e**ferences list.

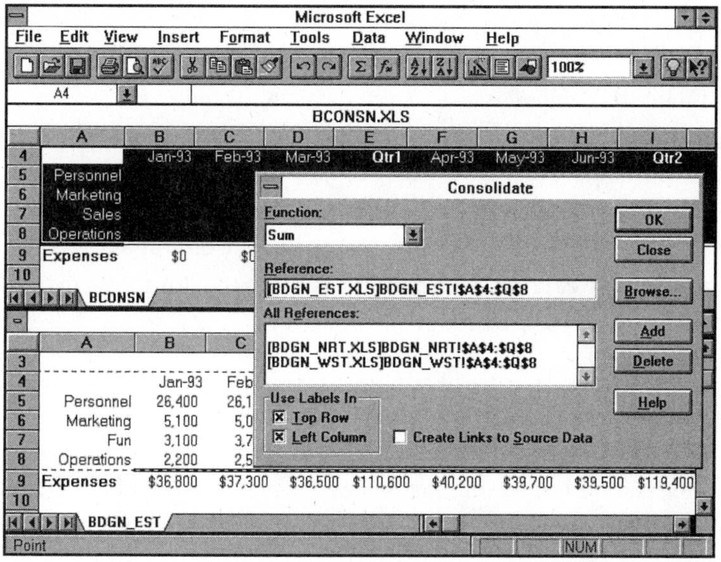

Fig. 25.17
Consolidation by heading enables you to reorder the consolidation layout.

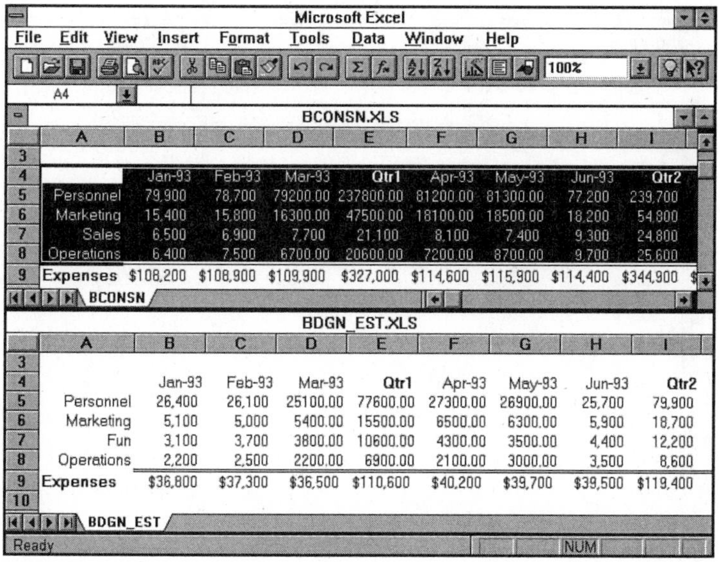

Fig. 25.18
Consolidation by labels rather than position is less error prone.

Delete source ranges from future consolidations by selecting the source range in the All R**e**ferences list and then choosing the **D**elete button.

Edit a source area by selecting it from the All R**e**ferences list, editing it in the **R**eference text box, and then choosing the **A**dd button. Delete the original source area from the list, if necessary.

Linking Consolidated Worksheets

When you select the Create Links to **S**ource Data check box, Excel consolidates and inserts detailed rows/columns that are linked to the source data in rows and columns between the consolidated results. These inserted rows and columns contain external reference formulas that link cells in the consolidation area to cells in each source area. These new rows and columns become part of a worksheet outline. The highest level of the outline shows the consolidation; the lower levels of the outline contain the links to source worksheets. Chapter 18, "Outlining Worksheets," describes worksheet outlining in more detail.

Figure 25.19 shows a destination area in DCONLINK.XLS created with headings and linking selected. Figure 25.20 shows the same destination area with the outline feature turned on. The highest level of the outline is the consolidation. Lower levels contain links that feed into the consolidation.

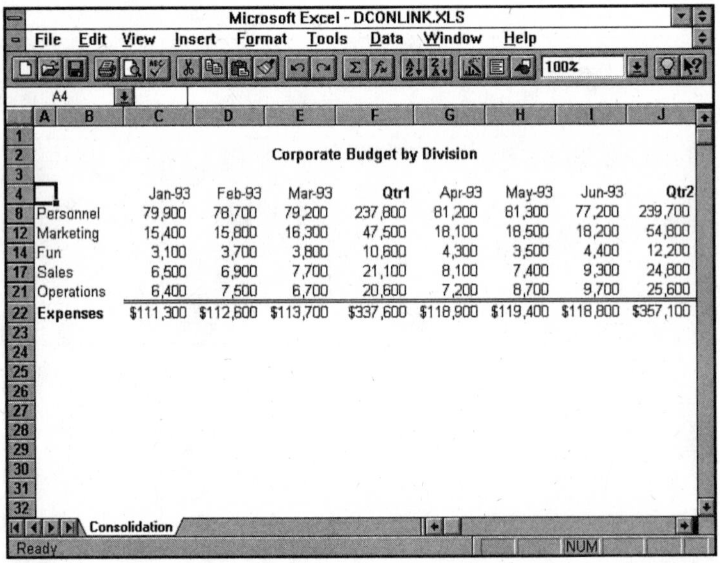

	Jan-93	Feb-93	Mar-93	Qtr1	Apr-93	May-93	Jun-93	Qtr2
Personnel	79,900	78,700	79,200	237,800	81,200	81,300	77,200	239,700
Marketing	15,400	15,800	16,300	47,500	18,100	18,500	18,200	54,800
Fun	3,100	3,700	3,800	10,600	4,300	3,500	4,400	12,200
Sales	6,500	6,900	7,700	21,100	8,100	7,400	9,300	24,800
Operations	6,400	7,500	6,700	20,600	7,200	8,700	9,700	25,600
Expenses	$111,300	$112,600	$113,700	$337,600	$118,900	$119,400	$118,800	$357,100

Fig. 25.19
This destination area does not have outlining turned on.

Formatting Consolidated Worksheets

You need to understand the relation of linked consolidations and outlines for two important reasons. You can give each level in an outline and the linked consolidation a different formatting style; you can expand or contract linked consolidations to show summary or detail views of the consolidated data.

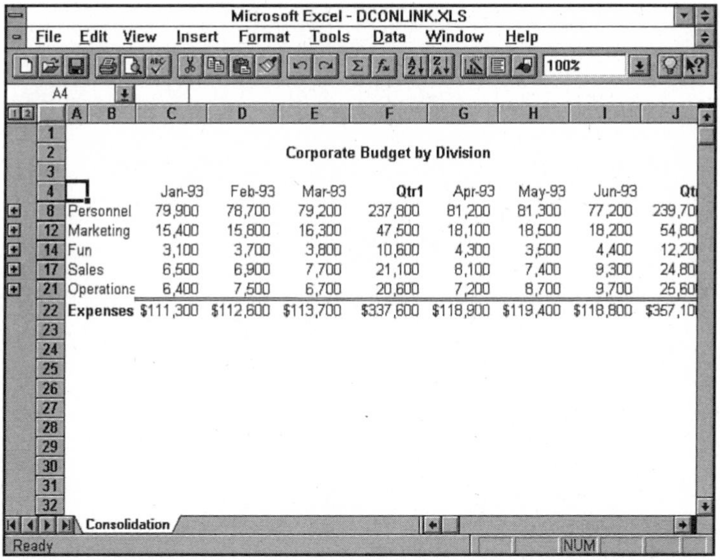

Fig. 25.20
Outlining makes it easy to show or hide detail in a consolidation.

By clicking the row-level buttons on the left side of the screen (shown with a plus sign, as in figure 25.20), the outline for rows opens to reveal the links that supply the consolidated cells. Figure 25.21 shows the hidden rows revealed. The consolidation results are actually SUM( ) functions that total the external references in these hidden rows.

If you double-click a detail row, its source worksheet will open and activate.

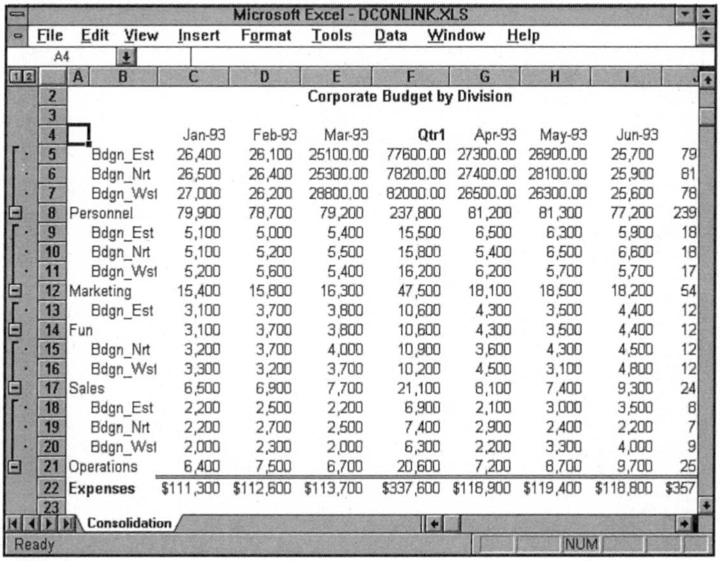

Fig. 25.21
Expanded outlines show the detail as well as the link to the source.

To apply outline styles to an existing linked consolidation, select the destination area, choose the **D**ata **G**roup and Outline S**e**ttings command. Select the **A**utomatic Styles option. Choose OK. Refer to Chapter 18, "Outlining Worksheets," for information on outlining. Refer to Chapter 10, "Formatting Worksheets," to learn how to change the definitions of outline styles to produce the outline formatting you want.

Consolidating Worksheets Manually

When you need to transfer only values between worksheets and you do not want these values automatically updated, use **E**dit Paste **S**pecial. With Paste **S**pecial, you combine the values from one worksheet into another. Paste **S**pecial enables you to combine data by pasting values or by adding, subtracting, multiplying, or dividing values with existing cell contents. Because a link is not established, values are not updated when the supporting worksheet changes.

To consolidate data between worksheets, use **E**dit **C**opy to copy cell contents from one worksheet. Activate the other worksheet and paste with the **E**dit Paste **S**pecial command. Select the **V**alues option to paste the values from the source worksheet. To perform a math operation with the data as it is pasted, select a math operation such as A**d**d from the Operation option group.

From Here...

Excel's capability of displaying multiple worksheets, linking pictures, and linking or consolidating open or disk-based worksheets gives your systems a great deal of flexibility and power.

Chapter 26

Auditing Workbooks and Worksheets

In this chapter, you learn how to:

- Troubleshoot error messages
- View cell information
- Use Excel's Auditing tools
- Check spelling
- Add notes and voice messages to the worksheet

Surveys show that 30 percent of all electronic worksheets contain errors. This statistic can be terrifying but believable when you consider that most users receive little or no training, and few are trained in designing or auditing worksheets. Few companies have policies for auditing or documenting worksheets.

Correct worksheets require careful planning and execution. Always be sure that you cross-check and review a new worksheet before using it for a critical decision. Excel has built-in commands, macros, and error values to help you discover trouble spots in your worksheets.

Troubleshooting Error Messages

Excel cannot evaluate a formula or function.

The program displays an error value in the offending cell. Error values begin with a pound sign (#). Excel has seven kinds of error values with self-explanatory names. Brief explanations of the seven error values follow.

`#DIV/0!` *The formula or macro is attempting to divide by zero.*

Examine cell references for blanks or zeros. You may have accidentally deleted an area of the worksheet needed by this formula. An incorrectly written formula may be attempting to divide by zero.

`#N/A` *The formula refers to a cell that has a #N/A entry.*

You can type *#N/A* in mandatory data-entry cells. Then, if data isn't entered to replace the *#N/A*, formulas that depend on this cell display #N/A. This error value warns you that not all the data was entered. Or it is possible that an array argument is the wrong size, and #N/A is returned in some cells. Another possibility is that HLOOKUP(), VLOOKUP(), LOOKUP(), MATCH(), or other functions have incorrect arguments. In some instances, these functions return an error value when they cannot find a match.

It's possible that you omitted an argument from a function. If Excel cannot correctly evaluate the arguments that you entered, some functions return #N/A. See the function's description in Chapter 6, "Using Functions," for more information about the function.

#NAME? *Excel does not recognize a name.*

Use the **I**nsert **N**ame **D**efine command to see whether the name exists. Create a name, if necessary. Verify the spelling of the name. Make sure that no spaces exist in the name.

As another possibility, verify that functions are spelled correctly. Spaces are fine except between the function name and the opening parenthesis. Novice users frequently type a space between the last character in the function name and the first parenthesis.

See whether you used text in a formula without enclosing the text in quotation marks. Excel considers the text as a name rather than as text.

Check whether you mistyped an address or range so that this information appears to Excel as a name, such as the cell ABB5 (two Bs) or the range B12C45 (a missing :).

See whether you referred to an incorrect or nonexistent name in a linked worksheet.

#NULL! *The formula specifies two areas that don't intersect.*

See whether the cell or range reference is entered incorrectly.

#NUM! *The formula has a problem with a number.*

See whether the numeric argument is out of the acceptable range of inputs, or whether the function can find an answer given the arguments you entered.

#REF! *The cell reference is incorrect.*

See whether you have deleted cells, rows, or columns referenced by formulas. Other causes may include indexes that exceed a range used in a function or offsets that are outside worksheet boundaries.

See whether external worksheet references are still valid. Chapter 25, "Linking, Embedding, and Consolidating Worksheets," covers linking worksheets.

See whether a macro has returned a #REF! value from an unopened or incorrect function macro.

See whether a Dynamic Data Exchange (DDE) topic is incorrectly entered or is not available.

#VALUE! *The value is not the kind expected by the argument or the result from an intersect operation when the ranges being evaluated do not intersect.*

Verify that values used as arguments are of the kind listed in Chapter 6, "Using Functions."

Viewing Worksheet Information

Changing what is displayed in your worksheet can help you audit a worksheet. You can, for instance, display the formulas (rather than the results), and you can display an information window that lists formulas, names, formats, notes, and other information associated with a cell.

Viewing Formulas

When auditing a worksheet, you want to see more than one formula or determine the range names that a cell is part of.

To switch the worksheet to display formulas, follow these steps:

1. Choose the **T**ools **O**ptions command.
2. Select the View tab.
3. Select the Fo**r**mulas option.
4. Choose OK.

Figure 26.1 shows a worksheet with the formulas displayed.

Fig. 26.1
By displaying the formulas, you can see how the information flows through a worksheet.

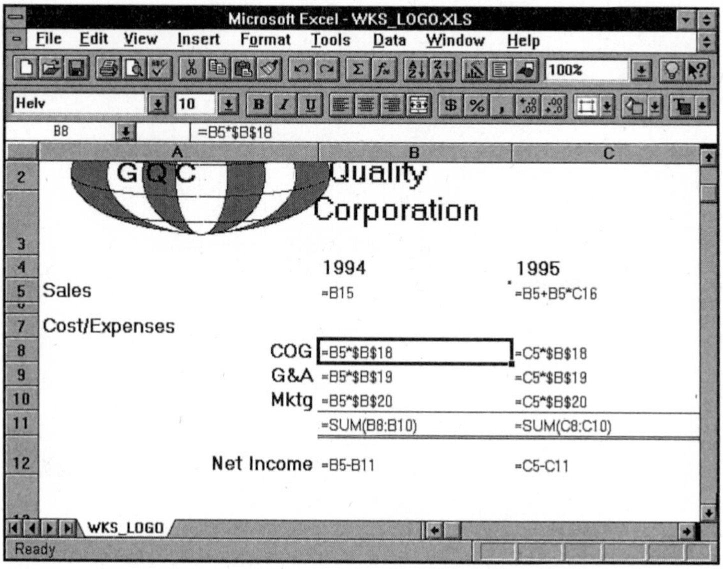

Tip
Press the shortcut key Ctrl+` (grave accent) to switch between viewing results and viewing formulas.

Open a second window to the worksheet with the **W**indow **N**ew Window command; and then format one worksheet to show results and the other to show formulas.

Viewing Cell Information

To see the range names, formulas, and formats that involve a cell, follow these steps:

1. Select the cell.
2. Choose the **T**ools **O**ptions command.
3. Choose the View tab.
4. Select the Info **W**indow check box to display an Information window. A new menu appears while the Info Window is active.
5. Choose OK.
6. From the **I**nfo menu, select the attributes you want to see about the active cell: **C**ell, Fo**r**mula, **V**alue, Forma**t**, Pr**o**tection, Na**m**es, **P**recedents, **D**ependents, and **N**ote.

Tip
Leave the Information window open. When you select a new cell, you can switch to the Info window for this cell by pressing Ctrl+F6.

Figure 26.2 shows an Info window with the cell, formula, and format listed.

If you selected exactly the same cells used by a range name, the name appears in the Reference area at the top left corner of the worksheet.

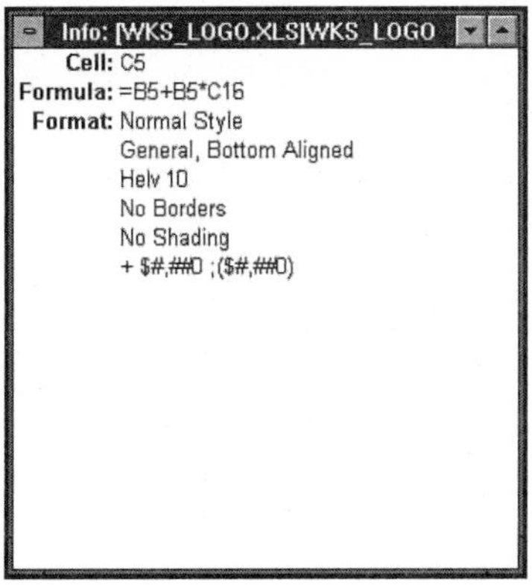

Fig. 26.2
The cell information can show you the formula, the selected format, and other information about the selected cell.

Finding Errors by Selecting Special Cells

The **E**dit **G**o To **S**pecial command is a powerful ally in auditing and troubleshooting a worksheet. From the Go To Special dialog box, you can select specific parts of a worksheet or cell contents. You can move to the specific cells and more easily correct any errors.

To select special cells, follow these steps:

1. Choose the **E**dit **G**o To command.
2. Choose the Special button. The Go To Special dialog box appears (see fig. 26.3).

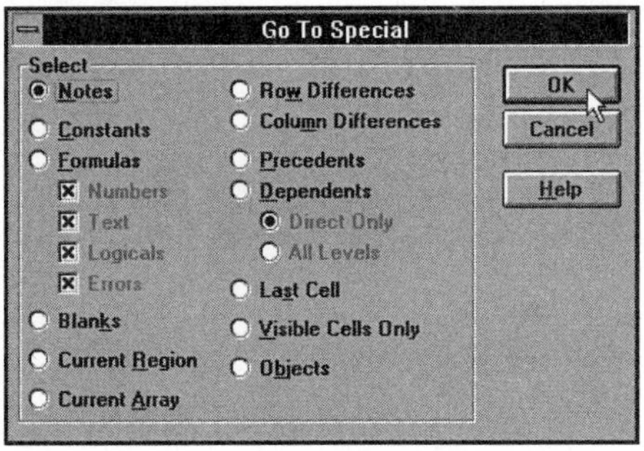

Fig. 26.3
Select the kinds of cells you want to select.

3. Select the options you want. Table 26.1 describes the options you can use when auditing a worksheet.
4. Choose OK.

Tip
Press F5 to select the Go To command.

Table 26.1 Formula Select Special Options Used in Auditing

Option	Action
Notes	Selects cells that contain notes.
Constants	Specifies that constants are selected.
Formulas	Specifies that formulas with results of the type you specify are selected. Other formula options:
N**u**mbers	Selects constants or formulas that result in numbers.
Text	Selects constants or formulas that result in text.
Logicals	Selects constants or formulas that result in logicals (true/false).
Errors	Selects cells with error values.
Blan**k**s	Selects blank cells.
Current **R**egion	Selects region.
Current **A**rray	Selects array.
Ro**w** Differences	Selects cells in the same row that have a different reference *pattern.*
Colu**m**n Differences	Selects cells in the same column that have a different reference *pattern.*
Precedents	Selects cells that support the active cell.
Dependents	Selects cells that depend on the active cell.
D**i**rect Only	Selects cells that immediately feed or depend on the active cell.
All **L**evels	Selects cells that feed into or depend on the active cell at all levels.
La**s**t Cell	Selects last cell that contains data formatting.
Visible Cells Only	Selects only cells presently visible on-screen.
O**b**jects	Selects all graphics objects.

Finding errors such as `#REF!` or `#N/A` in a worksheet or in a range is easy. Select the **F**ormulas option and deselect all check boxes except the **E**rrors check box.

When you debug a worksheet, find the cells that feed information in the active cell and the cells that depend on the results in the active cell. To see which cells feed into the active cell, select the **P**recedents option; to see cells that depend on the active cell, select the **D**ependents option. The D**i**rect Only option selects cells that immediately feed or depend on the active cell. The All **L**evels option selects cells that feed into or depend on the active cell at all levels. The D**i**rect Only option is like selecting only your parents or your children. The All **L**evels option is like selecting the entire family tree, backward or forward.

Tip
An easier way to trace precedents and dependents is to use the auditing tools, which are described in the section "Using Excel's Auditing Tools."

Caution

Typing a number over a formula is a common error in worksheets. To see cells that contain formulas and cells that contain values, select the range you want to troubleshoot and select the **C**onstants or **F**ormulas options from the Go To Special dialog box. Usually, you leave all the related check boxes selected. You may be surprised to find a constant value in the middle of what you believed were formulas!

For Related Information

■ "Selecting Cells by Type of Content," p. 83

Press Tab or Shift+Tab to move the active cell between the selected cells, while keeping all other cells selected. Read each cell's contents in the formula bar until you find the cell that contains an error.

Using Excel's Auditing Tools

EXCEL 5

Excel provides some auditing tools that enable you to visually troubleshoot and audit your worksheet. Tracer arrows show you the flow of formulas and results in a worksheet. Error tracers can help you track down errors.

To best display the arrows, turn off the worksheet gridlines by choosing the **T**ools **O**ptions command. Select the View tab; then uncheck the **G**ridlines check box.

While you are in the View tab of the Options dialog box, be sure that Show **A**ll or Show **P**laceholders from the Objects group is selected. If objects are hidden, you won't see the tracers.

Tracing the Flow of Data and Formulas

To trace the flow of data and formulas, follow these steps:

1. Select the cell you want to trace.

   This cell can either contain a formula, be referenced in a formula, or contain an error message.

2. Choose the **T**ools **A**uditing command.

3. Choose one of the following commands:

Trace Precedents	Choose this command when you have selected a formula and want to see which cells are used in the formula. Choose the command again to see the next level of precedents.
Trace **D**ependents	Choose this command when you have selected a cell referenced in other formulas. You see which formulas reference this cell. To see the next level of dependents, choose the command again.
Trace **E**rror	Choose this command when the cell contains an error message and you want to see what cells are referenced in the formula.

If the selected cell is not appropriate for the option you choose, you see a message telling you so. Click OK and select a different option.

The tracer lines show the flow of data through the worksheet by connecting the active cell with related cells. The line ends with an arrow pointing to a formula.

When the tracer arrow is tracing a formula, the line is solid blue. Figure 26.4 shows an example of tracing the first level of precedents. Figure 26.5 shows an example of tracing the first level of dependents.

When you trace an error, a red line points to the source of the first error value. Blue arrows may also point to possible wrong values that are included in the first formula. The tracer selects the cell where the error and formula arrows meet so that you can audit the formula.

If more than one error is along the path, the tracer stops at the intersection of the errors so that you can choose which way to continue.

When you trace a formula that references external data, the line is dashed black and displays an icon.

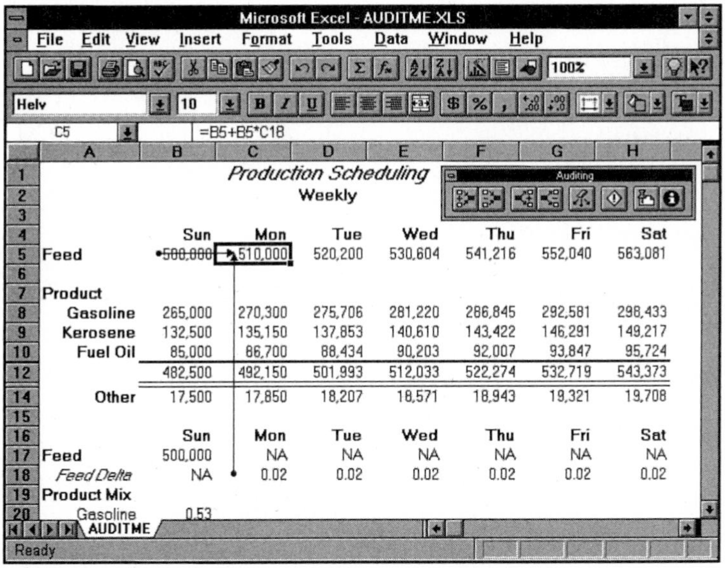

Fig. 26.4
Tracing the precedents in a formula.

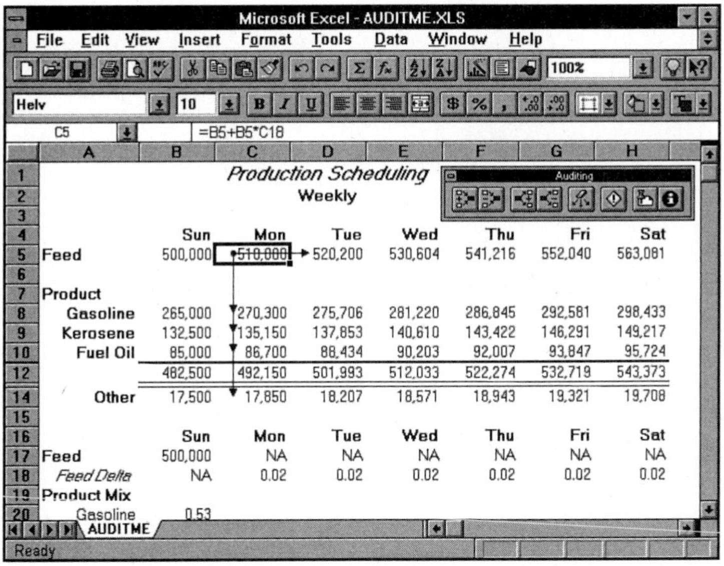

Fig. 26.5
Arrows trace the dependents. Double-click the arrow to move to the dependent.

You can move along the path drawn by the auditing tool by double-clicking the arrow.

Note

When you make some editing changes—such as change a formula in a tracer path, or insert or delete rows—the tracer arrows disappear.

Using the Auditing Toolbar

If you prefer to use the toolbar rather than the menu commands, you can. First, display the toolbar by choosing the **T**ools **A**uditing **S**how Auditing Toolbar command. Table 26.2 lists each button on the toolbar along with a description.

Table 26.2 Auditing Toolbar

Button	Name	Description
	Trace Precedents	Click this button once to show direct precedents. Click again to show additional levels of indirect precedents.
	Remove Precedent Arrows	Click this button to remove tracer arrows from one level of precedents. If more than one level is displayed, click the button again to remove next level of tracer arrows.
	Trace Dependents	Click this button once to show formulas that directly reference this cell. Click again to show additional levels of indirect dependents.
	Remove Dependent Arrows	Click this button to remove tracer arrows from one level of dependents. If more than one level is displayed, click the button again to remove the next level of tracer arrows.
	Remove All Arrows	Click this button to remove all tracer arrows in the worksheet.
	Trace Error	Click this button to display tracer arrows to the source of the error.
	Attach Note	Click this button to display the Cell Note dialog box and add a note.
	Show Info Window	Click this button to display the Info window.

Checking Spelling

Excel has a built-in spell checker that gives you the confidence your spelling matches the accuracy of your numbers. With Excel's dictionary, you can check one word, the entire worksheet, or even a chart. You also can check against a custom dictionary that contains abbreviations or words specific to your clients or industry.

Using the Standard Dictionary

When Excel checks the spelling on a worksheet, it checks more than just cell contents; it checks embedded charts, text boxes, and buttons.

To spell check a document, perform the following steps:

1. Select a single cell if you want to spell check the entire contents of a document. Select a range, embedded chart, or object to limit the check to the selected item. Select a single word or phrase in the formula bar to check individual words.

2. Choose the **T**ools **S**pelling command or click the Spelling button on the Standard toolbar.

   If a word cannot be found in the standard or custom dictionary, the Spelling dialog box, shown in figure 26.6, appears. The word appears at the top left corner after `Not in Dictionary`. Depending on the setting of the Alwa**y**s Suggest check box, the suggested alternate spelling may show in the Suggestio**n**s list.

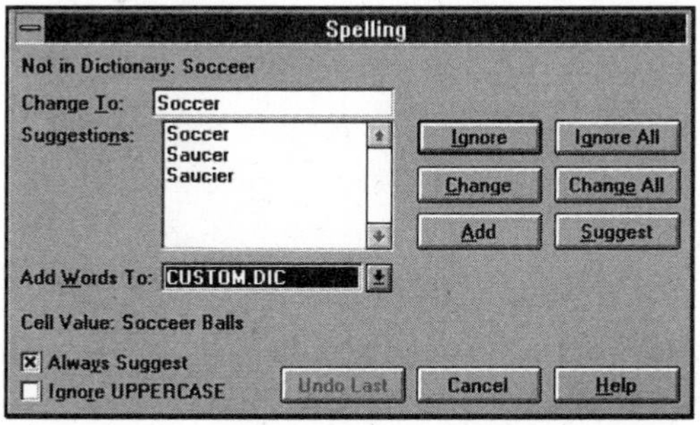

Fig. 26.6
When Excel finds a spelling error, you can choose to ignore, replace with the correct spelling in the Suggestions list, or add the word to the dictionary.

   If no misspelled words are found, the Spelling dialog box never appears. A dialog box appears and tells you that the word in the formula bar or the document has no misspelled words.

3. Accept or edit the word in the Change **T**o text box; and then choose the **C**hange button. Choose the Chang**e** All button to change this word throughout the document.

   Alternatively, select one of the words from the Suggestions list, and then choose the **C**hange button. Choose the Chang**e** All button to change this word throughout the document.

   You can also choose one of these alternatives:

Ignore	Ignore this word and continue.
I**g**nore All	Ignore this word throughout the document.
Add	Add this word to the current custom dictionary.
Suggest	Suggest some alternatives from the dictionary.
Cancel	Stop the spell check.
Help	Display a window of help on how to use spell checking.

   If Excel did not spell check the contents above the starting point, you are asked whether you want to continue the check from the top of the sheet.

4. If prompted, choose **Y**es to continue from the top of the document. You can choose Cancel at any time to stop spell checking.

5. When an alert box tells you that the entire worksheet has been checked, choose OK to complete the spell check.

Tip
Press F7 to choose the **T**ools **S**pelling command.

If you prefer to see possible correct words in the Suggestion list, select the Alwa**y**s Suggest check box. Spell checking may take longer when you request suggestions. If you want to skip over words that are in uppercase, such as part numbers, account codes, and IDs, select the Igno**r**e UPPERCASE check box.

Note

To use Excel's built-in spell checker, you must have installed the spell checking utility. If you did not install spell checking during initial installation, you can repeat the installation and select to install only spell checking.

Creating Custom Dictionaries. You may need a custom dictionary with your worksheets so that you are not frequently prompted to verify the spelling of client names, abbreviations, product codes, industry terms, and so on. When Excel checks spelling, it looks first at the standard dictionary. If Excel doesn't find the word there, it checks the custom dictionary. You can have multiple custom dictionaries; however, only one can be selected for each spell check.

Unless you specify otherwise, words you add go into the dictionary named CUSTOM.DIC. This name appears in the Add **W**ords To drop-down list in the Spelling dialog box. You can build your own custom dictionaries and select them from the list. You can have as many custom dictionaries as you like, but only one can operate at a time with the standard dictionary.

To create a new custom dictionary, perform the following steps:

1. Choose the **T**ools **S**pelling command.
2. Type the dictionary name in the Add **W**ords To text box.
3. Choose the **A**dd or Cancel button. Choosing **A**dd adds the current word to the dictionary.

   A dialog box appears, asking whether you want to create a new custom dictionary.
4. Choose **Y**es to create a new dictionary.

Tip
Custom dictionary files are stored in a spelling directory specified in the WIN.INI file. The default location for this directory is WINDOWS\MSAPPS\PROOF.

At any time when the Spell dialog box is open, you can change to a different custom dictionary by selecting the dictionary from the Add **W**ords To list.

To add words to your custom dictionary, start the spell check. When you want to add a word to a custom dictionary, select the dictionary from the Add **W**ords To list and choose the **A**dd button.

Adding Notes and Voice Messages

You can attach notes and voice messages to cells in a worksheet or database. Notes appear in special dialog boxes or are printed when you request. You attach notes to cells for two reasons: to preserve your sanity and to preserve your business.

You can attach voice messages to cells and play them back for the same purpose as text notes. They help you give more information than what is shown on the worksheet. Voice messages can add more emphasis and personality to a message. Voice also is the first of many ways in which Windows applications such as Excel will be able to enhance documents.

Using Text Notes

Include in notes any information that helps the next person using the worksheet. That next person might be you in two months, after you have forgotten how and why the worksheet operates.

You can put many things in a note. In cell A1, you can put the following:

- The author's name
- The auditor's name
- The date the worksheet was last audited

In data-entry cells, you can put the following:

- The worksheets assumptions
- Any data-entry limits
- The historical significance of a value (such as the high sale of the year)

In formula cells, you can put the following:

- The origin or verification of a formula
- Any analytical comments about a result

Creating Text Notes. To create a text note, perform the following steps:

1. Select the cell you want to contain the note.
2. Choose the **I**nsert No**t**e command or press Shift+F2 to display the Cell Note dialog box (see fig. 26.7).
3. Enter text in the **T**ext Note area.

   If you need to move to a new line, press Alt+Enter.
4. Choose OK when the note is completed.

A small red dot at the top right corner of a cell indicates that the cell contains a note.

Tip
To turn on or off the indicator dots in the display, choose the **T**ools **O**ptions command and select the View tab. Select or clear the **N**ote Indicator option.

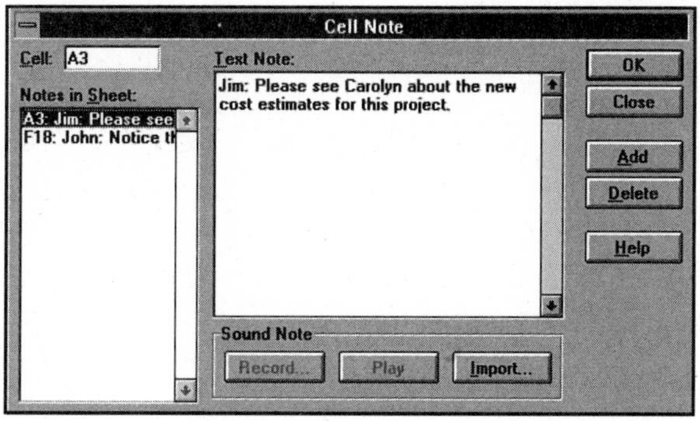

Fig. 26.7
Type the text of the note. From the Cell Note dialog box, you can also delete and view other notes in the worksheet.

The Notes in **S**heet box in the Cell Note dialog box lists all the notes in the worksheet preceded by their cell references. When you select a note from the list, the text appears in the **T**ext Note box, and the cell reference appears in the **C**ell box. You can view another note by selecting it from the Notes in **S**heet list.

The **A**dd button adds information from the **T**ext Note box to the cell shown in the **C**ell box. This method enables you to add new notes to cells without having to return to the worksheet. You can enter cell references in the **C**ell box by typing them, or by clicking the **C**ell box and then clicking the cell in the worksheet.

Displaying, Finding, and Printing Notes. If the **N**ote Indicator option is selected, a red dot appears in the top right corners of cells containing notes. To display the note behind a cell, select the cell and press Shift+F2. Select all the cells that contain notes by choosing the **E**dit **G**o To command and choosing the **S**pecial button. Then select the **N**otes option (you also can press Ctrl+Shift+?). Move between the cells containing notes with Tab or Shift+Tab.

Use the **E**dit **F**ind command to search quickly through cells and find a note that contains a pertinent word. Select the **L**ook in Notes option in the Find dialog box.

Tip
To quickly view the note attached to a cell, select the cell and then press Shift+F2.

You can print the notes in a worksheet by choosing the **F**ile Page Set**u**p command. Select the Sheet tab and then the **N**otes option. Then print the worksheet.

Editing a Text Note. To edit a note, select the cell and choose the **I**nsert No**t**e command. Edit the note as you normally edit text in Excel. Then choose OK. To delete a note, select it from the Notes in **S**heet box, and then choose the **D**elete button.

Using Sound Messages

Sound messages can carry greater emphasis than text notes. Leaving a voice explanation in Excel is one of the first examples of how personal computers can incorporate different media within a frequently used business application.

> **Note**
>
> To record sound messages, you need a Windows-compatible sound board installed in your computer and a microphone matched to that sound board. You also must be using Excel and Windows 3.0 with Microsoft's Multimedia Extensions 1.0 or later or Windows 3.1 or later. The Que book, *Using Windows 3.1*, Special Edition, describes how to install the drivers and use embedded voice messages in many Windows applications.

Recording Sound Messages. If your system is capable of recording sound, follow these steps to leave a message in a cell:

1. Select the cell to which you want to add a voice message.
2. Choose the **I**nsert No**t**e command.
3. Choose the **R**ecord button.

   The Record dialog box appears. You can record for up to 2 minutes. The scale shows you the length of your recording. The graph shows you your voice modulation.
4. Begin recording your message.
5. Choose the appropriate VCR-type button to replay, pause, rewind, or re-record your message.
6. Choose the **S**top button to stop the recording.

   You can replay your recorded message by choosing the rewind control and then choosing the Replay button.
7. Choose OK to enter the voice message.

Importing a Sound Message. If you used the Windows Sound Recorder accessory or other Windows multimedia software to record a voice or other sound message, you can import the .WAV file that contains the sound.

To import a sound file into a note:

1. Choose the **I**nsert No**t**e command.
2. Choose the **I**mport button from the Note dialog box.
3. When the Open file dialog box displays, select the sound file you want to import (see fig. 26.8).

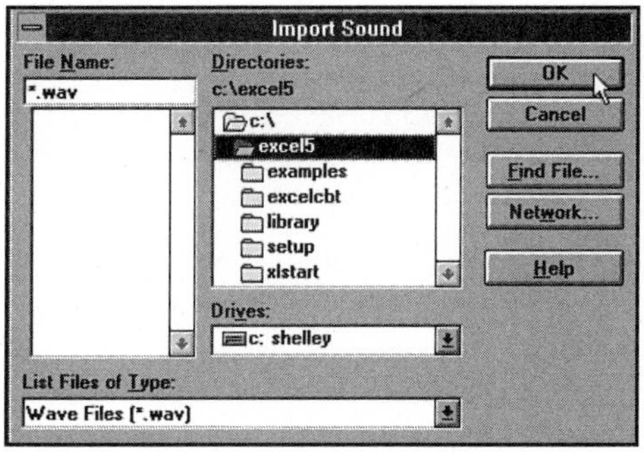

Fig 26.8
If you have WAV (sound files), you can import and attach them to a cell.

4. Choose OK.

Playing Sound Messages. Before you can play back a voice message, your computer must have a Windows-compatible sound board installed and have the sound board drivers correctly installed for Windows 3.0 with Multimedia Extensions or Windows 3.1 or later.

To play back a voice message, perform the following steps:

1. Select the cell.

   If there is no text note, the voice message immediately replays.

   If there is a text message and voice message, the Note dialog box appears.

2. Press Shift+F2.
3. Select the note from the Notes in **S**heet list. Sound messages display an asterisk (*).
4. Choose the **P**lay button.

Deleting Sound Messages. To erase a voice message, follow these steps:

1. Choose the **I**nsert No**t**e command.

2. Select the note from which you want to delete the voice message.

3. Choose the **E**rase button.

When you erase a voice message, the **E**rase button changes to **R**ecord so that you can record another message in the cell. The **I**mport button also becomes available.

From Here...

Excel provides many tools for special data analysis.

- Chapter 27, "Solving with Goal Seeking and Solver," covers solving problems with Goal Seeking and Solver.

- Chapter 28, "Testing Multiple Solutions with Scenarios," explains how to manage different scenarios with the Scenario Manager.

- Chapter 29, "Using the Analysis ToolPak," is a good resource if you want to use some of the functions provided in Excel's ToolPak.

Chapter 27

Solving with Goal Seeking and Solver

Excel provides many tools to help you analyze data on worksheets. Two powerful examples of these tools are the **T**ools **G**oal Seek command and the Solver add-in. The **G**oal Seek command helps find the input value that produces the answer you want in a formula cell. Solver is a mathematical tool that helps find the best answer in a formula cell when multiple input values exist or where the input values must conform to constraints.

EXCEL 5

In this chapter, you learn how to:

- Use Goal Seek to reach a desired value for a formula that depends on one input cell
- Use chart markers to seek goals for formula cells
- Use Solver to optimize a formula value that is subject to constraints
- Preserve multiple sets of constraints for a Solver problem
- Produce Solver reports

Deciding Which Tool To Use

Excel provides many tools for different problem solving situations. Some tools, such as Solver, are add-in programs. For information on how to install and activate add-in programs, see Chapter 22, "Taking Advantage of Excel's Add-Ins."

Goal Seek and Solver are tools that specifically address the problem of finding values for one or more *input* cells that optimize the value of a formula which depends on those cells.

Tool	When To Use the Tool
Goal Seek	When you want to generate a specific value in a formula cell by adjusting the value in *one* cell that influences its value.
Solver	If you have one or more input values, and have constraints on the solution; if you want to obtain an optimal solution; or both. The Scenario Manager remembers named solutions found by the Solver so that you can create reports of optimal solutions.

Using the Goal Seek Feature

When you know the answer you want, and you must work backward to find the input value that gives you that answer, choose **T**ools **G**oal Seek. With this command, you specify a solution and then the cell that should be changed to reach this solution. Excel finds the input value that results in the specific answer you want. To do so, the command operates as if it were making repeated educated guesses, narrowing in on the exact value.

The **G**oal Seek command saves you time when you need to *back into* solutions. You can use this command, for example, to determine the needed growth rate to reach a sales goal, or to determine how many units must be sold to break even.

When you choose the **T**ools **G**oal Seek command, the cell being changed must contain a value (not a formula) and must affect the cell you have specified as requiring a particular answer. Because you cannot put restraints on the command, you may end up with input values that make no sense, or you may specify a solution for which no input value is possible. If you face situations like these, you can use Data Tables or the Scenario Manager to test different input values, or you can use the Solver to find the optimal solution within constraints that you specify.

Solving for a Single Solution

Figure 27.1 shows a simple worksheet that forecasts future Sales, Cost/Expenses, and Net Income. The changeable data entry cells are the rates of Change in row 16 and the Cost ratios in cells B18:B20. The rates of Change are used to project the Sales figures, and the Cost ratios are used to estimate Cost/Expenses.

Suppose that you want to know the rate of Change for Sales that would be necessary in 1994 (cell D16) in order to reach Net income of $3,000 in 1996 (cell F12). You can have **G**oal Seek vary the value in cell D16 until cell F12 reaches the value $3,000.

> **Caution**
>
> If you have selected **P**recision as Displayed on the **T**ools **O**ptions Calculation tab, Excel may not be able to reach the goal exactly, even though that goal would otherwise be attainable. Clear the **P**recision as Displayed option on the Calculation tab before you use the **G**oal Seek command; afterward, you can return to enforced precision.

To solve for a specific answer using Goal Seek, follow these steps:

1. Select a goal cell that contains a formula that you want to force to produce a specific value. In the example, this goal cell is F12.

2. Choose the **T**ools **G**oal Seek command. The Goal Seek dialog box appears (this is also visible in fig. 27.1). Notice that the **S**et cell text box contains the cell selected in step 1.

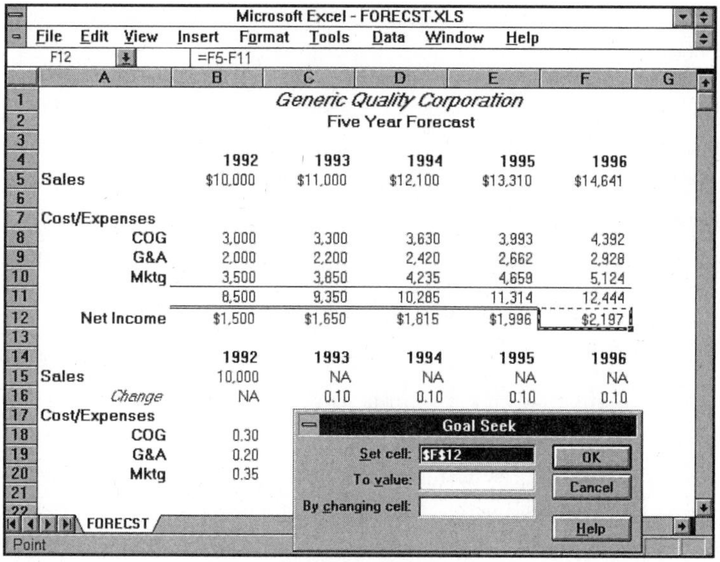

Fig. 27.1
The **S**et cell text box in the Goal Seek dialog box is automatically filled with the address of the active cell.

3. In the To **v**alue text box, type the solution you want to reach. In the example, the desired solution is $3,000, so you type **3000**.

4. In the By **c**hanging cell text box, enter the cell reference of the input cell. This cell must contribute to the value of the formula in the goal cell selected in step 1. In the example, the cell being changed is D16, so you type **D16**. In this instance cell D16 contributes to the goal formula value only indirectly—it helps determine the values of Sales in row 5, and the Sales cells contribute to the Net Income values in row 12.

Figure 27.2 shows the completed Goal Seek dialog box.

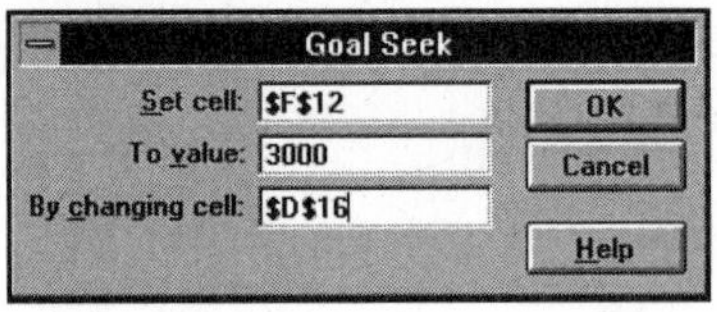

Fig. 27.2
This completed dialog box sets cell F12 to the value 3000 by changing cell D16 to an appropriate value.

5. Choose OK.

   Goal Seek begins substituting input values into cell D16. It substitutes high and low values, and converges them so that the solution becomes as close as possible to the solution you requested.

6. If you want to pause or cancel goal-seeking during a long goal-seeking process, in the Goal Seek Status dialog box, which is displayed during the calculations, choose **P**ause or Cancel. To step through the solution iterations, choose **S**tep in the Goal Seek Status dialog box. As you step, you see the current solution value in the dialog box. To continue at full speed after pausing, choose the **C**ontinue button.

The input cell selected in step 4 must contribute to the value of the formula in the goal cell and must not contain a formula. To see which cells are precedents (contributors) to the goal cell, select the goal cell. Choose **E**dit **G**o To and then choose **S**pecial. When the Select Special dialog box appears, select the **P**recedents All **L**evels option button, and choose OK. All cells that contribute to the value of the goal cell are selected. Press Tab or Enter to move among these cells; they remain selected.

After a solution has been found, choose OK to replace the values in the original worksheet with the new values shown on-screen, or choose Cancel to keep the original values.

Moving a Chart Marker To Seek a Goal

You can use a chart to search for a goal you want to meet. To do so, you must be in a 2-D column, bar, or line chart. When you drag a marker to a new value position, the Goal Seek dialog box and worksheet appear. Excel asks which input value cell you want changed to make the chart marker's new value true.

To find a solution graphically from a chart, complete the following steps:

1. Open the worksheet and the chart you want to manipulate. Activate the chart.

2. Hold down Ctrl and click the data series marker (column, bar, or line symbol) for which you want to change the value. Black handles appear on the marker, as shown in figure 27.3.

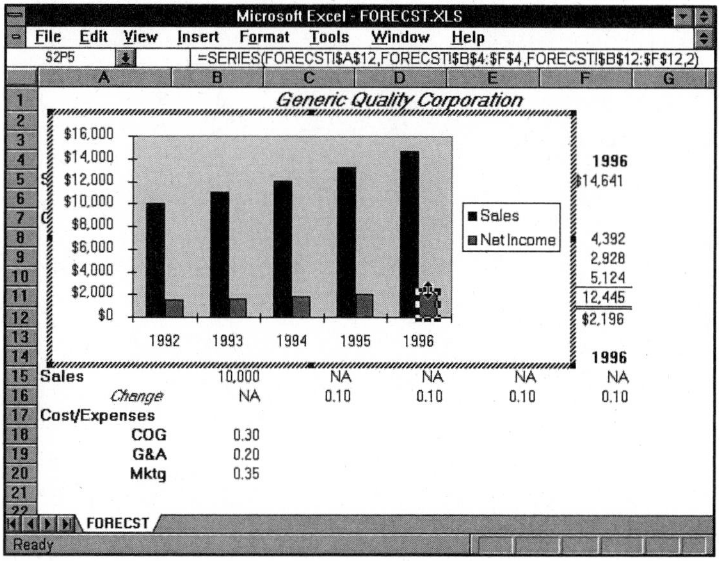

Fig. 27.3
Press Ctrl and click a bar to display the black handles on a chart marker.

3. Drag the black handles to move the end of the marker to a new value. In this example, drag the black handles up or down to change the height of the column.

As you drag the marker, notice that the numeric value of the marker appears in the reference area on the left end of the formula bar. This reference enables you to see the value of the marker change as you reposition the marker.

When you release the mouse button, the Goal Seek dialog box appears (see fig. 27.4).

Note

If the chart marker is linked to a cell that contains a number rather than a formula, the Goal Seek dialog box does not appear. Instead, the number in the worksheet changes to reflect the new marker value. This feature helps you to enter values easily into a worksheet when you need to make those values reflect a certain chart configuration.

- In the Goal Seek dialog box, the To **v**alue text box is filled with the new value of the chart marker.

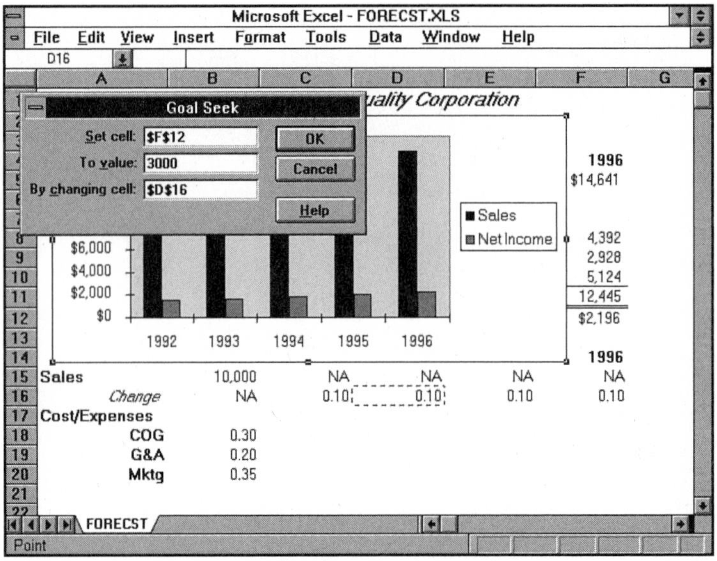

Fig. 27.4
Dragging a chart marker to a new value displays the Goal Seek dialog box, if the chart marker is linked to a cell that contains a formula.

4. Change the To **v**alue if you need a different value. The **S**et cell box contains the worksheet cell linked to the chart marker.
5. In the By **c**hanging cell text box, type the cell reference you want to change or click the input cell with the mouse.
6. Choose OK.

You can use the Goal Seek options described in step 6 in the previous set of instructions while Excel seeks the input value that most exactly produces your new desired value for the chart marker.

Finding the Best Solution with Solver

Many worksheets are too complex for the **T**ools **G**oal Seek command to find a solution. A valid solution in these more complex models may require multiple inputs and may have limiting constraints on some of the input values, or on the printed result.

Unlike the Goal Seek feature, which finds a specific solution, the Solver program finds an optimal solution by varying multiple input cells while ensuring that other formulas in the worksheet stay within limits you set. The Solver works the way problems in the real world work—more than one variable must be changed to find an answer, yet other areas of the problem must be watched to make sure that they stay within realistic limits.

Often, you may need to adjust your worksheet to fit the type of model with which Solver works best. To set up such a worksheet, you must have a good understanding of the relationships among variables and formulas. Solver's reward for your efforts, however, can be extremely high. Solver can save you from wasting resources with mismanaged schedules; help you earn higher rates through better cash management; and show you what mix of manufacturing, inventory, and products produces the best profit.

Understanding When To Use Solver

Use Solver to find the best solution to a problem. Solver is normally helpful for the following types of problems:

- *Product Mix.* Maximizing the return on products given limited resources to build those products.
- *Staff Scheduling.* Meeting staffing levels at minimum cost within specified employee satisfaction levels.
- *Optimal Routing.* Minimizing transportation costs between a manufacturing site and points-of-sale.
- *Blending.* Blending materials to achieve a certain quality level at minimal cost.

The types of problems with which Solver works best share three important facets. First, the problems have a single objective; for example, to maximize profit or to minimize time. Second, the problems have constraints that are typically given as inequalities; for example, the materials used cannot exceed inventory, or the machine hours scheduled cannot exceed 24 hours minus maintenance time. Third, the problems have input values that directly or indirectly affect both the constraints and the values being optimized.

These problems usually fall within two mathematical types: linear and nonlinear. Solver can solve either type. *Linear problems* are those in which the relationship between input and output, when graphed, results in a straight line or flat plane. If you have a linear problem, Solver has an option for finding solutions faster using linear programming techniques. Linear formulas are usually simple and have the following form:

X=A*Y1+B*Y2+C*Y3...

In this syntax, X is the result; A, B, and C are constants; and Y1, Y2, and Y3 are variables.

Solver also solves for the best solution in worksheets involving nonlinear relationships. The following are examples of *nonlinear problems*:

- Sales approach a certain volume and then level off.
- Product quality decreases as production-line staffing increases.
- Advertising response increases with ad frequency but then diminishes.
- Product costs vary with different sales volumes.

Some of the forms involving nonlinear relationships include the following:

X=Y1/Y2

X=Y1^.5 (which is the square root of Y1)

X=A+Y1*Y2

Here, X is the result, A is a constant, and Y1 and Y2 are input values.

Creating the Sample Worksheet

The worksheet in figure 27.5 illustrates a simple model built to work with Solver. In this worksheet, a city government has begun a service named Dirt Cheap, Inc. The service uses many existing resources to produce a positive income stream for the city. In addition, Dirt Cheap reduces and recycles garbage and landscape trimmings.

Tip
Excel uses names next to the set cell as constraints to generate printed reports. Avoid long or confusing names to promote clarity.

Dirt Cheap has a collection program for organic garbage, park trimmings, Christmas trees, and so on. The service mulches or composts these items, and combines them in different blends with soil and mineral additives to produce high-quality mulch, soil, and growing mixtures. Some of the labor is volunteer, and material costs, except for collection costs, are low.

The worksheet calculates the best combination of raw materials to produce the highest margin, shown in cell I17. Most real problems are not this simple, but Solver can work within the constraints of the real world to recalculate the best solution, given changing conditions.

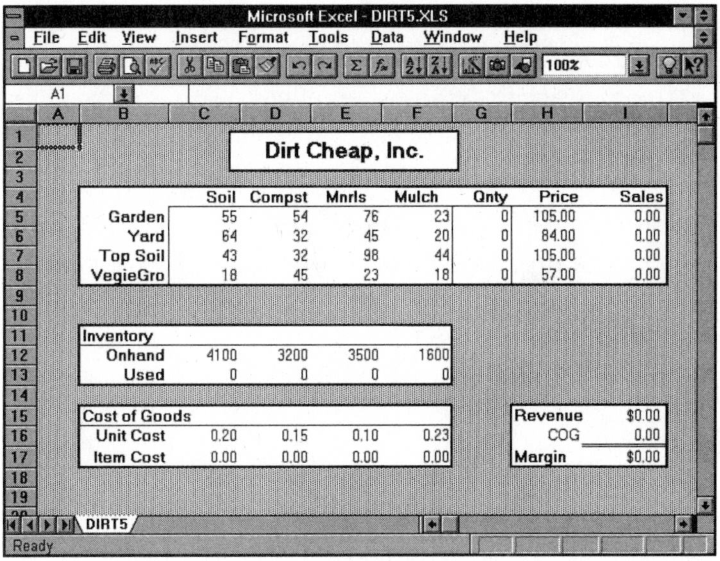

Fig. 27.5
Solver can use the Dirt Cheap worksheet to solve for the best combination of materials to reach the highest profit margin.

Much of the Dirt Cheap worksheet is text and constant numbers. To build the worksheet, type the text shown in figure 27.5 to use as a skeleton. Then enter the following numbers and formulas:

Cells	Item	Enter
C5:F8	Mixture amounts Row Headings:	Column Headings **C** **D** **E** **F** **5** 55 54 76 23 **6** 64 32 45 20 **7** 43 32 98 44 **8** 18 45 23 18
G5:G8	Product amount	0
H5:H8	Product price	Numbers 105, 84, 105, 57
I5:I8	Product $ sold	=G5*H5; G6*H6; G7*H7; G8*H8
C12:F12	Inv. on hand	Numbers 4100, 3200, 3500, 1600
C13	Inv. used	=$G5*C5+$G6*C6+$G7*C7+$G8*C8; then fill right into D13:F13
C16:F16	Unit cost	Numbers 0.20, 0.15, 0.10, 0.23
C17:F17	Item cost	=C16*C13; D16*D13; E16*E13; F16*F13
I15	Revenue	=SUM(I5:I8)
I16	Cost of goods	=SUM(C17:F17)
I17	Margin	=I15-I16

In the model, the values from C5:F5 are the mixture amounts necessary to create a soil product called *Garden Blend*. The retail price for a unit of Garden Blend is $105.00. Solver finds the best quantity to make of Garden Blend (G5). After the best quantity is found, the sales amount in I5 is calculated by multiplying G5 by H5. This technique is used for each soil product.

One constraint is that a limited amount of material exists with which to make the products. The on-hand inventory of materials—Soil, Compost, Minerals, and Mulch—is specified in cells C12:F12. Cells C13:F13 calculate the amount of each material used to find the best combination of products. Of course, the amount of materials used cannot exceed the amount of materials on hand.

The costs of materials used are found by multiplying the unit costs for the materials (C16:F16) by the amounts of materials used (C13:F13). The results of this cost formula are in C17:F17.

The revenue is calculated in cell I15 by totaling the sales, I5:I8. The cost of goods (COG) in cell I16 is the total of the item costs (C17:F17). The margin in I17 is total revenue minus total cost.

Before you run the Solver, save this worksheet to disk using the **F**ile Save **A**s command.

Installing Solver

Solver involves a special Dynamic Link Library that works with Excel. If you did not install Solver when you installed Excel, rerun the Excel installation procedure, and select the option to install Solver. You do not have to reinstall all of Excel or Windows.

After you install Solver, it is available as an Excel add-in. You can keep Solver more readily available by selecting it as an add-in. Add-ins are described in detail in chapter 22, "Taking Advantage of Excel's Add-ins."

To have Solver load when you start Excel, select it as an add-in by following these steps:

1. Choose the Tools Add-Ins command.
2. Select the Solver Add-In check box from the Add-ins Available list in the Add-Ins dialog box.
3. Choose OK.

If you do not usually use Solver, you need not do anything until you are ready to use it. When you choose **T**ools Sol**v**er, the Solver program starts.

Solving for the Best Solution

Suppose that for this model, the city council mandates that the goal is to find the optimal (maximum) dollar return in cell I17. This objective helps expand the recycling and composting done by Dirt Cheap and may reduce taxes.

The input values that are changed to find the best margin are the quantities of each soil product to be created. At this point, the city sells all the product it makes, so it does not have to worry about limits on a product. Limiting an item's production or availability of resources is explained in the sections "Changing Constraints" and "Changing a Limited Resource" that follow in this chapter. The input values for which Solver is solving are in G5:G8. For this example, the input values to begin with are all 0. In models that take a long time to calculate, you reduce calculation time by beginning with input values that you believe are near the best solution.

The constraint on the solution is that the inventory used cannot exceed the inventory on hand. In spreadsheet terms, the calculated totals in cells C13:F13 cannot exceed the corresponding values in C12:F12. In addition, the values in G5:G8 must be greater than 0 because you cannot produce a negative amount of soil.

After the Solver Parameters dialog box is filled in for this problem, the cell to be optimized, the cells to be changed, and the constraints on the solution appear as shown in figure 27.6.

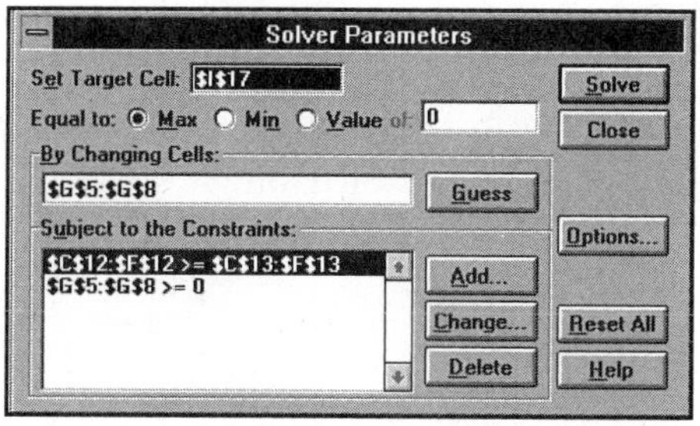

Fig. 27.6
The completed Solver Parameters dialog box for maximizing the Margin value in cell I17, given the Inventory constraints.

To solve for the best solution, complete the following steps:

1. Select the cell you want to optimize. In this example, the cell is I17.

2. Choose **T**ools Sol**v**er. The Solver loads (if it didn't when Excel was started), and the empty Solver Parameters dialog box appears (see fig. 27.7).

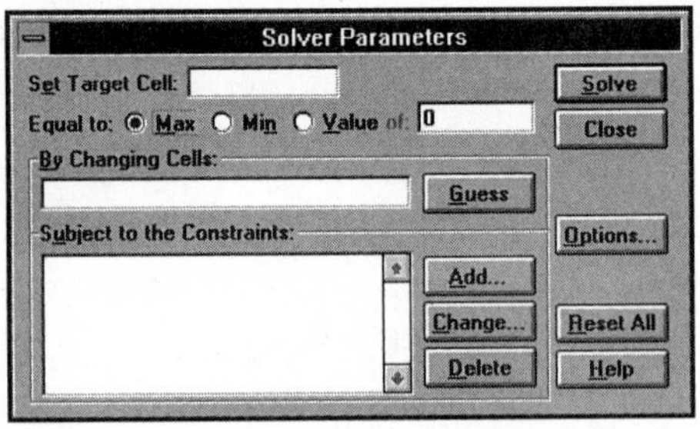

Fig. 27.7
The Solver Parameters dialog box before the problem is defined.

3. In the S**e**t Target Cell text box, reference the cell you want to optimize.

4. Define the type of relation between the S**e**t Target Cell and a solution value by selecting one of the following Equal To option buttons:

Max	Finds the maximum result for the target cell.
Mi**n**	Finds the minimum result for the target cell.
Value of	Finds exact values for the changed cells so that the target cell results in the amount typed in the Value of text box.

For this example, select **M**ax.

5. Select the **B**y Changing Cells text box; then select the adjustable cells that Solver should change while attempting to find the best answer. For this example, the cells are $G$5:$G$8. You can type the entry, select each cell using the keyboard, or drag across the cells. If the cells you need are not visible, you can move the Solver Parameters dialog box, or scroll the worksheet.

6. Choose **A**dd to add constraints to the list of constraints. The Add Constraint dialog box appears, as shown in figure 27.8.

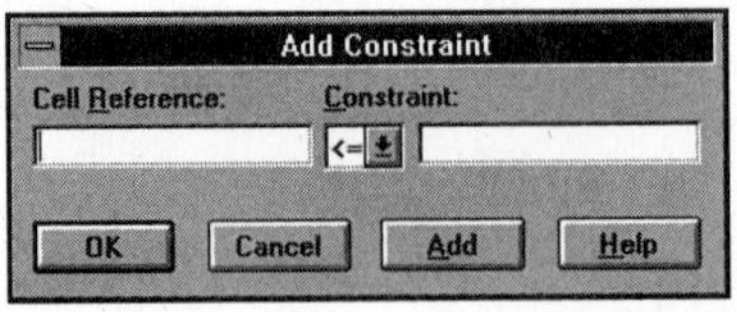

Fig. 27.8
The Add Constraint dialog box is used for each constraint in the Solver problem.

7. Enter the first constraint. In this example, the values in $G$5:$G$8 must be greater than 0. This constraint ensures that Solver considers only those solutions which produce a positive or zero quantity of soil.

In the Cell **R**eference text box, enter **$G$5:$G$8**. You can type the cell reference, select it using the keyboard, or drag across the cells. If the cells you need are not visible, you can move the Add Constraint dialog box, or scroll the worksheet.

Press Tab, or click the down arrow, to reach the operator symbol drop-down list. For this example, select the >= comparison sign.

In the **C**onstraint text box, enter **0**.

The completed Add Constraint dialog box for this example appears in figure 27.9.

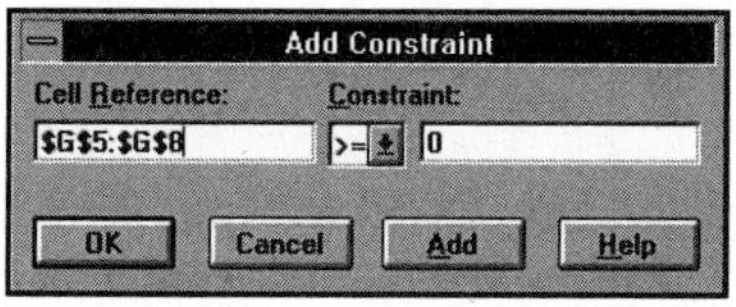

Fig. 27.9
A completed constraint places a condition on the value that may be generated in each cell of the Cell **R**eference field.

8. Choose **A**dd so that you can add another constraint. When the Add Constraint dialog box reappears, enter the second constraint. For this example, the constraint is $C$12:$F$12>=$C$13:$F$13, which indicates that the inventory used must always be less than, or equal to, the inventory on hand.

9. Choose OK. The completed Solver Parameters dialog box appears (refer to fig. 27.6).

10. Choose **S**olve to run Solver to find the optimal combination of soil products (the one that gives the maximum margin).

    When Solver finds a solution, the Solver Results dialog box appears, as shown in figure 27.10.

11. Select **K**eep Solver Solution to keep the offered solution, which is shown in the worksheet. Select Restore **O**riginal Values to return to the original worksheet values. For this example, select **K**eep Solver Solution and choose OK. In this dialog box, you also choose the reports you may want to generate, as explained later in this chapter, in "Printing Solver Reports."

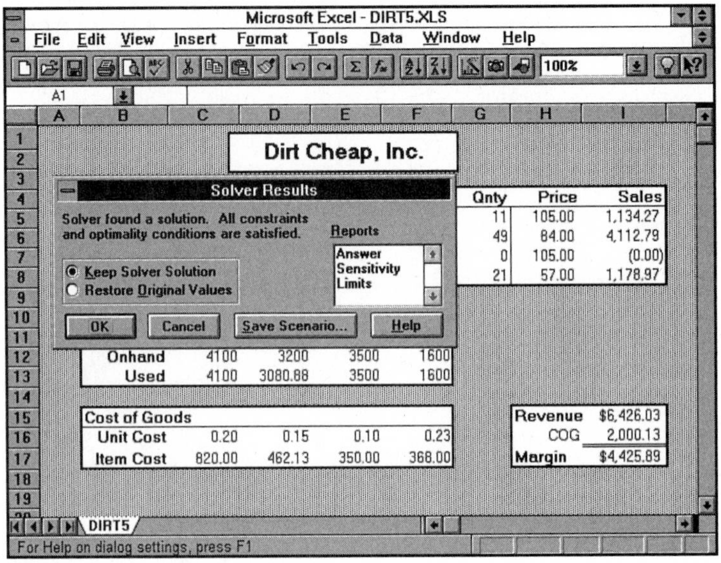

Fig. 27.10
The Solver Results dialog box gives you options for using the solution that Solver has calculated.

Solver tells you that you can achieve the best margin if you make 11 units of Garden, 49 units of Yard, no Top Soil, and 21 units of VegieGro. With this combination, the maximized margin is $4,425.89.

Note

With some linear-programming tools, you are required to set up constraints as comparison formulas that produce a TRUE or FALSE result. With Solver, you do not need to do so. If you have worksheets or mainframe data from programs requiring this method, however, you still can use them with Solver. In the S**u**bject to the Constraints box of the Solver Parameters dialog box, set the constraint equal to **TRUE** or **FALSE**. Do not use 1 or 0 to indicate TRUE or FALSE.

Note

Do not change the values on the worksheet if you want to try the exercises that follow in this chapter.

Tip
You can stop a long Solver calculation by pressing Esc.

Solver stores the dialog box settings in the worksheet that contains the problem. The settings are stored in named formulas. Because the Solver Parameters dialog box stores previous settings, rerunning Solver with different constraints is easy. You can reset the worksheet by entering zeros in G5:G8 and rerunning Solver. You then see the settings of your most recent solution. This procedure is explained later in this chapter, in the section "Saving and Loading Solver Data."

After you find a solution, you also can save the references used in **B**y Changing Cells for use in the **C**hanging Cells box of the Scenario Manager. If you want to use the Scenario Manager to run the solution found by Solver, choose the **S**ave Scenario button, shown in figure 27.10. When the Save Scenario dialog box appears, type the name you want. This name stores whatever input values the Solver determined for the cells listed in the **B**y Changing Cells text box. You can save several scenarios of answers, and then review and compare them using the Scenario Manager. Detailed instructions on using the Scenario Manager are presented in Chapter 28, in the section "Using the Scenario Manager."

If you want to store settings without running Solver, enter the settings as explained in the preceding instructions, and then choose Close.

Changing a Limited Resource

In real-world situations, the limits on production resources sometimes change. You can see the effects of such a change on Solver solutions by changing resource data in the worksheet, and rerunning Solver. The effect of such a change is known as the *dual value* or *shadow price*. A shadow price tells you what a change in inventory or resources does to the bottom line.

Suppose that the people at Dirt Cheap get a phone call telling them that they can have a hundred pounds of minerals for the cost of the gas required to haul them. For $10, Dirt Cheap can get 100 more pounds of minerals. This exchange throws off the average mineral price slightly, but are the minerals worth $10?

To find the return margin for 100 more pounds of minerals, change the mineral inventory in cell E12 from 3,500 to 3,600. Enter 0s in G5:G8. Rerun Solver by using the same settings as in the previous problem. Keep this solution so that your worksheet matches the next situation.

Adding 100 pounds of minerals takes the margin from 4,425.89 at 3,500 pounds of minerals to $4,464.24 with 3,600 pounds of minerals. The minerals cost $10.00, but contributed $38.35 to the margin; therefore, they are a good value.

Changing Constraints

The real world does not remain steady for long. Things are always changing. With Solver, however, you can resolve to find an optimal solution quickly, even when conditions change.

Suppose that a major purchaser of Dirt Cheap's soils calls to say that she must have 10 units of Top Soil. After checking the printout, Dirt Cheap's manager finds that no Top Soil is going to be mixed in this run. She decides to add a constraint that 10 units of Top Soil must be made for this customer. What effect does this change have on the margin?

To see the effect of requiring 10 units of Top Soil, choose the **T**ools Sol**v**er command to open the Solver Parameters dialog box. You need to add the new constraint, and then rerun Solver. To add the constraint, follow these steps:

1. Choose **A**dd, and then type the constraint:

   $G$7>=10

   This statement indicates that at least 10 units of top soil must be made. Choose OK.

2. Choose **S**olve to solve for the best margin.

The new solution, using a lower bound of 10 units of top soil, and including the additional 100 pounds of minerals, yields a result of $4,039.10. This amount is $325.14 less than the margin was after adding the 100 pounds of minerals. Thus, satisfying this long-term customer costs money in the short run but might gain loyalty and word-of-mouth advertising.

You can delete constraints by selecting them and choosing **D**elete. Choose **R**eset All to clear all settings in the Solver Parameters dialog box.

Setting Integer Constraints

According to cell G5, Solver currently is recommending that you make 1 unit of Garden Soil. If you select cell G5 and look on the formula bar, however, you can see that Solver actually calculated an optimal value of `0.879608026131586`. The value displayed was rounded to an integer because of the formatting of the cells. The answer in the Margin cell includes revenue from this portion of a unit of Garden Soil. To force Solver to allow only integer values for the units, choose the **T**ools Sol**v**er command to open the Solver Parameters dialog box. Then add an integer constraint, and rerun Solver. To add the integer constraint, follow these steps:

1. In the Solver Parameters dialog box, choose **A**dd.
2. Select cells $G$5:$G$8 as the cell reference.
3. Select `int` from the drop-down list of comparison signs. The contents of the **C**onstraint box change to Integer.
4. Choose OK. The constraint `$G$5:$G$8 = Integer` appears in the S**u**bject to the Constraints list.
5. Choose **S**olve. Solver calculates a solution in which all the unit values are integers. Integer constraints make many calculations much slower.

The new margin result is $4,023.11, and the recommended quantity of Garden Soil is now zero. The value is less than before, but in this case it is more precise and more realistic because all the quantities are true integers.

Changing Operational Settings

You can change the technique used by Solver to find answers, and change how long Solver works or how precise an answer it attempts to find. When you choose **O**ptions in the Solver Parameters dialog box, the Solver Options dialog box appears (see fig. 27.11). Use these options to control how Solver works. The default settings are appropriate for most problems, but table 27.1 shows other options and their capabilities.

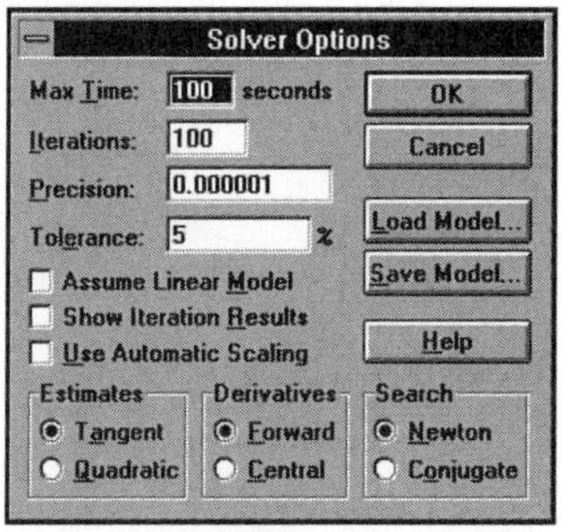

Fig. 27.11 The Solver Options dialog box enables you to control in various ways how Solver works to calculate a solution.

Table 27.1 Solver Option Settings

Option	Control
Max **T**ime	Specifies the maximum time in seconds that Solver can spend to find a solution.
Iterations	Specifies the number of times Solver can recalculate with new solution attempts.

(continues)

Table 27.1 Continued

Option	Control
Precision	Specifies how near to each other two trial solutions must be before a best solution is declared.
Tol**e**rance	Specifies by percentage how close the answer must be to the best possible solution when working with integer problems. Setting a higher tolerance can speed up calculation considerably when working with complex integer problems. Use only with integer models.
Assume Linear **M**odel	Sets Solver to use a linear programming solution method that speeds solutions that are linear. You are warned if the worksheet is not linear.
Show Iteration **R**esults	Pauses to display intermediate trial solutions and waits for you to choose to Continue or Stop.
Use Automatic Scaling	Enables the Solver to set some of the changing cells to radically larger or smaller values than others.
Estimates	Additional solution methods are T**a**ngent and **Q**uadratic. Use Quadratic if the worksheet involves complex formulas that are highly nonlinear.
Derivatives	Specifies the method of partial derivatives, using **F**orward or **C**entral differencing. Central differencing can take longer but may result in a closer solution.
Search	Specifies a quasi-**N**ewton or C**o**njugate gradient method of searching.

Printing Solver Reports

Solver generates reports that summarize the results of its solutions. These reports are helpful when comparing different constraint conditions, or calculating shadow prices that show the effects had by data changes on final results.

Solver can generate three reports: Answer, Sensitivity, and Limit reports. To generate a report after you solve a model, select one or more of the reports from the **R**eports list when the solution box appears (refer to fig. 27.10). To select more than one report from the list, select the first report, hold down Ctrl, and click one or both of the other reports. Each report is generated in its own sheet. Select a sheet tab, or press Ctrl+PgDn and Ctrl+PgUp to browse through the reports and the original data sheet.

Answer Report. The Answer report, shown in figure 27.12, shows the original and final values for the target cell and the adjustable cells. The constraint analysis tells the *Status* of each constraint: Binding, if the constraint is effectively constraining the pursuit of the value in the target cell; Not Binding, if the constraint is not limiting the value in the target cell; or Not Satisfied, if complying with the constraint is not possible. The *Slack* values in the report show the differences between the constraints and the final values. In the Dirt Cheap example, the Slack is the amount of inventory that remains unused in reaching the solution value.

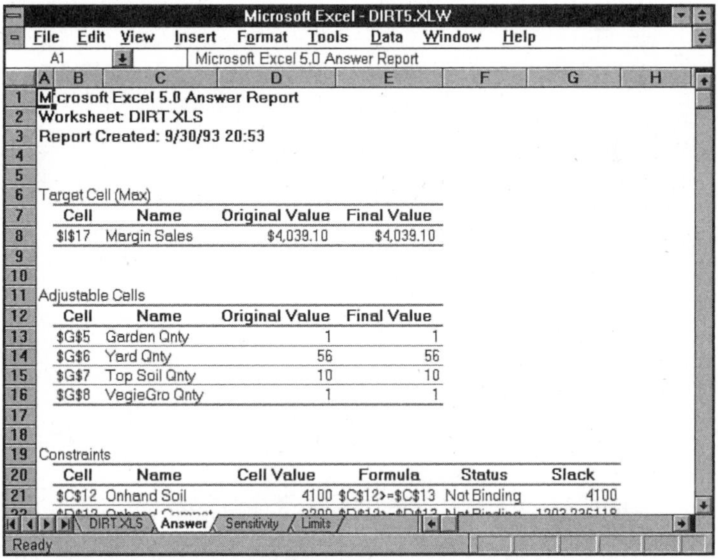

Fig. 27.12
The Answer report compares the original values and the final (solution) values.

Sensitivity Report. The Sensitivity report has two sections (see fig. 27.13). The first shows each adjustable cell, the cell name, the value, and the amount the target cell would increase (or decrease) for each unit change in that adjustable cell. The second section shows each constraint cell, its name, value, and the amount the target cell would increase (or decrease) for each unit change in that constraint. This report can show you how much difference it would make to change either the adjustable or constraint cell values. When Solver is working with a Linear Model, the Sensitivity report also shows how much the cell value could increase or decrease before the target cell would change at all.

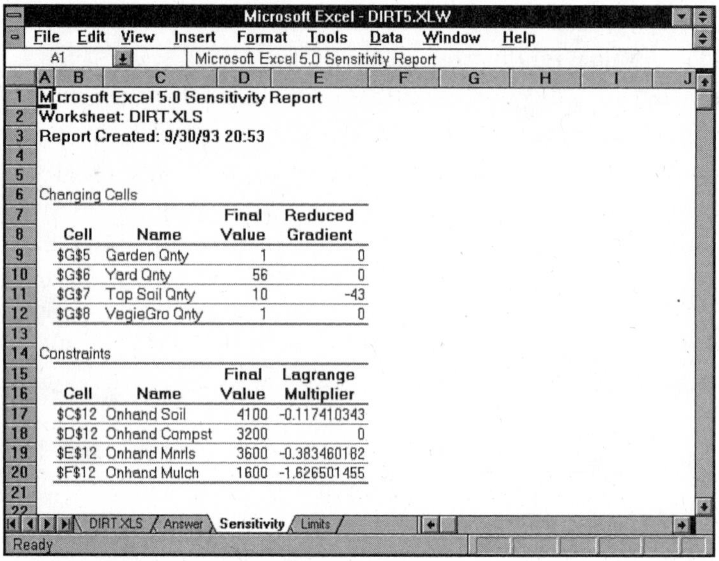

Fig. 27.13
The Sensitivity report shows the sensitivity of each element of the solution to changes in input or constraints.

Limits Report. The Limits report shows the set cell value, adjustable cell values, upper and lower limits, and the target result. The upper and lower limits specify how much the adjustable cell can change and still satisfy all constraints. The target result is the set cell value when the adjustable cell value is at its upper or lower limit. This report shows you how much variance is available in adjustable cells. Figure 27.14 shows the Limits report.

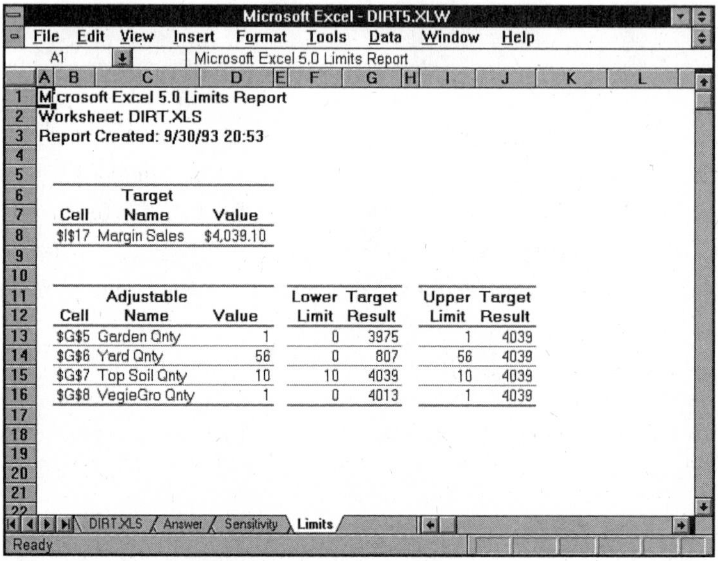

Fig. 27.14
The Limits report shows the maximum and minimum values the adjustable cells have within the constraints.

Saving and Loading Solver Data

Solver stores in the worksheet the last settings used to solve a problem (those that were in the Solver Parameters dialog box when you chose OK). As mentioned previously, the last settings used are stored in named formulas. The next time you open that worksheet and run Solver, the Solver Parameters dialog box appears as you last used it.

In some cases, you may want to store predefined settings for the Solver Parameters dialog box. You may, for example, have specific sets of constraints that you must consider. You can store each of these sets of constraints in cells on the worksheet and quickly load the settings you need.

You can save and load different Solver models (settings) by choosing **O**ptions in the Solver Parameters dialog box. To save Solver settings, complete the following steps:

1. Set up the Solver Parameters dialog box with the settings you want to save. Choose OK.

2. On the worksheet, select a range of cells equal to the number of constraints plus three cells.

   The range can be any shape. Making it too large doesn't hurt. Excel advises you (in step 4 below) if the range is not large enough, or if you select a single cell, Excel suggests a range.

3. Choose **T**ools Sol**v**er. When the Solver Parameters dialog box appears, choose **O**ptions.

4. Choose **S**ave Model. When the Solver Parameters dialog box reappears, choose Cancel.

The range is filled with the settings from the Solver Parameters dialog box. Figure 27.15 shows an example of saved settings.

Note

When you use the preceding steps to save the model, you save all the information needed for Solver to work: the adjustable cell references, the optimization type, the constraints, and any options. This information enables you to switch between completely different ways of looking at the problem. When you use **S**ave Scenario at the completion of a Solver calculation, you are saving only the values for the adjustable cells. You can use the Scenario Manager, explained in Chapter 28, to switch quickly among different results from different Solver problems, or to build a report of the alternate solutions.

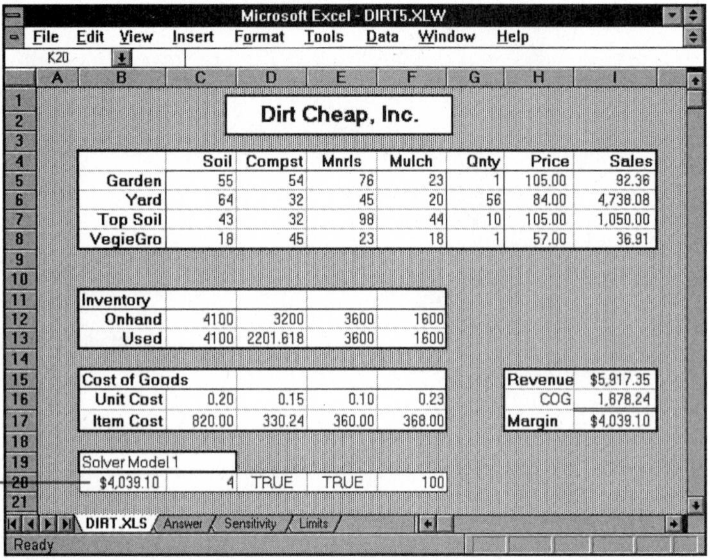

Fig. 27.15
The settings in the Solver Parameters dialog box can be saved as cell entries to make it easy to use those settings again in the future.

Solver parameters saved as cell entries

To load settings when you want to rerun a saved Solver model, follow these steps:

1. Select the range of cells that contains the model.
2. Choose **T**ools Sol**v**er.
3. Choose **O**ptions.
4. Choose **L**oad Model.
5. When the Solver Parameters dialog box reappears, with the settings loaded, you can run the Solver, or choose OK and run it later.

Understanding the Solver Samples

Excel comes with example worksheets that use Solver to find an optimal or best solution. Although simplified, these examples cover many of the types of problems for which Solver is designed. For these problems, Solver saves time over trial-and-error methods.

These example files are located in the \EXAMPLES\SOLVER directory, in the file named SOLVSAMP. The \EXAMPLES directory is located under the directory in which Excel is installed. Use the **F**ile **O**pen command to open the example file. There are six example sheets. Select the tab for a worksheet, and then choose **T**ools Sol**v**er. You can examine the settings in the Solver Parameters dialog box. You may want to write down the settings and limitations, and then return to the worksheet to see how they relate to the problem.

To run Solver on an example, open a worksheet, choose **T**ools Sol**v**er, and choose **S**olve. If you choose to keep the solutions that are found, save the worksheet with a different name to preserve the original example.

The following table lists the example worksheets and their purposes.

File name	Purpose
Product Mix	Finds the maximum profit by changing the production mix of electronic products, where the products share common parts and the sales margin diminishes with increased volume, due to increased sales costs.
Shipping Routes	Minimizes the shipping costs from a set of production plants to warehouses while meeting warehouse needs and not exceeding plant production.
Staff Scheduling	Finds an employee schedule that meets all shift requirements while minimizing unnecessary staffing.
Maximizing Income	Finds the best combination of certificates of deposit (CDs) and deposit times so that the interest earned is maximized, while ensuring that cash-on-hand is available for forecasted needs.
Portfolio of Securities	Finds the combination of stocks in a portfolio that gives the best rate of return for a specific level of risk.
Engineering Design	Finds the ohms value of a resistor that will discharge a circuit to a specific amount within a specific time frame.

From Here...

For additional information related to the solutions produced by the Goal Seek and Solver commands, consult the following chapters of this book:

- Chapter 22, "Taking Advantage of Excel's Add-ins," shows how to access the add-in tools.
- Chapter 23. "Manipulating and Analyzing Data," shows how to create simple and complex formulas for Goal Seek and Solver to optimize.
- Chapter 28, "Testing Multiple Solutions with Scenarios," shows how to record and display different combinations of values or solution sets for one or more cells.

Chapter 28

Testing Multiple Solutions with Scenarios

Worksheets are ideally suited for *what-if* analysis. You enter values into key cells and watch what happens to the results. Although this procedure enables you to easily enter new alternatives, reconstructing the preceding values is often tedious. In many situations, you need to look at several alternatives.

Microsoft Excel manages multiple scenarios by storing values for input data cells in names that you assign. These values are stored in the worksheet as hidden names. You can keep several versions—or *scenarios*—of input values and switch easily among them. When you want to view the results from a different scenario of input values, you just choose a different named scenario.

In this chapter, you learn how to:

- Create multiple scenarios in a worksheet model
- Use scenarios for what-if analysis
- Create summaries of results of various scenarios
- Keep track of changes in scenarios over time

Creating Scenarios

A model with named scenarios should have a clear set of one or more key input values and a clear set of one or more result values that will change based on the inputs. Figure 28.1 shows a Five Year Forecast worksheet. The results in rows 5 through 13 are from formulas that use the input values in the range D16:D19.

To convert the model to use growth rates for the forecast, complete the following steps:

1. Group the growth estimates in cells D16:D19, and put appropriate labels in C16:C19. Enter the numeric values as shown in figure 28.1. These values are the input values saved by the Scenario Manager.

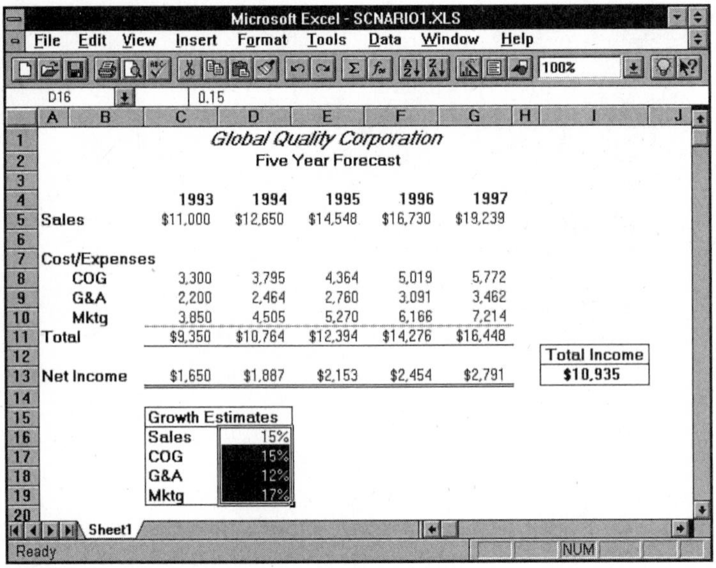

Fig. 28.1
A model for forecasting sales and expenses.

The Scenario Manager does not require the input cells to be in a block, but grouping them can help highlight the key input values for the model.

2. Enter the following numbers that will be used to project future sales, cost of goods sold (COGS), general and administrative expenses (G&A), and marketing expenses (Mktg). These constants are the starting values for the first year.

Item	Cell	Enter number
Sales	C5	$211,000
COGS	C8	3,300
G&A	C9	2,200
Mktg	C10	3,850

3. Enter the following formulas to calculate the growth of each item for the first year. Each formula has the appropriate absolute reference ($) so that it can be copied to the right across each row.

Item	Cell	Enter formula
Sales	D5	=C5*(1+$D$16)

Item	Cell	Enter formula
COGS	D8	=C8*(1+$D$17)
G&A	D9	=C9*(1+$D$18)
Mktg	D10	=D10*(1+$D$19)

4. Enter the formula **=SUM(C8:C10)** into cell C11, and enter the label **Total** into A11. Select cell C11 and drag the fill handle to column G.

5. Enter the formula **=C5C11** into cell C13, and enter the label **Net Income** into A13. Select cell C13 and drag the fill handle to column G.

6. Enter the formula **=SUM(C13:G13)** into cell I13, and enter the label **Total Income** into I12. You can watch this cell to see the overall effect of changes to the input variables.

7. Select cell I13 and choose the **I**nsert **N**ame **D**efine command. Type **Total_Income** in the Names in **W**orkbook box if it does not already show, and then choose OK.

When you type new numbers for the growth estimates in range D16:D19, the Income figures will adjust themselves automatically, and you can see the new Total Income in cell I13. You have a clear set of input values as well as a clear result value.

Using Named Cells

Before running a what-if scenario, you should give names to the input cells. Excel does not require that input cells have names, but if they do, the dialog boxes and reports in the Scenario Manager will display the names rather than difficult-to-understand cell addresses.

To name the input and result cells for the example worksheet shown in figure 28.1, complete the following steps:

1. Select cells C16:D19.

2. Choose the **I**nsert **N**ame **C**reate command, and select the **L**eft Column check box.

3. Choose OK.

4. Select cells I12:I13.

5. Choose the **I**nsert **N**ame **C**reate command, and select the **T**op Row check box.

6. Choose OK.

This process uses the text labels in the left column to create names for the cells in the right column. Steps 4 and 5 name the final result cell as Total_Income. To check the names you create, display the name list by clicking the arrow button in the formula bar and select one of the names. (Alternatively, press F5 to get to the GoTo dialog box, select the name, and then choose OK.) Notice that the label G&A on the sheet becomes G_A when Excel made it into a name. The active cell should move to the name you specified.

Note

The Scenario Manager will use a name instead of a cell reference if a name applies specifically to that cell. If a name applies to more than the single cell, the Scenario Manager ignores the name. To determine if a cell has a name, select the cell. If a name has been assigned to that cell, it will appear in the Name box at the extreme left of the formula bar. Otherwise the Name box will display the cell reference. To display a list of names in the worksheet, click the arrow adjacent to the Name box.

Adding Named Scenarios

Suppose that you need to create three scenarios for this model: a best-guess estimate, a best-case estimate, and a worst-case estimate. These estimates will enable you to get a sense of the range of options for the future. Excel offers two methods of adding named scenarios to the worksheet: using the Scenarios drop-down list box in the WorkGroup toolbar, and using the Scenario Manager.

Using the Scenario Drop-Down List Box. To use the Scenario drop-down list box to add the best-guess scenario to a worksheet like the example, follow these steps:

1. Select cells D16:D19, the input values, and enter the following best guess numbers into the cells: **15%** for Sales, **15%** for COGS, **12%** for G&A, and **17%** for Mktg.

   Keep these cells selected. When you create your scenario, Excel uses the currently selected cells, with their current values, as the default Changing Cells. If your scenario has only one Changing Cell and Excel selects another cell after you press Enter, reselect the Changing Cell.

Fig. 28.2
The WorkGroup toolbar contains a Scenarios drop-down list box (at right) that lists the names of scenarios you create.

2. Choose the **V**iew **T**oolbars command, and then select the WorkGroup toolbar from the **T**oolbars list. This displays the WorkGroup toolbar (see fig. 28.2).

3. Type **Best Guess** in the Scenarios box (at the right end of the WorkGroup toolbar), and then press Enter.

You now have a single scenario stored in the worksheet. Behind the scenes, Excel saves the set of values in the input cells as the Best Guess scenario under a hidden name.

Note

Because scenarios are often used in larger organizations, the Scenarios box is part of the WorkGroup toolbar. However, you don't have to be on a network or connected to a workgroup to use scenarios.

No other buttons on the WorkGroup toolbar—besides the Scenarios box—are directly relevant to creating scenarios.

If you save the worksheet, the input (changing) cells for the scenarios, as well as the scenario name and values, will be stored with the worksheet. A single scenario, however, doesn't enable you to do very much.

To add the Best Case scenario, follow these steps:

1. Select cells D16:D19 and change the values to those of the Best Case scenario: **20%** for Sales, **18%** for COGS, **18%** for G&A, and **19%** for Mktg.

2. Select the Scenarios drop-down list box in the WorkGroup toolbar. This highlights the Best Guess scenario name.

3. Type **Best Case** for the scenario name, and then press Enter. (This overwrites the Best Guess name, but don't worry; the Best Guess scenario is still in the workbook.)

Note

When you enter a new scenario name, you overwrite whatever scenario name previously appeared in the Scenarios box. Don't worry, though; this does not delete or change any existing scenarios in the workbook.

Using the Scenario Manager. You also can create scenarios with the Scenario Manager. The Scenarios drop-down list box is much faster, but if you are making numerous changes to your scenario structure, using the Scenario Manager dialog box is more efficient. You can choose the **A**dd, **E**dit, or **D**elete buttons at any time the Scenario Manager dialog box is displayed. To see how this works, type these worst-case values into cells D16:D19 in the worksheet: **12%** for Sales, **14%** for COGS, **18%** for G&A, and **20%** for Mktg.

To create a scenario with the Scenario Manager, follow these steps:

1. After entering or changing input values, select the input cells (D16:D19 in the Global Quality example in fig. 28.1).

2. Choose the **T**ools **Sc**enarios command. The Scenario Manager dialog box, shown in figure 28.3, appears.

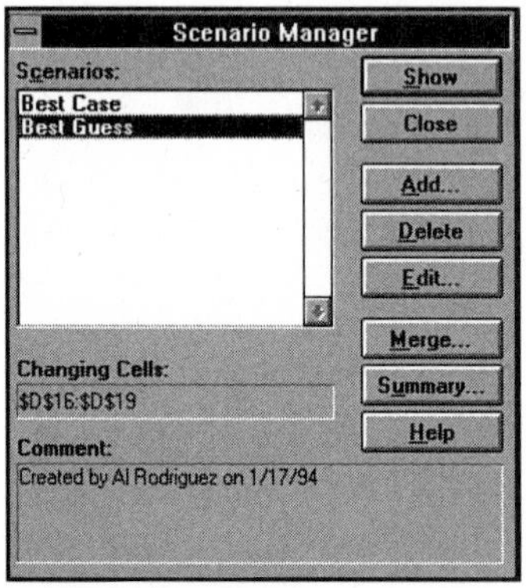

Fig. 28.3
In the Scenario Manager dialog box, you can add, change, or delete scenarios.

3. Click the **A**dd button. The Add Scenario dialog box appears. If your worksheet already contains a scenario whose set of changing cells corresponds to the current selection in the worksheet, the name, changing cells, and comments relating to that scenario will appear.

4. Type the name of the scenario in the Scenario **N**ame text box. (If you are following the example, type **Worst Case**, as shown in figure 28.4.)

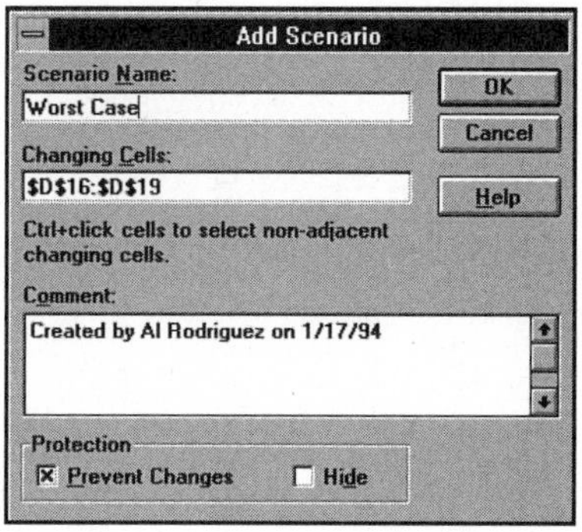

Fig. 28.4
Click the **Add** button in the Scenario Manager dialog box to bring up the Add Scenario text box.

5. If necessary, edit the addresses for the input cells in the Changing **C**ells text box.

6. Choose OK to accept the worst-case scenario. The Scenario Manager dialog box reappears—this time, with all three scenarios listed, as shown in figure 28.5.

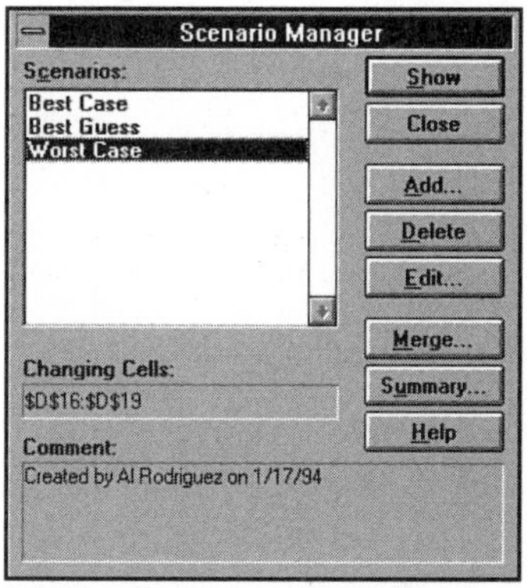

Fig. 28.5
The Scenario Manager after adding three scenarios.

7. Choose Close or press Esc to close the Scenario Manager dialog box.

You now have all three scenarios on the worksheet ready to review, but you must first save the updated worksheet to disk by using the **F**ile **S**ave command. Because the named scenarios are stored in hidden names in the worksheet when you save the worksheet, you save the scenarios you have just created.

Switching between Scenarios

Now that you have some named scenarios in the worksheet, you can quickly switch the model from one scenario to another. Simply select a different scenario from the Scenarios drop-down list box, as shown in figure 28.6. The values for the scenario you chose appear in the changing cells, and the worksheet is recalculated.

Fig. 28.6
Switch rapidly between scenarios by selecting from the Scenarios drop-down list box.

To switch between scenarios using the Scenario Manager, follow these steps:

1. Choose the **T**ools S**c**enarios command to display the Scenario Manager dialog box.

2. Drag the dialog box so that the most interesting parts of the screen remain visible.

   You can drag the dialog box over the Excel menu bars to reveal most of the screen. When you leave the Scenario Manager and then reactivate it, Excel remembers where you left the dialog box.

3. Double-click a different scenario. (Alternatively, you can select a scenario from the **S**cenarios list box and choose **S**how or press Enter.) The values for the scenario you chose appear in the changing cells, and the worksheet is recalculated.

4. When you have finished examining the scenarios, select the one you want to display , and then choose Close or press Esc.

Editing a Scenario

After you have named scenarios in your worksheet, you can go back and change the values for a given scenario.

To edit the values for a scenario using the Scenario drop-down list box, follow these steps:

1. Select the scenario you want to change in the Scenarios drop-down list box in the WorkGroup toolbar.

2. Make the changes to the input values in the worksheet.

3. Click the name of the scenario again in the Scenarios drop-down list box, and then press Enter.

4. Choose **Y**es to confirm the change.

To edit the values for a scenario using the Scenario Manager, follow these steps:

1. Choose the **T**ools S**c**enarios command to display the Scenario Manager dialog box.

2. Select the scenario you want to change from the S**c**enarios list box.

3. Choose the **E**dit button. The Edit Scenario dialog box appears.

4. If you want to specify different changing cells, edit the Changing **C**ells text box.

5. Choose OK. The Scenario Values dialog box appears (see fig. 28.7).

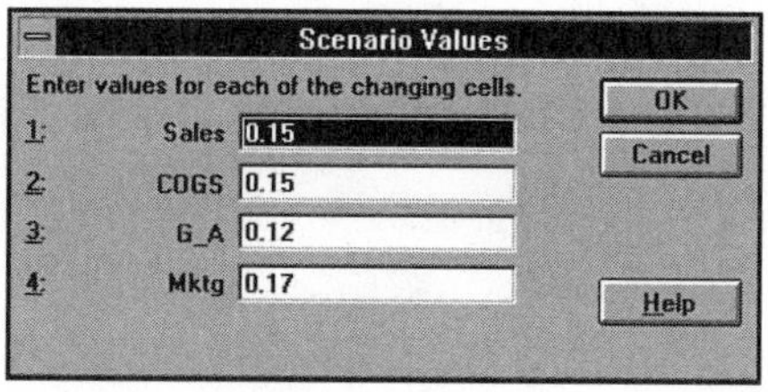

Fig. 28.7
You can change values for scenarios in the Scenario Values dialog box.

6. Make changes in the appropriate text box(es), and then choose OK.

7. In the Scenario Manager, choose **S**how to reflect the changes in the worksheet.

8. Choose Close or press Esc to close the dialog box.

To delete a scenario, display the Scenario Manager, select the scenario you want to delete and choose the **D**elete button.

Using Multiple Scenario Sets

The scenarios you have seen in the previous examples present a simplified view of a planning situation. In the example, growth rates for costs and expenses vary independently of the growth rate of sales. In reality, however, costs are related to the level of sales. The values in rows 8 through 10 are the product of the current year's sales and the appropriate percentage. To help reflect these complex dynamics, Version 5 of Excel enables you to have more than one set of scenarios on a worksheet at a time.

Consider the worksheet in figure 28.8. This worksheet is similar to the one in figure 28.1, with one exception. In figure 28.1, the annual growth rates specified in cells D17:D19 are applied to actual expense amounts for 1993 to arrive at the projected expense amounts for 1994 through 1997. In figure 28.8, the expenses for each year are computed as a ratio of that year's sales. The projected ratios are entered in cells D17:D19.

As you can see from looking at the formula bar in figure 28.8, COGS for 1993 is computed by multiplying 1993 sales (cell C5) by the amount for COGS as a percentage of sales (cell C17). Cell C8 was copied to cells C9:C10 and cells D8:G10. With this setup, you can deal with separate sets of assumptions for sales growth and *cost of goods sold* (COGS) levels.

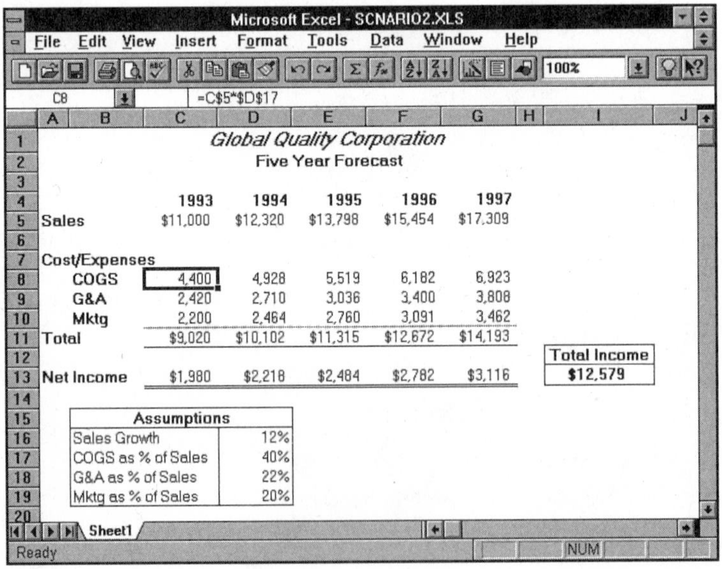

Fig. 28.8
A model for forecasting sales and expenses that relates projected expenses to projected sales.

If you create two sales growth scenarios in this workbook (High Sales and Low Sales) using cell D16 as the input cell, and create two scenarios for COGS (High Costs and Low Costs) using cell D17 as the input cell, you have two *sets* of scenarios in this workbook, resulting in four possible combinations. Suppose that you create these scenarios using the values summarized below:

Scenario Set	Input Cell	Scenarios Value
High Sales	D16	16%
Low Sales	D16	12%
High Costs (COGS)	D17	40%
Low Costs (COGS)	D17	34%

You can then combine sales and cost scenarios. To project results under the assumptions of high sales growth and high costs, you first select the High Sales scenario, and then select the High Costs scenario—or vice versa. Figure 28.9 shows the results.

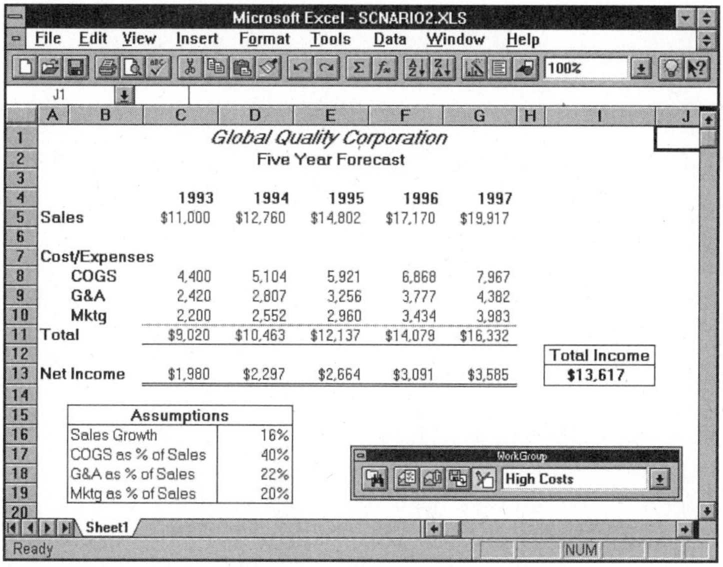

Fig. 28.9
Displaying the High Sales scenario for sales growth and the High Costs scenario for projected costs.

If you selected the Low Costs scenario, your worksheet would look like figure 28.10. As you can see, the sales figures have not changed. Because the High Costs and Low Costs scenarios do not impact the sales figures, the High Sales scenario persists in the worksheet until you select another scenario in that set.

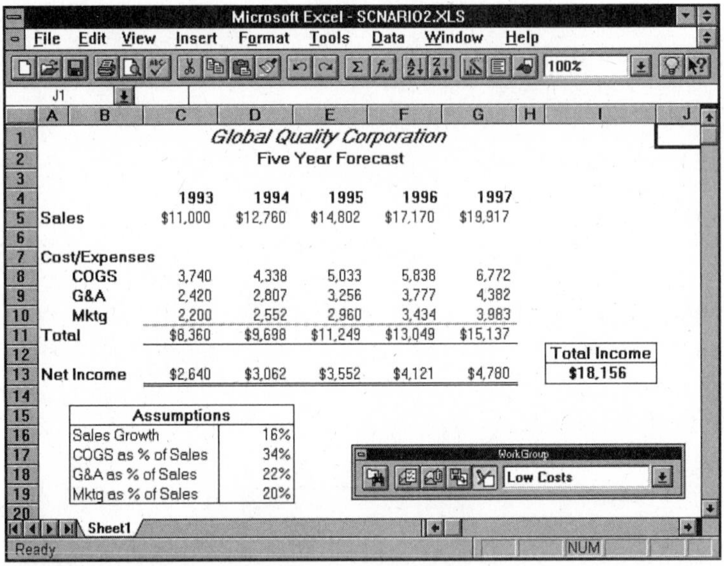

Fig. 28.10 Displaying the High Sales scenario for sales growth and the Low Costs scenario for projected costs.

Summarizing Scenarios in Tables

Switching among different scenarios is useful, but many times you also will need to see a single summary table with the results for all the scenarios. Excel produces two types of scenario reports. The scenario summary is suitable for models with a single scenario set. For models containing multiple scenario sets, Excel creates a pivot table report that computes results for all possible outcomes.

Creating a Scenario Summary Report

If your worksheet has only one scenario set and you want to see a summary of the inputs and results of all the scenarios, you should generate a scenario summary report.

To create a scenario summary report, follow these steps:

1. Choose the **T**ools S**c**enarios command.

2. Choose the **Summary** button. The Scenario Summary dialog box appears, as shown in figure 28.11.

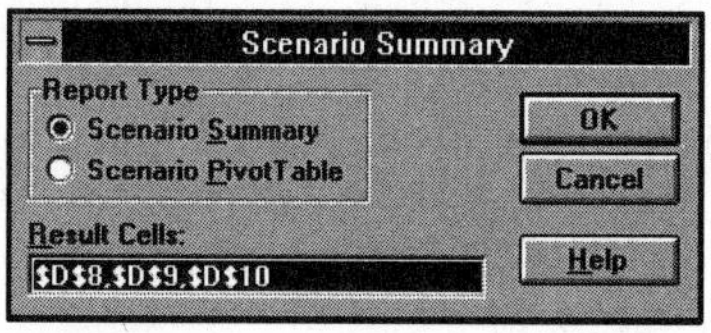

Fig. 28.11 Choosing the **Summary** button in the Scenario Manager brings up the Scenario Summary dialog box.

3. Under Report Type, select Scenario **Summary**, if it is not already selected.

4. If needed, change the contents of the **Result** Cells text box by pointing on the sheet. (If you are following the example, click cell I13.) The result cell is the cell that contains the answer to be printed. Use a reference or a name.

5. Choose OK. Excel displays a new sheet with a summary table of the scenario inputs and results.

Excel displays a new sheet containing a scenario summary report. Figure 28.12 shows a summary table created from the worksheet in figure 28.1 after creating the Best Case, Best Guess, and Worst Case scenarios, with cell I13 specified as the result cell.

Note

Because the summary is a separate sheet, you can print or close it, copy it to another workbook, or save it as part of the current workbook. The summary is not linked to the worksheet, however, so if you change any values or formulas on the worksheet, you need to create a new summary table. You can select more than one result cell for the summary report, but you should be sure to give each of the result cells a name in Excel before you create the report. Otherwise, the report will display cell addresses rather than readable names.

Creating a Scenario Pivot Table Report

With multiple scenario sets, you can analyze the results more thoroughly if you create a Pivot Table summary.

To create a Pivot Table summary report, follow these steps:

1. Choose the **Tools** **Scenarios** command.

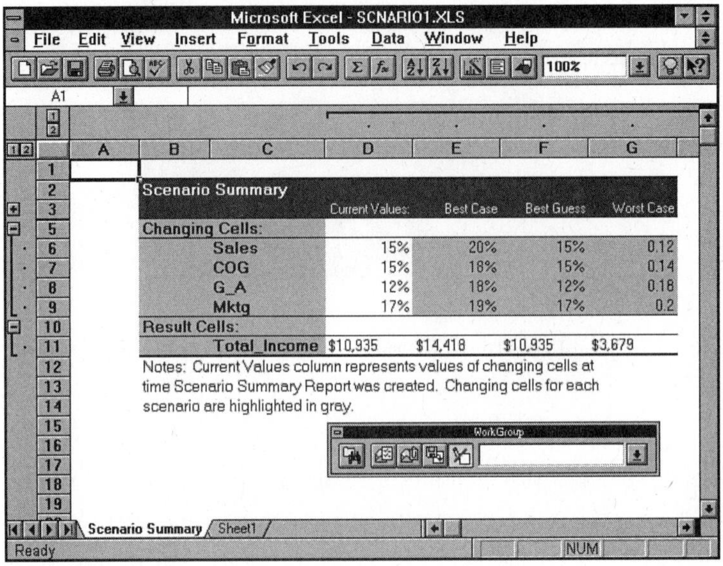

Fig. 28.12
You can summarize the results of several scenarios in a scenario summary report.

2. Choose the **Su**mmary button. In the Scenario Summary dialog box, select Scenario **P**ivotTable.

3. Enter or select the result cell(s) in the **R**esult Cells text box, if necessary. You must specify one or more result cells when creating a scenario pivot table.

4. Choose OK.

For Related Information

- "Naming Cells for Better Worksheets," p. 157
- "Reorganizing the Pivot Table," p. 1015

After a few seconds, Excel displays a new sheet that contains a summary in pivot table form. Figure 28.13 shows a pivot table summary of the model in figure 28.10 with cell I13 specified as the result cell. (The amounts in column C have been formatted to display whole dollars.)

You can manipulate the pivot table summary as you can any other pivot table. However, if you change a scenario, you cannot update an existing scenario pivot table; you must create a new one.

Managing Scenarios

If you work with what-if scenarios a great deal, you will notice that managing your various models and scenario sets can become complicated. To stay on top of your models and to get the most out of Excel scenarios, you need to master some scenario management features.

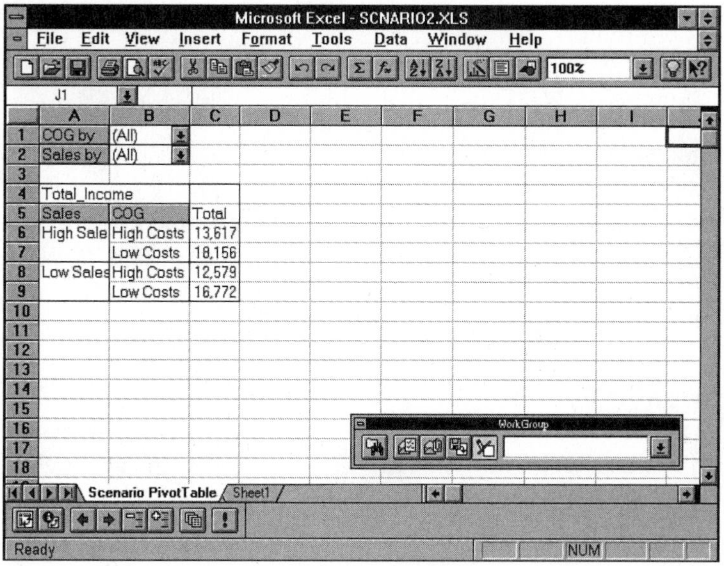

Fig. 28.13
You can summarize the results of multiple scenario sets in a scenario pivot table.

Merging Scenarios

If you have created scenarios in separate workbooks, you might occasionally need to bring scenarios into a given workbook from another workbook.

To merge scenarios, follow these steps:

1. Open all workbooks containing the scenarios you want to merge.
2. Choose the **T**ools S**c**enarios command.
3. Click the **M**erge button. The Merge Scenarios dialog box appears (see fig. 28.14).

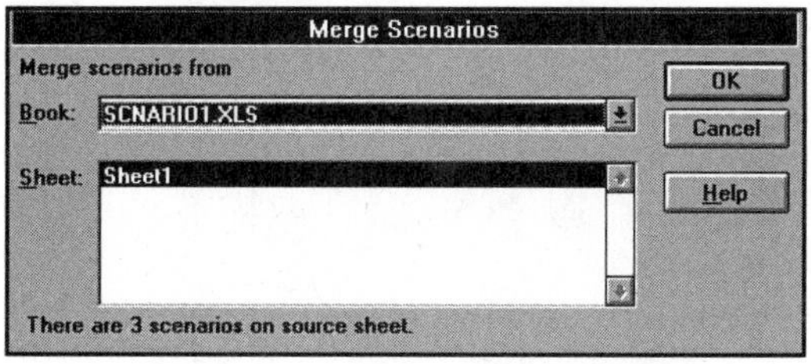

Fig. 28.14
Choosing the Merge button in the Scenario Manager displays the Merge Scenarios dialog box, where you can merge scenarios from other workbooks into the current workbook.

4. Select the name of the workbook and sheet containing the scenarios you want to merge from the **B**ook drop-down list box and **S**heet list box, respectively.

5. Choose OK.

Excel copies all the scenarios you created in the source sheet to the active worksheet and displays the Scenario Manager dialog box again. If you want to merge scenarios in other sheets, choose the **M**erge button again to redisplay the Merge Scenarios box.

Managing Scenario Names

Merging scenarios from one workbook into another creates the potential for duplicating scenario names. When this happens, Excel appends date identifiers to the scenario names to help you distinguish between them. If identically named scenarios were created on the same date, Excel appends sequential numbers as identifiers (for example, "Most Likely Estimate 3/15/94 1").

Using Scenario Manager in a WorkGroup

EXCEL 5

When a group of people collaborates on building a model, the capability to protect against unauthorized changes and to identify the source of changes to scenarios, can be critical to accuracy.

Any time a scenario is created or changed, Excel records the date and user name. When you display the Scenario Manager, Excel displays an activity log in the Comment box, as shown in figure 28.15.

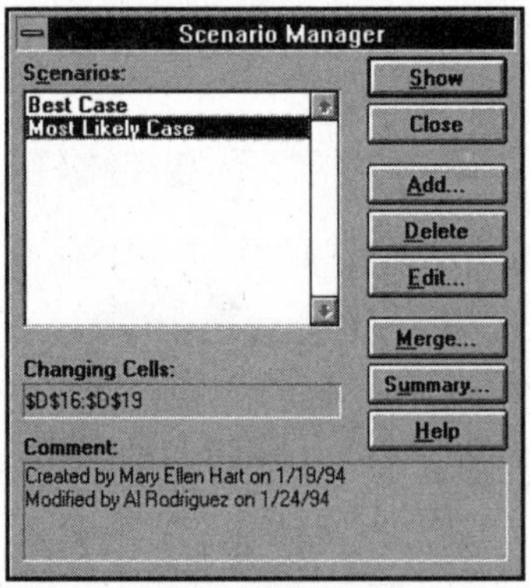

Fig. 28.15
The Scenario Manager tracks changes to and creation of scenarios, displaying them in the Comment box.

When you create or edit scenarios, you can protect your scenarios from being edited. These options only protect your scenarios; unless you also lock the input cells, another user can still edit the cells directly. However, you do need to activate sheet protection, using the following procedure, to make the protection effective.

1. Choose the **T**ools **P**rotection command.
2. Choose the **P**rotect Sheet option from the submenu to display the Protect Sheet dialog box.
3. If you want to require a password, enter it in the **P**assword box.
4. Make sure that the **S**cenarios option is selected, and then choose OK.

The Protection options are included in the Add Scenario and Edit Scenario dialog boxes (see fig. 28.16). Selecting **P**revent Changes prevents changes to the scenario you are editing or creating. Selecting Hi**d**e suppresses the display of the scenario name on the scenario list.

Fig. 28.16
The Protection options in the Add Scenario and Edit Scenario dialog boxes offer two ways to protect scenario data in workbooks.

Troubleshooting

The scenarios are changing the values in the wrong cells.

You probably inadvertently selected another cell after setting the input values. This can happen if your Excel setup moves the selected cell after you press Enter. To remedy the situation, choose the **E**dit button in the Scenario Manager dialog box, and enter the correct cell reference in the Changing **C**ells box.

Excel dosen't produce a summary report that includes all the scenarios created.

Check to see if one or more of your scenarios have changing cells that overlap but do not exactly coincide with, another scenario in the workbook. If you create multiple scenario sets (that is, scenarios that affect different changing cells), make sure that none of the sets of changing cells overlap. That will prevent unintended changes to key cells as you switch scenarios.

For Related Information

- "Protecting Sheets and Workbooks," p. 362
- "Naming and Saving a View," p. 540

From Here...

For additional information that relates to scenarios, browse through these chapters:

- Chapter 27, "Solving with Goal Seeking and Solver." Learn how to compute the inputs necessary to achieve a specified result and to find the optimal solution to problems involving constraints.
- Chapter 36, "Using Pivot Tables." Learn how to analyze information in a list and create reports by viewing and totaling the data from different perspectives.

Chapter 29

Using the Analysis ToolPak

The Analysis ToolPak is an extensive and powerful collection of tools added to Microsoft Excel 5. Once added with the help of add-in macro sheets, these features are implemented using dynamic link libraries, which are fast and efficient.

EXCEL 5

In this chapter, you learn how to:

- Use the Analysis Toolpak
- Install the tools to be available in worksheets
- Create sample data
- Analyze real data

Most of the commands and functions in the Analysis ToolPak are designed for specific, technical purposes. If you do not know what some mean, you probably do not need them. If you are not a highly technical user, however, do not simply skip this chapter. Some of these tools are useful for a wide variety of problems. This chapter helps you to sift through the Analysis ToolPak to find those parts you can put to use. Because these tools all work in a consistent way, highly technical users also learn in this chapter how to apply the tools they need.

First, you must have an idea of what the ToolPak is and how it works. The Analysis ToolPak contains two parts:

- Commands that are available through the **D**ata Analysis command on the **T**ools menu. The ToolPak includes 17 statistical commands and two engineering commands. (Table 29.1 at the end of this chapter lists all these commands.)
- Functions that you can use from a worksheet, just like any other functions. The ToolPak includes 49 mathematics and engineering functions and 41 financial functions. (Tables 29.2 and 29.3 at the end of this chapter list all these functions.)

Many statistical functions are directly built into Excel, and therefore technically are not part of the Analysis ToolPak. See Chapter 6, "Using Functions," for more information on built-in functions.

Using Data Analysis Tools Commands

Most of the Data Analysis Tools commands perform sophisticated statistical analyses on input data. These tools are for the statistician, researcher, scientist, or engineer. Hidden among these tools, however, are several tools that you can readily apply in a wide variety of situations. This section covers three common tasks you can accomplish by using the Data Analysis Tools:

- Creating realistic sample data
- Evaluating performance
- Smoothing time-series data

Creating Realistic Sample Data

Random numbers have many uses. A common use is to create realistic sample data while a model is under development. Suppose that you want to create a model to analyze Dirt Cheap's orders. You have one chart that is a histogram of the number of orders per day. Eventually, you will have actual data to put into the model, but for now you want to create a prototype chart to show your managers how the model results appear. A *histogram* is a table that reflects how data is distributed. A histogram is comprised of "bins," each containing a number of items that satisfy a certain requirement. The requirements usually entail a specific numeric range or a range of dates, but bins also can be used for text items. In the example, each bin holds the number of orders for that day.

You know that your company sales force makes approximately 200 calls per day, and that about 10 percent of the people who are called purchase your product, so the company averages 20 orders per day. You could just create a sample data series with average data figures for each day, but that histogram forms a single spike. You know that this pattern doesn't reflect actual daily sales. Most days, Dirt Cheap gets between 10 and 30 orders. You can use the Analysis ToolPak to create a series of random numbers between 10 and 30 to make the sample histogram appear more realistic.

To create a uniform random series, take these steps:

1. Find a location on the worksheet where you can enter the set of random numbers in a range. Note the top-left corner as well as the number of rows and columns needed.

2. Choose the **T**ools **D**ata Analysis command. The Data Analysis dialog box appears, as shown in figure 29.1.

> **Note**
>
> If the Data Analysis option is not available, choose the Tools Add-Ins Analysis command.

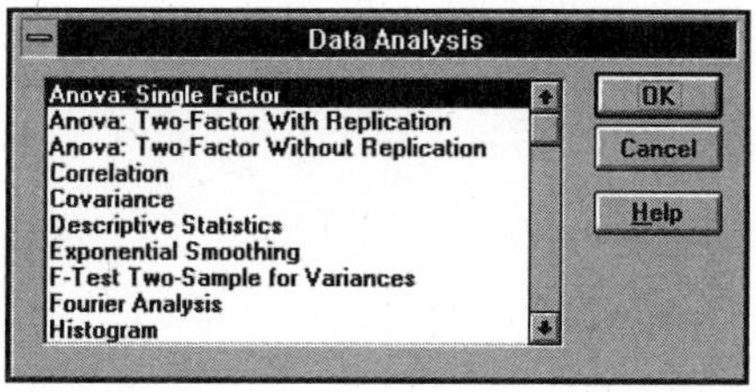

Fig. 29.1
Select a tool from the Data Analysis dialog box.

3. Select Random Number Generation from the list. Choose OK.

   The Random Number Generation dialog box appears, as shown in figure 29.2.

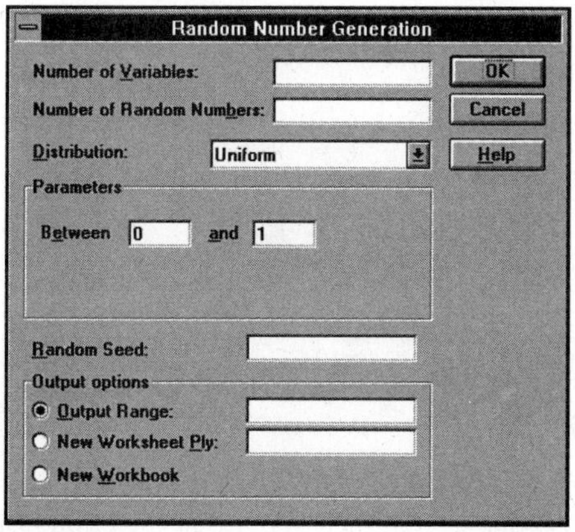

Fig. 29.2
Use settings in the Random Number Generation dialog box to specify the type of random numbers to generate.

4. Select Uniform from the **D**istribution drop-down list.

5. Type **1** in the Number of **V**ariables box. This is the number of columns into which you want random numbers placed.

6. Type **180** in the Number of Random Num**b**ers box. This is the number of rows of random numbers you want to simulate six months of daily orders.

7. Type **10** and **30** for the upper- and lower-limit values in the B**e**tween box and the **a**nd box, respectively. This shows you expect between 10 and 30 orders each day.

8. Type a number in the **R**andom Seed box if you want to create the same series of random numbers more than once. The seed can be used again to duplicate this series. Otherwise, leave the box blank.

9. Type a reference to the top-left cell of the range where you want the random numbers in the **O**utput Range box. (You specified the number of rows and columns in steps 5 and 6.)

10. Choose OK. If data exists already in the output range, Excel asks whether you are sure you want it replaced.

Excel generates random numbers and fills the column with them. From this column, you can create a histogram that graphically shows the distribution of these numbers. The next section, "Creating Histograms and Frequency Distributions," describes how to create frequency tables and the chart shown in figure 29.3.

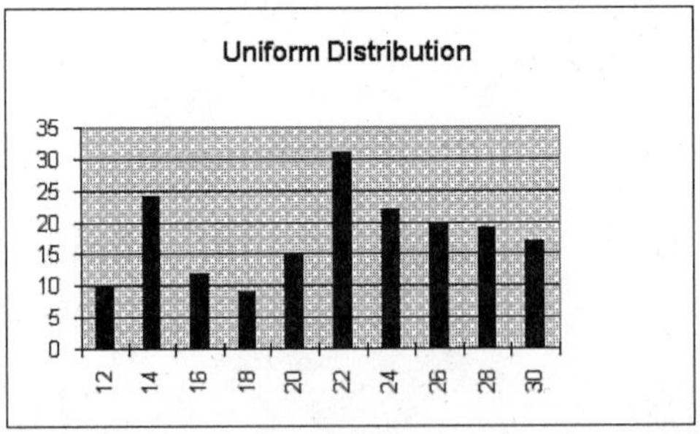

Fig. 29.3
A histogram with uniformly distributed random numbers.

The Random Number Generator can create other kinds of random numbers that may be closer to your needs. One potentially useful choice is the Normal distribution. The Normal distribution creates what is commonly known as a *bell curve*. For the Normal distribution, you specify the desired average along with a standard deviation. Most of the data falls within the standard deviation on either side of the average. The Normal distribution works well for data such as test scores or performance rankings.

For Dirt Cheap's orders, however, there is an even better choice. In this sample situation, 200 customers each day choose to order or not to order, and 10 percent on average choose to order. This situation is similar to that of tossing a coin—but a *loaded* coin. The Binomial distribution exactly models this situation. For the Binomial distribution, you specify how many coin tosses you want for each sample, and what percentage of them on average should be heads.

To create 180 random numbers using the Binomial distribution, follow these steps:

1. Choose the **T**ools **D**ata Analysis command.

2. Select Random Number Generation from the list and choose OK.

3. Select Binomial from the **D**istribution drop-down list. Select the distribution type before entering values for any parameters, or you may lose the parameter values. Figure 29.4 shows the Random Number Generation dialog box with the parameters for the Binomial distribution.

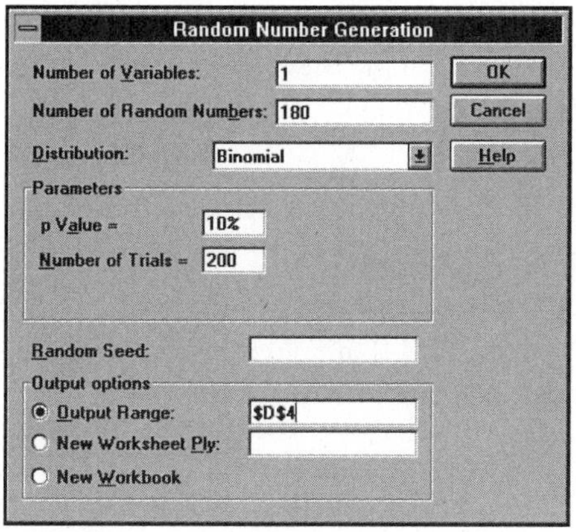

Fig. 29.4
The parameters for the Random Number Generation dialog box vary with each Distribution type.

4. Type **1** in the Number of **V**ariables box.

5. Type **180** in the Number of Random Num**b**ers box.

6. Type **10%** for the p V**a**lue and **200** in the **N**umber of Trials box. This shows that 10 percent of 200 calls result in orders.

7. Type a reference to the top-left cell of the range where you want the random numbers in the **O**utput Range box.

8. Choose OK. Excel generates random numbers and enters them in the sheet.

When you create a histogram of these numbers, the numeric distribution is very realistic, as you can see in figure 29.5. This chart gives management a good sense of what the final charts look like. (Creation of a histogram chart and frequency distribution table is described in the following section.)

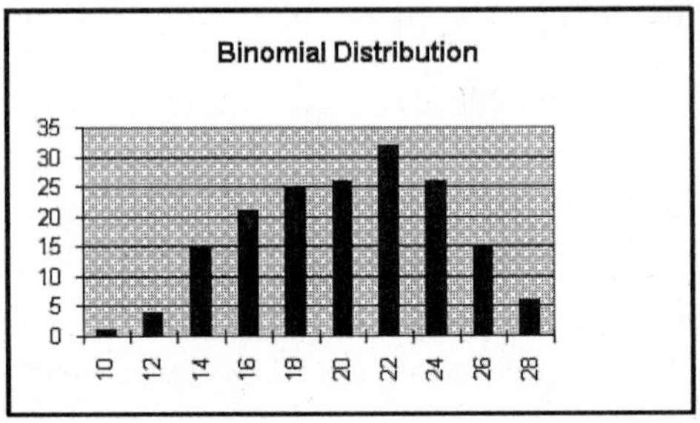

Fig. 29.5
A histogram of random numbers created with a binomial distribution.

Creating Histograms and Frequency Distributions

Tip
The histogram in Excel does essentially the same thing as the Data Distribution command in 1-2-3.

Just about any performance measure compares one item with others. It is often necessary to see how people or widgets or orders per day fit into performance bands. One of the tools in Excel's Analysis ToolPak—the histogram—provides this capability. Here, a *histogram* is a table where values in a data set are counted into bins. A histogram sometimes is called a *frequency distribution.* You use histograms to get a picture of the spread of data, whether the number of orders per day or the number of students who fall into grade categories. Figure 29.6 shows a worksheet that contains random orders per day.

To categorize the orders into bins or to find out how many days had x orders placed, follow these steps:

1. Create a set of numbers to use as bins. These numbers do not have to be a regular series, but they do need to be sorted in ascending order. In figure 29.6, the numbers defining the bins are in E4 through E14.

2. Select the input data for the histogram. In the figure, this is all numerical data in column C. The Data Analysis Tools use the current selection as the default input range.

3. Choose the **T**ools **D**ata Analysis command.

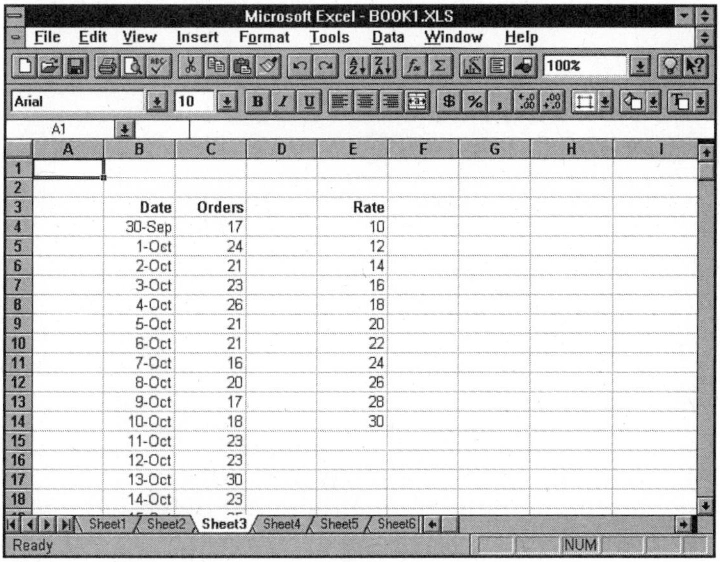

Fig. 29.6
Random orders per day ready to be grouped with a histogram. The Bins are the numbers under the Rate heading.

4. Select Histogram from the list, and choose OK. The Histogram dialog box in figure 29.7 appears.

5. Type the reference **$E$4:$E$14** in the **B**in Range box; or select the box, and in the sheet drag across the range E4:E14.

6. Type a reference to the top-left cell of the range where you want the output in the **O**utput Range box; or select the box, and in the sheet click the top-left cell of the range.

   The resulting report fills down and right, so be certain that you reference an area where there is sufficient room. The Histogram command provides titles in the first row, and copies the bin values to the first column.

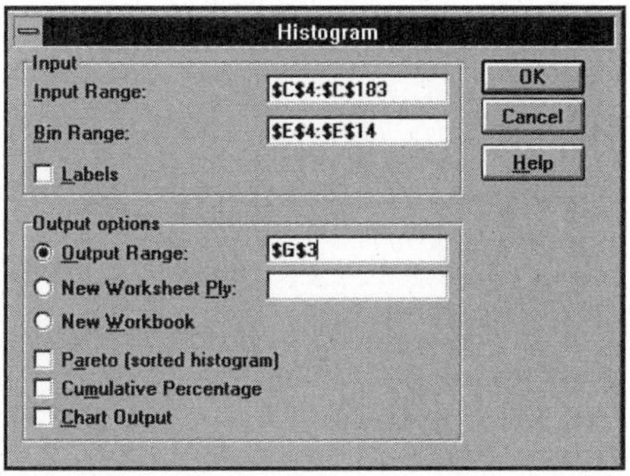

Fig. 29.7
Use the Histogram dialog box to specify how the data is analyzed.

7. Leave the other dialog box items blank, and choose OK.

   The report is generated, as shown in figure 29.8.

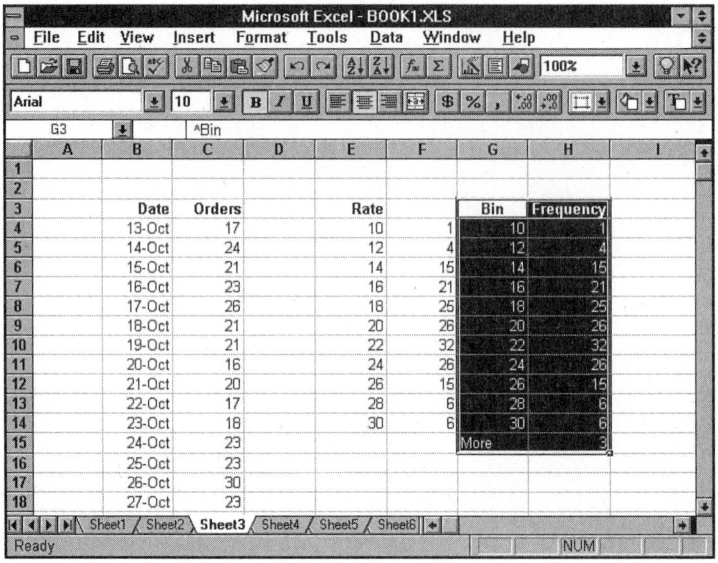

Fig. 29.8
The completed histogram report shows the distribution of data in each category.

The check boxes in the Histogram dialog box add powerful capabilities to the Histogram command. Selecting the P**a**reto check box creates an extra copy of the report; that copy is sorted by the number of items each bin contains, from greatest to smallest. Selecting the Cu**m**ulative Percentage check box puts into the output report an additional column that shows the cumulative percentage of the total for each bin—if a chart is requested, the percentages are used for the chart (refer to fig. 29.7). If the **C**hart Output check box is selected, Excel creates a new chart based on the report results.

Note

The Analysis ToolPak add-in must be loaded for add-in functions, such as FREQUENCY( ), RANK( ), and PERCENTRANK( ), to work.

The Histogram command is convenient because it walks you through the steps of creating a histogram. The values in the Frequency column of the report, however, are frozen values, not linked formulas. With a little work, you can use one of Excel 5's new built-in statistical functions to create a hot-linked histogram that actually changes when the input data changes.

To create a histogram table with linked formulas, follow these steps:

1. Select from cell C3 to the bottom of the data. The formula is much easier to create if the input and bin ranges are named.

2. Choose the **I**nsert **N**ame **C**reate command.

3. Choose OK.

4. Select the range E3:E14 and choose the **I**nsert **N**ame **C**reate command again. This step assigns the name at the top of each column to the cells below.

5. Select cells F4:F14. This range is where the function for the histogram is placed.

6. Choose the **I**nsert **F**unction command.

7. Select Statistical Function **C**ategory.

8. Select FREQUENCY from the Function **N**ame list, as shown in figure 29.9.

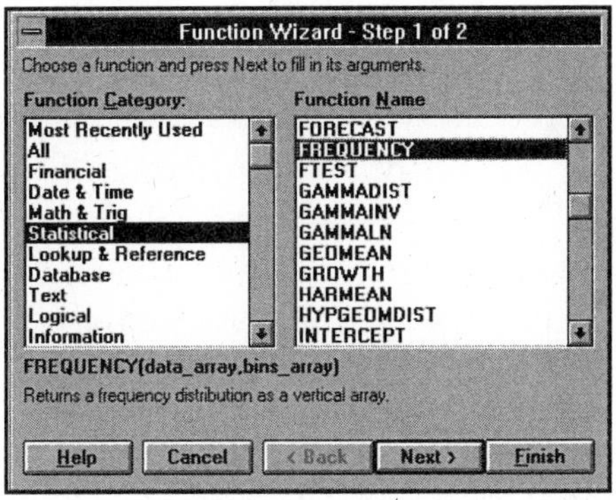

Fig. 29.9
Choose the FREQUENCY function to specify that you want to add the proper formula to the selected cells.

9. Choose the **F**inish button. `FREQUENCY( )` appears in the formula bar, with the data_array parameter highlighted and ready to be edited.

10. Replace the data_array parameter with **Orders**, the name of the input range. Double-click the bins_array parameter to select it, and then replace it with **Rate**, the name of the bin's range.

11. Press Shift+Ctrl+Enter to enter the function as an array. See Chapter 5, "Working with Formulas," for more information about array formulas.

Tip
Press F3 to show a list that allows you to select from defined range names rather than typing the range names.

The FREQUENCY( ) function fills the cells. These values are linked to the data, however; so if the underlying data values change, the histogram is automatically updated.

Note

Another useful command for evaluating performance is the Rank and Percentile command. This command works much like the Histogram command, but produces a report that shows both ordinal ranking and percentile ranking—the percentage of items in the sample scoring that are the same or worse than the current sample. You can use the command version in the Analysis ToolPak or, if you prefer hot-linked formulas, use the RANK( ) and PERCENTRANK( ) statistical functions.

Smoothing Time-Series Data

As you begin to track and chart Dirt Cheap's orders over time, you may see orders fluctuate a great deal. Sometimes it is difficult to tell whether orders are improving over time, or dropping off. You need a way to smooth out the random variations in orders to see the underlying trends more clearly. The Analysis ToolPak provides two commands to help smooth time-series data: Moving Average and Exponential Smoothing.

The Moving Average command puts the average of the previous few periods into each period. You can specify how many periods to include in this average. Exponential Smoothing averages the smoothed value for the previous period and the actual data for the previous data point. This feature automatically includes all previous periods in the average. You can specify how greatly to weight the current period.

Figure 29.10 shows a worksheet with the last month of Dirt Cheap orders. As you can see, it is difficult to see any trends in the data in the chart. Try the Moving Average and Exponential Smoothing commands.

To smooth the line with a moving average, follow these steps:

1. Select the ordered data to smooth.

2. Choose the **T**ools **D**ata Analysis command, select Moving Average, and then select OK. The Moving Average dialog box appears (see fig. 29.11).

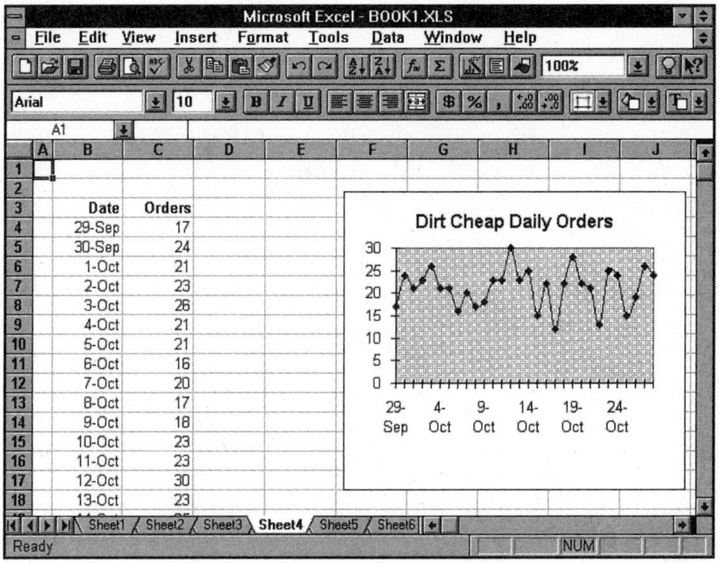

Fig. 29.10
The last month of Dirt Cheap orders, needing to be smoothed.

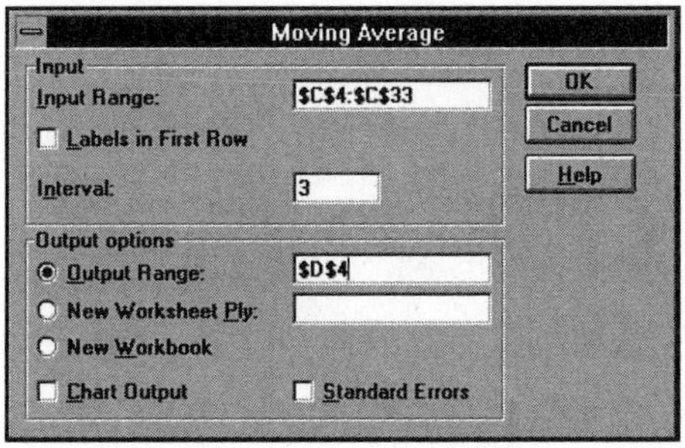

Fig. 29.11
The Moving Average dialog box enables you to smooth data by averaging changes over a specified interval.

3. Edit and select boxes as necessary. Figure 29.11 shows a completed box. The following list explains some of the available options:

Input Range	Contains the data being smoothed.
Output Range	Contains the top cell where you want the smoothed data entered. The results will be one column wide and as long as the input range.

Interval	Enables you to control the number of past periods included in the average. Increasing the interval smooths the curve more but increases the inertia of the line so that the line does not reflect changes in trends as quickly. Enter **3** for the example.
Standard Errors	Creates an additional column of error statistics. Do not select this check box for the example.
Chart Output	Creates a chart. Because the example already has a chart, it is unnecessary to select this check box for the example.

4. Choose OK.

The smoothed data fills the worksheet, beginning in cell D4. The first two periods say #N/A because there were not yet three periods of data available to average. The number #N/A reflects the number you used for the interval; until there are enough data periods to sample, the data cannot be smoothed.

Now you need to add the exponential smoothing. To smooth the data using exponential smoothing, follow these steps:

1. Verify that the data to be smoothed is selected.
2. Choose the **T**ools **D**ata Analysis command.
3. Select Exponential Smoothing from the list, and choose OK. The Exponential Smoothing dialog box, shown in figure 29.12, appears.
4. Select **I**nput Range and type the range of orders being smoothed.
5. Select **D**amping factor and type **3**. The **D**amping factor gives the amount of weighting to be applied to the prior average. A higher damping factor produces a smoother line.
6. Select the **O**utput Range and click cell E4.
7. Choose OK.

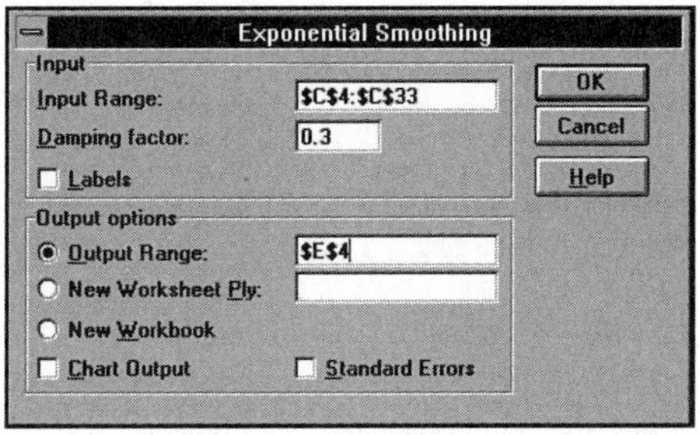

Fig. 29.12 The Exponential Smoothing dialog box.

The exponentially smoothed data for the example is entered, beginning in cell E4.

If you use these two lines of data (the moving average and the exponentially smoothed data) in the chart, you get something close to what is shown in figure 29.13. With the smoothed data on the chart, you can see that Dirt Cheap orders dropped during the first half of the month, but have been picking up during the second half.

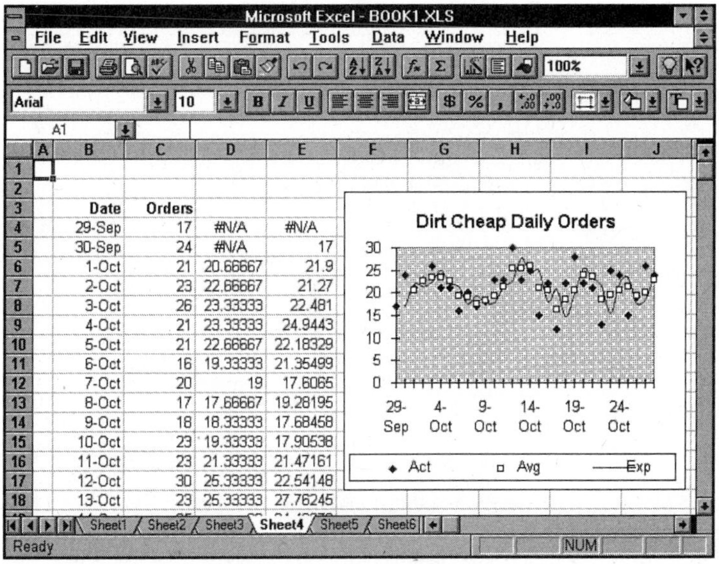

Fig. 29.13 The worksheet with both types of smoothing, and a chart comparing the different types of data.

Note

Moving Average and Exponential Smoothing are the only Data Analysis Tools that put formulas in cells. If you change input values, the smoothed data is updated.

Overview of ToolPak Commands and Functions

The Analysis ToolPak contains many commands and functions. The following tables give an overview of the new commands and functions, the new built-in statistical functions, and the existing add-in functions from Excel 4.

> **Note**
>
> The Analysis ToolPak consists of functions available through the **I**nsert **F**unction command, and commands available through the **T**ools **D**ata Analysis command. Installing the Analysis ToolPak provides access to most of these functions and commands.

Table 29.1 Analysis ToolPak Commands

Command	Description	Macro*
ANOVA: Single Factor	Simple Analysis of Variance.	ANOVA1
ANOVA: Two-Factor with Replication	Analysis of Variance including more than one sample for each data group.	ANOVA2
ANOVA: Two-Factor Without Replication	Analysis of Variance not including more than one sample for each data group.	ANOVA3
Correlation	Measurement-independent correlation between data sets.	MCORREL
Covariance	Measurement-dependent correlation between two sets.	MCOVAR
Descriptive Statistics	Report of univariate statistics for sample.	DESCR
Exponential Smoothing	Smooths data, weighting more recent data heavier.	EXPON
F-Test: Two-Sample for Variances	Two-Sample F-Test to compare population variances.	FTEST
Histogram	Counts occurrences in each of several data bins.	HISTOGRAM
Moving Average	Smooths data series by averaging the last few periods.	MOVEAVG

Command	Description	Macro*
Random Number Generation	Creates any of several types of random numbers.	RANDOM
Uniform	Uniform random numbers between upper and lower bounds.	
Normal	Normally distributed numbers based on the mean and the standard deviation.	
Bernoulli	Ones and zeros with a specified probability of success.	
Binomial	Sum of several Bernoulli trials.	
Poisson	A distribution of random numbers given a desired lambda.	
Patterned	A sequence of numbers at a specific interval (cf. Data Series).	
Discrete	Probabilities based on predefined percents of total.	
Rank and Percentile	Creates a report of ranking and percentile distribution.	RANKPERC
Regression	Creates a table of statistics that result from least-squares regression.	REGRESS
t-Test: Paired Two-Sample for Means	Paired two-sample student's t-test.	PTTESTM
t-Test: Two-Sample Assuming Equal Variances	Paired two-sample t-test assuming equal means.	PTTESTV
t-Test: Two-Sample Assuming Unequal Variances	Homoscedastic t-test.	TTESTM
z-Test: Two-Sample for Means	Two-sample z-test for means with known variances.	ZTESTM
Engineering Commands		
Fourier Analysis	DFT or FFT method, including reverse transforms.	FOURIER
Sampling	Samples a population randomly or periodically.	SAMPLE

* *The Macro column gives the command name in case you want to run it from a macro.*

Table 29.2 Analysis ToolPak Engineering Functions

Function	Description
BESSELI	Returns the modified Bessel function In(x).
BESSELJ	Returns the Bessel function Jn(x).
BESSELK	Returns the modified Bessel function Kn(x).
BESSELY	Returns the Bessel function Yn(x).
BIN2DEC	Converts a number from binary notation to decimal.
BIN2HEX	Converts a number from binary notation to hexadecimal.
BIN2OCT	Converts a number from binary notation to octal.
COMPLEX	Converts real and imaginary coefficients into a complex number.
CONVERT	Converts a number from one measurement system to another.
DEC2BIN	Converts a number from decimal notation to binary.
DEC2HEX	Converts a number from decimal notation to hexadecimal.
DEC2OCT	Converts a number from decimal notation to octal.
DELTA	Returns 1 if two numbers are equal, 0 if not.
ERF	Returns the error function between limits.
ERFC	Returns the complementary ERF function.
FACTDOUBLE	Returns the double factorial.
GCD	Returns the greatest common divisor of two numbers.
GESTEP	Returns 1 if a number is greater than a threshold value.
HEX2BIN	Converts a number from hexadecimal notation to binary.
HEX2DEC	Converts a number from hexadecimal notation to decimal.
HEX2OCT	Converts a number from hexadecimal notation to octal.
IMABS	Returns the absolute value of a complex number.
IMAGINARY	Returns the imaginary component of a complex number.
IMARGUMENT	Returns an angle, expressed in radians, of a complex number.
IMCONJUGATE	Returns the complex conjugate of a complex number.

Function	Description
IMCOS	Returns the cosine of a complex number.
IMDIV	Divides one complex number by another.
IMEXP	Returns the exponential of a complex number.
IMLN	Returns the natural logarithm of a complex number.
IMLOG10	Returns the base-10 logarithm of a complex number.
IMLOG2	Returns the base-2 logarithm of a complex number.
IMPOWER	Returns a complex number raised to an integer power.
IMPRODUCT	Returns the product of two complex numbers.
IMREAL	Returns the real coefficient of a complex number.
IMSIN	Returns the sine of a complex number.
IMSQRT	Returns the square root of a complex number.
IMSUB	Returns the difference of two complex numbers.
IMSUM	Returns the sum of two complex numbers.
ISEVEN	Returns 1 if a number is even, 0 if it is odd.
ISODD	Returns 1 if a number is odd, 0 if it is even.
LCM	Returns the least common multiple of 1-12 integers.
MROUND	Rounds a number to a multiple of a specified number.
MULTINOMIAL	Divides the factorial of several added numbers by the product of the factorial of each number.
OCT2BIN	Converts a number from octal notation to binary.
OCT2DEC	Converts a number from octal notation to decimal.
OCT2HEX	Converts a number from octal notation to hexadecimal.
QUOTIENT	Returns the integer part of the answer to a division. Equivalent to TRUNC(x/y).
SERIESSUM	Returns the sum of a power series.
SQRTPI	Returns the square root of a specified number times PI. Equivalent to SQRT(PI( )*x).

Table 29.3 Analysis ToolPak Financial Functions

Function	Description
ACCRINT	Returns the accrued interest for a security.
ACCRINTM	Returns the accrued interest for a security that pays at maturity.
AMORDEGRC	Returns the depreciation for each accounting period (for the French accounting system). The function is similar to AMORLINC, except that a depreciation coefficient is applied in the calculation depending on the life of the assets.
AMORLINC	Returns the depreciation for each accounting period (for the French accounting system).
COUPDAYBS	Returns the number of days for a coupon before settle-ment.
COUPDAYS	Returns the number of days for a coupon in its last period.
COUPDAYSNC	Returns the difference between COUPDAYS and COUPDAYSBS.
COUPNCD	Returns the next coupon date after the settlement date.
COUPNUM	Returns the number of coupons between the settlement date and the maturity date.
COUPPCD	Returns the previous coupon date before the settlement date.
CUMIPMT	Returns the cumulative interest on a loan between two periods.
CUMPRINC	Returns the cumulative principal on a loan between two periods.
DISC	Returns the discount rate for a security.
DOLLARDE	Converts fractional dollars to decimal dollars.
DOLLARFR	Converts decimal dollars to fractional dollars.
DURATION	Returns the annual duration of a security.
EDATE	Returns the serial number date that is the indicated number of months before or after a specified start date.
EFFECT	Returns the effective interest rate of a loan.
EOMONTH	Returns the serial number date for the last day of the month that is the indicated number of months before or after a specified start date.

Function	Description
INTRATE	Returns the interest rate for a fully invested security.
MDURATION	Returns the modified duration of a security.
NETWORKDAYS	Returns the net count of working days between two dates.
NOMINAL	Returns the nominal interest rate of a loan.
ODDFPRICE	Returns the price per $100 of a security with an odd first period.
ODDFYIELD	Returns the yield of a security with an odd first period.
ODDLPRICE	Returns the price per $100 of a security with an odd last period.
ODDLYIELD	Returns the yield of a security with an odd last period.
PRICE	Returns the price per $100 of a security.
PRICEDISC	Returns the price per $100 of a discounted security.
PRICEMAT	Returns the price per $100 of a security that pays at maturity.
RECEIVED	Returns the amount received at maturity.
TBILLEQ	Returns the bond-equivalent yield for a treasury bill.
TBILLPRICE	Returns the price per $100 of a treasury bill.
TBILLYIELD	Returns the yield for a treasury bill.
WORKDAY	Returns a date that is a specified number of work days from a base date.
XIRR	Returns the IRR for irregular cash flows.
XNPV	Returns the NPV for irregular cash flows.
YEARFRAC	Returns the fraction of a year between two dates.
YIELD	Returns the yield of a security.
YIELDDISC	Returns the yield of a discounted security.
YIELDMAT	Returns the yield of a security that pays at maturity.

Table 29.4 Built-in Statistical Functions*

Function	Description
AVEDEV	Returns the average absolute deviation from the mean.
BETADIST	Returns the cumulative beta probability density function.
BETAINV	Returns the inverse of the cumulative beta probability density function.
BINOMDIST	Returns the individual term binomial distribution probability.
CEILING	Returns a number rounded up to the next highest multiple of a specified value.
CHIDIST	Returns the chi-square distribution.
CHIINV	Returns the inverse of the chi-square distribution.
CHITEST	Returns the test for independence.
COMBIN	Returns the number of ways that a specified number of objects can be chosen from another specified number of objects.
CONFIDENCE	Returns the confidence interval for a population mean.
CORREL	Returns the correlation coefficient of two arrays.
COVAR	Returns the covariance for data point pairs.
CRITBINOM	Returns the smallest integer where the cumulative binomial distribution is less than a specified value.
DEVSQ	Returns the sum of squares of deviations.
EVEN	Returns a number rounded up to the next even integer.
EXPONDIST	Returns the exponential distribution function.
FDIST	Returns the F probability distribution.
FINV	Returns the inverse of the F probability distribution.
FISHER	Returns the Fisher transformation.
FISHERINV	Returns the inverse of the Fisher transformation.
FLOOR	Returns a number rounded down to the next lower multiple of a specified value.
FORECAST	Returns the predicted value for *x* based on a linear regression.

Function	Description
FREQUENCY	Returns a histogram distribution for a given set of values and bins.
FTEST	Returns the results of an F-test.
GAMMADIST	Returns the gamma distribution function.
GAMMAINV	Returns the inverse of the gamma cumulative distribution.
GAMMALN	Returns the natural logarithm of the gamma function.
GEOMEAN	Returns the geometric mean of an array.
HARMEAN	Returns the harmonic mean of an array.
HYPGEOMDIST	Returns the hypergeometric distribution.
INTERCEPT	Returns the intercept of a linear regression line.
KURT	Returns the kurtosis of a data set.
LARGE	Returns the value found a specified position from the largest value in a data set.
LOGINV	Returns the inverse of the lognormal cumulative distribution function.
LOGNORMDIST	Returns the lognormal cumulative distribution function.
MEDIAN	Returns the median of a set of numbers.
MODE	Returns the mode of a set of numbers.
NEGBINOMDIST	Returns the negative binomial distribution.
NORMDIST	Returns the normal cumulative distribution.
NORMINV	Returns the inverse of the normal cumulative distribution.
NORMSDIST	Returns the standard normal cumulative distribution.
NORMSINV	Returns the inverse of the standard normal cumulative distribution.
ODD	Returns a number rounded up to the next larger odd number.
PEARSON	Returns the Pearson product moment correlation coefficient.
PERCENTILE	Returns the value from an array at the specified percentile.

(continues)

Table 29.4 Continued

Function	Description
PERCENTRANK	Returns the percentage rank of a value in a data set.
PERMUT	Returns the number of permutations of a number chosen from another number.
POISSON	Returns the Poisson probability distribution.
PROB	Returns the probability that values in a range are between a lower and upper limit.
QUARTILE	Returns the specified quartile value from a data set.
RANK	Returns the rank of a number in a data set.
RSQ	Returns the square of the Pearson product moment correlation coefficient.
SKEW	Returns the skewness of a distribution.
SLOPE	Returns the slope of a linear regression line.
SMALL	Returns the value a specified position from the smallest value in a data set.
STANDARDIZE	Returns a normalized value from a distribution.
STEYX	Returns the standard error of the regression of *y* on *x*.
SUMSQUARES	Returns the sum of the squares of a set of numbers.
SUMX2MY2	Returns the sum of the difference of squares of corresponding values in two arrays.
SUMX2PY2	Returns the sum of squares' sums of corresponding values in two arrays.
SUMXMY2	Returns the sum of squares' differences of corresponding values in two arrays.
TDIST	Returns the student's distribution.
TINV	Returns the inverse of the student's distribution.
TRIMMEAN	Returns the average of a set, excluding a specified percentage of data points from the tails.
TTEST	Returns the probability associated with a student's t-test.
WEIBULL	Returns the Weibull distribution.
ZTEST	Returns the *p* value of a two-tailed z-test.

**These functions are built into Excel and are always available.*

Table 29.5 Additional Related Functions

Function	Description
DEGREES	Converts a number from radians to degrees.
RADIANS	Converts a number from degrees to radians.
RANDBETWEEN	Returns a random number between specified limits.

For Related Information

- "Entering Worksheet Functions," p. 178
- "Excel Function Dictionary," p. 184

From Here...

The tools described in this chapter extend far beyond the capabilities of most electronic spreadsheets. They give you the ability to solve problems that only a few years ago required minicomputers.

The Analysis ToolPak is a specialized tool that brings Excel to professionals that require hard-coded programs to solve specific financial, statistical, or scientific problems. With the Analysis ToolPak, disciplines with specialized needs have many advanced functions they can use in a worksheet.

- Chapter 5, "Working with Formulas." Reviews the basics of entering and editing formulas.
- Chapter 6, "Using Functions." Explains how to use the hundreds of available built-in functions without adding the ToolPak.
- Chapter 26, "Auditing Workbooks and Worksheets." Discusses the tools for preventing and finding errors in calculations after your worksheets are created.

Part V

Managing Lists or Databases

30 **Designing a List or Database**

31 **Entering Data in a List or Database**

32 **Sorting Data**

33 **Finding, Filtering, and Editing Lists and Databases**

34 **Working with Filtered Data**

35 **Retrieving Data from External Databases**

36 **Using Pivot Tables**

37 **Analyzing and Reporting with Pivot Tables**

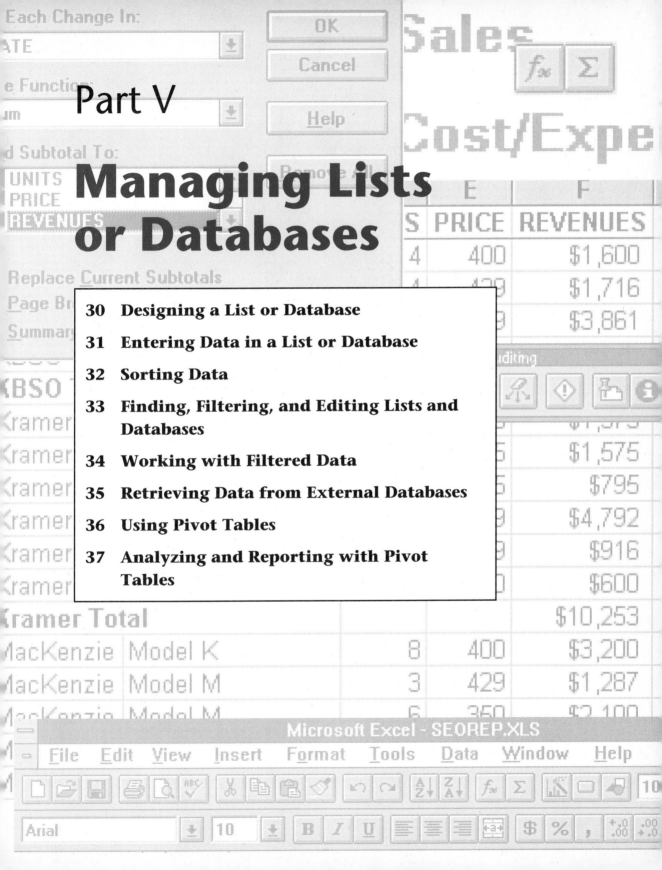

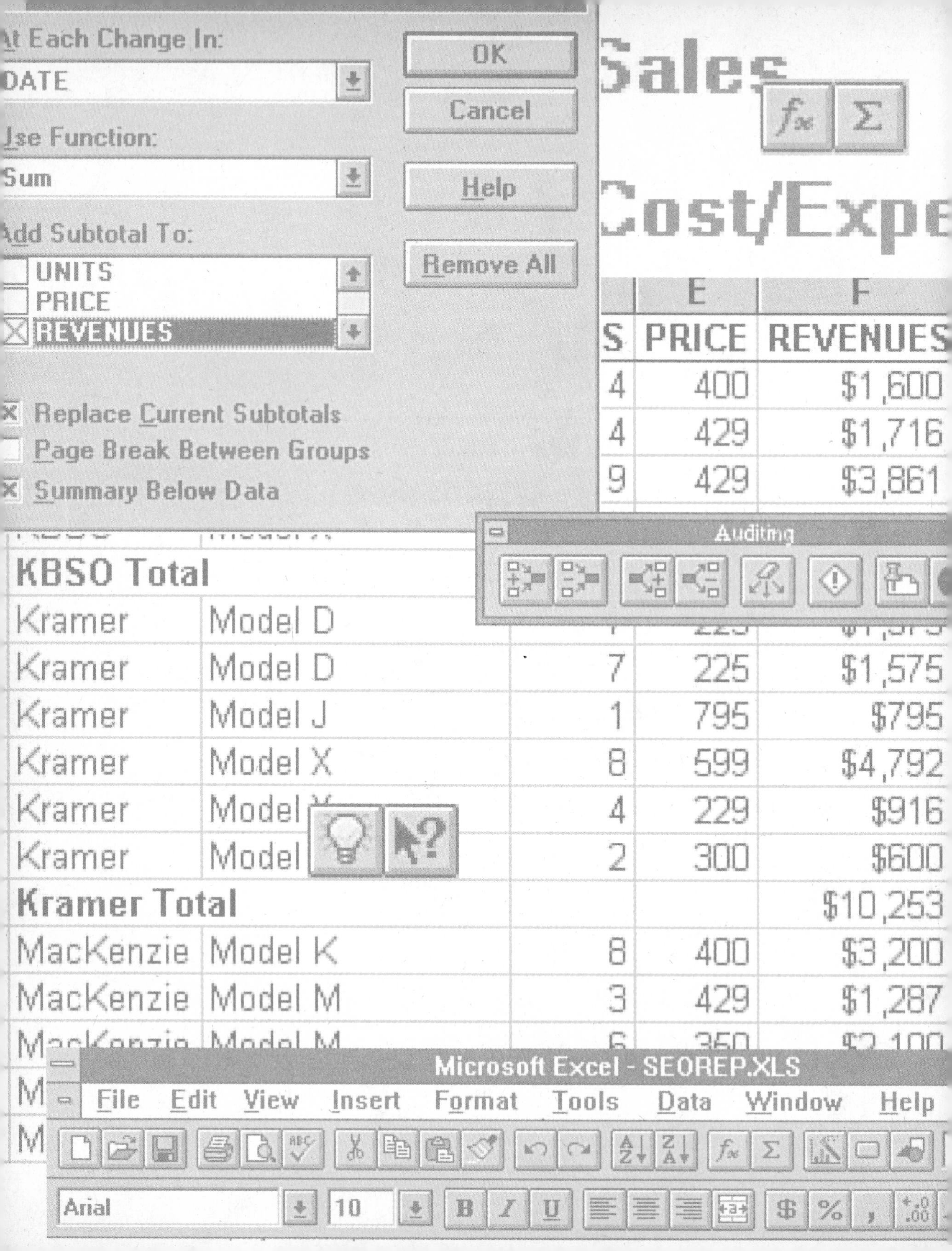
At Each Change In:
DATE
Use Function:
Sum
Add Subtotal To:
UNITS
PRICE
REVENUES
Replace Current Subtotals
Page Break Between Groups
Summary Below Data
OK
Cancel
Help
Remove All
Sales
Cost/Expe
E
F
PRICE
REVENUES
400
$1,600
429
$1,716
429
$3,861
Auditing
KBSO Total
Kramer Model D
Kramer Model D 7 225 $1,575
Kramer Model J 1 795 $795
Kramer Model X 8 599 $4,792
Kramer 4 229 $916
Kramer 2 300 $600
Kramer Total $10,253
MacKenzie Model K 8 400 $3,200
MacKenzie Model M 3 429 $1,287
Microsoft Excel - SEOREP.XLS
File Edit View Insert Format Tools Data Window Help
Arial
10

Chapter 30

Designing a List or Database

This chapter helps you understand important terms used when talking about Excel lists. (Note this change in terminology; in Excel Version 4.0, Microsoft used the term *database*.) This chapter advises how to choose the contents for a list and shows you how to lay out a list in the worksheet. Chapters 30 through 37 explain the details of building and working with lists.

In this chapter, you learn:

- The definition of a list
- The parts of a list including a database range, a criteria range, and the extract range
- Suggestions for naming and creating your list
- How to organize a list

You are already familiar with lists of information. You probably keep lists of names and addresses, to-do lists, and shopping lists. Excel works with simple lists of information—such as a shopping list—or can work with larger, more complex lists, also known as databases. A *database* in Excel is just a list that contains one or more columns. (Excel Version 5 now refers to databases as *lists*.)

With Excel's features, you can sort information in the list, find information that meets certain requirements, make copies of specific information, or even extract copies of information from larger databases located on a network or mainframe computer.

What Is a List?

The first example of a business list that most people encounter is the familiar rolling card file (see fig. 30.1). You can flip through a card file quickly to find information such as a client's address, phone number, or favorite restaurant. Card files are easy to use provided that the cards are kept in alphabetical order according to a single key word, such as the client's name. Card files can present problems, however, when you want to do more than just find a client by name. If you wanted to find all the financial analysts in San Francisco, for example, using a card file could take considerable time.

Excel's list feature handles basic functions, such as finding, quickly and easily, the kind of information you usually write on a card. Excel also handles complex jobs, such as analyzing and extracting information in the list.

Fig. 30.1
Cards in a card file are easy to use but time-consuming and inefficient to find.

Turnigan, Kathleen	(415) 579-2650
Financial Analyst	
Brown, James & Assoc.	
213 California St.	
San Francisco, CA 94003	
Background:	Interned w/Peterman; MBA Stanford
Expertise:	Bond portfolio analysis
Computer experience:	Excel and Visual Basic

The file card for Kathleen Turnigan contains information related to Kathleen Turnigan. In an Excel list, the information on one file card is known as a *record*. All the information from each file card goes into one row of related information. In this row, individual items are stored in *fields*—each field is a column in the worksheet. A field contains the same kind of information for each row in the list.

Each piece of data in the record (row) must be entered in a separate cell. Kathleen's first name, for example, goes in one cell (the First Name field), her last name in another cell (the Last Name field), the firm name in a third cell (the Firm field), and so on. To keep the information organized, each field is typed in a specific column. For example, you might put first names in column A, last names in column B, and so on. Each column is given a unique *field name*. These names, which go across the top of a list, are called the *header row*. Figure 30.2 shows how part of Kathleen's card is entered in the first record of an Excel list in row 10.

Your Excel list may have many records. When you need to find information, you need to tell Excel what field (column) to search in for matching information that you need. Using Excel's **D**ata **F**ilter command, you can do this in two ways: you can use the Auto**F**ilter feature, or you can create a criteria range that uses the exact field names used in the header row over your list. To find the records in a list for everyone in San Francisco, for example, you may tell Excel to search a field named City. Field names must be text or text formulas. Figure 30.2 shows how the field names and data are arranged within an Excel worksheet.

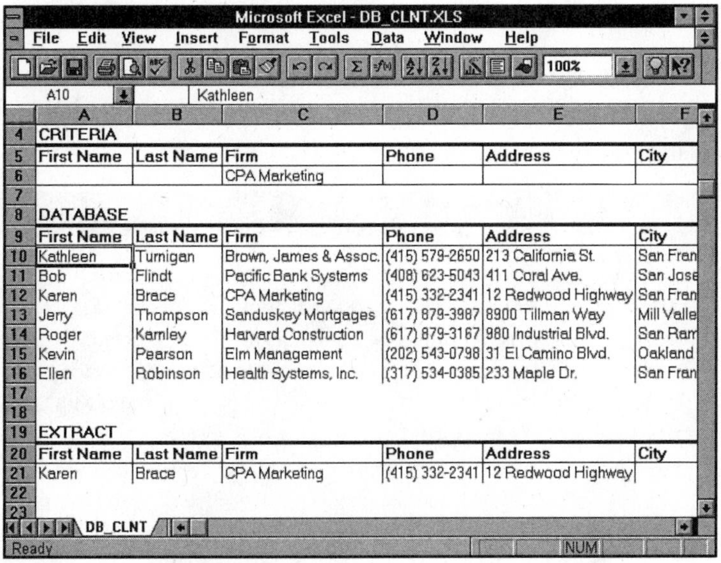

Fig. 30.2
An Excel list usually contains a header row that describes each column and data in the rows underneath.

Figure 30.2 shows that the information from the card in figure 30.1 now appears in a single record (row) of the list; each cell in the row contains a different field of data. From the field names at the top of each column, you can easily tell the data each field contains.

Your list may be simple, or it may be a multiple column list with thousands of rows of information. If you have a simple list or only need to find information using simple specifications, you can use the AutoFilter feature. To create a more robust list, you need to understand a few simple terms, as described in the following section.

Identifying the Parts of a List

To use many of the list management features, you only need to have the list. Figure 30.3 show the three parts of a fully functional list: Criteria, Database, and Extract ranges. The following list describes these ranges:

Tip
With Microsoft Query, Excel's new database program that replaces Q&E from Excel 4, you can link Excel to databases on a hard disk, SQL server, or mainframe.

- *Database Range.* Where list information is kept. An Excel list is kept in a worksheet; related information is entered in rows. Each column of information has a unique field name.

- *Criteria Range.* Where you indicate what you want to find or analyze in the list by specifying criteria. This range should contain field names and an area in which you type a specification that describes the information you want.

- *Extract Range.* Where Excel copies desired information from the list. This range should contain field names of the data you want and an area in which the copy is pasted.

Note

Excel 5 doesn't require the database, criteria, and extract range to have specific names as in Excel 4. A list can be any table of information you select. Likewise, the Criteria range may be any range, named or selected. The range to which you copy extracted data doesn't have to be named Extract, it can be any range. The advantages and disadvantages of naming ranges with Database, Criteria, and Extract are described in following chapters.

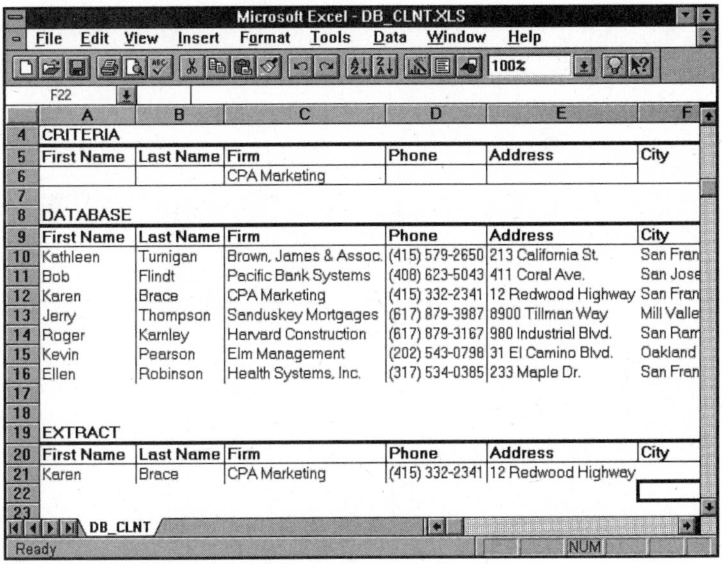

Fig. 30.3
The three parts of a fully functional list. The selected Database range contains both the field names and data.

Identifying the Database Range

Before you can use a list with Excel, it must be able to find the list. Excel uses a couple of rules to determine where the list is located. Excel finds the location of the list in one of the following ways:

- If you assigned the name Database to a range in the worksheet, Excel assumes that this range is the list. The top row is assumed to be field names and the rows below the field names are data.

- If you selected a range of cells before choosing a command from the **D**ata menu, then Excel uses the range you selected as the list.

- If you choose a **D**ata command that requests a range on which to operate, you can enter a range reference or a range name of a reference.

- Excel finds and selects the list you want to work on if the above rules do not apply and you selected a cell within a list. Excel examines cells above the active cell to find a row that meets the rules for text field names. All filled cells that touch and are below these field names then are selected.

The easiest way to work with Excel lists is to create lists that abide by the following rules:

- Always place a row of field names across the top of your list. Each column in the list must have a label at the top.
- If you have only one list in a worksheet, use the **I**nsert **N**ame **D**efine command to assign it the name Database.
- If you do not name the list with the name Database, then create each list so that it has a *moat* of empty cells above the field names and to the left of, right of, and below the data. As long as this *moat* of empty cells remains around the list, you can use features from the **D**ata menu by selecting a single cell within the list.
- If you cannot create or ensure that empty cells remain around each list, use the **I**nsert **N**ame **D**efine command to assign a name to each list or database range. Understand that if the user adds information to the bottom of the list, you may need to redefine the name.

After you create a list, you can add, delete, edit, sort, and find information within it. As you learn in the following chapter, choosing the **D**ata F**o**rm command automatically creates a database form with buttons. The form enables you to view one record at a time. Figure 30.4 shows the form created for the list in figure 30.3. Notice that the form shows all the fields that were not immediately visible and the fields on-screen.

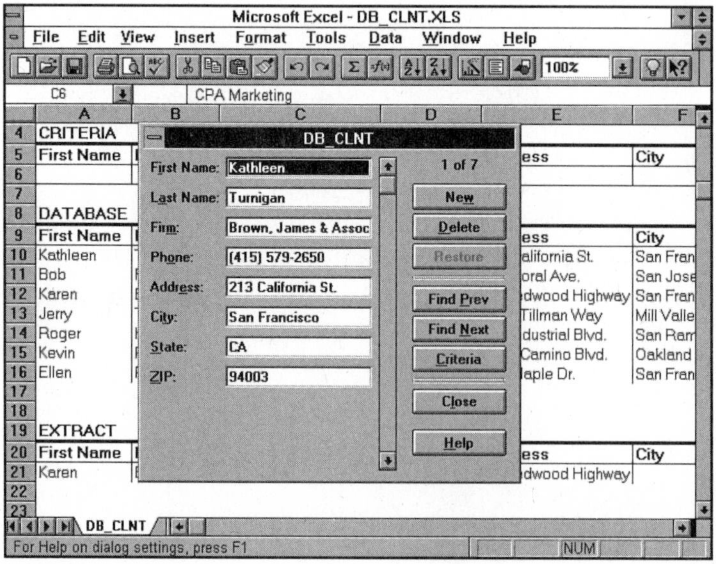

Fig. 30.4
Choose the **D**ata F**o**rm command to create a data entry and edit form for the current list or the range named Database.

Excel's AutoFilter feature enables you to quickly find information within any list, whether or not you named the list. As figure 30.5 shows, when you use AutoFilter the field names in the current list change to pull-down lists. Selecting from one or more of these pull-down lists in the header causes Excel to only display information in the list that matches your selection.

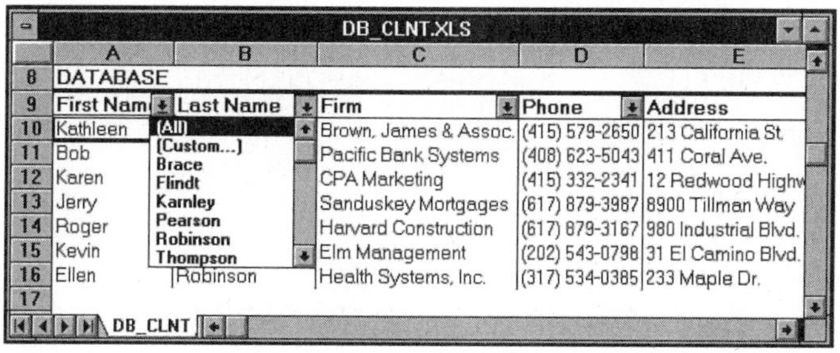

Fig. 30.5
When you use AutoFilter, the field names change to pull-down lists. Selecting from a pull-down list filters the list.

Identifying the Criteria Range

To conduct complex searches or extract a copy of information from the list, you need to specify a criteria range. A *criteria range* is where you enter the specifications that determine the complex data for which you are searching. The criteria range can be a reference, a named range, or a range named as Criteria. If you use the AutoFilter, then a criteria range is optional. But you need a criteria range to do more complex filters or analysis.

The criteria range can be any range. If you assign the range the name, Criteria, then by default, Excel assumes that the criteria is contained in the range named Criteria. Figure 30.6 shows a criteria range selected. This range contains a simple set of criteria that filters the list below it. A criteria filters information in the database so that you find or display only records (rows) in the list that match the criteria.

The criteria range must contain the field names on top and at least one blank row beneath. The criteria range doesn't need to include all the fields in the list, it only needs to include the field names for which you are filtering. The field names must be exactly the same as the field names in the list. In the blank row below the field names, you specify the information you want to find.

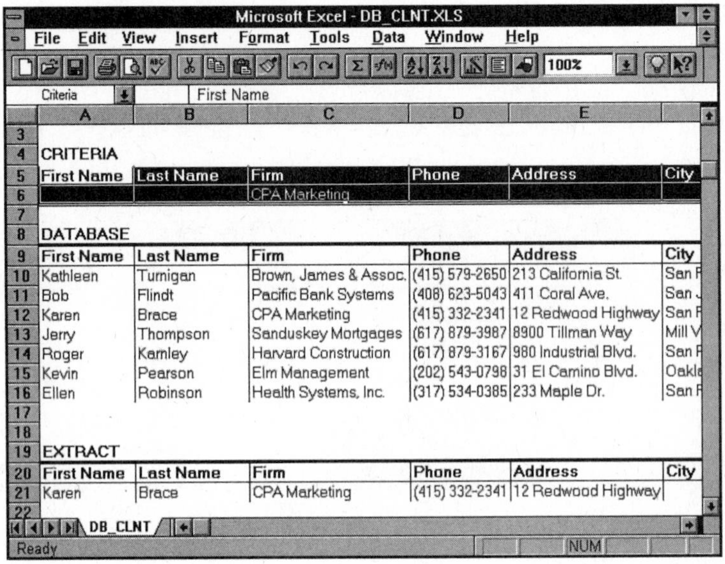

Fig. 30.6
When you need to filter data with more stringent specifications than AutoFilter, use a criteria range to specify how you want the list filtered.

Identifying the Extract Range

The last list term you need to know is the extract range. An *extract range* is optional and is where Excel copies records that meet the filter you specified. You can, for example, request an extract of all addresses in a specific ZIP code. Excel will copy the addresses into the extract range. The original list or database is left unchanged. Another excellent use of this feature is to create smaller lists or reports from the original list. The extract range doesn't have to be in the same worksheet as the original worksheet.

A *limited extract* range is a range where you define the field name row and then specify the number of rows your extract range can have. For example, if you want to limit output to 10 rows, you can select rows 20-30 as part of your extract range.

An *unlimited extract* range defines only the row of field names. When you extract information from the database, Excel can fill in information from the row of field names to the bottom of your worksheet (row 16384).

Figure 30.6 (in the preceding section) shows a single row of headings (row 20 in the figure) that will be used as the row headers for an extract. The only information that will be extracted from the list or database will be rows that match the filter in the criteria range (CPA Marketing in row 6) and columns that match the field names in the extract range.

For Related Information

- "Naming Cells for Better Worksheets," p. 157
- "Using the AutoFilter," p. 913
- "Using the Advanced Filter," p. 916

Choosing the Contents for a List

You can save time and trouble by planning your list before building it. As a simple checklist for what data to include in a list and how to name it, consider these points:

- List the groups of data you want, such as Company Info and Personal Info.
- Break these groups of data into the smallest elements that you will ever consider using. Address, for example, might be divided into separate fields such as Street, City, State, and Zip. This technique makes searching the list easier and enables you to reorder data in new structures. Use only text or text formulas in field names. Do not use numeric or date values.
- Eliminate fields you probably will never use. For example, don't use fields that can be calculated in a report. Why waste disk space storing information that you can calculate?

Choose small fields that contain the most usable part of the data. Rather than using Name as a single field containing an entire name, for example, you may want to use three fields: Prefix, First_Name, and Last_Name. This technique gives you the option of reordering the data in many different combinations. Suppose that your data looks like the following:

Prefix	First_Name	Last_Name
Ms.	Kathleen	Turnigan

From this data, you later can use Excel's text functions and concatenate cell contents to create any of the following combinations:

Ms. Turnigan

Kathleen

Ms. Kathleen Turnigan

Kathleen Turnigan

Stay on the lean side when including data fields. Many business information systems lie unused because some well-meaning person wanted the list to contain too much information. The result is an expensive, time-consuming,

Tip

Never include ZIP codes in the city and state fields. Demographic and market data may be tied to the ZIP code. You can lower postage costs by sorting mailings by ZIP code.

For Related Information

■ "Manipulating Text," p. 685

and tedious-to-maintain database. When a list isn't maintained, it isn't used. Include only data you can use and keep up-to-date.

Organizing Your List

Before building a list, consider how it fits with the rest of the worksheet and how to coordinate it with other worksheets and lists for your business. Remember that you can link together Excel lists and worksheets in different files. The following list shows additional points to consider:

- Locate the list so that at least one blank row exists above the field names and below the last row of data. Make sure that at least one blank column remains on the left and right side of the list, which will aid you in selecting an unnamed list.

- Do not put formulas or important data to the left or right of a list. Information on the sides of a list may be hidden when you apply a filter to the list. If important data is in these rows, you cannot see it while the filter is on.

- Lists may be easier to work with if you use only one list per worksheet. Your workbook, however, can have many worksheets, each containing different lists.

- Draw diagrams of other lists and worksheets in your business, and notice where the data is stored twice. Can the data be stored in separate files and recombined as needed with the aid of Excel or Microsoft Query? If you need to join lists or if the lists involve more than a few thousand records (rows), use a relational database such as Microsoft Access instead of a worksheet like Excel. Microsoft Access can store the data and then export as an Excel worksheet the filtered data you need. If you need to automate procedures, the Excel Visual Basic is similar to the Access Basic development language.

- Be certain that nothing lies below an unlimited extract range. Extracting to an unlimited extract range clears all cells below the extract field names.

- Position the list so that room is available for downward expansion. If you use the data form to add records (rows) to your list, records are added without pushing down the information below the list. If not enough room is available to insert data for the new records, the data form does not let you add a new record.
- If you use a list that was assigned the name Database, then you need to rename the range for the list if you add data to the bottom of the database range. You can preserve the correct range if you insert cells in the middle of the list to add data or if you use the data form to add data.

From Here...

For information relating directly to designing and building your list, you may want to review the following chapters of this book:

- Chapter 31, "Entering Data in a List or Database," teaches you how to set up the list and efficiently enter data.
- In Chapter 32, "Sorting Data," you learn how to select a list and sort on one or more columns.
- Chapter 33, "Finding, Filtering, and Editing Lists and Databases," explains how the AutoFilter works to quickly find information. When you need a complex search, then learn how to use the Criteria range.
- Chapter 34, "Working with Filtered Data," shows how to extract the data you need from large lists or databases and put the data in another worksheet.

Chapter 31

Entering Data in a List or Database

Although Excel is primarily a spreadsheet, it has list management capability that can help you analyze stock market trends, track client names and addresses, monitor expense account data, and store sales figures. The combination of list functions, powerful worksheet analysis capabilities, and charting capabilities makes Excel an excellent tool for business analysis and management systems.

Note

Excel 5 uses the term list to refer to related information stored in rows and columns. If you are familiar with previous versions of Excel or with other software, you may be more familiar with the term database.

This and the following chapters describe how to build and use a list that resides in an Excel worksheet. A list is like an automated card-file system that enables you to find information quickly and then edit, sort, extract, and print or analyze it. In the most simple form of an Excel list, you only need a set of information topped by a row of headings to use some of Excel's list management features.

In this chapter, you learn how to build a list and how to enter information. If you want to find and edit information in a data-entry form, you will find the discussion on the automatic data form interesting. If you want to enter information directly into a list on the worksheet, you will prefer the other methods.

In this chapter, you learn how to:

- Enter the field names that are in the first rows of a list
- Name the range containing a list
- Enter data in a form using the **D**ata F**o**rm command
- Efficiently enter data directly in cells on a worksheet
- Enter data using data-entry shortcut keys
- Format a list using the AutoFormat command

Entering the Field Names

The list must have field names in a single row across the top of the list if you want to use Excel's capability of filtering out unwanted data. To use Excel's advanced filter capabilities, each field name also must be unique. The field names identify each column of data. The list must have at least one row of data directly below the field names.

Figure 31.1 shows the only mandatory part of a list: the single row of field headings (here, shown in row 10) and the data (shown in rows 11–19). Figure 31.2 shows a sample list and the criteria range where questions that filter the data are entered. The formatting shown in the figure is not a requirement; it serves to enhance the list's appearance and to reduce errors. The text labels that appear in row 9 are not part of the field names. Only the row next to the data can contain the unique field names.

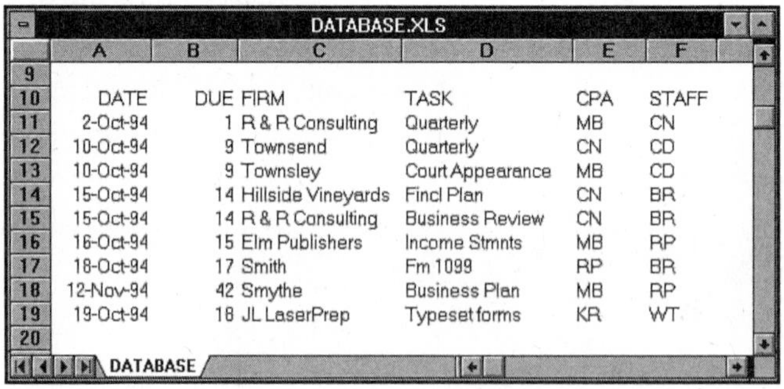

	A	B	C	D	E	F
9						
10	DATE	DUE	FIRM	TASK	CPA	STAFF
11	2-Oct-94	1	R & R Consulting	Quarterly	MB	CN
12	10-Oct-94	9	Townsend	Quarterly	CN	CD
13	10-Oct-94	9	Townsley	Court Appearance	MB	CD
14	15-Oct-94	14	Hillside Vineyards	Fincl Plan	CN	BR
15	15-Oct-94	14	R & R Consulting	Business Review	CN	BR
16	16-Oct-94	15	Elm Publishers	Income Stmnts	MB	RP
17	18-Oct-94	17	Smith	Fm 1099	RP	BR
18	12-Nov-94	42	Smythe	Business Plan	MB	RP
19	19-Oct-94	18	JL LaserPrep	Typeset forms	KR	WT
20						

Fig. 31.1
To filter or sort data, all you need is a list with headings at the top.

When you enter field names across the top of the list, keep the following points in mind:

- Field names can include up to 255 characters, but short names are easier to see in a cell.

- Only the names in the row directly above the data are used as field names. You can add explanatory names—such as the names in cells A9 and B9 of figure 31.2—but only the field names in the row directly above the data are used by Excel.

- Names must be different from each other if you want to use Excel's data filter.

- Do not put a row of dashed lines or blanks under the row of field names.

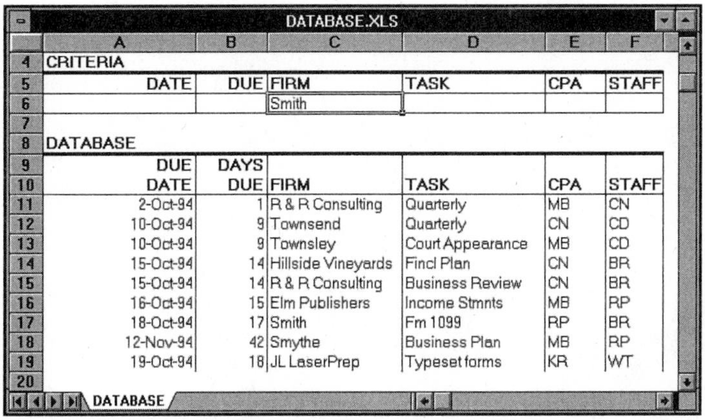

Fig. 31.2
A list must have field names in the top row and one row of data. A criteria range is necessary only for advanced filters.

After you create field names, you need to add at least one row of data before building the rest of the list. Add rows of data with standard worksheet entry techniques. After you create the list, you can use more convenient methods of entering data, which are described later in this chapter.

Naming the List or Database Range

Excel 5 can recognize lists and list headings without naming the database range, as was required in previous versions of Excel. (Names are English text, used in place of a cell reference or range reference.) You can select a cell within a list or database and, when you choose a Data command, Excel selects the headings and data that surround the active cell.

If you select a cell within a range that has the name, Database—for example, in a list from a previous version of Excel—then the Advanced Filter dialog box automatically recognizes all existing ranges defined with the name Database, Criteria, or Extract.

If you have many lists and decide not to use the name Database, you still may want to use names to move quickly between lists. Assign a name to one cell in each list's field names. With this capability, you can go quickly to the named cell and choose the **D**ata command. The **D**ata command then selects all touching cells. The following paragraph describes how to name a cell.

To name the entire list, you need to select the list range (see fig. 31.3). Notice that although two rows of titles exist in the figure, only the row of field names directly above the data is selected. Use the following procedure to name the entire list.

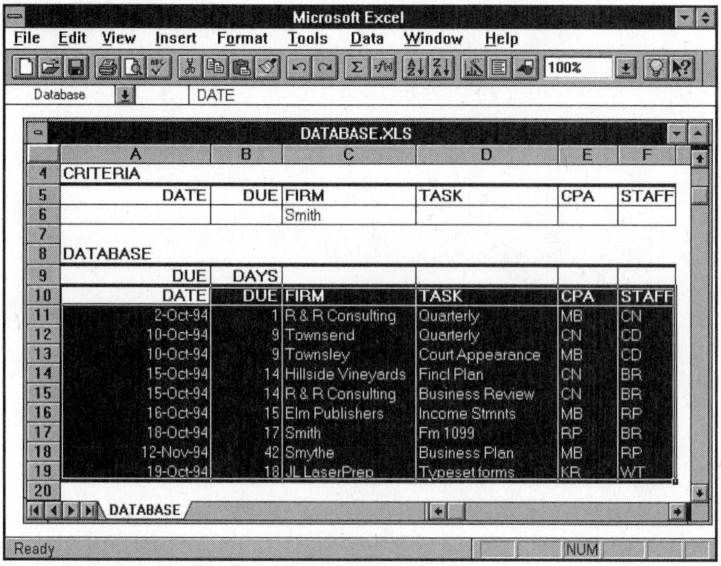

Fig. 31.3
The list range, A10:F19, includes data and a single row of field names above the data.

To name a single cell or the selected range that contains a list, take these steps:

1. Select a single cell in the field names or select the field names and all the data underneath.
2. Choose the **I**nsert **N**ame **D**efine command.
3. In the **N**ame edit box, type a descriptive name. Begin with a letter and do not use spaces.
4. Choose OK.

Now that you have named the range, you can select the range easily by choosing **E**dit **G**o To, or pressing F5, and then selecting the name from the Go To dialog box.

If you want to delete the name Database, Criteria, or Extract that were used in previous versions of Excel, choose the **I**nsert **N**ame **D**efine command, select the name from the Names in **W**orkbook list, and then choose **D**elete and Close.

For Related Information

■ "Naming Cells for Better Worksheets," p.157

Entering the Data

Now that you have entered the field headings and initial data for your list, you can use many methods for entering data, including the following methods:

- You can use Excel's automatic data form to enter data. This is a quick and easy method of entering data.
- You can enter data in blank rows or cells inserted through a list. This preserves any range name that you gave to the list.
- Use Visual Basic for Applications to display a data-entry sheet or dialog box that asks for data, checks the data, and transfers the new data into a blank row of the list.

Using the Data Form

The easiest method of entering data is with Excel's automatically generated data form. You can use Excel's automatic data form once you create a list that contains field names and a row of data.

To enter data using an automatic form, take these steps:

Tip
Use the data-entry shortcut keys in table 31.2 for faster data entry.

1. If you named the list range Database, skip to step 2; otherwise, select a cell within the list. A quick way to select a range is to press F5, select the range name, and choose OK.
2. Choose the **D**ata F**o**rm command.

   A data form similar to figure 31.4 appears over the worksheet.

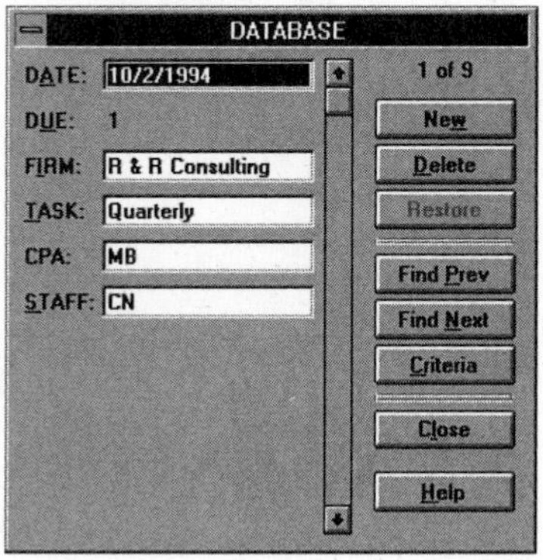

Fig. 31.4
Display an automatic data-entry and edit form by using **D**ata F**o**rm on any list.

3. Choose the New button.

4. Type data in the fields. You can see, but not type in fields containing calculated results.

5. To enter additional records, repeat steps 3 and 4.

6. Choose Close to return to the worksheet.

   The data form displays calculated field results, but you cannot edit the contents. To hide fields in the form, hide the calculated field's column in the worksheet.

Choosing the New button places the new record you typed in the form into the list and empties the fields in the data form so you can type a new record. You can return to a record's original data by choosing the **R**estore button before you move to another record. After choosing the Close button, you may want to save the workbook to record the additions on disk.

The records added with the data form are placed below the last row of the list. Information below the list is not pushed down.

Caution

The data form does not let you add new records if there are not enough blank cells below the current list range. You receive the warning, `Cannot extend database`, when there is no more room to expand downward. When you create your list, choose a location in the worksheet with enough room to expand.

Note

If you used the name Database to name the range of your data, then entering data through the data form automatically extends the range Database.

You can change the data in the new record until you choose New or Close to add the record to the list. After you add the new data, use any of the filter and edit techniques described in Chapter 33, "Finding, Filtering, and Editing Lists and Databases," to make changes.

To delete a record using the data form, just display in the form the record you want to delete and then choose the **D**elete button. A dialog box asks if you are sure you want to delete the record; choose OK to confirm that you want to delete the record.

Entering Data Directly

A second method for entering data is typing the data directly into rows in the worksheet. Before you use this data-entry method, you must make room in the list for new records.

If you named the range that contains your list, insert new rows or cells between existing records (rows). Inserting new cells through the list automatically copies formats from the cells above into the new cells. For this reason, it is usually best to insert cells below the first row of data. If you insert new rows or cells below the last record of the list, those rows or cells are not included in the list range. If you insert new rows or cells directly under the field headings, the format of the heading is copied into the new row, not the format of other data cells.

If you named the list range and added new records below the last row of the existing data instead of between records, you must redefine the range name. To redefine the range, reselect the field names next to the data, including the new data, and choose the **I**nsert **N**ame **D**efine command. Retype the original name—*do not select the name from the list*—and choose OK.

> **Note**
>
> To move through a list quickly from top to bottom or side to side, use Ctrl+arrow key. This action moves the active cell across filled cells until the edge of the list is reached. To select cells as you move, also hold down Shift (therefore, Shift+Ctrl+arrow key). You can move across filled cells with the mouse by holding Ctrl as you double-click the side of the active cell. To select as you move, hold down Shift and Ctrl at the same time, and double-click the side of the active cell.

Inserting entire rows through the list moves everything in the worksheet below that row. To move down just those cells directly below the list, select only a range that matches the list's columns before inserting rows. Insert cells in the list when you don't want to disturb areas to the right or left of the list.

In figure 31.5, the cells of the middle two records have been selected so that they can be moved down to allow for the addition of two more records. Cells outside the list are not selected. Notice that the markers in column G indicate the cell locations outside the selected cells.

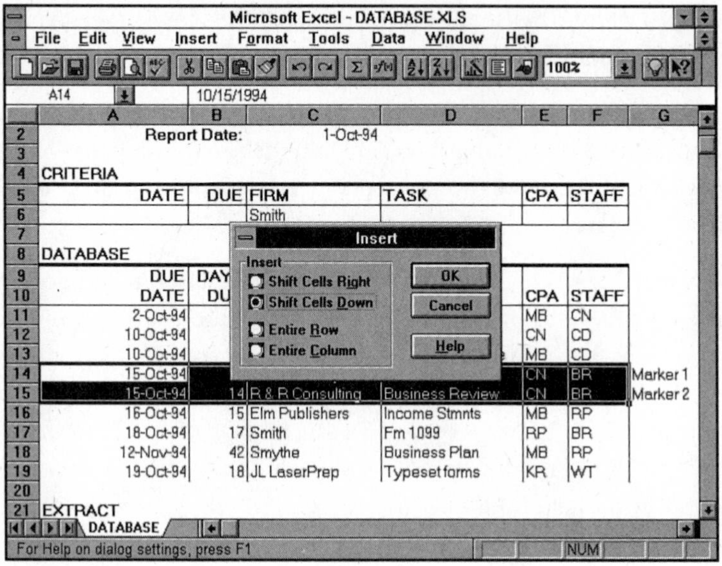

Fig. 31.5
Select cells in the middle of a list and choose **I**nsert C**e**lls to open cells for data entry while preserving a named range.

After you select cells from one side of the list to the other, press Shift+Ctrl+ + (plus) or choose **I**nsert C**e**lls to display the Insert dialog box. Select the Shift Cells **D**own option button to insert cells and push down the list. Any data or worksheet contents below these cells are also pushed down. As the markers in column G of figure 31.6 show, areas to the side of the inserted cells do not move.

To enter data in the blank cells that you inserted, take these steps:

1. Select the cells to receive data. If you just inserted them, they still are selected.
2. Type data in the active cell.
3. Press one of the keys shown in table 31.1 to enter the data and move the active cell while still retaining the selected range. Return to step 2 to enter more data.
4. After all the data is entered, press an arrow key to deselect the range.
5. Format the columns of data if necessary.
6. Create and copy formulas down the appropriate columns.

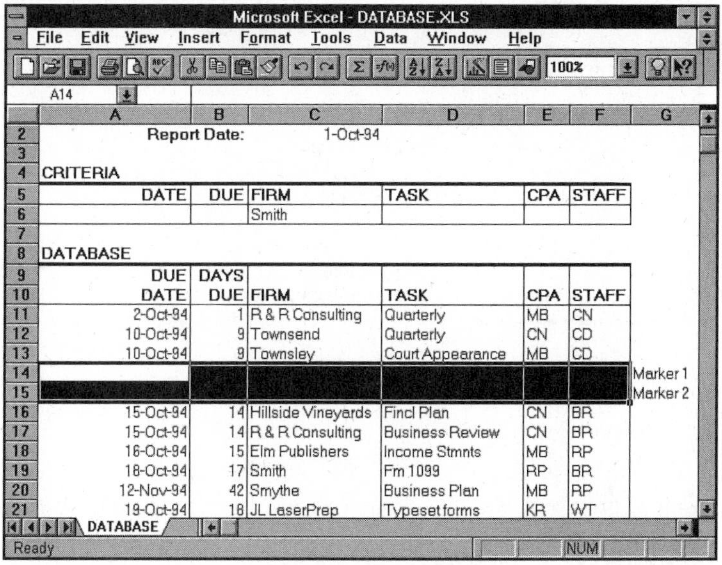

Fig. 31.6
Inserting cells through the middle of a list preserves range names, copies formats down, and does not affect cells to the side.

Table 31.1 Data-Entry Keys

Key	Action
Tab	Enters data and moves right
Shift+Tab	Enters data and moves left
Enter	Enters data and moves down
Shift+Enter	Enters data and moves up

While you are working within a selected data-entry range, the active cell remains in the data-entry area. The active cell wraps from one edge of the selected range to the next edge.

Excel has five shortcut key combinations that can speed data-entry work. The key combinations are shown in table 31.2.

Table 31.2 Shortcut Keys for Data Entry

Key combination	Action
Ctrl+; (semicolon)	Enters the computers current date
Ctrl+: (colon)	Enters the computers current time

(continues)

Table 31.2 Continued

Key combination	Action
Ctrl+' (apostrophe)	Copies the formula from the cell above without adjusting cell references
Ctrl+" (double quotation marks)	Copies the value from the cell above
Ctrl+arrow	Moves over filled cells to the last filled cell, or moves over blank cells to the first filled cell

Speeding Up Data Entry

In large lists that contain many formulas, constant recalculation can slow data entry. While Excel is calculating, you can continue to enter data; Excel stops calculation momentarily to accept an entry or command.

To speed data entry, turn off automatic recalculation by choosing the **T**ools **O**ptions command, selecting the Calculation tab, and selecting the **M**anual option. If automatic calculation is off and you plan to read the list while it remains on disk through worksheet links or through Microsoft Query, be certain that you press F9 or choose the Recalculate Before **S**ave check box that is in the same Calculation tab. Recalculating before the save, when the **M**anual option is on, ensures that the list is accurate even while saved on disk.

While Excel is in manual calculation mode, the program doesn't update the formulas as you enter data. When you make a change that affects a formula in the worksheet, a Calculate indicator appears in the status bar at the bottom of the Excel screen. When you see the Calculate indicator, do not trust formula results displayed on-screen.

To recalculate all open worksheets while staying in manual calculation mode, press F9 or choose the **T**ools **O**ptions command, select the Calculation tab, and choose the Calc **N**ow button. To calculate the active document, choose the Calc D**o**cument button or press Shift+F9.

After making list entries, you can return to automatic calculation by choosing the **T**ools **O**ptions command, selecting the Calculation tab and the **A**utomatic option.

Troubleshooting

The list doesn't work correctly with dates.

Be certain that dates are entered in a format that Excel understands as a date. Excel can read these formats, such as m/d/yy, convert the date to a serial date number, and format the cell. Without a serial date number, the column sorts as text not in date order, and list functions treat the date entry as text or as a number.

A quick way to clear a cell is selecting it and pressing the space bar. Will this cause a problem in a database or list?

Blank spaces (the space bar character) in what appears to be a blank cell causes problems when you search or extract data. To Excel, the space bar character is a character, not a blank cell, which can cause problems when you sort or search. A space bar character, which is treated as text, also causes some list analysis and reporting functions to give what appear to be incorrect results.

For Related Information

- "Entering Dates and Times," p. 93
- "Entering Text," p. 89
- "Entering Numbers," p. 90

Formatting Your List or Database

In Excel, a list doesn't need to look drab. You can quickly format a list to make it easier to read and more attractive. Figure 31.7 shows a list formatted with one command.

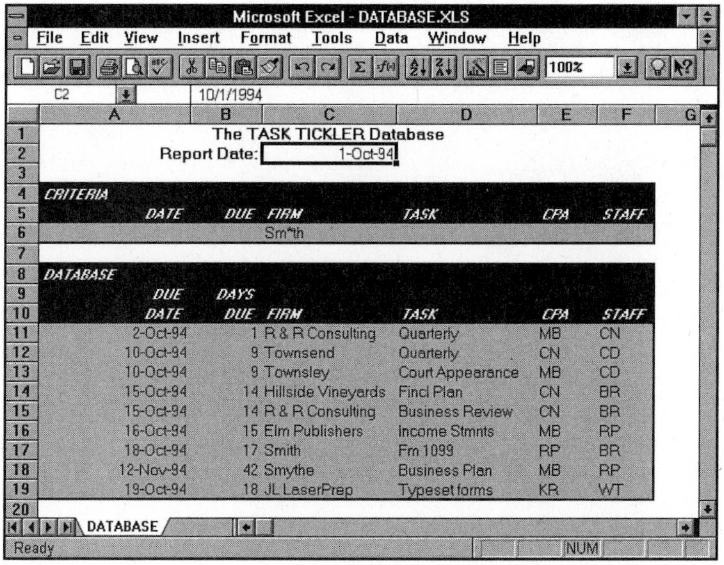

Fig. 31.7
Use Format AutoFormat to quickly apply attractive formats to a list.

To format your list, take these steps:

1. Select a cell within the list.

2. Choose the F**o**rmat **A**utoFormat command.

3. Select a format you like from the **T**able Format list. Watch the Sample area for an example of the effect.

4. For most lists, you don't want AutoFormat to affect the alignment or column width because you have formatted them manually, so choose the **O**ptions button, then deselect the **A**lignment and **W**idth/Height check boxes.

5. Choose OK.

If you do not like the format you choose, immediately choose the **E**dit **U**ndo command and try a different format.

For Related Information

■ "Formatting with Autoformats," p. 303

From Here...

For information relating directly to creating the list or database and entering data, you may want to examine these other chapters for helpful information:

- Chapter 4, "Entering and Editing Data." This chapter describes data-entry techniques that can speed up your data entry. Look here to learn how to enter dates correctly.

- Chapter 10, "Formatting Worksheets." Excel has impressive data formatting ability. This chapter describes Excel's formatting commands and includes numerous tips on normal and custom formatting.

Chapter 32

Sorting Data

Sorting organizes your data in ascending or descending alphabetic and numeric order. Excel can sort the rows of a list, or database, or the columns of a worksheet.

Excel sorts thousands of rows or columns in the time it would take you to manually sort just a few, sorting on three fields at a time in case duplicates exist in one of the sorted fields.

In this chapter, you learn how:

- Excel orders and sorts different types of data
- To sort by command or with the sort buttons on the toolbar
- To sort a range or selected portion
- To return a range to its original sorted order
- To sort as many columns or rows as you want
- To sort using custom sort lists

What You Need To Know about Sorting

When you choose **D**ata **S**ort, Excel displays the Sort dialog box, shown in figure 32.1. The items that you can select in the box include the sort keys (the columns or rows that you want to determine the new order), the sort order, and whether the data has a row of labels as a header.

The Sort By entries determine which fields Excel uses for sorting. In a telephone book, for example, the first field sorted is Last Name and the second is First Name. If several people have the name Smith, their first names are used to put all the Smiths in sorted order. In the dialog box shown in figure 32.2, the first sort field is column A (DATE), the second field is column E (CPA), and the third field is column F (STAFF).

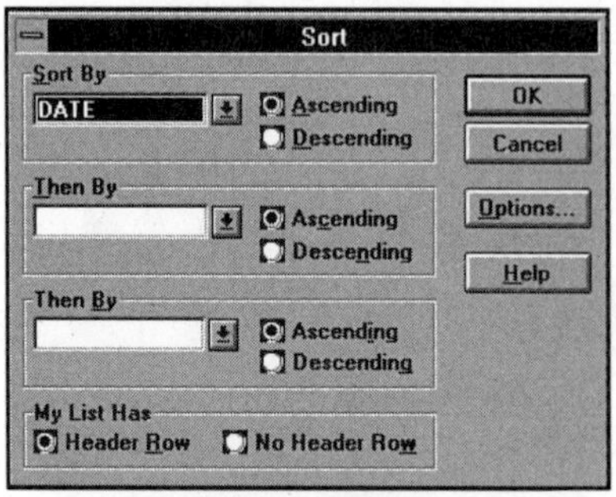

Fig. 32.1
Select a cell in the list or database, and choose **D**ata **S**ort to sort on one or more columns.

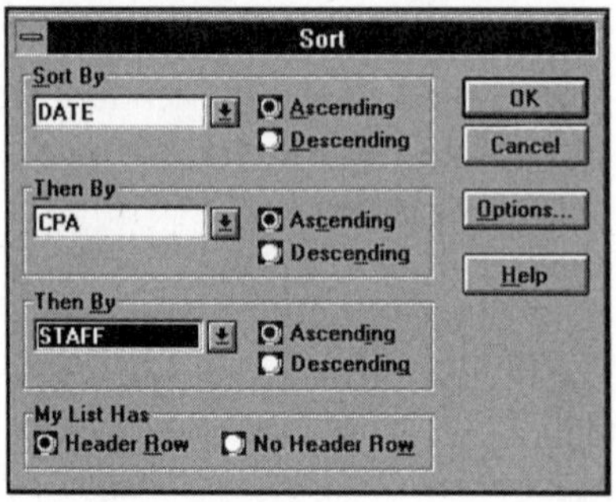

Fig. 32.2
Excel sorts on up to three columns or rows at a time.

The **A**scending and **D**escending option buttons next to each sort field tell Excel to sort in ascending (A to Z) or descending (Z to A) order. Excel sorts in ascending order from top to bottom for rows, or left to right for columns. The Descending option reverses this order (Z to A from top to bottom or from left to right). Blanks always sort to the bottom in ascending or descending sort. In addition, the program uses the following order of priority:

Numbers from largest negative to largest positive

Text

FALSE results

TRUE results

Error values

Blanks

With Excel 5, you can specify whether you want Excel to take case into consideration when sorting. Excel can ignore the difference between upper- and lowercase letters, or it can be case-sensitive. You also can adapt Excel to sort certain text lists in a nontext order—for example, Sunday, Monday, Tuesday, Wednesday, and so on. Although this order is not alphabetical, it is the order in which we expect this particular data to sort.

If you set international character settings through the Windows Control Panel, Excel sorts in the order used by the country specified.

Caution

Be careful when you sort lists or databases that contain formulas. When the rows in the list or database change order, formulas in the rows adjust to the new locations, which may produce references that provide incorrect results. To avoid this problem, remember that a formula in a list or database row should refer to other cells in the same row. If the formula references a cell outside the sort range, that reference should be an absolute reference or a named reference so that it doesn't change during sorting.

If you want numbers to sort as text, enter them as text by typing an apostrophe before the number. In the following list of numbers, for example, the first three are sorted as numbers. The others sort as text. Notice how the numbers entered as text mix with the alphanumeric combinations.

1	number
2	number
3	number
1	left-aligned text preceded by '
1a	left-aligned text preceded by '
2	left-aligned text preceded by '
2a	left-aligned text preceded by '
3	left-aligned text preceded by '
3a	left-aligned text preceded by '

You also can enter numbers as text formulas, for example:

```
="321"
```

Note

Although Excel treats numbers entered with a preceding apostrophe (') as regular numbers in some calculations, they still sort as alphabetic entries.

Sorting by Command

Sorting is easy to use and is helpful for any list or database. In fact, you can create quick and valuable reports by sorting database-like information so that the information you need ends up in adjacent rows. Excel's Data Subtotals command also works with sorted data to create subtotals and grand totals in sorted lists.

To sort a list or database with a layout similar to the one in figure 32.1, follow these steps:

1. Choose the **F**ile Save **A**s command or press F12. Save the worksheet with a different file name in case you scramble the data during sorting.

2. Select the cells to be sorted in one of two ways:

   To select the entire range of data when the range is surrounded on all sides by blank cells, click in one cell inside the data. The sort command selects the range.

   To sort a specific portion of a range, such as a column or row, select that specific portion.

3. Choose **D**ata **S**ort.

4. If the list or database has text field names in the top row, select the My List Has Header **R**ow option button. This ensures that the field names are not sorted in with the data. If the list or database lacks field names, select the My List Has No Header Ro**w** option button. Usually, Excel correctly selects this option.

5. Choose **S**ort By and select the label of the column that you want to sort first. This column is also called the *first sort key*.

   If the data lacks labels in a header row, select the worksheet column letter for the column you want to sort.

6. Select **A**scending or **D**escending sort order.

7. Choose **T**hen By; select the label of the column that you want to use as a second sort field.

   If the data lacks labels in a header row, select the worksheet column letter for the column you want to use.

   The second sort field is used only if duplicate data exists in the first sort field. The third sort field is used only if duplicate data exists in the first and second sort fields.

   Repeat step 6.

8. Choose Then **B**y, and repeat the procedures in step 7 to select a third sort field.

9. Choose OK.

Caution

Make sure that you select the full width of a list or database before sorting. If you select manually, make sure that you get all columns, not just the columns visible on-screen. If you select a single cell and let Excel select the range, make sure that no blank columns separate the list or database. If the full width is not selected, part of the list or database is sorted and part is not, resulting in scrambled data. A database must have the full width selected before sorting, but not necessarily the full height. If you sort a list of names, phone numbers, and addresses, for example, and you select the First Name and Last Name fields in the sort area but do not include the Phone and Address fields, the First Name and Last Name cells sort into a different order than the Phone and Address cells.

If you need to sort a list in a left-to-right order rather than a top-to-bottom order, follow the preceding procedure, but before selecting the fields to sort in the Sort dialog box, choose **O**ptions to display the Sort Options dialog box shown in figure 32.3. Select Sort **L**eft to Right, and choose OK.

The major danger in sorting is in failing to select all parts of the database and therefore scrambling the database—having part in a different order than the rest of the database. The problem of scrambling a database occurs most frequently when the database extends past the right of the screen, and you select only the cells visible on-screen. If you sort by columns, the same problem

Tip
Excel can be case-sensitive when sorting. If you want a case-sensitive sort, choose **O**ptions and select **C**ase Sensitive. In an ascending case-sensitive sort, uppercase sorts before lowercase.

can occur if you do not select the full column height. If you immediately recognize that the sort has created a problem, choose the **E**dit **U**ndo Sort command. If you cannot undo a problem, hope that you did not skip step 1. If you see a problem, retrieve the copy of the file.

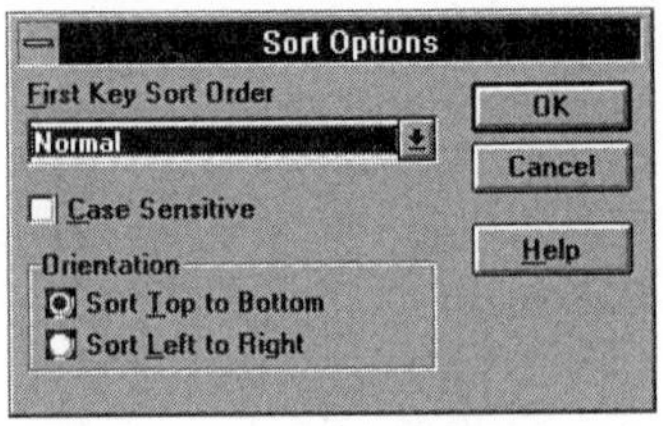

Fig. 32.3
Choosing Options enables you to sort left to right or to require a case-sensitive sort.

Sorting with the Toolbar

The Standard toolbar contains two buttons that sort in ascending or descending order. These buttons show A over Z for an ascending sort and Z over A for a descending sort.

To sort a list or database with sorting buttons, follow these steps:

1. Select a cell in the column you want to use as the sort key.
2. Click the Ascending or Descending sort button.

The sort buttons sort with only one key field (the field you selected before clicking the button). They use the settings for case-sensitivity, special sort order, and orientation that were last selected in the Sort Options dialog box.

Returning a Sort to the Original Order

When you want to sort a list or database but later return it to the original order, you need to add a record index to the list. A record index assigns a number to each record according to the record's position, its date and time of entry, or some other unique numeric record indicator. Figure 32.4 shows an index in column A for a database. You can insert a column or cells to make room for an index next to any list or database. (This method does not help databases that have been split by incorrect sorting.)

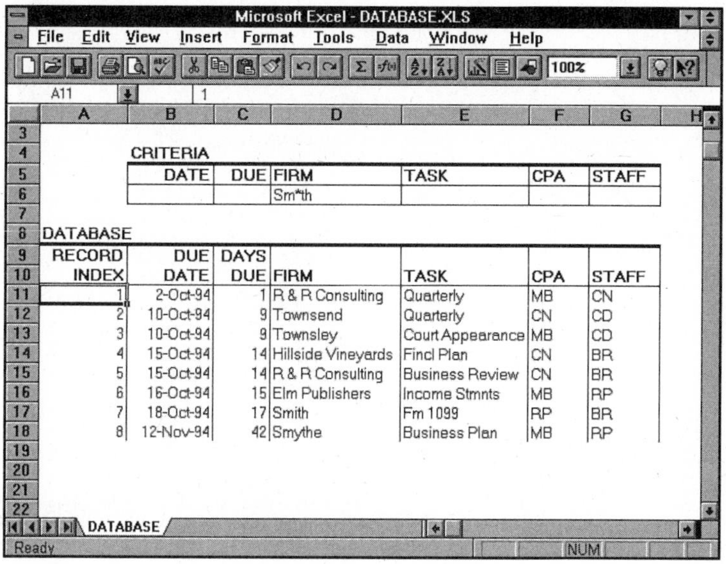

Fig. 32.4
A record index enables you to return the database to its previous order.

To index the database records so that you can return them to a previous order, follow these steps:

1. Insert a column adjacent to the list or database. (If you named the list or database range, you need to redefine the name to include the new cells.)

2. Type a number, such as **1**, in the top cell of the column. Type **2** in the second cell.

3. Select the cells containing 1 and 2 and drag the fill-handle down the length of the list. When you release the mouse button, a series of numbers fill in next to each row. These are the *index numbers.*

When you sort, always make sure that you include the column containing the index numbers. When you want to return to the original order, select the column of index numbers in the **S**ort By list and select **A**scending.

Sorting in a Special Order

In some cases, you may need to sort items that should not appear in normal alphabetical order. For example, items such as the following text examples (not Excel dates) do not sort correctly if you sort in alphabetical order:

Sun, Mon, Tue, Wed, Thu, Fri, Sat

Sunday, Monday, Tuesday, Wednesday, Thursday, Friday, Saturday

Jan, Feb, Mar, Apr, May, Jun, Jul, Aug, Sep, Oct, Nov, Dec

January, February, March, April, May, June, July, August, September, October, November, December

When you are faced with these non-normal sort orders, choose **O**ptions to display the Sort Options dialog box. Choose **F**irst Key Sort Order and select from the drop-down list box how you want the first key sorted, then choose OK, which works for the sort order only on the key you selected in the **S**ort By drop-down list box.

You can return to normal sorting order on the first field by selecting Normal from the **F**irst Key Sort Order drop-down list box.

Note

Limiting special sort orders to the first key does not prevent you from sorting in special order on any key. For example, if you want the Last Name field sorted first and the Day field sorted second using a special sort order, you first sort by the Day field only using it as the first key. After this sort, sort with the Last Name field using a normal sort order. For more information on sorting multiple times, read the upcoming section titled "Sorting on More Than Three Fields."

Sorting by Date and Time

For Related Information

- "Entering Dates and Times," p. 93
- "Formatting Dates and Times," p. 341
- "Manipulating Text," p. 685

Excel sorts date fields using the serial number created by dates and times entered in cells. Sorting works correctly on only dates and times entered with a date and time format that Excel recognizes or created with date or time functions. If you enter dates and times that Excel does not recognize, Excel stores them as text and sorts them in text order, unless you use a special sorting order as described in the previous section.

In many cases, you can change text dates into serial date numbers by inserting a column and entering a formula into the column that converts the adjacent date entry. Chapter 23, "Manipulating and Analyzing Data," describes several functions that may be helpful in this process. TRIM() removes unwanted blanks; DATE() converts month, day, and year to a serial number;

and LEFT(), RIGHT(), MIDDLE(), and LEN() can take apart text so that pieces from within text can be used to calculate the date or time.

Sorting Account Codes, Service Codes, or Part Numbers

Sorting account codes, service codes, and part numbers can seem confusing at first because these codes can contain a prefix, body, and suffix. For example, your business may use codes, such as the following:

AE-576-12

02-88022-09

0001-6589

PRE-56983-LBL

Sorting part and service codes can be difficult because a segment of one code can overlap the character position of a different segment of another code. The result is incorrect sorting. For example, different sections of a code can have different numbers of characters for different items, such as AE-999-12 and AE-1000-12 (representing parts 999 and 1000). In this case, AE-999-12 sorts after AE-1000-12, and that's not what you want.

You can solve this problem in two ways. One way is to ensure that each code segment has exactly the same number of characters. You can, for example, enter the examples in the preceding paragraph as AE-0999-12 and AE-1000-12. Because you have added a zero to the middle section of the first code, both codes have the same number of characters. Another way is to have the information center (IC) download part numbers with each part code segment so that each part code segment loads into a different cell. Using the previous example, AE is in the first cell, 999 or 1000 is in the second cell, and 12 is in the third cell. You can then use Excel's capability of sorting on an unlimited number of columns to sort by all code segments or a single code segment.

Another problem that can exist is a number that drops the leading zero. For entries that require a specific number of zero placeholders, you can use the custom numeric formats described in Chapter 10, "Formatting Worksheets."

Following are three methods of entering the number 0056:

What Is Typed	Numeric Format	Display
56	0000	0056
="0056"	Any format	0056
'0056	Any format	0056

The first method is a number formatted to display leading zeros, and it is sorted before text, as are normal numbers. The second and third methods change the numbers to text. The text sorts with alphabetic characters.

Sorting on More than Three Fields

With Excel's Data Sort command, you can sort on as many fields as you want. You are not limited to three. You can re-sort on additional fields as often as necessary without losing the ordered result from previous sorts. The guideline for sorting on more than three keys is to sort the lowest levels first, working your way up to the highest level.

If you want to sort, for example, column A as the first key, column B as the second key, column C as the third key, and so on for six keys, you would need a sort like the following:

Column	A	B	C	D	E	F
Key	1	2	3	4	5	6

Although Excel has only three sort keys, you still can sort the six columns needed. Your first sort uses the lowest level columns, such as the following:

Column	A	B	C	D	E	F
Key				1	2	3

A second sort sorts the higher level columns with the following keys:

Column	A	B	C	D	E	F
Key	1	2	3			

Sorting Calculated Results

You are not confined to sorting on the entire contents of a given cell. You can include in your list or database formulas that calculate new data that represents just part of the existing data in a cell.

In figure 32.5, column F contains the following function:

=RIGHT(E8,5)

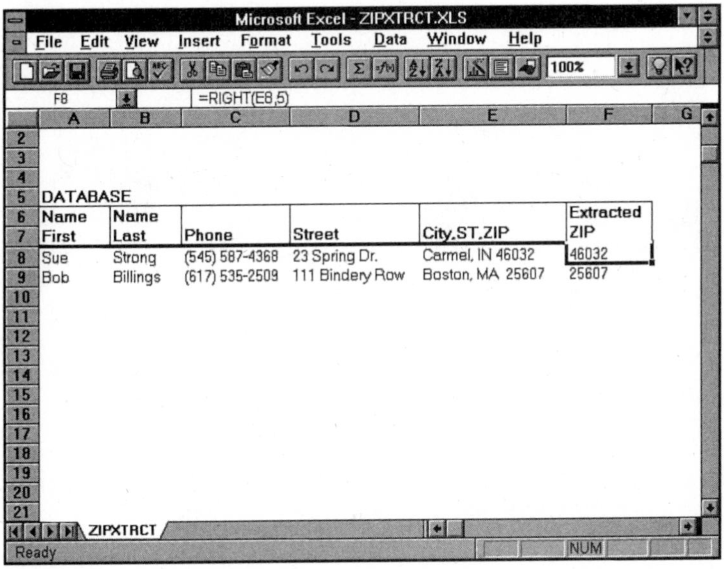

Fig. 32.5
You can sort calculated results as shown with this RIGHT() function that extracts a ZIP code from the address in column E.

This function extracts the last five characters of cell E8, the ZIP. After you have the ZIPs in column F, you can sort on column F. If you want to convert these calculated ZIPs into text permanently, copy them and paste them over the originals by using Edit Paste Special with Values selected.

For Related Information

- "Manipulating Text," p. 685
- "Entering Formulas," p. 127

Rearranging Worksheet, List, or Database Columns

Excel can sort columns as well as rows. This capability enables you to rearrange the columns in your list or database without extensive cutting and pasting.

Figure 32.6 shows the sample database about to be sorted into a new column order. Row 7 contains numbers indicating the desired column order. Notice that the DAYS DUE column must remain directly to the right of DUE DATE in order for the formula in DAYS DUE to calculate correctly. The formula in cell B11 of the DAYS DUE column is

=A11–$C$2

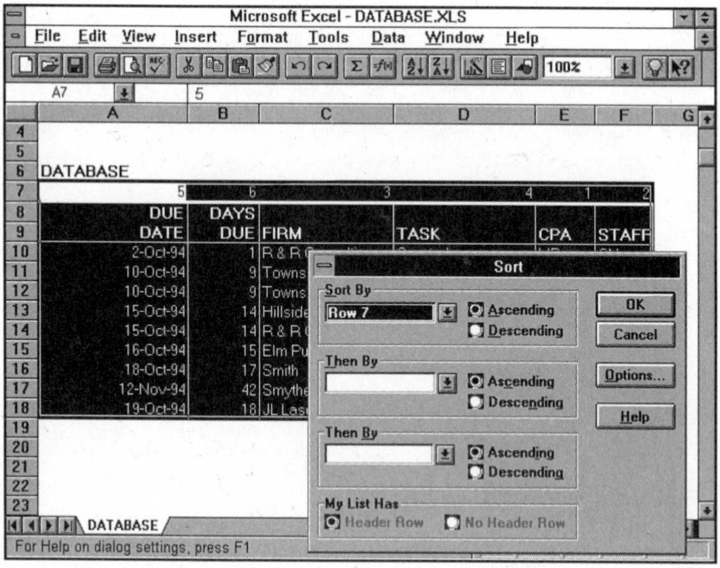

Fig. 32.6
Sort left to right on a row of numbers (row 7) to rearrange the list or database columns.

To do this sort, you must enter the numbers in row 7, then manually select the range from A7:F18. You cannot just select a single cell and let Excel do the range selection because Excel does not understand that the numbers in row 7 should be included in the sort range. Choose **D**ata **S**ort. After the Sort dialog box appears, choose **O**ptions and select Sort **L**eft to Right; choose OK. The Sort dialog box looks like figure 32.6. Notice the **S**ort By field is Row 7, the row containing the numeric order in which you want the columns. Choose OK in the sort dialog box.

Figure 32.7 shows the database after the columns are sorted in the order specified in row 7. If the DAYS DUE column did not stay directly to the right of the DUE DATE column, the formulas would display the error `#VALUE!`. This error appears because the formulas in DAYS DUE would then refer to cells containing text and not dates.

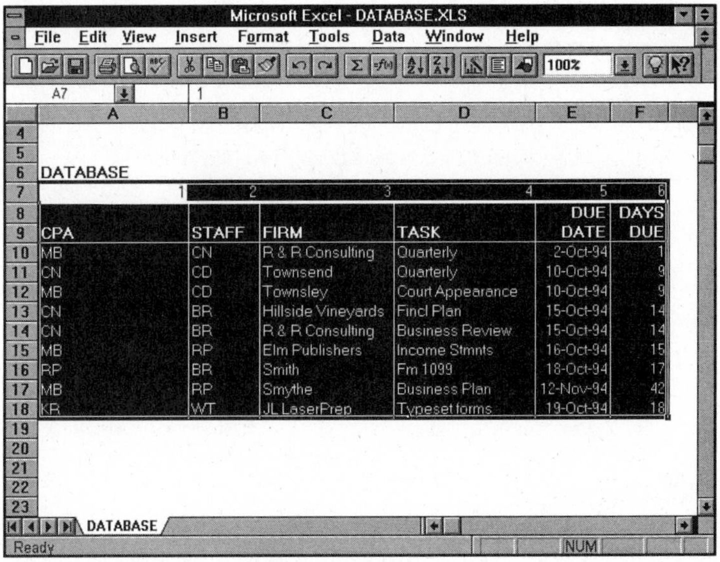

Fig. 32.7
After sorting, the columns are in a different order.

Note

You probably will have to adjust column widths after you reorder columns in a database. If columns are too narrow to display a number or date in the required format, the cell displays #####.

Be careful when you perform a column sort on a worksheet. After the sort, formulas refer to the same relative addresses (for example, two cells left) or absolute address that they did before the sort. When you shift worksheet columns around, the appropriate cell may no longer be where it is expected.

Troubleshooting

After sorting, the calculated data in the database shows errors or is incorrect.

You can use formulas to calculate data within a list or database, but sorting can cause a problem with these formulas unless you remember two rules. First, *in most cases*, formulas that refer to other cells within the list or database should refer only to cells within the database and in the same row as the formula. Second, formulas inside the database that reference cells outside the database should use absolute references, for example $G$32.

(continues)

Troubleshooting (Continued)

I sorted a list, but some of the records in the list did not sort.

Rows or columns may have been hidden during the sort. Rows or columns that are hidden do not sort, except for hidden rows or columns in an outline.

Data on the left side of the records does not align with the appropriate data on the right side.

The database may have split in half and been scrambled by a sort that did not include all columns. No way exists to repair the problem. Use a previously saved version.

From Here...

For information relating directly to sorting and formulas that can help you sort, review the following chapters in this book:

- Chapter 19, "Creating Automatic Subtotals." After you sort a list or database, this chapter shows you how to insert subtotals or grand totals. You also learn a few tricks on how to hide rows or columns depending on their content.
- Chapter 33, "Finding, Filtering, and Editing Lists and Databases." This chapter describes how to filter your database to show only the information in which you are interested.

Chapter 33

Finding, Filtering, and Editing Lists and Databases

In this chapter you learn:

- How to use the data form to find and edit data
- How to use AutoFilter to create simple criteria
- How to use wild cards and formulas to create complex criteria to filter data
- How to use Advanced Filters to create complex criteria

Lists or databases are used most frequently to find or analyze a collection of information. Finding data in a list or database involves selecting the row or rows of information satisfying some *criteria*, a set of questions, that you asked. Frequently you will want to see all the rows of information that satisfy criteria. In Excel you can also *filter* a list or database. Filtering temporarily hides all rows in the list that do not satisfy the criteria. After performing a filter, your list collapses to show only the row(s) satisfying the criteria you specified.

Note

In Excel 5, the term *database* has generally been replaced with *list*, and the **D**ata menu provides list management features that are analogous to the database management features in Excel 4 and earlier versions.

In Excel you can find or filter data by using three mechanisms: the data form, the AutoFilter, or the Advanced Filter. The data form is an easy way to search for and edit individual records. The AutoFilter is a very easy way of collapsing a list to show only the row(s) satisfying your questions. The Advanced Filter is only slightly more complex, but enables you to ask very complex questions that must satisfy multiple conditions and even calculated criteria.

Tip
The worksheet editing commands **E**dit **F**ind and **E**dit R**e**place find and replace individual words or phrases in a worksheet or list. Refer to Chapter 4, "Entering and Editing Data."

By using the information in this chapter, you can find and edit any type of data in your list. The concepts on building filters and queries are important to following chapters. In Chapter 34, "Extracting Data," you learn how to extract information from your list and move it to another location. Chapter 35, "Linking Excel to External Databases," uses these queries' concepts to demonstrate how to use Microsoft Query, which comes with Excel, to link Excel worksheets to data on disk, in SQL servers, or in mainframe relational databases.

Specifying Criteria

No matter which of the three methods of finding or filtering data you use, you need to learn how to specify the data you want to find. The specifications for what you want to find are called *criteria*. Criteria can be in many forms. It may be simply a name, such as *John*, or a comparison, such as *Amounts>500*; or it may involve a calculation, such as *=AND(B12>500,B12<1000)*.

You enter criteria in different locations, depending on whether you are using the data form, an AutoFilter, or the Advanced Filter. The concepts are all the same. Later sections of this chapter describe where to enter the information in each type of find or filter.

Finding Simple or Exact Matches

Comparative criteria involve finding exact matches or simple ranges of greater-than or less-than comparisons. Comparative criteria do not involve mathematical calculations or logical operators such as AND or OR. You can use comparative criteria in all of Excel's data find and filter methods. If you need to use complex or calculated criteria, you must use the AutoFilter with a criteria range. (See the sections "Matching Calculated Criteria" and "Matching Compound Criteria with AND and OR Conditions" later in this chapter.)

The simplest and easiest criteria specify text for which you are searching. Figures 33.1 and 33.2 show how text criteria for the name *John* is entered in the data form (fig. 33.1) and in the AutoFilter pull-down list (fig. 33.2). In figure 33.3, simple criteria are entered into the criteria range before using the Advanced Filter.

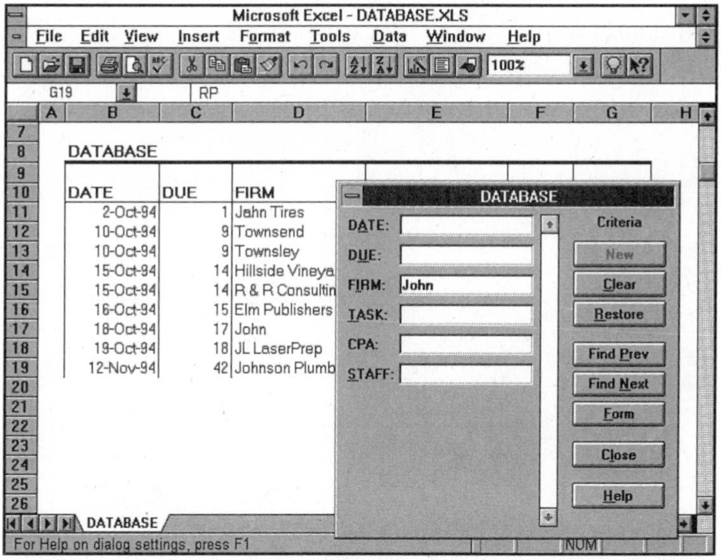

Fig. 33.1
Use the data form to find and edit, using simple criteria.

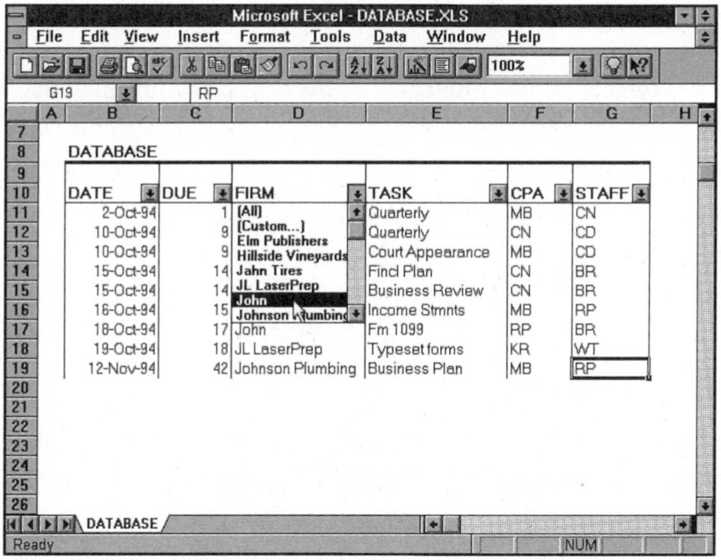

Fig. 33.2
Select what you want to see from the pull-down list in an AutoFilter.

Caution

Do not clear cells by pressing the space bar and then pressing Enter. This procedure enters a blank character in the criteria row. Excel then attempts to find records that contain a blank character in this field.

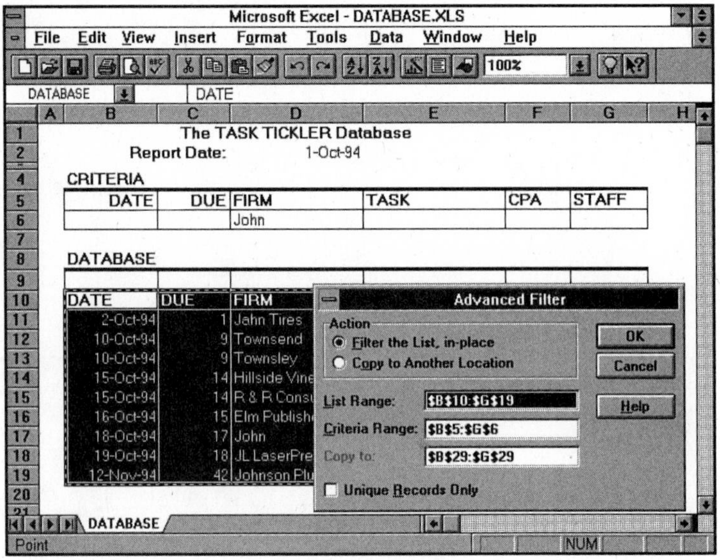

Fig. 33.3
Type a simple name or date into the criteria range of an Advanced Filter.

Tip
You can use comparisons to find ranges of both text and numbers. To find all text entries that start with T or letters after T, you can use the criteria >=T.

Using Numeric Comparisons

To find an exact match for a number, enter the number in the criteria area of the data form, select the number from the pull-down AutoFilter list, or enter the number in the Advanced Filter criteria range directly below the appropriate field name.

If you want to find numbers greater than or less than a number, enter comparison criteria, such as the criteria in figures 33.4 and 33.5. In this case, the expression <15 tells Excel to search the DUE field (column) for records where the value is less than 15. Table 33.1 shows other comparison operators that you can use in the criteria range or data form.

Table 33.1 Comparison Operators

Operator	Meaning	Example	Finds
=	Equals	=200	Fields equal to 200
=	Equals	=	Fields equal to blank
>	Greater than	>200	Fields greater than 200
>=	Greater than or equal to	>=200	Fields greater than or equal to 200
<	Less than	<200	Fields less than 200

Operator	Meaning	Example	Finds
<=	Less than or equal to	<=200	Fields less than or equal to 200
<>	Not equal to	<>200	Fields not equal to 200

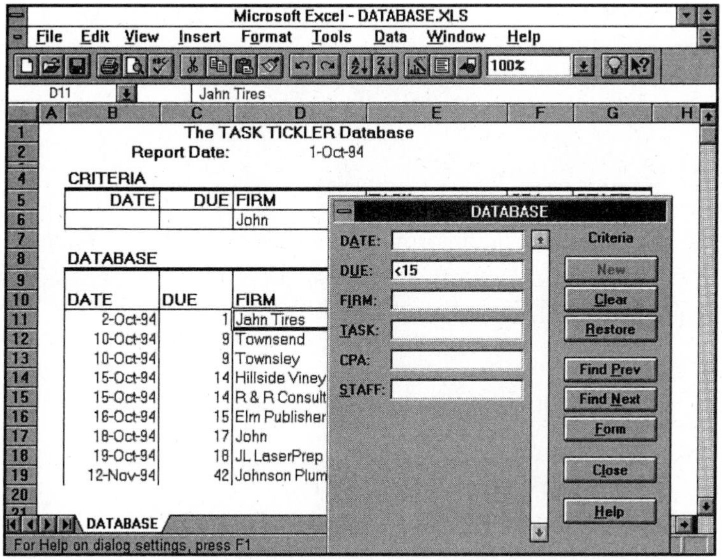

Fig. 33.4
Enter a simple numeric comparison in a data form.

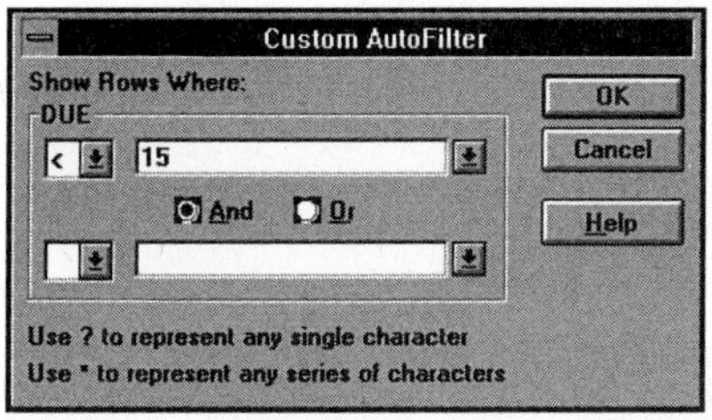

Fig. 33.5
Use the Custom AutoFilter dialog box to enter numeric comparisons.

Note

Find blank fields by using the = comparison operator followed by nothing. Find filled fields by using the not equal to operator, < >, followed by nothing.

Finding Date and Time Matches

When you search for dates by using comparison criteria, use the comparative operators from table 33.1. Type dates the same way you would type them into a worksheet cell. For example, to search the list shown in figure 33.3 for dates greater than October 11, 1994, you can enter the following criteria for the DATE field in the data form, the Custom AutoFilter dialog box, or the criteria range of an Advanced Filter:

>10/11/94

or

>11 Oct 94

You can use a date that exists in any of Excel's predefined date formats in the criteria.

Finding Near Matches with Wild Cards

If you are not sure of the spelling of a word in the list, or you need to find records that contain similar but not identical text, you need a couple of extra cards up your sleeve. In Excel, these cards are known as *wild cards*, and they are part of the searching game.

You can use the two text criteria wild cards: the asterisk (*) and the question mark (?). The two wild cards represent the following characters:

?	Any single character in the same position
*	Any group of characters in the same position

You can use the question mark (?) if you are uncertain how to spell the word you want to match. If a name in the FIRM field may be John or Jahn, for example, you enter the criteria as shown in the following example:

J?hn

The ? matches any single letter between the *J* and *h*.

The asterisk (*) matches groups of characters. You can use it at any location in the text criteria: beginning, middle, or end. To locate data in a field with a name like Gallon Cans, you might use the criteria * *paint*. This criteria finds the following matches:

blue paint

red paint

yellow paint

If you need to find the actual symbols * or ? in a list, then type a tilde (~) before the * or ?. The tilde indicates that you are not using the * or ? as a wild card.

Matching Multiple Criteria with AND and OR Conditions

You can specify multiple criteria when you need to find records that satisfy more than one criterion. For example, in your personal contact list you might need to find all your California clients with whom you have not talked in the last 30 days.

In the data form, you specify multiple criteria by entering criteria in more than one of the criteria edit fields. In the AutoFilter, you use a Custom AutoFilter dialog box in which you can enter two criteria. With an Advanced Filter you can enter many combinations of multiple criteria.

Excel handles multiple criteria using two logical conditions, AND and OR. The rules for AND and OR criteria are

AND	All of the multiple specifications must match for the criteria to be TRUE. Only if a record matches all of the AND criteria will the record be found or be displayed by the filter. (Think of the questions as "This one must be true *AND* this one must be true *AND*....")
OR	One or more of the multiple specifications must match for the criteria to be TRUE. If any criteria matches from the multiple criteria that are OR'd together, then the entire record will be found or be displayed by the filter. (Think of the question as "Either this one must be true *OR* this one must be true *OR* ....")

It is important to understand the difference between AND and OR, or you will not get the answers you want. A few general rules will help:

- If you are dealing with allowed ranges *in the same field,* for example, Amount>10 and Amount<35, you should be using an AND condition.
- If you are dealing with *separate fields where all must meet their conditions in the same record,* for example, LName=Thompson and State=CA, you should be using an AND condition.

- If you are dealing with the *same field that can meet multiple conditions*, for example, State=WA or State=NY or State=MA, you should be using an OR condition. (This one is often confused because it is different from how we speak.)
- If you are dealing with *different fields where if any of the conditions are met you want a match*, for example, State=WA or LName=Thompson or Due>500, use an OR condition.

Choosing the Best Search Method

With three methods of finding or filtering in a list, and the different capabilities of each method, it may at first seem daunting when you must decide which method to use. The following table shows some of the limits and capabilities of each method. It may help you decide when to use different methods.

Capability	Data Form	AutoFilter	Advanced Filter
Displays	Single record	List on sheet	List on sheet
Editing	Form	On sheet	On sheet
Mouse required	No	Yes	No
Single comparison	Yes	Yes	Yes
AND comparisons	Yes, simple multifield or one AND within field	Yes, across multiple fields	Yes, advanced
OR comparisons	No	Yes, in same field	Yes, advanced
Mixed AND and OR	No	No	Yes, advanced
Calculated/complex comparisons	No	No	Yes
Exact match, ease of use		Easiest	
Find blanks, ease of use		Easiest	
Find nonblanks, ease of use		Easiest	

Capability	Data Form	AutoFilter	Advanced Filter
Automatic copy of found/filtered data to another location	No	No	Yes
Limit to the number of fields (columns)	Yes, limited by form size and screen resolution	256 columns	256 columns

Using the Data Form

Excel's data form is excellent for finding and editing records that satisfy simple or multiple comparisons. You enter criteria in a blank form and request the next or previous record that matches your criteria. The data form then displays the next or previous record that matches your criteria.

Finding Data with the Data Form

To use the data form to find records, follow these steps:

1. Select a cell within the list. If the list has adjacent filled cells or has more than two rows of headings, select the range that contains the list and the row of field names next to the data.

2. Choose the **D**ata F**o**rm command to display the data form for the selected list (see fig. 33.6).

   Note

   If you want to see all records, ignore the next step or leave the criteria fields blank.

3. Select the **C**riteria button.

   Selecting **C**riteria changes the buttons on the form and clears the text box next to each field (see fig. 33.7).

4. Select the text box next to the field in which you want a criterion. Type the criterion. Click in another box or press Tab for the next box, Shift+Tab for the previous box, or the Alt+key combination for a particular field.

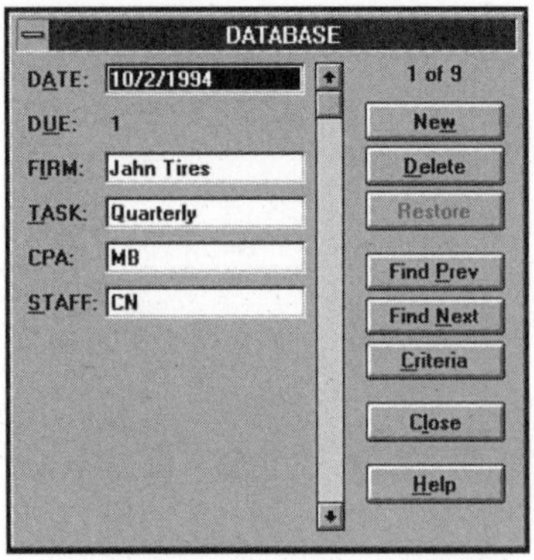

Fig. 33.6
The data form shows each of the fields in the list.

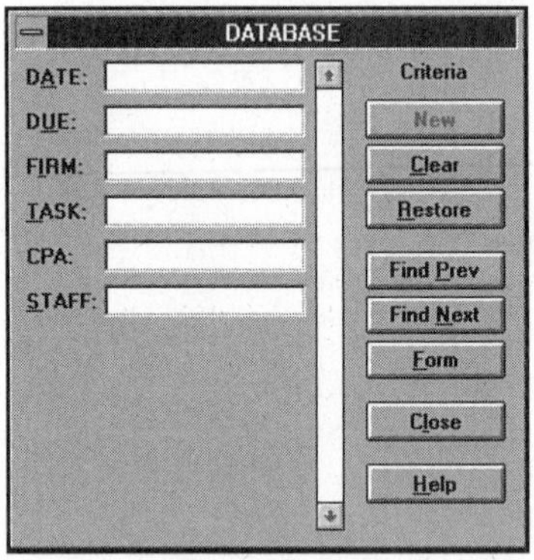

Fig. 33.7
After selecting the **C**riteria button you can enter criteria.

Note

Each key combination (Alt+A, Alt+B, and so on) is available only once. After you have used up key combinations, the field may have no key combination. For example, in figure 3.7, CPA has no combination because C has been used for **C**lear, P for Find **P**rev, and A for the field D**A**TE.

5. Choose Find **N**ext or Find **P**rev to move from the current record to the next record in the indicated direction that meets the entered criteria.

Figure 33.8 shows a data form with criteria entered that will match records where the CPA has the initials MB. You also can find records that must satisfy criteria in more than one field. For example, the criteria in figure 33.9 specify a search for records with a CPA who has initials CN, the date DUE less than 15 days, and the FIRM name starting with H.

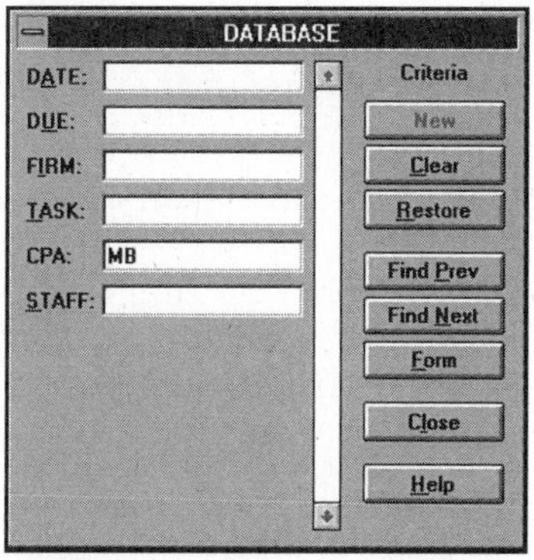

Fig. 33.8
This simple set of criteria specifies that the CPA field must have the initials MB.

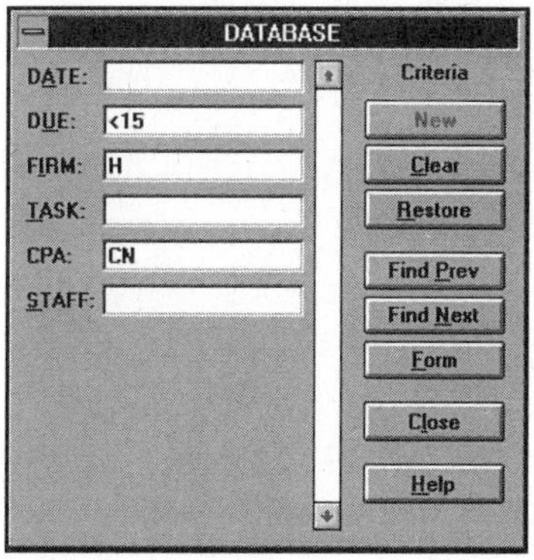

Fig. 33.9
These criteria specify that the CPA field must have the initials CN, the date DUE is less than 15, and the FIRM name starts with H.

Typing multiple comparisons produces an AND condition, as described at the beginning of this chapter. All comparisons in the criteria must be true for a record to be found. For example, in figure 33.9, the only records that will be found are those where *all three* criteria are true. You cannot do an OR condition using the data form. You can use the form to find only simple or multiple comparisons. You cannot use the form to find calculated criteria or complex AND and OR comparisons. If you want to filter using two comparisons in the same field in an OR, use the AutoFilter. If you need an unlimited number of AND and OR conditions, use the Advanced Filter.

You can use the data form on only one list at a time. You can use the data form even while the list is filtered. Although you can see only filtered data on the sheet, you will be able to find, scroll through, and edit all records using a data form.

Because the data form is so easy to use, you may be able to search for data after just a few minutes of practice. If you want to see data in the worksheet while doing simple searches, use the AutoFilter. If you need to do more complex searches and see the filtered data in the worksheet, use the Advanced Filter.

Caution

When you enter a simple text criteria in the data form, the form assumes that the text criteria ends with the * wild card. This ensures that it finds data that may have been entered with a space at the end. However, it also means that if you typed in *John*, you will also find *Johnson*.

Tip
If you click in the form's vertical scroll bar, you move to another record, but it may not be a record meeting the criteria you have specified.

Editing with the Data Form

The data form provides an easy way to edit individual records. If you can find the record by using the simple comparative criteria available in the data form, use the form to do your editing.

To edit data using the data form, take these steps:

1. Select a cell within the database or the range containing the list.
2. Choose the **D**ata F**o**rm command.
3. Select the **C**riteria button.
4. Type the criteria you want and then choose the Find **P**rev or Find **N**ext button to find a matching record.
5. Edit the data if necessary. If you make changes and want to undo your changes before you have moved to the next record, choose the **R**estore button.
6. Repeat steps 4 and 5 until you have found and edited the records you want.
7. Select C**l**ose to save the changes to the last record and return to the worksheet.

If you need to delete a record you have found with the form, choose the **D**elete button on the form. An alert message warns that you are about to delete the current record. Choose OK to complete the deletion. Keep in mind that deleted records cannot be recovered.

Using the AutoFilter

The AutoFilter gives you quick access to a great deal of list management power. By pointing and clicking, you can quickly filter out data you do not want to see or print. Unlike the data form, the AutoFilter displays the data in the worksheet. Rows of data that do not match the criteria you specify are filtered out and hidden. The entire row of data that does not match the criteria is hidden.

> **Caution**
>
> If you have worksheet information to the side of a list, filtering the list may hide rows within the worksheet information to the side. When rows are hidden in the list, they are hidden across the entire worksheet. To prevent a filter from hiding parts of your worksheet results, put the list in its own worksheet or be sure to keep the sides of lists clear.

When you use the AutoFilter you can use either of two methods of finding data. You can use the pull-down menus to find exact matches, or you can create simple or two-field comparisons by selecting the (Custom) subcommand from the pull-down menu (see fig. 33.10). Figure 33.11 shows the Custom AutoFilter dialog box in which you can enter simple or two-condition criteria. Because the AutoFilter hides rows containing records that do not match the criteria you select, row numbers appear to be skipped (see fig. 33.12).

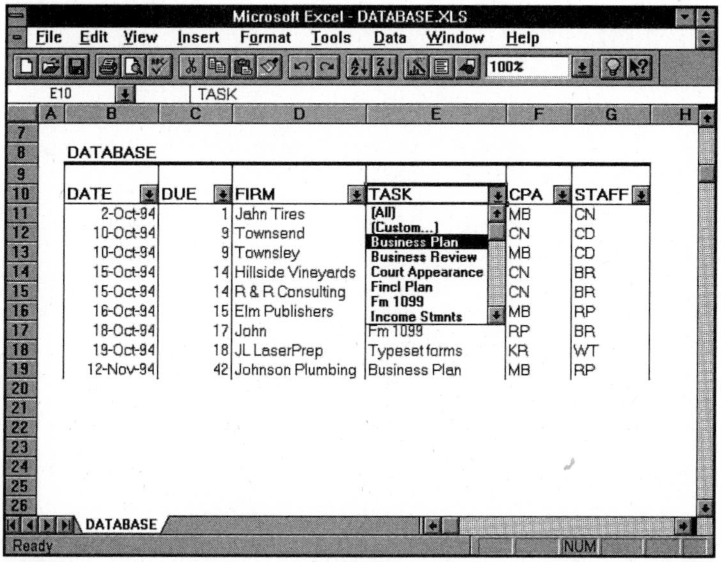

Fig. 33.10
Click the AutoFilter's pull-down list for exact matches on one or more comparisons.

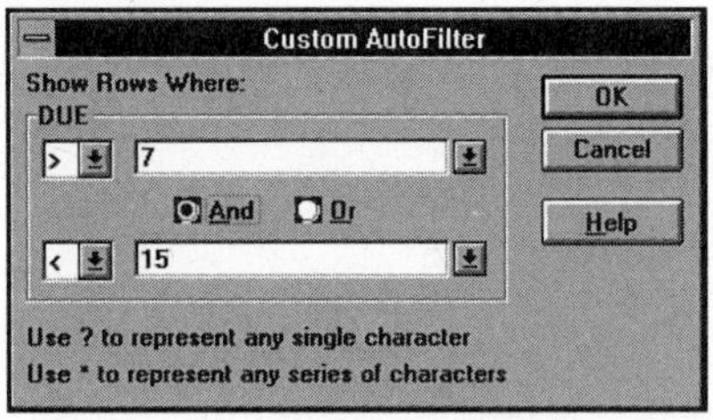

Fig. 33.11
Select (Custom...) from the AutoFilter pull-down list to enter one or two criteria.

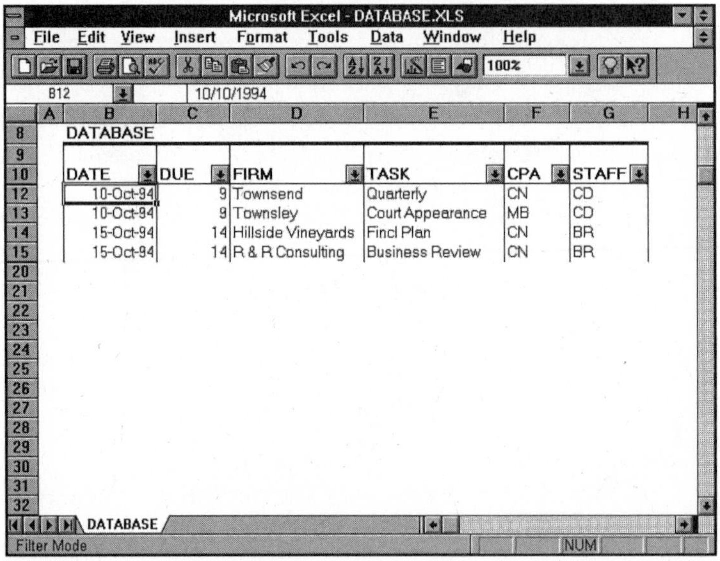

Fig. 33.12
This filter hid rows less than 15 days due. Notice the missing row numbers between rows 15 and 20.

Finding Data with the AutoFilter

Before using AutoFilter, make sure that it is turned off from any previous list. Choose the **D**ata **F**ilter command. If there is a check mark next to the Auto**F**ilter command, it is on for another list. Choose the Auto**F**ilter command to turn it off before using AutoFilter on another list.

To create an AutoFilter on a list, take these steps:

1. Select a cell within the list. If the list has filled cells touching it, select just the range containing the list.

2. Choose the **D**ata **F**ilter Auto**F**ilter command.

As figure 33.10 above shows, the field names at the top of the list become pull-down lists.

To filter out rows that do not match your criteria, follow these steps:

1. Click the pull-down list for the column in which you want to enter criteria.

2. Select the criteria you want for that field. Select from the following options:

(All)	Allows all records in this field.
(Custom...)	Displays the Custom AutoFilter dialog box enabling you to create AND or OR criteria.
Exact values	Displays only records with this exact value in this field. If you need to select more than one exact value, use the (Custom...) subcommand.
(Blanks)	Displays all records with blanks in this field.
(NonBlanks)	Displays all records with nonblanks (records that contain data) in this field.

3. Complete the Custom AutoFilter dialog box if you selected this subcommand. A description follows these steps.

4. Return to step 1 and click other pull-down lists if you want filters on other fields.

As soon as you make an AutoFilter selection from the pull-down lists, the worksheet hides rows that do not meet your criteria. You immediately see the results of your filter.

As you select criteria from each pull-down list it is ANDed with the criteria you have selected for other fields. In other words, for a record to display it must meet all the criteria for all the fields from which you made a selection.

Note

Short labels used as field names may be hidden by the arrows from pull-down AutoFilter lists. To make these field names visible, select the cell and format it for left alignment by clicking the Align Left button in the Formatting toolbar or by choosing the F**o**rma**t** C**e**lls command and selecting the Alignment tab.

If you don't like the filtered result from a selection you make, you can immediately reselect the same pull-down and choose the (All) subcommand for that field.

To display all records and remove the criteria from all AutoFilters, choose the **D**ata **F**ilter **S**how All command.

To exit AutoFilter, choose the **D**ata **F**ilter Auto**F**ilter command.

When AutoFilter is on, a checkmark appears in the menu next to the Auto**F**ilter command.

Finding Near Matches or AND/OR Matches

AutoFilter is very easy to use when you want to find an exact match for one or more fields. Through the use of its Custom AutoFilter dialog box, it is also easy to specify near matches or to match many AND and OR conditions.

Tip
Use AND when finding records within a *range*; for example, between one date AND another date. Use OR when you want one *exact* item OR another exact item.

To enter comparative criteria, select a comparison operator from the first pull-down list, and then type the value or select one from the list to its right. If you have a second comparison, select the And or Or option; then select the second comparison operator and the second comparison value. Remember that if you try it and don't like the results, you can choose the (All) subcommand to remove what you entered.

The examples in figures 33.13, 33.14, and 33.15 show some of the ways you can use the Custom AutoFilter to filter data.

Using the Advanced Filter

Although using the **D**ata **F**ilter **A**dvanced Filter command involves more work than using the data form or AutoFilter, the command enables you to search for data that must match calculated criteria or matches involving complicated AND and OR criteria. In addition, the command prepares you to use more powerful features, such as extracting a copy of filtered data from a list. The command also uses the same concepts required for using Excel's analysis functions and data tables as described in Chapter 23, "Manipulating and Analyzing Data." It also uses similar criteria concepts to those used by Microsoft Query, as in Chapter 35, "Retrieving Data from External Databases," to link Excel to external databases.

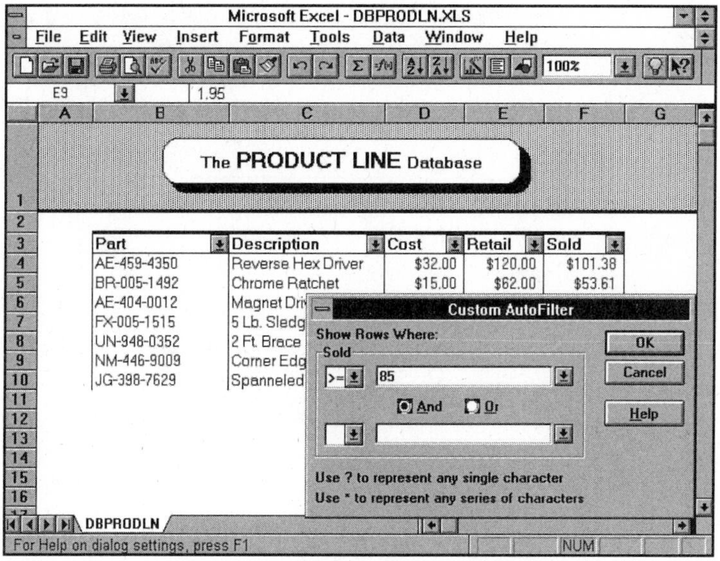

Fig. 33.13
Display records where the amount Sold is greater than or equal to $85.

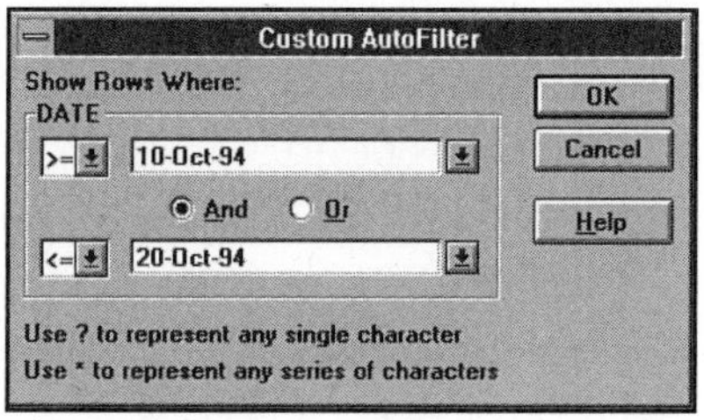

Fig. 33.14
Display inclusive dates between 10-Oct-94 and 20-Oct-94. Notice the use of AND for a range.

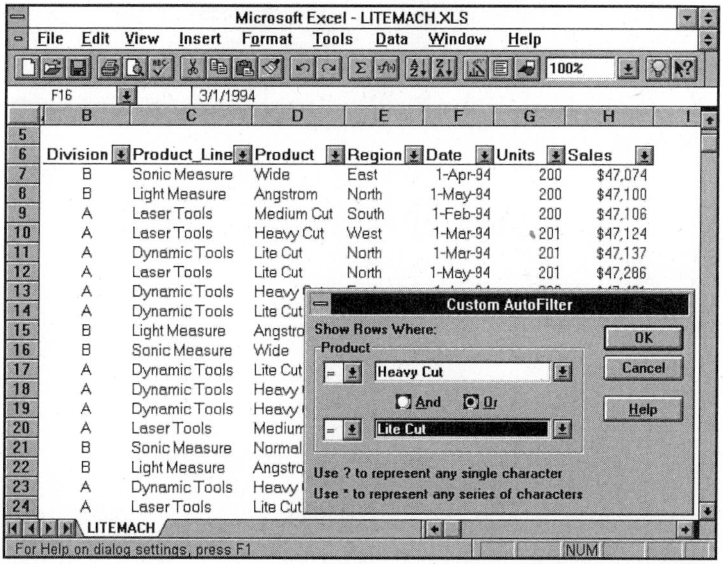

Fig. 33.15
Display records of either or both Heavy Cut or Lite Cut.

> **Caution**
>
> If you have worksheet information to the side of a list, filtering the list may hide rows within the worksheet information to the side. When rows are hidden, they are hidden across the entire worksheet.

Understanding the Advanced Filter

If you plan to use advanced filters, you need to create a criteria range. The criteria range specifies the conditions that filtered data must meet. The top row of the criteria range contains field names that must be spelled exactly the same as the field names above the list. You do not need to include every field name from the list in the criteria range. The criteria range also includes at least one blank row below the field names. You enter in this row criteria that the records you are searching for must match. Excel matches the criteria under a field name in the criteria range against the data under the same field name in the list.

Figure 33.16 shows a selected criteria range. (In this example, the selected cells were outlined with the F**o**rmat C**e**lls command and the options on the Border tab.) Do not use more than one blank row in the criteria range unless you will be entering multiple criteria in all the rows, as explained in the earlier section "Matching Multiple Criteria with AND and OR Conditions." If you leave a line blank in your criteria range, the filter does not work, and Excel displays all data in the list.

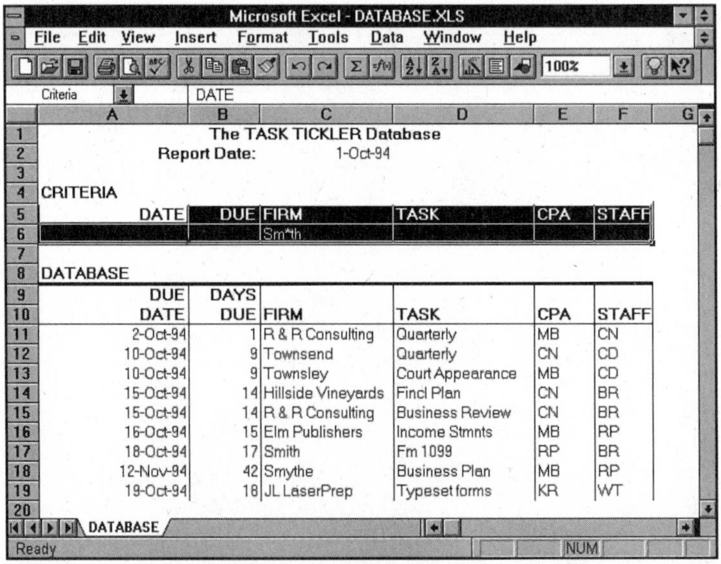

Fig. 33.16
The criteria range must have a blank row and field names spelled exactly like those above the list. To ensure that the field names match, use the **C**opy command.

You do not need to name the criteria range, but you will find it easier to enter the criteria range—and you will make fewer errors—if you assign the criteria range a name by using the **I**nsert **N**ame **D**efine command.

Note

If you assign the name Criteria to the criteria range, the Advanced Filter dialog box automatically picks up and enters the correct range in its **C**riteria Range edit box. This does not prevent you from changing the range in the **C**riteria Range edit box to any other range.

If the field names at the top of the criteria range do not match those in the list, the **D**ata **F**ilter **A**dvanced Filter command will not work. To be certain that your criteria field names match the list field names exactly, copy them from the list with the **E**dit **C**opy and **E**dit **P**aste commands or with shortcut keys or toolbar buttons. You do not need to include every field name in the criteria range, and you can include the names in any order you like, as long as they exactly match the field names used in the list.

Tip
Unlike earlier versions of Excel, Excel 5 can use text, numbers, or formula results as field names in lists and criteria ranges.

Note

Do not include unused blank rows in the criteria range. Blank rows in the criteria range tell Excel to match against all records in the list. You can see the size of the criteria range by choosing the **D**ata **F**ilter **A**dvanced Filter command, selecting the **C**riteria Range, and checking the range on-screen that is surrounded by the moving dashed line. If unneeded blank rows are in the criteria range, redefine the criteria range without the blank rows.

Finding Data with the Advanced Filter

After you prepare a criteria range, you are ready to filter records in the list.

Tip
AutoFilter criteria don't affect the operation of the Advanced Filter. The two methods operate independently. If the AutoFilter is on, the Advanced Filter turns it off.

To enter criteria and use the Advanced Filter, take these steps:

1. Use the Del key or **E**dit Cle**a**r command to clear old criteria from the criteria range.

2. Enter new criteria in the blank row of the criteria range as in that shown in figure 33.16.

The criteria range can contain simple criteria, such as *Townsend,* below the FIRM field name if you are looking for just Townsend in that column. The criteria range also can contain entries that match ranges of numbers, calculate criteria, and contain TRUE/FALSE comparisons. Later sections in this chapter describe other matching conditions.

To run an Advanced Filter, follow these steps:

1. Select a cell within the list. If the list has filled cells touching it, select the range containing the list. If you select a cell within a range that has the name Database, this range is assumed to be the list you want to filter.

2. Choose the **D**ata **F**ilter **A**dvanced Filter command to display the Advanced Filter dialog box shown in figure 33.17.

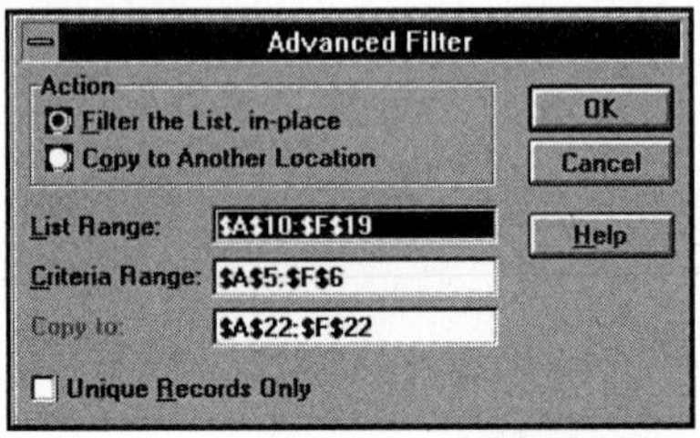

Fig. 33.17
Use the Advanced Filter dialog box to indicate the criteria and database ranges.

3. Select the **F**ilter the List, in-place option so that you see only matching items in the list area of the worksheet. If you want to place the data in another area of the worksheet for printing or to work with so you don't disturb the original data, select C**o**py to Another Location.

4. Select the **L**ist Range edit box and enter the range of the list if it did not automatically appear or if you want to change the displayed range.

   Enter the list range and the criteria range in the **L**ist Range and **C**riteria Range edit boxes by first selecting the edit box, and then typing the reference or dragging across the range on-screen.

5. Select the **C**riteria Range edit box and enter the range of the criteria if it did not automatically appear or if you want to change the displayed range.

6. Select the Unique **R**ecords Only check box if you want to filter out duplicate records. This shows only the first record that meets the

criteria and eliminates duplicates. If you do not select this option, all records that meet the criteria display.

7. Choose OK.

The list changes to display only those records that meet the criteria. Rows containing records that do not meet the criteria are hidden. This may hide rows on either side of the list.

If you enter a simple match in the criteria range, you may get more returned than you expected. For example, if you filter a list and have the letter L under the Product_Line header in the criteria range, Excel displays all entries for the Product_Line that start with L. The Advanced Filter acts as though there is an * (asterisk) wild card at the end of each simple match.

Note

When the Transition **F**ormula Evaluation check box is selected by choosing the **T**ools **O**ptions command and selecting the Transition tab, Excel criteria follow the database search rules used by Lotus 1-2-3. If your list does not seem to be using the rules listed here, check whether the Transition **F**ormula Evaluation check box is cleared.

Using Multiple Comparisons in a Criteria Range

When using the Advanced Filter, you can enter multiple criteria on the same row in the criteria range. When you enter multiple criteria on the same criteria row, *all* the criteria must be met in order for a record to qualify as a match. Figure 33.18 shows a criteria range where DAYS DUE must be greater than 14 *and* CPA must be MB. Because both of these criteria are in the same row of the criteria range, a record must meet both criteria for Excel to find the record. The records in rows 16 and 18 will be displayed.

To find records where one *OR* the other criteria is met, create a criteria range with more than one row. Insert an additional row in the criteria range for each criterion. Be certain that the extra row is included in the criteria range if you name the range or when you choose the **D**ata **F**ilter **A**dvanced Filter command. Figure 33.19 shows a criteria range with two rows for criteria. The criteria entries shown below CPA tell Excel to find records where the CPA is MB *OR* the CPA is CN.

Fig. 33.18
All criteria on the same row must be met.

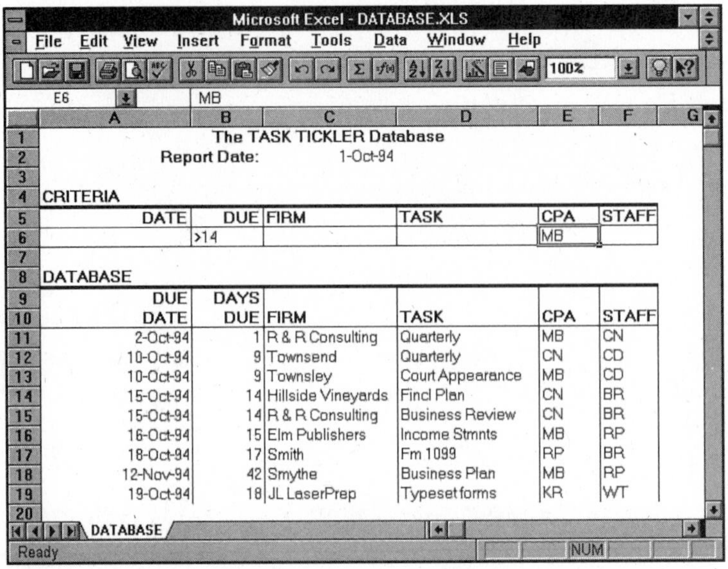

Fig. 33.19
Either one or the other of criteria on separate rows can be true.

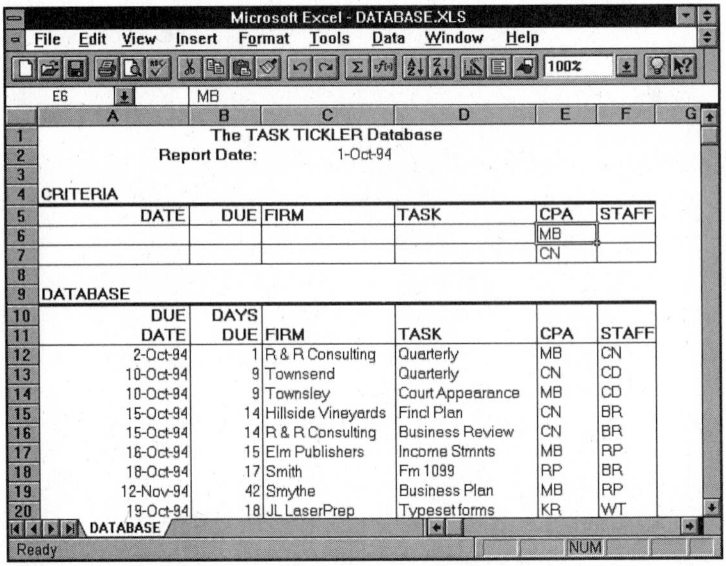

Note

Be careful when you use two or more rows in the criteria range. A blank row tells Excel to find all records in the list. Therefore, if you leave a row blank in the criteria range, Excel filters nothing and displays all records.

Figure 33.20 shows how you can combine simple criteria to ask complex questions of your list. The criteria range uses two rows so that you can find records matching one value or the other. A record must match all the criteria in one row *or* the other if it is to match and be displayed. The English equivalent of the criteria range in the figure is the following expression.

Find all records where

> The DAYS DUE are less than 15 AND the CPA is CN.
>
> OR
>
> The DUE DATE is 18-Oct-94 AND the FIRM name is Smith.

Excel finds the records that meet these criteria in rows 13, 15, 16, and 18.

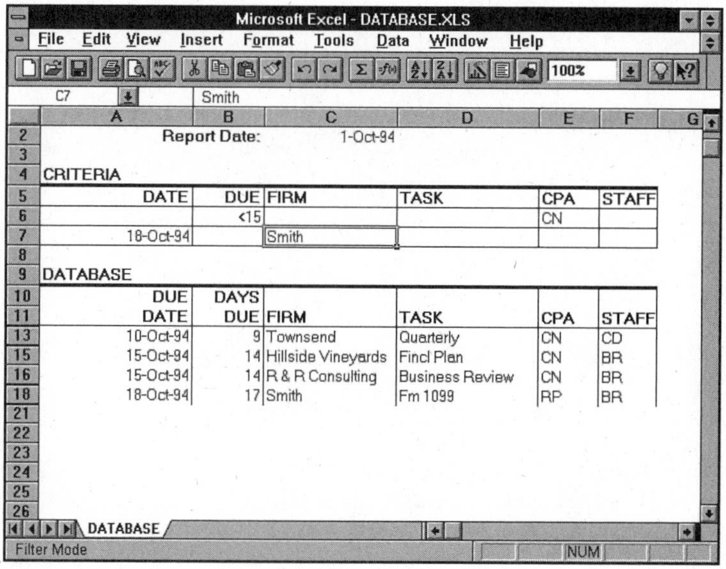

Fig. 33.20
Use multiple rows with multiple criteria for complex searches.

Calculating What You Want To Find

Using comparative criteria and ANDs and ORs through the use of additional rows in the criteria range is helpful and quick, but in some cases you need to specify more exact data. You may want to find dates between two ranges, or even use formulas to calculate what you are searching for. In these cases, you need to use calculated criteria.

Matching Calculated Criteria. You can select records according to any calculation that results in a TRUE or FALSE logical value when it is tested against the contents of a record. Calculated criteria that result in TRUE are a match.

Calculated criteria are needed, for example, when you want to find records where inventory quantities are less than a calculated reorder quantity, where a range of dates is needed but some dates within the range are excluded, or where a mailing list has the ZIP code included with the City and State field.

Figure 33.21 shows an example of calculated criteria that find Parts that were sold for less than 90 percent of Retail price. Notice that the calculated criteria, `=F9<0.9*E9`, must be entered in the criteria range below a *field name that does not exist* in the list. In this example, the name Calc was inserted in the middle of the criteria range; Calc is not used as a field name in the list. *You can use any text name above the calculated criteria, if it has not been used in the list as a field name.*

> **Note**
>
> You must enter calculated criteria in the criteria range below names that are not used as field names in the list. Use a field name that is different from any field name in the list.

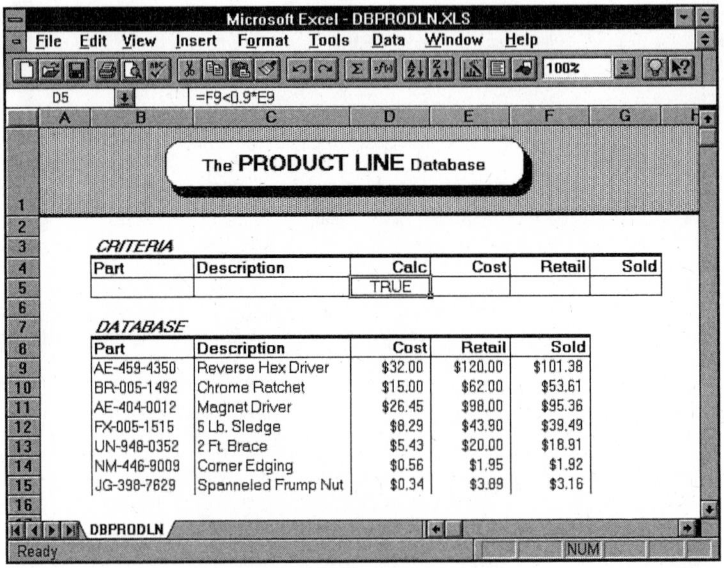

Fig. 33.21
Use a formula to calculate criteria that can be found in no other way. (The formula for this example is visible in the formula bar, near the top of the screen.)

In your calculated criteria formula, use cell references that refer to a cell in the top data row of the list. Use relative reference addresses (without $ signs) for references within the list, as shown in figure 33.21. Use absolute cell references to refer to any cell outside the list that is involved in the calculated criteria.

Calculated criteria can involve multiple fields and equations, but the result must produce a TRUE or FALSE condition. The Advanced Filter displays those records that produce a TRUE result. Some simple calculated criteria, where the first data row is row 36, are illustrated in the following table:

Criteria	Explanation
=B36=G36	Compares the values of fields in the same record. Selects the record when the value in column B equals the value in column G.
=B36<G36/2	Compares the value in B36 to one half the value in G36. Both cells are in the same record. Selects the record when the value in column B is less than half of the value in column G.
=B36G36>10	Compares two values in the same record. Selects the record when a value in column B minus a value in column G is greater than 10.

Note

Remember that calculated criteria must compare the value found in the first row of data in the list. The filter will produce incorrect results if your calculation compares a cell that is not in the first row of data.

More complex but extremely useful calculated criteria include comparisons between values in a record with other records or with values outside the list. These types of criteria are useful when you want to compare records or use criteria calculated elsewhere in the worksheet. The following table shows some examples of these types of criteria; assume that the first data row (record) is row 36:

Criteria	Explanation
=B36–G37>10	Compares values in adjacent records. Selects the record when the value in column B of one record is more than 10 greater than the value in column G of the next record. Usually you will want to sort the list before doing this type of comparison so that columns B and G are in an order that makes sense for the comparison.
=B36=$C$24	Compares a value in a record to a value outside the list. Selects the record when the value in column B equals the value in $C$24, where C24 is a cell outside the list. This is how you can refer to criteria calculated or entered elsewhere in the worksheet.

Tip
If you use the correct syntax when you enter a calculated criteria formula, Excel displays TRUE or FALSE in the cell after you enter the formula. TRUE or FALSE applies to the specific cells you used in the formula.

As you can see from the examples, calculated criteria can involve cell references that are outside the list. You must use an absolute reference to refer to any location outside the list.

Matching Compound Criteria with AND and OR. You can use Excel's AND( ), OR( ), and NOT( ) functions to create complex compound criteria. These are the AND( ), OR( ), and NOT( ) functions that are used as worksheet and macro functions. This method is useful for specifying complex criteria that cannot be handled by inserting additional rows in the criteria range. The conditions that are being matched are used as arguments within the functions. For an AND( ), OR( ), or NOT( ) function to be TRUE so that a record matches, the arguments within them must match the following conditions:

AND	All conditions (arguments) must be TRUE.
OR	One condition (argument) out of all the conditions must be TRUE.
NOT	The condition used with NOT is reversed. TRUE changes to FALSE; FALSE changes to TRUE.

Just as you can enter calculated criteria that result in a TRUE or FALSE value, you can enter AND( ), OR( ), and NOT( ) functions that evaluate to TRUE or FALSE. For example, consider the list in figure 33.22. The following calculated criteria could be used under the dummy field name, Calc, in the criteria range. Notice that each compound criteria uses the cell reference of the first cell in the column being tested. These are all in row 11.

For each of the following queries stated in English syntax, the associated compound criteria formula is presented, and the resulting records that Excel finds are listed:

English statement:	The CPA is CN AND the STAFF is BR.
Compound criteria:	=AND(E11="CN",F11="BR")
Result:	Finds the records in rows 14 and 15.
English statement:	The FIRM is Townsley OR the FIRM is Smith.
Compound criteria:	=OR(C11="Townsley",C11="Smith")
Result:	Finds the records in rows 13 and 17.
English statement:	The FIRM is NOT Townsley AND the DAYS DUE is 9.
Compound criteria:	=AND(NOT(C11="Townsley"),B11=9)
Result:	Finds the record in row 12.

For Related Information

- "Logical Functions", p. 207
- "Using Formulas to Make Decisions," p. 687
- "Using Formulas to Look Up Data in Tables," p. 693

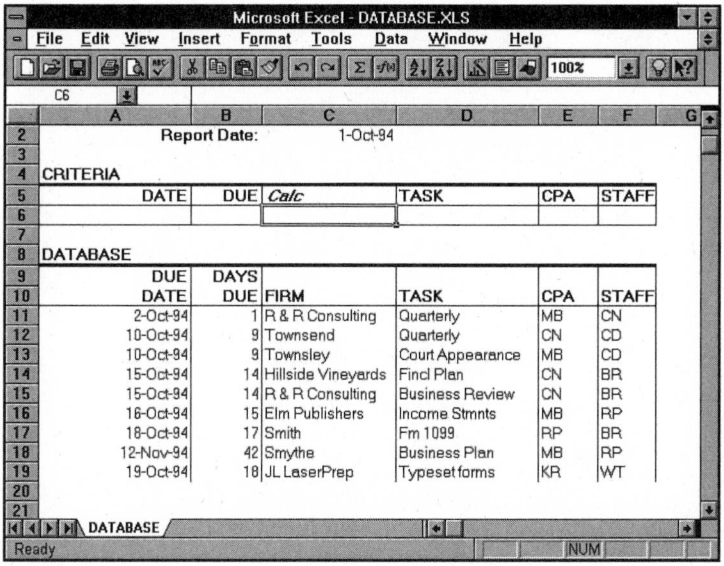

	A	B	C	D	E	F
2	Report Date:		1-Oct-94			
3						
4	CRITERIA					
5	DATE	DUE	*Calc*	TASK	CPA	STAFF
6						
7						
8	DATABASE					
9	DUE	DAYS				
10	DATE	DUE	FIRM	TASK	CPA	STAFF
11	2-Oct-94	1	R & R Consulting	Quarterly	MB	CN
12	10-Oct-94	9	Townsend	Quarterly	CN	CD
13	10-Oct-94	9	Townsley	Court Appearance	MB	CD
14	15-Oct-94	14	Hillside Vineyards	Fincl Plan	CN	BR
15	15-Oct-94	14	R & R Consulting	Business Review	CN	BR
16	16-Oct-94	15	Elm Publishers	Income Stmnts	MB	RP
17	18-Oct-94	17	Smith	Fm 1099	RP	BR
18	12-Nov-94	42	Smythe	Business Plan	MB	RP
19	19-Oct-94	18	JL LaserPrep	Typeset forms	KR	WT
20						
21						

Fig. 33.22
The Calc field is being used as a dummy name for calculated or compound criteria.

Note

AND( ) and OR( ) are easy to confuse. If you are searching a single field for two different text entries (for example, Smith and Jones), use the OR( ) function. An OR( ) function specifies that one name OR the other can be found (TRUE). An AND( ) function specifies that Smith AND Jones must be in the field at the same time—something that will not happen.

Viewing and Editing Filtered Lists

If you have a long or wide list, it may cover thousands of rows and more columns than fit on-screen. As you scroll down or across, the field headers at the top of the list or data in left columns scroll out of sight.

There is an easy way to prevent this. You can fix the top rows and left columns of a screen so that they do not scroll from view as you scroll any direction in the data. This enables you to see field headers at the top of a list and one or two columns of pertinent information like names along the left side.

To freeze panes in a window so the headers and left columns stay in sight, follow these steps:

1. Position your list on-screen so the field headers are near the top of the screen. Any columns you want to remain in sight should be along the left edge of the screen.

2. Select the cell that is directly under the field header row and directly right of the columns you want to remain visible.

3. Choose the **W**indow **F**reeze Panes command.

For Related Information

- "Entering and Editing Data," p. 87
- "Moving or Copying Data and Formulas," p. 235

The window splits into four panes. You can scroll the lower right pane using normal scrolling techniques. To return to normal window scrolling, choose the **W**indow Un**f**reeze Panes command.

To edit a filtered list, use the techniques you normally use to edit in a worksheet.

Troubleshooting

Entries in the criteria range that once worked no longer work.

Check to see whether you may have changed the Transition Formula Evaluation check box found in the Transition tab of the Options dialog box. Choose the Tools Options command to see this dialog box. When this check box is selected, queries use the database rules used by Lotus 1-2-3.

*Excel doesn't correctly select the list when a **D**ata Filter command is chosen.*

Use the following checklist to troubleshoot the layout of your list:

- Check to ensure that the list is surrounded on all sides by empty cells.
- Make sure that no completely blank rows or columns exist that run through the list.

*The **D**ata commands do not work at all.*

Use the following checklist of steps to find the problem:

- It may be that the list had a preexisting filter that prevented you from seeing all the data. If you are using the AutoFilter, choose the **D**ata **F**ilter command, and choose **S**how All from the submenu. Then redo the filter.
- If you have named the database or criteria range, choose the Edit Go To command or press F5, select the Database range name or the Criteria range, and choose OK. Be certain that each range includes a single row of field names at the top of the selected range. The Criteria range should contain at least one row in addition to field names. The Database range should include one row of field names and all data.
- Select the rows under the field names in the criteria range, and use **E**dit Clear to remove any hidden space characters in the criteria range.
- Be certain that field names in the criteria and extract ranges are spelled exactly the same as they are in the database range.

Parts of the worksheet disappear after filtering.

Filtering hides rows that don't meet the filter's criteria. Rows are hidden all the way across the breadth of the worksheet. If there is data to either side of the list, the data outside the list is hidden.

(continues)

Tip

If you have many changes to make that are the same, use the **E**dit R**e**place command to search and replace through the list. If you deselect the Match **C**ase and Find Entire Cells **O**nly options you can find and replace pieces within larger words, part numbers, IDs, abbreviations, formulas, and so on.

Troubleshooting (Continued)

Calculated criteria does not produce an expected result.

Calculated criteria must be entered in the criteria range beneath a heading that is *not* a field name. To use calculated criteria, create a new field heading that is *different* from any field name in the list. Replace an existing field heading in the criteria range with this new heading, or extend the criteria range to make room for the additional heading. The cell reference in the calculated criteria must be to the top data cell in the columns you are comparing.

Formulas in the list that refer to values outside the list return incorrect results.

Be certain that formulas referring to cells or names outside the list use absolute references.

*The **D**ata **F**ilter commands do not act on records that obviously satisfy criteria for an advanced filter.*

Complete the following steps:

1. Be certain that the field names at the top of the criteria rows are exactly the same as the field names that head each list column. Use **E**dit **C**opy and **E**dit **P**aste to duplicate field names.

2. Use **E**dit Cle**a**r to erase all blank cells in the criteria range. Cells may appear blank, even when they contain blank characters entered with the space bar. Excel tries to find fields that match these blank characters.

3. Check whether the data is misspelled or contains leading or internal space characters that are different than what is typed for the criteria.

Complex criteria using AND and OR do not work as expected.

AND statements must satisfy the first condition *and* the second condition simultaneously. OR statements can satisfy *one* of the conditions *or* both conditions. Consider the following example:

    =AND(A15>500,A15<750)

This formula finds records where the data in column A is between 500 and 750. Those are the only values where both conditions are true. Remember that if you are searching for values between two points, such as in a numeric or date range, use AND. If you are searching for multiple text occurrences, such as two names, use OR.

The list does not work correctly with dates.

Be certain that dates have been entered with a method that produces a serial date number. Without a serial date number, list management functions treat your date entry as text or as a number. For more information, read the sections on entering dates in Chapter 4, "Entering and Editing Data."

Troubleshooting (Continued)

Data at the bottom of the list is not found or extracted.

If you named the list with the name Database, Excel uses that range. However, data may have been entered below that range and the range not expanded to include the new data. Use **E**dit **G**o To to be certain that the bottom rows are included in the database range. To display each corner of the selected range, press Ctrl+**.** (period). If the range does not include all records, reselect the range and use **I**nsert **N**ame **D**efine to rename it.

From Here...

For information relating directly to finding or editing data, you may want to review the following chapters:

- Chapter 4, "Entering and Editing Data." Learn how to enter text, numbers, and dates. There are many shortcuts described in this chapter.
- Chapter 10, "Formatting Worksheets." You don't have to manually format your lists—you can use AutoFormat. This chapter also describes how to create your own custom formats for numbers and dates.
- Chapter 32, "Sorting Data." Sorted lists are much easier to work with.
- Chapter 34, "Working with Filtered Data." After you find the data you want, you may want to chart it or copy it to another sheet.

Chapter 34

Working with Filtered Data

This chapter shows you how to work with data in a list, after you have filtered out unwanted information.

There are many reasons for filtering a list. You may want to examine or edit only certain information. By filtering out unwanted information, you can make a list easier to work in. After you filter information in your list, you may want to do more than just examine it. You may want to sort it, subtotal it, or create a chart from it. It is convenient and safer to work with a copy of filtered data that you have placed on a separate worksheet or workbook. Because the information in your list is probably valuable to you, you should learn how to maintain its integrity and safety.

EXCEL 5

In this chapter you learn how to:

- Edit, sort, subtotal, print, and chart filtered lists
- Copy filtered data to a new worksheet or workbook
- Remove duplicate records from filtered lists
- Remove records you no longer want

Editing, Sorting, Subtotaling, and Charting the Filtered Data

You probably filtered a list with the purpose of doing something with it. You may need to sort, print, chart, or subtotal the list. When you work on filtered lists, you can use most Excel commands on the data displayed *after* the filter is complete.

Whether you use the AutoFilter or the Advanced Filter, you can manipulate the visible data while the filter is on. To tell if the filter is on, watch the row headings for hidden row numbers. Row numbers in the list turn blue, and the status bar shows the message `Filter Mode`.

Editing Filtered Data

Editing and deleting in filtered data affects only the data in which you work. While you work in Filter mode, some commands are not available to you. These commands are grayed. The editing and formatting commands that are available act as you may expect. The following table shows how these commands act while the Filter mode is on.

Command or Feature	Action
Edit Fill	Fills visible cells. You cannot fill series of data.
Edit Clear	Clears visible cells.
Edit Copy	Copies visible cells.
Edit Delete Row	Deletes an entire row of the filtered list.
Delete Row (Shortcut menu)	Deletes an entire row of the filtered list.
Insert Row (Shortcut menu)	Inserts an entire row through the filtered list.
Insert Paste Row (Shortcut menu)	Inserts an entire row through the filtered list and pastes in the copied data. Copy a selection, and then before you paste, select a cell in the same column the active cell was in when you copied.
Format Cells	Formats visible cells.

Sorting, Subtotaling, and Printing Filtered Data

When you sort a filtered list, only the visible records are affected. After you sort, you can use the **D**ata Su**b**totals command to create subtotals in the filtered list. If you change the filter, the subtotals update to reflect the new set of filtered data.

When you print a worksheet, only the filtered data prints. To print the entire list, check the status bar to make sure Excel is not in Filter mode. To show all data, choose the **D**ata **F**ilter **S**how All command.

Charting Filtered Data

To chart filtered data, apply the filter to the list. Then create a chart by using any of the techniques described in Chapters 12 through 15. If you do not want specific columns of data in a chart, hide those columns by choosing the

F**o**rmat **C**olumn **H**ide command. Then create the chart. After you change the filter, the chart updates to show the new data displayed using the new filter criteria.

If you do not want a chart to change when the criteria change, use the Select Visible Cells button to select only the cells shown at the time of the chart's creation. Before you can do this, you need to add the Select Visible Cells button to a toolbar. Display a toolbar that you use when charting, such as the Chart toolbar. Choose the **V**iew **T**oolbars command and then choose the **C**ustomize button. From the Customize dialog box, drag the Select Visible Cells button onto the toolbar. Choose the Close button to close the Customize dialog box.

For Related Information

- "Entering Data," p. 87
- "Creating Simple Subtotals," p. 607
- "Creating an Embedded Chart," p. 407
- "Using the AutoFilter," p. 913

To create a chart that doesn't update when the filter changes, follow these steps:

1. Apply the filter to the list.
2. Select the cells you want to chart. Include field names in the selection if you want labels in the chart.
3. Click the Select Visible Cells button that was just described.
4. Draw the chart using the techniques described in Chapters 12 and 13.

Copying Filtered Data to a New Location

Many reasons exist for working with copies of a subset of your data. A co-worker, for example, may need a filtered portion of the list. Rather than give the co-worker the entire list, you can filter out the unnecessary information. You also may need to make extensive changes to the format or insert formulas, and you don't want to endanger the original list. In this case, it makes sense to use a filtered copy that contains only the data you need.

You can copy data to another worksheet in two ways. First, you can manually copy and paste, which is the method to use if you want to use a simple AutoFilter or if you have a small amount of data. Second, you can copy the data to another location by using the Advanced Filter. With this method, you can handle more complex filters. When you create a copy, you can specify that the copy contains only unique records and that all duplicates are filtered out. The original list remains intact after you extract a copy of the data that matches the criteria.

Note

You may want to keep large lists on a disk and extract filtered portions of them using Microsoft Query. Microsoft Query comes free with Excel. Microsoft Query works with files in many formats. For more information about Microsoft Query, refer to Chapter 35, "Retrieving Data from External Databases."

Creating a Copy with AutoFilter

To make a copy of data, describe the data by using the AutoFilter method, filter the data, and then copy and paste the filtered data to another sheet.

To copy a list using the AutoFilter, follow these steps:

1. Apply an AutoFilter to the list so that only the data you want to copy is shown. Chapter 33 describes how to use an AutoFilter.

2. Select the data and choose the **E**dit **C**opy command or click the Copy button. The Copy command copies only the data shown by the filter.
3. Activate the sheet in which you want the data.
4. Select the cell that will be the top left corner of the new list.

5. Choose the **E**dit **P**aste command or click the Paste button.

Copying to the Same Sheet with an Advanced Filter

You should use the Advanced Filter method of copying data if the criteria you need to use is too complex for the AutoFilter.

To use the Advanced Filter to copy, you must use the Advanced Filter dialog box, which requires a range for the list, a range for the criteria, and a range that specifies where the copied data goes.

Note

When you display the Advanced Filter dialog box, it recognizes the ranges it needs to know if you select a cell within the list and you previously used the **I**nsert **N**ame **D**efine name command to name the ranges Database, Criteria, and Extract. The Extract named range can either include just the field names or the field names and the rows for the data. If the Extract range includes only field names, you can copy an unlimited number of records. If the Extract range includes field names and a limited number of rows underneath, only as many records are copied as will fit in the range.

The Advanced Filter method of copying filtered data needs a new range in which the data will be copied—the *Copy to Range or Extract range.* In the Advanced Filter dialog box of figure 34.1, you can see edit boxes for the **L**ist Range, **C**riteria Range, and Copy **t**o range. The Copy To range receives a copy of the filtered data. The Copy **t**o edit box appears only after you select the C**o**py to Another Location option button. For a description of the list range and criteria range, refer to Chapters 30 and 33.

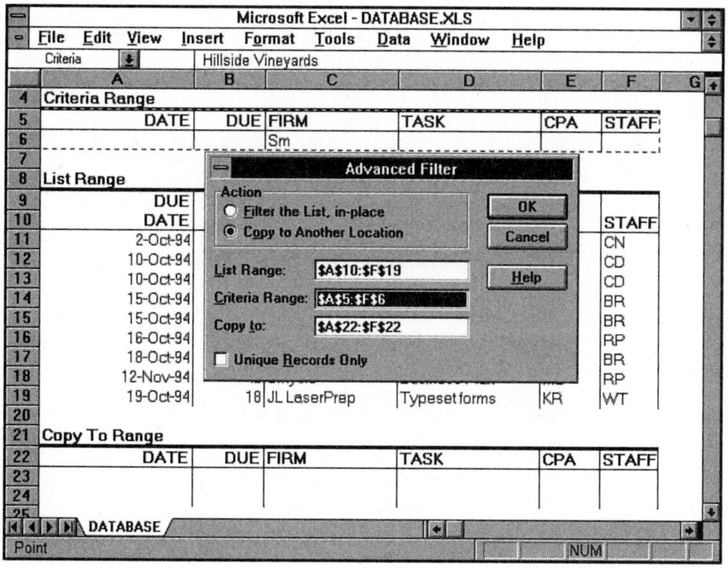

Fig. 34.1
The Advanced Filter dialog box. You need a List range, Criteria range, and a Copy to range to copy data when you use the Advanced Filter method.

A set of field names can head the top of the Copy To range. The field names must be exactly the same as the field names at the top of the Database or List range. These field names tell Excel which data you want extracted and how you want the columns arranged. Figure 34.1 shows a small list with the three parts that are important to extracting: the Criteria range in `$A$5:$F$6`, the Database range in `$A$10:$F$19`, and the field names for the Copy To range in `$A$22:$F$22`. In figure 34.2, the data that meets the criteria that FIRM entries must start with "Sm" is copied from the list and pasted below the field names in the Copy To range.

If you specify a blank and unheaded Copy To range, a dialog box appears, asking whether you want to extract data to this range. You can accept or deny the extract.

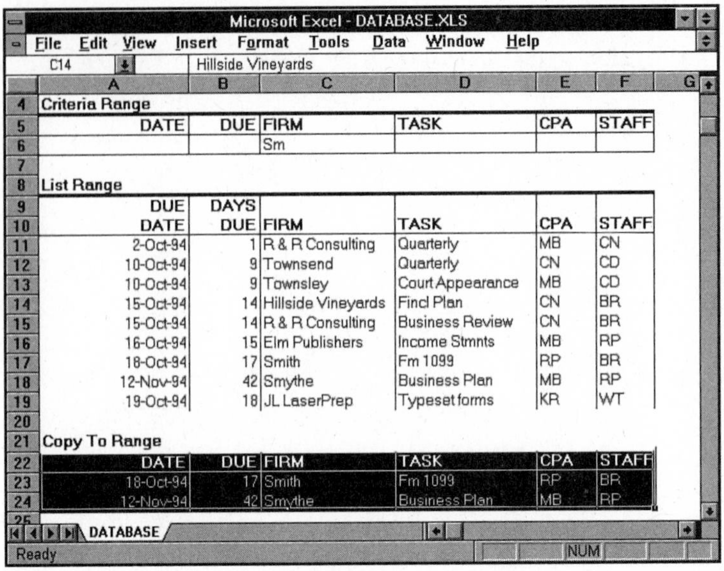

Fig. 34.2
Data matching the criteria is copied from the list to the Copy To range.

The Copy To range is separate and distinct from the Criteria and List ranges. In figures 34.1 and 34.2, notice that three ranges are used. The row of field names selected as the Copy To range must be separate from the rows of field names that head the Database and Criteria ranges.

The field names at the top of the Extract range must be identical to the field names used at the top of the List range. The best way to prepare your Copy To range is to copy the field names that you want from the top of the list.

As figures 34.3 and 34.4 illustrate, however, you don't have to include in the Copy To range *all* the field names from the List range, nor must the field names be in the same order as they appear in the list. You can create reports with only the information you need and in the column order you want. Use selected field names and reorder the names as you want them to appear in the copied data.

Caution

If you insert or delete field names in the Copy To or Criteria range, make sure that you recheck the ranges listed in the Advanced Filter dialog box before copying data to another location. By inserting or deleting within the previous ranges, you may have moved the end points of the ranges.

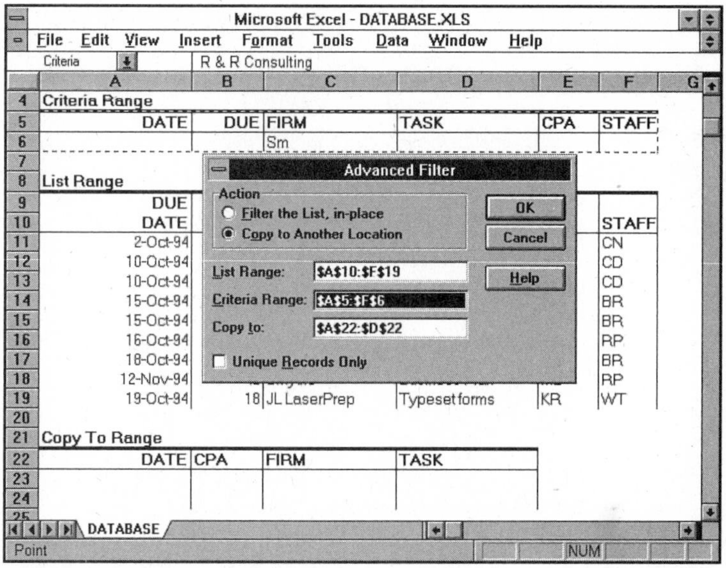

Fig. 34.3
Put the Copy To field names in a different order from those in the list.

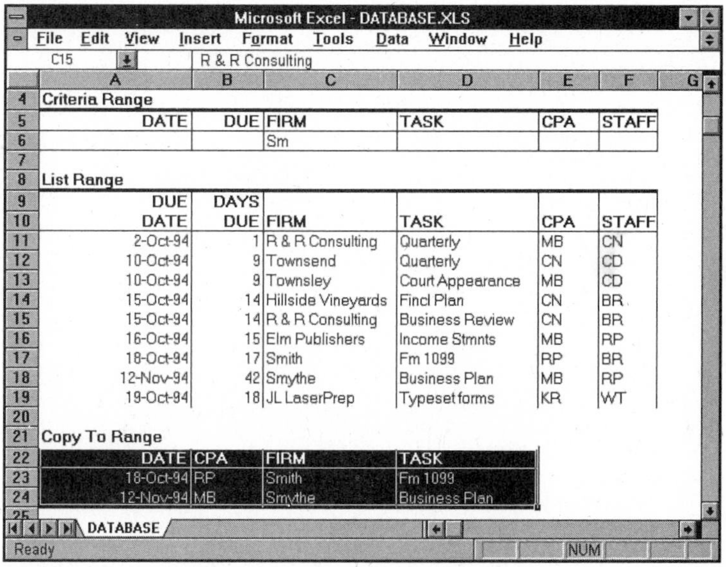

Fig. 34.4
Reordering Copy To field names enables you to structure reports.

You can define the Copy To range in two ways. You can use the **I**nsert **D**efine **N**ame command to assign a name to the Copy To range, or you can display the Advanced Filter dialog box and select the range by selecting the Copy **t**o box and dragging it across the range on the sheet. If you assign the name *Extract* to the Copy To range, Excel recognizes the Copy To range and enters the correct cell references in the Copy **t**o box.

You can specify two sizes of Copy To ranges, limited and unlimited. A *limited Copy To range* includes the field names at the top of the range and a limited number of cells below the names. The copied information fills only the cells available in the Copy To range. Excel leaves out copied data that does not fit and gives you a warning message.

In an *unlimited Copy To range*, you select only the field names or name only the field names. You can fill the resulting range with data, beginning with the field names and extending to the bottom of the worksheet. If you don't know how much data will be copied, use an unlimited Copy To range.

Caution

The worksheet area below unlimited extracts is erased—old data or parts of the worksheet below the field names of an unlimited extract range are cleared. Do not put anything below the field names of an unlimited Copy To range. Excel does not warn you that all cells below the Extract range headings will be cleared. After you complete an unlimited copy, Excel clears this area to avoid mingling the old data with the new.

Tip
You may need to recalculate before you copy filtered data. If Excel is set to recalculate formulas manually and the worksheet needs recalculating, `Calculate` appears at the bottom of the screen. Press F9 (Calculate).

Tip
To copy both limited and unlimited numbers of records, create multiple names, each with the field names as the top of the range.

Use the following basic procedure to copy filtered data from the list to a new location. Each step is described in greater detail in the sections that follow.

1. Create field names for the Copy To range by copying the single row of field names from the top of the list. Arrange the field names in the order you want the columns of data to appear.
2. Enter the criteria in the Criteria range.
3. If you do not copy filtered information very often, you may not want to take the time to use names. You can select the Copy To range from within the Advanced Filter dialog box. If you will use this Copy To range frequently, however, name the range with one of the following methods:
   - To copy an unlimited number of data records, select only the field names at the top of the Copy To range as shown in figure 34.5, Choose the **I**nsert **N**ame **D**efine command, enter the name in the Names in **W**orkbook box, and then choose OK.
   - To limit the number of records copied, select the field names at the top of the Copy To range and select as many additional cells directly below the names as you want records (see fig. 34.6). Choose the **I**nsert **N**ame **D**efine command, enter the name in the Names in **W**orkbook box, and then choose OK.

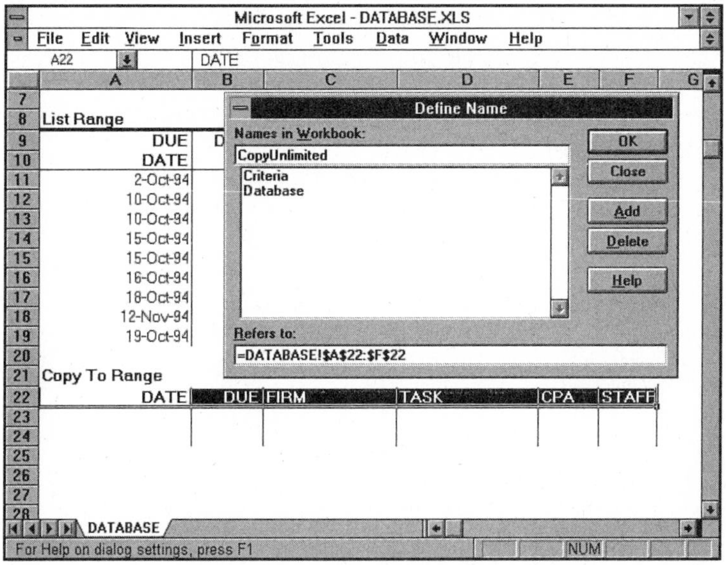

Fig. 34.5
Define just the field names to copy an unlimited number of records.

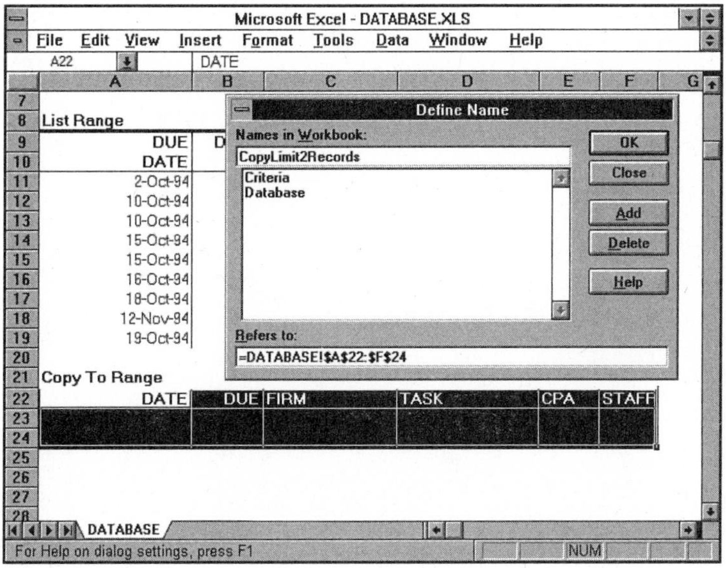

Fig. 34.6
Select and name a limited number of cells under the field name to limit the amount of copied data.

4. Choose the **D**ata **F**ilter **A**dvanced Filter command to display the Advanced Filter dialog box (refer to fig. 34.1).

5. Choose the C**o**py to Another Location option.

6. Select the **L**ist Range box and type in the range name, or drag across the worksheet area containing the list.

7. Select the **C**riteria Range box and type in the range name, or drag across the worksheet area containing the criteria range.

8. Select the Copy **t**o box and type in the range name, or drag across the worksheet area containing the area to receive the filtered copy.

9. If you want no duplicate records, select the Unique **R**ecords Only check box.

10. Choose OK.

Note

Use a unique copy of a filtered list to cross-check lists for typographical errors. Suppose that you created a list of 320 records, with 16 different part names. To cross-check for misspelled part names, you can extract unique records by using a Copy To range that is headed by the field name containing the part names. Each of the 16 correctly spelled part names appears once in the extract range. Any misspelled part name appears in the Copy To range as an additional item. Use **D**ata F**o**rm or **E**dit **F**ind to locate the misspelled part name within the list. You can use **E**dit R**e**place command to search for and replace the mistake.

Tip

Before you print hundreds of mailing labels from an Excel list, use a unique extract to make sure that you don't print duplicate labels.

Copying Filtered Data between Worksheets or Workbooks

You often can benefit greatly from copying filtered data to another worksheet before you use the data. You can avoid contaminating original data, and the worksheet in which you are working will have a smaller list, using less memory, so it can run faster. You also can generate reports more easily because you don't have to worry about rearranging columns, changing column widths, or reorganizing the structure on a new worksheet.

An easy way to copy a filtered list between worksheets is to filter the list by using either AutoFilter or Advanced Filter and then copy it from one sheet and paste it into another sheet. You can, however, use the **A**dvanced Filter command to move filtered data between sheets.

In the following example, all items with a Quantity field greater than 10 are extracted from the list on the FLIMINV.XLS worksheet and placed in the Copy To range on the FLIMXTRC.XLS worksheet.

Figure 34.7 shows the two worksheets in different workbooks. The FLIMINV.XLS worksheet contains a list in the range A5:C14 that was named *Database*. Using named ranges becomes convenient when you copy between sheets or workbooks because remembering the long syntax of external references is difficult. Remembering a name is much easier.

The FLIMXTRC.XLS worksheet contains a Criteria range and a Copy To range. The Criteria range of A5:C6 was named *Criteria.* The field names that act as headings for the extract in FLMXTRC.XLS are in cells A9:C9. The Copy To range was named *Extract.*

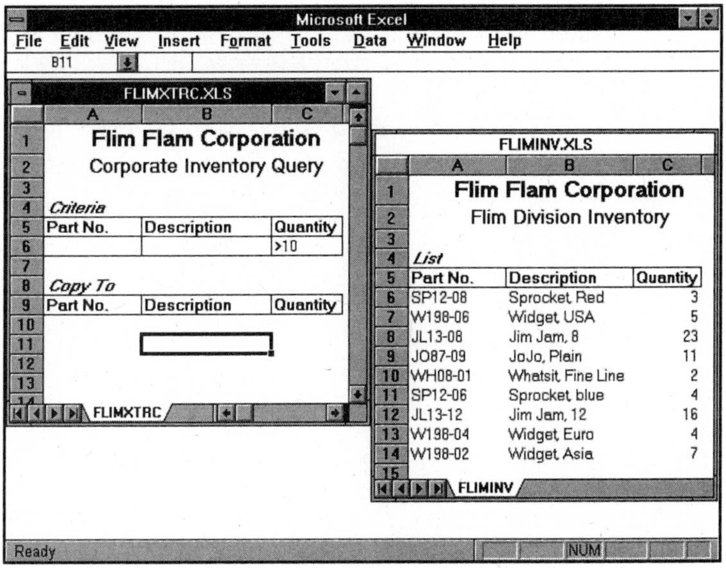

Fig. 34.7
You can copy filtered lists from one worksheet to any other worksheet.

To copy filtered data between worksheets, follow these steps:

1. Open the worksheets containing the Criteria, List, and Copy To ranges.
2. Activate the worksheet containing the Copy To range (refer to fig. 34.7). To extract only some of the columns of data, enter field names that specify the desired data.
3. Select a blank cell that is not touching filled cells. This prevents Excel from attempting to find a list range on the worksheet to receive the extracted data.
4. Choose the **D**ata **F**ilter **A**dvanced Filter command to display the Advanced Filter dialog box (refer to fig. 34.1).
5. Choose the C**o**py to Another Location option.
6. Select the **L**ist Range box and then activate the sheet containing the list. Drag across the database range, or click one cell in the sheet and edit the reference to include the name of the list. The external reference to the list on another sheet in another workbook looks like

```
[FLIMINV.XLS]FLIMINV!Database
```

where the syntax is

```
[Workbookname]Sheetname!Rangename
```

If the other sheet is in the same workbook, omit the workbook name.

7. Select the **C**riteria Range box and enter a range by activating the sheet containing the Criteria range and dragging across that range.

8. Select the Copy **t**o range box and enter the Copy To range from the original worksheet that was active in step 2 by activating the original worksheet and dragging across the field names to use as headers for the extracted data.

9. Select the Unique **R**ecords Only check box if you want to remove duplicates. Figure 34.8 shows a completed Advanced Filter dialog box.

10. Choose OK.

Figure 34.9 shows the result of copying a filtered list on FLIMINV.XLS onto the FLIMXTRC.XLS sheet. The Criteria and Copy To range were on one sheet and the list was on another.

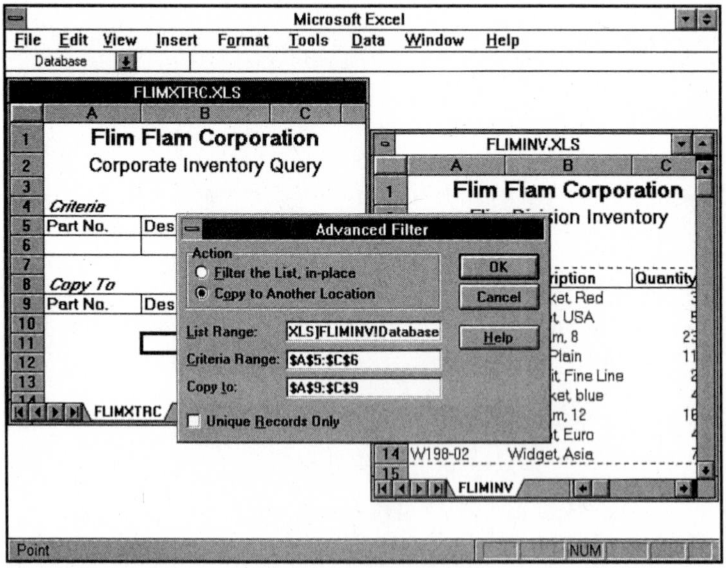

Fig. 34.8
Select Criteria, List, and Copy To ranges from any sheets.

Maintaining Data

Lists have a tendency to grow. Eventually, memory and speed limitations dictate that you clean up. As part of this process, you need to make backup copies of the old information before removing it from the working list or database.

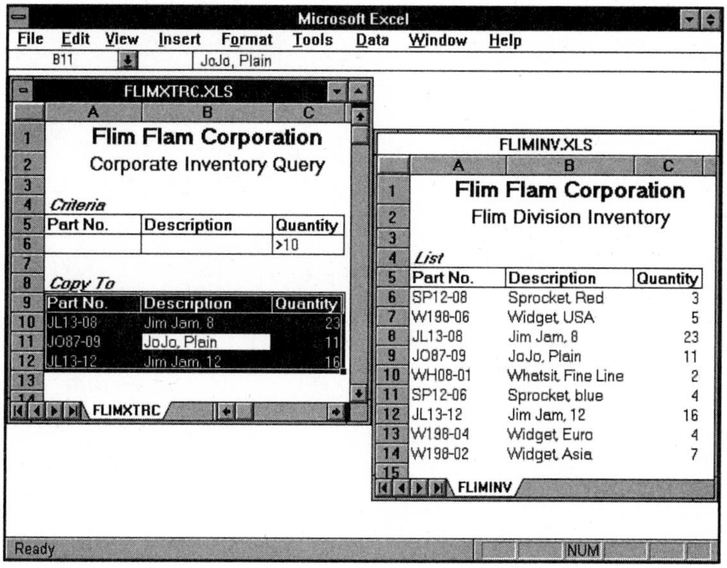

Fig. 34.9
You can copy filtered lists from any worksheet or workbook to any other worksheet or workbook.

Backing Up Data

An unpleasant surprise awaits you if you continually save a worksheet to the same file name. When you choose the **F**ile **S**ave commmand, the current Excel file replaces the original file on disk. This practice is fine, provided that you never make a mistake. You may accidentally delete the wrong records, make a number of incorrect edits, or add some incorrect data. If you save a bad file over good, you are left with only a bad file.

If you want more security, save the list you are editing every 15 to 30 minutes by using the **F**ile Save **A**s command. Each time you save with **F**ile Save **A**s, edit the file name to make it different from the previous name. You may want to use a sequence of file names, such as the following:

ACCT_01.XLS

ACCT_02.XLS

ACCT_03.XLS

The last two characters before the extension indicate the file's version number. This numbering technique enables you to return to an older file to recover previous data. When files are too old to use again, choose the **F**ile **D**elete command to erase the files from the disk, or switch to the File Manager and erase multiple files at the same time.

Keep more than one copy of all important list files, and do not keep the backup copy in the same building as the original. Take the backup files to a different building or to a bank vault. If your building burns or a thief takes the computers and disks, you still have your data.

Deleting a Group of Records

Your list is of little use unless someone maintains it. You must edit, add, and delete single records, but Excel can help you delete groups of records. To delete a group of records, apply a filter to show only the records you want to delete. Select those records and then delete them with the **E**dit **D**elete command.

If you have only a few records to delete or records that may be difficult to describe with criteria, you may want to delete them manually. Use **D**ata F**o**rm to find the records and then select the **D**elete button on the form to delete the current record.

From Here...

Copying filtered lists can help when you create reports or analyze large sets of data. Excel contains many other features to help you in this same area. Refer to the following chapters for powerful features:

- Chapter 18, "Outlining Worksheets," shows you how to show or hide different levels of detail in reports, which is helpful when you need to see different groups and levels of data.

- Chapter 19, "Creating Automatic Subtotals," teaches how to put subtotals and grand totals in lists. You can use subtotals on filtered lists.

- Chapter 23, "Manipulating and Analyzing Data," is where you begin to learn how to analyze data in a list.

- Chapter 36, "Using Pivot Tables," shows you how to create reports and analyses of your list by examining it from different perspectives.

Chapter 35

Retrieving Data from External Databases

Excel is supplied with the stand-alone program Microsoft Query. By using Microsoft Query, you can retrieve specific information from external databases (such as dBASE, Access, Paradox, and SQL Server) and then insert that data into your current worksheet. You can sort, format, or edit the data before inserting it into your worksheet.

This chapter describes how Microsoft Query works and then explains some of the database terms that you need to know. Next, the chapter describes how to make Microsoft Query available from Excel and explains how to start Microsoft Query, retrieve data from an external source, and insert that data into your Excel worksheet. This chapter also describes how to format and edit data in Microsoft Query, how to update the results of a query in your worksheet, and how to copy the data to other worksheets.

EXCEL 5

In this chapter, you learn to:

- Create data sources for a query
- Create and perform queries and specify criteria for selecting data
- Insert retrieved information into your worksheets and update the retrieved information

Understanding Microsoft Query and ODBC

To successfully retrieve data from external databases, you need to understand a few basic terms. A basic understanding of how Microsoft Query connects to external databases and how Excel connects to Microsoft Query is also useful.

Microsoft Query is a self-contained program that you can use with or without Excel. This chapter focuses on using Microsoft Query from within Excel, although you can use Microsoft Query by itself. Use Microsoft Query to bring data into Excel from external databases for reporting, charts, or analysis; you can also use Microsoft Query to obtain data from other Excel workbooks or worksheets.

You can use Microsoft Query for the following tasks:

- Retrieve information from multiple external databases, based on criteria that you specify
- Select specific items of information for display
- Display, edit, sort, or otherwise organize the retrieved information before inserting the data into Excel

Excel communicates with Microsoft Query through Dynamic Data Exchange (DDE) messages; Microsoft Query, in turn, communicates with external databases through various *ODBC drivers*. (ODBC stands for Open Database Connectivity, a standard developed by Microsoft explicitly for the task of obtaining information from databases created by different applications.) An ODBC driver is a special set of program routines, stored in a Dynamic Link Library (DLL), that enables an application to use Structured Query Language (SQL) to access data stored in another format.

You use the Microsoft Query graphical interface to design a query; Microsoft Query then creates the SQL statements necessary to retrieve the data from the external database. You do not need to learn SQL or any other programming or macro language in order to use Microsoft Query successfully.

After you retrieve the data from the external database, you can alter the way the data displays, and format or sort the data. When you are satisfied with the data and its formatting, you insert the data into your Excel worksheet. (Inserting data into an Excel worksheet is called *returning* the data to Excel.)

After you return the retrieved data to your Excel worksheet, you can extract data, generate statistical totals, create reports or charts, format, sort, and filter the data just as you would with any other worksheet data. The returned data becomes part of the worksheet.

To retrieve data from an external database using Microsoft Query, you perform these basic steps:

1. Create and select a data source.
2. Create and perform a query, optionally specifying criteria to determine which information is retrieved.

3. Format, sort, or otherwise manipulate the retrieved information.

4. Return the result to an Excel worksheet.

Later sections of this chapter describe these steps in detail.

Database Types and Terms

To work successfully with Microsoft Query, you need to understand the database-related terms that Microsoft Query uses, and the basic types of database structures that you can access through Microsoft Query.

Database management systems (abbreviated DBMS) typically use one or more *tables* to store data. A database table is organized in a fashion similar to a worksheet. Each row of a database table is called a *record;* each column in a database row is a *field.* Fields are used to store specific items of information (numbers or text) such as a person's name, a phone number, dollar values, and so on. Not every DBMS uses the term *table;* some systems simply refer to the tables that contain data as *files.* Microsoft Query uses the terms on-screen that are correct for the DBMS you are querying.

Many of the databases from which you retrieve data are *relational databases.* Relational DBMSs include applications such as Access, FoxPro, Paradox, Oracle, and others. Relational databases get their name from the fact that the data is stored in several different tables or files. The different tables or files are connected (related) by having one or more fields in common. For example, a database may consist of one table that contains product descriptions, another table that contains inventory records for products, and a third table that contains sales figures for each product. In this example, each table in the database has a field containing the product number; this field is the *relational key* (also called the *linking field,* or just the *link*) used to connect the information in the tables.

Note

Don't confuse the term *link* or *linking field* used in connection with database tables with worksheet links or OLE links. A linking field in a database just means that the contents of that field are used to relate a record in one database table to one or more records in another table.

Relational database tables may include one or more *primary key* fields (sometimes referred to simply as *key* fields). Primary key fields can contain only unique values; if there is more than one primary key field, then the combination of values in the primary key fields must be unique. For example, a database table containing product numbers and product descriptions might use a primary key field for the product number to ensure that duplicate product numbers are never entered into the database. A database of names and addresses might use a combination of three primary key fields—last name, first name, and ZIP code—to ensure that duplicate names and addresses are never entered into the database. In this second example, because the *combination* of primary key fields must be unique, it is possible to have more than one person with the same first and last name (which is a likely circumstance), but it is not possible to have two people with the same first and last name in the same ZIP code.

Although primary key fields are often used as a relational link to another database, a database table can contain primary key fields that are not used as part of a relational link. Not all relational databases support the use of primary keys.

Many other databases from which you retrieve data by using Microsoft Query consist of only one table. Sometimes the full power and features of a relational DBMS are not needed, so all of the information is placed in a single database table. Some DBMSs just do not support the relational model of database construction and design, and can only place data in a single table.

Data Sources and Result Sets

Before you can query an external database and retrieve information from it, you need to define one or more data sources. A *data source* consists of the information that Microsoft Query needs to locate the database, and sometimes the names of the specific tables or files that are used in the query. The data source information is saved with a name that you assign to it; Microsoft Query uses the data source's name to identify the specific set of location and table information that it will use. A data source might consist of the name of an SQL Server database, the server on which the database resides, and the network used to access the server. Another data source might consist of a group of Paradox files and the disk directory in which the files reside. Creating and selecting data sources is described in "Specifying or Creating the Data Source," later in this chapter.

The information that Microsoft Query retrieves from the external database is called the *result set*. The result set may include some or all of the information in a single table, or a combination of information from records in different tables. Joining tables and specifying criteria for selecting specific records is described later in this chapter.

What Databases Can You Query?

The databases that you can query depend on the ODBC drivers you have installed on your computer. In order to retrieve information from a specific DBMS, you must have an ODBC driver for that DBMS installed.

Microsoft Query, as supplied with Excel, includes the ODBC drivers necessary to access information in the most common personal computer and mainframe computer database formats. The following table lists the database formats and versions from which you can retrieve data by using the supplied ODBC drivers.

File Extension	Database Type	Versions
DBF	dBASE	III+ and IV
DBF	Microsoft FoxPro	2.0, 2.5
MDB	Microsoft Access	1.0, 1.1
DB	Paradox	3.0, 3.5
n/a	SQL Server	1.1, 4.2, NT, and Synbase 4.x

Starting Microsoft Query

Before you can start Microsoft Query from Excel, you must have the Microsoft Query application installed (along with any ODBC drivers that you want to use), and you also must have installed and activated the Microsoft Query Add-in for Excel.

Installing Microsoft Query and the Microsoft Query Add-In

You install Microsoft Query, ODBC drivers, and the Microsoft Query Add-in by using the Excel Setup program. If you did not install these components when you first installed Excel, you can run Excel Setup at any time to add them.

To install Microsoft Query, all the ODBC drivers, and all the Excel add-ins, double-click the Microsoft Excel Setup icon in the Windows Program Manager to start Setup. After Setup starts, choose the **A**dd/Remove button, select the Data Access and Add-ins check boxes, and then choose the **C**ontinue button. Setup installs these components. Excel Setup needs to read your Excel distribution disks to finish installing the additional components. For more information on using Excel Setup, refer to the User's Guide supplied with Excel.

Installing the Microsoft Query Add-In in Excel

To make Microsoft Query available from Excel, you must use the Microsoft Query Add-in. The Microsoft Query Add-in is stored in a file named XLQUERY.XLA on your hard disk, in the \LIBRARY\MSQUERY subdirectory under your Excel directory.

The Microsoft Query Add-in adds the Get E**x**ternal Data command to the **D**ata menu. If this command is not present, then you need to activate the Microsoft Query Add-in. Refer to Chapter 22, "Taking Advantage of Excel's Add-Ins," for additional information about installing Excel Add-ins and other add-ins that are available.

To activate the Microsoft Query Add-in, follow these steps:

1. Choose the **T**ools Add-**I**ns command. The Add-ins dialog box appears.

2. Select the Xlquery add-in from the **A**dd-ins Available list so that an X appears in the box to its left. (Choose the **B**rowse button to search for the XLQUERY.XLA file in the \LIBRARY\MSQUERY directory, if Xlquery doesn't appear in the **A**dd-ins Available list.)

3. Choose OK.

Excel installs the Microsoft Query Add-in, adds the Get E**x**ternal Data command to the **D**ata menu, and adds the Get External Data button to the Query and Pivot toolbar. (Use the **V**iew **T**oolbars command to hide or display the Query and Pivot toolbar.)

Starting Microsoft Query from Excel

To start Microsoft Query from Excel, choose the **D**ata Get E**x**ternal Data command. The Microsoft Query application starts up; it displays the Microsoft Query window and the Select Data Source dialog box shown in figure 35.1. Creating and selecting data sources is described in the following section.

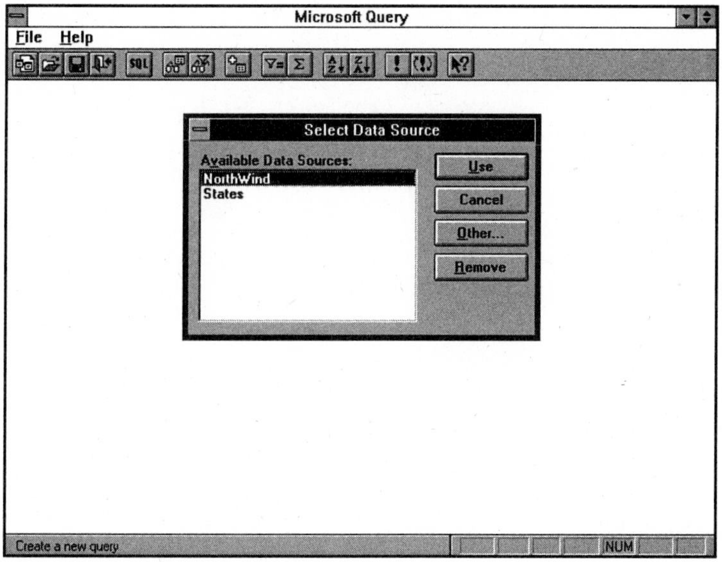

Fig. 35.1
Microsoft Query displays the Select Data Source dialog box when you first start the program.

Starting Microsoft Query from Program Manager

You can also start Microsoft Query directly from the Program Manager. If you start Microsoft Query from the Program Manager, instead of from inside Excel, you cannot return data directly to Excel as described in this chapter. Instead, you must use the procedures for pasting or linking data from other Windows applications, described fully in Chapter 38 and briefly later in this chapter.

To start Microsoft Query from Program Manager, make Program Manager the current application, and open the program group (Microsoft Excel 5.0 or Microsoft Office) that contains the Microsoft Query program icon. Double-click the Microsoft Query icon; Query starts up, and displays the window shown in figure 35.1, without the Select Data Source dialog box. The instructions on creating and selecting data sources, and opening, creating, and executing queries, are the same whether you start Microsoft Query from inside Excel or from Program Manager.

For Related Information

- "Starting and Quitting Excel," p. 25
- "Choosing Commands," p. 38
- "Displaying or Hiding Toolbars," p. 45
- "Using Add-In Programs," p. 675

Creating a Query

Tip
For step-by-step help in creating a query, choose **H**elp C**u**e Cards in Microsoft Query.

Creating a query begins with selecting the data source for the query. You can select an existing data source for your query, or create a new data source. You select and create data sources from the Select Data Source dialog box in Microsoft Query. To open the Select Data Source dialog box, use one of the following methods:

- Choose the **D**ata Get E**x**ternal Data command in Excel. Excel starts Microsoft Query, which opens the Select Data Source dialog box.

- Click the Get External Data button on the Query and Pivot toolbar in Excel.

- If Microsoft Query is already running, choose the **F**ile **N**ew Query command in Microsoft Query.

Note

When you choose the **D**ata Get E**x**ternal Data command, Excel waits for you to return data from Microsoft Query. While Excel is waiting for you to return data from Microsoft Query, Excel does not respond to either keyboard or mouse actions.

Specifying or Creating the Data Source

To select an existing data source in the Select Data Source dialog box, first select the name of the data source you want to use in the A**v**ailable Data Sources list. Then choose the **U**se button. Microsoft Query displays a blank query form on-screen, and then displays the Add Tables dialog box. Using the Add Tables dialog box is described in the later section, "Creating the Query Definition."

To create a new data source, choose the **O**ther button in the Select Data Source dialog box. Microsoft Query then displays the ODBC Data Sources dialog box shown in figure 35.2.

To finish creating the new data source, follow these steps:

1. Choose the **N**ew button in the ODBC Data Sources dialog box. Microsoft Query displays the Add Data Source dialog box (see fig. 35.3).

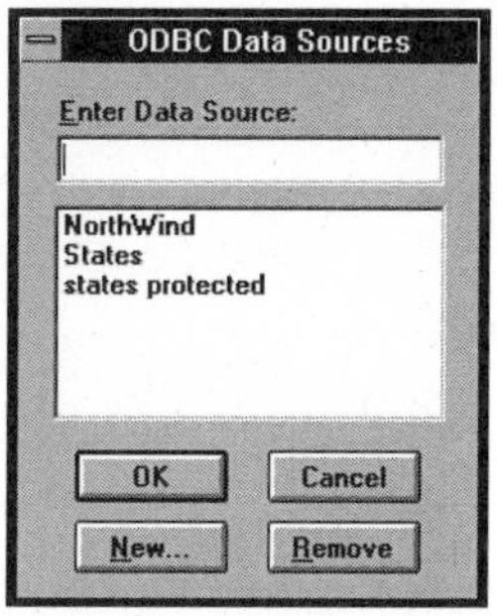

Fig. 35.2
Use the ODBC Data Sources dialog box to create new data sources.

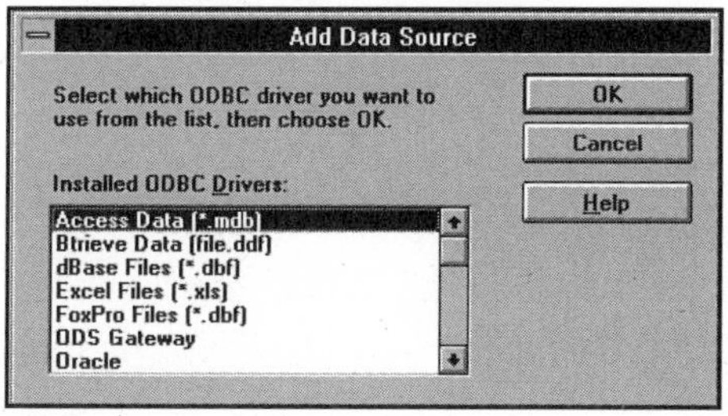

Fig. 35.3
Select the ODBC driver for the data source in the Add Data Source dialog box.

2. Select the ODBC driver that you want to use in the Installed ODBC **D**rivers list and choose OK.

   Microsoft Query now displays an ODBC Setup dialog box, similar to the one shown in figure 35.4. The exact title and appearance of the dialog box depends on the ODBC driver that you selected.

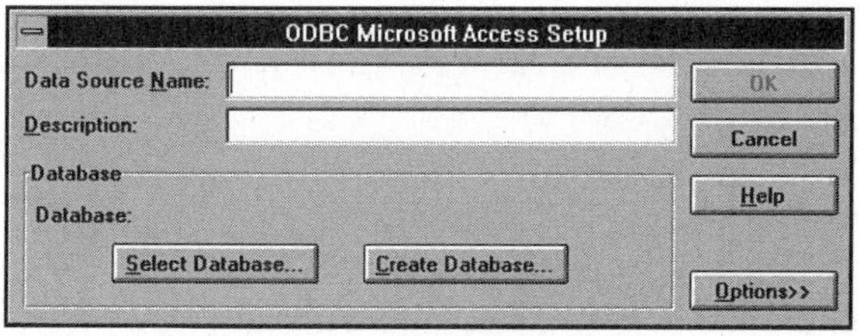

Fig. 35.4
The ODBC Setup dialog box for Microsoft Access. Microsoft Query displays different ODBC Setup dialog boxes, depending on the ODBC driver you selected.

3. In the Data Source **N**ame text box, type a name for the new data source and a brief description of the data source in the **D**escription text box.

4. Choose the **S**elect Database or **S**elect Directory button (the button available in the dialog box depends on the ODBC driver you chose).

Microsoft Query displays a Select Database or Select Tables dialog box, again depending on which ODBC driver you selected. The Select Database dialog box is similar in appearance to a standard File Open dialog box; the Select Tables dialog box displays a list of tables available (such as SQL Server or Oracle databases).

Note

If any of the databases that you include in the data source are password-protected, Microsoft Query displays a dialog box asking you to enter the password. Type your password, and then choose OK.

5. Fill in the dialog box options as appropriate for the particular dialog box displayed. Press F1 for help in filling in your specific dialog box.

6. Choose OK to return to the ODBC Setup dialog box. Choose OK again to return to the ODBC Data Sources dialog box.

   The newly created data source's name is added to the list of data sources, and the name is entered in the **E**nter Data Source text box.

7. Choose OK to add the new data source to the list of data sources in the Select Data Source dialog box.

8. Select the name of the data source in the A**v**ailable Data Sources list, and then choose the **U**se button.

   Microsoft Query displays a blank query form on-screen and then displays the Add Tables dialog box. Using the Add Tables dialog box is described later in this section; before you can add tables, you need to understand some basic Query window terminology.

Understanding the Query Window

A typical query window is shown in figure 35.5. As you can see from the figure, the query window is divided into several areas, called *panes*.

The *table pane* is the part of the query window that displays the tables from which the query retrieves data. In the figure, a table named *states* is the source of the data in the query result. The table pane may contain one or more tables. If the table pane has more than one table, the table pane also shows which fields are used to join together the different tables. (Joining multiple tables in a single query is described in the section "Joining Multiple Tables," later in this chapter.)

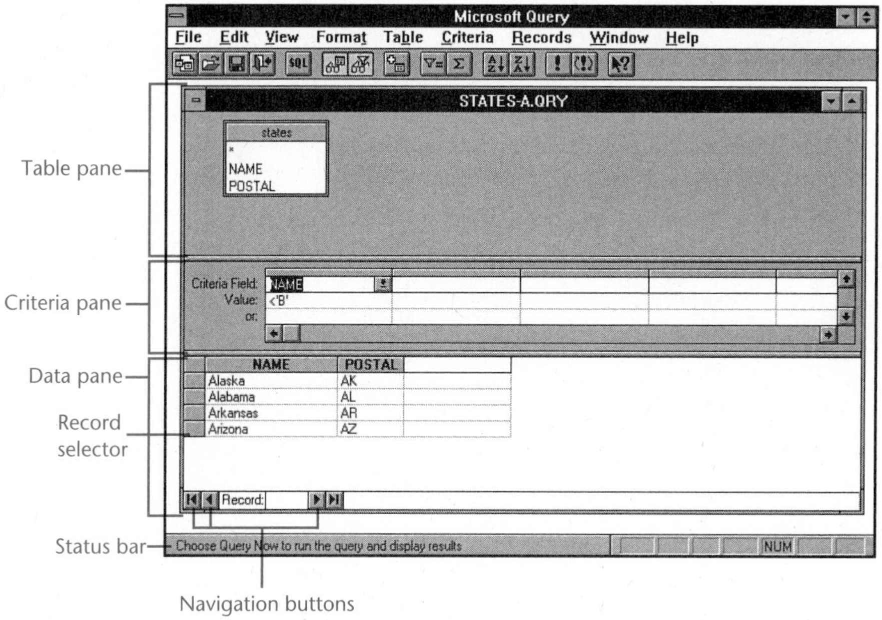

Fig. 35.5
A typical query window, showing query results and the criteria that produced those results.

The *criteria pane* displays the criteria used to select the records in the result set. The criteria pane does not display when you first create a new query because there are no criteria to display. Adding and editing criteria are described in a following section.

The *data pane* displays the results of the query. When you first create a query, the data pane is blank. You must add the fields that you want displayed to the data pane to add them to the result set. Each field in the data pane is one column; each record is one row. Use the record selector and navigation buttons to move from record to record. The data pane always displays a blank column at the right side so that you easily can tell where to add another field. Adding fields to the data pane is described in a following section.

A *status bar* displays at the bottom of the Microsoft Query application window. The status bar displays the status of the Num Lock, Caps Lock, and other editing keys; it also displays helpful information about what actions Microsoft Query expects you to perform next.

Tip
See the information displayed at the left side of the status bar for hints about which action to perform next.

To make more room in the query window available for viewing the result set in the data pane, you might want to hide either or both of the table and criteria panes.

Showing or Hiding the Table Pane. To hide or display the table pane, use one of the following methods:

- Choose the **V**iew **T**ables command. If the table pane is already hidden, it displays.
- Click the Show/Hide Tables button on the toolbar.

Showing or Hiding the Criteria Pane. To hide or display the criteria pane, use one of the following methods:

- Choose the **V**iew **C**riteria command. If the criteria pane is already hidden, it displays.
- Click the Show/Hide Criteria button on the toolbar.

Creating the Query Definition

Before you can retrieve information from an external database, you must build a query definition. A query definition consists of the following:

- Information that Microsoft Query uses to connect to the data source (such as the disk directory, network server, and so on). This information is contained in the data source you chose to base the query on.
- Information that Microsoft Query uses to determine which data to retrieve from the specified data sources. You provide this information by adding tables to the table pane, entering criteria in the criteria pane, and adding fields to the data pane.

After the query definition is completed, Microsoft Query uses the information in it to create an SQL statement that is then sent to the ODBC driver which extracts the appropriate data from the external database. Microsoft Query displays the resulting data in the data pane of the query window.

After you select the data source, Microsoft Query displays a query window with empty table and data panes, and the criteria pane hidden. Microsoft Query displays the Add Tables dialog box so that you can add tables to the new query definition, as described in the next section.

Adding and Removing Tables on the Table Pane. Only the tables you place on the table pane are used to supply data for the query, regardless of the number of tables or files in the directory you specify for the data source.

If you are creating a new query, Microsoft Query opens the Add Tables dialog box, and you can start adding tables to the table pane immediately. As you work with your query definition, however, you may decide that you want to add or remove tables from the table pane, especially if you are creating a multiple table query definition.

Note

The exact appearance of the Add Tables dialog box depends on the ODBC driver that you specify for use with the data source on which your query definition is based.

To open the Add Tables dialog box, choose the Ta**b**le **A**dd Tables command, or click the Add Tables button on the toolbar. To add tables to the table pane from the Add Tables dialog box, follow these steps:

1. In the Table **N**ame text box, type the name of the table to add, or select the table from the list under the Table Name text box or from the **T**able list. (The exact options depend on the ODBC driver in use.)
2. Select among any other options available in the Add Tables dialog box; the exact options depend on the particular ODBC driver used. Press F1 for help with the specific options in your Add Tables dialog box.
3. Choose the **A**dd button to add the table or file to the table pane in the query window.
4. Repeat steps 1 through 3 for each table you want to add to the table pane.
5. Choose the **C**lose button to close the Add Tables dialog box.

When you place a table on the table pane, it is displayed as a *field list.* The field list is a window with the name of the table in the title bar, and contains a list of all the fields in that particular table.

To remove a table from the table pane, click anywhere on the table in the table pane, and then press Del. Microsoft Query removes the table from the table pane.

Adding, Inserting, and Deleting Fields on the Data Pane. To display any data in the data pane, you must first place one or more fields on the data pane. When you execute the completed query, data from fields in the database display in the corresponding field columns you have placed in the data pane. You can add fields to the data pane in any of several ways. You can add fields one at a time, all at once, or several at once.

Use any of the following three methods to add fields to the data pane:

- To add fields one at a time, double-click the field name in the field list in the table pane, or drag the field name from the field list in the table pane over the blank column in the data pane.
- To add all the fields at once, double-click the asterisk at the beginning of the field list on the table pane, or drag the asterisk over the blank column in the data pane.
- To add several, but not all fields at once, select the fields by holding down the Ctrl key as you click each field name you want to add to the data pane. After you select all the field names you want to add, drag them over the blank column on the data pane.

To insert a field between other fields on the data pane, drag the field (or several selected fields) over the column to the right of the point where you want to insert the field or fields. Microsoft Query inserts the fields to the left of the column, pushing all other fields on the data pane to the right.

To remove a field from the data pane, click the column heading for that field on the data pane to select the entire column, and then press Del. Microsoft Query removes the field from the data pane.

Specifying and Editing Criteria. Unless you specify otherwise, Microsoft Query includes all records from the source database(s) in the result set displayed in the data pane. In most cases, you are interested in a more specific group of records. To specify the data retrieved from the source tables or files, enter the criteria in the criteria pane. After you enter your search criteria, Microsoft Query only retrieves the records from the source database that match the criteria you specify.

You can specify criteria to select records based on the following types of criteria:

- A specific range of records, such as sales that occurred between December 1st and January 31st

- Records that have fields containing values that begin with, end with, or contain specific characters, such as all the products that have the word *improved* in their description, or all the customers whose phone numbers begin with *581*
- Records with fields that *don't* match a specified value, such as all products that are not discontinued
- Records that have empty fields, such as all the client records that don't have a phone number entered
- Records that have field values from a specified list, such as all the customers with area codes of *415*, *510*, or *707*

You can combine any of the above types of criteria to create even more specific result sets. For example, you might add criteria to retrieve only records for salespeople in Canada that have also sold over $10,000 in the second quarter of the year.

When you combine criteria, you can combine the criteria with an AND condition or an OR condition. In an AND condition, Microsoft Query retrieves only those records that match both criteria; in an OR condition, Microsoft Query retrieves those records that match either criteria.

Adding Criteria. To add criteria to a query definition, follow these steps:

1. Choose the **C**riteria **A**dd Criteria command. Microsoft Query displays the dialog box (see fig. 35.6).

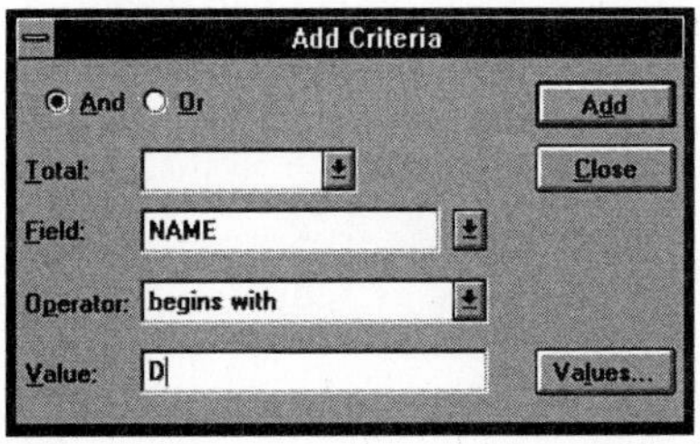

Fig. 35.6
Use the Add Criteria dialog box to select the field, condition, and value to match.

2. Select the field that contains the values you want to match in the **F**ield drop-down list box.
3. Select the comparison or condition that you want as part of the criteria ("is less than," "equals," "is greater than," and so on) in the O**p**erator drop-down list box.

4. Type the value that you want to match in the **V**alue text box, or choose the Va**l**ues button to select the contents of the **V**alue text box from a list of existing field values in the database.

   When you type the value to match in the **V**alue text box, you can use either of the following wild-card characters:

   - % represents any number of characters. Typing **D%o** in the **V**alue text box with "equals" in the O**p**erator box, for example, retrieves records where the field entry begins with the letter *D*, is followed by any number of characters, and ends with the letter *o*.

   - _ represents any single character. Typing **D_o** in the **V**alue text box with "equals" in the O**p**erator box, for example, retrieves records where the field entry begins with the letter *D*, is followed by any other single character, and ends with the letter *o*.

5. Choose whether to combine this criterion with other criteria in the query as either an AND condition or an OR condition by selecting the **A**nd or O**r** option, as desired.

   If this is the first criterion for the query definition, there are no other criteria to combine it with, and the **A**nd and O**r** options are disabled (grayed).

6. Choose the **A**dd button to add the new criterion to the criteria pane.

7. Repeat steps 2 through 6 for each criterion you want to add to the query definition.

8. Choose **C**lose when you are finished adding criteria.

Editing or Deleting Criteria. If your query definition does not produce the results you want, you may wish to change the criteria for the query definition. You cannot change the field used for the criterion by editing the criterion, however. If you want to change the field on which a particular criterion is based, you must delete the criterion and create a new one.

To edit a query criterion, follow these steps:

1. Choose the **V**iew **C**riteria command to display the criteria pane, if it is not already displayed.

2. Double-click on the criterion you want to edit. Microsoft Query displays the Edit Criteria dialog box (see fig. 35.7).

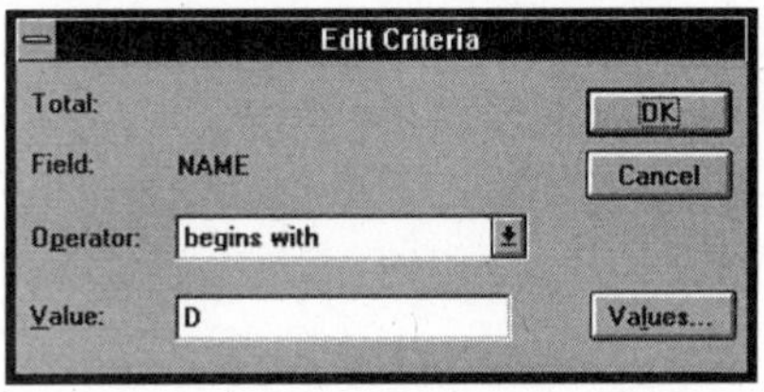

Fig. 35.7
Use the Edit Criteria dialog box to change your query's criteria.

3. Select a new operator in the O**p**erator drop-down list box.
4. Select a new matching value in the **V**alue text box; type the value directly into the text box, or choose the Va**l**ues button to select a value from existing values for that field.
5. Choose OK to change the criterion and close the Edit Criteria dialog box.

To delete a criterion, choose the **V**iew **C**riteria command to display the criteria pane, if it is not already displayed. Next, click the criterion you want to remove, and then press Del.

Executing a Query

To display or update the records in the data pane, the completed query definition must be executed. You can either execute the query manually, or have Microsoft Query execute the query each time you add or remove fields on the data pane, or whenever you make changes to the criteria pane.

To turn on Auto Query, click the Auto Query button on the toolbar. The button remains "down," to indicate that Auto Query is on. You also can choose the **R**ecords Automatic **Q**uery command to turn on Auto Query. To turn off Auto Query, choose the **R**ecords Automatic **Q**uery command again, or click the Auto Query button.

Tip
When you first create a query, or if you make extensive changes to a query, turn Auto Query off so that you can work faster, without waiting for the query to execute after each change you make.

When Auto Query is off, you must execute the query manually to update the data pane if you change the query criteria or fields on the data pane. To execute the query manually, click the Query Now button, or choose the **R**ecords Query **N**ow command.

Saving a Query

If you create a complex query definition or a query definition that you expect to use repeatedly, you may want to save the query definition for future use. In particular, you should save your query definition if you plan to later update or modify the result set.

To save a query definition, choose the **F**ile **S**ave Query command, or click the Query Save button on the toolbar. When you save a query for the first time, the Save As dialog box appears; type the name for the query in the File **N**ame text box, and choose the OK button. To save a query with a different name, follow these steps:

1. Choose the **F**ile Save **A**s command. Microsoft Query displays the Select Data Source dialog box.
2. Select QRY File in the Sa**v**e As list.
3. Choose the **S**ave button. Microsoft Query displays the Save As dialog box.
4. Type the name for the query in the File **N**ame text box. Use the **D**irectories and Dri**v**e lists to select another disk or directory in which to save the query, as you wish.
5. Choose OK.

Closing a Query

After you finish using a query definition in a working session, you can close the query. To close the query, choose the **F**ile **C**lose Query command. If you have made changes to the query definition, or if the query has never been saved before, Microsoft Query prompts you to save your changes. Choose **Y**es to save the query. If the query has never been saved before, a Save As dialog box appears. Type the name for the query in the File **N**ame text box, and then choose OK.

Opening a New Query Window

As you work in Microsoft Query and experiment with various result sets, you may want to create several query definitions at once. If you are already in Microsoft Query, choose the **F**ile **N**ew Query command or click the New Query button on the toolbar to create a new query definition; Microsoft Query opens a new query window and displays the Select Data Source dialog box. Follow the procedures described earlier in this chapter in the section, "Selecting or Creating a Data Source" to select a data source for the new query.

Using a Saved Query Definition

To use a saved query definition, you must open the query, and then execute the query. To open a saved query, follow these steps:

1. Choose the **F**ile **O**pen Query command; Microsoft Query displays the Open Query dialog box (see fig. 35.8).

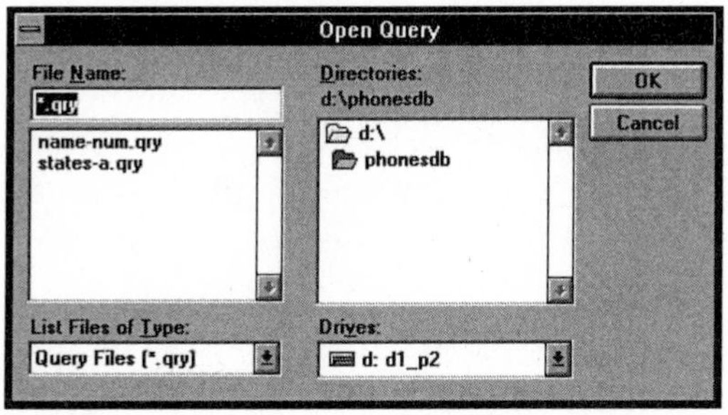

Fig. 35.8
Use the Open Query dialog box to open a saved query.

2. Type the name of the query in the File **N**ame text box, or select it from the list. If the query you want to open is not listed in the File **N**ame list, use the **D**irectories and Dri**v**es lists to select a different drive and directory to locate the query.
3. Choose OK.

For Related Information
- "Working in Dialog Boxes," p. 48
- "Manipulating Windows," p. 58

If the query was saved while Auto Query was turned on, the result set in the data pane is updated as the query is opened.

Working with SQL Queries

If you are an SQL expert, you may want to alter or add criteria, fields, or tables to the query by directly editing the SQL statement that Microsoft Query sends to the ODBC driver.

To view or edit the SQL statement, choose the **V**iew **S**QL command, or click the SQL button on the toolbar. Microsoft Query displays the SQL dialog box shown in figure 35.9. Add to or edit the SQL statement displayed in the SQL dialog box as you would the text in any other text box or worksheet cell. When you are satisfied with your changes, choose OK.

Joining Multiple Tables

Many of the databases from which you retrieve data will be relational databases. To retrieve all the information you need from the different tables that make up a relational database, you not only need to place multiple tables on the table pane, you also need to join together the tables through their linking fields. Tables on the table pane are connected by *join lines* that indicate the linking fields and how they join the tables. Figure 35.10 shows a table pane with one join line connecting two tables. In the figure, the Entry # fields are joined because the entry number is the linking field for these databases. Table *phaddr* contains the address information for the persons listed in the *phnames* table; in order to match the correct addresses with the names in *phnames*, the two tables must be joined by their linking fields.

Fig. 35.9
You can view or edit the SQL statement that Microsoft Query sends to the ODBC driver.

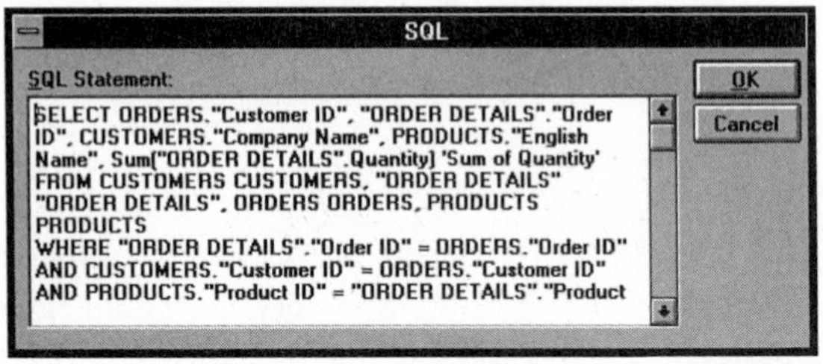

Fig. 35.10
Join lines connect the linking fields in a relational database.

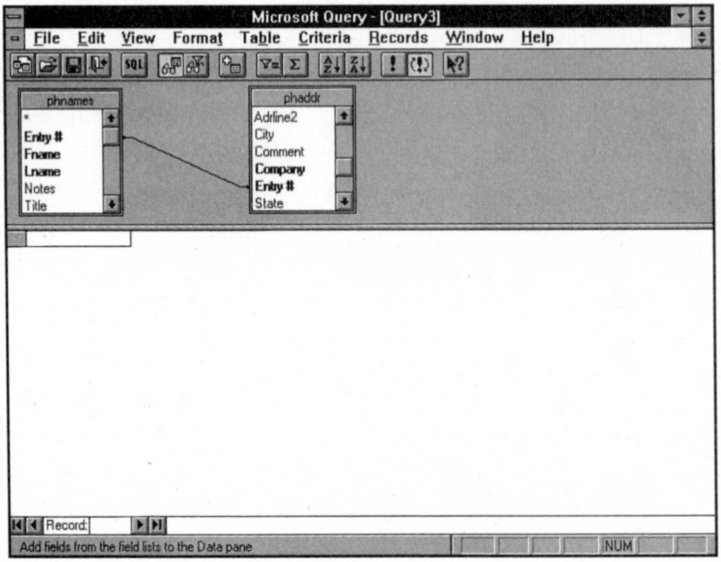

In some cases, Microsoft Query automatically places join lines on the table pane. If one of the tables on the table pane has a primary key, and you place another table on the table pane that has the same field containing the same type of data (date, text, or numbers), Microsoft Query adds a join line connecting the two fields. The join line shown in figure 35.10 was placed by

Microsoft Query. Some types of databases, such as dBASE, do not use primary keys; for these databases you must manually add join lines to connect related fields. You can create additional join lines or remove join lines at any time.

Adding Join Lines

You can add join lines to connect any two fields between tables on the table pane. To add a join line with the mouse, drag a field from one table over the field you want to join it to in another table. Microsoft Query adds the join line. If you attempt to join two fields that contain different types of data (one field contains text, the other field contains dates, for example), Microsoft Query asks you to confirm creating the link. In most cases, you should choose **N**o to creating a join line between fields that contain different data types. Because it is unlikely that the values in fields of dissimilar data type match up, a join line like this is not usually useful.

Join lines created with the mouse form an *inner join*. In an inner join, only records which have field values that exactly match each other are included in the result set.

You can also add join lines with the Joins dialog box by following these steps:

1. Choose the Ta**b**le **J**oins command. Microsoft Query displays the Joins dialog box (see fig. 35.11).

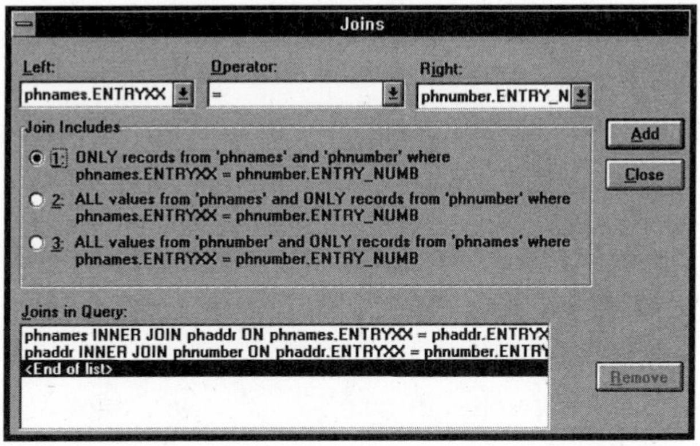

Fig. 35.11
Use the Joins dialog box to create different types of join lines.

2. Select the table and field for the left side of the join line in the **L**eft list box.

3. Select the table and field for the right side of the join line in the R**i**ght list box.

4. Select an operator in the **O**perator list box to determine the linking relationship between the fields. (The equal sign (=) is the most common operator.)

5. Select one of the Join Includes options to determine what the join includes.

   You cannot use the second and third join types (called *outer joins*) if there are more than two tables on the table pane.

6. Choose **A**dd to add the join line to the table pane.

7. Repeat steps 2 through 6 for each join line you want to create.

8. Choose **C**lose to close the Joins dialog box.

Removing Join Lines

You can remove join lines with the mouse or through the Joins dialog box. To remove a join line with the mouse, select the join line, and then press Del. Microsoft Query removes the join line. To remove a join line with the Joins dialog box, choose the Ta**b**le **J**oins command to display the Joins dialog box. Select the join you want to remove in the **J**oins in Query list at the bottom of the Joins dialog box, and then choose the **R**emove button to delete the join. Choose **C**lose to close the Joins dialog box.

For Related Information

■ "Using Operators in Formulas," p. 139

Working with Data in the Result Set

As you view the result set in the data pane, you may want to alter the way the information is ordered or formatted. You can hide or show columns, change the column widths and order, change the row height, sort data, change column headings, change the display formatting of data in the data pane, and even edit the data.

Working with Columns and Rows

You have a variety of formatting options available with the columns in the data pane. You may want to hide a column in the data pane to clarify your view of other data, without actually removing the column from the data pane.

To hide a column, click anywhere in the column you want to hide, and then choose the Forma**t** **H**ide Columns command. The column is removed from the data pane.

When you want to display the column again, choose the Forma**t** **S**how Columns command to display the Show Column dialog box. Hidden columns do not have a check mark next to them in the Co**l**umns list. Select the column you want to show in the Co**l**umns list, and choose the **S**how button. The column again is displayed on the data pane. Choose **C**lose to close the Show Columns dialog box.

Changing Column Width and Column Order. You can change the width of a column by either dragging the column border to resize the column, or by using the Column Width dialog box.

To use the Column Width dialog box, follow these steps:

1. Click anywhere in the column whose width you want to change.
2. Choose the Forma**t** Column Width command. Microsoft Query displays the Column Width dialog box.
3. Choose among the following dialog box options to select the width of the column:

Option	Description
Column Width	Type the number of characters to display in the column in the current font size; Microsoft Query may display a few more or less characters in the column if the field contains symbols or capital letters that take up more or less space.
Standard Width	Select this check box to return the column to the standard width that Microsoft Query chooses. This check box is automatically deselected if you type a number in the **C**olumn Width box or choose **B**est Fit.
Best Fit	Choose this button to have Microsoft Query change the size of the column so that the column is wide enough to display the entire contents of the longest entry in the selected column.

To change the order of the columns, click once on the column's title bar to select the column. Then drag the column by the title bar to a new location. As you drag the column, a thick vertical line appears, indicating the location where the column will be inserted.

Changing Column Headings. Often the field names in a database table are terse abbreviations of the description of the data contained in the field. You may want to change the column heading to show a more complete description of the contents of that field. For example, you may want to change the field name QRTR_SALES to a more complete and intelligible heading of "Quarterly Sales."

To change a column heading, follow these steps:

1. Choose the **R**ecords **E**dit Column command, or double-click the column heading. Microsoft Query displays the Edit Column dialog box, showing the name of the field which the column displays in the **F**ield drop-down list box.

2. Type the new heading name in the Column **H**eading text box.

3. Choose OK.

Changing Row Height. You can change the height of a row either by dragging the row border or by using the Row Height dialog box. Changing the row height affects all the rows in the data pane and the entire result set. To use the Row Height dialog box, choose the Forma**t** **R**ow Height command and specify the desired height.

Note

If you select **S**tandard Height, Microsoft Query changes the row height if the display font changes (larger or smaller) so that the full height of the characters remains visible. If you use a custom row height, the row height remains at that size regardless of the display font size. If you later change to a larger font, it may not fit in your custom row height, and the bottoms of the letters may be chopped off. If this happens, change the custom row height to display all the letters, or choose **S**tandard Height.

Sorting Data

Microsoft Query enables you to sort the data in the data pane based on the contents of one or several columns. You can sort in ascending (A–Z, 0–9) order or in descending (Z–A, 9–0) order.

Sorting with the Toolbar. To sort data on a single column by using the toolbar, click anywhere in the column that you want to use as the basis for the sort, and then click the Sort Ascending button to sort in ascending order, or click the Sort Descending button to sort in descending order. Finally, execute the query by clicking the Query Now button, if Auto Query is not turned on.

To further sort your data, you can sort on additional columns. The records remain in the sort order based on the first column you sorted on, but the records are further sorted within the columns you previously sorted.

To sort on an additional column, click anywhere on the next column you want to sort, and then hold down the Ctrl key as you click either the Sort Ascending or Sort Descending button. If you don't hold down the Ctrl key, the sort based on the new column replaces the previous sort.

To sort the data on the data pane based on several columns at once, first arrange the columns in the order you want the sorts performed, from right to left. Next, select the columns you want to sort. Finally, click either the Sort Ascending or Sort Descending button.

Sorting with the Sort Dialog Box. To sort the data on the data pane with the Sort dialog box, follow these steps:

1. Choose the **R**ecords **S**ort command. Microsoft Query displays the Sort dialog box (see fig. 35.12).

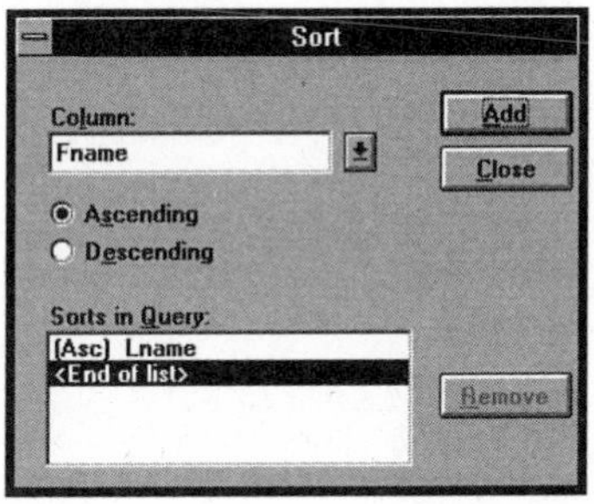

Fig. 35.12 Choosing the sort order.

2. Select the column you want to base the sort on in the Co**l**umn drop-down list box. Only columns that have not already been used in the sort order are listed in the Co**l**umn drop-down list.
3. Select the A**s**cending or D**e**scending option, as desired.
4. Choose the **A**dd button. Microsoft Query sorts the data on that column and adds the column to the Sorts in **Q**uery list.
5. Repeat steps 2 through 4 for each column you want to sort on.
6. Choose **C**lose to close the Sort dialog box.

Removing a Sort Order. To remove a sort order, follow these steps:

1. Choose the **R**ecords **S**ort command. Microsoft Query displays the Sort dialog box.
2. Select the column whose sort order you want to remove in the Sorts in **Q**uery list.
3. Choose the **R**emove button. The values in the column return to the order they were in before you sorted them.
4. Choose **C**lose to close the Sort dialog box.

Working with Records and Fields

Before you can copy, edit, or format any data in the data pane, you must be able to move from one record or field to another, and select all or part of the contents of a record or field.

Moving to Another Record. The current record contains the insertion point and has an arrow in its record selector. Use the up- and down-arrow keys or the navigation buttons to move from one record to another. To move to a specific record, place the insertion point in the record number box, type the record number, and press Enter. If you can see any part of the record on-screen, you can move to the record by clicking anywhere on it.

Selecting Records. To select a single record, click the record selector to the left of the record, or press Shift+space bar to select the current record. To select several records at once, click the first record selector, and drag to the last record, or press Shift+space bar and then press Shift+down arrow or Shift+up arrow until all the desired records are selected. To select all the records, click in the upper-left corner of the data pane, or press Ctrl+Shift+space bar.

Moving to Another Field. If you can see the field you want to move to, click anywhere in that field to move to it. The following table lists the keystrokes for moving from field to field by using the keyboard:

Key	Action
Tab, right-arrow, or Enter	Move to next field
Shift+Tab, left-arrow	Move to previous field
Home	Move to first field of record
End	Move to last field of record

Selecting Fields. You may select all or part of a field. To select an entire field, click the field or move to the field. Moving the insertion point to a field selects the entire field. To use the mouse to select part of the data in a field, double-click the field, and then drag across the data you want to select. To select part of the data in a field with the keyboard, move to that field, press F2, move the insertion point to the place you want to start selecting, and then press Shift+right-arrow key or Shift+left-arrow key to select data.

Formatting Data

In Microsoft Query, you can only change the display font for the entire result set in the data pane. You cannot change the character formatting for individual fields or records. You can, however, select any font available from the installed fonts on your computer for the display font.

To change the display font, choose the Forma**t** **F**ont command. Microsoft Query displays a standard font selection dialog box. Select the font and styles (bold, italic, and so on), and then choose OK.

Editing Data

Depending on the specific database and ODBC driver you are using, you may be able to edit the data in the data pane. To edit data, however, you first must tell Microsoft Query to allow editing. To turn editing on or off, choose the **R**ecords **A**llow Editing command. When this option is turned on, a check mark appears next to the command on the **R**ecords menu.

> **Caution**
>
> Editing data in the data pane *does* affect the data in the source documents. If you edit, add, or delete records in the data pane, you are actually editing, adding, or deleting records in the source databases. Be very careful when you use this feature.

Adding Records. Whenever you turn on the Allow Editing option, Microsoft Query adds a blank record at the end of the result set. An asterisk appears in the record selector to the left of the blank record.

To enter a new record, follow these steps:

1. Choose the **R**ecords **A**llow Editing command to turn on editing, if it is not on already.
2. Move to the first field of the record, and type a value for the field.
3. Press Tab to move to the next field, and type in the value for the field.

4. Repeat step 3 until all the fields in the record are filled in.

5. Press Tab to move to the first field of the next blank record.

   If the result set is sorted, the new record moves to the proper location in the sort order.

   Note

   If you have selection criteria entered in the query pane and you enter a new record that does *not* match the specified criteria, the new record is added to the source database(s), but is not displayed in the data pane.

6. Repeat steps 2 through 5 until you are finished adding records.

Editing Data in Fields. To edit data in a field, first make sure that the Allow Editing option is turned on, then perform one of the following actions:

Tip
If you need more room to type changes, choose the **V**iew **Z**oom Field command (or double-click with the right mouse button) to expand the field in a zoom box so that you can see the entire field's contents.

- To replace all or part of a field's contents, select the data you want to replace, and then type your changes.

- To insert data in a field, double-click where you want to begin inserting; or move to the field, press F2, and then use the arrow keys to position the insertion point where you want to begin inserting. Finally, type your changes.

Note

Not all source databases allow their data to be changed. If the source database does not allow data to be changed, you cannot edit the data in Microsoft Query.

Saving Data. When you edit records and fields in Microsoft Query, you do not need to perform any special action to save your changes. Whenever you leave the current record, Microsoft Query saves the changes for that record in the source database(s). Microsoft Query also saves changes to the database whenever the query is closed.

Whenever you are adding or changing a record, a pencil displays in the record selector at the left of the record, indicating that there is unsaved data in the record. As soon as you leave the record or close the query, the record is saved in the source database(s) and the pencil disappears.

Copying or Moving Data. You can copy or move all or part of the data from one field in the data pane to another, or you can copy or move data to another application. Copying and moving data to another application is described later in this chapter, in the section "Transferring Data to Excel."

To copy or move data, follow these steps:

1. Select the data you want to copy. You may select an entire record, field, or part of a field.
2. Choose the **E**dit **C**opy command if you want to copy the data, or choose the **E**dit Cu**t** command if you want to move the data.
3. Move to the record or field where you want to insert the data.
4. Choose the Edit Paste command to insert the data.

Note

If the Allow Editing option is not turned on, the **E**dit Cu**t**, **C**opy, Copy **S**pecial, **P**aste, and **D**elete commands are not available. Use the **R**ecords **A**llow Editing command to turn on the Allow Editing option and enable these **E**dit commands. (Some of the **E**dit menu commands may remain disabled for other reasons, even if Allow Editing is on; **P**aste, for example, remains disabled if there is nothing in the Clipboard to paste.)

Deleting Data. You may want to delete data that you no longer use from the source database. From Microsoft Query, you can delete all or part of the data in a field, or delete one or more whole records. To delete data, the Allow Editing option must be turned on as described at the beginning of this section.

For Related Information

- "Entering Data," p. 87
- "What You Need to Know About Sorting," p. 887
- "Changing Character Fonts, Sizes, Styles, and Colors," p. 312

To delete data, select the record, field, or part of a field you want to delete, and then press Del. If you are deleting one or more entire records, Query asks you to confirm the deletion.

Undoing Changes. You can undo your most recent changes; that is, you can undo only the last change you made. To undo the most recent addition or deletion, choose the Edit Undo command.

Transferring Data to Excel

After you finish selecting, sorting, organizing, and formatting the data in Microsoft Query, you are ready to transfer that data to Excel. If you started

Microsoft Query from Excel with the **D**ata Get E**x**ternal Data command, you can only transfer data to Excel by using the Microsoft Query **F**ile **R**eturn Data to Excel command. If you started Microsoft Query directly from Program Manager, you can use the Microsoft Query **E**dit **C**opy or **E**dit Copy **S**pecial command to copy data from Microsoft Query to the Windows Clipboard; you then use the **E**dit **P**aste or Edit Paste **S**pecial command in Excel or another Windows application to paste the data into that application. Pasting and linking data from other Windows applications also is described in Chapter 38.

Returning Data from Microsoft Query

To return data from Microsoft Query to Excel, you must have started Microsoft Query from Excel. When you start Microsoft Query from Excel, the **R**eturn Data to Excel command appears on Microsoft Query's **F**ile menu, and the Return Data button appears on Microsoft Query's toolbar. When you return data to Excel, all the data in the data pane goes to your Excel worksheet. Returning data to Excel doesn't close Microsoft Query.

> **Note**
>
> When you return data to Excel, the data inserted in your worksheet is a *copy* of the data retrieved by Microsoft Query. You must update the information in the worksheet manually (or execute the query and return the data again) to have the data in the worksheet reflect changes in the source data that occur after the first time you return data to Excel from that particular database.

When you return data to Excel, all the data in the data pane is copied to your worksheet; you do not need to select any data in the data pane before returning the data to Excel. To return data to Excel, follow these steps:

1. Choose the **F**ile **R**eturn Data to Excel command, or click the Return Data button on the toolbar. Excel displays the Get External Data dialog box (see fig. 35.13).

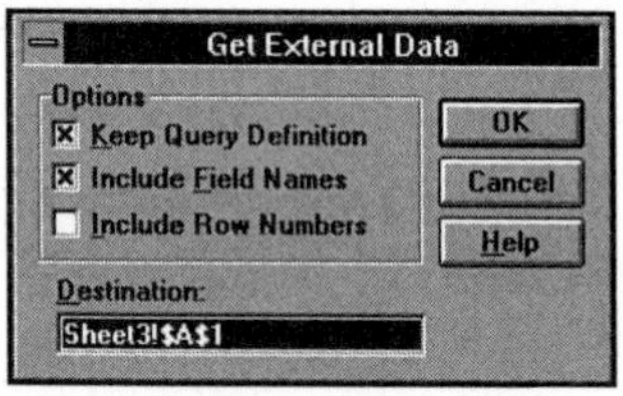

Fig. 35.13
Use the Get External Data dialog box to return data to Excel.

2. Enter the Excel sheet name and cell coordinates for the upper-left corner of the returned data in the **D**estination text box. If you don't change the location, the result set is inserted in the worksheet at the current location.

3. Select among the following options:

Keep Query Definition	Select this check box to keep the query that you used to create the result set that you are inserting. The query information is stored in the Excel worksheet.
Include **F**ield Names	Select to include the field names in the Excel worksheet as column headings for the data.
Include Row Numbers	Select to include row numbers.

4. Choose OK. Excel inserts the data from Microsoft Query into the worksheet.

Caution

If you have text labels or cell formulas at the bottom or right side of the area filled by data returned from Microsoft Query, and you change the query so that it returns more columns or rows, the returned data overwrites the formulas or text labels covered by the larger returned data set. To avoid this problem, return the data to an empty worksheet, and then copy or move it to its final location.

The area on the worksheet that contains the data pasted (returned) from Microsoft Query is called a *data range*. The worksheet cell specified in the **D**estination text box of the Get External Data dialog box is the upper-left corner of the data range.

Pasting or Linking Data from Microsoft Query

You can only paste or link data to Excel if you started Microsoft Query directly from Program Manager. You cannot perform these operations if you started Microsoft Query with Excel's **D**ata Get E**x**ternal Data command.

When you paste data from Microsoft Query (or any other Windows application) into Excel, you have two options. First, you can simply paste the data into Excel as a copy of the data in the original source. This has essentially the same effect as returning data to Excel, as described in the preceding section.

If the source data changes, the data in your Excel worksheet does not change; you must manually update the information by copying it from the source and pasting it into Excel again.

The second option links the data from the source application (Microsoft Query, in this case) to the Excel worksheet. After you link data to your Excel worksheet, you can automatically update the information if the source data changes. Updating linked or embedded information is described in Chapter 38.

Pasting Data. Pasting data into Excel manually has one minor advantage over returning data to Excel. By using the copy-and-paste method described here, you can transfer single fields or parts of a single field to your worksheet. When you return data to Excel (as described earlier in this section), all the data in Microsoft Query's data pane is copied to Excel.

To paste data into an Excel worksheet from Microsoft Query, follow these steps:

1. Select the information (records, fields, or part of a field) you want to place into the worksheet from the data pane in Microsoft Query. Use any of the selection methods described earlier in this chapter.

2. Choose the **E**dit **C**opy command or the **E**dit Copy **S**pecial command. Use the Edit Copy **S**pecial command if you want to include column headings or row numbers in the information you are copying.

   Microsoft Query copies the selected information to the Windows Clipboard.

3. Use the Windows Task Manager to make Excel the current application. (Refer to your Windows documentation for information on the Task Manager.)

4. Make current the worksheet cell that you want to be the upper-left corner of the data range that you paste into Excel.

5. Choose the **E**dit **P**aste command. Excel pastes the information from the Windows Clipboard into your worksheet.

Remember that the information you insert into a worksheet this way is just a copy of the information in the source application. You must repeat this copy-and-paste operation to update the information in your worksheet.

Linking Data. Linking data to Excel is essentially the same as pasting data into Excel, except that Excel records the origin of the data, and can use the DDE or OLE link to update the information in your worksheet. Updating DDE and OLE links is described in Chapter 38.

To link data to an Excel worksheet from Microsoft Query, follow these steps:

1. Select the information you want to place in the worksheet from the data pane in Microsoft Query. Use any of the selection methods described earlier in this chapter.

2. Choose the **E**dit **C**opy command or the **E**dit Copy **S**pecial command. Use the Edit Copy **S**pecial command if you want to include column headings or row numbers in the information you are linking.

   Microsoft Query copies the selected information to the Windows Clipboard.

3. Use the Windows Task Manager to make Excel the current application, or press Alt+Tab until Excel becomes the current application.

4. Make current the worksheet cell that you want to be the upper-left corner of the data range that you link to Excel.

5. Choose the **E**dit Paste **S**pecial command. Excel displays the Paste Special dialog box.

6. To link the data to your worksheet, choose the Paste **L**ink option in the Paste Special dialog box. (The **P**aste option produces the same effect as using the **E**dit **P**aste command described previously.)

7. Choose OK. Excel inserts the linked information into your worksheet.

To update the linked information, use the **E**dit Lin**k**s command. See Chapter 38 for more information on updating links.

Note

If you insert data from Microsoft Query into your Excel worksheet using the linking procedure described here, remember that the link you are creating is a link to Microsoft Query, *not* a link to the original data source.

Opening Worksheets Linked to Databases

Whenever you open a worksheet or workbook that contains linked data, Excel offers you the choice of updating the information produced by the links as the worksheet is opened. Choose **Y**es to update the links, or choose **N**o if you know that the links do not need to be updated.

Closing Microsoft Query

To close Microsoft Query, you must choose the E**x**it command from the Microsoft Query **F**ile menu. The E**x**it command does not appear on the Microsoft Query **F**ile menu if you started or switched to Microsoft Query by choosing the **D**ata Get E**x**ternal Data command; instead, the Return Data to Excel command appears. Returning data to Excel does not close Microsoft Query. To close Microsoft Query, first return data to Excel, then switch back to Microsoft Query by using the Windows Task Manager or pressing Alt+Tab, and finally choose the **F**ile E**x**it command. Closing Microsoft Query does not close Excel.

Moving Data and Query Definitions to Another Worksheet or Workbook

You may want to use the same external data in more than one workbook, or in more than one worksheet. Also, if you want to preserve any formatting or formulas that you have added to a data range inserted in your worksheet by returning data from Microsoft Query, you need to copy the data to another worksheet before updating the query; otherwise, the new returned data replaces the old data and all its formatting. If the new result set is larger than the old result set, cells that contain formulas may be overwritten by data in the new result set.

To copy data from Microsoft Query to another workbook, follow these steps:

1. Save the query definition in Microsoft Query.
2. Choose the **F**ile **R**eturn Data to Excel command to return the data to your current workbook.
3. Open a new workbook in Excel.
4. Choose the **D**ata Get E**x**ternal Data command.

5. Open the saved query file, and choose the **R**ecords Query **N**ow command to execute the query.

6. Choose the **F**ile **R**eturn Data to Excel command to return the data to the new workbook.

To copy data returned from Microsoft Query to another worksheet in the same workbook, select the data you want to copy, and use the **E**dit **C**opy command to copy the data to the Clipboard. Next, move to the worksheet and cell you want to copy the data to, and choose the **E**dit **P**aste command.

For Related Information

- "Copying Data between Applications," p. 1045
- "Linking Data between Applications," p. 1047

Editing Existing Query Results in a Worksheet

You can format, edit, extract data, create reports, create charts, sort, filter, or otherwise manipulate the returned data from Microsoft Query just as you would any other data in your worksheet. Data returned from Microsoft Query behaves just like data you typed into the worksheet yourself.

There is one exception, however. If you later perform another query with Microsoft Query and return the result to Excel, the new result set replaces the old result set, and any special formatting you may have applied is lost. To preserve any changes or editing you made to the data in the result set, copy the result set to another worksheet before performing another query.

Updating Query Results

If you use the data returned from an external database as the source of periodic reports, you may want to update the returned data at some time or other.

If you only want to update the results of the query that you used previously, place the insertion point anywhere in the data range occupied by the result set, and choose the **D**ata **R**efresh Data command. Excel runs Microsoft Query, instructs it to execute the query, and then immediately returns the result set to Excel.

If you want to change the query definition that produced the result set and update the result set, perform these steps:

1. Move to any cell in the returned result set, and choose **D**ata Get E**x**ternal Data. Excel displays the Get External Data dialog box.

2. Choose the **E**dit Query button. Excel starts Microsoft Query with the query definition for this result set open.

3. Edit the query as desired.

4. If Auto Query is not on, choose **R**ecords Query **N**ow or click the Query Now button on the toolbar to execute the query.

5. Return the result set to Excel.

From Here...

Microsoft Query is a powerful Windows applications that gives Excel and Word for Windows access to databases from other personal computer applications, to SQL Server or networked databases, and even to the most commonly used mainframe databases. If a driver, the connecting software, for your databases did not come with Excel, check with your database software manufacturer for an ODBC driver and installer. For related information, please see these chapters:

- Chapter 38, "Using Excel with Windows Applications." This chapter describes how to copy and paste, link, or embed data from other Windows applications into Excel.

- Chapter 39, "Using Excel with DOS and Mainframe Applications." Learn how Excel can import data from many DOS or mainframe applications without using Microsoft Query.

Chapter 36

Using Pivot Tables

Pivot tables, new with Excel Version 5 for Windows, allow you to analyze data in lists and tables. Pivot tables offer more flexible and intuitive analysis of data than Excel 4's crosstab tables, which they replace.

EXCEL 5

In this chapter, you learn how to:

- Use the PivotTable Wizard to summarize data in a pivot table
- Filter data in a pivot table with a page field
- Create a chart from a pivot table

Pivot tables do more than just group and summarize data; they add depth to the data. In creating a pivot table, you tell Excel which of the fields (in the list) are to be arranged in rows and columns. You can also designate a *page field* that seems to arrange items in a stack of pages. You can rearrange the position of pivot table fields in a split second—in effect twisting the data around. (That's where the word "pivot" comes in.)

Most Excel lists appear something like that in figure 36.1. These lists contain rows of information arranged in columns that hold a specific type of information. The list in figure 36.1, for example, contains information about the daily sales of different kinds of snack foods. The items in the list are sorted by date.

This database contains a wealth of information, but it is difficult to form any type of a comprehensive view. That is where pivot tables come in.

Like the crosstab tables of Excel 4, pivot tables display the finished result of a database analysis. With them, you can analyze values in a database according to related fields. Figure 36.2, for example, shows a pivot table showing how each of the products is selling in each of the four sales regions. The PivotTable Wizard helps build this complex report.

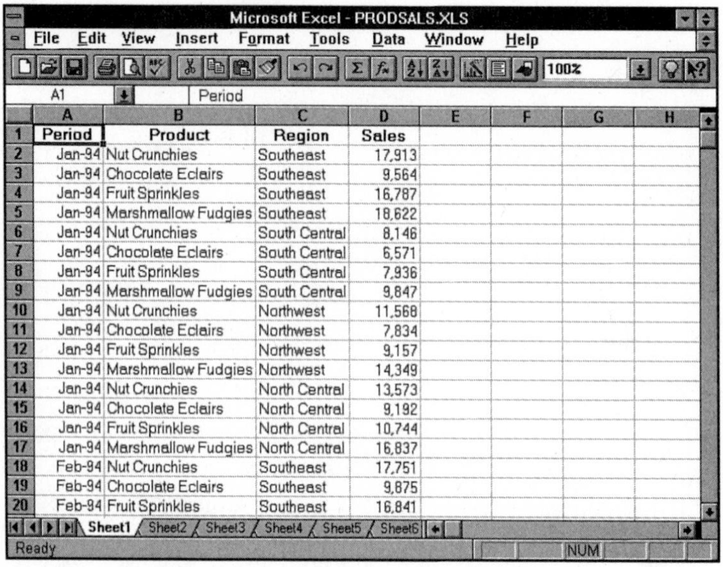

	Period	Product	Region	Sales
2	Jan-94	Nut Crunchies	Southeast	17,913
3	Jan-94	Chocolate Eclairs	Southeast	9,564
4	Jan-94	Fruit Sprinkles	Southeast	16,787
5	Jan-94	Marshmallow Fudgies	Southeast	18,622
6	Jan-94	Nut Crunchies	South Central	8,146
7	Jan-94	Chocolate Eclairs	South Central	6,571
8	Jan-94	Fruit Sprinkles	South Central	7,936
9	Jan-94	Marshmallow Fudgies	South Central	9,847
10	Jan-94	Nut Crunchies	Northwest	11,568
11	Jan-94	Chocolate Eclairs	Northwest	7,834
12	Jan-94	Fruit Sprinkles	Northwest	9,157
13	Jan-94	Marshmallow Fudgies	Northwest	14,349
14	Jan-94	Nut Crunchies	North Central	13,573
15	Jan-94	Chocolate Eclairs	North Central	9,192
16	Jan-94	Fruit Sprinkles	North Central	10,744
17	Jan-94	Marshmallow Fudgies	North Central	16,837
18	Feb-94	Nut Crunchies	Southeast	17,751
19	Feb-94	Chocolate Eclairs	Southeast	9,875
20	Feb-94	Fruit Sprinkles	Southeast	16,841

Fig. 36.1 Excel can accumulate large amounts of tabular data, but looking at the data in this detailed format makes it difficult to analyze.

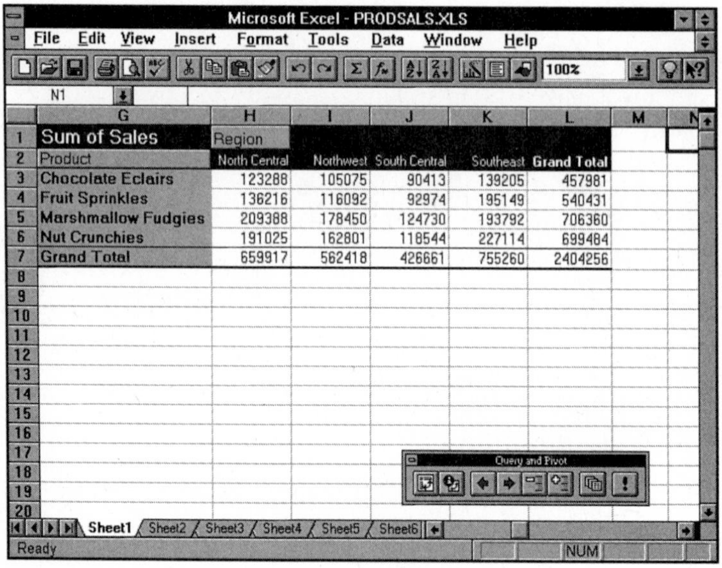

Sum of Sales	Region				
Product	North Central	Northwest	South Central	Southeast	Grand Total
Chocolate Eclairs	123288	105075	90413	139205	457981
Fruit Sprinkles	136216	116092	92974	195149	540431
Marshmallow Fudgies	209388	178450	124730	193792	706360
Nut Crunchies	191025	162801	118544	227114	699484
Grand Total	659917	562418	426661	755260	2404256

Fig. 36.2 The PivotTable Wizard builds complex reports with multifield analysis and subtotals.

Working with Pivot Tables

Pivot tables are analytical and reporting tools that are useful for a number of purposes, including the following:

- *Creating summary tables.* As you saw in figure 36.2, pivot tables can summarize lists and databases to provide a big-picture view of the data.

They can, for instance, group a large number of transactions into account totals, or display averages and statistics for records in a list or external database.

- *Reorganizing tables with drag and drop.* More dynamic than crosstabs, pivot tables can provide a better impression of trends and relationships in and among data elements. Figure 36.3 shows the same pivot table shown in figure 36.2 after being rearranged to summarize regional sales by month. You reorganize pivot tables by dragging text labels to different locations on-screen.

- *Filtering and grouping data in the pivot table.* When you are examining data, sometimes you want to see grand totals. At other times, you want to look at a subset of the data. Pivot tables enable you to zero in on the data. Figure 36.4, for example, shows the same data as in figure 36.3 except that the sales amount for only one product, Nut Crunchies, is shown.

- *Charting from pivot tables.* Pivot tables are great presentation tools, but charts can still add punch. It is easy to create charts from pivot tables (see fig. 36.5). The charts change dynamically as you manipulate the pivot table.

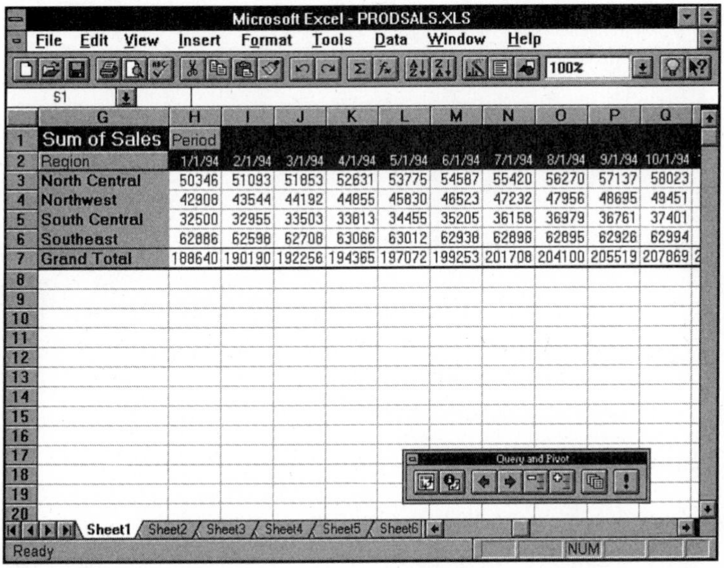

Sum of Sales	Period									
Region	1/1/94	2/1/94	3/1/94	4/1/94	5/1/94	6/1/94	7/1/94	8/1/94	9/1/94	10/1/94
North Central	50346	51093	51853	52631	53775	54587	55420	56270	57137	58023
Northwest	42908	43544	44192	44855	45830	46523	47232	47956	48695	49451
South Central	32500	32955	33503	33813	34455	35205	36158	36979	36761	37401
Southeast	62886	62598	62708	63066	63012	62938	62898	62895	62926	62994
Grand Total	188640	190190	192256	194365	197072	199253	201708	204100	205519	207869

Fig. 36.3
This is the same pivot table as in figure 36.2, rearranged to get a different view of the data.

V

Managing Lists

Fig. 36.4
You can define a filtered view of the data. This pivot table summarizes sales for the Nut Crunchies product.

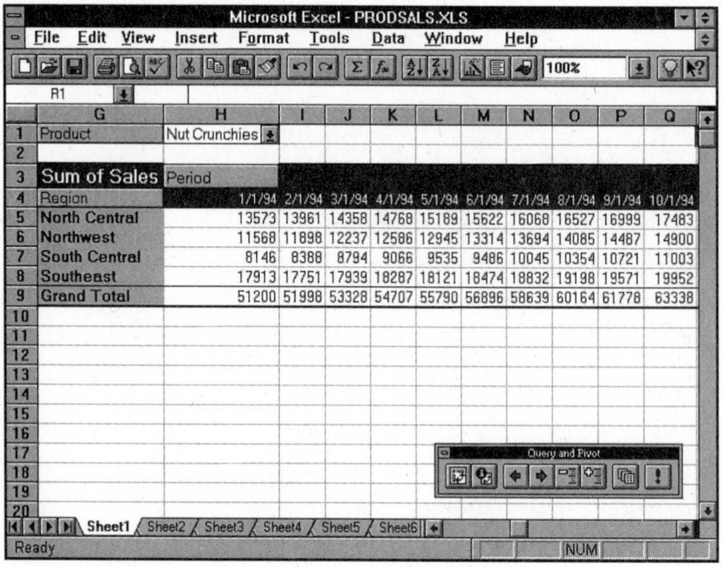

Region	1/1/94	2/1/94	3/1/94	4/1/94	5/1/94	6/1/94	7/1/94	8/1/94	9/1/94	10/1/94
North Central	13573	13961	14358	14768	15189	15622	16068	16527	16999	17483
Northwest	11568	11898	12237	12586	12945	13314	13694	14085	14487	14900
South Central	8146	8388	8794	9066	9535	9486	10045	10354	10721	11003
Southeast	17913	17751	17939	18287	18121	18474	18832	19198	19571	19952
Grand Total	51200	51998	53328	54707	55790	56896	58639	60164	61778	63338

Fig. 36.5
The chart at the bottom was created from the pivot table at the top of the screen.

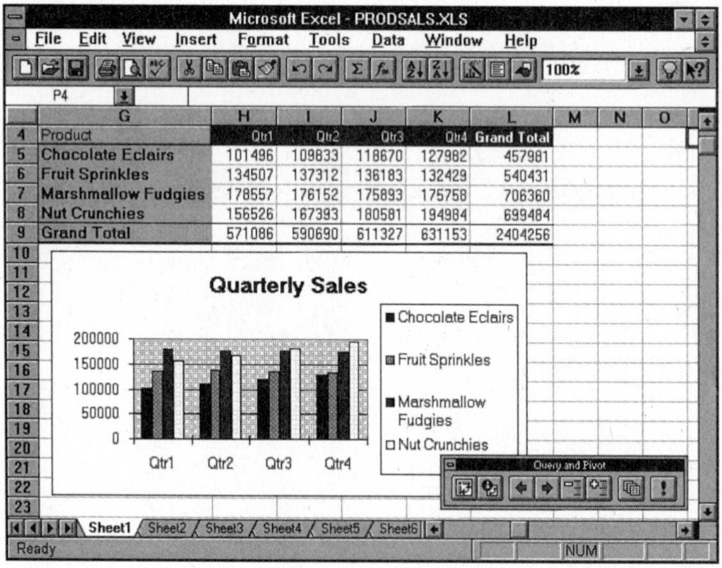

Product	Qtr1	Qtr2	Qtr3	Qtr4	Grand Total
Chocolate Eclairs	101496	109833	118670	127982	457981
Fruit Sprinkles	134507	137312	136183	132429	540431
Marshmallow Fudgies	178557	176152	175893	175758	706360
Nut Crunchies	156526	167393	180581	194984	699484
Grand Total	571086	590690	611327	631153	2404256

Understanding Pivot Tables

A pivot table is a device for organizing data. You determine exactly how the data is organized by specifying which *fields* and *items* you want to appear in the pivot table. A field is a generic category; an item is an individual value or instance within that category. In the pivot table in figure 36.6, for instance, *District* and *Grade* are fields; the individual districts and grade levels are items.

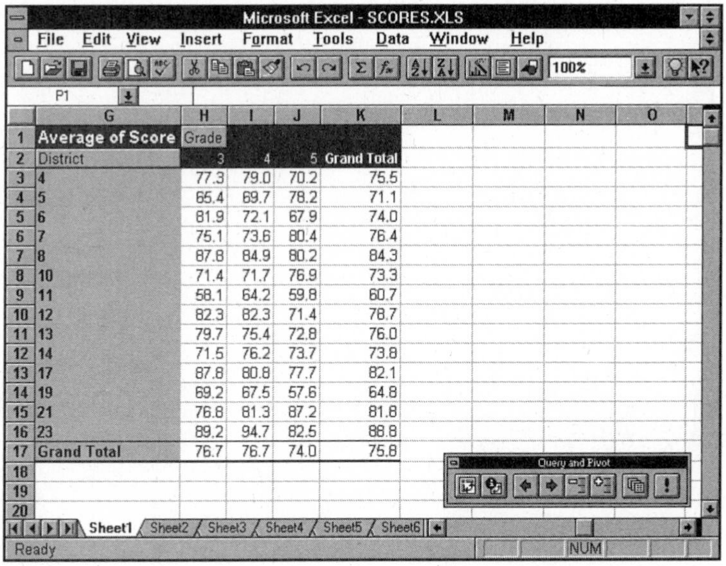

Fig. 36.6
A pivot table summarizing test score performance at various grade levels by district.

The source of the data can be a list or table in an Excel worksheet, or even data created in another program. Multiple data sources can feed data into a pivot table. In this chapter, the term *list* means a list in an Excel worksheet. Terms like *tabular data* and *multicolumn table* refer generically to data in tabular form, whether in an Excel worksheet or a file created in another program. *External data* refers to data created in another program.

When you create a pivot table, you specify row, column, and page fields, as illustrated in figure 36.7. Naturally, you can see the rows and columns only in the two-dimensional table. Although you can view only a single page field at a time, you can think of the pages as being stacked in the "through" dimension, as noted in the illustration.

Although the data displayed in pivot tables looks like any other worksheet data, you cannot directly enter or change the data in the data area of a pivot table. The pivot table itself is linked to the source data, and what you see in the cells of the table are read-only amounts. You can, however, change the formatting and select from a variety of computation options.

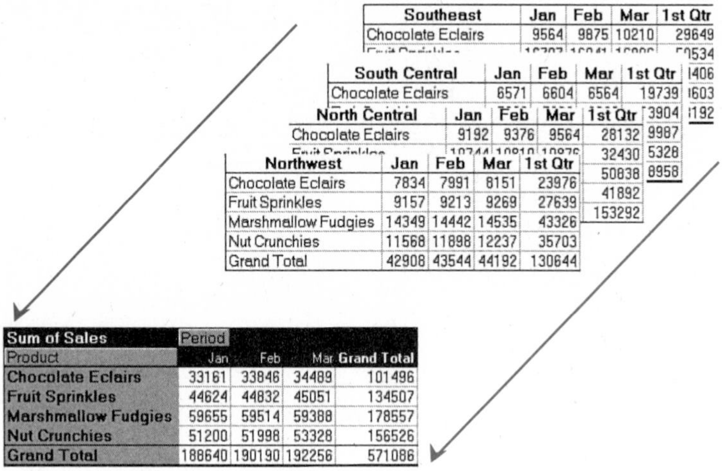

Southeast | Jan | Feb | Mar | 1st Qtr
Chocolate Eclairs | 9564 | 9875 | 10210 | 29649
South Central | Jan | Feb | Mar | 1st Qtr
Chocolate Eclairs | 6571 | 6604 | 6564 | 19739
North Central | Jan | Feb | Mar | 1st Qtr
Chocolate Eclairs | 9192 | 9376 | 9564 | 28132
Northwest | Jan | Feb | Mar | 1st Qtr
Chocolate Eclairs | 7834 | 7991 | 8151 | 23976
Fruit Sprinkles | 9157 | 9213 | 9269 | 27639
Marshmallow Fudgies | 14349 | 14442 | 14535 | 43326
Nut Crunchies | 11568 | 11898 | 12237 | 35703
Grand Total | 42908 | 43544 | 44192 | 130644
Sum of Sales | Period
Product | Jan | Feb | Mar | Grand Total
Chocolate Eclairs | 33161 | 33846 | 34489 | 101496
Fruit Sprinkles | 44624 | 44832 | 45051 | 134507
Marshmallow Fudgies | 59655 | 59514 | 59388 | 178557
Nut Crunchies | 51200 | 51998 | 53328 | 156526
Grand Total | 188640 | 190190 | 192256 | 571086

Fig. 36.7
Pivot tables arrange data in three dimensions, each of which can contain multiple fields.

Creating a Pivot Table

You create pivot tables with the PivotTable Wizard. It involves only a few steps, but it does require you to think about how you want to summarize the data. Consider the data in figure 36.8. This workbook contains time-sheet data for a consulting firm. Each record (row) in this table contains data for the following fields:

Field	Description
Date	The date the work was performed
Staff	The name of the staff person doing the work
Project	The name of the client or project
Work Code	A code indicating the type of work performed
Hours	The number of hours worked

The primary purpose of recording this information is to determine how much to bill the firm's clients for work performed. The information has other uses, though—a manager could use it to evaluate staff performance or to estimate how much longer it will take to complete a project. You'll see shortly how Excel's pivot tables are tailor-made to provide the variety of perspectives on this data required by sound business practices.

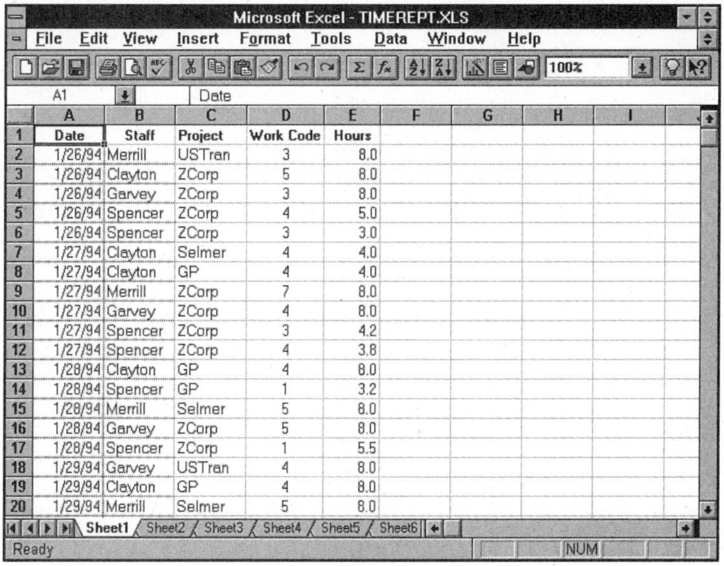

Fig. 36.8
Time-sheet entries in Excel are a good example of a transaction database that can be summarized with a pivot table.

Note

As you follow this initial example, please be aware that it does not cover every option. Any pivot table option not explained in this example will be explained in subsequent examples in this chapter or the next.

To use the PivotTable Wizard to begin creating a pivot table, follow these steps:

1. Choose the **D**ata **P**ivotTable command. This brings up the first dialog box in the PivotTable Wizard (see fig. 36.9). From this point until the pivot table appears in the worksheet, you are working in the PivotTable Wizard.

   The buttons along the bottom enable you to move forward or backward through the PivotTable Wizard:

Button	Result
Help	Displays an explanation of the options for the current screen; close the Help window to return to the normal screen
Cancel	Cancels the PivotTable Wizard and returns to the worksheet

(continues)

Button	Result
< Back	Moves to the preceding dialog box
Next >	Moves to the next dialog box
Finish >	Uses current options and moves to the last dialog box

2. Under the heading Create Pivot Table from data in, you specify the source of the tabular data:

Option	Type of Data
Microsoft Excel List or Database	List or range with labeled columns in an Excel worksheet
External Data Source	Files or tables created in other programs, such as Paradox, dBase, Access, or SQL Server
Multiple **C**onsolidation Ranges	Multiple ranges with labeled rows and columns in Excel worksheets
Another Pivot Table	An existing pivot table within the active workbook

Choose **M**icrosoft Excel List or Database (if it is not already selected); then click Next > to display the second PivotTable Wizard screen (see fig. 36.10).

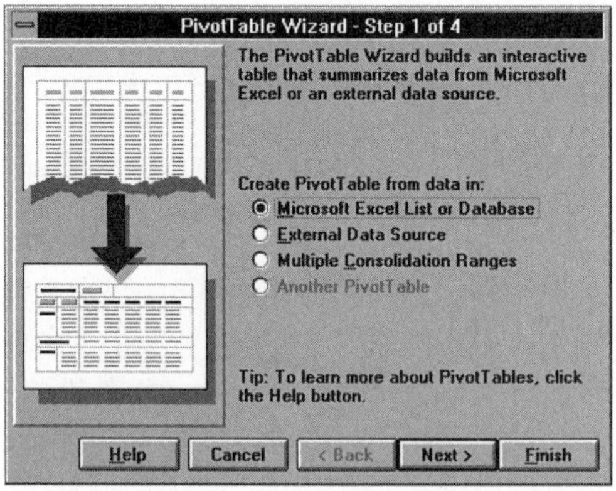

Fig. 36.9
The first screen in the PivotTable Wizard asks you to specify the source of the data you will summarize in the pivot table.

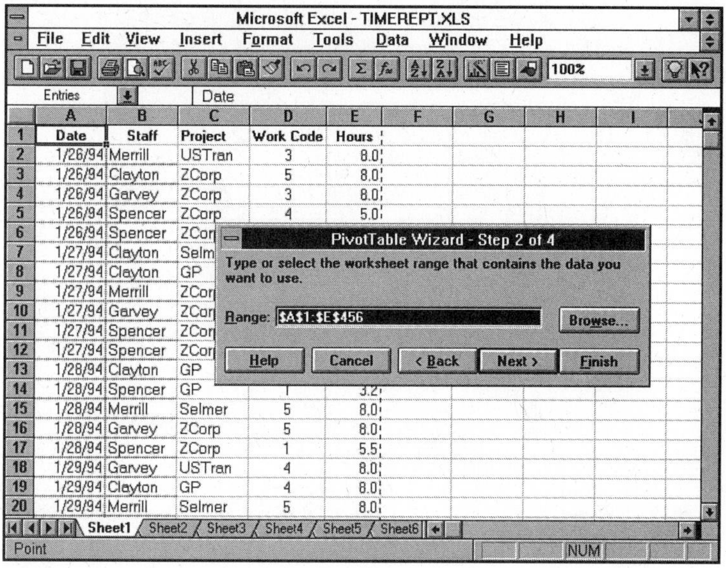

Fig. 36.10
The second PivotTable Wizard step where you select a range.

3. You can enter or select the range that contains the data in the **R**ange box in the Step 2 box of the Wizard. If the active cell is within a range that you named Database, the Wizard selects this range. Choose Next >.

Excel now displays the Step 3 screen of the PivotTable Wizard (see fig. 36.11).

Remember reading about row, column, and page fields earlier in the chapter? This is where you employ those concepts. What you do here controls what data will be displayed and where it is positioned in the table. Do not be intimidated, though; the beauty of pivot tables is that whatever you do here can be modified after you display the table on-screen.

To define the layout and create the pivot table within Step 3 of the Wizard, follow these steps:

1. Determine which field contains the data you want summarized, and then drag the corresponding buttons into the **D**ATA area. You often do not have much choice in this step. In the time-reporting example, the objective is to summarize hours worked. Consequently, the data field must be Hours; you have no logical alternative in this case.

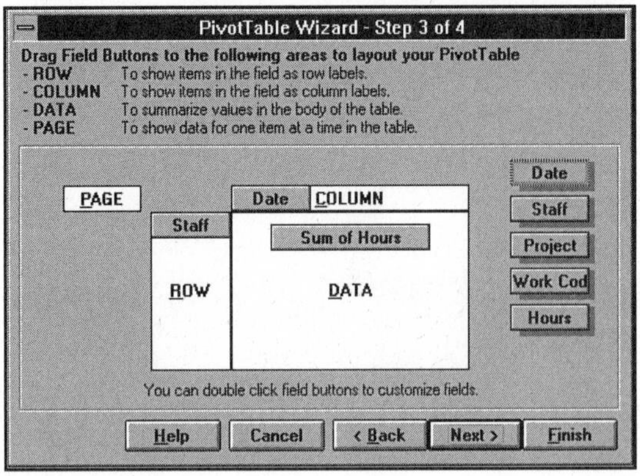

Fig. 36.11
The third PivotTable Wizard screen, where you design the layout by dragging buttons into the **R**OW, **C**OLUMN, **P**AGE, and **D**ATA areas.

2. Determine how you want the data arranged:

   - To arrange the items in a field in *columns*, with labels across the top, drag the button for that field to the **C**OLUMN area. Figure 36.11 needs the hours in columns according to the dates worked, so drag the Date button to the **C**OLUMN area.

   - To arrange the items in a field in *rows*, with labels along the side, drag the button for that field to the **R**OW area. Because figure 36.11 needs a list of all staff members as row headings, the Staff button is dragged to the **R**OW area.

   - The effect of using the **P**AGE area of the screen is explained later in this chapter in the section, "Filtering Data by Creating Page Fields."

   Figure 36.12 illustrates how to lay out a pivot table that creates a summary of the consulting firm's time-reporting data by staff member and date.

3. Choose Next >.

Tip
Putting pivot tables on a separate sheet makes them easier to find and less likely to overwrite other parts of a sheet.

4. In the final PivotTable Wizard screen (see fig. 36.13), you tell Excel where to put the pivot table. You can put the pivot table in any worksheet in any workbook. (Just be careful not to put the table where it might overwrite data.) Enter the upper-left cell of the table in the PivotTable **S**tarting Cell (or click the cell). One option in the final Wizard screen is including totals and subtotals, which Excel usually recommends. If you deselect totals, you can rerun the Wizard later and reselect this option.

You also can save data with the pivot table. Saving the data with the pivot table stores—on the sheet with the pivot table—a copy of the data being analyzed, which has the advantage that the original source needn't be open to change the pivot table. The disadvantages are that the file containing the pivot table can grow very large and that you cannot create a pivot table from a pivot table.

Choose Finish to complete the pivot table.

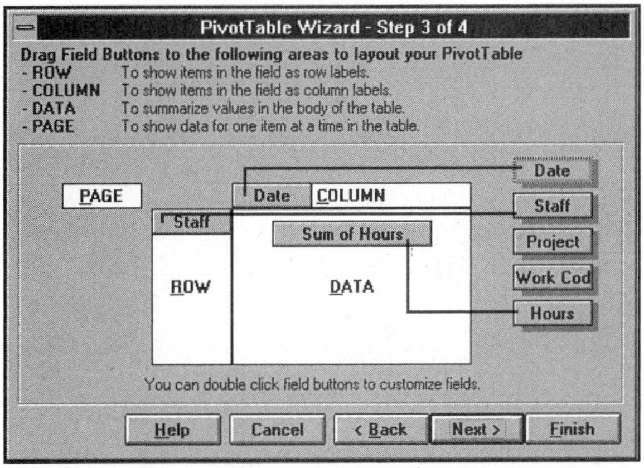

Fig. 36.12
To lay out the pivot table, drag the field buttons into the proper places in the PivotTable Wizard Step 3 screen.

Fig. 36.13
In Step 4 of the PivotTable Wizard, you tell Excel where to put the pivot table and, optionally, change some global options.

Figure 36.14 displays the pivot table resulting from the specifications in figure 36.12.

After you create a pivot table, the Query and Pivot toolbar appears in the document, as shown in figure 36.15. (However, if you previously displayed and removed the Query and Pivot toolbar, Excel will not display it.) You learn how to use this toolbar later in this chapter and in the next chapter.

For Related Information

■ "What Is a List," p. 863

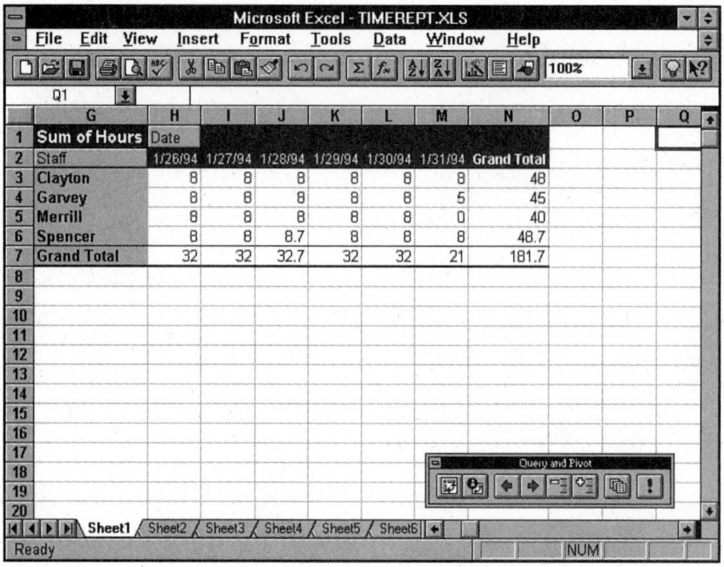

Fig. 36.14
The pivot table resulting from the layout in 36.12. With this report, the payroll department can record hours worked over the past week.

Fig. 36.15
The Query and Pivot toolbar appears after you create a pivot table.

Editing Your Pivot Table

As you learned earlier, pivot tables are devices for displaying information, so amounts appearing in the body of the table cannot be changed. Excel does provide a number of tools to control the type of summary information, as well as the formatting, in the table. (You'll learn how to use those tools in Chapter 37, "Analyzing and Reporting with Pivot Tables.")

Tip
You can change the names of pivot table fields by typing over them.

You can change the names of pivot table fields and items. Simply select the field or item, and type the new name (see fig. 36.16). Naturally, Excel will not let you duplicate names. If you inadvertently enter an existing field or item name, Excel will rearrange the pivot table, moving the item with that name to the location where you typed the name.

Note

Changing field or item names in a pivot table does not change the names in the source list or database.

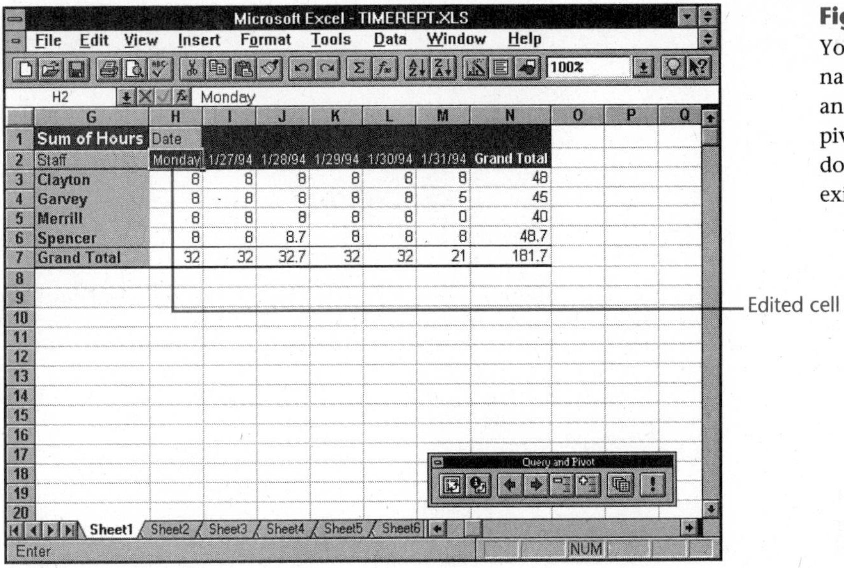

Fig. 36.16
You can type new names for fields and items into pivot tables, if you do not duplicate existing names.

Updating a Pivot Table

The pivot table display does not change when you change the data in the source list or table. You can update, or refresh, the pivot table for the following types of changes to the source data by selecting any cell within the pivot table and clicking the Refresh Data button on the Query and Pivot toolbar:

- Changes to data in a data field
- New or changed items
- Insertions or deletions of fields or items

If you add new fields to the source list, they will not show up in the pivot table unless you display Step 3 of the PivotTable Wizard.

Caution

Updating a pivot table after you add new fields to the source list can expand the size of the pivot table. Leave plenty of "growing room" below and to the right of pivot tables so that you do not overwrite other data in the worksheet. By putting a pivot table on a separate sheet, you alleviate this problem.

Note

Excel will not let you insert rows into an Excel source list if those rows intersect with a pivot table, because Excel protects the integrity of pivot tables. You can, however, insert a range into a source list if the range does not intersect with a pivot table.

If you have changed any field or item names by direct entry into the pivot table, the changes will remain in effect after you update the table.

Sometimes you may want to preserve a pivot table in its current form even though the source data may change in the future. To take a "snapshot" of a pivot table, copy it and paste it to another location by choosing the **E**dit Pas**t**e Special command and then selecting the **V**alues option.

Caution

Refreshing a pivot table removes any formatting applied to the cells in the pivot table, other than formats applied with the **A**utoFormat command on the F**o**rmat menu. For more information, see the section "Formatting the Pivot Table" in the next chapter.

Specifying the Source Data

The example presented in figures 36.7 through 36.16 glosses over some options in step 1 of the PivotTable Wizard, but it is now time to come back to that step. In addition to a list or table in an Excel worksheet, you can use data created in other programs as a source for pivot tables. You can also use multiple lists from one or more Excel worksheets.

Using a List or Database in the Workbook

To create a pivot table from an existing list in the current Excel workbook, select the **M**icrosoft Excel List or Database option in the first PivotTable Wizard screen, if it is not already selected.

The source list must include column labels. Make sure that you include the column labels in the range you enter in step 2 of the PivotTable Wizard. Excel uses the values in the first row of the specified range as field names.

Using a List or Database in Another Workbook

To specify a source list in another workbook, follow these steps:

1. Choose the Browse button in step 2 of the PivotTable Wizard. This opens the Browse dialog box.
2. Select the file containing the list you want, and then choose OK to return to the PivotTable Wizard. The step 2 screen reappears, with the file name in the **R**ange box.
3. Enter the name or the range address of the source list.
4. Choose Next > to complete the remaining screens in the PivotTable Wizard.

Using External Databases

To use an external data source, select the **E**xternal Data Source option in the first PivotTable Wizard screen, and then choose Next > to bring up the step 2 screen, shown in figure 36.17.

Fig. 36.17
The PivotTable Wizard step 2 screen after selecting the **E**xternal Data Source option in step 1.

Choose the **G**et Data button. This starts the Microsoft Query program and displays a dialog box similar to the one shown in figure 36.18.

In Microsoft Query, you perform a series of operations to define the data you want to bring into Excel. Figure 36.19 shows an example query definition table. Finding and retrieving data from other programs using Microsoft Query is explained in detail in Chapter 35, "Retrieving Data from External Databases."

After you have defined your query, choose the **R**eturn Data to Microsoft Excel command from the Microsoft Query **F**ile menu. This returns you to step 2 of the PivotTable Wizard, which resembles figure 36.20.

Updating a pivot table linked to an external data source causes Excel to query the data source again.

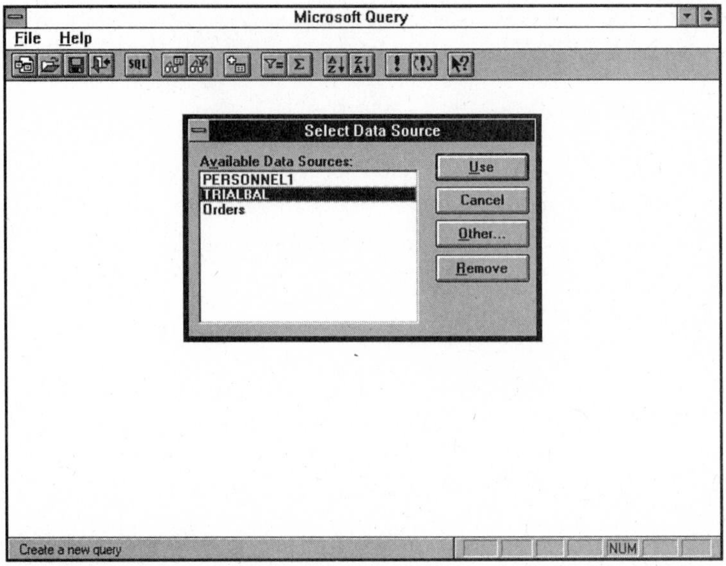

Fig. 36.18
The PivotTable Wizard uses Microsoft Query to retrieve data created in other programs.

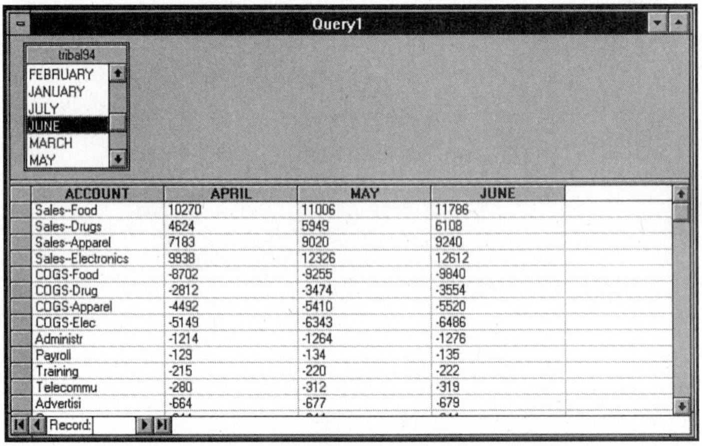

Fig. 36.19
You fill out a query definition table to tell the PivotTable Wizard what data to retrieve from the specified source.

Fig. 36.20
The PivotTable Wizard step 2 screen after querying an external database.

Converting Crosstab Tables from Version 4

If you have created crosstab tables in Excel 4, you probably want to convert these to pivot tables.

To convert a crosstab table to a pivot table, follow these steps:

1. Open the worksheet (created in version 4) that contains the crosstab table.

2. Choose the **D**ata PivotT**a**ble command. This brings up the step 3 screen in the PivotTable Wizard.

3. Complete the remaining steps in the PivotTable Wizard in the usual manner.

> **Caution**
>
> Converting a crosstab table is an irrevocable operation, so make sure that you convert from a copy if you foresee any possible need to use the crosstab table again in version 4 of Excel.

For more information on crosstab tables, refer to Chapter 35, "Retrieving Data from External Databases."

Filtering Data by Creating Page Fields

Since it is humanly impossible to read text and figures in three-dimensions, all the fields you want to see in your pivot tables must be shoehorned into either the row or column position during step 3 of the PivotTable Wizard.

You can, however, set up a third dimension to provide additional flexibility in examining the data. Creating a page field creates a viewing filter of sorts. To see how this works, look first at the pivot table in figure 36.21. This pivot table does not display the Work Code or Project field names. That is because the displayed data reflects the hours spent on all work codes and all projects.

To add the option of flipping through the projects or work codes to display the amounts for any individual item in either of these fields, you create a page field.

To create a page field when you create a pivot table, follow these steps:

1. Start the PivotTable Wizard and complete steps 1 and 2 of the PivotTable Wizard's four steps.

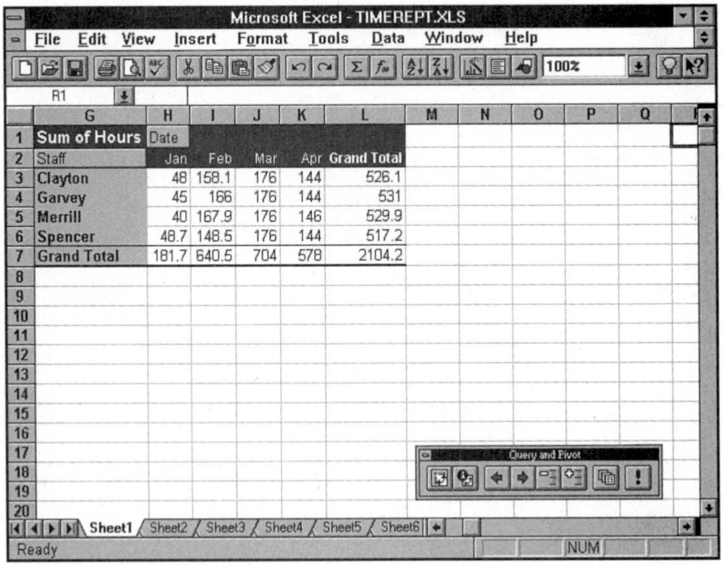

Fig. 36.21
The total time from individual staff members is shown by date worked, but detailed information by project or work code is not available on this pivot table.

2. In the PivotTable Wizard's step 3 screen, move the field you want to filter to the **P**age area. This can be a field not previously displayed, or one displayed in the row or column position.

3. Choose OK, and then continue with the remaining screens in the PivotTable Wizard.

After you add a page field, the pivot table looks like figure 36.22, which displays only the hours for the ZCorp project.

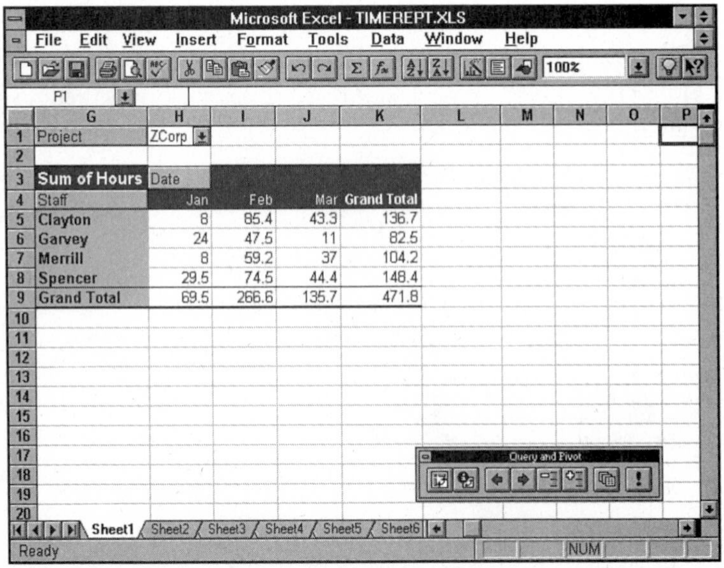

Fig. 36.22
The same pivot table as in figure 36.21, after adding Project as a page field and selecting the ZCorp project from the list in the page field.

Clicking the arrow in the page field displays a list of all items in the page field along with a selection for totals, as shown in the figure. Simply select the item you want to view, and the pivot table displays that page.

For Related Information

- "Using the AutoFilter," p. 913
- "Paging or Filtering a Pivot Table," p. 1028

Consolidating Data Using a Pivot Table

Often, the data you wish to summarize is located in more than one range—sometimes even in several different worksheets. If the ranges have a similar structure, and common row and column labels, you can group them together for analysis in a single pivot table.

Figure 36.23 shows a workbook with regional sales information for a snack food company. The figures for the regions are contained in separate sheets, which are named after the respective regions.

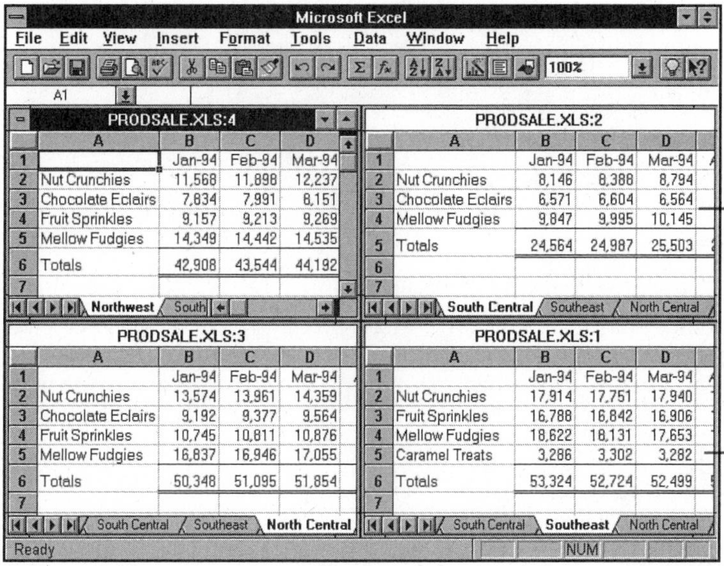

Fig. 36.23
Each sheet in this workbook contains sales figures for a different region. You can create a pivot table that consolidates this data.

The data to be consolidated does not have to reside in separate sheets; you can consolidate data in separate ranges in a single sheet, in separate sheets, or in a combination of both locations.

Using a pivot table, you can consolidate data from multiple ranges. This is similar to using the **D**ata Co**n**solidate command; an advantage is that you can manipulate the pivot table to view the results of the consolidation in a variety of ways.

To create a pivot table from multiple worksheet ranges, start the PivotTable Wizard, and then select the Multiple **C**onsolidation Ranges option. This brings up the step 2a screen (see fig. 36.24). You can have Excel create a single page field, or you can create the page field(s) yourself.

To create a pivot table from multiple worksheet ranges, with Excel creating the page field automatically, follow these steps:

1. In step 2a, select the **C**reate a single page field for me option button, and then choose Next >.

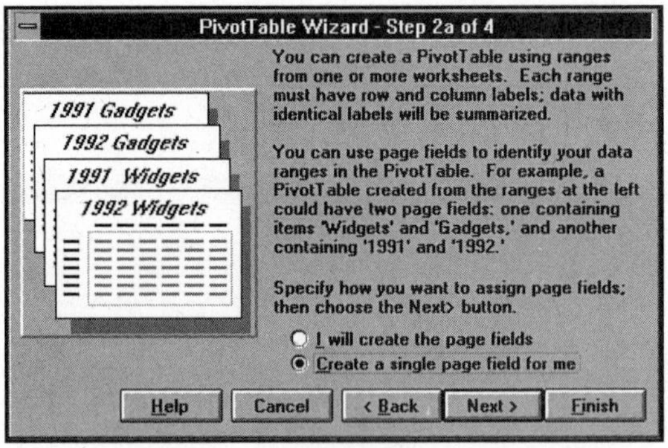

Fig. 36.24 When you use multiple source ranges, selecting Create a single page field for me in step 2a of the PivotTable Wizard automatically assigns the ranges to a page field.

2. Excel displays step 2b of the PivotTable Wizard. Enter or select all the source ranges (selecting the ranges usually is faster). After you select each range, choose **A**dd; the selected range is added to the A**l**l Ranges list. Figure 36.25 shows the dialog box after all the ranges displayed in figure 36.23 have been added.

   Choose Next >.

Caution

If your source ranges include totals, do not include the total rows or columns when you select the ranges; this causes the PivotTable Wizard to include the totals as items in the pivot table. This is why, in the example, only the first four rows in the South Cental region worksheet are selected.

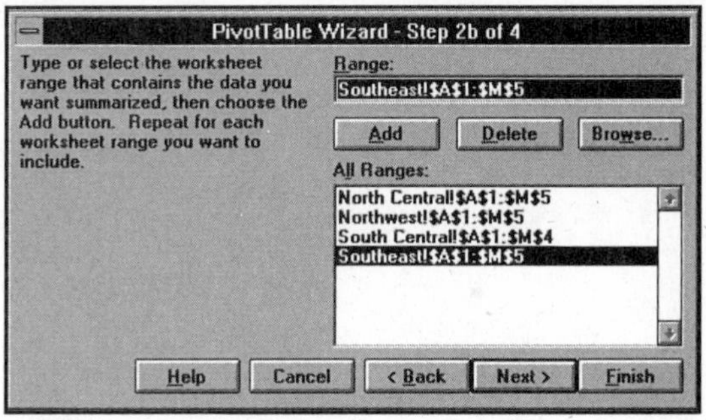

Fig. 36.25
Adding source ranges in the PivotTable Wizard.

3. In step 3 of the PivotTable Wizard, choose Next > to accept the default field positions. When you use multiple source ranges, Excel does not have the information it needs to determine the field names, so it uses generic descriptions ("Page1," "Row," and so on). You can specify field names later.

4. Complete step 4 of the PivotTable Wizard in the usual manner, and choose **F**inish to create the pivot table.

Figure 36.26 shows the pivot table created from the example data. Now you can enter field names in the appropriate cells. The following table lists the changes you would make to the pivot table in the example:

Field Name To Replace	Cell	New Field Name
Page1	A1	Region
Column	B3	Period
Row	A4	Product

Click the arrow in cell B1. Instead of displaying the names of the regions, Excel displays placeholder names—Item1, Item2, and so on. When Excel creates the page field, you save some time initially, but you have to replace the placeholders with meaningful names—in this case, the names of the four regions. Naturally, this would be very time consuming if your pivot table contains numerous items.

If you expect to use the resulting pivot table extensively, you should select the **I** will create the page fields option button in step 2a of the PivotTable Wizard. In that event, step 2b of the PivotTable Wizard displays a dialog box where you assign names to each item in the field.

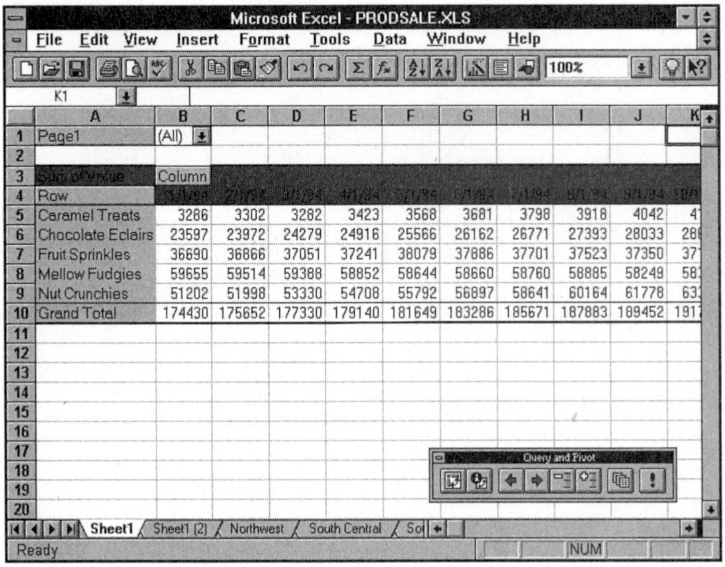

Fig. 36.26
The pivot table created from the multiple source ranges shown in figure 36.23.

To view consolidated totals, choose the (All) option from the list adjacent to the page field button. This displays all five products, including Caramel Treats (which is sold only in the Southeast). The PivotTable Wizard uses the same intelligent consolidation method as the **D**ata Co**n**solidate command (for more information on consolidating, see Chapter 25, "Linking, Embedding, and Consolidating Worksheets"). The PivotTable Wizard, however, reads the text labels and aggregates the totals correctly according to the text labels, not the cell addresses.

To select the page fields yourself while creating a pivot table, follow these steps:

1. In step 2a of the PivotTable Wizard, select the **I** will create the page fields option button.

2. In step 2b (see fig. 36.27), enter or select all the source ranges, and add them to the A**l**l Ranges list as explained in the previous example.

3. Select the **1** option button just below the A**l**l Ranges box to indicate that you want one page field. (To create two or more page fields, select the appropriate option, or select **0** if you do not want a page field.)

4. For each of the ranges in the A**l**l Ranges list, select the range, and then type a label for it in the Field **O**ne box. When you have entered labels for the appropriate number of ranges, choose Next >.

For Related Information

■ "Consolidating Worksheets," p. 763

5. Complete the rest of the PivotTable Wizard screens in the usual manner.

When Excel creates the pivot table, your labels for the ranges are included in the pull-down list adjacent to the Page1 button.

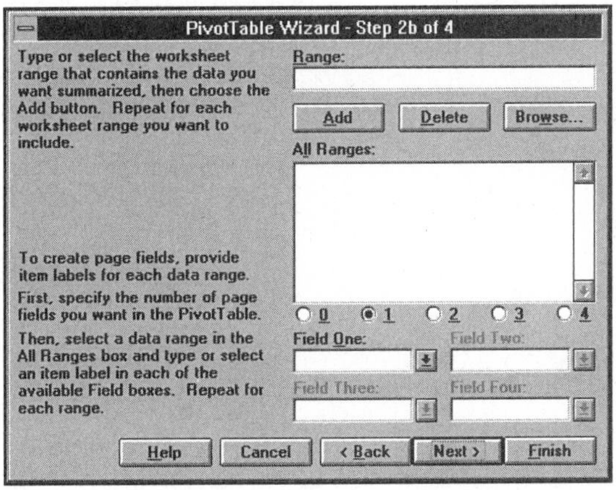

Fig. 36.27
In step 2b of the PivotTable Wizard, you specify how many page fields to include in the pivot table, and enter labels for the individual items.

Using More Than One Data Field

In all the examples so far, the data field label (located above the row heading and to the left of the column heading) has shown the type of summary calculation (such as Sum of) and the name of a data field (such as Hours). This indicates that the pivot table contains only one data field.

You can include more than one data field in step 3 of the PivotTable Wizard. In the time reporting example, for instance, you might want to view the chargeable dollars along with the hours spent on projects. When a pivot table has more than one data field, the data field label does not appear. Instead, the pivot table displays a Data button, and labels for each data field. Figure 36.28 shows a pivot table with two data fields, Hours and Dollars. Notice the Data button in cell H2.

Chapter 37, "Analyzing and Reporting with Pivot Tables," contains information related to the specific task of adding fields to pivot tables.

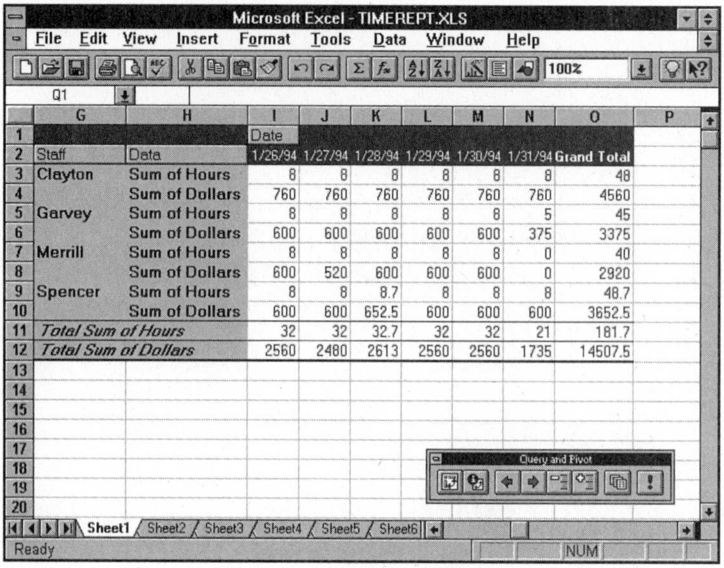

Microsoft Excel - TIMEREPT.XLS
File Edit View Insert Format Tools Data Window Help
100%
Q1
G H I J K L M N O P
Date
Staff Data 1/26/94 1/27/94 1/28/94 1/29/94 1/30/94 1/31/94 Grand Total
Clayton Sum of Hours 8 8 8 8 8 8 48
Sum of Dollars 760 760 760 760 760 760 4560
Garvey Sum of Hours 8 8 8 8 8 5 45
Sum of Dollars 600 600 600 600 600 375 3375
Merrill Sum of Hours 8 8 8 8 8 0 40
Sum of Dollars 600 520 600 600 600 0 2920
Spencer Sum of Hours 8 8 8.7 8 8 8 48.7
Sum of Dollars 600 600 652.5 600 600 600 3652.5
Total Sum of Hours 32 32 32.7 32 32 21 181.7
Total Sum of Dollars 2560 2480 2613 2560 2560 1735 14507.5
Query and Pivot
Sheet1 Sheet2 Sheet3 Sheet4 Sheet5 Sheet6
Ready
NUM

Fig. 36.28
A pivot table with two data fields, Hours and Dollars, displayed in the row position.

Creating a Pivot Table from Another Pivot Table

Pivot tables can become complex if you decide to display much detail—so complex that you might want to summarize the data further by creating a pivot table based on the existing pivot table.

Tip
To create one pivot table from another, you must have selected the Save **D**ata with Table Layout check box in the PivotTable Wizard.

To create a pivot table using source data in another pivot table in the same workbook, follow these steps:

1. Make sure that no part of a pivot table is selected. (If the active selection includes any part of a pivot table, Excel will assume you want to make changes to that pivot table.)

2. Start the Pivot Table Wizard.

3. Select the **A**nother Pivot Table option, and then choose Next >. The PivotTable Wizard displays a list of pivot tables in the active workbook.

4. Select the pivot table you want to use as your data source, and then choose Next >.

5. Complete the remaining screens in the PivotTable Wizard in the usual manner.

Excel creates the second pivot table in the location you specify. The two pivot tables are updated simultaneously whenever you refresh either of them.

To create a pivot table using source data from a pivot table in another workbook, copy the existing pivot table into the current workbook. The copied data, if it meets the definition of a list, can be used as a source list for a new pivot table. You should know, however, that the new pivot table loses any links to the original source data that exist for the old pivot table. As a result, you are not able to manipulate the new pivot table as you would if the source data resided in the same workbook.

Creating a Chart from a Pivot Table

You can create a chart linked to a pivot table. The chart changes dynamically as you change the layout of your pivot table. Figure 36.29 shows a pivot table and a chart created from that table.

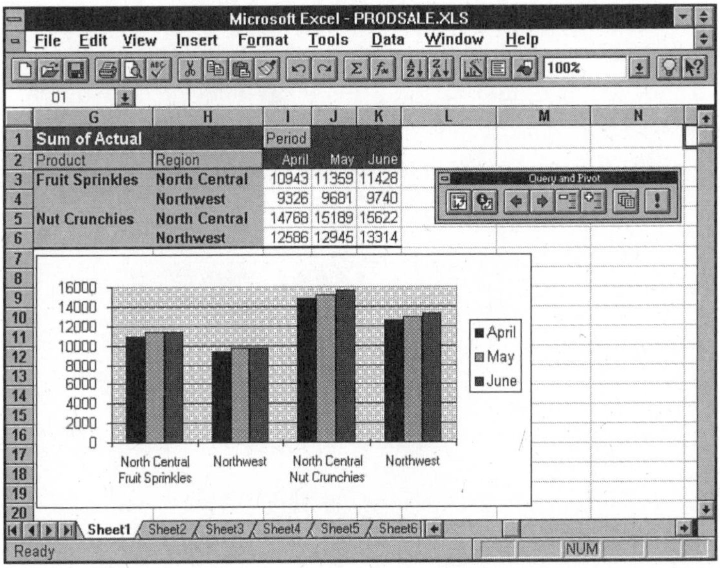

Fig. 36.29
This chart was created from the pivottable above it.

Notice that this pivot table has two row fields and one column field. In such cases, Excel displays the items in the row fields along the category (X) axis of the chart. It groups the chart series according to the grouping in the pivot table (first Fruit Sprinkles, and then Nut Crunchies).

Whichever field type (row or column) has the greater number of fields is assigned to the category axis. To avoid confusion, use at most two row fields and two column fields in pivot tables from which you plan to create charts.

To create a chart from a pivot table, follow these steps:

1. Select the pivot table. As you do so, avoid selecting any columns containing totals. You must also avoid dragging any of the field tabs, or Excel will think that you want to move the row field.

2. Click the ChartWizard button on the Standard toolbar. Follow the instructions in the ChartWizard screens.

The ChartWizard does not display items in page fields on a chart. However, if you select an item in a page field, a chart created from the pivot table changes dynamically to display the data for the selected item.

For Related Information

- "Creating an Embedded Chart," p.407 and "Creating a Chart Automatically," p. 415
- "Analyzing Pivot Table Data with Charts," p. 1027

Saving Files with Pivot Tables

Sometimes files with pivot tables are surprisingly large. This is because Excel creates a copy of the source data, and stores it as hidden data with the worksheet that contains the pivot table. If your pivot table references a large amount of data in another file, you store the same data twice whenever you save the file that contains the pivot table.

> **Caution**
>
> If you are working with a pivot table linked to a large list in an Excel worksheet, consider putting the pivot table in a separate workbook and linking to a closed sheet to conserve memory.

To avoid this, deselect the Save **D**ata With Table Layout check box in step 4 of the PivotTable Wizard. Excel then saves the pivot table layout, but omits the copy of the source data. When you make changes to—or refresh—the pivot table, Excel updates it directly from the source data. Pivot tables that have this check box deselected cannot be used as a source for other pivot tables.

Troubleshooting

Step 3 of the PivotTable Wizard displays numbers and nonsensical field names.

You didn't include the row with the field names when you specified the source range in step 2. Choose the Back button and redefine the range.

Excel displays a `PivotTable field name not valid` *message.*

In defining the range containing your source data, you have included a column that has an invalid field name. This happens most often when you inadvertently select a blank column in defining the range in step 2.

The pivot table shows values of "1" in every cell.

Most likely, the pivot table is showing a count of the items rather than the sum, average, or other summary function you want. See the section, "Analyzing the Data," in Chapter 37 for instructions on changing the summary function in a pivot table.

The pivot table is empty (or nearly empty).

This happens when your pivot table contains at least one page field for which the value of the first item in the field is blank or zero. To see if this is true, select (All) in the page field list, and notice whether the pivot table displays more values.

From Here...

For information relating directly to pivot tables, review the following chapter:

- Chapter 37, "Analyzing and Reporting with Pivot Tables." You learn how to change the layout of pivot tables to critically analyze the data and format the data to make it easier to read and to understand.

Chapter 37

Analyzing and Reporting with Pivot Tables

The concept of breaking things down and separating them into components is inherent in the term *analysis*. Just as an aspiring automobile mechanic learns how an engine works by taking it apart and reassembling it, you "break down" the data and reassemble it in different ways as you strive to discern the operative forces that underlie the data.

EXCEL 5

In this chapter, you learn how to:

- Group detailed breakdowns in pivot tables into summary and subtotal figures
- Narrow your view of summary data to dig out important details
- Display different summary calculations (such as totals, averages and changes over time) for the same data

In the example presented in Chapter 36, the billing department needs the data broken down in a certain way so it can create invoices for clients. On the other hand, project managers, cost accounting, and payroll need their own particular breakdowns of the time data.

In many organizations, relational databases and accounting programs provide sufficient management reports and summaries for users to carry out their routine duties. But when you need up-to-the-minute information for important decisions, or when you have to look at the data a number of ways to enrich your understanding, bring it into an Excel pivot table.

Adding and Removing Data

When you are seeking "the truth, the whole truth, and nothing but the truth," your first task is to determine what data is worth viewing. Excel has several convenient methods for adding or deleting data categories and items.

To master data analysis in pivot tables, you must understand how fields fit into the row, column, and page positions (see fig. 37.1). A field is not a row, column, or page field by nature. The Project field in figure 37.1 is a page field only because it was defined as such in the PivotTable Wizard, or because it was positioned there after the pivot table was created. As you will see in the section, "Reorganizing the Pivot Table," dragging a field to a different position changes the layout of the pivot table.

Fig. 37.1
Positions of fields in pivot tables.

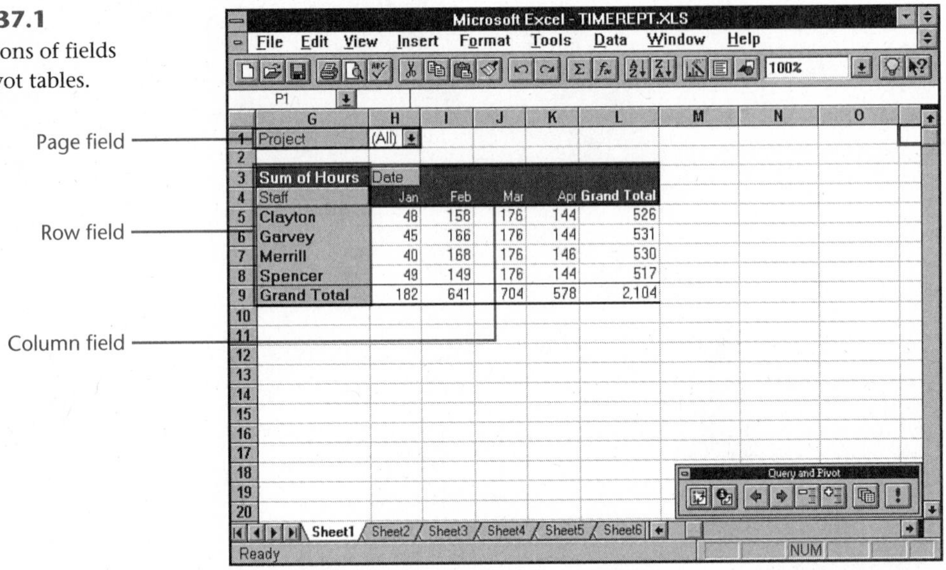

As you continue through this chapter, notice that the amounts in most of the diagrams are rounded to even numbers, whereas your pivot tables might display decimals. The pivot tables were formatted so the examples would be clearer.

Adding New Rows, Columns, or Pages

To enhance the amount of detail available in a pivot table, you add more fields. Adding row and column fields expands the pivot table and widens the view. In contrast, adding a page field narrows the scope and helps you zero in on details.

To add a row, column, or page field to a pivot table, follow these steps:

1. Select a cell in the pivot table.

2. Click the PivotTable Wizard button in the Query and Pivot toolbar.

3. In the PivotTable Wizard step 3 screen, move the button for the desired field to the appropriate area (**R**OW, **C**OLUMN, or **P**AGE), as illustrated in figure 37.2.

4. Choose **F**inish.

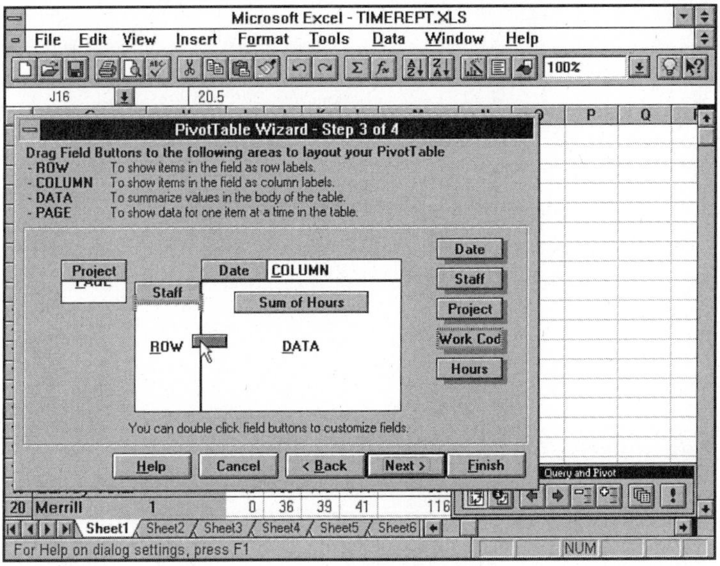

Fig. 37.2
To add a field, move the field button to the appropriate area of the step 3 screen, as shown on the left.

Figure 37.3 indicates the added field in the pivot table.

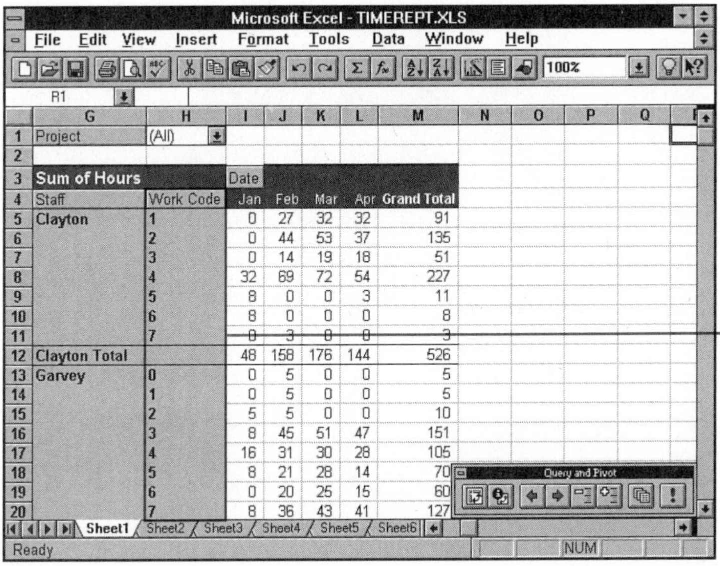

Fig. 37.3
The pivot table after adding the Work Code field.

> **Note**
>
> A quicker way to add a row or column field is to double-click an item in a row or column field in the pivot table. If the pivot table already contains more than one field in that (row or column) position, make sure you double-click the innermost field.

Removing Rows, Columns, or Pages

To remove a row, column, or page field, drag it outside the boundaries of the pivot table. A large X appears on the field as you drag it. When you release the button, the field disappears from the pivot table.

Alternatively, you can select a cell in the field, click the PivotTable Field button in the Query and Pivot toolbar, and choose **D**elete.

Adding Data To Analyze

Sometimes you want to look at more than one kind of data. You might want to see unit sales and dollar sales, verbal and math test scores, or blood pressure and cholesterol levels. Figure 37.4 shows a pivot table with two data fields.

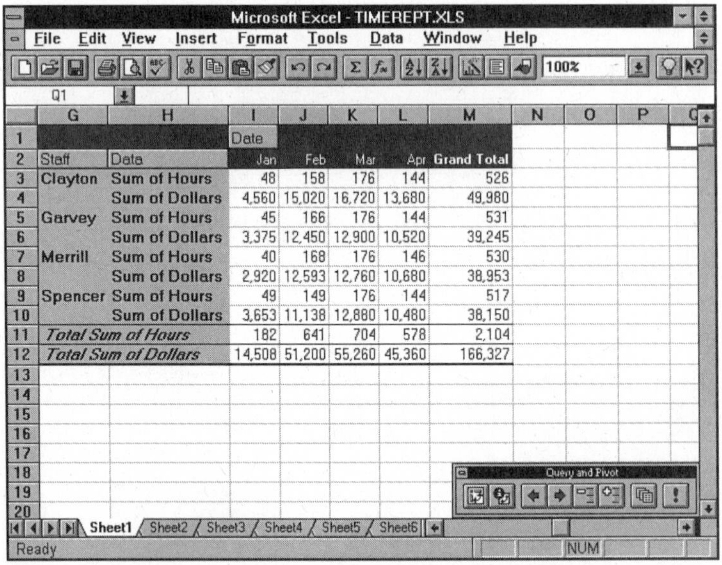

Staff	Data	Jan	Feb	Mar	Apr	Grand Total
Clayton	Sum of Hours	48	158	176	144	526
	Sum of Dollars	4,560	15,020	16,720	13,680	49,980
Garvey	Sum of Hours	45	166	176	144	531
	Sum of Dollars	3,375	12,450	12,900	10,520	39,245
Merrill	Sum of Hours	40	168	176	146	530
	Sum of Dollars	2,920	12,593	12,760	10,680	38,953
Spencer	Sum of Hours	49	149	176	144	517
	Sum of Dollars	3,653	11,138	12,880	10,480	38,150
Total Sum of Hours		182	641	704	578	2,104
Total Sum of Dollars		14,508	51,200	55,260	45,360	166,327

Fig. 37.4
A pivot table with two data fields.

Tip
Add a data field by double-clicking on a row or column field then selecting the field you want to add from the dialog box that appears.

To add another data field to a pivot table, follow these steps:

1. Select a cell in the pivot table.

2. Click the PivotTable Wizard button on the Query and Pivot toolbar.

3. In the PivotTable Wizard step 3 screen, move the button for the data field you want to add to the **D**ATA area.

4. Choose **F**inish.

Reorganizing the Pivot Table

Another way to break down data in a pivot table is to change the orientation of the table. You do this by dragging the field tabs into different positions. This enables you to examine selected cross-sections of the data.

Flipping the Orientation

Suppose you are a project manager for a consulting firm. You are trying to find the right staff people to work on a project, and you are looking at the pivot table shown in figure 37.5. In its current form, the pivot table won't provide the information you need to hunt down qualified staffers because you are primarily interested in the hours your people have spent on certain activities. You want to see a breakdown by staff and work code.

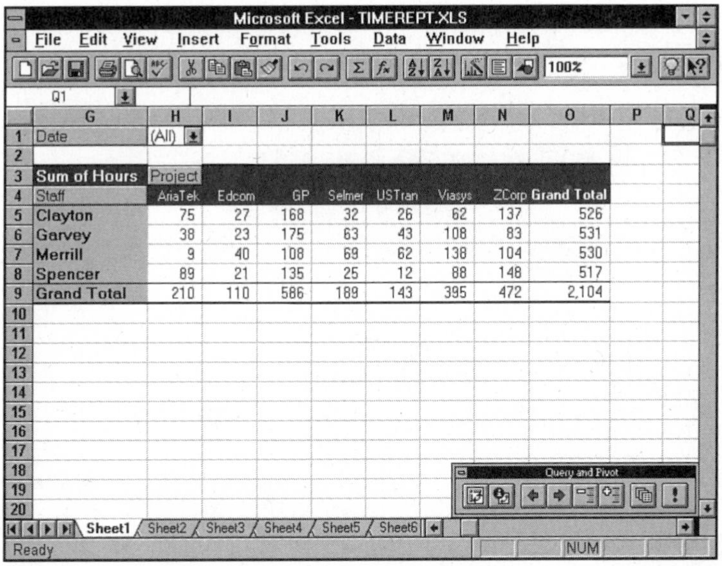

Fig. 37.5
A pivot table showing hours worked by staff and project.

To move a pivot table field, drag the row, column, or page field to the desired position. As you do so, an *insert marker* appears. The shape of the marker depends on the position. Figure 37.6 shows a row field being moved to the column position. When the insert marker appears, release the mouse button.

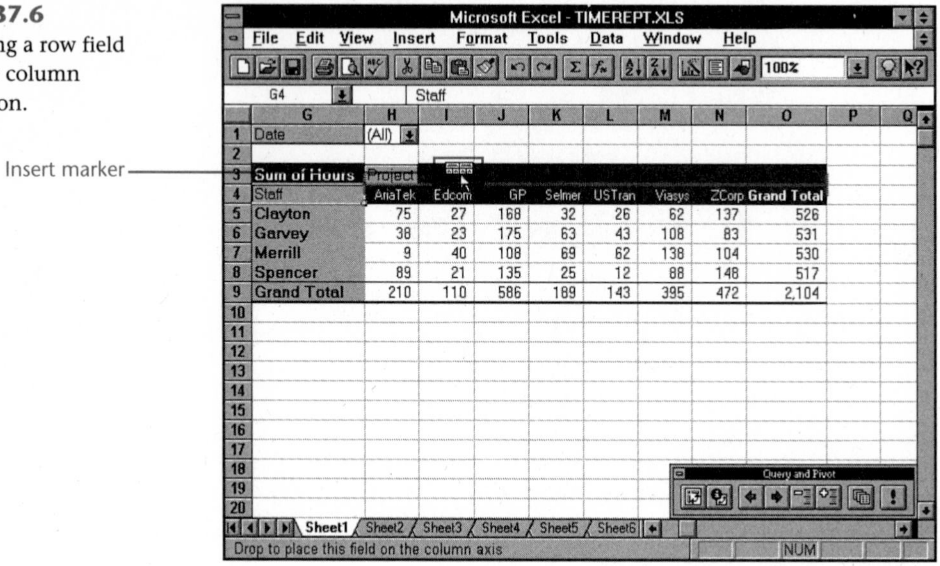

Fig. 37.6
Moving a row field to the column position.

To reorient the pivot table in figure 37.5 to show work codes across the top, follow these steps:

1. Drag the Work Code field tab from the page position to the column position. The pivot table becomes very wide and shallow.

2. Drag the Project field tab to the page position. When the insert marker changes to an image of rectangles stacked in a staggered fashion, release the button.

3. Select (All) from the page field.

The time reporting pivot table now looks like figure 37.7.

Moving Individual Items within a Field

To change the sequence of items in a pivot table, drag them into the desired positions.

To move an item in a pivot table, simply drag the item label to another location within the same field. As you drag, a gray border appears around the item. When the border is properly positioned, release the button. Excel inserts the selected item—carrying its data with it—in the target location, moving subsequent items down or to the right.

You can also sort items in a pivot table. Please see the section "Sorting Items" later in this chapter.

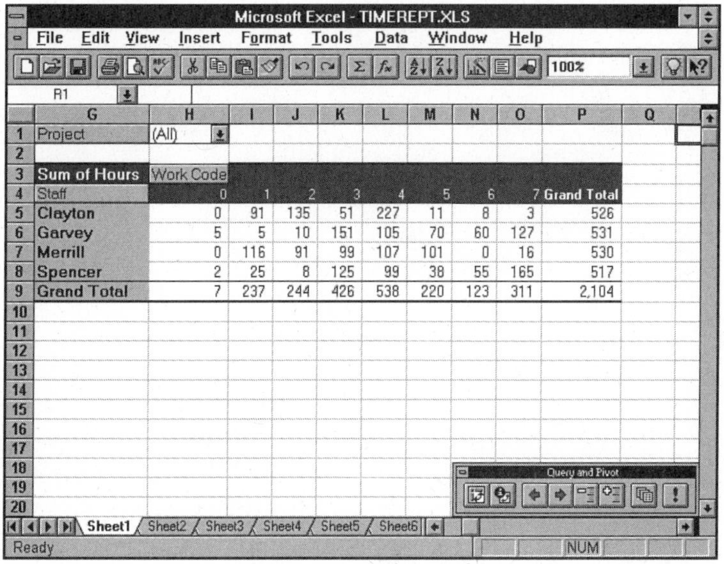

Fig. 37.7
The pivot table from figure 37.5, after rearranging the layout to show Work Codes as the row field.

V

Managing Lists

Moving Data Fields

Ordinarily, you cannot move data fields to the row, column, or page position. However, when a pivot table contains more than one data field, you can drag the Data button from the row position to the column position and vice versa. Figure 37.8 shows the time-reporting pivot table with the data fields (Hours and Dollars) displayed in a row orientation. Figure 37.9 shows the same pivot table with the data fields in a column orientation.

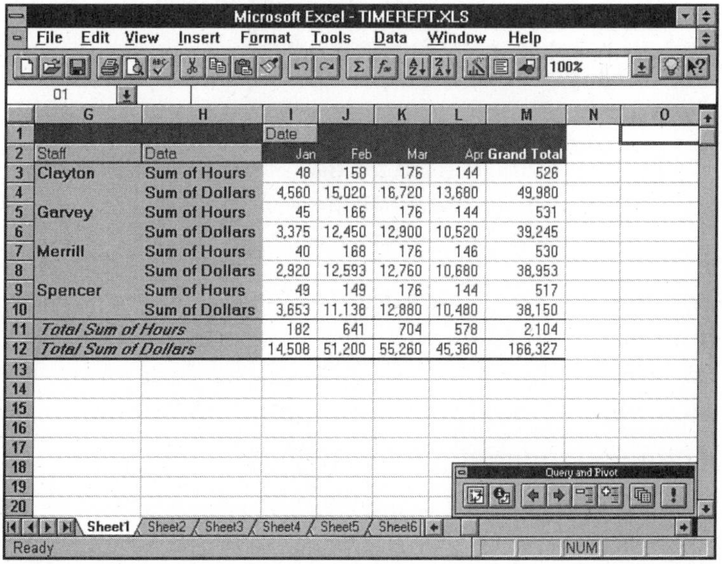

Microsoft Excel - TIMEREPT.XLS
File Edit View Insert Format Tools Data Window Help
100%
O1
G H I J K L M N O
1 Date
2 Staff Data Jan Feb Mar Apr Grand Total
3 Clayton Sum of Hours 48 158 176 144 526
4 Sum of Dollars 4,560 15,020 16,720 13,680 49,980
5 Garvey Sum of Hours 45 166 176 144 531
6 Sum of Dollars 3,375 12,450 12,900 10,520 39,245
7 Merrill Sum of Hours 40 168 176 146 530
8 Sum of Dollars 2,920 12,593 12,760 10,680 38,953
9 Spencer Sum of Hours 49 149 176 144 517
10 Sum of Dollars 3,653 11,138 12,880 10,480 38,150
11 Total Sum of Hours 182 641 704 578 2,104
12 Total Sum of Dollars 14,508 51,200 55,260 45,360 166,327
Query and Pivot
Sheet1 Sheet2 Sheet3 Sheet4 Sheet5 Sheet6
Ready
NUM

Fig. 37.8
This pivot table displays multiple data fields in a row orientation.

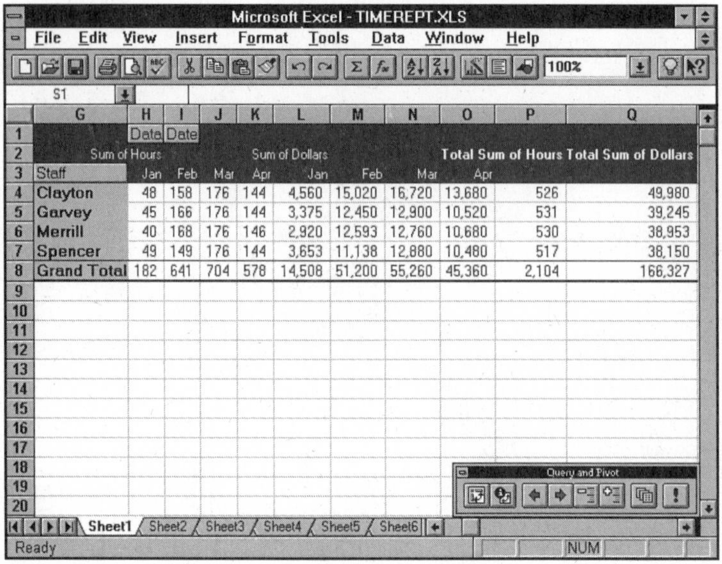

	G	H	I	J	K	L	M	N	O	P	Q
1		Data	Date								
2		Sum of Hours				Sum of Dollars				Total Sum of Hours	Total Sum of Dollars
3	Staff	Jan	Feb	Mar	Apr	Jan	Feb	Mar	Apr		
4	Clayton	48	158	176	144	4,560	15,020	16,720	13,680	526	49,980
5	Garvey	45	166	176	144	3,375	12,450	12,900	10,520	531	39,245
6	Merrill	40	168	176	146	2,920	12,593	12,760	10,680	530	38,953
7	Spencer	49	149	176	144	3,653	11,138	12,880	10,480	517	38,150
8	Grand Total	182	641	704	578	14,508	51,200	55,260	45,360	2,104	166,327

Fig. 37.9 After you move the Data button into the column position, the pivot table displays multiple data fields in a column orientation.

Instead of displaying multiple data fields, you can show multiple summary calculations for a single data field. You learn how to do this in the section "Using Custom Calculations" later in this chapter.

Grouping Items

Occasionally you might have to sift through large quantities of organized data, such as financial results for a large company, or demographic data from a national survey. To properly analyze such information, you have to determine the level you can work with best. Whether you need a lot of detail, or want to see the overall picture, Excel's pivot tables give you the means to view only the data you need.

Grouping Items by Their Labels. Consider a large retailer with stores in several countries. At the highest level, it tracks results by country. Each country—the United States, for instance—is divided into several regions. Each region contains several states, and the company has numerous stores in every state. Store, state, region, country, and company are *aggregation levels* arranged in a hierarchy—with the company at the highest level. You define these grouping levels in the pivot table.

To group several items into a higher level category, follow these steps:

1. Multiple-select the items (within the same field) you want to group together. (The best way to do this is to select one item and then hold down the Ctrl key as you click additional items.)

2. Click the Group button on the Query and Pivot toolbar. Excel adds the new group field to the pivot table and inserts place holder labels for the new items.

3. Replace the place holder labels with labels for each of the new groups.

Figure 37.10 shows a pivot table with a group field for work codes added.

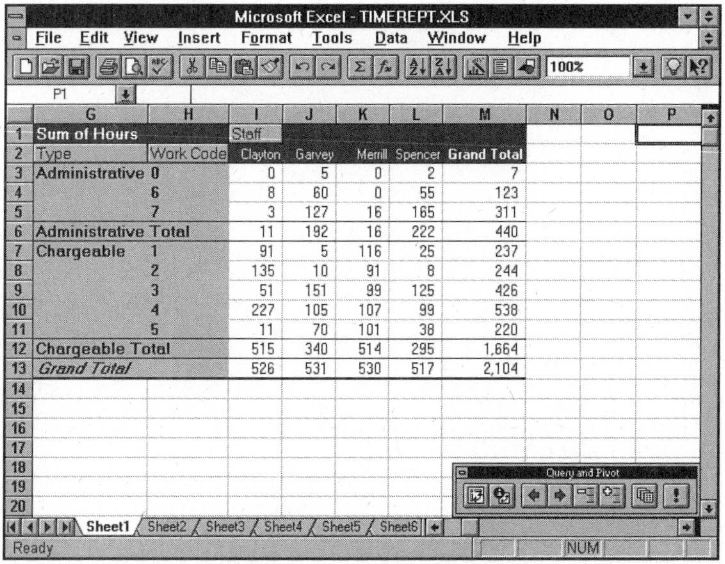

	G	H	I	J	K	L	M
1	Sum of Hours		Staff				
2	Type	Work Code	Clayton	Garvey	Merrill	Spencer	Grand Total
3	Administrative	0	0	5	0	2	7
4		6	8	60	0	55	123
5		7	3	127	16	165	311
6	Administrative Total		11	192	16	222	440
7	Chargeable	1	91	5	116	25	237
8		2	135	10	91	8	244
9		3	51	151	99	125	426
10		4	227	105	107	99	538
11		5	11	70	101	38	220
12	Chargeable Total		515	340	514	295	1,664
13	*Grand Total*		526	531	530	517	2,104

Fig. 37.10
You can group items in the same field together. This pivot table aggregates subtotals for administrative time and chargeable time.

Note

Excel cannot infer groupings from the source data. Even if your source list has fields for both city and state, Excel cannot automatically group the cities by state; you have to create the state groups yourself.

Hiding and Redisplaying Detail. It's helpful to begin the process of analysis by viewing summary figures. After you have acquired the big picture, you can work your way down to a more detailed level. Excel offers a quick method for moving between detail and summary views.

You can hide or show detail in pivot table groupings. A grouping may consist of several items you have grouped together, or it can be the outermost field within a position (row or column). The higher level groupings, or *summary items,* are located at the upper or outer edge of the pivot table. In figure 37.10, the summary items are the group fields Administrative and Chargeable. In figure 37.11, the Staff field is a summary item.

Fig. 37.11
In this pivot table, the Staff field is a summary item. The work code detail can be displayed or hidden.

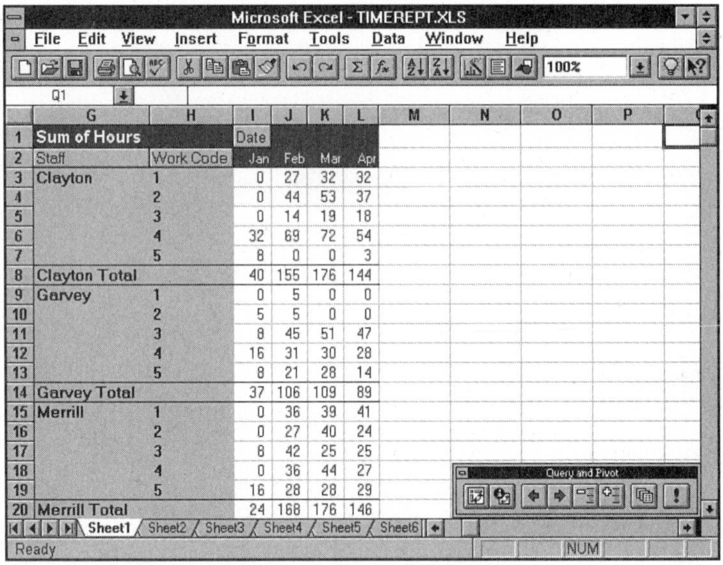

To hide the detail items in a summary item, double-click the item in the outer row (or column) field. Double-clicking Clayton and Garvey in succession, for example, collapses the detail for those groups, as shown in figure 37.12.

Fig. 37.12
The pivot table in figure 37.11 after hiding the detail for Clayton and Garvey.

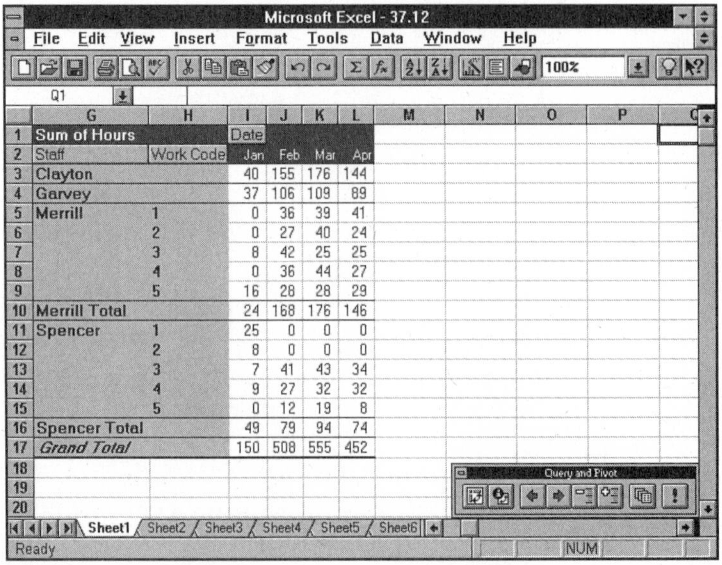

You also can hide detail in a pivot table such as the one in figure 37.13, which contains three geographic grouping levels (Region, State, and City). Double-clicking the summary item Pennsylvania in the State field yields the pivot table shown in 37.14.

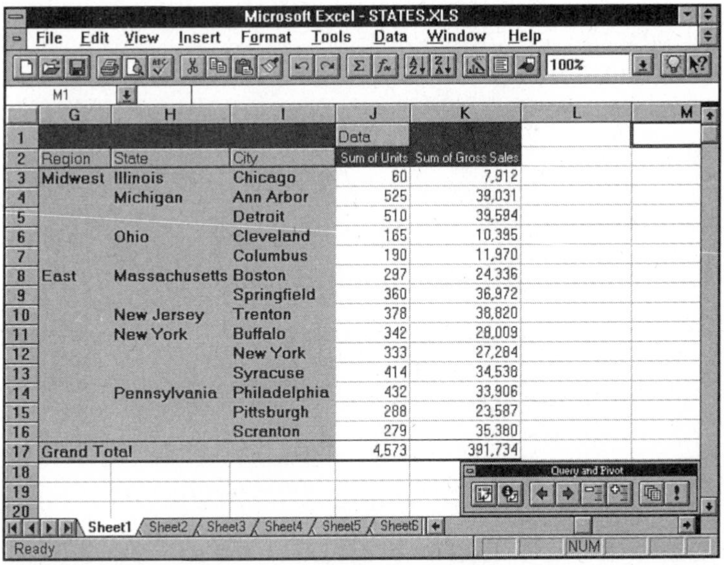

Region	State	City	Sum of Units	Sum of Gross Sales
Midwest	Illinois	Chicago	60	7,912
	Michigan	Ann Arbor	525	39,031
		Detroit	510	39,594
	Ohio	Cleveland	165	10,395
		Columbus	190	11,970
East	Massachusetts	Boston	297	24,336
		Springfield	360	36,972
	New Jersey	Trenton	378	38,820
	New York	Buffalo	342	28,009
		New York	333	27,284
		Syracuse	414	34,538
	Pennsylvania	Philadelphia	432	33,906
		Pittsburgh	288	23,587
		Scranton	279	35,380
Grand Total			4,573	391,734

Fig. 37.13
In this pivot table, results for cities are grouped by state, and the states are grouped by region.

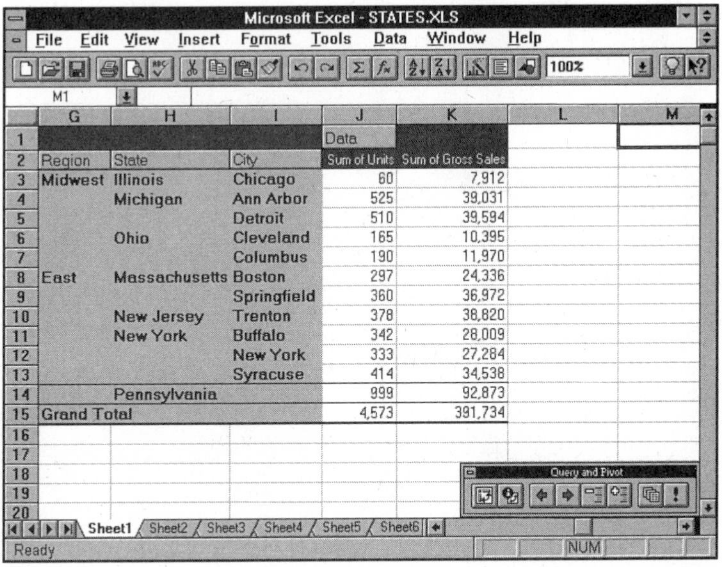

Region	State	City	Sum of Units	Sum of Gross Sales
Midwest	Illinois	Chicago	60	7,912
	Michigan	Ann Arbor	525	39,031
		Detroit	510	39,594
	Ohio	Cleveland	165	10,395
		Columbus	190	11,970
East	Massachusetts	Boston	297	24,336
		Springfield	360	36,972
	New Jersey	Trenton	378	38,820
	New York	Buffalo	342	28,009
		New York	333	27,284
		Syracuse	414	34,538
	Pennsylvania		999	92,873
Grand Total			4,573	391,734

Fig. 37.14
Double-clicking the summary item Pennsylvania collapses the city detail into totals for the state.

You can also use the Query and Pivot toolbar to show or hide detail items. To hide an item, select the item, then click the Hide Detail button on the Query and Pivot toolbar. To show detail for a summary item, select the item, and then click the Show Detail button on the Query and Pivot toolbar.

To hide detail for more than one item, the Hide Detail button on the Query and Pivot toolbar is more efficient than double-clicking. You can select multiple items, and then click the Hide Detail button on the Query and Pivot toolbar to hide detail for all selected items. This is handy when you want to remove an entire grouping level from a pivot table. The pivot table in figure 37.15 shows the results of selecting all items in the State field in the pivot table in figure 37.13.

To show or hide detail items with commands, follow these steps:

1. Select the summary item whose detail items you want to hide.
2. Choose the **G**roup and **O**utline command from the **D**ata menu (or from the shortcut menu).
3. Choose the option you want (**S**how Detail or **H**ide Detail).

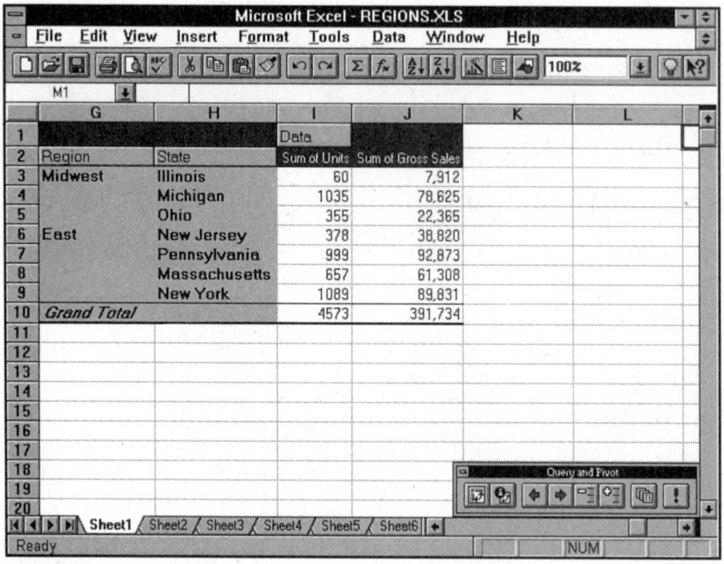

Fig. 37.15
The pivot table in figure 37.13 after hiding detail for all states.

Displaying More Detail. You will be surprised at how much detail you can get with the help of pivot tables. In the previous section you learned that double-clicking the outermost rows and columns (those containing the summary items) limits the amount of detail displayed. Double-clicking on the innermost row or column has the opposite effect: it displays even more detail.

To add more detail to a pivot table, follow these steps:

1. Double-click the detail (innermost) row or column for which you want to show more detail as shown in figure 37.16.

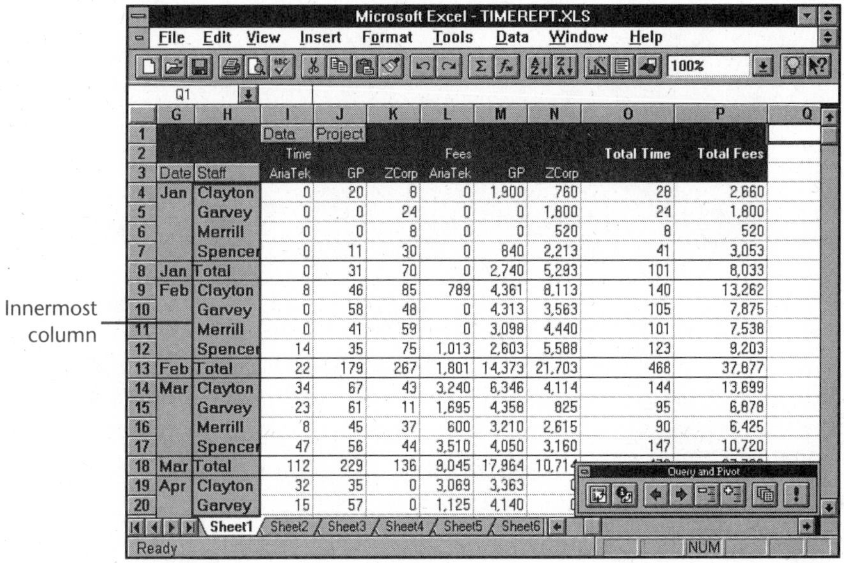

Fig. 37.16 To add more fields to a pivot table, double-click the innermost row or column (areas indicated in the diagram).

This brings up the Show Detail dialog box containing a list of available fields (see fig. 37.17).

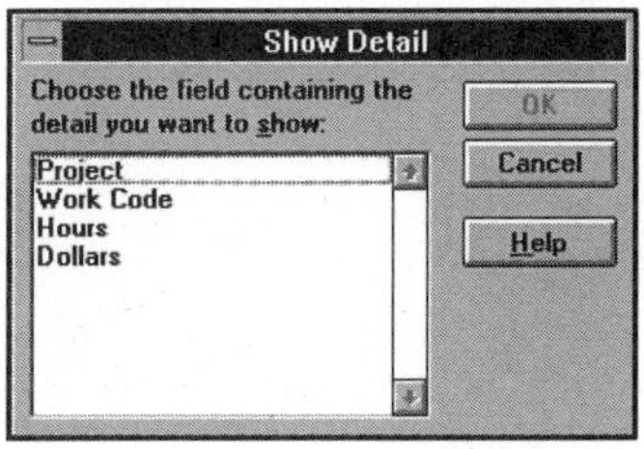

Fig. 37.17 In the Show Detail dialog box, you can select a field to provide a more detailed break-down of figures in a pivot table.

2. Select the field you want to add.

Figure 37.18 shows the result of adding work-code detail to the pivot table in figure 37.16. (This was done by double-clicking Spencer and then selecting Work Code in the Show Detail dialog box.)

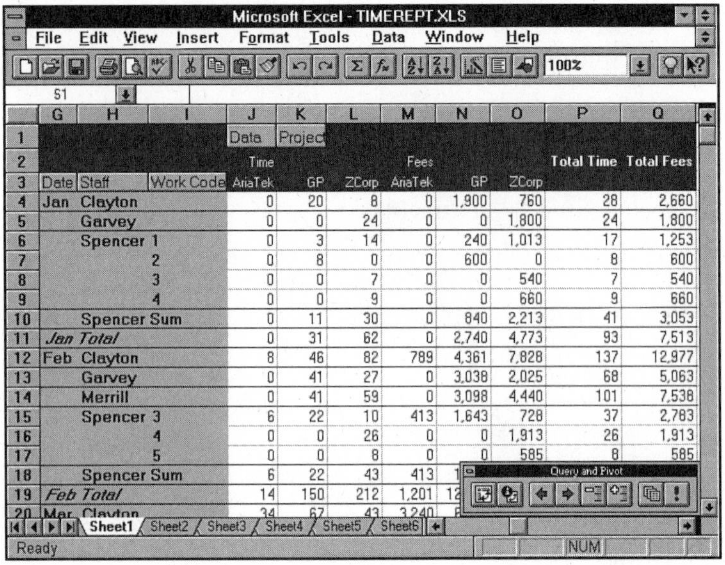

	G	H	I	J	K	L	M	N	O	P	Q
1				Data	Project						
2				Time			Fees			Total Time	Total Fees
3	Date	Staff	Work Code	AriaTek	GP	ZCorp	AriaTek	GP	ZCorp		
4	Jan	Clayton		0	20	8	0	1,900	760	28	2,660
5		Garvey		0	0	24	0	0	1,800	24	1,800
6		Spencer	1	0	3	14	0	240	1,013	17	1,253
7			2	0	8	0	0	600	0	8	600
8			3	0	0	7	0	0	540	7	540
9			4	0	0	9	0	0	660	9	660
10		Spencer Sum		0	11	30	0	840	2,213	41	3,053
11	*Jan Total*			0	31	62	0	2,740	4,773	93	7,513
12	Feb	Clayton		8	46	82	789	4,361	7,828	137	12,977
13		Garvey		0	41	27	0	3,038	2,025	68	5,063
14		Merrill		0	41	59	0	3,098	4,440	101	7,538
15		Spencer	3	6	22	10	413	1,643	728	37	2,783
16			4	0	0	26	0	0	1,913	26	1,913
17			5	0	0	8	0	0	585	8	585
18		Spencer Sum		6	22	43	413	1			
19	*Feb Total*			14	150	212	1,201	12			
20	Mar	Clayton		34	67	43	3,240				

Fig. 37.18
The pivot table in figure 37.16 after adding work-code detail for Spencer.

Sometimes while viewing a pivot table you may want to investigate the source data. Simply double-click a cell in the data area of the pivot table (the area of the pivot table excluding the field and item labels). Excel inserts a new worksheet and displays a copy of the source data that was used to calculate the value appearing in the cell. Figure 37.19 shows the displayed source data for the sales entries for Detroit.

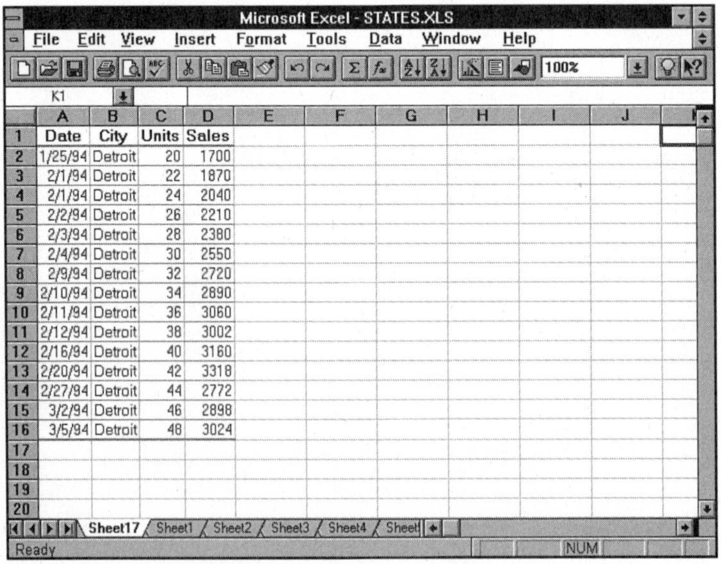

	A	B	C	D
1	Date	City	Units	Sales
2	1/25/94	Detroit	20	1700
3	2/1/94	Detroit	22	1870
4	2/1/94	Detroit	24	2040
5	2/2/94	Detroit	26	2210
6	2/3/94	Detroit	28	2380
7	2/4/94	Detroit	30	2550
8	2/9/94	Detroit	32	2720
9	2/10/94	Detroit	34	2890
10	2/11/94	Detroit	36	3060
11	2/12/94	Detroit	38	3002
12	2/16/94	Detroit	40	3160
13	2/20/94	Detroit	42	3318
14	2/27/94	Detroit	44	2772
15	3/2/94	Detroit	46	2898
16	3/5/94	Detroit	48	3024

Fig. 37.19
This pivot table was produced by double-clicking either the Units or Sales cell for Detroit in the pivot table shown in figure 37.18.

To display source data for a cell in the data area with the toolbar, follow these steps:

1. Select the cell whose related source data you want to display.
2. Click the Show Detail button on the Query and Pivot toolbar.

To display source data for a cell in the data area with commands, follow these steps:

1. Select the cell whose related source data you want to display.
2. Choose the **G**roup and Outline command from the **D**ata menu (or from the shortcut menu).
3. Choose the Show Detail button.

Tip
The data you display is only a copy; making changes to this copy does not change the source data.

Grouping Items with Numeric Labels into Ranges. Sometimes you are faced with pivot tables containing items identified by numeric labels. In the example in figure 37.20, the District field contains numeric codes. Excel can group these items into ranges based on the initial digit in the account number.

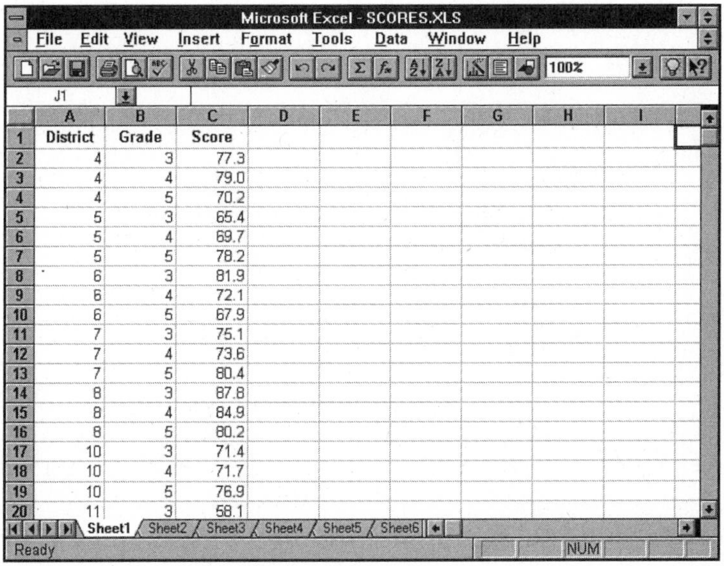

	A	B	C
1	District	Grade	Score
2	4	3	77.3
3	4	4	79.0
4	4	5	70.2
5	5	3	65.4
6	5	4	69.7
7	5	5	78.2
8	6	3	81.9
9	6	4	72.1
10	6	5	67.9
11	7	3	75.1
12	7	4	73.6
13	7	5	80.4
14	8	3	87.8
15	8	4	84.9
16	8	5	80.2
17	10	3	71.4
18	10	4	71.7
19	10	5	76.9
20	11	3	58.1

Fig. 37.20
A source list with numeric codes (column A).

To group items with numeric labels into ranges, follow these steps:

1. Select one of the numeric item labels.

2. Click the Group button on the Query and Pivot toolbar. (Alternatively, you can choose the **G**roup and Outline command from the **D**ata menu or the shortcut menu.) Excel displays a dialog box like the one in figure 37.21.

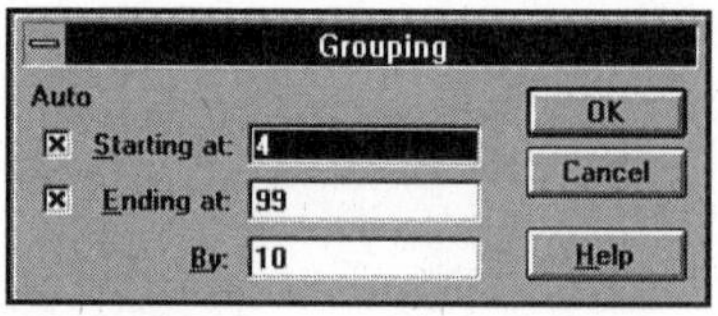

Fig. 37.21
A Grouping dialog box when the items in the group are labeled by identifying numbers with a maximum of two digits.

3. Excel guesses how you want to group the items and enters proposed values in the **S**tarting at, **E**nding at, and **B**y boxes. To accept the defaults, choose OK. To define the grouping method yourself, continue with steps 4 through 7.

4. In the **S**tarting at box, enter the first number in the sequence you want to break into groups.

5. In the **E**nding at box, enter the last number in the sequence you want to break into groups.

6. In the **B**y box, enter the size of the numeric ranges you want.

7. Choose OK.

Figure 37.22 shows the pivot table in figure 37.20 after grouping the districts.

	G	H	I	J	K
1	Average of Score	Grade			
2	District	3	4	5	Grand Total
3	1-11	76.5	75.2	75.6	75.8
4	11-21	74.8	74.4	68.8	72.7
5	21-31	83.0	88.0	84.9	85.3
6	91-101	87.4	83.3	84.0	84.9
7	Grand Total	77.4	77.1	74.7	76.4

Fig. 37.22
The pivot table in figure 37.20, after grouping the districts.

Note

The options under Auto in the Grouping dialog box are selected by default, but are cleared if you enter values in the boxes. Selecting one or both of the Auto options restores the starting and/or ending values in the source list.

Grouping Items by Date or Time Intervals. If one of your fields contains items based on time periods, and the items you want to group are in one of Excel's date or time cell formats, Excel displays the dialog box shown in figure 37.23. Select the desired time interval for grouping items from the **B**y box.

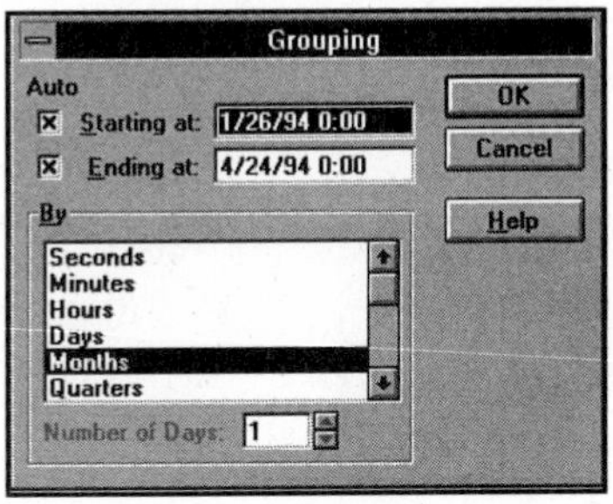

Fig. 37.23
You can create time period groups in this dialog box.

Troubleshooting

When grouping a date field, Excel creates a new group field instead of displaying the Group dialog box.

If the selection includes dates, make sure all the cells in the date column in the source list are formatted in a date or time format.

An error message appears when I try to group a selection.

Check to see if you included a blank row or column in the source range you specified in step 2 of the PivotTable Wizard.

Analyzing the Data

After you get a look at your data through the pivot table, you will likely want to modify a number of elements to display the data in a useful and informative way. You can choose to view high-level summaries or show a lot of detail. You can change the sequence of items, and you can classify your data by values in the data area rather than by item.

Analyzing Pivot Table Data with Charts

Moving pivot table fields to a different position (row to column or vice versa) generally does not affect charts created from pivot tables. The field with the greater number of fields is assigned to the category axis, regardless of whether it is a row or a column field.

Tip
It can be difficult to fit all the item labels into charts created from pivot tables. If the pivot table contains many items, substitute short names for the labels in the pivot table.

One of the most effective ways to examine pivot table data is to add a page field, and then create a chart from the pivot table. You can then flip through the items in the page field while viewing the chart to obtain a visual impression of the numbers.

Sorting Items

As you might expect, you can sort items in a pivot table field by their labels. In addition, you can sort based on values in the data fields or use a custom sort order.

When you create a pivot table, all items are automatically sorted by label in ascending order. However, if you've added new items or moved fields—or if you want to sort the items in descending order—you can redo the field.

To sort items by labels with the Standard toolbar, select the desired field, and then click the Sort Ascending or Sort Descending button, as appropriate.

To sort items by labels with menu commands, follow these steps:

1. Select the field you want to sort.
2. Choose the **D**ata **S**ort command.
3. Make sure the **L**abels option in the Sort area is selected.
4. Select the sort order you want (**A**scending or **D**escending button). Notice that a thumbnail description of the sort parameters is displayed at lower left in the dialog box (see fig. 37.24).
5. Choose OK.

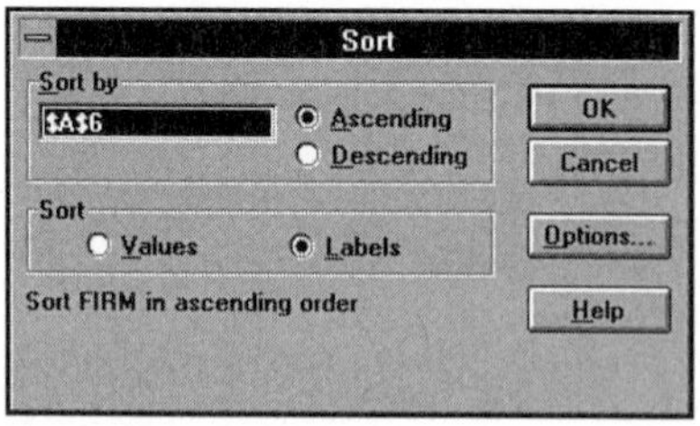

Fig. 37.24
Choose **D**ata **S**ort while a field in a pivot table is selected to display this dialog box.

Paging or Filtering a Pivot Table

As you learned in Chapter 36, "Using Pivot Tables," page fields selectively filter data in a pivot table. To display a particular item in a page field, click the arrow to the right of the page field, and then select the desired item from the list, as shown in figure 37.25.

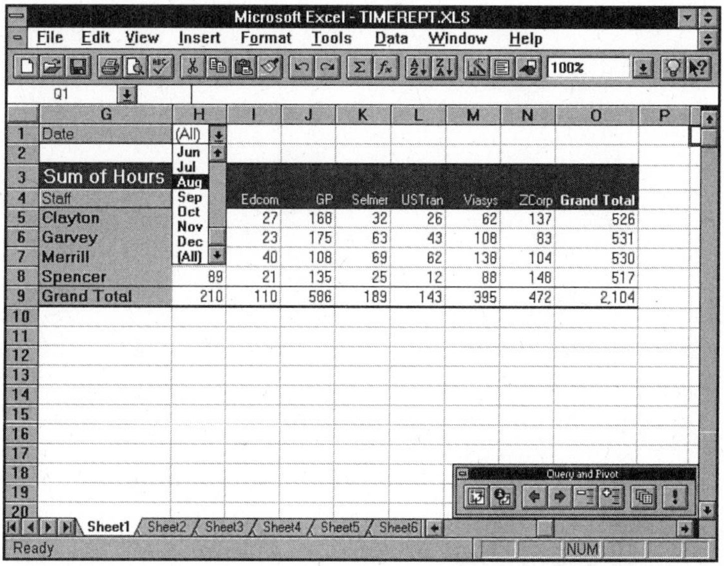

Fig. 37.25
Select an item from the list attached to a page field to display data for that item only.

To display totals for the entire field, select (All) from the list. The displayed totals include data for all items in the field, including hidden items.

Using More Than One Page Field. By adding more page fields, you can filter your data very finely. The pivot table in figure 37.26 displays time spent by Merrill on the GP project.

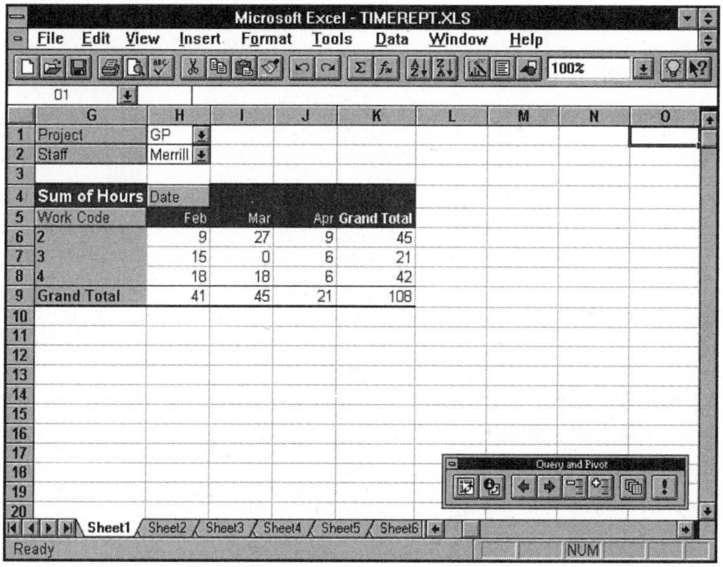

Fig. 37.26
With two page fields, you can look at very specific slices of data.

To add a page field to a pivot table, follow these steps:

1. Select a cell in the pivot table.

2. Click the PivotTable Wizard button in the Query and Pivot toolbar.
3. Move the desired field button to the **P**AGE area.
4. Choose the **F**inish button.

To create a page field from an existing field in a pivot table, drag the field button from the row or column past the upper left corner of the main body of the pivot table. When the insert marker turns to stacked rectangles, release the mouse button.

Tip

Show multiple pivot tables on one printed sheet by pasting fixed copies with the **E**dit Paste **S**pecial command and the **V**alues and Forma**t**s options.

Breaking Pages into Separate Worksheets. You can display individual pages in a pivot table in separate worksheets. This is useful if you want to print all the pages or move among the pages using the worksheet tabs. Before you can do this, however, the pivot table must already have at least one page field.

To break pages in a pivot table into separate worksheets, follow these steps:

1. Select a cell in the pivot table.

2. Click the Show Pages button in the Query and Pivot toolbar, or choose the Show Pages command on the shortcut menu.
3. The Show Pages dialog box displays a list of the page fields in the pivot table. Select the field whose items you want to display on separate worksheets, and then choose OK. (If the pivot table displays only one field, it is selected by default.)

Excel inserts a new worksheet into the workbook for each item in the page field, naming the worksheets after the respective items. Each of the worksheets contains a pivot table with the appropriate item selected in the page field.

Managing Totals and Subtotals

By default, Excel automatically displays grand totals for rows and columns in pivot tables. If the pivot table contains multiple row or multiple column fields, it will also display subtotals, as shown in figure 37.27.

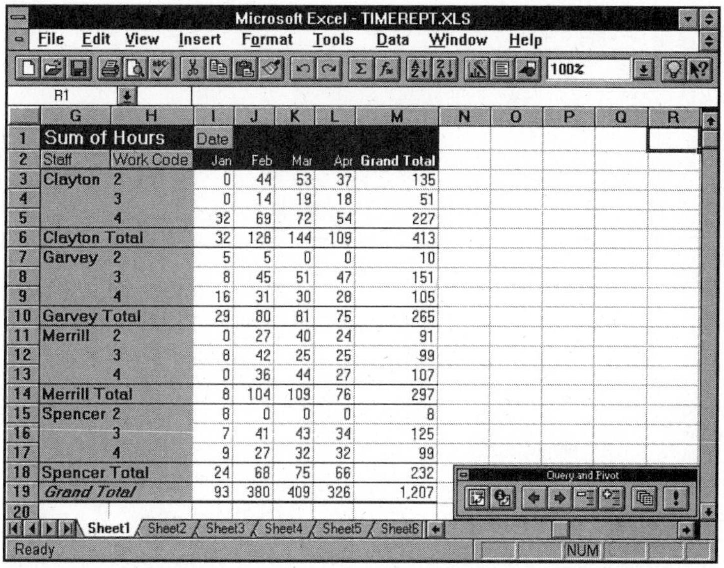

	G	H	I	J	K	L	M
1	Sum of Hours		Date				
2	Staff	Work Code	Jan	Feb	Mar	Apr	Grand Total
3	Clayton	2	0	44	53	37	135
4		3	0	14	19	18	51
5		4	32	69	72	54	227
6	Clayton Total		32	128	144	109	413
7	Garvey	2	5	5	0	0	10
8		3	8	45	51	47	151
9		4	16	31	30	28	105
10	Garvey Total		29	80	81	75	265
11	Merrill	2	0	27	40	24	91
12		3	8	42	25	25	99
13		4	0	36	44	27	107
14	Merrill Total		8	104	109	76	297
15	Spencer	2	8	0	0	0	8
16		3	7	41	43	34	125
17		4	9	27	32	32	99
18	Spencer Total		24	68	75	66	232
19	*Grand Total*		93	380	409	326	1,207

Fig. 37.27 Excel automatically displays subtotals and grand totals in pivot tables.

Hiding Grand Totals. To hide grand totals, turn off the first two check boxes in step 4 of the PivotTable Wizard (see fig. 37.28).

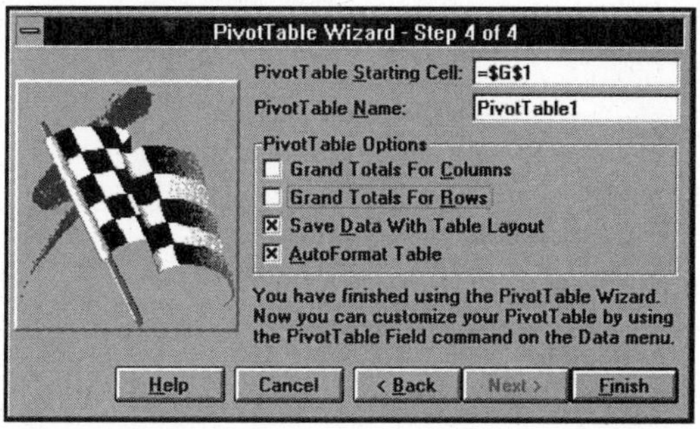

Fig. 37.28 Turning off the Grand Totals For Rows and Grand Totals For Columns options in the PivotTable Wizard suppress the display of grand totals.

When the pivot table contains more than one data field, it displays grand totals for each data field. You can display grand totals for all or none of the fields in the row or column position.

Hiding Subtotals. Subtotals are associated with individual fields, so you hide or display them individually.

To hide subtotals for a field:

1. Click the PivotTable Field button on the Query and Pivot toolbar. (Alternatively, you can double-click the desired field in the pivot table or choose the PivotTable Field command from the shortcut menu.)

2. In the Subtotals area of the PivotTable Field dialog box, select **N**one, and then choose OK.

To redisplay subtotals, bring up the dialog box and select Au**t**omatic.

Displaying Subtotals for Multiple Fields in a Row or Column. When a row or column contains more than one field, and automatic subtotals are selected, the pivot table displays subtotals for the outermost field only. You can, however, display subtotals for the innermost field, as shown in figure 37.29.

Fig. 37.29
You can display block totals for the innermost field, as shown here for the Work Code field, by creating custom subtotals.

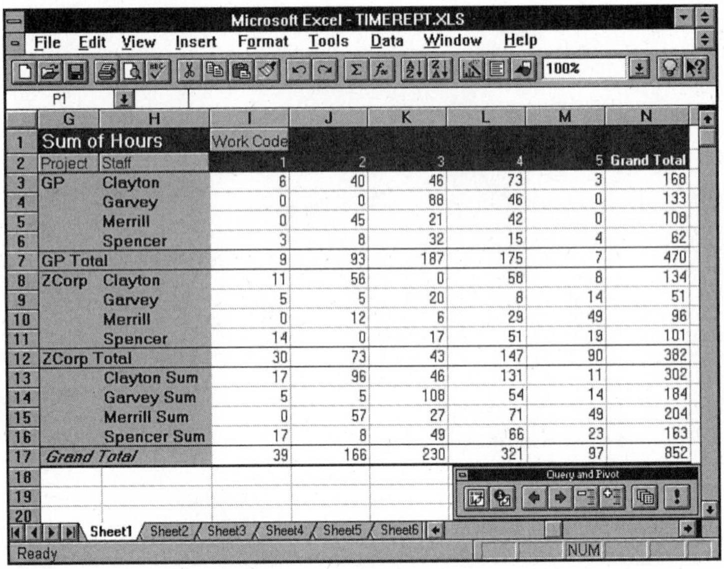

	G	H	I	J	K	L	M	N
1	Sum of Hours		Work Code					
2	Project	Staff	1	2	3	4	5	Grand Total
3	GP	Clayton	6	40	46	73	3	168
4		Garvey	0	0	88	46	0	133
5		Merrill	0	45	21	42	0	108
6		Spencer	3	8	32	15	4	62
7	GP Total		9	93	187	175	7	470
8	ZCorp	Clayton	11	56	0	58	8	134
9		Garvey	5	5	20	8	14	51
10		Merrill	0	12	6	29	49	96
11		Spencer	14	0	17	51	19	101
12	ZCorp Total		30	73	43	147	90	382
13		Clayton Sum	17	96	46	131	11	302
14		Garvey Sum	5	5	108	54	14	184
15		Merrill Sum	0	57	27	71	49	204
16		Spencer Sum	17	8	49	66	23	163
17	*Grand Total*		39	166	230	321	97	852
18								
19								
20								

To display subtotals for an innermost field, follow these steps:

1. Select the field for which you want to display subtotals.

2. Click the PivotTable Field button on the Query and Pivot toolbar. (Alternatively, you can double-click the button for the desired field in the pivot table or choose the PivotTable Field command from the shortcut menu.) This brings up the PivotTable Field dialog box (see fig. 37.30).

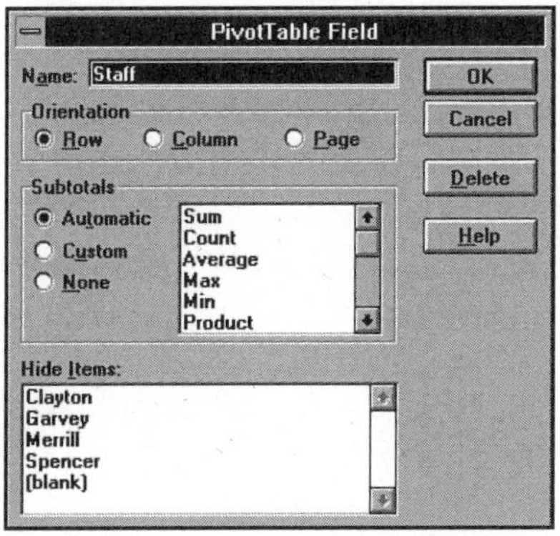

Fig. 37.30
You can change the function Excel uses to summarize data in the PivotTable Field dialog box.

3. In the Subtotals area of the PivotTable Field dialog box, select C**u**stom.

4. Select the type of subtotal calculation, such as Sum, from the adjacent list, and then choose OK.

Using Other Functions for Data Analysis

Most of the pivot tables you've looked at so far have presented summary totals of the numeric values contained in the data source. Sometimes, though, you will want to view other computations, such as averages.

Changing the Summary Function. Unless you specify otherwise, Excel summarizes data by summing numeric values when creating a pivot table. (If the data fields contain text, the pivot table displays counts of the values.)

You can change the summary function, or calculation type, from Sum to Average.

To change the summary calculation in a pivot table in the PivotTable Wizard, follow these steps:

1. Select a cell in the data area of the pivot table.

2. Click the PivotTable Wizard button in the Query and Pivot toolbar.

3. Double-click the field button in the **D**ATA area.

4. In the **S**ummarize by list, select the desired summary function.

   Table 37.1 describes Excel's most commonly used pivot table calculation types.

Table 37.1 Summary Functions for Pivot Tables

Summary function	How Excel computes amount in pivot table from source data for a given cell
Sum	Totals all numeric values
Count	Counts all values
Average	Computes sum of all numeric values, divided by number of records in the source data
Max	Finds highest value
Min	Finds lowest value
Product	Multiplies all numeric values
Count Nums	Counts all numeric values

5. Choose OK to return to the PivotTable Wizard, and then choose **F**inish.

Using Different Summary Functions in the Same Pivot Table. You can use a different summary function for each data field in the pivot table. Figure 37.31 shows a pivot table summarizing total hours worked and average dollars (fees) generated.

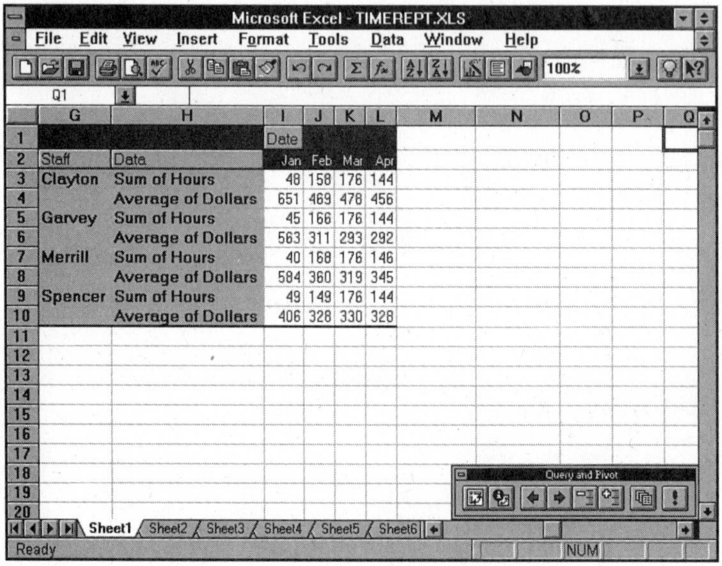

Fig. 37.31
In this pivot table, the hours are summarized using the Sum function and the dollars are summarized using the Average function.

You also can use a different summary function for the same data field if you add the data field to the pivot table twice.

Tip

Summarize the same data different ways by adding the data field twice and using the PivotTable Field button to change each summary method

Using Custom Calculations. Sometimes you might want a pivot table to calculate values in a nonstandard way. Excel provides several calculation types that calculate values based on other values in the data area of the pivot table. Figure 37.32 illustrates a pivot table that calculates values as a percentage of the grand totals for the rows, rather than as numeric totals.

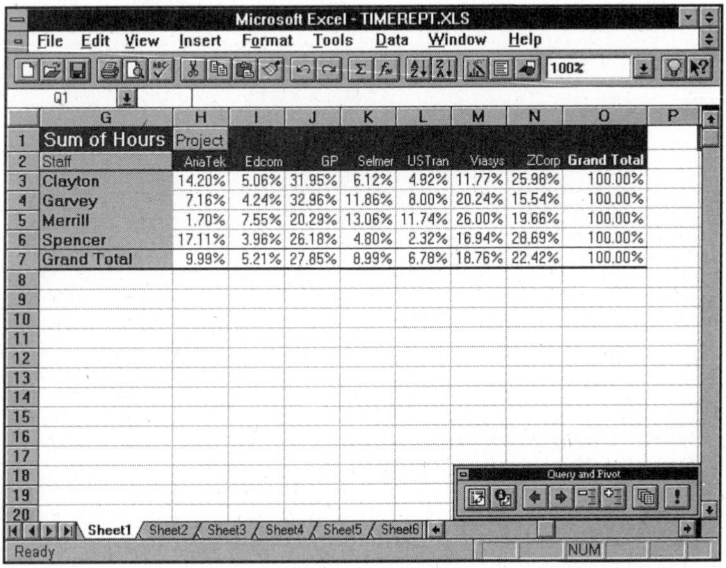

Fig. 37.32
This pivot table uses the % of row custom-calculation type.

To change the calculation type for a data field, follow these steps:

1. Select a pivot table cell in the field you want to change.
2. Click the PivotTable Field button in the Query and Pivot toolbar.

3. In the PivotTable Field dialog box, choose **O**ptions.
4. Select the desired calculation type from the Show D**a**ta as list. See Table 37.2 for explanations of the various calculation types. In the Description column, the term "result" refers to the computed result of the summary function for a given cell in the pivot table.

Table 37.2 Calculation Types for Pivot Tables

Calculation Type	What Appears in the Pivot Table Cell
Difference From	The difference between the result and a field and item you specify in the Base Field and Base Item boxes
% Of	The result divided by the specified base field and item, expressed as a percentage
% Difference From	The difference between the result and a specified field and item, divided by that base field and item, expressed as a percentage
Running Total in	For the specified base field, totals which cumulate the result for successive items
% of row	The result divided by the row's total, expressed as a percentage
% of column	The result divided by the column's total, expressed as a percentage
% of total	The result divided by the pivot table grand total, expressed as a percentage
Index	The value computed by the following formula: Result x Grand Total/Grand Row Total x Grand Column Total

5. If necessary, select the field and item you want in the Base **F**ield and Base **I**tem boxes, respectively. (You learn how this works in a moment.) You do not need to specify a base field for the % of row calculation type illustrated in figure 37.31, because this calculation does not use a base field.

6. Choose OK.

To illustrate how base fields and items work, imagine you are working for a snack food company, and you are studying long-term sales trends. You have source data going back to 1987, and you'd like to show sales by product for that period and year-by-year percentage changes.

To display sales results over time with percentage changes, follow these steps:

1. Create a pivot table with two data fields for Sales.

2. In the Step 3 screen of the PivotTable Wizard, double-click the Sum of Sales2 button in the **D**ATA area. This brings up the PivotTable Field dialog box.

3. Change the name of the field to *Increase* in the Na**m**e box.

4. If necessary, choose **O**ptions to expand the dialog box.

5. Choose the % Difference From option from the Show d**a**ta as list. The PivotTable Field dialog box then looks like figure 37.33.

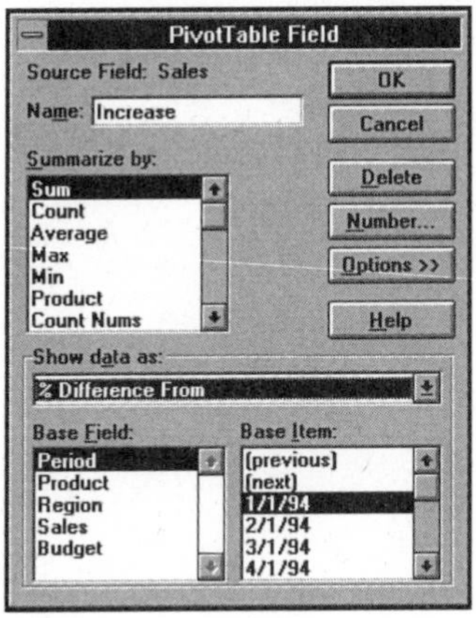

Fig. 37.33
Calculating sales as a percentage difference compared to the previous period.

6. In the Base **F**ield box, select Period.

7. In the Base **I**tem box, select (previous).

8. Choose OK.

9. Choose **F**inish.

Excel then displays a pivot table like the one in figure 37.34.

Formatting the Pivot Table

The pivot table is a unique animal in the Excel menagerie. In one sense, it's simply a range of cells containing numeric constants. In another sense, it's a single unified entity that's linked to one or more other cell ranges. Pivot Tables' unique characteristics dictate special formatting methods.

Tip
Preserve the data and appearance of a pivot table by copying it and pasting it to another location with the **E**dit Paste **S**pecial command. Paste with the **V**alues option, then with Forma**t**s.

AutoFormatting Pivot Tables

Although you can apply formatting to individual cells in a pivot table, the effort usually goes for naught, because Excel reformats the table as a whole whenever the layout is changed or the table is refreshed. To reformat the table, select any cell in the table and choose the F**o**rmat **A**utoFormat command. Then select the desired format from the AutoFormat dialog box.

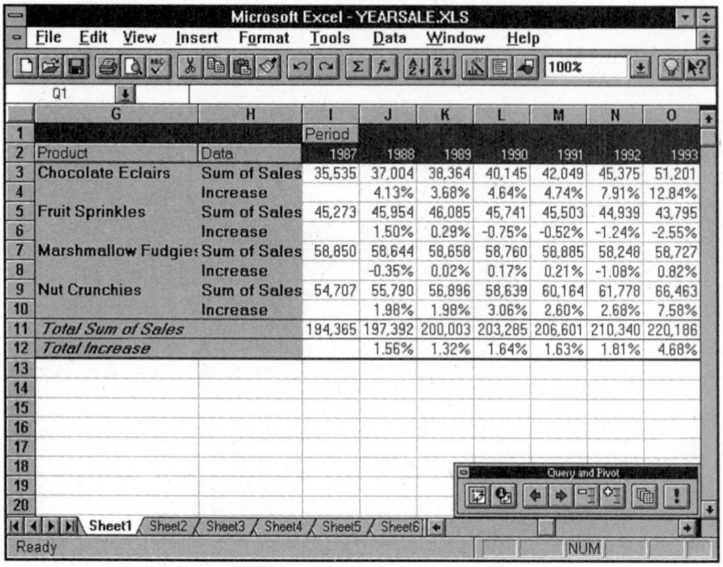

	G	H	I	J	K	L	M	N	O
1			Period						
2	Product	Data	1987	1988	1989	1990	1991	1992	1993
3	Chocolate Eclairs	Sum of Sales	35,535	37,004	38,364	40,145	42,049	45,375	51,201
4		Increase		4.13%	3.68%	4.64%	4.74%	7.91%	12.84%
5	Fruit Sprinkles	Sum of Sales	45,273	45,954	46,085	45,741	45,503	44,939	43,795
6		Increase		1.50%	0.29%	-0.75%	-0.52%	-1.24%	-2.55%
7	Marshmallow Fudgie:	Sum of Sales	58,850	58,644	58,658	58,760	58,885	58,248	58,727
8		Increase		-0.35%	0.02%	0.17%	0.21%	-1.08%	0.82%
9	Nut Crunchies	Sum of Sales	54,707	55,790	56,896	58,639	60,164	61,778	66,463
10		Increase		1.98%	1.98%	3.06%	2.60%	2.68%	7.58%
11	*Total Sum of Sales*		194,365	197,392	200,003	203,285	206,601	210,340	220,186
12	*Total Increase*			1.56%	1.32%	1.64%	1.63%	1.81%	4.68%

Fig. 37.34
A pivot table using the % Difference From calculation type for Sales makes it easy to spot trends over time.

Tip
Use AutoFormat on pivot tables to preserve their appearance when they change or update.

When you reorganize or refresh the pivot table, it retains the autoformat you applied.

Formatting Numbers

When you create a new pivot table, Excel applies the number format for the worksheet's Normal cell style to the cells in the data area. You can change that format, however.

To apply a different number format to the data area of a pivot table, follow these steps:

1. Select a cell in the data area of the pivot table.

2. Click the PivotTable Field button in the Query and Pivot toolbar. This brings up the PivotTable Field dialog box.

3. Choose **N**umber. This brings up the Number tab in the Format Cells dialog box.

4. Select the desired number format in the usual manner, and then choose OK.

The number format you select stays with all the cells in the data area, regardless of whether the data area changes shape.

Changing Field and Item Names

You can change any of the text labels surrounding the data area in the conventional way: selecting the cell and typing a new name.

For Related Information

■ "Formatting with Autoformats," p. 303

From Here...

For information relating directly to analyzing data in pivot tables, you may want to review the following major sections of this book:

- Chapter 36, "Using Pivot Tables." This chapter gives you basic information about pivot tables: how to create pivot tables and how to understand various data sources.

Part VI

Integrating Excel with Other Applications

38 Using Excel with Windows Applications

39 Using Excel with DOS and Mainframe Applications

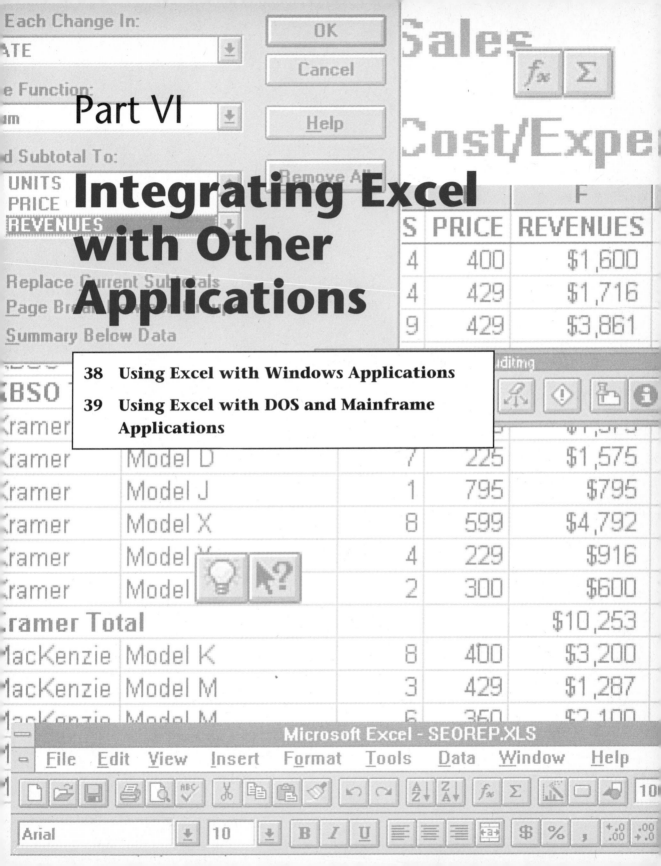

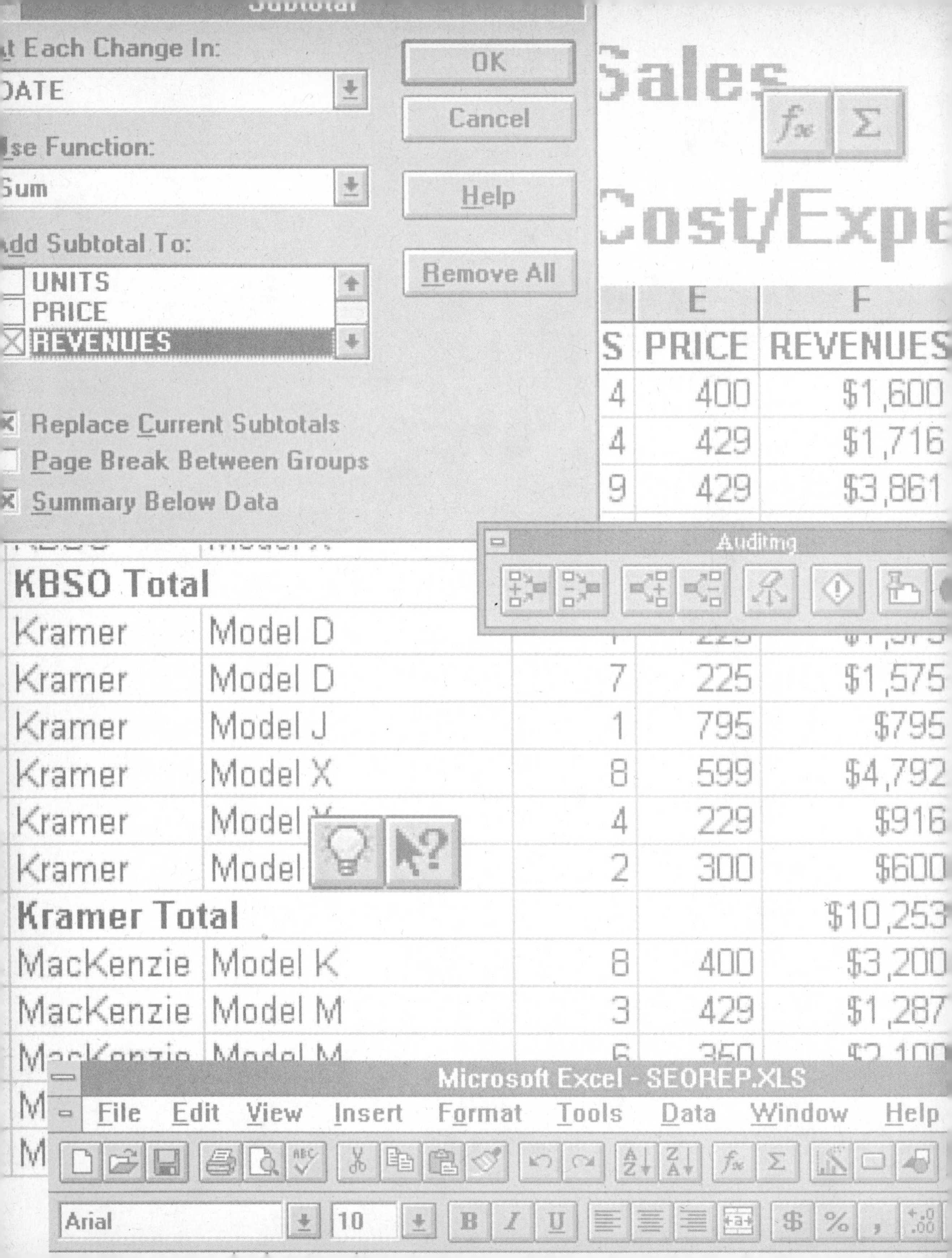

Subtotal
At Each Change In:
DATE
Use Function:
Sum
Add Subtotal To:
UNITS
PRICE
REVENUES
Replace Current Subtotals
Page Break Between Groups
Summary Below Data
OK
Cancel
Help
Remove All
Sales
Cost/Expe
E
F
S PRICE REVENUES
4 400 $1,600
4 429 $1,716
9 429 $3,861
Auditing
KBSO Total
Kramer Model D
Kramer Model D 7 225 $1,575
Kramer Model J 1 795 $795
Kramer Model X 8 599 $4,792
Kramer Model 4 229 $916
Kramer Model 2 300 $600
Kramer Total $10,253
MacKenzie Model K 8 400 $3,200
MacKenzie Model M 3 429 $1,287
Microsoft Excel - SEOREP.XLS
File Edit View Insert Format Tools Data Window Help
Arial
10

Chapter 38

Using Excel with Windows Applications

In this chapter, you learn how to:

- Link Excel charts and tables to word processors
- Exchange graphics with drawing programs
- Embed Excel worksheets and charts into presentation graphics programs
- Copy Excel screen shots into page layout programs

Excel is part of the new generation of software taking advantage of greater processor power and the new Windows software environment.

This environment has many advantages when you are working with multiple applications:

- Easy to learn: operating procedures in Windows, OS/2, and Macintosh applications are similar, and there are many similarities between applications within the same operating environment. Microsoft Excel for Windows and Word for Windows, for example, have many similarities in the way they operate.
- Capability of running multiple Windows and DOS applications.
- Capability of cutting and pasting static information between Windows and DOS applications.
- Capability of creating hot links that pass live data between Windows or Presentation Manager applications.
- Use of embedded objects that enable you to create a compound document composed of objects created in different Windows applications. You then can edit each object by using the application that originally created it.

This chapter first presents the general concepts of how to use Excel with other Windows applications. The chapter then describes examples, using specific Windows applications.

Understanding the Clipboard

For Windows applications, the *Clipboard* makes sharing information possible within documents in the same application and among documents in different applications. The Clipboard is a reserved part of memory in Windows not part of any individual application that holds one item at a time. The Clipboard holds the text, graphics, numbers, or other data that you copy or cut in the application you are using. After you store something in the Clipboard, you can move to another location in your file or switch to a file in another application and paste the information from the Clipboard.

You can view the contents of the Clipboard at any time by opening the Clipboard Viewer. Open the Main Program group in Program Manager to access the Clipboard Viewer.

Because the Clipboard belongs to Windows rather than to an application, the information it contains can be shared among applications. Because Windows applications use similar commands and in many cases, identical commands, to move data into and out of the Clipboard, sharing data among applications is easy.

You can transfer data within and among applications in three ways, depending on the application and how you copy and paste the data. The first way is a simple copy and paste operation: you select and copy the data (using the **E**dit **C**opy command), switch to another location or another document, and then paste the data (using the **E**dit **P**aste command). In a simple copy and paste operation, the data retains no tie to the originating document.

The second and third ways to transfer data by using the Clipboard depend on a Windows technology known as *object linking and embedding*, or OLE. In this technology, the data transferred is known as an object and may be text, numbers, a graphic, or any other type of data. The object can be embedded in a document or linked into a document. An embedded object includes all the information necessary to update that object from within the document in which it is pasted. A linked object remains linked to the originating document and can be updated when the original document changes.

In the language of OLE, documents and applications function as *servers*, which create the data that is embedded or linked into another document, or as *clients*, which receive the data that is embedded or linked from another document or application. Some applications, including Excel, can function as a server and as a client. Excel also can handle multiple clients and multiple servers. Chapters 17, "Adding Graphics Elements to Sheets," and 25, "Linking, Embedding, and Consolidating Worksheets," describe other situations where linking is used in Excel.

Data transferred by the Clipboard can assume several formats, which you can specify. In this way, you can control whether the data is copied and pasted or whether the data is embedded or linked.

You also can control how the data looks or behaves when pasted into another application. When you copy data from an Excel worksheet, for example, you can paste that data into a Word for Windows document as an embedded object, as linked or unlinked text that is formatted or unformatted, or as a linked or unlinked picture or bit map. These choices are described later in the section "Pasting Embedded Objects."

Copying Data between Applications

Using Excel with Windows is like having a large integrated software system, with the information from different applications linked together, even if the applications come from different vendors. With the Windows Clipboard, you can cut or copy information from one Windows or DOS application and paste it into another. Chapter 39, "Using Excel with DOS and Mainframe Applications," explains the many ways to exchange Excel data and charts with common DOS applications and mainframe computers.

Copying and Pasting Text

To copy or cut text information from Excel and paste it into another Windows application, such as Word for Windows, complete the following steps:

1. Select the range of cells you want to transfer, and choose the **E**dit **C**opy or the **E**dit Cu**t** command.

   When you cut data, it is removed from the original location and placed in the Clipboard. When you copy data, the data remains in the original location, and a copy of it is placed in the Clipboard.

2. Activate the Windows application into which you want to paste the information. If the Windows application is not running, activate the Program Manager and start the application.

Tip
Learning how to switch between applications and start them is covered in Chapter 2, "Getting around in Excel and Windows."

3. Move the insertion point to the location in the application where you want to insert the Excel data.

4. Choose the **E**dit **P**aste command for the receiving Windows application.

The Excel data is pasted into the receiving application. The data is not linked back to Excel. Refer to "Linking Data between Applications," later in this chapter, for information on linking.

Copying and Pasting Charts, Images, and Screens

You can capture an entire Excel chart, a bitmapped picture of a worksheet range, or an image of the screen and paste it into other Windows applications, such as Aldus PageMaker (a page layout application), Word for Windows (a word processing application), or Microsoft Draw (a free graphics application that comes with some Microsoft applications).

To copy an Excel chart into another application, follow these steps:

1. Activate the Excel chart that you want to copy.

2. Select the entire chart by clicking the chart background or by pressing the up- or down-arrow keys until the chart is selected.

3. Choose the **E**dit **C**opy command.

4. Activate the other Windows application.

5. Choose the application's **E**dit **P**aste or **E**dit Paste **S**pecial command. Applications that do not have linking capability do not have an **E**dit Paste **S**pecial command.

Capturing a screen image (screen shot) can be valuable for technical documentation or training materials. If you do not have a Windows application for documents, such as Aldus PageMaker or Word for Windows, you can create short training or technical documents with Excel. Paste screen shots into Excel worksheets, and then use Excel text boxes or word-wrapped text in cells to create multicolumn text descriptions.

To capture an image of an entire Windows or Excel screen that you can paste into Windows applications, follow these steps:

1. Prepare the Windows or Excel screen the way you want it to appear in the screen shot.

2. Press the Print Screen key to copy a bitmap of the screen image into the Clipboard. Alternatively, press the Alt+Print Screen key combination to copy an image of just the active window. The Print Screen key may be shown on the key cap as PrtScrn. This keystroke may not work on Toshiba portables. On older computers, pressing Print Screen may not work; use the Alt+Print Screen combination instead.

3. Activate the Windows application into which you want to paste the screen shot. The application must be capable of accepting graphics from the Clipboard.

4. Choose the **E**dit **P**aste command. The image now becomes an object that you can format or manipulate in the receiving program.

To copy a portion of the worksheet as a bitmapped image, follow these steps:

1. Select the worksheet range that you want to copy.

2. Hold down the Shift key and choose the **E**dit **C**opy Picture command. This command appears on the **E**dit menu only when you hold down the Shift key as you select the menu. The Copy Picture dialog box appears.

3. Select the As Shown when **P**rinted option if you want to paste into another Windows application and preserve the highest quality.

4. Choose OK.

5. Activate the other Windows application.

6. Select where you want the graphic image of the worksheet range, and then choose that applications **E**dit **P**aste command.

For Related Information

■ "Filling or Copying Cells Contents," p. 241

■ "Combining Data and Charts on the Same Page," p. 571

Linking Data between Applications

Many Windows applications can communicate with each other through linking. Through linking, a Windows application can send data to or receive data from other linking-capable Windows applications.

Linking takes place in two ways: linking Excel to other applications by using a remote reference formula—much as you link Excel workbooks together by using external references—or by using macros to control the Dynamic Data

Exchanges that produce links. You can type a remote reference formula into a cell if you know the correct syntax, or you can paste the formula into a cell by using the **E**dit Paste **S**pecial command.

Linking Excel to Data in Other Windows Applications

Excel can receive data from other Windows applications through hot links to other DDE-capable Windows applications. As data in the server application changes, the data in Excel (the client) can update automatically. Applications in which this feature is important include tracking prices in stock transactions, continuous monitoring of manufacturing line inventory, and analyzing laboratory data that is read from monitors.

Links also can update under manual control. This usually is done in most business situations if you need to update data in a worksheet or update a link between Excel and a word processor such as Word for Windows.

You can create links through the **E**dit menu, through typed formulas that duplicate the external reference formula created by the menu, or through macros. Link control through the use of macros is beyond the scope of this book.

Excel can create links through its **E**dit **C**opy and **E**dit Paste **S**pecial commands if the other Windows application also has link commands available on the menu. In this case, creating links is no more difficult than linking two worksheets.

Follow these steps to link Excel as a client to another OLE or DDE-capable Windows application:

1. Open Excel and the other Windows application. Activate the Windows application that will send information to the server.
2. Select the text, cell, range, value, graphic object, or data fields that you want to link.
3. Choose the **E**dit **C**opy command.
4. Activate Excel, and select where you want the linked data to appear.
5. Choose the **E**dit Paste **S**pecial command or its equivalent.
6. Select the Paste **L**ink option.
7. Choose OK.

You may have a choice of whether the linked data should update automatically or only when you manually request an update. Windows applications operate faster if you use manually updated links.

Note

The server application may not support linking through a Paste Link command. If Excel's **E**dit Paste **S**pecial command with the Paste **L**ink button is not available after you copy data from another Windows application, the application from which you copied does not support linking through menus; you cannot paste the link into Excel.

Turning Links On and Off

If you want Excel to use the last worksheet values it received and not request remote reference updates from other applications, choose the **T**ools **O**ptions command, select the Calculation tab, and clear the Update **R**emote References option. You can put the remote reference links back in effect by selecting the Update **R**emote Reference option.

Saving External Link Values

When you link an Excel worksheet to an external document—for example, a database—the values from the linked document are normally saved with the worksheet. Because the values are saved with the worksheet, the next time you open the worksheet, Excel doesn't have to reread the linked document to update the values in the worksheet. However, if the linked document is very large—for example, a large database—saving the values from the external document will result in much larger Excel files and can increase the time it takes to open the worksheet file. To cut down on the file size or the time to open a worksheet linked to an external document, choose the **T**ools **O**ptions command, select the Calculation tab, deselect the Save External **L**ink Values, and choose OK. Be aware that the next time you open this worksheet, if you opt to update the worksheet, Excel will have to reread the external document, which may require a substantial amount of time.

Excel can send information through DDE to other Windows applications just as it can initiate information requests. You can turn off Excel's capability of updating data links to other applications by choosing the **T**ools **O**ptions command, selecting the General tab, and then selecting the **I**gnore Other Applications option. To enable remote requests and allow information to pass out of Excel, deselect the **I**gnore Other Applications option.

For Related Information

- "Moving Cell Contents," p. 235
- "Creating an Embedded Chart," p. 407
- "Linking Workbook Cells and Ranges," p. 750

Embedding Data from Other Applications into Worksheets

You can embed data into an Excel worksheet from any OLE server application. After being embedded, the data is part of the Excel worksheet; to edit the embedded data, you can start the server application from within Excel. (If the server is not available—as it may not be if you give the document to someone who does not have the application—Windows tries to substitute a different application that uses the same data to do the update.)

In some ways, embedding an object into an Excel worksheet is like linking an object. In both cases, you retain some connection to the server application used to create the object, enabling you to update the object in Excel by changing the original object. Embedding and linking are very different in other ways, however. Some of the advantages and disadvantages of embedding follow:

Advantages

- You don't have to maintain links to the server document. (In a link, Excel always must know where to find the server document or it cannot update the linked object.)
- You don't have to save a separate server document because the server document becomes part of the client document.
- You can start the server application from within Excel to update the embedded object.
- An embedded object updates only when you choose to update it (some links are updated automatically).

Disadvantages

- Excel worksheets containing embedded objects are larger than documents with links, because the entire embedded object is saved inside the Excel document.
- If you update an embedded object using an application other than the server application, the resulting object may have lower resolution, or may lose formatting.

- You must update each embedded object individually; whereas a single source document that is linked into many Excel worksheets can update all its clients at one time.

Use linking when you have one server document to link to several Excel client documents, when you want to update many links at one time, or when you want instant updating when the server document changes. Use embedding when you want to keep the worksheet and data together, when you have only a single server object to embed, or when you want to control the updates manually from within Excel.

You can embed an object into an Excel document in two ways. You can insert the object by using an **I**nsert command and actually creating the embedded object from within Excel. Alternatively, you can open an application that contains an existing object, copy the object, and paste it into Excel.

Inserting New Embedded Objects

You can use two types of applications to insert new embedded objects into an Excel worksheet. The first is any OLE-capable Windows server application, such as Word for Windows or Windows Paintbrush.

The second includes applets that come free with some Windows applications, such as Word for Windows. If you install an application on your computer that comes with free applets, the applets become available to Excel and other client applications. Applets are not stand-alone applications; they can be used only from within a client application such as Excel.

To insert a new embedded object into an Excel worksheet, follow these steps:

1. Choose the **I**nsert **O**bject command and select the Create New tab to display the dialog box shown in figure 38.1.

2. Select from the **O**bject Type list the server application you want to use to create an embedded object.

3. Choose OK. The server application starts on top of the Excel workbook.

4. Create the object you want to embed.

5. In the server application, choose a command such as **F**ile **U**pdate or **F**ile **R**eturn Data to add the object to your Excel worksheet. You then can close the document or exit the application. As an alternative, you can choose **F**ile E**x**it (sometimes **F**ile E**x**it and Return to document) to exit

the server application and update the Excel document. Respond to a dialog box asking you to confirm that you want to update the Excel document by choosing **Y**es.

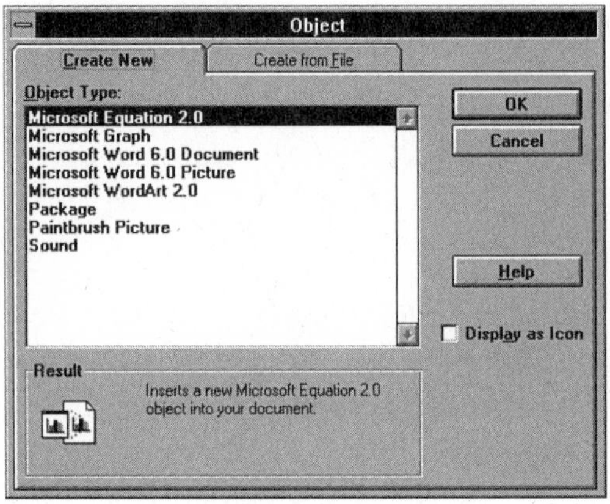

Fig. 38.1
The Object dialog box with the Create New tab selected.

Objects embedded in Excel—even text objects—appear as pictures that you can resize and move. See Chapter 17, "Adding Graphics Elements to Sheets," for more information on working with graphics in a worksheet.

Excel 5 supports the new version of object linking and embedding, OLE 2. If the applications you use in conjunction with Excel also support OLE 2, you can take advantage of the benefits of this new version of OLE. Microsoft Word for Windows 6 and some of the applets that come with Word support OLE 2. If you choose an OLE 2-compatible server application from the Object dialog box, you will notice several differences from the original OLE 1:

- The server application does not open on top of the Excel workbook. The Excel workbook remains visible, and a hatched border appears around the embedded object.
- The name in the title bar changes from `Microsoft Excel` to the name of the server application. This change reminds you that you are working in the server application and not in Excel.
- With the exception of the File and Window menus, the server application's menus replace the Excel menus.
- The toolbars for the server application replace the Excel toolbars.

The ability to view and work with the embedded object while viewing the document it is embedded in is called *in-place activation* and is a benefit of OLE 2. You don't have to move back and forth between the server and client applications to see what the embedded application looks like in the original document. When you double-click the embedded object, the menu commands and tools you need to edit the embedded object are available from within the client application—in this case, Excel. You can view the embedded object in context as you edit it. Figure 38.2 shows a Word 6 document being edited within an Excel 5 worksheet. Notice the Word menus and toolbars appear within Excel while the user is working within the Word document. To return to Excel, click anywhere outside the embedded object.

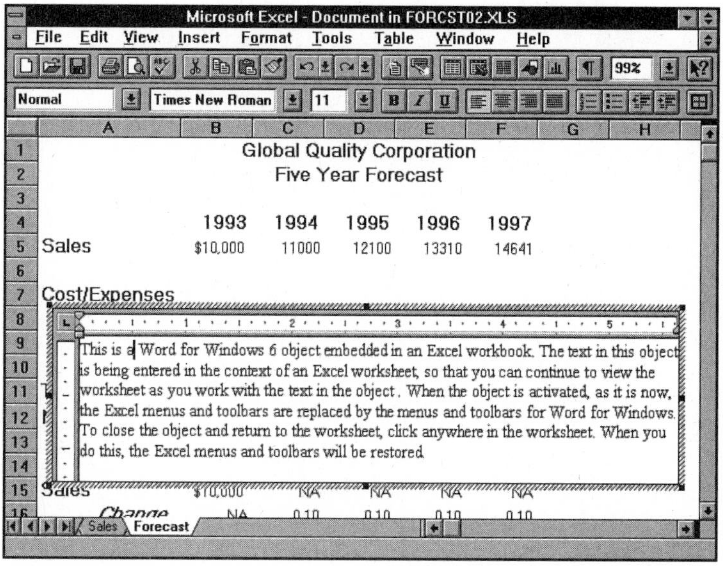

Fig. 38.2
OLE 2 enables you to use other applications to edit objects while in your Excel workbook.

Another feature of OLE 2 is that you can drag-and-drop data between two applications that both support OLE 2. Dragging data has the same results as using the **E**dit **C**opy/**E**dit **P**aste commands to copy data from one application to another. If you press Shift while you drag the data, the data is inserted at the cursor or in the active cell of the receiving document. Pressing Ctrl while you drag the data is like using the **E**dit Cu**t**/**E**dit **P**aste commands; the data is removed from the source document and pasted in the destination document.

Tip
Use drag and drop to embed one OLE document into another OLE document.

Inserting Existing Files as Embedded Objects

You can use the **I**nsert **O**bject command to insert an existing file as an embedded object in an Excel worksheet. When you do this, the entire file is stored with the worksheet file and can be changed without affecting the original file.

To insert an existing file as an embedded object, follow these steps:

1. Choose the **I**nsert **O**bject command and select the Create from File tab to display the dialog box shown in figure 38.3.

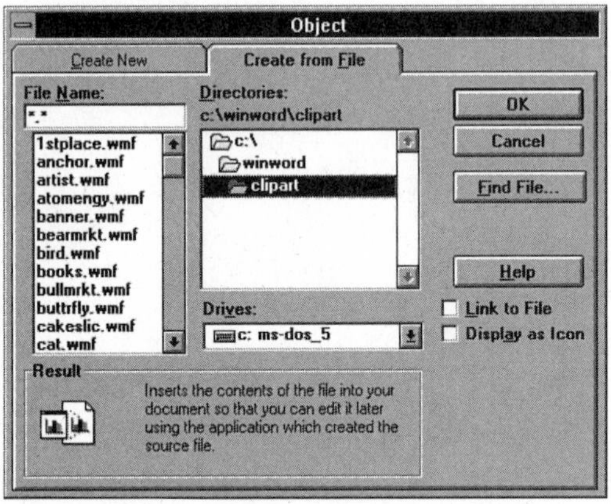

Fig. 38.3
The Object dialog box with the Create from File tab selected.

2. Select the source file from the File **N**ame list box.

   If the file you want to insert is located in another directory, select the correct directory from the **D**irectories list box.

   If you don't know where the file is located, choose the **F**ind File button and use the Find File dialog box to find the file (see Chapter 9, "Managing Files," for more information on finding files).

3. If you want to link the file to the worksheet, select the **L**ink to File option.

   If you do not select this option, there will be no link to the original file. If the data in the original file changes, it will not be updated in the worksheet.

4. Choose OK.

Pasting Embedded Objects

Another way to embed objects in Excel worksheets is to open the server application containing the data you want to embed, copy the object, and paste it into Excel as an embedded object. This technique for embedding is useful if you want to embed only part of a document from another application. You cannot use this technique with an applet because applets can start only from within a client document.

Windows applications that are not fully OLE compliant may not appear in the Insert Object dialog box. You still may be able to use these applications to create an OLE object and embed it into your worksheet.

To embed an object by using the Paste Special command, complete the following steps:

1. Start the server application in which you will create the document to embed.
2. Select the portion of the document you want to embed.
3. Choose the **E**dit **C**opy command.
4. Switch to Excel, activate the worksheet or macro sheet in which you want to paste the object, and select the cell where you want the object's top-left corner.
5. Choose the **E**dit Paste **S**pecial command. The Paste Special dialog box appears (see fig. 38.4).

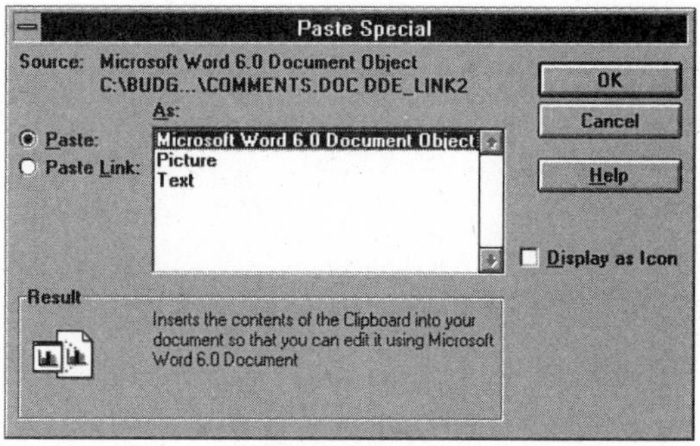

Fig. 38.4
The Paste Special dialog box is used to link embedded objects from other applications into Excel.

6. Select one of the options from the **A**s list:

   Selecting the name of server application inserts the Clipboard contents as an embedded object that can be edited by using the server application.

Selecting Picture inserts the Clipboard contents as a simple graphic that is not linked to the application that created the picture. The object takes up less space in the workbook because the information linking the graphic to its source application is not stored with the file. You cannot edit the picture as you can an embedded object. Picture is a better choice than Bitmap for high-quality printing.

The Bitmap option is similar to the Picture option, except you get an exact representation of what you see on-screen. Bitmaps can be linked to the server application, but take up more memory and disk space than Picture format.

7. Select either the **P**aste option, if you do not want to link the object to its source application, or the Paste **L**ink option if you do want to link the object to the source.

8. Choose OK.

The object appears in the worksheet or macro sheet. You can format it, size it, or move it as you would any graphic object. The data types that appear in the list depend on the application from which you are bringing information. If you want to embed an object, select the name of the application in which the object was created from the As list. If, for example, you copied data from the XYZ database, you would see XYZ in the list. Other data types in the list depend on the types of data the server application is capable of transferring. Some of the other data types you might see include the following:

Data Type	Meaning
Formatted Text (RTF)	Formatted text
Unformatted Text	Unformatted text
Picture	Graphic composed of drawing elements. Editable with Windows Draw or other major Windows drawing applications.
Bitmap	Graphic using screen dots. Editable with Windows Paintbrush.

Note

If you do not see the name of the source application as one of the data types in the list, the application you copied from is not capable of embedding OLE objects. In this case, you may be able to paste the copied information with a link; if not, you can copy it only as simple unlinked, unembedded data.

You can also use the **I**nsert **P**icture command to insert graphics into a worksheet. See Chapter 17, "Adding Graphics Elements to Sheets" for more information on using the **I**nsert **P**icture command.

For Related Information

- "Inserting Graphics," p. 557
- "Creating Graphic Objects," p. 560

Embedding Objects as Icons

You have the option of displaying an embedded object as an icon rather than displaying the actual object. For example, you can embed a Word for Windows document in an Excel worksheet and display it as a icon, so the user can double-click the icon to open Word and display the document. This feature is useful if you want to make information related to your worksheets readily available when needed without having to actually display the information in your worksheets.

To display an embedded object as an icon, select the Display as Icon option in the Paste **S**pecial or **O**bject dialog box, depending on which you are using to insert an embedded object (see earlier sections on inserting embedded objects).

Converting Embedded Objects

If you attempt to edit an embedded object that was created by an application that is not installed on your computer, Excel will look on your computer for applications of the same type. If it finds suitable applications that are able to convert the object, it will display the Convert dialog box, from which you can select from a list of these applications the one you want to use to edit the embedded object. The embedded object is converted to the format for the selected application. Another way to access the Convert dialog box is to select the object, choose the **E**dit Lin**k**s command, and choose the **C**onvert button in the Links dialog box.

Printing Embedded Objects

Unless you specify otherwise, embedded objects are printed as they appear on-screen in a workbook. If you don't want an object to print, select the object, choose the F**o**rmat Obj**e**ct command, and select the Properties tab. Clear the **P**rint Object option and choose OK.

Editing Linked and Embedded Objects

The advantage to linking or embedding an object into an Excel worksheet is that you can edit the object or the linked data by using the data's original application. This technique enables you to use features designed for this specific type of data.

To edit an embedded object, double-click the object or display the shortcut menu and choose either the Object command (appears when server application supports OLE 2) or the Edit Object command (appears when server application doesn't support OLE 2). You can also choose the **O**bject command from the **E**dit menu. If the server application supports OLE 2, a submenu will appear when you select the Object command. Choose Edit to activate the object within the workbook, where you can edit the object by using the menus and toolbars from the source application. When you finish editing the object, click anywhere in the worksheet to return to the worksheet and restore the Excel menus and toolbars. Choose the Open command to open the source application in its own window. When you are done editing the object, close the application window by choosing the **C**lose and Return to command.

If the application doesn't support OLE 2, choosing the **E**dit **O**bject command or Edit Object from the shortcut menu will open the source application in its own window. Make the changes and then choose a command such as **F**ile **U**pdate or **F**ile E**x**it to close the source application and return to Excel.

Tip
To quickly access all the commands that apply to an embedded object, click the object with the right mouse button to display the shortcut menu for the object.

You can edit a linked object by changing and then updating the original object or by editing the link itself.

By default, objects linked into Excel are set to update automatically; when you change the server document and save the file, the object embedded in Excel updates to reflect the change. If the embedded object is set to update manually, however (you learn how in the next few paragraphs), you can update the linked object by following these steps:

1. Select the linked object.

2. Choose the **E**dit Lin**k**s command. The Links dialog box appears (see fig. 38.5).

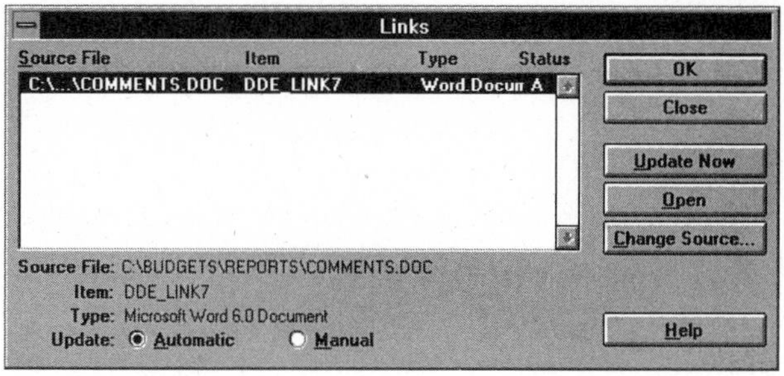

Fig. 38.5
The Links dialog box can be used to update or edit links with embedded objects.

3. Choose the **U**pdate Now button.

   If you have additional links to update, select them in the Source File list and then choose **U**pdate Now for each.

4. To open the linked object—for example, to edit it—choose the **O**pen button.

5. If you change the link to the object, choose the **C**hange Source button and enter the new file name and path for the object. Choose OK.

6. Select the **M**anual Option if you want the linked data to be updated only when you choose the **U**pdate now button.

   You also can select the **A**utomatic option to update the linked data automatically.

7. Choose OK to close the Links dialog box or Close to cancel the command.

For Related Information

- "Linking Pictures of Worksheet Cells," p. 744
- "Linking Workbook Cells and Ranges," p. 750
- "Changing and Updating Links," p. 759

You also can edit the link directly by editing the external reference in the formula bar. For example, you can change the document or range to which the object is linked.

Examples of Transferring and Linking Data

The following examples show you how useful it can be to pass data between Windows applications or to create integrated systems.

Copying Excel Screen Shots into PageMaker

Aldus PageMaker was one of the first powerful applications written for Windows. It brought the power of extremely expensive typesetting and page-layout systems to personal computers at an affordable price. PageMaker is designed to produce text-oriented materials that require graphic features beyond the capability of word processors. In PageMaker for Windows, you can mix text and graphics in any arrangement. The application's powers include the capability to place multicolumn formats on the same page; to insert, move, size, and crop graphics; to wrap text around graphics and add text callouts; and to print to typesetting equipment.

The instructions in this section specify Aldus PageMaker; however, you can use these techniques to copy any applications screen shots into other applications. You can copy screen shots into Word for Windows, Windows Paintbrush, or an Excel worksheet, for example.

To capture a screen shot of Excel and paste it into Aldus PageMaker, follow these steps:

1. Start PageMaker and open the document that will receive the screen shot.
2. Activate Excel. Display the subjects you want to capture in the screen shot.
3. Press the Print Screen key to shoot the whole screen. On some computers, you may need to press Alt+Print Screen, which shoots only the active window. (These key combinations may not work on Toshiba portables.) This action copies a bit-mapped image of the screen into the Clipboard.
4. Activate PageMaker.
5. Choose the **E**dit **P**aste command.

   PageMaker receives the image as a selected object, which you can move to any location.

After you paste the screen shot, you can move, resize, crop, or format it by using the commands available in Aldus PageMaker.

Linking Charts and Tables into Word for Windows

Excel and Word for Windows work side by side to create documents that combine the table and chart capabilities of Excel with the text-manipulation and layout features of a powerful word processor. Word for Windows' menus and commands are very similar to Excel's. Word for Windows' toolbars and ruler at the top of the screen are similar to Excel's toolbar, so you can do most of the formatting without using menu commands.

One of the advantages of using Word for Windows with Excel is the capability of Word for Windows to incorporate Excel charts and worksheets into text documents. You can paste this incorporated data as unlinked items or link the items to the original Excel documents. Linking to the Excel document enables you to update the Word document easily.

Pasting Unlinked Worksheet Data. To paste unlinked Excel worksheet data into Word for Windows and create a table, follow these steps:

1. Select the range in the Excel worksheet that you want to transfer.
2. Choose the **E**dit **C**opy command in Excel.
3. Activate Word for Windows and the document into which you want to paste the Excel data. Move the insertion point to where you want the table to appear.
4. Choose the **E**dit **P**aste command in Word for Windows.

As figure 38.6 shows, the Excel range becomes a table when pasted in Word for Windows. Character, border formatting, and column widths are preserved. The information in this table is not linked to the Excel worksheet. Each cell from the worksheet becomes a cell in the Word for Windows table.

Note

You can quickly activate other Microsoft Applications by using the Microsoft toolbar. You can open Microsoft Word, PowerPoint, Access, FoxPro, Project, Schedule+, and Mail from the Microsoft toolbar. To display the Microsoft toolbar, click any displayed toolbar with the right mouse button to display the shortcut menu and select Microsoft, or choose the **V**iew **T**oolbars command, select Microsoft from the **T**oolbars list, and choose OK.

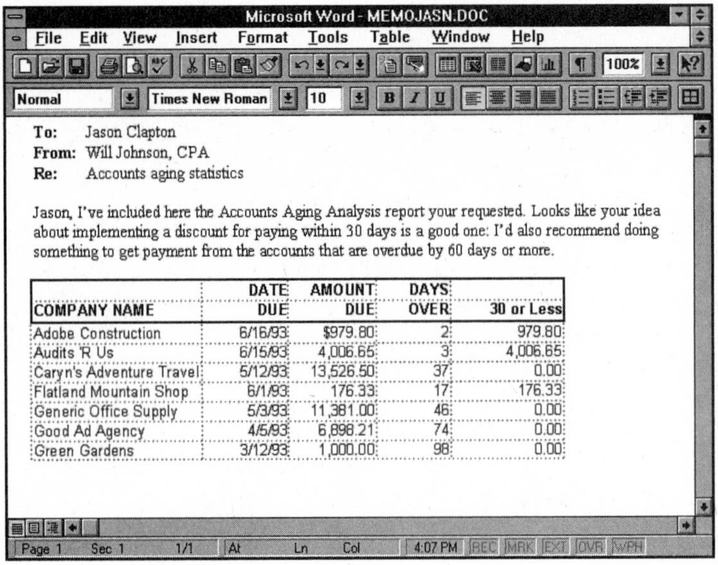

Fig. 38.6
Data pasted from Excel into Word for Windows becomes a table.

Pasting Linked Worksheet Data. To link an Excel worksheet range in a Word for Windows document, follow these steps:

1. Select the range in the Excel worksheet.
2. Choose the **E**dit **C**opy command in Excel.
3. Activate Word for Windows and the document into which you want to paste Excel data. Move the insertion point to where you want the data to appear.
4. Choose the **E**dit Paste **S**pecial command in Word for Windows. The Paste Special dialog box appears (see fig. 38.7).

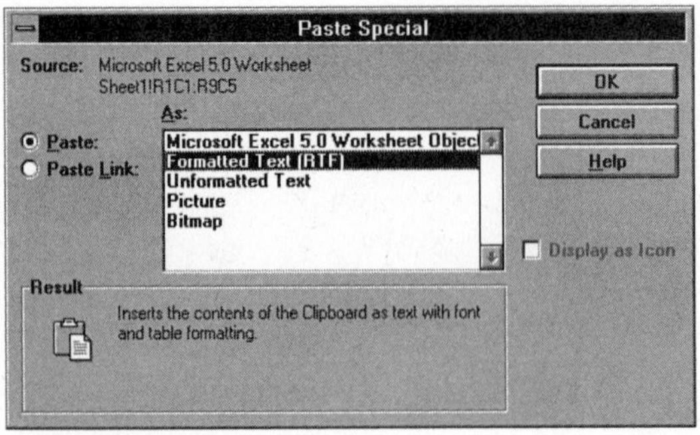

Fig. 38.7
The Paste Special dialog box in Word for Windows.

5. Select the Paste **L**ink option.

6. Choose Microsoft Excel 5.0 Worksheet Object from the **A**s list.

7. Choose OK.

A range from Excel linked to a Word for Windows document (the one in figure 38.6, for example) also appears in a table. This table is linked to the Excel range.

By default, the table in the Word for Windows document updates whenever data in the worksheet changes. This form of link slows performance and is needed only by systems requiring continuous updates. For most business applications, change the links to manual.

When you paste the linked data into Word for Windows, you actually insert a hidden field code in the document that looks similar to the following code:

Word for Windows 6:

{LINK Excel.Sheet.5 "C:\\EXCEL\\FINANCE\\ACCOUNTS.XLS"
"Receivable!R1C1:R9C5 \a\p}

To see the code behind the table, select the entire table. Then press Shift+F9, or choose the **T**ools **O**ptions command, select the View tab, select the **F**ield Codes option, and choose OK.

Note

Links are easier to maintain if you edit the Excel range in Words field code. You can change the range R5C2:R15C6, for example, to an Excel range name that defines the same cells, such as BUDGET. Using named Excel ranges in the links enables you to rearrange the Excel worksheet and still preserve the link to Word.

Including a Worksheet File. To include a disk-based worksheet file or range from a file in a Word for Windows document without opening Excel, follow these steps:

1. Position the insertion point in the Word document.

2. Choose the **I**nsert Fi**l**e command. The File dialog box appears.

3. Change the file specification in the File **N**ame box to *.XLS.

4. Press Enter to see the worksheet names.

5. Select the worksheet file from the File **N**ame list box and type a range name into the **R**ange box if you are importing a range from the worksheet.

   If you want the Word document to maintain a permanent link to the Excel worksheet, select the **L**ink to File check box.

   If you select the **C**onfirm Conversions option, the Convert File dialog box will appear when you choose OK with a list of file formats that Word can convert from. If the correct file type is selected in the list, choose OK. Otherwise, select the correct file type from the list and then choose OK.

6. Choose OK. The Open Workbook dialog box appears.

7. Select the worksheet that you want to import from the list of worksheets and choose **O**pen.

8. Select either Entire Worksheet or a named range from the **N**ame or Cell Range list that appears.

   If you want to format the imported data so that it can be used in a Word for Windows mail merge operation, select the **F**ormat for Mail Merge option.

9. Choose OK.

   If you select the **L**ink to File option in step 5, an {INCLUDETEXT} field is inserted in the Word document. If the information in the source worksheet changes, you can update the imported data in the Word document by selecting the table and pressing F9, the Field Update key.

Note

If your Word for Windows conversion files are not as current as the recent version of Excel, the Excel file may not be recognized. If your Excel file is not recognized, save the Excel worksheet to a different name and select an earlier Excel file format from the Save as File Type list in the Save As dialog box. Call Microsoft to update Word for Windows conversion files. See the appendix for Microsoft's phone number.

Pasting Excel Charts. To paste or link an Excel chart into a Word for Windows document, follow these steps:

1. Activate the Excel chart and save the Excel chart in the directory where you expect it to remain.

2. Select the entire chart by clicking the chart background or by pressing the up- or down-arrow keys until the chart is selected.

3. Choose the **E**dit **C**opy command.

4. Activate the Word for Windows document, and position the insertion point where you want the chart to appear.

5. Choose the **E**dit **P**aste command to paste a picture of the chart. Choose the **E**dit Paste **S**pecial command, and then select either Microsoft Excel 5.0 Chart Object, Picture, or Bitmap from the **A**s list in the Paste Special dialog box.

   Select Paste **L**ink to paste a picture that is linked to the worksheet.

6. Choose OK.

7. Use Word for Windows techniques to move, resize, and format the chart in the document. If the frame enclosing the chart is too large to select a right edge for resizing, select the picture and choose the F**o**rmat Pictu**r**e command; set the Height and Width in the Scaling group to 50 percent. You then should be able to see and select the chart's scaling handles.

Figure 38.8 shows a linked chart in a Word for Windows document. Pasting a chart with a link into Word for Windows creates a field code that looks like the following:

Word for Windows 6:

```
{LINK Excel.Sheet.5
"EXCEL\\SALES\\FINANCE.XLS""Revenue![FINANCE.XLS]Revenue
Chart 1" \a\p}
```

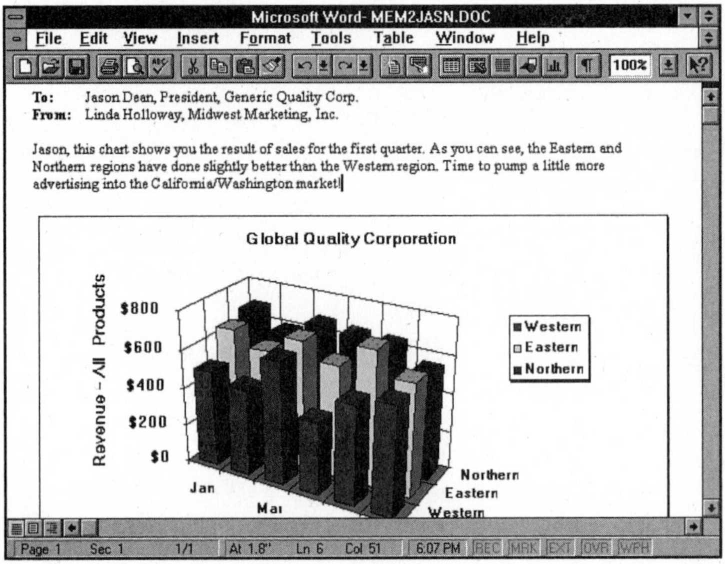

Fig. 38.8
Link Excel charts into Word for Windows documents.

Note

Resizing a chart's window in Excel changes the size and cropping you may have performed on the chart in Word for Windows. The chart in Word changes size the next time its link is updated. To prevent this size change, activate the chart in Excel and choose the **T**ools **P**rotection **P**rotect Sheet command. Leave the **C**ontents box checked and choose OK. You do not need to enter a password. This procedure locks the size and position of the chart window and prevents it from changing in Excel. This procedure also prevents the linked chart in Word for Windows from changing.

Embedding Objects in a Worksheet

If you have any applets installed on your computer, you can use them to create embedded objects in your Excel worksheet. If you have installed Word for Windows on your computer, for example, you also received the applets WordArt and Microsoft Equation for free. (You also got Microsoft Graph, but its capabilities are a subset of Excel's charting capabilities.) You can use any of these applets in Excel.

For Related Information

- "Creating an Embedded Chart," p. 407
- "Creating Graphic Objects," p. 560
- "Linking Workbook Cells and Ranges," p. 750

(For creating logos and fancy titles, you cannot beat the applet WordArt that comes with Word for Windows. WordArt is a simple applet that uses its own set of graphic fonts to twist and turn words into interesting shapes. WordArt objects appear as movable, sizable graphic objects in your Excel documents.

To embed a Microsoft WordArt object in an Excel document, follow these steps:

1. Choose the **I**nsert **O**bject command. The Object dialog box appears.

2. From the Object Type list, select MS WordArt 2.0.

3. Choose OK to start the WordArt applet.

   WordArt 2.0 is an OLE 2 application, supporting in-place activation. Therefore, when you insert a WordArt 2.0 object, the Excel menus and toolbars are replaced by WordArt's menus and toolbar, as shown in fig. 38.9. You can create and edit your WordArt object in the context of the worksheet the object is embedded in.

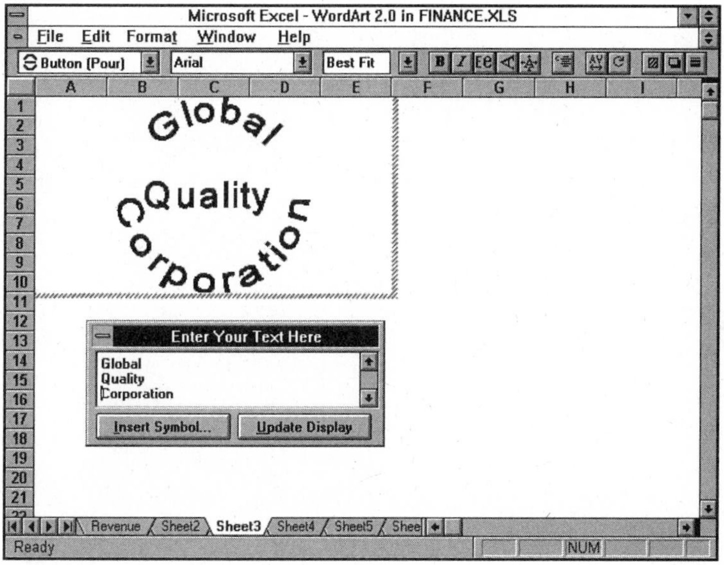

Fig. 38.9
The WordArt menus and toolbar replace Excel's menus and toolbars when you activate WordArt.

   For more information on using WordArt 2.0, see *"Using Word Version 6 for Windows,"* a Que publication.

4. Create your logo or fancy title by typing your text in the Enter Your Text Here box. Format your text the way you want using the menus and toolbar. Choose the **U**pdate Display button to apply the selections you make to the object in the worksheet, so you can see what the text will look like.

5. When you are done creating the WordArt object, click anywhere in the worksheet to restore the Excel menus and toolbars.

When you use WordArt, play with the different options to see how they change your logo.

To edit your WordArt object, double-click it or display the shortcut menu and choose WordArt 2.0 Object Edit. (Display the shortcut menu by clicking the object with the right mouse button or by selecting the object and pressing Shift+F10.)

From Here...

Being able to integrate and work easily with multiple applications is one of the great advantages to using Windows. It is not uncommon for experienced Windows users to be working with three or four applications in one session. To learn more about using Excel with other applications, refer to these chapters:

- Chapter 17, "Adding Graphics Elements to Sheets." This chapter describes how to import or insert pictures and graphics into your worksheets.
- Chapter 35, "Retrieving Data from External Databases." You learn how to use Microsoft Query to bring data into Excel worksheets from a wide variety of PC, network, or mainframe databases.
- Chapter 39, "Using Excel with DOS and Mainframe Applications." This chapter shows how to import or copy data from non-Windows applications into Excel.

Chapter 39

Using Excel with DOS and Mainframe Applications

If you use DOS applications such as dBASE, Paradox, Lotus 1-2-3, WordPerfect, or Microsoft Word, sharing information with Excel will be easy for you. Excel also simplifies the exchange of ASCII (text) files with mainframes.

In this chapter, you learn how to:

- Copy and paste information between Excel and DOS applications
- Save Excel worksheets in file formats that can be read by other applications
- Open files created by other applications and save the data in Excel format
- Transfer information to or from Excel and DOS or mainframe applications by using text files

Note

Many DOS applications also are available in Windows versions. If you use WordPerfect for Windows, 1-2-3 for Windows, or a Windows version of any other application mentioned in this chapter, use the methods discussed in Chapter 38, "Using Excel with Windows Applications," to share data. The information in this chapter relates to DOS applications only.

Excel loads and saves many file formats, such as dBASE, 1-2-3, and Multiplan. Excel also loads or creates text files for information transfer with applications, such as Quicken, that do not use one of the common formats as an interchange.

Understanding How Windows Runs DOS Applications

Tip
To review switching between open DOS and Windows applications, see "Switching between Applications," in Chapter 2.

Windows enables you to load more than one DOS or Windows application simultaneously. If you run Windows on a 386-based computer with more than 2M of memory, Windows operates in Enhanced mode and the computer continues to run DOS applications even when the applications are in the *background*. On a 286 computer or in Windows 3.1 Standard mode, DOS applications are placed on hold when they are not in the *foreground*.

If you are running Windows in 386 Enhanced mode, you can run DOS applications full-screen or in a window. To switch the active DOS application between full-screen and window display, press Alt+Enter.

For Related Information

- "Understanding Windows and Excel Terms," p. 34
- "Manipulating Windows," p. 58

Copying and Pasting between Applications

You can copy and paste text and numerical data between Excel and DOS applications, such as the applications mentioned in previous sections of this chapter. You can do so with Windows in Standard or 386 Enhanced mode.

Copying and Pasting in Standard Mode

When Windows runs in Standard mode—the mode for 286 computers—DOS applications must run full-screen, and you must copy an entire screen of text from DOS applications to paste into Excel for Windows. Often, pasting an entire screen of data from a DOS application to Excel is impractical, especially if you want only a small part of the on-screen information from the DOS application. Instead, you may want to paste the screen from the DOS application into a text editor, such as the Windows Notepad, and then reselect and paste only the information you want. (Refer to Chapter 38 for information on copying and pasting data between Windows applications.) You can paste, however, specifically selected data from Excel for Windows to DOS applications.

Note

If you have more than one screen of data to transfer between Excel and a DOS application, try saving the data in a file format that Excel for Windows and the DOS application have in common or use a text file to transfer the information. Both transferal methods are covered in following sections of this chapter.

If you run Windows with the minimum memory configuration for Excel (4M), you might not be able to run a DOS application and Excel simultaneously. To copy and paste between the DOS application and Excel, you may have to add more extended memory.

To copy from a full-screen DOS application when in Standard mode and paste into Excel, perform the following steps:

1. Activate the DOS application, and position the screen to show the desired data.
2. Press the Print Screen key to copy the DOS application's screen to the Windows clipboard. On PCs with older ROM BIOS, you may need to press Alt+Print Screen.
3. Switch to Excel, if it is already running, by using any application-switching method described in Chapter 2; otherwise, start Excel now. (If you need help starting Excel, refer to "Starting Windows and Excel," also in Chapter 2.)
4. Open the Excel workbook into which you want to paste the data from the DOS application, if it is not already open.
5. Select the cell in which you want the first line from the DOS application screen.
6. Choose the **E**dit **P**aste command.

Excel places each line of text or numbers into separate cells below the cell selected in step 5. Each line from the DOS application's screen goes into a single cell. Text and numbers from the line of data are not separated into individual cells.

Remove unwanted data by using Excel's editing or clearing techniques. Separate lines of data into individual cells by using the parsing technique described in the section "Separating (Parsing) Text into Columns with the Text Wizard" later in this chapter.

To copy selected data from Excel and paste the data into a DOS application, complete the following steps:

1. Select the cell or range in Excel.
2. Choose the **E**dit **C**opy command.

3. Switch to the DOS application. If it is already running, start the application now.

4. Position the DOS application's typing cursor (the insertion point) where you want to paste the Excel data.

5. Reduce the DOS application to an icon by pressing Alt+Esc.

6. With the DOS application's icon selected (press Alt+Esc to select it, if necessary), press Alt+space bar to display the icon's Control menu, and then choose the **P**aste command. The application reactivates to full-screen, and the data from Excel is pasted at the location chosen in step 4.

Tip
You may need to minimize or move the Excel window or other application windows to see the DOS application's icon.

Pasted lines of data end with a *carriage return* (the character produced when you press the Enter key). Some applications, such as 1-2-3, do not always move the cursor to a new cell or line when they receive a carriage return. When you paste multiple lines of data from Excel into these applications, all the pasted data goes into the same cell or line as a single, continuous line; all line breaks are lost. You must therefore paste Excel data into 1-2-3 and similar applications one cell or line at a time. Other applications, however, move the cursor to a new line or cell when they receive a carriage return, so multiple lines of data pasted from Excel retain their formatting as separate lines.

Copying and Pasting in 386 Enhanced Mode

Tip
Exporting data to 1-2-3 is easier if you save a copy of the Excel sheet in one of the 1-2-3 file formats that Excel can read or write.

When Windows is in 386 Enhanced mode, you can run DOS applications full-screen or in a window. DOS applications in a window can be moved on-screen the same way as true Windows applications. DOS applications in a window operate with the same commands and display that the applications use when running under DOS. While you run DOS applications in a window, you can copy selected text or numbers from a DOS application screen and then switch to another DOS or Windows application to paste the selection.

To copy from a DOS application and paste into Excel, perform the following steps:

1. If the application is running full-screen, press Alt+Enter to place it into a window. (Alt+Enter toggles the DOS application between full-screen and window display.)

2. Press Alt+space bar, and choose the **E**dit Mar**k** command. Select the data you want copied by dragging across the data with the mouse.

If using a keyboard, press the cursor-movement keys to move to one corner of the data you want to select, and then press Shift+cursor-movement keys to select the data.

3. Press Alt+space bar again, and choose the **E**dit Cop**y** Enter command to copy the selected data to the Windows clipboard.

Note

You cannot operate a DOS application while in Mark mode. To return to the DOS application without copying any data to the Windows clipboard, press Esc.

4. Switch to Excel, if it is already running; otherwise, start Excel now.
5. Open the Excel workbook into which you want to paste the DOS data, if it is not already open.
6. Select the cell where you want to paste the data.
7. Choose the **E**dit **P**aste command.

When you copy numbers from a DOS application into Excel, you can copy a single number or a column of numbers. The number or column pastes into a single cell or a column of cells. If you copy entire lines, the numbers do not separate for pasting into individual cells in the row. (Long lines of data with uniform separators can be pasted into multiple cells using the technique described in the "Separating (Parsing) Text into Columns with the Text Wizard" section later in this chapter.)

To copy data from Excel and paste it into a DOS application, complete the following steps:

1. Select the cell or range in Excel that you want to copy.
2. Choose the **E**dit **C**opy command.
3. Switch to the DOS application's, if it is already running; otherwise, start it now.
4. Position the application's cursor where you want the data located.
5. Press Alt+space bar, and choose the **E**dit **P**aste command.

Data enters the DOS application as though you had typed it there. Excel places a tab between each cell's contents, which makes tables of data easy to align once pasted into a word processor. You only need to set tabs for the area that contains Excel data so that the columns of data align. Use right- or decimal-alignment tabs for the best alignment of numbers.

For Related Information

- "Manipulating Windows," p. 58
- "Filling or Copying Cell Contents," p. 241
- "Copying Data between Applications," p. 1045

Exporting Data

Excel can share data and charts with other applications. When you need to transfer information between Excel and a DOS application, either export data from Excel to a file that the other application can read or import data from the other application into a file that Excel can read, depending on which direction the data is going. Excel reads and writes many file formats from other applications.

Understanding File Formats

Excel imports (reads) and exports (writes) many file formats used by DOS, Macintosh, and mainframe applications. If no specific file format is available for Excel to transfer information directly, you can create a text file format that transfers text and numbers.

The file formats Excel can read and write are listed in table 39.1.

Table 39.1 File Formats Read and Written by Excel

File Format	File Extension	Description
Excel 2.1	XLS	Excel 2.1
Excel 3.0	XLS	Excel 3.0
Excel 4.0	XLS	Excel 4.0 Worksheet
Excel 4.0	XLW	Excel 4.0 Workbook (saves only worksheets, chart sheets, and Excel 4 macro sheets)
Excel 4.0	XLC	Excel 4.0 Chart
Excel 4.0	XLM	Excel 4.0 Macro

File Format	File Extension	Description
Formatted Text	TXT, PRN	Space Delimited, also called column-delimited or fixed-width. Cells of data are arranged in columns of fixed width, with no special delimiters used; rows end with a carriage return.
Text	TXT	Tab Delimited; tabs separate cells of data; rows end with a carriage return; in some text files, characters other than a tab or comma are used as delimiters.
CSV(*variation*)	CSV	Comma Separated Values: cells are separated by commas. Text or number values are enclosed in quotation marks if they contain a comma; for example, *"$5,000"*, *"10,367"*, or *"Smith, Susan"*. Remove unwanted quotation marks from a worksheet with the **E**dit Re**p**lace command.
WKS	WKS	1-2-3 Release 1, 1A, and Symphony; Microsoft Works (open, but can't save Works format).
WK1	WK1, FMT, ALL	1-2-3 Release 2x.
WK3	WK3, FM3	1-2-3 Release 3 (saves only worksheets and chart sheets).
Quattro	WQ1	Quattro 2.0 and Quattro Pro for DOS.
DIF	DIF	Data Interchange Format: common low-level worksheet format (VisiCalc).
DBF 2	DBF	dBASE II.
DBF 3	DBF	dBASE III.
DBF 4	DBF	dBASE IV.
SYLK	SLK	Symbolic Link: Multiplan, Microsoft Works.

If you are unsure of the appearance of a CSV or text file, create an Excel worksheet and save it under different names, using CSV and text file formats. Use a word processor such as Windows Write to open the saved files and see how Excel encloses data in tabs, commas, and quotes.

Unless otherwise specified in table 39.1, Excel 5 can both open and save the listed file formats. Also, unless otherwise specified, only the active sheet is saved when you save to another file format (as described in the following section). For more information on text file formats, see the section, "Importing Text Files with the Convert Text Import Wizard," later in this chapter.

Saving Excel Worksheets in a Different Format

To save Excel worksheets in a different format, perform the following steps:

1. Choose the **F**ile Save **A**s command. The Save As dialog box appears, as shown in figure 39.1. Type the file name in the text box, but do not add a file extension, and do not press Enter.

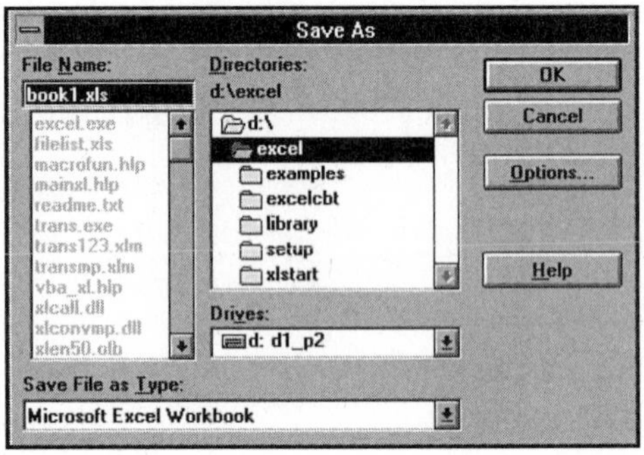

Fig. 39.1
The Save As dialog box enables you to save worksheets in different file formats.

2. From the Save File as **T**ype list, select the format in which you want to save the file.

   Table 39.1 lists these formats and the related descriptions.

3. If necessary, select from the **D**irectories list the directory to which you want to save these files, and select from the Dri**v**es list the desired drive.

4. Choose the OK button.

If you save an Excel 5 workbook in Excel 4 format, only the worksheets, chart sheets, and version 4 macro sheets are saved. If you save an Excel 5 workbook in Lotus 1-2-3 version 3.0 format, only the worksheets and chart sheets are saved. All other formats save only the current worksheet.

Exporting Text

You can export data to many DOS or mainframe applications by saving the file in one of the many formats used by Excel. Most DOS or mainframe applications can translate from one of these formats into their own formats. You can use the formats from table 39.1 to exchange data between Excel and applications as small as Quicken's check register or as large as Cullinet mainframe accounting software.

Common file formats for exchanging data with databases or mainframes are CSV and Text. Both of these file types separate the data into worksheet cells with delimiters. Formulas are changed to results. The character set used when saving depends on which type of CSV or Text file you select. Seven different sets are defined in the list: Formatted Text (Space delimited), Text (Tab delimited), CSV (Comma delimited), Text (Macintosh), Text (OS/2 or MS-DOS), CSV (Macintosh), and CSV (OS/2 or MS-DOS).

Text files separate cell contents with a delimiter, or arrange the cell data in fixed columns across the page, aligning the columns with space characters. Saving a file with Text (Tab delimited) format produces a text file with cell contents separated by tab characters. Saving a file with Formatted Text (Space delimited) format produces a text file with the cell contents arranged in fixed-width columns. This second type of text file is also sometimes called a *fixed-width* or *column-delimited* text file. To see a sample Text format file, save a worksheet in either tab- or space-delimited Text format. Then open the worksheet using an application, such as Word for Windows, in which you can see tab markers (you must turn on the display of nonprinting characters to see tab characters).

Comma Separated Value (CSV) files separate each cell's contents with a comma. Cells that contain commas are enclosed in quotation marks and then separated by commas. Any text or numbers that contain a comma are enclosed in quotation marks so that the commas that are part of the cell data are distinguished from the separator commas. Again, you can see the type of format Excel imports and exports by saving a worksheet with this format and then opening it in a word processor.

Linking Excel Data to WordPerfect 6

Excel worksheets or ranges can be read directly into some programs, such as WordPerfect. Rather than using a file format as an intermediary, WordPerfect and some other word processors have the capability of reading data directly from an Excel worksheet file. WordPerfect however, does not currently have a file converter for version 5 of Excel, so you need to save your Excel documents in Excel 4 format, if you plan to read them into WordPerfect.

To import Excel data into a WordPerfect 6 file, complete the following steps:

1. Save your Excel data in Excel 4 worksheet format using the steps detailed in the previous section, "Saving Excel Worksheets in a Different Format."

Note

WordPerfect 6 imports several spreadsheet file formats that Excel exports, including Excel 2.1, 3.0, and 4.0; and Lotus 1-2-3, versions 1.0 through 3.1.

2. Switch to WordPerfect, if it is already running; otherwise, start it now. (Refer to Chapter 2 for information on switching between applications.)
3. Open the WordPerfect file in which you want to use the Excel data, if it is not already open, and then position the cursor where you want the Excel data to appear.
4. Choose the **T**ools command, or press Alt+F7; then choose **S**preadsheet **I**mport.
5. Choose **F**ilename, type the full path name, and then press Enter.
6. Choose the **R**ange command, and enter the data range or range name. If you don't specify a data range or range name, the entire worksheet is imported.
7. Choose the **T**ype command, and select Import as Table or Import as Text. You may need to reformat fonts and columns in tables to fit the data on the page.

Tip
You can use WordPerfect's File List or QuickList to find the file you need.

Tip
To preserve Excel's mathematical functions so that WordPerfect can recalculate the data if you make changes, choose the Import as T**a**ble command.

Caution

Some mathematical functions in Excel may not translate into WordPerfect, so check the results carefully.

8. Choose the **I**mport command.

WordPerfect inserts the data.

Newer Macintosh computers are capable of reading and writing Windows' Excel files directly from an MS-DOS disk. For older Macintosh computers, you need to transfer the data between computers. A transfer between computers is performed with a null-modem serial cable (a non-normal serial cable) and a Macintosh-to-PC communication application. A number of good applications can accomplish such a transfer.

Tip

If dates are four years off after importing from or exporting to a Macintosh Excel worksheet, change Excel's date.

Exporting Files to Macintosh Excel

If you are transferring between Macintosh and Windows versions of Excel 5, you do not need to convert the file. If one computer uses Excel 3 or 4 and the other Excel 5, you need to save files to the older version before transferring. If the Macintosh version is earlier than Excel 3, you need conversion software, which usually comes with the file transfer software.

For Related Information

- "Saving Workbooks," p. 272

Importing Data

Excel is used by many businesses to analyze data stored in other applications. If you want to automate your system or create links between Excel and a database, you should explore the use of Microsoft Query and Excel (see Chapter 35, "Linking Excel to External Databases"). Many other Windows applications can link Excel to network servers and mainframe databases.

Opening Files Saved in Another File Format

The easiest way to import data into Excel is to import the data directly through one of the many file formats that Excel can read, and then resave the data in Excel 5 format. The file formats that Excel can read are listed in table 39.1, earlier in this chapter.

To open a non-Excel file, follow these steps:

1. Choose the **F**ile **O**pen command. Excel displays the standard File Open dialog box.

2. Select the file format for the type of file you want to import in the List Files of **T**ype drop-down list box.

3. Select the file you want to import in the File **N**ame list box. Locate the file using the **D**irectories and Dri**v**es lists to switch the directory and drive, if necessary.

4. Choose the OK button. Excel imports the file.

When Excel loads a non-Excel file, Excel remembers the format in which the file came. When you save the file, Excel displays the Save As dialog box. To save the file in the original non-Excel format, choose the OK button; Excel asks you to confirm replacing the original file.

Usually, however, you will want to save the file in Excel 5 workbook format. To save the file as an Excel 5 workbook, choose Microsoft Excel Workbook in the Save File as **T**ype drop-down list box. If you close a non-Excel file that you have made changes in, Excel asks if you want to save changes before closing the file and reminds you that the file is not in Excel 5 format. Choose the Yes button to save changes; Excel displays the Save As dialog box. Follow the procedure described in the preceding paragraph to save the file in the original non-Excel format or as an Excel workbook.

Caution

Saving to a non-Excel format can result in the loss of formulas, functions, special features, and formatting that are unique to Excel.

Note

If you need to selectively read information from an Excel, dBASE, Access, or Paradox file, or from another file laid out in row and column format, or in a database table, you may want to use Microsoft Query. Using Microsoft Query, you can selectively extract information from a large file on disk without importing the entire file. Microsoft Query is described in Chapter 35, "Retrieving Data from External Databases." Microsoft Query comes with Excel.

Importing Data from Mainframe Computers

If the database management system (DBMS) of the mainframe from which you want to import data supports Structured Query Language (SQL) and is connected to your computer through a network, you should be able to use Microsoft Query to retrieve data easily and quickly from the mainframe database. Microsoft Query is capable of accessing data in a variety of mainframe and personal computer database formats. Refer to Chapter 35, "Retrieving Data from External Databases," for more information on using Microsoft Query and Excel to retrieve data from external databases.

If you want to access data from a mainframe database that is not available to your computer through a network, or if the mainframe database uses a format that Microsoft Query cannot read, then you must use an intermediary text file to import the data into Excel.

Many corporations download text files from their mainframes into Text, Formatted Text, or CSV format. Excel can *parse* (separate) text lines up to 255 characters long into individual cells in the worksheet. Parsing is described in the section, "Separating (Parsing) Text into Columns with the Text Wizard," later in this chapter.

Importing Text Files with the Convert Text Import Wizard

Use text files to pass data when Excel cannot read an applications file format. Most applications can save or print data to a text file, and specify how the text file is laid out. For information on performing this task in DOS or mainframe applications, check the index of your application's manual under the headings *ASCII, ANSI, report generator, text file,* or *printing to disk.*

Excel imports three types of text files: CSV, text, and column-delimited (formatted text). Excel automatically separates data fields from CSV and Text formats into cells. Each row of imported data is placed into an Excel row. Each comma-separated or tab-separated segment of data appears in its own cell. You can specify the type of delimiter used in the text file you are importing.

To see the CSV or Text format that Excel reads automatically, create an Excel worksheet with sample data in cells. To save that worksheet, choose the **F**ile Save **A**s command, drop down the Save File as **T**ype list, and select the Text or CSV format of the character set you need (ANSI, ASCII, or Macintosh). Choose the OK button. Then use Windows Write or another word processor to examine that file and see how commas, quotes, or tabs are placed around data. When you create a text or CSV file for import to Excel, use commas, tabs, and quotes in the same way.

The third type of text file Excel reads is known as a *column-delimited* or *fixed-length* text file. Each data field is assigned to specific character locations in a line of text. For example, first names may be stored from position 1 to 12, last names from position 13 to 25, and so on. Unused positions are filled with space characters so that all of the data lines up in columns of a fixed width. Choose the **D**ata T**e**xt to Columns command to separate lines of data into cells according to each cell's range of column positions. Refer to the section "Separating (Parsing) Text into Columns with the Text Wizard," later in this chapter, for a description of this command.

You can view, edit, print, and save text files using the Windows Notepad. Windows Notepad saves all files as text files. Notepad does not add formatting to the text in the file.

EXCEL 5

To import a text file into Excel, perform the following steps:

1. Choose the **F**ile **O**pen command, and then select Text (*.prn, *.txt, *.csv) in the List Files of **T**ype drop-down list box.

2. Select the text file you want to open in the File **N**ame list box. Locate the file using the **D**irectories and Dri**v**es lists to switch the directory and drive, if necessary.

3. Choose the OK button.

   Excel automatically opens the Text Import Wizard to import the text file. The dialog box shown in figure 39.2 appears.

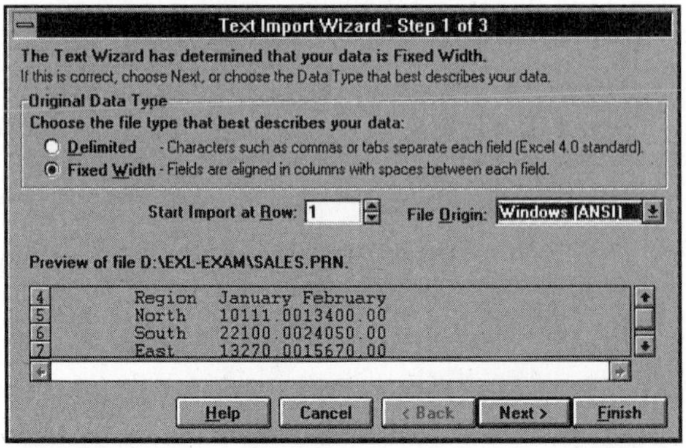

Fig. 39.2
The Text Import Wizard helps you to describe how text is separated in the imported file.

4. Select in the File **O**rigin list box the type of application or system from which the data is coming. Select **M**acintosh, **W**indows (ANSI), or **D**OS or OS/2 (PC-8) to tell Excel the type of character set being used. Macintosh applications use Macintosh; Windows applications use ANSI; and DOS and OS/2 applications use PC-8. Text data from a mainframe computer is most likely to use the PC-8 character set, although some mainframe text files may use the ANSI character set.

5. Select the **D**elimited option button if the text file you are importing is delimited with spaces, tabs, commas, or some other character; select the Fixed **W**idth option button instead if the text file is space-delimited, fixed-length, or column-delimited. Most Formatted Text files can be successfully imported using the Fixed **W**idth option.

   A sample of the text file is displayed at the bottom of the dialog box to help you determine the file's format as you fill in the Text Import Wizard options.

> **Note**
>
> If the sample data displayed in the preview window at the bottom of the Text Import Wizard dialog box contains odd-looking characters, or appears to be "garbage," you may not have selected the correct File **O**rigin character set. Try using different character sets until the data in the preview window looks correct.

6. Select the starting row for the text import in the Start Import at **R**ow text box.

   Many text files contain titles or notes in the first few lines of the file. In most cases, you will not want to import these lines along with the data. As an example, if the first two lines of a text file contain notes, you begin the import with row (line) 3.

7. Choose the Next button.

   The Text Import Wizard displays a dialog box for the second step of the importing process. The exact dialog box that Text Import Wizard displays depends on whether you selected **D**elimited or Fixed **W**idth in step 6. Refer to the following sections, "Choosing Delimited Text Import Options" and "Choosing Fixed-Width Text Import Options," for instructions on filling in the appropriate dialog boxes.

8. When you have finished filling in the Text Import Wizard options, choose **F**inish. Excel imports the file.

After you have imported the text file, use the **F**ile Save **A**s command to save the file as an Excel 5 workbook. Be sure that you choose Microsoft Excel Workbook in the Save File as **T**ype drop-down list box when you save the imported file.

Choosing Delimited Text Import Options. If, in step 1 of the Text Import Wizard (refer to fig. 39.2), you indicate that the text file you are importing is a delimited file, the Text Import Wizard displays the dialog box shown in figure 39.3.

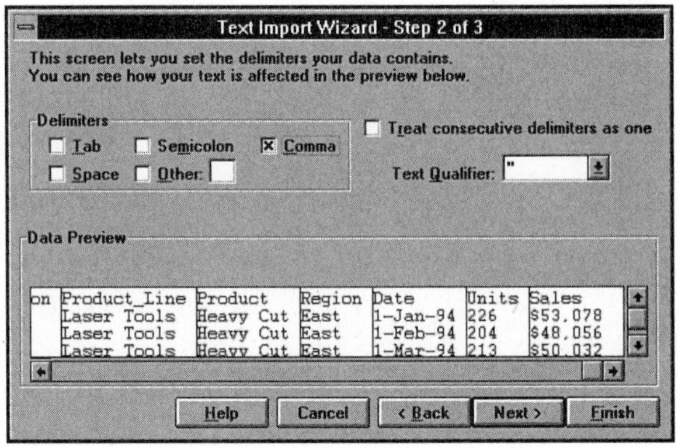

Fig. 39.3 Select the delimiter character, text qualifier, and whether to count multiple separators as a single column.

Follow these steps to finish importing a delimited text file:

1. In the Delimiters section of the Text Import Wizard dialog box, select the appropriate check boxes for the delimiters in the text file. You may select more than one delimiter, in any combination.

   The Text Import Wizard divides each row of text into columns, based on the location of the delimiters. The preview window at the bottom of the dialog box indicates where each column begins and ends with a solid black vertical line.

2. Select the T**r**eat consecutive delimiters as one check box if you want to ignore empty columns of data as the file is imported. Usually, however, you should leave this check box empty.

3. Select the appropriate text qualifier from the Text **Q**ualifier drop-down list.

   The text qualifier is used to enclose number or text values that include the delimiting character, in order to distinguish the delimiting character from the data. The most common text qualifier is the double quotation mark.

4. Use the Data Preview area at the bottom of the dialog box to verify that the column breaks appear in the correct locations. If they do not, alter

the delimiter and text qualifier choices until they do. If you cannot align the columns, choose the **B**ack button and try importing the file as a fixed-width file.

5. Choose the Next button. The Text Import Wizard now displays the dialog box shown in figure 39.4.

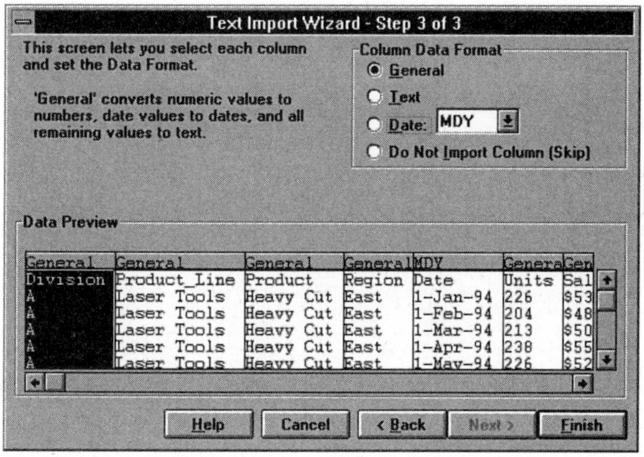

Fig. 39.4
Choose the data formats for each imported column of data.

6. Select the data format for each column of data. Click the button over each column to select that column, or use the arrow keys to select each column. After selecting the column, choose the appropriate Column Data Format options. These options are summarized in the following table:

General	Select to have Excel convert numeric values to numbers, date values to dates, and all other values to text.
Text	Select to format all data in the column as text.
Date	Use to format all data in the column as a date in the specified format.
Do Not Import Column (Skip)	Select if you do not want to import the data in the column. The Text Import Wizard skips the selected column when data is imported.

7. Choose the **F**inish button to import the data.

Choosing Fixed-Width Text Import Options. If, in step 1 of the Text Import Wizard (refer to fig. 39.2), you indicate that the text file you are importing is a fixed-width file, the Text Import Wizard displays the dialog box shown in figure 39.5.

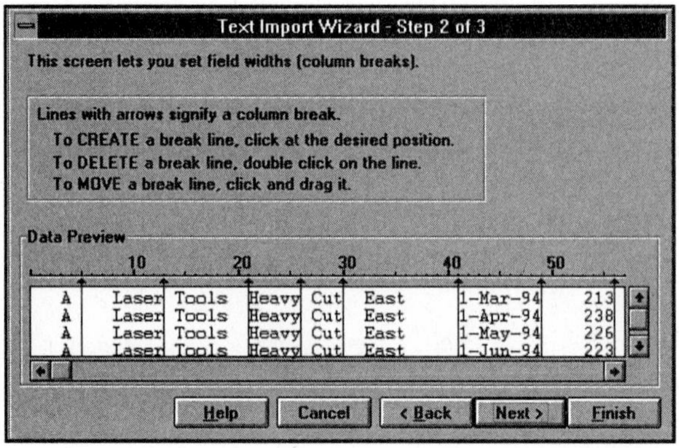

Fig. 39.5
Position the column breaks for a fixed-width text file.

The Data Preview at the bottom of the dialog box shows suggested column breaks. If the column breaks are not correct, drag them to the correct positions. Create a new column break by clicking the ruler at the top of Data Preview window; delete a column break by double-clicking it.

To complete the fixed-width file import, follow these steps:

1. After the column breaks are satisfactorily positioned, choose the Next button. The Text Import Wizard displays the dialog box shown previously in figure 39.4.

2. Select the data format for each column of data. Click the button over each column to select that column, or use the arrow keys to select each column. After selecting the column, choose the appropriate Column Data Format options.

3. Choose the **F**inish button to import the data.

Separating (Parsing) Text into Columns with the Text Wizard
Occasionally, you may import a text file that is not properly delimited, or is improperly formatted as a fixed-length file. When this happens, your only choice is to import the file as a single column. If you paste data into Excel from another application, it sometimes may be easier to paste a whole line, instead of making several paste operations—one for each portion of the line.

In either case, an entire row of data is entered into a single cell in your Excel worksheet; if you import a text file, each line of the text file is in a separate cell, and all cells form a single column. No data is separated into individual cells. To separate the long lines into cells, you must *parse*, or separate, each line into its individual parts. Figure 39.6 shows a worksheet with several lines of text entered into single cells, which then form a single column. The data in the imported text file, as you can see, was not lined up properly for a fixed-width import, and the data items are not delimited in any way.

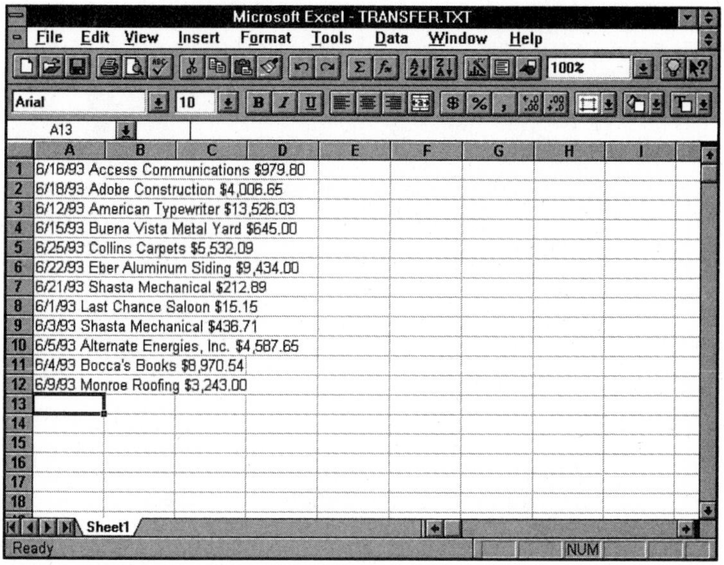

Fig. 39.6
If imported text data is not in a fixed-length or delimited format, or you paste long lines of text, you must parse the text into columns.

To parse the text shown in figure 39.6, perform the following steps (if you have just imported a text file, choose the **F**ile Save **A**s command to save it in Excel format before you begin these steps):

1. Select the cell or cells of text you want to convert to columns. If you select more than one cell, all cells you select must be in the same column.

2. Choose the **D**ata T**e**xt to Columns command. The Convert Text to Columns Wizard dialog box appears, as shown in figure 39.7.

   The three steps of the Convert Text to Columns Wizard dialog boxes are exactly the same as the Import Text Wizard dialog boxes with one exception. In the Convert Text to Columns Wizard, the dialog box for step 3 of the conversion has one additional option: the Destination text box. Use the Destination text box to optionally specify a destination for the parsed data other than the cell containing the line you are parsing. If you do not change the destination, the parsed data is inserted beginning with the cell containing the line you are converting to columns. Follow the instructions in the preceding section, "Importing Text Files with the Convert Text Import Wizard," to fill in the other options in the Convert Text to Columns Wizard dialog boxes. Choose the Next button after each step.

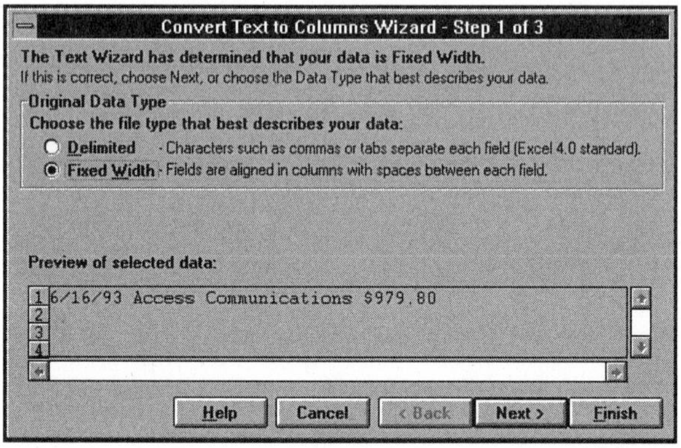

Fig. 39.7
The Convert Text to Columns Wizard helps you to change text in a single cell into data that spans several columns.

3. When you have filled in all three steps in the other options Convert Text to Columns Wizard, choose the **F**inish button. The text in the selected cell or cells is separated into individual columns.

   Figure 39.8 shows the worksheet from figure 39.6, with the first seven rows parsed into columns, and with the column widths adjusted to show the entire contents of the cells.

Note

Be certain that sufficient blank columns to hold the parsed data exist to the right of the single column that contains your selected cells. Parsed data overwrites cells to the right, with no consideration for their current contents.

For Related Information
- "Opening an Existing Workbook," p. 268

If your file is like the one in figure 39.6, you cannot convert all the lines at once, because the text is not aligned in columns and does not contain delimiters. When this is the case, you must convert each line to columns individually. If at least some of the text is aligned in columns, you can select a range of rows to convert all at once.

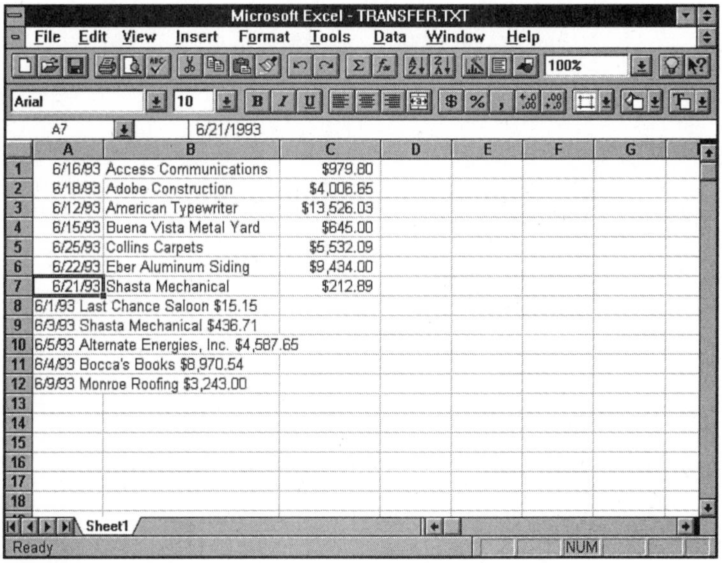

Fig. 39.8
The first seven rows have been parsed into individual cells.

From Here...

Using Excel with your existing DOS applications, or with downloaded files from a mainframe, offers several advantages. Many corporations maintain corporate and division sales, marketing, and financial data on their mainframe computers, and then download the data as text files to Excel for analysis, charting, and report generation. For more information about retrieving data from other sources, you may want to read the following chapter:

- Chapter 35, "Retrieving Data from External Databases." Learn how to use Microsoft Query to import external database information into your Excel worksheets.

Part VII

Customizing Excel

40 Customizing the Excel Screen

41 Creating Custom Toolbars and Menus

42 Creating Templates and Controlling Excel's Startup

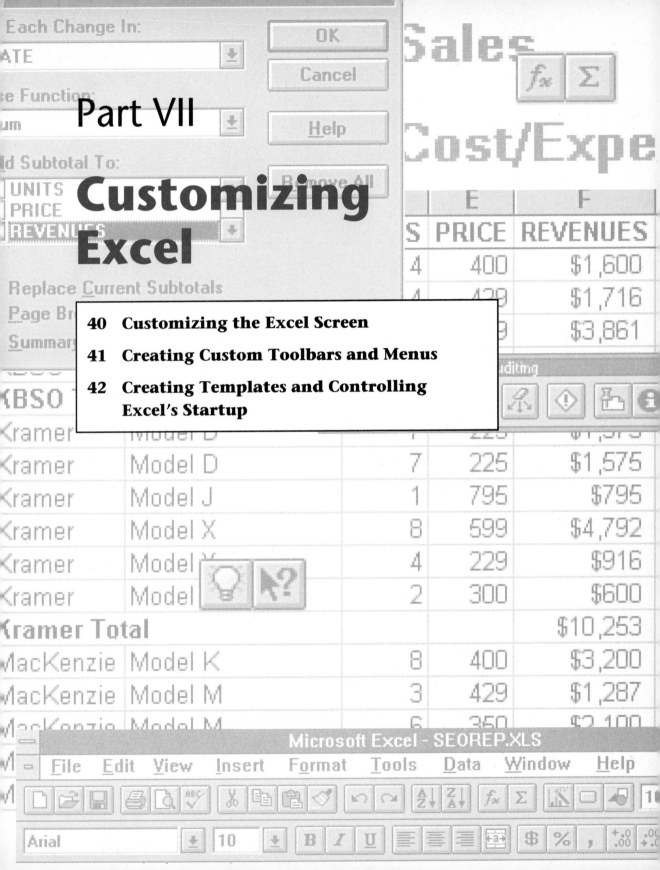

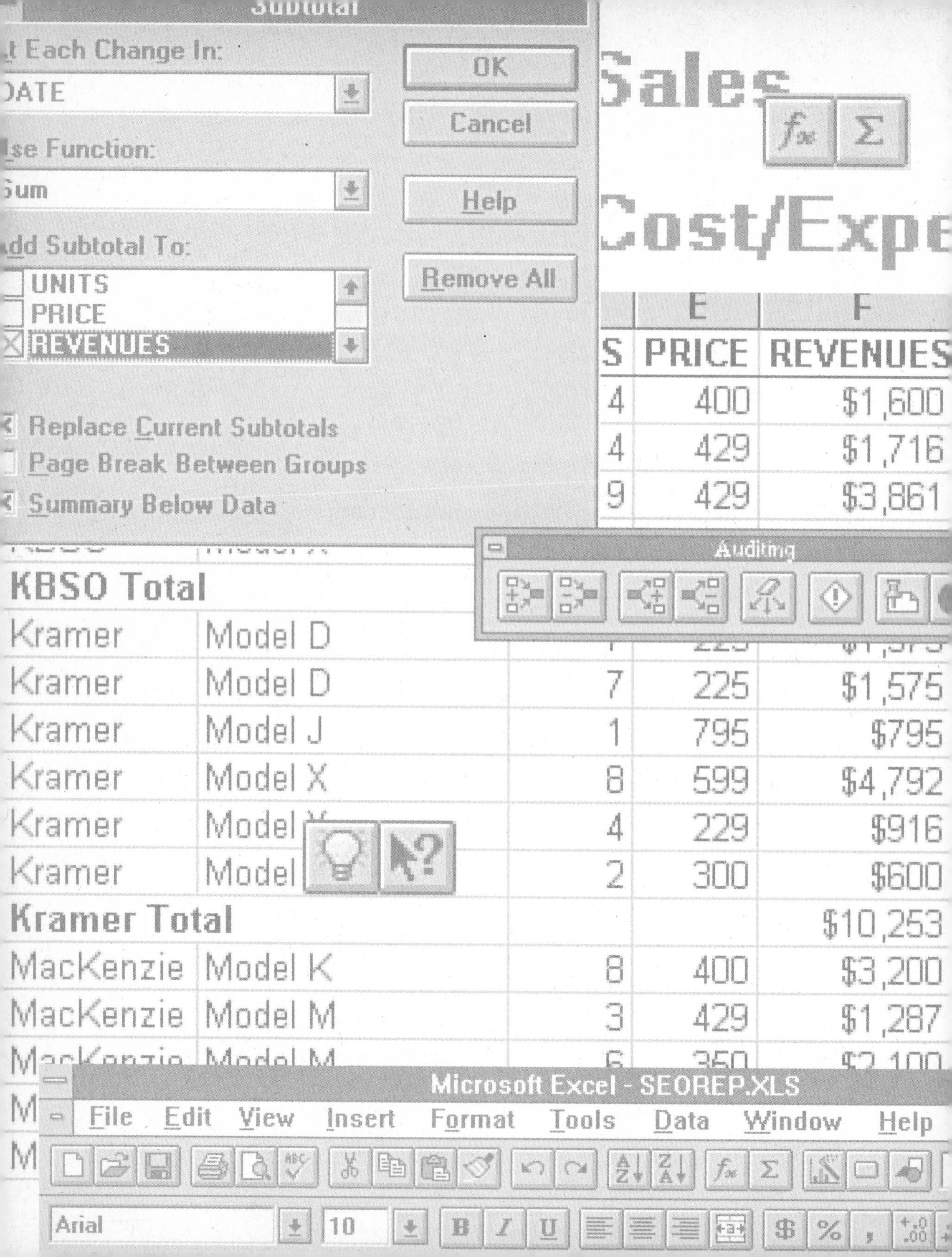

Subtotal
At Each Change In:
DATE
Use Function:
Sum
Add Subtotal To:
UNITS
PRICE
REVENUES
Replace Current Subtotals
Page Break Between Groups
Summary Below Data
OK
Cancel
Help
Remove All
Sales
Cost/Expe
E
F
PRICE
REVENUES
Auditing
KBSO Total
Kramer
Model D
Model J
Model X
Kramer Total
$10,253
MacKenzie
Model K
Model M
Microsoft Excel - SEOREP.XLS
File
Edit
View
Insert
Format
Tools
Data
Window
Help
Arial
10

Chapter 40

Customizing the Excel Screen

The graphical user interface of Windows offers the ideal environment in which to work because of its ease of use. Excel extends this capability by allowing you to customize your workspace.

As you learned from previous chapters, Excel allows you to change many of the elements of the Excel workspace, including creating custom toolbars, turning off the display of such features as the scroll bars and cell gridlines, and creating your own cell formats and styles. In this chapter, you learn how to change Windows settings to better suit your needs.

In this chapter, you learn how to:

- Access Excel's customization features
- Change the Windows colors and backgrounds
- Modify the color palettes in Excel
- Modify the international character sets
- Change the mouse operation

Exploring Customization Features

This chapter describes ways of customizing Excel that were not yet covered in this book. You may want to go back and explore the following features and topics covered in other chapters:

- *Ten-key accounting pad.* Choose the **T**ools **O**ptions command, select the **E**dit tab, and choose the Fi**x**ed Decimal option so that you can type numbers on the numeric pad and have the decimal automatically entered. For more information see chapter 4, "Entering and Editing Data."

- *Automatic rounding of formatted numbers.* Choose the **T**ools **O**ptions command, select the **C**alculation tab, and choose the **P**recision as Displayed option to make Excel calculate with the formatted number you see on-screen. For more information see, chapter 4, "Entering and Editing Data."

- *Worksheet templates.* Create default workbook templates that you use frequently. Templates are quick to access in the **F**ile **O**pen box. Templates can contain worksheet formulas, text, graphics, formats, macros, and display settings you want. You also can create chart templates that contain the chart type, formats, and scales for each of the chart types you use frequently. Chapter 42, "Creating Templates and Controlling Excel's Startup," describes templates.

- *Toolbars.* Customize existing or create your own Toolbars with the **V**iew **T**oolbars command. You can add and remove buttons, design and create custom buttons and toolbars, and assign macros to buttons. Chapter 41, "Creating Custom Toolbars and Menus," discusses how to customize Toolbars.

- *File loading on start-up.* Load workbooks and workspace files automatically by storing them in the XLSTART directory. When you use the same worksheets frequently, this setup enables you to get to your work quickly and easily. Chapter 42, "Creating Templates and Controlling Excel's Startup," describes different methods of starting Excel.

- *Run Custom Visual Basic procedures.* Assign macros to the Tools menu, buttons, and graphics objects in a workbook. Chapter 44, "Recording and Modifying VBA Models," and Chapter 45, "Programming in Visual Basic," cover Excel's Visual Basic programming language.

- *Custom menus.* Use custom menu bars, menus, and commands to change the control system of Excel completely. You use macros to change the menu structure. Chapter 41, "Creating Custom Toolbars and Menus," describes how to use the Menu Editor to change Excel's menus.

- *Custom dialog boxes.* Create custom dialog boxes and then use those boxes to retrieve information from users under Visual Basic control. Chapter 45, "Programming in Visual Basic," discusses dialog boxes in detail.

- *Workspace tools.* Choose the **T**ools **O**ptions command, and select the **V**iew tab to add or remove workspace tools, such as the formula bar, scrolling bars, status bar, sheet tabs, and so on. Chapter 16, "Managing the Worksheet Display" for more information.

- *Hidden elements.* Choose the **W**indows **H**ide command to hide active workbook windows. Choose the F**o**rmat S**h**eet **H**ide command to hide sheets within a workbook. Choose the F**o**rmat C**e**lls Protection command to hide formulas in the Formula Bar. Chapter 10, "Formatting Worksheets," and chapter 16, "Managing the Worksheet Display," describe how to hide elements.

- *Protection.* Use the **T**ools **P**rotection commands to protect worksheets and workbooks from being altered without a password. Use the **F**ile Save **A**s **O**ptions command to prevent a worksheet from being opened without a password. Chapter 9, "Managing Files," and chapter 10, "Formatting Worksheets," describe how to protect worksheets.

Creating Your Own Colors

Excel 5 has a palette of 56 colors available for use in worksheet and chart patterns. Although this palette is filled with a standardized set of colors when you get Excel, you can change the palette to use colors that you choose. After you define a set of colors, you can copy those colors to other workbooks or save a workbook as a template so that you can reuse the palette.

Note

If you have a monochrome video driver installed, you cannot customize the colors in the palette.

Caution

Before you change colors on the palette, consider that your changes may affect objects you have already colored. If, for example, you have created a text box with the fourth color on the palette as the background color, changing the fourth color on the palette also changes the background color of your text box.

To choose your own colors for the color palette, complete the following steps:

1. Open the workbook in which you want custom colors.

2. Choose the **T**ools **O**ptions command and select the Color tab. Figure 40.1 shows the Options Color tab. On a color monitor, you can see the actual colors.

For Related Information

- "Entering Numbers with a Fixed Decimal Place," p. 120
- "Working While Excel Recalculates," p. 122
- "Creating and Saving a Workbook Template," p. 1128
- "Customizing and Creating Toolbars," p. 1108
- "Controlling How Excel Starts," p. 1132
- "Creating Custom Menus," p. 1117
- "Creating Custom Dialog Boxes," p. 1212
- "Controlling the Worksheet Display," p. 533
- "Protecting Sheets and Workbooks," p. 362
- "Password-Protecting your Workbooks," p. 279

3. On the palette, select the color you want to change. Click that color box, or press the arrow keys to select the color.

4. Choose the **M**odify button to display the Color Picker dialog box shown in figure 40.2. The **M**odify button is unavailable if you are using a monochrome monitor; you cannot customize the colors in the color palette.

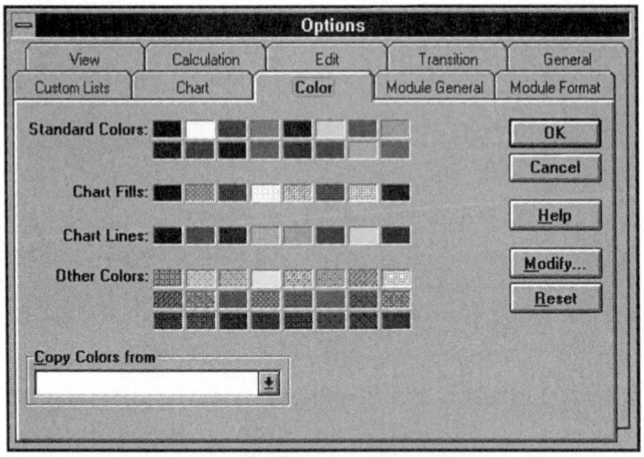

Fig. 40.1
The Color tab displays 56 colors you can change.

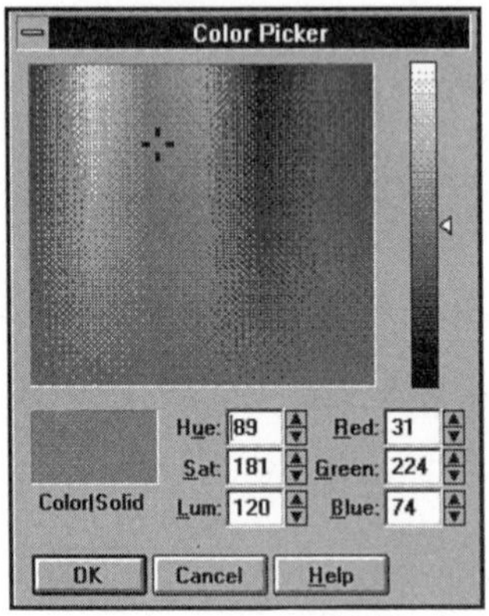

Fig. 40.2
Choose a custom color for a new color on your palette.

5. Select the new color you want for the selection you made in step 3 by performing one of the following:

   Click in the color box on the color you want. To change the luminosity, drag the pointer up or down along the right column. Watch the sample color in the Color/Solid box below the color box.

You also can choose mixtures of red, green, and blue. To mix these colors, select the **R**ed, **G**reen, and **B**lue boxes and enter a number from 0 to 255; 255 represents the greatest amount of the color. To change the hue of a color, select **H**ue and enter a number from 0 to 239; in the color box, 0 hue is the color at the left edge and 239 hue is the color at the right edge. Use the same method to change the saturation (**S**at); 0 saturation is the color at the bottom edge of the color box and 240 saturation is the color at the top edge. To change the luminosity (**L**um), enter a number from 0 to 240, which is the maximum luminosity at the top of the right column.

6. Choose OK to close the Color Picker dialog box.
7. Choose OK to accept your color change.

If you want to return the palette to its original set of 56 colors, choose the **T**ools **O**ptions command, and select the Color tab. Then choose the **R**eset button.

Note

When you copy a colored object from one workbook to another, the object carries with it the palette number of its color. When the object is pasted into the new workbook, the object uses the color assigned to that number on the palette of that new workbook. In other words, objects may change color when copied between documents that have different palettes.

To copy a color palette from one workbook to another, take the following steps:

1. Open both the workbook from which you want to copy and the workbook to which you are copying. Activate the workbook that will receive the new palette.
2. Choose the **T**ools **O**ptions command and select the Color tab.
3. In the **C**opy Colors from list box, select the name of the document from which you are copying colors.
4. Choose OK.

Colored objects in the document receiving the new palette change to reflect the new palette.

For Related Information

- "Adding a Pattern or Color," p. 351
- "Changing Object Colors, Patterns, and Borders," p. 480

Setting Preferences

Excel contains a number of features that enable you to customize Excel for your work preferences. These features enable you to change such options as enabling Lotus 1-2-3 movement keys or disabling Excel features such as drag-and-drop editing. Other preferences, such as turning off the display of the status bar or changing worksheet grid colors, are described in chapter 16, "Managing the Worksheet Display."

Operating with 1-2-3 Keys

If you are familiar with Lotus 1-2-3, you can use your knowledge to learn Excel. You can modify Excel to aid you in your switch from 1-2-3.

To use operating methods similar to 1-2-3 as you learn Excel:

1. Choose the **T**ools **O**ptions command and select the Transition tab (see fig. 40.3).
2. Type a slash character (/) in the Microsoft Excel **M**enu or Help Key text box.
3. Select the **L**otus 1-2-3 Help option.
4. Choose OK.

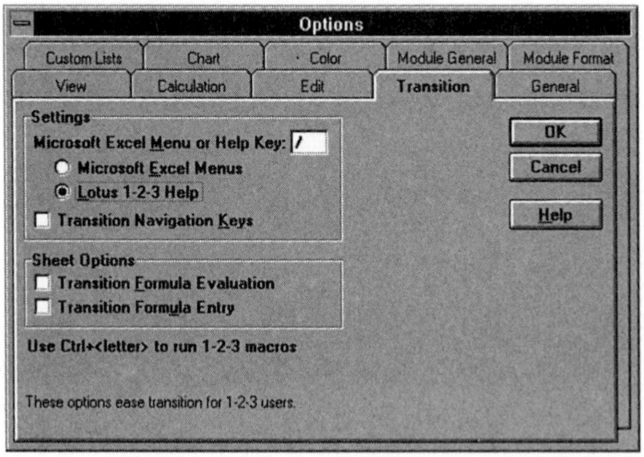

Fig. 40.3
Ease the transition to Excel from 1-2-3 with 1-2-3 Help.

Tip
To access more help when making the switch from 1-2-3 press F1, select Switching from Other Applications from the Using Microsoft Excel topic. Choose Switching from Lotus 1-2-3 for more topics.

These choices will display Excel's help for users whenever you press the slash key. While in a worksheet, you can press the keys that you would use for a 1-2-3 process, and Excel will demonstrate the equivalent Excel keystrokes. This method, described in the Introduction, enables you to use 1-2-3 knowledge while you continue to work productively and learn Excel.

Select the Transition Navigation **K**eys check box to use many of the 1-2-3 cell movement methods, such as End, arrow. However, Excel has all the equivalent navigation keys, so unless you are intimately familiar with 1-2-3 keystrokes, you should learn the Excel navigation keystrokes.

Moving the Active Cell after Entering Data

When you type data, Excel moves the active cell to the next lower cell after you press the Enter key. If you want the active cell to stay in place, follow these steps:

1. Choose the **T**ools **O**ptions command.
2. Select the Edit tab.
3. Clear the **M**ove Selection After Enter check box.
4. Choose OK.

Editing Data Directly in a Cell

When you double-click a cell entry, Excel activates the formula bar so that you can make changes to the entry. If you'd prefer to enter Edit mode manually, follow these steps:

1. Choose the **T**ools **O**ptions command.
2. Select the Edit tab.
3. Remove the check mark from **E**dit Directly in Cell.
4. Choose OK.

For Related Information

- "Getting Help," p. 55
- "Controlling the Worksheet Display," p. 533

Customizing Excel with the Windows Control Panel

You can customize Excel's features and appearance with the Windows Control Panel. The Control Panel runs from the Main group of the Windows Program Manager. In the Control Panel, you can set the computer's date and time, install or delete printers and fonts, change colors used in Windows borders and backgrounds, select international date and currency formats, and more.

To start the Control Panel from the Program Manager, take these steps:

1. Switch to the Program Manager if necessary by pressing Ctrl+Esc or by choosing **S**witch To from the application Control menu.

2. Activate the Main group window in the Program Manager by pressing Ctrl+F6, clicking the Main group window, or double-clicking its icon. The Main window is shown in figure 40.4.

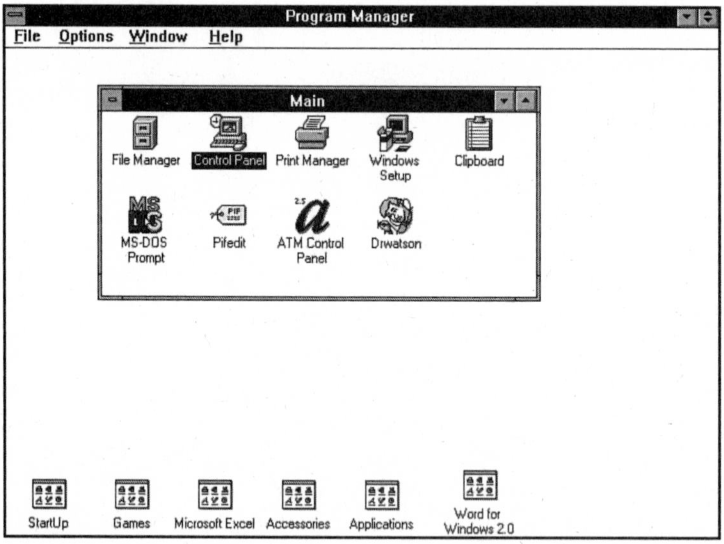

Fig. 40.4
The Main Group window contains the Control Panel icon.

3. Choose the Control Panel icon to start the Control Panel. Double-click the icon, or press the arrow keys to select the Control Panel and press Enter. Figure 40.5 shows the open Control Panel.

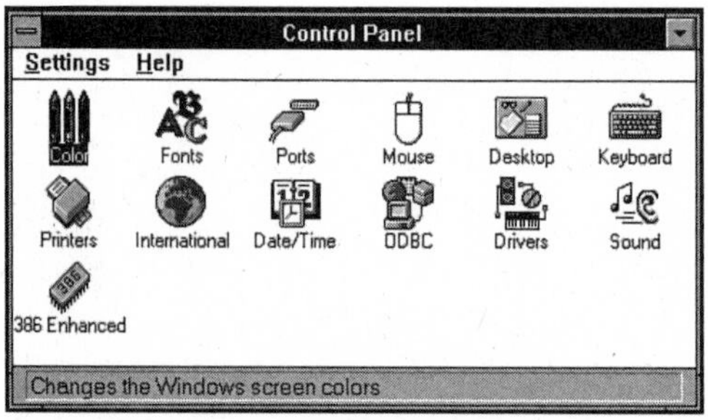

Fig. 40.5
The Control Panel contains utilities that allow you to customize Windows.

For information on how to use programs found in the Control Panel, press F1 or choose the **H**elp **C**ontents command. To display the topic you want information about, click the appropriate underlined name, or use the **S**earch button to search on a keyword. Each of the dialog boxes also displays a Help button where you can get context-sensitive Help on the current program.

Changing the Screen Appearance

You can change the color or gray scale for most portions of the Excel screen. You can select from predefined color combinations or create your own color combinations for different screen parts in Windows and Windows applications. To choose from the predefined color combinations, complete the following steps:

1. Choose the Color icon from the Control Panel by double-clicking the icon or by pressing the arrow keys to select the color, and then pressing Enter. Figure 40.6 shows the Color dialog box.

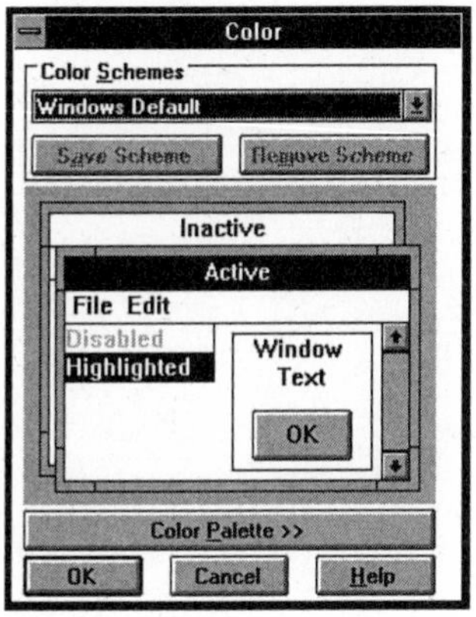

Fig. 40.6
Choose a predefined color scheme or create your own in the Color dialog box.

2. Select a color combination from the Color **S**chemes drop-down list.

3. Check the appearance of this color combination in the sample window in the Color dialog box. Select a different color to fit your mood or environment. Monochrome is best for monochrome screens. The default Windows color combination has the name Windows Default.

4. Choose OK to accept the new colors.

Changing the Desktop

All Windows applications and the Program Manager reside on a desktop. You can customize Windows to show patterns or pictures on this desktop. Windows comes with a number of patterns and pictures you can use; or you can draw your own pictures by using the Windows Paintbrush application that comes free with Windows.

To change the pattern, or *wallpaper,* of the desktop background complete the following steps:

1. Choose the Desktop icon from the Control Panel by double-clicking the icon or by pressing the arrow keys to select the icon and pressing Enter. Figure 40.7 shows the Desktop dialog box that appears in Windows 3.1.

Fig. 40.7
Choose a Windows background from the Desktop dialog box.

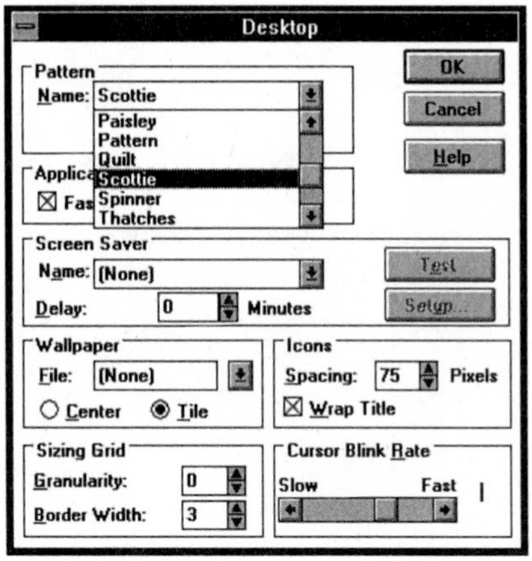

2. Select a pattern from the **N**ame drop-down list. Patterns are two-color patterns that fill the background behind a Window.

   Or select a wallpaper (picture) from the **F**ile drop-down list. Wallpapers are pictures or digitized images stored in a BMP (bit-map) file. Wallpaper takes precedence over desktop patterns.

3. Choose OK.

If the wallpaper is centered on-screen and does not fill the screen background, repeat the preceding steps and choose the **T**ile option. This option repeats the bit-mapped image to fill the screen. Take the time to experiment and look at some of these wallpapers and color combinations. They will keep you awake on those long, dreary February workdays.

Note

You can create wallpapers by drawing pictures in the Windows Paintbrush accessory and saving the picture to the Windows directory with the BMP format. Reopen the Desktop dialog box, and your drawing will be one of the listed wallpapers.

Customizing the Mouse

If you are left-handed and want to switch the left- and right-button functions, you can use the Control Panel to make the switch. You also can use the Control Panel to control the rate of motion and the click speed for the mouse. If you have an LCD display with a laptop computer (and you are using Windows 3.1), you can improve the visibility of the mouse pointer by turning on mouse trails.

To customize the mouse, follow these steps:

1. Choose the Mouse icon from the Control Panel by double-clicking the icon or by pressing the arrow keys to select the icon and pressing Enter. The Mouse dialog box appears (see fig. 40.8).

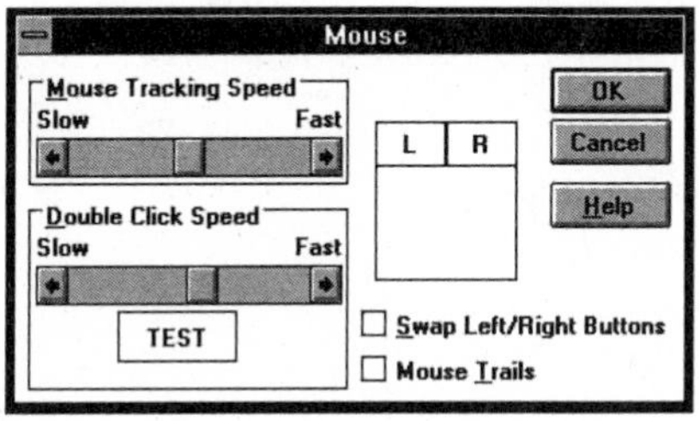

Fig. 40.8 Change the way the mouse operates with the Mouse dialog box.

2. You can change any of the following options:

   Mouse Tracking Speed: The speed the on-screen pointer moves with respect to your movement of the hand-held mouse. If you are a Windows beginner, you may want to start on the Slow side.

   Double-click Speed: The speed with which you must double-click for a double-click to be accepted. Use a slower rate if your are new to Windows. Test the double-click rate by double-clicking the TEST square. The TEST square changes color when it recognizes a double-click.

Mouse Trails: Produces a shadowed trail of mouse pointers that makes the pointer easier to see on LCD panel displays (used in laptop computers). This option is available in Windows 3.1 only.

3. Choose OK.

Changing International Character Sets

When you work in Windows, you can switch among different international character sets, time and date displays, and numeric formats. The international settings you choose show up in the formatting in your Excel worksheets. The F**o**rmat **C**ells Number list, for example, shows number and date/time formats for the country you have selected.

To specify the international settings you want to use, choose the International icon from the Control Panel by double-clicking the icon or by pressing the arrow keys to select the icon and pressing Enter. Figure 40.9 shows the International dialog box from which you can select country, language, date, currency, and other formats. Windows may need your original installation disks to change some settings.

Fig. 40.9
Select the international formatting options you need from the International dialog box.

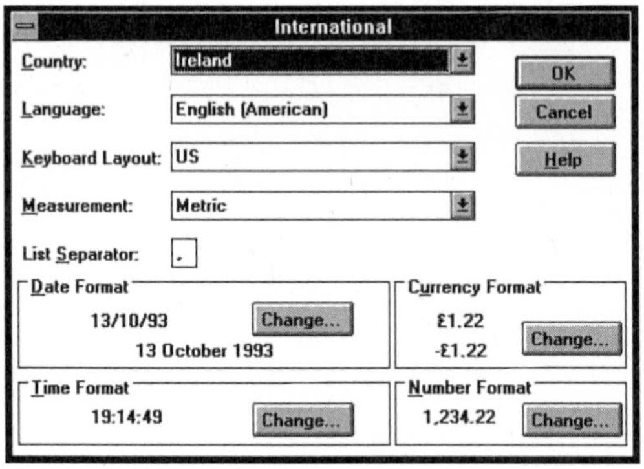

Select from the **C**ountry, **L**anguage, **K**eyboard Layout, and **M**easurement lists the format you need to use. Review the contents of the format text boxes in the lower part of the dialog box to ensure that they show the format you want.

If you need country settings that are not in the **C**ountry or **L**anguage lists, choose the Change button in each Format group, and make changes to individual formats as needed.

Troubleshooting

I am running Excel on a laptop with an LCD screen. The mouse pointer randomly disappears and then reappers while I am working. Is there anyway I can rectify this problem?

You can customize the mouse settings to improve the visibility of the mouse pointer. Switch to the Windows Program Manager, open the Control Panel, and choose the Mouse icon. In the Mouse dialog box, select Mouse **T**rails and click OK.

When I enter data in a cell and press Enter, the active cell moves down a cell. I prefer that the active cell remain in the same place. Can I change this setting in Excel?

The Tools Option command enables you to change many of the operations in Excel to work in a manner in which your accustomed, including preventing the active cell from moving when you enter data. Choose **T**ools **O**ptions, and select the Edit tab. Select **M**ove Selection After Enter to clear the check box and OK.

When I double-click an entry that contains a note, Excel enters Edit mode, and I can't see the note. How do you view a note in Excel 5.0?

A new feature in Excel 5.0 is the ability to edit a cell's contents directly in the cell. As you've discovered, this feature prevents you from viewing the note. You can turn this feature off by choosing **T**ools **O**ptions, selecting the Edit tab, and removing the check box from the **E**dit Directly in Cell option.

Another way to view a note in a worksheet cell is by using the **I**nsert No**t**e command. To try it, choose **I**nsert No**t**e and select the cell reference that contains the note you wish to view from the Notes in sheet list. The text of the note appears in the Text note window. Choose Close when you've finished viewing the note.

I have recently upgraded to Excel from Lotus 1-2-3. I was under the impression that Excel makes it easy for 1-2-3 users to make the switch, specifically, that I could use the slash (/) to get help on using 1-2-3 commands in Excel. However, when I press the slash key, it activates Excel menu bar. Have I been misled?

No, you haven't. In order to use the slash key to access help on 1-2-3, you must first let Excel know your intentions by choosing **T**ools **O**ptions, selecting the Transition tab, choosing **L**otus 1-2-3 Help in the Settings area of the dialog box, and choosing OK. Now, when you press the slash key, the Help for 1-2-3 Users dialog box appears.

From Here...

Windows and Excel are flexible work environments that make customizing your workspace easy. Take advantage of Windows by setting it up the way you want it. Examine the following chapters to learn more about customizing Excel:

- Chapter 10, "Formatting Worksheets." This chapter shows you how to change the standard font and create your own custom numeric and date formats.

- Chapter 16, "Managing the Worksheet Display." In this chapter, you learn how to control the appearance of worksheets and windows.

- Chapter 41, "Creating Custom Toolbars and Menus." This chapter teaches how to customize the toolbar and add your own buttons as well as how to change the menu by using the Menu Editor.

- Chapter 42, "Creating Templates and Controlling Excel's Startup." If you use the same type of document frequently, read this chapter to learn about templates and save yourself some time.

Chapter 41

Creating Custom Toolbars and Menus

Part of the power of Excel for Windows comes from its flexibility; you can change its shape to fit your work habits. You can create and modify toolbars, buttons, menu bars, and menus. You can add Excel commands that don't normally appear on the toolbar or menu. You can even assign macros and Visual Basic procedures to commands, tools, or buttons. This flexibility allows you to create your own customized workbook such as the on-screen policy manual as shown in figure 41.1.

In this chapter, you learn how to:

- Add and change toolbar buttons
- Create and modify toolbars
- Add and modify menus
- Attach macros to buttons and menus

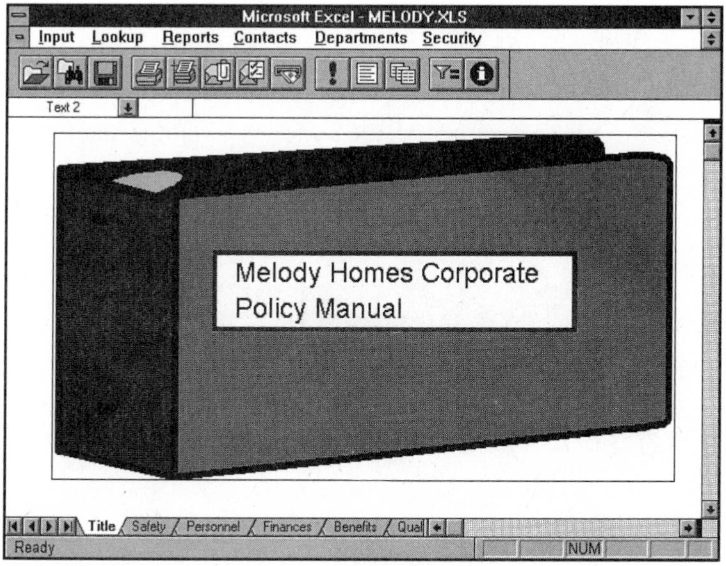

Fig. 41.1
Customize menus and toolbars. You even can assign your own macros or procedures.

Customizing and Creating Toolbars

Tip
Visual Basic procedures as well as Excel 4 macros can be assigned to menu commands and buttons.

Excel enables you to customize toolbars and create your own toolbars and buttons. Specifically, you can do the following:

- Change any of the built-in toolbars
- Design and edit your own toolbars
- Assign macros to custom buttons on custom toolbars

To make your work easier, you can create your own toolbars, rearrange existing toolbars, add or delete buttons, and even assign macros to custom buttons by using supplied icons or by drawing your own custom button faces.

Adding Buttons

The following example shows how you can add the Find File button to the Standard toolbar. To add a new button to any toolbar, complete the following steps:

1. Use the right mouse button to click on a toolbar and choose Toolbars from the shortcut menu, or choose the **V**iew **T**oolbars command.
2. The Toolbars dialog box appears, shown in figure 41.2. Make sure the check box to the left of the toolbar you want to change is selected.
3. Choose the **C**ustomize button. You see the Customize dialog box, shown in figure 41.3. The pointer is on the Find File button.
4. Choose the category containing the button you want to add to the toolbar. The Find File button is in the File category. "Using the Toolbars" in Chapter 2, "Getting Around in Excel and Windows," contains a diagram of the buttons and their categories.

Note

If you are unsure of a tool's function, click the tool. Look at the bottom of the Customize dialog box to see a definition of the function. Release the mouse button without dragging the button from the Customize dialog box. The same technique works on toolbars in the workspace (information appears at the bottom of the screen); however, move the pointer off the button before releasing or you will execute the command. You also can turn on mouse explanations of buttons by selecting the **S**how ToolTips check box on the Toolbars dialog box. When you have this option checked, a help pop-up shows when you point to each button.

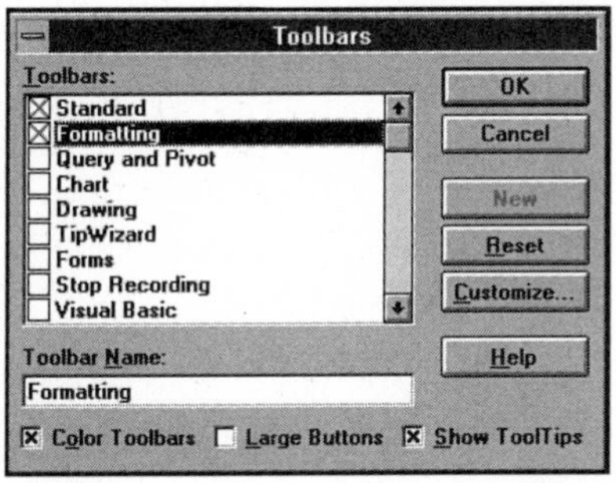

Fig. 41.2
Check the box next to each toolbar in the Toolbars dialog box to display the toolbar.

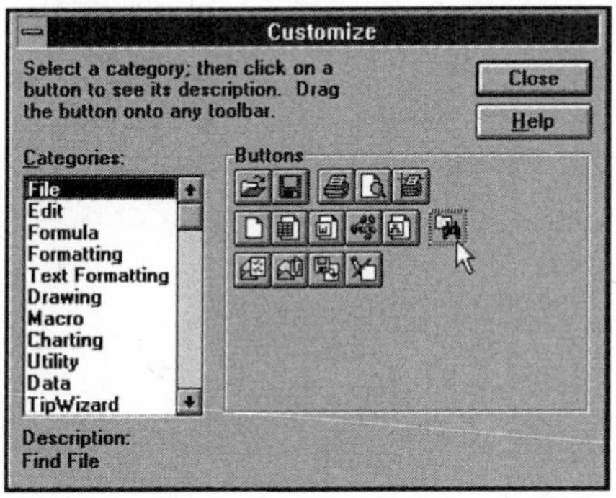

Fig. 41.3
The mouse pointer appears on the Find File button in the Customize dialog box. Find File appears in the Description area.

5. Drag the button you want to add, in this case the File Find button shown in figure 41.3, so that its center is over the location on the toolbar where you want the button to appear. The button is added to the toolbar.

6. Release the mouse button.

At this point, the standard toolbar may appear a bit crowded, especially if you are working with a standard VGA screen. (Some buttons may have vanished off the right end of the screen.) You can eliminate this crowding by removing buttons, changing the spacing between buttons, and changing the width of a pull-down list.

Note

You also can add buttons to a toolbar by moving or copying them from another toolbar. Display the toolbar containing the button you want to copy or move and the toolbar to which you want to copy or move the button, and then display the Customize dialog box. To move a button, drag it from one toolbar to another. To copy a button, hold down the Ctrl key while you drag the button from one toolbar to another.

Reorganizing Buttons

Tip
You can always return a predefined toolbar to its originally installed condition by selecting it in the Toolbars dialog box and choosing the **R**eset button.

When a toolbar gets crowded, you need to remove buttons, resize buttons so you can fit more buttons on the bar, or reorganize the buttons.

To change the width of a pull-down list, like the Font button, complete the following steps:

1. Click the right mouse button on the toolbar and choose Customize from the shortcut menu; or choose the **V**iew **T**oolbars command, and when the Toolbars dialog box appears, choose the **C**ustomize button.
2. With the Customize dialog box displayed, click a pull-down button in the toolbar, such as the Font or Style button.
3. Move the mouse pointer to the right side of the button. When the double arrow appears, drag the arrow left or right to resize the list box (see fig. 41.4).

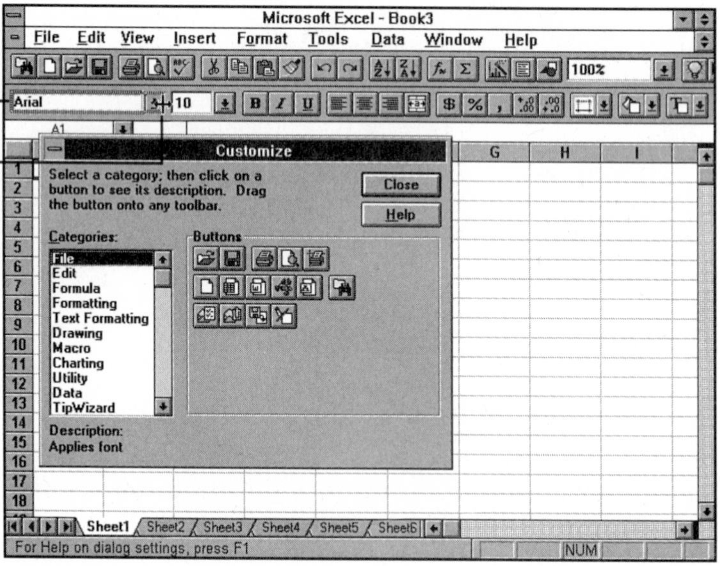

Font button being resized

Double arrow

Fig. 41.4
The double arrow allows you to change the size of the Font list on the Customize dialog box.

4. Choose **C**lose.

If you want to remove a button, complete the following steps:

1. Click the right mouse button on the toolbar and choose Customize from the shortcut menu; or choose the **V**iew **T**oolbars command, and when the Toolbars dialog box appears, choose the **C**ustomize button.

2. With the Customize dialog box displayed, drag the button off the toolbar into the worksheet area. Do not drag the button onto another toolbar.

3. Release the mouse button.

To reorganize a toolbar and move buttons into new locations, complete the following steps:

1. Click the right mouse button on the toolbar and choose Customize from the shortcut menu; or choose the **V**iew **T**oolbars command, and when the Toolbars dialog box appears, choose the **C**ustomize button.

2. With the Customize dialog box displayed, drag the button so that its center is between the buttons where you want it to be.

3. Release the mouse button.

Creating Your Own Toolbar

In addition to modifying the built-in toolbars, you also can design your own toolbar. To create your own toolbar, complete the following steps:

1. Click the right mouse button on any displayed toolbar and choose Toolbars from the shortcut menu, or choose the **V**iew **T**oolbars command.

2. In the Toolbar **N**ame edit box, type the name you want to give to the new toolbar such as My Toolbar (see fig. 41.5). The name can be any length and can contain spaces.

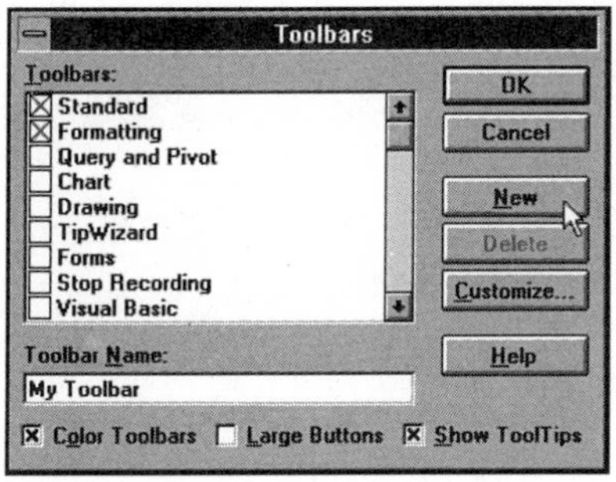

Fig. 41.5
To create your own toolbar, type the name in the Toolbar **N**ame text box and select the **N**ew command button.

3. Choose the **N**ew button to add the toolbar to the screen.

   The Customize dialog box is displayed. Your new toolbar is large enough for only one button.

4. Drag desired buttons from the Customize dialog box or from displayed toolbars into the new toolbar.

5. Choose **C**lose when you are finished. The new toolbar contains the buttons you copied into it (see fig. 41.6).

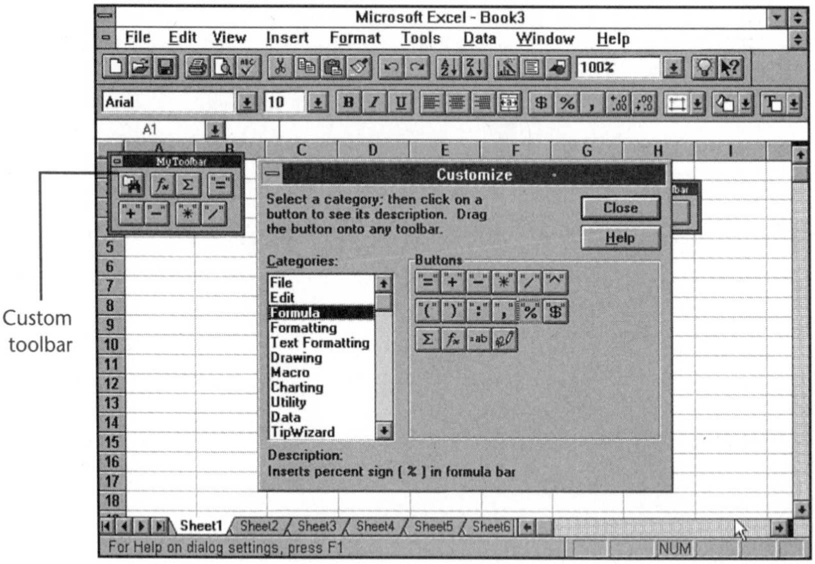

Fig. 41.6 This custom toolbar adds the Find File button and buttons instead of keys on the keyboard for creating formulas.

A quick way to create a toolbar is to display the Customize dialog box and drag one of the buttons onto your worksheet. A custom toolbar called Toolbar1, or 2, or the next sequential number appears. You cannot rename a toolbar. Your new toolbar's name now appears at the bottom of the list of toolbars. You can treat it like any other toolbar.

Note

To delete a custom toolbar, click the right mouse button on the toolbar, and choose Toolbars from the Shortcut menu; or choose the **V**iew **T**oolbars command, and select the custom toolbar from the **T**oolbars list. Then choose the **D**elete button.

Assigning a Macro or Visual Basic Procedures to a Button

In addition to providing fast access to often-used Excel commands, you also can use the toolbar to run macros. The Custom category in the Customize list contains blank buttons that you can add your macros to. When you want to assign a macro to a button, drag one of these custom button faces onto a toolbar and assign your macro to it.

To assign a macro to a toolbar, perform these steps:

1. Display the toolbar that contains the button you want to assign to a macro.
2. Click the right mouse button on the toolbar and choose Customize from the shortcut menu; or choose the **V**iew **T**oolbars command, and when the Toolbars dialog box appears, choose the **C**ustomize button.
3. With the Customize dialog box displayed, select Custom from the **C**ategories list.
4. Drag one of the custom buttons onto your toolbar. The Assign Macro dialog box appears, as shown in figure 41.7.

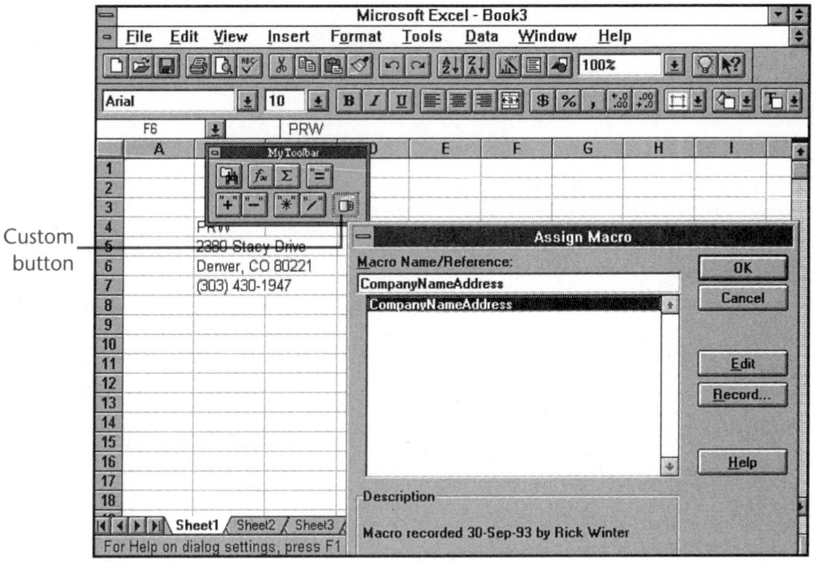

Fig. 41.7
This custom button adds the company name and address through the Assign Macro dialog box.

5. In the **M**acro Name/Reference list, choose the macro you want associated with the button and click OK, or choose **R**ecord to record a new macro.

Drawing Your Own Button Faces

To further customize a toolbar, you can draw your own button faces by using a graphics application, such as Windows Paintbrush. You then copy the picture from the graphics application and paste it onto a button. You get the best results if you make the picture you draw the same size as the existing button face; the easiest way is to copy an existing button face into the graphics application and make your new button face the same size.

Figure 41.8 shows a flag face button that has been added to a toolbar.

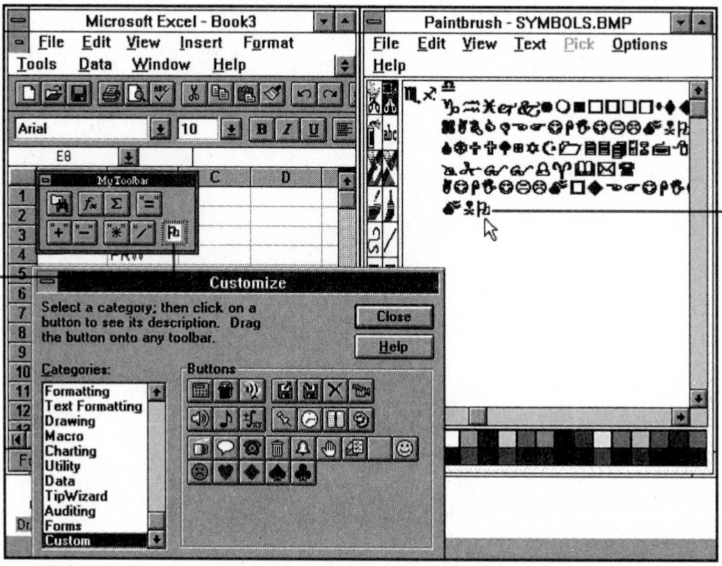

Fig. 41.8
The flag button was created from Paintbrush symbol font characters.

To draw a custom button face, perform the following steps:

1. Click the right mouse button on the toolbar and choose Customize from the shortcut menu; or choose the **V**iew **T**oolbars command, and when the Toolbars dialog box appears, choose the **C**ustomize button.

2. In the toolbar, click the button face you want to customize. (The Customize dialog box must be displayed, or clicking the button face activates the button.)

3. Choose the **E**dit **C**opy Button Image command.

4. Switch to your graphics application, and choose the **E**dit **P**aste command. Change the button face as you like.

5. Select your new button face, and choose the **E**dit **C**opy command. Be certain that you select just the button face—not any blank space around it.

6. Switch back to Excel.

7. Choose the **E**dit **P**aste Button Image command.

8. Choose Close to close the Customize dialog box.

As an alternative, you can use Excel's freehand buttons to create a button face. Display the Drawing button bar, and use the buttons to create a button face.

After you create the button, select the drawing, and choose **E**dit **C**opy. Then display the Customize dialog box, and in a toolbar, click the button whose face you want to customize. Choose the **E**dit **P**aste Button Image command.

You also can copy a button face to a different button. Display the Customize dialog box, and click the button whose face you want to copy. Choose **E**dit **C**opy Button Image. Click the button to which you want to copy the face, and choose **E**dit **P**aste Button Image. Choose Close to close the Customize dialog box.

To reset a button face back to its original appearance, display the Customize dialog box, and click with the right mouse button on the button whose face you want to reset. From the shortcut menu, select Reset Button Image.

Transferring Toolbars to Other Users

If you want to share a toolbar you created with another user, you can attach the toolbar to a workbook and then give a copy of the workbook file to them.

To attach a toolbar to a workbook, follow these steps:

1. Open the file to which you want to attach the toolbar.
2. Enter the Visual Basic module by selecting a workbook tab for a Visual Basic module or by choosing the **I**nsert **M**acro **M**odule command.
3. Choose the **T**ools Attach **T**oolbar command. The Attach Toolbars dialog box appears as shown in figure 41.9.

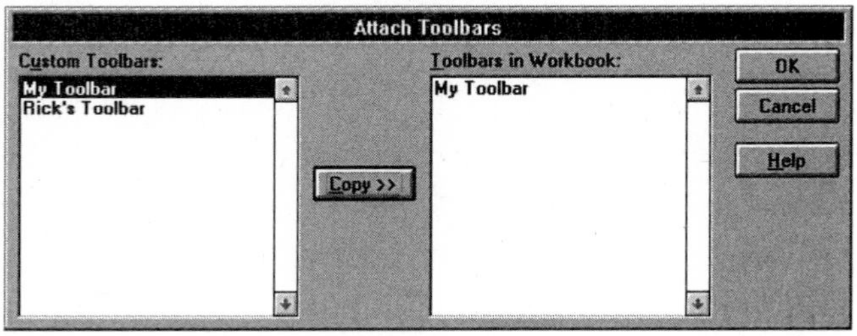

Fig. 41.9 The Attach Toolbars dialog box allows you to attach custom toolbars to workbooks.

4. Select the toolbars in the C**u**stom Toolbars list box.

5. Select the **C**opy command button. The name or names of the toolbars appear in the **T**oolbars in Workbook list box.

6. Choose OK.

7. Make sure you save the workbook after you complete this procedure.

Troubleshooting

Toolbars end up in wrong places on-screen.

Because manipulating toolbars is so easy, you can create problems with your screen, especially because the toolbar changes remain on-screen after you exit and return to Excel. The program does not prompt you if you want to save changes to toolbars, nor does Excel have a reset option to return the screen to its original display.

Without realizing it, a user can drag the standard toolbar to the middle of the screen, and move the formatting toolbar to the top of the screen. This can really become frustrating and confusing to a new user. To return toolbars to the top of the screen, drag any portion of the toolbar that is not a tool. As you drag, a gray outline appears. Drag this outline onto the menu bar. The toolbar reappears directly below the menu bar.

The wrong toolbar appears on-screen.

To remove a toolbar from the screen, click the right mouse button on the toolbar and select the toolbar that is marked with a check mark.

The toolbar is a mess—too many buttons.

If you add a bunch of junk buttons to one of Excel's toolbars (as opposed to a custom toolbar you created) and you later want to return the toolbar to its original form, select the toolbar and then select the **R**eset command button on the Toolbars dialog box.

For Related Information

■ "Using the Toolbars," p. 41

Creating Custom Menus

In addition to changing toolbars, you can also change menus to fit your needs. You can add items to existing menus, create new menus, and even create new menu bars. With the flexibility to change Excel this way, you can enhance your productivity with procedures you do often and can create custom applications for your business.

You can modify menus with two different procedures. You can change menus through Excel's Visual Basic module Menu Editor, or by programming directly in Visual Basic. This chapter focuses on the Menu Editor. For more information on programming in Visual Basic, see Chapters 43–46 in Part VIII, "Automating with Visual Basic for Applications."

Running the Menu Editor

The Menu Editor is available when a Visual Basic module is active. If you already have a module sheet as part of your workbook, select the sheet tab containing the module; otherwise, you need to add a Visual Basic module sheet to your workbook.

To insert a Visual Basic module sheet, follow these steps:

1. Select a sheet on your workbook. (The Visual Basic module sheet will be added before this sheet.)

2. Choose the **I**nsert **M**acro **M**odule command. You enter a blank sheet, and the sheet tab says Module1 as shown in figure 41.10. If you have existing Modules, the sheet tab says Module2, Module3, and so forth. Along with the blank sheet, the Visual Basic toolbar appears.

3. Click the Menu Editor button on the Visual Basic toolbar or choose the **T**ools Men**u** Editor command.

   The Menu Editor dialog box appears as shown in figure 41.11.

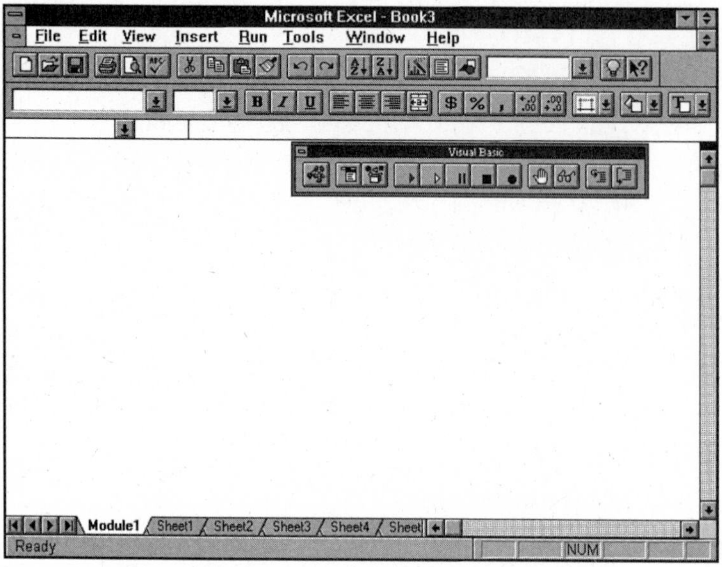

Fig. 41.10
When you add a new Visual Basic module sheet, the sheet is blank with a new Module1 sheet tab.

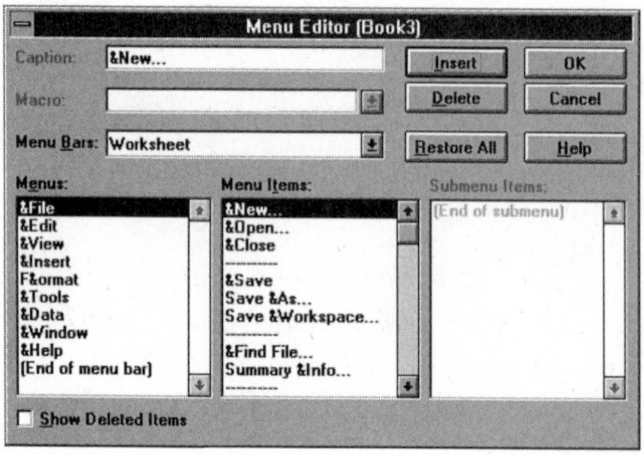

Fig. 41.11
Use the Menu Editor to add, delete, or modify existing or new menu items.

Understanding Menu Terms

To use the Menu Editor, you need to be familiar with four terms: menu bar, menu, menu item, and submenu item. The first term, the *menu bar,* is the main menu for the window or a shortcut menu that appears when you click the right mouse button on an object. Seven built-in menu bars are available, and you can create up to 15 custom menu bars at one time. When you select the Menu **B**ars pull-down list on the Menu Editor, you can select from the built-in or custom menu bars to modify. The built-in menus are described in table 41.1.

Table 41.1 The Built-In Menu Bars

Menu bar	Description
Worksheet	The menu bar appearing when a worksheet is active
Chart	The menu bar appearing when a chart is active
Visual Basic Module	The menu bar appearing at the top of the Visual Basic module
Shortcut Menus 1	Menus appearing when you click the right mouse button on a toolbar, cell, column, row, workbook tab, window title bar, or desktop
Shortcut Menus 2	Menus appearing when you click the right mouse button on a drawing object, button, or text box
Shortcut Menus 3	Menus appearing when you click the right mouse button on parts of a chart

Figure 41.12 shows the parts of a menu bar. A *menu* drops down when you select one of the choices on the menu bar. Most menu bars start with the **F**ile menu and end with **H**elp menu. A *menu item* is a choice on a menu. Menu items are separated into sections on the menu by *separator bars*. Menu items with an *ellipsis* bring up a dialog box. If a menu item has further choices, an arrow indicates *submenu items* are available.

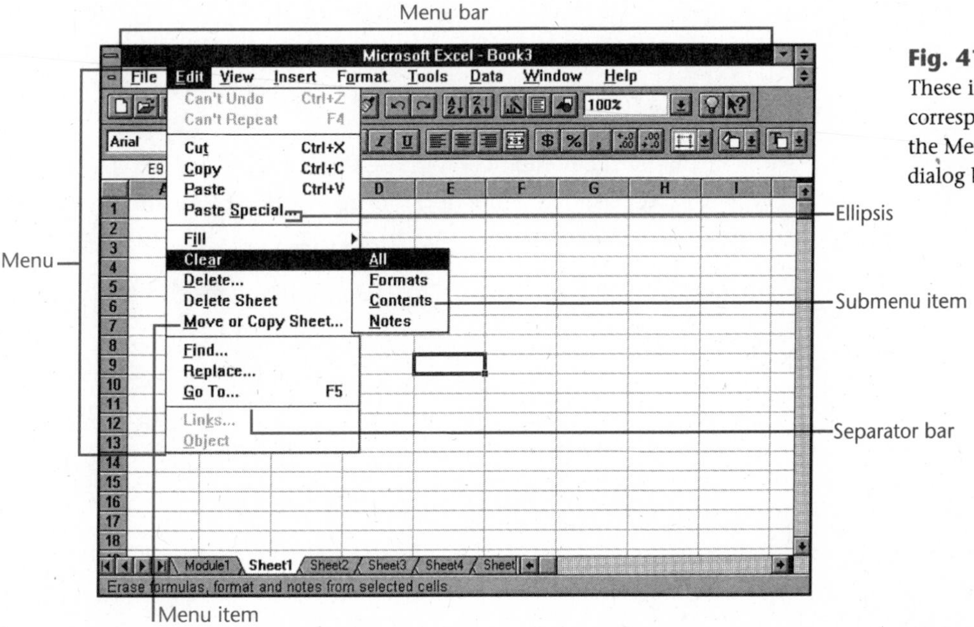

Fig. 41.12 These items correspond to the Menu Editor dialog box.

Building Menus from the Top Down

The following steps describe how to add to existing menu structures, create new menu structures, or modify exisiting menu structures. The following steps describe how to add each level of a menu's structure. One way to build a menu structure is to create one layer at a time: first create all the menu items, and so on. Another way is to build each menu and related menu items completely, one at a time.

No matter which method you use, it is important to remember to select upper levels of the menu structure from their list boxes before you can work on the levels underneath. If you want to create a new menu item, for example, and assign a procedure to it, you first must select a menu bar from the Menu Bars list, then select the related menu from the Menu's list, then finally select from the Menu Items list the item before which you want the new item to appear.

Creating a New Menu

To add a menu to a menu bar, select the Menu Bars list in the Menu Editor dialog box and then select one of the built-in menu bars listed in table 41.1 or a custom menu.

To add a menu to the selected menu, follow these steps:

1. Select from the M**e**nus list box the menu before which you want the new menu to appear. If you want a menu at the end of the menu bar, select [End of menu bar].

2. Choose the **I**nsert command button.

3. Type the name of the menu to add in the **C**aption text box. To create an accelerator key (underlined letter) for the menu, type an ampersand (&) before the character.

4. To add more menus, return to step 1. To stop creating menus, choose OK.

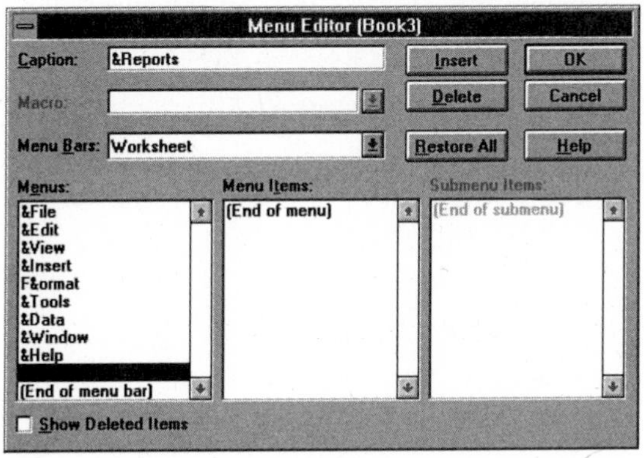

Fig. 41.13
The **Insert** button inserts a space for the new menu, and the **Caption** text box becomes available.

Note

Although you can have words with spaces for menu names, keep menu names to one word without spaces to preserve space on the menu bar and to avoid confusion since the name of each menu is separated by spaces on a horizontal line.

Adding Items to a Menu

After you select the menu bar and menu selected in the M**e**nus list, you can add menu items or separator bars to a menu.

To add an item or separator bar to a menu selected in the M**e**nus list, follow these steps:

1. Select from the Menu I**t**ems list the menu item before which you want your menu item to appear. If you want a menu item at the bottom of the menu, select [End of menu].

2. Choose the **I**nsert command button. A blank appears and the **C**aptions text edit box becomes available.

3. Type the name of the menu item in the **C**aption text box. To create an accelerator key (underlined letter) for the menu, type an ampersand (&) before the character. To create a separator bar, type a dash (-).

4. To add another menu item to the same menu, return to step 1. To add a procedure or macro to this menu item, follow the steps titled, "Assigning a Procedure to an Item." To add one or more subitems, follow the steps titled, "Creating a submenu." To stop creating menus, choose OK.

Creating a Submenu

After you select the menu bar, menu, and menu item, you can add submenu items to a menu item, as shown in figure 41.14.

Tip

You cannot directly rename a menu or menu item. To change the procedures associated with a built-in menu or menu item, delete the selection with the **D**elete command button and then **I**nsert the duplicate name.

To create a submenu under the currently selected menu item, follow these steps:

1. Select from the S**u**bmenu Item list box the Submenu item before which you want the item to appear. If you want a menu item at the bottom of the submenu, select [End of submenu].
2. Choose the **I**nsert command button. A blank appears in the Submenu Item list.
3. Type the name of the submenu item in the **C**aption text box. To create an accelerator key (underlined letter) for the menu, type an ampersand (&) before the character. To create a separator bar, type a dash (-).
4. To add another submenu item to the same menu item, return to step 1. To add a procedure or macro to this menu item, follow the steps titled, "Assigning a Procedure to an Item." To stop creating menus, choose OK.

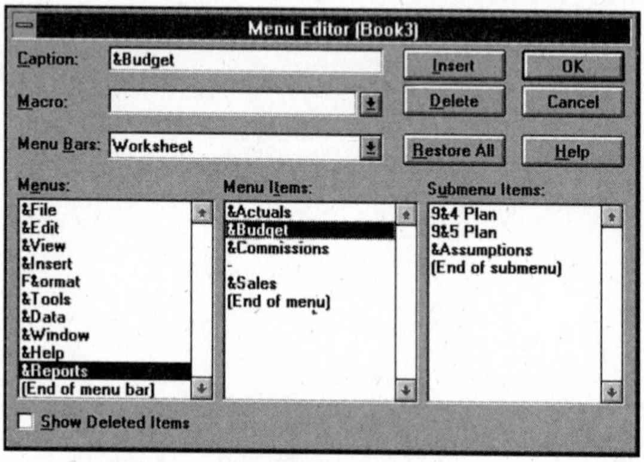

Fig. 41.14
The changes on the Menu Editor add a Reports menu with Actuals, Budget, Commissions, and Sales on the menu. The Budget menu has three submenu items: 94 Plan, 95 Plan, and Assumptions.

Note

To delete a menu, menu item, or submenu item, select the choice in the appropriate list box and select the **D**elete command button. If you want to reset all built-in menus to the default items, select the **R**estore All command button.

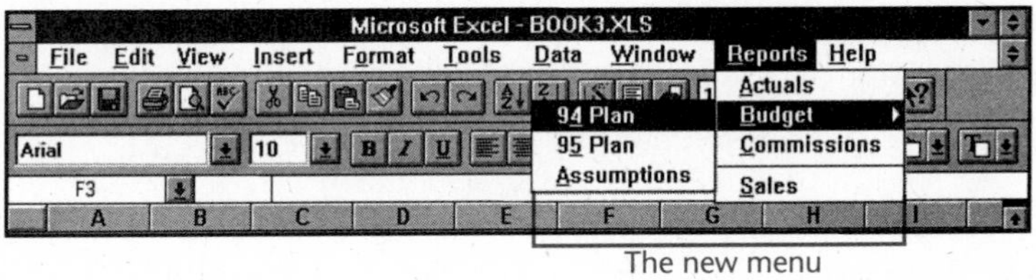

Fig 41.15
The menu created from the Menu Editor changes shown in figure 41.14.

Assigning a Procedure to an Item

After you create a menu item or menu subitem, you can attach a macro or Visual Basic subroutine.

To assign a procedure or macro to a selected menu item or subitem, take the following steps:

1. Select from the Menu **It**ems or S**u**bmenu Items list box.

2. Type or select the procedure or macro name in the **M**acro pull-down list as shown in figure 41.16.

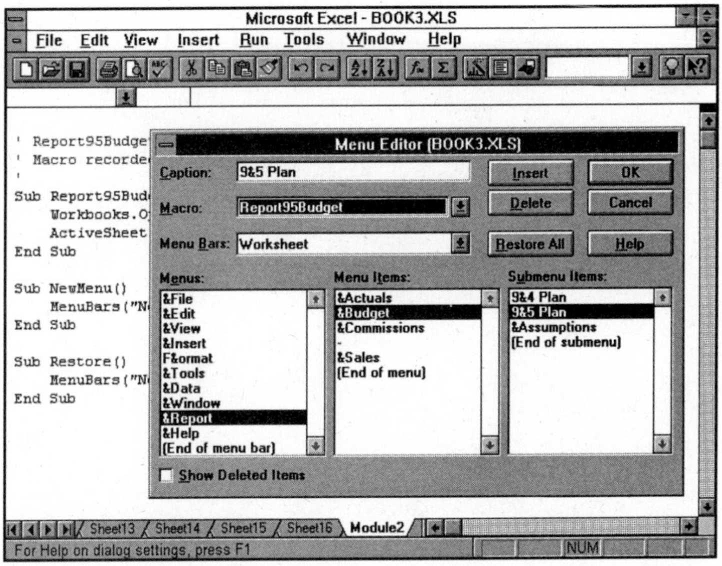

Fig. 41.16
You can assign to the menu item the macro or procedure you want.

3. To assign more procedures or macros, return to step 1. When finished editing the menus, choose OK.

   A menu is created (see fig. 41.15).

Creating a New Menu Bar

In some instances, you may want to create an entirely new menu bar. This may be true for your own accounting or data entry system.

To create a new menu bar, follow these steps:

1. Select Menu **B**ars in the Menu Editor and select any of the menu bars. It doesn't matter which one. The Menu **B**ars text box should be selected.

> **Caution**
>
> If you don't select the Menu **B**ars text box, the text item you type in the **C**aption text box becomes a menu item on the menu that is selected in the Menus box.

2. Choose the **I**nsert command button, which inserts a blank in the Menu Bars list. A Blank Menu Editor dialog box appears as shown in figure 41.17.

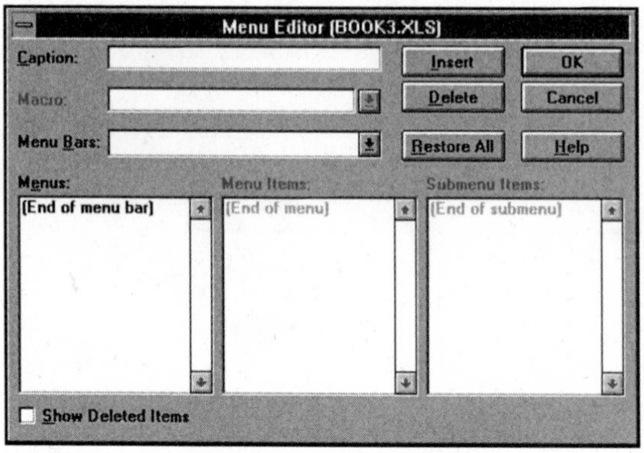

Fig. 41.17
Make sure the Menu Editor displays blank boxes for M**e**nus, Menu I**t**ems, and S**u**bmenu Items.

For Related Information

- "Choosing Commands," p. 38
- "Creating Custom Menus," p. 1117

3. Type the name of the new menu bar in the **C**aption text box.

4. Create menus, menu items, submenu items, and attach commands as described in the sections above.

5. Choose OK to finish the menu bar.

6. To display the menu, you need to create and run a Visual Basic subroutine with the command:

```
Menu Bars("name of menu").Activate
```

This command is shown in figure 41.18.

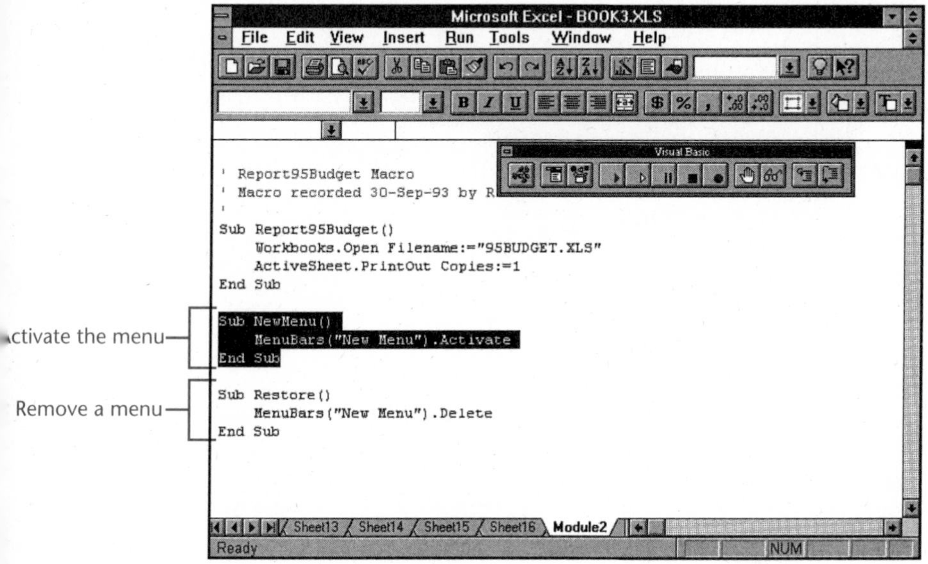

Fig. 41.18
The Subroutine NewMenu activates a menu bar called "New Menu."

Troubleshooting

You played with a menu so much that you messed it up.

If you end up with a menu mess and want to completely reset your menu, select **R**estore All on the Menu editor dialog box.

You cannot get the default menu back.

If, after you activate the Visual Basic NewMenu command, you cannot restore your menu, exit and return to Excel.

Tip
To remove a menu bar, you can use the Menu Editor or the Visual Basic command MenuBars ("name of menu"). Delete as shown in figure 41.18. Excel displays the built-in menu bar.

From Here...

For additional information that relates to toolbars and menus, you should browse through these chapters:

- Chapter 44, "Recording and Modifying VBA Modules." This chapter teaches you how to record and then modify Visual Basic procedures. You can assign these procedures to your toolbar buttons or menu items.

- Chapter 45, "Programming in Visual Basic for Applications." This chapter adds more detail and specific programming commands for writing Visual Basic procedures.

Chapter 42

Creating Templates and Controlling Excel's Startup

After you use Excel a while, you may find yourself making repetitive "housekeeping" changes to every document you open. Perhaps you don't like Excel's default page header, or you are always applying the #,##0_);(#,##0) number format to the entire workbook. By creating a special document called a *template*, you can tell Excel to incorporate these preferences in new worksheets, freeing you to focus on the task at hand.

Templates also are useful when you repeatedly create worksheets that incorporate the same data, such as labels and summary formulas. In organizations that use Excel extensively, templates can enhance accuracy and compliance with internal design standards.

If you work often with a certain document or group of documents, you may find it useful to move these files to an Excel startup directory so that Excel opens the files automatically. Finally, you can create macros and Visual Basic for Applications modules that run when Excel starts or when you open a given document.

EXCEL 5

In this chapter, you learn how to:

- Create template documents
- Save templates as autotemplates
- Cause Excel to open specified files when the program starts
- Create macros and Visual Basic modules

Creating Workbook and Worksheet Templates

A template is a file used as a form to create other workbooks. Documents created from a template contain the same layout, text, data formulas, settings, styles, formats, names, macros, worksheet controls, and Visual Basic modules as the features you find in the template.

Each workbook created from a template is a repeated image of others from the template. Templates are useful for forms, such as data entry and expense accounts, or for ensuring consistency in departmental budget presentations.

Understanding the Concept of Templates

A template differs from ordinary workbooks in two fundamental respects:

- Opening a template opens a replica of the template, rather than the physical template document.
- Template files use an XLT extension.

These two exceptions aside, a workbook template is like any other workbook.

Creating and Saving a Workbook Template

The phrase "creating a template" is a bit of a misnomer. Actually, you start by creating an Excel worksheet, chart, or other document type. You then add data, formatting, and other desired information to the document. Finally, you save the document as a Template document type.

To create a template, follow these steps:

1. Open or create a workbook that you want the template to use as a pattern. Include the worksheet elements (such as data, formulas, formatting and controls) you want.
2. Choose the **F**ile Save **A**s command.
3. Enter the template's name and select the directory in the usual manner.
4. Select the Template format from the Save File as **T**ype list. This step adds an XLT extension (the extension for template documents to the file name).
5. Choose OK.

Excel recognizes the type of document you are saving.

Note

Editing a file extension to become XLT doesn't save the file as a template. You must select Template from the Save File as **T**ype list in the Save As dialog box.

Creating Workbooks from Templates

Opening a template creates a new document based on the template. The template remains unchanged. The new document has a temporary name. If, for example, the template's file name is DATA.XLT, the documents based on the template are DATA1, DATA2, and so on.

You can make templates readily accessible by saving them in the XLSTART directory, which is a subdirectory of the EXCEL directory. Templates saved in XLSTART appear in the list shown in the New dialog box from the **F**ile **N**ew command. You learn more about the XLSTART directory in a following section of this chapter.

You can open a template stored in any directory; however, only the templates in the XLSTART directory appear in the New dialog box.

Note

You can change two important default worksheet attributes without resorting to templates. In the General tab in the Options dialog box, you can change the default number of sheets (**S**heets in New Workbook) and the standard font (St**a**ndard Font).

Creating Autotemplates

To change Excel's default font, formatting, protection, or other workbook attributes, create an *autotemplate*. You could, for example, create a workbook autotemplate with a footer that includes your name or the current date. If you then save the autotemplate in the XLSTART directory, it serves as the basis for all new workbooks you create. The autotemplate actually controls both the look and the contents of all new workbooks.

To create a workbook autotemplate, follow these steps:

1. Open or create a workbook that you want to use as the pattern for all new workbooks. Include the data, formulas, and formatting you want.

2. Choose the **F**ile Save **A**s command.

3. In the File **N**ame box, type **BOOK**.

4. In the **D**irectories box, select the XLSTART directory.

5. Select the Template format from the Save File as **T**ype list. This step adds an XLT extension to the file name.

6. Choose OK.

Now, whenever you create a new workbook (either by clicking the New Workbook button or choosing the **F**ile **N**ew command), that new workbook uses the options and formatting you created in the autotemplate.

At this point, you should review the key differences between ordinary templates and autotemplates:

- Ordinary templates can be useful regardless of where they are saved or how they are named. However, you must save a template in the XLSTART directory if you want it to appear in the New dialog box when you choose the **F**ile **N**ew command.

- An autotemplate, in general, is only useful if you save it under the name BOOK.XLT in the XLSTART directory. With that done, creating a new workbook opens a copy of the autotemplate. It isn't necessary to display the New dialog box.

Editing Templates

From time to time, naturally, you may want to revise your templates to reflect changes in your preferences. You can edit templates as you edit ordinary workbooks. You have to use a special procedure, however, in opening the template—otherwise you will open a copy, rather than the template itself.

To open a template to edit the template document:

1. Click the Open File button.

2. In the Open dialog box, select the template you want to edit.

3. Hold down the Shift key and choose OK.

Because you held down the Shift key as you choose OK, Excel opens up the true template rather than a copy of the template. After you edit the template, save by choosing the **F**ile **S**ave command. Excel saves the edited document in template format.

Inserting Sheet Templates

After a while, you might assemble several different types of worksheets in your workbook templates. You may want to use templates for individual sheets as well as for entire workbooks. You can tap into your collection of sheets that you stored as a template in the XLSTART subdirectory when inserting new sheets in a workbook.

To insert a sheet from a template into the current workbook, follow these steps:

1. Click the right mouse button on the sheet tab where you want to insert the worksheet, which brings up the sheet tab shortcut menu.
2. Choose the Insert command. Excel displays the Insert dialog box (see fig. 42.1, which displays the Time template used in an earlier example).
3. Select the template whose sheet you want to insert.
4. Choose OK.

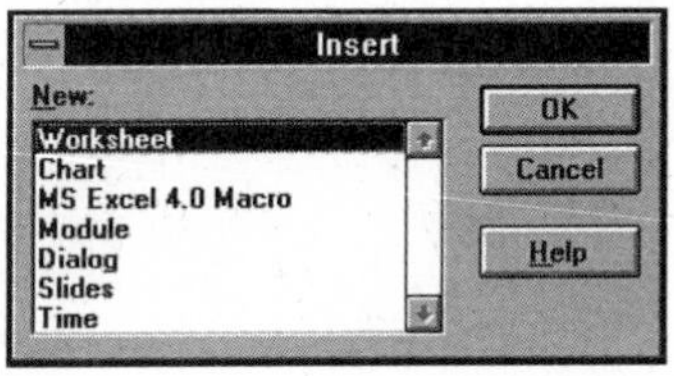

Fig. 42.1
Templates that you saved in the XLSTART directory are available in the Insert dialog box.

Figure 42.2 shows a time reporting sheet inserted from a template.

> **Caution**
>
> When you insert sheets from a template, Excel inserts all sheets in that template. This insertion can get messy if the template you select contains several sheets. For this reason, delete all blank sheets from workbook templates.

Troubleshooting Templates

A template was created, but rather than creating a workbook with the name of the template followed by the letter "l" when opened, Excel opens the actual template document.

You must have neglected to change the document type in the Save As dialog box when you first saved the template. Choose **F**ile Save **A**s, select Template from the Save File as **T**ype list, then choose OK.

(continues)

For Related Information

- "Changing Disks and Directories," p. 270
- "Saving Workbooks," p. 272

Troubleshooting (Continued)

After creating an autotemplate, every time Excel starts, it creates a workbook with the name of the template followed by the letter "1."

You probably saved the autotemplate as a regular Excel workbook in the XLSTART directory. Choose the File Save As command, and save the workbook as a template document.

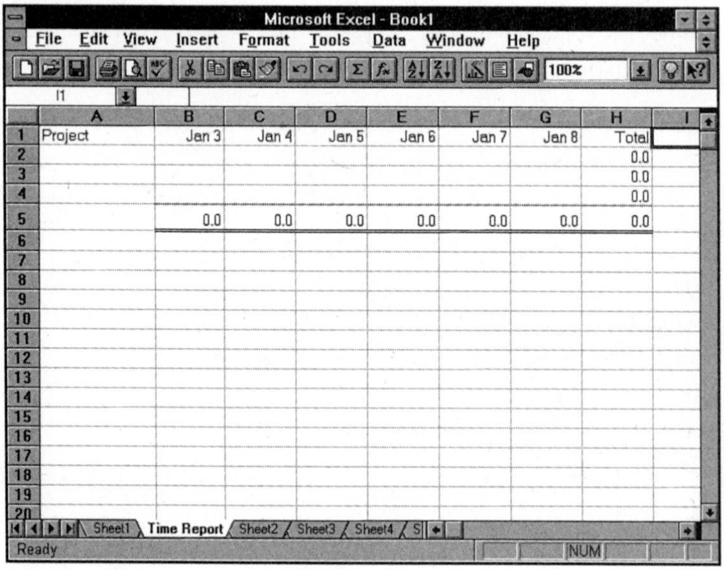

Fig. 42.2
The Time Report sheet inserted from the TIME.XLT template.

Controlling How Excel Starts

When Excel starts, it opens all workbooks, charts, and workspace files found in the XLSTART subdirectory. This feature is useful for automatically starting workbooks, macro-driven applications, and macro add-ins.

But you may also find it useful to have a separate start-up directory for temporary working files or for a private start-up directory on a network.

To specify one additional start-up directory, follow these steps:

1. Use the File Manager to create the directory that you want to use as a start-up directory.

2. Activate Excel and choose the **T**ools **O**ptions command.

3. Select the General tab (see fig. 42.3).

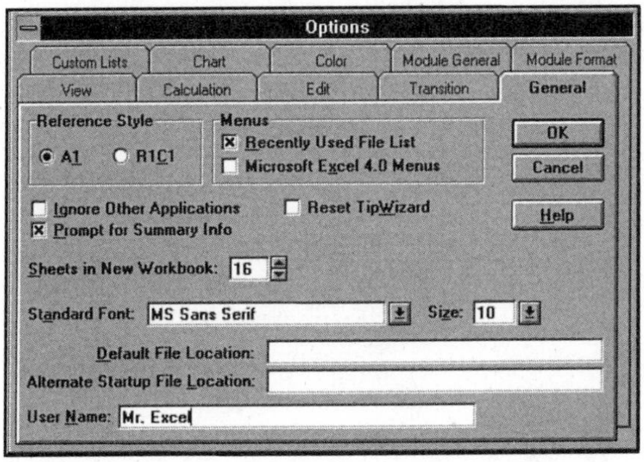

Fig. 42.3
Setting up an additional start-up directory in the General tab of the Options dialog box.

4. Enter the path for the additional start-up directory in the Alternate Startup File **L**ocation box.

5. Choose OK.

You also can specify the working directory—the directory selected when you display the Save or Open dialog boxes—in the General tab of the Options dialog box. The first time you start Excel, the working directory is the directory in which you installed Excel.

To set the working directory, display the General tab of the Options dialog box; then enter the directory path in the **D**efault File Location box.

Controlling How Excel Starts in the Windows Program Manager

You also can set startup options by using *startup switches* in the Properties dialog box in the Program Manager. Be aware, however, that any startup options you specified in the Options dialog box take precedence over the settings you enter in the Program Manager.

To control Excel startup by using switches, follow these steps:

1. Click the Excel icon in the Program Manager window.

2. Choose the **F**ile **P**roperties command. This brings up the Program Item Properties dialog box (see fig. 42.4).

3. If you want Excel to open a specific file at startup, type the path and name of the file in the **C**ommand Line box.

4. To specify a working directory, type the path and directory in the **W**orking Directory box.

5. Choose OK.

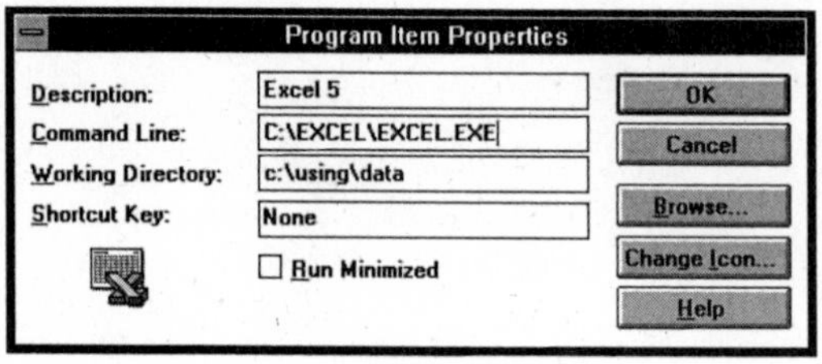

Fig. 42.4
Setting Excel startup options in the Program Item Properties dialog box.

Creating Custom Icons for Startup

You can customize Excel icons by task in the Program Manager. Suppose that much of your work in Excel is spent generating detailed proposals. To save time loading files, you can create individual Excel icons, with each icon associated with a different workbook, as shown in figure 42.5.

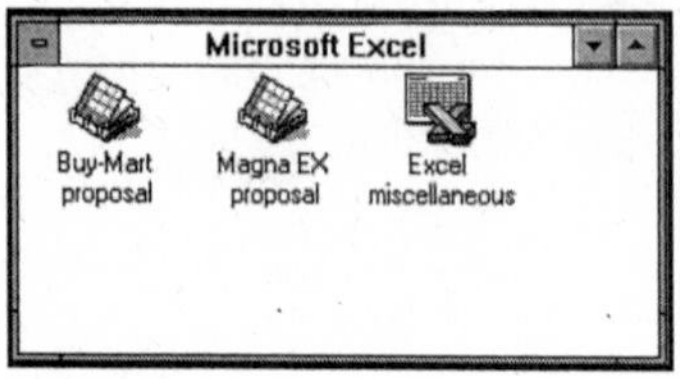

Fig. 42.5
You can create task-specific Excel icons. Each of these icons loads a different workbook or workspace file on startup.

To create custom Excel icons for specific tasks, take these steps:

1. In the Windows Program Manager, copy the Excel icon to the desired group window.

2. Choose the **F**ile **P**roperties command.

3. In the Program Item Properties window, make the desired revisions to the **C**ommand Line or **W**orking Directory options. For example, you can specify a file to load in the **C**ommand Line box. You also can choose the Change **I**con button and select a different Excel icon, as in figure 42.5.

4. When you are done making changes, choose OK.

Starting Excel with a Group of Workbooks

If you frequently work with a group of several workbooks, you can save the entire group as a *workspace file*. A workspace file is a special file that essentially contains a list of workbooks. By opening the workspace file, you open all the associated workbooks, which occupy the same window positions as when you last saved them.

To save a group of open workbooks as a workspace file, take these steps:

1. Close all workbook files that you do not want to include in the workspace file (see fig. 42.6).

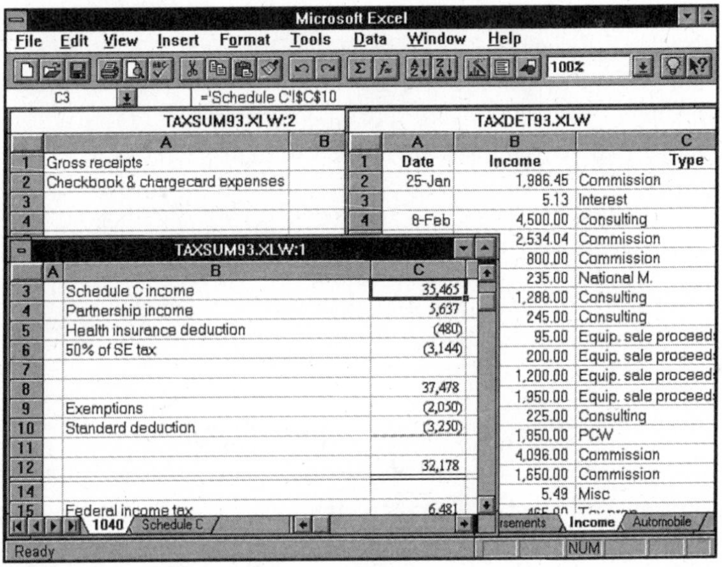

Fig. 42.6
If you save this group of open workbooks as a workspace file named TAX, you can later open them as a group by opening TAX.XLW.

2. Choose the **F**ile Save **W**orkspace command. Excel displays the Save Workspace dialog box.

3. Enter the file name in the File **N**ame box. If necessary, select the directory in the **D**irectories box.

4. Choose OK.

> **Caution**
>
> Be careful not to move files included in a workspace file to other directory locations. If you do, Excel will not be able to find them.

For Related Information

- "Starting and Quitting Excel," p. 25
- "Recording a Macro," p. 1157
- "Programming in Visual Basic for Applications," p. 1173

Running Macros and Procedures on Startup

Auto-Open and Auto-Close macros and procedures in a workbook run whenever you open the workbook, which provides another way to automate Excel startup. If you open a book or sheet autotemplate that contains an Auto-Open macro or procedure, the latter will run whenever you start Excel.

For more information on Auto-Open and Auto-Close macros, please refer to Chapter 13 of the *Visual Basic for Applications User's Guide* in the Microsoft Excel documentation.

From Here...

Creating customized applications at first may not seem worth the extra effort required. But features such as templates and startup directories can save considerable time if you do a great deal of repetitive work. For more information about starting and customizing Excel, refer to these chapters:

- Chapter 16, "Managing the Worksheet Display." Learn about how to hide, display, and customize elements on the Excel screen.
- Chapter 40, "Customizing the Excel Screen." When you want to change colors, modify the mouse, or customize your Windows environment, take a look in this chapter.
- Chapter 41, "Creating Custom Toolbars and Menus." If you find that you frequently use certain commands, you may want to add them to existing toolbars or make your own toolbars. If you record or program macros or Visual Basic procedures, you can add them to custom commands on menus.
- Chapter 44, "Recording and Modifying VBA Modules." Learn how to automate processes or tasks you do frequently.

Part VIII

Automating with Visual Basic for Applications

43 Introducing Visual Basic for Applications

44 Recording and Modifying VBA Modules

45 Programming in Visual Basic for Applications

46 Exploring Visual Basic for Applications Examples

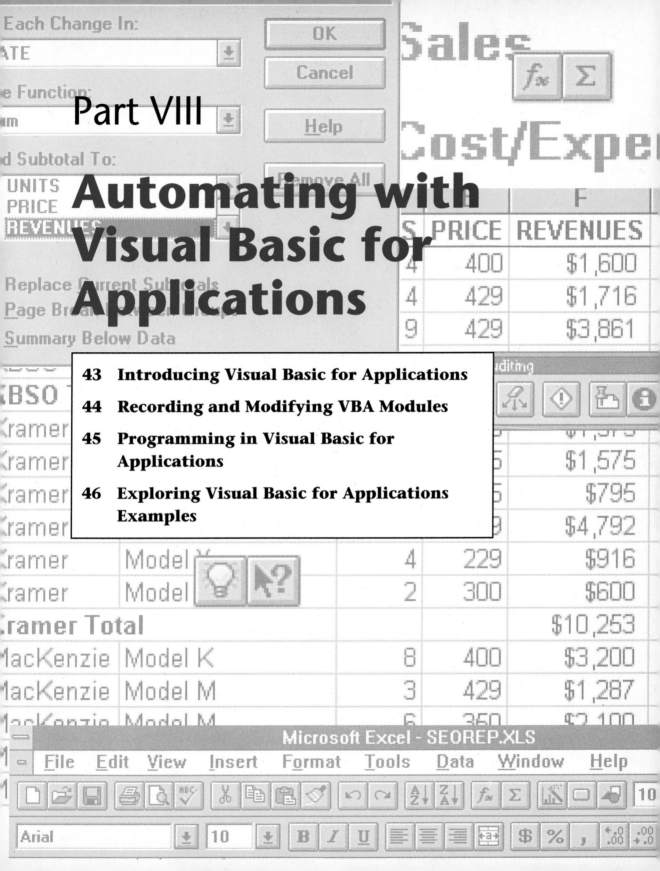

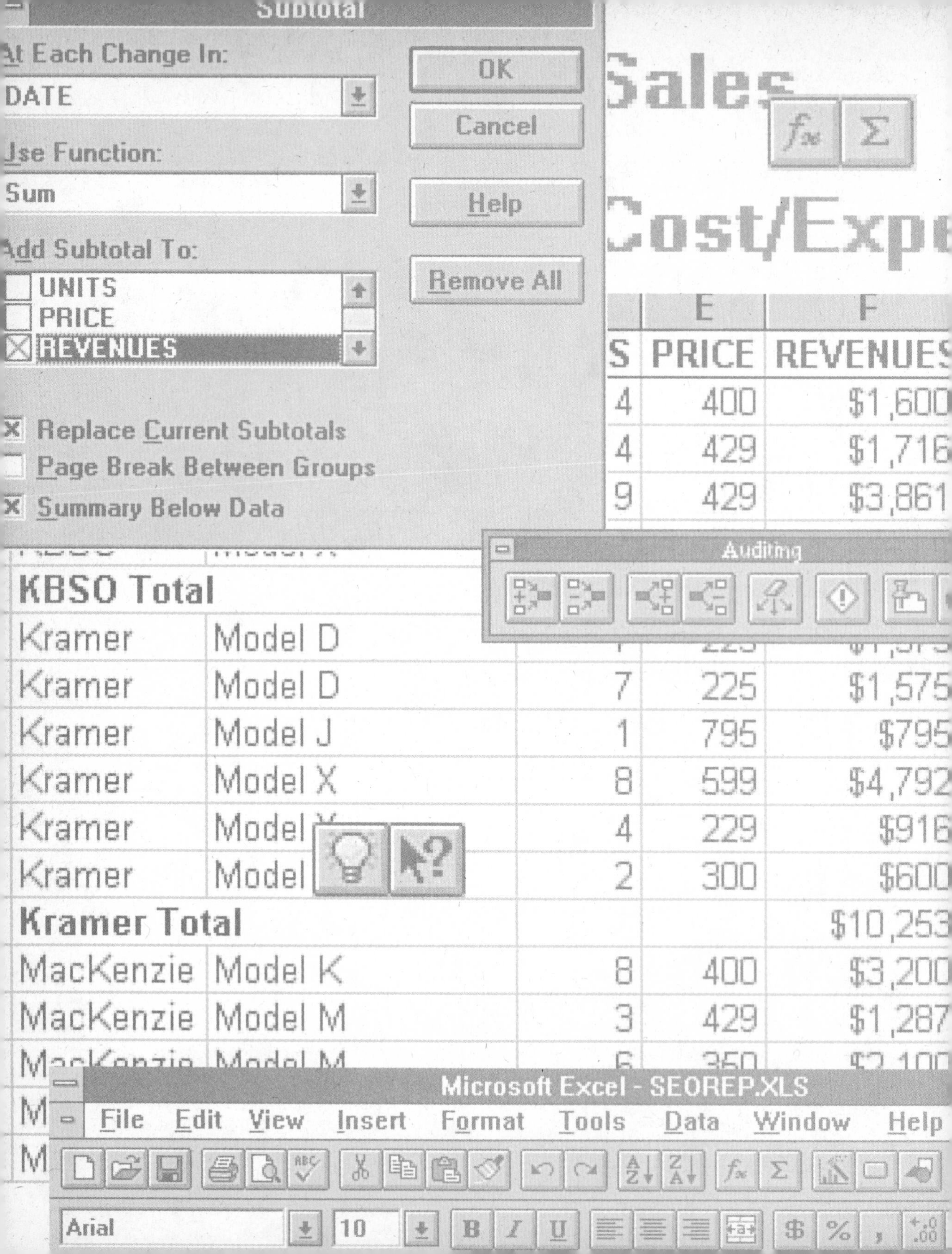
Subtotal
At Each Change In:
DATE
Use Function:
Sum
Add Subtotal To:
UNITS
PRICE
REVENUES
Replace Current Subtotals
Page Break Between Groups
Summary Below Data
OK
Cancel
Help
Remove All
Sales
Cost/Expe
E
F
S
PRICE
REVENUES
4
400
$1,600
4
429
$1,716
9
429
$3,861
Auditing
KBSO Total
Kramer
Model D
Kramer
Model D
7
225
$1,575
Kramer
Model J
1
795
$795
Kramer
Model X
8
599
$4,792
Kramer
4
229
$916
Kramer
2
300
$600
Kramer Total
$10,253
MacKenzie
Model K
8
400
$3,200
MacKenzie
Model M
3
429
$1,287
Microsoft Excel - SEOREP.XLS
File
Edit
View
Insert
Format
Tools
Data
Window
Help
Arial
10
B
I
U
$
%

Chapter 43

Introducing Visual Basic for Applications

In this chapter, you will learn:

- The differences between Excel 4 macros and VBA
- The concepts in the Visual Basic object model
- About objects, properties, methods, statements, and functions
- How to reference a cell, range, worksheet, or workbook
- How to change objects without selecting them
- How to attach Visual Basic procedures to commands or buttons on toolbars

For a number of years, Microsoft has hinted to the press and developers that their long-range strategy included a common application programming language used in all their applications. This language would be founded on BASIC, the most widely known computer language, and would provide power users and developers with a common application language (also known as macro language) between applications. This feature would reduce learning time and support costs. In addition, this language would provide the means for developers to develop systems that integrate multiple applications—enabling multiple applications to work together to solve a business problem.

That long awaited language is Visual Basic for Applications. The first Microsoft product to include the language is Excel 5. It offers power users and developers the ability to use the most common Windows programming language, Visual Basic, and apply it to Excel problems. It also enables users to more easily control other Microsoft applications. Once all the major Microsoft applications, such as Access and Word, include Visual Basic for Applications, it will be significantly easier to create integrated applications.

If you are an experienced Excel 4 macro programmer, you may face the transition to Visual Basic for Applications with mixed feelings. You probably have Excel systems that use the existing Excel 4 language as well as having hundreds of hours of learning and development in the Excel 4 language. Part of what you feel may be ambivalence. You are looking forward to a more powerful, easier-to-use language shared between Microsoft applications, yet at the same time you hate to think of redeveloping applications and learning an entirely new language.

The process of switching to Excel 5's Visual Basic for Applications is not going to be effortless, but it will be easier than when you first learned Excel macros. You won't have to make an immediate switch from the Excel macro language to Visual Basic for Applications. You can run your current Excel macro applications and program with the Excel macro language. Microsoft has promised that Excel 6 also will be able to run Excel macros.

You may want to begin the transition to Visual Basic for Applications immediately. Some of the reasons for using Visual Basic for Applications are:

- Learning and support synergy, because Visual Basic for Applications is the first example of Visual Basic for Applications, a common application language to be shared by all major applications.
- The language is based on Visual Basic, one of the most widely used Windows development language.
- Applications you write in Visual Basic for Applications can be copied into Visual Basic, compiled there, and run as Visual Basic programs that control Excel.
- Objects do not have to be selected in order to change their properties. For example, if you want to bold or clear a range on a worksheet using Visual Basic for Applications, you don't have to activate the worksheet and select the range.

Major Differences

There are major differences between the old Excel macro language and the new Visual Basic. However, if you are familiar with BASIC or Pascal, you will probably find Visual Basic fairly straightforward. These differences are discussed in this chapter.

When you write or record a Visual Basic program, the individual program is known as a *procedure*. Each procedure is like a macro in Excel 4. Procedures are kept on a Visual Basic sheet known as a *module*. You can have as many modules and procedures in a workbook as you want.

Understanding the Visual Basic Object Model

The Visual Basic for Applications language has a different structure than the Excel 4 macro language. The Visual Basic for Applications language is based on the Visual Basic programming language with extensions that enable it to control the different types of objects in Excel.

The Visual Basic for Applications language can be viewed as having two components—the Visual Basic language constructs and the Excel object model. The Visual Basic language portion contains statements and functions that are part of the Visual Basic language. *Statements* are commands that produce some action such as controlling the flow of the program. One of Visual Basic's statements is `If...Then...Else`. This tests whether a condition is true. `If` that condition is true, `Then` do some action. `If` it is not true (`Else`), do a different action.

Functions are Visual Basic commands that return a result, such as `Date`, that returns the current date in the computer system.

The Excel object models contains objects, properties, and methods that describe Excel and its contents. Excel *objects* are items in Excel that can be changed, such as a workbook, worksheet, chart title, range on a worksheet, and so forth. Each object has its own set of *properties* that describe it. These properties are its attributes or characteristics. If you want to set the value of cell A1 to 5, for example, you use a line like

```
Range("A1").Value=5
```

In this example, `Value` is a property of `Range`. Other properties of `Range` are `Font`, `Formula`, `Height`, `Hidden`, `Style`, and `Left`.

Each object also has related *methods*. Methods are actions inherent to an object. To remove the contents of the cell that just had its value changed, for example, you can use

```
Range("A1").Clear
```

where `Clear` is a method of `Range`. Actions that are inherent parts of `Range` that can take place on `Range`. Other methods that you can use on `Range` are `Activate`, `AutoFill`, `Borders`, `CheckSpelling`, `Copy`, `Delete`, and `Sort`.

You can obtain additional information on the topics discussed in this section from Excel Help. Choose **H**elp **C**ontents. Select Programming with Visual Basic, and then choose one from the following topics: Functions, Methods, Objects, Properties, or Statements.

Using Containers To Specify Objects

Objects may be confusing because there can be so many of them in Excel. In addition, you may find some code examples confusing because the programmer or Visual Basic has left out some of the objects in a line of code. As a result, the code shows only a property or method and not the object being acted upon.

Think of each object as a container that can hold smaller objects, and those objects within it can contain smaller objects, and so on.

The largest object is the *Application object.* When run from within Excel, the Application object always refers back to Excel, the application from which the procedure ran. This helps your Visual Basic program understand which program is being controlled when the Visual Basic procedure is controlling other applications as well as Excel.

One of the objects within Application is `Workbooks`. Workbooks is a *collection.* A collection is a group of objects. In this case, the Workbooks object contains a collection of all the open workbooks. You can use a Visual Basic `For Each...Next` statement, for example, to loop through each workbook in the collection Workbooks. If you want to refer to a specific workbook, you can use

```
Application.Workbooks("Book3")
```

To refer to a specific worksheet in Book3, you can add

```
Application.Workbooks("Book3").Worksheets("Sheet1")
```

To specify the first row, use

```
Application.Workbooks("Book3").Worksheets("Sheet1").Rows(1)
```

To specify the first cell in the first row, use

```
Application.Workbooks("Book3").Worksheets("Sheet1").Rows(1).Cells(1)
```

And, finally, to set the Formula property to `"Hi"` in the first cell of the first row, use

```
Application.Workbooks("Book3").Worksheets("Sheet1").Rows(1).Cells(1).
➥Formula="Hi"
```

This gets cumbersome quickly if you have to continually specify this many objects. But you don't. If you are referring to objects within Excel, you don't have to specify Application at the beginning of each line. And if the worksheet you are working on is active, you don't need to specify the Workbooks and Worksheets object. If the cell in which you want to put information is active, you don't have to specify the row or cell position. You can use a form such as

```
ActiveCell.Formula="Hi"
```

There are many shortcuts to using the object model. You can refer to active objects with the following shortcut object names:

```
ActiveWorkbook
ActiveSheet
ActiveWindow
ActiveCell
```

Another shortcut is to use the object `Selection` to refer to the currently selected object. For example,

```
Selection.Font.Size=24
```

Using *With* To Reduce Code Size

One additional way in which you can reduce the amount of Visual Basic code you write is to use the `With` clause. The `With` clause enables you to repeat several operations on the same object. If you turn on the Visual Basic recorder when you format selected cells with the F**o**rmat C**e**lls command, you see the following code:

```
Sub Formatter()
    With Selection
        .HorizontalAlignment = xlLeft
        .VerticalAlignment = xlBottom
        .WrapText = False
        .Orientation = xlHorizontal
        .AddIndent = False
    End With
    With Selection.Font
        .Name = "Arial"
```

```
            .FontStyle = "Bold"
            .Size = 11
            .Strikethrough = False
            .Superscript = False
            .Subscript = False
            .OutlineFont = False
            .Shadow = False
            .Underline = xlNone
            .ColorIndex = xlAutomatic
        End With
    End Sub
```

In the first `With` clause, the object (the current selection) has the selection's properties changed by the options in the Alignment tab of the Format Cells dialog box. In the second `With` clause, the Font tab of the Format Cells dialog box changes properties. By using the `With` clause, you do not have to repeat `Selection` or `Selection.Font` on each line.

Changing Objects without Selecting Them

As you probably inferred from the object model description, Visual Basic for Applications does not require that you select cells to change them or put something in a cell or range. As the example in the previous topic illustrated, however, specifying an object when it is not active can result in long lines.

Getting and Giving Information Using Parallel Syntax

One of the things that makes Excel 4 macros difficult to remember is that there is little or no parallel structure between changing an object property and finding what the current property is. Notice in the following example how changing the boldness of a cell uses a different function and syntax than determining whether a cell is already bold. In an Excel 4 macro, you make a cell bold with

```
FORMAT.FONT(,,TRUE)
```

where the third argument in this form of the `FONT` function is bold. To determine whether a cell is bold, Excel 4 macros use this function

```
GET.CELL(20)
```

where `GET.CELL` returns `True` if the active cell is bold and `False` if the active cell is not.

Because the actual words FORMAT.FONT and GET.CELL are unrelated, it makes the Excel 4 language difficult to remember or learn. And you always have to have a function reference manual available to make sure you have the right type number inside GET.CELL.

To do the same thing with Visual Basic is much easier. Both changing a cell to bold and finding out whether it is bold use the same syntax. In this example, the object is the range A1. The property to be changed is Font.Bold. To change cell A1 to bold, you use

```
Sub BoldMaker()
    Range("A1").Font.Bold = True
Sub End
```

If you want to determine whether A1 is already bold, you use the same object and properties, just on a different side of the equal sign. In the following code, the variable b stores the True or False result of whether A1 is bold. The code looks like

```
Sub BoldChecker()
    b = Range("A1").Font.Bold
    MsgBox "Is the cell bold? " & b
Sub End
```

In this example, Font.Bold determines whether the object Range("A1") is bold and returns True or False. If the cell is bold, the MsgBox function displays the message

```
Is the cell bold? True
```

As an aside, the MsgBox function can display only results that are text. The MsgBox normally cannot display the logical values of True or False from b. By joining the text message in quotes with the True or False result stored in b, the b is coerced into becoming text that MsgBox can display.

Referencing Ranges and Cells Is Easier in Visual Basic

Excel 4 macros use what appeared to new users as a bewildering collection of methods to refer to cells, ranges, or external references on nonactive worksheets. In Excel 4, you can use A1, R1C1, names, and refer to cells on the active worksheet with ! or on a specific worksheet with *filename!cellreference*.

In Visual Basic, you do not have to select an object before you find out its properties or before you change its properties. But you still need to refer to a cell or range in order to change it.

Note

Visual Basic objects, like the `Range` and `Cells` described here, cannot be used as a line of code by themselves. Use them to specify the object on which to apply the property or method, as in

```
Cells(1,2).Formula="Hello World"
```

or to specify where information is coming from, as in

```
Content = Cells(1,2).Formula
```

You can refer to the active cell as

```
ActiveCell
```

To refer to a cell or range using a text reference, use one of the following forms:

```
Range("B12")
Range("B12:C35")
Range("MonthReport")
```

The first is the single cell `B12` on the active sheet. The second is the range `B12:C35` on the active sheet. And the `MonthReport` is a named range on the active sheet. None of these objects can be used by themselves; they must be followed by a property or method.

If you need to refer to a cell or range by numeric position or a numeric offset in a row or column, use `CELLS` as follows:

```
CELLS(1,3)
CELLS(x,y)
```

If you need a specific location on a specific sheet in the active workbook, use the containers that surround the object you want to specify, such as in

```
Worksheets("Sheet6").Rows(3).Cells(2)
```

Other objects that are useful are `Rows` and `Columns`. If you need to offset the top left corner of a range use the `Offset` method. To resize a range, use the `Resize` method.

Note

A shortcut to writing cell or range objects on the active worksheet is to use the brackets ([ ]) as an abbreviation. For example,

```
[C14].Value=5
```

puts 5 in cell C14 on the active worksheet. You can even use the shortcut notation

```
[C14]=[B12]*3
```

where the result is that three times the content of B12 on the active worksheet is stored in cell C14 on the active worksheet.

Using Variables To Store Information

In Excel 4, macro names have multiple uses. They can define a range on a worksheet, or store a value, formula, or reference. Any name can store any type of value. In addition, any Excel 4 name is available for use by any other worksheet or macro.

In Excel 5, names define ranges on a worksheet, but variables store value, formulas, or references. You also can type variables so they store only specific types of data—for example, text or integer numbers. Data typing can reduce troubleshooting problems later because it prevents you from putting the incorrect type of data in a variable.

Another advantage to Excel 5 variables is that they can be *scoped* so they are available only within the Visual Basic procedure containing them, to other procedures within the module, or to other modules globally.

Storing Objects

In Excel 4 macros, you can store a reference or a calculated reference in a name. The name can be used later when you need to refer to that reference. To store the calculated reference that is offset from the name Budget on the active worksheet, you use

```
=SET.NAME("FutureRef",OFFSET(!Budget,2,3))
```

You run into the same need in Excel if you have objects that you want to refer to over and over throughout your Visual Basic procedure. To store an object for later use, use the `Set` statement:

```
Set FutureObj=ActiveWorkbook.Sheets("Sheet6").Range("B36")
```

You can use the variable later in place of typing the full object specification; for example,

```
FutureObj.Font.Bold=True
```

Creating Dialog Boxes in Visual Basic for Applications

Dialog boxes are significantly easier to draw and display in Excel 5. In Excel 4, you use the Dialog Editor to draw a dialog box. When the dialog box is pasted into a worksheet, it becomes a table of numbers and text describing the dialog box.

In Excel 5, you insert dialog sheets into a workbook and then draw the dialog directly on the sheet. Excel has more items that can be placed on a dialog. In addition to all the dialog items that are available in Excel 4, you also can include spinners and scroll bars (sliders). (The use of spinners and scroll bars on worksheets is described in Chapter 24, "Building Forms with Controls.") Spinners (increment/decrement arrows) are double-headed arrows that enable you to quickly scroll through numbers. Scroll bars enable a user to drag the box in a scroll bar to a new position, thereby entering a number. You use scroll bars for numbers that vary over a wide range.

Excel 4 has a simple method of displaying a dialog box and waiting for user input. To pause a dialog box in Excel 4 macros, just type a question mark between the dialog box macro function and its parenthesis. To display and pause the Font dialog box in an Excel 4 macro, use the following function:

```
=FORMAT.FONT?()
```

In Excel 5, the equivalent function is

```
=FONT.PROPERTIES?()
```

To make a built-in dialog box display in Visual Basic you use the `Dialogs` method combined with one of Excel's constants. These constants are part of the Excel object model. To select a range of cells with the name Total and then display the Format Number dialog box so a user can choose a numeric format, you use the following:

```
Range("Total").Activate
Application.Dialogs(xlDialogFormatNumber).Show
```

To see the possible Excel constants that display built-in dialog boxes, open a Visual Basic module and type the code

```
Application.Dialogs(
```

then stop and press F2, or choose the **V**iew **O**bject Browser command. This displays the Object Browser dialog box. From the **L**ibraries/Workbooks drop-down list, choose Excel. From the O**b**jects/Modules list choose `ExcelConstant`. The right-hand list, **M**ethods/Properties, shows a listing of all constants related to Excel. Drag the scroll box in the right scroll bar down until you see the list beginning with `xlDialog`. Select an `xlConstant` that is named after a dialog box you have seen Excel display. (Some of these `xlDialog` constants do not display a dialog box.) Choose the **P**aste button to paste in the constant. Finish the code by typing a closing parenthesis and ending with the `Show` method.

The final line should look like this:

```
Application.Dialogs(xlDialogFormatNumber).Show
```

Creating Menus and Toolbars

Excel 5 menus and menu items (commands) are much easier to create than they are in Excel 4. In Excel 5, you can create custom menu bars, menus, and menu items, including side or cascading menus. In addition you can create or modify toolbars. All these customized menus, commands, and toolbar buttons can have your Visual Basic for Application procedures assigned to them—instead of running built-in Excel commands, they run your procedures.

These menu bars, menus, menu items, and toolbars are a part of the workbook. Instead of using tables on a macro sheet to create menus, Excel 5 uses a menu editor. Toolbars are customized with the **V**iew **T**oolbars command.

To see the Menu Editor, insert a dialog sheet into the workbook, and then select the dialog sheet. Choose the **T**ools Men**u** Editor command. Chapter 41, "Creating Custom Toolbars and Menus," goes into detail on how to attach Visual Basic procedures to custom menu items.

Getting In-Depth Help On-Line

One of the best sources of technical information on Visual Basic is the On-Line Help. To get to the Help index for programming, choose the **H**elp **C**ontents command, and then choose Programming with Visual Basic. The Visual Basic Reference screen displays. One good place to begin learning details is to click the Objects link. This displays an alphabetized list of all objects. Selecting an object from the list displays the object description and examples. When you are looking at an object help screen, you can choose the `Methods` or `Properties` link at the top of the help screen to learn more about related methods or properties. Watch for links that say `Example`. These are links to a segment of sample code that you can copy from the help file, paste into a module sheet, and run.

Debugging Tools

In Excel 4, you are pretty much limited to two debugging tools, the Step box and the resultant values in cells. By placing a `STEP` function in your macro, you can force Excel to run the macro one step at a time. As it runs one step at a time, you can watch how the macro proceeds. By clicking the Evaluate button in the Step box, you can display partial results of macro functions. You use the second debugging tool for after-the-fact examination. With the macro displayed on-screen, you can press Ctrl+' (grave accent mark) to switch the display from showing macro functions to showing results. This enables you to see errors or functions that have not run correctly.

Visual Basic has far more debugging capability than Excel 4 macros. It contains three tools to help you debug. The following table describes these tools.

Tool	Description
Breakpoints	Breakpoints are conditions you specify that stops the procedure from running and puts the program into break mode. It does this before it runs the code containing the breakpoint. This is similar to using the `IF` function with a step to throw Excel 4 macros into step mode when a condition is met; for example, `=IF(B12>56,STEP())`
Debugging Buttons	The Visual Basic toolbar contains debugging buttons that display whenever a module (Visual Basic sheet) is active. Using these buttons you can run one statement or procedure, set breakpoints, or examine values.

Tool	Description
Debug Window	The Debug window displays over your application as it runs. It enables you to watch the resulting values and expressions as your procedure runs. You can change values in this window to see how it affects your procedure.

Running Excel 4 Macros in Visual Basic

As you move from Excel 4 macros to Visual Basic, you do not have to leave behind old systems or macros. You can run Excel 4 macros from Visual Basic.

To run an Excel 4 macro from Visual Basic, use the `Run` method. If you just want to run an Excel 4 macro, you use

```
RUN("macrosheetname!macroname")
```

If you want to send arguments to the Excel 4 macro and have the result of the macro returned to a variable in Visual Basic, you use the following :

```
myvariable=RUN("MacroSheet!PrintReport",3,"GQC")
```

In this example, the macro being run is `PrintReport`, located on the Excel 4 macro sheet named `MacroSheet` in the same workbook as the Visual Basic procedure. The arguments `3` and `"GOC"` are passed to the `PrintReport` macro. The result of the `PrintReport` macro is returned to Visual Basic and stored in the variable `myvariable`.

From Here...

To learn more about Visual Basic for Applications, read the chapters in this book that describe recording and programming in Visual Basic. While you are first using Visual Basic, you will want to make constant use of the on-line Programming Reference for Visual Basic that is available under the **H**elp **C**ontents command.

- Chapter 44, "Recording and Modifying VBA Modules." Learn how to use the recorder to create Visual Basic procedures. With a few modifications, you can make recordings ask for input and pause dialog boxes.

- Chapter 45, "Programming in Visual Basic for Applications." This chapter gives you an overview of programming in Visual Basic. You learn about scoping variables and the object model, and how to write your first Visual Basic procedure and display dialog boxes.

- Chapter 46, "Exploring Visual Basic for Applications Examples." The examples in this chapter give you working procedures to experiment with, which also are solutions to some of the more commonly faced problems when programming in Excel.

Chapter 44

Recording and Modifying VBA Modules

EXCEL 5

In this chapter, you learn how to:

- Create a procedure with the Macro Recorder
- Run a procedure
- Edit a procedure
- Obtain data from the worksheet
- Use data entry boxes
- Display a message

As an introduction to Visual Basic for Applications modules, you are going to let Excel write the first module. Excel's Macro Recorder records all your interactions with a worksheet as a sequence of Visual Basic commands. These commands form a macro procedure that you can execute to replay your interactions. This capability is especially useful for formatting complex worksheets, because after you have recorded the formatting, you only have to replay the procedure to format another sheet.

Automating with Visual Basic for Applications

The addition to Excel of Visual Basic for Applications is one of the most important improvements available in Excel 5. This improvement is a marriage of one of the most common programming languages with all the computational power of the Excel application. The language is not merely tacked onto Excel, but has full access to all of Excel's commands and structure.

Previously, you had to do all programming in Excel with the somewhat arcane Excel Macro Language. Although adequate for most tasks, it is anything but intuitive and bears little resemblance to any modern programming language (except possibly Lisp, but then Lisp programming is a career in itself).

If you are like many people, you are suffering from programming language and operating system overload. Every time you turn around, there is a new language to learn. Over the last few years, it seems as if every major application, including Excel, has come out with its own macro language, and each of these macro languages is totally different from all the others.

With Visual Basic for Applications, Microsoft is breaking that trend by including a variation of one of the most common programming languages, BASIC, as the macro language for Excel. Although this is BASIC, it is much, much more than the simple BASICA, GW-BASIC, or even QBasic. Visual Basic for Applications is a variant of the popular Visual Basic for Windows programming language, which is a modern programming language built on the BASIC language core. It has all the structured programming constructs and defined data types expected in a modern language, including object-oriented programming. In addition, there are built-in functions that give you complete control of Excel.

If you happen to like the older Excel macro language, or have a significant amount of code written in it, don't worry. Excel can still accommodate you. The ease of using Visual Basic for Applications, however, may quickly convince you to use it. Converting from Excel macros to Visual Basic is discussed in Chapter 43, "Introducing Visual Basic for Applications."

This chapter introduces you to Visual Basic for Applications by showing you how to use the Excel Macro Recorder to record the creation of a worksheet. In this way, Excel writes the Visual Basic code for you. Using this recorded code module, you learn the connection between the Visual Basic programming language and the Excel interface. In Chapter 45, "Programming in Visual Basic for Applications," you look at the most important aspects of the Visual Basic for Applications language. For a full explanation of all language elements, select the Programming Language Summary from the Programming with Visual Basic section of the table of contents of Excel's on-line help. The Programming Language Summary contains a complete alphabetical list of the Visual Basic language elements.

The following chapters use the terms *Visual Basic for Applications* and *Visual Basic* interchangeably. As far as these chapters are concerned, these terms are the same. Technically, however, Visual Basic is the programming language, and Visual Basic for Applications is the extended version that can manipulate Excel. In the near future, Visual Basic for Applications will be available for all major Microsoft products, including Word and Project.

To begin, you need to look at some terminology changes. In Excel 4 and earlier versions, the programming language is the Excel macro language, a program is known as a macro, and macros are written on a macro sheet. The term *macro* generally refers to the capability to replay a sequence of keystrokes (or mouse clicks); however, the Excel macro language extends far beyond that. With the switch from the Excel macro language to Visual Basic for Applications, a macro is now called a *procedure*, and macro sheets are called *modules*. This change brings the terminology more in line with modern programming practice.

As the terms are now defined, a procedure is a block of Visual Basic statements that perform a specific function. Visual Basic statements are not usually executed alone, but rather as part of a procedure; thus a procedure is the smallest executable block of Visual Basic code. Procedures are generally short blocks of code with a straightforward, verifiable purpose. The more complicated a procedure is, the more difficult it is to read and understand; and if you cannot understand a procedure, you cannot ensure that it is doing what it is supposed to be doing.

You can store one or more procedures together in a module. Storing procedures in modules is a convenient way to arrange and store them. Also, procedures in a module can share data with other procedures in the same module.

In the following sections, you familiarize yourself with Visual Basic for Applications by recording the creation of a simple worksheet. The worksheet has an input cell and a calculated output cell. The input cell accepts a cost, and the output cell calculates the discounted cost. The discount rate is displayed in a third cell.

Starting the Recorder

Before starting the Macro Recorder, prepare the worksheet by doing everything to it that you do not want included in the macro. This may include such things as opening a new worksheet or scrolling to a specific location. Once you start the Macro Recorder, everything you do to Excel is stored in a procedure.

To prepare the worksheet and display the Record New Macro dialog box, follow these steps:

1. Open a new workbook by executing the **F**ile **N**ew command.

2. Display the Record New Macro dialog box shown in figure 44.1 by choosing the **T**ools **R**ecord Macro **R**ecord New Macro command and then pressing the Options button, or by clicking the Record Macro button on the toolbar.

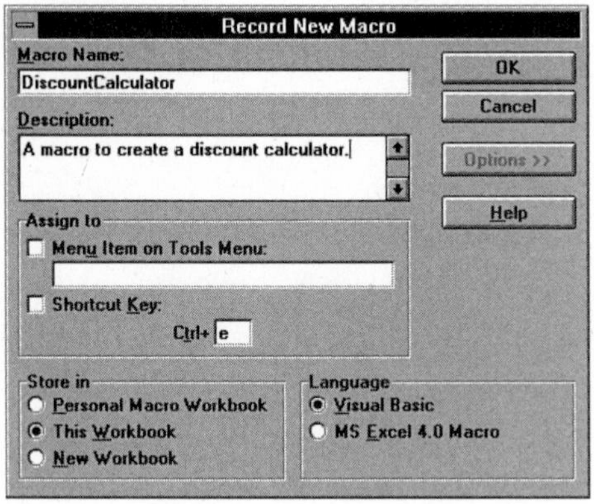

Fig. 44.1
The Record New Macro dialog box enables you to set the name and other options for a new procedure.

The Record New Macro dialog box shown in figure 44.1 is where you set the options for the Macro Recorder. The **M**acro Name and **D**escription fields are where you name your macro and add a description. Including a good, brief description here is important if you intend to keep this macro for more than a few days. If you do not use a good description, you probably will not remember what the macro does when you want to use it a year or so from now.

The Assign To field is where you attach the new macro to the **T**ools menu, or add a Shortcut **K**ey. You do not have to attach a macro to anything, because you can always run it by using the **T**ools **M**acro command. You should only attach macros that you use all the time so you can access them quickly. Also, you do not need to attach the macro now. You can come back later and attach the macro to a menu or button.

The Store in field is where you specify a place to put this new macro. If you select **P**ersonal Macro Workbook, Excel attaches the macro to a hidden notebook that opens whenever you start Excel. Thus, the macro becomes a global macro that is available to all open worksheets. Use the **W**indow-**U**nhide command to see the global macro sheet. The This **W**orkbook option places the macro in a new module sheet attached to the current workbook. The **N**ew Workbook option opens a new workbook and places the macro there in a new module sheet.

The Language field enables you to choose between Visual Basic for Applications and the Excel macro language. Use the Excel macro language only if you must keep your Excel 5 macros compatible with earlier versions of Excel.

To fill in the dialog box and start the Macro Recorder, follow these steps:

1. In the **M**acro Name field, type **DiscountCalculator**.
2. In the **D**escription field, type **A macro to create a discount calculator.**
3. Leave the other fields at their default values, as shown in figure 44.1, and click OK.

The Stop Recording button appears as a floating toolbar, and the Macro Recorder now records what you do. It records all your keystrokes and mouse clicks until you click the Stop Recording button.

Recording a Macro

You now can create the macro by simply creating the worksheet as you normally do.

To create the worksheet, follow these steps:

1. Choose the **T**ools **O**ptions command.
2. Select the View tab and clear the **G**ridlines check mark to turn off the gridlines. Then click OK.
3. Select cell B5, and type **Retail price:**.
4. Select cell C5, and choose the F**o**rmat C**e**lls command.
5. Select the Protection tab, and deselect the Locked check box. This change turns off protection for the cell so that later, when you enable protection for the worksheet, you still are able to change the value in this cell.
6. Select the Number tab, select the currency format $#,##0.00_);($#,##0.00), and click OK.
7. Select cell B7, and type **Discounted value:**.
8. Select cell B9, and type **Discount rate:**.
9. Click the vertical bar between columns B and C, and drag column B to be wide enough so that the whole label in cell B7 fits within the column.

10. Select cells B5:B9, and choose the F**o**rmat C**e**lls command. Then click the Alignment tab, select the **R**ight option button, and click OK. This right justifies the text in the cells.

11. Select cell C7, and choose the F**o**rmat C**e**lls command. Select the Number tab and the currency format $#,##0.00_);($#,##0.00), and then click OK.

12. Type the formula **=(1-C9)*C5**.

13. Select cell C9, and choose the F**o**rmat C**e**lls command. Then select the Number tab, the Percentage format 0.00%, and click OK.

14. Set a discount rate by typing **.05**.

15. To protect the cells in the worksheet, choose the **T**ools **P**rotection **P**rotect Sheet command and then choose OK.

The worksheet should now look like figure 44.2.

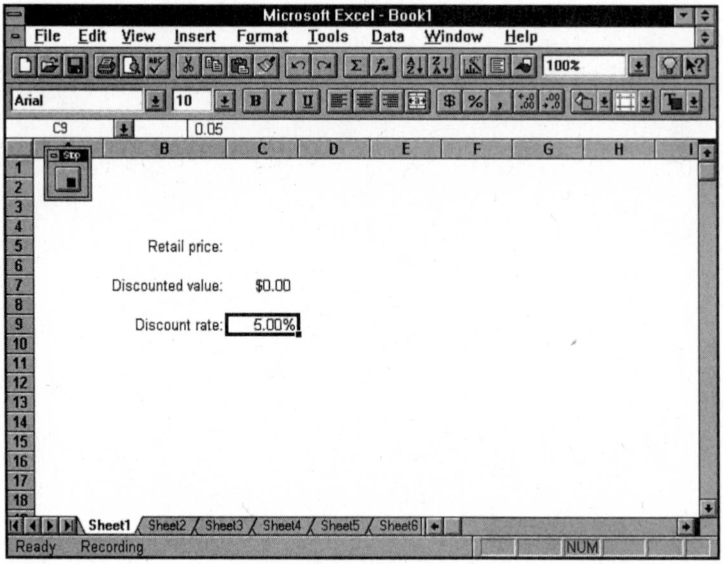

Fig. 44.2
The completed worksheet before turning off the Macro Recorder. Notice the Stop Recording button on the left side.

Stopping the Recorder

Stopping the recorder is easy, just click the Stop Recording button.

To resume recording at a later time, choose the **T**ools **R**ecord Macro R**e**cord at Mark command. The macro recording then continues from where it left off. You also can click the Resume Macro button.

If you have just opened this sheet and want to continue recording, select the Module containing the macro and click the last line of the macro. Then choose the **T**ools **R**ecord Macro **M**ark Position for Recording command. This forces the Macro Recorder to begin recording at that point. Switch back to the worksheet, and start recording by choosing the **T**ools **R**ecord Macro R**e**cord at Mark command.

Test the worksheet by typing **10** in cell C5. A `$9.50` should appear in cell C7, as shown in figure 44.3. If you try typing anywhere else on the worksheet, Excel displays a box telling you that you cannot do this on a protected worksheet.

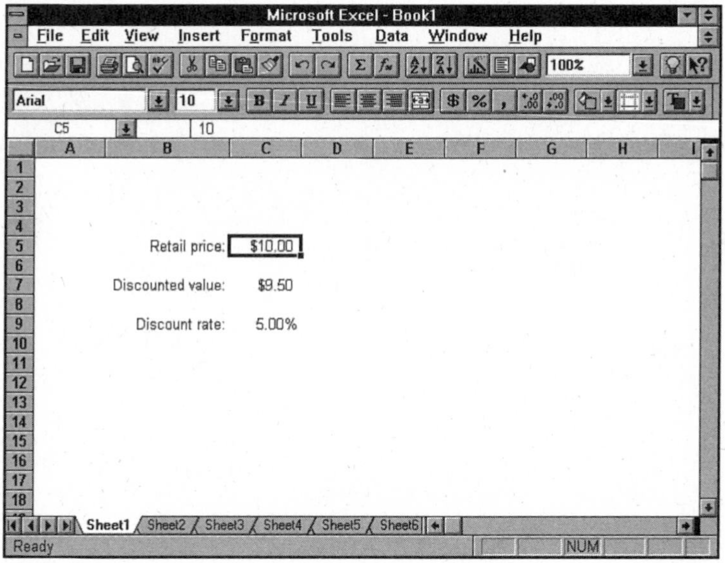

Fig. 44.3
The completed Discount Calculator worksheet with a test value of $10.00.

Examining the Procedure

To examine your newly created procedure, find the Module1 tab at the bottom of the screen and click it. Your procedure appears on-screen and looks like figure 44.4.

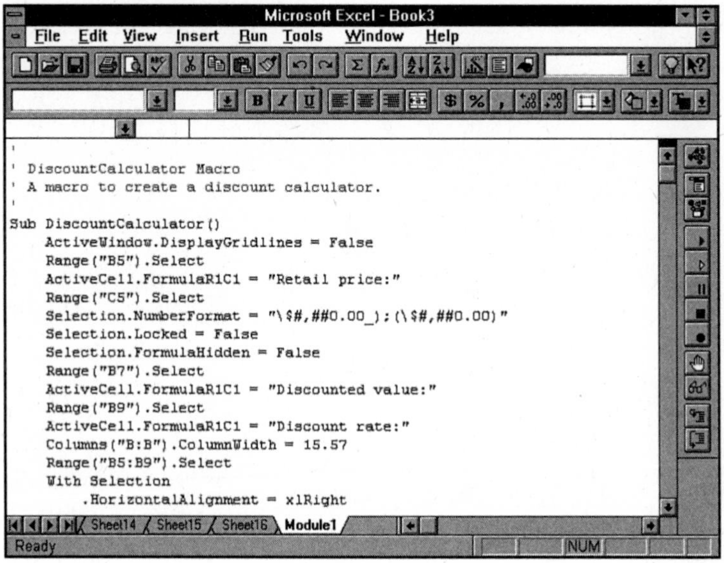

Fig. 44.4
The Excel Macro Recorder places the recorded commands in a module as shown here for the Discount Calculator.

The listing of the procedure is:

```
'
' DiscountCalculator Macro
' A macro to create a discount calculator.
'
Sub DiscountCalculator()
    ActiveWindow.DisplayGridlines = False
    Range("B5").Select
    ActiveCell.FormulaR1C1 = "Retail price:"
    Range("C5").Select
    Selection.NumberFormat = "\$#,##0.00_);(\$#,##0.00)"
    Selection.Locked = False
    Selection.FormulaHidden = False
    Range("B7").Select
    ActiveCell.FormulaR1C1 = "Discounted value:"
    Range("B9").Select
    ActiveCell.FormulaR1C1 = "Discount rate:"
    Columns("B:B").ColumnWidth = 15.57
    Range("B5:B9").Select
    With Selection
        .HorizontalAlignment = xlRight
        .VerticalAlignment = xlBottom
        .WrapText = False
        .Orientation = xlHorizontal
        .AddIndent = False
    End With
    Range("C7").Select
    Selection.NumberFormat = "\$#,##0.00_);(\$#,##0.00)"
    ActiveCell.FormulaR1C1 = "=(1-R[2]C)*R[-2]C"
    Range("C9").Select
    Selection.NumberFormat = "0.00%"
    ActiveCell.FormulaR1C1 = "0.05"
    ActiveSheet.Protect DrawingObjects:=True, Contents:=True, _
```

```
    Scenarios:=True
End Sub
```

If you examine this listing and the steps you just took, you see that each step results in one or more lines of code inserted in the procedure. Many extra lines also are in the procedure that set parameters that you did not explicitly set when you created the worksheet. These extra lines result when you click OK in a dialog box that sets several parameters. Although you may change only one parameter in the dialog box, closing the box sets all the parameters displayed in that box and inserts corresponding lines in the procedure being recorded. The "Understanding and Editing the Procedure" section later in this chapter discusses removing some of these lines.

The procedure appears in color, with comments in green, keywords in blue, and everything else in black. At the top right of the procedure window is the Visual Basic toolbar. The function of each toolbar button is shown in figure 44.5. You have already seen the operation of the command equivalents of the Record Macro and Stop Macro buttons. The functions of the other tools are covered in the contexts in which you use them.

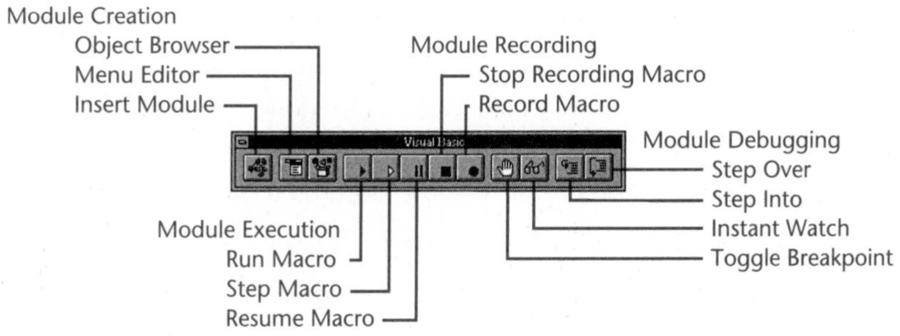

Fig. 44.5 The Visual Basic toolbar controls the execution and debugging of a program.

VIII

Automating with VBA

Running the Procedure

To run this procedure, first select an unused sheet. Be sure the sheet is unused, or has nothing useful in the B5:C9 range because this procedure overwrites that area. If you want to reuse the sheet where you created the procedure, be sure to turn off protection before you run the procedure, because the protected sheet cannot be changed. Next, choose the **T**ools **M**acro command. The Macro dialog box shown in figure 44.6 appears, showing all procedures available on this sheet and on the global sheet (currently none here). In the dialog box, select the DiscountCalculator procedure and choose **R**un. The worksheet appears and the procedure runs, setting the contents and formatting of the worksheet cells. The completed worksheet is identical to the one you created with the recorder running.

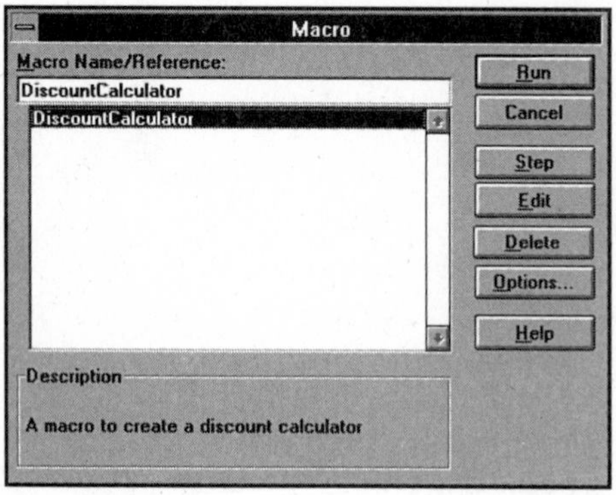

Fig. 44.6
The Macro dialog box allows you to select and execute procedures. The dialog box also provides an easy way to locate, edit, or delete procedures.

Attaching Procedures to Buttons, Menus, and Objects

In addition to running procedures with the **T**ools **M**acro command, you can attach them to menus, toolbar tools, buttons, or to other objects attached to the worksheet. One of the options when starting the Macro Recorder is to attach the recorded procedure to the **T**ools menu (refer to fig. 44.1). If you don't attach the procedure to a menu when you record it, you later can choose the **O**ptions button on the Macro dialog box to open a second dialog box from which you can then attach the macro to a menu.

Most people attach procedures to button objects, but you can attach them to almost any object attached to the worksheet, including embedded charts and objects, such as lines or circles, drawn with the drawing tools. To attach a procedure to an object on a worksheet, select the object and choose the **T**ools Assig**n** Macro command. When the dialog box appears, select the procedure you want to attach to the object.

For example, switch to an unused worksheet and choose the **V**iew **T**oolbars command. Select the Drawing toolbar and choose OK. The Drawing toolbar now is on-screen. Click the Create Button button and draw a button on the worksheet as shown in figure 44.7. The Assign Macro dialog box appears. Select the DiscountCalculator macro, and then choose OK. The macro now is attached to the button and executes when you choose the button. As long as a button has the six editing handles surrounding it, you can delete it, edit its text, move it around, or reassign the attached macro. After you have deselected the button, clicking it executes the macro. To select an object without executing its attached macro, hold down the Ctrl key when you click the object, or use the Select tool from the Drawing toolbar.

Click elsewhere on the worksheet to deselect the button; then click the button and the procedure executes, re-creating the Discount Calculator.

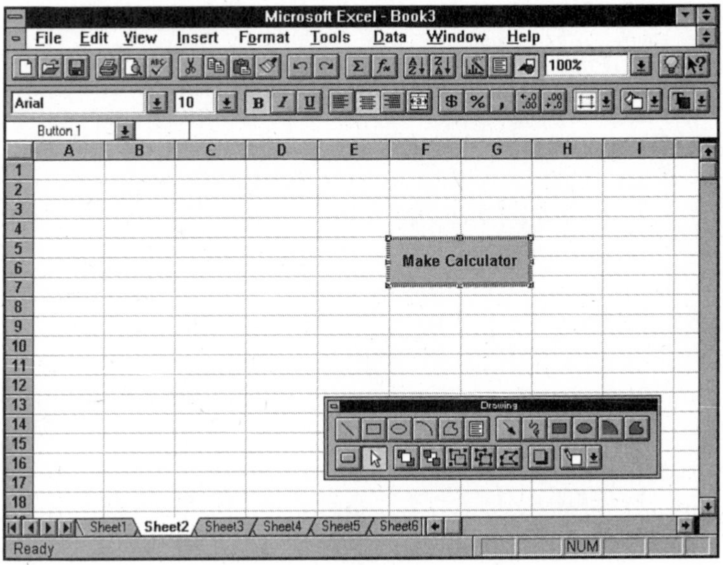

Fig. 44.7
Attaching a button to the worksheet and a procedure to the button makes it simple to execute the procedure quickly.

Understanding and Editing the Procedure

Now go back and take a closer look at the listing of the procedure by selecting the Module 1 tab. As mentioned previously, closing an editing dialog box inserts all the options in the recorded procedure, not just the one you changed. In most cases, when you select a formatting dialog box, you want to change only the formatting you select and leave all others alone. This way, you can apply a procedure in other situations, and not have it change all existing formatting, but only the specific item(s) you want changed. To make the procedure do so, you need to remove those other settings. In addition to making the procedure not do any more than you want it to do, removing extra lines also saves space and results in a more compact procedure. The following listing shows the procedure with settings you can remove marked in **bold**. You can remove these lines from the procedure, and it still operates the same.

```
'
' DiscountCalculator Macro
' A macro to create a discount calculator.
'
Sub DiscountCalculator()
    ActiveWindow.DisplayGridlines = False
    Range("B5").Select
    ActiveCell.FormulaR1C1 = "Retail price:"
    Range("C5").Select
    Selection.NumberFormat = "\$#,##0.00_);(\$#,##0.00)"
    Selection.Locked = False
    Selection.FormulaHidden = False
    Range("B7").Select
    ActiveCell.FormulaR1C1 = "Discounted value:"
    Range("B9").Select
    ActiveCell.FormulaR1C1 = "Discount rate:"
    Columns("B:B").ColumnWidth = 15.57
    Range("B5:B9").Select
    With Selection
        .HorizontalAlignment = xlRight
        .VerticalAlignment = xlBottom
        .WrapText = False
        .Orientation = xlHorizontal
        .AddIndent = False
    End With
    Range("C7").Select
    Selection.NumberFormat = "\$#,##0.00_);(\$#,##0.00)"
    ActiveCell.FormulaR1C1 = "=(1-R[2]C)*R[-2]C"
    Range("C9").Select
    Selection.NumberFormat = "0.00%"
    ActiveCell.FormulaR1C1 = "0.05"
    ActiveSheet.Protect DrawingObjects:=True,_
        :Contents:=True, Scenarios =True
End Sub
```

Now consider this procedure in a little more detail. Don't worry too much about the syntax of the statements yet. The next chapter, "Programming in Visual Basic for Applications," covers them all in greater detail. For now, get a feel for reading a Visual Basic procedure to gain a general understanding of what it does.

Using Comments

The first four lines of the procedure, shown here, are comments:

```
'
' DiscountCalculator Macro
' A macro to create a discount calculator.
'
```

Any characters that follow a single quotation mark in a Visual Basic procedure are comments. Comments in a Visual Basic procedure are totally ignored when the procedure executes, so adding them or deleting them has no effect on how a procedure runs. Comments, however, have a great effect on how understandable your procedures are. Use comments liberally in any procedures you plan to use more than once or twice. Although comments take extra time now, they save you much more time a year from now when you have to read and understand your procedures again so that you can make corrections or changes. Comments can comprise a whole line, as those above do. You also can place comments on the right, following any valid Visual Basic statement. Everything from the single quotation mark to the right end of the line is included in the comment.

Procedure Headers and Footers

The next line is the procedure header, and the last line in the procedure is the procedure footer. These two lines in a procedure define the procedure's limits in Visual Basic.

```
Sub DiscountCalculator()
.
.
.
End Sub
```

The first line of a procedure defines the procedure's name, type, and arguments. The type of a procedure is *Sub* or *Function*, and it determines whether the procedure returns a value. Function procedures operate in the same way as worksheet functions, which perform a calculation and return a value. Sub procedures do not return a value in the procedure's name, although they can return values through their arguments and through any global variables. The *arguments* of a procedure are placed within parentheses and form a connection between values in this procedure and those in a procedure that calls this one. Our example macro procedure is a `Sub` procedure, its name is `DiscountCalculator`, and it has no arguments.

The procedure footer simply marks the end. When a procedure reaches the last line, the execution point in a program returns to the procedure that called it. If no procedure called it, control returns to the desktop.

Controlling Characteristics

The first thing you did when creating this procedure was to turn off the gridlines in a window. The next line, shown here, does this:

```
ActiveWindow.DisplayGridlines = False
```

This line is a Visual Basic statement, and it sets to False the Display Gridlines property of the active window. The active window is whichever window is in front. In this way, you don't have to code the name of the worksheet with which you are working into a procedure. This procedure applies equally well to whichever window is currently active.

Accessing Worksheet Cells

The next two lines select cell B5 and place a text label in it:

```
Range("B5").Select
ActiveCell.FormulaR1C1 = "Retail price:"
```

Worksheet cells are accessed with cell objects, and cell objects are defined with `Range`, `Cell`, `Offset`, and `ActiveCell`. `Range` takes a cell reference as an argument and then refers to that cell. The `Select` method tells the indicated cell to become selected as the active cell. `Cell` operates in a similar manner, but takes two numbers as arguments. The two numbers specify the row and column of the selected cell. For example, `Cell(5, 2)` refers to the same cell as `Range("B5")`. `Offset` is similar to `Cell`, but the two numbers locate a cell relative to the active cell instead of to the upper-left corner of the worksheet. `ActiveCell` always refers to the current active cell on the active worksheet.

Tip
Placing a cell reference in square brackets—for example, **[B5]**—also references that cell.

In the preceding statements, the first statement makes B5 the active cell, and the second inserts a label in the active cell. The next few lines of the procedure select cell C5, apply a number format of \$#,##0.00_);(\$#,##0.00) to it, and turn off locking and hiding. You can delete the last statement in this group because you only need to turn off the Locked property and not the Hidden property.

```
Range("C5").Select
Selection.NumberFormat = "\$#,##0.00_);(\$#,##0.00)"
Selection.Locked = False
Selection.FormulaHidden = False
```

The next four lines select and insert text in cells B7 and B9:

```
Range("B7").Select
ActiveCell.FormulaR1C1 = "Discounted value:"
Range("B9").Select
ActiveCell.FormulaR1C1 = "Discount rate:"
```

One or more columns are selected with `Columns`, which takes a column reference as an argument. You can then use the `ColumnWidth` property to set the width of the columns. One or more rows can be selected in the same manner using `Rows`.

```
Columns("B:B").ColumnWidth = 15.57
```

The `With` clause is used to apply multiple statements to the same object. In the following lines, cells B5:B9 are selected, and the `With` clause applies the subsequent five statements, down to the `End With` statement, to the selected range:

```
Range("B5:B9").Select
With Selection
    .HorizontalAlignment = xlRight
    .VerticalAlignment = xlBottom
    .WrapText = False
    .Orientation = xlHorizontal
    .AddIndent = False
End With
```

These statements also could have been written as follows, with identical results. The `With` clause cuts down on the amount of typing, however, and makes the program more readable by grouping in a block all statements that apply to a single selection.

```
Range("B5:B9").Select
Selection.HorizontalAlignment = xlRight
Selection.VerticalAlignment = xlBottom
Selection.WrapText = False
Selection.Orientation = xlHorizontal
Selection.AddIndent = False
```

The next six statements select, format, and insert values or formulas into cells C7 and C9:

```
Range("C7").Select
Selection.NumberFormat = "\$#,##0.00_);(\$#,##0.00)"
ActiveCell.FormulaR1C1 = "=(1-R[2]C)*R[-2]C"
Range("C9").Select
Selection.NumberFormat = "0.00%"
ActiveCell.FormulaR1C1 = "0.05"
```

The final statement turns on protection for the active sheet:

```
ActiveSheet.Protect DrawingObjects:=True, _
    Contents:=True, Scenarios:=True
```

Note

The last statement consists of a single long line broken into two shorter lines. The underscore (_) character at the end of the first line is the Visual Basic line-continuation mark. It is used to shorten long lines so that they fit on-screen and are easier to read. The two following blocks of code give identical results:

```
ActiveSheet.Protect DrawingObjects:=True, Contents:=True, _
    Scenarios:=True

ActiveSheet.Protect DrawingObjects:=True, _
    Contents:=True, Scenarios:=True
```

Getting Data with a Data-Entry Box

In a Visual Basic procedure, you are not limited to the simple playback of keystrokes. You can create dialog boxes to get new values from the user to customize the procedure to different situations. For example, you might want to make several different discount-rate calculators, each calculating with a different discount rate. By inserting a `MsgBox` function at the appropriate place, you can pause the procedure and request that the user enter a discount rate to use in the calculation.

To add a dialog box to the DiscountCalculator procedure, follow these steps:

1. Select the Module1 tab, select the whole procedure by clicking and dragging across it, and choose **E**dit **C**opy.

2. Choose the **I**nsert **M**acro **M**odule command, which creates Module 2. You also can click the Insert Module button on the Visual Basic toolbar.

3. Choose the **E**dit **P**aste command to paste a copy of the DiscountCalculator macro into the new module.

4. In the fifth line of the procedure, change its name to DiscountCalculator2.

5. Delete the lines of the procedure that are not needed. (See the listing in the preceding section, "Understanding and Editing the Procedure," where unnecessary lines are marked in bold.)

6. In the line where the discount rate is inserted into cell C9 as `0.05` (5%), add an `InputBox` function as shown in the following listing. The changes are in bold.

```
'
' DiscountCalculator2 Macro
' A macro to create a discount calculator.
'
Sub DiscountCalculator2()
    ActiveWindow.DisplayGridlines = False
    Range("B5").Select
    ActiveCell.FormulaR1C1 = "Retail price:"
    Range("C5").Select
    Selection.NumberFormat = "\$#,##0.00_);(\$#,##0.00)"
    Selection.Locked = False
    Range("B7").Select
    ActiveCell.FormulaR1C1 = "Discounted value:"
    Range("B9").Select
    ActiveCell.FormulaR1C1 = "Discount rate:"
    Columns("B:B").ColumnWidth = 15.57
```

```
        Range("B5:B9").Select
        With Selection
            .HorizontalAlignment = xlRight
        End With
        Range("C7").Select
        Selection.NumberFormat = "\$#,##0.00_);(\$#,##0.00)"
        ActiveCell.FormulaR1C1 = "=(1-R[2]C)*R[-2]C"
        Range("C9").Select
        Selection.NumberFormat = "0.00%"
        ActiveCell.FormulaR1C1 = _
            InputBox("Input the discount rate as a fraction")
        ActiveSheet.Protect DrawingObjects:=True, _
            Contents:=True, Scenarios:=True
    End Sub
```

The `InputBox` function takes a caption as an argument and causes a dialog box to display on-screen. When you type a value in the dialog box and choose OK, the function returns the value you typed to the program, which inserts it in cell C9. Try this new procedure by selecting an unused worksheet and then choosing the **T**ools **M**acro command. In the Macro dialog box, select the DiscountCalculator2 macro and choose **R**un. The procedure starts making the worksheet and then displays the dialog box shown in figure 44.8. Type the value **0.2** (20% discount) in the dialog box, as shown in the figure, and choose OK. When the procedure finishes, type **10** into cell C5 to test the worksheet as you did before. The worksheet now looks like figure 44.9, with the 20% you typed into the dialog box inserted in cell C9.

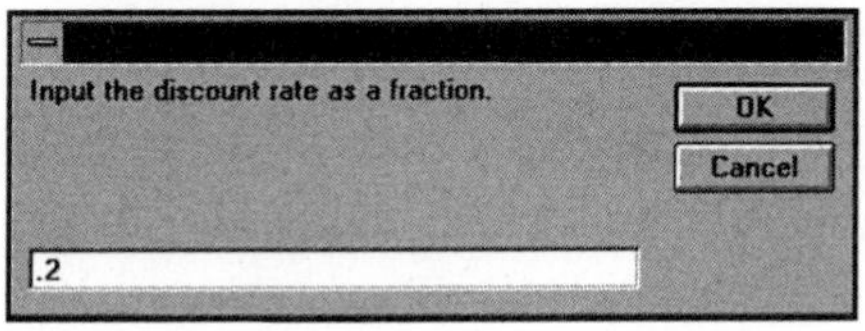

Fig. 44.8
A dialog box created with the `InputBox` function to input the discount rate.

Displaying a Message

In some instances, you may want to send a message to your user. You can use the `InputBox` function as shown in the previous section, but the input area might be confusing to another user. To simply send a message, use the `MsgBox` function, which works similarly to the `InputBox` function, but does not have an input area or Cancel button. It has only an OK button for the user to acknowledge the message.

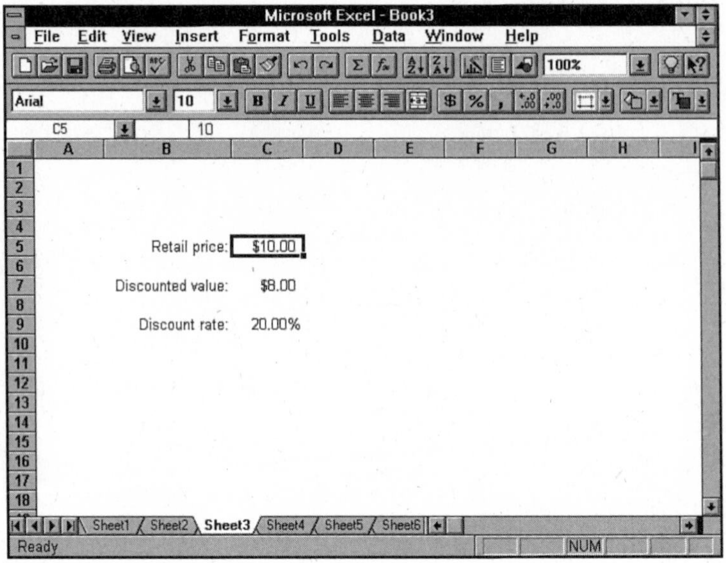

Fig. 44.9
The Discount Calculator created with the revised procedure using a dialog box to set the discount rate.

You can add a short message to the end of the current example to tell the user that the formatting has been completed. Copy the previous listing to a new module and name it DiscountCalculator3. Add the bold text in the following listing to the procedure, select a blank worksheet, and run the procedure:

```
'
' DiscountCalculator3 Macro
' A macro to create a discount calculator.
'
Sub DiscountCalculator3()
    ActiveWindow.DisplayGridlines = False
    Range("B5").Select
    ActiveCell.FormulaR1C1 = "Retail price:"
    Range("C5").Select
    Selection.NumberFormat = "\$#,##0.00_);(\$#,##0.00)"
    Selection.Locked = False
    Range("B7").Select
    ActiveCell.FormulaR1C1 = "Discounted value:"
    Range("B9").Select
    ActiveCell.FormulaR1C1 = "Discount rate:"
    Columns("B:B").ColumnWidth = 15.57
    Range("B5:B9").Select
    With Selection
        .HorizontalAlignment = xlRight
    End With
    Range("C7").Select
    Selection.NumberFormat = "\$#,##0.00_);(\$#,##0.00)"
    ActiveCell.FormulaR1C1 = "=(1-R[2]C)*R[-2]C"
    Range("C9").Select
    Selection.NumberFormat = "0.00%"
```

```
    ActiveCell.FormulaR1C1 = _
        InputBox("Input the discount rate as a fraction")
    ActiveSheet.Protect DrawingObjects:=True, _
        Contents:=True, Scenarios:=True
    MsgBox ("The discount calculator maker has completed _
        building the worksheet.")
End Sub
```

The first dialog box appears, asking you for the discount rate. When the formatting is done, the second dialog box appears, as shown in figure 44.10, telling you that the procedure has completed its run.

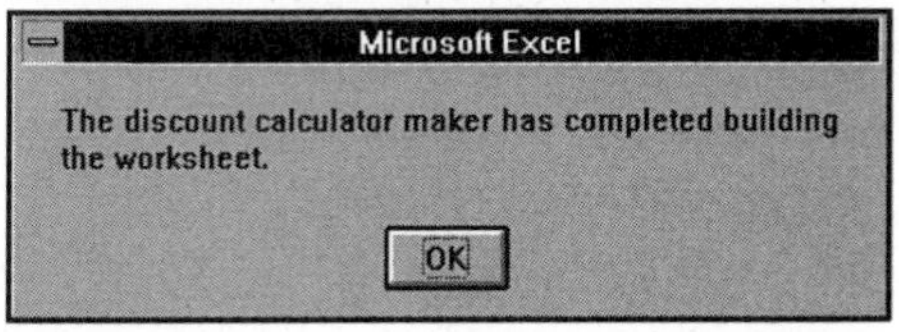

Fig. 44.10
The MsgBox function creates a dialog box telling you that the macro has completed.

From Here...

This chapter has given you a brief introduction to the operation of Excel macro procedures and the Macro Recorder. To learn more about Visual Basic, go on to Chapter 45, "Programming in Visual Basic for Applications," which discusses how to program using this language. In addition, you can access the on-line help package and choose the Visual Basic section from the table of contents.

Chapter 45

Programming in Visual Basic for Applications

In the last chapter, you got a taste of Visual Basic for Applications controlling an Excel worksheet. In this chapter, you learn a great deal more about Visual Basic and the Visual Basic object model (see fig. 45.1). The objects of Visual Basic can be visualized as a series of containers. The largest container is the application object, within the application object are menu objects, control objects, and workbook objects. Within the workbook objects are sheet objects (worksheets, macro sheets, modules, dialog sheets, and so forth), and within the sheet objects are range objects (cell ranges).

In this chapter, you learn:

- The intricacies of the Visual Basic object model
- How to use an object's properties and methods
- How to access the worksheet from Visual Basic
- How to read and create files
- How to create custom dialog boxes

Learning More with On-Line Help

There is a lot more to Visual Basic than this chapter describes, especially the unique syntaxes and special options of all the Visual Basic commands and functions. To learn about the details of all these functions, use the on-line help facility within Excel. At the contents window of the on-line help, select the *Programming with Visual Basic* section. When you are in the Visual Basic section of on-line help, you can select the *Programming Language Summary* for an alphabetical list of all of the language elements or select one of the individual language elements sections to display an alphabetical list of just those elements. You can also use the search capability to locate specific topics.

Fig. 45.1
The Visual Basic object model; containers within containers.

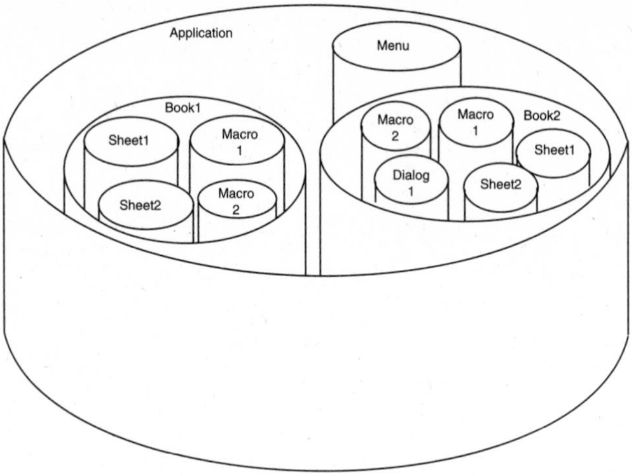

Understanding Objects

Tip
The search capability in on-line help will not locate Visual Basic language elements until you are in the Visual Basic section of on-line help.

Visual Basic and Visual Basic for Applications both use an object-oriented programming model. If you understand object-oriented programming (OOP), understanding Visual Basic's implementation of it is easy. If you don't, don't worry—it is not as complicated as it sounds.

Visual Basic *objects* provide a convenient way of storing and hiding data and code in a program. Instead of writing a program to manipulate some data values, you encapsulate the data and the code that manipulates that data in a Visual Basic object. From then on, you have only to access the object to use or manipulate its data. You don't write code to manipulate the data—you send the object a message, and it does the work for you. Think of an object as a light bulb in a table lamp. You don't need to know how a light bulb works to be able to make the lamp give light; you only need to give it electricity (the message), and it does the rest for you.

Just as there is more than one way to make a light bulb illuminate, there is more than one way to make an object perform its function. A light bulb can be a simple, inexpensive incandescent bulb or one of those low-energy, high-cost fluorescent replacements. Both are turned on in the same way—just add electricity to the base—but each creates light in a very different way. But you don't need to know or care how they work, only that they do. Using object-oriented code is the same. You don't need to know how an object works; you only need to know how to send a message to it to make it do the work.

Visual Basic objects include such things as buttons, menu items, ranges of worksheet cells, or even a worksheet itself. Most everything you can see on-screen while Excel is running is a Visual Basic object.

As with physical objects, programming objects can be made up of many simpler objects, which, in turn, are made up of even more simpler objects, and so on. The more complex object that holds the simpler objects is called the *container* (refer to fig. 45.1). Going back to the light bulb example, several light bulb objects may be screwed into a floor lamp object, which is the container of the light bulb objects. The floor lamp also has a switch object and a plug object. If you send the floor lamp two messages by first plugging it in and then pressing the switch, the lamp sends the light bulbs a message (electricity), and they illuminate. Again, the encapsulation now makes it unnecessary for you to know how to make a light bulb work. You only need to know how to plug in the lamp and press its switch. This encapsulation can go on for quite some time, as the lamp is contained in the room object, which is contained in a house object, which is one of many houses contained in a city object, and so on.

The highest level container in Visual Basic for Applications is the *application* itself (Microsoft Excel). Within the application object are workbook objects, menu objects, toolbar objects, and so forth. Within the workbook objects are worksheet objects, module sheet objects, chart sheet objects, and dialog sheet objects. Within a worksheet object are range (cell range) objects.

Note

Individual cells are not objects in Visual Basic, but are accessed as range objects, which contain a cell or cell range.

Accessing Objects

To access a specific object in Visual Basic, you start with the outermost container object's name, followed by a period, followed by the next inner container object's name, followed by a period, and so forth until you reach the object you are interested in. For example, to access cell B5 on a worksheet named Sheet3 in a workbook named Book2, you could use the following reference:

```
Application.Workbooks("Book2").Worksheets("Sheet3").Range("B5")
```

This reference is somewhat cumbersome, so Visual Basic makes an assumption that allows you to leave out some of these containers. For each container not included on the left side of a reference to an object (such as the workbook or worksheet reference), Visual Basic assumes that the currently active object of that type is the one being referenced.

Thus, the application can almost always be left out, as can the workbook. Be careful though; be sure you know what objects are active before you leave them out of the specification. Leaving out the containers has the positive effect of making your procedures more portable. If you leave out all but the range object, your code always applies to the currently active sheet, so you don't have to change the sheet name in order to apply your code to a different sheet. In addition to the named sheets and workbooks, you can use the objects `ActiveWorkbook`, `ActiveSheet`, `ActiveCell` to reference the currently active objects without having to know their names.

Note

Keep in mind that if you use specific workbook and sheet names in your procedures, the procedures will only work in those named workbooks and procedures. By leaving out parts of an object's specification, you make your code applicable to all objects of the type you left out.

The following list contains some of the more commonly used objects in Visual Basic. For a comprehensive list of Visual Basic and Excel objects, see the Visual Basic section of on-line help, and select the objects section of the programming language summary. You can also use the Object Browser, described later in this chapter, to locate objects.

Use the `Use With` statement to explicitly specify the outer containers for blocks of code. The `Use With` statement is described later in this chapter.

Some common Visual Basic objects are

```
AddIn
Application
Arc
AxisTitle
Button
Chart
ChartObject
CheckBox
DataLabel
DialogFrame
```

```
DialogSheet
Drawing
DropDown
EditBox
Font
GroupBox
GroupObject
Label
Line
ListBox
Module
OLEObject
OptionButton
Oval
Picture
PivotField
PivotItem
PivotTable
Range
Rectangle
Scenario
ScrollBar
Series
Spinner
Style
TextBox
Toolbar
ToolbarButton
Trendline
Workbook
Worksheet
```


Understanding Classes and Collections

A *class* of objects is a reference to a general type or classification of objects, such as all light bulbs belong to the Light Bulbs class. A specific light bulb is an *instance* of a class called an object. In Visual Basic, for example, each cell or cell range on a worksheet is an instance of the Range class. Visual Basic does not refer to classes often, but error messages occasionally refer to them.

If you combine all the specific light bulbs in a floor lamp into a group, that group is known as a *collection*. A collection in code is a list of references to all similar objects in a container object. Thus, all the workbooks in the application object are in the collection Workbooks, and all the worksheets in a workbook are in the collection Worksheets. All the worksheets are also in the collection Sheets, which includes all sheets (worksheet, chart, module, dialog) in a workbook.

Accessing Collections

Collections are very useful for locating a specific object, especially if you don't know the number of, or names of, objects of a specific class. For example, you don't often know how many worksheets there are in a workbook, but you can still access them because they are all contained in the collection Worksheets. To access a specific member of a collection, follow the collection name by either a string containing the object name or an integer in parentheses. Thus, `Worksheets("Sheet1")` refers to the sheet named Sheet1, and `Worksheets(2)` refers to the second worksheet in the collection of all worksheets in the active workbook. For example, if you want to access cell B5 on the third worksheet in a workbook named Book2, you can use the following reference:

```
Workbooks("Book2").Worksheets(3).Range("B5")
```

If you leave out the number and parentheses in the reference to a collection, the reference is to all the members of the collection. The following list contains some common collections.

Caution

Be careful when using numbers to select objects in a collection. If you add or delete members from a collection, the numbering of all the other members of that collection can change, and your number may select a different object.

Some common Visual Basic collections are

```
Buttons            Modules
Charts             OLEObjects
ChartObjects       OptionButtons
CheckBoxes         Ovals
DataLabels         Pictures
Drawings           Rectangles
DropDowns          ScrollBars
EditBoxes          Sheets
GroupBoxes         Spinners
GroupObjects       TextBoxes
Labels             Workbooks
Lines              Worksheets
ListBoxes
```

Understanding Properties

An object contains data, and data that you can access from the outside of an object is a *property* of that object. Most properties are readable, but not all can be written to or changed. In the light bulb example, the manufacturer and the wattage are read-only properties printed on the side of the bulb. The on/off property is also read only, but it changes when the light is turned on or off. If a light is plugged into a light dimmer, the intensity setting of the light dimmer is a readable or writable (changeable) property of the dimmer switch.

For a range object (one or more worksheet cells), the font, color, font size, contents, and so forth are read/write properties, although the location is read only (cells don't move.) Properties can refer to the direct data contained in an object, such as the value of a cell, or to data values that control how an object looks and behaves, such as color.

Property values can be strings of text, numbers, logicals (True or False), or enumerated lists. An *enumerated list* is a numbered list of values, where the number selects the specific value. For example, the Color property of most objects is an enumerated list where 0 is none, 1 is black, 2 is white, 3 is red, 4 is green, 5 is blue, and so forth. For the enumerated lists, Visual Basic and Excel both contain lists of constants to use in place of the numbers. Using the constants is much more informative than the numbers. The constants are listed in the description of the property in on-line help. You can get a list of constants by searching for "constants" or "variables" in the on-line help and selecting the Variables and Constants Keywords Summary and Visual Basic Constants topics. You can also use the Object Browser (described in this chapter) to search the Excel and VBA libraries for the `ExcelConstant` object.

The following list contains all the properties of the range object. These properties control almost all aspects of a worksheet cell. You rarely use more than a few of these properties in a program, with `Formula` (the formula in a cell) and `Value` (the displayed value of a cell) being the most common. The other properties are most easily set by turning on the Macro Recorder, making the changes in the worksheet, turning off the recorder, and then copying the recorded property changes into your program. See the Visual Basic section of on-line help for a comprehensive list of all properties. In the description of each object is a list of the properties that apply to it.

Properties of the range object are

```
Application            Next
Column                 Note
ColumnWidth            NumberFormat
Count                  NumberFormatLocal
Creator                Orientation
CurrentArray           OutlineLevel
CurrentRegion          PageBreak
Dependents             Parent
DirectDependents       PivotField
DirectPrecedents       PivotItem
EntireColumn           PivotTable
EntireRow              Precedents
Font                   PrefixCharacter
Formula                Previous
FormulaArray           Row
FormulaHidden          RowHeight
FormulaLocal           ShowDetail
FormulaR1C1            SoundNote
FormulaR1C1Local       Style
HasArray               Summary
HasFormula             Text
Height                 Top
Hidden                 UseStandardHeight
HorizontalAlignment    UseStandardWidth
Interior               Value
Left                   VerticalAlignment
LocationInTable        Width
Locked                 Worksheet
Name                   WrapText
```

Accessing Properties

You access properties with the following syntax:

```
object.property
```

where `object` is the object whose properties you want to change, and `property` is the name of the property. If the preceding construct is on the right side of a statement, then you are reading the value of the property from the object. If the construct is on the left side of a statement, then you are setting the value of the property. For example, to set the value of the `Formula` property (the contents of the cell) of cell B5 to `=ABS(B4)` when cell B5 is on the Sheet1 worksheet (which is in the Book2 workbook), you can use the statement

```
Workbooks("Book2").WorkSheets("Sheet1").Range("B5")
➥.Formula = "=ABS(B4)"
```

To read the same property from the same cell and store it in `myFormula`, you can use the statement

```
myFormula =Workbooks("Book2").WorkSheets("Sheet1").Range("B5")
➥.Formula
```

The rules concerning omitting container objects (described previously) apply here. Because you must include an object with the property, you cannot leave off the range object to get the formula in whatever cell is the active cell. For these and similar cases involving other objects, there are some special properties that return the currently active or selected object. Table 45.1 lists these special properties. For example, to get the formula contained in the active cell of the Sheet3 worksheet, you can use the statement

```
myFormula = Workbooks("Book2").WorkSheets("Sheet3").ActiveCell
➥.Formula
```

If Book2 and Sheet3 are the currently active workbook and worksheet, you can use

```
myFormula = ActiveCell.Formula
```

If Book2 is the active workbook but Sheet3 is not necessarily the active worksheet, you can use

```
myFormula = WorkSheets("Sheet3").ActiveCell.Formula
```

If you want to access cell B5 on whatever worksheet is active in Book2, you use

```
myFormula = WorkBooks("Book2").ActiveSheet.Range("B5").Formula
```

Everything to the left of the last period must evaluate to an object or a collection of objects.

Table 45.1 Special Properties That Return the Active Objects

Property	Description
`ActiveCell`	The active cell on the active window
`ActiveChart`	The active chart in a workbook
`ActiveDialog`	The active dialog sheet in a workbook
`ActiveSheet`	The active worksheet, chart, module, or dialog sheet in a workbook
`ActiveWorkbook`	The active workbook in an application
`Selection`	The currently selected object on the currently selected sheet

Understanding Methods

Visual Basic *methods* are the blocks of code stored in an object that know how to manipulate the object's data. For the `Range` object, for example, the Calculate method causes the formulas in the selected cells to be recalculated, and the Clear method clears the cell's contents. Methods do things to cells, as opposed to properties, which set values. The following list contains all the methods that apply to the range object. To learn more about the specifics of different methods, and to find out what methods apply to what objects, see the Visual Basic section of on-line help. You can also use the Object Browser to see what methods are available for what objects.

The methods of the range object are

```
Activate
Address
AddressLocal
AdvancedFilter
ApplyNames
ApplyOutlineStyles
Areas
AutoFill
AutoFilter
AutoFit
AutoFormat
AutoOutline
BorderAround
Borders
Calculate
Cells
Characters
CheckSpelling
Clear
ClearContents
ClearFormats
ClearNotes
ClearOutline
ColumnDifferences
Columns
Consolidate
Copy
CopyPicture
CreateNames
CreatePublisher
Cut
DataSeries
Delete
DialogBox
End
FillAcrossSheets
FillDown
FillLeft
FillRight
FillUp
Find
FindNext
FindPrevious
FunctionWizard
GoalSeek
Group
Insert
Item
Justify
ListNames
NavigateArrow
Offset
Parse
Paste
PasteSpecial
PrintOut
PrintPreview
RemoveSubtotal
Replace
Resize
RowDifferences
Rows
Run
Select
Show
ShowDependents
ShowErrors
ShowPrecedents
Sort
SpecialCells
SubscribeTo
Subtotal
Table
TextToColumns
Ungroup
```

Accessing Methods

You access or execute an object's methods in nearly exactly the same way that you access an object's properties. The main difference being that a property is always accessed as part of a formula, but a method need only be part of a formula if it returns a value. For example, the `Rows` method returns a collection containing all the rows in the range. To use it to set the `RowHeight` property of all the rows in the currently selected range to 20, use a formula like the following:

```
Selection.Rows.RowHeight = 20
```

To get the number of rows in the current selection, you could use the `Rows` method to return a collection and the `Count` property to return the number of items in the collection:

```
numRows = Selection.Rows.Count
```

Some methods require arguments to make them work. For example, the `Insert` method, when applied to a range object, needs an argument to tell it how to move the cells that are already in the selection; the `Rows` method needs an index number to select a single row from the collection of rows. If the method is part of a formula, the arguments must go in parentheses. For example, to get the `RowHeight` of the second row in the collection of rows, you can use

```
theHeight = Selection.Rows(2).RowHeight
```

If the method is just being executed and is not part of a formula, place the arguments to the right of the reference to the method. For example, to use the `Insert` method to insert blank cells for the current selection and to move the current selection down to make room, you can use

```
Selection.Insert xlDown
```

The argument is actually an integer, but use the built-in constants to make your code more readable. You can get the built-in constants that apply to a method in the description of the method in on-line help, or you can search for "constants" or "variables" in the on-line help and select the Variables and Constants Keywords Summary or the Visual Basic Constants topics. To see the Excel constants, use the Object Browser described next to search the Excel library for the Constants object.

Finding Objects with the Object Browser

With all these objects floating around, keeping track of what all the objects are named and where they are located gets a bit difficult. For the Visual Basic and Excel objects, the on-line help is a good reference. For other libraries and applications (and for Excel and Visual Basic as well), you can use the Object Browser. To use the Object Browser, switch to a module sheet and select the **V**iew **O**bject Browser command. The Object Browser dialog box appears as shown in figure 45.2. In the Libraries/Workbooks: window at the top, you can select Excel, VBA (Visual Basic for Applications), or Module 1. If there are more libraries or modules attached to the current open session of Excel, they appear here also. As more applications support Visual Basic for Applications, they also appear in the Object Browser's list.

If you select Excel, as shown in figure 45.2 , all the objects and modules contained in Excel appear in the O**b**jects/Modules window on the left. If you select one of the objects, such as the `Range` object, all the properties and methods appear in the **M**ethods/Properties window on the right. If you select one of the methods or properties, such as `Insert`, the method—along with its syntax—appears at the bottom. If you press the button with the question mark on it at the bottom left of the window, you are taken directly to the on-line help topic explaining that method or property. If you select the **P**aste button, the selected object or method is inserted in the active module at the current insertion point.

Understanding Functions and Procedures

In the last chapter, the macro you created was called a *procedure*. A procedure is the smallest programming object in Visual Basic. There are two types of procedures in Visual Basic, subprocedures and function procedures.

Subprocedures

Subprocedures are generally just called procedures. Subprocedures can be sent arguments and can change those arguments. The procedures created in the last chapter are subprocedures. The procedure header and footer from the DiscountCalculator example is as follows:

```
Sub DiscountCalculator()
.
.
.
End Sub
```

Subprocedures always start with a procedure header that starts with the keyword `Sub`, followed by the procedure name and parentheses. The names of any arguments to be passed to the procedure are placed between the parentheses. Arguments are the data values that a calling procedure is giving to this procedure to work on. They also represent the values that a procedure can pass back to the procedure that called it. Subprocedures must end with the `End Sub` procedure footer. Between the procedure header and footer are declarations, statements, and commands that the procedure executes. Subprocedures are executed by selecting them in the Macro dialog box, calling them from another procedure, or pressing a button or other object to which the procedure is attached.

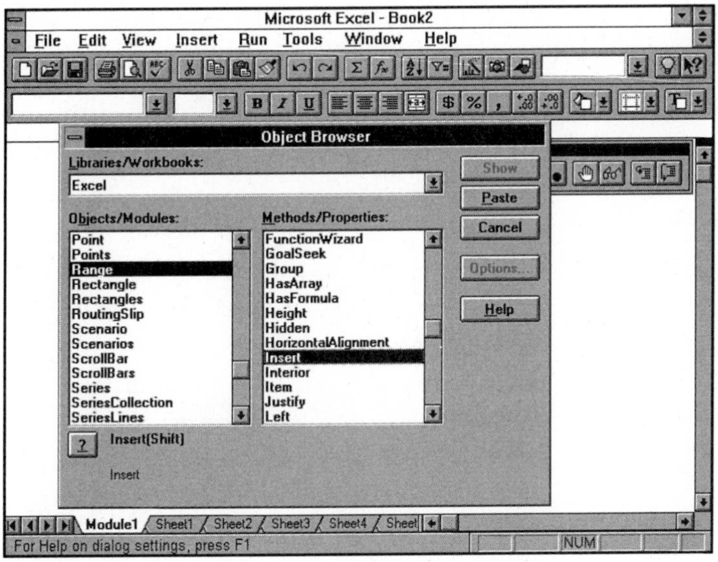

Fig. 45.2
The Object Browser with the Excel application selected.

User-Defined Functions

Functions are very similar to procedures, except that the function's name returns a value. These functions are identical in operation to worksheet functions—you can define new functions with Visual Basic and then use them on the worksheet. There is one main restriction on functions that are used on the worksheet, though—they can only do calculations. These functions cannot access and change other cells on the worksheet, nor can they execute menu commands.

Functions have a procedure header and footer similar to that used for subprocedures, and they must assign a value to the procedure name before completing.

```
Function myFunction(arguments)
.
.
.
myFunction = something
End Function
```

After you define a function, you can use it on the worksheet.

For example, the following listing creates a simple function that performs the same calculation as the example in the last chapter. The function accepts two numbers as arguments, a retail price and a percentage. It then calculates and returns the discounted price.

```
'
' Calculate the discounted price from
' a retail price and a discount percentage.
'
Function DisPrice(Retail, Rate)
   DisPrice = Retail * (1 - Rate)
End Function
```

Start with a new workbook, create a module with the **I**nsert **M**acro **M**odule command. Type the listing above into the module as shown in figure 45.3. Select Sheet 1, and set it up as shown in figure 45.4, with the retail amount in cell B2 formatted as currency, the percentage in cell B3 formatted as percent, and the following formula in cell B4, formatted as currency:

```
=DisPrice(B2,B3)
```

The new function defined in Module 1 is now usable in the worksheet just like any of the built-in functions.

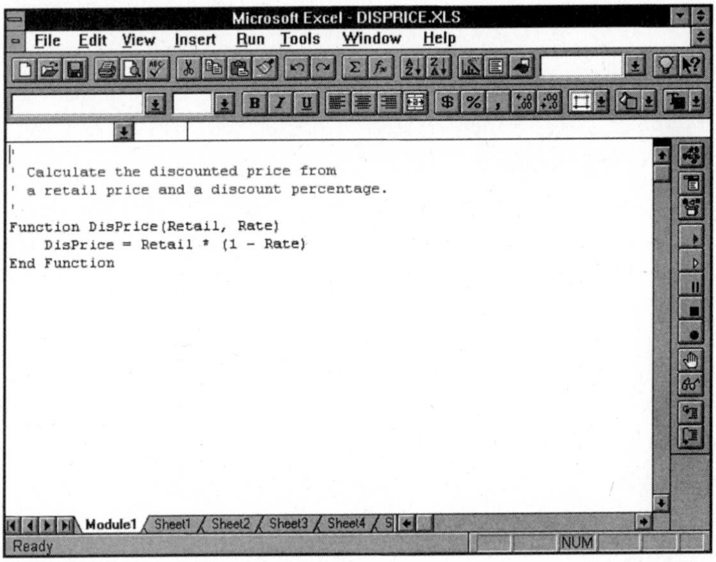

Fig. 45.3
A user-defined function named `DisPrice` defined in a module.

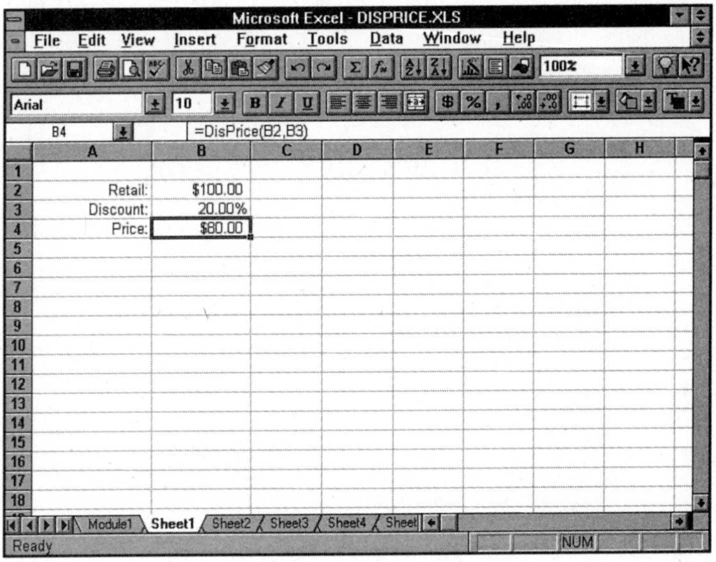

Fig. 45.4
The user-defined function `DisPrice` being used in a worksheet.

Creating an Application

Now that you know all about objects, properties, and methods, you can start putting some of that together to create an application. The application you are going to create is a simple electronic personal organizer. A worksheet serves as the input form, and a Visual Basic program stores and retrieves the data. The program has four user-accessible functions: accept new data, scan up one record, scan down one record, and search for a record. It also has an initialization function to reset the data and prepare the program for use.

A program like this forms the basis for a database program. It has a data entry capability for inserting new records into the database, a browsing capability to allow you to scan through the records, and a search capability to allow you to locate a specific record based on some criteria. A variation of this program could be set up to store sales records by date, or by region, or to store inventory by product.

First, you must create the worksheet data input form, which has a Name field, an Address field, a City field, a State field, a Zip field, and a Telephone field. There are five buttons on the worksheet to initialize the program and to execute the four database functions.

To create the worksheet, follow these steps:

1. Start with a new workbook, and select Sheet1.
2. Select cell B1, and type **Personal Organizer**.
3. Select cell A3, and type **Name:**.
4. Select cell A4, and type **Address:**.
5. Select cell A5, and type **City:**.
6. Select cell A6, and type **State:**.
7. Select cell A7, and type **Zip:**.
8. Select cell A8, and type **Telephone:**.
9. Select the bar between columns A and B, and make column A 11 characters wide.
10. Select the bar between columns B and C, and make column B 20 characters wide.

11. Select cells A3:A8, select the F**o**rmat C**e**lls command, select the Alignment tab, click the **R**ight option button, and select OK.

12. Select cells B3:B8, select the F**o**rmat C**e**lls command, select the Border tab, select the single thin line, and select the Left, Right, Top, and Bottom check boxes. Select the Number tab, and select the @ from the **F**ormat Codes list box. Select the Protection tab, uncheck the Locked check box, and select OK.

13. Choose the **V**iew **T**oolbars command, select the Drawing toolbar, and select OK. The Drawing toolbar should appear.

14. Select the Button tool from the Drawing toolbar, draw a button over cell D2. After the Assign To dialog box appears, type **AddName** for the macro and select OK.

15. The button still should be selected; if not, select the Selection tool from the Drawing toolbar and select the button. Select the text on top of the button and change it to **Add**.

16. Create another button over cell D4, attach it to the macro **UpOne**, and make the title **Up**.

17. Create another button over cell D6, attach it to the macro **DownOne**, and make the title **Down**.

18. Create another button over cell D8, attach it to the macro **FindIt**, and make the title **Find**.

19. Create another button over cell D10, attach it to the macro **InitIt**, and make the title **Init**.

20. Remove the Drawing toolbar by clicking its close button (upper left corner).

21. Reduce the size of the worksheet to just contain the buttons and input cells.

22. Choose the **T**ools **O**ptions command, select the View tab, uncheck the **G**ridlines and Row & Column H**e**aders check boxes, and select OK.

23. Save the workbook as ROLLO1.XLS.

The worksheet should now look like figure 45.5. When you finish the procedures, you will come back and turn off the scroll bars and tabs, and turn on sheet protection. Next, you need to create the five procedures to attach to the buttons.

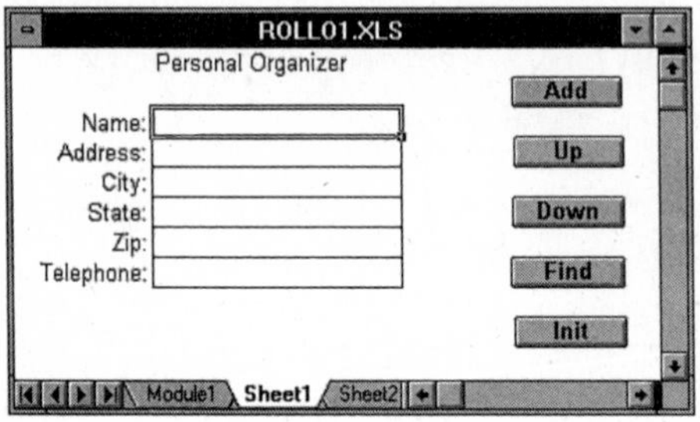

Fig. 45.5
The user interface for the personal organizer.

To create the procedures, perform the following steps:

1. Select the **I**nsert **M**acro **M**odule command to create and open a new module.

2. Type Listing 45.1 into the module. Don't worry that you do not understand what you are typing; all of it is discussed later.

Listing 45.1 The ROLLO1 program

```
'Force defining of all variables
Option Explicit
'Definefined type to hold the data
Type myType
   Name As String
   Address As String
   City As String
   State As String
   Zip As Long
   Phone As String
End Type
'Define a constant to indicate the maximum number of entries
Const maxEntries = 100
'Declare an array to hold the entries
Dim theData(maxEntries) As myType
'Declare some more module level variables
Dim numEntries As Integer, displayedEntry As Integer
'
'Initialize the procedure
'
```

```
Sub InitIt()
numEntries = -1  'initialize numentries
End Sub
'
'Add the current worksheet Data to the List
'
Sub AddName()
numEntries = numEntries + 1  'Increment the entry number
If numEntries > maxEntries Then
   MsgBox ("Too many entries, can't insert any more")
   numEntries = numEntries - 1
   Exit Sub
End If
'Copy the data from the worksheet to the array.
theData(numEntries).Name = ActiveSheet.Range("Name").Value
theData(numEntries).Address = ActiveSheet.Range("Address").Value
theData(numEntries).City = ActiveSheet.Range("City").Value
theData(numEntries).State = ActiveSheet.Range("State").Value
theData(numEntries).Zip = Val(ActiveSheet.Range("Zip").Value)
theData(numEntries).Phone = ActiveSheet.Range("Telephone").Value
displayedEntry = numEntries
End Sub

'
'Display the next set of data on the worksheet
'
Sub UpOne()
If displayedEntry < numEntries Then
   displayedEntry = displayedEntry + 1
Else
   displayedEntry = numEntries
End If
DisplayIt displayedEntry
End Sub
'
'Display the previous set of data on the worksheet
'
Sub DownOne()
If displayedEntry > 0 Then
   displayedEntry = displayedEntry - 1
Else
   displayedEntry = 0
End If
DisplayIt displayedEntry
End Sub
'
'Search for an entry and display it
'
Sub FindIt()
Dim I As Integer
For I = 0 To numEntries
```

(continues)

Listing 45.1 Continued

```
    If InStr(1, theData(I).Name, ActiveSheet.Range("Name").Value, 1) >
    ➥0 Then
       Exit For
    End If
    Next I
    If I = numEntries + 1 Then
       MsgBox ("Not found")
    Else
       DisplayIt I
    End If
    End Sub

    Sub DisplayIt(theEntry As Integer)
    With ActiveSheet
      .Range("Name").Value = theData(theEntry).Name
      .Range("Address").Value = theData(theEntry).Address
      .Range("City").Value = theData(theEntry).City
      .Range("State").Value = theData(theEntry).State
      .Range("Zip").Value = Str(theData(theEntry).Zip)
      .Range("Telephone").Value = theData(theEntry).Phone
    End With
End Sub
```

The module should now look like figure 45.6, with the six procedures in Module 1. There is quite a bit here, and you will see how it all works as you learn about the different parts of the Visual Basic language.

3. Select the Sheet1 tab.

4. Choose the **T**ools **O**ptions command, select the View tab, uncheck Horizon**t**al Scroll Bar, **V**ertical Scroll Bar, and Sheet Ta**b**s, and select OK.

5. Choose the **T**ools **P**rotection **P**rotect Sheet command, and select OK.

6. Save the workbook.

The worksheet should now look like figure 45.7. If all was done correctly, you can store some names and addresses in the database. Go ahead, select the Init button to initialize it, type a name and address into the worksheet, and select the Add button to store it. Type another name and address by selecting the fields, typing over the previous data, and selecting Add. After storing several addresses, use the Up and Down buttons to scroll through the list.

Type a partial name in the name field (a last name for instance), and select the Find button. The procedure should be able to locate the record containing that text and display the address. If you want to look at the procedures, you must reverse steps 4 and 5 so you can select the tabs and use the scroll bars.

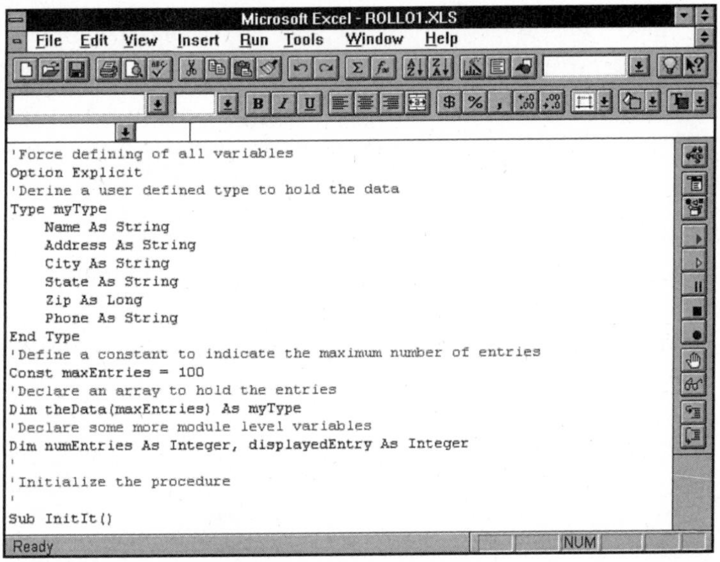

Microsoft Excel - ROLLO1.XLS
File Edit View Insert Run Tools Window Help
'Force defining of all variables
Option Explicit
'Derine a user defined type to hold the data
Type myType
Name As String
Address As String
City As String
State As String
Zip As Long
Phone As String
End Type
'Define a constant to indicate the maximum number of entries
Const maxEntries = 100
'Declare an array to hold the entries
Dim theData(maxEntries) As myType
'Declare some more module level variables
Dim numEntries As Integer, displayedEntry As Integer
'Initialize the procedure
Sub InitIt()
Ready
NUM

Fig. 45.6
The procedures stored in Module 1 of the personal organizer.

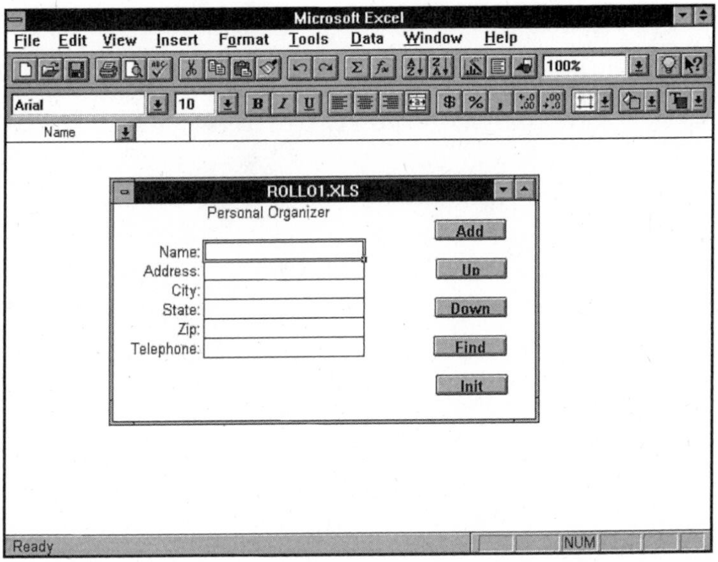

Fig. 45.7
The user interface for version 1 of the personal organizer.

Understanding Variables and Assignment Statements

Variables are named places in memory for storing data. Like naming cells on a worksheet, using variables to name storage locations in memory makes a program much more readable. You don't have to explicitly name a specific location in memory to use a variable, Visual Basic takes care of that for you. Simply using a name in a formula causes Visual Basic to define storage for it. After the storage location is defined, you can use a variable in assignment statements to store data.

An *assignment statement* consists of a variable or property name on the left, an equal sign, and a constant value or formula on the right. A formula can consist of a single constant value or a mixture of variables, constants, mathematical operators, and functions. The following are all assignment statements:

```
myFormula = ActiveSheet.Range("B5").Formula
Selection.Rows.RowHeight = 20
myVeriable = 17
someThing = Log(3.5)
yourVariable = myVariable * 33
```

Using Declarations and Visual Basic Data Types

Not all data values are the same type in Visual Basic. If you don't declare any variables, then all variables have a data type of `Variant`. The `Variant` type is useful because it can store anything from strings to pictures to floating point numbers. The problem with a `Variant` type variable is that in order to hold anything, it must check every time to see what kind of data is being stored in it—and have a lot of memory available to store it. Therefore, a variable of the `Variant` data type wastes time and memory. For a few small items, this waste won't matter, but it becomes important if you are storing many data items.

If you declare the type of a variable before you use it, Visual Basic does not have to check every time to see what it is and then reserve space for it. If it is declared, the type is known and the space is reserved ahead of time. Another reason to declare all variables is to help ensure that you have not misspelled something, creating a program *bug*. Visual Basic does not force you to declare everything, but you can do it yourself by placing an `Option Explicit` at the top of a module (see the start of Listing 45.1). If you do this, Visual Basic forces you to explicitly declare the data type of every variable in that module before you use it.

Note

If you have not yet encountered a program bug, you are living a charmed life. But, never fear, you will undoubtedly see many in the near future. A bug in a program is actually an error of some sort caused by using improper syntax (syntax errors), improper calculations or assignments (runtime errors), or improper program logic (logical errors).

Visual Basic has several built-in data types, shown in table 45.2. Of these, the `Variant` is the most general, but is the least conservative in terms of resources. A few things, such as pictures, must be stored in variables with a `Variant` type, but most numeric and string values should be stored in the appropriate variable type to save time and space.

Table 45.2 The Built-In Data Types in Visual Basic

Data Type	Size (bytes)	Digits	Range
`Boolean`	2	1	True or False
`Integer`	2	5	-32,768 to 32,767
`Long`	4	10	-2.15E9 to 2,15E9
`Single`	4	7	-3.402E38 to 3.402E38
`Double`	8	15	-1.797E308 to 1.797E308
`Currency`	8	19	-9.22E14 to 9.22E14
`Date`	8		
`String`	1+1th per character		
`Object`	4		
`Array`	Depends on type and number of elements		
`Variant`	Depends on the type of data stored in it		

To declare the type of a variable, use the `Dim` statement. At the top of a procedure or module, type the keyword `Dim` followed by a variable name, and then type the keyword `As` followed by the variable's data type. If the type is not specified, the variable is the `Variant` type. You can put more than one variable type declaration on a single line, separated by commas. The following are all variable declaration statements.

```
Dim myVariable As Integer, yourVariable As Single
Dim aFileName As String
Dim Cost As Currency, Rate As Single
```

Variables passed as arguments to a procedure are declared in the procedure header. For example, the following procedure header defines the arguments being passed to a procedure as an integer and a string:

```
Sub myProcedure(aVariable As Integer, AnotherVariable As String)
```

The type of value returned by a function procedure is declared by placing the type at the right side of the function header. For example, the following function takes a `Single` type value as an argument and returns a `Double` type value.

```
Function myFunction(aVariable As Single) As Double
```

Arrays

Arrays are not really a new data type, but are lists of one of the existing types such as integer or string. An *array* is an indexed list of variables, where the variable name is followed by one or more integers in parentheses. The integer selects the specific *element* of the array. The number of integers in the parentheses determines the *dimension* of the array.

A one-dimensional array has a single-integer index and is a linear list of values. The index selects which element of the list to use, counting from the beginning. For example, the statement

```
Dim myArray(10) As Integer
```

declares a list of 11 memory elements for storing integers (elements 0 through 10). In a formula, the value `myArray(3)` selects the fourth integer in that list, and `myArray(7)` selects the eighth.

A two-dimensional array uses two integers in the parentheses and is a two-dimensional table of numbers with the first index selecting the row and the second selecting the column. Higher order arrays are allowed, but they are a little difficult to imagine once the dimension goes over three. The following are declarations for arrays:

```
Dim anArray(5) As Single, thedigits(50,2) As Integer
Dim anOther(5,3,10) As Long
```

Note

Everything may seem to be off by one when examining array indexes. This occurs because the default starting point for an array index is 0, which makes the number of elements in an array one more than the value of the upper limit specified in the Dim statement. You can modify the default property by placing an `Option Base` statement at the top of a module, which changes the default starting point to 1. You can also use constructions like `Dim anArray(5 to 7)` to force the index to range between specific limits.

User-Defined Types

In addition to the built-in data types, you can define your own data types to make it more convenient for you to store your data. In the personal organizer example, you want to store five strings and an integer. You could store them in five different variables, but it makes sense to create a new data type that combines them together into a single *user-defined type*. A user-defined type is a data type that you create to fit the specific circumstances of whatever program you are creating. A user-defined type can be nearly any combination of the existing data types, including other user-defined types.

To create a user-defined data type, place a `Type` statement at the top of the procedure or module that needs the type. The `Type` statement consists of a `Type` header containing the keyword `Type` followed by the new type name, one or more named subvariables with `As` type clauses, and an `End Type` statement. For the personal organizer example, you must store the Name, Address, City, State, Zip, and Telephone number as four strings, an integer, and another string. The new user-defined data type is defined as follows:

```
Type myType
   Name As String
   Address As String
   City As String
   State As String
   Zip As Integer
   Phone As String
End Type
```

To use this type, you must declare a variable in a `Dim` statement and use the new type name as the type. For example,

```
Dim theData(100) As myType
```

creates an array of 101 elements of `myType` variables. To access the parts of a user-defined type, follow the variable name with a period and the part name.

For example, to get the ZIP code part from element 34, you would use the following example:

```
theData(34).Zip
```

The Scope of Variables

In Listing 45.1, the type definition and variable declaration is placed at the top of the module outside the procedures. The type definition and declaration are placed here so that the variables `theData`, `numEntries`, and `displayedEntry` are available to all the procedures within the module. If the declarations are placed within a procedure, then the values stored in the variables are available only within that procedure. The same variable can be defined in each of the five procedures, and each of those variables is then completely independent from the other four, even though they have the same name. If you have more than one module in a program, and you want a variable to be available to all the procedures in all the modules, you must declare that variable at the module level and use `Public` instead of `Dim` in the declaration.

Constants

There is one more declaration at the top of the module, and that declaration is

```
Const maxEntries = 100
```

An entry of this type declares a constant. When a constant is declared at the top of a module, it is available to all the procedures in a module. Note that a constant is not a variable, so you cannot change its value in a running program. When you use a constant, it behaves exactly as if you had typed the value of the constant everywhere the name is used. Using constants makes programs easier to understand and easier to change. If you want to increase the size of the array `theData`, you need to change only the value of the constant. If you didn't use the constant, you have to change the code everywhere the length of the data array is used.

Branching and Decision Making

As you read down the first list to the beginning of the `AddName` subprocedure, the first statement adds one to the value of `numEntries`. You do this because `numEntries` contains the number of entries stored in the array, and the `AddName` procedure adds another one:

```
numEntries = numEntries + 1  'Increment the entry number
```

Following that is a block `If` statement comprising five lines of code:

```
If numEntries > maxEntries Then
   MsgBox ("Too many entries, can't insert any more")
   numEntries = numEntries - 1
   Exit Sub
End If
```

These lines of code test the new value of `numEntries` to see if it has gotten too big. If `numEntries` is greater than `maxEntries`, the new data won't fit in the array. This potential problem is tested for using a block `If` statement. The two procedures `UpOne` and `DownOne` increase and decrease the value of `displayedEntry`. Both procedures have block `If` statements at the beginning to test the value of `displayedEntry` to be sure it is in the range `0` to `numEntries`. If an attempt is made to move beyond either end of the range, the block `If` statements set the value of `displayedEntry` to the end of the range.

Block If Statements

A block `If` statement allows you to use a logical condition equation to make a decision as to which block of code to execute. When the `If` statement is executed, *`condition1`* is tested, and if it is True, the block *`statements1`* is executed. If *`condition1`* is False, *`condition2`* is tested, and if it is True the block *`statements2`* is executed. There can be multiple `ElseIf` clauses, and each is tested in turn looking for one whose condition is True. If none of the conditions are True, the statements following the `Else` clause are executed. Only the block of statements following the first condition that returns True is executed; all the others are skipped, even if their conditions would have returned True.

Note

A block `If` statement is a structure that tests one or more conditions and selects a block of code to execute depending on which condition is True.

```
If condition1 Then
   statements1
ElseIf condition2
   statements2
Else
   statements3
End If
```

In the example, there are no `ElseIf` or `Else` clauses, so the block of three statements is executed only if the value of `numEntries` is greater than (>) `maxEntries`. If that condition is True, then you cannot add another entry, and the code displays a dialog box telling you that you can't add another entry, subtracts 1 from `numEntries`, and executes the `Exit Sub` statement. The `Exit Sub` statement immediately terminates a subprocedure, skipping all other statements in the procedure.

Logical Formulas

The conditions used in the `If` statements are logical values, formulas that result in a logical value, or numeric formulas that result in a value of `0` (False) or non-zero (True). Logical formulas are usually created by comparing two values using one of the comparison operators shown in table 45.3. Logical expressions may also be combined with the Boolean operators given in table 45.4. Search for "comparison operators" and "logical" in the Visual Basic section of on-line help for more information.

Table 45.3 The Comparison Operators

Operator	Description
=	Equal to
<>	Not equal to
>	Greater than
<	Less than
>=	Greater than or equal to
<=	Less than or equal to

Table 45.4 The Logical Operators

Operator	Description
`And`	Logical and
`Eqv`	Logical equivalence
`Imp`	Logical implies
`Not`	Logical negation
`Or`	Logical or
`Xor`	Logical exclusive or

Select Case

The `Select Case` statement performs a similar function to the block `If` statement, in that an expression is used to select a particular block of statements. In `Select Case`, the expression returns a value and that value is used to determine which block of statements to execute.

Note

The `Select Case` statement uses a value to select a block of code to execute.

```
Select Case expression
Case list1
   statements1
Case Else
   statements2
End Select
```

When the `Select Case` statement is executed, *`expression`* is evaluated. Following the `Select Case` statement are one or more `Case` statements. The value of *`expression`* is compared to the comma delimited list of values *`list1`*. If one of the values matches, the block *`statements1`* is executed. Otherwise, it skips over that block to the next `Case` statement. If none of the `Case` statements result in a match, the block *`statements2`* following the `Case Else` statement is executed. As with the block `If` statement, only one of the blocks of statements is executed.

Accessing Worksheet Cells

In the example, the next block of statements copies the data from the cells on the worksheet into the data array:

```
'Copy the data from the worksheet to the array.
theData(numEntries).Name = ActiveSheet.Range("Name").Value
theData(numEntries).Address = ActiveSheet.Range("Address").Value
theData(numEntries).City = ActiveSheet.Range("City").Value
theData(numEntries).State = ActiveSheet.Range("State").Value
theData(numEntries).Zip = Val(ActiveSheet.Range("Zip").Value)
theData(numEntries).Phone = ActiveSheet.Range("Telephone").Value
```

You use a `Range` reference to get the value of a named cell using the `Value` property. Notice that the `Value` property contains the value of a cell—that is, the number displayed on the worksheet. To get what was typed into a cell, use the `Formula` property. In this case, because none of the cells contain formulas, the `Value` and `Formula` properties are the same.

The `Range` reference refers to a named cell. This reference is preferable to referencing an explicit cell because you can rearrange the worksheet and the code will still get the value from the correct cell. You can reference the cells using a cell reference or reference a cell by row and column using `Cell`, which also returns a range object. The following three statements all reference the same cell in the example:

```
theData(numEntries).Name = ActiveSheet.Range("Name").Value
theData(numEntries).Name = ActiveSheet.Range("B3").Value
theData(numEntries).Name = ActiveSheet.Cell(3,2).Value
```

The fifth statement in the block is slightly different. The worksheet cell containing the ZIP code is formatted as a string, but the variable where `Zip` is to be stored is an integer. Excel can make this conversion for you and change the string into a number before storing it in the variable. However, if you don't type a number in the ZIP code cell, Excel passes a string to your program and the procedure crashes with a type mismatch error. The `Val()` function explicitly converts a string into a number and returns a value of 0 if the string can't be converted into a number. By applying the `Val()` function to the value returned from the cell, you ensure that a value of the correct type is always stored in the variable preventing your code from crashing:

```
theData(numEntries).Zip = Val(ActiveSheet.Range("Zip").Value)
```

The procedure `DisplayIt` reverses the action of the statements above, takes values from the array `theData`, and places those values in the worksheet cells.

```
With ActiveSheet
   .Range("Name").Value = theData(theEntry).Name
   .Range("Address").Value = theData(theEntry).Address
   .Range("City").Value = theData(theEntry).City
   .Range("State").Value = theData(theEntry).State
   .Range("Zip").Value = Str(theData(theEntry).Zip)
   .Range("Telephone").Value = theData(theEntry).Phone
End With
```

The statements are simply reversed from those in the `AddOne` procedure with the left and right sides of the formulas changing sides. Notice the statement transferring `Zip`. The numeric value of the code stored in the array is converted into a string value before being inserted into the `Value` property of the range. The `Str` function performs that conversion.

This block of statements also demonstrates the use of the `With` statement to block cells together and to save some typing. The statements are logically blocked together because they all refer to the same object, and they save some typing because you only have to type the first object once. The object following the With clause (ActiveSheet) is assumed to attach before the period to all the statements between the With and End With statements.

Calling Procedures

The DisplayIt procedure is an example of a subprocedure that is called by other procedures. The three procedures UpOne, DownOne, and FindIt need to be able to display the contents of one element of the data array on the worksheet. Because all three procedures need this function, it makes sense to place it in a separate procedure and then call it whenever it is needed. Otherwise, you have to type the identical block of statements in three different procedures.

```
Sub DisplayIt(theEntry As Integer)
With ActiveSheet
  .Range("Name").Value = theData(theEntry).Name
  .Range("Address").Value = theData(theEntry).Address
  .Range("City").Value = theData(theEntry).City
  .Range("State").Value = theData(theEntry).State
  .Range("Zip").Value = Str(theData(theEntry).Zip)
  .Range("Telephone").Value = theData(theEntry).Phone
End With
End Sub
```

The procedure needs one integer argument named theEntry in the DisplayIt procedure. In the UpOne procedure, the DisplayIt procedure is called with the following statement:

```
DisplayIt displayedEntry
```

Because this procedure call is not part of a formula, there are no parentheses required around the argument. Notice that in this procedure, the argument is an integer variable named displayedEntry. This variable points to a memory location, and that memory location is passed to the DisplayIt procedure where it is named theEntry. Both names point to the same memory location, so if the value of theEntry were changed in DisplayIt, the value of displayedEntry would be changed in UpOne when the procedure returned.

In some cases, you want to make sure that a procedure does not change an argument, so you must pass the argument as a value instead of a memory address. You can do this in the procedure heading or in the calling program. For example, the procedure heading precedes the argument with the keyword ByVal:

```
Sub DisplayIt(ByVal theEntry As Integer)
```

The other way is to turn the argument in the calling program into a formula. Instead of the addresses of any of the variables, the address where the result of the formula is stored is then sent to the procedure. You make a variable into a formula by simply surrounding the variable name with parentheses:

```
DisplayIt (displayedEntry)
```

Using Loops

The `FindIt` procedure has to search through the data array searching for a name that matches the name in the name box on the worksheet. If you were to write out all 101 of the array elements, you could search through each one, but you probably don't want to spend your time typing the same statement over and over again. To handle cases like this, you use loops. The most common loop is the `For/Next` loop that executes a block of statements a specified number of times.

For/Next

In the For/Next loop, *`loopvariable`* is a standard variable. The first time the loop executes, *`loopvariable`* has the value *`start`*, and all the statements down to the `Next` statement are executed. The second time the loop executes, *`stepval`* is added to *`loopvariable`* and that value is compared with *`end`*. If *`loopvariable`* is greater than *`end`*, the loop terminates; otherwise the statements within the loop are executed again. The `Step` *`stepval`* clause can be omitted, in which case the *`stepval`* is 1. If *`stepval`* is negative, the loop counts down instead of up, until *`loopvariable`* is less than *`end`*.

> **Note**
>
> A `For/Next` loop is a counted loop that executes a block of statements a specified number of times.
>
> ```
> For loopvariable = start To end Step stepval
> .
> .statements
> .
> Next loopvariable
> ```

The FindIt procedure uses a For/Next loop to search the array for a matching name.

```
'
'Search for an entry and display it
'
Sub FindIt()
Dim I As Integer
For I = 0 To numEntries
If InStr(1, theData(I).Name, ActiveSheet.Range("Name").Value, 1) >
0 Then
   Exit For
End If
Next I
If I = numEntries + 1 Then
   MsgBox ("Not found")
Else
   DisplayIt I
End If
End Sub
```

In this example, I is the loop variable, and it ranges from 0 to numEntries. Each time the loop executes, a different element of the array theData is checked. The block If statement uses the InStr function to search for an instance of the contents of the Name cell on the worksheet in the contents of the Name field of the array. If InStr finds the string, it returns the character number where the instance starts; otherwise, it returns 0. By checking for a non-zero return, you know when the matching value is found. In this case, the block If statement executes the Exit For statement, which immediately exits the loop.

The second block If statement checks the value of I, the loop variable. If the loop completes without finding a match, the value of the loop variable will be one more than the ending value of the For/Next loop. By testing for that condition, you know whether a match is found. If a match is not found, a dialog box saying "Not Found" appears; otherwise, the procedure calls the DisplayIt procedure to display the record it found.

While/Wend

The While/Wend loop uses a condition to determine how many times to execute the loop. As long as the condition is True, the loop continues executing.

Note

The `While/Wend` loop repeatedly executes a block of statements until a condition changes to False.

```
While condition
.
statements
.
Wend
```

`While/Wend` loops are used when you don't know how many times to execute a block of statements, but do know some condition that tells you that you are done. If you are calculating an amortization table for a loan, for example, you know that you must keep calculating a payment and reducing the principle until the principle is gone. If you did this with a `While/Wend` loop, your condition would be to see if the principle is greater than zero. If it is, the condition is True and the loop continues. When the principle is less than zero, the condition is False, the loan is paid, and the loop terminates.

Do/Loop

Like the `While/Wend` loop, the `Do/Loop` loop also uses a condition to determine how many times to execute the loop. The difference is that the condition can be tested at the beginning or the end of the loop, and the loop can continue while the condition is True (`While`) or while the condition is False (`Until`). `Do/Loop` loops are more flexible than `While/Wend` loops. The first syntax shown in the sidebar executes identically to the `While/Wend` loop with the same condition. The other variations of the syntax are used in different situations, depending on your needs.

Note

The `Do/Loop` loop calculates a block of statements until a condition changes from True to False, or False to True.

```
Do While condition
.
.  statements
.
Loop
```

or

```
Do Until condition
.
.  statements
.
Loop
```

or

```
Do
.
.  statements
.
Loop While condition
```

or

```
Do
.
.  statements
.
Loop Until condition
```

For Each

The `For Each` loop applies to arrays and collections only. The loop executes once for each element in the array or collection. This loop is very useful when you don't know (or don't care) how many elements there are in a collection. The loop variable *`element`* is of the data type of the elements in the *`group`* collection. Each time the loop is calculated, *`element`* takes on the value of another member of the collection.

Note

The `For Each` loop is used to perform some action for all the elements of an array or collection.

```
For Each element In group
   statements
Next element
```

Accessing Disk Files

If you have been playing with the example, you may have noticed that all the data values go away if you close the worksheet or change the procedures.

What is missing is a way to save the data so that it can be retrieved again the next time you need to use the program. You actually have a couple of options here. You can store the data in another worksheet so it is saved with the workbook, or you can open a disk file and store the data immediately. Both methods have different advantages, depending on what you are planning to do with the data. If you save it in a worksheet, you can apply all of Excel's database functions to it. If you save it in a disk file, then other programs can open it directly. In this example, you are going to save it in a disk file. To save the data, add code to the `InitIt` procedure to open a disk file and load the data, and add code to the `AddName` procedure to open a disk file and save the data whenever a new record is added.

To make these changes, perform the following steps:

1. Use the **F**ile Save **A**s command to save the workbook with the name ROLLO2.XLS.
2. Select the **T**ools **P**rotection Un**p**rotect Sheet command.
3. Select the **T**ools **O**ptions command, select the View tab, and check Horizon**t**al Scroll Bar, **V**ertical Scroll Bar, and Sheet Ta**b**s. Select OK.
4. Select the Module1 tab, and add the following constant to the module header next to the other `Const` statement

```
Const theFilename = "rollo.dat"
```

5. Change the `InitIt` and `AddName` procedures as shown in Listing 45.2. The changes are marked in bold.

Listing 45.2 The ROLLO2 program

```
'Force defining of all variables
Option Explicit
'Define a user defined type to hold the data
Type myType
    Name As String
    Address As String
    City As String
    State As String
    Zip As Long
    Phone As String
End Type
'Define a constant to indicate the maximum number of entries
Const maxEntries = 100
Const theFilename = "rollo.dat"
'Declare an array to hold the entries
Dim theData(maxEntries) As myType
```

```
'Declare some more module level variables
Dim numEntries As Integer, displayedEntry As Integer
'
'Initialize the procedure
'
Sub InitIt()
Dim I As Integer
'See if there is a data file, if there is, open it
'if not, initialize things.
If Dir(theFilename) <> "" Then
   'Open the datafile and load the data into the array
   Open theFilename For Input As #1
   Input #1, numEntries
   For I = 0 To numEntries
   Input #1, theData(I).Name
   Input #1, theData(I).Address
   Input #1, theData(I).City
   Input #1, theData(I).State
   Input #1, theData(I).Zip
   Input #1, theData(I).Phone
   Next I
   Close #1
Else
   MsgBox ("No data file found")
   numEntries = -1  'initialize numentries
End If
End Sub
'
'Add the current worksheet Data to the List
'
Sub AddName()
Dim I As Integer
numEntries = numEntries + 1  'Increment the entry number
If numEntries > maxEntries Then
   MsgBox ("Too many entries, can't insert any more")
   numEntries = numEntries - 1
   Exit Sub
End If
'Copy the data from the worksheet to the array.
theData(numEntries).Name = ActiveSheet.Range("Name").Value
theData(numEntries).Address =
ActiveSheet.Range("Address").Value
theData(numEntries).City = ActiveSheet.Range("City").Value
theData(numEntries).State = ActiveSheet.Range("State").Value
theData(numEntries).Zip = Val(ActiveSheet.Range("Zip").Value)
theData(numEntries).Phone =
ActiveSheet.Range("Telephone").Value
displayedEntry = numEntries
'Save the new database
Open theFilename For Output As #1
Write #1, numEntries
For I = 0 To numEntries
   Write #1, theData(I).Name
   Write #1, theData(I).Address
   Write #1, theData(I).City
   Write #1, theData(I).State
```

(continues)

Listing 45.2 Continued

```
   Write #1, theData(I).Zip
   Write #1, theData(I).Phone
Next I
Close #1
End Sub
'
'Display the next set of data on the worksheet
'
Sub UpOne()
If displayedEntry < numEntries Then
    displayedEntry = displayedEntry + 1
Else
    displayedEntry = numEntries
End If
DisplayIt displayedEntry
End Sub
'
'Display the previous set of data on the worksheet
'
Sub DownOne()
If displayedEntry > 0 Then
    displayedEntry = displayedEntry - 1
Else
    displayedEntry = 0
End If
DisplayIt displayedEntry
End Sub
'
'Search for an entry and display it
'
Sub FindIt()
Dim I As Integer
For I = 0 To numEntries
If InStr(1, theData(I).Name, ActiveSheet.Range("Name").Value,
1) > 0 Then
    Exit For
End If
Next I
If I = numEntries + 1 Then
    MsgBox ("Not found")
Else
    DisplayIt I
End If
End Sub

Sub DisplayIt(theEntry As Integer)
With ActiveSheet
    .Range("Name").Value = theData(theEntry).Name
    .Range("Address").Value = theData(theEntry).Address
    .Range("City").Value = theData(theEntry).City
    .Range("State").Value = theData(theEntry).State
    .Range("Zip").Value = Str(theData(theEntry).Zip)
    .Range("Telephone").Value = theData(theEntry).Phone
End With
End Sub
```

The additions to the `AddName` procedure open a disk file named ROLLO.DAT for output, with a file number of 1. The file number is used when reading, writing, and closing the file to identify which file to access because you may have more than one file open. The first `Write` statement saves the number of data items, and the block of `Write` statements save the data. The complementary changes in the `InitIt` procedure open the same file for input if it exists and read the data out of it back into the data array.

6. Select the Sheet1 tab.

7. Choose the **T**ools **O**ptions command, select the View tab, and uncheck Horizon**t**al Scroll Bar, **V**ertical Scroll Bar, and Sheet Ta**b**s. Select OK.

8. Choose the **T**ools **P**rotection **P**rotect Sheet command, and select OK.

9. Save the workbook.

The program still looks like that in figure 45.7, but now the data is saved between opening and closing the worksheet. For more information about reading and writing files, search for "input" in the Visual Basic section of on-line help, and select the Input and Output Keyword Summary topic.

Using Excel's Dialog Boxes

You have already used the two Visual Basic built-in dialog boxes to send or get information from the user. There are also two Excel dialog boxes (`GetSaveAsFilename` and `GetOpenFilename`) that you can use to enhance your programs when opening and saving files. You can add these to the personal organizer program to select the file to open instead of using the fixed file name.

The `GetSaveAsFilename` method displays the standard File Save As dialog box and gets a file name from the user. The dialog box does not really save anything, it only gets you a path and file name to use. You must then use the `Open` statement to actually create the file and save something in it. The `GetOpenFilename` method operates in the same way, but it displays the standard File Open dialog box instead.

Creating Custom Dialog Boxes

Besides the built-in dialog boxes, you can create custom dialog boxes and attach them to a Visual Basic program. The Personal Organizer program can easily have its data entry form switched from a worksheet to a custom dialog box.

To make this change, perform the following steps:

1. Open the ROLLO2.XLS workbook and save it as ROLLO3.XLS.
2. Choose the **T**ools **P**rotection Un**p**rotect Sheet command.
3. Choose the **T**ools **O**ptions command, select the View tab, and check Horizon**t**al Scroll Bar, **V**ertical Scroll Bar, and Sheet Ta**b**s. Select OK.
4. Select the **I**nsert **M**acro **D**ialog command. Your worksheet should look like figure 45.8, with a blank custom dialog box.

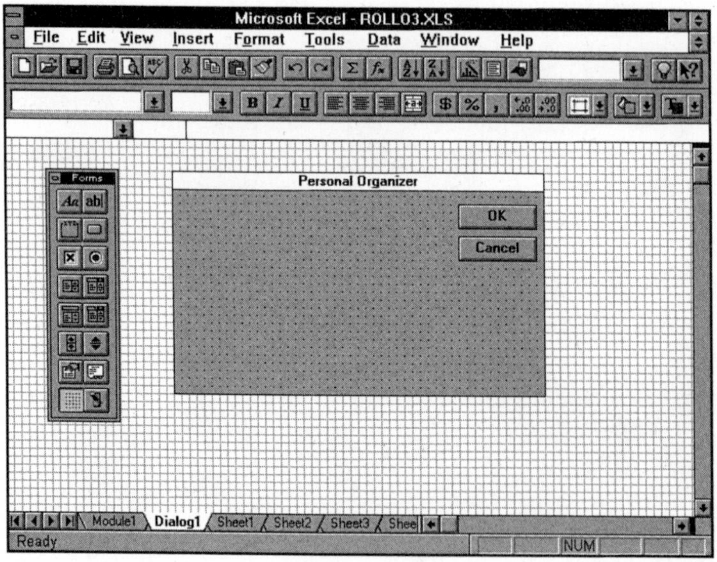

Fig. 45.8
A custom dialog box before editing.

5. Select the dialog caption and type **Personal Organizer**.
6. Select the Cancel button, select the F**o**rmat Obj**e**ct command, uncheck **C**ancel, and select OK.
7. Change the caption of the Cancel button to **Add**.

8. Using the Button tool, draw three more buttons on the dialog and label them as shown in figure 45.9.

9. Using the Label button, draw six labels on the dialog box and change their captions as shown in figure 45.9.

10. Using the Edit box button, draw six edit boxes on the dialog box as shown in figure 45.9.

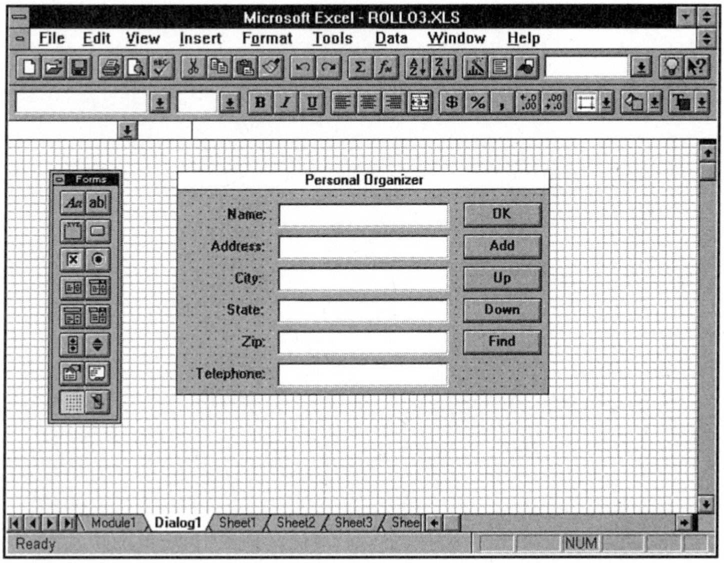

Fig. 45.9
Layout for the Personal Organizer dialog box.

11. Select the edit box next to the Name label and name it **DlName**.

12. Select the edit box next to the Address label and name it **DlAddress**.

13. Select the edit box next to the City label and name it **DlCity**.

14. Select the edit box next to the State label and name it **DlState**.

15. Select the edit box next to the Zip label and name it **DlZip**.

16. Select the edit box next to the Telephone label and name it **DlTelephone**.

17. Select the Add button, select the **T**ools Assig**n** Macro command, select the `AddName` macro, and select OK.

18. Select the Up button, select the **T**ools Assig**n** Macro command, select the `UpOne` macro, and select OK.

19. Select the Down button, select the **T**ools Assig**n** Macro command, select the `DownOne` macro, and select OK.

20. Select the Find button, select the **T**ools Assig**n** Macro command, select the `FindIt` macro, and select OK.

21. Select the edit box next to the Zip label and select F**o**rmat Obj**e**ct, check the Number type for checking, and select OK.

22. Select the module, and make the changes shown in Listing 45.3 to the procedures. The changes are in bold.

Listing 45.3 The ROLLO3 Program

```
'Force defining of all variables
Option Explicit
'Defined type to hold the data
Type myType
   Name As String
   Address As String
   City As String
   State As String
   Zip As Long
   Phone As String
End Type
'Define a constant to indicate the maximum number of entries
Const maxEntries = 100
Const theFilename = "rollo.dat"
'Declare an array to hold the entries
Dim theData(maxEntries) As myType
'Declare some more module level variables
Dim numEntries As Integer, displayedEntry As Integer
'
'Initialize the procedure
'
Sub InitIt()
Dim I As Integer
'See if there is a data file, if there is, open it
'if not, initialize things.
If Dir(theFilename) <> "" Then
  'Open the datafile and load the data into the array
   Open theFilename For Input As #1
   Input #1, numEntries
   For I = 0 To numEntries
   Input #1, theData(I).Name
Input #1, theData(I).Address
   Input #1, theData(I).City
   Input #1, theData(I).State
   Input #1, theData(I).Zip
   Input #1, theData(I).Phone
   Next I
   Close #1
Else
```

```
    MsgBox ("No data file found")
    numEntries = -1  'initialize entry number
End If
'Display the Dialog
DialogSheets("Dialog1").Show
End Sub
'
'Add the current worksheet Data to the List
'
Sub AddName()
Dim I As Integer
numEntries = numEntries + 1  'Increment the entry number
If numEntries > maxEntries Then
    MsgBox ("Too many entries, can't insert any more")
    numEntries = numEntries - 1
    Exit Sub
End If
'Copy the data from the worksheet to the array.
With DialogSheets("Dialog1")
  theData(numEntries).Name = .EditBoxes("DlName").Text
  theData(numEntries).Address = .EditBoxes("DlAddress").Text
  theData(numEntries).City = .EditBoxes("DlCity").Text
  theData(numEntries).State = .EditBoxes("DlState").Text
  theData(numEntries).Zip = Val(.EditBoxes("DlZip").Text)
  theData(numEntries).Phone = .EditBoxes("DlTelephone").Text
End With
displayedEntry = numEntries
'Save the new database
Open theFilename For Output As #1
Write #1, numEntries
For I = 0 To numEntries
    Write #1, theData(I).Name
    Write #1, theData(I).Address
    Write #1, theData(I).City
    Write #1, theData(I).State
    Write #1, theData(I).Zip
    Write #1, theData(I).Phone
Next I
Close #1
End Sub

'
'Display the next set of data on the worksheet
'
Sub UpOne()
If displayedEntry < numEntries Then
    displayedEntry = displayedEntry + 1
Else
    displayedEntry = numEntries
End If
DisplayIt displayedEntry
End Sub
'
'Display the previous set of data on the worksheet
'
Sub DownOne()
```

(continues)

Listing 45.3 Continued

```
If displayedEntry > 0 Then
   displayedEntry = displayedEntry - 1
Else
   displayedEntry = 0
End If
DisplayIt displayedEntry
End Sub
'
'Search for an entry and display it
'
Sub FindIt()
Dim I As Integer
For I = 0 To numEntries
If InStr(1, theData(I).Name,
DialogSheets("Dialog1").EditBoxes("DlName").Text, 1) > 0 Then
   Exit For
End If
Next I
If I = numEntries + 1 Then
   MsgBox ("Not found")
Else
   DisplayIt I
End If
End Sub

Sub DisplayIt(theEntry As Integer)
With DialogSheets("Dialog1")
  .EditBoxes("DlName").Text = theData(theEntry).Name
  .EditBoxes("DlAddress").Text = theData(theEntry).Address
  .EditBoxes("DlCity").Text = theData(theEntry).City
  .EditBoxes("DlState").Text = theData(theEntry).State
  .EditBoxes("DlZip").Text = Str(theData(theEntry).Zip)
  .EditBoxes("DlTelephone").Text = theData(theEntry).Phone
End With
End Sub
```

23. Save the workbook.

The first change in the procedure is in the `InitIt` procedure. This procedure is still attached to the Init button on the worksheet because you must have a running code to give a dialog box the `Show` method in order to see the dialog box. You also can do this with an autoexecute macro or by running the `InitIt` macro from the Macro dialog box. The change is to add the `Show` method to display your new dialog box:

```
DialogSheets("Dialog1").Show
```

The `DialogSheets` collection selects the dialog box and the `Show` method displays it. To get rid of a dialog box, use the `Hide` method. The next change is in the `AddName` method:

```
'Copy the data from the worksheet to the array.
With DialogSheets("Dialog1")
  theData(numEntries).Name = .EditBoxes("DlName").Text
  theData(numEntries).Address = .EditBoxes("DlAddress").Text
  theData(numEntries).City = .EditBoxes("DlCity").Text
  theData(numEntries).State = .EditBoxes("DlState").Text
  theData(numEntries).Zip = Val(.EditBoxes("DlZip").Text)
  theData(numEntries).Phone = .EditBoxes("DlTelephone").Text
End With
```

The `With` statement shortens the lines a little; the references to the cells on the worksheet change to the edit boxes on the dialog sheet. Again, in the `DisplayIt` procedure the references to the worksheet change to the dialog sheet. The last change is in the `FindIt` procedure—the reference from the Name cell on the worksheet changes to the `DlName` edit box on the dialog sheet.

The programming is almost identical, except the references changed to access the dialog sheet instead of the worksheet. When you run the program by pressing the Init button on the worksheet, the dialog box appears as shown in figure 45.10. You operate it in the same manner as the worksheet version, and press the OK button to end it.

Using the Debugging Tools

Program bugs are a fact of life for computer programmers. No matter how careful you are, bugs almost always show up and must be found and removed from your codes. The simplest bugs are syntax errors where you have put a comma in the wrong place or used a keyword improperly. Syntax errors are normally found by Visual Basic as soon as you type them. Next are the runtime errors, which are caused by using the wrong type of variable, or by performing an improper numeric calculation (for example, taking the square root of -1). These errors are also found by Visual Basic as soon as the improper statement is executed. Lastly are the logical errors, where a program runs just fine, but does not do what you want it to. Logical errors are the most difficult to find because everything seems to work, it just works wrong.

Visual Basic has a built-in set of powerful debugging tools to help you find and correct program bugs. You can set breakpoints anywhere in your programs to force them to stop executing at that point. After you stop your program, use the Instant Watch command to view the value of any variable or expression. You can then continue executing a program or step through it one statement at a time until you find your problems. You also can set watchpoints that automatically break a program when a variable or expression reaches a certain value.

Fig. 45.10
The Personal Organizer dialog box.

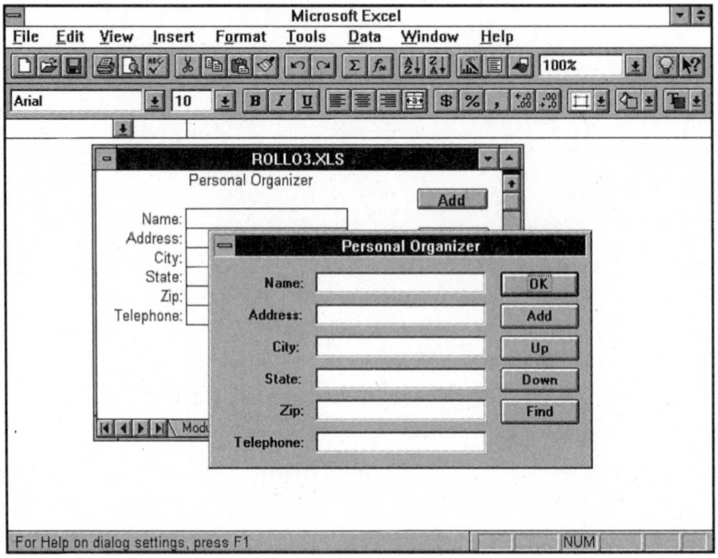

Using Break Mode

Break mode is where an executing program is halted with all its variables are still intact. A running program enters break mode when you press Ctrl+Break, when it encounters an error, or when it encounters a breakpoint or watchpoint. When a program enters break mode by encountering an error or by your pressing Ctrl+Break, the Macro Error dialog box appears as shown in figure 45.11, giving you the choice to quit, continue, or open the Debug window.

Setting Breakpoints

Breakpoints and watchpoints also put a program into break mode. A breakpoint is a marker on a line of code that forces a program to stop executing when Visual Basic attempts to execute the marked line. A watchpoint is a marker on the value of a variable or a simple formula. When the value of a watchpoint changes in some specific way, the program is stopped and placed in break mode.

To set a breakpoint, open the module containing your procedure and select the line of code where you want the program to stop. Select the **R**un Toggle **B**reakpoint command to set a breakpoint. Select the command again to remove a selected breakpoint, or select the **R**un **C**lear All Breakpoints command to remove all of them. Then run your code. When it reaches a breakpoint, it stops and enters break mode. When a program enters break mode by encountering a breakpoint or watchpoint, it goes directly to the Debug window discussed next.

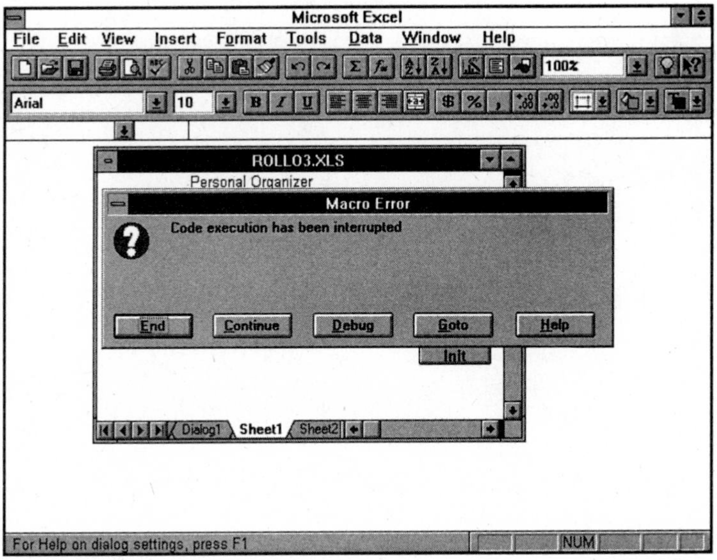

Fig. 45.11
The Macro Error dialog box.

The Debug Window

If you select **D**ebug on the Macro Error dialog box, or encounter a breakpoint or watchpoint, the Debug window appears. The Debug window is a split window, with the currently executing procedure in the bottom half and either the Immediate pane or the Watch pane at the top (see fig. 45.12). In the bottom half of the window, you can select lines of code, add, or remove breakpoints and select code for watchpoints. The Debug window shown in figure 45.12 shows the code stopped at a breakpoint set on the `If` statement highlighted in the Code pane. The Watch pane shows the current value of `thefilename` watch variable. At this point, you can continue execution of a procedure, set or delete more watchpoints, examine the value of variables, or step through the procedure, one statement at a time.

The Immediate Pane

In the Immediate pane of the Debug window, you can type and execute almost any Visual Basic command. The only restriction is that it must be only one line long. The Immediate pane also receives any printed values caused by the `Debug.Print` statement, used to print values from a running program.

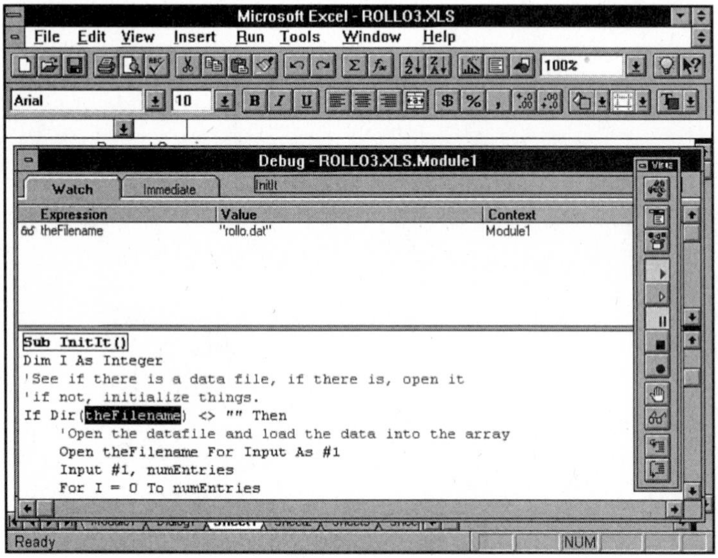

Fig. 45.12
The Debug window shows the Watch and Code panes. The Immediate pane is behind the Watch pane and is selected with the tab at the top. The highlighted line of code in the code pane is the breakpoint that stopped the execution. The Watch pane shows a watch variable and its current value.

The Watch Pane and Watch Variables

The Watch pane displays the current value of watchpoints and watch variables. Watchpoints, watch variables displayed in the Watch pane, continuously show the value of the variable or expression. the difference between these two is that while both show the value of a variable, a watchpoint can stop your code if the selected value changes in some specified way. The Instant watch is used to show the current value of a variable or expression without placing it in the Watch pane. Figure 45.13 shows the results of selecting the variable I in the Debug window and selecting the **T**ools Instant **W**atch command. If you select the **A**dd button, the instant watch variable is changed into a watch variable and added to the Watch pane.

The Step Commands

There are two step commands that you can use at this point to execute one line of your program and stop again in break mode: **R**un Step **I**nto and **R**un Step **O**ver. The **R**un Step **I**nto command makes the program execute one line at a time. If the program reaches a procedure call, the next step occurs in that called procedure.

The **R**un Step **O**ver command is similar, but when it reaches a procedure call, it executes the procedure completely before stopping and going into break mode again. Thus, the Step **O**ver command appears to step over procedure calls in the procedure you are executing.

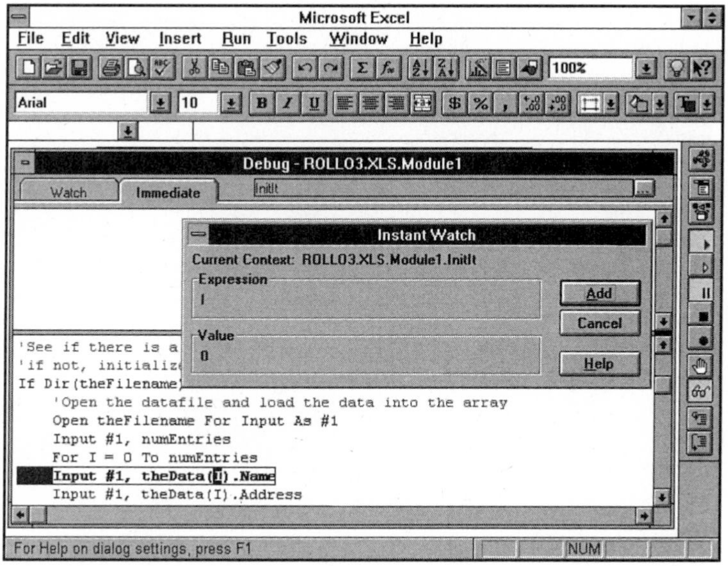

Fig. 45.13
An Instant Watch dialog box.

The Calls Window

The Calls window is on the upper right side of the Debug window shown in figure 45.12. The Calls window shows the name of the procedure that contains the current point of execution. If you select the Calls window, it expands and lists all the active procedures in this program. Active procedures are those that have not completed running yet, either because they contain the current execution point or because they were one of the calling procedures that eventually called the procedure that contains the execution point.

From Here...

One of the best sources of information for the syntax and usage of the Visual Basic commands and functions is the on-line help. Be sure that you select the Visual Basic section; then you can explore all the different functions and methods available there. The Object Browser is another helpful feature because it looks at the actual library files and extracts the real procedure names and properties directly from the procedures themselves. Finally, Chapter 46, "Exploring Visual Basic for Applications Examples," has several examples of working code that you can examine and run.

Chapter 46

Exploring Visual Basic for Applications Examples

VIII

Automating with VBA

In this chapter you learn how to:

- Examine values and format worksheet cells
- Locate and open workbooks
- Move objects on the worksheet
- Use OLE
- Use worksheet functions in Visual Basic
- Pass arrays to the worksheet

This chapter contains several operating Visual Basic procedures for you to examine and modify for your own use. It is split into two main sections—procedures and functions. Procedures are programs that do something to a worksheet, and the functions perform calculations and return one or more values. In each of these main sections are several procedures or functions to demonstrate the different aspects of Visual Basic for Applications.

Creating Command Procedures

In this section, you examine procedures that do things to Excel worksheets, such as formatting, inserting tables, and moving objects. The procedures in this section were either manually programmed, programmed using the macro recorder, or a combination of both. In general, if you know what you want to do on a worksheet, use the Macro Recorder to record the actions and then go back and edit the recording to do exactly what you want. In situations where you have been hand coding a procedure, and you come to a place where you want to manipulate a worksheet, use the **T**ools **R**ecord Macro **M**ark Position For Recording command to mark the current cursor location as the place to insert a new recording. Next, switch to the worksheet, choose the **T**ools **R**ecord Macro R**e**cord at Mark command to start the recorder, and perform the editing. Select Stop when you are done, and then go back and edit the inserted statements.

Examining Procedures

The simplest way to try out the procedures in this chapter is to attach them to a button on a worksheet. You can then easily execute the procedure from the worksheet and watch the results of its execution. To attach a procedure to a button, follow these steps:

1. Open a module sheet.
2. Type the procedure as shown in this text.
3. Switch to a worksheet.
4. Choose the **V**iew **T**oolbars command and select the Drawing toolbar.
5.  Click the Create Button button on the Drawing toolbar and draw a button on the worksheet where it won't interfere with what is already on the worksheet or with what the attached procedure is going to do.
6. When the Assign Macro dialog box appears, select the procedure name from the list and choose OK.

You can now execute the procedure by pressing the button you just attached to the worksheet.

Examining Worksheet Data with If Statements

This first example uses If statements to examine the contents of cells on the worksheet and to mark the statements if they have certain characteristics. In this case, non-numeric cells are yellow, cells with negative values are red, and cells with values greater than a goal (10,000 here) are green. A procedure of this kind can be used to flag negative values in a table of sales and highlight sales greater than a sales goal. The procedure also is used to audit a worksheet to locate incorrect values.

```
'
Option Explicit
Const Red = 3 'Name some constants
Const Green = 4
Const Yellow = 6
Const None = 0
Const Goal = 10000
'
' MakeRed Macro
'Examine all the cells in the current selection and
'make the background red for those that have a value
'less than zero, make the background yellow for non-numeric
'values, and make the background green for those values above
'the goal of 10000.
```

```
'
Sub MakeRed()
Dim theCell 'Defines a Variant type
'Loop over the cells in the selection
For Each theCell In Selection
If Not (IsNumeric(theCell.Value)) Then 'Test for non-numeric values
 With theCell.Interior 'If non-numeric make it yellow.
 .Pattern = xlSolid
 .ColorIndex = Yellow
 End With
ElseIf theCell.Value < 0 Then 'If negative, make red
 With theCell.Interior
 .Pattern = xlSolid
 .ColorIndex = Red
 End With
ElseIf theCell.Value > Goal Then 'If greater than goal, make green
 With theCell.Interior
 .Pattern = xlSolid
 .ColorIndex = Green
 End With
Else 'If positive number, clear the background
 With theCell.Interior
 .Pattern = xlNone
 .ColorIndex = None
 End With
End If
Next theCell
End Sub
```

This procedure starts with the `Option Explicit` statement to force you to define all the variables. Following this are constants defined at the module level so they apply to all the procedures in this module. The procedure then starts a loop over all the cells in the current selection, using the `For Each` loop. A block `If` statement first checks for non-numeric values, and colors yellow any cells that don't contain a numeric value. The second part of the block `If` statement locates cells with numeric values less than zero, and colors them red. The third block of the `If` statement locates cells with values greater than the value of the constant `Goal`, and colors them green. If none of the blocks selects the cell, it reaches the last block of the `If` statement, which clears the cell of any colors or patterns.

To use the procedure, select some cells on a worksheet and execute the procedure. The procedure then checks each cell in the selection and colors their background accordingly (see fig. 46.1).

Entering Data with a Location and Offset

Occasionally, you may want to do something to cells outside of the current selection, but located near the active cell. For example, inserting a table down and to the right of the current active cell. The following procedure does this:

```
'
' MakeTable Macro
' Make a table attached to the upper-left cell of the
' selection. Make two columns; Months and $. use a
' dialog to get the $
'
Sub MakeTable()
Dim topLeft As Object, gotString As String
Dim theMonth As Integer

'Everything is referenced to the active cell, so save a reference
'to it. Must use Set because it is an object.
Set topLeft = ActiveCell
'Select the range for the table
Range(topLeft, topLeft.Offset(12, 1)).Select
Selection.Clear 'Clear the range then outline it
Selection.BorderAround Weight:=xlThin, ColorIndex:=xlAutomatic
'Select and outline the table headings
Range(topLeft, topLeft.Offset(0, 1)).Select
Selection.BorderAround Weight:=xlThin, ColorIndex:=xlAutomatic
'Insert Month and Sales in the table heading
Range(topLeft, topLeft).Formula = "Month"
Range(topLeft.Offset(0, 1), topLeft.Offset(0, 1)).Formula = "Sales"
' Loop over 12 months, insert the date for the month in the first
' column
' does not know about the Date type.
For theMonth = 1 To 12
 topLeft.Offset(theMonth, 0).Value = (DateSerial(0, theMonth, 1))
Next theMonth
'Select the first column and format it to display only the months
Range(topLeft.Offset(1, 0), topLeft.Offset(12, 0)).Select
Selection.NumberFormat = "mmm"
'Select the second column and format it as currency
Range(topLeft.Offset(1, 1), topLeft.Offset(12, 1)).Select
Selection.NumberFormat = "$#,##0.00_);($#,##0.00)"
'Loop over the rows and put up a dialog box requesting the sales
'for a month. The dialog uses the name of the month from the first
'column as a title.
For theMonth = 1 To 12
 gotString = InputBox("Input the sales", Format(topLeft.Offset
    (theMonth, 0).Value, "mmm"))
 If gotString = "" Then 'Test for no input or cancel pressed
 Exit For 'Quit if no input or Cancel
 Else
 'Copy the value from the dialog box and insert it into the cell.
 topLeft.Offset(theMonth, 1).Value = Val(gotString)
 End If
Next theMonth
End Sub
```

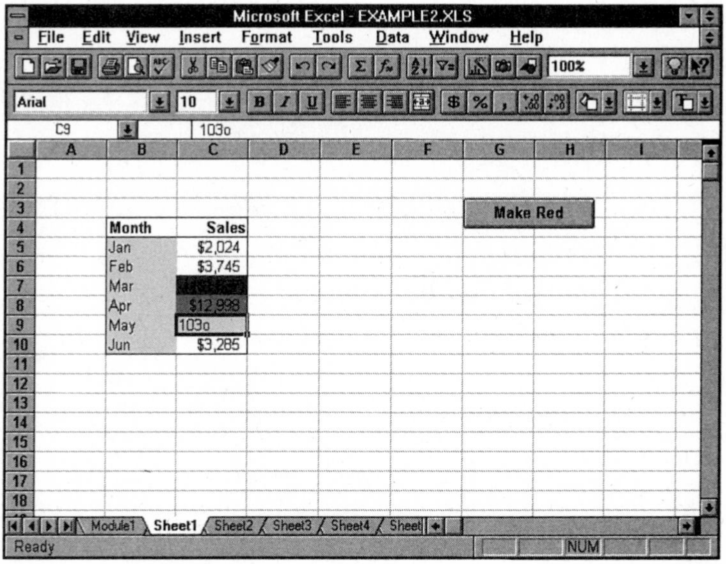

Fig. 46.1
A table of text and numbers colored with the MakeRed procedure. Note the number located by the procedure (yellow) where the letter **o** was typed instead of the number 0.

The `MakeTable` procedure clears a 13-by-2 range on a worksheet, using the current selection as the upper-left corner. The address of the current selection is saved and used with the `Offset` method to locate the rest of the parts of the table. The procedure then outlines the table and the headings, insets the headings, and fills the first column with dates from Jan. to Dec. It then opens a dialog box using the `InputBox()` function to request the values from you to put in the second column. To use this procedure, select a cell on the worksheet and execute the procedure. When the procedure completes, the worksheet will look like figure 46.2.

Printing Worksheet Cells with a Procedure

Often you are printing many different things on a worksheet, but it can be tedious to continually set the print area with the **F**ile Page Se**t**up command, and then printing with the **F**ile **P**rint command. It's much easier to have a button on the worksheet or toolbar that prints the current selection. The following procedure does this:

```
'
' Macro PrintRange
' Print the current selection
'
Sub PrintRange()
Selection.PrintOut
End Sub
```

As you can see, printing a range on the worksheet is almost trivial. Apply the `PrintOut` method to an Object such as the current selection, and it is printed on the printer. Create a button on the worksheet, or on a toolbar, and attach this procedure to it to make it convenient to access.

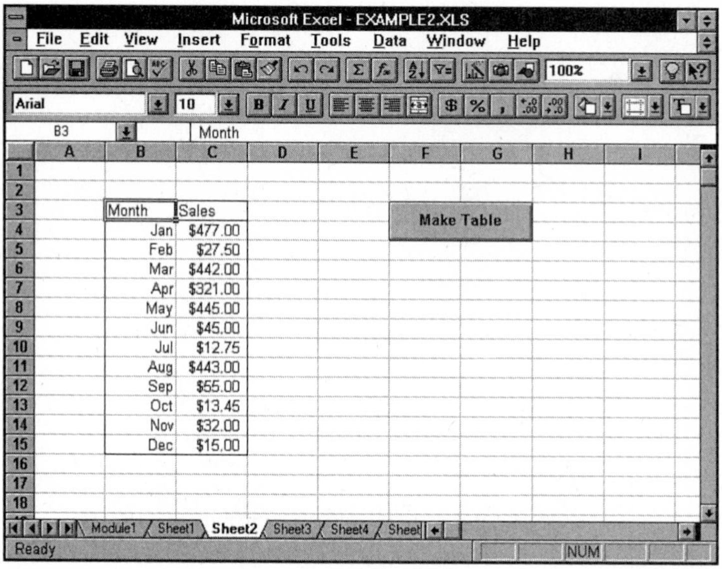

Fig. 46.2 The table inserted and formatted with the MakeTable procedure.

Testing for an Open Workbook and Opening It

Custom procedures often need to open a specific workbook file. The problem is that the file may not be in the current directory and the user must locate it. The following procedure uses the Workbooks collection to search for an open workbook with the name SALES.XLS. If it isn't open, the procedure displays the open dialog for you to locate the missing file. When you find the file, the procedure opens it.

```
'
' GetBook Macro
' See if a workbook is open, If not, open it.
'
Sub GetBook()
Dim fileToOpen As Variant, book As Object
Dim theFileName As String
' Search through the Collection of workbook names for one that
matches
' SALES.XLS
theFileName = "SALES.XLS" 'The name of the file to open
For Each book In Workbooks
 If book.Name = theFileName Then 'The workbook is open if we get a
    match.
```

```
  book.Activate 'Activate it, and then quit.
  Exit Sub
  End If
 Next book
 'If we got here, the workbook is not open, so have the user locate
 it.
 fileToOpen = Application.GetOpenFilename("Locate: " & theFileName &
 "," & theFileName)
 If fileToOpen = False Then 'If the user pressed cancel, then quit.
  Exit Sub
 Else
  Workbooks.Open fileToOpen 'Open the workbook
 End If
 End Sub
```

The procedure first uses the `For Each` loop to check every workbook in the Workbooks collection. If the name of one of the open workbooks matches the file name it is looking for, the workbook is activated and the procedure ends. If the workbook is not open, the Open dialog box is displayed using the `GetOpenFilename` procedure as shown in figure 46.3. The procedure returns the path and file name if the file is found, or `False` if the user selects Cancel. If Cancel was selected, the procedure exits; otherwise the Open method of the Workbooks collection is used to open the selected workbook.

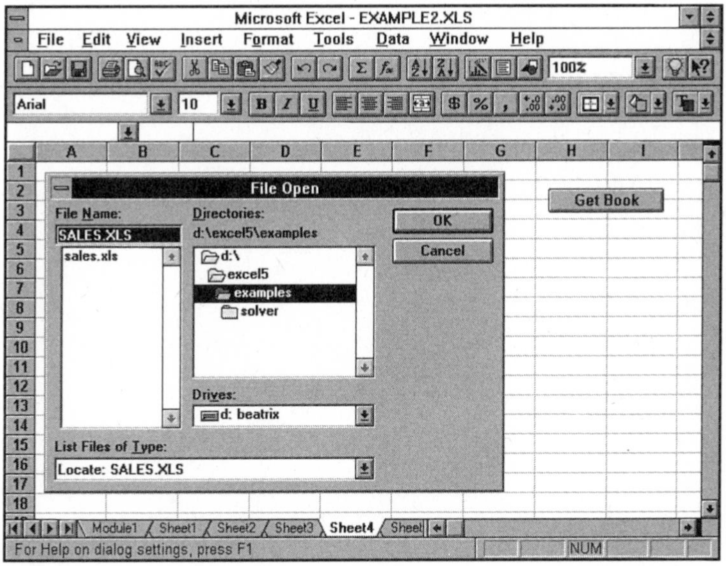

Fig. 46.3
The Open dialog displayed with the `GetBook` procedure.

Moving Objects on the Worksheet

As part of a special, on-line presentation, or a workbook designed to amaze your peers, you can make objects on a worksheet move. Movable objects include any attached object created with the drawing palette. To help you understand moving objects on the worksheet, the following two procedures move the buttons to which they are attached. The first procedure makes its button jump to a random location on the worksheet in a single motion. The second procedure makes its button slide to the new location.

```
'
' Procedure jumpingButton
' Demonstrates moving an object on the worksheet
'
Sub jumpingButton()
Dim x As Single, y As Single
ActiveSheet.DrawingObjects("JButton").Select 'Select the button
x = Rnd(1) * 400 'Randomly select a new x-y location
y = Rnd(1) * 150
With Selection
 .Visible = False 'Make the Button disappear
 .Left = x  'Change the Button's location
 .Top = y
 .Visible = True 'Make the button reappear
End With
ActiveSheet.Cells(1, 1).Select 'Deselect the button by selecting a cell.
End Sub
'
' procedure slidingButton
' Similar to jumpingbutton but the button slides to the new location
'
Sub slidingButton()
Dim x As Single, y As Single
Dim xOld As Single, yOld As Single
Dim xNew As Single, yNew As Single
Dim deltaX As Single, deltaY As Single
ActiveSheet.DrawingObjects("SButton").Select 'Select the button
With Selection
 xOld = .Left
 yOld = .Top
End With
xNew = Rnd(1) * 400 'Randomly select a new x-y location
yNew = Rnd(1) * 150
deltaX = (xNew - xOld) / 10 'Break the path into 10 steps
deltaY = (yNew - yOld) / 10
x = xOld
y = yOld
While Abs(x - xNew) > Abs(deltaX) / 2 'Step along the path to the new
location
 x = x + deltaX
 y = y + deltaY
 With Selection
 .Visible = False 'Hide the button
 .Left = x  'Change the Button's location
 .Top = y
 .Visible = True 'Show the button
 End With
ActiveSheet.DrawingObjects("SButton").Select 'Reselect the button
Wend
ActiveSheet.Cells(1, 1).Select 'Deselect the button by selecting a cell.
End Sub
```

To use these procedures, attach two buttons to a worksheet and name them JButton and SButton using the **I**nsert **N**ame **D**efine command. The `jumpingButton` procedure is attached to the button named JButton. It first uses the DrawingObjects collection to locate and select JButton. Next, it uses two random numbers to calculate a new location for the button. To move the button, it sets the `Visible` property to False to hide the button, changes the `Top` and `Left` properties to the new location, and sets the `Visible` property back to True to make it visible again. Finally, a worksheet cell is selected to deselect the button.

The `slidingButton` procedure works in much the same way as the `jumpingButton` procedure, except that it is attached to the button named SButton, which is slid from the first location to the next. A line between the current and new location is divided into 10 parts, and then the button is slid along that line, one step at a time using a `While/Wend` loop. The loop terminates when the button comes within deltaX/2 of the final location. Terminating the loop in this way, instead of terminating it when the button is exactly at the final location, takes care of any error that may occur when adding the 10 values of `deltaX` and `deltaY`. The round-off error could make the button move to a location very close to—but not exactly at—the final location, and a test for being exactly at the final location would fail and the button would continue moving off the side of the page. Try running this with the `.Visible = False`, and the `.Visible = True` statements commented out. The button zigzags from one location to the next.

OLE Automation

The Object Linking and Embedding (OLE) capabilities of Excel makes it possible to control another application using Visual Basic. Microsoft Word for Windows 6 (*not* Word for Windows 2) is an OLE-compliant application, and the following procedure starts Word 6, copies the current selection, and pastes it into Word 6 as an OLE object.

```
'
' InsertTable procedure
' This procedure uses OLE to start Word Version 6 for Windows from
  Excel and insert the current selection as a table.
'
Sub InsertTable()
Dim msWord As Object
'Open the Word application and access WordBasic
Set msWord = CreateObject("Word.Basic")
```

```
'Copy the current selection
Selection.Copy
'Send commands to Word.
With msWord
 .appmaximize  'Maximize to full screen
 .filenewdefault 'Create a new blank document
 .editpaste  'Paste the copied selection
End With
End Sub
```

The procedure first creates a link to the Word application, copies the current selection, and then pastes it into a new document in Word. To use this procedure, attach it to a button on the worksheet, select something and select the button.

Creating User Defined Functions

User defined functions are functions that you define with Visual Basic, and then use in a worksheet just like any of the built-in functions. Use user defined functions to provide special capabilities or variations of existing capabilities unavailable with Excel's built-in functions.

Using Worksheet Functions in Visual Basic

When you calculate a loan payment, you usually have the yearly interest rate in percent, the number of years to pay off the loan, and the amount of the loan. When you use the Excel Pmt function to calculate the payment, you must convert the interest rate per year into the fractional rate per month, and the years into months. In addition, you have to remember that the negative value returned by the Pmt function means paid out. It would be nice to have a worksheet function that uses the values you have so you don't have to convert everything. The following glue function does just that. It's called a *glue function* because it connects, or glues, the arguments of a function you want into a function you have.

```
'
' MPmt function
' A variation of the Excel Pmt function that
' uses the yearly interest rate and number of years
' as arguments instead of the monthly interest rate and
' the number of payments.
'
Function MPmt(yearlyRate As Single, numYears As Integer, PresVal As
Currency)
'The Excel function expects the rate per period and the
'number of periods, but most loans are specified as rate
'per year and number of years, even though they are paid monthly.
'Pmt(rate, nper, pv, fv, type)
```

```
'In addition, most loans are paid off (fv=0), the payment
'occurs at the end of the period (type=0), and you want a positive
'value, rather than the negative value returned by the function.
'This is called a glue function, to connect or glue a function
'you have to a function you want.
MPmt = -Application.Pmt(yearlyRate / 1200, numYears * 12, PresVal, 0, 0)
End Function
```

The function `MPmt` needs only the yearly interest rate, the number of years, and the loan balance as arguments, and returns the payment as a positive value. Because the `Pmt` function already exists, there is no need to rewrite i; however it exists only on the worksheet, and not in Visual Basic for Applications. To find it, use the Object Browser, and the Excel library. You will find it in the Application object along with all the other worksheet functions. To use it, or any of the worksheet functions in Visual Basic for Applications, preface the function name with the application object. To use this function on the worksheet, you use something like:

```
=MPmt(6.875,15,131000)
```

You also can use cell ranges for arguments, and the glue function adjusts the values for you.

Selecting a Calculation with an Index

The following function calculates the area of conic sections. The type of conic is selected with a numeric index.

```
'
' ConicVolume Function
' Return the volume of an object.
' The type argument selects the geometric shape
' 1 - Cylinder
' 2 - Cone
' 3 - Sphere
Function ConicVolume(Height As Single, Radius As Single, theType As
Integer) As Single
Const Cylinder = 1
Const Cone = 2
Const Sphere = 3
Const Pi = 3.14159
Select Case theType
 Case Cylinder
 ConicVolume = Pi * Radius ^ 2 * Height
 Case Cone
 ConicVolume = Pi * Radius ^ 2 * Height / 3
 Case Sphere
 ConicVolume = (4 / 3) * Pi * Radius ^ 3
 Case Else
 ConicVolume = CVErr(xlErrValue)
End Select
End Function
```

There are three possible calculations with this function, and the correct one is chosen using an index. First, four constants are defined so that the words Cylinder, Cone, and Sphere can be used instead of the index numbers, making the function procedure much more readable. Next, a `Select Case` statement is used to select the particular calculation based on the index number sent as an argument of the function. If an incorrect index is used, the error `#Value` is returned. To use this function in a worksheet, type in a cell

```
=ConicVolume(height,radius,type)
```

where *height* is the height of the conic, *radius* is it's radius, and *type* is `1` for a `cylinder`, `2` for a `cone`, and `3` for a `sphere`. You also can use this function in a more complicated worksheet formula. To register a function so it appears in the Function Wizard dialog box, Select the **V**iew **O**bject Browser command, select the function from the list, and select options. In the Function Category box, select the category to use, or type a new one, and choose OK. The function is now in the Function Wizard dialog box.

Passing Excel Arrays

Excel allows the use of arrays of values with functions as well as single values. Excel functions also can return an array instead of a single value (see Chapter 6, "Using Functions"), that you enter into an array of cells by holding down Ctrl+Shift when entering the function. The following function procedure demonstrates both possibilities by accepting an array or a range reference as an argument, and returning the row and column number of the cell that contains the smallest value.

```
'
' FindSmall
' find the smallest element of an array and return its location
'
Function FindSmall(theArray)
'The function must be a variant to return an array
Dim I As Integer, J As Integer
Dim Imin As Integer, Imax As Integer
Dim Jmin As Integer, Jmax As Integer
Dim theResult(1) As Integer
Dim theValue, theRange
'First, see what is being passed in theArray.
'If it is a Range object, it must be converted into an array.
If TypeName(theArray) = "Range" Then
 'Must transfer the data from a range to an array
 'Save the range object
 Set theRange = theArray
 Imax = theRange.Columns.Count 'Find the number of columns and rows
 Jmax = theRange.Rows.Count
 ReDim theArray(1 To Imax, 1 To Jmax) 'Change theArray into an array
 'Copy the data from the range into the array
```

```
  For I = 1 To Imax
  For J = 1 To Jmax
   'Use the Cells method to select the elements of the Range
   theArray(I, J) = theRange.Cells(I, J).Value
  Next J
  Next I
 ElseIf VarType(theArray) < 8192 Then
  'Not an array so return an error and quit
  FindSmall = Array(CVErr(xlErrValue), CVErr(xlErrValue))
  Exit Function
 End If 'If it is already an array, don't need to change it
 Imin = LBound(theArray, 1) 'Find the range of the array indices
 Imax = UBound(theArray, 1)
 Jmin = LBound(theArray, 2)
 Jmax = UBound(theArray, 2)
 theValue = theArray(1, 1) 'Pick an initial value
 theResult(0) = 1
 theResult(1) = 1
 For I = Imin To Imax 'Search for the minimum value
  For J = Jmin To Jmax
  If theValue > theArray(I, J) Then
   theResult(0) = I 'If a smaller value is found,
   theResult(1) = J 'save its indices and value
   theValue = theArray(I, J)
  End If
  Next J
 Next I
 'Store theResult array in the variant function name
 'This is a variant containing an array, not an array of variants
 FindSmall = theResult
 End Function
```

Since this function must operate on either an Excel array, such as {1,2,3;4,5,6;7,8,9}, or a range reference such as B5:D7, the function first must see what was passed to it. First, it uses the `TypeName` function to see if the argument contains a `Range` object. If it does, the function saves the object, erases the argument, and redefines it as an array. The values from the range object are then copied into the array. If it is not a range object, then the `VarType` function is used to see if it is an array. Arrays cause `VarType` to return a value of `8192` or larger, so if the value returned is less than `8192`, the argument is not an array and the function returns an error.

If the argument is an array, or a range converted to an array, an initial value is selected from the array, and then the rest is searched for a smaller value. When the loop completes, the array `theResult` contains the row and column number of the smallest element in the array. The array `theResult` then is equated to the variant function name so that the function returns a two element array.

To use this function, select two cells on a worksheet, and type

```
=FindSmall(array)
```

Hold down Ctrl-Shift when pressing Enter to insert it into both cells as an array (see fig. 46.4). The argument *array* can be either a cell range, or an Excel array. For example,

```
=FindSmall({2,2,3;4,1,5;7,8,9})
```

would return the value 2 in both cells, pointing to the value 1 in the second row and second column of the array. Another example,

```
=FindSmall(B5:D7)
```

would return two numbers between 1 and 3 that locate the smallest value in the range B5:D7.

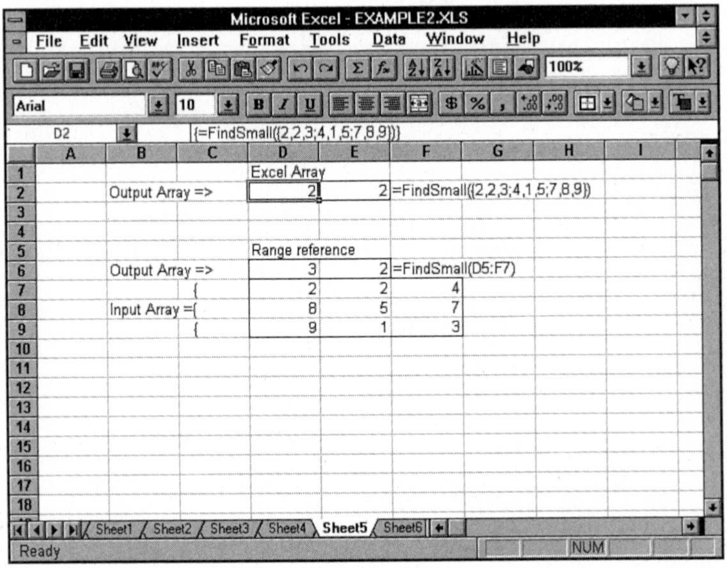

Fig. 46.4 Passing arrays with the FindSmall procedure. At the top an explicit Excel array is passed to the procedure, and below that is an array sent as a range of cells to the procedure. The two returned values (Output Array) in each case are also Excel arrays.

From Here...

The best way to learn this programming is to do it, so try writing your own procedures and see how they work. If they don't seem to work, use the Debug window to set break points, and examine values until you understand how things work. Use the Visual Basic on-line Help with the Visual Basic section selected for more information on functions, and the Object Browser for locating objects and properties. See Chapter 45, "Programming in Visual Basic for Applications," for information on programming with Visual Basic.

Appendix

Support Services

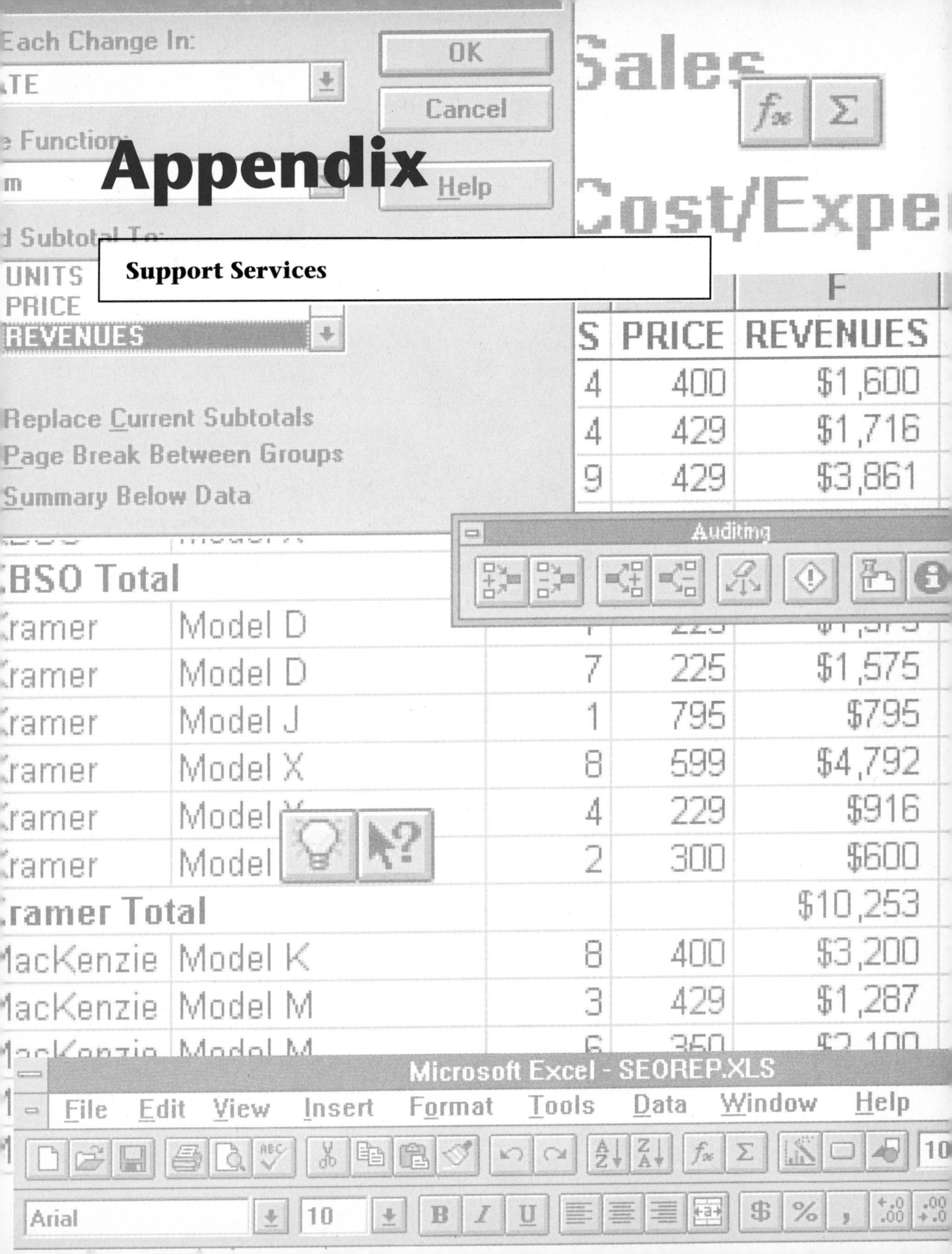

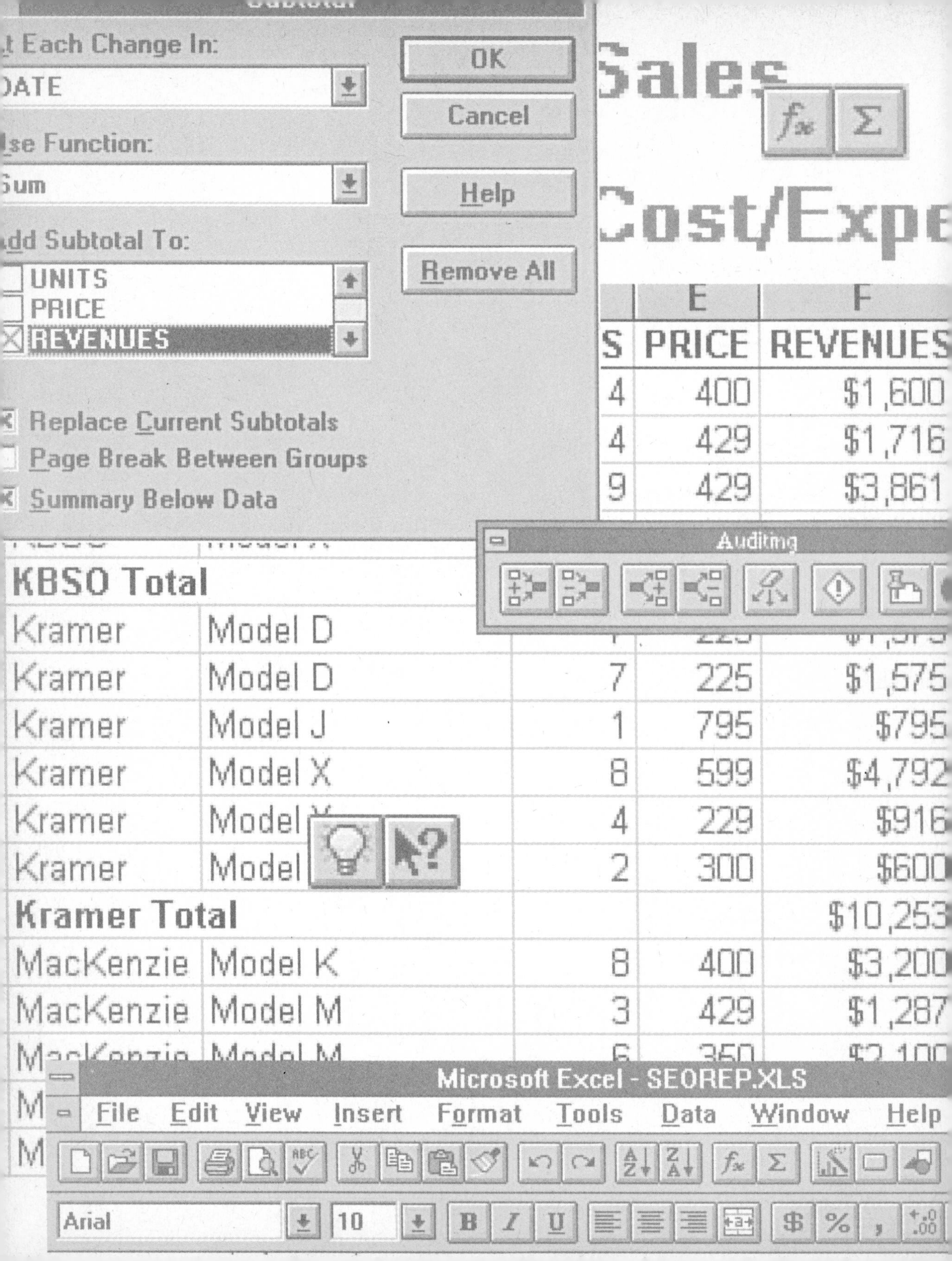
At Each Change In:
DATE
Use Function:
Sum
Add Subtotal To:
UNITS
PRICE
REVENUES
Replace Current Subtotals
Page Break Between Groups
Summary Below Data
OK
Cancel
Help
Remove All
Sales
Cost/Expe
E
F
S
PRICE
REVENUES
4
400
$1,600
4
429
$1,716
9
429
$3,861
Auditing
KBSO Total
Kramer
Model D
Kramer
Model D
7
225
$1,575
Kramer
Model J
1
795
$795
Kramer
Model X
8
599
$4,792
Kramer
4
229
$916
Kramer
2
300
$600
Kramer Total
$10,253
MacKenzie
Model K
8
400
$3,200
MacKenzie
Model M
3
429
$1,287
Microsoft Excel - SEOREP.XLS
File
Edit
View
Insert
Format
Tools
Data
Window
Help
Arial
10

Appendix

Support Services

This directory represents only a sampling of the products and resources designed to work with Excel. However, the directory gives you an indication of the many products and services available.

Microsoft Corporation

Microsoft Corporation
One Microsoft Way
Redmond, WA 98052-6399

206-882-8080, Corporate

800-426-9400, Customer Service (Sales and Upgrade)

206-635-7070, Excel support line

206-635-7071, Excel FastTips

206-462-9673, Word for Windows support line

206-637-7098, Windows support line

800-426-9400, Microsoft product-support line

6 a.m.-6 p.m., M-F, Pacific time

Microsoft maintains a telephone support line for technical questions concerning Windows, Excel, and Word for Windows.

CompuServe

CompuServe
5000 Arlington Centre Boulevard
P.O. Box 20212
Columbus, OH 43220

800-848-8199

CompuServe is a computer service available to your computer through a telephone connection. With CompuServe, you can access databases, sample files, and question-and-answer forums that concern hundreds of topics and industries. CompuServe contains an Excel forum, a troubleshooting service, and libraries of worksheets and macros.

The Excel and Microsoft Windows services are provided by Microsoft Corporation. To access the many Windows forums and libraries, type **GO MSOFT** at any menu prompt. To directly access the applications forums and libraries, type **GO MSAPP** at any menu prompt. For information on how to use CompuServe, contact CompuServe directly.

Que Corporation

Que Corporation
201 W. 103rd Street
Indianapolis, IN 46290
317-581-3500
800-428-5331, outside Indiana

Que Corporation is the worldwide leader in computer book publishing. Other books available about Windows applications by Ron Person or Karen Rose include *Using Word Version 6 for Windows,* Special Edition; *Using Windows 3.1,* Special Edition; and *Windows 3.1 QuickStart.* Call Que for a free catalog. Corporate and volume discounts are available.

Ron Person & Co.

Ron Person & Co.
P.O. Box 5647
Santa Rosa, CA 95402

415-989-7508	Voice
707-539-1525	Voice
707-538-1485	Fax

Ron Person & Co., based in San Francisco, has attained Microsoft's highest rating for Microsoft Excel and Word for Windows consultants, as one of the original Microsoft Consulting Partners. The firm also is a Microsoft Registered Developer for Excel and Word for Windows. In addition to writing three best-selling books on Windows applications, they are recognized leaders in training corporate developers and support personnel in Microsoft Visual Basic for Applications and other Microsoft application languages.

Index

Symbols

(pound sign) in error values, 145
#DIV/0! error message, 777
#N/A error message, 777
#NAME error message, 778
#NULL! error message, 778
#NUM! error message, 778
#REF! error message, 778
#VALUE! error message, 779
$ (dollar sign) in absolute cell references, 133
% (percentage) operator, 140
& (concatenation) operator, 140, 685
... (ellipsis) in commands, 39, 48
* (asterisk)
  multiplication operator, 140
  wild card, 906-907
    finding/replacing data, 99, 101
+ (plus sign)
  addition operator, 139
  closed folders, 292
- (minus sign)
  negation operator, 139
  open folders, 292
  subtraction operator, 139
/ (division) operator, 140
< (less than) operator, 140, 904
<= (less than/equal to) operator, 140
<> (not equal) operator, 140
= (equal sign) in formulas, 125, 127
= (equal to) operator, 140, 904
> (greater than) operator, 140, 904
>= (greater than/equal to) operator, 140, 904
? wild card, 99, 101, 906-907
^ (exponentiation) operator, 140
2-D charts, 447
286 Standard mode, 1070-1072
3-D cell names, 166
3-D cell references, 138-139
3-D charts
  formatting, 497-501
  rotating
    by commands, 500-501
    by dragging, 497-499
  surface, 450
3-D View command (Format menu), 500-501
3-D View dialog box, 500
386 Enhanced mode, 1072-1074

A

ABS( ) function, 216
absolute cell references, 131-134
  $ (dollar sign), 133
  editing, 136
accessing
  disk files, 1207-1211
  methods, 1183
  objects, 1175-1177
  properties, 1180-1181
  worksheet cells, 1201-1203
accessing worksheet cells, 1166-1167
ACCRINT( ) function, 854
ACCRINTM( ) function, 854
ACOS( ) function, 232
ACOSH( ) function, 232
activating
  embedded charts, 414, 428
  links (OLE), 1049
  panes (windows), 546
  workbooks, 67
active cell, 73
  data entry, 121
  moving, 73-74, 1099
active window, 29
active workbook window, 30
Add Criteria command (Microsoft Query, Criteria menu), 961
Add Custom AutoFormat dialog box, 451
Add Data Source dialog box, 954
Add Scenario dialog box, 824, 835
Add Tables command (Microsoft Query, Table menu), 959
Add Tables dialog box, 954, 959
add-ins
  Analysis ToolPak, 676-677
  AutoSave, 677
  installing, 672-675, 952
  Report Manager, 678
  Slide Show, 660-666, 678
  Solver, 679, 795, 800-817
  starting, 675
  View Manager, 679-680
Add-Ins Analysis command (Tools menu), 839
Add-Ins command (Tools menu), 672, 675-680, 952
Add-ins dialog box, 676-680, 952

AddIn object, 1176
adding summary information, 297-298
addition (+) operator, 139
ADDRESS( ) function, 209
Advanced Filter, 916-919, 930
  comparison criteria, 902-909
  data
    copying, 936-942
    copying between workbooks or worksheets, 942-944
    finding, 919-931
Advanced Filter command (Data menu), 708
Advanced Filter dialog box, 708, 943
aligning
  cell contents, 319-327
  controls, 737
  text in charts, 486
ALL (1-2-3 Release 2x) file name extension, 1075
Allow Editing command (Microsoft Query, Records menu), 973-982
AMORDEGRC( ) function, 854
AMORLINC( ) function, 854
Analysis ToolPak, 676-677
  commands, 850-851
    Exponential Smoothing, 848-849
    Histogram, 843-846
    Moving Average, 846- 848
    Random Number Generation command, 839-842
  functions, 859
    engineering, 852-853
    financial, 854-855
    statistical, 856-858
  histograms, 842-846
  series, 838-842
  time-series data, 846-849
analyzing worksheets, 710-716
  fill handles, 711-713
  Fill Series command, 713-714
  worksheet functions, 715-716
AND comparisons, 907-908, 916, 930
AND( ) function, 207, 689, 926-928
ANOVA: Single Factor command (Analysis ToolPak), 850
ANOVA: Two-Factor command (Analysis ToolPak), 850
Answer reports (Solver), 813
appending
  commands to custom menus, 1121
  controls to worksheets, 724-736
  dialog boxes to procedures, 1168-1169
  fields, 1014
  pivot tables, 1012-1015
applets, 559
  embedded objects, 1066
application icon, 28
Application object, 1142, 1176
application window, 28, 59
  switching between, 59
applications, 1175
  copying data across applications, 1045-1047
  creating, 1188-1193
  cycling, 59
  DOS
    copying/pasting Excel data, 1070-1074
    exporting Excel data, 1077
    Windows, 1070
  embedding data across applications, 1050-1057
  exchanging data across applications, 1059-1068
  linking data across applications, 1047-1049
  mainframe, 1080-1081
  switching between, 59
applying
  Autoformats to charts, 441-442
  names to cells, 169-170
Arc object, 1176
Arc tool, 562
arcs, 564-565
AREAS( ) function, 209
arguments, 174-176
  database functions, 704
  functions, 182
  procedures, 1165
  subprocedures, 1184
arithmetic operators, 139-140
  % (percentage), 140
  * (multiplication), 140
  + (addition), 139
  – (negation), 139
  – (subtraction), 139
  / (division), 140
  ^ (exponentiation), 140
Arrange command (Window menu), 548
arranging windows, 548-549
array argument, 175
arrays, 152-156, 1196-1197
  calculations, 155-156
  dimensions, 1196
  elements, 1196
  formulas
    editing, 156
    entering, 152-154
  functions, editing, 156
  passing, 1234-1236
  ranges, 154-155
Arrow tool, 562
arrows (charts), 405, 437
  formatting, 496-497, 579-581
  inserting, 474
arrows on commands, 39
ascending order sort, 888, 970
ASIN( ) function, 232
ASINH( ) function, 232
assessing collections (objects), 1178
Assign Macro command (Tools menu), 570, 1162-1213
Assign Macro dialog box, 569, 1162
assigning
  macros/program code to toolbar buttons, 1112-1113
  procedures to commands, 1123
assignment statements, 1194
ATAN( ) function, 232
ATAN2( ) function, 232
ATANH( ) function, 233
Attach Note (Auditing toolbar), 786
Attach Toolbar command (Tools menu), 1115
Attach Toolbars dialog box, 1115
attaching
  procedures to buttons, 1224
  procedures to objects, 1162-1163
  toolbars to workbooks, 1115-1117

attributes
cells, 252-255
text, 643
worksheets, 1129
auditing worksheets, 777-794
Auditing command (Tools menu), 19, 784
Auditing toolbar, 43, 786
Auto Outline command (Outline menu), 598
Auto-Close macros, 1136
Auto-Open macros, 1136
AutoFill, 17, 111-119
AutoFilter, 21
comparison criteria, 902-909
copying data, 936, 942-944
finding data, 913-916
AutoFilter command (Data menu), 865, 914
AutoFormat, 303-307
charts, 441-453
AutoFormat command (Format menu), 305-307, 441-453, 502-503, 614, 886, 996, 1037
AutoFormat dialog box, 305, 441, 451, 1037
automatic
backups, 278-279
chart creation, 415-421
data entry in lists, 879-881
formats (numbers), 92
formatting, 328, 651-656
starting Excel, 26
subtotals, 607
workbook saving, 277-278
Automatic Outlining, 598-599
Automatic Query command (Microsoft Query, Records menu), 963
AutoSave add-in, 277-278, 677
AutoSave command (Tools menu), 277, 677
AutoSave dialog box, 677
autotemplates, 1129-1130
AVEDEV( ) function, 222, 856
Average function (pivot tables), 1034
AVERAGE( ) function, 221
averages, 513
axes
charts, 405, 437
category axis, 403
customizing, 493-494
scaling, 494-496
secondary, 509-510
X axis labels, 416
AxisTitle object, 1176

B

backgrounds (charts), 437
backups, 945-946
automatic, 278-279
bell curves, 840
Bernoulli command (Analysis ToolPak), 851
BESSELI( ) function, 852
BESSELJ( ) function, 852
BESSELK( ) function, 852
BESSELY( ) function, 852
BETADIST( ) function, 222, 856
BETAINV( ) function, 222, 856
BIN2DEC( ) function, 852
BIN2HEX( ) function, 852
BIN2OCT( ) function, 852
BINOMDIST( ) function, 222, 856
Binomial command (Analysis ToolPak), 851
Binomial distribution, 841
bins in histograms, 838
bitmaps, copying across applications, 1047
black and white printing, 383
blending materials, 801
block If statements, 1199-1200
blocks
moving to edge, 74-75
selecting adjacent cells, 80-82
BMP (Windows Bitmaps) file name extension, 557
bold text, 643
borders, 624-626
charts, 488
formatting, 581-583
objects, 480-482
underlining subtotals, 354
worksheeets, 352-354
Borders button, 354
boxes, 644-646
branching programs, 1198-1201
block if statements, 1199-1200
logical formulas, 1200
Select Case statement, 1201
break mode, 1218
breakpoints, 1150, 1217-1219
Bring to Front tool, 562
Browse dialog box, 997
bugs, 1194, 1217-1221
building
charts, 416-418
data tables, 698-700
forms, 719-741
built-in data types (Visual Basic), 1195
built-in formulas, *see* functions
built-in menus, 1118-1119
Button object, 1176
buttonface customization, 1113-1115
buttons
appending to toolabrs, 1108-1109
attaching procedures, 1162-1163
Borders, 354
Color Palette, 352
edit, 120-123
Format Painter, 311-312
macro, 568-571
reorganizing, 1110-1111
Slide Show, 662

C

calculated criteria, 924-931
calculations, 122-123
arrays, 155-156
data tables, 703
formulas, 126
lists, 884-886
calling procedures, 1203-1204
Calls window (Debug window), 1221
case-sensitive sorts, 888
category axis, 403
CEILING( ) function, 216, 856
cell contents, aligning, 319-327
Cell Note dialog box, 790, 791
cell objects, defining, 1166
cell references, 128-139
3-D references, 138-139
absolute references, 131-136
changing style, 135-136
entering by pointing, 129-130
external references, 138
formulas, 130-131
mixed references, 135
relative references, 131-133, 136
workbook sheets, 137, 138
CELL( ) function, 201-203
cells, 66
accessing, 1201-1203
accessing with Visual Basic procedures, 1166-1167
active cell, 73

attributes, pasting, 252-255
blocks, *see* blocks
copying
between worksheets, 252
inserting, 251-252
into slide shows, 662-664
data entry, 89, 121
deleting, 103-107
editing, 95-97, 1099
undoing/repeating changes, 97
filling
fill handles, 241-242
with Ctrl+Enter keys, 242
with custom fill, 244-245
with Fill commands, 243
formatting, 18
characters, 314-319
colors, 351-354
dates/times, 341-345
lines, 352-354
numbers, 328-341
patterns, 351-354
styles, 355-362
formulas, hiding, 363-364
input scenarios, 819-822
inserting
with commands, 238-239, 251-252
with mouse, 237-238
linking to chart text, 523-527
moats, 868
moving
between worksheets, 239-241
Go To command, 75-76
with commands, 236-237
with keyboard, 73-74
with mouse, 235-236
names, 157-171
pasting multiple copies, 247-250
protected forms, 740-741
protecting, 362-365
Range references, 1201
ranges, *see* ranges
referencing, 1145-1147
seed, 111
selecting
by content, 83-85
Go To command, 75-76
marquee, 237
single cell, 73-74
sorting calculated fields, 897
text
centering across cells, 320-322
joining with numbers, 323
rotating, 326-327
tabs/line breaks, 324
wrapping, 322
viewing, 780
Cells Border command (Format menu), 353
Cells command
Format menu, 314-319, 644, 1158
Patterns option, 351-352
Protection option, 363
Insert menu, 106
centering
headings, 636
text across cells, 320-322
vertically, 638
CGM (Computer Graphics Metafile) file name extension, 557
changing
chart type, 509
directories, 270
default, 271
opening files, 269
disks, 270
names, 167
CHAR( ) function, 227
characters
centering, 638
formatting, 18
in cells, 314-319
Chart As New Sheet command (Insert menu), 259
Chart command (Insert menu), 415
Chart object, 1176
Chart On This Sheet command (Insert menu), 407
chart sheets (workbooks), 66, 267
creating charts, 415
renaming charts, 415
Chart toolbar, 42, 440
Chart Type command (Format menu), 438-453
Chart Type dialog box, 439, 503
chart types
ChartWizard, 410
groups, 507
charting filtered data, 934-935
ChartObject object, 1176
charts, 20, 403-407, 435, 438-440
2-D, 447
3-D
formatting, 497-501
surface, 450
adding data, 458-459
arrows, 405, 474
Autoformats, 451-452
axes, 405
category axis, 403
customizing, 493-494
scaling, 494-496
building, 416-418
changing types, 452-453
combination charts, 505-510
copying
into slide shows, 662-664
across applications, 1046
creating, 406-407
automatically, 415-421
ChartWizard, 407
from outlines, 519-521
in chart sheets, 415
manually, 421-426
with shortcut keys, 415
data labels, 469-472
data points, 405, 416
data ranges (ChartWizard), 459-460
data series, 406
editing, 462-464
inserting, 410
series formulas, 461-462
trendlines, 514
defaults, 454-456
deleting
data, 461
data series, objects, or formats, 501-502
dragging and dropping data, 18
embedded charts, 405
activating, 428
adding data, 456-458
deleting, 414
formatting, 414
error bars, 517-519
formatting, 21, 477-478
arrows, 496-497
ChartWizard, 410-411
data series, 488-491
markers, 491-492
numbers, 483-487
text, 483-486
transferring formats, 503

gridlines, 475
handles, 413
hierarchical, 522
layout, 411-412, 421-422
legends, 404-406
ChartWizard, 412
inserting, 472-473
line charts, 453-454
linking into Word for Windows, 1061-1068
links, 427
margins, 430
markers, 406, 798-800
objects
borders, 480-482
colors, 480-482
moving, 478-480
patterns, 480-482
selecting, 436-437
shortcut menus, 435-436
sizing, 478-480
opening, 428-429
outlines, 603-605
pasting, 1065-1066
picture charts, 524-529
pivot tables, 1007-1008, 1027-1028
plot area, 406
printing, 429-432, 678
saving, 426-427
scatter (XY) charts, 494
series, 416
series formula, 406
spelling, 469
text, 406
floating text, 468-469
linking to cells, 523-524
tick marks, 406
titles
ChartWizard, 412-414
inserting, 466-467
toolbar, 406
trendlines, 21, 513
data series, 514-516
y-intercept value, 514
trends, 513-516
troubleshooting, 453
types, 502-503
What-If analysis, 510-513
worksheets, 648-651
embedding, 571-572
moving, 413
pasting, 571-573
positioning, 413
sizing, 413
XY (scatter), 453-454
see also embedded charts
ChartWizard, 572
chart layout, 411-412
chart types, 410
combination charts, 506
creating charts, 407
data range, 409-410, 459-460
dialog boxes, 408-409
embedded charts, 407-408
formats, 410-411
legends, 412
titles, 412-414
ChartWizard button (Standard toolbar), 1008
check boxes, 20
dialog boxes, 49-50
IF function, 728
worksheets, 727-728
CheckBox object, 1176
CHIDIST( ) function, 222, 856
CHIINV( ) function, 222, 856
CHITEST( ) function, 222, 856
CHOOSE( ) function, 209-210, 730
choosing, *see* selecting
circular errors (formulas), 148
classes (objects), 1177
CLEAN( ) function, 227
Clear All Breakpoints command (Run menu), 1219
Clear command (Edit menu), 103, 122
All option, 501-502, 703
Contents option, 102
Series option, 461
clearing outlines, 600
clicking mouse, 35
clients (OLE), 1044
clip art, 526, 556
Clipboard, 1044-1045
Close command (File menu), 62, 282
Close Query command (Microsoft Query, File menu), 964
closing
dialog boxes, 54
files, 62
Microsoft Query, 980
queries, 964
windows, 61-62
Help window, 58
multiple, 552
workbook window, 61-62
workbooks, 282
code segment sorts, 895-896
CODE( ) function, 227
codes for headers/footers, 381
collapsing outlines, 596
collections (objects), 1177
color, 318
gridlines, 536-537
printing, 383
color palette, 1095-1097
hue changes, 1097
mixing colors, 1097
Color Palette button, 352
Color Picker dialog box, 1096
colors
borders, 579-581
charts, 488
lines, 579-581
markers, 491-492
objects, 480-482
printing worksheets, 646-648
worksheets, 338-339, 351-354
Column command (Format menu)
Hide option, 348, 935
Standard Width option, 350
Width option, 346-347
Column Width command (Microsoft Query, Format menu), 969
Column Width dialog box, 346, 969
COLUMN( ) function, 210
column-delimited files, 1077, 1081-1086
see also fixed-length text files
columns, 633-634
formatting, 346-347
headings, 969-970
hiding, 535
printing, 377-378
hiding, 348, 968-969
inserting/deleting, 103-107
joining worksheets, 770-772
labels, 634-635
order, 969
parsing text into, 1086-1088
printing, 387
selecting, 82-83
sorting, 897-900
View Manager, 350
white space, 635-636
width, 391-392, 969
Columns command (Insert menu), 107
COLUMNS( ) function, 210
COMBIN( ) function, 216, 856

combination charts, 447, 505-510
  axes, 509-510
  changing type, 509
  predefined chart types, 508
combining database functions with tables, 707-710
Comma Separated Value (CSV) files, 1077, 1081-1086
Comma style, 355
command buttons (dialog boxes), 49
commands, 29
  ... (ellipsis), 39, 48
  Analysis ToolPak, 850-851
    Exponential Smoothing, 848-849
    Histogram, 843-846
    Moving Average, 846-848
    Random Number Generation command, 839-842
  arrows, 39
  assigning procedures to in custom menus, 1123
  Data menu, 613-614
    Advanced Filter, 708
    AutoFilter, 865, 914
    Consolidate, 764-776, 1001
    External Data, 980-982
    Filter, 20
    Filter Advanced Filter, 916-928, 943
    Filter AutoFilter, 914
    Form, 868, 879, 909-912
    Get External Data, 952-954
    Group, 598-599, 602-603
    Group and Outline, 1022
    PivotTable, 989
    Refresh Data, 981
    Sort, 20, 612-613, 887, 898, 1028
    Subtotals, 20, 608-614, 934
    Table, 109, 698
  dimmed, 39
  Edit menu
    Clear, 103, 122
    Clear All, 501-502, 703
    Clear Contents, 102
    Clear Series, 461
    Copy, 97, 102, 247, 250-253, 459, 753, 1045
    Copy Button Image, 1114-1115
    Copy Picture, 1047
    Copy Sheet, 261-263
    Cut, 102, 237-239, 1045
    Delete, 102-107, 122
    Delete Sheet, 260
    Fill Right/Left/Up/Down, 243
    Fill Series, 109-119, 123, 245, 702, 710, 713-714
    Find, 97-99
    Go To, 75-76, 103, 781-783
    Links, 748-749, 759-763, 1057-1058
    Mark, 1072
    Move, 261-263
    Object, 1058
    Paste, 97, 102, 237, 240, 247, 250-252, 459, 1046
    Paste Button Image, 1115
    Paste Link, 753
    Paste Special, 252-255, 459, 753, 1048
    Repeat, 97
    Replace, 99-101
    Undo, 97, 236-237
    Undo Delete, 106
    Undo Replace, 101
    Undo Sort, 892
  File menu
    Close, 62, 282
    Exit, 27
    Find, 17
    Find File, 282-292
    New, 267
    New SLIDES, 678
    Open, 268
    Page Setup, 374
    Print, 370, 395
    Print Preview, 389
    Print Report, 396, 678
    Properties, 1133
    Save As, 275
    Save Workspace, 280
    Summary Info, 276
  Format menu
    3-D View, 500-501
    AutoFormat, 305-307, 441-453, 502-503, 614, 886, 996, 1037
    Cells, 314-319, 644, 1158
    Cells Border, 353
    Cells Patterns, 351-352
    Cells Protection, 363
    Chart Type, 438-453
    Column Hide, 348, 935
    Column Standard Width, 350
    Column Width, 346-347
    Format Cells Aligment, 319-327
    Format Cells Number, 331, 344-345
    Group, 488-490
    Object, 568, 580, 601
    Placement Bring to Front, 590
    Placement Send to Back, 590
    Row Height, 348
    Row Unhide, 350
    Selected item, 490-496
    Selected Object, 478-480, 484-487
    Selected Series, 461-464, 478
    Sheet Hide, 740
    Sheet Rename, 264
    Sheet Unhide, 740
    Style, 355-362
    Styles, 651-656
  Help menu
    Contents, 1150
    Search for Help on, 673
  Insert menu
    Cells, 106
    Chart, 415
    Chart As New Sheet, 259
    Chart On This Sheet, 407
    Columns, 107
    Copied Cells, 251
    Cut Cells, 239
    Data Labels, 471-472
    Error Bars, 518
    File, 1063
    Function, 144, 182-183, 677, 845, 850
    Gridlines, 475
    Legend, 472
    Macro Dialog, 259, 1212
    Macro Module, 259, 1115-1117, 1168
    Macro MS Excel 4.0, 259
    Name Apply, 169
    Name Create, 163, 758, 821, 845
    Name Define, 159-162, 167, 758, 868, 878, 881
    Name Paste, 143, 182

New Data, 457
Note, 792
Object, 1051, 1067
Page Break, 386
Picture, 557
Rows, 107
Titles, 466-467
Trendline, 513-514
Worksheet, 259
menus
shortcut menus, 39-40
submenus, 39
Microsoft Query
Criteria Add Criteria, 961
Edit Copy, 975, 978-979
Edit Cut, 975
Edit Links, 979
Edit Paste, 978
Edit Paste Special, 979
File Close Query, 964
File New Query, 954, 964
File Open Query, 965
File Return Data to Excel, 976-981
File Save Query, 964
Format Column Width, 969
Format Font, 973
Format Hide Columns, 968
Format Row Height, 970
Records Allow Editing, 973-975
Records Automatic Query, 963
Records Edit Column, 970
Records Sort, 971
Table Add Tables, 959
Table Joins, 967-968
View Criteria, 958-963
View SQL, 965
View Tables, 958
names, 167-168
Outline menu
Auto Outline, 598
Group, 599, 602-603
Run menu
Clear All Breakpoints, 1219
Step Into, 1220
Step Over, 1221
Toggle Breakpoint, 1218
selecting, 38-41
Shift key, 41
shortcut menus, 39-40
sort operatons, 890-892
step commands, 1220-1221
submenus, 39
Tools menu
Add-Ins, 672, 675-680, 952
Add-Ins Analysis, 839
Assign Macro, 570, 1162, 1213
Attach Toolbar, 1115
Auditing, 19, 784
AutoSave, 677
Autosave, 277
Data Analysis, 677, 837, 839-850
Goal Seek, 443-444, 795-800
Goals Seek, 512
Macro, 1161
Menu Editor, 1149
Options, 126, 258, 456, 689, 1192
Options Color, 480
Options Custom Lists, 244
Options Edit, 1099
Options Transition, 1098
Protection, 364, 835
Protection Protect Sheet, 1192
Protection Protect Sheet command, 590
Protection Unprotect Sheet command, 590, 1208
Record Macro Mark Position for Recording, 1159
Record Macro Record at Mark, 1159
Scenarios, 824-826
Selected Series, 481
Solver, 679, 805
Spelling, 469, 789
Spreadsheet Import, 1078
Toolbars, 120
Toolbars WorkGroup, 823
View menu
Formula Bar, 177
Full Screen, 16, 535
Object Browser, 1149
Toolbars, 45, 440, 474, 483, 721, 1061, 1108, 1149
Toolbars Standard, 177, 179
View Manager, 542, 680
Window menu
Arrange, 548
Freeze Panes, 546, 928
Hide, 550
New Window, 547, 723
Split, 545
UnFreeze Panes, 546, 928
comments (procedures), 1164-1165
comparative criteria in lists
AND or OR, 907-908
dates/times, 905-906, 930
multiple, 921-931
numeric, 904-905
text, 902-903
wild cards, 906-907
comparison operators, 1200
< (less than), 140
<= (less than/equal to), 140
<> (not equal), 140
> (greater than), 140
>= (greater than/equal to), 140
= (equal to), 140
COMPLEX( ) function, 852
compound criteria, 926-928
compressing printing, 392-394
CompuServe, 1239-1240
Computer Graphics Metafile (CGM) file name extension, 557
CONCATENATE( ) function, 227, 686, 856
concatenation, 323, 685
concatenation (&) operator, 140
conditional formatting, 339
conditional formulas, 687-690
CONFIDENCE( ) function, 222, 856
conic sections, 1233-1234
Consolidate command (Data menu), 764-776, 1001
Consolidate dialog box, 768
consolidating data with pivot tables, 1001-1005
constant values, 87, 90-92
constants, 1198
constraints (Solver), 810-811
containers, 1175
applications, 1175
specifying objects, 1142-1143
Contents command (Help menu), 1150

controlling
recalculation, 737-738
sheet display, 533-538
controls
aligning, 737
cell contents/calculations, 723-725
check boxes, 727-728
copying, 737
deleting, 725, 736
dimming, 739
forms, 719-723
Forms toolbar, 721-723
modifying, 736-737
moving, 725, 736
option buttons, 728-730
printing forms without controls, 739
protected forms, 740-741
resizing, 736
scroll bars, 734-736
scrolling/pull-down lists, 730-733
spinners, 733-734
worksheets, 724-736
worksheets versus dialog boxes, 720-721
Convert dialog box, 1057
CONVERT( ) function, 852
converting crosstab tables, 998-999
Copied Cells command (Insert menu), 251
Copy command (Edit menu), 97, 102, 247, 250-253, 459, 753, 1045
Button Image option, 1114-1115
Picture option, 1047
Sheet, 261-263
Copy command (Microsoft Query, Edit menu), 975, 978-979
Copy dialog box, 261
Copy Picture dialog box, 1047
copying
cells
between worksheets, 252
inserting, 251-252
controls, 737
data, 975
across applications, 1045-1047
between Excel and DOS applications, 1070-1074
into slide shows, 662-664
fields, 972-973
files, 301-302
filtered data, 935-936
between worksheets or workbooks, 942-944
with Advanced Filter, 936-942
with AutoFilter, 936
formats, 311-312
formulas
cell names, 168
ranges, 254
with commands, 247
graphics, 558-560, 583-584
outlines, 603-605
records, 972-973
screens to PageMaker, 1060
sheets in workbooks, 260-262
styles, 358-359
troubleshooting, 255
with commands, 247
with mouse, 246
CORREL( ) function, 222, 856
Correlation command (Analysis ToolPak), 850
COS( ) function, 233
COSH( ) function, 233
Count function (pivot tables), 1034
Count Nums function (pivot tables), 1034
COUNT( ) function, 223
COUNTA( ) function, 223
COUNTIF( ) function, 706
COUPDAYBS( ) function, 854
COUPDAYS( ) function, 854
COUPDAYSNC( ) function, 854
COUPNCD( ) function, 854
COUPNUM( ) function, 854
COUPPCD( ) function, 854
COVAR( ) function, 222, 856
Covariance command (Analysis ToolPak), 850
Create Button tool, 562, 568-571
creating
charts, 406-407
automatically, 415-421
chart sheets, 415
ChartWizard, 407
embedded charts, 407-408
from outlines, 519-521
hierarchical charts, 522
manually, 421-426
shortcut keys, 415
footers, 378-382
headers, 378-382
links, 427
names
3-D, 166
cells, 159-162
from worksheet text, 162-166
panes (windows), 545
views, named views, 541
workbooks, 267
CRITBINOM( ) function, 222, 856
criteria
lists
comparative, 902-909, 921-931
ranges, 918-919, 929
matching
calculated, 924-931
compound, 926-928
panes, 957-963
query definitions
adding, 961-962
deleting, 962-963
editing, 962-963
Criteria command (Microsoft Query, View menu), 958, 962-963
criteria range, 866, 869
cross-application data embedding, 1050-1057
converting embedded objects, 1057
embedding objects as icons, 1057
existing files, 1054
new objects, 1051-1053
pasting embedded objects, 1055-1057
printing embedded objects, 1057
cross-application data exchanges, 1059-1068
cross-application data links, 1047-1049
activating/disabling links, 1049
client role, 1048-1049
external link values, 1049
cross-application data transfers, 1045-1047
bitmaps, 1047
charts, 1046
screens, 1046-1047
text, 1045-1046

crosstab tables, 998-999
CSV (Comma delimited) files, 1077, 1081-1086
CSV (Comma Separated Valued) file name extension, 1075
CSV (Macintosh) files, 1077
CSV (OS/2 or MS-DOS) files, 1077
CUMIPMT( ) function, 854
CUMPRINC( ) function, 854
Currency style, 355
custom
- Autoformats, 451-452
- dialog boxes, 1212-1217
- dictionaries, 789
- fill, 244-245
- footers, 379
- headers, 379
- icons, 1134
- lists, 118
- menus, 1117-1125
  - appending commands, 1121
  - assigning procedures to commands, 1123
  - creating, 1120-1121
  - creating menu bars, 1124-1125
  - Menu Editor, 1117
  - submenus, 1122
  - terminology, 1118-1119
  - troubleshooting, 1125
- sort orders, 893-894
- toolbars, 1108-1116
  - assigning macros/ program code to toolbars, 1112-1113
  - attaching to workbooks, 1115-1117
  - buttonfaces, 1113-1115
  - buttons, 1108-1109

Custom AutoFilter dialog box, 916
Customize dialog box, 1108
customizing
- chart axes, 493-494
- color palette, 1095-1097
- Excel, 1093-1106
- formats
  - dates/times, 344-345
  - number, 333-341
- with Windows Control Panel, 1099-1105
  - desktop, 1102-1103
  - international settings, 1104
  - mouse, 1103-1104
  - screen appearance, 1101
- work preferences, 1098-1099

Cut command (Edit menu), 102, 237-239, 1045
Cut command (Microsoft Query, Edit menu), 975
cutting cells, 235-241
cycling applications, 59

D

data
- backups, 945-946
- copying/pasting between Excel and DOS applications, 1070-1074
- dragging and dropping, 18
- editing
  - in cells, 95-97
  - in formula bar, 94
  - with data form, 912
- exporting to DOS or mainframe applications, 1077-1079
- finding
  - criteria, 908-909
  - with Advanced Filter, 919-931
  - with AND or OR, 907-908
  - with AutoFilter, 913-916
  - with data form, 909-912
  - with wild cards, 906-907
- linking from Microsoft Query to Excel, 978-979
- queries
  - editing in worksheets, 981
  - updating, 981-982
- tracing, 783-785
- transferring between Microsoft Query, 975-981

Data Analysis command (Tools menu), 677, 837-850
Data Analysis dialog box, 839
data analysis functions (pivot tables), 1033-1037
data entry, 87-88
- array formulas, 152-154
- cell references
  - inserting in existing formulas, 130
  - pointing, 129-130
- cells, 89, 121
- dates/times, 93-94
- formula bar, 88
- formulas, 127-128
  - date and time, 144
  - text, 144
- header/footer information, 380
- lists
  - accelerating, 884-886
  - directly into rows, 881-884
  - recalculating, 884-886
  - troubleshooting, 885
  - with data form, 879-881
- numbers, 90
  - fixed decimal places, 120
- recalculating, 122-123
- series, 110-119
- shortcut keys, 121, 883-884
- text, 89-90, 116-119
- troubleshooting, 122-123

data forms
- comparison criteria, 902-909
- data
  - editing, 912
  - finding, 909-912
- lists, 879-881

data integrity (worksheets), 690-692
data labels (charts), 469-472
Data Labels command (Insert menu), 471-472
data layout (charts), 421-422
Data menu commands
- Advanced Filter, 708
- AutoFilter, 865, 914
- Consolidate, 764-776, 1001
- External Data, 980-982
- Filter, 20
  - Advanced Filter option, 916-928, 943
  - AutoFilter option, 613-614, 914
- Form, 868, 879, 909-912
- Get External Data, 952, 954
- Group, 598-599, 602-603
- Group and Outline, 1022
- PivotTable, 989
- Refresh Data, 981
- Sort, 20, 612-613, 887, 898, 1028
- Subtotals, 20, 608-614, 934
- Table, 109, 698

data panes, 957
- adding/deleting fields, 959
- columns/rows, 968-970
- editing data, 973-975
- fields, 972-973

formatting data, 973
records, 972-973
sorting data, 970-972
data points (charts), 405, 416
data ranges
ChartWizard, 409-410
returned from Microsoft Query, 977
data series (charts), 241-242 406, 416, 437
AutoFill, 17
changing chart type, 507
deleting, 501-502
editing, 462-464
formatting, 488
error bars, 491
trendlines, 490
inserting, 410
markers
rearranging, 464-465
series formulas, 461-462
trendlines, 514-516
data sources, 950-951, 954-958
data tables
building, 698-700
calculating, 703
editing, 701-703
trends, 710-716
fill handles, 711-713
Fill Series command, 713-714
worksheet functions, 715-716
data types (Visual Basic), 1195-1200
data-entry screens (View Manager), 679
database functions, 185-187, 704-705
arguments, 704
combining with tables, 707-710
COUNTIF( ) function, 706
DCOUNT( ), 704
DCOUNTA( ), 704
DSUM( ), 707-708
DSUM( ), 704
SUMIF( ), 706
database management systems, *see* DBMS
database range, 866-869
DataLabel object, 1176
date series, 115
DATE( ) function, 188, 894
dates/times, 885
data entry, 93-94
finding, 905-906, 930
formatting, 341-345
formulas, 144
functions, 187-192
searches, 290-291
sorts, 894-895
DATEVALUE( ) function, 188-189
DAVERAGE( ) function, 185-186
DAYS360( ) function, 189
DBF (dBASE II, III, IV) file name extension, 1075
DBMS (database management systems), 949-950, 1080-1081
DCOUNT( ) function, 186, 704
DCOUNTA( ) function, 186, 704
DDE (Dynamic Data Exchange), 948
deactivating Macro Recorder, 1158-1159
Debug Window, 1151, 1219
Calls window, 1221
Immediate pane (Debug window), 1219-1220
Watch pane (Debug window), 1220
Debugging Buttons, 1150
debugging tools, 1150-1151
break mode, 1218
breakpoints, 1218-1219
step commands, 1220-1221
DEC2BIN( ) function, 852
DEC2HEX( ) function, 852
DEC2OCT( ) function, 852
decimal places, 120
declaring variables, 1196
decreasing margins, 387
defaults
charts, 454-456
directory, changing, 271
margins, 375
printer, 372
settings, 665
sheets in workbooks, 258
style (Normal), 361
defining
cell objects, 1166
names (cells), 159-160
print area, 384-392
styles, 357
defining queries, *see* query definitions
DEGREES( ) function, 859
Delete command (Edit menu), 102-107, 122
Delete dialog box, 105-107
Delete Sheet command (Edit menu), 260
deleting
cells, 103-107
chart data, 461
charts, 414
columns, 103-107
controls, 725, 736
data, 934, 975
data series, 501-502
fields from data pane, 959-963
files, 302
formats, 337, 501-502
join lines, 968
links, 772-773
names (cells), 167
objects, 501-502, 579
print area, 385
records, 946
rows, 103-107
sheets from workbooks, 260
sound messages, 794
styles, 361
subtotals, 610
tables from table pane, 958-959
text box characters, 52
views, 543
see also clearing
DELTA( ) function, 852
dependent variables, 715
descending sorts, 888, 970-972
Descriptive Statistics command (Analysis TookPak), 850
desktop
customizing with Windows Control Panel, 1102-1103
wallpapers, 1103
desktop publishing, 651-656
DEVSQ( ) function, 222, 856
DGET( ) function, 186
dialog box sheets, 66
dialog boxes, 14, 48-54, 1211
3-D View, 500
Add Custom AutoFormat, 451
Add Data Source, 954
Add Scenario, 824, 835
Add Tables, 954, 959
Add-ins, 676-680, 952
Advanced Filter, 708, 943
appending to procedures, 1168-1169
Assign Macro, 569, 1162
Attach Toolbars, 1115
AutoFormat, 305, 441, 451, 1037

AutoSave, 677
Browse, 997
Cell Note, 790-791
Chart Type, 439, 503
ChartWizard, 408-409
check boxes, 49-50
closing, 54
Color Picker, 1096
Column Width, 346, 969
command buttons, 49
Consolidate, 768
controls, 720-721
Convert, 1057
Copy, 261
Copy Picture, 1047
creating with Visual Basic, 1148-1149
custom, 1212-1217
Custom AutoFilter, 916
Customize, 1108
Data Analysis, 839
Delete, 105-107
Edit Column, 970
Edit Criteria, 962
Edit Scenario, 827, 835
Edit Slide, 664-665
File, 1063
Find, 98-101
Fonts, 309
Format, 478, 484-487, 490-491
Format Axis, 494-496
Format Cells, 314, 357, 360-363, 1038, 1144
Format Data Series, 481, 491
Format Number, 1148
Format Object, 568, 580, 725, 729
Format Title, 486
Forms toolbar, 721-723
Function Wizard, 677, 1234
Get External Data, 976-980, 982
Go To Special, 103, 781
Goal Seek, 797-800
Goal Seek Status, 798
Group, 599
Grouping, 1026
Help, 57
Histogram, 843
Insert Paste, 239
Joins, 967-968
Links, 748-749, 759-763, 1057-1058
list boxes, 49, 52-54
Macro, 1161, 1218
Macro Error, 1218-1219
Macro Recorder, 1157
Menu Editor, 1120
Merge Styles, 358
Mouse, 1103
Move, 261
Moving Average, 846
New Data, 457-458
Note, 793
Number Format, 333
Object, 1067
Object Browser, 1149, 1184
ODBC Data Sources, 954-956
ODBC Setup, 955
Open Query, 965
Open Workbook, 1064
option buttons, 49-51
Options, 258, 724
Paste Special, 503, 753, 979
Pattern, 481-482
Patterns, 582
Picture, 557
PivotTable Field, 1033-1038
Program Item Properties dialog box, 1133
Protect Sheet, 835
Random Number Generation, 839
Record, 792
Record New Macro, 1155
Rename Sheet, 264
Replace, 100-101
Row Height, 348, 970
Save Workspace, 1135
Scenario Manager, 824-827
Search, 284
Select Data Source, 953-954, 964-965
Select Database, 956
Select Special, 798
Select Tables, 956
Series, 245
Sets Defaults, 665
Show Pages, 1030
Solver Parameters, 805-817
Sort, 887, 891, 898, 971-972
Sort Options, 891, 894
Style, 355-362
Subtotal, 608-612
Table, 700-701
tabs, 49-50
text boxes, 49
  deleting characters, 52
  editing in, 51-52
Toolbars, 440, 721, 1108
TrueType, 310
User-Defined AutoFormats, 451
DialogFrame object, 1176
DialogSheet object, 1177
dictionaries, 789
DIF (Data Interchange Format) file name extension, 1075
Dim statement (declaring variables), 1196
dimensions (arrays), 1196
dimmed commands, 39
dimming controls, 739
directories
  changing, 270
  default, 271
  opening files, 269
  path names, 274
  searches, 285-286
disabling links (OLE), 1049
DISC( ) function, 854
Discrete command (Analysis ToolPak), 851
disk files, accessing, 1207-1211
disks, changing, 270
display
  settings (View Manager), 679
  sheets, 533-539
displaying
  formulas, 126, 147, 537-540
  panes (query window), 958
  sheets
    full screen, 533-535
    in separate windows, 547-548
  text with numbers, 337
  toolbars, 45-46
  user messages (Visual Basic), 1169-1171
  views, 543
division (/) operator, 140
DLLs (Dynamic Link Libraries), 948
DMAX( ) function, 186
DMIN( ) function, 186
Do/Loop loops, 1206-1207
docking toolbars, 46
documents, opening, 547
dollar sign ($) in absolute cell references, 133
DOLLAR( ) function, 227
DOLLARDE( ) function, 854
DOLLARFR( ) function, 854

DOS applications
copying/pasting Excel data, 1070-1074
exporting Excel data, 1077
Windows, 1070
double-clicking mouse, 35
DPRODUCT( ) function, 186
Draft Quality printing, 395
dragging cells, 235-236
dragging and dropping
chart data, 18
rotating 3-D charts, 497-501
dragging mouse, 35
drawing controls, 725
Drawing object, 1177
Drawing toolbar, 43, 561-563
drawing tools, 561-563
Freehand, 565-567
drivers, installing, 951-952
drives, searches, 285-286
drop lines (charts), 437
Drop Shadow tool, 563
drop-down lists, 20
DropDown object, 1177
DRW (Micrografx Designer) file name extension, 557
DSTDEV( ) function, 186
DSTDEVP( ) function, 187
DSUM( ) function, 187, 704, 707-708
dual values, 809
DURATION( ) function, 854
DVAR( ) function, 187
DVARP( ) function, 187
Dynamic Data Exchange (DDE) messages, 948
Dynamic Link Libraries (DLLs), 948
Solver, 804

E

EDATE( ) function, 189, 854
edit buttons, 120-123
Edit Column command (Microsoft Query, Records menu), 970
Edit Column dialog box, 970
Edit Criteria dialog box, 962
Edit menu commands
Clear, 103, 122
All option, 501-502, 703
Contents option, 102
Series option, 461
Copy, 97, 102, 247, 250-253, 459, 753, 1045
Button Image option, 1114-1115
Picture option, 1047
Sheet option, 261-263
Cut, 102, 237-239, 1045
Delete, 102-107, 122
Sheet option, 260
Fill
Right/Left/Up/Down options, 243
Series option, 109-119, 123, 245, 702, 710, 713-714
Find, 97-99
Go To, 75-76, 103, 781-783
Links, 748-749, 759-763, 1057-1058
Mark, 1072
Move, 261-263
Object, 1058
Paste, 97, 102, 237, 240, 247, 250-252, 459, 1046
Button Image option, 1115
Link option, 753
Special option, 252-255, 459, 753, 1048
Repeat, 97
Replace, 99-101
Undo, 97, 236-237
Undo Delete, 106
Undo Replace, 101
Undo Sort, 892
Edit Scenario dialog box, 827, 835
Edit Slide dialog box, 664-665
EditBox object, 1177
editing
cell references, 136
cells, 1099
contents, 95-97
chart titles, 467
criteria, 960-963
data forms, 912
data series, 462-464
data tables, 701-703
embedded objects, 1058-1059
fields, 972-973
filtered data, 934
formula bar data, 94
formulas, 156
functions, 182-183
array functions, 156
groups of sheets, 264-266
linked objects, 1058-1059
links, 427, 772-773
lists, filtered, 928-931
notes, 792
pivot tables, 994
procedures, 1163-1167
query data in worksheets, 981
records, 972-973
scenarios, 826-827
slide shows, 668
transitions, 665
SQL statements, 965
summary information, 297-298
templates, 1130
text boxes (dialog boxes), 51-52
workbooks, 761-763
worksheet layouts, 101-107
EFFECT( ) function, 854
elements (arrays), 1196
Ellipse tool, 562
ellipses, 564-565
ellipsis (...) in commands, 39, 48
embedded charts, 405, 571-572
activating, 428
adding data, 456-458
creating with ChartWizard, 407-408
deleting, 414
formatting, 414
saving, 426-427
embedded objects
applets, 1066
editing, 1058-1059
embedded pictures of charts, 571
embedding data across applications, 1050-1057
converting embedded objects, 1057
embedding objects as icons, 1057
existing files, 1054
new objects, 1051-1053
pasting embedded objects, 1055-1057
printing embedded objects, 1057
Encapsulated PostScript (EPS) file name extension, 557
engineering analysis (Analysis ToolPak), 676-677

engineering commands, 837, 851
engineering functions, 837, 852-853
Enhanced mode, 1072-1074
enlarging printing, 382
enumerated lists, 1179
EOMONTH( ) function, 190, 854
EPS (Encapsulated PostScript) file name extension, 557
equal sign (=) in formulas, 125-127
equal to (=) operator, 140
ERF( ) function, 852
ERFC( ) function, 852
error bars (charts), 517-519
  formatting, 491
Error Bars command (Insert menu), 518
error messages
  #DIV/0!, 777
  #N/A, 777
  #NAME?, 778
  #NULL!, 778
  #NUM!, 778
  #REF!, 778
  #VALUE!, 779
error tracking (worksheets), 781-783
error values, 87
ERROR.TYPE( ) function, 203-204
errors in formulas, 145-152
evaluation order of operators, 142
EVEN( ) function, 217, 856
EXACT( ) function, 228
Excel
  customizing, 1093-1106
  quitting, 25-27
  starting, 25-27, 1132-1136
  transferring Microsoft Query data, 975-980
  version 4, 41, 272
  Windows applications interaction, 1043-1068
exchanging data across applications, 1059-1068
Exit command (File menu), 27
exiting Excel, 25-27
EXP( ) function, 216
expanding outlines, 596
EXPONDIST( ) function, 222, 856
Exponential Smoothing command (Analysis ToolPak), 848-850
exponentiation (^) operator, 140
exporting
  data to DOS or mainframe applications, 1077
  Windows Excel to Macintosh Excel, 1079
Extend mode, 78
extensions (file names), 270
  BMP (Windows Bitmaps), 557
  BMP (Windows Paintbrush), 557
  CGM (Computer Graphics Metafile), 557
  DRW (Micrografx Designer), 557
  EPS (Encapsulated PostScript), 557
  HGL (HP Graphic Language), 557
  PCT (Macintosh Picture), 557
  PCX (PC Paintbrush), 557
  TIF (Tagged Image File Format), 557
  WMF (Windows Metafile), 557
  WPG (DrawPerfect), 557
external cell references, 138
external data, 987
External Data command (Data menu), 980-982
external link values, 1049
external reference formulas, 747, 751-753, 757-758
extract range, 866, 870

F

FACT( ) function, 217
FACTDOUBLE( ) function, 852
FALSE( ) function, 207
FDIST( ) function, 222, 856
field arguments (database functions), 704
fields, 865, 949, 972-973
  appending, 1014
  data panes, 959-963
  lists, naming, 876-877
  tables, join lines, 967-968
File command (Insert menu), 1063
File dialog box, 1063
file formats, 280
  exporting/importing data, 1074-1076
  importing non-Excel data, 1079-1080
File menu commands
  Close, 62, 282
  Exit, 27
  Find, 17
  Find File, 282-292
  New, 267
  New SLIDES, 678
  Open, 268
  Page Setup, 374
  Print, 370, 395
  Print Preview, 389
  Print Report, 396, 678
  Properties, 1133
  Save As, 275
  Save Workspace, 280
  Summary Info, 276
file name extensions, 270, 274
  BMP (Windows Bitmaps), 557
  BMP (Windows Paintbrush), 557
  CGM (Computer Graphics Metafile), 557
  DRW (Micrografx Designer), 557
  EPS (Encapsulated PostScript), 557
  HGL (HP Graphic Language), 557
  PCT (Macintosh Picture), 557
  PCX (PC Paintbrush), 557
  TIF (Tagged Image File Format), 557
  WMF (Windows Metafile), 557
  WPG (DrawPerfect), 557
files, 267, 949
  closing, 62
  copying, 301-302
  deleting, 302
  formats, 556-557
    reading/writing by Excel, 1074-1076
  listing, 293-294
  opening
    changing directories, 269
    Excel 4, 272
    Find File, 300
    on network, 271-272
    on networks, 269

printing, 300-301
saving, 677
with pivot tables, 1008-1009
searches, 286-287
selecting
Find File, 293, 299-300
multiple, 299
text, 1081-1086
viewing information, 292-293, 296
workspace files, 280-281, 1135
fill handles, 241-242
calculating worksheet trends, 711-713
series, 117
Fill Right/Left/Up/Down command (Edit menu), 243
Fill Series command (Edit menu), 109-119, 123, 245, 702, 710, 713-714
Filled Arc tool, 562
Filled Ellipse tool, 562
Filled Freeform tool, 562
Filled Rectangle tool, 562
filling cells
fill handles, 241-242
with Ctrl+Enter keys, 242
with custom fill, 244-245
with Fill commands, 243
Filter command (Data menu), 20
Advanced Filter option, 916-928, 943
AutoFilter option, 613, 914
Filter mode, 934-935
filtered data, 933-946
backups, 945-946
charting, 934-935
copying, 935-936
between worksheets or workbooks, 942-944
with Advanced Filter, 936-942
with AutoFilter, 936
deleting, 934
editing, 934
printing, 934
subtotaling, 934
subtotals, 613-614
filtered lists, 928-931
filters
Advanced Filter, 916-931, 936-942
AutoFilter, 913-916, 936
financial analysis (Analysis ToolPak), 676-677
financial functions, 192-201, 837, 854-855
Find command (Edit menu), 97-99
Find command (File menu), 17
Find dialog box, 98-101
Find File
copying files, 301-302
deleting files, 302
file information, 292-293, 296
opening files, 300
previewing workbooks, 294-296
printing files, 300-301
selecting files, 299-300
sorting file lists, 293-294
summary information
adding, 297-298
editing, 297-298
viewing, 296-297
workbooks, 292-293
Find File command (File menu), 282-292
FIND( ) function, 228
finding
data
criteria, 908-909
text, numbers, or formulas, 97-99
with Advanced Filter, 919-931
with AND or OR, 907-908
with AutoFilter, 913-916
with data form, 909-912
with wild cards, 906-907
dates/times, 905-906
files, *see* searches
goals/solutions, 796-800
numbers, 904-905
objects (Object Browser), 1184
solutions with Solver, 800-817
text, 902-903
FindIt procedure, 1204
FINV( ) function, 222, 856
FISHER( ) function, 222, 856
FISHERINV( ) function, 222, 856
fixed decimal places, numbers, 120
FIXED( ) function, 228
fixed-length text files, 1081-1086
fixed-width text files, 1077, 1086
flipping pivot table orientation, 1015-1016
floating text (charts), 468-469
floating toolbars, 46
FLOOR( ) function, 217, 856
FM3 (1-2-3 Release 3) file name extension, 1075
FMT (1-2-3 Release 2x) file name extension, 1075
folders, 292
Font command (Microsoft Query, Format menu), 973
Font object, 1177
fonts, 638-642
charts, 485-486
printer, 308
printer fonts, 308
screen, 308
TrueType, 309-311
Fonts dialog box, 309
footers
codes, 381
creating, 378-382
custom, 379
formats, 378
previewing, 380
printing, 381
For Each loops, 1207
For/Next loops, 1204-1205
FORECAST( ) function, 222, 856
Form command (Data menu), 868, 879, 909-912
form-like worksheets, 723-724
Format Axis dialog box, 494-496
Format Cells command (Format menu)
Alignment option, 319-327
Number option, 331, 344-345
Format Cells dialog box, 314, 357, 360-363, 1038, 1144
Format Data Series dialog box, 481, 491
Format dialog box, 478, 484-487, 490-491
Format menu commands
3-D View, 500-501
AutoFormat, 305-307, 441-453, 502-503, 614, 886, 996, 1037
Cells, 314-319, 644, 1158
Border option, 353
Patterns option, 351-352
Protection option, 363
Chart Type, 438-453

Column
Hide option, 348, 935
Standard Width option, 350
Width option, 346-347
Format Cells
Aligment option, 319-327
Number option, 331, 344-345
Group, 488-490
Object, 568, 580, 601
Placement
Bring to Front option, 590
Send to Back option, 590
Row
Height option, 348
Unhide option, 350
Selected Item, 490-496
SelectedObject, 478-480, 484-487
Selected Series, 461-464, 478
Sheet
Hide option, 740
Rename option, 264
Unhide option, 740
Styles, 355-362, 651-656
Format Number dialog box, 1148
Format Object dialog box, 568, 580, 725, 729
Format Painter button, 311-312
Format Painter tool, 18
Format Title dialog box, 486
formats, 620
charts
ChartWizard, 410-411
default, 454-456
copying, 311-312
files, 280, 556-557
importing non-Excel data, 1079-1080
reading/writing by Excel, 1074-1076
footers, 378
headers, 378
multiple, *see* styles
numbers, 92
pasting, 311-312
predefined, 91
styles, 307
Formatted Text (Space delimited) files, 1077, 1081-1086
formatting
arrows, 579-581
Autoformat, 303-307
borders, 581-583
cells, 18
borders/lines, 352-354
characters, 314-319
colors/patterns, 351-354
dates/times, 341-345
numbers, 328-341
patterns/colors, 351-354
charts, 21, 477-478
3-D, 497-501
arrows, 496-497
data series, 488-491
deleting formats, 501-502
embedded charts, 414
markers, 491-492
numbers, 483, 485-487
objects, 480-482
text, 483-486
transferring formats, 503
color, 338
columns
hiding, 348
width, 346-347
conditional, 339
data, 973
embedded charts, 414
error bars, 491
fields, 972-973
groups of sheets, 264-266
hiding zeros, 339
lines, 579-581
lists, 885-886
outlines, 602-603
patterns, 581-583
pivot tables, 1037-1039
AutoFormatting, 1037-1038
numbers, 1038
records, 972-973
reports, 614
rows, 348-350
sheets in workbooks, 365-366
tables (AutoFormat), 305-307
trendlines, 490
worksheets, 620-623, 627-648, 651-656, 774-776
Formatting toolbar, 42, 316-317, 483
buttons
Borders, 354
Color Palette, 352
numbers, 332
forms
building, 719-741
controls, 719-723
printing without controls, 739
protecting, 740
Forms toolbar, 43, 721-723
Formula Bar, 31, 126-128, 177-178
editing data, 94
data entry, 88
hiding, 536
Formula Bar command (View menu), 177
formulas, 125-127
= (equal sign), 125-127
3-D, 765
array formulas
editing, 156
entering, 152-154
built-in, *see* functions
calculation, 126
cell references, 128-139, 167-168
inserting, 130
pasting, 143-144
pointing, 129-130
cells, hiding, 363-364
changing to values, 144-145
circular errors, 148
compound criteria, 927
conditional, 687-690
copying
cell names, 168
ranges, 254
with commands, 247
with mouse, 246
dates, 144
displaying, 126, 147, 537-540
entering
formula bar, 127-128
in-cell, 127-128
errors, 145-152
external reference, 747
finding, 97-99
Function Wizard, 18
functions, 143-144
linked, 845
names, 170-171
operators, 139-142
parentheses, 142, 147
pasting multiple copies, 247-250
querying tables, 693-697
exact matches, 695
LOOKUP( ) functions, 693-695
MATCH/INDEX functions, 695-697

recalculation, 126
replacing, 99-101
series formulas, 406, 461-464
text, 686
text entry, 144
times, 144
tracing, 783-785
troubleshooting, 147-152
viewing, 125, 779-780
Fourier Analysis command (Analysis TookPak), 851
frames, 577
Freeform tool, 562
freehand buttons, 1115
Freehand drawing tool, 565-567
freehand objects, 584
Freehand tool, 562
Freeze Panes command (Windows menu), 546, 928
freezing
panes (windows), 546, 928-931
workbooks, 763
frequency distribution, *see* histograms
FREQUENCY( ) function, 222, 844, 846, 857
FTEST( ) function, 222, 857
Full Screen command (View menu), 16, 535
full screen sheet display, 533-535
Full Screen toolbar, 44
Function command (Insert menu), 144, 182-183, 677, 845, 850
function keys, 36-38
Function Wizard, 18
editing functions, 182-183
Help, 183
inserting functions, 180-182
Function Wizard dialog box, 677, 1234
functions, 126, 173-175, 178, 1185-1186
3-D cell references, 139
ABS( ), 216
ACCRINT( ), 854
ACCRINTM( ), 854
ACOS( ), 232
ACOSH( ), 232
ADDRESS( ), 209
AMORDEGRC( ), 854
AMORLINC( ), 854
Analysis ToolPak, 676-677, 837
AND( ), 207, 689, 926-928
AREAS( ), 209
arguments, 175-176
array functions, 156
ASIN( ), 232
ASINH( ), 232
ATAN( ), 232
ATAN2( ), 232
ATANH( ), 233
AVEDEV( ), 222, 856
AVERAGE( ), 221
BESSELI( ), 852
BESSELJ( ), 852
BESSELK( ), 852
BESSELY( ), 852
BETADIST( ), 222, 856
BETAINV( ), 222, 856
BIN2DEC( ), 852
BIN2HEX( ), 852
BIN2OCT( ), 852
BINOMDIST( ), 222, 856
CEILING( ), 216, 856
CELL( ), 201-203
CHAR( ), 227
CHIDIST( ), 222, 856
CHIINV( ), 222, 856
CHITEST( ), 222, 856
CHOOSE( ), 209-210, 730
CLEAN( ), 227
CODE( ), 227
COLUMN( ), 210
COLUMNS( ), 210
COMBIN( ), 216, 856
COMPLEX( ), 852
CONCATENATE, 686
CONCATENATE( ), 227
CONFIDENCE( ), 222, 856
CONVERT( ), 852
CORREL( ), 222, 856
COS( ), 233
COSH( ), 233
COUNT( ), 223
COUNTA( ), 223
COUPDAYBS( ), 854
COUPDAYS( ), 854
COUPDAYSNC( ), 854
COUPNCD( ), 854
COUPNUM( ), 854
COUPPCD( ), 854
COVAR( ), 222, 856
CRITBINOM( ), 222, 856
CUMIPMT( ), 854
CUMPRINC( ), 854
database, 185-187
DATE( ), 188, 894
date/time, 187-192
DATEVALUE( ), 188-189
DAVERAGE( ), 185-186
DAYS360( ), 189
DCOUNT( ), 186
DCOUNTA( ), 186
DEC2BIN( ), 852
DEC2HEX( ), 852
DEC2OCT( ), 852
DEGREES( ), 859
DELTA( ), 852
DEVSQ( ), 222, 856
DGET( ), 186
DISC( ), 854
DMAX( ), 186
DMIN( ), 186
DOLLAR( ), 227
DOLLARDE( ), 854
DOLLARFR( ), 854
DPRODUCT( ), 186
DSTDEV( ), 186
DSTDEVP( ), 187
DSUM( ), 187
DURATION( ), 854
DVAR( ), 187
DVARP( ), 187
EDATE( ), 189, 854
editing, 182-183
EFFECT( ), 854
EOMONTH( ), 190, 854
ERF( ), 852
ERFC( ), 852
ERROR.TYPE( ), 203-204
EVEN( ), 217, 856
EXACT( ), 228
EXP( ), 216
EXPONDIST( ), 222, 856
FACT( ), 217
FACTDOUBLE( ), 852
FALSE( ), 207
FDIST( ), 222, 856
financial, 192-201
FIND( ), 228
FINV( ), 222, 856
FISHER( ), 222, 856
FISHERINV( ), 222, 856
FIXED( ), 228
FLOOR( ), 217, 856
FORECAST( ), 222, 856
FREQUENCY( ), 222, 844-846, 857
FTEST( ), 222, 857
Function Wizard, 180-182
FV( ), 195
GAMMADIST( ), 222, 857
GAMMAINV( ), 222, 857
GAMMALN( ), 222, 857

GCD( ), 852
GEOMEAN( ), 222, 857
GESTEP( ), 852
GROWTH( ), 223, 715
HARMEAN(( ), 222
HARMEAN( ), 857
Help, 183
HEX2BIN( ), 852
HEX2DEC( ), 852
HEX2OCT( ), 852
HLOOKUP( ), 210-211, 693-695
HOUR( ), 190
HYPGEOMDIST( ), 222, 857
IF, 728
IF( ), 207, 339, 687-690
IMABS( ), 852
IMAGINARY( ), 852
IMARGUMENT( ), 852
IMCONJUGATE( ), 852
IMCOS( ), 853
IMDIV( ), 853
IMEXP( ), 853
IMLN( ), 853
IMLOG10( ), 853
IMLOG2( ), 853
IMPOWER( ), 853
IMPRODUCT( ), 853
IMREAL( ), 853
IMSIN( ), 853
IMSQRT( ), 853
IMSUB( ), 853
IMSUM( ), 853
INDEX, 695-697, 732
INDEX( ), 211, 693
INDEX(MATCH( )), 695
INDIRECT( ), 212
INFO( ), 204
information, 201-206
InputBox(), 1169, 1227
INT( ), 217
INTERCEPT( ), 222, 857
INTRATE( ), 855
IPMT( ), 195
IRR( ), 196
ISEVEN( ), 853
ISfunction( ), 204-205
ISNA( ), 692
ISODD( ), 853
KURT( ), 222, 857
LARGE( ), 222, 857
LCM( ), 853
LEFT( ), 228
LEN( ), 229
LINEST( ), 223-224, 715
LN( ), 217
LOG( ), 217
LOG10( ), 218
LOGEST( ), 224-225, 715
logical, 207-208
LOGINV( ), 222, 857
LOGNORMDIST( ), 222, 857
lookup, 208-215
LOOKUP( ), 212-213, 692-693
LOWER( ), 229
MATCH( ), 213, 691-697
mathematical, 216-221
MAX( ), 225
MDETERM( ), 218
MDURATION( ), 855
MEDIAN( ), 222, 225, 857
MID( ), 229
MIN( ), 225
MINUTE( ), 190
MINVERSE( ), 218
MIRR( ), 196-197
MMULT( ), 218
MOD( ), 218
MODE( ), 222, 857
MONTH( ), 190
MROUND( ), 853
MsgBox, 1169
MULTINOMIAL( ), 853
N( ), 205-206
NA( ), 206
NEGBINOMDIST( ), 857
NEGMINOMDIST( ), 222
NETWORKDAYS( ), 190, 855
NOMINAL( ), 855
NORMDIST( ), 222, 857
NORMINV( ), 222, 857
NORMSDIST( ), 222, 857
NORMSINV( ), 222, 857
NOT( ), 208, 926-928
NOW( ), 191
NPER( ), 198
NPV( ), 198
OCT2BIN( ), 853
OCT2DEC( ), 853
OCT2HEX( ), 853
ODD( ), 218, 857
ODDFPRICE( ), 855
ODDFYIELD( ), 855
ODDLPRICE( ), 855
ODDLYIELD( ), 855
OFFSET( ), 213-214
OR( ), 208, 926-928
pasting to formulas, 143-144
PEARSON( ), 222, 857
PERCENTILE( ), 222, 857
PERCENTRANK( ), 222, 844-846, 858
PERMUT( ), 222, 858
PI( ), 219
Pmt function, 1232-1233
PMT( ), 174-175, 199
POISSON( ), 222, 858
PPMT( ), 199
PRICE( ), 855
PRICEDISC( ), 855
PRICEMAT( ), 855
PROB( ), 222, 858
PRODUCT( ), 219
PROPER( ), 229
PV( ), 199
QUARTILE( ), 222, 858
QUOTIENT( ), 853
RADIANS( ), 859
RAND( ), 219
RANDBETWEEN( ), 859
RANK( ), 222, 844-846, 858
RATE( ), 200
RECEIVED( ), 855
reference, 208-215
REPLACE( ), 229
REPT( ), 229
RIGHT( ), 230
ROUND( ), 219
ROW( ), 214-215
ROWS( ), 215
RSQ( ), 222, 858
SEARCH( ), 230
SECOND( ), 191
selecting calculations with an index, 1233-1234
SERIESSUM( ), 853
SIGN( ), 219
SIN( ), 233
SINH( ), 233
SKEW( ), 222, 858
SLN( ), 200
SLOPE( ), 222, 858
SMALL( ), 222, 858
SQRT( ), 220
SQRTPI( ), 853
STANDARDIZE( ), 222, 858
statistical, 221-226
STDEV( ), 225
STDEVP( ), 226
STEP, 1150
STEYX( ), 222, 858
SUM( ), 179-180, 220
SUMPRODUCT( ), 220

SUMSQ( ), 220
SUMSQUARES( ), 858
SUMX2MY2( ), 220, 858
SUMX2PY2( ), 220, 858
SUMXMY2( ), 221, 858
SYD( ), 200
T( ), 230
TAN( ), 233
TANH( ), 233
TBILLEQ( ), 855
TBILLPRICE( ), 855
TBILLYIELD( ), 855
TDIST( ), 222, 858
text, 226-231
TEXT( ), 90-91, 231, 687
TIME( ), 191
TIMEVALUE( ), 191
TINV( ), 222, 858
TODAY( ), 192
toolbars, 177-178
TRANSPOSE( ), 215
TREND( ), 226, 715-716
trigonometric, 232-233
TRIM( ), 231, 894
TRIMMEAN( ), 222, 858
TRUE( ), 208
TRUNC( ), 221
TTEST( ), 222, 858
TYPE( ), 206, 207
typing, 179
UPPER( ), 231
user defined, 1232
Val(), 1202
VALUE( ), 231
VAR( ), 226
VARP( ), 226
VDB( ), 201
VLOOKUP( ), 215-216, 693-695
WEEKDAY( ), 192
WEIBULL( ), 222, 858
with Visual Basic, 1232-1233
WORKDAY( ), 855
XIRR( ), 855
XNPV( ), 855
YEAR( ), 192
YEARFRAC( ), 192, 855
YIELD( ), 855
YIELDDISC( ), 855
YIELDMAT( ), 855
ZTEST( ), 222, 858
FV( ) function, 195

G

GAMMADIST( ) function, 222, 857
GAMMAINV( ) function, 222, 857
GAMMALN( ) function, 222, 857
GCD( ) function, 852
GEOMEAN( ) function, 222, 857
GESTEP( ) function, 852
Get External Data command (Data menu), 952, 954
Get External Data dialog box, 976-982
GetOpenFilename method, 1211
GetOpenFilename procedure, 1229
GetSaveAsFilename method, 1211
Go To command (Edit menu), 75-76, 103, 781-783
Go To Special dialog box, 103, 781
Goal Seek command (Tools menu), 443-444, 795-800
Goal Seek dialog box, 797-800
Goal Seek Status dialog box, 798
goals, 796-800
Goals Seek command (Tools menu), 512
graphic objects, 560
copying, 583-584
deleting, 579
grouping, 588
hiding, 591
moving, 583-584
positioning, 584-587
printing, 591
protecting, 590
reordering layers, 589-590
selecting, 577-579
sizing, 583-584
graphics
charts, 524
copying, 558-560
into slide shows, 662-664
inserting, 557-558
greater than (>) operator, 140
greater than/equal to (>=) operator, 140
gridlines (charts), 437
color, 536-537
hiding, 536-537
inserting, 475
printing, 377-378
Gridlines command (Insert menu), 475
Group and Outline commands (Data menu), 1022
Group button (Query and Pivot toolbar), 1019
Group command
Data menu, 598-599, 602-603
Format menu, 488-490
Outline menu, 599, 602-603
Group dialog box, 599
Group tool, 562
group windows, 25
GroupBox object, 1177
grouping
graphic objects, 588
sheets, 264-266
Grouping dialog box, 1026
grouping in pivot tables, 1018-1027
by label, 1018-1019
displaying/hiding detail, 1019, 1022-1025
numeric labels, 1025-1026
time intervals, 1027
GroupObject object, 1177
groups
chart type groups, 507
sheets, formatting, 365-366
growth series, 113-115
GROWTH( ) function, 223, 715

H

handles, 577
charts, 413
hard disks, 17
HARMEAN( ) function, 222, 857
header rows, 865
Header/Footer tab (Page Setup), 375
headers
codes, 381
creating, 378-382
custom, 379
entering information, 380
formats, 378
previewing, 380
printing, 381
headers/footers (procedures), 1165

headings
- centering in worksheets, 636
- columns, 535, 969-970
- data entry, 116-119
- printing, 377-378
- rows, hiding, 535

Help, 55-58
- functions, 183
- on-line help, 1173
- toolbars, 44-45
- Visual Basic, 1150

Help menu commands
- Contents, 1150
- Search for Help on, 673

Help window, 58
HEX2BIN( ) function, 852
HEX2DEC( ) function, 852
HEX2OCT( ) function, 852
HGL (HP Graphic Language) file name extension, 557
hi-lo lines (charts), 437
Hide Columns command (Microsoft Query, Format menu), 968
Hide command (Window menu), 550
Hide Detail button (Query and Pivot toolbar), 1022
hiding
- columns, 348, 968-969
- formula bar, 536
- formulas in cells, 363-364
- graphic objects, 591
- gridlines, 536-537
- headings, 535
- levels (outlines), 600-602
- numbers with custom formats, 338
- panes (query window), 958
- rows, 349-350
- scroll bars, 535-536
- sheet tabs, 536
- sheets, 550-551
- status bar, 536
- symbols (outlines), 600
- toolbars, 45-46
- totals (pivot tables), 1031-1032
- windows, 550-551
- zeros, 339-340

hierarchical charts, 522
Histogram command (Analysis ToolPak), 843-846, 850
Histogram dialog box, 843
histograms, 838, 842-846
HLOOKUP( ) function, 210-211, 693-695
HOUR( ) function, 190
HP Graphic Language (HGL) file name extension, 557
hue changes (color palette), 1097
HYPGEOMDIST( ) function, 222, 857

I

icons
- application icon, 28
- custom, 1134
- maximize icon, 29
- minimize icon, 29
- restore icon, 29
- workbook control icon, 31
- workbook icon, 31

If statements, 1224-1225
IF( ) function, 207, 339, 687-690, 728
IMABS( ) function, 852
IMAGINARY( ) function, 852
IMARGUMENT( ) function, 852
IMCONJUGATE( ) function, 852
IMCOS( ) function, 853
IMDIV( ) function, 853
IMEXP( ) function, 853
IMLN( ) function, 853
IMLOG10( ) function, 853
IMLOG2( ) function, 853
Immediate pane (Debug window), 1219-1220
importing
- mainframe application data, 1080-1081
- non-Excel data, 1079-1080
- sound message, 793
- text files, 1081-1086

IMPRODUCT( ) function, 853
IMREAL( ) function, 853
IMSIN( ) function, 853
IMSQRT( ) function, 853
IMSUB( ) function, 853
IMSUM( ) function, 853
in-cell formula entry, 127-128
in-place activation (OLE 2), 1053
inactive window, 29-31
independent variables, 715
index numbers, 893
INDEX( ) function, 211, 693-697, 732
indicators (modes), 31
INDIRECT( ) function, 212
INFO( ) function, 204
information functions, 201-206
inner joins, 967
input cells, 819-822
InputBox( ) function, 1169, 1227
Insert Cells command (Edit menu), 239
Insert menu commands
- Cells, 106
- Chart, 415
- Chart As New Sheet, 259
- Chart On This Sheet, 407
- Columns, 107
- Copied Cells, 251
- Cut Cells, 239
- Data Labels, 471-472
- Error Bars, 518
- File, 1063
- Function, 144, 182-183, 677, 845, 850
- Gridlines, 475
- Legend, 472
- Macro Dialog, 259, 1212
- Macro Module, 259, 1115, 1117, 1168
- Macro MS Excel 4.0, 259
- Name
  - Apply option, 169
  - Create option, 163, 758, 821, 845
  - Define option, 159-162, 167, 758, 868, 878, 881
  - Paste option, 143, 182
- New Data, 457
- Note, 792
- Object, 1051, 1067
- Page Break, 386
- Picture, 557
- Rows, 107
- Titles, 466-467
- Trendline, 513-514
- Worksheet, 259

Insert method (range objects), 1183
Insert Paste dialog box, 239
inserting
- arrows (charts), 474
- cells, 103-107
  - with commands, 238-239, 251-252
  - with mouse, 237-238
- columns, 103-107
- data series in charts, 410

error bars (charts), 518-519
fields into data panes, 959-963
functions, 180-182
graphics, 557-558
gridlines (charts), 475
legends (charts), 472-473
rows, 103-107
sheets in workbooks, 259-260
text in charts, 466-472
trendlines (charts), 514-516
insertion point, 88
installing
add-ins, 672-675, 951-952
drivers, 951-952
printers, 372
Solver, 804-809
instances (objects), 1177
INT( ) function, 217
integer constraints (Solver), 810-811
INTERCEPT( ) function, 222, 857
international settings, 1104
INTRATE( ) function, 855
IPMT( ) function, 195
IRR( ) function, 196
ISEVEN( ) function, 853
ISfunction( ) function, 204-205
ISNA( ) function, 692
ISODD( ) function, 853
italic text, 643

J-K

join lines, 967-968
joining worksheets, 763-767
by physical layout, 767-770
by row and column headings, 770-772
formatting, 774-776
linking, 774
manually, 776
with 3-D formulas, 765
Joins command (Microsoft Query, Table menu), 967-968
Joins dialog box, 967-968
jumping to Help topics, 57

key combinations, 36
keyboard, 35-38
function keys, 36-38
moving cells, 73-74
scrolling worksheets, 71-72
selecting
commands, 40-41
files, 300
ranges, 76-79
tabs, 50
Shift key in commands, 41
starting Excel, 26
zooming display, 539
KURT( ) function, 222, 857

L

Label object, 1177
labels
columns, 634-635
legends, 417
titles, 417
X axis, 416
LARGE( ) function, 222, 857
laser printers, 375
layouts, 620
charts, 411-412
joining worksheets, 767-770
outlines, 595-596
pages, 744-745
worksheets, 620-624, 627-648
borders, 624-626
editing, 101-107
pages, 626-627
white space, 624
LCM( ) function, 853
LEFT( ) function, 228
left-handed mouse, 32
Legend command (Insert menu), 472
legends (charts), 404-406, 437
ChartWizard, 412-414
inserting, 472-473
labels, 417
LEN( ) function, 229
less than (>) operator, 140
less than/equal to (<=) operator, 140
limited extract range, 870
limited resources (Solver), 809
Limits reports (Solver), 814
line charts, 453-454
formatting, 491-492
Line object, 1177
Line tool, 562
line-continuation (Visual Basic), 1167
linear optimization, 679
linear problems, 801-802
linear series, 110-116
lines, 564-565, 644-646
formatting, 579-581
worksheets, 352-354
LINEST( ) function, 223-224, 715
linked formulas, 845
linked objects, 1058-1059
linked pictures of cells, 574-577
linked pictures of charts, 572
linked worksheets, 980
linking
across applications, 1047-1049
cells, 750-753
by typing, 757-758
editing, 761-763, 772-773
freezing, 763
saving, 763
to chart text, 523-524
updating, 759-761
with Copy/Paste Link commands, 753-755
data from Microsoft Query to Excel, 979
Excel data to WordPerfect 6.0, 1077-1079
into Word for Windows, 1061-1068
pictures of worksheet cells, 744-749
worksheets, 774
linking fields, *see* relational keys
links
creating, 427
editing, 427-428
Links command
Edit menu, 748-749, 759-763, 1057-1058
Microsoft Query, Edit menu, 979
Links dialog box, 748-749, 759-763, 1057-1058
list boxes (dialog boxes), 49, 52-54
ListBox object, 1177
listing
files, 293-294
names (cells), 166-167
listing procedures, 1159-1161
lists, 863-866
as worksheet controls, 730-733
comparative criteria, 902-909, 930

criteria ranges, 918-919
data categories, 871-872
data entry
accelerating, 884-886
directly into rows, 881-884
troubleshooting, 885
with data forms, 879-881
fields, 876-877
filtered, 928-931
formatting, 885-886
organizing, 872-873
Pivot tables, 983-1009
ranges
criteria, 866, 869
database, 866-869
extract, 866, 870
recalculating, 884-886
records
editing, 912
finding with Advanced Filter, 919-931
finding with AutoFilter, 913-916
finding with data form, 909-912
summarizing data, 705-710
LN( ) function, 217
loans, 1232-1233
locating, *see* finding
locking windows, 551-552
LOG( ) function, 217
LOG10( ) function, 218
LOGEST( ) function, 224-225, 715
logical argument, 175
logical formulas, 1200
logical functions, 207-208
logical operators, 1200
logical values, 87
LOGINV( ) function, 222, 857
LOGNORMDIST( ) function, 222, 857
lookup functions, 208-215
LOOKUP( ) function, 212-213, 692-695
loops, 1204-1207
Do/Loop, 1206-1207
For Each, 1207
For/Next loops, 1204-1205
While/Wend, 1205-1206
Lotus 1-2-3, 1098-1099
LOWER( ) function, 229

M

Macintosh Excel, 1079
Macintosh Picture (PCT) file name extension, 557
macro buttons, 568-571
Macro command (Tools menu), 1161
Macro dialog box, 1161, 1216
Macro Dialog command (Insert menu), 259, 1212
Macro Error dialog box, 1218-1219
macro language versus Visual Basic, 1140
Macro Module command (Insert menu), 259, 1115-1117, 1168
Macro MS Excel 4.0 command (Insert menu), 259
Macro Recorder, 1153-1157
Macro Recorder dialog box, 1157
macro sheets (workbooks), 66, 267
macros, 1154
IF( ) functions, 687
parallel syntax, 1144-1145
recording, 1157-1158
running in Visual Basic, 1151
starting Macro Recorder, 1155-1157
STEP function, 1150
terminating recording process, 1158-1159
mainframe applications
exporting, 1077
importing data, 1080-1081
manipulating text, 685-687
manual chart creation, 421-426
manual page breaks, 385-386
margins, 375-377
charts, 430
decreasing, 387
footers, 378
headers, 378
laser printers, 375
print preview, 391-392
Margins tab (Page Setup), 375
Mark command (Edit menu), 1072
markers
charts, 406, 437, 798-800
data series, 461-465
formatting, 491-492
sheets, 511-513
marquees, 237
MATCH( ) function, 213, 691-697
matches
AND or OR conditions, 907-908
criteria, 908-909, 930
dates/times, 905-906
numeric, 904-905
text, 902-903
wild cards, 906-907
mathematical functions, 216-221, 837
Max function (pivot tables), 1034
MAX( ) function, 225
maximize icon, 29
maximizing windows, 60
MDETERM( ) function, 218
MDURATION( ) function, 855
MEDIAN( ) function, 222, 225, 857
memory (Clipboard), 1044-1045
menu bars, 29, 1124-1125
Menu Editor, 1117-1119
Menu Editor command (Tools menu), 1149
Menu Editor dialog box, 1120
menus, 13, 29
built-in menus, 1118-1119
creating with Visual Basic, 1149
custom, 1117-1125
appending commands, 1121
assigning procedures to commands, 1123
creating, 1120-1121
creating menu bars, 1124-1125
Menu Editor, 1117
submenus, 1122
terminology, 1118-1119
pull-down, 39
shortcut, 39-40
Drawing, 563
objects, 435-436
submenus, 39
troubleshooting, 1125
Merge Styles dialog box, 358
merging
scenarios, 833-834
styles, 356-359
methods, 1182
accessing, 1183
PrintOut, 1228
range objects, 1182

Micrografx Designer (DRW) file name extension, 557
Microsoft Corporation products/technical support, 1239
Microsoft Excel 5.0—Complete/ Custom dialog box, 673
Microsoft Query, 22, 936, 947-949
  closing, 980
  commands
    Criteria Add Criteria, 961
    Edit Copy, 975, 978-979
    Edit Cut, 975
    Edit Links, 979
    Edit Paste, 978
    Edit Paste Special, 979
    File Close Query, 964
    File New Query, 954, 964
    File Open Query, 965
    File Return Data to Excel, 976-981
    File Save Query, 964
    Format Column Width, 969
    Format Font, 973
    Format Hide Columns, 968
    Format Row Height, 970
    Records Allow Editing, 973-975
    Records Automatic Query, 963
    Records Edit Column, 970
    Records Sort, 971
    Table Add Tables, 959
    Table Joins, 967-968
    View Criteria, 958, 962-963
    View SQL, 965
    View Tables, 958
  data panes
    columns/rows, 968-970
    editing data, 973-975
    formatting data, 973
    records/fields, 972-973
    sorting data, 970-972
  data sources, 950-951
  editing data results in worksheets, 981
  importing data from DBMSs, 1080-1081
  installing, 951-952
  queries
    closing, 964
    data sources, 954-956
    defining, 958-963
    executing, 963
    reusing, 964-965
    saving, 963-964
  query window, 956-958, 964
  starting, 953
  tables, 965-967
    join lines, 967-968
  terminology, 949-950
  transferring data to Excel, 975-980
  updating data results, 981-982
Microsoft toolbar, 44
MID( ) function, 229
Min function (pivot tables), 1034
MIN( ) function, 225
minimize icon, 29
minimizing windows, 60
minus sign (-) on open folders, 292
MINUTE( ) function, 190
MINVERSE( ) function, 218
MIRR( ) function, 196-197
mixed cell references, 135
mixing colors (color palette), 1097
MMULT( ) function, 218
moats, empty cells, 868
MOD( ) function, 218
MODE( ) function, 222, 857
models (Analysis ToolPak), 676-677
modes
  286 Standard, 1070-1072
  386 Enhanced, 1072-1074
  Filter, 934-935
  indicators, 31
modifying controls, 736-737
Module object, 1177
modules (Visual Basic), 1155
MONTH( ) function, 190
mouse, 31-35
  adding chart data, 456-457
  column width, 346
  copy operations, 246, 260
  creating panes, 545
  customizing with Windows Control Panel, 1103-1104
  filling cells, 241-242
  hiding columns, 348
  inserting cells, 237-239
  moving
    cells, 235-236
    sheets in workbooks, 262
  pointer, 29, 32-33
  row height, 349
  scrolling worksheets, 71
  selecting
    files, 299
    ranges, 76
    tabs, 50
    text box characters, 51
  starting Excel, 26
  troubleshooting, 34
  zooming display, 539
Mouse dialog box, 1103
Move command (Edit menu), 261-263
Move dialog box, 261
moving
  active cells, 74-75, 1099
  between workbooks, 67
  between worksheets, 68
  cells
    between worksheets, 239-241
    Go To command, 75-76
    with commands, 236-237
    with keyboard, 73-74
    with mouse, 235-236
  charts in worksheets, 413
  controls, 725, 736
  data, 975
  fields in pivot tables, 1017-1018
  graphic objects, 583-584
  markers, 511-513
  objects, 478-480
  sheets in workbooks, 262-263
  to other fields, 972
  to other records, 972-973
  toolbars, 46-47
  windows, 60-61
  worksheet objects (Visual Basic procedures), 1229-1231
Moving Average command (Analysis ToolPak), 846, 848, 850
Moving Average dialog box, 846
moving averages, 513
MROUND( ) function, 853
MsgBox function, 1169
multicolumn tables, 987
MULTINOMIAL( ) function, 853
multiple field sorts, 896
multiple fields (pivot tables), 1005
multiple page fields, 1029-1030
multiple sets, scenarios, 828-830
multiple-input data tables in sensitivity analysis, 700-701
multiplication (*) operator, 140

N

N( ) function, 205-206
NA( ) function, 206
Name command (Insert menu)
  Apply option, 169
  Create option, 163, 758, 821, 845
  Define option, 159-162, 167, 758, 868, 878, 881
  Paste option, 143, 182
named views, 541-543
names
  3-D names, 166
  cells, 157-171
    applying, 169-170
    changing, 167
    commands, 167-168
    creating, 159-162
    defining, 159-161
    deleting, 167
    formulas, 167-168
    scenario input cells, 821-822
    sheet-level, 162
    workbook level, 162
  charts, 415
  creating from worksheet text, 162-166
  files, 270
  formulas, 170-171
  listing, 166-167
  lists, 876-877
  pasting to formulas, 143-144
  scenarios, 834
  values, 170-171
  views, 540-543
  workbooks, 273-302
navigating worksheets, 70-72
negation (-) operator, 139
NEGBINOMDIST( ) function, 857
NEGMINOMDIST( ) function, 222
NETWORKDAYS( ) function, 190, 855
networks, 269, 271-272
New command (File menu), 267
New Data command (Insert menu), 457
New Data dialog box, 457-458
New Query command (Microsoft Query, File menu), 954, 964
New SLIDES command (File menu), 678
New Window command (Window menu), 547, 723
New Workbook button (Standard toolbar), 267
NOMINAL( ) function, 855
nonlinear optimization, 679
nonlinear problems, 801-802
Normal command (Analysis TookPak), 851
Normal distribution, 840
Normal style, 355, 361
NORMDIST( ) function, 222, 857
NORMINV( ) function, 222, 857
NORMSDIST( ) function, 222, 857
NORMSINV(( ) function, 222
NORMSINV( ) function, 857
not equal (< >) operator, 140
NOT( ) function, 208, 926-928
Note command (Insert menu), 792
Note dialog box, 793
notes (worksheets), 396, 789-794
NOW( ) function, 191
NPER( ) function, 198
NPV( ) function, 198
num arguments, 175
Number Format dialog box, 333
numbers
  cells
    formatting, 328-341
    joining with text, 323
    rotating, 326-327
  charts, 483-487
  data entry, 90
  displaying with text, 337
  finding, 97-99, 904-905
  fixed decimal places, 120
  replacing, 99-101
  rounding, 1093
numeric comparisons, 904-905

O

Object Browser, 1184
Object Browser command (View menu), 1149
Object Browser dialog box, 1149, 1184
Object command
  Edit menu, 1058
  Format menu, 568, 580, 601
  Insert menu, 1051, 1067
Object dialog box, 1067
Object Linking and Embedding, *see* OLE
object model, 1141-1142
objects, 1174-1175
  accessing, 1175-1177
  Application object, 1142
  applications, 1188-1193
  assessing collections, 1178
  attaching procedures, 1162-1163
  borders, 480-482
  changing, 1144
  charts, 501-502
  classes, 1177
  collections, 1177
  colors, 480-482
  containers, 1175
  deleting, 501-502, 579
  embedded, 1058-1059
  functions, 1185-1186
  graphic, 577-579
  instances, 1177
  linked, 1058-1059
  methods, 1182
  moving, 478-480
  Object Browser, 1184
  patterns, 480-482
  procedures, 1184
  properties, 1179-1180
  selecting, 436-437
  shortcut menus, 435-436
  sizing, 478-480
  specifying with containers, 1142-1143
  storing, 1147-1148
  subprocedures, 1184-1185
  Visual Basic, 1146, 1176-1177
  Workbooks object, 1142
  see also graphic objects
OCT2BIN( ) function, 853
OCT2DEC( ) function, 853
OCT2HEX( ) function, 853
ODBC (Open Database Connectivity), 948
  installing drivers, 951-952
ODBC Data Sources dialog box, 954, 956
ODBC Setup dialog box, 955
ODD( ) function, 218, 857
ODDFPRICE( ) function, 855
ODDFYIELD( ) function, 855
ODDLPRICE( ) function, 855
ODDLYIELD( ) function, 855
Offset method of entering worksheet data, 1225-1227
OFFSET( ) function, 213, 214

OLE (Object Linking and Embedding)
automation, 19
clients, 1044
Visual Basic procedures, 1231-1232
OLE 2, 1052-1053
OLEObject object, 1177
on-line Help, 183, 1173
Visual Basic, 1150
on/off property, 1179
one-dimensional arrays, 1196
Open command (File menu), 268
Open Database Connectivity, see ODBC
Open Query command (Microsoft Query, File menu), 965
Open Query dialog box, 965
Open Workbook dialog box, 1064
opening
charts, 428-429
documents, 547
files
changing directories, 269
Excel 4, 272
Find File, 300
networks, 269
on network, 271-272
query windows, 964
workbooks, 268-272
linked, 758-759
multiple, 269
Visual Basic procedures, 1228-1229
worksheets, 980
operational settings (Solver), 811-812
operators
arithmetic, 139-140
% (percentage), 140
+ (addition), 139
* (multiplication), 140
- (negation), 139
- (subtraction), 139
/ (division), 140
^ (exponentiation), 140
comparison, 904-905, 1200
< (less than), 140
<= (less than/equal to), 140
<> (not equal), 140
> (greater than), 140
>= (greater than/equal to), 140
= (equal to), 140
evaluation order, 142
formulas, 139-142
logical operators, 1200
reference, 141
reference operators, 141
text operators, 140
optimal routing, 801
option buttons, 20, 49-51, 728-730
OptionButton object, 1177
Options Color command (Tools menu), 480
Options command (Tools menu), 126, 258, 456, 689, 1192
Options Custom Lists command (Tools menu), 244
Options dialog box, 258, 724
Options Edit command (Tools menu), 1099
Options Transition command (Tool menu), 1098
OR comparisons, 907-908, 916, 930
OR( ) function, 208, 926-928
order of columns, 969
order of evaluation (operators), 142
ordering
page layout, 382
sequences (reports), 398
orientation (printing), 377
outer joins, 968
Outline menu commands
Auto Outline, 598
Group, 599, 602-603
outlines, 593-595
chart creation, 519-521
charting data, 603-605
clearing, 600
copying data, 603-605
creating
manually, 599-600
with Automatic Outlining, 598-599
formatting, 602-603
layout, 595-596
levels, 600-602
subtotals, 612-613
symbols, 597, 600
Oval object, 1177

P

Page Break command (Insert menu), 386
page breaks, 384-386
page fields, 1029-1030
pivot tables, 983, 999-1001
page layout order, 382
Page Setup, 374-383
Header/Footer tab, 375
Margins tab, 375
Page tab, 374
Sheet tab, 375
Page Setup command (File menu), 374
Page tab (Page Setup), 374
PageMaker, 1060
paging through pivot tables, 1028-1030
palettes, 47-49
panes
criteria, 957, 960-963
query window, 958
table, 956, 958-959
windows, 544-546
activating, 546
creating with mouse, 545
freezing, 546, 928-931
resizing, 546
scrolling, 544-546
paper size (printing), 377
parallel syntax, 1144-1145
parentheses in formulas, 142, 147
parsing text, 1081, 1086-1088
passing arrays, 1234-1236
passwords, 279-280, 551
cell protection, 364, 365
workbooks, 269
Paste Button Image command (Edit menu), 1115
Paste command
Edit menu, 97, 102, 237, 240, 247, 250, 252, 459, 1046
Microsoft Query, Edit menu, 978
Paste Link command (Edit menu), 753
Paste Special command
Edit menu, 252-255, 459, 753, 1048
Microsoft Query, Edit menu, 979

Paste Special dialog box, 503, 753, 979
pasting, 247
  attributes into cells, 252-255
  between Excel and DOS applications, 1070-1074
  cells, 235-241
  charts, 571-573, 1065-1066
  embedded objects, 1055-1057
  formats, 311-312
  from Microsoft Query into Excel, 978
  functions to formulas, 143-144
  multiple copies, 247-250
  names (cells) to formulas, 143-144
  names list, 166-167
  undoing, 237
path names, 274
Pattern dialog box, 481-482
Pattern tool, 563
Patterned command (Analysis TookPak), 851
patterns
  charts (data series), 488
  formatting, 581-583
  objects, 480-482
  worksheeets, 351-354
Patterns dialog box, 582
pausing slide shows, 667
PC Paintbrush (PCX) file name extension, 557
PCT (Macintosh Picture) file name extension, 557
PCX (PC Paintbrush) file name extension, 557
PEARSON( ) function, 222, 857
Percent style, 355
percentage (%) operator, 140
PERCENTILE( ) function, 222, 857
PERCENTRANK( ) function, 222, 844, 846, 858
PERMUT( ) function, 222, 858
PI( ) function, 219
picture charts, 524-529
Picture command (Insert menu), 557
Picture dialog box, 557
Picture object, 1177
Pivot Table summary report, 831-832
pivot tables, 22, 983-1009
  appending, 1012-1015
  AutoFormatting, 1037-1038
  based on pivot tables, 1006-1007
  charts, 1007-1008, 1027-1028
  consolidating data, 1001-1005
  converting crosstab tables, 998-999
  creating, 988-993
  current workbook data, 996
  custom calculations, 1035-1037
  data analysis functions, 1033-1037
  data sources in other workbooks, 997
  editing, 994
  external databases, 997
  formatting, 1037-1039
  formatting numbers, 1038
  grouping, 1018-1027
    by label, 1018-1019
    displaying/hiding detail, 1019, 1022-1025
    numeric labels, 1025-1026
    time intervals, 1027
  label changes, 1039
  moving fields, 1017-1018
  multiple fields, 1005
  orientation, 1015-1016
  page fields, 983, 999-1001
  paging through, 1028-1030
  removing items, 1014
  saving files, 1008-1009
  sequence, 1016
  snapshots, 996
  sorting, 1028
  specifying source data, 996-999
  totals/subtotals, 1030-1033
  updating, 995-996
PivotField object, 1177
PivotItem object, 1177
PivotTable command (Data menu), 989
PivotTable Field button (Query and Pivot toolbar), 1038
PivotTable Field dialog box, 1033, 1035, 1037, 1038
PivotTable object, 1177
PivotTable Wizard, 983-1009
Placement command (Format menu)
  Bring to Front option, 590
  Send to Back option, 590
playing sound message, 793
plot area (charts), 406, 437
plus sign (+) on closed folders, 292
Pmt function, 1232-1233
PMT( ) function, 174-175, 199
point tables, troubleshooting, 1009
pointers (mouse pointer), 29, 32-33
pointing to cell references, 129-130
points, *see* data points
Poisson command (Analysis TookPak), 851
POISSON( ) function, 222, 858
polygon objects, 584
positioning
  charts in worksheets, 413
  graphic objects, 584-587
pound sign (#) in error values, 145
PPMT( ) function, 199
predefined chart types, 508
predefined formats, 91
  date/time, 341-342
  dates, 91
  number, 328-330
predefined styles, 355
previewing
  printing, 389-391
    charts, 430
    headers/footers, 380
  workbooks, 294-296
PRICE( ) function, 855
PRICEDISC( ) function, 855
PRICEMAT( ) function, 855
primary key fields, 950
print area
  defining, 384-385
  multiple, 387-392
  page breaks, 384
  removing, 385
Print command (File menu), 370, 395
print preview, 389-391
  charts, 430
  column width adjustment, 391-392
  margins, 391-392
Print Preview command (File menu), 389

print quality, 383
print queue, 369
print range, 383-388
Print Report command (File menu), 396, 678
print settings, 540-543
print spool, 369
printer fonts, 308
Printer Setup dialog box, 372
printers
- default, 372
- installation, 372
- laser printers, 375
- selecting, 372-374
- setup, 371-375

printing, 369-371, 385-387, 395-396
- black and white, 383
- cells (Visual Basic procedures), 1227-1228
- charts, 429-432, 678
- color, 383
- columns, 387
- compressing, 392-394
- Draft Quality, 395
- enlarging, 382
- files, 300-301
- filtered data, 934
- footers, 378-382
- forms without controls, 739
- graphic objects, 591
- gridlines, 377-378
- headers, 378-382
- headings for rows/columns, 377-378
- margins, 375-377, 430
- notes, 396
- orientation, 377
- page breaks, 385
- page layout (ordering), 382
- Page Setup, 374-383
- paper size, 377
- previewing headers/footers, 380
- reducing, 382
- reports
  - Report Manager, 396-399
  - sequences, 399
  - Solver, 812-814
  - with subtotals, 614
- selections, 395
- titles, 389
- troubleshooting, 388
- views, 369
- worksheets, 678

PrintOut method, 1228
PRN (Formatted Text) file name extension, 1075
PROB( ) function, 222, 858
problems
- linear/nonlinear, 801-802
- Solver add-in, 800-817

procedures (Visual Basic), 1155, 1184
- accessing worksheet cells, 1166-1167
- appending to dialog boxes, 1168-1169
- arguments, 1165
- attaching to buttons, 1224
- attaching to objects, 1162-1163
- calling, 1203-1204
- comments, 1164-1165
- data entry, 1225-1227
- displaying user messages, 1169-1171
- editing, 1163-1167
- FindIt, 1204
- GetOpenFilename, 1229
- headers/footers, 1165
- If statements, 1224-1225
- listing, 1159-1161
- moving objects, 1229-1231
- OLE automation, 1231-1232
- opening workbooks, 1228-1229
- running, 1161-1162
- subprocedures, 1184-1185
- Visual Basic, 1223-1236
  - creating, 1223-1232
  - printing cells, 1227-1228
- window gridlines, 1165-1166

Product function (pivot tables), 1034
product mixes, 801
PRODUCT( ) function, 219
products, 1239
Program Item Properties dialog box, 1133
Program Manager, 953
programming
- accessing disk files, 1207-1211
- accessing worksheet cells, 1201-1203
- arrays, 1196-1197
- assignment statements, 1194
- block if statements, 1199-1200
- branching, 1198-1201
- break mode, 1218
- breakpoints, 1218-1219
- calling procedures, 1203-1204
- changing objects, 1144
- collections, 1178
- constants, 1198
- containers specifying objects, 1142-1143
- custom dialog boxes, 1212-1217
- Debug window, 1219
- debugging tools, 1217-1221
- Excel dialog boxes, 1211
- functions, 1185-1186
- logical formulas, 1200
- loops, 1204-1207
  - Do/Loop, 1206-1207
  - For Each, 1207
  - For/Next, 1204-1205
  - While/Wend, 1205-1206
- methods, 1182-1183
- Object Browser, 1184
- objects, 1174-1177
- on-line help, 1173
- parallel syntax, 1144-1145
- procedures, 1184-1185
- properties, 1179-1181
- scope of variables, 1198
- Select Case statement, 1201
- step commands, 1220-1221
- variables, 1194
- Visual Basic object model, 1141-1142
- With clause, 1143-1144

programming languages, 23
programs
- breakpoints, 1217
- Microsoft Query, 947-949
- ROLLO1 (listing 45.1), 1190-1192
- ROLLO2 (listing 45.2), 1208-1210
- ROLLO3 Program (listing 45.3), 1214-1216
- watchpoints, 1218
- *see also* add-ins; applications

PROPER( ) function, 229
properties
- accessing, 1180-1181
- enumerated lists, 1179
- objects, 1179-1180
- range objects, 1180
- returning active codes, 1181

Properties command (File menu), 1133
Protect Sheet dialog box, 835

protecting
forms, 740
graphic objects, 590
scenarios, 834-835
sheets in workbooks, 362-365
Protection command (Tools menu), 364, 835
protection of data backups, 945-946
Protection command (Tools menu)
Protect Sheet option, 590, 1192
Unprotect Sheet option, 590, 1208
pull-down lists, 730-733
pull-down menus, 39
PV( ) function, 199

Q

QUARTILE( ) function, 222, 858
queries
data sources, 954-956
databases, 951
Query and Pivot toolbar, 42, 954
Group button, 1019
Hide Detail button, 1022
PivotTable Field button, 1038
Refresh Data button, 995
Show Pages button, 1030
query definitions, 958-963
adding criteria, 961-962
closing, 964
deleting criteria, 962-963
editing criteria, 962-963
executing, 963
opening new window, 964
reusing, 964-965
saving, 963-964
Query, *see* Microsoft Query
query window, 956-958
querying tables with formulas, 693-697
exact matches, 695
LOOKUP( ) functions, 693-695
MATCH/INDEX functions, 695-697
queue (print queue), 369
quitting Excel, 25-27
QUOTIENT( ) function, 853

R

RADIANS( ) function, 859
RAND( ) function, 219
RANDBETWEEN( ) function, 859
Random Number Generation command (Analysis ToolPak), 839-842, 851
Random Number Generation dialog box, 839
random series, 838-842
range objects, 1177-1179
Insert method, 1183
methods, 1182
properties, 1180
Range references, 1201
ranges
arrays, 154-155
criteria, 866, 869
data returned from Microsoft Query, 977
database, 866-869
extract, 866, 870
formatting
characters, 314-319
styles, 355-362
formulas, 254
linking cells, 750-753
by typing, 757-758
editing, 761-763
freezing, 763
saving, 763
updating, 759-761
with Copy/Paste Link commands, 753-755
print range, 383-388
protecting, 362-365
referencing, 1145-1147
selecting, 76-82
multiple, 79-80
shortcut keys, 78-79
Rank and Percentile command (Analysis TookPak), 851
RANK( ) function, 222, 844, 846, 858
RATE( ) function, 200
recalculation
controlling, 737-738
formulas, 126
see also calculation
RECEIVED( ) function, 855
Record dialog box, 792
Record Macro Mark Position for Recording command (Tools menu), 1159
Record Macro Record at Mark command (Tools menu), 1159
Record New Macro dialog box, 1155
recording sound messages, 792
recording macros, 1157-1158
records, 949, 972-973
deleting, 946
editing, 912
finding
with Advanced Filter, 919-931
with AutoFilter, 913-916
with data form, 909-912
Rectangle object, 1177
Rectangle tool, 562
rectangles, 564-565
reducing printing, 382
reference argument, 175
reference functions, 208-215
reference operators, 141
referencing cells/ranges, 128-139, 1145-1147
Refresh Data button (Query and Pivot toolbar), 995
Refresh Data command (Data menu), 981
Regression command (Analysis TookPak), 851
regression types, 515
relational databases, 949
relational keys, 949
relational tables, 965-968
relative cell references, 131-133, 136
Remove All Arrows (Auditing toolbar), 786
Remove Dependent Arrows (Auditing toolbar), 786
Remove Precedent Arrows (Auditing toolbar), 786
removing
breakpoints, 1219
items from pivot tables, 1014
split window, 545
see also deleting
Rename Sheet dialog box, 264
renaming
chart sheet, 415
sheets (workbooks), 264, 274-275
reordering
layers of graphic objects, 589-590
sequences (reports), 398
slide shows, 665-666

reorganizing
groups of sheets, 264-266
toolbar buttons, 1110-1111
Repeat command (Edit menu), 97
Replace command (Edit menu), 99-101
Replace dialog box, 100-101
REPLACE( ) function, 229
replacing data, 99-101
Report Manager, 678
printing reports, 396-399
sequences, 397-398
reports
formatting, 614
outlining, 593-596
printing, 396-399
Solver, 812-814
with subtotals, 614
scenarios
summary, 830-831
summary, Pivot Table, 831-832
View Manager, 679
see also Report Manager
REPT( ) function, 229
Reshape tool, 563, 565
reshaping objects, 584
reshaping toolbars, 46-47
resizing
controls, 736
panes (windows), 546
toolbars, 46-47
see also sizing
restore icon, 29
restoring original sort order, 892-893
restoring windows, 60
Return Data to Excel command (Microsoft Query, File menu), 976-981
ribbon charts, *see* line charts, 3-D
RIGHT( ) function, 230
ROLLO1 program (Listing 45.1), 1190-1192
ROLLO2 program (Listing 45.2), 1208-1210
ROLLO3 Program (Listing 45.3), 1214-1216
rotating
3-D charts
by commands, 500-501
by dragging, 497-499
text/numbers in cells, 326-327
ROUND( ) function, 219
rounding numbers, 1093
Row Height command
Format menu, 348
Microsoft Query, Format menu, 970
Row Height dialog box, 348, 970
Row Unhide command (Format menu), 350
ROW( ) function, 214-215
rows, 633-634
formatting, 348-350
headings
hiding, 535
printing, 377-378
height, 970
inserting/deleting, 103-107
joining workseets, 770-772
lists, 881-884
selecting, 82-83
sorting, 897-900
View Manager, 350
white space, 635-636
Rows command (Insert menu), 107
ROWS( ) function, 215
RSQ( ) function, 222, 858
Run menu commands
Clear All Breakpoints, 1219
Step Into, 1220
Step Over, 1221
Toggle Breakpoint, 1218
running procedures, 1161-1162

S

Sampling command (Analysis TookPak), 851
Save As command (File menu), 275
Save Query command (Microsoft Query, File menu), 964
Save Workspace command (File menu), 280
Save Workspace dialog box, 1135
saving, 974
charts, 426-427
embedded charts, 426-427
files, 677
formats, 280
pivot tables, 1008-1009
queries, 963-964
search criteria, 291-292
slide shows, 668
Solver data, 815-816
templates, 1128-1129
views, 540-543
windows, 552
workbooks, 272-281
automatically, 277-278
linked, 763
naming, 273-274
renaming, 274-275
summary information, 275-277
worksheets in format other than Excel, 1076
scaling axes in charts, 494-496
scatter (XY) charts, 453-454, 494
Scenario Manager, 820, 824-825
Scenario Manager dialog box, 824-827
Scenario object, 1177
scenarios, 819-821
adding, 822-825
editing, 826-827
input cells, 821-822
merging, 833-834
multiple sets, 828-830
naming, 834
protecting, 834-835
summary reports, 830-832
switching between, 826
troubleshooting, 835
Scenarios command (Tools menu), 824, 826
scientific analysis (Analysis ToolPak), 676-677
scope (variables), 1198
screen
icons, 29
menu bar, 29
scroll bar, 29
sheet tabs, 31
status bar, 29, 31
title bar, 29
screen fonts, 308
screens
copying across applications, 1046-1047
copying to PageMaker, 1060
customizing with Windows Control Panel, 1101
viewing, 16
scroll bar, 29, 31, 535-536, 734-736, 1148
ScrollBar object, 1177

scrolling
- lists, 730-733
- panes (windows), 544-546
- sheet tabs, 31, 68
- worksheets
  - with keyboard, 71-72
  - with mouse, 71

search criteria, 284
Search dialog box, 284
Search for Help on command (Help menu), 673
SEARCH( ) function, 230
searches, 284-292
- date saved/created, 290-291
- directories, 285-286
- drives, 285-286
- file types, 286-287
- files, 286-287
- Find File command, 282-284
- Help topics, 56-57
- limiting, 284
- saving criteria, 291-292
- summary information, 287-290
- text, 287-290

SECOND( ) function, 191
secondary axes, 509-510
security, *see* protection
seed cells, 111
Select Case statement (Visual Basic), 1201
Select Data Source dialog box, 953-954, 964-965
Select Database dialog box, 956
Select Special dialog box, 798
Select Tables dialog box, 956
Select tool, 562
Selected item command (Format menu), 490-496
Selected Object command (Format menu), 478-480, 484-487
Selected Series command (Format menu), 461-464, 478
Selected Series command (Tools menu), 481
selecting, 34, 85-86
- blocks, 80, 82
- cells
  - by content, 83-85
  - Go To command, 75-76
  - marquee, 237
  - single cell, 73-74
- chart objects, 436-437
- chart type, 438-440
- charts, 413
- columns, 82-83
- commands, 38-41
- fields, 973
- files
  - Find File, 293, 299-300
  - multiple, 299
- printers, 372-374
- ranges, 76-82
  - array ranges, 154-155
  - multiple, 79-80
  - shortcut keys, 78-79
- rows, 82-83
- tabs, 50
- text, 318
- text box characters, 51
- worksheets, 69-70

selecting calculations with an index, 1233-1234
Send to Back tool, 562
sensitivity analysis (worksheets), 697-703
- multiple-input data tables, 700-701
- single-input data tables, 698-700

Sensitivity reports (Solver), 813
sequences (reports), 397-398
- printing, 399
- reordering, 398

serial_number argument, 175
series
- data entry, 110-119
- uniform random, 838-842

Series dialog box, 245
series formula (charts), 406, 461-465
Series object, 1177
series, *see* data series
SERIESSUM( ) function, 853
servers (OLE), 1044
Sets Defaults dialog box, 665
settings (print settings), 540-543
setup (printers), 371-375
shading, 644-646
shadow prices, 809
Sheet Hide command file (Format menu), 740
Sheet Rename command (Format menu), 264
Sheet tab (Page Setup), 375
sheet tabs, 31
- hiding, 536
- scrolling, 31
- scrolling buttons, 68
- split box, 31

sheet templates, 1131-1133
Sheet Unhide command file (Format menu), 740
sheet-level cell names, 162
sheets, 66
- chart sheets, 66, 415
- dialog box sheets, 66
- displaying
  - controlling, 533-538
  - full screen, 533-535
  - in separate windows, 547-548
  - zooming, 538-539
- hiding, 550-551
- macro sheets, 66
- protecting, 834-835
- values (markers), 511-513
- *see also* worksheets

sheets in workbooks, 258
- chart sheets, 267
- copying, 260-262
- default, 258
- deleting, 260
- formatting
  - groups, 365-366
  - startup options, 366-367
- grouping to edit, format, or reorganize, 264-266
- inserting, 259-260
- macro sheets, 267
- moving, 262-263
- protecting, 362-365
- renaming, 264
- styles, 355-362
- worksheets, 267

Shift key in commands, 41
shortcut keys
- creating charts, 415
- data entry, 121, 883-884
- editing
  - formulas, 95-96
  - worksheet layouts, 102
- formatting
  - cells or characters, 317
  - dates/times, 344
  - numbers, 332
- selecting ranges, 78-79

shortcut menus, 39-40
- Drawing, 563
- objects, 435-436

Show Info Window (Auditing toolbar), 786
Show Pages button (Query and Pivot toolbar), 1030
Show Pages dialog box, 1030
SIGN( ) function, 219
SIN( ) function, 233

single-input data tables (sensitivity analysis), 698-700
SINH( ) function, 233
size of fonts, 638-642
sizing
  charts, 413
  graphic objects, 583-584
  objects, 478-480
  panes (windows), 546
  toolbars, 46-47
  windows, 61
  see also resizing
SKEW( ) function, 222, 858
Slide Show add-in, 660-661, 678
slide shows
  creating, 661-665
  editing, 665, 668
  pausing, 667
  reordering, 665-666
  restarting, 667
  saving, 668
  starting, 666-667
  stopping, 667
sliders, 1148
slides, 318
SLK (Symbolic Link: Multiplan, Microsoft Works) file name extension, 1075
SLN( ) function, 200
SLOPE( ) function, 222, 858
SMALL( ) function, 222, 858
smoothing data (time-series), 846-849
snapshots (pivot tables), 996
Solver add-in, 679, 795, 800-804
  constraints, 810
  installing, 804-809
  limited resources, 809
  printing reports, 812-814
  samples, 816-817
  saving/loading data, 815-816
  settings
    integer constraints, 810-811
    operational, 811-812
Solver command (Tools menu), 679, 805
Solver Parameters dialog box, 805-817
Sort command
  Data menu, 20, 612, 887, 898, 1028
  Microsoft Query, Records menu, 971-972
Sort dialog box, 887, 891, 898, 971-972
Sort Options dialog box, 891, 894
sorting, 887-890, 970-972
  ascending/descending sorts, 888
  calculated fields, 897
  case-sensitivity, 888
  code segment sorts, 895-896
  command method, 890-892
  custom sort orders, 893-894
  date/time sorts, 894-895
  file lists, 293-294
  filtered data, 934
  multiple field sorts, 896
  pivot tables, 1028
  restoring original sort order, 892-893
  rows/columns, 897-900
  toolbar method, 892
  troubleshooting, 899-900
  undoing sorts, 892
sound messages
  deleting, 794
  importing, 793
  playing, 793
  recording, 792
source workbooks, 751-753
specifying objects with containers, 1142-1143
specifying source data (pivot tables), 996-999
spell checker, 787-790
spelling in charts, 469
Spelling command (Tools menu), 469, 789
Spinner object, 1177
spinners, 690, 1148
  worksheets, 733-734
split box (scroll bar), 29
Split command (Window menu), 545
splitting windows, 545
spool (print spool), 369
Spreadsheet Import command (Tools menu), 1078
SQL (Structured Query Language), 948, 965
SQL command (Microsoft Query, View menu), 965
SQRT( ) function, 220
SQRTPI( ) function, 853
Standard Dictionary, 787-790
Standard mode, 1070-1072
Standard toolbar, 42, 177-178
  ChartWizard button, 1008
  Format Painter tool, 18
  New Workbook button, 267
STANDARDIZE( ) function, 222, 858
starting
  add-ins, 675
  Excel, 25-27
    options, 1132-1136
  Macro Recorder, 1155-1157
  Microsoft Query
    from Excel, 953
    from Program Manager, 953
  slide shows, 666-667
startup
  formats, 366-367
  icons, 1134
  switches, 1133
statistical analysis (Analysis ToolPak), 676-677
statistical commands, 837
statistical functions, 221-226, 838, 856-858
statistics (charts), 514
status bar, 29, 31
  hiding, 536
  query window, 957
STDEV( ) function, 225
STDEVP( ) function, 226
step commands, 1220-1221
STEP function, 1150
Step Into command (Run menu), 1220
Step Over command (Run menu), 1221
step value, 115
STEYX( ) function, 222, 858
Stop Recording toolbar, 43
stop value, 115
stopping slide shows, 667
storing objects, 1147-1148
Structured Query Language, *see* SQL
Style command (Format menu), 355-362
Style dialog box, 355-362
Style object, 1177
styles, 354-355, 361-362
  applying to collection of formats, 355-362
  creating, 356-359
  deleting, 361
  desktop publishing, 651-656
  formats, 307

merging, 358-359
redefining, 359-361
Styles command (Format menu), 651-656
submenus, 39, 1122
subprocedures, 1184-1185
subprocedures, *see* procedures
Subtotal dialog box, 608-612
subtotals, 607-610
deleting, 610
filtered data, 613-614, 934
multiple calculations, 611-612
nesting, 611
outlines, 612-613
reports, 614
underlining, 354
Subtotals command (Data menu), 20, 608, 611, 614, 934
subtraction (-) operator, 139
Sum function (pivot tables), 1034
SUM( ) function, 179-180, 220
SUMIF( ) function, 706
summarizing subtotals, 607-614
summarizing list data, 705-710
Summary Info command (File menu), 276
summary information (Find File)
adding, 297-298
editing, 297-298
searches, 287-290
viewing, 296-297
workbooks, 275-277
summary report scenarios, 830-832
SUMPRODUCT( ) function, 220
SUMSQ( ) function, 220
SUMSQUARES( ) function, 858
SUMX2MY2( ) function, 220, 858
SUMX2PY2( ) function, 220, 858
SUMXMY2( ) function, 221, 858
surface charts (3-D), 450
switching
applications, 59
between workbooks, 59, 67
between worksheets, 68
windows, 547
SYD( ) function, 200
symbols
date and time format, 342-343
formatting, 335-336
outlines, 597, 600

T

T( ) function, 230
t-Test: Paired Two-Sample for Means command (Analysis ToolPak), 851
t-Test: Two-Sample Assuming Unequal Variances command (Analysis ToolPak), 851
Table command (Data menu), 109, 698
Table dialog box, 700, 701
tables, 949
AutoFormat, 305-307
columns/rows, 968-970
combining with database functions, 707-710
data
editing, 973-975
formatting, 973
sorting, 970-972
fields, 972-973
histogram, 845
histograms, 838
linking into Word for Windows, 1061-1068
panes, 956
adding/deleting tables, 958-959
displaying/hiding, 958
fields, 967-968
pivot tables, 22, 983-1009
appending, 1012-1015
AutoFormatting, 1037-1038
based on pivot tables, 1006-1007
charts, 1007-1008, 1027-1028
consolidating data, 1001-1005
converting crosstab tables, 998-999
creating, 988-993
current workbook data, 996
custom calculations, 1035-1037
data analysis functions, 1033-1037
data sources in other workbooks, 997
editing, 994
external databases, 997
formatting, 1037-1039
formatting numbers, 1038
grouping, 1018-1027
label changes, 1039
moving fields, 1017-1018
multiple fields, 1005
orientation, 1015-1016
page fields, 999-1001
paging through, 1028-1030
removing items, 1014
saving files, 1008-1009
sequence, 1016
snapshots, 996
sorting, 1028
specifying source data, 996-999
totals/subtotals, 1030-1033
updating, 995-996
querying with formulas, 693-697
exact matches, 695
LOOKUP() functions, 693-695
MATCH/INDEX functions, 695-697
records, 972-973
see also relational tables
Tables command (Microsoft Query, View menu), 958
tabs
cells, 324
dialog boxes, 49-50
scrolling buttons, 68
selecting, 50
see also sheet tabs
tabular data, 987
Tagged Image File Format (TIF) file name extension, 557
TAN( ) function, 233
TANH( ) function, 233
target workbooks, 751-753
TBILLEQ( ) function, 855
TBILLPRICE( ) function, 855
TBILLYIELD( ) function, 855
TDIST( ) function, 222, 858
tear off palettes, 15, 47-49
technical support
CompuServe, 1239-1240
Microsoft Corporation, 1239
Que Corporation, 1240
Ron Person & Co, 1240
templates, 362, 1127-1132
autotemplates, 1129-1130
creating from workbooks, 1129

editing, 1130
saving, 1128-1129
sheet templates, 1131-1133
troubleshooting, 1131-1132
ten-key accounting pad, 1093
text
attributes, 643
cells
centering across, 320-322
joining with numbers, 323
rotating, 326-327
tabs/line breaks, 324
charts, 406, 437
aligning, 486
data labels, 469-472
floating text, 468-469
formatting, 483-487
linking to cells, 523-524
spelling, 469
titles, 466-467
concatenation, 685
copying across applications, 1045-1046
data entry, 89-90, 116-119
displaying with numbers, 337
exporting from Excel to DOS or mainframe applications, 1077
finding, 97-99, 902-903
formulas, 144
in formulas, 686
parsing, 1081, 1086-1088
replacing, 99-101
searches, 287-290
selecting, 318
sorting, 887-890
spell checker, 787-789
wrapping, 322
Text (Macintosh) files, 1077
Text (OS/2 or MS-DOS) files, 1077
Text (Tab delimited) files, 1077, 1081-1086
text argument, 175
Text Box tool, 562
text boxes (dialog boxes), 49, 567-568
deleting characters, 52
editing, 51-52
selecting characters, 51
text files, importing, 1081-1086
text functions, 226-231
Text Import Wizard, 1081-1086
text operators, 140
Text Wizard, 1086-1088
TEXT( ) function, 90-91, 231, 687
TextBox object, 1177
TextWizard, 21
tick marks (charts), 406
TIF (Tagged Image File Format) file name extension, 557
time, *see* date and time
time sorts, 894-895
TIME( ) function, 191
time-series data, 846-849
times/dates
data entry, 93-94
finding, 905-906
TIMEVALUE( ) function, 191
TINV( ) function, 222, 858
TipWizard, 15, 42, 58
title bar, 29
titles
charts
ChartWizard, 412-414
editing, 467
inserting, 466-467
labels, 417
printing, 389
Titles command (Insert menu), 466-467
TODAY( ) function, 192
Toggle Breakpoint command (Run menu), 1218
Tool menu commands
Options Transition, 1098
Spelling, 789
Toolbar object, 1177
ToolbarButton object, 1177
toolbars, 31, 41-48, 1094
appending buttons, 1108-1109
assigning macros/program code to buttons, 1112-1113
attaching to workbooks, 1115-1117
Auditing toolbar, 43, 786
button faces, 1113-1115
Chart toolbar, 42
charts, 406
creating, 1111-1112, 1149
custom, 1108-1116
displaying, 45-46
docking, 46
Drawing toolbar, 43, 561-563
floating, 46
Formatting toolbar, 42, 483
Borders button, 354
Color Palette button, 352
Forms toolbar, 43
Formula Bar, 177-178
freehand buttons, 1115
Full Screen toolbar, 44
Help, 44-45
hiding, 45-46
Microsoft, 44
moving, 46-47
Query and Pivot toolbar, 42, 954
reorganizing buttons, 1110-1111
reshaping, 46-47
resizing, 46-47
sort operatons, 892
sorting data, 970-971
Standard toolbar, 42, 177-178
Format Painter, 18
Stop Recording toolbar, 43
tear-off palettes, 47-49
TipWizard toolbar, 42
troubleshooting, 48, 1116
Visual Basic toolbar, 43
WorkGroup, 823
WorkGroup toolbar, 43
Toolbars command
Tools menu, 120
View menu, 45, 440, 474, 483, 721, 1061, 1108, 1149
Toolbars dialog box, 440, 721, 1108
Toolbars Standard command (View menu), 177, 179
Toolbars WorkGroup command (Tools menu), 823
tools
drawing, 561-563
Format Painter, 18
see also drawing tools
Tools menu commands
Add-Ins, 672, 675-680, 952
Analysis option, 839
Assign Macro, 570, 1162, 1213
Attach Toolbar, 1115
Auditing, 19, 784
AutoSave, 277, 677
Data Analysis, 677, 837-850
Goal Seek, 443-444, 512, 795-800
Macro, 1161
Menu Editor, 1149

Options, 126, 258, 456, 689, 1192
Color option, 480
Custom Lists option, 244
Edit option, 1099
Protection, 364, 835
Protect Sheet option, 590, 1192
Unprotect Sheet option, 590, 1208
Record Macro Mark Position for Recording, 1159
Record Macro Record at Mark, 1159
Scenarios, 824, 826
Selected Series, 481
Solver, 679, 805
Spelling, 469
Spreadsheet Import, 1078
Toolbars, 120
Toolbars WorkGroup, 823
ToolTips, 15
topics (Help), 56-57
totals, 354
Trace Dependents (Auditing toolbar), 786
Trace Error (Auditing toolbar), 786
Trace Precedents (Auditing toolbar), 786
tracing data/formulas, 783-785
transferring
data from Microsoft Query to other worksheets/ workbooks, 980-981
Microsoft Query data to Excel, 975-980
transitions (slide shows), 665
TRANSPOSE( ) function, 215
transposing, 254
TREND( ) function, 226, 715-716
Trendline command (Insert menu), 513-514
Trendline object, 1177
trendlines (charts), 21, 513
data series
inserting, 514-516
formatting, 490
regression types, 515
y-intercept value, 514
trends (charts), 513-516
trends (worksheets), 710-716
fill handles, 711-713
Fill Series command, 713-714
worksheet functions, 715-716
trigonometric functions, 232-233
TRIM( ) function, 231, 894
TRIMMEAN( ) function, 222, 858
troubleshooting
AutoFormat, 307
cells
copying, 255
moving, 241
charts, 453
customization operations, 1105
data entry, 122-123, 885
formatting
aligning cell contents, 327
characters, 319
dates/times, 345
fonts, 311, 319
numbers, 341
rows/columns, 350
startup options for workbooks/worksheets, 367
formulas, 147-152
menus, 1125
mouse, 34
outlines, 601-603
pivot tables, 1009
printing, 388
scenarios, 835
sheet display, 538
sorting worksheets, 899-900
starting Excel, 27
templates, 1131-1132
toolbars, 48, 1116
worksheet error messages, 777-779
worksheet viewing, 70
worksheets, 265-266
TRUE( ) function, 208
TRUE/FALSE responses (worksheets), 727-728
TrueType dialog box, 310
TrueType fonts, 309-311
TRUNC( ) function, 221
TTEST( ) function, 222, 858
two-dimensional arrays, 1196
TXT (Formatted Text) file name extension, 1075
TXT (Text) file name extension, 1075
Type statement (Visual Basic), 1197
TYPE( ) function, 206-207
typeface, *see* fonts

U

underlined text, 643
underlining subtotals, 354
Undo (Ctrl+Z) shortcut key, 236
Undo command (Edit menu), 97, 236-237
Undo command (Edit menu)
Delete option, 106
Replace option, 101
Sort option, 892
undoing
changes, 97
pasting, 237
UnFreeze Panes command (Window menu), 546, 928
Ungroup Sheets (sheet tab shortcut menu), 265
Ungroup tool, 563
ungrouping sheets, *see* grouping
unhiding sheets, 551
Uniform command (Analysis ToolPak), 851
uniform random series, 838-842
unlimited extract range, 870
unlinked pictures of cells, 574-577
unlinked pictures of charts, 571-573
updating
pivot tables, 995-996
query data in worksheets, 981-982
worksheets
linked, 759-761
linked cell pictures, 747-748
UPPER( ) function, 231
user-defined functions, 1185-1186, 1232, 1234-1236
user messages (Visual Basic), displaying, 1169-1171
User-Defined AutoFormats dialog box, 451
user-defined data types (Visual Basic), 1197-1200

V

Val( ) function, 1202
value arguments, 175
VALUE( ) function, 231
values
  changing to formulas, 144-145
  constant, 90-92
  dual, 809
  names, 170-171
  sheets
    markers, 511-513
VAR( ) function, 226
variables, 1147, 1194
  arrays, 1196-1197
  declaring, 1196
  scope, 1198
  watch variables, 1220
VARP( ) function, 226
VDB( ) function, 201
View Manager, 540-543
  rows/columns, 350-351
View Manager add-in, 679-680
View Manager command (View menu), 542, 680
View menu commands
  Formula Bar, 177
  Full Screen, 16, 535
  Object Browser, 1149
  Toolbars, 45, 440, 474, 483, 721, 1061, 1108, 1149
  Toolbars Standard, 177, 179
  View Manager, 542, 680
viewing
  cells, 780
  Clipboard, 1044
  file information, 292-293, 296
  formulas, 125, 779-780
  lists, filtered, 928-931
  screens, 16
  SQL statements, 965
  summary information, 296-297
  workbooks, 292-293
  worksheets, 70
views
  creating named views, 541
  deleting named views, 543
  displaying named views, 543
  naming, 540-543
  printing, 369
  saving, 540-543
  saving settings, 540-543
Visual Basic, 23, 1139-1140, 1153-1155
  (underscore) _ character, 1167
  built-in data types, 1195
  changing objects, 1144
  collections, 1178
  debugging tools, 1150-1151
  dialog boxes, 1148-1149
  displaying user messages, 1169-1171
  GetOpenFilename method, 1211
  GetSaveAsFilename method, 1211
  InputBox function, 1169
  menus, 1149
  module modification, 1153-1171
  modules, 1155
  objects, 1146, 1176-1177
  On-Line Help, 1150
  parallel syntax, 1144-1145
  procedures, 1155, 1223-1236
    accessing worksheet cells, 1166-1167
    attaching to buttons, 1224
    comments, 1164-1165
    creating, 1223-1232
    data entry, 1225-1227
    editing, 1163-1167
    headers/footers, 1165
    If statements, 1224-1225
    listing, 1159-1161
    moving objects, 1229-1231
    OLE automation, 1231-1232
    opening workbooks, 1228-1229
    printing cells, 1227-1228
    running, 1161-1162
  running macros, 1151
  Select Case statement, 1201
  Show method, 1218
  storing objects, 1147-1148
  structure, 1141-1142
  terminology, 1154-1155
  toolbars, 1149
  Type statement, 1197
  user-defined data types, 1197-1200
  variables, 1147
  versus macro language, 1140
  With clause, 1143-1144
  worksheet functions, 1232-1233
Visual Basic module sheets, 1117
Visual Basic toolbar, 43
VLOOKUP( ) function, 215-216, 693-695
voice messages (worksheets), 789-794

W

wallpapers, 1103
Watch pane (Debug window), 1220
watch variables, 1220
watchpoints (programs), 1218
WEEKDAY( ) function, 192
WEIBULL( ) function, 222, 858
What-If analysis, 510-513, 819
While/Wend loops, 1205-1206
white space, 624, 635-636
wild cards, 99, 101, 906-907
Window menu commands
  Arrange, 548
  Freeze Panes, 928
  Hide, 550
  New Window, 547, 723
  Split, 545
  UnFreeze Panes, 928
  Unfreeze Panes, 546
Windows
  Control Panel, 1099-1105
  DOS applications, 1070
windows, 58-62
  active window, 29
  application windows, 28, 59
  arranging, 548-549
  closing, 552
  Debug window, 1219
  gridlines, 1165-1166
  group windows, 25
  Help window, 58
  hiding, 550-551
  inactive window, 29
  locking, 551-552
  maximizing, 60
  minimizing, 60
  moving, 60-61
  multiple, 546-552
  panes, 544-546
    activating, 546
    freezing, 546, 928-931
    resizing, 546
    scrolling, 544-546
  query, 956-958
  restoring, 60

saving, 552
sizing, 61
splitting, 545
switching, 547
unhiding, 550
workbook window, 30, 59
active workbook window, 30
closing, 61-62
inactive workbook window, 31
Windows applications interaction, 1043-1068
Windows Bitmaps (BMP) file name extension, 557
Windows Metafile (WMF) file name extension, 557
Windows Paintbrush (BMP) file name extension, 557
With clause, 1143-1144
wizards
PivotTable, 983-1009
Text Import, 1081-1086
Text Wizard, 1086-1088
WK1 (1-2-3 Release 2x) file name extension, 1075
WK3 (1-2-3 Release 3) file name extension, 1075
WKS (1-2-3 Release 1, 1A) file name extension, 1075
WKS (Microsoft Works) file name extension, 1075
WKS (Symphony) file name extension, 1075
WMF (Windows Metafile) file name extension, 557
Word for Windows, 1061-1068
WordPerfect 6.0, 1077-1079
work preferences, 1098-1099
workbook control icon, 31
workbook icon, 31
Workbook object, 1177
workbook window, 30, 59
active window, 30
closing, 61-62
inactive workbook window, 31
switching between, 59
workbook-level cell names, 162
workbooks, 66
activating, 67
closing, 282
copying filtered data between, 942-944
creating, 267
from templates, 1129
linked
editing, 762-763, 772-773
freezing, 763
saving, 763
linking
cells and ranges, 750-763
editing, 761-762
moving between, 67
naming, 273-275
opening, 268-272
linked, 758-759, 980
multiple, 269
Visual Basic procedures, 1228-1229
passwords, 269, 279-280
previewing, 294-296
renaming, 274-275
saving, 272-281
automatically, 277-278
naming, 273-302
renaming, 274-275
summary information, 275-277
sheets, 258
chart sheets, 267
copying, 260-262
default, 258
deleting, 260
grouping, 264-266
inserting, 259-260
macro sheets, 267
moving, 262-263
moving between, 68
protecting, 362-365
renaming, 264
startup formats, 366-367
styles, 355-362
worksheets, 267
starting Excel, 1135
summary information, 275-277
switching between, 59, 67
tab scrolling buttons, 68
templates, 1127-1132
transferring data from Microsoft Query, 980-981
viewing, 292-293
worksheets, 16-17
see also worksheets
Workbooks object, 1142
WORKDAY( ) function, 855
WorkGroup toolbar, 43, 823
workgroups (scenarios), 834-835
Worksheet command (Insert menu), 259
Worksheet object, 1177
worksheet templates, 1094
worksheets, 16-17
3-D formulas, 265-266
accessing cells, 1201-1203
attribute changes, 1129
auditing, 777-794
borders, 352-354
calculating data tables, 703
cell attributes, 252-255
cells, copying between, 252
charts, 648-651
embedding, 571-572
moving, 413
pasting, 571-572, 573
positioning, 413
sizing, 413
check boxes, 727-728
colors, 351-354
controlling recalculation, 737-738
controls, 720-736
copying filtered data between, 942-944
data
adding to charts, 458-459
moving between, 236-237, 239-241
data integrity, 690-692
database functions, 704-705
deactivating Macro Recorder, 1158-1159
desktop publishing guidelines, 620-623
dialog boxes, 20
dimming controls, 739
editing layout, 102
embedded charts, 414
error messges, 777-779
error tracking, 781-783
form-like, 723-724
format startup options, 366-367
formatting, 620-623, 627-648, 651-656
Forms toolbar, 721-723
functions, 178-180
headings, centering, 636
joining, 763-767
by physical layout, 767-770
by row and column headings, 770-772
formatting, 774-776
linking, 774
manually, 776
with 3-D formulas, 765

layouts, 623-624, 627-648
  borders, 624-626
  editing, 101-107
  pages, 626-627
  white space, 624
lines, 352-354
linked, 429
linking
  cells and ranges, 750-763
  pictures of cells, 744-749
links
  creating, 427
  editing, 427
modifying controls, 736-737
moving between, 68
names (cells), 162-166
navigating, 70-72
notes, 789-794
opening linked, 980
option buttons, 728-730
outlining, 596
patterns, 351-352, 354
printing, 678
protecting forms, 740
query data
  editing, 981
  updating, 981-982
recalculating lists, 884-886
recording macros, 1157-1158
saving in format other than Excel, 1076
scroll bars, 734-736
scrolling
  with keyboard, 71-72
  with mouse, 71
selecting, 69-70
sensitivity analysis, 697-703
  multiple-input data tables, 700-701
  single-input data tables, 698-700
sorting, 887-890
  calculated fields, 897
  code segment sorts, 895-896
  command method, 890-892
  custom sort orders, 893-894
  date/time sorts, 894-895
  multiple field sorts, 896
  restoring original sort order, 892-893
  rows/columns, 897-900
  toolbar method, 892
  troubleshooting, 899-900
sound messages, 792-794
spell checker, 787-790
spinners, 690, 733-734
styles, 355-362, 651-656
summarizing list data, 705-710
templates, 1128-1132
transferring data from Microsoft Query, 980-981
trends, 710-716
  fill handles, 711-713
  Fill Series command, 713-714
  worksheet functions, 715-716
undoing sorts, 892
View Manager, 679
viewing, 70, 779-780
voice messages, 789-794
see also sheets; workbooks
workspace files, 280-281, 1135
WPG (DrawPerfect) file name extension, 557
WQ1 (Quattro) file name extension, 1075
wrapping text, 322

X

x arguments, 715
X axis labels, 416
XIRR( ) function, 855
XLC (Excel 4.0 Chart) file name extension, 1074
XLM (Excel 4.0 Macro) file name extension, 1074
XLS (Excel 2.1, 3.0, 4.0) file name extension, 1074
XLT files, 1128
XLW (Excel 4.0 Workbook) file name extension, 1074
XNPV( ) function, 855
XY (scatter) charts, 453-454

Y

y arguments, 715
Y axis, 506
y-intercept value (trendline), 514
YEAR( ) function, 192
YEARFRAC( ) function, 192, 855
YIELD( ) function, 855
YIELDDISC( ) function, 855
YIELDMAT( ) function, 855

Z

z-Test: Two-Sample for Means command (Analysis ToolPak), 851
zeros, 339-340
zooming, 390
  sheet display, 538-539
ZTEST( ) function, 222, 858